SAXON MATH™
Course 2

Teacher's Manual
Volume 2

Stephen Hake

A Harcourt Achieve Imprint

www.SaxonPublishers.com
1-800-284-7019

Acknowledgements

This book was made possible by the significant contributions of many individuals and the dedicated efforts of a talented team at Harcourt Achieve.

Special thanks to:

- Melody Simmons and Chris Braun for suggestions and explanations for problem solving in Courses 1-3,
- Elizabeth Rivas and Bryon Hake for their extensive contributions to lessons and practice in Course 3,
- Sue Ellen Fealko for suggested application problems in Course 3.

The long hours and technical assistance of John and James Hake on Courses 1-3, Robert Hake on Course 3, Tom Curtis on Course 3, and Roger Phan on Course 3 were invaluable in meeting publishing deadlines. The saintly patience and unwavering support of Mary is most appreciated.

– Stephen Hake

Staff Credits

Editorial: Jean Armstrong, Shelley Farrar-Coleman, Marc Connolly, Hirva Raj, Brooke Butner, Robin Adams, Roxanne Picou, Cecilia Colome, Michael Ota

Design: Alison Klassen, Joan Cunningham, Deborah Diver, Alan Klemp, Andy Hendrix, Rhonda Holcomb

Production: Mychael Ferris-Pacheco, Heather Jernt, Greg Gaspard, Donna Brawley, John-Paxton Gremillion

Manufacturing: Cathy Voltaggio

Marketing: Marilyn Trow, Kimberly Sadler

E-Learning: Layne Hedrick, Karen Stitt

ISBN 978-1-5914-1838-2
ISBN 1-5914-1838-0

5 6 7 8 9 0868 12 11 10 09

Course 2
Content Overview

ABOUT THE AUTHOR

Stephen Hake has authored five books in the Saxon Math series. He writes from 17 years of classroom experience as a teacher in grades 5 through 12 and as a math specialist in El Monte, California. As a math coach, his students won honors and recognition in local, regional, and statewide competitions.

Stephen has been writing math curriculum since 1975 and for Saxon since 1985. He has also authored several math contests including Los Angeles County's first Math Field Day contest. Stephen contributed to the 1999 National Academy of Science publication on the Nature and Teaching of Algebra in the Middle Grades.

Stephen is a member of the National Council of Teachers of Mathematics and the California Mathematics Council. He earned his BA from United States International University and his MA from Chapman College.

EDUCATIONAL CONSULTANTS

Nicole Hamilton
Consultant Manager
Richardson, TX

Joquita McKibben
Consultant Manager
Pensacola, FL

John Anderson
Lowell, IN

Beckie Fulcher
Gulf Breeze, FL

Heidi Graviette
Stockton, CA

Brenda Halulka
Atlanta, GA

Marilyn Lance
East Greenbush, NY

Ann Norris
Wichita Falls, TX

Melody Simmons
Nogales, AZ

Benjamin Swagerty
Moore, OK

Kristyn Warren
Macedonia, OH

Mary Warrington
East Wenatchee, WA

Table of Contents

Integrated and Distributed Units of Instruction

TABLE OF CONTENTS

Section 1 — *Lessons 1–10, Investigation 1*

Math Focus:
Number & Operations • Algebra

Distributed Strands:
Number & Operations • Algebra • Geometry • Measurement • Problem Solving

Maintaining & Extending

Section 2 *Lessons 11–20, Investigation 2*

Math Focus:
Number & Operations • Problem Solving

Distributed Strands:
Number & Operations • Algebra • Geometry • Measurement • Problem Solving

Maintaining & Extending

Power Up

Facts pp. 75, 82, 88, 93, 100, 107, 114, 120, 128, 134

Mental Math Strategies pp. 75, 82, 88, 93, 100, 107, 114, 120, 128, 134

Problem Solving Strategies pp. 75, 82, 88, 93, 100, 107, 114, 120, 128, 134

Enrichment

Early Finishers pp. 81, 87, 92, 113, 127, 133, 142

TABLE OF CONTENTS

Section 3 Lessons 21–30, Investigation 3

Math Focus:
Number & Operations • Problem Solving

Distributed Strands:
Number & Operations • Geometry • Problem Solving

Maintaining & Extending

Power Up

Facts pp. 149, 157, 163, 169, 175, 182, 188, 194, 200, 208

Mental Math Strategies pp. 149, 157, 163, 169, 175, 182, 188, 194, 200, 208

Problem Solving Strategies pp. 149, 157, 163, 169, 175, 182, 188, 194, 200, 208

Enrichment

Early Finishers pp. 162, 168, 187, 199, 207, 215

Section 4 *Lessons 31–40, Investigation 4*

Math Focus:
Number & Operations • Data Analysis & Probability

Distributed Strands:
Number & Operations • Geometry • Measurement • Data Analysis & Probability

Maintaining & Extending

Power Up

Facts pp. 221, 228, 235, 241, 247, 255, 264, 273, 280, 285

Mental Math Strategies pp. 221, 228, 235, 241, 247, 255, 264, 273, 280, 285

Problem Solving Strategies pp. 221, 228, 235, 241, 247, 255, 264, 273, 280, 285

Enrichment

Early Finishers pp. 234, 246, 254, 263, 292

Extensions p. 295

Section 5 Lessons 41–50, Investigation 5

Math Focus:
Number & Operations

Distributed Strands:
Number & Operations • Measurement • Data Analysis & Probability

Maintaining & Extending

Power Up

Enrichment

Section 6 Lessons 51–60, Investigation 6

Math Focus:
Number & Operations • Problem Solving

Distributed Strands:
Number & Operations • Algebra • Geometry • Problem Solving

Maintaining & Extending

Power Up
Facts pp. 363, 369, 375, 380, 386, 393, 400, 406, 413, 420

Mental Math Strategies pp. 363, 369, 375, 380, 386, 393, 400, 406, 413, 420

Problem Solving Strategies pp. 363, 369, 375, 380, 386, 393, 400, 406, 413, 420

Enrichment
Early Finishers pp. 374, 379, 385, 392, 412, 419, 426

Section 7 Lessons 61–70, Investigation 7

Math Focus:
Number & Operations • Geometry

Distributed Strands:
Number & Operations • Algebra • Geometry • Measurement

Maintaining & Extending

Power Up

Section 8 *Lessons 71–80, Investigation 8*

Math Focus:
Number & Operations • Algebra

Distributed Strands:
Number & Operations • Algebra • Geometry • Measurement

Maintaining & Extending

Power Up

Facts pp. 502, 507, 513, 518, 523, 529, 534, 540, 545, 550

Mental Math Strategies pp. 502, 507, 513, 518, 523, 529, 534, 540, 545, 550

Problem Solving Strategies pp. 502, 507, 513, 518, 523, 529, 534, 540, 545, 550

Enrichment

Early Finishers pp. 512, 517, 522, 528, 539, 544, 549

Extensions p. 561

TABLE OF CONTENTS

Section 9 *Lessons 81–90, Investigation 9*

Math Focus:
Algebra

Distributed Strands:
Number & Operations • Algebra • Geometry • Measurement

Maintaining & Extending

Power Up

Facts pp. 562, 569, 575, 580, 586, 592, 598, 604, 610, 618

Mental Math Strategies pp. 562, 569, 575, 580, 586, 592, 598, 604, 610, 618

Problem Solving Strategies pp. 562, 569, 575, 580, 586, 592, 598, 604, 610, 618

Enrichment

Early Finishers pp. 568, 574, 585, 603, 609, 617, 623

Section 10 *Lessons 91–100, Investigation 10*

Math Focus:
Algebra • Geometry

Distributed Strands:
Number & Operations • Algebra • Geometry • Measurement • Data Analysis & Probability

Maintaining & Extending

Power Up

Facts pp. 631, 636, 642, 648, 653, 660, 668, 677, 686, 693

Mental Math Strategies pp. 631, 636, 642, 648, 653, 660, 668, 677, 686, 693

Problem Solving Strategies pp. 631, 636, 642, 648, 653, 660, 668, 677, 686, 693

Enrichment

Early Finishers pp. 635, 641, 659, 667, 676, 685, 692

Section 11 Lessons 101–110, Investigation 11

Math Focus:
Algebra

Distributed Strands:
Number & Operations • Algebra • Geometry • Measurement • Problem Solving

Maintaining & Extending

Power Up

Enrichment

Section 12 *Lessons 111–120, Investigation 12*

Math Focus:
Algebra • Measurement • Problem Solving

Distributed Strands:
Number & Operations • Algebra • Geometry • Measurement • Problem Solving

Maintaining & Extending

Power Up

Facts pp. 778, 784, 791, 799, 804, 809, 817, 825, 832, 837

Mental Math Strategies pp. 778, 784, 791, 799, 804, 809, 817, 825, 832, 837

Problem Solving Strategies pp. 778, 784, 791, 799, 804, 809, 817, 825, 832, 837

Enrichment

Early Finishers pp. 783, 790, 798, 803, 824, 831

Extensions p. 845

Contents by Strand

This chart gives you an overview of the instruction of math concepts by strand in *Saxon Math* Course 2. The chart shows where in the textbook each topic is taught and references the New Concepts section of a lesson or the instructional part of an Investigation.

	LESSONS
NUMBER AND OPERATIONS	
Numeration	
read and write whole numbers and decimals	1, 5, 31
place value to trillions	5
place value to hundred trillions	5
number line (integers, fractions)	4, 8, 29, 34, 59, 64, 68
number line (rational and irrational numbers)	78, 86
expanded notation	4
comparison symbols ($=, <, >$)	4, 33
comparison symbols ($=, <, >, \leq, \geq$)	4, 78, 93
compare and order rational numbers	33, 86
compare and order real numbers	100
scientific notation	51, 57, 69, 83, 111
Basic operations	
add, subtract, multiply, and divide integers	1, 2 ,3, 4, 6, 11, 12, 13, 52, 68, 73, 91,98, 103
add, subtract, multiply, and divide decimal numbers	1, 35, 45, 83, 111
add, subtract, multiply, and divide fractions and mixed numbers	9, 10, 14, 23, 24, 25, 26, 39, 49, 73, 111; Investigation 1
add, subtract, multiply, and divide algebraic terms	84, 87, 102, 103, 106
mental math strategies	1-120
regrouping in addition, subtraction, and multiplication	2, 23
multiplication notations: $a \times b$, $a \cdot b$, $a(b)$	1
division notations: division box, division sign, and division bar	1
division with remainders	10, 42, 44
Properties of numbers and operations	
even and odd integers	4
factors, multiples, and divisibility	6, 118
prime and composite numbers	21
greatest common factor (GCF)	6, 21, 24
least common multiple (LCM)	27, 30
divisibility tests (2, 3, 5, 9, 10)	6
divisibility tests (4, 6, 8)	6
prime factorization of whole numbers	21, 24, 30, 103, 115
positive exponents of whole numbers, decimals, fractions	20, 83
positive exponents of integers	47, 103
negative exponents of whole numbers	57
square roots	20, 100, 103, 106, 109
cube roots	106
order of operations	2, 52, 63, 85
inverse operations	2, 9, 106

	LESSONS
Estimation	
round whole numbers, decimals, mixed numbers	**29, 33**
estimate sums, differences, products, quotients	**29**
estimate squares and square roots	**29, 100**
determine reasonableness of solution	**29**
approximate irrational numbers	**29, 100**
ALGEBRA	
Ratio and proportional reasoning	
fractional part of a whole, group, set, or number	**8, 14, 22, 60, 71, 72, 74**
equivalent fractions	**15, 24, 27, 48**
convert between fractions, terminating decimals, and percents	**8, 43, 48; Investigation 1**
convert between fractions, repeating decimals, and percents	**43, 48**
reciprocals of numbers	**9, 25**
complex fractions involving one term in numerator/denominator	**25, 76**
identify/find percent of a whole, group, set, or number	**8, 14, 77**
percents greater than 100%	**8**
percent of change	**92**
solve proportions with unknown in one term	**39, 81**
find unit rates and ratios in proportional relationships	**36, 46, 53**
apply proportional relationships such as similarity, scaling, and rates	**46, 54, 55**
estimate and solve application problems involving percent	**81, 110**
estimate and solve application problems involving proportional relationships such as similarity and rate	**46, 54, 98**
Patterns, relations, and functions	
generate a different representation of data given another representation of data	**56, 116, 120; Investigation 9**
use, describe, extend arithmetic sequence (with a constant rate of change)	**4**
input-output tables	**16, 56**
analyze a pattern to verbalize a rule	**4**
analyze a pattern to write an algebraic expression	**56, 87**
evaluate an algebraic expression to extend a pattern	**4, 56**
compare and contrast linear and nonlinear functions	**120**
Variables, expressions, equations, and inequalities	
solve equations using concrete and pictorial models	**87; Investigation 7**
formulate a problem situation for a given equation with one unknown variable	**11, 12, 13, 14**
formulate an equation with one unknown variable given a problem situation	**11, 12, 13, 14, 101**
solve one-step equations with whole numbers	**41; Investigation 7**
solve one-step equations with fractions and decimals	**90; Investigation 7**
solve two-step equations with whole numbers	**93, 102, 108, 109**

	LESSONS
solve two-step equations with fractions and decimals	**93, 108, 110**
graph an inequality on a number line	**78, 86**
solve inequalities with one unknown	**93**
validate an equation solution using mathematical properties	**102, 106, 109**
GEOMETRY	
Describe basic terms	
point	**7, 117**
segment	**7, 117**
ray	**7, 117**
line	**7, 117**
angle	**7, 117**
plane	**7, 117**
Describe properties and relationships of lines	
parallel, perpendicular, and intersecting	**7, 61, 117**
horizontal, vertical, and oblique	**117**
slope	**107, 116, 117**
Describe properties and relationships of angles	
acute, obtuse, right	**7, 62**
straight	**7**
complementary and supplementary	**40**
angles formed by transversals	**102**
angle bisector	**Investigation 10**
vertical angles	**40**
adjacent angles	**40**
calculate to find unknown angle measures	**101, 102**
Describe properties and relationships of polygons	
regular	**18**
interior and exterior angles	**61, 89**
sum of angle measures	**40**
diagonals	**89**
effects of scaling on area	**Investigation 11**
effects of scaling on volume	**98; Investigation 11**
similarity and congruence	**18, 97**
classify triangles	**62**
classify quadrilaterals	**75; Investigation 6**
Use Pythagorean theorem to solve problems	
Pythagorean theorem involving whole numbers	**99, 112**
3-Dimensional figures	
represent in 2-dimensional world using nets	**67; Investigation 12**
draw 3-dimensional figures	**67**

	LESSONS
Coordinate geometry	
name and graph ordered pairs	**56; Investigation 3**
intercepts of a line	**116**
determine slope from the graph of line	**116, 117**
identify reflections, translations, rotations, and symmetry	**58, 80**
graph reflections across the horizontal or vertical axes	**80**
graph translations	**80**
graph linear equations	**56; Investigation 9**
MEASUREMENT	
Measuring physical attributes	
use customary units of length, area, volume, weight, capacity	**16, 70, 79, 82**
use metric units of length, area, volume, weight, capacity	**32, 70, 79, 82, 114**
use temperature scales: Fahrenheit, Celsius	**16, 32**
use units of time	**49**
Systems of measurement	
convert units of measure	**16, 49, 50, 114**
convert between systems	**32**
convert between temperature scales	**108**
unit multipliers	**50, 88**
Solving measurement problems	
perimeter of polygons, circles, complex figures	**19, 65**
area of triangles, rectangles, and parallelograms	**20, 37**
area of trapezoids	**75**
area of circles	**82**
area of semicircles and sectors	**104**
area of complex figures	**75**
surface area of right prisms and cylinders	**105**
surface area of spheres	**105**
estimate area	**79**
volume of right prisms, cylinders, pyramids, and cones	**95, 113, 117, 119**
volume of spheres	**113, 119**
estimate volume	**117, 119**
Solving problems of similarity	
scale factor	**98; Investigation 11**
similar triangles	**97**
indirect measurement	**97**
scale drawings: two-dimensional	**98**
Use appropriate measurement instruments	
ruler (U.S. customary and metric)	**8; Investigation 10**
compass	**Investigations 2, 10**
protractor	**17, 96**
thermometer	**32**

	LESSONS
DATA ANALYSIS AND PROBABILITY	
Data collection and representation	
collect and display data	38; Investigation 5
tables and charts	110; Investigation 9
frequency tables	38
pictographs	38
line graphs	38; Investigation 5
histograms	Investigation 5
bar graphs	38; Investigation 5
circle graphs	38; Investigation 5
Venn diagrams	86
line plots	56
stem-and-leaf plots	Investigation 4
box-and whisker plots	Investigation 4
choose an appropriate graph	38
identify bias in data collection	38
draw and compare different representations	38; Investigation 5
Data set characteristics	
mean, median, mode, and range	28; Investigation 4
select the best measure of central tendency for a given situation	77, 79; Investigation 4
determine trends from data	38
predict from graphs	Investigation 5
recognize misuses of graphical or numerical information	38; Investigation 5
evaluate predictions and conclusions based on data analysis	38
Probability	
experimental probability	Investigation 8
make predictions based on experiments	Investigation 8
accuracy of predictions in experiments	Investigation 8
theoretical probability	Investigation 8
sample spaces	36
simple probability	14
probability of compound events	Investigation 8
probability of the complement of an event	14
probability of independent events	94; Investigation 8
probability of dependent events	94
PROBLEM SOLVING	
Four-step problem-solving process	1-120
Problem-solving strategies	1-120

Section 7 Overview

Lessons 61–70, Investigation 7

Lesson Planner

LESSON	NEW CONCEPTS	MATERIALS	RESOURCES
61	• Area of a Parallelogram • Angles of a Parallelogram	Manipulative Kit: straightedges and protractors Paper, scissors, plastic straws, string, paper clips, graph paper	**Power Up L**
62	• Classifying Triangles	Manipulative Kit: rulers, protractors Colored pencils or markers	**Power Up M** **Lesson Activity 17 Transparency**
63	• Symbols of Inclusion	Calculators, graph paper	**Power Up L** **Investigation Activity 13**
64	• Adding Positive and Negative Numbers	Manipulative Kit: positive and negative number cards 60–100 index cards used to create "number cards"	**Power Up N** **Investigation Activity 13** **Lesson Activity 15 Transparency**
65	• Circumference and Pi	Manipulative Kit: metric tape measure or meter stick and string Circular objects such as paper cups, jar lids and so on; calculators	**Power Up M** **Geometric Formulas** concept poster
66	• Ratio Problems Involving Totals		**Power Up N**
67	• Geometric Solids	Manipulative Kit: Relational GeoSolids	**Power Up M**
68	• Algebraic Addition	Colored pencils	**Power Up N** **Investigation Activity 13** **Investigation Activity 15**
69	• Proper Form of Scientific Notation		**Power Up M**
70	• Volume	Manipulative Kit: wooden color cubes, color tiles	**Power Up N**
Inv. 7	• Balanced Equations	Manipulative Kit: color tiles Balance scale	

Lesson Highlights

Lessons 61–70, Investigation 7

Problem Solving

Strategies

- **Find a Pattern** Lesson 69
- **Make a Table** Lesson 64
- **Make It Simpler** Lessons 66, 68, 69
- **Make an Organized List** Lessons 61, 63
- **Use Logical Reasoning** Lessons 64, 65, 70
- **Draw a Diagram** Lesson 68
- **Write an Equation** Lessons 62, 67
- **Guess and Check** Lessons 65, 66, 70

Real-World Applications

pp. 434, 437–440, 444, 446, 447, 452, 455–457, 462, 463, 465–468, 471, 472, 476–480, 483, 486, 489, 492, 493

4-Step Process

Teacher Edition Lessons 61–70 (Power-Up Discussions)

Communication

Discuss

pp. 432, 433, 435, 448, 466, 485, 497, 500

Summarize

pp. 466, 497, 501

Explain

pp. 444, 467, 468, 470, 482, 486

Formulate a Problem

pp. 470, 484

Connections

Math and Other Subjects

Math and History p. 489
Math and Science pp. 450, 456, 468, 482, 489, 495
Math and Sports pp. 437, 479, 486, 493
Math and Social Studies p. 444

Math to Math

- **Problem Solving and Measurement,** Lessons 61–70
- **Algebra and Problem Solving,** Lessons 61–64, 67, 69, 70, Inv. 7
- **Fractions, Decimals, Percents, and Problem Solving,** Lessons 61–70, Inv. 7
- **Fractions and Measurement,** Lessons 61, 63, 65–70
- **Measurement and Geometry,** Lessons 61–70
- **Probability and Statistics,** Lessons 63, 64, 66, 67, 69, 70

Representation

Manipulatives/Hands On

pp. 433–435, 442, 443, 452, 460, 474, 475, 497

Model

pp. 445, 446, 450, 452, 476, 499

Represent

pp. 437, 444, 449, 452, 468, 477, 487

Formulate an Equation

pp. 437, 444, 451, 458, 478, 488, 494, 501

Technology

Student Resources

- **eBook**
- **Calculator** Lessons 63, 65
- **Online Resources** at www.SaxonPublishers.com/ActivitiesC2
  - **Graphing Calculator Activity** Lesson 65
  - **Real-World Investigation 3** after Lesson 65
  - **Online Activities**
  - **Math Enrichment Problems**
  - **Math Stumpers**

Teacher Resources

- **Resources and Planner CD**
- **Adaptations CD** Lessons 61–70
- **Test & Practice Generator CD**
- **eGradebook**
- **Answer Key CD**

Content Highlights

Lessons 61–70, Investigation 7

Students engage in activities as they connect geometry and measurement skills. Students are introduced to ratio problems that involve totals. They revisit the order of operations and a lesson on symbols of inclusion as these topics are key to success in algebra.

Geometry and Measurement

Geometric concepts are emphasized through student activities.

Students participate in two activities in Lesson 61 as they study parallelograms and learn to calculate their areas. In Lesson 62 students classify triangles by angles and by sides. Students engage in an activity in Lesson 65 to find the ratio of the circumference to the diameter of a circle to experientially determine a value of pi. In Lesson 67 students identify and draw geometric solids and their nets, and they learn to calculate volumes of rectangular solids in Lesson 70.

Problem Solving and Proportional Thinking

Students continue to translate and solve ratio problems.

Solving ratio problems that involve totals can be challenging for students. In Lesson 66 students continue to use a graphic organizer to sort the numbers in the ratio problems to identify the proportion that solves the problem.

Equivalence

Students represent scientific notation in proper form.

Students will learn to solve problems in scientific notation. However, those calculations often generate answers that are not in scientific notation. In Lesson 69 students learn a method for expressing scientific notation in proper form.

Problem Solving and Algebraic Thinking

Special attention is given to "symbols of inclusion" as this is a trouble spot for many students.

There is a growing emphasis on algebra in the second half of this course. Extending order of operations, students work to simplify expressions with multiple grouping symbols in Lesson 63. They learn algebraic methods for adding and subtracting positive and negative numbers in Lessons 64 and 68. In Investigation 7 students view and solve problems displayed as balanced equations while they learn to simplify equations using inverse operations.

Assessment

A variety of weekly assessment tools are provided.

After Lesson 65:
- Power-Up Test 12
- Cumulative Test 12
- Performance Activity 12

After Lesson 70:
- Power-Up Test 13
- Cumulative Test 13
- Customized Benchmark Test
- Performance Task 13

Content Trace

Lessons 61–70, Investigation 7

LESSON	NEW CONCEPTS	PRACTICED	ASSESSED
61	• Area of a Parallelogram	Lessons 61, 63, 66, 72, 74, 85, 87, 90, 94, 96, 99, 102, 117	Tests 13, 17
	• Angles of a Parallelogram	Lessons 61, 63, 64, 66, 68, 72, 74, 87, 102, 103	Test 13
62	• Classifying Triangles	Lessons 62, 63, 64, 65, 66, 67, 68, 69, 71, 73, 74, 76, 79, 89, 91, 99, 113	Test 14
63	• Symbols of Inclusion	Lessons 63, 64, 65, 66, 67, 68, 71, 72, 74, 75, 77, 78, 79, 81, 85, 88, 89, 93, 95, 106, 107, 108, 110, 112, 113	Tests 13, 17, 19, 22
64	• Adding Positive and Negative Numbers	Lessons 64, 65, 66, 67, 72, 75, 87, 90, 93, 94, 97, 99, 111, 112, 113, 114, 115, 116	Tests 13, 17
65	• Circumference and Pi	Lessons 65, 66, 67, 68, 69, 70, 71, 72, 73, 74, 75, 76, 77, 78, 79, 80, 82, 83, 84, 85, 86, 87, 88, 89, 90, 91, 92, 93, 96, 97, 98, 100, 101, 102, 103, 104	Tests 14, 15, 16
66	• Ratio Problems Involving Totals	Lessons 66, 67, 69, 71, 73, 74, 76, 77, 78, 79, 80, 81, 83, 84, 85, 86, 91, 92, 93, 94, 99, 102, 105, 106, 107, 108, 109, 114, 115, 119	Tests 13, 14, 15, 16, 17, 19, 22
67	• Geometric Solids	Lessons 67, 68, 69, 70, 71, 72, 73, 74, 76, 77, 78, 79, 80, 83, 84, 85, 86, 88, 90, 91, 92, 93, 94, 96, 101, 104, 105	Test 14
68	• Algebraic Addition	Lessons 68, 69, 70, 71, 72, 73, 74, 75, 76, 77, 78, 79, 81, 82, 83, 84, 91, 92, 93, 94, 95	Tests 14, 15, 16
69	• Proper Form of Scientific Notation	Lessons 69, 70, 71, 72, 73, 75, 78, 79, 80, 81, 82	Test 14
70	• Volume	Lessons 70, 71, 72, 73, 74, 75, 77, 78, 79, 80, 82, 83, 85, 87, 88, 89, 93, 94, 101, 102, 104, 105, 114, 119, 120	Tests 14, 15, 17, 18
Inv. 7	• Balanced Equations	Lessons 71, 72, 73, 74, 75, 76, 77, 78, 79, 80, 81, 82, 83, 84, 85, 86, 87, 88, 89, 90, 91, 92	Tests 14, 15, 16, 17, 18

• Area of a Parallelogram
• Angles of a Parallelogram

Objectives
- Find the area of a parallelogram.
- Find the measures of the angles of a parallelogram.

Lesson Preparation

Materials
- **Power Up L** in (*Instructional Masters*)
- **Manipulative kit: straightedges and protractors**
- **Teacher-provided material: paper, scissors, plastic straws, string, paper clips, graph paper**

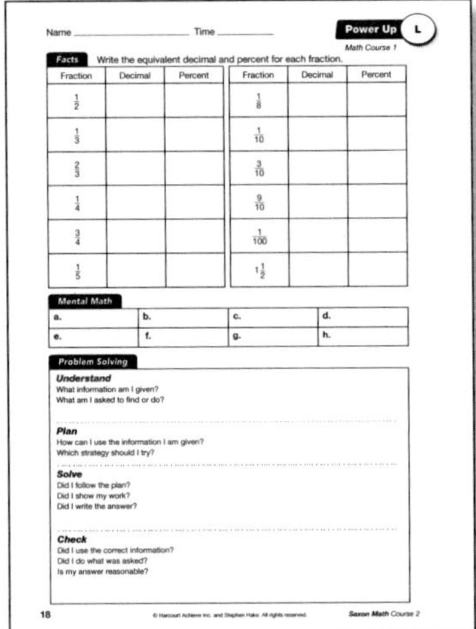
Power Up L

Math Language
English Learners (ESL)
mesh

Technology Resources
Student eBook Complete student textbook in electronic format.

Resources and Planner CD Assessment, reteaching, and instructional masters, plus a pacing calendar with standards.

Test and Practice Generator CD Create additional practice sheets and custom-made tests.

www.SaxonPublishers.com Visit for more student activities and planning materials.

Inclusion

Adaptations CD Adapted lessons, investigations, practice and assessments.

Meeting Standards

National Council of Teachers of Mathematics (NCTM)

Geometry

GM.1a Precisely describe, classify, and understand relationships among types of two- and three-dimensional objects using their defining properties

GM.1b Understand relationships among the angles, side lengths, perimeters, areas, and volumes of similar objects

GM.4d Use geometric models to represent and explain numerical and algebraic relationships

Measurement

ME.2b Select and apply techniques and tools to accurately find length, area, volume, and angle measures to appropriate levels of precision

ME.2c Develop and use formulas to determine the circumference of circles and the area of triangles, parallelograms, trapezoids, and circles and develop strategies to find the area of more-complex shapes

Power-Up Discussion *For use with Power Up, p. 432*

Problem-Solving Strategy: Make an Organized List

A large sheet of paper is 0.1 mm thick. If we tear it in half and stack the two pieces, the resulting stack is 2 pieces of paper, or 0.2 mm high. If we tear that stack of paper in half and stack the remaining halves, the resulting stack is 4 pieces of paper, or 0.4 mm high. If we could continue to tear-in-half and stack, how high would our stack be after 20 times? 25 times?

Understand — *Understand the problem.*

"What information are we given?"

A sheet of paper 0.1 mm thick is torn in half and stacked several times.

"What are we asked to do?"

We are asked to determine about how high the stack of paper would be after it has been torn in half and stacked 20 times and 25 times.

Plan — *Make a plan.*

"What problem-solving strategy will we use?"

We will *make an organized list* and record all the relevant information.

"What information needs to be included in our list?"

We will record the number of tears, the resulting number of the layers, and the height of the resulting stack.

Solve — *Carry out the plan.*

"We begin by filling in the numbers of tears, then we fill in the layers of paper and height of the stack."

Number of Tears:	0	1	2	3	4	5	6	7	8	9	10
Layers of Paper:	1	2	4	8	16	32	64	128	256	512	1024
Height of Stack:	0.1 mm	0.2	0.4	0.8	1.6	3.2	6.4	12.8	25.6	51.2	102.4

Teacher's Note: Take this opportunity to point out that we are only looking for the approximate height of the stack, so we may round 102.4 mm to 100 mm, which is 0.1 m. We adjust to meters and continue doubling. From this point on, the numbers of layers and heights of the stacks are approximations.

Number of Tears:	10	11	12	13	14	15	16	17	18	19	20
Layers of Paper:	1000	2000	4000	8000	16000	32000	64000	128000	256000	512000	1 mil
Height of Stack:	0.1 m	0.2	0.4	0.8	1.6	3.2	6.4	12.8	25.6	51.2	100 m

Number of Tears:	21	22	23	24	25
Layers of Paper:	2 mil	4 mil	8 mil	16 mil	32 mil
Height of Stack:	200 m	400 m	800 m	1600 m	3200 m

Check — *Look back.*

"Did we do what we were asked to do?"

Yes, after 20 tears the stack would be about 100 m tall (roughly the length of a football field), and after 25 tears, the stack would be about 3200 m tall (about 2 miles high).

"How can we use exponents to show the number of layers of paper after 20 and 25 tears?"

2^{20}, 2^{25}

1 Power Up

Facts

Distribute **Power Up L** to students. See answers below.

Mental Math

Encourage students to share different ways to mentally compute these exercises. Strategies for exercises **b** and **h** are listed below.

b. Move the Decimal Point

Place the decimal point in the product.

$2.4 \times 10^{-1} = 0.24$

Divide by 10

$2.4 \times 10^{-1} = 2.4 \times \frac{1}{10^1}$ or $\frac{1}{10}$

$\frac{2.4}{10} = 0.24$

h. Multiply by 6%

$\$20 \times 0.06 = 6 \times 20 = 120$

Move left 2 decimal places: $1.20

$\$20.00 + \$1.20 = \$21.20$

Multiply by 5% and 1%

$\$20 \times 0.05 = \$1$

$\$20 \times 0.01 = \$0.20$

$\$1 + \$0.20 = \$1.20$

$\$20.00 + \$1.20 = \$21.20$

Problem Solving

Refer to **Power-Up Discussion,** p. 432F.

2 New Concepts

Instruction

Begin by asking students to name some real world examples of parallelograms. Examples may include carpets, crackers, and picture frames.

Remind students that in Investigation 6 they learned that all rectangles are parallelograms, but not all parallelograms are rectangles. Explain that the non-rectangular parallelograms are the focus of this lesson.

(continued)

LESSON 61

• Area of a Parallelogram
• Angles of a Parallelogram

Power Up *Building Power*

facts Power Up L

mental math

a. **Decimals:** 50×4.6 230

b. **Decimals/Exponents:** 2.4×10^{-1} 0.24

c. **Ratio:** $\frac{a}{20} = \frac{12}{8}$ 30

d. **Measurement:** Convert 1.5 km to m. 1500 m

e. **Exponents:** $3^2 - 2^3$ 1

f. **Fractional Parts:** $\frac{7}{10}$ of $3.00 $2.10

g. **Geometry:** What type of triangle has three equal sides? equilateral

h. **Calculation:** What is the total cost of a $20 item plus 6% sales tax? $21.20

problem solving

A large sheet of paper is 0.1 mm thick. If we tear it in half and stack the two pieces, the resulting stack is 2 pieces of paper, or 0.2 mm, high. If we tear that stack of paper in half and stack the remaining halves, the resulting stack is 4 pieces of paper, or 0.4 mm high. If we could continue to tear-in-half and stack, how high would our stack be after 20 times? 25 times? 100 m; 3200 m

New Concepts *Increasing Knowledge*

area of a parallelogram

Thinking Skill

Discuss

Why is the figure on the right not a parallelogram? The sides of the third figure are not parallel. If they were extended upward, they would meet.

Recall from Investigation 6 that a parallelogram is a quadrilateral in which both pairs of opposite sides are parallel.

Parallelogram   Parallelogram   Not a parallelogram

In this lesson we will practice finding the areas of parallelograms, but first we will review a couple of terms. Recall that the dimensions of a rectangle are called the length and the width. When describing a parallelogram, we do not use these terms. Instead we use the terms **base** and **height.**

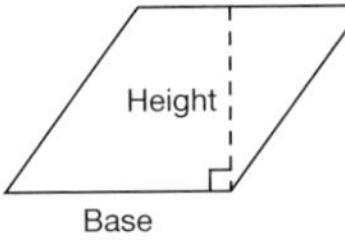

Facts Write the equivalent decimal and percent for each fraction.

Fraction	Decimal	Percent	Fraction	Decimal	Percent
$\frac{1}{2}$	0.5	50%	$\frac{1}{8}$	0.125	$12\frac{1}{2}\%$
$\frac{1}{3}$	$0.\overline{3}$	$33\frac{1}{3}\%$	$\frac{1}{10}$	0.1	10%
$\frac{2}{3}$	$0.\overline{6}$	$66\frac{2}{3}\%$	$\frac{3}{10}$	0.3	30%
$\frac{1}{4}$	0.25	25%	$\frac{9}{10}$	0.9	90%
$\frac{3}{4}$	0.75	75%	$\frac{1}{100}$	0.01	1%
$\frac{1}{5}$	0.2	20%	$1\frac{1}{2}$	1.5	150%

Notice that the height is not one of the sides of the parallelogram (unless the parallelogram is a rectangle). Instead, **the height is perpendicular to the base.**

Activity 1

Area of a Parallelogram

Materials needed:

- Paper
- Scissors
- Straightedge

Cut a piece of paper to form a parallelogram as shown. You may use graph paper if available.

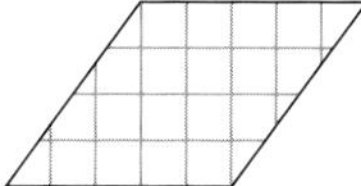

Next, sketch a segment perpendicular to two of the parallel sides of the parallelogram. The length of this segment is the height of the parallelogram. Cut the parallelogram into two pieces along the segment you drew.

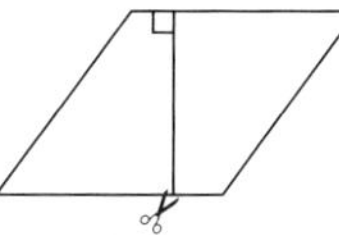

Finally, reverse the positions of the two pieces and fit them together to form a rectangle. The area of the original parallelogram equals the area of this rectangle.

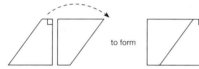

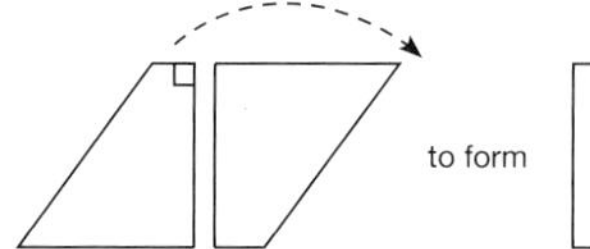

To conclude this activity, answer these questions:

1. What dimensions of the original parallelogram match the length and width of this rectangle? The base of the original parallelogram corresponds to the length of the rectangle. Its height corresponds to the width of the rectangle.
2. How would you find the area of the rectangle? To find the area of the rectangle, we would multiply the length and the width.
3. Discuss How would you find the area of the original parallelogram?

To find the area of the original parallelogram, we would multiply the base and the height.

Activity 1

Instruction

Ask students to recall what the term **perpendicular** means and how it can be represented in a figure. Perpendicular is a word that describes two lines or line segments that meet or intersect to form a right angle. It can be represented by the right angle symbol.

Explain to students that the height of a parallelogram can be found inside or outside the parallelogram just as long as it is perpendicular to the base.

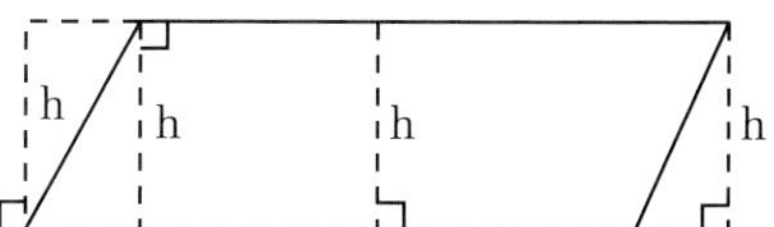

Problem 3 Discuss

"Is the perimeter of the rectangle equal to the perimeter of the parallelogram? Explain how you know." no, two sides of the parallelogram are longer than two sides of the rectangle.

Math Background

Can the areas of a triangle and a parallelogram be related?

Yes, the areas are related if the base and height of the triangle have the same measure as the base and height of the parallelogram. The area of the parallelogram is twice the area of the triangle. This relationship can be determined with a physical model of two congruent triangles. Show cutouts of two congruent triangles individually. Then place the triangles together, turning one triangle to align with the corresponding side of the other triangle to make a parallelogram with the same base and height as each triangle. Also, consider the formulas for the area of a triangle and a parallelogram, respectively: $A = \frac{1}{2}bh$ and $A = bh$.

2 New Concepts (Continued)

Example 1

Instruction

Before starting example 1, remind students that perimeter is expressed in units of length, such as inches or centimeters, while area is described in square units, such as square inches (in.^{2}) or square centimeters (cm^2)

(continued)

Activity 2

Instruction

Students may find it easier to thread the string through their straws if they attach the string to an opened, lightweight paper clip.

(continued)

As we see in Activity 1, the area of the rectangle equals the area of the parallelogram we are considering. Thus we find the area of a parallelogram by multiplying its base by its height.

Area of a parallelogram = base · height

$$A = bh$$

Example 1

Parallelogram Park is a small park in town with the dimensions shown. Find a. the perimeter of the park and b. its area.

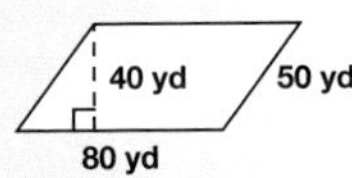

Solution

a. The perimeter is the distance around the park. We add the lengths of the sides. Opposite sides of a parallelogram are the same length.

50 yd + 80 yd + 50 yd + 80 yd = **260 yd**

b. We multiply the base and height to find the area.

80 yd × 40 yd = **3200 sq. yd**

angles of a parallelogram

Figures J and K of Investigation 6 illustrated a "straw" rectangle shifted to form a parallelogram that was not a rectangle. Two of the angles became obtuse angles, and the other two angles became acute angles.

Figure J   Figure K

In other words, two of the angles became more than 90°, and two of the angles became less than 90°. Each angle became greater than or less than 90° *by the same amount.* If, by shifting the sides of the straw rectangle, the obtuse angles became 10° *greater than* 90° (100° angles), then the acute angles became 10° *less than* 90° (80° angles). The following activity illustrates this relationship.

Activity 2

Angles of a Parallelogram

Materials needed:

- Protractor
- Paper
- Two pairs of plastic straws (The straws within a pair must be the same length. The two pairs may be different lengths.)
- Thread or lightweight string
- Paper clip for threading the straws (optional)

Teacher Tip

Make a **sample straw rectangle** before class to use as a demonstration tool. You may want to tape two or three straws together so it is large enough for the whole class to see.

Make a "straw" parallelogram by running a string or thread through two pairs of plastic straws. If the pairs of straws are of different lengths, alternate the lengths as you thread them (long-short-long-short).

Bring the two ends of the string together, pull until the string is snug but not bowing the straws, and tie a knot.

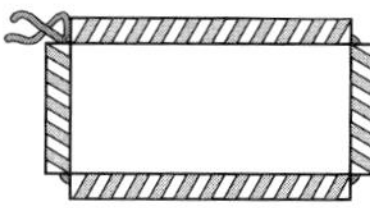

You should be able to shift the sides of the parallelogram to various positions.

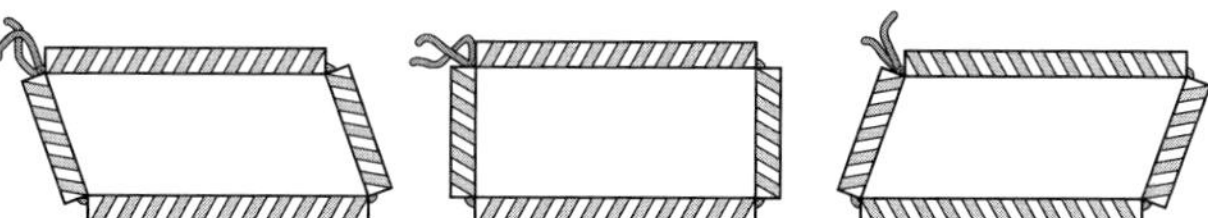

Lay the straw parallelogram on a desktop with a piece of paper under it. On the paper you will trace the parallelogram. Shift the parallelogram into a position you want to measure, hold the straws and paper still (this may require more than two hands), and carefully trace with a pencil around the *inside* of the parallelogram.

Set the straw parallelogram aside, and use a protractor to measure each angle of the traced parallelogram. Write the measure inside each angle. Some groups may wish to trace and measure the angles of a second parallelogram with a different shape before answering the questions below.

1. What were the measures of the two obtuse angles of one parallelogram?
2. What were the measures of the two acute angles of the same parallelogram?
3. What was the sum of the measures of one obtuse angle and one acute angle of the same parallelogram?

If you traced two parallelograms, answer the three questions again for the second parallelogram.

Record several groups' answers on the board.

Discuss Can any general conclusions be formed?

Yes. Samples: Opposite angles of a parallelogram are equal.; A parallelogram contains two acute angles and two obtuse angles.

The quality of all types of measurement is affected by the quality of the measuring instrument, the material being measured, and the person performing the measurement. However, even rough measurements can suggest underlying relationships. The rough measurements performed in activity 2 should suggest the relationships between the angles of a parallelogram shown on the next page.

Activity 2 *(Continued)*

Instruction

You may wish to post each group's answers in one large chart on the board. Using several examples, generalize the relationships between the angles. Use the terms *adjacent angles* and *nonadjacent angles* as you analyze the data.

Have students explain why a parallelogram cannot have four acute angles. Sample: The sum of the measures of the angles in a parallelogram equals 360°. Therefore, if all of the angles were less than 90°, the sum of these four angles would be less than 360°.

2 New Concepts (Continued)

Example 2

Instruction

Ask students to write an equation for the total angle measure of the parallelogram.
Sample: $2(110°) + 2(180° - 110°) = 360°$

Practice Set

Problems a–c Generalize

"How can you identify which measurement of each parallelogram is the height?" Sample: The height is perpendicular to the base so a right angle symbol indicates which segment is the height.

Problems d–g Conclude

Ask student volunteers how they determined the measure of each angle.

"What is the relationship between ∠d and the 75° angle?" supplementary angles

1. Nonadjacent angles (angles in opposite corners) have equal measures.
2. Adjacent angles (angles that share a common side) are supplementary—that is, their sum is 180°.

Conclude What is the sum of the measures of the angles of the parallelogram? How does this sum compare to the sum of the measures of the angles of a rectangle? 360°, they are equal

Example 2

In parallelogram *ABCD*, m∠*D* is 110°. Find the measures of angles *A*, *B*, and *C* in the parallelogram.

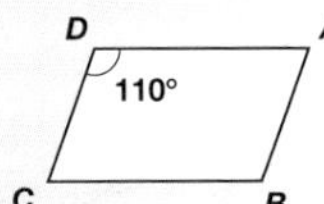

Solution

Nonadjacent angles, like ∠*B* and ∠*D*, have equal measures, so **m∠*B* = 110°.** Adjacent angles are supplementary, and both ∠*A* and ∠*C* are adjacent to ∠*D*, so **m∠*A* = 70°** and **m∠*C* = 70°.**

Practice Set ▶ Generalize Find the perimeter and area of each parallelogram. Dimensions are in centimeters.

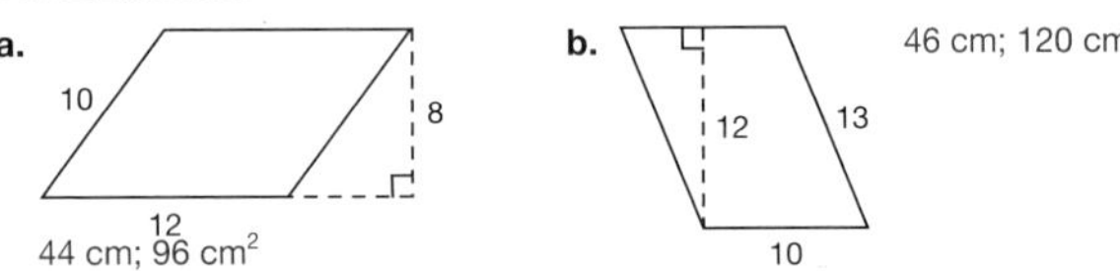

a. 44 cm; 96 cm^2

b. 46 cm; 120 cm^2

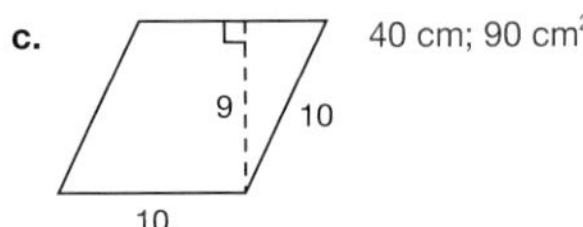

c. 40 cm; 90 cm^2

▶ Conclude For problems **d–g,** find the measures of the angles marked *d*, *e*, *f*, and *g* in this parallelogram.

d. 105°
e. 75°
f. 105°
g. 75°

Figure *ABCD* is a parallelogram. Refer to this figure to find the measures of the angles in problems **h–j.**

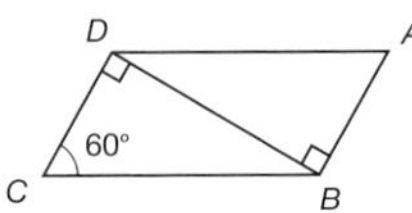

h. ∠*A* 60° **i.** ∠*ADB* 30° **j.** ∠*ABC* 120°

▶ See Math Conversations in the sidebar.

i. No; the boards remained the same length. Yes; The area did change (from 2400 in.^{2} to 2250 in.^{2}) As the frame shifts, the area decreases. If the frame is shifted completely, the area becomes zero.

k. Write a formula for the area of a parallelogram. $A = bh$

l. Sid built a rectangular door frame 80 inches tall and 30 inches wide. The frame was bumped before it was installed so that the top was only 75 inches above the base. Did the perimeter of the frame change? Did the area within the frame change? Explain your answers.

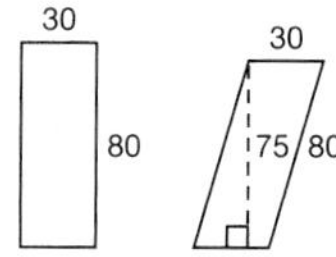

Written Practice

Strengthening Concepts

▶ **1.** (16, 46) **Justify** If $\frac{1}{2}$ gallon of milk costs \$1.64, what is the cost per pint? \$0.41 per pint

*** 2.** (54) Use a ratio box to solve this problem. The muffin recipe called for oatmeal and brown sugar in the ratio of 2 to 1. If 3 cups of oatmeal were called for, how many cups of brown sugar were needed? $1\frac{1}{2}$ cups

▶ *** 3.** (55) **Analyze** Ricardo ran the 400-meter race 3 times. His fastest time was 54.3 seconds. His slowest time was 56.1 seconds. If his average time was 55.0 seconds, what was his time for the third race? 54.6 seconds

4. (46) It is $4\frac{1}{2}$ miles to the end of the bicycle trail. If Sakari rides to the end of the trail and back in 60 minutes, what is her average speed in miles per hour? 9 miles per hour

▶ **5.** (51) Sixty-three million, one hundred thousand is how much greater than seven million, sixty thousand? Write the answer in scientific notation. 5.604×10^7

6. (36, 48) Only three tenths of the print area of the newspaper carried news. The rest of the area was filled with advertisements.

a. What percent of the print area was filled with advertisements? 70%

b. What was the ratio of news area to advertisement area? $\frac{3}{7}$

c. If, without looking, Kali opens the newspaper and places a finger on the page, what is the probability that her finger will be on an advertisement? $\frac{7}{10}$

▶ *** 7.** (51, 57) **a.** **Represent** Write 0.00105 in scientific notation. 1.05×10^{-3}

b. Write 3.02×10^5 in standard form. 302,000

▶ **8.** (24) **a.** Use prime factorization to reduce $\frac{128}{192}$. $\frac{2}{3}$

b. What is the greatest common factor of 128 and 192? 64

▶ See Math Conversations in the sidebar.

3 Written Practice

Math Conversations

Discussion opportunities are provided below.

Problem 1 Justify

Before students answer this problem, have them recall the units for capacity and their equivalences. Be sure to discuss gallons, quarts, and pints.

"What does a gallon cost?" \$3.28

"What does a quart cost?" \$0.82

Problem 3 Analyze

Most students will solve this as a three-step problem. Ask them to describe the process they used. Sample: add 54.3 and 56.1 and subtract it from the product of 55 × 3

Then challenge students to write one equation that can be used to solve the problem. Let t represent Ricardo's time for the third race. $\frac{54.3 + 56.1 + t}{3} = 55.0$

Problem 7 Represent

Sometimes newspapers use the terms 1.8 million or 1.8 billion.

"How would you write 1.8 million in standard form? Explain how you know your answer is correct." Sample: 1.8 million is the same as 1.8×10^6 because there are 6 zeros after the 1 in 1 million. Move the decimal point six places to the right. 1.8 million = 1.8×10^6 or 1,800,000

"How would you write 1.8 billion using scientific notation?" 1.8 billion = 1.8×10^9 or 1,800,000,000

Errors and Misconceptions

Problem 5

If students are having difficulty, suggest that they write the numbers in standard numerical form to find the difference. They can then rewrite the answer in scientific notation.

Problem 8

Watch for students who do not completely simplify the fraction. The prime factorizations are:

numerator: $2 \cdot 2 \cdot 2 \cdot 2 \cdot 2 \cdot 2 \cdot 2$

denominator: $2 \cdot 2 \cdot 2 \cdot 2 \cdot 2 \cdot 2 \cdot 3$

(continued)

English Learners

To help with the meaning of the word **mesh** in problem l, say:

"A mesh is used to separate small objects from large objects. A wire mesh uses pieces of wire that are woven together like this."

Draw a rectangle on the board and cover it with a series of crossed lines. Ask students for examples of things they could separate with a mesh. Samples: large rocks from small rocks, spaghetti from water, tea leaves from tea

3 Written Practice (Continued)

Math Conversations

Discussion opportunities are provided below.

Problem 10 Classify

Suggest that students draw this figure on their paper and label all the segments. Encourage students to trace figures *ECBF* and *ECBA* to help distinguish between the two quadrilaterals.

Problem 11 Analyze

"The area of triangle ABF plus the area of triangle EDC is equal to what fractional part of the area of rectangle ABDE?" one fourth

Problem 14c Analyze

"Does the parallelogram have line symmetry" No

"Explain your answer." No line drawn on the parallelogram will create mirror-image figures. If the sides of the parallelogram were equal in length, it would have line symmetry.

Errors and Misconceptions

Problem 11a

For students who don't know how to begin solving this problem, help them to determine the height and base of *BCEF*.

(continued)

9. (50) Use a unit multiplier to convert 1760 yards to feet.
1760 yards $\frac{3 \text{ feet}}{1 \text{ yard}}$ = 5280 feet

In the figure below, quadrilateral *ABDE* is a rectangle and $\overline{EC} \parallel \overline{FB}$. Refer to the figure to answer problems **10–12.**

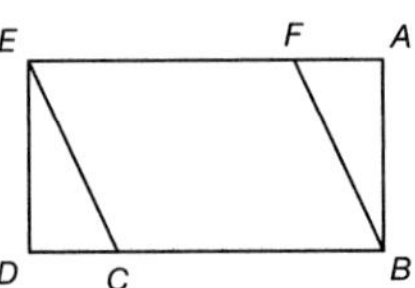

▶ * **10.** (Inv. 6) Classify What type of quadrilateral is:

a. quadrilateral *ECBF* parallelogram

b. quadrilateral *ECBA* trapezoid

* **11.** (37, 61) Analyze If *AB* = *ED* = 4 m, *BC* = *EF* = 6 m, and *BD* = *AE* = 8 m, then

▶ **a.** what is the area of quadrilateral *BCEF*? 24 m^2

b. what is the area of triangle *ABF*? 4 m^2

c. what is the area of quadrilateral *ECBA*? 28 m^2

12. (7) Classify each of the following angles as acute, right, or obtuse:

a. ∠*ECB* obtuse angle **b.** ∠*EDC* right angle **c.** ∠*FBA* acute angle

13. (Inv. 4) The following is an ordered list of the number of used cars sold in 19 days during the month of May. Find the following for this set of numbers:

a. median 8 **b.** first quartile 6

c. third quartile 9 **d.** any outliers the number 2

2, 5, 5, 6, 6, 6, 7, 7, 7, 8, 8, 8, 8, 9, 9, 10, 10, 10, 10

* **14.** (Inv. 6, 61) A park in the shape of a parallelogram has the dimensions shown in this figure. Refer to the figure to answer **a–c.**

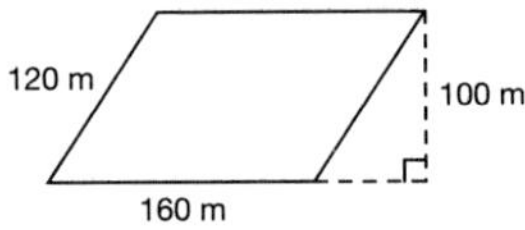

a. If Clyde walks around the park once, how far does he walk? 560 m

b. What is the area of the park? 16,000 m^2

▶ **c.** Analyze Does the parallelogram have rotational symmetry? yes, order 2

* **15.** (40, 61) The parallelogram at right is divided by a diagonal into two congruent triangles. Find the measure of

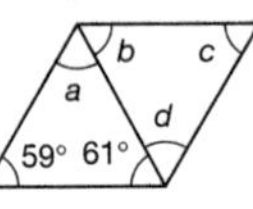

a. ∠*a.* 60° **b.** ∠*b.* 61°

c. ∠*c.* 59° **d.** ∠*d.* 60°

▶ See Math Conversations in the sidebar.

16. Tara noticed that the tape she was using to wrap packages was (50) 2 centimeters wide. How many meters wide was the tape? 0.02 meter

17. A circle is drawn on a coordinate plane with its center at the origin. The (Inv. 3) circle intersects the x-axis at (5, 0) and (−5, 0).

a. At what coordinates does the circle intersect the y-axis? (0, 5), (0, −5)

b. What is the diameter of the circle? 10 units

18. The scale is balanced so the 3 items on the left have a total mass of 50 g. The labeled masses total 15 g, so the cube must be 35 g because 35 g + 15 g = 50 g.

18. On one tray of a balanced scale was a 50-g (3) mass. On the other tray were a small cube, a 10-g mass, and a 5-g mass. What was the mass of the small cube? Describe how you found your answer.

▶* 19. **Analyze** The trail Paula runs begins at 27 feet below sea level and (59) ends at 164 feet above sea level. What is the gain in elevation from the beginning to the end of the trail? 191 feet

Generalize Simplify:

▶ 20. $10 + 10 \times 10 - 10 \div 10$ 109 (52)

* 21. $2^0 - 2^{-3}$ $\frac{7}{8}$ (57)

22. 4.5 m + 70 cm = 5.2 m (34)

* 23. $2.75 \text{ L} \cdot \frac{1000 \text{ mL}}{1 \text{ L}}$ 2750 mL (50)

24. $5\frac{7}{8} + \left(3\frac{1}{3} - 1\frac{1}{2}\right)$ $7\frac{17}{24}$ (23, 30)

25. $4\frac{4}{5} \cdot 1\frac{1}{9} \cdot 1\frac{7}{8}$ 10 (26)

26. $6\frac{2}{3} \div \left(3\frac{1}{5} \div 8\right)$ $16\frac{2}{3}$ (26)

27. $12 - (0.8 + 0.97)$ 10.23 (35)

28. $(2.4)(0.05)(0.005)$ 0.0006 (35)

29. $0.2 \div (4 \times 10^2)$ 0.0005 (47)

30. $0.36 \div (4 \div 0.25)$ 0.0225 (45)

Early Finishers
Real-World Application

Ida's Country Kitchen Restaurant has 6 different main courses.

Chicken and dumplings \$9.00
Fish and wild rice \$11.00
Steak with baked potato \$28.00
Vegetable Stew with tofu \$9.00
Pasta with vegetables \$8.00
Spinach Salad with garlic bread \$7.00

Use the mean, median, mode, and range to describe the meal prices. Which measure best describes the price of a typical meal at this restaurant? Justify your choice. mean \$12; median \$9; mode \$9; range \$21; Sample: The median or mode gives the best description because most of the meals are between \$7 and \$9.

▶ See Math Conversations in the sidebar.

3 Written Practice (Continued)

Math Conversations

Discussion opportunities are provided below.

Problem 19 Analyze

Discuss with students why they should add the two numbers rather than subtract them.

Problem 20 Generalize

Have student explain why parentheses are not required for this problem. order of operations indicates that you multiply and divide from left to right before you add and subtract from left to right; multiply 10 × 10 and divide 10 ÷ 10 before you add and subtract

Looking Forward

Understanding the area and angles of a parallelogram prepares students for:

- **Lesson 75,** finding the area of complex figures.
- **Lesson 82,** finding the area of circles.

• Classifying Triangles

Objectives

- Classify a triangle by its angles.
- Order the sides of a triangle from shortest to longest when given only the measures of the angles.
- Classify a triangle by its sides.

Lesson Preparation

Materials

- **Power Up M** (in *Instructional Masters*)

Optional

- **Manipulative kit: rulers, protractors**
- **Lesson Activity 17** (in *Instructional Masters*)
- **Teacher-provided material: colored pencils or markers**

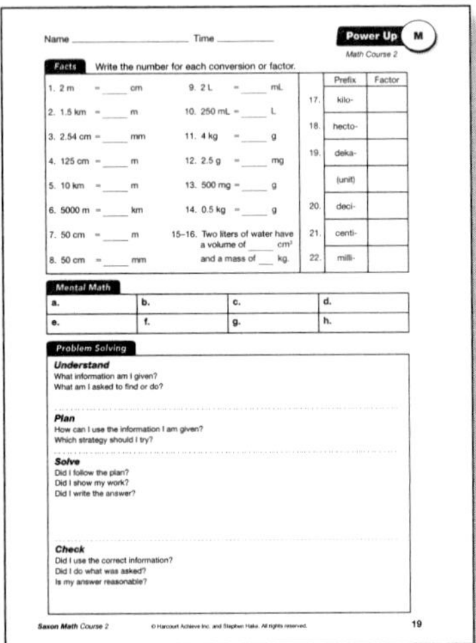

Name ____________ Time ________

Power Up M
Math Course 2

Facts Write the number for each conversion or factor.

1. 2 m = ____ cm
2. 1.5 km = ____ m
3. 2.54 cm = ____ mm
4. 125 cm = ____ m
5. 10 km = ____ m
6. 5000 m = ____ km
7. 50 cm = ____ m
8. 50 cm = ____ mm
9. 2 L = ____ mL
10. 250 mL = ____ L
11. 4 kg = ____ g
12. 2.5 g = ____ mg
13. 500 mg = ____ g
14. 0.5 kg = ____ g

15–16. Two liters of water have a volume of ____ cm^3 and a mass of ____ kg.

	Prefix	Factor
17.	kilo-	
18.	hecto-	
19.	deka-	
	(unit)	
20.	deci-	
21.	centi-	
22.	milli-	

Mental Math

a.	b.	c.	d.
e.	f.	g.	h.

Problem Solving

Understand
What information am I given?
What am I asked to find or do?

Plan
How can I use the information I am given?
Which strategy should I try?

Solve
Did I follow the plan?
Did I show my work?
Did I write the answer?

Check
Did I use the correct information?
Did I do what was asked?
Is my answer reasonable?

Saxon Math Course 2 © Harcourt Achieve Inc. and Stephen Hake. All rights reserved. 19

Power Up M

Math Language

New		English Learners (ESL)
acute triangle	obtuse triangle	opposite
equilateral triangle	right triangle	
isosceles triangle	scalene triangle	

Technology Resources

Student eBook Complete student textbook in electronic format.

Resources and Planner CD Assessment, reteaching, and instructional masters, plus a pacing calendar with standards.

Test and Practice Generator CD Create additional practice sheets and custom-made tests.

www.SaxonPublishers.com Visit for more student activities and planning materials.

Inclusion

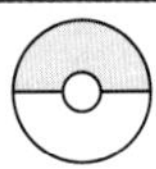

Adaptations CD Adapted lessons, investigations, practice and assessments.

Meeting Standards

National Council of Teachers of Mathematics (NCTM)

Geometry

GM.1a Precisely describe, classify, and understand relationships among types of two- and three-dimensional objects using their defining properties

GM.4a Draw geometric objects with specified properties, such as side lengths or angle measures

GM.4e Recognize and apply geometric ideas and relationships in areas outside the mathematics classroom, such as art, science, and everyday life

Communication

CM.3a Organize and consolidate their mathematical thinking through communication

CM.3b Communicate their mathematical thinking coherently and clearly to peers, teachers, and others

Power-Up Discussion *For use with Power Up, p. 440*

Problem-Solving Strategy: Write an Equation

Michelle's grandfather taught her this method for converting kilometers to miles: "Divide the kilometers by 8, and then multiply by 5." Michelle's grandmother taught her this method: "Multiply the kilometers by 0.6." Use both of these methods to convert 80 km to miles. Do both methods produce the same result?

Understand — *Understand the problem.*

"What information are we given?"

Michelle's grandparents taught her two methods for converting kilometers to miles:

1. Divide the km by 8 and then multiply by 5.
2. Multiply the km by 0.6.

"What are we asked to do?"

We are asked to use both methods to convert 80 km into miles.

Plan — *Make a plan.*

"What problem-solving strategy will we use?"

We will *write an equation* to solve with both methods.

"Is a mile larger or smaller than a kilometer?"

A mile is larger.

"Therefore, do we expect the number of miles to be greater than or less than the number of kilometers?"

less than

Solve — *Carry out the plan.*

"How would we write each equation?"

Grandfather's method: $(K \div 8) \times 5 = M$
Grandmother's method: $K \times 0.6 = M$

"How many miles is 80 kilometers using the grandfather's method?"

$(80 \div 8) \times 5 = 10 \times 5 = 50$ miles

"How many miles is 80 kilometers using the grandmother's method?"

$80 \times 0.6 = 48$ miles

"Do both methods produce the same result?"

No, but they are close. For the purposes of approximation, either method appears to work.

Check — *Look back.*

"Did we do what we were asked to do?"

Yes, we analyzed the methods that Michelle's grandparents taught her and determined that they do not produce the same result.

"One kilometer approximately equals 0.621 miles. Are the approximations we found reasonable?"

Yes, using 1 km $\approx$ 0.621 mi, 80 km $\approx$ 49.68 mi, which is close to both our approximations. Our approximations are both reasonable.

LESSON 62

• Classifying Triangles

1 Power Up

Facts

Distribute **Power Up M** to students. See answers below.

Mental Math

Encourage students to share different ways to mentally compute these exercises. Strategies for exercises **a** and **e** are listed below.

a. Distributive Property

$5 \times 8.6 = (5 \times 8) + (5 \times 0.6)$

$40 + 3.0$ or 43

Equivalent Expression

$5 \times 8.6 = 10 \times 4.3$ or 43

e. Subtract the Exponents

$10^{3-3} = 10^0$ or 1

Divide and Cancel

$\frac{\overset{1}{\cancel{10}} \cdot \overset{1}{\cancel{10}} \cdot \overset{1}{\cancel{10}}}{\underset{1}{\cancel{10}} \cdot \underset{1}{\cancel{10}} \cdot \underset{1}{\cancel{10}}} = \frac{1}{1}$ or 1

Problem Solving

Refer to **Power-Up Discussion,** p. 440B.

2 New Concepts

Instruction

Draw several angles on the board. Have students label them *acute, right,* and *obtuse.* Then have another set of students erase the arrowheads from the rays of the angles. Ask them to connect these ends with a line segment to make triangles from the angles. Point out that the labels are still correct.

Emphasize that a triangle must have three acute angles to be called an acute triangle.

Illustrate on the board that a triangle cannot have two angles equal to or greater than a right angle.

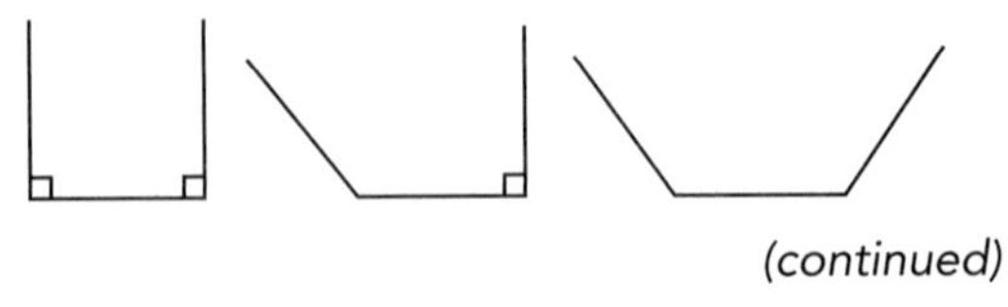

(continued)

Power Up — *Building Power*

facts Power Up M

mental math

a. **Calculation:** 5×8.6 43

b. **Decimals/Exponents:** 2.5×10^{-2} 0.025

c. **Algebra:** $10x + 2 = 32$ 3

d. **Measurement:** Convert 2500 g to kg. 2.5 kg

e. **Exponents:** $10^3 \div 10^3$ 1

f. **Fractional Parts:** $\frac{2}{3}$ of \$24.00 \$16.00

g. **Geometry:** What is the name for a regular quadrilateral? square

h. **Calculation:** 8^2, -4, $\div 2$, $\times 3$, $+10$, $\sqrt{\ }$, $\times 2$, $+5$, $\sqrt{\ }$, -4, square that number, -1 0

problem solving

Michelle's grandfather taught her this method for converting kilometers to miles: "Divide the kilometers by 8, and then multiply by 5." Michelle's grandmother taught her this method: "Multiply the kilometers by 0.6." Use both of these methods to convert 80 km to miles. Do both methods produce the same result? Grandfather's method: 50 miles. Grandmother's method: 48 miles.

New Concept — *Increasing Knowledge*

Recall from Lesson 7 that we classify angles as acute angles, right angles, and obtuse angles.

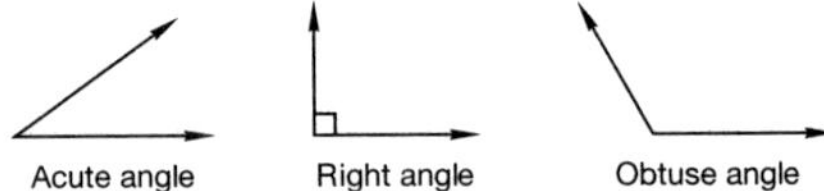

Thinking Skills

Analyze

Can a triangle have two obtuse angles? Explain. No; Sample: A triangle has three angles whose sum is 180°. The sum of two obtuse angles would be greater than 180°.

We use the same words to describe triangles that contain these angles. If every angle of a triangle measures less than 90°, then the triangle is an **acute triangle.** If the triangle contains a 90° angle, then the triangle is a **right triangle.** An **obtuse triangle** contains one angle that measures more than 90°.

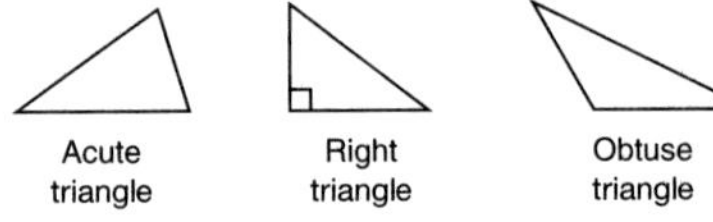

Facts Write the number for each conversion or factor.

1. 2 m = 200 cm	9. 2 L = 2000 mL	
2. 1.5 km = 1500 m	10. 250 mL = 0.25 L	
3. 2.54 cm = 25.4 mm	11. 4 kg = 4000 g	
4. 125 cm = 1.25 m	12. 2.5 g = 2500 mg	
5. 10 km = 10,000 m	13. 500 mg = 0.5 g	
6. 5000 m = 5 km	14. 0.5 kg = 500 g	
7. 50 cm = 0.5 m	15–16. Two liters of water have a volume of 2000 cm³	
8. 50 cm = 500 mm	and a mass of 2 kg.	

	Prefix	Factor
17.	kilo-	1000
18.	hecto-	100
19.	deka-	10
	(unit)	1
20.	deci-	0.1
21.	centi-	0.01
22.	milli-	0.001

When describing triangles, we can refer to the sides and angles as "opposite" each other. For example, we might say, "The side opposite the right angle is the longest side of a right triangle." The side opposite an angle is the side the angle opens toward. In this right triangle, $\overline{AB}$ is the side opposite $\angle C$, and $\angle C$ is the angle opposite side AB.

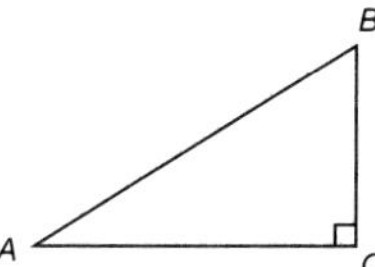

The lengths of the sides of a triangle are in the same order as the measures of their opposite angles. This means that the longest side of a triangle is opposite the largest angle, and the shortest side is opposite the smallest angle.

Example 1

Name the sides of this triangle in order from shortest to longest.

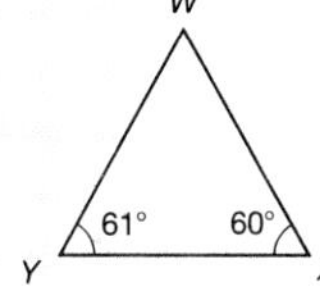

Solution

The sum of the measures of all three angles is 180°, so the measure of $\angle W$ is 59°. Since $\angle W$ is the smallest of the three angles, the side opposite $\angle W$, which is $\overline{XY}$, is the shortest side. The next angle in order of size is $\angle X$, so $\overline{YW}$ is the second longest side. The largest angle is $\angle Y$, so $\overline{WX}$ is the longest side. So the sides in order are

$$\overline{XY}, \overline{YW}, \overline{WX}$$

If two angles of a triangle are the same measure, then their opposite sides are the same length.

Example 2

Which sides of this triangle are the same length?

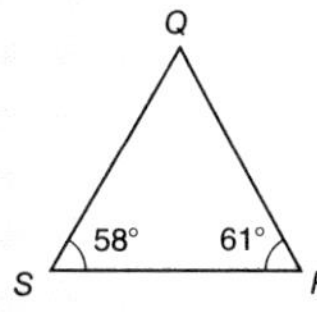

Solution

First we find that the measure of $\angle Q$ is 61°. So angles Q and R have the same measure. This means their opposite sides are the same length. The side opposite $\angle Q$ is $\overline{SR}$. The side opposite $\angle R$ is $\overline{SQ}$. So the sides that are the same length are $\overline{SR}$ and $\overline{SQ}$.

2 New Concepts (Continued)

Instruction

Copy $\triangle ABC$ on the board. Then model how to identify the side opposite each angle in the triangle. Remind students that each side can be correctly named two ways. For example, $\overline{AB}$ of $\triangle ABC$ may also be called $\overline{BA}$.

Example 1

Instruction

Ask a student volunteer to model this example at the board step by step.

Step 1: Write in the measures of all 3 angles. Have the student explain how to find the angle measure of the unknown angle.

Step 2: Write the word *shortest* near side $\overline{XY}$. Have the student explain why it is the shortest side.

Step 3: Write the word *longest* near side $\overline{WX}$. Have the student explain why it is the longest side.

Then, have the student write the side names in order from shortest to longest.

Example 2

Instruction

"Since you are looking for two sides that are the same length, what do you know about $\angle Q$?" It must be equal to one of the other angles.

"What kind of a triangle has all 3 sides the same length and all 3 angles the same measure?" equilateral

(continued)

Math Background

Can any three lengths form a triangle?

No, a triangle has 3 sides but not three sides of any length.

Three lengths can form a triangle only if the lengths are positive numbers and the sum of the lengths of any two sides is greater than the length of the third side.

- Side lengths of 3 inches, 4 inches, and 5 inches form a triangle because $3 + 4 > 5$; $4 + 5 > 3$; and $3 + 5 > 4$
- Side lengths of 3 inches, 4 inches, and 4 inches form a triangle because $3 + 4 > 4$ and $4 + 4 > 3$
- Side lengths of 3 inches, 4 inches, and 8 inches do not form a triangle because $3 + 4 < 8$

English Learners

Before example 1 explain the meaning of **opposite**. Say:

"The side opposite an angle is the side across from or facing the angle."

Ask students what is opposite their desk, classroom, school, and house.

2 New Concepts (Continued)

Example 3

After discussing the solution to example 3, ask students to answer the following questions:

"Are all equilateral triangles similar? Explain." Yes, they all have the same shape.

"Are all equilateral triangles congruent? Explain." No, not all equilateral triangles are the same size.

Instruction

As you discuss the diagram of the isosceles and equilateral triangles, ask students to pay close attention to the tick marks on the triangles. These tick marks indicate angles of equal measure and sides of equal length.

Students may find it helpful to discuss the origin of the math vocabulary words.

isos·ce·les: *isos* from the Greek word for equal; *skelos* from the Greek word for leg

An isosceles trapezoid has two sides the same length.

sca·lene: from the Greek word *skalenos* meaning to hoe the ground and make it uneven

(continued)

If all three angles of a triangle are the same measure, then all three sides are the same length.

Example 3

In triangle JKL, $JK = KL = LJ$. Find the measure of $\angle J$.

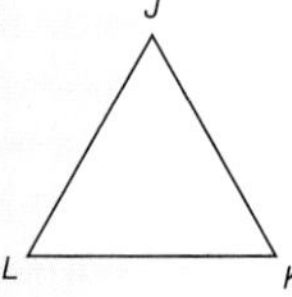

Solution

If two or more sides of a triangle are the same length, then the angles opposite those sides are equal in measure. In $\triangle JKL$ all three sides are the same length, so all three angles have the same measure. The angles equally share 180°. We find the measure of each angle by dividing 180° by 3.

$$180° \div 3 = 60°$$

We find that the measure of $\angle J$ is **60°.**

The triangle in example 3 is a regular triangle. We usually call a regular triangle an **equilateral triangle.** As shown below, the three angles of an equilateral triangle each measure 60°, and the three sides are the same length. The tick marks on the sides indicate sides of equal length, while tick marks on the arcs indicate angles of equal measure.

Equilateral triangle

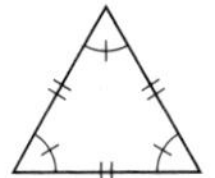

- Three equal sides
- Three equal angles

If a triangle has at least two sides of the same length (and thus two angles of the same measure), then the triangle is called an **isosceles triangle.** The triangle in example 2 is an isosceles triangle, as are each of these triangles:

Isosceles triangles

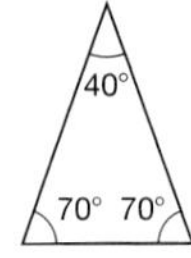

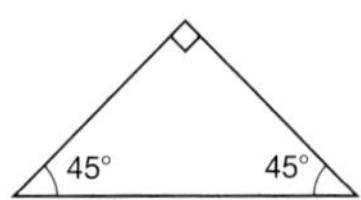

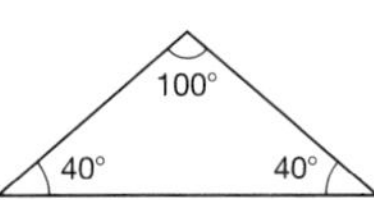

- At least two sides have the same length.
- At least two angles have the same measure.

Manipulative Use

Materials: Lesson Activity 17 Angle–Side Relationships in Triangles, ruler, colored pencils or markers

Some students may need help visualizing the angle measure/side length relationship of a triangle. If so students should

- use a ruler to measure and label the lengths of the sides of each triangle,
- mark the largest angle and longest side in one color and the smallest angle and shortest side in another color.

Remind them that the longest side is always opposite the largest angle and the shortest side is always opposite the smallest angle.

Math Language

On geometric figures, identical tick marks mean that angles or sides are equal. The isosceles triangle has two angles and two sides that are equal. All equilateral triangles are isosceles because they have at least 2 equal sides. Some isosceles triangles are equilateral, and some are not.

If the three sides of a triangle are all different lengths (and thus the angles are all different measures), then the triangle is called a **scalene triangle.**

Scalene triangle

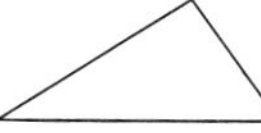

- All sides have different lengths.
- All angles have different measures.

Classify Are all equilateral triangles isosceles triangles? Are all isosceles triangles equilateral triangles? Explain.

Example 4

The perimeter of an equilateral triangle is 2 feet. How many inches long is each side?

Solution

All three sides of an equilateral triangle are equal in length. Since 2 feet equals 24 inches, we divide 24 inches by 3 and find that the length of each side is **8 inches.**

Example 5

Draw an isosceles right triangle.

Solution

Isosceles means the triangle has at least two sides that are the same length. *Right* means the triangle contains a right angle. We sketch a right angle, making both segments equal in length. Then we complete the triangle.

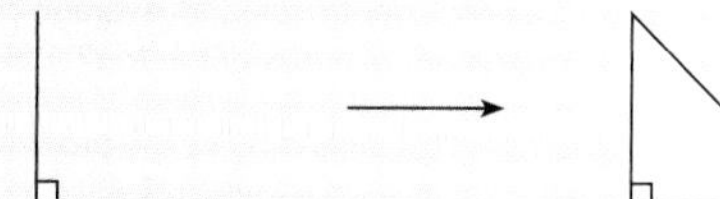

Analyze What is the measure of each of the angles opposite the sides you drew? 45°

Practice Set ▸ Classify Describe each triangle by its angles.

a. 
right triangle

b. 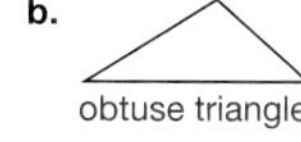
obtuse triangle

c. 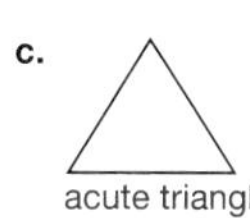
acute triangle

Classify Describe each triangle by its sides.

d. 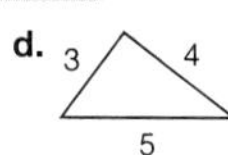

scalene triangle

e. 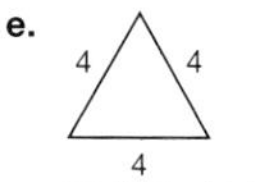

equilateral triangle

f. 5 5 8
isosceles triangle

▸ See Math Conversations in the sidebar.

2 New Concepts (Continued)

Example 4

Instruction

Remind students that an equilateral triangle is a regular triangle. Regular triangles and all other regular geometric figures have sides equal in length and angles equal in measure. Draw a regular and an irregular hexagon on the board. Ask students which figure is regular and why.

Example 5

Instruction

Ask students to explain why the side opposite the right angle in a right triangle is always the longest side. The sum of the other two angles will always equal the measure of the right angle. Therefore, the right angle will always be the largest angle and the side opposite it will be the longest side of the triangle.

Practice Set

Problems a–f Classify

Remind students that a triangle can be classified in many ways. Ask questions such as:

"Can a right triangle be isosceles? Scalene?" yes; yes

"Can an obtuse triangle be isosceles? Scalene?" yes; yes

"Can an equilateral triangle be isosceles? Scalene?" isosceles but not scalene

Have student volunteers draw examples at the board.

(continued)

2 New Concepts (Continued)

Practice Set

Problem g Explain

"If you know that a triangle is isosceles, what do you know about the measures of the angles and the lengths of the sides?" Sample: Two angles have the same measure, and 2 sides have the same length.

Problem h Classify

"If you know that all the angle measures of a triangle are less than 90°, what do you know about the triangle?" It is acute.

3 Written Practice

Math Conversations

Discussion opportunities are provided below.

Problem 5 Represent

If necessary, review ratio boxes with students. Then draw the following ratio box and have students complete it to solve the problem.

	Ratio	Actual Count
Mammal Books		
Plant Books		

Problem 7 Formulate

Remind students to change $3\frac{1}{3}$ to an improper fraction before solving the equation.

"How do you prove your answer is correct?" Sample: $\frac{1}{6} \times \frac{10}{3} = \frac{5}{9}$; $2\frac{7}{9} + \frac{5}{9} = 2\frac{12}{9}$; $2\frac{12}{9} = 3\frac{3}{9}$ or $3\frac{1}{3}$

Errors and Misconceptions

Problem 1

If students are struggling with this multi-step problem, break the problem into steps.

Step 1: Find out how many minutes Ms. Kwan has paid for.

Step 2: Add 10 minutes.

Step 3: Convert this time in minutes to hours and minutes.

Step 4: Add the answer to 1:30 to find the time the meter will expire.

(continued)

---

g. 11 cm; Since the triangle is isosceles, two sides are the same length, either 3-3-4 or 3-4-4. Since the perimeter is not 10 cm (3-3-4), the perimeter must be 11 cm (3-4-4).

h. The triangle is acute because all the angles are acute. The triangle is scalene because the three angles are different measures so the three sides are different lengths.

▶ **g.** Explain If we know that two sides of an isosceles triangle are 3 cm and 4 cm and that its perimeter is not 10 cm, then what is its perimeter? Explain how you know.

▶ **h.** Classify If the angles of a triangle measure 55°, 60°, and 65°, then what two names describe the type of triangle it is? Explain how you know.

i. Name the angles of this triangle in order from smallest to largest. ∠L, ∠N, ∠M

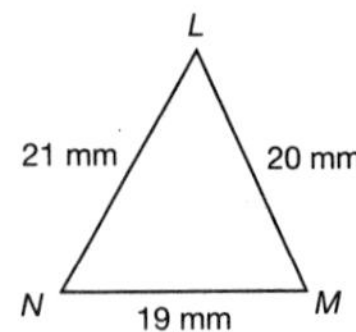

Written Practice *Strengthening Concepts*

▶ **1.** (28) At 1:30 p.m. Ms. Kwan found a parking meter that still had 10 minutes until it expired. She put 2 quarters into the meter and went to her meeting. If 10 cents buys 15 minutes of parking time, at what time will the meter expire? 2:55 p.m.

Use the information in the paragraph below to answer problems **2** and **3.**

The Barkers started their trip with a full tank of gas and a total of 39,872 miles on their car. They stopped 4 hours later and filled the gas tank with 8.0 gallons of gas. At that time the car's total mileage was 40,092.

2. (12) How far did they travel in 4 hours? 220 miles

3. (46) The Barkers' car traveled an average of how many miles per gallon during the first 4 hours of the trip? 27.5 miles per gallon

4. (41) When 24 is multiplied by w, the product is 288. What is the quotient when 24 is divided by w? 2

▶ *** 5.** (54) Represent Use a ratio box to solve this problem. There were 144 books about mammals in the library. If the ratio of books about mammals to books about plants was 9 to 8, how many books about plants were in the library? 128 books about plants

6. (22, 48) Read this statement. Then answer the questions that follow.

Exit polls showed that 7 out of 10 voters cast their ballot for the incumbent.

a. According to the exit polls, what percent of the voters cast their ballot for the incumbent? 70%

b. According to the exit polls, what fraction of the voters did not cast their ballot for the incumbent? $\frac{3}{10}$

▶ *** 7.** (60) Formulate Write an equation to solve this problem: $W_N = \frac{5}{6} \times 3\frac{1}{3}$; $2\frac{7}{9}$

What number is $\frac{5}{6}$ of $3\frac{1}{3}$?

▶ See Math Conversations in the sidebar.

8. $21,700; Sample: Find 8.5% of $20,000: 0.085 × $20,000 = $1700. Then add the amount of sales tax to the price of the car to find the total price including sales tax: $20,000 + $1700 = $21,700

11.

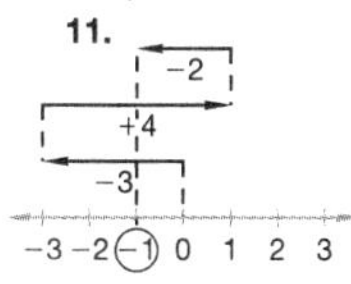

8. (46) What is the total price of a $20,000 car plus 8.5% sales tax? How do you know?

9. (51) Write 1.86×10^5 in standard form. Then use words to write the number. 186,000; one hundred eighty-six thousand

10. (32) Compare: 1 quart ⊘ 1 liter (<)

▶* **11.** (59) **Model** Show this addition problem on a number line:

$$(-3) + (+4) + (-2)$$

12. (48) Complete the table.

Fraction	Decimal	Percent
$\frac{5}{8}$	**a.** 0.625	**b.** $62\frac{1}{2}$%
c. $2\frac{3}{4}$	**d.** 2.75	275%

13. (52) Evaluate: $x + \frac{x}{y} - y$ if $x = 12$ and $y = 3$ 13

▶* **14.** (47, 57) **Generalize** Find each missing exponent:

a. $2^5 \cdot 2^3 = 2^{\square}$ 8　　**b.** $2^5 \div 2^3 = 2^{\square}$ 2

c. $2^3 \div 2^3 = 2^{\square}$ 0　　**d.** $2^3 \div 2^5 = 2^{\square}$ −2

▶* **15.** (62) **Classify** In the figure below, angle *ZWX* measures 90°.

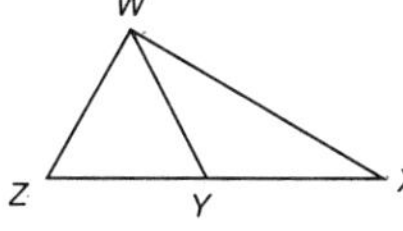

a. Which triangle is an acute triangle? △*ZWY*

b. Which triangle is an obtuse triangle? △*WYX*

c. Which triangle is a right triangle? △*ZWX*

16. (19, 37) In the figure at right, dimensions are in inches and all angles are right angles.

a. What is the perimeter of the figure? 21 in.

b. What is the area of the figure? 22 in.^{2}

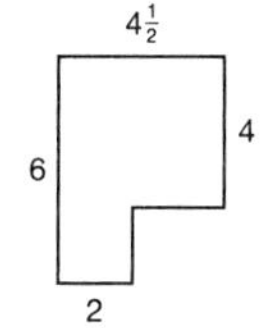

▶* **17.** (37, 62) **a.** Classify this triangle by its sides. isosceles triangle

b. What is the measure of each acute angle of the triangle? 45°

c. What is the area of the triangle? 18 cm^2

d. The longest side of this triangle is opposite which angle? ∠*C*

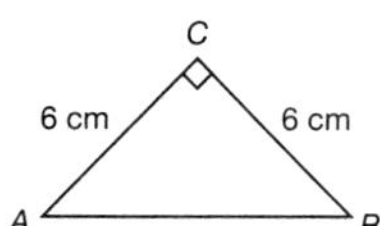

▶ See Math Conversations in the sidebar.

2 New Concepts (Continued)

Math Conversations

Discussion opportunities are provided below.

Problem 11 Model

Ask a student volunteer to draw at the board. Point out that we can show a negative number by drawing a left-pointing arrow and a positive number by drawing a right-pointing arrow. Have the student explain the answer.

Problem 14 Generalize

Before students complete these exercises, elicit that when multiplying exponential numbers with the same base, we add the exponents. Also, elicit that when dividing exponential numbers with the same base, we subtract the exponents.

Problem 15 Classify

Ask questions to help students form conclusions about the triangle.

"If you know ∠ZWX is 90° what do you know about the triangle?" △*ZWX* is a right triangle

"If you know ∠ZWX is 90°, what do you know about angles ZWY and YWX?" each angle is acute

Problem 17

Extend the Problem

Ask students how they can divide this isosceles triangle so it forms two right angles. draw a line that bisects the right angle and is perpendicular to the base, side *AB*

You might want to point out to students that in mathematics *dissect* means divide into two or more sections while *bisect* means to divide into two equal sections.

(continued)

3 Written Practice (Continued)

Math Conversations

Discussion opportunities are provided below.

Problem 28 Model

To be accurate, students will need a ruler and a protractor to answer this problem. Have them use a protractor to draw a 60° angle. They can then use a ruler to make two congruent sides on the rays of this angle. Connecting the endpoints of these segments produces an equilateral triangle.

Lead a discussion about symmetry and triangles. Have student volunteers draw examples at the board.

- An equilateral triangle can be divided into two congruent halves by three different lines, therefore it has 3 lines of symmetry.
- An isosceles triangle that is not equilateral can be divided into two congruent halves by only 1 line, therefore it has 1 line of symmetry.
- A scalene triangle cannot be divided into two congruent halves by a line, therefore it has no line of symmetry.

Errors and Misconceptions

Problem 20

If students simplify 5^2 and/or 2^5 to 10, remind them that the exponent indicates how many times the base is used as a factor, not as an addend.

Problem 23

If students are struggling with this exercise, suggest they convert 1 L to mL by using the unit multiplier: $\frac{1000 \text{ mL}}{1 \text{ L}}$.

Solve:

18. (35) $7q = 1.428$ 0.204

19. (39) $\frac{30}{70} = \frac{w}{\$2.10}$ \$0.90

Simplify:

▶ **20.** (20, 52) $5^2 + 2^5 - \sqrt{49}$ 50

21. (52) $3(8) - (5)(2) + 10 \div 2$ 19

22. (49) 1 yd 2 ft $3\frac{3}{4}$ in. + 2 ft $6\frac{1}{2}$ in.

22. 2 yd 1 ft $10\frac{1}{4}$ in.

▶ **23.** (32) 1 L − 50 mL = 950 mL

24. (50) $\frac{60 \text{ mi}}{1 \text{ hr}} \cdot \frac{1 \text{ hr}}{60 \text{ min}}$ $1 \frac{\text{mi}}{\text{min}}$

25. (30) $2\frac{7}{24} + 3\frac{9}{32}$ $5\frac{55}{96}$

26. (26) $2\frac{2}{5} \div \left(4\frac{1}{5} \div 1\frac{3}{4}\right)$ 1

27. (23, 26) $20 - \left(7\frac{1}{2} \div \frac{2}{3}\right)$ $8\frac{3}{4}$

▶* **28.** (58, 62) **a.** Model Draw an equilateral triangle and show its lines of symmetry.

28.

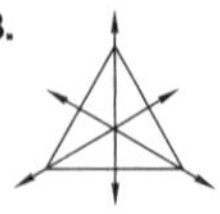

b. Does an equilateral triangle have rotational symmetry? yes, order 3

* **29.** (52, 59) Conclude Evaluate: $|x - y|$ if $x = 3$ and $y = 4$ 1

30. (3, 32) On one tray of a balanced scale was a 1-kg mass. On the other tray were a box and a 250-g mass. What was the mass of the box? 750 g

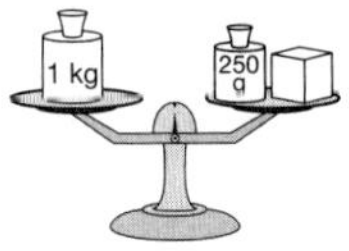

Early Finishers
Math Applications

Melody said she could use properties to make simplifying each expression easier. Is Melody correct? Use properties to validate your conclusion.

$\frac{1}{2} \cdot 41 + \frac{1}{2} \cdot 35 + \frac{1}{2} \cdot 24$ $\frac{1}{4} \cdot 20.5 + \frac{1}{4} \cdot 3.5 + \frac{1}{4} + 5.25 + \frac{3}{4}$

Yes. See student work. Sample:

$\frac{1}{2} \cdot 41 + \frac{1}{2} \cdot 35 + \frac{1}{2} \cdot 24 =$

$\frac{1}{2}(41 + 35 + 24) =$ Distributive Property

$\frac{1}{2}(100) = 50$

$\frac{1}{4} \cdot 20.5 + \frac{1}{4} \cdot 3.5 + \frac{1}{4} + 5.25 + \frac{3}{4} =$

$\frac{1}{4}(20.5 + 3.5) + \frac{1}{4} + 5.25 + \frac{3}{4} =$ Distributive Property

$\frac{1}{4}(24) + \frac{1}{4} + \frac{3}{4} + 5.25 =$

$6 + 1 + 5.25 = 12.25$

▶ See Math Conversations in the sidebar.

Looking Forward

Understanding how to classify triangles prepares students for:

- **Lesson 99,** finding an unknown length of a side of a right triangle using the Pythagorean theorem.
- **Investigation 10,** classifying the triangles formed when inscribing regular octagons in circles.
- **Lesson 107,** finding the slope of lines using right triangles.
- **Lesson 112,** applying the Pythagorean theorem to real situations to determine missing measurements.

• Symbols of Inclusion

Objectives

- Identify symbols of inclusion.
- Simplify expressions that have multiple symbols of inclusion.
- Use a calculator to perform calculations with parenthesis keys.

Lesson Preparation

Materials

- **Power Up L** (in *Instructional Masters*)
- **Teacher-provided material: calculators, graph paper**

Optional

- **Investigation Activity 13**

Name ________ Time ________ **Power Up L** *Math Course 1*

Facts Write the equivalent decimal and percent for each fraction.

Fraction	Decimal	Percent	Fraction	Decimal	Percent
$\frac{1}{2}$			$\frac{1}{8}$		
$\frac{1}{3}$			$\frac{1}{10}$		
$\frac{2}{3}$			$\frac{3}{10}$		
$\frac{1}{4}$			$\frac{9}{10}$		
$\frac{3}{4}$			$\frac{1}{100}$		
$\frac{1}{5}$			$1\frac{1}{2}$		

Mental Math

a.	b.	c.	d.
e.	f.	g.	h.

Problem Solving

Understand
What information am I given?
What am I asked to find or do?

Plan
How can I use the igformation I am given?
Which strategy should I try?

Solve
Did I follow the plan?
Did I show my work?
Did I write the answer?

Check
Did I use the correct information?
Did I do what was asked?
Is my answer reasonable?

18 *Saxon Math Course 2*

Power Up L

Math Language

	Maintain	English Learners (ESL)
	symbols of inclusion	**elevation**

Technology Resources

Student eBook Complete student textbook in electronic format.

Resources and Planner CD Assessment, reteaching, and instructional masters, plus a pacing calendar with standards.

Test and Practice Generator CD Create additional practice sheets and custom-made tests.

www.SaxonPublishers.com Visit for more student activities and planning materials.

Inclusion

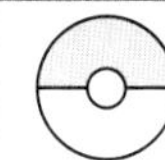

Adaptations CD Adapted lessons, investigations, practice and assessments.

Meeting Standards

National Council of Teachers of Mathematics (NCTM)

Numbers and Operations

NO.2a Understand the meaning and effects of arithmetic operations with fractions, decimals, and integers

Communication

CM.3a Organize and consolidate their mathematical thinking through communication

CM.3d Use the language of mathematics to express mathematical ideas precisely

Power-Up Discussion *For use with Power Up, p. 447*

Problem-Solving Strategy: Make an Organized List

Jamillah has two standard number cubes. If she rolls the cubes together once, what totals does she have a $\frac{5}{36}$ chance of rolling?

Understand ***Understand the problem.***

"What information are we given?"

Jamillah has two standard number cubes that she will roll together.

"What are we asked to do?"

We are asked to find what totals she has a $\frac{5}{36}$ chance of rolling.

Plan ***Make a plan.***

"What problem-solving strategy will we use?"

We will *make an organized list* of the possible totals, and the pairs of faces that result in those totals. Then we will record the number of ways to roll each total.

Solve ***Carry out the plan.***

"How do we begin our list?"

We will write the possible totals (2–12) in a column. Then we will record the pairs of faces that add to those totals in a second column. We will write the pairs "A, B", where A is the face showing on the first cube and B is the face showing on the second cube. Finally, we will count the ways each total can be achieved and record that number in a third column.

Sum	Rolls that will achieve the sum	Total number of ways to achieve the sum
2	1,1	1
3	1,2 2,1	2
4	1,3 2,2 3,1	3
5	1,4 2,3 3,2 4,1	4
6	1,5 2,4 3,3 4,2 5,1	5
7	1,6 2,5 3,4 4,3 5,2 6,1	6
8	2,6 3,5 4,4 5,3 6,2	5
9	3,6 4,5 5,4 6,3	4
10	4,6 5,5 6,4	3
11	5,6 6,5	2
12	6,6	1
		36–There are 36 possible outcomes for rolling 2 number cubes.

"Which sums have a $\frac{5}{36}$ probability of being rolled?"

There are 36 total possible outcomes, so we look for totals that can be achieved in 5 different ways: 6 and 8.

Check ***Look back.***

"Did we do what we were asked to do?"

Yes, we found the two totals Jamillah has a $\frac{5}{36}$ probability of rolling.

"Was it necessary to list all the possible outcomes?"

No, but it helped us ensure that we did not overlook any possible outcomes when calculating probabilities.

LESSON 63

• Symbols of Inclusion

Power Up — *Building Power*

facts Power Up L

mental math

a. **Calculation:** 5 × 246 1230

b. **Exponents:** 4×10^{-3} 0.004

c. **Equivalent Fractions:** $\frac{15}{20} = \frac{x}{8}$ 6

d. **Measurement:** Convert 0.5 L to mL. 500 mL

e. **Square Roots:** $\sqrt{196}$ 14

f. **Fractional Parts:** $\frac{3}{8}$ of $24.00 $9.00

g. **Geometry:** What type of triangle has 2 equal sides? isosceles

h. **Calculation:** Instead of multiplying 50 and 28, double 50, find half of 28, and multiply those numbers. 1400

problem solving Jamillah has two standard number cubes. If she rolls the cubes together once, what totals does she have a $\frac{5}{36}$ chance of rolling? 6 and 8

New Concept — *Increasing Knowledge*

parentheses, brackets, and braces

Parentheses are called **symbols of inclusion.** We have used parentheses to show which operation to perform first. For example, to simplify the following expression, we add 5 and 7 before subtracting their sum from 15.

$$15 - (5 + 7)$$

Math Language
A *symbol of inclusion* is a symbol that groups or includes numbers together.

Brackets, [ ], and **braces,** { }, are also symbols of inclusion. When an expression contains multiple symbols of inclusion, we simplify within the innermost symbols first.

To simplify the expression

$$20 - [15 - (5 + 7)]$$

we simplify within the parentheses first.

$20 - [15 - (12)]$ simplified within parentheses

Next we simplify within the brackets.

$20 - [3]$ simplified within brackets

17 subtracted

Facts Write the equivalent decimal and percent for each fraction.

Fraction	Decimal	Percent	Fraction	Decimal	Percent
$\frac{1}{2}$	0.5	50%	$\frac{1}{8}$	0.125	$12\frac{1}{2}$%
$\frac{1}{3}$	$0.\overline{3}$	$33\frac{1}{3}$%	$\frac{1}{10}$	0.1	10%
$\frac{2}{3}$	$0.\overline{6}$	$66\frac{2}{3}$%	$\frac{3}{10}$	0.3	30%
$\frac{1}{4}$	0.25	25%	$\frac{9}{10}$	0.9	90%
$\frac{3}{4}$	0.75	75%	$\frac{1}{100}$	0.01	1%
$\frac{1}{5}$	0.2	20%	$1\frac{1}{2}$	1.5	150%

1 Power Up

Facts

Distribute **Power Up L** to students. See answers below.

Mental Math

Encourage students to share different ways to mentally compute these exercises. Strategies for exercises **d** and **f** are listed below.

d. Use Reasoning

0.5 L means one-half liter
1000 mL = 1 L so,
500 mL = one half liter

Move the Decimal Point

1000 mL = 1 L
Move the decimal point 3 places.
0.5 × 1000 = 500

f. Divide First

$24 ÷ 8 = $3
$3 × 3 = $9

Multiply First

3 × $25 = $75
$75 − 3 = $72
$72 ÷ 8 = $9

Problem Solving

Refer to **Power-Up Discussion,** p. 447B.

2 New Concepts

Instruction

The symbols of inclusion we use are symbols that must be used in a particular order. Sometimes they enclose one or more additional pairs of grouping symbols. It can be helpful for students to locate each pair before starting to solve a problem. This helps determine where to begin and end solving.

Write these four expressions on the board.

$20 - [15 - (5 + 7)]$ 17
$20 - 15 - (5 + 7)$ −7
$20 - [15 - 5 + 7]$ 3
$20 - 15 - 5 + 7$ 7

Point out that each expression uses the same numbers in the same order, but the grouping symbols are altered. The result is four different answers.

(continued)

2 New Concepts (Continued)

Example 1

Instruction

"If we remove the parentheses in example 1, will the answer change?" no

"If we remove the brackets but not the parentheses, will the answer change?" yes; 35

"If we remove both the parentheses and the brackets, will the answer change?" yes; 35

Example 2

Instruction

Remind students that **absolute value** is the distance of a number from zero on a number line. Explain that when absolute value symbols are used as symbols of inclusion, two steps are necessary: simplifying the expression inside the symbols and then determining the absolute value of the result.

Example 3

Instruction

If students have difficulty understanding how a division bar can be a symbol of inclusion, demonstrate by rewriting the division horizontally:

$$(4 + 5 \times 6 - 7) \div [10 - (9 - 8)]$$

Be sure students understand that they need to simplify above and below the division bar before they actually divide.

(continued)

Example 1

Simplify: $50 - [20 + (10 - 5)]$

Solution

First we simplify within the parentheses.

$50 - [20 + (5)]$	simplified within parentheses
$50 - [25]$	simplified within brackets
25	subtracted

Discuss Compare the vertical arrangement of solution steps above with the same steps arranged in horizontal form:

$$50 - [20 + (10 - 5)] = 50 - [20 + (5)] = 50 - [25] = 25$$

Discuss which method is more helpful in understanding how the problem is solved. Sample: The vertical format makes each step of the solution process easy to identify. It is easier to follow and makes checking the solution easier.

Example 2

Simplify: $12 - (8 - |4 - 6| + 2)$

Solution

Absolute value symbols may serve as symbols of inclusion. In this problem we find the absolute value of 4 − 6 as the first step of simplifying within the parentheses.

$12 - (8 - 2 + 2)$	found absolute value of 4 − 6
$12 - (8)$	simplified within parentheses
4	subtracted

division bar As we noted in Lesson 52, a division bar can serve as a symbol of inclusion. We simplify above and below the division bar before we divide. We follow the order of operations within the symbol of inclusion.

Example 3

Simplify: $\dfrac{4 + 5 \times 6 - 7}{10 - (9 - 8)}$

Solution

We simplify above and below the bar before we divide. Above the bar we multiply first. Below the bar we simplify within the parentheses first. This gives us

$$\frac{4 + 30 - 7}{10 - (1)}$$

We continue by simplifying above and below the division bar.

$$\frac{27}{9}$$

Now we divide and get

$$3$$

Math Background

Symbols of inclusion, such as parentheses, brackets, and braces are often called *grouping symbols.* These symbols organize expressions and operations into groups.

Nesting these symbols, as in {[( )]}, indicates the order in which each group should be simplified. The order is easy to remember: The innermost set gets simplified first. This means that we begin simplifying in the inside and work our way outward, deleting the grouping symbols as we go.

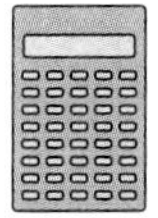

Some calculators with parenthesis keys are capable of dealing with many levels of parentheses (parentheses within parentheses within parentheses). When performing calculations such as the one in example 1, we press the "open parenthesis" key, (, for each opening parenthesis, bracket, or brace. We press the "close parenthesis" key,), for each closing parenthesis, bracket, or brace.

For the problem in example 1, the keystrokes are

5 0 − (2 0 + (1 0 − 5)) =

To perform calculations such as the one in example 3 using a calculator, we follow one of these two procedures:

1. We perform the calculations above the bar and record the result. Then we perform the calculations below the bar and record the result. Finally, we perform the division using the two recorded numbers.
2. To perform the calculation with one uninterrupted sequence of keystrokes, we picture the problem like this:

$$\frac{4 + 5 \times 6 - 7}{10 - (9 - 8)} =$$

We press the equals key after the 7 to complete the calculations above the bar. Then we press ÷ for the division bar. We place all the operations below the division bar within a set of parentheses so that the denominator is handled by the calculator as though it were one number.

If you have a calculator with parenthesis keys and algebraic logic, perform these calculations and note the display at the indicated location in the sequence of keystrokes.

4 + 5 × 6 − 7 =

What number is displayed and what does this number represent? 27; This is the numerator.

Continue the calculation using the following sequence of key strokes.

÷ (1 0 − (9 − 8)) =

What number is displayed and what does this number represent? 3; This is the quotient.

Practice Set

Represent Simplify, then show and justify each step in your solution using vertical form.

▸ **a.** $100 - 3[2(6 - 2)]$ 76; (See below.)

Simplify:

b. $30 - [40 - (10 - 2)]$ −2

▸ **c.** $\frac{10 + 9 \cdot 8 - 7}{6 \cdot 5 - 4 - 3 + 2}$ 3

d. $\frac{1 + 2(3 + 4) - 5}{10 - 9(8 - 7)}$ 10

e. $12 + 3(8 - |-2|)$ 30

a.

Step:	Justification:
100 − 3[2(6 − 2)]	Given problem
100 − 3[2(4)]	Simplified within parentheses
100 − 3[8]	Simplified within brackets
100 − 24	Multiplied
76	Subtracted

▸ See Math Conversations in the sidebar.

2 New Concepts (Continued)

Instruction

Here is a quick way for students to find out if their calculators have algebraic logic. Begin by having them find the value of the following expression using the rules for order of operations and no grouping symbols:

$$120 + 9 \div 3^2$$

The value is 121. Now have students enter the same expression into their calculators with no grouping symbols. If the answer is 121, the calculator has algebraic logic, meaning that it divides before it adds.

Practice Set

Problem a Represent

Ask a student volunteer to work at the board and explain the steps of the solution.

Problem c Error Alert

If students wrote $\frac{5}{29}$ as the answer, they computed from left to right without following the order of operations.

"What is the first step in simplifying the numerator?" multiply 9×8

"What is the first step in simplifying the denominator?" multiply 6×5

Teacher Tip

Almost all **calculators** handle **grouping symbols** in a similar manner. When you press the "open parentheses" key, the calculator "waits" until you press the "close parentheses" key before it calculates what is between the grouping symbols. Calculators vary in how many nested grouping symbols they process. Suggest that students try several examples to find out how their calculators treat nested grouping symbols.

3 Written Practice

Math Conversations

Discussion opportunities are provided below.

Problem 4

Extend the Problem

"About how many miles would a hiker need to travel each day to walk the entire Appalachian Trail in 3 months?" about 24 miles per day

Problem 5 **Analyze**

Check that students know that *net gain or loss* means the total change in elevation between the beginning and the end of the day.

Ask a student volunteer to sketch a vertical number line at the board to model this problem. Discuss the model with the class.

Problem 8 **Connect**

Ask students how they know their answers are correct. Answers will vary.

Problem 11 **Model**

Be sure students understand that they need to draw a number line from −3 to +5 to show the addition.

Errors and Misconceptions

Problem 2

If students are having difficulty with this problem, point out that this is a multiple-step problem. One approach is to figure out Marisol's heart rate while she is at rest for half an hour and then when she is jogging for half an hour. Then students can find the difference. Another way to solve this problem is by first finding the difference between the minute rates and then multiplying that difference by 30 minutes.

Problem 12

If students write 33% for $\frac{1}{3}$, show students:

$$\frac{1}{3} = 3\overline{)1.00} = .333 = 0.\overline{3}$$

$$\begin{array}{r} 9 \\ \hline 10 \\ 9 \\ \hline 10 \\ 9 \\ \hline 1 \end{array}$$

33% = 0.33

Thus, $33\frac{1}{3}\%$ is greater than 33%.

(continued)

Written Practice *Strengthening Concepts*

1. (28) Jennifer and Jason each earn $11 per hour doing yard work. On one job Jennifer worked 3 hours, and Jason worked $2\frac{1}{2}$ hours. Altogether, how much money were they paid? $60.50

▶ 2. (28, 53) When Marisol is resting, her heart beats 70 times per minute. When Marisol is jogging, her heart beats 150 times per minute. During a half hour of jogging, Marisol's heart beats how many more times than it would if she were resting? 2400 times

3. (54) Use a ratio box to solve this problem. The ratio of pairs of dress shoes to pairs of running shoes sold at the Shoe-Fly Buy store last Saturday was 2 to 9. If 720 pairs of running shoes were sold, how many pairs of dress shoes were sold? 160 pairs of dress shoes

▶ 4. (55) During the first 5 days, a hiker on the Appalachian Trail averaged 17 miles a day. During the next two days the hiker traveled 13 and 19 miles. The trail is a little more than 2174 miles long. About how much farther does the hiker have to travel? about 2057 miles

▶ * 5. (59) **Analyze** Yesterday, the hiker began hiking at 2850 feet above sea level, climbed over a 5575 foot-high summit and descended 2695 feet before stopping for the night. What was the hiker's net gain or loss of elevation during the day? How did you get your answer?

5. a gain of 30 feet; Sample: I subtracted 2695 from 5575 to see that the hiker ended up at 2880 feet above sea level.

6. (51) The average distance from Earth to the Sun is 1.496×10^8 km. Use words to write that distance. one hundred forty-nine million, six hundred thousand kilometers

7. (22, 48) Read this statement. Then answer the questions that follow.

Twelve of the 40 cars pulled by the locomotive were tankers.

a. What fraction of the cars were tankers? $\frac{3}{10}$

b. What percent of the cars were not tankers? 70%

▶ * 8. (57) **Connect** To convert inches to meters, we can multiply the number of inches by $2.54 \cdot 10^{-2}$. Use this fact to convert 1 yard to meters. 1 yard = 36 inches = 0.9144 meters

9. (50) Use a unit multiplier to convert 1.5 km to m. $1.5 \text{ km} \cdot \frac{1000 \text{ m}}{1 \text{ km}} = 1500 \text{ m}$

10. (45) Divide 4.36 by 0.012 and write the answer with a bar over the repetend. $363.\overline{3}$

▶ * 11. (59) **Model** Show this addition problem on a number line:

$$(-3) + (+5) + (-2)$$

11.

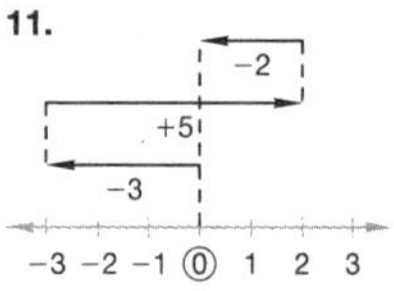

▶ 12. (48) Complete the table.

Fraction	Decimal	Percent
a. $\frac{33}{100}$	**b.** 0.33	33%
$\frac{1}{3}$	**c.** $0.\overline{3}$	**c.** $33\frac{1}{3}\%$

▶ See Math Conversations in the sidebar.

English Learners

Direct the students' attention to problem 5. Explain the meaning of **elevation.** Say:

"Elevation tells the height of something. If you climb a mountain, the elevation is how high you are."

Draw a vertical line on the board. Label 2850 feet and 5575 feet on the line. Ask students which elevation is higher.

▶* **13.** (56) **Formulate** Describe the rule of this function. Then write the rule as an equation using x for the input and y for the output. Begin by writing $y =$. Sample: Divide x, the Input number, by 3 to find y, the Output number. $y = \frac{1}{3}x$ or $y = \frac{x}{3}$

x Input	y Output
3	1
12	4
6	2
15	5

14. (14, 36) A deck of 26 cards has one letter of the alphabet on each card. What is the probability of drawing one of the letters in the word "MATH" from the deck? $\frac{2}{13}$

In the figure below, $AB = AD = BD = CD = 5$ cm. The measure of angle ABC is 90°. Refer to the figure for problems **15–17.**

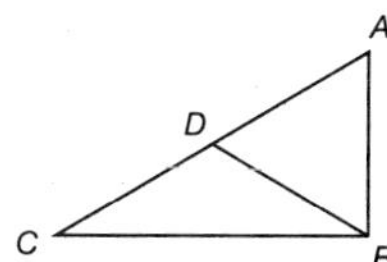

* **15.** (62) **a.** Classify $\triangle BCD$ by its sides. isosceles triangle

b. What is the perimeter of the equilateral triangle? 15 cm

c. Which triangle is a right triangle? $\triangle ABC$

16. (40) Find the measure of each of the following angles:

a. $\angle BAC$ 60° **b.** $\angle ADB$ 60°

c. $\angle BDC$ 120° **d.** $\angle DBA$ 60°

e. $\angle DBC$ 30° **f.** $\angle DCB$ 30°

17. (36) What is the ratio of the length of the shortest side of $\triangle ABC$ to the length of the longest side? $\frac{1}{2}$

Solve:

18. (30) $\frac{5}{18} = x + \frac{1}{12}$ $\frac{7}{36}$

19. (45) $2 = 0.4p$ 5

▶ **Generalize** Simplify:

* **20.** (63) $3[24 - (8 + 3 \cdot 2)] - \frac{6 + 4}{|-2|}$ 25

21. (52) $3^3 - \sqrt{3^2 + 4^2}$ 22

22. (49)
$$\begin{array}{r} 1 \text{ week } 2 \text{ days } 7 \text{ hr} \\ - \quad 5 \text{ days } 9 \text{ hr} \\ \hline 3 \text{ days } 22 \text{ hr} \end{array}$$

23. (50) $\frac{20 \text{ mi}}{1 \text{ gal}} \cdot \frac{1 \text{ gal}}{4 \text{ qt}}$ $5\frac{\text{mi}}{\text{qt}}$

24. (30) $4\frac{2}{3} + 3\frac{5}{6} + 2\frac{5}{9}$ $11\frac{1}{18}$

25. (26) $12\frac{1}{2} \cdot 4\frac{4}{5} \cdot 3\frac{1}{3}$ 200

26. (26, 30) $6\frac{1}{3} - \left(1\frac{2}{3} \div 3\right)$ $5\frac{7}{9}$

27. (52) Evaluate: $x^2 + 2xy + y^2$ if $x = 3$ and $y = 4$ 49

▶ See Math Conversations in the sidebar.

3 Written Practice (Continued)

Math Conversations

Discussion opportunities are provided below.

Problem 13 Formulate

Ask students to name a real world situation that could be represented by this equation. Sample: converting feet to yards where x = the number of feet and y = the number of yards; predicting the number of wheels on tricycles where y = the number of tricycles and x = the number of wheels

Problems 20–26 Generalize

Ask students to choose between mental math or paper and pencil to solve each problem. Have them explain their choice. Answers will vary.

(continued)

Lesson 63 451

3 Written Practice (Continued)

Math Conversations

Discussion opportunities are provided below.

Problem 29 Represent

Students will need graph paper or a copy of **Investigation Activity 13** Coordinate Plane to answer this problem.

"Explain how you found your answer."

Sample 1: count squares and multiply by 25, $12 \times 25 = 300$; Sample 2: subtract the x-coordinates and multiply the difference by 5, $4 \times 5 = 20$, then subtract the y-coordinates and multiply the difference by 5, $3 \times 5 = 15$, finally multiply $15 \times 20 = 300$

Problem 30

Extend the Problem

Write the following on the board.

● = 24

♥ = ● + 6

■ = ● − 8

Then ask students to use all 3 shapes to formulate an equation that has a value of 6. Mention that they can use symbols of inclusion to set up the equation.

Some students may find it easier to work if they write the values inside the shapes. Sample

♥ − (●−● / ■) − ● = 6

$$30 - \frac{24 - 24}{16} - 24 = 30 - \frac{0}{16} - 24$$

$$30 - \frac{0}{16} - 24 = 30 - 0 - 24 = 6$$

28.

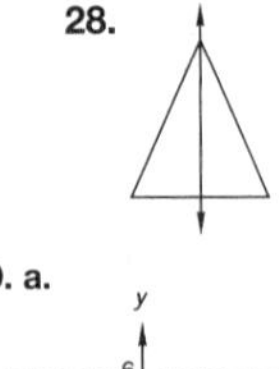

29. a.

* **28.** (58, 62) Model Draw an isosceles triangle that is not equilateral, and show its line of symmetry.

▸* **29.** (61) Della and Ray are planning to build a patio in the shape of a parallelogram. They sketched the patio on graph paper. Each square on the grid represents a 5 foot square. The coordinates of the four vertices are (0,0), (4,0), (1, −3), and (−3,−3).

a. Represent Graph the parallelogram.

b. What is the area of the patio they are planning? 300 ft^2

▸ **30.** (3) Three identical boxes are balanced on one side of a scale by a 750-g mass on the other side of the scale. What is the mass of each box? 250 g

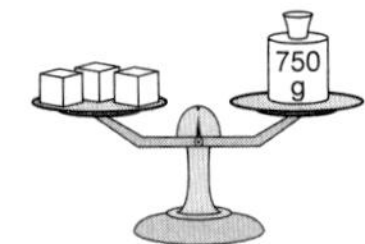

Early Finishers
Real-World Application

Dexter works at a clothing store and receives a 15% employee discount. He wants to buy a corduroy blazer that is on sale for 30% off the original price of $79.

a. Write and solve a proportion to find the price of the blazer without the employee discount. Sample: $\frac{70}{100} = \frac{x}{79}$; $55.30

b. Write and solve an equation to find the price Dexter would pay using his employee discount. Sample: 0.85 × $55.30 = e; e = $47.01

c. What percent of the original price did Dexter save by buying the blazer on sale and using his employee discount? Round your answer to the nearest whole percent. Show your work. 40 or 41%; Dexter paid 85% of 70% = 59.5%. Dexter saved 100% − 59.5% = 40.5%

▸ See Math Conversations in the sidebar.

Looking Forward

Simplifying expressions having symbols of inclusion prepares students for:

- **Lesson 85,** simplifying expressions using the order of operations with positive and negative numbers.

452 **Saxon** Math Course 2

• Adding Positive and Negative Numbers

Objectives

- Add positive and negative numbers without drawing a number line.

Lesson Preparation

Materials

- **Power Up N** (in *Instructional Masters*)
- **Lesson Activity 15 Transparency** (in *Instructional Masters*)
- **Investigation Activity 13** (in *Instructional Masters*) or **graph paper**
- **Manipulative kit: positive and negative number cards**

Optional

- **Teacher-provided material: 60–100 index cards** used to create "number cards"

Math Language

English Learners (ESL)
employ

Technology Resources

Student eBook Complete student textbook in electronic format.

Resources and Planner CD Blackline masters, plus a pacing calendar with standards.

Test and Practice Generator CD Create additional practice sheets and custom-made tests.

www.SaxonPublishers.com Visit for more student activities and planning materials.

Inclusion

Adaptations CD Adapted lessons, investigations, practice and assessments.

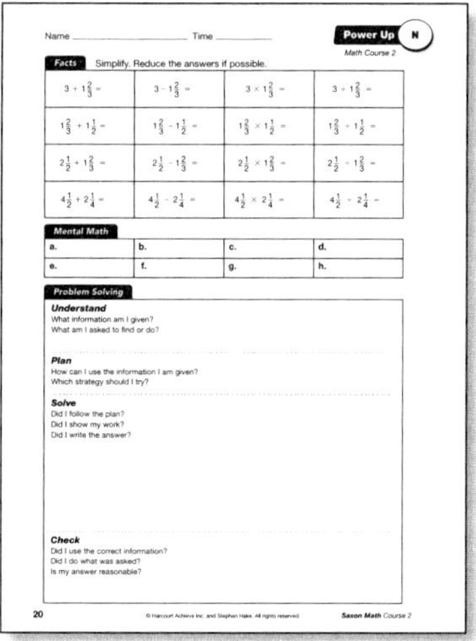

Power Up N

Lesson Activity 15

Meeting Standards

National Council of Teachers of Mathematics (NCTM)

Numbers and Operations

NO.1g Develop meaning for integers and represent and compare quantities with them

NO.2a Understand the meaning and effects of arithmetic operations with fractions, decimals, and integers

NO.3b Develop and analyze algorithms for computing with fractions, decimals, and integers and develop fluency in their use

Algebra

AL.1b Relate and compare different forms of representation for a relationship

Problem Solving

PS.1b Solve problems that arise in mathematics and in other contexts

Representation

RE.5b Select, apply, and translate among mathematical representations to solve problems

Power-Up Discussion *For use with Power Up, p. 453*

Problem-Solving Strategy: Use Logical Reasoning/Make a Table

Candice has a red notebook, a yellow notebook, and a blue notebook. She uses one notebook for school, one notebook for sketching, and one notebook for her journal. Her yellow notebook is not used for sketching. She does not use her red notebook for school. She does not use her blue notebook for her journal. If her blue notebook is not used for school, what notebook does Candice use for each purpose? Make a table to show your work.

Understand Understand the problem.

"What information are we given?"

Candice has a red notebook, a yellow notebook, and a blue notebook. She uses each notebook for one of three things: school, sketching, and her journal. We are given four facts about her notebooks:
Fact 1: Her yellow notebook is not used for sketching.
Fact 2: Her red notebook is not used for school.
Fact 3: Her blue notebook is not used for her journal.
Fact 4: Her blue notebook is not used for school.

"What are we asked to do?"

We are asked to make a table showing which notebook Candice uses for each purpose.

Plan Make a plan.

"What problem-solving strategy will we use?"

We have been asked to *make a table* to show our work. We will *use logical reasoning* to fill in the table.

"To which notebook can we already assign a purpose?"

Her blue notebook is not used for her journal or for school, so it must be used for sketching.

Solve Carry out the plan.

"How do we begin?"

We set up our table with columns labeled "school", "sketching", and "journal", and rows labeled "red", "yellow", and "blue". We use the four facts from the problem to fill in some of the table. Since blue is not used for school or her journal, it must be used for sketching. Therefore, red is not used for sketching, so red must be her journal. Thus, yellow is for school.

	school	**sketching**	**journal**
red	NO (Fact 1)	NO	**YES**
yellow	**YES**	NO (Fact 2)	NO
blue	NO (Fact 4)	**YES**	NO (Fact 3)

Check Look back.

"Did we do what we were asked to do?"

Yes, we found which notebook Candice uses for each purpose.

"How can we verify the solution is correct?"

We can re-read the facts while reviewing the table to make sure each one holds true.

LESSON 64

Adding Positive and Negative Numbers

Power Up *Building Power*

facts Power Up N

mental math

a. **Decimals:** 3.6×50 180

b. **Decimals/Exponents:** 7.5×10^2 750

c. **Algebra:** $4x - 5 = 35$ 10

d. **Measurement:** Convert 20 cm to mm. 200 mm

e. **Square Roots:** $\sqrt{9 + 16}$ 5

f. **Fractional Parts:** $\frac{5}{9}$ of $1.80 $1.00

g. **Geometry:** What is the name for a regular triangle? equilateral triangle

h. **Calculation:** 1.5 + 1, × 2, + 3, ÷ 4, − 1.5 0.5

problem solving Candice has a red notebook, a yellow notebook, and a blue notebook. She uses one notebook for school, one notebook for sketching, and one notebook for her journal. Her yellow notebook is not used for sketching. She does not use her red notebook for school. She does not use her blue notebook for her journal. If her blue notebook is not used for school, what notebook does Candice use for each purpose? Make a table to show your work. yellow notebook: school; blue notebook: sketching; red notebook: journal

	Red	Yellow	Blue
School	No		No
Sketching	No	No	
Journal		No	No

New Concept *Increasing Knowledge*

From our practice on the number line, we have seen that when we add two negative numbers, the sum is a negative number. When we add two positive numbers, the sum is a positive number.

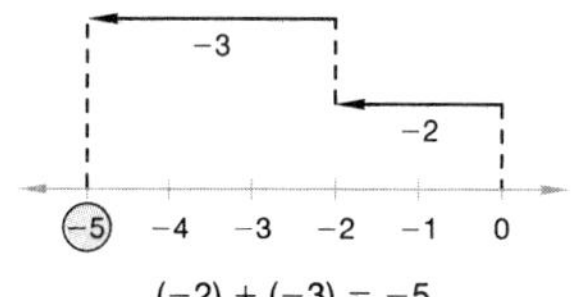

(−2) + (−3) = −5

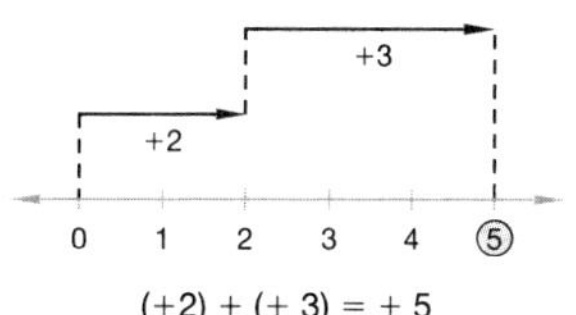

(+2) + (+ 3) = + 5

Math Language
The **absolute value** of a number is the distance on the number line of that number from zero and is always positive.

We have also seen that when we add a positive number and a negative number, the sum is positive, negative, or zero depending upon which, if either, of the numbers has the greater absolute value.

Facts Simplify. Reduce the answers if possible.

$3 + 1\frac{2}{3} = 4\frac{2}{3}$	$3 - 1\frac{2}{3} = 1\frac{1}{3}$	$3 \times 1\frac{2}{3} = 5$	$3 \div 1\frac{2}{3} = 1\frac{4}{5}$
$1\frac{2}{3} + 1\frac{1}{2} = 3\frac{1}{6}$	$1\frac{2}{3} - 1\frac{1}{2} = \frac{1}{6}$	$1\frac{2}{3} \times 1\frac{1}{2} = 2\frac{1}{2}$	$1\frac{2}{3} \div 1\frac{1}{2} = 1\frac{1}{9}$
$2\frac{1}{2} + 1\frac{2}{3} = 4\frac{1}{6}$	$2\frac{1}{2} - 1\frac{2}{3} = \frac{5}{6}$	$2\frac{1}{2} \times 1\frac{2}{3} = 4\frac{1}{6}$	$2\frac{1}{2} \div 1\frac{2}{3} = 1\frac{1}{2}$
$4\frac{1}{2} + 2\frac{1}{4} = 6\frac{3}{4}$	$4\frac{1}{2} - 2\frac{1}{4} = 2\frac{1}{4}$	$4\frac{1}{2} \times 2\frac{1}{4} = 10\frac{1}{8}$	$4\frac{1}{2} \div 2\frac{1}{4} = 2$

1 Power Up

Facts
Distribute **Power Up N** to students. See answers below.

Mental Math
Encourage students to share different ways to mentally compute these exercises. Strategies for exercise **b** is listed below.

b. Multiply by 100

$10^2 = 100$

$7.5 \times 100 = 750$

Insert 2 decimal places: 750

Move the Decimal Point

$10^2 = 100$

Move the decimal point 2 places: 750

Problem Solving
Refer to **Power-Up Discussion,** p. 453B.

2 New Concepts

Instruction
Use the transparency of **Lesson Activity 15** Number Lines as you walk through the addition examples with students. Guide them to discover the rules for adding positive and negative numbers.

Direct attention to the addition $(-2) + (-3) = -5$.

"We start at −2 on the number line. To add −3, do we move left or right?" left

Direct attention to the addition $(+2) + (+3) = +5$.

"We start at +2 on the number line. To add +3, do we move left or right?" right

"What do you notice about the signs of the addends in these two equations?" The signs of the addends are the same.

"What do you notice about the signs of the sums in these two equations?" They are the same as the addends.

(continued)

2 New Concepts (Continued)

Instruction

Before continuing, be sure students understand that to add numbers with the same sign, they should add the absolute values and use the same sign.

Continue working with the number line to add numbers with opposite signs. Direct attention to the addition $(+3) + (-5) = -2$.

"We start at +3. To add −5, which direction do we move?" left

Direct attention to the addition $(-3) + (+5) = +2$.

"We start at −3. To add +5, which direction do we move?" right

"What do you notice about the sign of the sum in each equation?" It has the same sign as the addend with the greater absolute value.

Students should understand that to add numbers with different signs, they subtract their absolute values and use the sign of the number with the greater absolute value.

Be sure students understand that opposites refer to a positive number and a negative number whose absolute values are equal. The sum of two opposites is always zero. +3 and −3 are opposites and their sum is 0.

Example 1

Instruction

After students have completed example 1, give students an opportunity to determine the signs. Write these problems on the board.

(_9) + (_11) = −2 +9, −11
(_16) + (_25) = +9 −16, +25
(_5) + (_15) = −20 −5, −15

(continued)

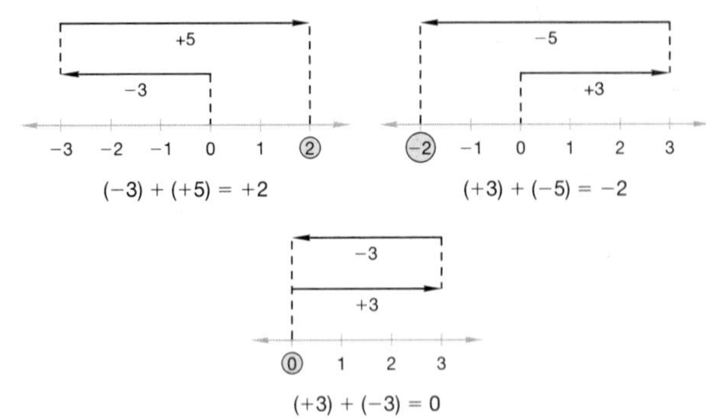

We can summarize these observations with the following statements.

1. The sum of two numbers with the same sign has an absolute value equal to the sum of their absolute values. Its sign is the same as the sign of the numbers.
2. The sum of two numbers with opposite signs has an absolute value equal to the difference of their absolute values. Its sign is the same as the sign of the number with the greater absolute value.
3. The sum of two opposites is zero.

We can use these observations to help us add positive and negative numbers without drawing a number line.

Thinking Skill
Apply
Will the sum of (−34) + (+43) be positive or negative? Explain? positive; +43 has a greater absolute value than −34 does.

Example 1

Find each sum:

a. $(-54) + (-78)$ **b.** $(+45) + (-67)$ **c.** $(-92) + (+92)$

Solution

a. Since the signs are the same, we add the absolute values and use the same sign for the sum.

$$(-54) + (-78) = \mathbf{-132}$$

b. Since the signs are different, we find the difference of the absolute values and keep the sign of −67 because its absolute value, 67, is greater than 45.

$$(+45) + (-67) = \mathbf{-22}$$

c. The sum of two opposites is zero, a number which has no sign.

$$(-92) + (+92) = \mathbf{0}$$

Example 2

Find the sum: $(-3) + (-2) + (+7) + (-4)$

Math Background

Grasping the concept of negative numbers is an important step in constructing a sophisticated understanding of mathematics. In this lesson, students build on their growing familiarity with negative numbers and learn to manipulate positive and negative numbers in addition problems. It is important for students to learn general rules that they can memorize and apply automatically.

While counting on a number line is a useful conceptual tool, it is too slow and inefficient to use in test-taking or real world situations. A facility with positive and negative signs in expressions and equations is fundamental for students to succeed in algebra and more advanced mathematics.

Solution

We will show two methods.

Method 1: Adding in order from left to right, add the first two numbers. Then add the third number. Then add the fourth number.

$(-3) + (-2) + (+7) + (-4)$	problem
$(-5) + (+7) + (-4)$	added -3 and -2
$(+2) + (-4)$	added -5 and $+7$
$\mathbf{-2}$	added $+2$ and -4

Method 2: Employing the commutative and associative properties, rearrange the terms and add all numbers with the same sign first.

$(-3) + (-2) + (-4) + (+7)$	rearranged
$(-9) + (+7)$	added
$\mathbf{-2}$	added

Example 3

Find each sum:

a. $\left(-2\frac{1}{2}\right) + \left(-3\frac{1}{3}\right)$ **b.** $(+4.3) + (-7.24)$

Solution

These numbers are not integers, but the method for adding these signed numbers is the same as the method for adding integers.

a. The signs are both negative. We add the absolute values and keep the same sign.

$$\left(-2\frac{1}{2}\right) + \left(-3\frac{1}{3}\right) = \mathbf{-5\frac{5}{6}}$$

$$\begin{array}{r} 2\frac{1}{2} = 2\frac{3}{6} \\ +\ 3\frac{1}{3} = 3\frac{2}{6} \\ \hline 5\frac{5}{6} \end{array}$$

b. The signs are different. We find the difference of the absolute values and keep the sign of -7.24.

$$(+4.3) + (-7.24) = \mathbf{-2.94}$$

$$\begin{array}{r} \overset{6\ 1}{7.24} \\ -\ 4.3 \\ \hline 2.94 \end{array}$$

Example 4

On one stock trade Mr. Figuera lost \$450. On a second trade Mr. Figuera gained \$800. What was the net result of the two trades?

Thinking Skill
Conclude
What if Mr. Figuera made a third trade and lost \$350. What is the net result of the three trades? \$0.00

Solution

A loss may be represented by a negative number and a gain by a positive number. So the results of the two trades may be expressed this way:

$$(-450) + (+800) = \mathbf{+350}$$

2 New Concepts (Continued)

Example 2
Instruction

Emphasize that the Commutative and Associative Properties can be used because this is an addition problem. Even though we sometimes think of adding a negative number as another way of subtracting, writing the expression as an addition problem allows us to use the properties of addition.

Example 3
Instruction

Encourage students to rewrite the expressions in vertical form before solving.

If students are still unsure how to proceed, have them revert to the number line method. Then have them try another problem involving positive and negative fractions, decimals, or whole numbers.

Example 4
Instruction

If students are confused by the term *net result,* explain that the *net result* is the final number after all of the gains and losses are added.

(continued)

Manipulative Use

Materials: Positive and negative number cards

If students need extra practice adding positive and negative numbers, have them play the **Integer Game.** Prepare number cards labeled -1 to -10 in red and 1 to 10 black. Use about 60 to 100 per deck, depending upon how many students will play.

- Shuffle the deck and divide the cards evenly among the players.
- Each player takes the top two cards from his or her stack and lays them number-side up on the table.
- The player whose cards have the greatest sum gets to keep all the cards.
- If two or more players have the same sum, each player turns over a third card to add to his or her sum.

The object of the game is to get the most cards.

English Learners

In example 2 explain the term **employ.** Say:

"Employ means to put to use. When asked to employ the commutative and associative properties, it means to use these properties to find the answer."

Write 23 + 17 on the board. Ask students what operation they should employ to solve this problem.

2 New Concepts (Continued)

Practice Set

Problem f Generalize

Encourage students to use two different methods to find the sum. Have them refer back to example 2 to review the two methods.

Problem i Connect

Ask students to explain why we don't say that Mrs. Francois lost -300 dollars, since we write the expression using a negative sign. The word "lost" tells us that we must add a negative amount of money. In the real world, it is impossible to "lose" a negative amount of money. We can only gain or lose positive amounts of money.

3 Written Practice

Math Conversations

Discussion opportunities are provided below.

Problem 2 Analyze

You might want to work through the solution with the students. Start with the total amount of money Eric paid the driver. Subtract the cost of the first mile and then determine the cost of each additional tenth of a mile. Students should realize that they need to subtract 1 mile (the first mile) from the total distance of the trip and then find the cost of the remaining (additional) tenths of a mile.

Problem 7 Formulate

Ask students to write a word problem that can be solved using this equation. Answers will vary.

(continued)

Practice Set Generalize Find each sum:

a. $(-56) + (+96)$ $+40$

b. $(-28) + (-145)$ -173

c. $(-5) + (+7) + (+9) + (-3)$ $+8$

d. $(-3) + (-8) + (+15)$ $+4$

e. $(-12) + (-9) + (+16)$ -5

▶ **f.** $(+12) + (-18) + (+6)$ 0

g. $\left(-3\frac{5}{6}\right) + \left(+5\frac{1}{3}\right)$ $+1\frac{1}{2}$

h. $(-1.6) + (-11.47)$ -13.07

▶ **i.** Connect On three separate stock trades Mrs. Francois gained \$250, lost \$300, and gained \$525. Write an expression that shows the results of each trade. Then find the net result of the trades. $(+250) + (-300) + (+525)$; The net result was a gain of \$475.

Written Practice *Strengthening Concepts*

1. (51) Two trillion is how much more than seven hundred fifty billion? Write the answer in scientific notation. 1.25×10^{12}

▶ ***2.** (28) Analyze The taxi cost \$2.25 for the first mile plus 15¢ for each additional tenth of a mile. For a 5.2-mile trip, Eric paid \$10 and told the driver to keep the change as a tip. How much was the driver's tip? \$1.45

3. (44) Mae-Ying wanted to buy packages of crackers and cheese from the vending machine. Each package cost 35¢. Mae-Ying had 5 quarters, 3 dimes, and 2 nickels. How many packages of crackers and cheese could she buy? 4 packages

4. (21) The two prime numbers p and m are between 50 and 60. Their difference is 6. What is their sum? Tell how you found your answer. 112; Explanations will vary.

5. (28) What is the mean of 1.74, 2.8, 3.4, 0.96, 2, and 1.22? 2.02

6. (22, 48) Diagram this statement. Then answer the questions that follow.

Over the summer, Ty earned \$120 babysitting. He spent $\frac{3}{5}$ of the money to buy a new bike and saved the rest.

6. \$120: $\frac{2}{5}$ saved: \$24, \$24; $\frac{3}{5}$ spent on bike: \$24, \$24, \$24

a. How much did he spend on the bike? \$72

b. What percent of his earnings did he save? 40%

▶ ***7.** (60) Formulate Write an equation to solve this problem:

What number is $\frac{5}{9}$ of 100? $W_N = \frac{5}{9} \times 100$; $55\frac{5}{9}$

***8.** (51, 57) Connect Use words to write each measure.

a. The temperature at the center of the sun is about 1.6×10^7 degrees Celsius. sixteen million degrees Celsius

b. A red blood cell is about 7×10^{-6} meter in diameter. seven millionths meter

▶ See Math Conversations in the sidebar.

Inclusion

Students can model the addition of integers by drawing circle counters and labeling them + or −. For $(+3) + (-5)$ have the students draw eight circles. Then write + in three of the circles and − in five. Instruct them to circle each pair of + and −.

"What does each + and − pair equal?" zero

"What counters are not paired up?" two negatives

Discuss how the model represents that -2 is the result of $(+3) + (-5)$.

▶ * **9.** (57) *Analyze* Compare:

a. 1.6×10^7 ⊘ 7×10^{-6} $>$

b. 7×10^{-6} ⊘ 0 $>$

c. 2^{-3} ⊘ 2^{-2} $<$

10. (44) Divide 456 by 28 and write the answer

a. as a mixed number. $16\frac{2}{7}$

b. as a decimal rounded to two decimal places. 16.29

c. rounded to the nearest whole number. 16

* **11.** (64) *Generalize* Find each sum:

a. $(-63) + (-14)$ -77

b. $(-16) + (+20) + (-32)$ -28

c. $\left(-\frac{1}{2}\right) + \left(-\frac{1}{2}\right)$ -1

* **12.** (64) On two separate stock trades Ms. Miller lost $327 and gained $280. What was the net result of the two trades? a loss of $47

▶ * **13.** (Inv. 2, 62) The figure shows an equilateral triangle inscribed in a circle.

a. What is the measure of the inscribed angle *BCA*? 60°

b. *Justify* Select a chord of this circle, and state whether the chord is longer or shorter than the diameter of the circle and why.

13. b. The chords are $\overline{AB}$ (or $\overline{BA}$), $\overline{BC}$ (or $\overline{CB}$), and $\overline{CA}$ (or $\overline{AC}$). Each chord is shorter than the diameter, which is the longest chord of a circle.

Math Language

Review

A **chord** is a line segment with endpoints that lie on the circle.

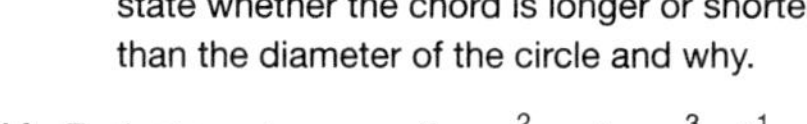

14. (52) Evaluate: $x + xy$ if $x = \frac{2}{3}$ and $y = \frac{3}{4}$ $1\frac{1}{6}$

Refer to the hexagon below to answer problems **15** and **16.** Dimensions are in meters. All angles are right angles.

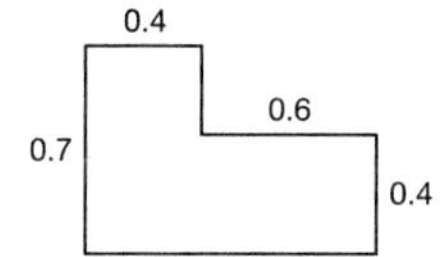

15. (19) What is the perimeter of the hexagon? 3.4 m

16. (37) What is the area of the hexagon? 0.52 m^2

▶ * **17.** (36) *Analyze* What is the probability of rolling 10 with a pair of number cubes? (Hint: see the sample space in Lesson 36). $\frac{3}{36} = \frac{1}{12}$

▶ **18.** (Inv. 3) The center of a circle with a radius of three units is (1, 1). Which of these points is on the circle? **B**

A (4, 4) **B** (−2, 1) **C** (−4, 1) **D** (3, 0)

▶ See Math Conversations in the sidebar.

3 Written Practice (Continued)

Math Conversations

Discussion opportunities are provided below.

Problem 9 Connect

You may need to remind students how to work with negative exponents.

Problem 13a Justify

Ask students to justify their answer to part **a.** Sample: We know that angle *BCA* measures 60° because it is one angle of an equilateral triangle. The three angles in an equilateral triangle are all equal. Since there are 180° in any triangle, each of the three angles of an equilateral triangle has a measure of 60°.

Problem 13b Justify

Extend the Problem

Asks students how many lines of symmetry this figure has. 3

Problem 17 Analyze

Ask students how they know their answers are correct. Sample: There are 36 possible outcomes ($6 \times 6 = 36$). There are 3 ways to roll a 10 ($6 + 4$, $4 + 6$, $5 + 5$). 3 out 36 $= \frac{1}{12}$

Problem 18

Extend the Problem

After students name the point on the circle, ask them to determine if the other points are inside or outside the circle. a. outside, c. outside, d. inside

Errors and Misconceptions

Problem 17

If students are having difficulty determining the sample space, suggest that they draw a table or a tree diagram.

Problem 18

Most students will need to graph the circle in order to determine which point is on the circle. Have them use a safety compass and graph paper (or a copy of **Investigation Activity 13** Coordinate Plane) to draw a circle with a radius of 3 units whose center is at (1, 1). They should label the points that are "on" the circle.

(continued)

3 Written Practice (Continued)

Math Conversations

Discussion opportunities are provided below.

Problem 27 Formulate

If students are unsure how to begin, have them focus on one x, y pair. Ask them to identify which number represents the x coordinate. first number

Then ask them to explain the relationship between the first number in the pair and the second number. The second number is twice the first number.

Errors and Misconceptions

Problem 21

Watch for students who think the answer is 1. Work through the steps and point out that after they have applied the exponents, they need to find the square root of the sum in the denominator.

Problem 23

If students answer 42 or 54, they probably simplified 4^0 as 0 or as 4. Remind students that any number (other than 0) to the zero power equals 1.

Solve:

19. (15) $\frac{4}{9} = y - \frac{2}{9}$ $\frac{2}{3}$

20. (44) $25x = 10$ 0.4 or $\frac{2}{5}$

Generalize Simplify:

▸* **21.** (63) $\frac{3^2 + 4^2}{\sqrt{3^2 + 4^2}}$ 5

22. (26) $2\frac{4}{5} \div \left(6 \div 2\frac{1}{2}\right)$ $1\frac{1}{6}$

▸* **23.** (57, 63) $100 - [20 + 5(4) + 3(2 + 4^0)]$ 51

24. (49)
5 gal 2 qt 1 pt 7 oz
+ 1 gal 1 qt 1 pt 9 oz
7 gal 1 pt

25. (26, 30) $\left(1\frac{1}{2}\right)^2 - \left(4 - 2\frac{1}{3}\right)$ $\frac{7}{12}$

26. (35) $0.1 - (0.01 - 0.001)$ 0.091

▸* **27.** (56) Formulate Write the rule of the graphed function in an equation. Begin the equation with $y =$. Then name another (x, y) pair not named on the graph that satisfies the function.

27. $y = 2x$; any x, y pair in which y is twice x satisfies the function, such as (4, 8) and (−1, −2).

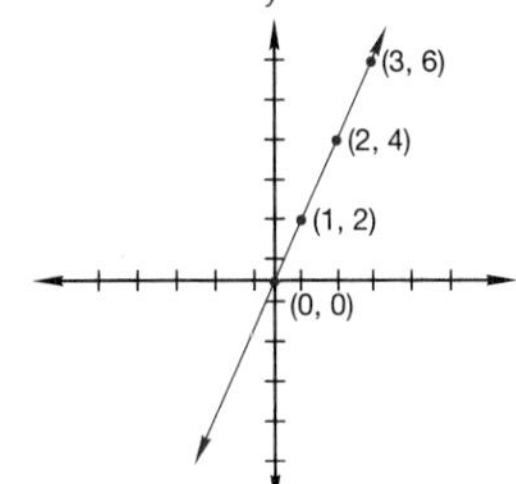

28. (43) Write $3\frac{1}{5}$ as a decimal number, and subtract it from 4.375.   1.175

29. (14) What is the probability of rolling an even prime number with one toss of a die? $\frac{1}{6}$

***30.** (61) Figure $ABCD$ is a parallelogram. Find the measure of

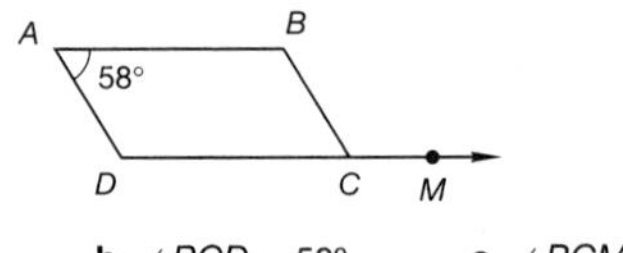

a. $\angle B$.   122°   **b.** $\angle BCD$.   58°   **c.** $\angle BCM$.   122°

▸ See Math Conversations in the sidebar.

Looking Forward

Learning to add positive and negative numbers prepares students for:

- **Lesson 68,** using algebraic addition to simplify subtraction expressions.
- **Lesson 73,** multiplying and dividing positive and negative numbers.
- **Lesson 83,** multiplying numbers in scientific notation with exponents of positive and negative numbers.
- **Lesson 85,** using the order of operations to simplify expressions with positive and negative numbers.
- **Lesson 96,** using the Distributive Property to simplify expressions with algebraic terms.

• Circumference and Pi

Objectives

- Find an approximate value of pi (π) by measuring the circumference and diameter of different circular objects.
- Use the formula $C = \pi d$ to calculate the circumference of a circle given the length of the diameter or radius.
- Represent the constant pi (π) as a fraction and a decimal.

Lesson Preparation

Materials

- **Power Up M** (in *Instructional Masters*)
- **Manipulative kit: metric tape measure** or meter stick and string
- **Teacher-provided material: circular objects such as paper cups, jar lids and so on; calculators**

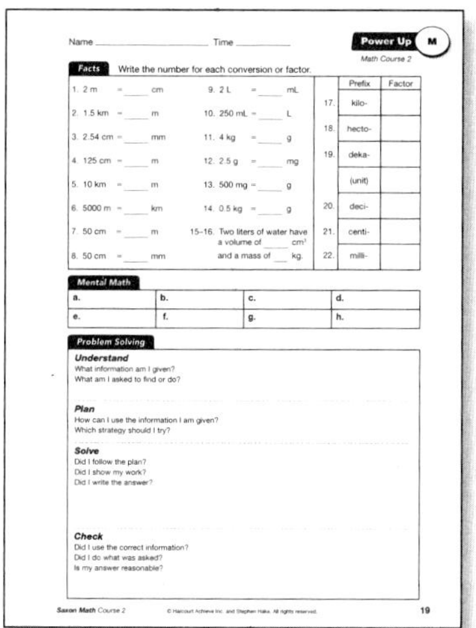

Name ________ Time ________ **Power Up M** *Math Course 2*

Facts Write the number for each conversion or factor.

1. 2 m = ___ cm	9. 2 L = ___ mL	
2. 1.5 km = ___ m	10. 250 mL = ___ L	
3. 2.54 cm = ___ mm	11. 4 kg = ___ g	
4. 125 cm = ___ m	12. 2.5 g = ___ mg	
5. 10 km = ___ m	13. 500 mg = ___ g	
6. 5000 m = ___ km	14. 0.5 kg = ___ g	
7. 50 cm = ___ m	15–16. Two liters of water have a volume of ___ cm^3	
8. 50 cm = ___ mm	and a mass of ___ kg.	

	Prefix	Factor
17.	kilo-	
18.	hecto-	
19.	deka-	
	(unit)	
20.	deci-	
21.	centi-	
22.	milli-	

Mental Math

a.	b.	c.	d.
e.	f.	g.	h.

Problem Solving

Understand
What information am I given?
What am I asked to find or do?

Plan
How can I use the information I am given?
Which strategy should I try?

Solve
Did I follow the plan?
Did I show my work?
Did I write the answer?

Check
Did I use the correct information?
Did I do what was asked?
Is my answer reasonable?

Saxon Math Course 2 © Harcourt Achieve Inc. and Stephen Hake. All rights reserved. 19

Power Up M

Math Language

New	Maintain	English Learners (ESL)
constant	circumference	constant
pi	diameter	
	radii	
	radius	

Technology Resources

Student eBook Complete student textbook in electronic format.

Resources and Planner CD Assessment, reteaching, and instructional masters, plus a pacing calendar with standards.

Test and Practice Generator CD Create additional practice sheets and custom-made tests.

www.SaxonPublishers.com Visit for more student activities and planning materials.

Inclusion

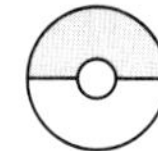

Adaptations CD Adapted lessons, investigations, practice and assessments.

Meeting Standards

National Council of Teachers of Mathematics (NCTM)

Geometry

GM.1a Precisely describe, classify, and understand relationships among types of two- and three-dimensional objects using their defining properties

GM.4d Use geometric models to represent and explain numerical and algebraic relationships

Measurement

ME.2c Develop and use formulas to determine the circumference of circles and the area of triangles, parallelograms, trapezoids, and circles and develop strategies to find the area of more-complex shapes

Power-Up Discussion

For use with Power Up, p. 459

Problem-Solving Strategy: Use Logical Reasoning/ Guess and Check

Copy this problem and fill in the missing digits:

```
     _ _ _ _ R 5
  _)_ _ _ _
    8
    _ _
    16
     _ _
     24
      _ _
      _
       _
```

Understand ***Understand the problem.***

"What information are we given?"

We are shown a division problem with several digits missing.

"What are we asked to do?"

We are asked to find the missing digits.

Plan ***Make a plan.***

"What problem-solving strategy will we use?"

We will *use logical reasoning* and number sense to help us intelligently *guess and check* for the missing digits.

"What can we deduct about the divisor?"

The divisor is a single-digit factor of 8, 16, and 24.

"What are the possible divisors?"

2, 4, or 8.

"Can 2 or 4 be the divisor?"

No, because the remainder is 5, and the remainder should never be larger than the divisor. Therefore, the divisor is 8.

Solve ***Carry out the plan.***

"How do we begin?"

We fill in the divisor, and we know that the final subtrahend must be 8 also. We know that the remainder is 5, so that makes the final minuend 13 and the ones place of the dividend 3. We continue to fill in digits in this manner, checking our arithmetic as we go.

```
   _ _ _ _ R 5     _ _ _ _ R 5     _ _ _ _ R 5     _ _ _ _ R 5     _ _ _ _ R 5     1231 R 5
8)_ _ _ _       8)_ _ _ 3       8)_ _ 53        8)_ 853         8)9853          8)9853
  8               8               8               8               8               8
  _ _             _ _             _ _             18              18              18
  16              16              16              16              16              16
   _ _             _ _             25              25              25              25
   24              24              24              24              24              24
    _               13              13              13              13              13
    8                8               8               8               8               8
    _                5               5               5               5               5
```

Check ***Look back.***

"Did we do what we were asked to do?"

Yes, we found the missing digits.

"How can we verify the solution is correct?"

We can use the inverse operation of division to check our answer: $1231 \times 8 = 9848 + 5 = 9853$.

LESSON 65

• Circumference and Pi

Power Up

Building Power

facts Power Up M

mental math

a. **Decimals:** 0.42 × 50   21

b. **Decimals/Exponents:** 1.25×10^{-1} 0.125

c. **Ratio:** $\frac{9}{w} = \frac{15}{10}$ 6

d. **Measurement:** Convert 0.75 m to mm.   750 mm

e. **Exponents:** $5^3 - 10^2$ 25

f. **Fractional Parts:** $\frac{9}{10}$ of \$4.00   \$3.60

g. **Geometry:** A circle has a diameter of 7 ft. What is the radius of the circle? $3\frac{1}{2}$ ft

h. **Calculation:** What is the total cost of a \$20.00 item plus 7% sales tax?   \$21.40

problem solving Copy this problem and fill in the missing digits:

```
 ____ R 5          1231 R 5
_)____            8)9853
  8                 8
  __                18
  16                16
  __                 25
   24                24
   __                 13
    _                  8
    _                  5
```

New Concept

Increasing Knowledge

Recall from Investigation 2 that a **circle** is a smooth curve, every point of which is the same distance from the **center.** The distance from the center to the circle is the **radius.** The plural of radius is **radii.** The distance across a circle through the center is the **diameter.** The distance around a circle is the **circumference.**

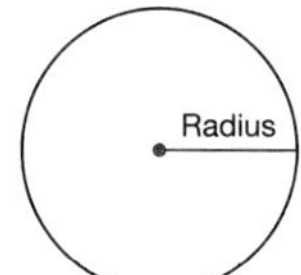

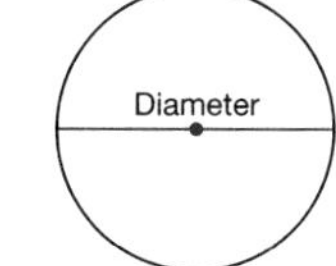

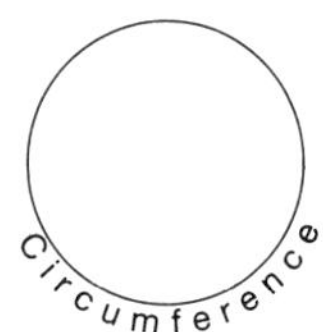

1 Power Up

Facts

Distribute **Power Up M** to students. See answers below.

Mental Math

Encourage students to share different ways to mentally compute these exercises. Strategies for exercises **c** and **d** are listed below.

c. Cross Multiply

$15w = 90$

$90 \div 15 = 180 \div 30$ or 6

$w = 6$

Equivalent Fractions

$\frac{15}{10} = \frac{3}{2}$ and $\frac{3}{2} = \frac{9}{6}$

$w = 6$

d. Move the Decimal Point

1000 mm = 1 m

Move the decimal point 3 places.

$0.75 \times 1000 = 750$

Use Reasoning

1000 mm = 1 m

0.75 is three-fourths of 1.0

750 is three-fourths of 1000

Problem Solving

Refer to **Power-Up Discussion,** p. 459B.

2 New Concepts

Instruction

Lead a class discussion about circles. Have students consider where they see circular objects in everyday life. Some answers may include:

- wheels or tires on cars or bicycles
- lids on jars or bottles
- circular fans

"How can you find the distance a bicycle travels in one turn of the wheel?"

Find the distance around the wheel or the circumference of the wheel.

Explain to students that an understanding of circumference and pi will help them solve such problems about circular objects.

(continued)

Facts Write the number for each conversion or factor.

1. 2 m = 200 cm	9. 2 L = 2000 mL	
2. 1.5 km = 1500 m	10. 250 mL = 0.25 L	
3. 2.54 cm = 25.4 mm	11. 4 kg = 4000 g	
4. 125 cm = 1.25 m	12. 2.5 g = 2500 mg	
5. 10 km = 10,000 m	13. 500 mg = 0.5 g	
6. 5000 m = 5 km	14. 0.5 kg = 500 g	
7. 50 cm = 0.5 m	15–16. Two liters of water have a volume of 2000 cm^3	
8. 50 cm = 500 mm	and a mass of 2 kg.	

	Prefix	Factor
17.	kilo-	1000
18.	hecto-	100
19.	deka-	10
	(unit)	1
20.	deci-	0.1
21.	centi-	0.01
22.	milli-	0.001

Activity

Instruction

If metric tape measures are not available, show students how to use string and a meter stick to measure the circumference and diameter of circular objects.

If the ratio of circumference to diameter is not close to 3.14 for any objects that students measure, have them measure the circumference and diameter of the objects again and check their computation.

2 New Concepts (Continued)

Instruction

Have students use the method illustrated in the book to show another way to find how many diameters equal circumference. Draw different-sized circles on the board. Ask volunteers to cut a piece of string the length of the diameter of each circle. Have them find how many lengths of the string reach around each circle. Students should conclude that a little more than three diameter-lengths equal circumference.

Ask a volunteer to demonstrate and explain the calculations that prove $3\frac{1}{7} = \frac{22}{7}$, or about 3.14. Seven times 3 plus 1 equals 22. Write 22 over 7. Twenty-two divided by 7 equals 3.14 rounded to two decimal places.

(continued)

We see that the diameter of a circle is twice the radius of the circle. In the following activity we investigate the relationship between the diameter and the circumference.

Activity

Investigating Circumference and Diameter

Materials needed:

- Metric tape measure (or string and meter stick)
- Circular objects of various sizes
- Calculator (optional)

Working in a small group, select a circular object and measure its circumference and its diameter as precisely as you can. Then calculate the number of diameters that equal the circumference by dividing the circumference by the diameter. Round the quotient to two decimal places. Repeat the activity with another circular object of a different size. Record your results on a table similar to the one shown below. Extend the table by including the results of other students in the class. Are your ratios of circumference to diameter basically the same?

Sample Table

Object	Circumference	Diameter	$\frac{\text{Circumference}}{\text{Diameter}}$
Waste basket	94 cm	30 cm	3.13
Plastic cup	22 cm	7 cm	3.14

How many diameters equal a circumference? Mathematicians investigated this question for thousands of years. They found that the answer did not depend on the size of the circle. The circumference of every circle is slightly more than three diameters.

Another way to illustrate this fact is to cut a length of string equal to the diameter of a particular circle and find how many of these lengths are needed to reach around the circle. No matter what the size of the circle, it takes three diameters plus a little extra to equal the circumference.

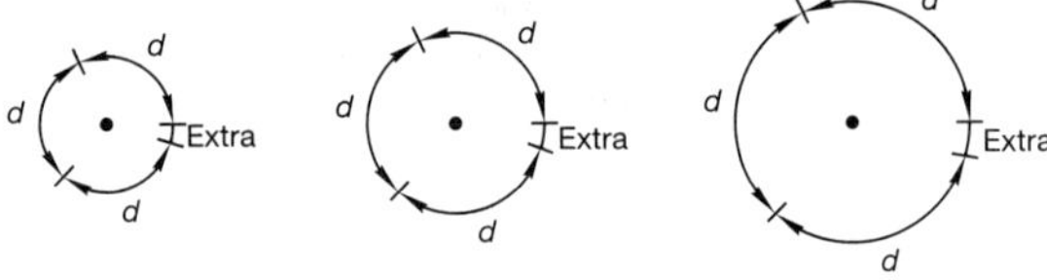

The extra amount needed is about, but not exactly, one seventh of a diameter. Thus the number of diameters needed to equal the circumference of a circle is about

$$3\frac{1}{7} \quad \text{or} \quad \frac{22}{7} \quad \text{or} \quad 3.14$$

Math Background

Is there an exact value for pi?

By definition, pi is the ratio of the circumference of a circle to its diameter. This ratio is always the same, no matter which circle you use to compute it. Mathematicians have worked for centuries to compute an exact value of pi. They have concluded that all the digits of pi can never be fully known. Pi, to thirty decimal places is 3.141592653589793238462643383279. Because pi is a number that cannot be expressed as a ratio of two integers, it is said to be an irrational number. Students will study irrational numbers in Lesson 100.

Neither $3\frac{1}{7}$ nor 3.14 is the exact number of diameters needed. They are approximations. There is no fraction or decimal number that states the exact number of diameters in a circumference. (Some computers have calculated the number to more than 1 million decimal places.) We use the symbol π, which is the Greek letter **pi** (pronounced like "pie"), to represent this number. Note that π is not a variable. Rather, π is a **constant** because its value does not vary.

The circumference of a circle is π times the diameter of the circle. This idea is expressed by the formula

$$C = \pi d$$

In this formula C stands for circumference and d for diameter. To perform calculations with π, we can use an approximation. The commonly used approximations for π are

3.14 and $\frac{22}{7}$

For calculations that require great accuracy, more accurate approximations for π may be used, such as

3.14159265359

Sometimes π is left as π. Unless directed otherwise, we use 3.14 for π for calculations in this book.

Example 1

The radius of a circle is 10 cm. What is the circumference?

Solution

If the radius is 10 cm, the diameter is 20 cm.

$$\begin{aligned}\text{Circumference} &= \pi \cdot \text{diameter}\\ &\approx 3.14 \cdot 20 \text{ cm}\\ &\approx 62.8 \text{ cm}\end{aligned}$$

Thinking Skill

Connect

For any calculation that uses an inexact value for π, the answer is approximate and we use the $\approx$ symbol.

The circumference is about **62.8 cm.** In the solution we used the symbol $\approx$, which means "approximately equals," because the value for π is not exactly 3.14.

Generalize How could you write the formula for the circumference of a circle using the radius (r) instead of the diameter (d)? Accept all correct answers, such as $C = \pi \cdot 2 \cdot r$, $2r\pi$, or $2\pi r$, which is the standard form.

Example 2

Find the circumference of each circle:

a.

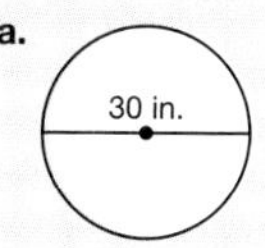

Use 3.14 for π.

b.

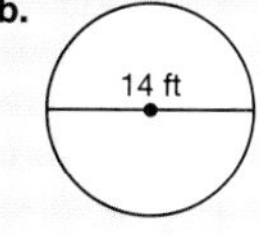

Use $\frac{22}{7}$ for π.

c.

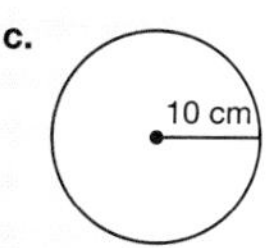

Leave π as π.

2 New Concepts (Continued)

Instruction (continued)

Point out to students that C and d are variables because the value of circumference and diameter varies with each circle. Explain to students that although π is a constant, there are several approximate values that can be used for π when calculating the circumference of a circle.

Tell students that the approximation of $\frac{22}{7}$ for π is often used to find circumference when the diameter is a whole number that is a multiple of 7, or a fraction whose numerator is a multiple of 7.

Example 1

Instruction

Have students justify their formula. Diameter is 2 times radius, so $C = \pi 2r$.

Example 2

Instruction

Point out to students that the solution to problem c has an *is equal to* sign, not an *is approximately equal to* sign. Explain to students that when the symbol π is left as π in the answer, the circumference is an exact value, not an approximation.

Ask students to determine which approximation they would use to find the circumference of circles with the following dimensions. Have them explain their reasoning.

- diameter: $\frac{21}{25}$ cm $\frac{22}{7}$; The numerator of the diameter is a multiple of 7.
- radius: 28 ft $\frac{22}{7}$; The radius is a whole number that is a multiple of 7.
- diameter: $\frac{32}{35}$ m 3.14; The numerator of the diameter is *not* a multiple of 7.

(continued)

English Learner

The word **constant** has multiple meanings. You may need to explain the mathematical meaning of this term. Say:

"If something is a constant, it does not change. The number of days in a week is constant. Is the number of days in a month constant?" no

"Why not?" The number of days in each month is not the same.

Teacher Tip

Take this opportunity to review these **symbols.** Write them on the board.

$\approx$ "is approximately equal to"

$\sim$ "is similar to"

$\cong$ "is congruent to"

Ask students to formulate an equation using each symbol as you point to it.

2 New Concepts (Continued)

Practice Set

Problems a–c Generalize

Have students identify what the dimension given in each circle represents. a. radius; b. diameter; c. radius

"How do you find circumference when the diameter of a circle is given?" Use the formula $C = \pi d$.

"How do you find circumference when the radius of a circle is given?" Multiply the radius by 2 to find the diameter and use the formula $C = \pi d$; or use the formula $C = 2\pi r$.

Problem d Explain

"If you doubled the radius, would the circumference double? Why or why not?" Yes; Since the relationship of the circumference to the diameter is a ratio and the diameter is twice the radius, the circumference will increase proportionately as the radius increases.

3 Written Practice

Math Conversations

Discussion opportunities are provided below.

Errors and Misconceptions

Problem 3

Watch for students who use the value of the radius instead of the value of the diameter in the formula $C = \pi d$. Remind them that they need to double the radius to find the circumference.

(continued)

(continued)

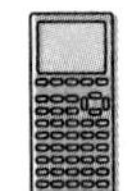

Visit www.SaxonPublishers.com/ActivitiesC2 *for a graphing calculator activity.*

Solution

a. $C = \pi d$
$C \approx 3.14(30 \text{ in.})$
$C \approx$ **94.2 in.**

b. $C = \pi d$
$C \approx \frac{22}{7}(14 \text{ ft})$
$C \approx$ **44 ft**

c. $C = \pi d$
$C = \pi(20 \text{ cm})$
$C =$ **20πcm**

Note the form of answer **c:** first 20 times π, then the unit of measure.

Discuss When might it be better to use $\frac{22}{7}$ instead of 3.14 for π? Use $\frac{22}{7}$ for π when the radius or diameter is a multiple of 7 to make the calculation easier.

Practice Set

▶ **Generalize** Find the circumference of each circle:

a.

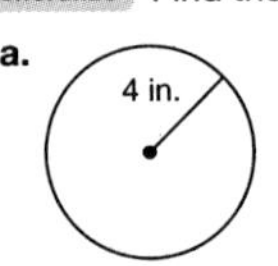

Use 3.14 for π.
25.12 in.

b.

Use $\frac{22}{7}$ for π.
132 mm

c.

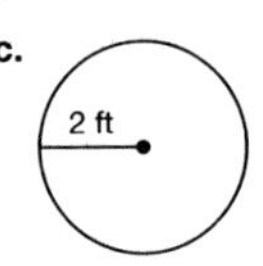

Leave π as π.
4π ft

▶ **d.** **Explain** Sylvia used a compass to draw a circle. If the point of the compass was 3 inches from the point of the pencil, how can she find the circumference of the circle? (Use 3.14 for π.) The distance from the point of the compass to the point of the pencil is the radius of the circle. Since the radius is 3, the diameter is 2×3 or 6. Sylvia can substitute this value into the formula $C = \pi d$ and solve for C. $C = 3.14 \times 6 = 18.84$ inches.

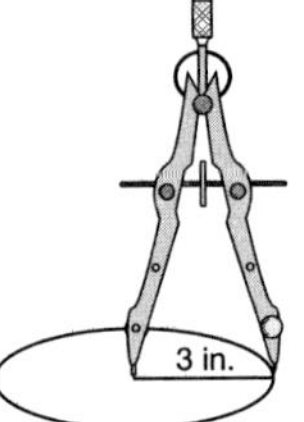

Written Practice *Strengthening Concepts*

1. (46) If 5 pounds of apples cost $4.45, then

a. what is the price per pound? $0.89 per pound

b. what is the cost for 8 pounds of apples? $7.12

2. (41) **a.** Simplify and compare: 0.27 = 0.27

(0.3)(0.4) + (0.3)(0.5) ◯ 0.3(0.4 + 0.5)

b. What property is illustrated by this comparison? Distributive Property

▶ ***3.** (65) Find the circumference for each circle.

a.

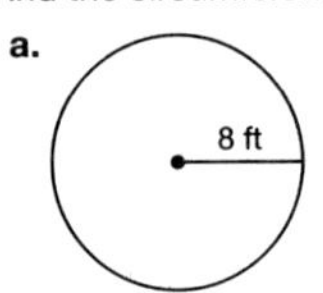

Leave π as π.
16π ft

b.

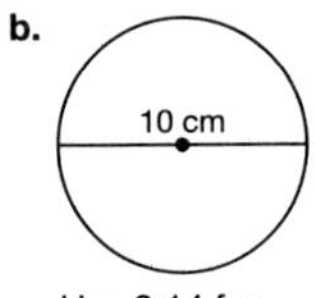

Use 3.14 for π.
31.4 cm

c.

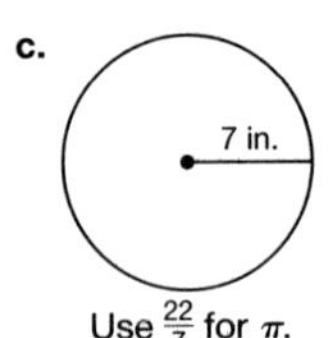

Use $\frac{22}{7}$ for π.
44 in.

▶ See Math Conversations in the sidebar.

4. (44, 46) The car traveled 350 miles on 15 gallons of gasoline. The car averaged how many miles per gallon? Round the answer to the nearest tenth. $23.3\,\frac{\text{miles}}{\text{gallon}}$

5. (28) The average of 2 and 4 is 3. What is the average of the reciprocals of 2 and 4? $\frac{3}{8}$

6. (51) Write 12 billion in scientific notation. 1.2×10^{10}

7\. 60 computers

$\frac{1}{6}$ were shipped.	10 computers
$\frac{5}{6}$ were not shipped.	10 computers
	10 computers
	10 computers
	10 computers
	10 computers

▶ **7.** (22, 36) **Model** Diagram this statement. Then answer the questions that follow.

One sixth of the five dozen computers were shipped.

a. How many computers were not shipped? 50 computers

b. What was the ratio of computers shipped to those that were not shipped? $\frac{1}{5}$

c. What percent of the computers were shipped? $16\frac{2}{3}\%$

8\. a. one possibility: D C A B

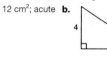

▶ * **8.** (Inv. 6) **a.** **Represent** Draw segment AB. Draw segment DC parallel to segment AB but not the same length. Draw segments between the endpoints of segments AB and DC to form a quadrilateral.

b. **Classify** What type of quadrilateral was formed in **a?** trapezoid

9. (37) Find the area of each triangle. (Dimensions are in centimeters.) Then classify each triangle as acute, obtuse, or right.

a. 12 cm²; acute **b.** 12 cm²; right

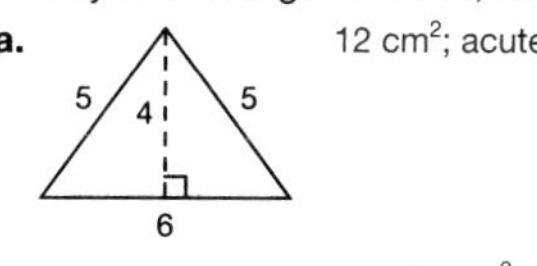

c. 12 cm²; obtuse

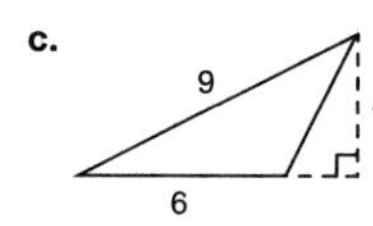

▶ **10.** (28, 34) What is the average of the two numbers indicated by arrows on the number line below? 0.82

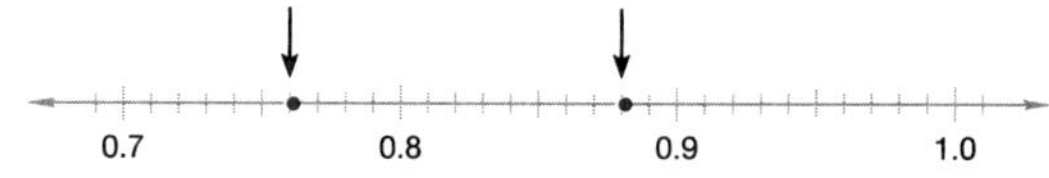

Write equations to solve problems **11** and **12.**

11. (60) What number is 75 percent of 64? $W_N = 0.75 \times 64$; 48

12. (46) What is the tax on a \$7.40 item if the sales-tax rate is 8%? $t = 0.08 \times \$7.40$; \$0.59

* **13.** (64) **Generalize** Find each sum:

a. $(-3) + (-8)$ -11

b. $(+3) + (-8)$ -5

▶ **c.** $(-0.3) + (+0.8) + (-0.5)$ 0

▶ See Math Conversations in the sidebar.

3 Written Practice (Continued)

Math Conversations

Discussion opportunities are provided below.

Problem 7 Model

Extend the Problem

"Sketch a circle to show the computers that were shipped and those that were not shipped. Label the circle with fractions and percents."

Sample

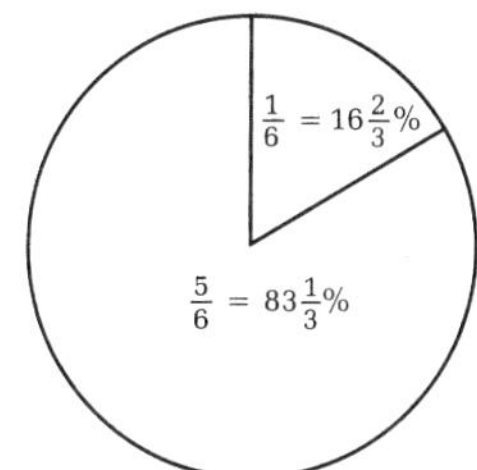

Problem 8 Represent

Have students share the different quadrilaterals that could be formed for this problem. Answers will vary.

Problem 13c Generalize

"Would using the Commutative Property make simplifying this expression easier? Why or why not?" Answers may vary.

Errors and Misconceptions

Problem 10

Some students might have difficulty identifying the numbers indicated by the arrows. Be sure students understand that the number line is divided into hundredths; 0.7 = 0.70 and so on.

(continued)

3 Written Practice (Continued)

Math Conversations

Discussion opportunities are provided below.

Problem 15 Evaluate

Have students explain how they could use mental math to convert 0.95 liters to milliliters. There are three zeros in 1000 milliliters, so move the decimal point in 0.95 three places to the right.

Problem 20 Analyze

Have students explain their reasoning for each problem.

Problem 21

Extend the Problem

Tell students that the mean of the data is 16.75.

"Why are the mean and median close in value?" The data is closely grouped with no values far from the median on one side to pull the mean one way or the other.

(continued)

Math Language
The **origin** is the point (0, 0) on a coordinate plane.

14. (Inv. 3) A circle is drawn on a coordinate plane with its center at the origin. One point on the circle is (3, 4). Use a compass and graph paper to graph the circle. Then answer **a** and **b.**

a. What are the coordinates of the points where the circle intersects the x-axis? (5, 0), (−5, 0)

b. What is the diameter of the circle? 10 units

▸ **15.** (50) Evaluate Use a unit multiplier to convert 0.95 liters to milliliters.
0.95 liters $\cdot \frac{1000 \text{ milliliters}}{1 \text{ liter}}$ = 950 milliliters

16. (52) Evaluate: $ab + a + \frac{a}{b}$ if $a = 5$ and $b = 0.2$ 31

17. (13) How many small blocks were used to build this cube? 27 blocks

18.
a. ∠*COD* or ∠*DOC*
b. ∠*AOB* or ∠*BOA*

18. (40) Recall that one angle is the complement of another angle if their sum is 90°, and that one angle is the supplement of another if their sum is 180°. In this figure, **a** which angle is a complement of ∠*BOC* and **b** which angle is a supplement of ∠*BOC?*

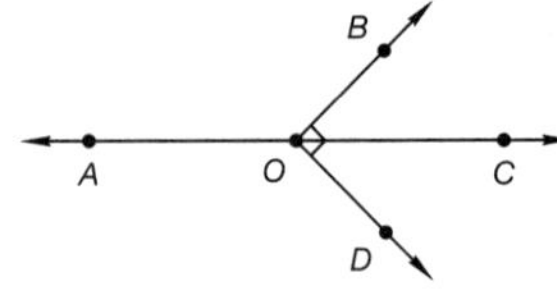

19. (29, 33) Round each number to the nearest whole number to estimate the product of 19.875 and $4\frac{7}{8}$. 100

▸ **20.** (58, 62) Analyze Refer to △*ABC* at right to answer the following questions:

C A 62° 59° B

a. What is the measure of ∠*A?* 59°

b. Which side of the triangle is the longest side? $\overline{AB}$ or $\overline{BA}$

c. Triangle *ABC* is an acute triangle. It is also what other type of triangle? isosceles triangle

d. Triangle *ABC*'s line of symmetry passes through which vertex? C

21. a. Arrange the numbers in order, and look for the middle number. Since there is an even number of scores, there are two middle numbers. So the median is the mean of the two middle numbers.

▸ **21.** (Inv. 4) **a.** Describe how to find the median of this set of 12 scores.

18, 17, 15, 20, 16, 14, 15, 16, 17, 18, 16, 19

b. What is the median of the set of scores? 16.5

22. (62) Answer true or false:

a. All equilateral triangles are congruent. false

b. All equilateral triangles are similar. true

▸ See Math Conversations in the sidebar.

23. (32, 34) The high jump bar was raised from 2.15 meters to 2.2 meters. How many centimeters was the bar raised? 5 centimeters

▶ **Generalize** Simplify:

24. (47) $\frac{10^3 \cdot 10^3}{10^2}$ 10^4 or 10,000

25. (49)

	4 days	5 hr	15 min
−	1 day	7 hr	50 min
	2 days	21 hr	25 min

26. (45) $4.5 \div (0.4 + 0.5)$ 5

27. (52) $\frac{3 + 0.6}{3 - 0.6}$ 1.5

28. (26) $4\frac{1}{5} \div \left(1\frac{1}{6} \cdot 3\right)$ $1\frac{1}{5}$

29. (52) $3^2 + \sqrt{4 \cdot 7 - 3}$ 14

30. (63) $|-3| + 4[(5 - 2)(3 + 1)]$ 51

Early Finishers *Real-World Application*

Central Park is a rectangular shaped park in the middle of New York City. The area of the park is 3.41 km^2.

a. If the width of the park is 800 meters, what is its length to the nearest meter? Show your work. Sample: $0.8x = 3.41$; 4263 meters

b. How many acres is the park to the nearest acre? (Note: 1 km^2 ≈ 247 acres) Use a unit multiplier and show your work. $\frac{3.41 \text{ km}^2}{1} \times \frac{247 \text{ acres}}{1 \text{ km}^2} \approx$ 842 acres

▶ See Math Conversations in the sidebar.

3 Written Practice *(Continued)*

Math Conversations

Discussion opportunities are provided below.

Problems 24–30 Generalize

Have students choose whether they would use mental math or paper and pencil to simplify each problem. Ask them to explain their choice. Answers will vary.

Errors and Misconceptions

Problem 30

If students have difficulty with this problem, point out that $5 - 2$ and $3 + 1$ are in parentheses enclosed by brackets. Remind students to perform the operations in parentheses first and the operations in brackets next. Then follow the order of operations to complete the problem.

Looking Forward

Understanding circumference and pi prepares students for:

- **Lesson 82,** finding the area of circles.
- **Lesson 95,** finding the volume of right circular cylinders.
- **Lesson 104,** finding the perimeter of figures that contain semicircles and the perimeter of sectors of circles.
- **Lesson 105,** finding the surface area of right circular cylinders (cans).

Assessment

30–40 minutes *For use after Lesson 65*

Distribute **Cumulative Test 12** to each student. Two versions of the test are available in *Saxon Math Course 2 Course Assessments Book*. Have students complete the **Power-Up Test** first. Allow 10 minutes. Then have students work the 20 numbered items on the **Cumulative Test.** Students may use copies of the answer sheet to record their work. Track individual and class progress with the **Test Analysis** forms.

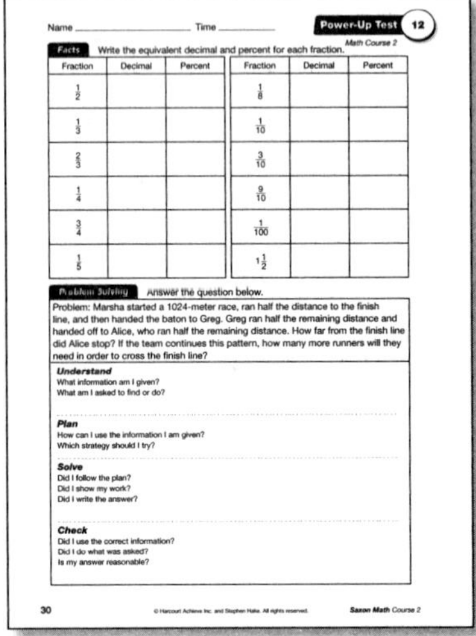

Name ______ Time ______

Power-Up Test 12
Math Course 2

Facts Write the equivalent decimal and percent for each fraction.

Fraction	Decimal	Percent	Fraction	Decimal	Percent
$\frac{1}{2}$			$\frac{1}{8}$		
$\frac{1}{3}$			$\frac{1}{10}$		
$\frac{2}{3}$			$\frac{3}{10}$		
$\frac{1}{4}$			$\frac{9}{10}$		
$\frac{3}{4}$			$\frac{1}{100}$		
$\frac{1}{5}$			$1\frac{1}{2}$		

Problem Solving Answer the question below.

Problem: Marsha started a 1024-meter race, ran half the distance to the finish line, and then handed the baton to Greg. Greg ran half the remaining distance and handed off to Alice, who ran half the remaining distance. How far from the finish line did Alice stop? If the team continues this pattern, how many more runners will they need in order to cross the finish line?

Understand
What information am I given?
What am I asked to find or do?

Plan
How can I use the information I am given?
Which strategy should I try?

Solve
Did I follow the plan?
Did I show my work?
Did I write the answer?

Check
Did I use the correct information?
Did I do what was asked?
Is my answer reasonable?

30 © Harcourt Achieve Inc. and Stephen Hake. All rights reserved. ***Saxon Math** Course 2*

Power-Up Test 12

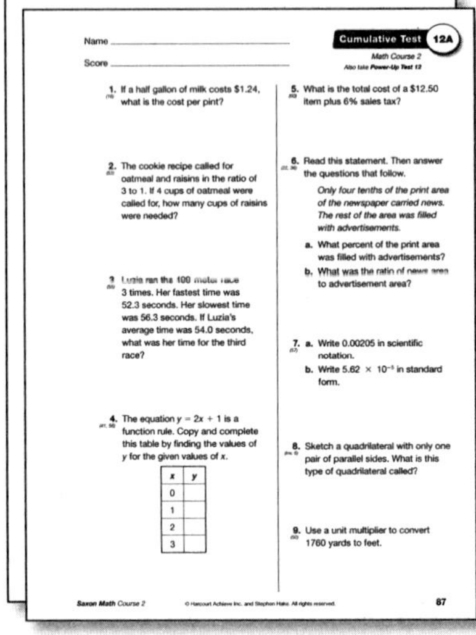

Name ______
Score ______

Cumulative Test 12A
Math Course 2
*Also take **Power-Up Test 12***

1. If a half gallon of milk costs $1.24, what is the cost per pint?

2. The cookie recipe called for oatmeal and raisins in the ratio of 3 to 1. If 4 cups of oatmeal were called for, how many cups of raisins were needed?

3. Luzia ran the 100 meter race 3 times. Her fastest time was 52.3 seconds. Her slowest time was 56.3 seconds. If Luzia's average time was 54.0 seconds, what was her time for the third race?

4. The equation $y = 2x + 1$ is a function rule. Copy and complete this table by finding the values of y for the given values of x.

x	y
0	
1	
2	
3	

5. What is the total cost of a $12.50 item plus 6% sales tax?

6. Read this statement. Then answer the questions that follow.

Only four tenths of the print area of the newspaper carried news. The rest of the area was filled with advertisements.

a. What percent of the print area was filled with advertisements?
b. What was the ratio of news area to advertisement area?

7. a. Write 0.00205 in scientific notation.
b. Write 5.62×10^{-5} in standard form.

8. Sketch a quadrilateral with only one pair of parallel sides. What is this type of quadrilateral called?

9. Use a unit multiplier to convert 1760 yards to feet.

***Saxon Math** Course 2* © Harcourt Achieve Inc. and Stephen Hake. All rights reserved. 87

Cumulative Test 12A

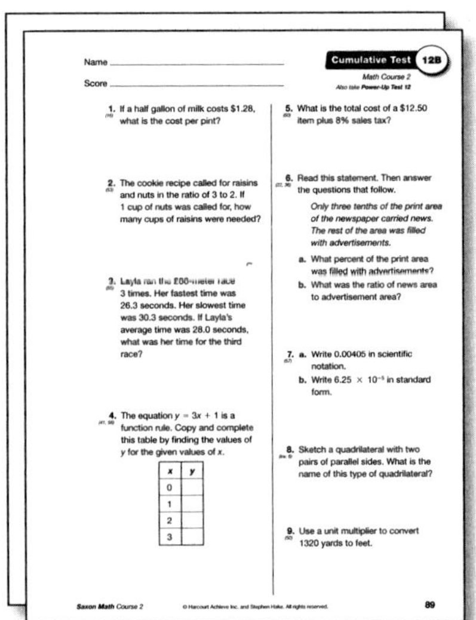

Name ______
Score ______

Cumulative Test 12B
Math Course 2
*Also take **Power-Up Test 12***

1. If a half gallon of milk costs $1.28, what is the cost per pint?

2. The cookie recipe called for raisins and nuts in the ratio of 3 to 2. If 1 cup of nuts was called for, how many cups of raisins were needed?

3. Layla ran the 200-meter race 3 times. Her fastest time was 26.3 seconds. Her slowest time was 30.3 seconds. If Layla's average time was 28.0 seconds, what was her time for the third race?

4. The equation $y = 3x + 1$ is a function rule. Copy and complete this table by finding the values of y for the given values of x.

x	y
0	
1	
2	
3	

5. What is the total cost of a $12.50 item plus 8% sales tax?

6. Read this statement. Then answer the questions that follow.

Only three tenths of the print area of the newspaper carried news. The rest of the area was filled with advertisements.

a. What percent of the print area was filled with advertisements?
b. What was the ratio of news area to advertisement area?

7. a. Write 0.00405 in scientific notation.
b. Write 6.25×10^{-5} in standard form.

8. Sketch a quadrilateral with two pairs of parallel sides. What is the name of this type of quadrilateral?

9. Use a unit multiplier to convert 1320 yards to feet.

***Saxon Math** Course 2* © Harcourt Achieve Inc. and Stephen Hake. All rights reserved. 89

Alternative Cumulative Test 12B

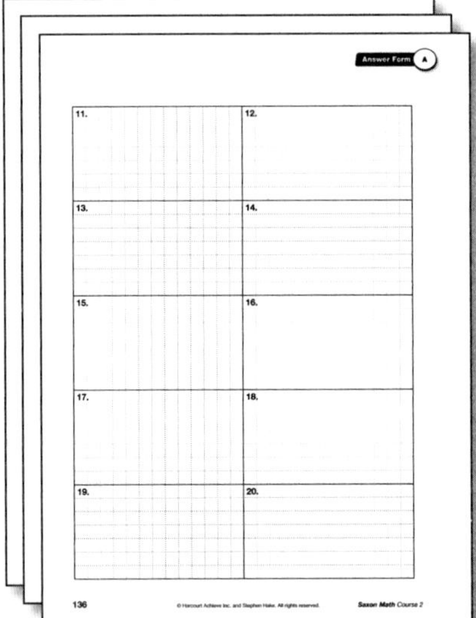

Answer Form A

11. 12.
13. 14.
15. 16.
17. 18.
19. 20.

136 © Harcourt Achieve Inc. and Stephen Hake. All rights reserved. ***Saxon Math** Course 2*

Optional Answer Forms

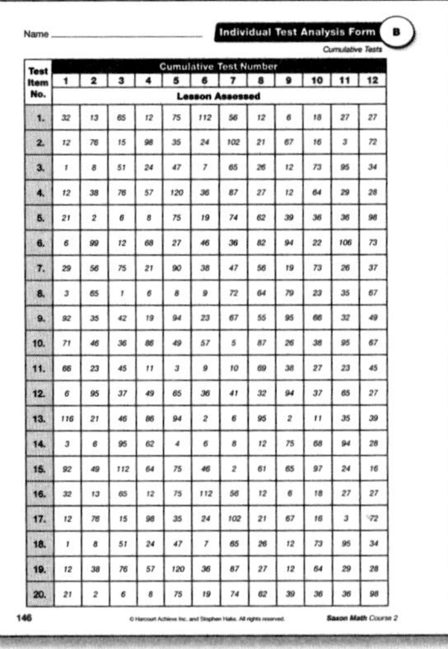

Name ______

Individual Test Analysis Form B
Cumulative Tests

Test Item No.	Cumulative Test Number 1	2	3	4	5	6	7	8	9	10	11	12
	Lesson Assessed											
1.	32	13	65	12	75	112	56	12	6	18	27	27
2.	12	76	15	98	35	24	102	21	67	16	3	72
3.	1	8	51	24	47	7	65	26	12	73	95	34
4.	12	38	76	57	120	36	87	27	12	64	29	28
5.	21	2	6	8	75	19	74	62	39	36	36	98
6.	6	99	12	68	27	46	36	82	94	22	106	73
7.	29	56	75	21	90	38	47	56	19	73	26	37
8.	3	65	1	6	8	9	72	64	79	23	35	67
9.	92	35	42	19	94	23	67	55	95	66	32	49
10.	71	46	36	86	49	57	5	87	26	38	95	67
11.	66	23	45	11	3	9	10	69	38	27	23	45
12.	6	95	37	49	65	36	41	32	94	37	65	27
13.	116	21	46	86	94	2	6	95	2	11	35	39
14.	3	6	95	62	4	6	8	12	75	68	94	28
15.	92	49	112	64	75	46	2	61	65	97	24	16
16.	32	13	65	12	75	112	56	12	6	18	27	27
17.	12	76	15	98	35	24	102	21	67	16	3	72
18.	1	8	51	24	47	7	65	26	12	73	95	34
19.	12	38	76	57	120	36	87	27	12	64	29	28
20.	21	2	6	8	75	19	74	62	39	36	36	98

146 © Harcourt Achieve Inc. and Stephen Hake. All rights reserved. ***Saxon Math** Course 2*

Individual Test Analysis Form

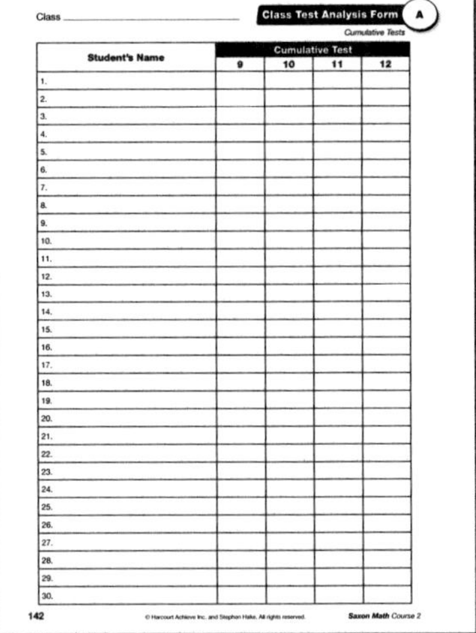

Class ______

Class Test Analysis Form A
Cumulative Tests

Student's Name	Cumulative Test 9	10	11	12
1.				
2.				
3.				
4.				
5.				
6.				
7.				
8.				
9.				
10.				
11.				
12.				
13.				
14.				
15.				
16.				
17.				
18.				
19.				
20.				
21.				
22.				
23.				
24.				
25.				
26.				
27.				
28.				
29.				
30.				

142 © Harcourt Achieve Inc. and Stephen Hake. All rights reserved. ***Saxon Math** Course 2*

Class Test Analysis Form

Reteaching

Students who score below 80% on the assessment may be in need of reteaching. Look for the causes of student mistakes. If errors are conceptual, refer to the *Reteaching Masters* for reteaching.

Performance Activity 12

Predicting–2

Assign after Lesson 65 and Test 12

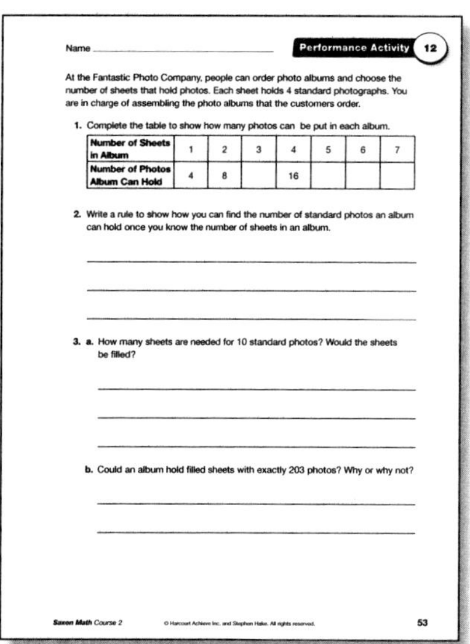

Name ____________ **Performance Activity 12**

At the Fantastic Photo Company, people can order photo albums and choose the number of sheets that hold photos. Each sheet holds 4 standard photographs. You are in charge of assembling the photo albums that the customers order.

1. Complete the table to show how many photos can be put in each album.

Number of Sheets in Album	1	2	3	4	5	6	7
Number of Photos Album Can Hold	4	8		16			

2. Write a rule to show how you can find the number of standard photos an album can hold once you know the number of sheets in an album.

3. a. How many sheets are needed for 10 standard photos? Would the sheets be filled?

   b. Could an album hold filled sheets with exactly 203 photos? Why or why not?

Saxon Math Course 2

53

Performance Activity 12

Objectives

- Complete a function table.
- Write a rule for a function table.
- Communicate their ideas through writing.

Materials

Performance Activity 12

Preparation

Make copies of **Performance Tasks 12.** (One each per student.)

Time Requirement

15–30 minutes; Begin in class and complete at home.

Activity

Explain to students that for this activity they will be finding out how many photos various albums of different sizes can hold for the Fantastic Photo Company. They will complete a table and write a rule to show how many photos an album will hold given the number of sheets in the album. They will also explain why it is impossible to have an album that holds exactly 10 photos. Explain that all of the information students need is on **Performance Activity 12.**

Criteria for Evidence of Learning

- Accurately completes the table.
- Accurately writes a rule.
- Communicates mathematical ideas clearly and accurately.

Meeting Standards

National Council of Teachers of Mathematics (NCTM)

Algebra

AL.1a Represent, analyze, and generalize a variety of patterns with tables, graphs, words, and, when possible, symbolic rules

AL.3a Model and solve contextualized problems using various representations, such as graphs, tables, and equations

Representation

RE.5b Select, apply, and translate among mathematical representations to solve problems

Ratio Problems Involving Totals

Objectives

- Use ratio boxes to organize the data in ratio problems involving totals.
- Use proportions to solve ratio word problems involving totals.

Lesson Preparation

Materials

- **Power Up N** (in *Instructional Masters*)

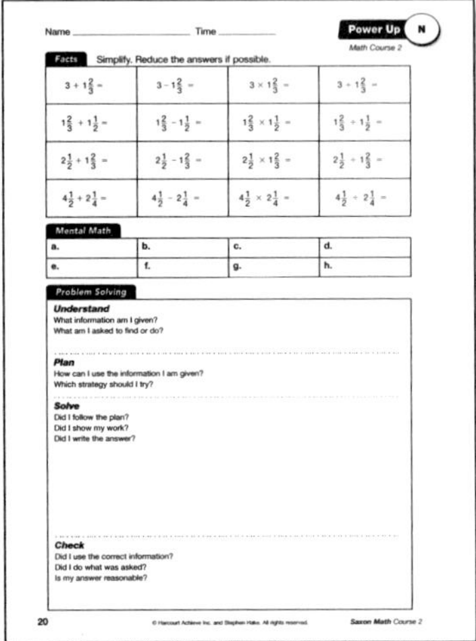

Power Up N

Math Language

English Learners (ESL)
collect

Technology Resources

Student eBook Complete student textbook in electronic format.

Resources and Planner CD Assessment, reteaching, and instructional masters, plus a pacing calendar with standards.

Test and Practice Generator CD Create additional practice sheets and custom-made tests.

www.SaxonPublishers.com Visit for more student activities and planning materials.

Inclusion

Adaptations CD Adapted lessons, investigations, practice and assessments.

Meeting Standards

National Council of Teachers of Mathematics (NCTM)

Numbers and Operations

NO.1d Understand and use ratios and proportions to represent quantitative relationships

NO.3d Develop, analyze, and explain methods for solving problems involving proportions, such as scaling and finding equivalent ratios

Problem Solving

PS.1b Solve problems that arise in mathematics and in other contexts

Power-Up Discussion

For use with Power Up, p. 466

Problem-Solving Strategy: Make It Simpler/ Guess and Check

A palindrome is a number or word that can be read the same forward or backward, such as "42324" or "Madam, I'm Adam." Start with a 4-digit whole number, and then add to it the number formed by reversing its digits. To the sum, add the number formed by reversing the sum's digits. Continue this process, and eventually you will have a sum that is a palindrome. Why do you think this will always be the case?

Understand Understand the problem.

"What information are we given?"

A palindrome is a number, word, or phrase that can be read the same forwards and backwards. We are given a process to create a palindrome starting with a 4-digit number.

"What are we asked to do?"

Determine why a palindrome always eventually results when we sum numbers with reversed digits.

Plan Make a plan.

"What problem-solving strategy will we use?"

We will look at *simpler*, but similar problems to see if we can determine how palindromes are made. Then we will *guess and check* to see if our hypothesis is correct.

Solve Carry out the plan.

Teacher Note: Allow students time to try 4-digit problems of their own making.

"Can palindromes be formed if we begin with a single-digit number?"

Yes (i.e. 8 + 8 = 16 + 61 = 77)

"How are palindromes formed from 2-digit numbers using digits less than 5?"

24 + 42 = 66

"How are palindromes formed from 3-digit numbers using digits less than 5?"

301 + 103 = 404

"How quickly can we achieve a palindrome when using digits less than 5?"

In one step.

"Why?"

Because there is never any regrouping involved.

"How are palindromes formed from 2-digit numbers using digits greater than 5?"

78 + 78 = 156 + 651 = 807 + 708 = 1515 + 5151 = 6666

"How many steps does it take to achieve a palindrome when using digits greater than 5?"

It varies.

"Why?"

Because regrouping is often involved.

"What property of arithmetic makes this process work?"

The Commutative Property tells us that 1 + 5 is the same as 5 + 1. By reversing a number's digits we place digits at both ends of the sum that add to the same total.

Check Look back.

"Did we do what we were asked to do?"

Yes, we determined why palindromes are eventually formed when you reverse a number's digits and add it to itself (the Commutative Property of Addition).

1 Power Up

Facts

Distribute **Power Up N** to students. See answers below.

Mental Math

Encourage students to share different ways to mentally compute these exercises. Strategies for exercises **a** and **f** are listed below.

a. Add Left to Right

$3.65 + 1.2 = 4.85$

$4.85 + 2 = 6.85$

Add Whole Numbers First

$3 + 1 + 2 = 6$

$0.65 + 0.2 = 0.85$

$6 + 0.85 = 6.85$

f. Multiply by a Fraction

$\frac{1}{4} \times 24 = 24 \div 4$ or 6

Equivalent Expressions

$0.25 \times 24 = 0.5 \times 12$

$0.5 \times 12 = 1 \times 6$ or 6

Problem Solving

Refer to **Power-Up Discussion,** p. 466B.

2 New Concepts

Instruction

Remind students that they have already learned about ratio word problems and how to use a ratio box to write a proportion. Explain that this lesson takes them a step further, to solving ratio problems where totals are used.

"Since we know that the total number of students is 180, what do we know about the value of B and G?" Both will be less than 180 since their sum is 180. From the given ratio we know that *B* is greater than *G*. Since the ratio numbers are close in size we expect *B* and *G* also to be relatively close in size.

(continued)

LESSON 66

• Ratio Problems Involving Totals

Power Up — *Building Power*

facts Power Up N

mental math

a. **Decimals:** $3.65 + 1.2 + 2$ 6.85

b. **Decimals/Exponents:** 1.2×10^{-3} 0.0012

c. **Algebra:** $9y + 3 = 75$ 8

d. **Measurement:** Convert 20 decimeters (dm) to meters. 2 meters

e. **Power/Roots:** $\sqrt{144} + 2^3$ 20

f. **Percent:** 25% of 24 6

g. **Geometry:** A circle has a radius of 8 mm. What is the circumference of the circle? 50.24 mm

h. **Estimation:** Estimate the product of 3.14 and 25. 75

problem solving A palindrome is a number or word that can be read the same forward or backward, such as "42324" or "Madam, I'm Adam." Start with a 4-digit whole number, and then add to it the number formed by reversing its digits. To the sum, add the number formed by reversing the sum's digits. Continue this process, and eventually you will have a sum that is a palindrome. Why do you think this will always be the case? The Commutative Property tells us that 1 + 5 is the same as 5 + 1. By reversing a number's digits we place digits at both ends of the sum that add to the same number.

New Concept — *Increasing Knowledge*

Some ratio problems require that we use the total to solve the problem. Consider the following problem:

The ratio of boys to girls at the assembly was 5 to 4. If there were 180 students in the assembly, how many girls were there?

We begin by making a ratio box. This time we add a third row for the total number of students.

	Ratio	Actual Count
Boys	5	*B*
Girls	4	*G*
Total	9	180

Sample: The third row gives the total ratio number and the total actual count. We use it when solving ratio problems in which the total is given.

Thinking Skills

Summarize

What is the purpose of the third row in the ratio box? How can we use it?

Discuss How is this ratio box different from the ratio boxes we have been using? There is a third row entitled "Total" and more than one unknown.

Facts Simplify. Reduce the answers if possible.

$3 + 1\frac{2}{3} = 4\frac{2}{3}$	$3 - 1\frac{2}{3} = 1\frac{1}{3}$	$3 \times 1\frac{2}{3} = 5$	$3 \div 1\frac{2}{3} = 1\frac{4}{5}$
$1\frac{2}{3} + 1\frac{1}{2} = 3\frac{1}{6}$	$1\frac{2}{3} - 1\frac{1}{2} = \frac{1}{6}$	$1\frac{2}{3} \times 1\frac{1}{2} = 2\frac{1}{2}$	$1\frac{2}{3} \div 1\frac{1}{2} = 1\frac{1}{9}$
$2\frac{1}{2} + 1\frac{2}{3} = 4\frac{1}{6}$	$2\frac{1}{2} - 1\frac{2}{3} = \frac{5}{6}$	$2\frac{1}{2} \times 1\frac{2}{3} = 4\frac{1}{6}$	$2\frac{1}{2} \div 1\frac{2}{3} = 1\frac{1}{2}$
$4\frac{1}{2} + 2\frac{1}{4} = 6\frac{3}{4}$	$4\frac{1}{2} - 2\frac{1}{4} = 2\frac{1}{4}$	$4\frac{1}{2} \times 2\frac{1}{4} = 10\frac{1}{8}$	$4\frac{1}{2} \div 2\frac{1}{4} = 2$

In the ratio column we wrote 5 for boys and 4 for girls, then *added these to get 9 for the total ratio number*. We were given 180 as the actual count of students. This is a total. We can use two rows from this table to write a proportion. Since we were asked to find the number of girls, we will use the "girls" row.

Because we know both total numbers, we will also use the "total" row. Using these numbers, we solve the proportion.

	Ratio	Actual Count
Boys	5	B
Girls	4	G
Total	9	180

$$\frac{4}{9} = \frac{G}{180}$$
$$9G = 720$$
$$G = 80$$

We find there were 80 girls. We can use this answer to complete the ratio box.

	Ratio	Actual Count
Boys	5	100
Girls	4	80
Total	9	180

Example

The ratio of football players to soccer players in the room was 5 to 7. If the football and soccer players in the room totaled 48, how many were football players?

Solution

We use the information in the problem to form a table. We include a row for the total number of players.

Explain How do we find the number to put into the total ratio box in the table? Add the two ratios for football and soccer players: 5 + 7 = 12.

	Ratio	Actual Count
Football Players	5	F
Soccer Players	7	S
Total Players	12	48

$$\frac{5}{12} = \frac{F}{48}$$
$$12F = 240$$
$$F = 20$$

To find the number of football players, we write a proportion from the "football players" row and the "total players" row. We solve the proportion to find that there were **20 football players** in the room.

2 New Concepts *(Continued)*

Instruction

Students should focus on the variable in the Girls row only. Remind them to use cross products to find G. After they have determined the value of G they can simply subtract the number of girls from the total to find the number of boys.

Ask students whether they could find the number of boys without finding the number of girls. yes

Ask a volunteer to write the proportion and solve the problem on the chalkboard. You could use the proportion $\frac{5}{9} = \frac{B}{180}$, then subtract 100 from 180 to get the number of girls.

Point out the connection between finding the totals in both columns of the ratio box. Just as they can find the total in the Actual Count column by adding the other two terms, they can find the total in the Ratio column by adding.

Example

Instruction

Once students understand how to find the number of football and soccer players, ask them what factor each actual number was divided by to get the ratio. 4

(continued)

Math Background

Why it is important to use ratio boxes to set up proportion problems?

Drawing a model is a helpful problem-solving technique. The ratio box helps students focus visually on the data and establish the relationship between what is given and what is unknown. Ratio boxes help students to read the problem carefully and to organize the data before performing calculations.

Since so many mathematical relationships are proportional, ratios are applicable across a broad spectrum of mathematical content. Ratio boxes serve as a versatile tool for students who are in the process of becoming proportional thinkers.

For students who have difficulty setting up proportions, the ratio box is an important guide. With so many different equations possible, it is easy to become confused. With time and practice most students will replace the ratio box with a mental image.

Inclusion

Help students visualize the part and whole of the example ratio by asking 12 students to stand up. Then ask 5 of the 12 to be football players. Have each keep his/her arm up as if passing a football. Ask:

"Are the football players separate or part of the total group?" part

"What other part is in the total group?" the soccer players

Have each of those students keep his/her leg extended outward as if kicking a ball.

2 New Concepts (Continued)

Practice Set

Problem a *Explain*

Ask students what letters they can use in the ratio box to represent the number of racing bikes and the number of mountain bikes. Have them explain their reasoning for choosing each variable. Sample: m for mountain bikes and r for racing bikes.

Problem b *Represent*

Students should notice that they will be looking for the total number of items recycled, not the actual number of bottles. The actual number of cans is given and can be used in the proportion to find the answer without having to find the number of bottles.

3 Written Practice

Math Conversations

Discussion opportunities are provided below.

Problem 4 *Represent*

Ask a student volunteer to draw a ratio box on the board and explain how to set up the proportion.

	Ratio	Actual Count
Dimes	5	d
Quarters	8	q
Total	13	520

For Dimes $\frac{5}{13} = \frac{d}{520}$ **For Quarters** $\frac{8}{13} = \frac{q}{520}$

Ask students how would they write expressions for finding the dollar values for the dimes and quarters.
Sample: $200 \times 0.10 = d$; $320 \times 0.25 = q$

Summarize with the solution to the problem.
200 dimes = \$20; 320 quarters = \$80; \$100 is in the machine

Errors and Misconceptions

Problem 2

If students wrote $6\frac{1}{4}$ miles as the answer, they did not take the round trip into consideration. Point out that Ahmad walked $1\frac{1}{4}$ miles *each* way for 5 days. If he walked $6\frac{1}{4}$ miles one way for 5 days, how would you find the distance he walked round trip? double $6\frac{1}{4}$ or $12\frac{1}{2}$ miles round trip

(continued)

From this information we can complete the ratio box.

	Ratio	Actual Count
Football Players	5	20
Soccer Players	7	28
Total Players	12	48

Practice Set *Represent* Solve these problems. Begin by drawing a ratio box.

a. I can make a ratio box with 3, 5, and 8 in the first column and M, R, and 72 in the second column. Then I can write and solve a proportion: $\frac{5}{8} = \frac{R}{72}$; $R =$ 45 racing bikes.

▸ **a.** *Explain* The bicycle store has mountain bikes and racing bikes on the showroom floor at a ratio of 3 to 5. If there are a total of 72 bicycles on the showroom floor, how can you find the number of racing bikes? Use your method to find the answer.

▸ **b.** The Recycling Club collects cans and bottles for recycling. The ratio of cans to bottles collected was 8 to 9. If they collected 240 cans, how many items to be recycled did they collect in all? 510 items

c. The ratio of big fish to little fish in the pond was 4 to 11. If there were 1320 fish in the pond, how many big fish were there? 352 big fish

Written Practice *Strengthening Concepts*

1. (38, 60) Use the circle graph to answer **a** and **b**.

How Mr. Gains Spent His Income

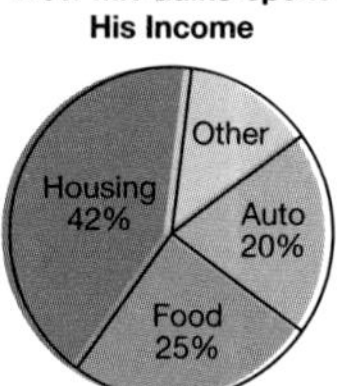

a. What percent of Mr. Gains's income was spent on items other than food and housing? 33%

b. If his income was \$25,000, how much did he spend on food? \$6250

▸ **2.** (28) It is $1\frac{1}{4}$ miles from Ahmad's house to school. How far does Ahmad travel in 5 days walking to school and back? $12\frac{1}{2}$ miles

3. (35) When the sum of 1.9 and 2.2 is subtracted from the product of 1.9 and 2.2, what is the difference? 0.08

▸ *** 4.** (66) *Represent* Use a ratio box to solve this problem. There were a total of 520 dimes and quarters in the bottled water vending machine.

a. If the ratio of dimes to quarters was 5 to 8, how many dimes were there? 200 dimes

b. Use your answer to **a** to find the total amount of money in the machine. \$100

5. (51) Saturn's average distance from the Sun is about 900 million miles. Write that distance in scientific notation. 9×10^8 miles

▸ See Math Conversations in the sidebar.

English Learners

Direct the students' attention to problem b and explain the meaning of the term **collect**. Say:

"If you collect cans, you gather or get together a group of cans."

Ask students to tell about something they collect or would like to collect.

6. Read this statement. Then answer the questions that follow.
(22, 48)

Three tenths of the 400 acres were planted with alfalfa.

a. What percent of the land was planted with alfalfa? 30%

b. How many of the 400 acres were not planted with alfalfa? 280 acres

7. c. It is more likely the sheet will have a name in cursive because less than half the sheets have names that are printed.

7. Twelve of 30 students printed their name at the top of their homework sheet. The rest wrote their names in cursive.
(14, 48)

a. What fraction of the students printed their names? $\frac{2}{5}$

b. What percent of the students printed their names? 40%

c. If one of the homework sheets is selected at random, which is more likely: the name at the top is printed or the name at the top is in cursive? Defend your answer.

▶ *** 8.** **Verify** Find the circumference of each circle:
(65)

a. 65.94 in.

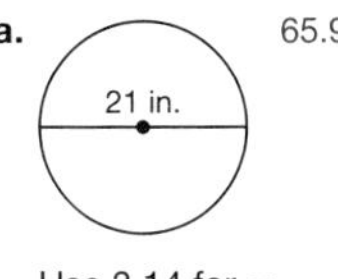

Use 3.14 for π.

b. 66 in.

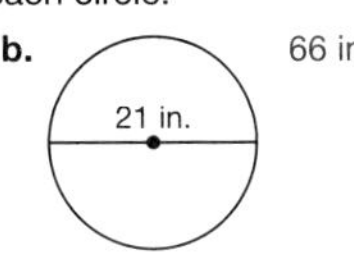

Use $\frac{22}{7}$ for π.

▶ *** 9.** **Analyze** Refer to the figure at right to answer **a–c.** Dimensions are in centimeters.
(37, 61)

a. What is the area of the parallelogram? 336 cm^2

b. The two triangles are congruent. What is the area of one of the triangles? 168 cm^2

c. Each triangle is isosceles. What is the perimeter of one of the triangles? 64 cm

10. Write 32.5 billion in scientific notation. 3.25×10^{10}
(51)

Write equations to solve problems **11** and **12.**

11. What number is 90 percent of 3500? $W_N = 0.9 \times 3500$; 3150
(60)

12. What number is $\frac{5}{6}$ of $2\frac{2}{5}$? $W_N = \frac{5}{6} \times 2\frac{2}{5}$; 2
(60)

13. Complete the table.
(48)

Fraction	Decimal	Percent
a. $\frac{9}{20}$	0.45	**b.** 45%
c. $\frac{3}{40}$	**d.** 0.075	7.5% or $7\frac{1}{2}$%

▶ *** 14.** **Generalize** Find each sum:
(64)

a. (5) + (−4) + (6) + (−1) 6

b. 3 + (−5) + (+4) + (−2) 0

c. (−0.3) + (−0.5) −0.8

▶ See Math Conversations in the sidebar.

3 Written Practice (Continued)

Math Conversations

Discussion opportunities are provided below.

Problem 8 Verify

"The circles are the same size, why are the answers different?" Using different numbers for π causes a difference in the actual answer. $\frac{22}{7}$ is a little greater than π and 3.14 is a little less than π.

Problem 9 Analyze

Extend the Problem

"If you attached a third congruent triangle to the parallelogram, what type of quadrilateral would you form?" trapezoid

"What number could you multiply times the area of the parallelogram to get the area of the trapezoid?" $1\frac{1}{2}$ or $\frac{3}{2}$

Problem 14 Generalize

Ask student volunteers to explain their thinking for each problem.

(continued)

3 Written Practice (Continued)

Math Conversations

Discussion opportunities are provided below.

Problem 16 Conclude

Ask students to describe the steps they took to find $\angle b$. Since $\angle a$ and $\angle b$ are vertical angles, $m\angle b$ must also be 55°.

Problems 21–27 Generalize

Ask student to decide whether they would use mental math or paper and pencil to solve each problem. Have them explain their choice. Answers will vary.

Errors and Misconceptions

Problem 17

Some students may not understand that rounding to one nonzero digit is the same as rounding to the greatest place value.
2876 rounds to the nearest thousand or 3000;
513 rounds to the nearest hundred or 500;
18 rounds to the nearest ten or 20;
$3000 \times 500 \times 20 = 30{,}000{,}000$

Problem 20

If students don't know how to start, suggest that they isolate the variable. You might also remind them to rename the fractions with common denominators.

(continued)

---

15. $1.4 \text{ kg} \cdot \frac{1000 \text{ g}}{1 \text{ kg}}$
$= 1400$ g

16. f. The sum of the angles of a triangle is 180°; The sum of the angles of a parallelogram is 360° and the opposite angles are equal.

18.

15. (50) Use a unit multiplier to convert 1.4 kilograms to grams.

▶ * **16.** (40, 61) **Conclude** Refer to the figure at right to answer **a–f.** In the figure, two sides of a parallelogram are extended to form two sides of a right triangle. The measure of $\angle M$ is 35°. Find the measure of these angles.

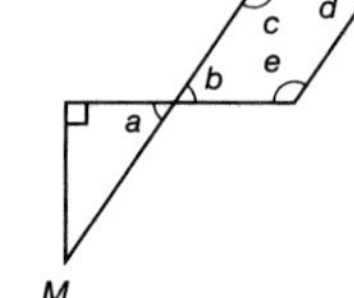

M

a. $\angle a$ 55°

b. $\angle b$ 55°

c. $\angle c$ 125°

d. $\angle d$ 55°

e. $\angle e$ 125°

f. **Explain** What did you have to know about a right triangle in order to solve **a?** What did you have to know about a parallelogram in order to solve **c?**

▶ **17.** (29) Estimate this product by rounding each number to one nonzero digit before multiplying: 30,000,000

(2876)(513)(18)

18. (Inv. 3) The coordinates of the vertices of square *ABCD* are (2, 2), (2, −2), (−2, −2), and (−2, 2). The coordinates of the vertices of square *EFGH* are (2, 0), (0, −2), (−2, 0), and (0, 2). Draw both squares on the same coordinate plane and answer **a–d.**

a. What is the area of square *ABCD?* 16 units²

b. What is the length of one side of square *ABCD?* 4 units

c. Counting two half squares on the grid as one square unit, what is the area of square *EFGH?* 8 units²

d. Remembering that the length of the side of a square is the square root of its area, what is the length of one side of square *EFGH?* $\sqrt{8}$ units

Solve:

19. (39) $\frac{0.9}{1.5} = \frac{12}{n}$ 20

▶ **20.** (30) $\frac{11}{24} + w = \frac{11}{12}$ $\frac{11}{24}$

▶ **Generalize** Simplify:

21. (57) $2^1 - 2^0 - 2^{-1}$ $\frac{1}{2}$

22. (49)
4 lb 12 oz
\+ 1 lb 7 oz
6 lb 3 oz

23. (50) $\frac{3 \text{ ft}}{1 \text{ yd}} \cdot \frac{12 \text{ in.}}{1 \text{ ft}}$ $36\frac{\text{in.}}{\text{yd}}$

24. (45) $16 \div (0.8 \div 0.04)$ 0.8

* **25.** (63) $0.4[0.5 - (0.6)(0.7)]$ 0.032

26. (26) $\frac{3}{8} \cdot 1\frac{2}{3} \cdot 4 \div 1\frac{2}{3}$ $1\frac{1}{2}$

* **27.** (63) $30 - 5[4 + (3)(2) - 5]$ 5

28. (13) Write a word problem for this division: \$2.88 ÷ 12 Sample: If a dozen flavored icicles cost \$2.88, what is the price of each flavored icicle?

▶ See Math Conversations in the sidebar.

▶ **29.** Two identical boxes balance a 9-ounce weight. What is the weight of each box? $4\frac{1}{2}$ ounces
(3)

*** 30.** *Analyze* Refer to the circle with center at point *M* to answer **a–c.**
(Inv. 2, 62)

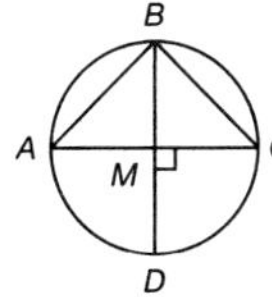

a. Name two chords that are not diameters. $\overline{AB}$ (or $\overline{BA}$), $\overline{BC}$ (or $\overline{CB}$)

▶ **b.** Classify $\triangle AMB$ by its sides. isosceles triangle

▶ **c.** What is the measure of inscribed angle *ABC*? 90°

Early Finishers
Real-World Application

On the first day of the month the balance in Ronda's checking account is \$500. Every day for the next fourteen days, she withdraws \$30. On the fifteenth day Ronda deposits two \$712 checks. Over the next three days she makes three withdrawals that total \$65.

a. Write an expression that represents the total amount in deposits. Write another expression that represents the total amount in withdrawals. sample: 2×712; $14 \times 30 + 65$

b. Write an expression that represents the change from the deposits and withdrawals to the original balance. What is the balance in Ronda's account after all the transactions? sample: $500 + (2 \times 712) - (14 \times 30 + 65)$; \$1439

▶ See Math Conversations in the sidebar.

3 Written Practice *(Continued)*

Math Conversations

Discussion opportunities are provided below.

Problem 29

Extend the Problem

Ask students to write an equation that corresponds to the scale. Sample: $2w = 9$; $w = 4\frac{1}{2}$

Problem 30b Analyze

"Why isn't the answer a right triangle?"

The problem asks for the triangle to be classified by its sides.

Problem 30c Analyze

Ask students to justify their answer. Since the center angles of both triangles are 90°, the remaining angles in each isosceles triangle measures 45°. So, inscribed angle *ABC* consists of two 45° angles and a 90° angle.

Looking Forward

Using ratio boxes and proportions to solve ratio problems involving totals prepares students for:

- **Lesson 72,** solving implied ratio problems.
- **Lesson 81,** solving percent problems using ratio boxes and proportions.
- **Lesson 97,** using ratio boxes and proportions to solve indirect measure problems.
- **Lesson 98,** solving scale model or drawing problems using ratio boxes and proportions.
- **Lesson 110,** solving successive discount problems using ratio boxes and proportions.

• Geometric Solids

Objectives

- Identify geometric solids.
- Describe polyhedrons by their faces, edges, or vertices.
- Identify a three-dimensional figure from its flat pattern.

Lesson Preparation

Materials

- **Power Up M** (in *Instructional Masters*)
- **Manipulative kit: Relational GeoSolids**

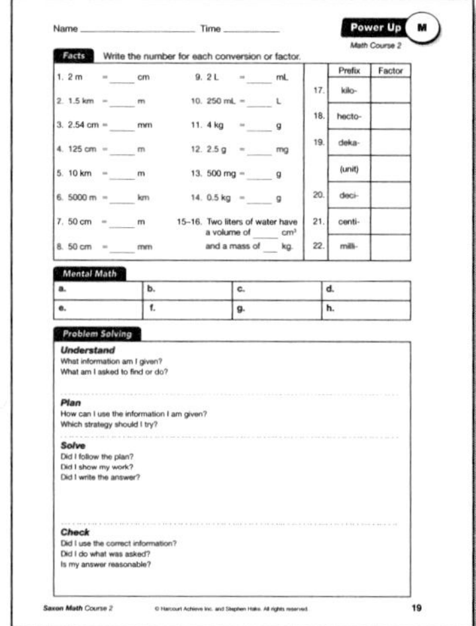

Name ________ Time ________ **Power Up M** *Math Course 2*

Facts Write the number for each conversion or factor.

1. 2 m = ____ cm
2. 1.5 km = ____ m
3. 2.54 cm = ____ mm
4. 125 cm = ____ m
5. 10 km = ____ m
6. 5000 m = ____ km
7. 50 cm = ____ m
8. 50 cm = ____ mm
9. 2 L = ____ mL
10. 250 mL = ____ L
11. 4 kg = ____ g
12. 2.5 g = ____ mg
13. 500 mg = ____ g
14. 0.5 kg = ____ g

15–16. Two liters of water have a volume of ____ cm^3 and a mass of ____ kg.

	Prefix	Factor
17.	kilo-	
18.	hecto-	
19.	deka-	
	(unit)	
20.	deci-	
21.	centi-	
22.	milli-	

Mental Math

a.	b.	c.	d.
e.	f.	g.	h.

Problem Solving

Understand
What information am I given?
What am I asked to find or do?

Plan
How can I use the information I am given?
Which strategy should I try?

Solve
Did I follow the plan?
Did I show my work?
Did I write the answer?

Check
Did I use the correct information?
Did I do what was asked?
Is my answer reasonable?

Saxon Math Course 2 © Harcourt Achieve Inc. and Stephen Hake. All rights reserved. 19

Power Up M

Math Language

New	Maintain	English Learners (ESL)
edge	vertex (vertices)	pattern
face		
geometric solids		
polyhedron (polyhedra)		
prism		
surface area		

Technology Resources

Student eBook Complete student textbook in electronic format.

Resources and Planner CD Assessment, reteaching, and instructional masters, plus a pacing calendar with standards.

Test and Practice Generator CD Create additional practice sheets and custom-made tests.

www.SaxonPublishers.com Visit for more student activities and planning materials.

Inclusion

Adaptations CD Adapted lessons, investigations, practice and assessments.

Meeting Standards

National Council of Teachers of Mathematics (NCTM)

Geometry

GM.1a Precisely describe, classify, and understand relationships among types of two- and three-dimensional objects using their defining properties

GM.4d Use geometric models to represent and explain numerical and algebraic relationships

Reasoning and Proof

RP.2c Develop and evaluate mathematical arguments and proofs

Power-Up Discussion *For use with Power Up, p. 472*

Problem-Solving Strategy: Write an Equation

Paul reads 4 pages in 3 minutes, and Art reads 3 pages in 4 minutes. If they both begin reading 120-page books at the same time, then Paul will finish how many minutes before Art?

Understand — *Understand the problem.*

"What information are we given?"

Paul reads 4 pages in 3 minutes and Art reads 3 pages in 4 minutes. They are both reading 120-page books. We assume they read to the end of the books without interruption.

"What are we asked to do?"

We are asked to determine how many minutes Paul will finish the book before Art.

Plan — *Make a plan.*

"What problem-solving strategy will we use?"

We will *write an equation* to find Paul's and Art's reading times.

Solve — *Carry out the plan.*

"Write a proportion to find Paul's reading time."

$\frac{4 \textit{ pages}}{3 \text{ min}} = \frac{120 \textit{ pages}}{x \text{ min}}$ $4x = 3(120)$

$4x = 360$, $x = 90$ minutes

"Write a proportion to find Art's reading time."

$\frac{3 \textit{ pages}}{4 \text{ min}} = \frac{120 \textit{ pages}}{x \text{ min}}$ $3x = 4(120)$

$3x = 480$, $x = 160$ minutes

"How much sooner will Paul finish the book than Art?"

$160 - 90 = 70$ minutes

Check — *Look back.*

"Did we do what we were asked to do?"

Yes, we found how many more minutes it will take Art to finish the book.

1 Power Up

Facts
Distribute **Power Up M** to students. See answers below.

Mental Math
Encourage students to share different ways to mentally compute these exercises. Strategies for exercises **d** and **e** are listed below.

d. Solve a Proportion

1 m = 10 dm

$\frac{1}{10} = \frac{20}{d}$

$d = 200$

Multiply

1 m = 10 dm so,

20 m = 20 × 10 or 200 dm

e. Subtract the Exponents

$10^3 \div 10^1 = 10^{3-1} = 10^2$ or 100

Multiply

$10^3 = 1000$

1000 ÷ 10 = 100

Problem Solving
Refer to **Power-Up Discussion,** p. 472B.

2 New Concepts

Instruction
Invite students to look around the room and describe some of the geometric solids they see. Some examples might include the following:

- book (rectangular prism)
- pen or pencil (cylinder)
- globe (sphere)

To help students recognize the *vertices*, *faces*, and *edges* of polyhedra, pass around models of the cube, the rectangular prism, and the pyramid from the manipulative kit.

Use the shapes to discuss how geometric solids are identified. For example, a cube has 6 faces and eight vertices, so we know it is a rectangular prism.

(continued)

LESSON 67

• Geometric Solids

Power Up — *Building Power*

facts Power Up M

mental math

a. **Decimals:** 43.6 − 10 33.6

b. **Decimals/Exponents:** 3.85×10^3 3850

c. **Ratio:** $\frac{5}{10} = \frac{2.5}{m}$ 5

d. **Measurement:** Convert 20 m to decimeters (dm). 200 dm

e. **Exponents:** $10^3 \div 10$ 100

f. **Percent:** 75% of 24 18

g. **Measurement:** 4 pints is what fraction of a gallon? $\frac{1}{2}$

h. **Mental Math:** A mental calculation technique for multiplying is to double one factor and halve the other factor. The product is the same. Use this technique to multiply 45 and 16. 720

$$\begin{array}{r} 35 \\ \times\ 14 \\ \hline 490 \end{array} \xrightarrow[\div 2]{\times 2} \begin{array}{r} 70 \\ \times\ 7 \\ \hline 490 \end{array}$$

problem solving Paul reads 4 pages in 3 minutes, and Art reads 3 pages in 4 minutes. If they both begin reading 120-page books at the same time, then Paul will finish how many minutes before Art? 70 minutes

New Concept — *Increasing Knowledge*

Geometric solids are shapes that take up space. Below we show a few geometric solids.

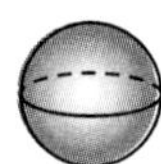
Sphere

Cylinder

Cone

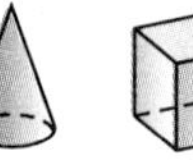
Cube

Triangular prism

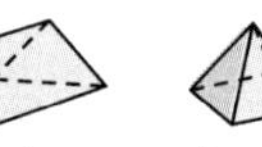
Pyramid

Polyhedrons (Cube, Triangular prism, Pyramid)

Some geometric solids, such as spheres, cylinders, and cones, have one or more curved surfaces. If a solid has only flat surfaces that are polygons, the solid is called a **polyhedron.** Cubes, triangular prisms, and pyramids are examples of polyhedrons.

When describing a polyhedron, we may refer to its faces, edges, or vertices. A **face** is one of the flat surfaces. An **edge** is formed where two faces meet. A **vertex** (plural, **vertices**) is formed where three or more edges meet.

Facts Write the number for each conversion or factor.

				Prefix	Factor
1. 2 m = 200 cm	9. 2 L = 2000 mL		17.	kilo-	1000
2. 1.5 km = 1500 m	10. 250 mL = 0.25 L		18.	hecto-	100
3. 2.54 cm = 25.4 mm	11. 4 kg = 4000 g		19.	deka-	10
4. 125 cm = 1.25 m	12. 2.5 g = 2500 mg			(unit)	1
5. 10 km = 10,000 m	13. 500 mg = 0.5 g		20.	deci-	0.1
6. 5000 m = 5 km	14. 0.5 kg = 500 g		21.	centi-	0.01
7. 50 cm = 0.5 m	15–16. Two liters of water have a volume of 2000 cm^3				
8. 50 cm = 500 mm	and a mass of 2 kg.		22.	milli-	0.001

Thinking Skill

Analyze

How many faces does a cube have? How many edges? How many vertices?

6; 12; 8

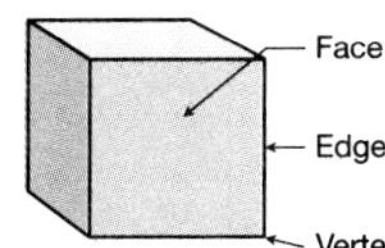

A **prism** is a special kind of polyhedron. A prism has a polygon of a constant size "running through" the prism that appears at opposite faces of the prism and determines the name of the prism. For example, the opposite faces of this prism are congruent triangles; thus this prism is called a **triangular prism.**

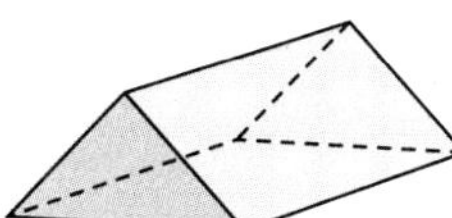

Notice that if we cut through this triangular prism perpendicular to the base, we would see the same size triangle at the cut.

To draw a prism, we draw two identical and parallel polygons, as shown below. Then we draw segments connecting corresponding vertices. We use dashes to indicate edges hidden from view.

Rectangular prism: We draw two congruent rectangles. Then we connect the corresponding vertices (using dashes for hidden edges).

Triangular prism: We draw two congruent triangles. Then we connect corresponding vertices.

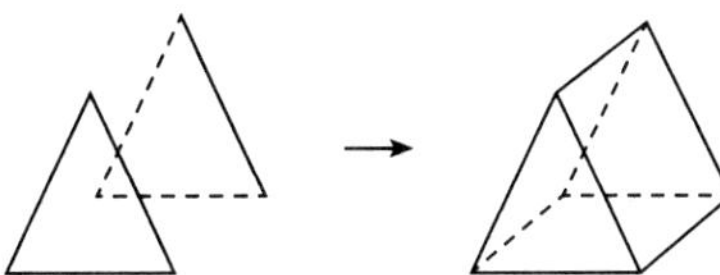

Geometric solids have three dimensions: length, width, and height (or depth). Each dimension is perpendicular to the others.

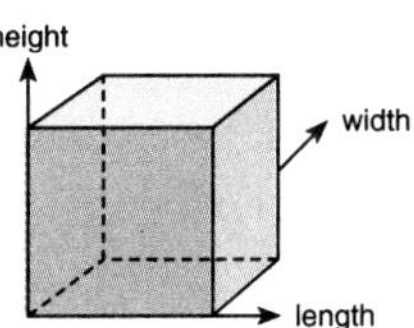

If a two-dimensional figure like a circle or polygon is moved through the third dimension, it sweeps out a three-dimensional figure. For example, if we press a quarter into soft clay, the circular shape of the quarter carves a hole the shape of a cylinder.

2 New Concepts (Continued)

Instruction

You may want to demonstrate the concept that a prism has a polygon of constant size "running through it." With a plastic knife, make a cut parallel to one of the bases of a rectangular eraser or some other rectangular object. When you separate the two sections the new face will be congruent to the base of the prism.

Have students look at the polyhedrons on the previous page and ask them to visualize what each figure would look like if it were cut in half parallel to its base. Ask a student volunteer to work at the board and draw the plane shape that would be formed by the cut.

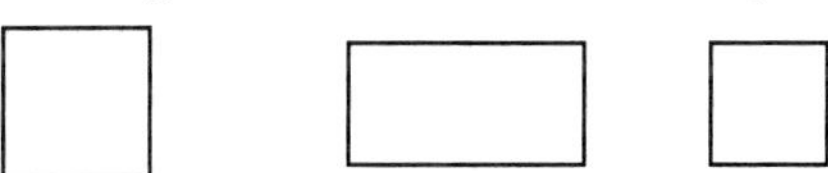

cube triangular prism pyramid

"Look at the pyramid. What do you notice about the square formed by the cut?" It is smaller than its square base.

"Explain your observation." Because the figure is a pyramid rather than a prism, it tapers to a point. Cuts made farther from the base, yet still parallel to the base will produce smaller and smaller squares.

(continued)

Math Background

A polyhedron is a 3-dimensional solid with faces that are polygons joined at the edges. It is important that students understand and be able to recognize the attributes of polyhedra and other solids. Students will build on this knowledge in later lessons to measure volume and surface area. The key properties of some common polyhedra are in the chart below.

Polyhedron	Faces	Vertices	Edges
Cube/Rectangular Prism	6 square or rectangular	8	12
Triangular Prism	2 triangular and 3 rectangular	6	9
Square/Rectangular Pyramid	4 triangular and 1 square/rectangular	5	8
Triangular Pyramid	4 triangular	4	6

Inclusion

Students who have difficulty drawing a three-dimensional figure may find it useful to model the figure with wire pipe cleaners. For example, instruct the students to connect 12 wire segments to create a cube. You can have them use different color wire for the top, bottom, and side edges to help them transfer what they see from the model to paper. Have the students hold their models up at an angle so that they can see every edge. Then have the students draw what they see from the model.

2 New Concepts (Continued)

Example 1

Instruction

1. Draw these shapes on the board.

 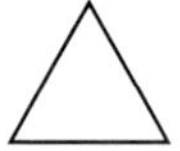 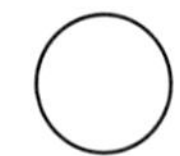

2. Ask students to visualize pushing each plane shape through a piece of clay.

"What 3-dimensional shape would each form?" cube or rectangular prism; triangular prism; cylinder

Example 2

Instruction

1. Use the same shapes on the board.

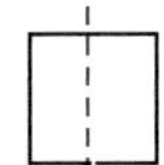 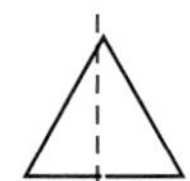 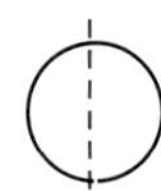

2. Ask students to visualize rotating (spinning) each plane shape around the indicated line of symmetry.

"What 3-dimensional shape would each form as it spins?" cylinder; cone; sphere

3. Ask students to compare and contrast these shapes as they translate or rotate through space.

	Translation	Rotation
Square	rectangular prism	cylinder
Triangle	triangular prism	cone
Circle	cylinder	sphere

Example 4

Instruction

Before discussing example 4, make sure students understand that perpendicular faces intersect to form a 90-degree angle. Faces that are parallel do not intersect.

1. Draw these figures on the board.

	1	2	3	4
Top				
Side				
Shape	Rectangular Prism	Pyramid	Cylinder	Cone

2. Ask students to sketch the 3-dimensional solid that would be formed by the top and side views given. Invite a student volunteer to work at the board.

(continued)

Example 1

Imagine pressing a flat rectangular object into clay. What would be the shape of the hole that is formed?

Solution

As the rectangular object is pressed into the clay, it would carve a hole the shape of a **rectangular prism.**

Example 2

Use the name of a geometric solid to describe the shape of each object:

a. basketball **b. can of beans** **c. shoe box**

Solution

a. sphere **b. cylinder** **c. rectangular prism**

Example 3

A cube has how many:

a. faces **b. edges** **c. vertices**

Solution

a. 6 faces **b. 12 edges** **c. 8 vertices**

Example 4

Draw a cube and answer the following questions.

a. Look at one edge of the cube. How many edges are perpendicular to that edge and how many are parallel to it?

b. Look at one face of the cube. How many faces are perpendicular to that face and how many faces are parallel to it?

Solution

A cube is a special kind of rectangular prism. All faces are squares.

a. For each edge there are **four perpendicular edges and three parallel edges.**

b. For each face there are **four perpendicular faces and one parallel face.**

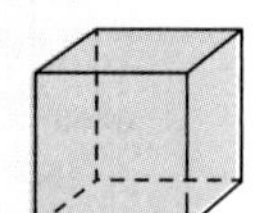

Connect How do you know that all cubes are rectangular prisms, but not all rectangular prisms are cubes? All cubes are rectangular prisms because all the square faces are rectangles. However, rectangular prisms are not cubes because not all rectangular faces are squares.

474 **Saxon** Math Course 2

Manipulative Use

Materials: Relational GeoSolids or a ball, box, can, and cube

As you work through the examples on this page, allow students to work in small groups. Have them use the **Relational GeoSolids** or other models of polyhedra to verify the solutions.

Workers involved in the manufacturing of packaging materials make boxes and other containers out of flat sheets of cardboard or sheet metal. If we cut apart a cereal box and unfold it, we see the six rectangles that form the faces of the box.

Thinking Skill
Connect

The unfolded box is a 2-dimensional representation of a 3-dimensional figure. This type of representation is sometimes called a *net*.

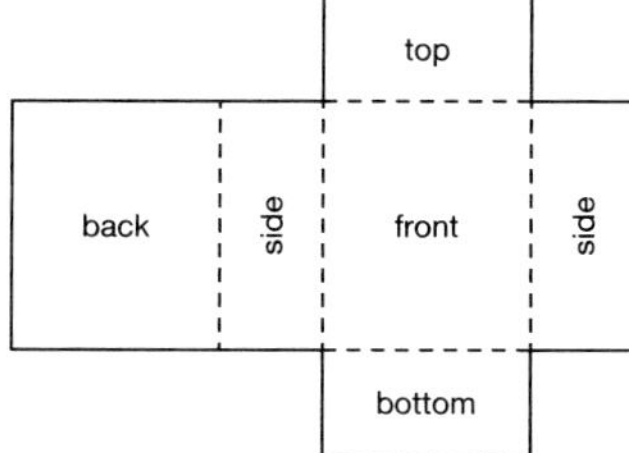

If we find the area of each rectangle and add those areas, we can calculate the surface area of the cereal box.

Example 5

Which of these patterns will not fold to form a cube?

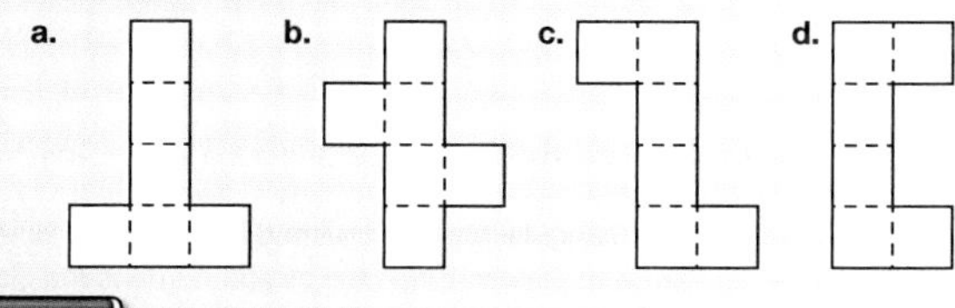

Solution

Pattern d will not fold into a cube.

Example 6

If each edge of a cube is 5 cm, what is the surface area (the combined area of all of the faces) of the cube?

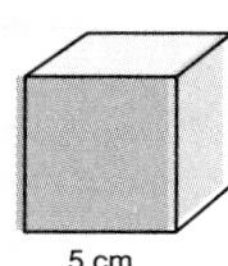

Solution

A cube has six congruent square faces. Each face of this cube is 5 cm by 5 cm. So the area of one face is 25 cm^2, and the area of all six faces is

$$6 \times 25 \text{ cm}^2 = \mathbf{150\ cm^2}$$

Infer If the surface area of a cube is 54 $in.^2$, how can we find the dimensions of the cube? Sample: First, find the area of each face by dividing the surface area by 6, the number of faces on a cube: 54 $in.^2 \div 6 = 9$ $in.^2$. Next, insert the area of one side, 9 $in.^2$ into the formula for the area of a square: $A = s^2$, 9 $in.^2 = s^2$. Then solve for s: $s = \sqrt{9} = 3$. The dimensions are 3 in. by 3 in. by 3 in.

2 New Concepts (Continued)

Instruction

After students have reviewed this paragraph, pass around a cereal box opened to show the six faces. Allow students to fold and unfold the box to understand how a rectangular prism can be made from a flat pattern (net) and how a net can fold up to make a rectangular prism.

Be sure students understand that the dashed lines in the net represent the folds or edges of the solid figure. They separate the faces of the solid.

Example 5

Instruction

Use one-inch graph paper to make samples of the four patterns in example 5. Ask volunteers to show how patterns A through C fold into a cube. Show students that it is impossible to fold pattern D into a cube. Have students draw another net that will fold into a cube.

Sample answer:

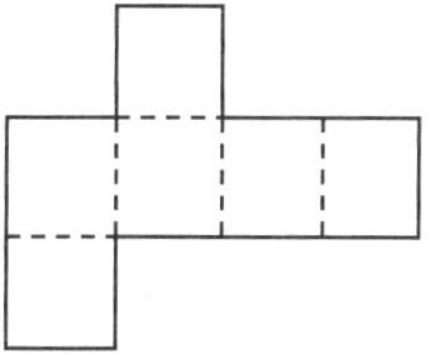

Example 6

Instruction

Use these questions to help students work through the surface area question.

"If you know the surface area, or area of all 6 faces, how do you find the area of one face?" Divide the surface area by 6.

"If you know the area of one square face, how do you find the length of one side?" Find the square root of the area.

(continued)

Teacher Tip

Tell students that **pyramids** and **prisms** are named for plane shapes of their bases. A pyramid with a base that is a pentagon is a pentagonal pyramid, and a prism that has a base that is a hexagon is a hexagonal prism.

Pentagonal pyramid

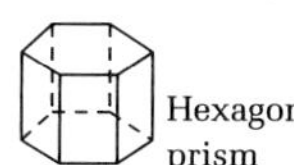

Hexagonal prism

Some students may enjoy finding other pyramids and prisms on the Internet and bringing them to class to share with other students.

English Learners

In example 5 explain the meaning of the term **pattern**. Say:

"A pattern is a plan or model used for making something. Example 5 has patterns for a cube."

Ask students to give other examples of things you might need a pattern to make. (clothes, house, tile designs)

2 New Concepts (Continued)

Practice Set

Problems a and c Classify

After students answer, have them describe the difference between a triangular prism and a rectangular prism. They have bases that are different in shape. The bases of a triangular prism are triangles. The bases of a rectangular prism are rectangles.

Problem j Predict

Remind students that the dotted lines represent folds in the net, and so separate the faces of the solid. Suggest that students consider the number and shape of these faces to predict the solid that will be formed.

Problem m Conclude

Have students draw the top and front views of the solids in Problems a, b, and c.

a. top front

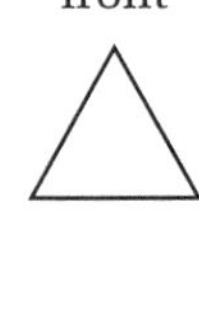

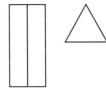

b. top front

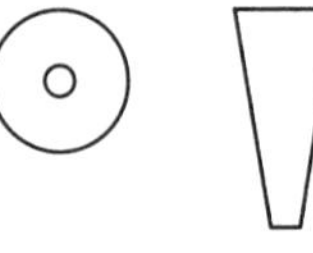

c. top front

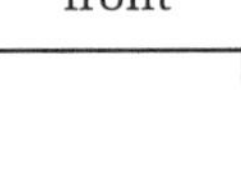

Practice Set Classify Use the name of a geometric solid to describe each shape:

a. Tent
triangular prism

b. 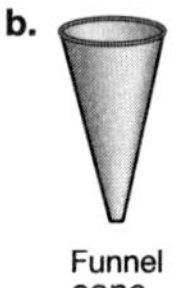

Funnel
cone

c. 

Box
rectangular prism

A triangular prism has how many of each of the following?

d. Faces 5 faces **e.** Edges 9 edges **f.** Vertices 6 vertices

Model Draw a representation of each shape. (Refer to the representations at the beginning of this lesson.)

g. Sphere

h. Rectangular prism 

i. Cylinder

j. Predict What three dimensional figure could be formed by folding this pattern?
triangular prism

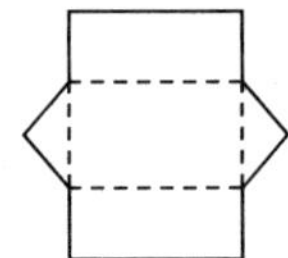

k. Calculate the surface area of a cube whose edges are 3 cm long.
54 cm^2

l. A flat triangular shape is pushed into clay. The hole that is formed is filled with plaster. When the plaster hardens the clay is removed. What is the shape of the hardened plaster? triangular prism

m. Conclude If we refer to the faces of a rectangular solid as front, back, top, bottom, left, and right, then which face is parallel to the top face?
the bottom face

Written Practice *Strengthening Concepts*

1. (14) The bag contains 20 red marbles, 30 white marbles, and 40 blue marbles.

a. What is the ratio of red to blue marbles? $\frac{1}{2}$

b. What is the ratio of white to red marbles? $\frac{3}{2}$

c. If one marble is drawn from the bag, what is the probability that the marble will not be white? $\frac{2}{3}$

2. (30) When the product of $\frac{1}{3}$ and $\frac{1}{2}$ is subtracted from the sum of $\frac{1}{3}$ and $\frac{1}{2}$, what is the difference? $\frac{2}{3}$

3. (12, 23) With the baby in his arms, Mr. Greer weighed 180 pounds. Without the baby, he weighed $165\frac{1}{2}$ pounds. How much did the baby weigh?
$14\frac{1}{2}$ pounds

▶ See Math Conversations in the sidebar.

Teacher Tip

Architects often design buildings that are made up of simple geometric solids like the ones in this lesson. Encourage students to **observe buildings and homes** in their area or find examples of buildings on line. Ask them to find an example of each solid they learned about in this lesson. They should record the names of the solids and where they found them. If possible, they should sketch pictures of the solids and share their findings with the class.

* **4.** (28, 55) Jerome read 42 pages of a book each day for five days. On the next 3 days he read 44 pages, 35 pages, and 35 pages.

  a. What was the average number of pages he read on the last 3 days? 38 pages

  ▸ **b.** What was the average number of pages he read for all 8 days? 40.5 pages

▸ * **5.** (66) **Represent** Use a ratio box to solve this problem. A collection of sedimentary rocks contained sandstone and shale in the ratio of 5 to 2. If there were 210 rocks in the collection, how many were sandstone? 150 sandstone

6. (22, 48) Read this statement. Then answer the questions that follow.

The market sold four-fifths of the 360 frozen turkeys during the second week of November.

  a. How many of the turkeys were sold during the second week of November? 288 turkeys

  b. What percent of the turkeys were not sold during the second week of November? 20%

▸ * **7.** (67) **Analyze** The three-dimensional figure that can be formed by folding this pattern has how many

  a. edges? 12 edges

  b. faces? 6 faces

  c. vertices? 8 vertices

▸ * **8.** (58, 62) **Analyze** Refer to the triangles below to answer **a–d.** Dimensions are in meters.

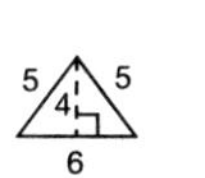

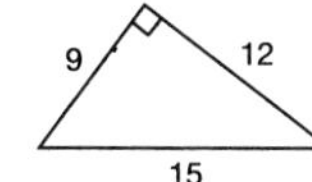

  a. What is the area of the scalene triangle? 54 m^2

  b. What is the perimeter of the isosceles triangle? 16 m

  c. If one acute angle of the right triangle measures 37°, then the other acute angle measures how many degrees? 53°

  d. Which of the two triangles is not symmetrical? The right triangle is not symmetrical.

9. (28, 34) What is the average of the two numbers marked by arrows on the number line below? 7.74

▸ See Math Conversations in the sidebar.

3 Written Practice

Math Conversations

Discussion opportunities are provided below.

Problem 4b

Extend the Problem

Most students will solve this problem using multiple steps. Challenge students to write one expression that can be used to find the total average. $\frac{(42 \times 5) + 44 + (35 \times 2)}{8}$

Problem 5 Represent

Ask a student volunteer to draw a ratio box at the board and explain how to set up the proportion.

	Ratio	Actual Count
Sandstone	5	a
Shale	2	h
Total	7	210

For sandstone $\frac{5}{7} = \frac{a}{210}$

For shale $\frac{2}{7} = \frac{h}{210}$

Problem 7 Analyze

"What is the name of the solid that would be formed if you folded this net?" rectangular prism

"Why isn't it a triangular prism?" four rectangles for sides not three; squares for bases not triangles

Problem 8 Analyze

"How can you identify the height of the right triangle?" The side labeled 9 m is perpendicular to the side labeled 12 m.

Problem 8a Analyze

"Can you multiply the area, 54 m^2, by 100 to convert the area from meters to centimeters? Why or why not?" No; The area of one square meter converted to centimeters is 100 × 100 or 10,000 cm^2. Multiply 54 by 10,000 to convert the area from meters to centimeters; 540,000 cm^2.

Errors and Misconceptions

Problem 8

If students are having difficulty, refer them to Classifying Triangles in the *Student Reference Guide.*

(continued)

3 Written Practice (Continued)

Math Conversations

Discussion opportunities are provided below.

Problem 16 Analyze

Suggest that students write an expression to solve this problem. Ask what symbols will be used for gains and losses. gains (+) and losses (−); −560 + 850 + (−280)

Problem 17 Formulate

Ask students to describe a situation where this equation could be used. Sample: the number of days in a given number of weeks where y = the number of days and x = the number of weeks

Problem 19 Generalize

"If you estimated the answer to this problem, would your answer be the same or different? Explain your reasoning."

Sample: π is about 3. 3 × 24 = 72 inches

Problem 20

Extend the Problem

Ask students to draw a figure that has both supplementary and complementary angles.

Sample:

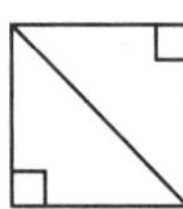

Errors and Misconceptions

Problem 10

If students write 2.5×10^3, remind them that since they moved the decimal point to the right, the exponent should be negative.

(continued)

▶ **10.** (57) Write twenty-five ten-thousandths in scientific notation. 2.5×10^{-3}

Write equations to solve problems **11** and **12.**

11. (60) What number is 24 percent of 75? $W_N = 0.24 \times 75$; 18

12. (60) What number is 120% of 12? $W_N = 1.2 \times 12$; 14.4

13. (64) Find each sum:

a. $\left(-\frac{1}{4}\right) + \left(+\frac{1}{4}\right)$ 0

b. (+2) + (−3) + (+4) 3

14. (48) Complete the table.

Fraction	Decimal	Percent
a. $\frac{1}{25}$	**b.** 0.04	4%
$\frac{7}{8}$	**c.** 0.875	**d.** 87.5%

or $87\frac{1}{2}$%

15. (50) Use a unit multiplier to convert 700 mm to cm. $700 \text{ mm} \cdot \frac{1 \text{ cm}}{10 \text{ mm}} = 70$ cm

▶ * **16.** (64) Analyze In three separate stock trades Dale lost $560, gained $850, and lost $280. What was the net result of the three trades? a gain of $10

▶ * **17.** (56) Formulate Describe the rule of the function in words and as an equation. Then find the missing number. Multiply the "in" number by 7 to find the "out" number. $y = 7x$

Input x	Output y
7	49
0	0
11	77
1	7

18. (33) Round 7856.427

a. to the nearest hundredth. 7856.43

b. to the nearest hundred. 7900

▶ * **19.** (65) Generalize The diameter of Debby's bicycle tire is 24 inches. What is the circumference of the tire to the nearest inch? 75 inches

▶ **20.** (40) Consider angles A, B, C, and D below.

A 30°
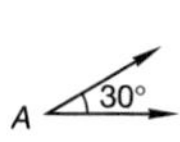

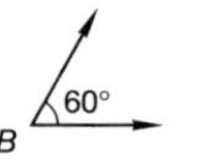

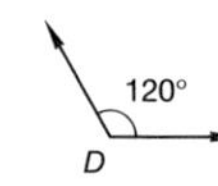

a. Which two angles are complementary? ∠A and ∠B

b. Which two angles are supplementary? ∠B and ∠D

21. (41) **a.** Show two ways to simplify 2(5 ft + 3 ft).

b. Which property is illustrated in **a?** Distributive Property

21. **a.** 2(5 ft + 3 ft)
2(8 ft)
16 ft
or
2(5 ft + 3 ft)
10 ft + 6 ft
16 ft

22. (39) Solve: $\frac{2.5}{w} = \frac{15}{12}$ 2

▶ See Math Conversations in the sidebar.

▶ **Generalize** Simplify:

* **23.** (63) $9 + 8\{7 \cdot 6 - 5[4 + (3 - 2 \cdot 1)]\}$ 145

* **24.** (49) 1 yd − 1 ft 3 in. 1 ft 9 in.

25. (35) $6.4 - (0.6 - 0.04)$ 5.84

26. (52) $\frac{3 + 0.6}{(3)(0.6)}$ 2

27. (30) $1\frac{2}{3} + 3\frac{1}{4} - 1\frac{5}{6}$ $3\frac{1}{12}$

* **28.** (26, 59) $\frac{3}{5} \div 3\frac{1}{5} \cdot 5\frac{1}{3} \cdot |-1|$ 1

29. (26) $3\frac{3}{4} \div \left(3 \div 1\frac{2}{3}\right)$ $2\frac{1}{12}$

30. (52, 57) $5^2 - \sqrt{4^2} + 2^{-2}$ $21\frac{1}{4}$

Early Finishers *Real-World Application*

The top three players on the basketball team scored a total of 1216 points this season in the ratio of 5 to 2 to 1.

a. Below is a ratio box for these ratios. How many points did each player score during the season?

Ratio	Points
5	760
2	304
1	152
8 (total)	1216

b. Find the percents of the total that each player scored. Verify your work by showing that the percentages you find total 100%. 62.5%, 25%, 12.5%; sample: 62.5% + 25% + 12.5% = 100%

▶ See Math Conversations in the sidebar.

3 Written Practice (Continued)

Math Conversations

Discussion opportunities are provided below.

Problems 23–30 Generalize

Ask students to decide whether they would use mental math or paper and pencil to solve each problem. Have them explain their choice.
Answers will vary.

Looking Forward

Understanding geometric solids prepares students for:

- **Lesson 70,** finding the volume of rectangular prisms.
- **Lesson 95,** finding the volume of right solids (square and triangular prisms and circular cylinders).
- **Lesson 105,** finding the surface area of right solids and spheres.
- **Lesson 113,** finding the volume of pyramids, cones, and spheres.

• Algebraic Addition

Objectives

- Use algebraic addition to simplify expressions.

Lesson Preparation

Materials

- **Power Up N** (in *Instructional Masters*)
- **Investigation Activity 13** (in *Instructional Masters*) or **graph paper**

Optional

- **Lesson Activity 15** (in *Instructional Masters*)
- **Teacher provided material: colored pencils**

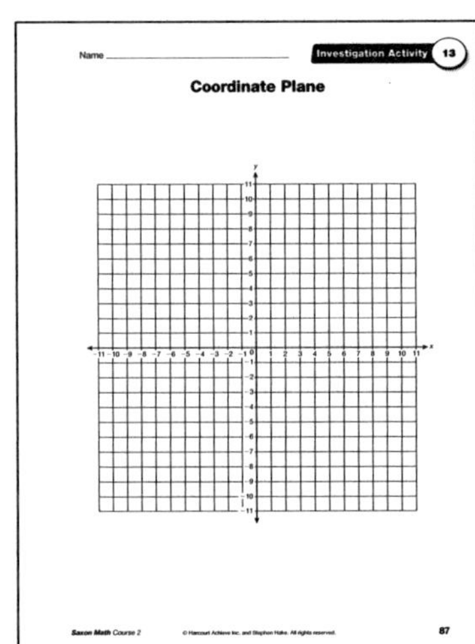

Power Up N

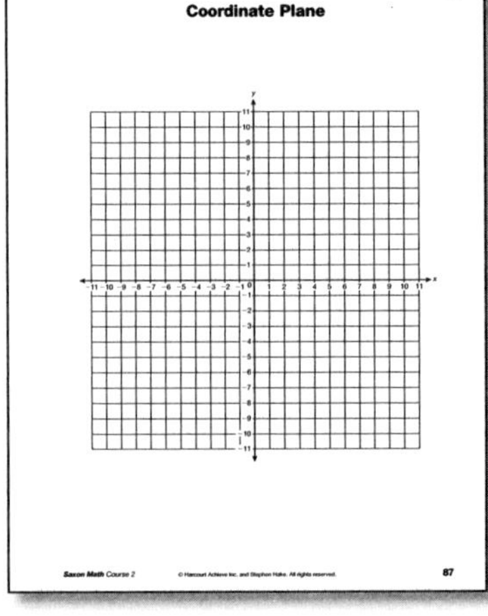

Investigation Activity 13

Math Language

New	English Learners (ESL)
algebraic addition	mass

Technology Resources

Student eBook Complete student textbook in electronic format.

Resources and Planer CD Blackline masters, plus a pacing calendar with standards.

Test and Practice Generator CD Create additional practice sheets and custom-made tests.

www.SaxonPublishers.com Visit for more student activities and planning materials.

Inclusion

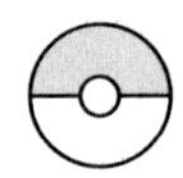

Adaptations CD Adapted lessons, investigations, practice and assessments.

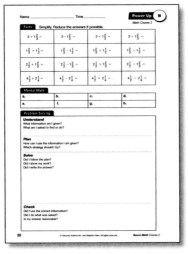

Meeting Standards

National Council of Teachers of Mathematics (NCTM)

Numbers and Operations

NO.1g Develop meaning for integers and represent and compare quantities with them

NO.2a Understand the meaning and effects of arithmetic operations with fractions, decimals, and integers

Connections

CN.4a Recognize and use connections among mathematical ideas

Power-Up Discussion *For use with Power Up, p. 480*

Problem-Solving Strategy: Make It Simpler/ Draw a Diagram

If you have five different colors of paint, how many different ways can you paint a clown mask if you make the hair, nose, and mouth each a different color?

Understand ***Understand the problem.***

"What information are we given?"

We have five colors of paint. We want to paint the mouth, nose, and hair of a clown mask each a different color.

"What are we asked to do?"

We are asked to determine how many different ways we can paint the mask.

Plan ***Make a plan.***

"What problem-solving strategy will we use?"

We will *make it simpler* by considering one starting color and finding the possible combinations for that color, then multiplying by the total number of colors. We will *draw a diagram* to record the possibilities for our starting color.

"What are the five colors of paint?"

It isn't stated, so we can choose our own. We will work through the problem using the colors red, blue, green, yellow, and purple.

Solve ***Carry out the plan.***

"How do we begin?"

We choose a mouth color to begin our diagram. We choose to paint the mouth red. There are four remaining colors from which to choose the nose color. We draw a branch on our tree diagram for each choice. For each nose color, there are three remaining colors from which to choose the hair color. We draw and label these branches on our tree diagram as well.

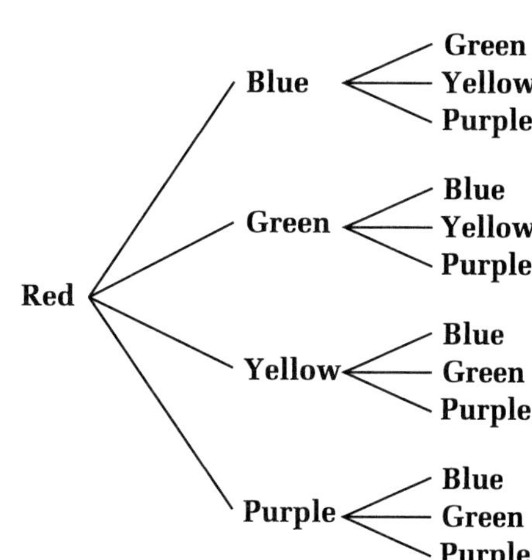

"If the mouth is red, how many different ways can you paint the mask?"

We count the branches and find that there are 12 ways to paint the mask with a red mouth.

"How can we find the total number of ways we can paint the mask?"

There exist similar tree diagrams with blue, green, yellow, and purple as the mouth color. We can multiply the number with a red mouth by 5 (the total number of colors) to find the total number of ways we can paint the mask.

"How many different color combinations could be used on the mask?"

$5 \times 12 = 60$

Check ***Look back.***

"Did we do what we were asked to do?"

Yes, we found that with five different colors of paint we can paint the clown mask in 60 different ways.

1 Power Up

Facts

Distribute **Power Up N** to students. See answers below.

Mental Math

Encourage students to share different ways to mentally compute these exercises. Strategies for exercises **g** and **h** are listed below.

g. Change the Unit of Measure

20 mm = 2 cm

3.14 × 2 = 6.28 cm

6.28 × 10 = 62.8 mm

Multiply by 10, Then Double

3.14 × 10 = 31.4 × 2 = 62.8 mm

h. Use Perimeter Formula

2(2 + 1.5) = 2 × 3.5 or 7 m

Add From Left to Right

2 + 2 + 1.5 + 1.5 = 7 m

Problem Solving

Refer to **Power-Up Discussion,** p. 480B.

2 New Concepts

Instruction

Introduce this lesson by telling students they are going to learn a new way to think about subtraction. Ask them to solve the following two expressions:

$$13 - 6$$
$$-6 + 13$$

Point out that the answers are the same. The addition of 13 and −6 is the same as the subtraction of 6 from 13. Tell them that this lesson teaches them how to rewrite subtraction problems as addition.

Supply students with several other examples of adding opposites. Elicit from students the generalization that adding opposites results in a sum of 0.

(continued)

LESSON 68

Algebraic Addition

Power Up *Building Power*

facts Power Up N

mental math

a. **Decimals:** 0.75 + 0.5 1.25

b. **Power/Roots:** $\sqrt{1} - (\frac{1}{2})^2$ $\frac{3}{4}$

c. **Algebra:** 4*w* − 1 = 35 9

d. **Mental Math:** 12 × 2.5 (halve, double) 30

e. **Measurement:** 20 dm to cm 200 cm

f. **Percent:** $33\frac{1}{3}$% of 24 8

g. **Geometry:** A circle has a diameter of 20 mm. What is the circumference of the circle? 62.8 mm

h. **Geometry:** Find the perimeter and area of a rectangle that is 2 m long and 1.5 m wide. 7 m; 3 m^2

problem solving If you have five different colors of paint, how many different ways can you paint a clown mask if you make the hair, nose, and mouth each a different color? 60

New Concept *Increasing Knowledge*

Math Language
A positive number and a negative number whose absolute values are equal are **opposites.**

Recall that the graphs of −3 and 3 are the same distance from zero on the number line. The graphs are on the opposite sides of zero.

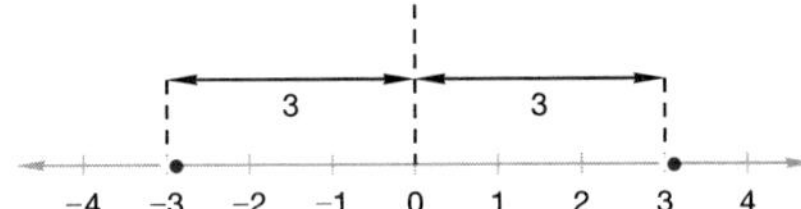

This is why we say that 3 and −3 are the opposites of each other.

3 is the opposite of −3

−3 is the opposite of 3

We can read −3 as "the opposite of 3." Furthermore, −(−3) can be read as "the opposite of the opposite of 3." This means that −(−3) is another way to write 3.

(−3) −(−3)

−4 −3 −2 −1 0 1 2 3 4

There are two ways to simplify the expression 7 − 3. The first way is to let the minus sign signify subtraction. When we subtract 3 from 7, the answer is 4.

$$7 - 3 = 4$$

Facts Simplify. Reduce the answers if possible.

$3 + 1\frac{2}{3} = 4\frac{2}{3}$	$3 - 1\frac{2}{3} = 1\frac{1}{3}$	$3 \times 1\frac{2}{3} = 5$	$3 \div 1\frac{2}{3} = 1\frac{4}{5}$
$1\frac{2}{3} + 1\frac{1}{2} = 3\frac{1}{6}$	$1\frac{2}{3} - 1\frac{1}{2} = \frac{1}{6}$	$1\frac{2}{3} \times 1\frac{1}{2} = 2\frac{1}{2}$	$1\frac{2}{3} \div 1\frac{1}{2} = 1\frac{1}{9}$
$2\frac{1}{2} + 1\frac{2}{3} = 4\frac{1}{6}$	$2\frac{1}{2} - 1\frac{2}{3} = \frac{5}{6}$	$2\frac{1}{2} \times 1\frac{2}{3} = 4\frac{1}{6}$	$2\frac{1}{2} \div 1\frac{2}{3} = 1\frac{1}{2}$
$4\frac{1}{2} + 2\frac{1}{4} = 6\frac{3}{4}$	$4\frac{1}{2} - 2\frac{1}{4} = 2\frac{1}{4}$	$4\frac{1}{2} \times 2\frac{1}{4} = 10\frac{1}{8}$	$4\frac{1}{2} \div 2\frac{1}{4} = 2$

The second way is to use the thought process of **algebraic addition.** To use algebraic addition, we let the minus sign mean that -3 is a negative number and we treat the problem as an addition problem.

$$7 + (-3) = 4$$

Notice that we get the same answer both ways. The only difference is in the way we think about the problem.

We can also use algebraic addition to simplify this expression:

$$7 - (-3)$$

We use an addition thought and think that 7 is added to $-(-3)$. This is what we think:

$$7 + [-(-3)]$$

But the opposite of -3 is 3, so we can write

$$7 + [3] = 10$$

We will practice using the thought process of algebraic addition because algebraic addition can be used to simplify expressions that would be very difficult to simplify if we used the thought process of subtraction.

Example 1

Thinking Skill

Generalize

What is the sum of $+7$ and -7? 0

Simplify: $-3 - (-2)$

Solution

We think addition. We think we are to *add* -3 and $-(-2)$. This is what we think:

$$(-3) + [-(-2)]$$

The opposite of -2 is 2 itself. So we have

$$(-3) + [2] = \mathbf{-1}$$

Example 2

Simplify: $-(-2) - 5 - (+6)$

Solution

We see three numbers. We think *addition,* so we have

$$[-(-2)] + (-5) + [-(+6)]$$

We simplify the first and third numbers and get

$$[+2] + (-5) + [-6] = \mathbf{-9}$$

Note that this time we write 2 as $+2$. Either 2 or $+2$ may be used.

Math Background

Students connect the concept of subtraction with "taking away." Therefore, when presented with "taking away" a negative number, having the result be a greater number than the one they started with, $7 - (-3) = 10$, can be confusing.

Algebraic addition allows students to think about subtraction in terms of combining two algebraic terms. So, in the example of $7 - (-3)$, they can treat the subtraction sign as a negative and visualize this expression as combining the terms 7 and $-(-3)$.

Given the information that the negative sign means opposite, simplifying the term $-(-3)$ to the "opposite of the negative of 3" is easily sorted out. The answer of 10 may then begin to make more sense to students in the context of addition.

2 New Concepts (Continued)

Example 1

Once students have mastered rewriting the subtraction sign as a negative: $-(-2)$, explain that they can also think of subtraction as adding an opposite. Copy the problem on the board and draw an arrow pointing to the subtraction sign.

$$-3 \overset{\downarrow}{-} (-2)$$

Tell them that they can change the subtraction sign to an addition sign and write the opposite of the number that was being subtracted (the opposite of -2 is $+2$).

$$-3 + (+2)$$

Then, have them follow the rules for adding.

Example 2

Instruction

"Why is the answer negative instead of positive?" because $-3 + -6 = -9$

(continued)

2 New Concepts (Continued)

Example 3

Instruction

Emphasize that the rules for operating on integers extend to positive and negative decimals. Students should also notice that as with positive decimals, students should line up the decimal points when adding and subtracting negative decimals.

Practice Set

Problems a–h Analyze

Before actually working the practice problems, have students rewrite each problem as an addition problem.

Problem i

Have students support their answer to this problem by simplifying each expression and graphing the answers on a number line.

3 Written Practice

Math Conversations

Discussion opportunities are provided below.

Problem 3

Extend the Problem

Ask students to write one expression that represents this situation.

$$\frac{\frac{1}{4}+\frac{1}{2}}{\frac{1}{4}\times\frac{1}{2}} = \frac{\frac{2}{8}+\frac{4}{8}}{\frac{1}{4}\times\frac{1}{2}} = \frac{\frac{6}{8}}{\frac{1}{8}} = \frac{6}{8}\times\frac{8}{1} = \frac{48}{8}, \text{ or } 6$$

Errors and Misconceptions

Problem 5b

Some students may need help breaking this problem into smaller steps. Ask students to first change the average speed in miles per hour to miles per minute. $\frac{1 \text{ mile}}{5 \text{ minutes}}$ Then have them rewrite this answer in minutes per mile $\frac{5 \text{ minutes}}{1 \text{ mile}}$, or 5 minutes per mile.

(continued)

Example 3

Simplify: (−1.2) − (+1.5)

Solution

We think addition.

$$(-1.2) + [-(+1.50)]$$

The opposite of positive 1.5 is negative 1.5.

$$(-1.2) + (-1.5) = \mathbf{-2.7}$$

Practice Set ▶ Generalize Use algebraic addition to simplify each expression.

a. (−3) − (+2) −5 **b.** (−3) − (−2) −1

c. (+3) − (2) 1 **d.** (−3) − (+2) − (−4) −1

e. (−8) + (−3) − (+2) −13 **f.** (−8) − (+3) + (−2) −13

g. $\left(-\frac{3}{5}\right) - \left(-\frac{1}{5}\right)$ $-\frac{2}{5}$ **h.** (−0.2) − (+0.3) −0.5

▶ **i.** Which is greater, 3 + (−6) or 3 − (−6)? Explain. 3 − (−6), Subtracting −6 is the same as adding +6 while adding −6 is the same as subtracting +6.

Written Practice *Strengthening Concepts*

1. (12) The combined mass of the beaker and the liquid was 1037 g. The mass of the empty beaker was 350 g. What was the mass of the liquid? 687 g

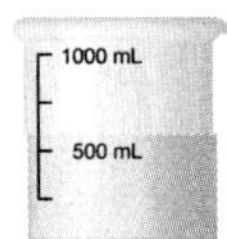

2. (54) Use a ratio box to solve this problem. Adriana's soccer ball is covered with a pattern of pentagons and hexagons in the ratio of 3 to 5. If there are 12 pentagons, how many hexagons are in the pattern? 20 hexagons

▶ **3.** (25, 30) When the sum of $\frac{1}{4}$ and $\frac{1}{2}$ is divided by the product of $\frac{1}{4}$ and $\frac{1}{2}$, what is the quotient? 6

4. (46) Pens were on sale 4 for $1.24.

a. What was the price per pen? $0.31 per pen

b. How much would 100 pens cost? $31.00

5. (46) Christy rode her bike 60 miles in 5 hours.

a. What was her average speed in miles per hour? 12 miles per hour

▶ **b.** What was the average number of minutes it took to ride each mile? 5 minutes per mile

6. (32, 53) Sound travels through air at about $\frac{1}{3}$ of a kilometer per second. If thunder is heard 6 seconds after a flash of lightning, about how many kilometers away was the lightning? about 2 kilometers

482 **Saxon** Math Course 2

▶ See Math Conversations in the sidebar.

Teacher Tip

Materials: Lesson Activity 15 Number Lines, colored pencils or markers

Some students may need extra practice with the concept of **"the opposite of an opposite."** Have these students draw a number line.

- Graph a positive number such as +4.
- Graph its opposite (−4).
- Graph the opposite of −4, or − (−4).
- Write this label, − (−4), above the +4 point on the number line.

Elicit from the students that +4 and − (−4) are equal. Then give them a series of numbers, such as −2, −6, 4, −3, 5. Have students graph and label each point and its opposite on the number line. Each set of points should be graphed in a different color and the opposites of negative numbers should be labeled as − (−*n*).

7. (Inv. 4) Mr. Chen had the following golf scores:

79, 81, 84, 88, 100, 88, 82

a. Which score was made most often? 88

b. What is the median of the scores? 84

c. What is the mean of the scores? 86

8. (28, 34) What is the average of the two numbers marked by arrows on the number line below? 9.1

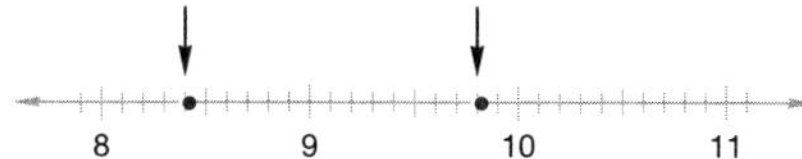

*** 9.** (67) This rectangular shape is two cubes tall and two cubes deep.

a. How many cubes were used to build this shape? 12 cubes

b. What is the name of this shape? rectangular prism

*** 10.** (66) Generalize Find the circumference of each circle:

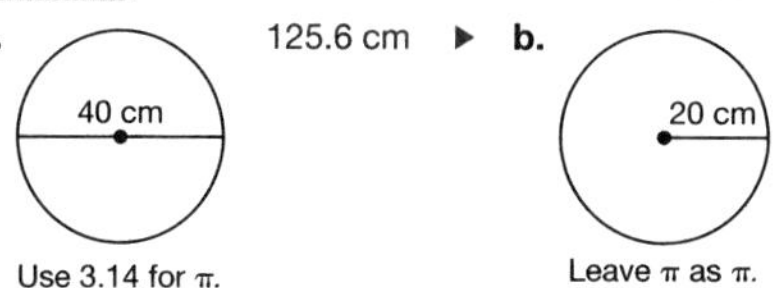

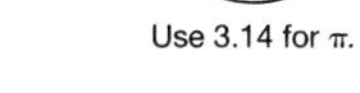

11.

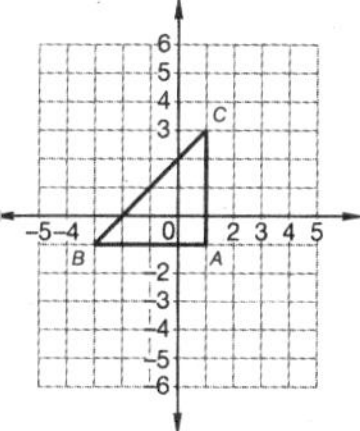

▶* 11. (58, 62) Analyze The coordinates of the vertices of $\triangle ABC$ are A (1, −1), B (−3, −1), and C (1, 3). Draw the triangle and answer these questions:

a. What type of triangle is $\triangle ABC$ classified by angles? right triangle

b. What type of triangle is $\triangle ABC$ classified by sides? isosceles triangle

c. Triangle ABC's one line of symmetry passes through which vertex? A

d. What is the measure of $\angle B$? 45°

e. What is the area of $\triangle ABC$? 8 sq. units

▶ 12. (51) Multiply twenty thousand by thirty thousand, and write the product in scientific notation. 6×10^8

13. (60) What number is 75 percent of 400? $W_N = 0.75 \times 400$; 300

*** 14.** (68) Simplify:

a. (−4) − (−6) 2

b. (−4) − (+6) −10

c. (−6) − (−4) −2

d. (+6) − (−4) 10

▶ See Math Conversations in the sidebar.

3 Written Practice (Continued)

Math Conversations

Discussion opportunities are provided below.

Problem 10b Generalize

"Why isn't the answer 20π cm?" The radius is given, so we multiply the radius 20 cm by 2 to get the diameter length, 40 cm.

Problem 11 Analyze

Before answering this problem, have students make a list of the different types of triangles classified by their angles. Then have them make another list of triangles as classified by their sides and use this list to answer parts **a** and **b.** Students will need graph paper or a copy of **Investigation Activity 13** Coordinate Plane to solve this problem.

Errors and Misconceptions

Problem 12

For students who are struggling to answer this problem, suggest that they write twenty thousand and thirty thousand in standard form before multiplying. Then have them write the product in standard form before changing it to scientific notation.

(continued)

English Learners

Point out the word **mass** in problem 1. Tell students:

"The mass is the weight of an object measured in grams or kilograms. In this exercise we are asked to find the mass of the liquid and beaker together (in grams)."

Ask students to give examples of times they needed to know the mass of an object. (vegetables at the grocery store, a package at the post office)

3 Written Practice (Continued)

Math Conversations

Discussion opportunities are provided below.

Problem 15 Generalize

Ask a student volunteer to explain how to solve this problem. Sample: find the area of one face and multiply it by 6

Problem 16 Connect

Ask a student to draw a number line on the board and estimate the position of each fraction on it.

Sample:

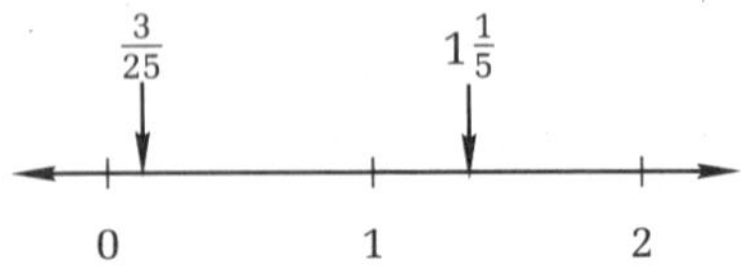

Problem 18 Classify

Extend the Problem

Have students draw the top view of each figure assuming the solids are in the same position as they are on the page.

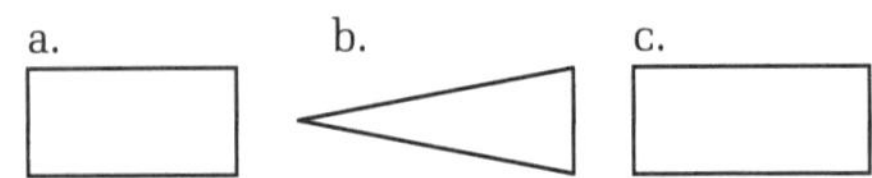

Problem 19 Predict

Extend the Problem

Suppose these shapes replace the triangular piece of metal.

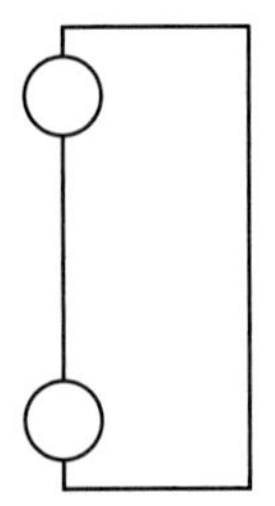

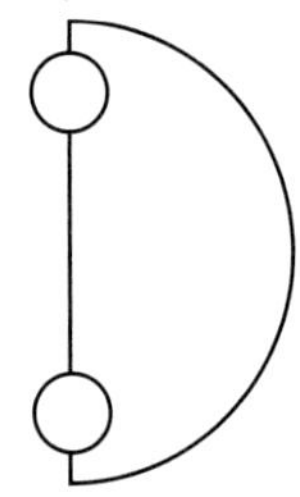

What geometric figures are traced by spinning the shapes? cylinder, sphere

▸ * **15.** (67) Generalize Find the surface area of a cube that has edges 4 inches long. 96 in.^{2}

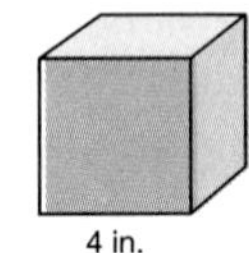

▸ **16.** (48) Connect Complete the table.

Fraction	Decimal	Percent
$\frac{3}{25}$	**a.** 0.12	**b.** 12%
c. $1\frac{1}{5}$	**d.** 1.2	120%

17. (52) Evaluate: $x^2 + 2xy + y^2$ if $x = 4$ and $y = 5$ 81

▸ * **18.** (52) Classify Use the name of a geometric solid to describe each object:

a.

rectangular prism

b.
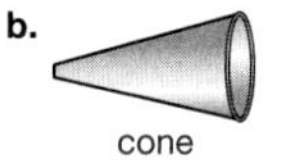
cone

c.

cylinder

▸ * **19.** (67) Predict A triangular piece of metal spins around a rod. As it spins, its path through space is shaped like which geometric solid in Problem 18? cone

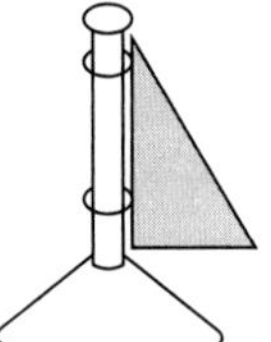

20. (40, 61) In this figure parallelogram *ABCD* is divided by a diagonal into two congruent triangles. Angle *DCA* and ∠*BAC* have equal measures and are complementary. Find the measure of

D A 60° C B

a. ∠*DCA*. 45° **b.** ∠*DAC*. 75°

c. ∠*CAB*. 45° **d.** ∠*ABC*. 60°

e. ∠*BCA*. 75° **f.** ∠*BCD*. 120°

21. (13) Write a word problem for this division: \$3.00 ÷ \$0.25
One possibility: How many \$0.25 pens can you buy with \$3.00?

Solve:

22. (39) $\frac{4}{c} = \frac{3}{7\frac{1}{2}}$ 10

23. (35) $(1.5)^2 = 15w$ 0.15

Simplify:

24. (56) 1 gal − 1 qt 1 pt 1 oz 2 qt 15 oz

25. (45) $16 \div (0.04 \div 0.8)$ 320

* **26.** (63) $10 - [0.1 - (0.01)(0.1)]$ 9.901

27. (30, 52) $\frac{5}{8} + \frac{2}{3} \cdot \frac{3}{4} - \frac{3}{4}$ $\frac{3}{8}$

28. (26) $4\frac{1}{2} \cdot 3\frac{3}{4} \div 1\frac{2}{3}$ $10\frac{1}{8}$

29. (52) $\sqrt{5^2 - 2^4}$ 3

* **30.** (63) Generalize $3 + 6[10 - (3 \cdot 4 - 5)]$ 21

484 **Saxon** Math Course 2

▸ See Math Conversations in the sidebar.

Looking Forward

Understanding algebraic addition prepares students for:

- **Lesson 73,** multiplying and dividing positive and negative numbers.
- **Lesson 85,** simplifying expressions by using the order of operations with positive and negative numbers.
- **Lesson 96,** simplifying expressions by using the Distributive Property with algebraic terms.

• Proper Form of Scientific Notation

Objectives

- Combine powers of 10 to write numbers in scientific notation.

Lesson Preparation

Materials

- **Power Up M** (in *Instructional Masters*)

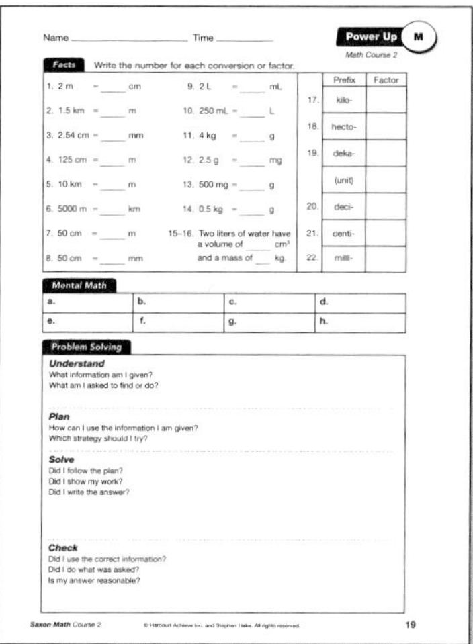

Name ______ Time ______

Power Up M
Math Course 2

Facts Write the number for each conversion or factor.

1. 2 m = ___ cm
2. 1.5 km = ___ m
3. 2.54 cm = ___ mm
4. 125 cm = ___ m
5. 10 km = ___ m
6. 5000 m = ___ km
7. 50 cm = ___ m
8. 50 cm = ___ mm
9. 2 L = ___ mL
10. 250 mL = ___ L
11. 4 kg = ___ g
12. 2.5 g = ___ mg
13. 500 mg = ___ g
14. 0.5 kg = ___ g

15–16. Two liters of water have a volume of ___ cm^3 and a mass of ___ kg.

	Prefix	Factor
17.	kilo-	
18.	hecto-	
19.	deka-	
	(unit)	
20.	deci-	
21.	centi-	
22.	milli-	

Mental Math

a.	b.	c.	d.
e.	f.	g.	h.

Problem Solving

Understand
What information am I given?
What am I asked to find or do?

Plan
How can I use the information I am given?
Which strategy should I try?

Solve
Did I follow the plan?
Did I show my work?
Did I write the answer?

Check
Did I use the correct information?
Did I do what was asked?
Is my answer reasonable?

Saxon Math Course 2 19

Power Up M

Technology Resources

Student eBook Complete student textbook in electronic format.

Resources and Planner CD Assessment, reteaching, and instructional masters, plus a pacing calendar with standards.

Test and Practice Generator CD Create additional practice sheets and custom-made tests.

www.SaxonPublishers.com Visit for more student activities and planning materials.

Inclusion

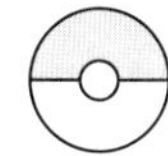

Adaptations CD Adapted lessons, investigations, practice and assessments.

Meeting Standards

National Council of Teachers of Mathematics (NCTM)

Numbers and Operations

NO.1e Develop an understanding of large numbers and recognize and appropriately use exponential, scientific, and calculator notation

NO.1g Develop meaning for integers and represent and compare quantities with them

Communication

CM.3d Use the language of mathematics to express mathematical ideas precisely

Power-Up Discussion For use with Power Up, p. 485

Problem-Solving Strategy: Make It Simpler/ Find a Pattern

A rectangle has a length of 10 meters and a width of 8 meters. A second rectangle has a length of 6 meters and a width of 4 meters. The rectangles overlap as shown. What is the difference between the areas of the two non-overlapping regions of the two rectangles?

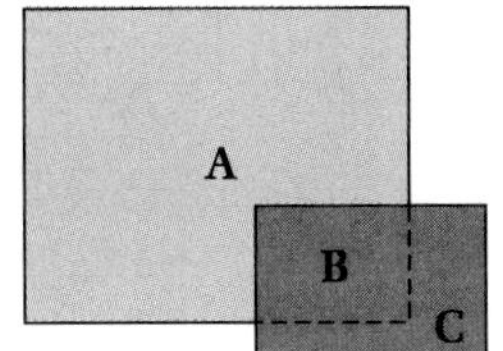

Understand ***Understand the problem.***

"What information are we given?"

We are given the dimensions of two rectangles.

"What are we asked to do?"

We are asked to find the difference in the areas of the non-overlapping regions of the two rectangles, which is the area of A minus C.

"What information do we not have that we might need to solve this problem?"

We do not know how much the two rectangles overlap, the area of B.

Plan ***Make a plan.***

"What problem-solving strategy will we use?"

We will *make it simpler* by first considering cases in which the two rectangles overlap completely and not at all. Then we will test a few different cases in which the rectangles overlap. We will see if we can *find a pattern* to help us find the difference in area between the two regions.

Solve ***Carry out the plan.***

"What is the difference in non-overlapping areas when the rectangles overlap completely?"

Area of region A: $(10 \text{ m} \times 8 \text{ m}) - (6 \text{ m} \times 4 \text{ m}) = 56 \text{ m}^2$
Area of region B: $6 \text{ m} \times 4 \text{ m} = 24 \text{ m}^2$
Area of region C: 0
Area A − Area C: $56 \text{ m}^2 - 0 = 56 \text{ m}^2$

"What is the difference in non-overlapping areas when the rectangles do not overlap at all?"

Area of region A: $10 \text{ m} \times 8 \text{ m} = 80 \text{ m}^2$
Area of region B: 0
Area of region C: $6 \text{ m} \times 4 \text{ m} = 24 \text{ m}^2$
Area A − Area C: $80 \text{ m}^2 - 24 \text{ m}^2 = 56 \text{ m}^2$

"What is the difference in non-overlapping areas when the rectangles overlap 1 m²?"

Area of region A: $80 \text{ m}^2 - 1 \text{ m}^2 = 79 \text{ m}^2$
Area of region B: 1 m^2
Area of region C: $24 \text{ m}^2 - 1 \text{ m}^2 = 23 \text{ m}^2$
Area A – Area C: $79 \text{ m}^2 - 23 \text{ m}^2 = 56 \text{ m}^2$

"What do we notice about the difference in areas in each case?"

The difference always equals 56 m^2.

"Do you think that the difference will always be the same?"

Yes, we are always subtracting the same amount of overlap from both areas, so the difference between the two remains constant.

Check ***Look back.***

"Did we do what we were asked to do?"

Yes, we found that the difference between the two non-overlapping regions is constant. The difference always equals 56 m^2.

LESSON 69

• Proper Form of Scientific Notation

Power Up — *Building Power*

facts Power Up M

mental math

a. **Decimals:** $4 - 1.5$ 2.5

b. **Exponents:** 75×10^{-3} 0.075

c. **Ratio:** $\frac{x}{4} = \frac{1.5}{3}$ 2

d. **Mental Math:** 18×35 (halve, double) 630

e. **Measurement:** 20 cm to dm 2 dm

f. **Percent:** $66\frac{2}{3}\%$ of 24 16

g. **Primes/Composites:** Name the first 5 prime numbers. 2, 3, 5, 7, 11

h. **Calculation:** 5^2, $\times 3$, $- 3$, $\div 8$, $\sqrt{\ }$, $\times 7$, $- 1$, $\div 4$, $\times 10$, $- 1$, $\sqrt{\ }$, $\div 2$ $3\frac{1}{2}$

problem solving

A rectangle has a length of 10 meters and a width of 8 meters. A second rectangle has a length of 6 meters and a width of 4 meters. The rectangles overlap as shown. What is the difference between the areas of the two non-overlapping regions of the two rectangles? 56 sq. m

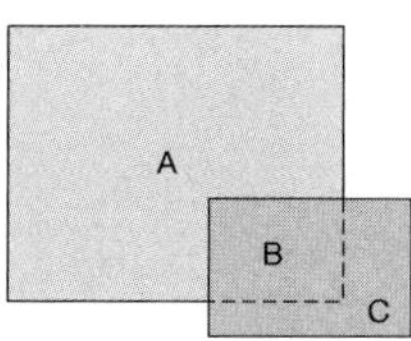

New Concept — *Increasing Knowledge*

When we write a number in scientific notation, we usually put the decimal point just to the right of the first digit that is not zero. To write

$$4600 \times 10^5$$

in scientific notation, we use two steps. First we write 4600 in scientific notation. In place of 4600 we write 4.6×10^3. Now we have

$$4.6 \times 10^3 \times 10^5$$

Thinking Skill
Discuss
By what number are we multiplying when we multiply by 10^3? By 10^5?
1000; 100,000

For the second step we change the two powers of 10 into one power of 10. We recall that 10^3 means the decimal point is 3 places to the right and that 10^5 means the decimal point is 5 places to the right. Since 3 places to the right and 5 places to the right is 8 places to the right, the power of 10 is 8.

$$4.6 \times 10^8$$

Discuss How can we check to see that 4600×10^5 is equal to 4.6×10^8?
Sample: $10^5 = 100{,}000$, $4600 \times 100{,}000 = 460{,}000{,}000$; $10^8 = 100{,}000{,}000$, $4.6 \times 100{,}000{,}000 = 460{,}000{,}000$

Facts Write the number for each conversion or factor.

			Prefix	Factor
1. 2 m = 200 cm	9. 2 L = 2000 mL	17.	kilo-	1000
2. 1.5 km = 1500 m	10. 250 mL = 0.25 L	18.	hecto-	100
3. 2.54 cm = 25.4 mm	11. 4 kg = 4000 g	19.	deka-	10
4. 125 cm = 1.25 m	12. 2.5 g = 2500 mg		(unit)	1
5. 10 km = 10,000 m	13. 500 mg = 0.5 g	20.	deci-	0.1
6. 5000 m = 5 km	14. 0.5 kg = 500 g	21.	centi-	0.01
7. 50 cm = 0.5 m	15–16. Two liters of water have a volume of 2000 cm^3	22.	milli-	0.001
8. 50 cm = 500 mm	and a mass of 2 kg.			

1 Power Up

Facts

Distribute **Power Up M** to students. See answers below.

Mental Math

Encourage students to share different ways to mentally compute these exercises. Strategies for exercises **c** and **e** are listed below.

c. Cross Multiply

$3x = 4 \times 1.5$

$3x = 6$; $x = 2$

Equivalent Fractions

$\frac{1.5}{3} \times \frac{2}{2} = \frac{3}{6} = \frac{1}{2}$; $\frac{1}{2} \times \frac{2}{2} = \frac{2}{4}$

$x = 2$

e. Solve a Proportion

$1 \text{ dm} = 10 \text{ cm}$

$\frac{20}{x} = \frac{10}{1}$

$10x = 20$

$x = 2$

Divide

10 cm = 1 dm so,

20 cm = 20 ÷ 10 or 2 dm

Problem Solving

Refer to **Power-Up Discussion,** p. 485B.

2 New Concepts

Instruction

Introduce this lesson by writing several real world examples on the board. Explain to students that scientific notation is often used to represent numbers that are very large or very small.

Speed of light in a vacuum
1.86×10^5 miles per second

One light year
9.46×10^{12} km

If students are unsure if 4600×10^5 is written in scientific notation, explain that only one nonzero digit is written to the left of the decimal point when a number is written in scientific notation.

(continued)

2 New Concepts (Continued)

Example 1

Instruction

If students are having difficulty writing numbers in proper scientific notation, break the process down. Explain that they must first convert the number into proper form. Then they can use what they know about combining powers of 10 to find the correct power of 10.

Example 2

Instruction

Encourage students to do a quick mental estimate to check that they have converted numbers into scientific notation correctly. Remind them that a number in scientific notation must equal the same number in standard form.

Practice Set

Problems a–f (Error Alert)

Encourage students who use the wrong exponent to show each step when writing these numbers in scientific notation.

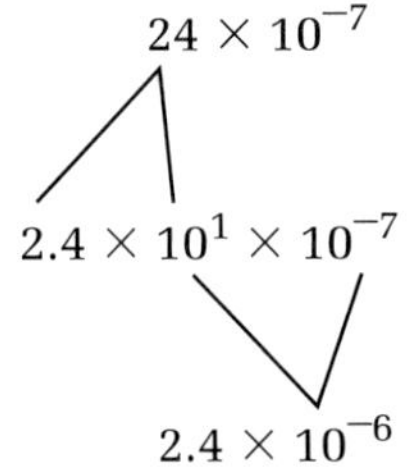

3 Written Practice

Math Conversations

Discussion opportunities are provided below.

Problem 1

Extend the Problem

Suppose a diver's quality score is calculated by removing the highest and lowest scores and finding the mean of the remaining five scores. What would be the quality score for this dive? $\frac{7.0 + 6.5 + 6.5 + 7.0 + 6.5}{5} = 6.7$

(continued)

Example 1

Write 25×10^{-5} in scientific notation.

Solution

First we write 25 in scientific notation.

$$2.5 \times 10^{1} \times 10^{-5}$$

Then we combine the powers of 10 by remembering that 1 place to the right and 5 places to the left equals 4 places to the left.

$$\mathbf{2.5 \times 10^{-4}}$$

Example 2

Write 0.25×10^{4} in scientific notation.

Solution

First we write 0.25 in scientific notation.

$$2.5 \times 10^{-1} \times 10^{4}$$

Since 1 place to the left and 4 places to the right equals 3 places to the right, we can write

$$\mathbf{2.5 \times 10^{3}}$$

With practice you will soon be able to perform these exercises mentally.

Thinking Skill
Explain
When 0.25 is written in scientific notation why does it have a negative exponent? A negative exponent indicates a number less than 1. Since we move the decimal point one place to get to 2.5, the exponent is −1.

Practice Set ▶ *Connect* Write each number in scientific notation. Show the steps you used to get each answer.

a. 0.16×10^{6} 1.6×10^{5} **b.** 24×10^{-7} 2.4×10^{-6}

c. 30×10^{5} 3×10^{6} **d.** 0.75×10^{-8} 7.5×10^{-9}

e. 14.4×10^{8} 1.44×10^{9} **f.** 12.4×10^{-5} 1.24×10^{-4}

Written Practice *Strengthening Concepts*

▶ **1.** (Inv. 4) The following is a list of scores received in a diving competition:

7.0	6.5	6.5	7.4	7.0	6.5	6.0

a. Which score was received the most often? 6.5

b. What is the median of the scores? 6.5

c. What is the mean of the scores? 6.7

d. What is the range of the scores? 1.4

*** 2.** (66) Use a ratio box to solve this problem. The team played 15 home games. The rest of the games were away games. If the team's ratio of home games to away games was 5 to 3, how many total games did the team play? 24 games

▶ See Math Conversations in the sidebar.

Math Background

Using scientific notation can help us compare two or more numbers.

For example, when comparing 1300×10^{3} and 0.85×10^{8}, it is not immediately obvious which number is greater.

At a glance, the coefficient 1300 is a much greater number than 0.85, but it is paired with a lesser power of 10.

If we rewrite the numbers in proper form 1.3×10^{6} and 8.5×10^{7}, we can see immediately which number is greater.

Neither decimal is greater than 10, therefore the number with the greater exponent of 10 is greater.

3. (54) Lucila swam 4 laps in 6 minutes. At that rate, how many minutes will it take Lucila to swim 10 laps? 15 minutes

*** 4.** (69) Write each number in scientific notation:

a. 15×10^5 1.5×10^6 **b.** 0.15×10^5 1.5×10^4

5. (14, 60) Refer to the following statement to answer **a–c:**

The survey found that only 2 out of 5 Lilliputians believe in giants.

a. According to the survey, what fraction of the Lilliputians do not believe in giants? $\frac{3}{5}$

b. If 60 Lilliputians were selected for the survey, how many of them would believe in giants? 24 Lilliputians

c. What is the probability that a randomly selected Lilliputian who participated in the survey would believe in giants? $\frac{2}{5}$

▶ *** 6.** (65) **Connect** The diameter of a circular tree stump was 40 cm. Find the circumference of the tree stump to the nearest centimeter. 126 cm

▶ *** 7.** (67) **Classify** Use the name of a geometric solid to describe the shape of these objects:

a. volleyball sphere **b.** water pipe cylinder **c.** tepee cone

*** 8.** (58, 62) **a.** What is the perimeter of the equilateral triangle at right? $1\frac{7}{8}$ in.

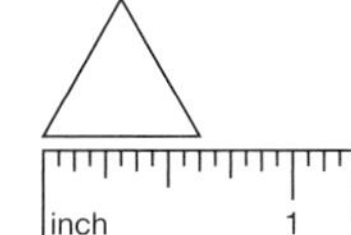

b. What is the measure of each of its angles? 60°

8. c.

▶ **c.** **Represent** Trace the triangle on your paper, and show its lines of symmetry.

▶ *** 9.** (68) **Generalize** Simplify:

a. $(-4) + (-5) - (-6)$ -3

b. $(-2) + (-3) - (-4) - (+5)$ -6

c. $(-0.3) - (-0.3)$ 0

*** 10.** (65) Find the circumference of each circle:

a. 21.98 cm

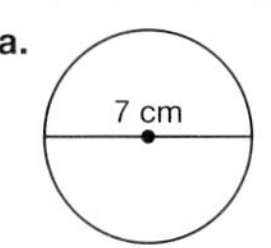

Use 3.14 for π.

b. 22 cm

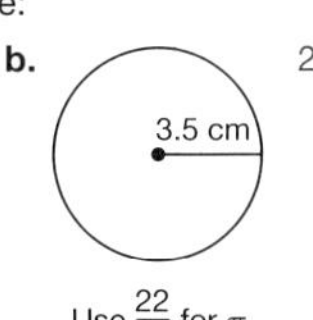

Use $\frac{22}{7}$ for π.

▶ See Math Conversations in the sidebar.

3 Written Practice (Continued)

Math Conversations

Discussion opportunities are provided below.

Problem 6 Connect

Ask students to estimate if they could put their arms around a tree stump that is 126 cm around. Answers will vary. 126 cm is about 50 inches

Problem 7 Classify

Draw these shapes on the board.

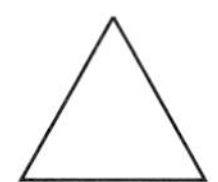

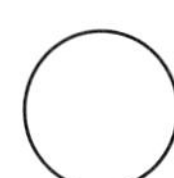

Explain to students that these are the *side views* of 3 dimensional figures. Ask them to sketch an example of the solid. Ask a student volunteer to work at the board.

Sample answers:

Square: cube, rectangular prism

Triangle: pyramid, triangular prism, cone

Circle: sphere, cylinder

Problem 8c Represent

"Does this triangle have rotational symmetry? Explain." yes; It will appear in its original form 3 times in a 360° turn.

Problem 9 Generalize

Ask student volunteers to explain their reasoning for each problem.

(continued)

3 Written Practice (Continued)

Math Conversations

Discussion opportunities are provided below.

Problems 11

Extend the Problem

"What is the area of the cut out section?"

$3 \text{ mm} \times 4 \text{ mm} = 12 \text{ mm}^2$

Problem 17

Extend the Problem

Ask students what set of numbers is generated by this equation. set of all odd numbers

Sample:

$y = 2x - 1$

$2(1) - 1 = 1$
$2(2) - 1 = 3$
$2(6) - 1 = 5$
$2(4) - 1 = 7$
$2(5) - 1 = 9$

(continued)

▸ **11.** (37) Refer to the figure to answer **a–c.** Dimensions are in millimeters. Corners that look square are square.

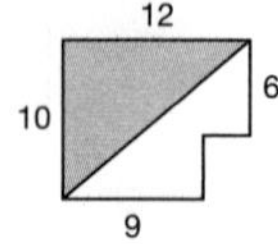

a. What is the area of the hexagon? 108 mm^2

b. What is the area of the shaded triangle? 60 mm^2

c. What fraction of the hexagon is shaded? $\frac{5}{9}$

Write equations to solve problems **12** and **13.**

12. (60) What number is 50 percent of 200? $W_N = \frac{1}{2} \times 200$; 100

13. (60) What number is 250% of 4.2? $W_N = 2.5 \times 4.2$; 10.5

14. (48) Complete the table.

Fraction	Decimal	Percent
$\frac{3}{20}$	**a.** 0.15	**b.** 15%
c. $1\frac{1}{2}$	**d.** 1.5	150%

15. (40) Refer to this figure to answer **a–c:**

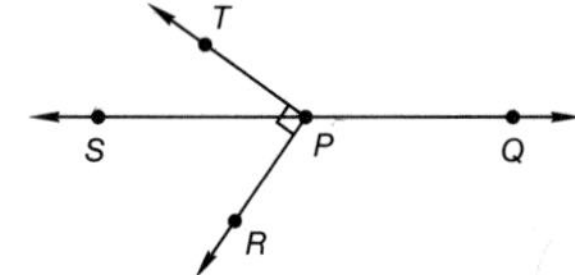

a. Which angle is supplementary to $\angle SPT$? $\angle TPQ$ or $\angle QPT$

b. Which angle is complementary to $\angle SPT$? $\angle SPR$ or $\angle RPS$

c. If $\angle QPR$ measures 125°, what is the measure of $\angle QPT$? 145°

16. (52, 57) Evaluate: $a^2 - \sqrt{a} + ab - a^0$ if $a = 4$ and $b = 0.5$ 15

▸ **17.** (56) Write the rule of this function with words and as an equation. Then complete the table. Multiply the "input" number by 2, then subtract 1 to find the "output" number. $y = 2x - 1$

Input x	Output y
8	15
6	11
10	19
4	7

18. (44) Divide 144 by 11 and write the answer

a. as a decimal with a bar over the repetend. $13.\overline{09}$

b. rounded to the nearest whole number. 13

▸ See Math Conversations in the sidebar.

19. (41) Anders Celsius (1701–1744) developed the Celsius scale. He used this formula to convert from degrees Celsius to degrees Fahrenheit:

$$F = 1.8\,C + 32$$

If the Celsius temperature (C) is 20°C, what is the Fahrenheit temperature (F)? 68°F

▶* **20.** (67) **Predict** Eva placed a quarter on its edge and gave it a spin. As it whirled, it moved through a space the shape of what geometric figure? sphere

Solve:

21. (30) $t + \frac{5}{8} = \frac{15}{16}$ $\frac{5}{16}$

22. (39) $\frac{a}{8} = \frac{3\frac{1}{2}}{2}$ 14

Estimate First estimate each answer to the nearest whole number. Then perform the calculation.

▶ **23.** (26) $\left(3\frac{3}{4} \div 1\frac{2}{3}\right) \cdot 3$ 6; $6\frac{3}{4}$

▶ **24.** (26, 30) $4\frac{1}{2} + \left(5\frac{1}{6} \div 1\frac{1}{3}\right)$ 9 or 10; $8\frac{3}{8}$

Simplify:

▶ **25.** (49)

```
  5 ft 7 in.
+ 6 ft 8 in.
 12 ft 3 in.
```

26. (50) $\frac{350\text{ m}}{1\text{ s}} \cdot \frac{60\text{ s}}{1\text{ min}} \cdot \frac{1\text{ km}}{1000\text{ m}}$ $21\frac{\text{km}}{\text{min}}$

27. (35) $6 - (0.5 \div 4)$ 5.875

28. (45) $7.50 ÷ 0.075 $100.00

▶ **29.** (24) **Generalize** Use prime factorization to reduce $\frac{432}{675}$. $\frac{16}{25}$

30. (43) ▶ **a.** Convert $2\frac{1}{4}$ to a decimal and add 0.15. 2.4

b. Convert 6.5 to a mixed number and add $\frac{5}{6}$. $7\frac{1}{3}$

Early Finishers
Math Applications

Suppose you spin each of these plane figures the same way you would spin a coin. Predict the three-dimensional figures that would be formed as the two figures move through space.

Figure A

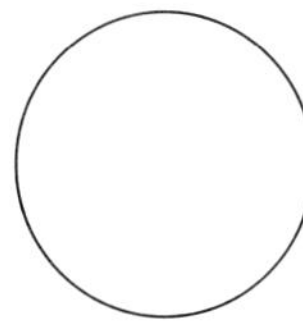
Figure B

Figure A, cone; Figure B, sphere

▶ See Math Conversations in the sidebar.

3 Written Practice (Continued)

Math Conversations

Discussion opportunities are provided below.

Problem 20 Predict

If students need help visualizing this problem, have them model it by holding a quarter or a counter with their thumb and forefinger and slowly spinning it on its edge.

Ask students to name other real world items that would form a sphere if they were rotated on their edges. Sample: plate, hockey puck, wheel

Problems 23 and 24 Estimate

Remind students that they are asked to give two answers for each of these problems, an estimated answer and an exact answer.

Problem 30a Evaluate

"How can you find the answer using mental math?" Sample: think of $\frac{1}{4}$ as 0.25 and add it to 0.15. 0.25 + 0.10 = 0.35 + 0.05 = 0.40; Then add this decimal to the whole number 2 with a result of 2.40.

Errors and Misconceptions

Problem 25

If students write the answer as 11 ft 15 in., remind them that answers should always be simplified if possible.

Problem 29

If students don't know how to begin, tell them to start by breaking the number apart using place value. For example:

$$432 = 400 + 32$$

Then they can start looking for factors.

$$(100 \times 4) + (8 \times 4)$$

Break each factor apart again.

$$(10 \times 10 \times 2 \times 2) + (4 \times 2 \times 2 \times 2)$$

Continue until all of the numbers are prime numbers.

$$(5 \times 2 \times 5 \times 2 \times 2 \times 2) + (2 \times 2 \times 2 \times 2 \times 2)$$

So the prime factorization of the numerator is:

$$5 \cdot 5 \cdot 2 \cdot 2 \cdot 2 \cdot 2 \cdot 2 \cdot 2 \cdot 2 \cdot 2 \cdot 2$$

Looking Forward

Understanding how to write numbers in proper scientific notation prepares students for:

- **Lesson 83,** multiplying powers of 10 and multiplying numbers in scientific notation.

Volume

Objectives

- Find the volume of rectangular prisms.

Lesson Preparation

Materials

- **Power Up N** (in *Instructional Masters*)
- **Manipulative kit: wooden color cubes and color tiles**

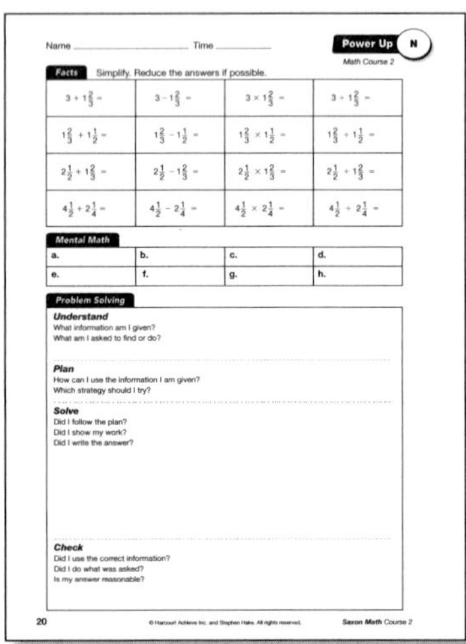

Power Up N

Math Language

New	English Learners (ESL)
volume	round trip

Technology Resources

Student eBook Complete student textbook in electronic format.

Resources and Planner CD Assessment, reteaching, and instructional masters, plus a pacing calendar with standards.

Test and Practice Generator CD Create additional practice sheets and custom-made tests.

www.SaxonPublishers.com Visit for more student activities and planning materials.

Inclusion

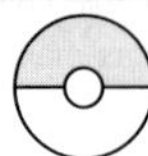

Adaptations CD Adapted lessons, investigations, practice and assessments.

Meeting Standards

National Council of Teachers of Mathematics (NCTM)

Geometry

GM.4b Use two-dimensional representations of three-dimensional objects to visualize and solve problems such as those involving surface area and volume

GM.4d Use geometric models to represent and explain numerical and algebraic relationships

Measurement

ME.1c Understand, select, and use units of appropriate size and type to measure angles, perimeter, area, surface area, and volume

ME.2d Develop strategies to determine the surface area and volume of selected prisms, pyramids, and cylinders

Power-Up Discussion *For use with Power Up, p. 490*

Problem-Solving Strategy: Guess and Check/ Use Logical Reasoning

Between the whole numbers 2 and 4 is the prime number 3. Between the whole numbers 4 and 8 are the prime numbers 5 and 7. Can you always find a prime number between a whole number greater than 1 and its double?

Understand Understand the problem.

"What information are we given?"

We are given two whole numbers and their doubles and are told that prime numbers exist between each number and its double.

"What are we asked to do?"

We are asked to determine whether we can always find a prime number between a whole number greater than 1 and its double.

Plan Make a plan.

"What problem-solving strategy will we use?"

We will *guess and check* in an organized manner, *using logical reasoning* to help us along the way.

Solve Carry out the plan.

"How do we begin?"

We will begin by evaluating whole numbers and their doubles in an ascending order. The prime number(s) will be in bold print.

2 **3** 4	3 **5** 6	4 **5** **7** 8	5 **7** 10
6 **7** **11** 12	7 **11** **13** 14	8 **11** **13** 16	9 **11** **13** **17** 18
10 **11** **13** **17** **19** 20	11 **13** **17** **19** 22	12 **13** **17** **19** **23** 24	13 **17** **19** **23** 26
14 **17** **19** **23** 24	15 **17** **19** **23** **29** 30	16 **17** **19** **23** **29** **31** 32	

"As the numbers and their doubles grow larger, what do we notice about the numbers of primes between them?"

There are more and more of them.

"Will there always be at least one prime between a whole number greater than 1 and its double?"

We can make a prediction that there will because as the number that you start with gets larger, its double gets further away thus leaving more chance that there will be prime numbers.

"What are the prime numbers between 1 and 100?"

2, 3, 5, 7, 11, 13, 17, 19, 23, 29, 31, 37, 41, 43, 47, 53, 59, 61,67, 71, 73, 79, 83, 87, 89, 97

"Is there at least one prime number in each decade (set of ten)?"

Yes. There are primes in the ones, tens, twenties, thirties, forties, fifties, etc. Therefore we can make a prediction that there will always be at least one prime between a whole number greater than 1 and its double.

"Can we prove it?"

no

Check Look back.

"Did we do what we were asked to do?"

Yes, we made the prediction that there will be at least one prime between each a whole number greater than 1 and its double.

"Is our conclusion reasonable?"

Yes. The larger the number is that is being doubled, the larger the range of numbers between the number and its double.

Teacher Note: To extend the problem, have students choose a large two-digit number and its double and then search for the prime numbers that are between them.

1 Power Up

Facts

Distribute **Power Up N** to students. See answers below.

Mental Math

Encourage students to share different ways to mentally compute these exercises. Strategies for exercises **a, d,** and **f** are listed below.

a. Add From Left to Right

$4.8 + 3 = 7.8$

$7.8 + 0.3 = 8.1$

Add Ones First

$4 + 3 = 7$

$0.8 + 0.3 = 1.1$

$7 + 1.1 = 8.1$

d. Halve, then Double

$\$2.40 \times 100 = \$240$

f. Equivalent Decimal

$0.6 \times 25 = 0.3 \times 50 = 15$

Equivalent Fraction

$\frac{60}{100} = \frac{6}{10} = \frac{3}{5}$

$\frac{3}{5} \times 25 = 25 \div 5 \times 3$ or 15

Problem Solving

Refer to **Power-Up Discussion,** p. 490B.

2 New Concepts

Instruction

"How would you determine how much water is needed to fill an aquarium?"

Elicit that this question involves finding volume. Explain to students that in this lesson, they will learn to find the volume of rectangular prisms.

Remind students that a prism is a polyhedron with two congruent parallel bases. Hold up a rectangular prism. Ask students to name the shape of the congruent bases of the box. rectangles

Point out to students that all the faces of a rectangular prism are rectangles.

Example 1

Instruction

If students have difficulty visualizing the solution, demonstrate how to model each layer of the prism with **wooden color cubes** from the Manipulative Kit.

LESSON 70

• Volume

Power Up — *Building Power*

facts Power Up N

mental math

a. Decimals: $4.8 + 3 + 0.3$ 8.1

b. Exponents: 25^2 625

c. Algebra: $5m - 3 = 27$ 6

d. Mental Math: $\$4.80 \times 50$ \$240.00

e. Measurement: 20 dm to mm   2000 mm

f. Percent: 60% of 25   15

g. Primes/Composites: What is the prime factorization of 10? 2×5

h. Geometry: Find the perimeter and area of a square that has sides 0.5 m long.   2 m; 0.25 m^2

problem solving Between the whole numbers 2 and 4 is the prime number 3. Between the whole numbers 4 and 8 are the prime numbers 5 and 7. Can you always find a prime number between a whole number greater than one and its double?   Yes.

New Concept — *Increasing Knowledge*

Recall from Lesson 67 that geometric solids are shapes that take up space. We use the word **volume** to describe the space occupied by a shape. To measure volume, we use units that occupy space. The units that we use to measure volume are cubes of certain sizes. We can use unit cubes to help us think of volume.

Thinking Skill *Predict*

A prism has 4 layers, each containing 9 cubes. Will it have the same volume as the prism on the right? Why or why not? Yes; 4 layers times 9 cubes per layer will be 36 cubes.

Example 1

This rectangular prism was constructed of unit cubes. Its volume is how many cubes?

Solution

To find the volume of the prism, we calculate the number of cubes it contains. We see that there are 3 layers of cubes. Each layer contains 3 rows of cubes with 4 cubes in each row, or 12 cubes. Three layers with 12 cubes in each layer means that the volume of the prism is **36 cubes.**

Facts Simplify. Reduce the answers if possible.

$3 + 1\frac{2}{3} = 4\frac{2}{3}$	$3 - 1\frac{2}{3} = 1\frac{1}{3}$	$3 \times 1\frac{2}{3} = 5$	$3 \div 1\frac{2}{3} = 1\frac{4}{5}$
$1\frac{2}{3} + 1\frac{1}{2} = 3\frac{1}{6}$	$1\frac{2}{3} - 1\frac{1}{2} = \frac{1}{6}$	$1\frac{2}{3} \times 1\frac{1}{2} = 2\frac{1}{2}$	$1\frac{2}{3} \div 1\frac{1}{2} = 1\frac{1}{9}$
$2\frac{1}{2} + 1\frac{2}{3} = 4\frac{1}{6}$	$2\frac{1}{2} - 1\frac{2}{3} = \frac{5}{6}$	$2\frac{1}{2} \times 1\frac{2}{3} = 4\frac{1}{6}$	$2\frac{1}{2} \div 1\frac{2}{3} = 1\frac{1}{2}$
$4\frac{1}{2} + 2\frac{1}{4} = 6\frac{3}{4}$	$4\frac{1}{2} - 2\frac{1}{4} = 2\frac{1}{4}$	$4\frac{1}{2} \times 2\frac{1}{4} = 10\frac{1}{8}$	$4\frac{1}{2} \div 2\frac{1}{4} = 2$

Reading Math
Read the measure 1 cm^3 as "one cubic centimeter."

Volumes are measured by using cubes of a standard size. A cube whose edges are 1 centimeter long has a volume of 1 cubic centimeter, which we abbreviate by writing 1 cm^3.

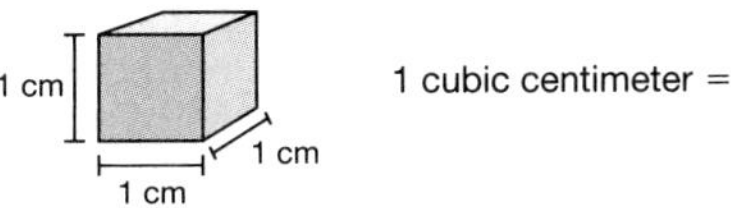

1 cubic centimeter = 1 cm^3

Similarly, if each of the edges is 1 foot long, the volume is 1 cubic foot. If each of the edges is 1 meter long, the volume is 1 cubic meter.

1 cubic foot = 1 ft^3 1 cubic meter = 1 m^3

To calculate the volume of a solid, we can imagine constructing the solid out of unit cubes of the same size. We would begin by constructing the base and then building up the layers to the specified height.

Example 2

Find the number of 1-cm cubes that can be placed inside a rectangular box with the dimensions shown.

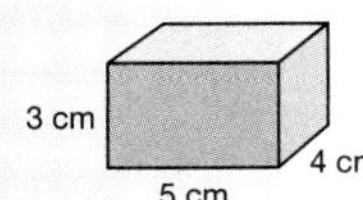

Solution

The base of the box is 5 cm by 4 cm, so we can place 5 rows of 4 cubes on the base. Thus there are 20 cubes on the first layer.

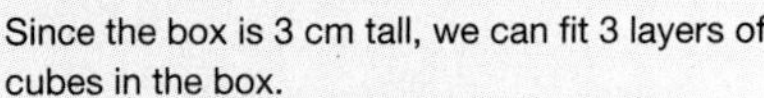

Since the box is 3 cm tall, we can fit 3 layers of cubes in the box.

$$\frac{20\text{ cubes}}{1\text{ layer}} \times 3\text{ layers} = 60\text{ cubes}$$

We find that **60 1-cm cubes** can be placed in the box.

Discuss How would we determine how many 1-cm cubes can be placed inside a rectangular box that is 4 cm high, 6 cm long, and 5 cm wide?

Sample: The base of the box is 6 cm by 5 cm so there would be 30 cubes on the first layer. Since the box is 4 cm tall we can fit 4 layers in the box. Since $4 \times 30 = 120$, 120 one-cm cubes can be placed in the box.

Example 3

What is the volume of this cube? Dimensions are in inches.

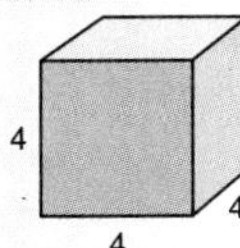

Solution

The base is 4 in. by 4 in. Thus 16 cubes can be placed on the base.

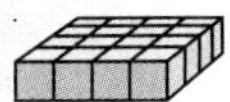

2 New Concepts (Continued)

Instruction

Point out to students that the raised 3 in 1 cm^3 is an exponent. An exponent shows how many times a base is used as a factor. Write $1\text{ cm} \times 1\text{ cm} \times 1\text{ cm} = 1\text{ cm}^3$ on the board. Tell students that when a base of 1 cm is used as a factor three times, the result is 1 cm^3. Point out that volume is always measured in cubic units.

Example 2

Instruction

Remind students that a cube is a rectangular prism with all square faces, so the procedure for finding the volume of a cube is the same as the procedure for finding the volume of other rectangular prisms.

(continued)

Math Background

How is it possible for 1 cubic yard to equal 27 cubic feet?

Picture a cube that measures 1 yard on each edge. This cube has a volume of 1 cubic yard or 1 yd^3. Since 1 yard is equivalent to 3 feet, this same cube measures 3 feet on each edge and therefore has a volume of $3\text{ ft} \times 3\text{ ft} \times 3\text{ ft} = 27$ cubic feet, or 27 ft^3. The volumes of the cubes below are equal because the dimensions are equal: 1 yd = 3 ft.

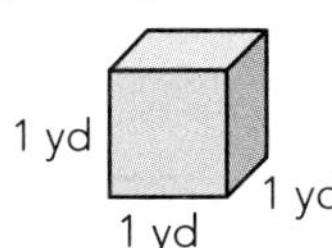

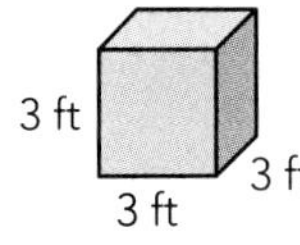

2 New Concepts (Continued)

Instruction

Guide students to discover the formula for finding the volume of a rectangular prism.

"What do the cubes in the first layer of a rectangular prism represent?" area of the base

"What do we multiply the area of the base by to find the volume of a rectangular prism?" height

"What is the formula for finding the volume of a rectangular prism?" *Volume = area of base × height*

"What dimensions do we use to find area?" length and width

"What is another way to write the formula for finding the volume of a rectangular prism?" *Volume = length × width × height or V = lwh*

Example 4

Instruction

Sketch the solid figure in example 4 on the board. Ask a volunteer to show another way to divide the solid into two blocks. Have students name the dimensions of each block.

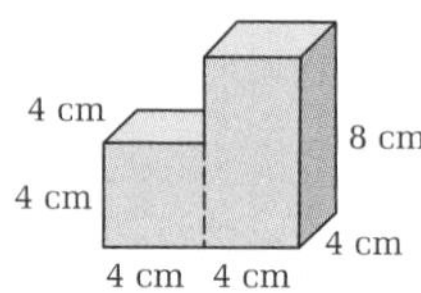

Now ask a volunteer to divide the solid into three blocks and name the dimensions of each block.

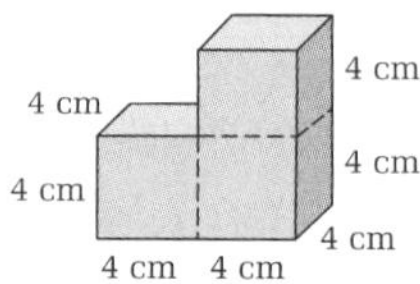

Lead students to conclude that no matter how the solid figure is divided, its volume does not change.

Practice Set

Problem a Generalize

Help students to recognize that they can count the cubes in the length, width, and height and multiply them to find the number of cubes in the whole prism.

Problem d Estimate

Ask student volunteers to record the data on the board as the activity progresses.

Problem e Formulate

Ask students to write problems about volume and share their problems and solutions with the class.

(continued)

Since the big cube is 4 in. tall, there are 4 layers of small cubes.

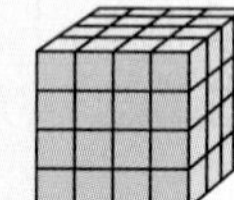

$$\frac{16 \text{ cubes}}{1 \text{ layer}} \times 4 \text{ layers} = 64 \text{ cubes}$$

Each small cube has a volume of 1 cubic inch. Thus the volume of the big cube is **64 cubic inches (64 in.^{3})**.

We refer to the dimensions of a rectangular prism as *length, width,* and *height.*

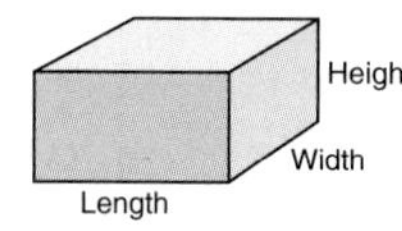

Write a formula that can be used to find the volume (V) of a rectangular prism if we know its length (l), its width (w), and its height (h).

Example 4

Find the volume of this solid.

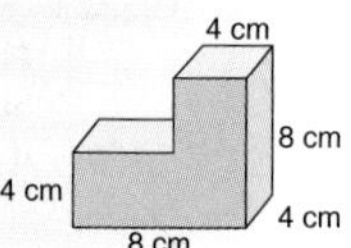

Solution

We divide the figure into two blocks and find the volume of each block.

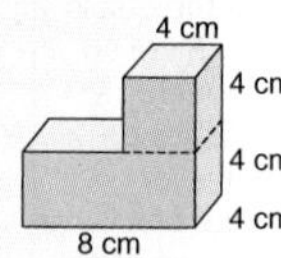

Lower: 8 cm × 4 cm × 4 cm = 128 cm^3
+Upper: 4 cm × 4 cm × 4 cm = 64 cm^3
Volume of both blocks = **192 cm^3**

Practice Set

▸ **a.** Generalize This rectangular prism was constructed of unit cubes. Its volume is how many unit cubes? 72 unit cubes

b. Find the number of 1-cm cubes that can be placed inside a box with dimensions as illustrated. 1000 1-cm cubes

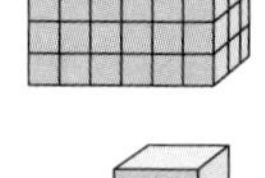

c. What is the volume of this rectangular prism? Dimensions are in feet. 240 ft^3

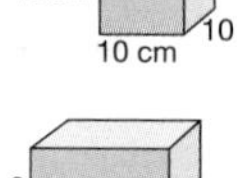

▸ **d.** Estimate As a class, estimate the volume of the classroom in cubic meters. Then use a meterstick to measure the length, width, and height of the classroom to the nearest meter, and calculate the volume of the room. Answers will vary.

▸ **e.** Formulate What is the formula for the volume of a rectangular prism? $V = lwh$

▸ See Math Conversations in the sidebar.

Inclusion

Materials: color tiles and cubes from the manipulative kit, small boxes with dimensions such that a box filled with cubes has no gaps

Some students may not understand the need to measure volume in *cubic units*. Have students cover the base of one box with the color tiles. Ask:

"If each tile is 1-inch by 1-inch, or 1 inch squared, what unit of measurement would you use for the space you covered with tiles? Explain." Sample: In.^{2}, because the tiles cover the 2-dimensional space of the box.

Have the students remove the color tiles from the box and then fill it with the color cubes. Ask them:

"If each cube is 1-inch by 1-inch by 1-inch, or 1 inch cubed, what unit of measurement would you use for space you filled with cubes? Explain." Sample: In.^{3}, because the tiles cover the 3-dimensional space of the box.

▸ f. **Generalize** Find the volume of this solid.
275 cm^3

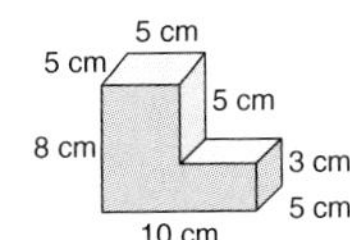

Written Practice *Strengthening Concepts*

1. (53) It was 19 kilometers from the campgrounds to the lake. Joel and Mario rode their bicycles from the campgrounds to the lake and back again. If the round trip ride took them 2 hours, what was their average speed in kilometers per hour? 19 kilometers per hour

2. (37, 58) The vertices of two angles of a triangle are (3, 1) and (0, −4). The y-axis is a line of symmetry of the triangle.
   a. What are the coordinates of the third vertex of the triangle? (−3, 1)
   b. What is the area of the triangle? 15 sq. units

3. A little too large. The actual value of π is greater than 3. Dividing the circumference, 600 cm, by π results in a measurement less than 200 cm.

▸ * 3. (66) **Verify** Using a tape measure, Gretchen found that the circumference of the great oak was 600 cm. Rounding π to 3, she estimated that the tree's diameter was 200 cm. Was her estimate for the diameter a little too large or a little too small? Why?

▸ 4. (46) Grapes were priced at 3 pounds for $5.28.
   a. What was the price per pound? $1.76 per pound
   b. How much would 10 pounds of grapes cost? $17.60

5. (35) If the product of nine tenths and eight tenths is subtracted from the sum of seven tenths and six tenths, what is the difference? 0.58

6. (22, 48) Three fourths of the batter's 188 hits were singles.
   a. How many of the batter's hits were singles? 141 hits
   b. What percent of the batter's hits were not singles? 25%

▸ 7. (8) On an inch ruler, which mark is halfway between the $1\frac{1}{2}$ inch mark and the 3 inch mark? $2\frac{1}{4}$ inch mark

▸ * 8. (70) **Generalize** Find the number of 1-cm cubes that can be placed in the box at right. 75 1-cm cubes

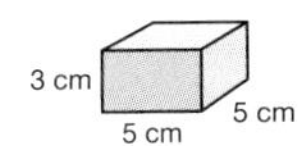

* 9. (65) Find the circumference of each circle:
   a. 2π in.
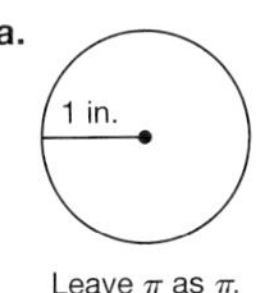

   Leave π as π.
   b. 3.14 in.
   $\frac{1}{2}$ in.
   Use 3.14 for π.

▸ * 10. (69) **Generalize** Write each number in scientific notation:
   a. 12×10^{-6} 1.2×10^{-5}
   b. 0.12×10^{-6} 1.2×10^{-7}

▸ See Math Conversations in the sidebar.

English Learners

Explain the meaning of the term **round trip** in problem 1. Say:

"If your round trip to school is 1 mile, it means that going to school and back home is 1 mile."

Ask students where they would like to go if they had free round trip tickets.

2 New Concepts (Continued)

Practice Set

Problem f (Error Alert)

Watch for students who do not include the exponent with 275 cm^3. Remind them that the answer is not correct unless the exponent 3 is included after the unit of measure.

3 Written Practice

Math Conversations

Discussion opportunities are provided below.

Problem 3 Analyze

Have students share their answers with the class. Then ask a volunteer to calculate the diameter of the tree using 3.14. about 191.1 cm

Problem 4 Verify

Extend the Problem

Ask students to write a formula to determine the cost of any number of pounds of grapes. Sample: $\$1.76n = t$ where n = the number of pounds of grapes and t = the total cost.

"Predict the price of 4.5 lb of grapes." $7.92

"How can you check that your formula works?" Sample: Use a doubling pattern. 1 pound is $1.76, 2 pounds is $3.52, 4 pounds is $7.04 + the price of a half pound, $0.88, equals $7.92.

Another method for checking is to write a proportion.

$\frac{1}{\$1.76} = \frac{4.5}{x}$; $x = 4.5 \times \$1.76$, or $7.92

Problem 8 Generalize

Lead a discussion that helps students see that since the dimensions of the prism are given in centimeters, they can multiply the length, width, and height and it will give both the volume and the number of centimeter cubes that the box contains.

Problem 10 Generalize

Have student volunteers work at the board to show the steps and explain the solutions.

Errors and Misconceptions

Problem 7

If students don't know how to begin this problem, let them refer to an inch ruler. Ask,

"How would you find the average of two numbers?" add and then divide by 2

After students find the average, have them compare the answer to the halfway mark on the ruler.

(continued)

3 Written Practice (Continued)

Math Conversations

Discussion opportunities are provided below.

Problem 13 Generalize

Ask student volunteers to review the rules for exponents.

Problem 16 Generalize

Have student volunteers explain how to simplify each problem using mental math.

Problem 20 Predict

Extend the Problem

Have students draw the top, bottom, front, and side views of the solid figure this pattern will form when it is folded.

Sample:

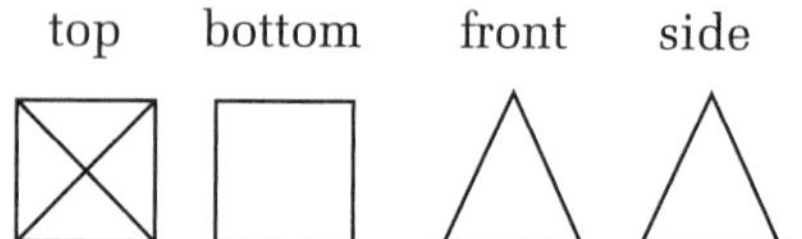

Errors and Misconceptions

Problem 20

If students have difficulty visualizing the three-dimensional figure, have them trace the pattern, cut it out, and fold it before they draw the three-dimensional figure.

Problem 21

Having just studied volume, some students may inadvertently find the volume of the cube. Point out that the problem asks for surface area.

(continued)

11. (28, 34) What is the average of the three numbers marked by arrows on the number line below? 0.85

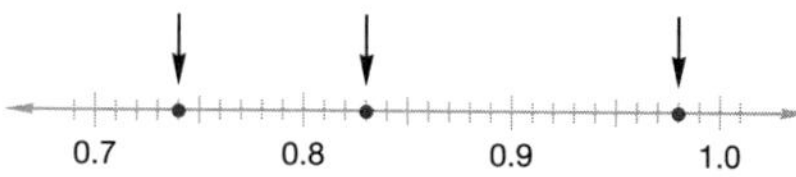

12. $1.25 \text{ kilograms} \cdot \frac{1000 \text{ grams}}{1 \text{ kilogram}}$ $= 1250$ grams

12. (50) Use a unit multiplier to convert 1.25 kilograms to grams.

▶* **13.** (47, 57) Generalize Find each missing exponent:

a. $2^6 \cdot 2^3 = 2^{\square}$ 9 **b.** $2^6 \div 2^3 = 2^{\square}$ 3

c. $2^3 \div 2^6 = 2^{\square}$ −3 **d.** $2^6 \div 2^6 = 2^{\square}$ 0

14. (60) Write an equation to solve this problem: What number is $\frac{1}{6}$ of 100? $W_N = \frac{1}{6} \times 100$; $16\frac{2}{3}$

15. (48) Complete the table.

Fraction	Decimal	Percent
a. $\frac{7}{50}$	**b.** 0.14	14%
$\frac{5}{6}$	**c.** $0.8\overline{3}$	**d.** $83\frac{1}{3}\%$

▶* **16.** (68) Generalize Simplify:

a. $(-6) - (-4) + (+2)$ 0

b. $(-5) + (-2) - (-7) - (+9)$ −9

c. $\left(-\frac{1}{2}\right) - \left(-\frac{1}{4}\right)$ $-\frac{1}{4}$

17. (52) Evaluate: $ab - (a - b)$ if $a = 0.4$ and $b = 0.3$ 0.02

18. (42) Round $29{,}374.6\overline{5}$ to the nearest whole number. 29,375

19. (29, 33) Estimate the product of 6.085 and $7\frac{15}{16}$. 48

▶* **20.** (67) Predict What three-dimensional figure can be formed by folding this pattern? Draw the three-dimensional figure. pyramid;

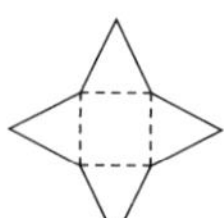

▶* **21.** (67) What is the surface area of a cube with edges 2 ft long? 24 ft²

Solve:

22. (35) $4.3 = x - 0.8$ 5.1

23. (39) $\frac{2}{d} = \frac{1.2}{1.5}$ 2.5

Simplify:

24. (49)

```
   10 lb
 − 6 lb 7 oz
   3 lb 9 oz
```

25. (53) $\frac{\$5.25}{1 \text{ hr}} \cdot \frac{8 \text{ hr}}{1 \text{ day}} \cdot \frac{5 \text{ days}}{1 \text{ week}}$ $\frac{\$210.00}{\text{week}}$

26. (26) $3\frac{3}{4} \div \left(1\frac{2}{3} \cdot 3\right)$ $\frac{3}{4}$

27. (30) $4\frac{1}{2} + 5\frac{1}{6} - 1\frac{1}{3}$ $8\frac{1}{3}$

494 **Saxon** *Math Course 2*

▶ See Math Conversations in the sidebar.

▶ **28.** (0.06 ÷ 5) ÷ 0.004 3
(45)

29. Write $9\frac{1}{2}$ as a decimal number, and multiply it by 9.2. 87.4
(35, 43)

30. A coin is tossed and the spinner is spun. One possible outcome is heads and A (HA).
(36)

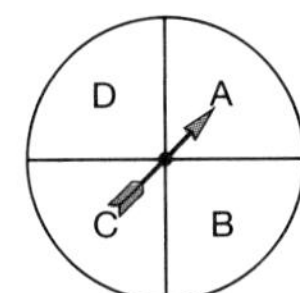

a. What is the sample space of the experiment? {HA, HB, HC, HD, TA, TB, TC, TD}

b. What is the probability of getting heads and a consonant? $\frac{3}{8}$

Early Finishers
Math and Science

Light travels at a speed of approximately 186,000 miles per second. Scientists use a unit of measurement known as a light-year for expressing distances from Earth to stars and other objects far away. A light-year is the distance light can travel in one year.

a. Express the given speed of light in scientific notation. 1.86×10^5 miles per second

b. Determine the number of seconds in one year (365 days). Express this result in scientific notation. 3.1536×10^7 seconds per year

c. Use the answers to **a** and **b** to find the distance light travels in one year. Express the answer in scientific notation. 5.865696×10^{12} miles

d. Round the answer to **c** to one non-zero digit, and then use words to name that distance. 6×10^{12} miles, six trillion miles

▶ See Math Conversations in the sidebar.

3 Written Practice (Continued)

Math Conversations

Discussion opportunities are provided below.

Problem 28

Extend the Problem

Discuss how this problem could be solved using fractions. Ask a student volunteer to record on the board as you lead the discussion.

Dividing by 5 is the same as multiplying by $\frac{1}{5}$.

$$\frac{6}{100} \div 5 = \frac{6}{100} \times \frac{1}{5} = \frac{6}{500}$$

$$\frac{6}{500} \div \frac{4}{1000} = \frac{\cancelto{3}{6}}{\cancelto{1}{500}} \times \frac{\cancelto{1}{\cancel{2}}\,\cancel{1000}}{\cancelto{1}{\cancel{2}}\,\cancel{4}} = 3$$

Looking Forward

Understanding volume prepares students for:

- **Lesson 95,** finding the volume of right solids (square and triangular prisms and circular cylinders).
- **Lesson 113,** finding the volume of pyramids, cones, and spheres.

Assessment

30–40 minutes *For use after Lesson 70*

Distribute **Cumulative Test 13** to each student. Two versions of the test are available in *Saxon Math Course 2 Course Assessments Book.* Have students complete the **Power-Up Test** first. Allow 10 minutes. Then have students work the 20 numbered items on the **Cumulative Test.** Students may use copies of the answer sheet to record their work. Track individual and class progress with the **Test Analysis** forms.

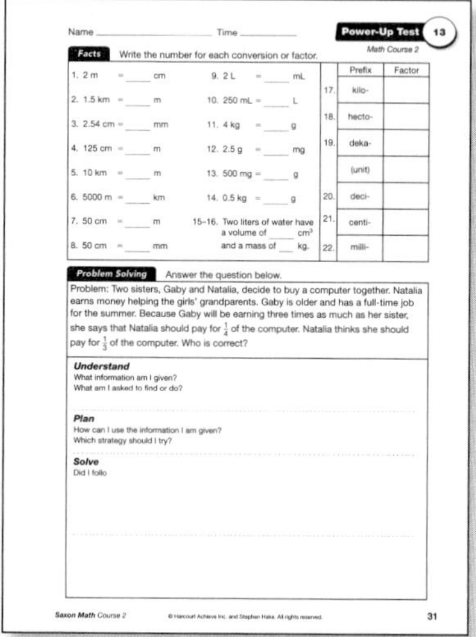

Power-Up Test 13

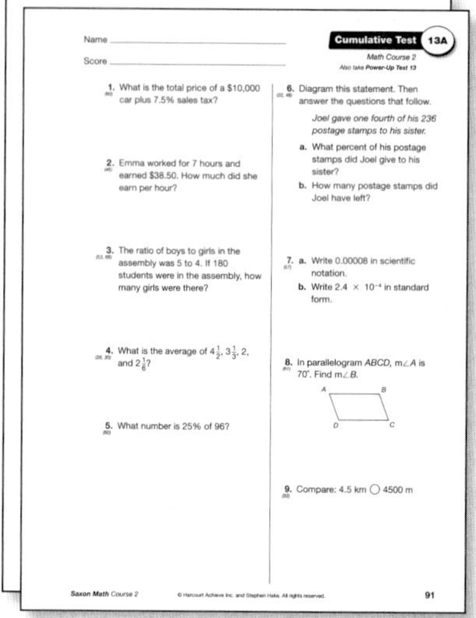

Cumulative Test 13A

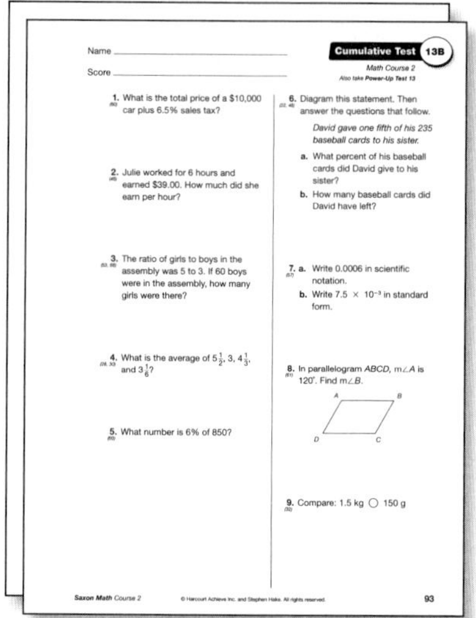

Alternative Cumulative Test 13B

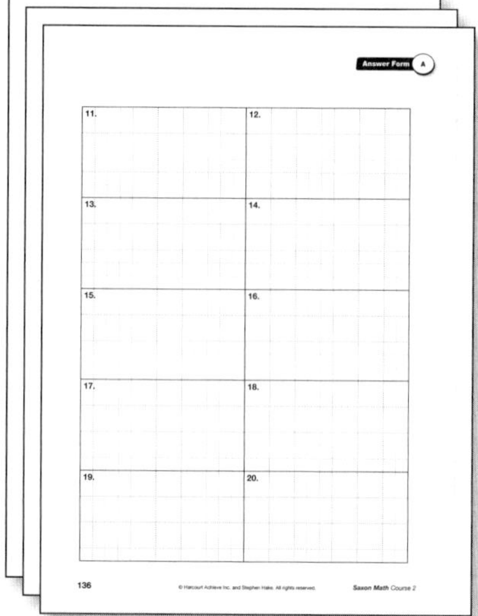

Optional Answer Forms

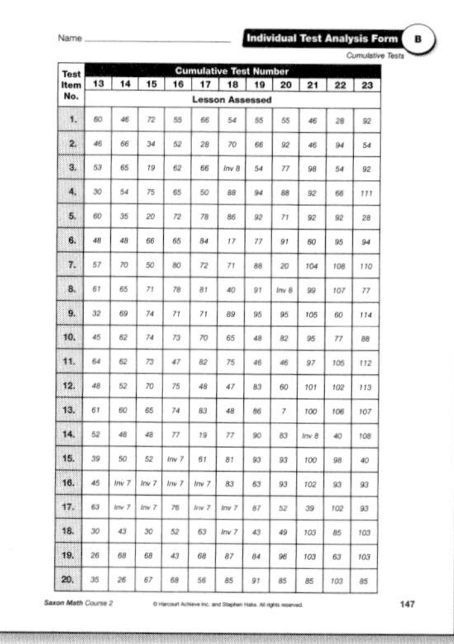

Individual Test Analysis Form

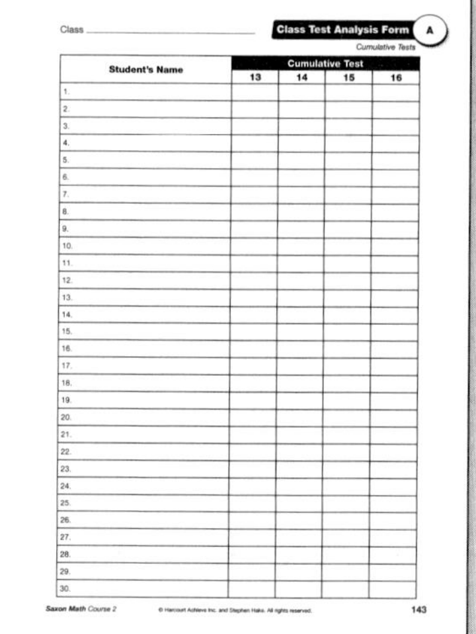

Class Test Analysis Form

Reteaching

Students who score below 80% on the assessment may be in need of reteaching. Look for the causes of student mistakes. If errors are conceptual, refer to the *Reteaching Masters* for reteaching.

Customized Benchmark Assessment

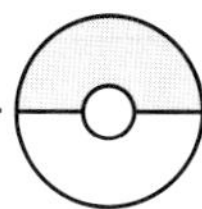

You can develop customized benchmark tests using the Test Generator located on the *Test and Practice Generator CD.*

This chart shows the lesson, the standard, and the test item question that can be found on the *Test and Practice Generator CD.*

LESSON	NEW CONCEPTS	LOCAL STANDARD	TEST ITEM ON CD
61	• Areas of a Parallelogram		7.61.1
	• Angles of a Parallelogram		7.61.2
62	• Classifying Triangles		7.62.1
63	• Symbols of Inclusion		7.63.1
64	• Adding Positive and Negative Numbers		7.64.1
65	• Circumference and Pi		7.65.1
66	• Ratio Problems Involving Totals		7.66.1
67	• Geometric Solids		7.67.1
68	• Algebraic Addition		7.68.1
69	• Proper Form of Scientific Notation		7.69.1
70	• Volume		7.70.1

Using the Test Generator CD

- Develop tests in both English and Spanish.
- Choose from multiple-choice and free-response test items.
- Clone test items to create multiple versions of the same test.
- View and edit test items to make and save your own questions.
- Administer assessments through paper tests or over a school LAN.
- Monitor student progress through a variety of individual and class reports —for both diagnosing and assessing standards mastery.

Performance Task 13

Analyze Temperature Data

Assign after Lesson 70 and Test 13

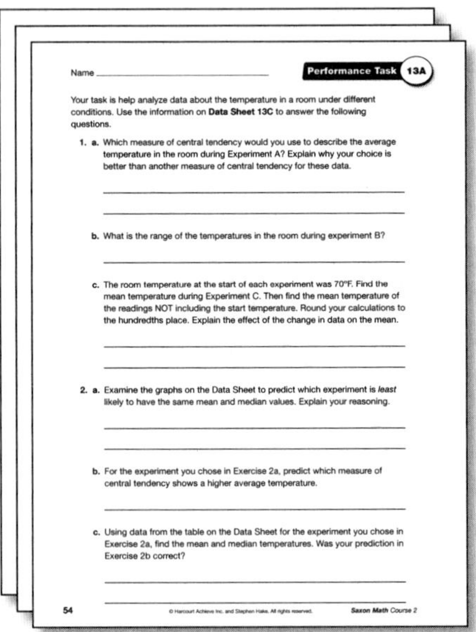

Name ____________

Performance Task 13A

Your task is help analyze data about the temperature in a room under different conditions. Use the information on **Data Sheet 13C** to answer the following questions.

1. **a.** Which measure of central tendency would you use to describe the average temperature in the room during Experiment A? Explain why your choice is better than another measure of central tendency for these data.

   b. What is the range of the temperatures in the room during experiment B?

   c. The room temperature at the start of each experiment was 70°F. Find the mean temperature during Experiment C. Then find the mean temperature of the readings NOT including the start temperature. Round your calculations to the hundredths place. Explain the effect of the change in data on the mean.

2. **a.** Examine the graphs on the Data Sheet to predict which experiment is *least* likely to have the same mean and median values. Explain your reasoning.

   b. For the experiment you chose in Exercise 2a, predict which measure of central tendency shows a higher average temperature.

   c. Using data from the table on the Data Sheet for the experiment you chose in Exercise 2a, find the mean and median temperatures. Was your prediction in Exercise 2b correct?

54 © Harcourt Achieve Inc. and Stephen Hake. All rights reserved. *Saxon Math Course 2*

Performance Task 13A, 13B, and 13C

Objectives

- Choose the best measure of central tendency or range to describe a set of data.
- Calculate mean, median, and mode, and find the range of a set of data.
- Find the effect on the mean of a change in the data.
- Communicate ideas through writing.

Materials

Performance Tasks 13A, 13B, and **13C**

Preparation

Make copies of **Performance Tasks 13A, 13B,** and **13C.** (One each per student.)

Time Requirement

30–60 minutes; Begin in class and complete at home.

Task

Explain to students that for this task they will examine data of temperature readings in a given room under different conditions. They will decide whether to use the mean, median, mode, or range to describe a set of data and they will justify their choices. They will also find the effect that a change in data has on the mean. Point out that all of the information students need is on **Performance Tasks 13A, 13B,** and **13C.**

Criteria for Evidence of Learning

- Chooses an appropriate measure of central tendency to describe a set of data and justifies the choice.
- Identifies the mean, median, mode, and range of a set of data correctly.
- Describes the effect that a change in the data has on the mean.
- Communicates ideas clearly through writing.

Meeting Standards

National Council of Teachers of Mathematics (NCTM)

Data Analysis and Probability

DP.2a Find, use, and interpret measures of center and spread, including mean and interquartile range

Problem Solving

PS.1b Solve problems that arise in mathematics and in other contexts

Communication

CM.3a Organize and consolidate their mathematical thinking through communication

Connections

CN.4c Recognize and apply mathematics in contexts outside of mathematics

Focus on

• Balanced Equations

Objectives

- Use a balance scale to model an equation.
- Solve and check equations that involve addition.
- Solve and check equations that involve multiplication.

Lesson Preparation

Materials

- **Manipulative kit: color tiles**
- **Teacher-provided material: balance scale**

Math Language

New

coefficient

Technology Resources

Student eBook Complete student textbook in electronic format.

Resources and Planner CD Assessment, reteaching, and instructional masters, plus a pacing calendar with standards.

Test and Practice Generator CD Create additional practice sheets and custom-made tests.

www.SaxonPublishers.com Visit for more student activities and planning materials.

Inclusion

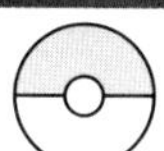

Adaptations CD Adapted lessons, investigations, practice and assessments.

Meeting Standards

National Council of Teachers of Mathematics (NCTM)

Numbers and Operations

NO.2c Understand and use the inverse relationships of addition and subtraction, multiplication and division, and squaring and finding square roots to simplify computations and solve problems

Algebra

AL.2d Recognize and generate equivalent forms for simple algebraic expressions and solve linear equations

Problem Solving

PS.1c Apply and adapt a variety of appropriate strategies to solve problems

Communication

CM.3b Communicate their mathematical thinking coherently and clearly to peers, teachers, and others

Representation

RE.5b Select, apply, and translate among mathematical representations to solve problems

INVESTIGATION 7

Have students consider the identity $15 = 15$. Discuss what happens if 2 is added to the left side of the equation. Is the resulting equation true or false? What if 2 is added to both sides of the equation? Is the resulting equation true or false? Elicit that the equation will remain a true equation if the same number is added to both sides.

Explain to students that in this investigation they will learn to balance equations.

Explain to students that if care is not taken to balance the equation when performing operations, the value that is found for the variable will be incorrect.

Point out that any letter can be used as the **variable** in an equation, although x is the variable that is most commonly used to write algebraic equations.

(continued)

INVESTIGATION 7

Focus on

• Balanced Equations

Equations are sometimes called **balanced equations** because the two sides of the equation "balance" each other. A balance scale can be used as a model of an equation. We replace the equal sign with a balanced scale. The left and right sides of the equation are placed on the left and right trays of the balance. For example, $x + 12 = 33$ becomes

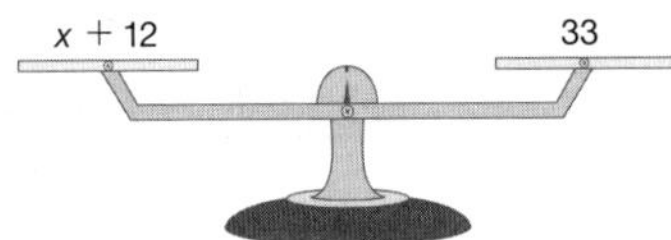

Using a balance-scale model we think of how to simplify the equation to get the unknown number, in this case x, alone on one side of the scale. Using our example, we could remove 12 (subtract 12) from the left side of the scale. However, if we did that, the scale would no longer be balanced. So we make this rule for ourselves.

> Whatever operation we perform on one side of an equation, we also perform on the other side of the equation to maintain a balanced equation.

We see that there are two steps to the process.

Step 1: Select the operation that will isolate the variable.

Step 2: Perform the selected operation on both sides of the equation.

We select "subtract 12" as the operation required to isolate x (to "get x alone"). Then we perform this operation on both sides of the equation.

Select operation:

To isolate x, *subtract 12.*

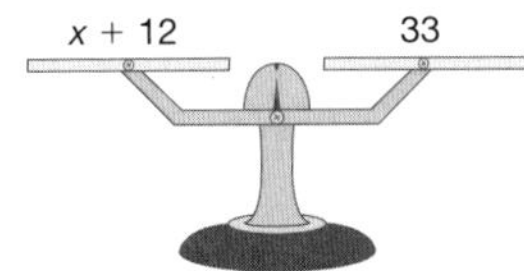

Math Background

Why should students be encouraged to show each step taken when solving equations?

Listing each step as it is being performed requires students to be more mindful of what is being done. This will not only make it easier to find a mistake, should one be made, but will also be helpful in preventing errors in the first place.

Another benefit to this action is that it will help students gain a firmer grasp on how to isolate a variable, making it easier to introduce more complex equations in future lessons.

Perform operation:

To keep the scale balanced, *subtract* 12 *from both sides of the equation.*

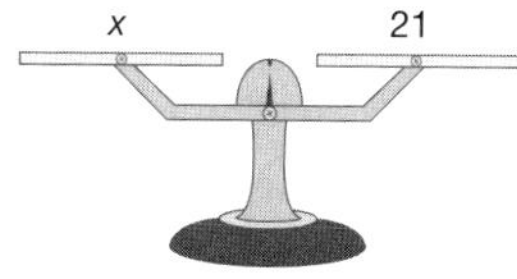

Sample: When we isolate a variable we perform an operation to get the variable alone on one side of the equal sign.

Summarize State what we do when we "isolate the variable."

After subtracting 12 from both sides of the equation, x is isolated on one side of the scale, and 21 balances x on the other side of the scale. This shows that $x = 21$. We check our solution by replacing x with 21 in the original equation.

$x + 12 = 33$	original equation
$21 + 12 = 33$	replaced x with 21
$33 = 33$	simplified left side

Both sides of the equation equal 33. This shows that the solution, $x = 21$, is correct.

Now we will illustrate a second equation $45 = x + 18$.

This time the unknown number is on the right side of the balance scale, added to 18.

▶ 1. **Analyze** Select the operation that will isolate the variable, and write that operation on your paper. subtract 18

2. Describe how to perform the operation and keep a balanced scale. Subtract 18 from both sides of the equation.

3. **Discuss** What will remain on the left and right side of the balance scale after the operation is performed. On the left side will be 27, and on the right side will be x.

We show the line-by-line solution of the equation below.

$45 = x + 18$	original equation
$45 - 18 = x + 18 - 18$	subtracted 18 from both sides
$27 = x + 0$	simplified both sides
$27 = x$	$x + 0 = x$

▶ See Math Conversations in the sidebar.

Instruction

After checking the solution to the equation $x + 12 = 33$, emphasize that students can assure a solution is correct by checking it. It is a way to find any computation or notation errors that have been made while solving the equation.

Math Conversations

Discussion opportunities are provided below.

Problem 1 Analyze

Make sure that students understand what "isolate the variable" means. Explain that the goal when solving an equation is to have the variable on one side of the equation and its value on the other side.

Encourage students to explain how they chose the operation that isolates the variable. Sample: We choose subtraction because it is the inverse of addition.

Ask a student volunteer to describe each step for solving this equation.

(continued)

Manipulative Use

Materials: balance scale, color tiles from the manipulative kit

Use a balance scale and tiles to demonstrate how performing the same operation to both sides of an equation will keep the scale balanced.

- Place four tiles on each side of the scale. Tell students that this balanced equation represents the equality $4 = 4$.
- Add and remove tiles to show that the scale remains balanced as long as the same number of tiles is added and removed from both sides of the scale.

Explain that equations are similar to scales. Any operation that is performed on one side of the equation must also be performed on the other side of the equation to maintain balance.

Instruction

Discuss how the multiplication equation is different from the addition equation. Make sure students understand why subtraction cannot be used to solve the equation. Remind students of inverse operations and challenge them to suggest a way to isolate x in a multiplication equation.

Perform and explain the line-by-line solution of a multiplication equation on an overhead projector. Have students copy the steps on their paper. Emphasize that the last step in solving an equation is to check the answer.

Math Conversations

Discussion opportunities are provided below.

Problem 4 Predict

Work through the steps to solve $132 = 2x$. Discuss how this problem and the example $2x = 132$ are the same. Emphasize that equal quantities can be written on either side of the equals sign.

(continued)

We check the solution by replacing x with 27 in the original equation.

$45 = x + 18$	original equation
$45 = 27 + 18$	replaced x with 27
$45 = 45$	simplified right side

By checking the solution in the original equation, we see that the solution is correct. Now we revisit the equation to illustrate one more idea.

▶ **4.** Predict Suppose the contents of the two trays of the balance scale were switched. That is, $x + 18$ was moved to the left side, and 45 was moved to the right side. Would the scale still be balanced? Write what the equation would be. Yes, the equation would stil be balanced. $x + 18 = 45$

Now we will consider an equation that involves multiplication rather than addition.

$$2x = 132$$

Since $2x$ means two x's ($x + x$), we may show this equation on a balance scale two ways.

Our goal is to isolate x, that is, to have one x. We must perform the operations necessary to get one x alone on one side of the scale. We do not subtract 2, because 2 is not added to x. We do not subtract an x, because there is no x to subtract from the other side of the equation. To isolate x in this equation, we *divide by 2*. To keep the equation balanced, we *divide both sides by 2*.

Select operation:

To isolate x, *divide by 2*.

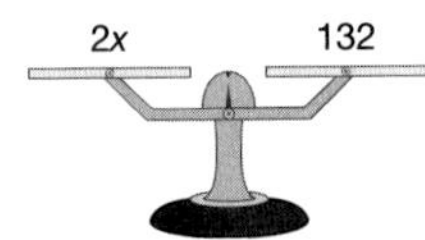

▶ See Math Conversations in the sidebar.

Teacher Tip

To prepare students for **solving** more **complex equations,** encourage them to show each step in their solutions. Emphasize to them how important it will be to them in future lessons to be able to successfully complete the equations being introduced here.

Perform operation:

To keep the equation balanced, divide *both sides by 2.*

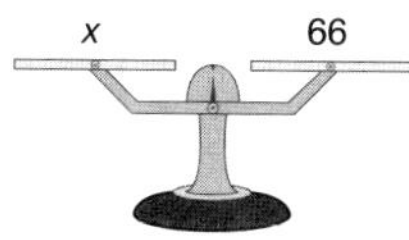

Here we show the line-by-line solution of this equation.

$2x = 132$	original equation
$\frac{2x}{2} = \frac{132}{2}$	divided both sides by 2
$1x = 66$	simplified both sides
$x = 66$	$1x = x$

Next we show the check of the solution.

$2x = 132$	original equation
$2(66) = 132$	replaced x with 66
$132 = 132$	simplified left side

This check shows that the solution, $x = 66$, is correct.

5. $3x$ 132

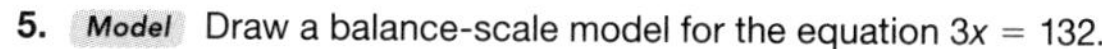

▸ **5.** Model Draw a balance-scale model for the equation $3x = 132$.

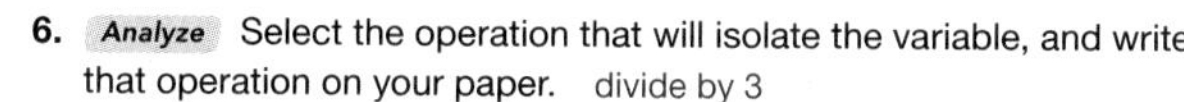

▸ **6.** Analyze Select the operation that will isolate the variable, and write that operation on your paper. divide by 3

7. Describe how to perform the operation and keep a balanced scale. Divide both sides of the equation by 3.

8. x 44

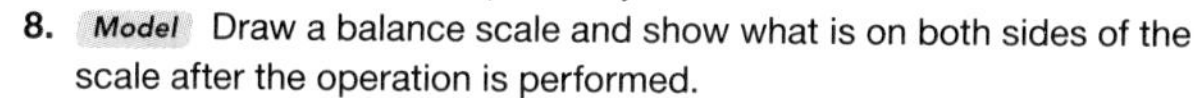

▸ **8.** Model Draw a balance scale and show what is on both sides of the scale after the operation is performed.

▸ **9.** Justify Write the line-by-line solution of the equation.

9. $3x = 132$
$\frac{3x}{3} = \frac{132}{3}$
$1x = 44$
$x = 44$

10. Show the check of the solution.

10. $3x = 132$
$3(44) = 132$
$132 = 132$ ✓

Most students choose to solve the equation $3x = 132$ by dividing both sides of the equation by 3. There is another operation that could be selected that is often useful, which we will describe next. First note that the number multiplying the variable, in this case 3, is called the **coefficient** of x. Instead of dividing by the coefficient of x, we could choose to **multiply by the reciprocal** of the coefficient. In this case we could multiply by $\frac{1}{3}$. In either case the goal is to make the coefficient 1.

$$3x = 132$$

$$\frac{1}{3} \cdot 3x = \frac{1}{3} \cdot 132$$

$$1x = \frac{132}{3}$$

$$x = 44$$

▸ See Math Conversations in the sidebar.

Math Conversations

Discussion opportunities are provided below.

Problem 5 Model

Tell students that they can use a triangle and a line segment to model a balance scale.

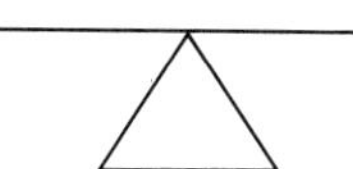

Problems 6 Analyze

"What is the inverse operation of multiplication?" division

Ask a student volunteer to illustrate that multiplication and division are inverse operations. Sample: $12 \div 3 = 4$ because $3 \times 4 = 12$; one operation undoes the other

Problems 8 Model

Ask a student volunteer to draw this scale on the board.

Problem 9 Justify

Show students how to work neatly and align equals signs for each step in solving the equation. Emphasize that this will help them to locate any errors.

Instruction

After introducing the term coefficient, have students look back at the equations $2x = 132$ and $x = 66$. Have them identify the coefficient in each equation. 2; 1

Emphasize that when the coefficient is not written in front of the variable, it is assumed to be 1. You may also want to review the coefficient of x in the addition equation $x + 12 = 33$. The coefficient is 1. The number 12 is called a **constant.**

Remind students that dividing by a number is the same as multiplying by its reciprocal. Discuss both methods of making the coefficient 1 and have students compare the solutions.

Encourage students to explain which method they prefer to solve a multiplication equation and why. Elicit that the method depends upon the form of the equation.

(continued)

Instruction

Some students may wonder how to use division to solve the equation. Demonstrate that division can still be performed as follows.

$$\frac{3}{4}x = \frac{9}{10}$$

$$\frac{3}{4} \div \frac{3}{4} = 1 \qquad \frac{9}{10} \div \frac{3}{4} = \frac{9}{10} \times \frac{4}{3} = \frac{6}{5}$$

$$1x = \frac{6}{5}$$

$$x = 1\frac{1}{5}$$

Math Conversations

Discussion opportunities are provided below.

Problem 11 Analyze

"Why can you multiply by $\frac{3}{4}$ rather than divide by $\frac{4}{3}$?" Since $\frac{3}{4}$ and $\frac{4}{3}$ are reciprocals, multiplying by $\frac{4}{3}$ is the same as dividing by $\frac{3}{4}$.

Problem 19 Evaluate

Have students explain what additional step is needed to solve for the variable in this equation. Write the fractions with common denominators to subtract.

(continued)

Discuss Why is $\frac{1}{3}$ the reciprocal of 3? Sample: 3 written as a fraction is $\frac{3}{1}$, and $\frac{3}{1} \times \frac{1}{3} = 1$

When solving equations with whole number or decimal number coefficients, it is usually easier to think about dividing by the coefficient. However, when solving equations with fractional coefficients, it is usually easier to multiply by the reciprocal of the coefficient. Refer to the following equation for problems 11–14:

$$\frac{3}{4}x = \frac{9}{10}$$

▶ **11.** **Analyze** Select the operation that will result in $\frac{3}{4}x$ becoming $1x$ in the equation. Tell why you chose the operation. multiply by $\frac{4}{3}$; See student work.

12. Describe how to perform the operation and keep the equation balanced. Multiply both sides of the equation by $\frac{4}{3}$.

13. Write a line-by-line solution of the equation.

14. Show the check of the solution.

We find that the solution to the equation is $\frac{6}{5}$ (or $1\frac{1}{5}$). In arithmetic we usually convert improper fractions to mixed numbers. In algebra we usually leave improper fractions in improper form unless the problem states or implies that a mixed number answer is preferable.

Evaluate For each of the following equations:

a. State the operation you select to isolate the variable.

b. Describe how to perform the operation and keep the equation balanced.

c. Write a line-by-line solution of the equation.

d. Show the check of the solution.

15. $x + 2.5 = 7$ **a.** subtract 2.5 **b.** Subtract 2.5 from both sides of the equation.

16. $3.6 = y + 2$ **a.** subtract 2 **b.** Subtract 2 from both sides of the equation.

17. $4w = 132$ **a.** divide by 4 **b.** Divide both sides of the equation by 4.

18. $1.2m = 1.32$ **a.** divide by 1.2 **b.** Divide both sides of the equation by 1.2.

▶ **19.** $x + \frac{3}{4} = \frac{5}{6}$ **a.** subtract $\frac{3}{4}$ **b.** Subtract $\frac{3}{4}$ from both sides of the equation.

20. $\frac{3}{4}x = \frac{5}{6}$ **a.** multiply by $\frac{4}{3}$ **b.** Multiply both sides of the equation by $\frac{4}{3}$.

19. c. $x + \frac{3}{4} = \frac{5}{6}$; $x + \frac{3}{4} - \frac{3}{4} = \frac{5}{6} - \frac{3}{4}$; $x + 0 = \frac{10}{12} - \frac{9}{12}$; $x = \frac{1}{12}$

d. $x + \frac{3}{4} = \frac{5}{6}$; $\frac{1}{12} + \frac{3}{4} = \frac{5}{6}$; $\frac{1}{12} + \frac{9}{12} = \frac{5}{6}$; $\frac{10}{12} = \frac{5}{6}$; $\frac{5}{6} = \frac{5}{6}$ ✓

20. c. $\frac{3}{4}x = \frac{5}{6}$; $\frac{4}{3} \cdot \frac{3}{4}x = \frac{4}{3} \cdot \frac{5}{6}$; $1x = \frac{20}{18}$; $x = \frac{10}{9}$

d. $\frac{3}{4}x = \frac{5}{6}$; $\frac{3}{4} \cdot \frac{10}{9} = \frac{5}{6}$; $\frac{30}{36} = \frac{5}{6}$; $\frac{5}{6} = \frac{5}{6}$ ✓

13.
$\frac{3}{4}x = \frac{9}{10}$
$\frac{4}{3} \cdot \frac{3}{4}x = \frac{4}{3} \cdot \frac{9}{10}$
$1x = \frac{36}{30}$
$x = \frac{6}{5}$ (or $1\frac{1}{5}$)

14.
$\frac{3}{4} \cdot \frac{6}{5} = \frac{9}{10}$
$\frac{18}{20} = \frac{9}{10}$
$\frac{9}{10} = \frac{9}{10}$ ✓

15. c.
$x + 2.5 = 7$
$x + 2.5 - 2.5 = 7 - 2.5$
$x + 0 = 4.5$
$x = 4.5$

d.
$x + 2.5 = 7$
$4.5 + 2.5 = 7$
$7 = 7$ ✓

16. c.
$3.6 = y + 2$
$3.6 - 2 = y + 2 - 2$
$1.6 = y + 0$
$1.6 = y$

d.
$3.6 = y + 2$
$3.6 = 1.6 + 2$
$3.6 = 3.6$ ✓

17. c.
$4w = 132$
$\frac{4w}{4} = \frac{132}{4}$
$1w = 33$
$w = 33$

d.
$4w = 132$
$4(33) = 132$
$132 = 132$ ✓

18. c.
$1.2m = 1.32$
$\frac{1.2m}{1.2} = \frac{1.32}{1.2}$
$1m = 1.1$
$m = 1.1$

d.
$1.2m = 1.32$
$1.2(1.1) = 1.32$
$1.32 = 1.32$ ✓

▶ See Math Conversations in the sidebar.

22. Sample: Subtraction: If two quantities are equal and the same number is subtracted from the quantities, then the differences are also equal; Multiplication: If two quantities are equal and both quantities are multiplied by the same number, the products are equal; Division: If two quantities are equal and both quantities are divided by the same nonzero number, then the quotients are also equal.

21. Formulate Make up your own equations. Solve and check each equation.

a. Make up an addition equation with decimal numbers. See student work.

▶ **b.** Make up a multiplication equation with a fractional coefficient. See student work.

We have used some **properties of equality** to solve the equations in this investigation. The following table summarizes properties of equality involving the four operations of arithmetic.

> **1.** Addition: If $a = b$, then $a + c = b + c$.
> **2.** Subtraction: If $a = b$, then $a - c = b - c$.
> **3.** Multiplication: If $a = b$, then $ac = bc$.
> **4.** Division: If $a = b$, and if $c \neq 0$, then $\frac{a}{c} = \frac{b}{c}$.

The addition rule means this: If two quantities are equal and the same number is added to both quantities, then the sums are also equal.

▶ **22.** Summarize Use your own words to describe the meaning of each of the other rules in the table.

extensions

▶ **a.** Justify Write an equation for each problem below. Then, choose between mental math, estimation, paper and pencil, or calculator to solve the equation. Justify your choice.

Marsha hiked a total of 12 miles on two trails in a national park. One trail was twice as long as the other. How long was each trail? Let s = the shorter trail. $s + 2s = 12$; longer trail = 8 mi; shorter trail = 4 mi.; See student work.

Jake earned $50. He put half of his money in the bank. He spent half of the money he did not put in the bank. How much money does Jake have left? Let m = the money Jake has left. $4m = \$50$; $m = \$12.50$; See student work.

Mr. Wang's business averages $14,250 in expenses each month. Company salaries average $26,395 each month. The rent for the company is $2,825 each month. How much should Mr. Wang budget for salaries, expenses, and rent for the year? Let a = the total budget. $12(\$14,250 + \$26,395 + \$2,825) = a$; $521,640; See student work.

b. Justify Look at the four equations below. Which equation does not belong? Explain your reasoning.

$4x = 8$ $\quad 132 = x + 130 \quad$ $22x = 66$ $\quad x + 12 = 14$

Accept any answer that students can support. Students may answer $22x = 66$ because it is the only equation that does not simplify to 2.

▶ See Math Conversations in the sidebar.

Math Conversations

Discussion opportunities are provided below.

Problem 21b Formulate

"Do you think the Properties of Equality work with all types of numbers?" They work for all rational numbers, which include both positive and negative fractions and decimals.

Problem 22 Summarize

Simplify these properties by explaining,

- Equals added to equals are equal.
- Equals subtracted from equals are equal.
- Equals multiplied by equals are equal.
- Equals divided by equals are equal.

Have students look back at the equations solved in the lesson and find examples of each of the properties. They should also find examples of equations with fractions and decimals.

Extensions

a. **Justify** Students should choose whatever method of calculation that is appropriate for them. There is no right or wrong choice.

Problem 1: Many students will use paper and pencil but some may use mental math.
Problem 2: Many students will use estimation.
Problem 3: Many students will use a calculator.

Looking Forward

Solving equations using the algebraic method of isolating a variable prepares students for:

- **Lesson 90,** solving equations with mixed number coefficients and negative coefficients.
- **Lesson 93,** solving two-step equations and inequalities.
- **Lesson 101,** translating expressions into equations and solving the equations.
- **Lesson 102,** simplifying equations by collecting like terms and applying the Distributive Property before solving the equations.
- **Lesson 109,** solving equations with exponents.

Section 8 Overview

Lessons 71–80, Investigation 8

Lesson Planner

LESSON	NEW CONCEPTS	MATERIALS	RESOURCES
71	• Finding the Whole Group When a Fraction Is Known		Power Up O
72	• Implied Ratios		Power Up N
73	• Multiplying and Dividing Positive and Negative Numbers	Two colors of tiles	Power Up O
74	• Fractional Part of a Number, Part 2		Power Up N
75	• Area of a Complex Figure • Area of a Trapezoid	Manipulative Kit: rulers Scissors, tape	Power Up O Investigation Activity 25
76	• Complex Fractions		Power Up P
77	• Percent of a Number, Part 2		Power Up P
78	• Graphing Inequalities		Power Up O Lesson Activity 15 Transparency
79	• Estimating Areas		Power Up P Investigation Activity 25
80	• Transformations	Transparency film, index cards	Power Up O Investigation Activity 13 Lesson Activity 19 Transparency
Inv. 8	• Probability and Odds • Compound Events • Experimental Probability	Coins	Investigation Activity 13 Investigation Activity 20

Lesson Highlights
Lessons 71–80, Investigation 8

Problem Solving

Strategies

- **Make an Organized List** Lessons 71, 73, 78
- **Use Logical Reasoning** Lessons 74, 75, 79, 80
- **Draw a Diagram** Lessons 72, 74, 80
- **Write an Equation** Lessons 77, 79
- **Guess and Check** Lessons 75, 76

Real-World Applications

pp. 503, 504, 506, 510, 512, 520, 521, 522, 526–528, 531, 532, 537, 539, 540, 542–544, 546–548, 556, 557, 559, 560

4-Step Process

Teacher Edition Lessons 71–80 (Power-Up Discussions)

Communication

Discuss

pp. 503, 516, 519, 531, 541, 546

Summarize

pp. 510, 514, 535

Explain

pp. 503, 519, 524, 525, 531, 533, 542, 556, 560

Formulate a Problem

p. 504

Connections

Math and Other Subjects

Math and Geography p. 510

Math and History p. 509

Math and Science pp. 504, 509, 515, 521, 532, 533, 542, 556

Math and Sports pp. 531, 560

Math to Math

- **Problem Solving and Measurement** Lessons 71–80
- **Algebra and Problem Solving** Lessons 71, 72, 74–80
- **Fractions, Decimals, Percents, and Problem Solving** Lessons 71–80, Inv. 8
- **Fractions and Measurement** Lessons 71, 72, 75, 76, 80
- **Measurement and Geometry** Lessons 71–80
- **Algebra, Measurement and Geometry** Lesson 75
- **Probability and Statistics** Lessons 73, 80, Inv. 8

Representation

Manipulatives/Hands On

pp. 506, 514, 524, 526, 538, 546, 552, 559, 560

Model

pp. 504, 505, 510, 515, 520, 527, 537, 538, 542, 543, 547

Represent

pp. 505, 510, 559

Formulate an Equation

pp. 505, 515, 519, 520, 538, 542, 548

Technology

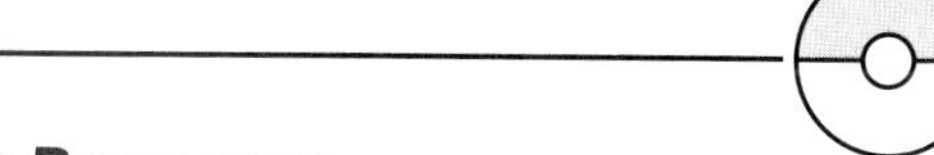

Student Resources

- **eBook**
- **Calculator** Lessons 63, 65
- **Online Resources** at www.SaxonPublishers.com/ActivitiesC2
  - **Graphing Calculator Activity** Lesson 76
  - **Real-World Investigation 4** after Lesson 79
  - **Online Activities**
  - **Math Enrichment Problems**
  - **Math Stumpers**

Teacher Resources

- **Resources and Planner CD**
- **Adaptations CD** Lessons 71–80
- **Test & Practice Generator CD**
- **eGradebook**
- **Answer Key CD**

Content Highlights

Lessons 71–80, Investigation 8

Students continue to experience different types of ratio problems and discuss ways to find the solutions. Estimating and calculating areas as well as transformations in the coordinate plane close this section.

Problem Solving and Proportional Thinking

Recognizing proportional relationships is a critical concept for students to develop.

In Lesson 72 students begin solving problems in which the ratio is implied but not explicitly stated. To understand problems about fractional parts it is helpful to draw a diagram. Students do so in Lesson 71 as they find the whole when knowing the fractional part. Students learn techniques for simplifying complex fractions in Lesson 76.

Problem Solving and Algebraic Thinking

Operations with integers continue as students write expressions and equations.

Students continue to develop algebra concepts. In Lesson 73 students multiply and divide positive and negative numbers. They solve percent problems with equations in Lesson 77 as they find the whole or the percent. In Lesson 78 they graph inequalities on the number line.

Geometry and Measurement

Solving area problems is the focus of these lessons.

In geometry students calculate the areas of complex figures in Lesson 75 and learn to find the area of a trapezoid. They practice techniques for estimating areas of figures in Lesson 79, and they describe geometric transformations in Lesson 80.

Probability and Statistics

Students record data resulting from probability experiments.

Probability is the topic in Investigation 8. Students differentiate between probability and odds. They find the probability of compound events, and they distinguish between theoretical and experimental probability.

Assessment

A variety of weekly assessment tools are provided.

After Lesson 75:

- Power-Up Test 14
- Cumulative Test 14
- Performance Activity 14

After Lesson 80:

- Power-Up Test 15
- Cumulative Test 15
- Customized Benchmark Test
- Performance Task 15

Content Trace

Lessons 71–80, Investigation 8

LESSON	NEW CONCEPTS	PRACTICED	ASSESSED
71	• Finding the Whole Group When a Fraction Is Known	Lessons 71, 72, 73, 77, 79, 80, 81, 82, 84, 85, 88, 89, 90, 91, 92, 94, 95, 101, 102, 109	Tests 15, 16, 17, 20
72	• Implied Ratios	Lessons 72, 73, 74, 75, 77, 78, 79, 80, 81, 82, 83, 84, 85, 86, 87, 88, 89, 91, 92, 96, 94, 95, 96, 97, 98, 99, 100, 101, 102, 103, 104, 105, 106, 107, 108, 109, 110, 112, 113, 115	Tests 15, 16, 17
73	• Multiplying and Dividing Positive and Negative Numbers	Lessons 73, 74, 75, 76, 77, 78, 79, 80, 81, 82, 83, 84, 85, 86, 87, 88, 89, 90, 91	Tests 15, 16
74	• Fractional Part of a Number, Part 2	Lessons 74, 75, 76, 77, 78, 80, 93, 98, 100, 104, 115	Tests 15, 16
75	• Area of a Complex Figure	Lessons 75, 76, 77, 79, 82, 84, 87, 93, 101	Tests 15, 16
	• Area of a Trapezoid	Lessons 75, 78, 80, 81, 83, 86, 88, 89, 91, 92, 95, 97, 109, 114, 116	Tests 15, 16, 18
76	• Complex Fractions	Lessons 76, 77, 78, 79, 81, 84, 85, 87, 88, 89, 91, 92, 93, 94, 96, 99, 111, 120	Tests 16, 21
77	• Percent of a Number, Part 2	Lessons 77, 78, 79, 80, 81, 86, 87, 88, 89, 90, 91, 92, 96, 97, 98, 99, 100, 103, 104, 105, 106, 107, 108, 109, 110, 112, 113, 114	Tests 16, 18, 19, 20, 22, 23
78	• Graphing Inequalities	Lessons 78, 79, 80, 81, 82, 83, 85, 90, 95, 98, 102, 119	Tests 16, 17
79	• Estimating Areas	Lesson 79	Test & Practice Generator
80	• Transformations	Lessons 80, 81, 82, 83, 85, 88, 90, 95, 96, 97, 98, 110, 111, 116, 117	Test 16
Inv. 8	• Probability and Odds	Lessons 82, 83, 85, 86, 88, 89, 112, Investigation 8	Test & Practice Generator
	• Compound Events	Investigation 8	Test & Practice Generator
	• Experimental Probability	Lessons 83, 85, 86, 88, 100, 102, 103, 106, 109, 114, 115, 116, 117, 118, 120, Investigation 8	Test & Practice Generator

• Finding the Whole Group When a Fraction Is Known

Objectives

- Draw diagrams to find the whole group when a fraction of the group is known.

Lesson Preparation

Materials

- **Power Up O** (in *Instructional Masters*)

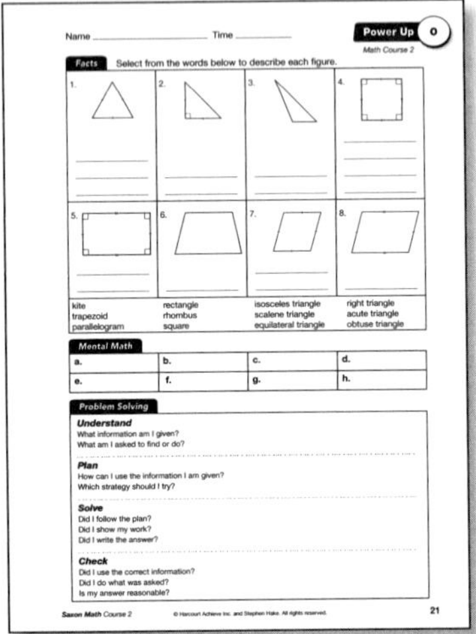

Name ______ Time ______ Power Up O
Math Course 2

Facts Select from the words below to describe each figure.

1.	2.	3.	4.
5.	6.	7.	8.
kite trapezoid parallelogram	rectangle rhombus square	isosceles triangle scalene triangle equilateral triangle	right triangle acute triangle obtuse triangle

Mental Math

a.	b.	c.	d.
e.	f.	g.	h.

Problem Solving

Understand
What information am I given?
What am I asked to find or do?

Plan
How can I use the information I am given?
Which strategy should I try?

Solve
Did I follow the plan?
Did I show my work?
Did I write the answer?

Check
Did I use the correct information?
Did I do what was asked?
Is my answer reasonable?

Saxon Math Course 2 © Harcourt Achieve Inc. and Stephen Hake. All rights reserved. 21

Power Up O

Technology Resources

Student eBook Complete student textbook in electronic format.

Resources and Planner CD Assessment, reteaching, and instructional masters, plus a pacing calendar with standards.

Test and Practice Generator CD Create additional practice sheets and custom-made tests.

www.SaxonPublishers.com Visit for more student activities and planning materials.

Inclusion

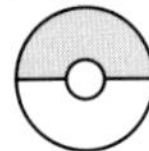

Adaptations CD Adapted lessons, investigations, practice and assessments.

Meeting Standards

National Council of Teachers of Mathematics (NCTM)

Numbers and Operations

NO.1a Work flexibly with fractions, decimals, and percents to solve problems

NO.1d Understand and use ratios and proportions to represent quantitative relationships

NO.2a Understand the meaning and effects of arithmetic operations with fractions, decimals, and integers

Problem Solving

PS.1c Apply and adapt a variety of appropriate strategies to solve problems

Power-Up Discussion *For use with Power Up, p. 502*

Problem-Solving Strategy: Make an Organized List

A rubber ball is dropped from a height of 12 meters. With each bounce the ball goes back up $\frac{2}{3}$ of its previous height. How many times will the ball bounce at least 12 cm high?

Understand — *Understand the problem.*

"What information are we given?"

A rubber ball is dropped from a height of 12 meters. The ball bounces back $\frac{2}{3}$ of its previous height each time. We stop counting after the ball makes a bounce that is less that 12 cm.

"What are we asked to do?"

We are asked to determine how many times the ball bounces at least 12 cm high.

Plan — *Make a plan.*

"What problem-solving strategy will we use?"

We will *make an organized list* to record the bounces and their height.

"What do you suspect the numbers in our chart will be?"

Because we are dividing repeatedly by 3, we will probably have non-terminating decimal values.

"When will it be appropriate to round values?"

Yes, we are looking for the number of bounces, so rounding the actual heights is appropriate since we are not looking for an exact number there. We can convert to centimeters if we encounter a number of meters that has several decimal places. We will continue to round to whole number places.

Solve — *Carry out the plan.*

"How will we structure our list?"

Our list will keep track of the number of bounces and the resulting height. We start with 12 meters and multiply by $\frac{2}{3}$ each time. When we multiply 8 by $\frac{2}{3}$ and get $5\frac{1}{3}$, we convert to cm and round to 533. We continue to multiply and record the products until we get to a bounce measuring less than 12 cm.

Bounce:	0	1	2	3	4	5	6	7	8	9	10	11	12
Height:	12 m	8 m	**533 cm**	356 cm	237 cm	158 cm	105 cm	70 cm	47 cm	31 cm	21 cm	14 cm	9 cm

"How many times will the ball bounce more than 12 cm high?"

11 bounces

Check — *Look back.*

"Did we do what we were asked to do?"

Yes, we found how many times the ball bounced at least 12 cm high.

1 Power Up

Fact Practice

Distribute **Power Up O** to students. See answers below.

Mental Math

Encourage students to share different ways to mentally compute these exercises. Strategies for exercises **d**, **f**, and **h** are listed below.

d. Halve, then Double

$6 \times 5 = 30$

f. Use a Fraction

$\frac{3}{4} \times 36$

$36 \div 4 = 9$; $3 \times 9 = 27$

Equivalent Expression

$75\% \times 36 = 150\% \times 18$

100% of $18 = 18$

50% of $18 = 9$

$18 + 9 = 27$

h. Use a Fraction

$\frac{8}{100} \times 30 = \$30 \div 100 \times 8$

$\$30 \div 100 = 0.30 \times 8 = \$2.40$

$\$30 + \$2.40 = \$32.40$

Use a Decimal

$\$30 \times 0.08 = \$2.40$

$\$30 + \$2.40 = \$32.40$

Problem Solving

Refer to **Power-Up Discussion**, p. 502F.

2 New Concepts

Instruction

Help students understand that the denominator of the fraction tells how many equal parts the diagram will have (5 parts) and that the numerator of the fraction indicates the number of parts bluegills will have in the diagram (3 parts). Since each of the 3 parts must have the same number of fish as each of the 5 parts, we divide $45 \div 3$ to find how many are in each part. Then we multiply 15×5 to find the total number of fish: 75.

(continued)

LESSON **71**

• Finding the Whole Group When a Fraction Is Known

Power Up *Building Power*

facts Power Up O

mental math

a. **Positive/Negative:** $(-3) + (-12)$ -15

b. **Decimals/Exponents:** 4.5×10^{-3} 0.0045

c. **Ratio:** $\frac{w}{100} = \frac{24}{30}$ 80

d. **Mental Math:** $12 \times 2\frac{1}{2}$ 30

e. **Measurement:** 50 cm to m 0.5 m

f. **Percent:** 75% of \$36 \$27

g. **Primes/Composites:** What is the prime factorization of 16? $2 \times 2 \times 2 \times 2$

h. **Calculation:** What is the total cost of a \$30 item plus 8% sales tax? \$32.40

problem solving A rubber ball is dropped from a height of 12 meters. With each bounce the ball goes back up $\frac{2}{3}$ of its previous height. How many times will the ball bounce at least 12 cm high? 11 times

New Concept *Increasing Knowledge*

Drawing diagrams of fraction problems can help us understand problems such as the following:

Three fifths of the fish in the pond are bluegills. If there are 45 bluegills in the pond, how many fish are in the pond?

The 45 bluegills are 3 of the 5 parts. We divide 45 by 3 and find there are 15 fish in each part. Since there are 15 fish in each of the 5 parts, there are 75 fish in all.

___ fish

$\frac{3}{5}$ were bluegills (45). — 15 fish, 15 fish, 15 fish

$\frac{2}{5}$ were not bluegills. — 15 fish, 15 fish

Facts Select from the words below to describe each figure.

1. equilateral triangle; acute triangle; isosceles triangle

2. isosceles triangle; right triangle

3. 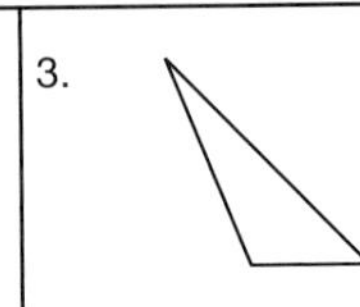
scalene triangle; obtuse triangle

4. 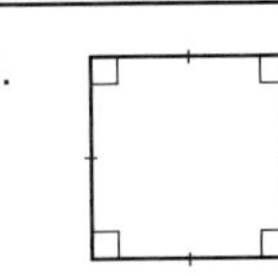
parallelogram; rectangle; rhombus; square

5. parallelogram; rectangle

6. trapezoid

7. parallelogram; rhombus

8. parallelogram

kite trapezoid parallelogram	rectangle rhombus square	isosceles triangle scalene triangle equilateral triangle	right triangle acute triangle obtuse triangle

Example 1

When Juan finished page 51, he was $\frac{3}{8}$ of the way through his book. His book had how many pages?

Solution

Juan read 51 pages. This is 3 of 8 parts of the book. Since 51 ÷ 3 is 17, each part is 17 pages. Thus the whole book (8 parts) totals 8 × 17, which is **136 pages.**

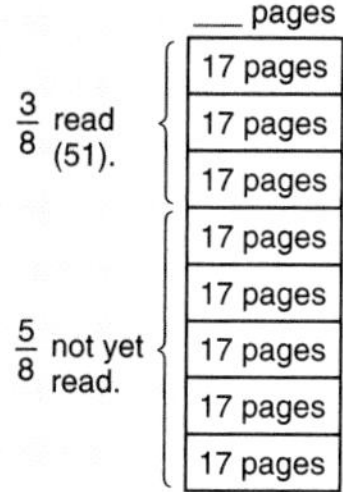

Justify How can we check that 136 pages is correct? Sample: Check that $\frac{3}{8}$ of 136 is 51: $\frac{3}{8} \times 136 = \frac{3}{1} \times 17 = 51$.

Example 2

The story in example 1 can be expressed with the following equation:

$$\frac{3}{8}P = 51$$

Solve the equation.

Solution

We change $\frac{3}{8}P$ to $1P$ by multiplying by $\frac{8}{3}$.

$$\frac{3}{8}P = 51$$

$$\frac{8}{3} \cdot \frac{3}{8}P = \frac{8}{3} \cdot 51$$

$$1P = \frac{408}{3} \qquad P = \mathbf{136}$$

Discuss Why do we multiply both sides of the equation by $\frac{8}{3}$? To keep the equation balanced. We multiply $\frac{3}{8}$ by $\frac{8}{3}$ to get 1.

Example 3

As Sakura went from room to room she found that $\frac{3}{5}$ of the lights were on and that 30 lights were off. How many lights were on?

Solution

Thinking Skill
Explain
How did we know that $\frac{2}{5}$ of the lights were off?
$\frac{5}{5}$ are all of the lights, if $\frac{3}{5}$ are on then $\frac{5}{5} - \frac{3}{5} = \frac{2}{5}$ are off.

Since $\frac{3}{5}$ of the lights were on, $\frac{2}{5}$ of the lights were off. Because $\frac{2}{5}$ of the lights was 30 lights, each fifth was 15 lights. Thus **45 lights** were on.

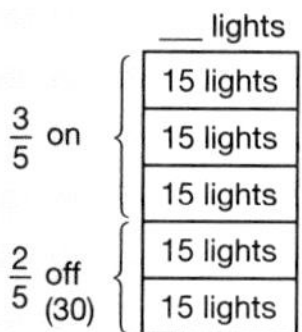

Math Background

When solving equations, why do we sometimes multiply by the reciprocal of the coefficient of the variable?

When solving equations like $\frac{3}{8}p = 51$ our goal is not to eliminate the coefficient. Rather, our goal is to make the coefficient 1. Therefore, we have the option of dividing by the coefficient or multiplying by its reciprocal.

2 New Concepts (Continued)

Example 1

Instruction

Discuss how to set up the equation from the word problem: $\frac{3}{8}$ of the total number of pages is equal to the number of pages Juan has already read. Make sure students understand how to translate the words in the problem to the equation.

Ask students to find how many pages Juan has left to read. Encourage them to find the answer using the diagram and parts of the whole rather than by subtraction. 85

Example 2

Instruction

Have students compare the equation in example 2 to the problem in example 1.

"What does the variable* P *represent in the equation?" the total number of pages in the book

Students should understand that to solve for P, we need to isolate the variable on one side of the equation.

To do that, we multiply both sides of the equation by $\frac{8}{3}$, the reciprocal of $\frac{3}{8}$. This will give us $1P$.

"Why is multiplying both sides of the equation by $\frac{8}{3}$ the same as using inverse operations to solve the equation?" When you divide both sides of the equation by $\frac{3}{8}$, you multiply by the reciprocal, which is $\frac{8}{3}$.

Example 3

Instruction

Students should realize that there are only two options for the lights—on or off. The fraction of the lights that was off is found using the fraction that was on. Ask students what important detail about the unknown fraction must always be true in an example like this. The fraction must always be the *only* other option.

(continued)

2 New Concepts (Continued)

Practice Set

Problems a–c Model

Remind students to include labels on their diagrams. This will help them distinguish the parts from the whole. For example, in problem **a,** the parts are girls and boys while the whole is made up of students.

Problem d Model

Discuss why the equation can be used to solve the problem. Ask students to identify what the variable H represents and to analyze the steps needed to solve the equation.

3 Written Practice

Math Conversations

Discussion opportunities are provided below.

Problem 3 Generalize

Challenge students to write a single equation that can be used to solve this problem. Discuss how to include 2 sets of inclusion symbols. $A = [2(80) + 3(90)] \div 5$

Problem 6 Model

Ask a student volunteer to draw a ratio box at the board and explain how to set up the proportion.

	Ratio	Actual Count
New	4	n
Used	7	u
Total	11	242

For New Pens $\frac{4}{11} = \frac{n}{242}$ For Used Pens $\frac{7}{11} = \frac{n}{242}$

Errors and Misconceptions

Problem 3

Students who get 85 as their answer have not taken the total number of tests into consideration. Ask students to list each test score separately.

(continued)

Practice Set ▶ Model Draw a diagram to solve problems **a–c:**

a. Three fifths of the students in the class are boys. If there are 15 boys in the class, how many students are there in all? 25 students

a. 25 students: 5 students, 5 students, 5 students ($\frac{3}{5}$ were boys (15).); 5 students, 5 students ($\frac{2}{5}$ were girls.)

b. Five eighths of the clowns had happy faces. If 15 clowns did not have happy faces, how many clowns were there in all? 40 clowns

b. 40 clowns: 5 clowns, 5 clowns, 5 clowns, 5 clowns, 5 clowns ($\frac{5}{8}$ had happy faces.); 5 clowns, 5 clowns, 5 clowns ($\frac{3}{8}$ did not have happy faces (15).)

c. Vincent was chagrined when he looked at the clock, for in $\frac{3}{4}$ of an hour he had only answered 12 homework questions. At that rate, how many questions would Vincent answer in an hour? 16 questions

▶ **d.** Model The story in problem **c** can be expressed with the equation $\frac{3}{4}H = 12$. Solve the equation.

e. Formulate Write and solve your own problem in which a fraction of a group is known and you must find the whole group. Use problems **a–c** as models. See student work.

Written Practice *Strengthening Concepts*

c.

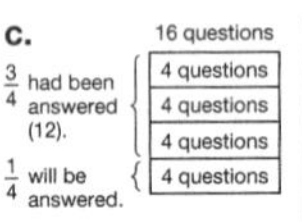

d. $\frac{3}{4}H = 12$

$\frac{4}{3} \cdot \frac{3}{4}H = \frac{4}{3} \cdot 12$

$1H = \frac{48}{3}$

$H = 16$

1. (32, 53) Nine seconds elapsed from the time Abigail saw the lightning until she heard the thunder. The lightning was about how many kilometers from Abigail? Sound travels about $\frac{1}{3}$ of a kilometer per second. about 3 kilometers

2. (28, 34) What is the average of the three numbers marked by arrows on the number line below? 3.43

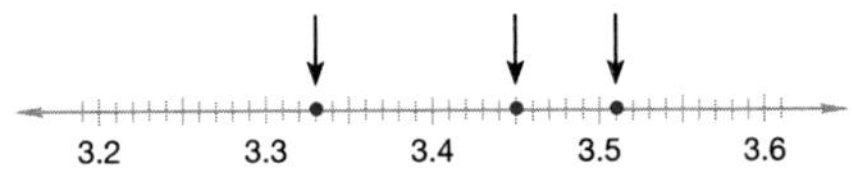

▶ *** 3.** (55) Generalize On his first 2 tests Nate's average score was 80 percent. On his next 3 tests Nate's average score was 90 percent. What was his average score for all 5 tests? 86 percent

4. (51) Twenty billion is how much more than nine billion? Write the answer in scientific notation. 1.1×10^{10}

5. (21) What is the sum of the first five prime numbers? 28

▶ *** 6.** (66) Model Use a ratio box to solve this problem. The ratio of new pens to used pens in the box was 4 to 7. In all there were 242 new pens and used pens in the box. How many new pens were in the box? 88 new pens

*** 7.** (71) Diagram this statement. Then answer the questions that follow.

When Rosario finished page 78, she was $\frac{3}{5}$ of the way through her book.

a. How many pages are in her book? 130 pages

b. How many pages does she have left to read? 52 pages

7. 130 pages: 26 pages, 26 pages, 26 pages ($\frac{3}{5}$ read (78).); 26 pages, 26 pages ($\frac{2}{5}$ not read.)

▶ See Math Conversations in the sidebar.

Inclusion

For students who have difficulty with the ratio box, you may want to try a different approach. Use the *Student Reference Guide* "Finding the Whole When a Fraction or Part Is Known" as an alternate approach.

▶ * 8. (67) **Generalize** Find the surface area of the box in problem **9** and tell how you found your answer. 96 in.^{2}; Sample: I found the area of one side of the cube and multiplied by 6 because the cube has 6 sides: $16 \times 6 = 96$.

* 9. (70) Find the number of 1-inch cubes that can be placed in this box. Dimensions are in inches. 64 1-inch cubes

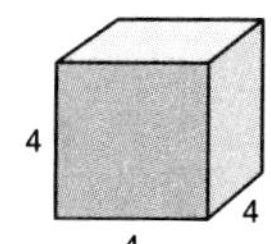

▶ * 10. (65) Find the circumference of each circle:

a. 87.92 cm

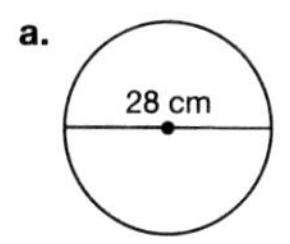

Use 3.14 for π.

b. 88 cm

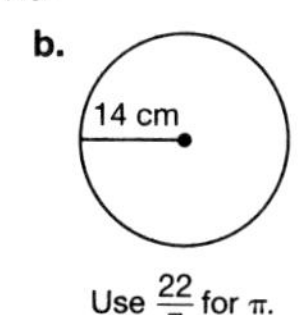

Use $\frac{22}{7}$ for π.

10. c. Sample: In **a,** I multiplied the diameter by 3.14. In **b,** I multiplied the radius by 2 to find the diameter. Then I multiplied the diameter by $\frac{22}{7}$.

c. **Connect** How did your method for finding the circumference for the circle in **a** differ from your method for finding the circumference of the circle in **b?**

* 11. (69) **Represent** Write each number in scientific notation:

a. 25×10^6 2.5×10^7

b. 25×10^{-6} 2.5×10^{-5}

12. (48) Complete the table.

Fraction	Decimal	Percent
a. $\frac{1}{10}$	0.1	**b.** 10%
c. $\frac{1}{200}$	**d.** 0.005	0.5%

13. (60) Write an equation to solve each problem:

a. What number is 35% of 80? $W_N = 0.35 \times 80$; 28

b. Three fourths of 24 is what number? $\frac{3}{4} \times 24 = W_N$; 18

14. (56) Write the rule of this function with words and as an equation. Then find the missing number. Add 7 to x to find y. $y = x + 7$

x	y
3	10
0	7
5	12
7	14

Thinking Skill

Infer

A **vertex** is a point on a figure where two or more line segments meet. What is the meaning of *vertices?* Vertices means more than one vertex.

▶ * 15. (67) **Model** Draw a rectangular prism. A rectangular prism has how many vertices? ; 8 vertices

16. (37, 62) Figure *ABCD* is a trapezoid. Dimensions are in centimeters.

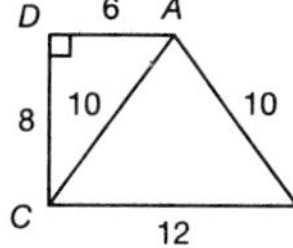

a. Find the perimeter of the trapezoid. 36 cm

b. Find the area of the right triangle. 24 cm^2

c. Find the area of the isosceles triangle. 48 cm^2

▶ See Math Conversations in the sidebar.

3 Written Practice (Continued)

Math Conversations

Discussion opportunities are provided below.

Problem 8 Generalize

"If you know the surface area of a cube, how would you find the length, width, and height?" divide by 6 and find the square root of the quotient

Problem 10 Connect

"If you know the circumference of a circle, how would you find the length of the radius?" divide by π and then divide the quotient by 2

Problem 15 Model

Have volunteers recall common items that are rectangular prisms. Ask them whether the specific shape of the rectangular prism affects the number of vertices that it has. no

(continued)

3 Written Practice (Continued)

Math Conversations

Discussion opportunities are provided below.

Problem 23 Conclude

Ask students to sketch the plane shape to represent this description.
Sample:

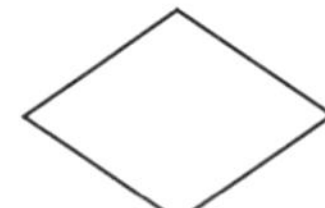

Problem 30

Extend the Problem

Discuss with students why it is easier to rewrite the decimal as a mixed number instead of rewriting the mixed number as a decimal. It is easier to rewrite 1.5 as a fraction than to rewrite $2\frac{2}{3}$ as a decimal because it is repeating.

Errors and Misconceptions

Problem 20

If students don't get the right answer to this problem, encourage students to substitute the numbers into the expression before they attempt to evaluate it. Remind them to apply the order of operations and multiply x and y before they subtract the product from y.

Problem 29a

Some students may get -4 as their answer. These students did not find the absolute value of -7 before trying to solve.

---

d. Combine the areas of the triangles to find the area of the trapezoid. 72 cm²

e. Analyze What information from your solutions to problems **a–c** was not needed to solve **d?** I did not need to know the perimeter of the trapezoid in order to find the area of the trapezoid.

17. (46) The restaurant bill was \$16.50. Marcia planned to leave a tip of about 15%. After paying for the meal, she had a few dollar bills and quarters left in her purse. About how much money should she leave for the tip? about \$2.50

18. (Inv. 4) The principal tallied the number of middle-grade classrooms in the school that had certain numbers of students. Make a box-and-whisker plot from this information.

26 27 28 29 30 31

Distribution of Students in Middle-Grade Classrooms

Number of Students	Tally of Classes
26	|
27	|||
28	||||
29	|||
30	||
31	|

19.

19. (Inv. 3) The coordinates of three vertices of triangle ABC are A (0, 6), B (8, −2), and C (−9, −3). Graph the triangle. Then use a protractor to find the measures of ∠A, ∠B, and ∠C to the nearest degree. m∠A = 90°; m∠B = 48°; m∠C = 42°

▸ **20.** (52) Evaluate: $y - xy$ if $x = 0.1$ and $y = 0.01$ 0.009

For problems **21** and **22,** solve and check each equation. Show each step. State the property of equality you used.

21. (Inv. 7) $m + 5.75 = 26.4$ 20.65 subtraction property of equality

22. (Inv. 7) $\frac{3}{4}x = 48$ 64 multiplication property of equality

▸* **23.** (Inv. 6) Conclude What is the name of a parallelogram whose sides are equal in length but whose angles are not necessarily right angles? rhombus

Simplify:

24. (63) $\dfrac{4^2 + \{20 - 2[6 - (5 - 2)]\}}{\sqrt{36}}$ 5

25. (56) $\begin{array}{r} 1 \text{ yd} \\ - \quad 1 \text{ ft } 1 \text{ in.} \\ \hline 1 \text{ ft } 11 \text{ in.} \end{array}$

26. (50) $3.5 \text{ hr} \cdot \dfrac{60 \text{ min}}{1 \text{ hr}} \cdot \dfrac{60 \text{ s}}{1 \text{ min}}$ 12,600 s

27. (26) $6\frac{2}{3} \div \left(4\frac{1}{2} \cdot 2\frac{2}{3}\right)$ $\frac{5}{9}$

28. (30) $7\frac{1}{2} - 5\frac{1}{6} + 1\frac{1}{3}$ $3\frac{2}{3}$

* **29.** (68) Generalize Simplify:

▸ **a.** $(-5) + (-6) - |-7|$ −18

b. $(-15) - (-24) - (+8)$ 1

c. $\left(-\frac{4}{5}\right) - \left(-\frac{1}{5}\right)$ $-\frac{3}{5}$

▸ **30.** (30, 43) Write 1.5 as a mixed number, and subtract it from $2\frac{2}{3}$. $1\frac{1}{6}$

506 Saxon Math Course 2

▸ See Math Conversations in the sidebar.

Looking Forward

Drawing diagrams to find the whole group when a fraction is known prepares students for:

- **Lesson 74,** finding the whole when a fraction is known.

• Implied Ratios

Objectives

- Solve implied ratio problems.

Lesson Preparation

Materials

- **Power Up N** (in *Instructional Masters*)

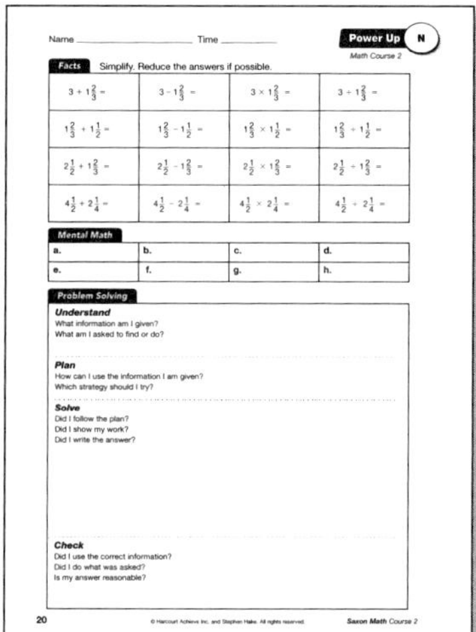

Power Up N

Math Language

	English Learners (ESL)
	swings

Technology Resources

Student eBook Complete student textbook in electronic format.

Resources and Planner CD Assessment, reteaching, and instructional masters, plus a pacing calendar with standards.

Test and Practice Generator CD Create additional practice sheets and custom-made tests.

www.SaxonPublishers.com Visit for more student activities and planning materials.

Inclusion

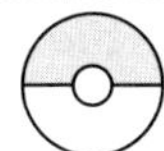

Adaptations CD Adapted lessons, investigations, practice and assessments.

Meeting Standards

National Council of Teachers of Mathematics (NCTM)

Numbers and Operations

NO.1d Understand and use ratios and proportions to represent quantitative relationships

NO.3d Develop, analyze, and explain methods for solving problems involving proportions, such as scaling and finding equivalent ratios

Algebra

AL.3a Model and solve contextualized problems using various representations, such as graphs, tables, and equations

Problem Solving

PS.1b Solve problems that arise in mathematics and in other contexts

PS.1c Apply and adapt a variety of appropriate strategies to solve problems

Power-Up Discussion *For use with Power Up, p. 507*

Problem-Solving Strategy: Draw a Diagram

Given that $\frac{1}{8}$ of a number is $\frac{1}{5}$, what is $\frac{5}{8}$ of that number?

Understand ***Understand the problem.***

"What information are we given?"

One-eighth of a certain number equals $\frac{1}{5}$.

"What are we asked to do?"

We are asked to determine what $\frac{5}{8}$ of the number is.

Plan ***Make a plan.***

"What problem-solving strategy will we use?"

We will *draw a diagram* representing the number as eight equal parts and use our diagram to find the value of $\frac{5}{8}$ of the number.

Solve ***Carry out the plan.***

"How do we begin?"

Since we know the value of $\frac{1}{8}$ of the number, we draw a diagram that depicts eighths, and then label one of the eighths $\frac{1}{5}$.

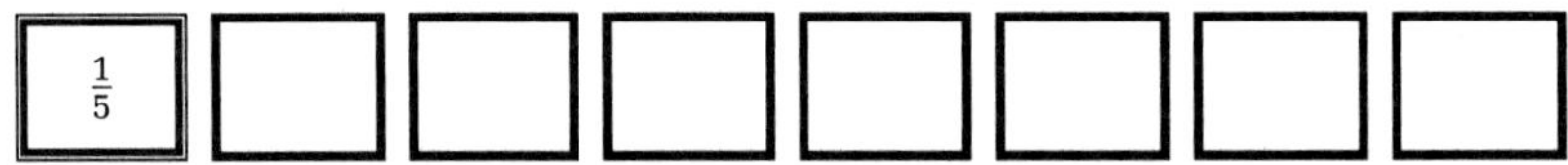

"If one of the eighths has the value $\frac{1}{5}$, what is the value of the other eighths?"

They are also $\frac{1}{5}$.

"We label each eighth as $\frac{1}{5}$. How can we find $\frac{5}{8}$ of this number?"

We can add the value of 5 of the eighths.

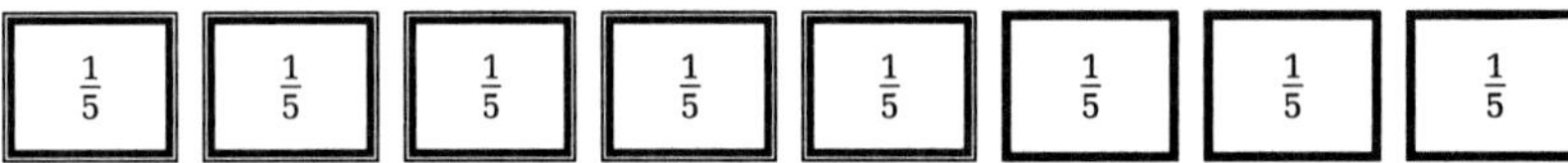

"What is $\frac{5}{8}$ of the number depicted?"

$\frac{1}{5} + \frac{1}{5} + \frac{1}{5} + \frac{1}{5} + \frac{1}{5} = 1$, or $5\left(\frac{1}{5}\right) = 1$.

Check ***Look back.***

"Did we do what we were asked to do?"

Yes, we found the value of $\frac{5}{8}$ of the number described in the problem.

Teacher's Note: Point out that the number depicted in our diagram ($\frac{8}{5}$) is the reciprocal of $\frac{5}{8}$.

LESSON **72**

• Implied Ratios

Power Up

Building Power

facts Power Up N

mental math

a. **Positive/Negative:** $(-10) + (+17)$ 7

b. **Exponents:** $\left(\frac{2}{3}\right)^2$ $\frac{4}{9}$

c. **Algebra:** $6x + 2 = 32$ 5

d. **Decimals:** What decimal is 10% of 36? 3.6

e. **Measurement:** 500 g to kg 0.5 kg

f. **Percent:** $33\frac{1}{3}$% of $36 $12

g. **Primes/Composites:** What is the prime factorization of 36? $2 \times 2 \times 3 \times 3$

h. **Calculation:** Find 15% of $30 by finding 10% of $30 plus half of 10% of $30. $4.50

problem solving Given that $\frac{1}{8}$ of a number is $\frac{1}{5}$, what is $\frac{5}{8}$ of that number? 1

New Concept

Increasing Knowledge

Consider the following problem:

If 12 math books weigh 40 pounds, how much would 30 math books weigh?

Thinking Skill

Predict

Would you expect the 30 books to weigh about 80, 100, or 120 pounds? Why? About 100 pounds. Since 30 is greater than 2×12, 80 pounds is too small. It is less than 3×12, so 120 pounds is too large.

We could solve this problem by finding the weight of one book and then multiplying that weight by 30. However, since the weight per book is constant we may write a proportion.

Notice that the problem describes two situations. In one case the number and weight of the books are given. In the other case the number is given and we are asked to find the weight. We will record the information in a ratio box. Instead of using the words "ratio" and "actual count," we will write "Case 1" and "Case 2." We will use p to stand for pounds.

	Case 1	Case 2
Books	12	30
Pounds	40	p

From the table we write a proportion and solve it.

$$\frac{12}{40} = \frac{30}{p} \quad \text{proportion}$$

We will cross multiply to solve the proportion, as shown on the following page.

Facts Simplify. Reduce the answers if possible.

$3 + 1\frac{2}{3} = 4\frac{2}{3}$	$3 - 1\frac{2}{3} = 1\frac{1}{3}$	$3 \times 1\frac{2}{3} = 5$	$3 \div 1\frac{2}{3} = 1\frac{4}{5}$
$1\frac{2}{3} + 1\frac{1}{2} = 3\frac{1}{6}$	$1\frac{2}{3} - 1\frac{1}{2} = \frac{1}{6}$	$1\frac{2}{3} \times 1\frac{1}{2} = 2\frac{1}{2}$	$1\frac{2}{3} \div 1\frac{1}{2} = 1\frac{1}{9}$
$2\frac{1}{2} + 1\frac{2}{3} = 4\frac{1}{6}$	$2\frac{1}{2} - 1\frac{2}{3} = \frac{5}{6}$	$2\frac{1}{2} \times 1\frac{2}{3} = 4\frac{1}{6}$	$2\frac{1}{2} \div 1\frac{2}{3} = 1\frac{1}{2}$
$4\frac{1}{2} + 2\frac{1}{4} = 6\frac{3}{4}$	$4\frac{1}{2} - 2\frac{1}{4} = 2\frac{1}{4}$	$4\frac{1}{2} \times 2\frac{1}{4} = 10\frac{1}{8}$	$4\frac{1}{2} \div 2\frac{1}{4} = 2$

1 Power Up

Facts

Distribute **Power Up N** to students. See answers below.

Mental Math

Encourage students to share different ways to mentally compute these exercises. Strategies for exercises **f** and **h** are listed below.

f. Multiply by a Fraction

$\frac{1}{3} \times 36$

$36 \div 3 = 12$

Divide by 3

$36 \div 3 = 12$

h. Use a Fraction

$\frac{1}{10} \times \$30 = \$3$; $\frac{1}{2} \times \$3 = \$1.50$

$\$3 + \$1.50 = \$4.50$

Use a Decimal

$\$30 \times 0.1 = \$3$

$\$3 \times 0.5 = \$1.50$

$\$3 + \$1.50 = \$4.50$

Problem Solving

Refer to **Power-Up Discussion,** p. 507B.

2 New Concepts

Instruction

Explain that in this lesson, students will use proportions to solve problems involving ratios. However, the word *ratio* will not appear as a clue to remind them to use a ratio. They will have to read each problem carefully to identify the ratio involved.

Write the following problem on the board:

The ratio of math books to pounds is 12 to 40. If there are 30 math books, how many pounds would they weigh?

Have students compare this problem to the problem at the beginning of this lesson.

"What is the difference between these two problems?" One problem states that the relationship between books and pounds is a ratio, and the other does not.

Explain that the problems in this lesson use the language students will hear in the real world.

(continued)

2 New Concepts (Continued)

Instruction

As students discuss the alternative strategy, have them try to solve the problem using the alternate strategy suggested. When you notice that they start to get bogged down by computation, have them stop and discuss which strategy would be easier.

Example 1

Instruction

Discuss why predicting the solution to a ratio problem is important. A large difference between the solution and the predicted or estimated solution could indicate that the numbers and variables were written in incorrect places in the ratio box or proportion. Also, predicting is a form of estimation that is useful in real-world situations when a quick, approximate answer is acceptable.

Example 2

Instruction

Ask students how they would solve this problem using hours instead of minutes.

3 minutes is $\frac{1}{20}$ of an hour

$$\frac{25}{\frac{1}{20}\text{ hr}} = \frac{x}{1\text{ hr}}$$

$$\frac{1}{20}x = 25$$

$$x = 25 \times 20 \text{ (Multiply both sides by 20)}$$

$$x = 500$$

Elicit that it is easier to use minutes to avoid fractional parts of an hour.

(continued)

$$12p = 40 \cdot 30 \quad \text{cross multiplied}$$

$$\frac{\overset{1}{\cancel{12}}p}{\underset{1}{\cancel{12}}} = \frac{40 \cdot 30}{12} \quad \text{divided by 12}$$

$$p = 100 \quad \text{simplified}$$

We find that 30 math books would weigh 100 pounds.

Example 1

If 5 pencils cost $1.20, how much would 12 pencils cost? Use a ratio box to solve the problem.

Solution

Since 12 pencils is a little more than two times 5 pencils, we estimate the cost would be a little more than two times $1.20, perhaps between $2.50 and $3.00.

Now we draw the ratio box. We use *d* for dollars.

	Case 1	Case 2
Pencils	5	12
Dollars	1.2	*d*

Now we write the proportion and solve for *d*.

Math Language
The term **cross multiply** means to multiply the numerator of one fraction in an equality by the denominator of the other fraction.

$$\frac{5}{1.2} = \frac{12}{d} \quad \text{proportion}$$

$$5d = 12(1.2) \quad \text{cross multiplied}$$

$$\frac{\overset{1}{\cancel{5}}d}{\underset{1}{\cancel{5}}} = \frac{12(1.2)}{5} \quad \text{divided by 5}$$

$$d = 2.88 \quad \text{simplified}$$

We find that 12 pencils cost **$2.88.**

Predict How could you predict the cost of 10 pencils without using a ratio box? Since 5 pencils cost $1.20 and 2 × 5 = 10, then 10 pencils would cost 2 × $1.20 or $2.40.

Example 2

Mrs. Campbell can tie 25 bows in 3 minutes. At that rate, how many bows can she tie in 1 hour?

Solution

We can use either minutes or hours but not both. *The units must be the same in both cases.* Since there are 60 minutes in 1 hour, we will use 60 minutes instead of 1 hour.

	Case 1	Case 2
Bows	25	*b*
Minutes	3	60

Math Background

Making ratio boxes and writing and solving proportions to solve problems involving ratios are not new to students. What is new in this lesson is that the ratio is implied rather than explicitly identified.

It is important that students understand how to solve this type of problem because real-world problems involving ratios rarely state the ratio explicitly. Problem solvers must be able to identify the ratio from what is implied.

Being able to estimate proportions is also an important real-life skill for students to master, because proportions are often inexact or difficult to measure. Encourage students to use estimation to preview or check their answers as they work through the lesson.

Next we write the proportion, cross multiply, and solve by dividing by 3.

$$\frac{25}{3} = \frac{b}{60} \quad \text{proportion}$$

$$25 \cdot 60 = 3b \quad \text{cross multiplied}$$

$$\frac{25 \cdot 60}{3} = \frac{\overset{1}{\cancel{3}}b}{\underset{1}{\cancel{3}}} \quad \text{divided by 3}$$

$$b = 500 \quad \text{simplified}$$

We see that Mrs. Campbell can tie **500 bows** in one hour.

Example 3

Six is to 15 as 9 is to what number?

Solution

Thinking Skill

Predict

Do you expect the answer will be greater than or less than 15? Why? The numerator 9 is greater than 6. So in an equivalent ratio 9 will be related to a number greater than 15.

We can sort the numbers in this question using a case 1–case 2 ratio box.

	Case 1	Case 2
First Number	6	9
Second Number	15	n

Now we write and solve a proportion.

$$\frac{6}{15} = \frac{9}{n}$$

$$6n = 9 \cdot 15$$

$$\frac{\overset{1}{\cancel{6}}n}{\underset{1}{\cancel{6}}} = \frac{9 \cdot 15}{6}$$

$$n = \mathbf{22\tfrac{1}{2}}$$

Predict Would the solution be different if the problem read: fifteen is to 6 as 9 is to what number? Why or why not?

Yes, because 15 is to 6 is not the same as the ratio 6 is to 15. The proportion would be $\frac{15}{6} = \frac{9}{n}$ instead of $\frac{6}{15} = \frac{9}{n}$ so the solution would be $3\frac{3}{5}$ rather than $22\frac{1}{2}$.

Practice Set

▸ **a.** *Estimate* Kevin rode 30 km in 2 hours. At that rate, how long would it take him to ride 75 km? Estimate an answer. Then use a case 1–case 2 ratio box to solve this problem. between 4 and 6 hours; 5 hours

	Case 1	Case 2
m	30	75
rs	2	h

b. If 6 bales are needed to feed 40 head of cattle, how many bales are needed to feed 50 head of cattle? $7\frac{1}{2}$ bales

▸ **c.** *Generalize* Five is to 15 as 9 is to what number? 27

Written Practice *Strengthening Concepts*

1. (12) The astronaut John Glenn first orbited Earth in 1962. In 1998, he returned to space for the last time aboard the space shuttle. How many years were there between his first and his last trip to space? 36 years

2. (55) In her first 4 basketball games Carolina averaged 4 points per game. In her next 6 games Carolina averaged 9 points per game. What was her average number of points per game after 10 games? 7 points

▸ See Math Conversations in the sidebar.

2 New Concepts (Continued)

Example 3

Instruction

This example is written in the form of an analogy. Provide several examples of analogies, such as "light is to dark as up is to down" and "square feet is to area as cubic feet is to volume." Explain that an analogy can be math related, but does not have to be. Then invite students to think of some analogies on their own.

Use this question to stress the importance of writing the numbers and the variable in a proportion in the correct place. If students are not sure whether the solution in example 3 would be different if the problem began "15 is to 6," have them write and solve a proportion using this ratio.

Practice Set

Problem a *Estimate*

Have students explain how they made their estimates.

Problem c *Generalize*

Some students may use mental math to solve this problem. Because $5 \times 3 = 15$, they can multiply 9×3 to find the solution. Encourage them to find more efficient ways to solve problems and share them with the class. This method works well when the numbers are easy to compute.

3 Written Practice

Math Conversations

Discussion opportunities are provided below.

Problem 4b Summarize

Ask students to write one expression to represent this situation.

$$\left(\frac{1}{2}+\frac{2}{5}\right)-\left(\frac{1}{2}\times\frac{2}{5}\right)$$

Ask a student volunteer to simplify this expression at the board.

Problem 6 Model

Ask a student to set up the ratio box at the board.

	Case 1	Case 2
Books	4	14
Pounds	9	p

$$\frac{4}{9}=\frac{14}{p}$$

$$4p = 9 \times 14$$
$$4p = 126$$
$$p = 31.5$$

Problem 8

Extend the Problem

Ask students to calculate how many full turns the tire would make if someone pedaled the bicycle for one mile. about 1005

Problem 11 Generalize

"Why can't you multiply the area of one face by 6 to find the total surface area?" Each face does not have the same dimensions.

Problem 12 Represent

Ask a student volunteer to solve these problems at the board. Discuss the solutions with the class.

Errors and Misconceptions

Problem 3

If students cannot find the correct multiplier, remind them that the prefix *milli-* means "one thousand." Have students break down the word *milliliter* into two pieces milli-liter.

Problem 12

If students use the wrong exponents in these problems, remind them to write 0.6 in scientific notation first. For problem 12a, 0.6×10^6 becomes $6 \times 10^{-1} \times 10^6$. Then help them to combine the powers of 10 by adding the exponents.

(continued)

▶ **3.** (50) Use a unit multiplier to convert 2.5 liters to milliliters. $2.5 \text{ liters} \cdot \frac{1000 \text{ milliliters}}{1 \text{ liter}} = 2500 \text{ milliliters}$

4. (30) **a.** If the product of $\frac{1}{2}$ and $\frac{2}{5}$ is subtracted from the sum of $\frac{1}{2}$ and $\frac{2}{5}$, what is the difference? $\frac{7}{10}$

▶ **b.** Summarize What math language did you need to know before you could solve part **a?**

4. b. Sample: I needed to know that a product is the answer in multiplication, that a sum is the answer when you add, and that difference is the answer when you subtract.

5. (54) Use a ratio box to solve this problem. The ratio of desktop to laptop computers in a school district is 7 to 2. If there are 126 desktop computers in the district, how many laptops are there? 36 laptops

▶ ***6.** (72) Model Use a ratio box to solve this problem. If 4 books weigh 9 pounds, how many pounds would 14 books weigh? $31\frac{1}{2}$ pounds

7. (60) Write an equation to solve each problem:

a. Two fifths of 60 is what number? $\frac{2}{5} \times 60 = W_N$; 24

b. How much money is 75% of $24? $M = 0.75 \times \$24$; $18

▶ ***8.** (65) The diameter of a bicycle tire is 20 in. Find the distance around the tire to the nearest inch. (Use 3.14 for π.) 63 in.

***9.** (71) Diagram this statement. Then answer the questions that follow.

Jasmine lives in New Jersey, which is located on the Atlantic coast. Jasmine has ridden her bike along 52 miles of the coastline. This is two-fifths of the total New Jersey coastline.

a. How many miles is the New Jersey coastline altogether? 130 miles

b. How many more miles would Jasmine have to travel to ride the entire state coastline? 78 miles

9. 130 miles: $\frac{2}{5}$ of coastline traveled: 26 mi, 26 mi; $\frac{3}{5}$ of coastline left to travel: 26 mi, 26 mi, 26 mi

***10.** (70) The volume of a block of ice with the dimensions shown is equal to how many 1-by-1-by-1-inch ice cubes? 480 ice cubes

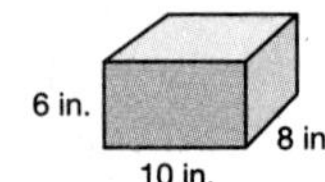

▶ ***11.** (67) Generalize Find the area of each of the six surfaces of the block of ice shown in problem **10.** Then add the areas to find the total surface area of the block of ice. 376 in.^{2}

▶ ***12.** (69) Represent Write each number in scientific notation:

a. 0.6×10^6 6×10^5 **b.** 0.6×10^{-6} 6×10^{-7}

13. (28, 34) What is the average of the three numbers marked by arrows on the number line below? How did you find the average? 1.46; Sample: I found the value of each point: 1.35, 1.44, and 1.59. I added the values and divided by 3.

1.3 1.4 1.5 1.6

▶ See Math Conversations in the sidebar.

14. (48) Complete the table.

Fraction	Decimal	Percent
$\frac{3}{5}$	**a.** 0.6	**b.** 60%
c. $\frac{1}{40}$	**d.** 0.025	2.5%

15. (21) **a.** Write the prime factorization of 8100 using exponents. $2^2 \cdot 3^4 \cdot 5^2$

b. Find $\sqrt{8100}$. 90

Thinking Skill

Conclude

What does the dashed line in the figure represent? the height of the parallelogram and the height of the shaded triangle

17. Only the triangular prism is a polyhedron, because it is the only figure whose faces are polygons.

16. (37, 61) **a.** Find the area of the parallelogram. 48 in.^{2}

b. Find the area of the shaded triangle. 24 in.^{2}

c. If each acute angle of the parallelogram measures 72°, what is the measure of each obtuse angle of the parallelogram? 108°

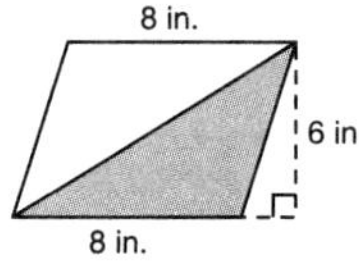

▶ 17. (67) Name each geometric solid and tell why only one of the figures is a polyhedron:

a. 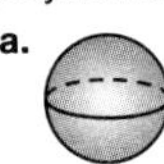 sphere

b. 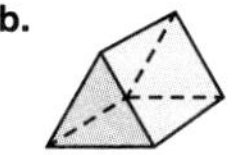 triangular prism

c cylinder

▶* 18. (67) *Connect* A rectangular piece of metal swings around a rod. As it spins, its path through space is shaded like which figure in problem 17? cylinder

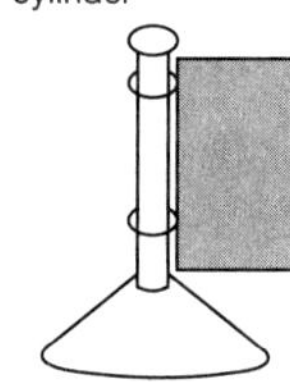

19. (65) Find the circumference of each circle:

a. 60π mm

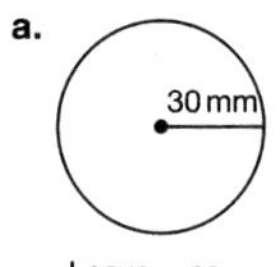

Leave π as π.

b. 188.4 mm

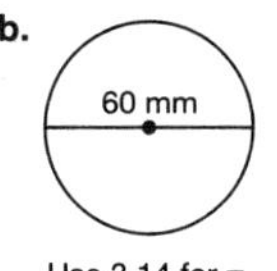

Use 3.14 for π.

20. (43) Compare: $\frac{2}{3}$ ⊘ 0.667

(the answer > is circled)

21. (52, 57) For $x = 5$ and $y = 4$, evaluate:

a. $x^2 - y^2$ 9

b. $x^0 - y^{-1}$ $\frac{3}{4}$

Analyze For problems **22** and **23,** solve and check each equation. Show each step.

▶* 22. (Inv. 7) $m - \frac{2}{3} = 1\frac{3}{4}$ $2\frac{5}{12}$

▶* 23. (Inv. 7) $\frac{2}{3}w = 24$ 36

▶ See Math Conversations in the sidebar.

3 Written Practice (Continued)

Math Conversations

Discussion opportunities are provided below.

Problem 17

Extend the Problem

Ask students to draw the bases of figures b and c.

Problem 18 *Represent*

Extend the Problem

Sketch the three-dimensional figure traced by this rectangle spinning around the rod. Assume the long side of the rectangle is the center of the rotation. Then sketch a second three-dimensional figure that would be traced by this figure if the rectangle were turned 90° and the short side of the rectangle was the center of the rotation.

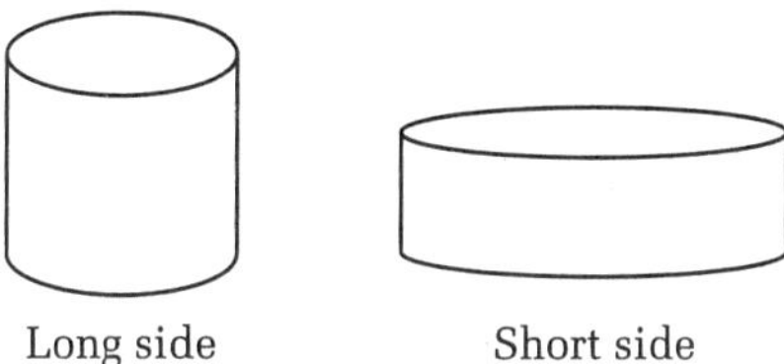

Problems 22 and 23 *Analyze*

Ask a volunteer to explain the steps of each solution while working at the board.

(continued)

English Learners

Direct the students' attention to problem 18. Explain the meaning of **swings.** Say:

"If the metal swings around the rod, it turns or moves in a curve around the rod."

Ask students to give examples of things you might swing such as a bat, a tennis racket, or a golf club.

3 Written Practice (Continued)

Math Conversations

Discussion opportunities are provided below.

Problem 24 Generalize

Point out that this problem uses four kinds of grouping symbols: parentheses, brackets, square root symbols, and the division bar. Remind students to simplify within parentheses before simplifying within the brackets.

Ask a student volunteer to simplify this problem at the board while explaining each step.

Generalize Simplify:

▶ * **24.** (63) $\dfrac{[30 - 4(5 - 2)] + 5(3^3 - 5^2)}{\sqrt{9} + \sqrt{16}}$ 4

25. (56) 2 gal 1 qt − 1 gal 1 qt 1 pt — 3 qt 1pt

26. (50) $\frac{1}{2}\text{ mi} \cdot \frac{5280 \text{ ft}}{1 \text{ mi}} \cdot \frac{1 \text{ yd}}{3 \text{ ft}}$ 880 yd

27. (26) $\left(2\frac{1}{2}\right)^2 \div \left(4\frac{1}{2} \cdot 6\frac{2}{3}\right)$ $\frac{5}{24}$

28. (30) $7\frac{1}{2} - \left(5\frac{1}{6} + 1\frac{1}{3}\right)$ 1

* **29.** (68) **a.** $(-7) + |+5| + (-9)$ −11

b. $(16) + (-24) - (-18)$ 10

c. $(-0.2) + (-0.3) - (-0.4)$ −0.1

30. (35, 43) Write the sum of $5\frac{1}{4}$ and 1.9 as a decimal. 7.15

Early Finishers
Real-World Application

A contractor built a lap pool for the Octave Family. The pool measures 10 ft by 40 ft by 4 ft. It can safely hold 95% of its volume with water.

a. Determine the volume of this pool in cubic feet. 1,600 ft^3

b. Determine the volume of water the pool can safely hold in cubic feet. 1520 ft^3

c. If one cubic foot equals about 7.48 gallons, determine the volume of water the pool can safely hold. 11,369.6 gallons

d. The contractor instructed the Octaves to fill the pool for 12 hours. If the rate of water flow is 20 gallons per minute, can they safely follow these instructions? Sample: No, because at 20 gal./min. for 12 hours is 14,400 gallons. This is greater than the 11,369.6 gallon limit and greater than the maximum capacity of the pool.

▶ See Math Conversations in the sidebar.

Looking Forward

Using proportions to solve implied ratio problems prepares students for:

- **Lesson 92,** solving problems that use percents to describe an amount of change.
- **Lesson 97,** finding the measure of objects indirectly.
- **Lesson 110,** finding successive discounts.

• Multiplying and Dividing Positive and Negative Numbers

Objectives

- Multiply positive and negative numbers.
- Divide positive and negative numbers.
- Learn the rules for multiplying and dividing positive and negative numbers.

Lesson Preparation

Materials

- **Power Up O** (in *Instructional Masters*)

Optional

- **Manipulative kit: two colors of color tiles**

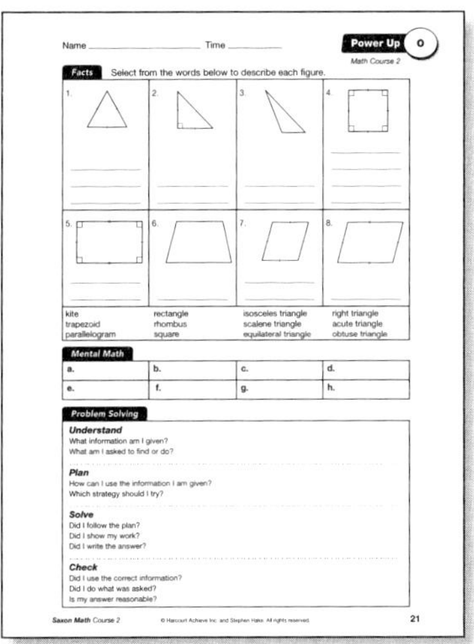

Power Up O

Technology Resources

Student eBook Complete student textbook in electronic format.

Resources and Planner CD Assessment, reteaching, and instructional masters, plus a pacing calendar with standards.

Test and Practice Generator CD Create additional practice sheets and custom-made tests.

www.SaxonPublishers.com Visit for more student activities and planning materials.

Inclusion

Adaptations CD Adapted lessons, investigations, practice and assessments.

Meeting Standards

National Council of Teachers of Mathematics (NCTM)

Numbers and Operations

NO.2a Understand the meaning and effects of arithmetic operations with fractions, decimals, and integers

NO.2c Understand and use the inverse relationships of addition and subtraction, multiplication and division, and squaring and finding square roots to simplify computations and solve problems

NO.3b Develop and analyze algorithms for computing with fractions, decimals, and integers and develop fluency in their use

Problem Solving

PS.1c Apply and adapt a variety of appropriate strategies to solve problems

Power-Up Discussion *For use with Power Up, p. 513*

Problem-Solving Strategy: Make an Organized List

Grayson is holding four cards in her hand: the ace of spades, the ace of hearts, the ace of clubs, and the ace of diamonds. Neeasha pulls two of the cards from Grayson's hand without looking. What is the probability that Neeasha has pulled at least one black ace?

Understand — Understand the problem.

"What information are we given?"

Grayson is holding four aces. We understand that two are black and two are red.

"What are we asked to do?"

We are asked to determine the probability that Neeasha will pull at least one black ace from Grayson's hand.

Plan — Make a plan.

"What problem-solving strategy will we use?"

We will *make an organized list* of the possible pairs of cards Neeasha could draw and use our list to help us calculate the probability of her drawing at least one black card.

Solve — Carry out the plan.

"Suppose Neeasha pulls the ace of spades first. How many choices does she have for her second pull?"

Three

"What are they?"

She could pull the ace of clubs, the ace of hearts, or the ace of diamonds.

"Using S for spade, C for clubs, H for hearts, and D for diamonds, write the pairs of cards Neeasha could draw if she pulls the ace of spades first."

SC, SH, SD

"Can we write similar lists of hands for choosing clubs, hearts, or diamonds first?"

Yes:
Clubs first: CS, CH, CD
Hearts first: HS, HC, HD
Diamonds first: DS, DC, DH

"How many different draw orders are there?"

12

"How many of the draw orders contain at least one black card (S or C)?"

10

"What is the probability that Neeasha draws at least one black card?"

$\frac{10}{12} = \frac{5}{6}$

Check — Look back.

"Did we do what we were asked to do?"

Yes, we found that the probability of Neeasha drawing at least one black card is $\frac{5}{6}$.

"How might we test our solution?"

If cards are available, we might perform this experiment several times, recording whether at least one black card was drawn. We can then calculate the experimental probability and compare it to the theoretical probability we calculated. The more times we repeat the experiment, the closer the experimental probability should be to the theoretical probability.

LESSON 73

• Multiplying and Dividing Positive and Negative Numbers

Power Up — *Building Power*

facts Power Up O

mental math

a. **Positive/Negative:** $(+15) + (-25)$ -10

b. **Decimals/Exponents:** 8.75×10^3 8750

c. **Ratio:** $\frac{12}{x} = \frac{2.5}{7.5}$ 36

d. **Mental Math:** $3\frac{1}{2} \times 18$ 63

e. **Measurement:** 500 mL to L 0.5 L

f. **Percent:** $66\frac{2}{3}\%$ of \$36 \$24

g. **Primes/Composites:** What is the prime factorization of 48? $2 \times 2 \times 2 \times 2 \times 3$

h. **Calculation:** Estimate 15% of 39 by finding 10% of 40 plus half of 10% of 40. 6

problem solving Grayson is holding four cards in her hand: the ace of spades, the ace of hearts, the ace of clubs, and the ace of diamonds. Neeasha pulls two of the cards from Grayson's hand without looking. What is the probability that Neeasha has pulled at least one black ace? $\frac{5}{6}$

New Concept — *Increasing Knowledge*

We can develop the rules for multiplying and dividing signed numbers if we remember that multiplication is a shorthand notation for repeated addition. Thus, 2 times -3 means $(-3) + (-3)$, so

$$2(-3) = -6$$

This illustration shows that $2(-3)$ is -6. It also shows that if -6 is divided into two equal parts, each part is -3. We also see that the number of -3s in -6 is 2. We show these multiplication and division relationships below.

$$2(-3) = -6 \qquad \frac{-6}{2} = -3 \qquad \frac{-6}{-3} = +2$$

Notice that multiplying or dividing two numbers whose signs are different results in a negative number. But what happens if we multiply two negative numbers such as -2 and -3? We can read $(-2)(-3)$ as "the opposite of 2 times -3." Since 2 times -3 equals -6, then the *opposite of* 2 times -3 equals the *opposite of* -6, which is 6.

$$(-2)(-3) = +6$$

Facts Select from the words below to describe each figure.

1.	2.	3.	4.
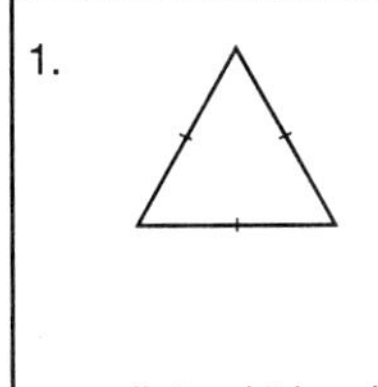 equilateral triangle, acute triangle, isosceles triangle	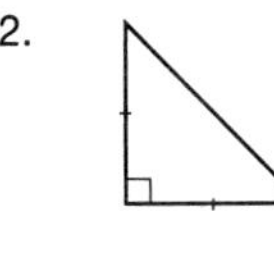 isosceles triangle, right triangle	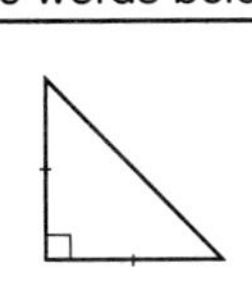 scalene triangle, obtuse triangle	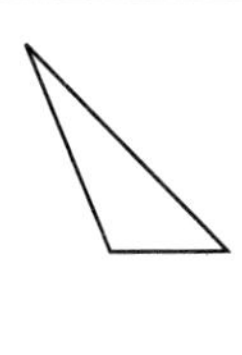 parallelogram, rectangle, rhombus, square
5.	**6.**	**7.**	**8.**
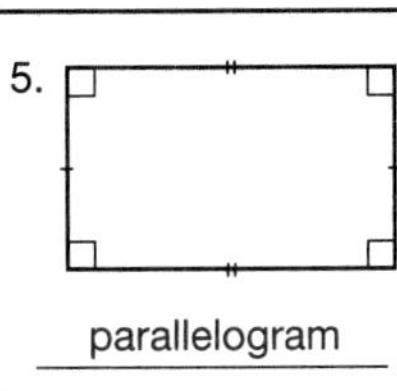 parallelogram, rectangle	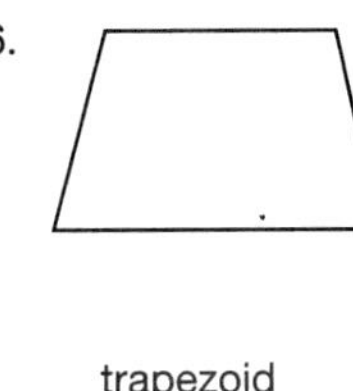 trapezoid	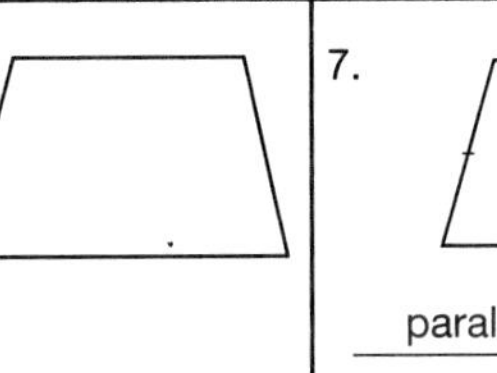 parallelogram, rhombus	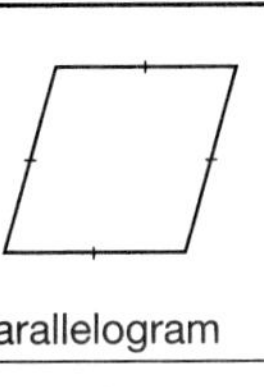 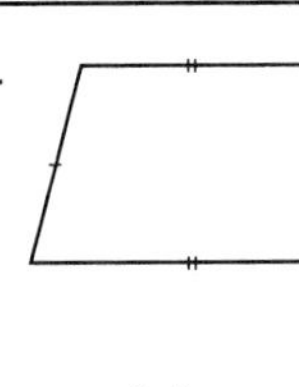 parallelogram
kite, trapezoid, parallelogram	rectangle, rhombus, square	isosceles triangle, scalene triangle, equilateral triangle	right triangle, acute triangle, obtuse triangle

1 Power Up

Facts

Distribute **Power Up O** to students. See answers below.

Mental Math

Encourage students to share different ways to mentally compute these exercises. Strategies for exercises **c** and **d** are listed below.

c. Cross Multiply

$\frac{2.5}{7.5} \div \frac{2.5}{2.5} = \frac{1}{3}$

$\frac{12}{x} = \frac{1}{3}$

$x = 3 \times 12$ or 36

Equivalent Fractions

$\frac{2.5}{7.5} \div \frac{2.5}{2.5} = \frac{1}{3}; \frac{1}{3} \times \frac{12}{12} = \frac{12}{36}$

$x = 36$

d. Double the First Factor, Halve the Second

$7 \times 9 = 63$

Halve the First Factor, Double the Second

$1\frac{3}{4} \times 36 = \frac{7}{4} \times 36$

$36 \div 4 = 9$

$9 \times 7 = 63$

Problem Solving

Refer to **Power-Up Discussion,** p. 513B.

2 New Concepts

Instruction

Some students may benefit from looking at patterns that show the products of positive and negative numbers.

Write these on the board.

$4 \times 2 = 8$	$4 \times (-2) = -8$
$3 \times 2 = 6$	$3 \times (-2) = -6$
$2 \times 2 = 4$	$2 \times (-2) = -4$
$1 \times 2 = 2$	$1 \times (-2) = -2$
$0 \times 2 = 0$	$0 \times (-2) = 0$
$(-1) \times 2 = -2$	$(-1) \times (-2) = 2$
$(-2) \times 2 = -4$	$(-2) \times (-2) = 4$
$(-3) \times 2 = -6$	$(-3) \times (-2) = 6$
$(-4) \times 2 = -8$	$(-4) \times (-2) = 8$

Have students discuss the patterns they observe.

(continued)

2 New Concepts (Continued)

Instruction

Invite students to rewrite and organize the multiplication and division examples so that the examples that have negative answers are in one column, and the examples that have positive answers are in another column. Have students discuss the patterns they observe, paying close attention to which numbers are positive and which are negative. Point out that the examples in the positive column all have similar signs, while examples in the negative column all have different signs.

Then invite students to answer the following question:

"If the result of the multiplication of two signed numbers is a positive number, can you tell if the factors are positive or negative? Explain." No. Either the factors are both positive or both negative.

Example 1

Instruction

Have students predict whether the product will be positive or negative before they multiply or divide.

(continued)

And since division undoes multiplication, these division problems must also be true:

$$\frac{+6}{-2} = -3 \quad \text{and} \quad \frac{+6}{-3} = -2$$

These conclusions give us the rules for multiplying and dividing signed numbers.

Rules For Multiplying And Dividing Positive And Negative Numbers

1. If the two numbers in the multiplication or division problem have the same sign, the answer is a positive number.
2. If the two numbers in the multiplication or division problem have different signs, the answer is a negative number.

Thinking Skill
Summarize
Use the symbols + and − to summarize the rules for multiplying and dividing signed numbers.
Example:
(+)(+) = (+)
Sample:
Multiplication
(+)(+) = (+)
(−)(−) = (+)
(+)(−) = (−)
(−)(+) = (−)
Division
(+)/(+) = (+)
(−)/(−) = (+)
(+)/(−) = (−)
(−)/(+) = (−)

Here are some examples:

Multiplication	Division
$(+6)(+2) = +12$	$\frac{+6}{+2} = +3$
$(-6)(-2) = +12$	$\frac{-6}{-2} = +3$
$(-6)(+2) = -12$	$\frac{-6}{+2} = -3$
$(+6)(-2) = -12$	$\frac{+6}{-2} = -3$

Conclude If the result of the multiplication of two numbers is a negative number, what can we say about the signs of the factors? One factor is positive and one is negative.

Example

Divide or multiply:

a. $\frac{-12}{-4}$ **b.** $\frac{-2.4}{4}$ **c.** $(6)(-3)$ **d.** $\left(-\frac{1}{2}\right)\left(-\frac{1}{2}\right)$

Solution

We divide or multiply as indicated. If both signs are the same, the answer is positive. If one sign is positive and the other is negative, the answer is negative. Showing the positive sign is permitted but not necessary.

a. 3 **b.** −0.6 **c.** −18 **d.** $\frac{1}{4}$

Practice Set

Generalize Divide or multiply:

a. $(-7)(3)$ −21 **b.** $(+4)(-8)$ −32 **c.** $(8)(+5)$ 40

d. $(-8)(-3)$ 24 **e.** $\frac{25}{-5}$ −5 **f.** $\frac{-27}{-3}$ 9

g. $\frac{-28}{4}$ −7 **h.** $\frac{+30}{6}$ 5 **i.** $\frac{+45}{-3}$ −15

Teacher Tip

Students that are having trouble remembering the **rules for multiplying and dividing positive and negative numbers** should take turns answering aloud questions about the rules. For example:

"If there are two negative factors, the product is..." positive

Manipulative Use

Materials: two-color tiles from the Manipulative Kit

Identify one color as positive (yellow) and one color as negative (red). Have students use the tiles to model multiplication of positive and negative integers.

- To model 2 × 3, have students create 2 groups each with 3 yellow counters for a total of 6 yellow counters, or +6.
- To model 2 × −3, have students create 2 groups each with 3 red counters for a total of 6 red counters, or −6.
- To model −2 × −3, have students create 2 groups each with 3 red counters for a total of 6 red counters. Then have them flip the tiles to account for multiplying by a negative number for a total of 6 yellow counters, or +6.

j. $\left(-\frac{1}{2}\right)\left(\frac{1}{4}\right)$ $-\frac{1}{8}$ k. $\frac{-1.2}{0.3}$ -4 l. $(-1.2)(-2)$ 2.4

m. **Model** Sketch a number line and show this multiplication: 3(−2).

m. −2 −2 −2

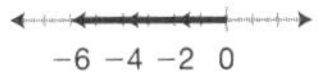

▶ n. Write two division facts illustrated by this number line.

$\frac{-8}{2} = -4$, $\frac{-8}{-4} = 2$

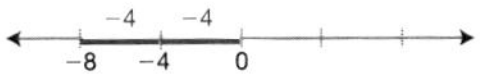

Written Practice *Strengthening Concepts*

▶ * 1. (72) **Model** Use a ratio box to solve this problem.

If Elena can wrap 12 packages in 5 minutes, how many packages can she wrap in 1 hour? 144 packages

▶ * 2. (55) **Analyze** Lydia walked 30 minutes a day for 5 days. The next 3 days she walked an average of 46 minutes per day. What was the average amount of time she spent walking per day during those 8 days? 36 minutes

3. (35, 45) If the sum of 0.2 and 0.5 is divided by the product of 0.2 and 0.5, what is the quotient? 7

▶ 4. (50) Use a unit multiplier to convert 23 cm to mm. 230 mm

5. (66) Use a ratio box to solve this problem. The ratio of paperback books to hardbound books in the school library was 3 to 11. If there were 9240 hardbound books in the library, how many books were there in all? 11,760 books

* 6. (69) Write each number in scientific notation:

a. 24×10^{-5} 2.4×10^{-4} b. 24×10^{7} 2.4×10^{8}

* 7. (71) **Model** Draw a diagram of this statement:

The 30 red-tailed hawks counted during fall migration amounted to $\frac{1}{4}$ of the hawks counted.

7.

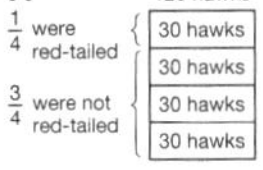

a. How many hawks were counted? 120 hawks

▶ b. How many of the hawks were not red-tails? 90 hawks

8. (60) Write an equation to solve each problem:

a. Five ninths of 45 is what number? $\frac{5}{9} \times 45 = W_N$; 25

b. What number is 80% of 760? $W_N = 0.8 \times 760$; 608

* 9. (73) Divide or multiply:

a. $\frac{-36}{9}$ -4 b. $\frac{-3.6}{-6}$ 0.6

c. $0.9(-3)$ -2.7 d. $(+8)(+7)$ 56

▶ See Math Conversations in the sidebar.

Inclusion

For multiplication, explain that the first number is the number of groups and the second number is the quantity in each group. For example, 6 × 3 means 6 groups of 3 numbers each. Explain that the first number tells you to keep the sign of the second or make the signs the opposite. Write (−6)(−3) on the board.

"How many groups of circles are there in this multiplication?" 6

"How many circles are in each group?" 3

"What does the negative mean with the 3?" each circle has a negative in it

Ask a student to draw on the board 6 groups with 3 circles in each group and write − in the each circle. Ask:

"What does the negative in front of the 6 tell you to do?" change the negative in each circle to positive

Have the student at the board change the − in each circle to +.

"What is the product for (−6)(−3) found from this model?" positive 18

2 New Concepts (Continued)

Practice Set

Problem n Connect

Point out to students that if −8 is divided into two equal parts, each part is −4.

$(-8 \div 2 = -4$, or $\frac{-8}{2} = -4)$

The number of −4s in −8 is 2.

$(-8 \div -4 = 2$, or $\frac{-8}{-4} = 2)$

3 Written Practice

Math Conversations

Discussion opportunities are provided below.

Problem 1 Model

Remind students that both of the times given in the problem must be written in the same units, either minutes or hours. You may want to suggest that students use minutes in order to eliminate fractional units of time.

Ask a student volunteer to set up and explain the proportion at the board.

	Case 1	Case 2
Packages	12	p
Minutes	5	60

$$\frac{12}{5} = \frac{p}{60}$$
$$5p = 12 \times 60$$
$$5p = 720$$
$$p = 144$$

Problem 2 Analyze

"Lydia said her average is 38 minutes. Is she right? Explain why or why not." no; She walked for 8 days not 2 days. $[(30 \times 5) + (46 \times 3)] \div 8 = 36$

Problem 7b Model

Have students explain how they used their diagrams to find their answer. Sample: Since $\frac{1}{4}$ of the hawks are red-tails, $\frac{3}{4}$ of the hawks are not red-tails. I added the total of 3 parts of the diagram: 30 + 30 + 30 = 90

Errors and Misconceptions

Problem 4

If students are having difficulty solving this problem, you may wish to point out that since there are 10 mm in 1 cm, the unit multiplier for this problem is 23 cm × $\frac{10 \text{ mm}}{1 \text{ cm}}$.

(continued)

3 Written Practice (Continued)

Math Conversations

Discussion opportunities are provided below.

Problem 12 Discuss

Encourage students to provide specific examples of multiplying signed numbers to explain their reasoning.

Problems 16–18 Classify

Point out to students that they are asked to give three answers for each of these problems. They are asked to:

- Classify each triangle by angles.
- Classify each triangle by sides.
- Find the area of each triangle.

For problem 18 remind students that the height need not be vertical, but it does need to be perpendicular to the base.

Extend the Problem

Have students say true or false for each statement. Ask them to explain their reasoning.

- The perimeter of triangle 17 and triangle 18 are about the same. true
- The area of triangle 17 is half the area of triangle 18. false
- All three triangles have one right angle. false
- The height of a triangle can be inside, outside, or on a triangle. true
- The area of triangle 16 is double the area of triangle 18. true

Errors and Misconceptions

Problem 11

Some students may not understand the meaning of the word *respectively*. Explain that the coordinates of $\angle R$ are (6, 0) and the coordinates of $\angle S$ are $(-2, -2)$.

(continued)

10. (21, 36) The face of the spinner is divided into eighths. If the spinner is spun once, what is the probability that it will stop on a composite number? $\frac{3}{8}$

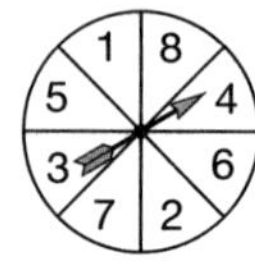

▶ **11.** (58, 62) The x-axis is a line of symmetry for $\triangle RST$. The coordinates of R and S are (6, 0) and $(-2, -2)$, respectively.

a. What are the coordinates of T? $(-2, 2)$

b. What type of triangle is $\triangle RST$ classified by sides? isosceles triangle

c. If the measure of $\angle R$ is approximately 28°, then what is the approximate measure of $\angle S$? 76°

▶* **12.** (73) Discuss Describe how to determine whether the product of two signed numbers is positive or negative.

12. If the signs of the two factors are the same—both positive or both negative—then the product is positive. If the signs of the two factors are different, the product is negative.

* **13.** (70) Find the number of 1-ft cubes that will fit inside a closet with dimensions as shown. 96 1-ft cubes

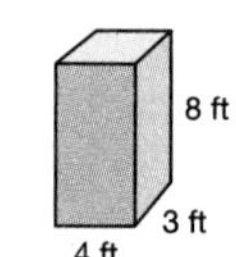

14. (65) Find the circumference of each circle:

a. 131.88 m

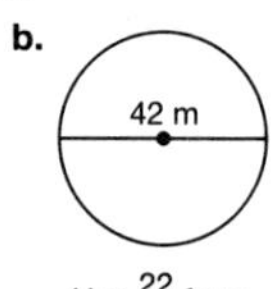

Use 3.14 for π.

b. 132 m

42 m

Use $\frac{22}{7}$ for π.

15. (48) Complete the table.

Fraction	Decimal	Percent
a. $2\frac{1}{2}$	2.5	**b.** 250%
c. $\frac{1}{500}$	**d.** 0.002	0.2%

▶ Classify Use the terms acute, right, or obtuse and equilateral, isosceles, or scalene to classify each triangle in problem **16–18.** Then find the area of each triangle. Dimensions are in centimeters.

* **16.** (37, 62)

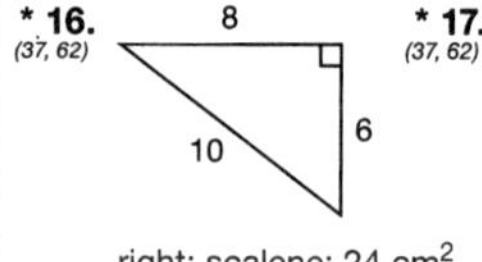

right; scalene; 24 cm²

* **17.** (37, 62)

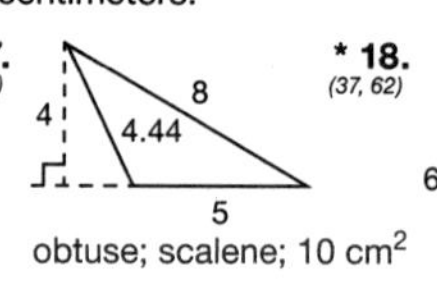

obtuse; scalene; 10 cm²

* **18.** (37, 62)

5
4
6
5

acute; isosceles; 12 cm²

▶ See Math Conversations in the sidebar.

Inclusion

For division, explain that the numerator tells us the total number of circles to draw and the sign to draw in each circle. The denominator tells us the number of circles to draw in each group and to keep the sign in the circles or make them the opposite sign. For $\frac{-12}{-4}$ ask a student to draw the groups of circles on the board. Guide him/her to draw 12 circles, separate them into 3 groups of 4 circles by drawing a larger circle around each group, and write + in each circle. Ask the students what the quotient of $\frac{-12}{-4}$ is from the model. 3

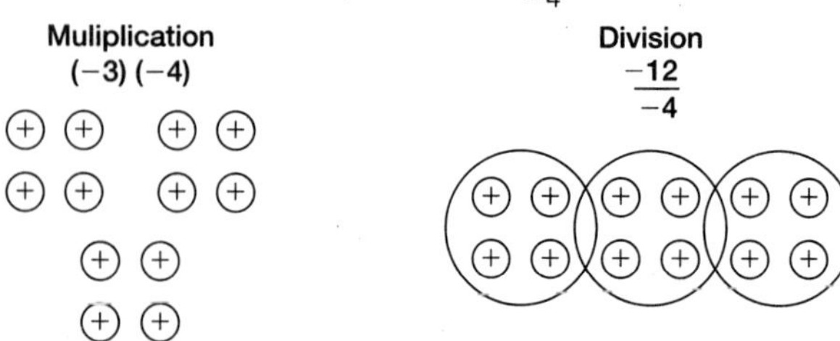

19. Name each three-dimensional figure:
(67)

a. 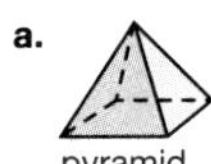
pyramid

b. 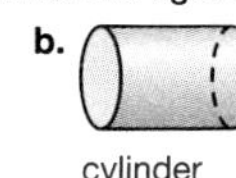
cylinder

c. 
cone

20. Compare: $\frac{2}{3}$ of 96 ⓒ $\frac{5}{6}$ of 84 $<$
(60)

▸ **21.** **Analyze** Find $ab - (a - b)$ if $a = \frac{5}{6}$ and $b = \frac{3}{4}$ $\frac{13}{24}$
(52)

Analyze For problems **22–24,** solve and check each equation. Show each step.

* **22.** $\frac{3}{5}w = 15$ 25
(Inv. 7)

▸* **23.** $b - 1.6 = (0.4)^2$ 1.76
(Inv. 7)

▸* **24.** $20w = 5.6$ 0.28
(Inv. 7)

Simplify:

25. (49)

$$\begin{array}{r} 2\text{ yd } 1\text{ ft } 7\text{ in.} \\ +\ 1\text{ yd } 2\text{ ft } 8\text{ in.} \\ \hline 4\text{ yd } 1\text{ ft } 3\text{ in.} \end{array}$$

26. $0.5\text{ m} \cdot \frac{100\text{ cm}}{1\text{ m}} \cdot \frac{10\text{ mm}}{1\text{ cm}}$ 500 mm
(50)

27. $12\frac{1}{2} \cdot 4\frac{1}{5} \cdot 2\frac{2}{3}$ 140
(26)

28. $7\frac{1}{2} \div \left(6\frac{2}{3} \cdot 1\frac{1}{5}\right)$ $\frac{15}{16}$
(26)

* **29.** **Generalize** Simplify.
(68)

▸ **a.** $(-8) + (-7) - (-15)$ 0

b. $(-15) + (+11) - |+24|$ −28

c. $\left(-\frac{1}{3}\right) - \left(-\frac{2}{3}\right)$ $\frac{1}{3}$

30. Find the product of 2.25 and $1\frac{1}{3}$. 3
(26, 43)

Early Finishers
Math Applications

Look at the three figures in problem 19 above.

a. What plane shape is formed if you make a vertical cut to divide each figure in half? Sketch the plane shape. triangle, circle, triangle; See student work.

b. What plane shape is formed if you make a horizontal cut? Sketch the plane shape. square, rectangle, circle; See student work.

▸ See Math Conversations in the sidebar.

3 Written Practice (Continued)

Math Conversations

Discussion opportunities are provided below.

Problem 21 Analyze

Have students substitute the value of each variable into the equation.

$$\left(\frac{5}{6} \times \frac{3}{4}\right) - \left(\frac{5}{6} - \frac{3}{4}\right)$$

"Why is using 24 as the common denominator easier than using the LCD 12?" because the product of $\frac{5}{6}$ and $\frac{3}{4}$ is $\frac{15}{24}$

Problems 23 and 24 Analyze

"If you changed the decimals in these equations to equivalent fractions, would the answers be the same or different? Explain why or why not." same; Decimals are another way to write a fraction.

Problem 29a Generalize

Remind students that when they subtract a negative number, they are actually adding the opposite of the number. In this problem, subtracting −15 is the same as adding 15.

Ask a student volunteer to explain the steps for simplifying this expression.

Early Finishers

Draw a cylinder on the board that has its bases top and bottom, not on right and left sides as shown in problem 19. Then draw a vertical dotted line through the middle. Say:

"When you make a vertical cut to divide a cylinder in half, the plane shape formed by the cut is a rectangle."

Draw a horizontal dotted line through the middle of the cylinder. Say:

"If you make a horizontal cut to divide the figure in half, the plane shape formed will be a circle."

Looking Forward

Multiplying and dividing positive and negative numbers prepares students for:

- **Lesson 85,** simplifying expressions by using the order of operations with positive and negative numbers.
- **Lesson 96,** using the Distributive Property to simplify algebraic expressions.
- **Lesson 103,** multiplying three or more positive and negative numbers, and simplifying powers of negative numbers.
- **Lesson 106,** finding positive and negative square roots of numbers, and finding cube roots of negative numbers.
- **Lesson 118,** understanding why dividing by zero is impossible.

• Fractional Part of a Number, Part 2

Objectives

- Solve a fractional-part-of-a-number problem when the total is unknown.

Lesson Preparation

Materials

- **Power Up N** (in *Instructional Masters*)

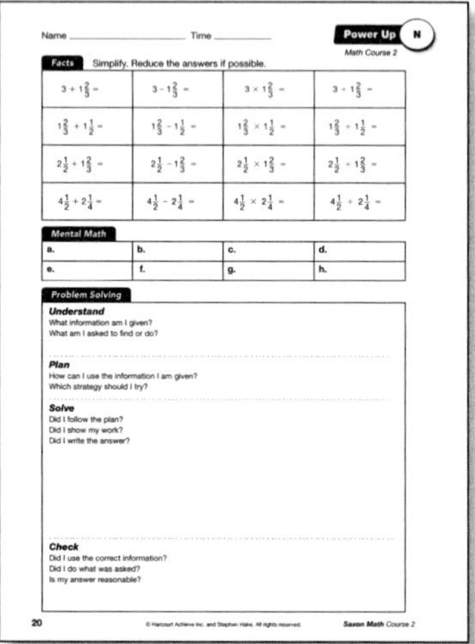

Name ______ Time ______ Power Up N
Math Course 2

Facts Simplify. Reduce the answers if possible.

$3 + 1\frac{2}{3} =$	$3 - 1\frac{2}{3} =$	$3 \times 1\frac{2}{3} =$	$3 \div 1\frac{2}{3} =$
$1\frac{2}{3} + 1\frac{1}{2} =$	$1\frac{2}{3} - 1\frac{1}{2} =$	$1\frac{2}{3} \times 1\frac{1}{2} =$	$1\frac{2}{3} \div 1\frac{1}{2} =$
$2\frac{1}{2} + 1\frac{2}{3} =$	$2\frac{1}{2} - 1\frac{2}{3} =$	$2\frac{1}{2} \times 1\frac{2}{3} =$	$2\frac{1}{2} \div 1\frac{2}{3} =$
$4\frac{1}{2} + 2\frac{1}{4} =$	$4\frac{1}{2} - 2\frac{1}{4} =$	$4\frac{1}{2} \times 2\frac{1}{4} =$	$4\frac{1}{2} \div 2\frac{1}{4} =$

Mental Math

a.	b.	c.	d.
e.	f.	g.	h.

Problem Solving

Understand
What information am I given?
What am I asked to find or do?

Plan
How can I use the information I am given?
Which strategy should I try?

Solve
Did I follow the plan?
Did I show my work?
Did I write the answer?

Check
Did I use the correct information?
Did I do what was asked?
Is my answer reasonable?

Power Up N

Technology Resources

Student eBook Complete student textbook in electronic format.

Resources and Planner CD Assessment, reteaching, and instructional masters, plus a pacing calendar with standards.

Test and Practice Generator CD Create additional practice sheets and custom-made tests.

www.SaxonPublishers.com Visit for more student activities and planning materials.

Inclusion

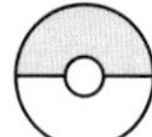

Adaptations CD Adapted lessons, investigations, practice and assessments.

Meeting Standards

National Council of Teachers of Mathematics (NCTM)

Numbers and Operations

NO.1a Work flexibly with fractions, decimals, and percents to solve problems

NO.3a Select appropriate methods and tools for computing with fractions and decimals from among mental computation, estimation, calculators or computers, and paper and pencil, depending on the situation, and apply the selected methods

Representation

RE.5b Select, apply, and translate among mathematical representations to solve problems

Power-Up Discussion *For use with Power Up, p. 518*

Problem-Solving Strategy: Use Logical Reasoning/ Draw a Diagram

In a class of 20 boys, 14 wear brown shoes, 12 wear watches, 11 are on a soccer team, and 10 are tall. How many tall, soccer-playing boys who wear watches and brown shoes could be in the class?

Understand Understand the problem.

"What information are we given?"

In a class of 20 boys, 14 wear brown shoes, 12 wear watches, 11 are on a soccer team, and 10 are tall.

"What are we asked to do?"

Determine how many boys in the class could be tall, play soccer, and wear brown shoes and watches.

Plan Make a plan.

"How can we find how many boys could fit the criteria?"

Find the greatest number that could fit the criteria and the least number that could fit the criteria.

"What problem-solving strategy will we use?"

We will *use logical reasoning* and *draw a diagram* to determine the number of boys that fit the criteria.

Solve Carry out the plan.

"We are given four categories and are told how many boys fit into each category. We are not told how much the categories overlap. Suppose that every tall boy is on the soccer team, wears a watch, and wears brown shoes (the categories overlap completely). How many boys fit the criteria?"

10

"Suppose the categories overlap as little as possible. We might draw a diagram to help us visualize this data:"

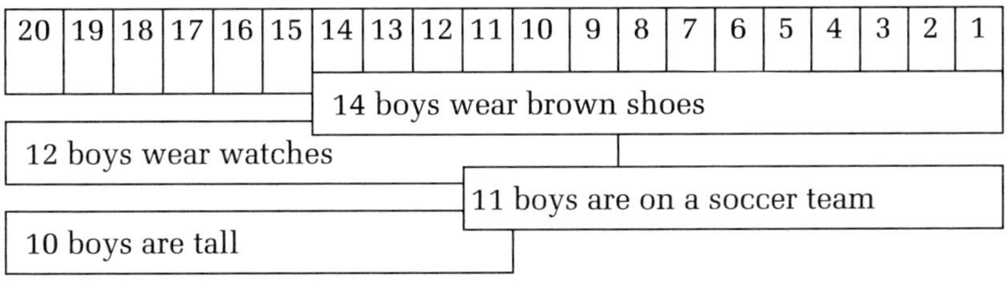

20	19	18	17	16	15	14	13	12	11	10	9	8	7	6	5	4	3	2	1

14 boys wear brown shoes

12 boys wear watches

11 boys are on a soccer team

10 boys are tall

"Use this diagram to determine how many boys fit the criteria in this instance."

1

"How many tall, soccer-playing boys wear watches and brown shoes?"

As few as one, or as many as 10.

Check Look back.

"Did we do what we were asked to do?"

Yes, we found the possible numbers of boys in the class who could be tall, play soccer, and wear brown shoes and watches.

1 Power Up

Facts

Distribute **Power Up N** to students. See answers below.

Mental Math

Encourage students to share different ways to mentally compute these exercises. Strategies for exercises **d** and **f** are listed below.

d. Use Fractions

$\frac{1}{10} \cdot \$20 = \$2$; $\frac{1}{2} \cdot \$2$ is $1

$\$2 + \$1 = \$3$

Move the Decimal Point

$\$20 \div 10 = \$2$; $\$2 \div 2 = \$1$

$\$2 + \$1 = \$3$

f. Use a Fraction

$\frac{4}{5} \times \$25 = \$25 \div 5 \times 4 = \$20$

$\$5 \times 4 = \$20$

Use 10%

10% of $25 = $2.50

$\$2.50 \times 8 = \$5 \times 4$ or $20

Problem Solving

Refer to **Power-Up Discussion,** p. 518B.

2 New Concepts

Instruction

Remind students that in Lesson 60 they learned to simplify fractional-part-of-a-number problems in which the unknown is the product isolated on one side of the equals (for example, $\frac{1}{3} \times 15 = W_N$).

In this lesson the concept is extended. Students learn to simplify fractional-part-of-a-number problems in which the unknown is a factor that is not isolated on one side of the equals sign (for example, $W_F \times 15 = 5$ or $\frac{1}{3} \times W_N = 5$).

Explain to students that they will use W_F (what fraction), W_D (what decimal), and W_N (what number) to represent the unknown part of the equation in these problems.

(continued)

LESSON 74

• Fractional Part of a Number, Part 2

Power Up *Building Power*

facts Power Up N

mental math

a. **Positive/Negative:** (−8) − (−12) 4

b. **Exponents:** 45×10^{-3} 0.045

c. **Algebra:** $7w + 1 = 50$ 7

d. **Estimate/Percent:** Estimate 15% tip on a $19.81 bill. $3.00

e. **Measurement:** 400 m to km 0.4 km

f. **Percent:** 80% of $25 $20

g. **Primes/Composites:** What is the prime factorization of 50? $2 \times 5 \times 5$

h. **Calculation:** 10% of 80, × 2, $\sqrt{\ }$, × 7, − 1, ÷ 3, $\sqrt{\ }$, × 12, $\sqrt{\ }$, ÷ 6 1

problem solving

In a class of 20 boys, 14 wear brown shoes, 12 wear watches, 11 are on a soccer team, and 10 are tall. How many tall, soccer-playing boys who wear watches and brown shoes could be in the class?
As few as one, or as many as 10.

New Concept *Increasing Knowledge*

In some fractional-part-of-a-number problems, the fraction is unknown. In other fractional-part-of-a-number problems, the total is unknown. As discussed in Lesson 60, we can translate these problems into equations by replacing the word "of" with a multiplication sign and the word "is" with an equal sign.

Example 1

What fraction of 56 is 42?

Solution

We translate this statement directly into an equation by replacing "what fraction" with W_F, "of" with a multiplication symbol, and "is" with an equal sign.

What fraction of 56 is 42? question

↓ ↓ ↓ ↓ ↓

$W_F \times 56 = 42$ equation

Facts Simplify. Reduce the answers if possible.

$3 + 1\frac{2}{3} = 4\frac{2}{3}$	$3 - 1\frac{2}{3} = 1\frac{1}{3}$	$3 \times 1\frac{2}{3} = 5$	$3 \div 1\frac{2}{3} = 1\frac{4}{5}$
$1\frac{2}{3} + 1\frac{1}{2} = 3\frac{1}{6}$	$1\frac{2}{3} - 1\frac{1}{2} = \frac{1}{6}$	$1\frac{2}{3} \times 1\frac{1}{2} = 2\frac{1}{2}$	$1\frac{2}{3} \div 1\frac{1}{2} = 1\frac{1}{9}$
$2\frac{1}{2} + 1\frac{2}{3} = 4\frac{1}{6}$	$2\frac{1}{2} - 1\frac{2}{3} = \frac{5}{6}$	$2\frac{1}{2} \times 1\frac{2}{3} = 4\frac{1}{6}$	$2\frac{1}{2} \div 1\frac{2}{3} = 1\frac{1}{2}$
$4\frac{1}{2} + 2\frac{1}{4} = 6\frac{3}{4}$	$4\frac{1}{2} - 2\frac{1}{4} = 2\frac{1}{4}$	$4\frac{1}{2} \times 2\frac{1}{4} = 10\frac{1}{8}$	$4\frac{1}{2} \div 2\frac{1}{4} = 2$

Thinking Skill

Explain

Why do we divide both sides of the equation by 56? Dividing both sides of the equation by 56 will isolate the variable W_F on one side of the equal sign.

To solve, we divide both sides by 56.

$$\frac{W_F \times 56}{56} = \frac{42}{56} \quad \text{divided by 56}$$

$$W_F = \frac{3}{4} \quad \text{simplified}$$

If the question had been "What decimal part of 56 is 42?" the procedure would have been the same, but as the last step we would have written $\frac{3}{4}$ as the decimal number 0.75.

$$W_D = 0.75$$

Discuss How do we change a fraction to an equivalent decimal? Sample: Divide the numerator by the denominator.

Example 2

Three fourths of what number is 60?

Solution

In this problem the total is the unknown. But we can still translate directly from the question to an equation.

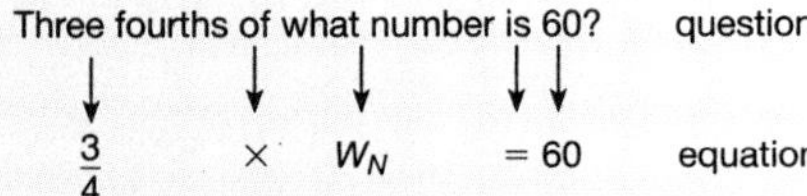

Three fourths of what number is 60? question

$\frac{3}{4} \times W_N = 60$ equation

To solve, we multiply both sides by $\frac{4}{3}$.

$$\frac{4}{3} \times \frac{3}{4} \times W_N = 60 \times \frac{4}{3} \quad \text{multiplied by } \frac{4}{3}$$

$$W_N = \mathbf{80} \quad \text{simplified}$$

Had the question been phrased using 0.75 instead of $\frac{4}{3}$, the procedure would have been similar.

Seventy-five hundredths of what number is 60? question

$0.75 \times W_N = 60$ equation

To solve, we can divide both sides by 0.75.

$$\frac{0.75 \times W_N}{0.75} = \frac{60}{0.75} \quad \text{divided by 0.75}$$

$$W_N = 80 \quad \text{simplified}$$

Practice Set ▶ **Formulate** Translate each statement into an equation and solve:

a. What fraction of 130 is 80? $W_F \times 130 = 80; \frac{8}{13}$

b. Seventy-five is what decimal part of 300? $75 = W_D \times 300; 0.25$

c. Eighty is 0.4 of what number? $80 = 0.4 \times W_N; 200$

d. Sixty is $\frac{5}{6}$ of what number? $60 = \frac{5}{6} \times W_N; 72$

e. Sixty is what fraction of 90? $60 = W_F \times 90; \frac{2}{3}$

▶ See Math Conversations in the sidebar.

2 New Concepts (Continued)

Example 1

Instruction

As students work through examples 1–3, it is important that they be able to identify which parts of the equation they are given, and which they are to find.

"What is the unknown?" the fraction

"Will the fraction be greater or less than 1?" less than 1

"How do you know?" Because 42 is less than 56, so 56 must be multiplied by a number less than 1.

After students explain how to rewrite a fraction as a decimal, ask them to explain how to rewrite decimals as fractions. The digits are placed over 100 and the fraction is reduced.

Example 2

Instruction

"What is the unknown?" the total

"Will the total be greater or less than 60?" greater than 60

"How do you know?" Because 60 is three fourths (part) of another number (the total), so that number must be greater than 60.

Remind students that they multiply by $\frac{4}{3}$ because it is the reciprocal of $\frac{3}{4}$.

Practice Set

Problems a–i Formulate

As students translate each statement directly into an equation, have them identify if they are to find the fraction, fractional part, or the total. Remind them to ask themselves similar questions.

"What is the unknown?"

"Will the fraction (decimal) be greater or less than 1?"

Math Background

How does the information about fractional parts of a number introduced in this lesson differ from that introduced in Lesson 60?

In this lesson, students build on the knowledge of fractional parts of numbers that they acquired in Lesson 60. In both lessons students translate words into expressions. Lesson 60 is more straightforward, having students complete simple multiplication expressions.

In this lesson students are asked to simplify algebraic expressions where they find a factor of multiplication rather than the product. It is essential that students be able to identify the three parts of the word problem—the total, the fraction, and the fractional part of the total—as well as which part they are to find.

3 Written Practice

Math Conversations

Discussion opportunities are provided below.

Problem 2

Extend the Problem

"Can you subtract $1.14 from $1.28 to find the greater unit price? Explain why or why not." no; One package is 12 ounces and the other package is 16 ounces; if both packages were 12 ounces, you could subtract $1.14 from $1.28 and divide the difference by 12 for an answer of 1.2¢.

Problem 5 Model

Ask a student volunteer to set up and explain the proportion at the board.

	Case 1	Case 2
Apples	5	8
Cost	$4.25	c

$$\frac{5}{\$4.25} = \frac{8}{c}$$
$$5c = 8 \times \$4.25$$
$$5c = \$34$$
$$c = \$6.80$$

Problems 7–11 Formulate

As students complete each problem, have them identify what part of the equation they are to find: the fraction, the fractional part, or the total. Then have them check if their answers are reasonable. Ask student volunteers to explain how they know their answers are reasonable.

(continued)

f. What decimal part of 80 is 60? $W_D \times 80 = 60$; 0.75

g. Forty is 0.08 of what number? $40 = 0.08 \times W_N$; 500

h. Six fifths of what number is 60? $\frac{6}{5} \times W_N = 60$; 50

i. For which of the above problems were you given the fractional part and asked to find the total or whole? Problems c; d; g; h

Written Practice *Strengthening Concepts*

1. (55) Miguel is reading the book *Call of the Wild,* by Jack London. During the first 3 days of the week he read an average of 15 pages per day. During the next 2 days, Miguel averaged 25 pages per day. For all five days, what was the average number of pages Miguel read per day? 19 pages

▶ **2.** (46) Twelve ounces of Brand X costs $1.14. Sixteen ounces of Brand Y costs $1.28. Brand X costs how much more per ounce than Brand Y? 1.5¢ per ounce

Math Language
A **unit multiplier** is a ratio equal to 1 that is composed of two equivalent measures.

3. (50) Use a unit multiplier to convert $4\frac{1}{2}$ feet to inches. $4\frac{1}{2}$ feet $\cdot \frac{12 \text{ inches}}{1 \text{ foot}} = 54$ inches

4. (66) Ira counted the number of car and food commercials during a one hour television program. The ratio was 2 to 3. If 18 of the commercials were for food, how many commercials did Ira count altogether? 30 commercials

▶ * **5.** (72) **Model** Use a ratio box to solve this problem. If 5 pounds of apples cost $4.25, how much would 8 pounds of apples cost? $6.80

6. 300 triathletes

	300 triathletes
$\frac{5}{6}$ completed the course.	50 triathletes
	50 triathletes
	50 triathletes
	50 triathletes
	50 triathletes
$\frac{1}{6}$ did not complete the course.	50 triathletes

6. (22, 36) Diagram this statement. Then answer the questions that follow.
Five sixths of the 300 triathletes completed the course.

a. How many triathletes completed the course? 250 triathletes

b. What was the ratio of triathletes who completed the course to those who did not complete the course? $\frac{5}{1}$

▶ **Formulate** Write equations to solve problems **7–11.**

* **7.** (74) Fifteen is $\frac{3}{8}$ of what number? $15 = \frac{3}{8} \times W_N$; 40

* **8.** (74) Seventy is what decimal part of 200? $70 = W_D \times 200$; 0.35

* **9.** (74) Two fifths of what number is 120? $\frac{2}{5} \times W_N = 120$; 300

10. (60) The store made a 60% profit on the $180 selling price of the coat. What was the store's profit? $P = 0.6 \times \$180$; $108

11. (60) The shoe salesperson received a 20% commission on the sale of a $35 pair of shoes. What was the salesperson's commission? $W_N = 0.2 \times \$35$; $7

* **12.** (67, 70) **a.** What is the volume of this cube? 27 in.^{3}

b. What is its surface area? 54 in.^{2}

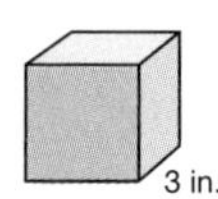

▶ See Math Conversations in the sidebar.

13. Find the circumference of each circle:
(65)

a. 44 m

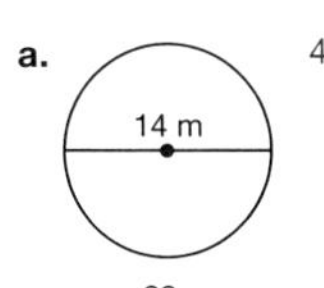

Use $\frac{22}{7}$ for π.

b. 14π m

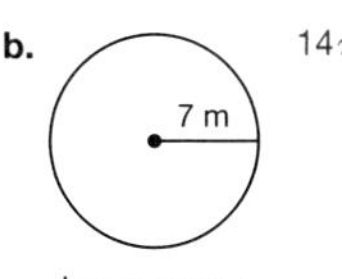

Leave π as π.

14. Complete the table.
(48)

Fraction	Decimal	Percent
$3\frac{1}{2}$	**a.** 3.5	**b.** 350%
c. $\frac{7}{20}$	**d.** 0.35	35%

15. Write the rule of this function with words and as an equation. Then find the missing number. To find y, multiply x by 3 and add 1. $y = 3x + 1$
(58)

x	y
0	1
2	7
4	13
5	16
8	25

16. The mean distance of the planet Mars from the Sun is 142 million miles. Write this distance in scientific notation. 1.42×10^8 mi
(51)

Classify Refer to the figure below to answer problems **17** and **18**. In the figure, $\overline{AE} \parallel \overline{BD}$, $\overline{AB} \parallel \overline{EC}$, and $EC = ED$.

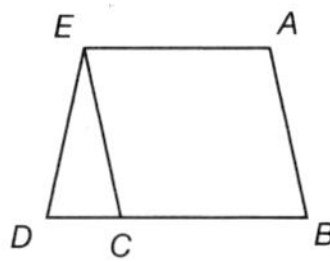

▶* **17.** **a.** What type of quadrilateral is figure $ABCE$? parallelogram
(Inv. 6, 62)

b. What type of quadrilateral is figure $ABDE$? trapezoid

c. What type of triangle is $\triangle ECD$ classified by sides? isosceles triangle

▶ **18.** If the measure of $\angle A$ is 100°, what is the measure of
(40, 61)

a. $\angle ABC$? 80° **b.** $\angle BCE$? 100° **c.** $\angle ECD$? 80°

d. $\angle EDC$? 80° **e.** $\angle DEC$? 20° **f.** $\angle DEA$? 100°

▶ **19.** Arrange these numbers in order from least to greatest:
(33)
0.0103, 0.013, 0.021, 0.1023
0.013, 0.1023, 0.0103, 0.021

20. Evaluate: $(m + n) - mn$ if $m = 1\frac{1}{2}$ and $n = 2\frac{2}{3}$ $\frac{1}{6}$
(52)

▶ See Math Conversations in the sidebar.

3 Written Practice (Continued)

Math Conversations

Discussion opportunities are provided below.

Problems 17 Classify

Extend the Problem

"If trapezoid ABDE were the side view of a 3-dimensonal solid, what would that solid look like? Is there more than one possibility? Ask students to sketch the 3-dimensional figure."

Sample:

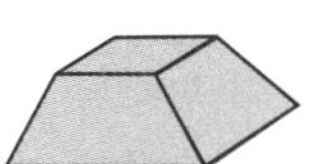

Allow students to describe the solid if they have difficulty sketching it. An example might include a prism or a truncated pyramid.

Problem 19

Extend the Problem

Have students place a negative sign in front of each decimal. Then ask them to write them in order from least to greatest.

"Will the order of the decimals change? Explain why or why not." yes; For negative numbers, the greater the distance from zero the lesser the value of the number, so the order is reversed.

Errors and Misconceptions

Problem 17

Some students may need to draw this figure on their paper and use tick marks to indicate the sides that are equal in length.

Problem 18

If students are having difficulty determining the measures of the angles, review the two kinds of angle relationships found in a parallelogram: adjacent (supplementary) and nonadjacent or opposite angles (equal).

(continued)

3 Written Practice (Continued)

Math Conversations

Discussion opportunities are provided below.

Problems 21 Analyze

Before beginning the problem, have students discuss how to add or subtract fractions with different denominators. Find the common denominator of the two fractions and rewrite each fraction with the common denominator.

Problem 26 Generalize

"How do you regroup minutes to seconds?"
1 minute equals 60 seconds

"How do you regroup hours to minutes?"
1 hour equals 60 minutes

Problem 30

Extend the Problem

Draw this arrow on the board.

Ask students to redraw the arrow from the original position to show the following clockwise terms.

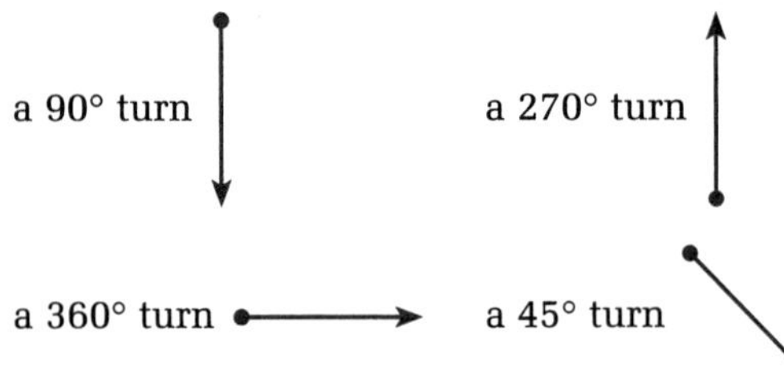

You might want set up a type of activity where students stand and turn to show the rotation. They can look at each other and discuss which way they should be facing.

Errors and Misconceptions

Problem 25

If students do not know how to begin simplifying this problem, revisit the order of operations and tell students that when an expression contains multiple symbols of inclusion, to always simplify within the inner most pair first.

Analyze For problems **21–24**, solve and check each equation. Show each step.

▶* **21.** $p + 3\frac{1}{5} = 7\frac{1}{2}$ $4\frac{3}{10}$ *(Inv. 7)*

* **22.** $3n = 0.138$ 0.046 *(Inv. 7)*

* **23.** $n - 0.36 = 4.8$ 5.16 *(Inv. 7)*

* **24.** $\frac{2}{3}x = \frac{8}{9}$ $\frac{4}{3}$ *(Inv. 7)*

Generalize Simplify:

▶* **25.** $\sqrt{49} + \{5[3^2 - (2^3 - \sqrt{25})] - 5^2\}$ 12 *(63)*

▶ **26.** *(49)*
$$\begin{array}{r} 4\text{ hr}\quad 5\text{ min}\quad 15\text{ s} \\ -\ 1\text{ hr}\quad 15\text{ min}\quad 30\text{ s} \\ \hline 2\text{ hr}\quad 49\text{ min}\quad 45\text{ s} \end{array}$$

* **27.** *(68)* **a.** $(-9) + (-11) - (+14)$ −34 **b.** $(26) + (-43) - |-36|$ −53

* **28.** *(73)* **a.** $(-3)(1.2)$ −3.6 **b.** $(-3)(-12)$ 36
c. $\frac{-12}{3}$ −4 **d.** $\frac{-1.2}{-3}$ 0.4

29. *(30, 43)* Write the sum of $8\frac{1}{3}$ and 7.5 as a mixed number. $15\frac{5}{6}$

▶ **30.** *(17)* Florence is facing north. If she turns 180°, which direction will she be facing? south

Early Finishers
Real-World Application

The bowling team is having a carwash to raise money for new bowling shoes. They are charging $3 per carwash, and they have raised $366 so far.

a. There are 15 members on the team and four-fifths of them need new shoes. If each pair of shoes costs $35, how much money does the team need to cover the cost of the shoes? $420

b. How many more carwashes does the team need to sell to raise this money? 18 more carwashes

522 **Saxon** *Math Course 2*

▶ See Math Conversations in the sidebar.

Looking Forward

Finding the fractional part of a number prepares students for:

- **Lesson 77,** solving problems involving percents by translating problems into equations and solving the equation.
- **Lesson 110,** solving problems involving successive discounts.

• Area of a Complex Figure
• Area of a Trapezoid

Objectives

- Find the areas of complex figures that include rectangular and triangular regions.
- Find the area of a trapezoid.

Lesson Preparation

Materials

- **Power Up O** (in *Instructional Masters*)

Optional

- **Investigation Activity 25** (in *Instructional Masters*) or **grid paper**
- **Manipulative kit: rulers**
- **Teacher-provided material: scissors, tape**

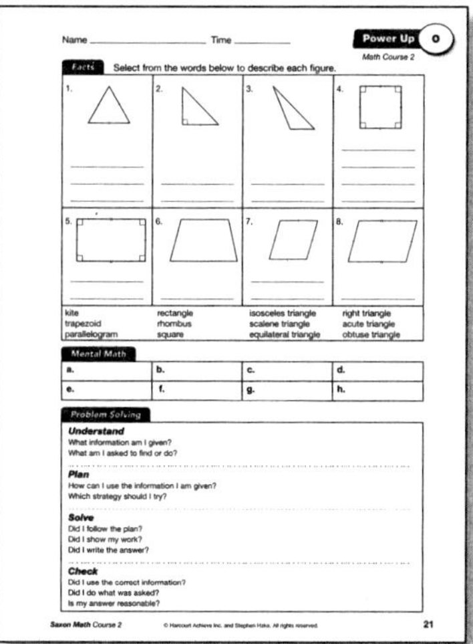

Power Up O

Math Language

English Learners (ESL)

corners that look square

Technology Resources

Student eBook Complete student textbook in electronic format.

Resources and Planner CD Assessment, reteaching, and instructional masters, plus a pacing calendar with standards.

Test and Practice Generator CD Create additional practice sheets and custom-made tests.

www.SaxonPublishers.com Visit for more student activities and planning materials.

Inclusion

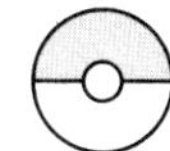

Adaptations CD Adapted lessons, investigations, practice and assessments.

Meeting Standards

National Council of Teachers of Mathematics (NCTM)

Geometry

GM.4d Use geometric models to represent and explain numerical and algebraic relationships

GM.4e Recognize and apply geometric ideas and relationships in areas outside the mathematics classroom, such as art, science, and everyday life

Measurement

ME.1c Understand, select, and use units of appropriate size and type to measure angles, perimeter, area, surface area, and volume

ME.2b Select and apply techniques and tools to accurately find length, area, volume, and angle measures to appropriate levels of precision

ME.2c Develop and use formulas to determine the circumference of circles and the area of triangles, parallelograms, trapezoids, and circles and develop strategies to find the area of more-complex shapes

Connections

CN.4b Understand how mathematical ideas interconnect and build on one another to produce a coherent whole

Power-Up Discussion   *For use with Power Up, p. 523*

Problem-Solving Strategy: Use Logical Reasoning/ Guess and Check

Copy this problem and fill in the missing digits:

$$\begin{array}{r} \_\,8\,\_ \\ \times \quad \_ \\ \hline 8\_\,\_\,8 \end{array}$$

Understand ***Understand the problem.***

"What information are we given?"

We are shown a multiplication problem with several digits missing.

"What are we asked to do?"

We are asked to find the missing digits.

Plan ***Make a plan.***

"What problem-solving strategy will we use?"

We will *use logical reasoning* to help us intelligently *guess and check* to find the missing digits.

Solve ***Carry out the plan.***

"What is the one-digit factor?"

Since we are multiplying a three-digit number by a one-digit number, and the product is a four-digit number greater than 8000, we know that the one-digit factor must be 9 (because any number less than 9 would result in a product less than 8000).

"How do we find the remaining digits?"

Since the ones digit of the product is 8, the ones digit of the upper factor must be 2. We continue to fill in digits in this manner, checking our arithmetic as we proceed.

Step 1:	Step 2:	Step 3:
$\begin{array}{r} ^{1} \\ 8\,\mathbf{2} \\ \times\,\mathbf{9} \\ \hline 8\_\,\_\,8 \end{array}$	$\begin{array}{r} ^{7\,1} \\ 8\,2 \\ \times\,9 \\ \hline 8\_\,\mathbf{3}\,8 \end{array}$	$\begin{array}{r} ^{7\,1} \\ \mathbf{9}\,8\,2 \\ \times\,9 \\ \hline 8\,\mathbf{8}\,3\,8 \end{array}$

Check ***Look back.***

"Did we do what we were asked to do?"

Yes, we found all the missing digits.

"How can we verify the solution is correct?"

We can use the inverse operation of multiplication to check our answer: $8838 \div 9 = 982$.

LESSON 75

• Area of a Complex Figure
• Area of a Trapezoid

Power Up — *Building Power*

facts Power Up O

mental math

a. **Positive/Negative:** $(-15) - (+20)$ -35

b. **Exponents:** 15^2 225

c. **Ratio:** $\frac{30}{40} = \frac{g}{12}$ 9

d. **Mental Math:** $25 \times \$2.40$ \$60.00

e. **Measurement:** 250 mg to g 0.25 g

f. **Percent:** 10% of \$35 \$3.50

g. **Statistics:** Find the average of the set of numbers: 80, 95, 75, 70. 80

h. **Decimals:** What decimal is half of 10% of 36? 1.8

problem solving Copy this problem and fill in the missing digits:

$$\begin{array}{r} \_8\_ \\ \times \quad \_ \\ \hline 8\_\_8 \end{array} \qquad \begin{array}{r} 982 \\ \times \quad 9 \\ \hline 8838 \end{array}$$

New Concepts — *Increasing Knowledge*

area of a complex figure

We have practiced finding the areas of figures that can be divided into two or more rectangles. In this lesson we will begin finding the areas of figures that include triangular regions as well.

Example 1

Find the area of this figure. Corners that look square are square. Dimensions are in millimeters.

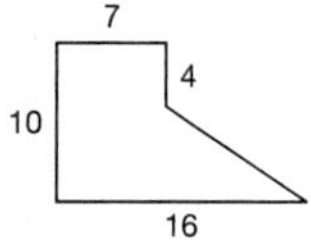

Solution

We divide the figure into smaller polygons. In this case we draw dashes that divide the figure into a rectangle and a triangle.

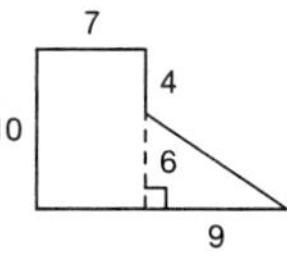

Area of rectangle	=	7×10 =	70 mm²
+ Area of triangle	=	$\frac{6 \times 9}{2}$ =	27 mm²
Total area		=	**97 mm²**

Math Language
To find the **area** of a triangle we use this formula: $A = \frac{1}{2}bh$.

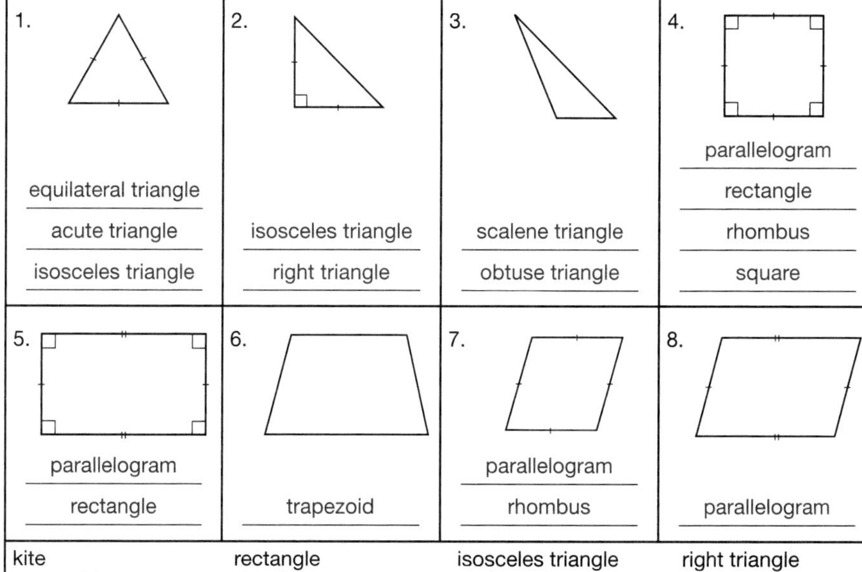

Facts Select from the words below to describe each figure.

1.	2.	3.	4.
equilateral triangle, acute triangle, isosceles triangle	isosceles triangle, right triangle	scalene triangle, obtuse triangle	parallelogram, rectangle, rhombus, square

5.	6.	7.	8.
parallelogram, rectangle	trapezoid	parallelogram, rhombus	parallelogram

kite trapezoid parallelogram	rectangle rhombus square	isosceles triangle scalene triangle equilateral triangle	right triangle acute triangle obtuse triangle

1 Power Up

Facts

Distribute **Power Up O** to students. See answers below.

Mental Math

Encourage students to share different ways to mentally compute these exercises. Strategies for exercises **b, d,** and **g** are listed below.

b. Decompose

$(15 \cdot 10) + (15 \cdot 5)$

$150 + 75 = 225$

Associative Property

$(5 \times 3)(5 \times 3)$

$(5 \times 5)(3 \times 3)$

$25 \times 9 = 25 \times 10 - 25$

$250 - 25 = 225$

d. Double, Halve

$50 \times \$1.20 = \$60$

g. Add Tens First

$80 + 90 + 70 + 70 = 310$

$310 + 5 + 5 = 320$

$320 \div 4 = 80$

Problem Solving

Refer to **Power-Up Discussion,** p. 523B.

2 New Concepts

Instruction

Discuss some real world examples of complex figures such as:

- the side of a house and its roof line.
- the area of an irregular garden.
- the area of a lake or pond.

Example 1

Instruction

"How do we know that the base of the triangle is 9 mm?" The side parallel to the 16 mm base has a length of 7 mm.
$16 - 7 = 9$ mm

"How do we know that the height of the triangle is 6 mm?" The side parallel to the height has a length of 10 mm. The section above the height has a length of 4 mm.
$10 - 4 = 6$ mm

(continued)

2 New Concepts (Continued)

Example 1 (continued)

Instruction

When solving area problems with complex figures, remind students to read carefully all given information about the figure, and to look at the drawing for more information, such as right angle symbols. It is also important to notice measurements that can be determined from given information.

Invite students to use the edge of their paper or a ruler to see that the dashed segment in the figure at the top of the page is not an extension of the slanted side.

Have students illustrate another way the figure might be divided to find its area. Here is one example.

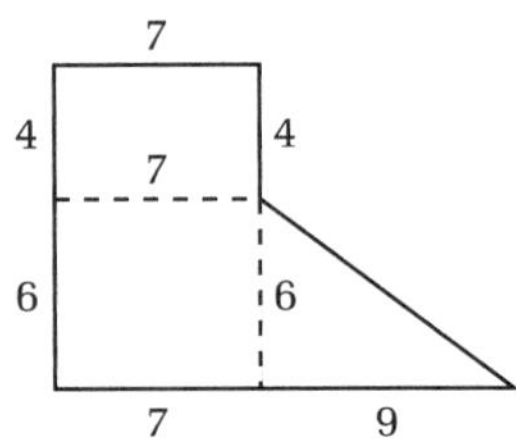

Ask students to give the dimensions of each shape.

Example 2

Instruction

Ask students to compare the processes for determining the area of the figure based on diagrams **a**, **b**, and **c**. Have them identify which process uses the fewest steps. In diagrams **a** and **b**, the figure is divided into three smaller figures. The area of each figure must be found and added to determine the area of the complex figure.

In diagram **c**, the figure has been added to, creating two figures. The area of the small triangle is subtracted from the area of the large square to determine the area of the complex figure. Using diagram **c** uses the fewest steps.

Instruction

Direct students to look at the figures that demonstrate multiplying only one of the bases by the height. In the figure on the left, multiplying by the lower base, b_2, produces an area that is larger than that of the trapezoid. Multiplying by the upper base, b_1, produces an area that is smaller than the area of the trapezoid.

(continued)

When dividing figures, we must avoid assumptions based on appearances. Although it may appear that the figure at right is divided into two triangles, the larger "triangle" is actually a quadrilateral. The slanted "segment" bends where the solid and dashed segments intersect. The assumption that the figure is divided into two triangles leads to an incorrect calculation for the area of the figure.

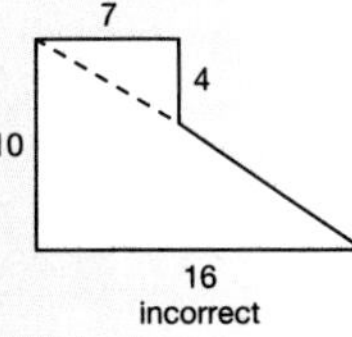

Example 2

Find the area of this figure. Corners that look square are square. Dimensions are in centimeters.

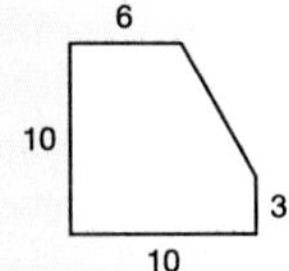

Solution

Thinking Skill

Explain

How would you find the area using method **a**?

Find the area of two rectangles and one triangle. Then find the sum of these areas.
Rect. 1:
$6 \times 7 = 42$
Rect. 2:
$3 \times 10 = 30$
Tri.:
$7 \times \frac{4}{2} = 14$
$42 + 30 + 14 = 86 \text{ cm}^2$

There are many ways to divide this figure.

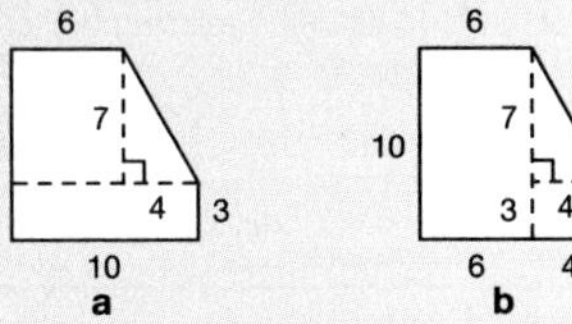

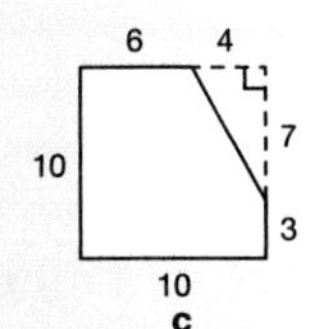

We decided to use **c**. We will find the area of the big rectangle and subtract from it the area of the triangle.

Area of rectangle	$= 10 \times 10 =$	100 cm^2
− Area of triangle	$= \frac{4 \times 7}{2} =$	14 cm^2
Total of figure	$=$	$\mathbf{86 \text{ cm}^2}$

area of a trapezoid

Now we will consider how to find the area of a trapezoid. The parallel sides of a trapezoid are both bases. The distance between the bases is the height. Multiplying one of the bases and the height does not give us the area of the trapezoid.

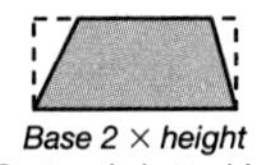

Base 2 × height
Rectangle is too big.

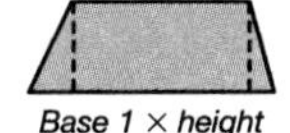

Base 1 × height
Rectangle is too small.

Math Background

What is the difference between the height of a triangle and the height of a trapezoid?

The height of a triangle is the perpendicular distance from any vertex of the triangle to the opposite side (base) of the triangle, or to the line containing the opposite side.

The height of a trapezoid is the perpendicular distance between the parallel sides, called bases.

A height in either a triangle or a trapezoid can be inside, outside, or on the figure.

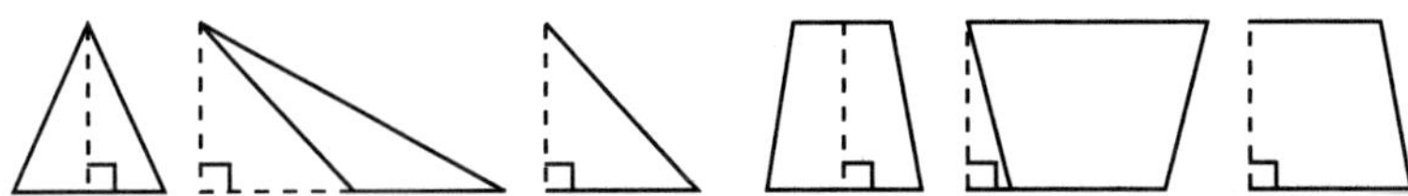

Recall that multiplying perpendicular lengths yields the area of a rectangle. Multiplying the base and height of a triangle results in the area of a rectangle, which we divide by 2.

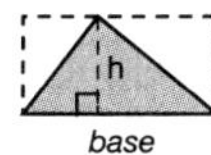

Also recall that multiplying the base and height of a parallelogram results in the area of a rectangle that equals the area of a parallelogram.

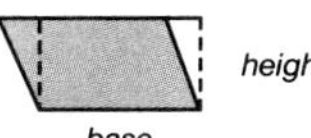

Instead of multiplying by one of the bases of a trapezoid, we multiply by the **average of the bases.** The trapezoid can be cut and rearranged to match the rectangle.

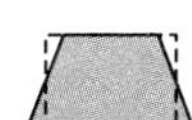

Average base × height
Area of rectangle equals area of trapezoid

Explain How would you find the average of the bases? Sample: Add the lengths of the bases and then divide by 2.

By understanding this concept we can generate a formula for area that applies to all trapezoids. We will begin with this formula:

Area = average of the bases × height

We will label the bases of a trapezoid b_1 and b_2 and the height h as we show in this illustration:

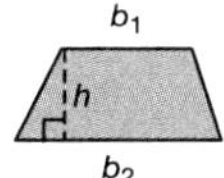

Use the labels in this illustration and the described formula to generate a formula for the area of a trapezoid.

Example 3

Find the area of this trapezoid. Dimensions are in centimeters.

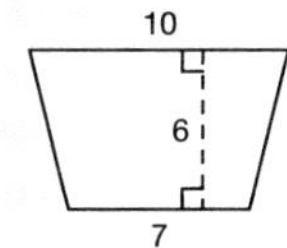

Solution

We multiply the average of the bases (7 cm and 10 cm) by the height (6 cm). We will use a formula.

$$A = \frac{1}{2}(b_1 + b_2)h$$

$$A = \frac{1}{2}(7\text{ cm} + 10\text{ cm})6\text{ cm}$$

$$A = \frac{1}{2} \cdot 17\text{ cm} \cdot 6\text{ cm}$$

$$A = \mathbf{51\ cm^2}$$

2 New Concepts (Continued)

Instruction

Explain that a trapezoid can be considered a complex figure like the ones discussed earlier in the lesson.

Explain that if we lined up b_1 and b_2 to form one line, the "average of the bases" would be the length halfway between the beginning and the end of the line. Multiplying the height by this average produces an area that is equal to the area of trapezoid.

Example 3

Instruction

Some students may mix up the numbers when substituting them into formulas. Have them link each number with the correct variable before beginning the substitution.

For example, $b_1 = 7$, $b_2 = 10$, and so on.

(continued)

Teacher Tip

Some students may need a more visual approach for **finding the area of a trapezoid.** They can divide the trapezoid into two triangles, find the area of each triangle, and then add the areas of the triangles.

For example:

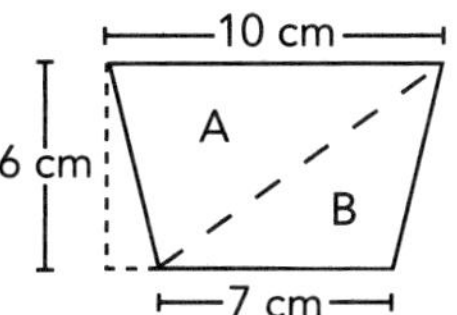

$$\begin{aligned} &\text{Area triangle A} = \tfrac{1}{2}(10 \times 6) &&= 30\text{ cm}^2 \\ +\ &\text{Area triangle B} = \tfrac{1}{2}(7 \times 6) &&= 21\text{ cm}^2 \\ \hline &\text{Total Area trapezoid} &&= 51\text{ cm}^2 \end{aligned}$$

English Learners

Demonstrate the meaning of **corners that look square** in example 2. Find a corner in your classroom to show students how the two walls meet to form a corner. Tell students:

"In example 2, the picture in your books shows a corner similar to this one. These corners look square because they form a 90° angle."

2 New Concepts (Continued)

Example 4

Instruction

Ask students how they would round a measurement of feet and inches. If the measure is 6 or more inches, the measurement is rounded up to the next foot. If the measure is less than 6 inches, ignore the inches and use the existing foot measure.

Practice Set

Problems a–c Generalize

Suggest that students trace these figures on their paper and use them when showing the steps for finding the areas. Ask student volunteers to explain the steps of the solution.

3 Written Practice

Math Conversations

Discussion opportunities are provided below.

Problem 5

Extend the Problem

Ask students to solve this problem.

The sum of Janet and Wayne's ages is 25. Janet is 7 years older than Wayne. How old is each of them? Sample: Draw a Diagram

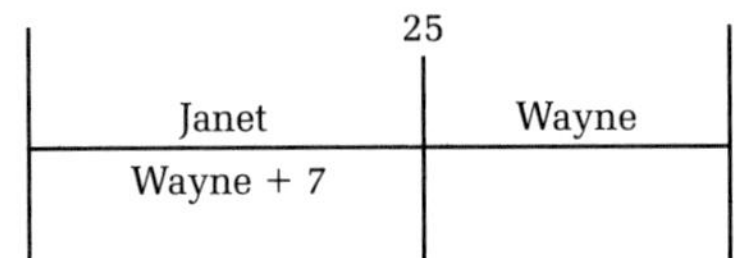

Since Wayne's age plus 7 years equals Janet's age, we see that Wayne's age plus Wayne's age plus 7 years totals 25 years.

$$w + w + 7 = 25$$

Therefore, Wayne's age is 9.

$$9 + 9 + 7 = 25$$

Janet is 7 years older than Wayne, so Janet is 16.

Errors and Misconceptions

Problem 5

If students write 40 years as their answer, explain that the question does not ask how old Chelsea is. It asks for the difference in the ages of the two women.

(continued)

Model Some people like to find the area of a trapezoid by dividing the trapezoid into two triangles. How could you divide the trapezoid in this example into two triangles? Sample: Draw a diagonal that divides the trapezoid into 2 triangles.

Example 4

Estimate the area of this trapezoid.

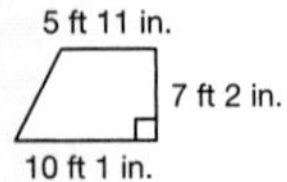

Solution

We round the two bases to 6 ft and 10 ft and the height to 7 ft. The average of the bases is 8 ft. We multiply that average by the height.

$$A = 8 \text{ ft} \cdot 7 \text{ ft} = \mathbf{56 \text{ ft}^2}$$

Practice Set ▸ Generalize Find the area of each figure. Dimensions are in centimeters. Corners that look square are square.

a. 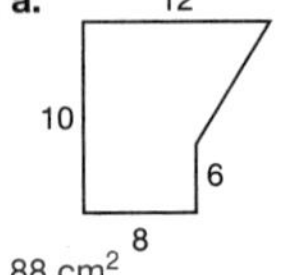

88 cm²

b. 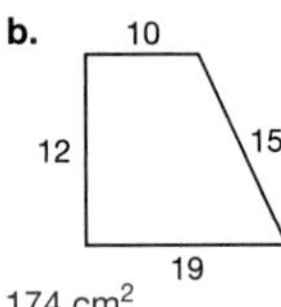

174 cm²

c. 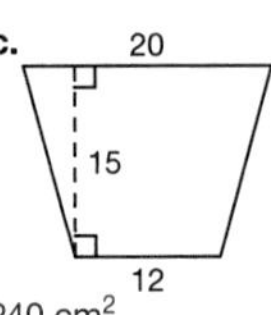

240 cm²

d. Write an equation for the area of a trapezoid.

d. $A = \frac{1}{2}(b_1 + b_2)h$ or $A = \frac{(b_1 + b_2)h}{2}$

e. Estimate In a photograph of a math book on a table, the cover appears to be a trapezoid. The parallel sides of the trapezoid are $2\frac{7}{8}$ in. and $5\frac{1}{8}$ in. The distance between the parallel sides is 3 in. Estimate the area of the photograph occupied by the cover of the book. Explain how you found the answer.

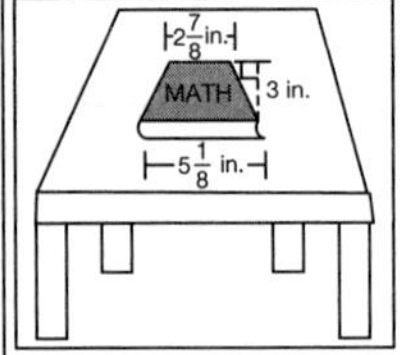

e. Round the bases to 3 inches and 5 inches. Find the average length of the base, which is 4 inches. Multiply the average base by the height. $A \approx (4 \text{ in.})(3 \text{ in.})$ $A \approx 12 \text{ in.}^2$

Written Practice *Strengthening Concepts*

1. (55) Paula is a dog walker. She walks 8 dogs each day. She walked each of the first 6 dogs for an average of 14 minutes each. For the rest of the dogs she averaged 18 minutes each. What was the average time per walk for the 8 walks? 15 minutes

2. (46) If 18 ounces of cereal costs \$3.69, what is the cost per ounce? 20.5¢ per ounce

3. (32) One thousand, five hundred meters is how many kilometers? 1.5 kilometers

4. (30) The sum of $\frac{1}{2}$ and $\frac{3}{5}$ is how much greater than the product of $\frac{1}{2}$ and $\frac{3}{5}$? $\frac{4}{5}$

▸ 5. (54) The ratio of Maela's age to her niece Chelsea's age is 3 to 2. If Maela is 60 years old, how many years older than Chelsea is she? 20 years

▸ See Math Conversations in the sidebar.

Manipulative Use

Suggest that students make an **isosceles trapezoid** by cutting an 8.5 × 11 sheet of paper and taping it together.

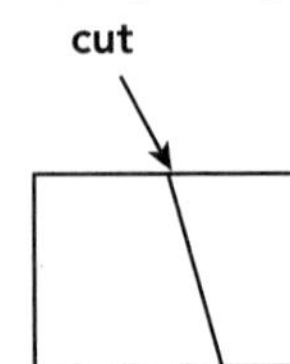

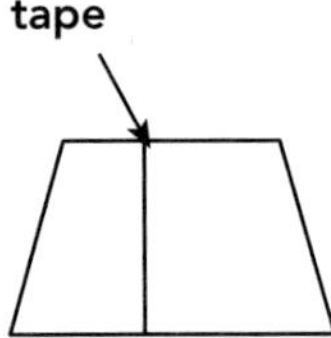

Students can then use these trapezoids to derive the methods for determining the area of a trapezoid.

▶ * **6.** (57, 69) **Analyze** Compare: $12.5 \times 10^{-4} \ (=) \ 1.25 \times 10^{-3}$

▶ * **7.** (72) **Model** Use a ratio box to solve this problem. Maria read 40 pages in 3 hours. At this rate, how long would it take Maria to read 100 pages? $7\frac{1}{2}$ hours

8. 21,000 books

$\frac{2}{5}$ were checked out.	4200 books
	4200 books
$\frac{3}{5}$ were not checked out.	4200 books
	4200 books
	4200 books

8. (22) Diagram this statement. Then answer the questions that follow.

Two fifths of the library's 21,000 books were checked out during the school year.

a. How many books were checked out? 8400 books

b. How many books were not checked out? 12,600 books

Connect Write equations to solve problems **9–12.**

▶ * **9.** (74) Sixty is $\frac{5}{12}$ of what number? $60 = \frac{5}{12} \times W_N$; 144

▶ **10.** (60) Seventy percent of $35.00 is how much money? $0.7 \times \$35.00 = M$; $24.50

▶* **11.** (74) Thirty-five is what fraction of 80? $35 = W_F \times 80$; $\frac{7}{16}$

▶* **12.** (74) Fifty-six is what decimal part of 70? $56 = W_D \times 70$; 0.8

* **13.** (73) Simplify:

a. $\frac{-120}{4}$ −30

▶ b. $\left(-\frac{1}{2}\right)\left(\frac{2}{3}\right)$ $-\frac{1}{3}$

c. $\frac{-120}{-5}$ 24

▶ d. $\left(-\frac{1}{3}\right)\left(-\frac{3}{4}\right)$ $\frac{1}{4}$

14. (70) Find the volume of this rectangular prism. Dimensions are in centimeters. What formula did you use? 3000 cm^3; $V = l \times w \times h$

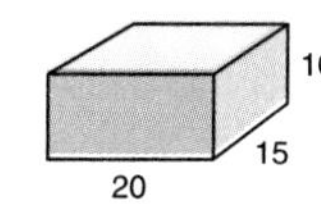

15. (65) The diameter of the plate was 11 inches. Find its circumference to the nearest half inch. $34\frac{1}{2}$ inches

16.
$A = \frac{1}{2}(b_1 + b_2)h$
$A = \frac{1}{2}(10 \text{ ft} + 14 \text{ ft})8 \text{ ft}$
$A = 96 \text{ ft}^2$

▶* **16.** (75) **Estimate** Kwan's room on the second floor has a wall the shape of a trapezoid with the dimensions shown in the illustration. Estimate the area of the wall in square feet. Show how you found the area using a formula.

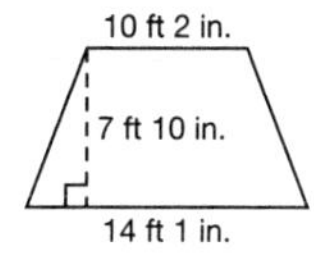

* **17.** (75) **Analyze** A corner was trimmed from a square sheet of paper to make the shape shown. Dimensions are in centimeters.

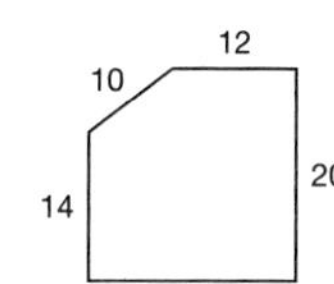

a. What was the length of each side of the square paper before the corner was trimmed? 20 cm

b. Find the perimeter of the figure. 76 cm

▶ c. Find the area of the figure. 376 cm^2

▶ See Math Conversations in the sidebar.

3 Written Practice (Continued)

Math Conversations

Discussion opportunities are provided below.

Problem 6 Analyze

Remind students that negative exponents denote a fractional form, where 1 is the numerator and the denominator is the base of the exponent to the positive power. Ask volunteers to explain how they know their answers are correct.

Problem 7 Model

Have a student work at the board to explain how to set up the proportion.

Problems 9–12 Connect

Ask students to identify what they know and what they are asked to find in each of these problems.

Problem 17c Analyze

Give students the opportunity to explain the different methods they could use to solve this part of the problem.

Errors and Misconceptions

Problem 13b and d

If students add these numbers instead of multiplying, point out that if this were an addition problem there would be a plus sign between the parentheses.

(continued)

3 Written Practice (Continued)

Math Conversations

Discussion opportunities are provided below.

Problems 21–23 Justify

Remind students that they need to isolate the variable to solve each equation. To do this, they must perform the inverse operation on both sides of the equation. Ask students to name the inverse operation they used to solve each equation.

Problem 29 Generalize

Ask students how they could simplify these expressions using mental math.

18. (48) Complete the table.

Fraction	Decimal	Percent
a. $1\frac{1}{4}$	**b.** 1.25	125%
$\frac{1}{8}$	**c.** 0.125	**d.** $12\frac{1}{2}\%$

19. (46) The taxicab bill was $12.50. Mr. Gomez tipped the driver 20%. Altogether, how much money did Mr. Gomez pay the driver? $15.00

20. (52) Evaluate: $x^3 - xy - \frac{x}{y}$ if $x = 2$ and $y = 0.5$ 3

▶ Justify For problems **21–23,** solve and check each equation. Show each step. See student work.

* **21.** (Inv. 7) $\frac{5}{8}x = 40$ 64

* **22.** (Inv. 7) $1.2w = 26.4$ 22

* **23.** (Inv. 7) $y + 3.6 = 8.47$ 4.87

Simplify:

* **24.** (63) $9^2 - [3^3 - (9 \cdot 3 - \sqrt{9})]$ 78

25. (49)
2 hr 48 min 20 s
− 1 hr 23 min 48 s
1 hr 24 min 32 s

26. (50) $100 \text{ yd} \cdot \frac{3 \text{ ft}}{1 \text{ yd}} \cdot \frac{12 \text{ in.}}{1 \text{ ft}}$ 3600 in.

27. (26) $5\frac{1}{3} \cdot \left(3 \div 1\frac{1}{3}\right)$ 12

28. (30) $3\frac{1}{5} + 2\frac{1}{2} - 1\frac{1}{4}$ $4\frac{9}{20}$

▶* **29.** (68) Generalize

a. $(-26) + (-15) - (-40)$ −1

b. $(-5) + (-4) - (-3) - (+2)$ −8

30. (47, 57) Find each missing exponent:

a. $5^5 \cdot 5^2 = 5^{\square}$ 7

b. $5^5 \div 5^2 = 5^{\square}$ 3

c. $5^2 \div 5^2 = 5^{\square}$ 0

d. $5^2 \div 5^5 = 5^{\square}$ −3

Early Finishers
Math Applications

Work with a partner and use 6 cubes to build a three-dimensional figure that matches all three of these views. Make a sketch of the figure you built.
See student work.

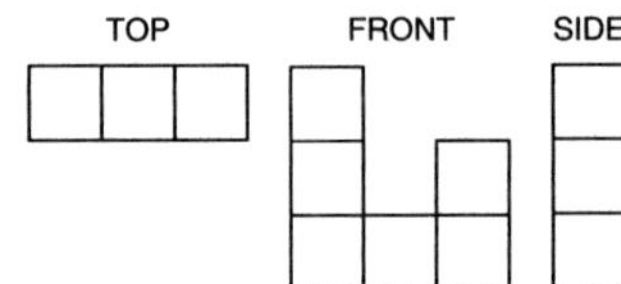

▶ See Math Conversations in the sidebar.

Looking Forward

Understanding how to find the areas of complex figures and trapezoids prepares students for:

- **Lesson 104,** finding the perimeters and areas of figures that contain semicircles.
- **Lesson 105,** finding the surface area of right solids.

Assessment

30–40 minutes *For use after Lesson 75*

Distribute **Cumulative Test 14** to each student. Two versions of the test are available in *Saxon Math Course 2 Course Assessments Book.* Have students complete the **Power-Up Test** first. Allow 10 minutes. Then have students work the 20 numbered items on the **Cumulative Test.** Students may use copies of the answer sheet to record their work. Track individual and class progress with the **Test Analysis** forms.

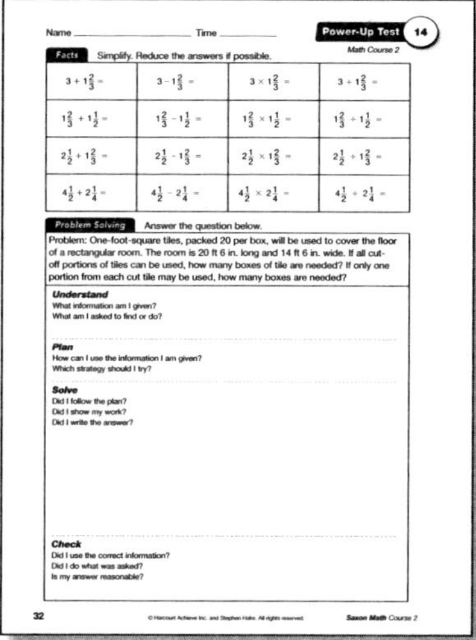

Power-Up Test 14

Facts: Simplify. Reduce the answers if possible.

Problem Solving: Answer the question below.

Problem: One-foot-square tiles, packed 20 per box, will be used to cover the floor of a rectangular room. The room is 20 ft 6 in. long and 14 ft 6 in. wide. If all cut-off portions of tiles can be used, how many boxes of tile are needed? If only one portion from each cut tile may be used, how many boxes are needed?

Understand: What information am I given? What am I asked to find or do?

Plan: How can I use the information I am given? Which strategy should I try?

Solve: Did I follow the plan? Did I show my work? Did I write the answer?

Check: Did I use the correct information? Did I do what was asked? Is my answer reasonable?

Power-Up Test 14

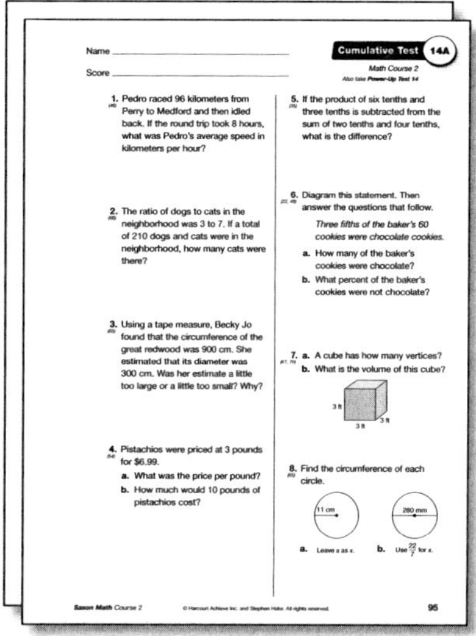

Cumulative Test 14A

1. Pedro raced 96 kilometers from Perry to Medford and then idled back. If the round trip took 8 hours, what was Pedro's average speed in kilometers per hour?

2. The ratio of dogs to cats in the neighborhood was 3 to 7. If a total of 210 dogs and cats were in the neighborhood, how many cats were there?

3. Using a tape measure, Becky Jo found that the circumference of the great redwood was 900 cm. She estimated that its diameter was 300 cm. Was her estimate a little too large or a little too small? Why?

4. Pistachios were priced at 3 pounds for $6.99.
a. What was the price per pound?
b. How much would 10 pounds of pistachios cost?

5. If the product of six tenths and three tenths is subtracted from the sum of two tenths and four tenths, what is the difference?

6. Diagram this statement. Then answer the questions that follow.
Three fifths of the baker's 60 cookies were chocolate cookies.
a. How many of the baker's cookies were chocolate?
b. What percent of the baker's cookies were not chocolate?

7. a. A cube has how many vertices?
b. What is the volume of this cube?

8. Find the circumference of each circle.

Cumulative Test 14A

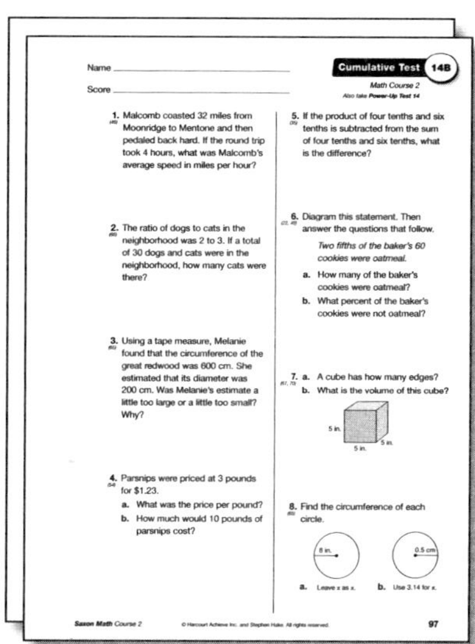

Cumulative Test 14B

1. Malcomb coasted 32 miles from Moonridge to Mentone and then pedaled back hard. If the round trip took 4 hours, what was Malcomb's average speed in miles per hour?

2. The ratio of dogs to cats in the neighborhood was 2 to 3. If a total of 30 dogs and cats were in the neighborhood, how many cats were there?

3. Using a tape measure, Melanie found that the circumference of the great redwood was 600 cm. She estimated that its diameter was 200 cm. Was Melanie's estimate a little too large or a little too small? Why?

4. Parsnips were priced at 3 pounds for $1.23.
a. What was the price per pound?
b. How much would 10 pounds of parsnips cost?

5. If the product of four tenths and six tenths is subtracted from the sum of four tenths and six tenths, what is the difference?

6. Diagram this statement. Then answer the questions that follow.
Two fifths of the baker's 60 cookies were oatmeal.
a. How many of the baker's cookies were oatmeal?
b. What percent of the baker's cookies were not oatmeal?

7. a. A cube has how many edges?
b. What is the volume of this cube?

8. Find the circumference of each circle.

Alternative Cumulative Test 14B

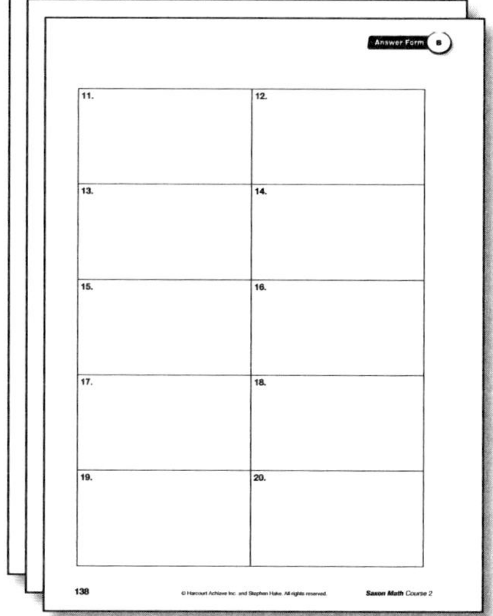

Optional Answer Forms

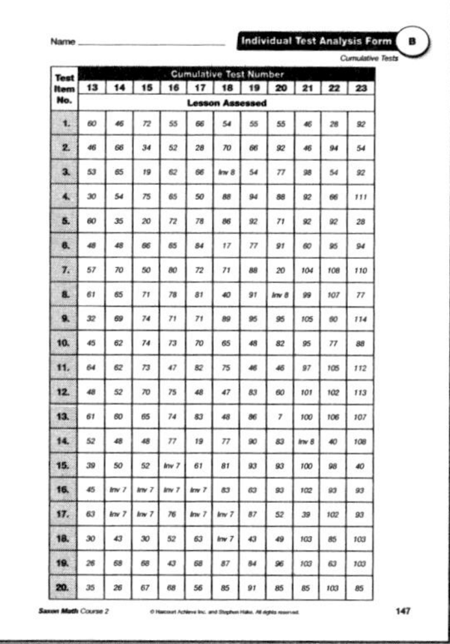

Individual Test Analysis Form

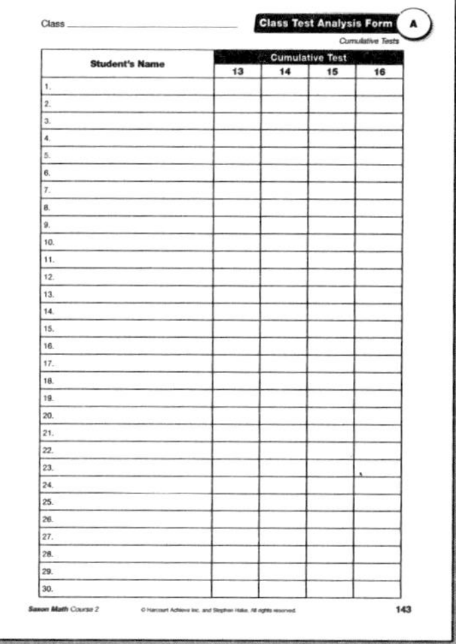

Class Test Analysis Form

Reteaching

Students who score below 80% on the assessment may be in need of reteaching. Look for the causes of student mistakes. If errors are conceptual, refer to the *Reteaching Masters* for reteaching.

Performance Activity 14

All About Circles

Assign after Lesson 75 and Test 14

Objectives

- Measure the diameter and circumference of a circle.
- Make a line graph that shows the relationship between the diameter and circumference of a circle.
- Communicate their ideas through writing.

Materials

Performance Activity 14

Ruler

Preparation

Make copies of **Performance Tasks 14.** (One each per student.)

Time Requirement

15–30 minutes; Begin in class and complete at home.

Name ______________________ **Performance Activity 14**

1. Find four circular objects with different diameters that are less than 7 inches. Complete the table below to show the diameter and circumference of each. (Use a tape or string to measure the circumference or roll the object along a ruler.)

Diameter	Circumference

2. Plot the points from Excercise 1 on the grid below.

Circumference

Diameter

3. Draw the line of fit through the points on the graph. Use the graph to describe the relationship between the diameter and the circumference of any circle?

____

____

Saxon Math Course 2 57

Performance Activity 14

Activity

Explain to students that for this activity they will be measuring the diameter and circumference of different circles and graphing the relationship between the diameter and the circumference. They will describe in words the relationship between the diameter and circumference. Explain that all of the information students need is on **Performance Activity 14.**

Criteria for Evidence of Learning

- Accurately measures the diameter and circumference of different circles.
- Graphs the relationship between the diameter and circumference of a circle accurately.
- Communicates mathematical ideas clearly.

Meeting Standards

National Council of Teachers of Mathematics (NCTM)

Algebra

AL.4a Use graphs to analyze the nature of changes in quantities in linear relationships

Measurement

ME.2b Select and apply techniques and tools to accurately find length, area, volume, and angle measures to appropriate levels of precision

Communication

CM.3d Use the language of mathematics to express mathematical ideas precisely

Representation

RE.5a Create and use representations to organize, record, and communicate mathematical ideas

• Complex Fractions

Objectives

- Simplify a complex fraction.

Lesson Preparation

Materials

- **Power Up P** (in *Instructional Masters*)

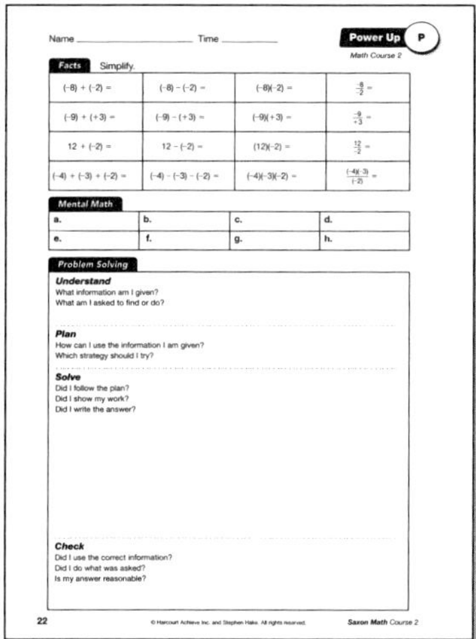

Power Up P

Math Language

New	English Learners (ESL)
complex fraction	alternative

Technology Resources

Student eBook Complete student textbook in electronic format.

Resources and Planner CD Assessment, reteaching, and instructional masters, plus a pacing calendar with standards.

Test and Practice Generator CD Create additional practice sheets and custom-made tests.

www.SaxonPublishers.com Visit for more student activities and planning materials.

Inclusion

Adaptations CD Adapted lessons, investigations, practice and assessments.

Meeting Standards

National Council of Teachers of Mathematics (NCTM)

Numbers and Operations

NO.1a Work flexibly with fractions, decimals, and percents to solve problems

NO.3a Select appropriate methods and tools for computing with fractions and decimals from among mental computation, estimation, calculators or computers, and paper and pencil, depending on the situation, and apply the selected methods

NO.3b Develop and analyze algorithms for computing with fractions, decimals, and integers and develop fluency in their use

Connections

CN.4b Understand how mathematical ideas interconnect and build on one another to produce a coherent whole

Power-Up Discussion *For use with Power Up, p. 529*

Problem-Solving Strategy: Guess and Check

The squares of the first nine counting numbers are each less than 100. Altogether, how many counting numbers have squares that are less than 1000?

Understand Understand the problem.

"What information are we given?"

The squares of the first nine counting numbers are each less than 100.

"What are the first nine squares?"

1, 4, 9, 16, 25, 36, 49, 64, and 81.

"What are we asked to do?"

We are asked to determine how many counting numbers have squares that are less than 1000.

Plan ***Make a plan.***

"What problem-solving strategy will we use?"

We will *guess and check* by starting with a counting number whose square is close to 1000, then testing numbers one-by-one until we find one greater than 1000.

Solve ***Carry out the plan.***

"There are nine squares between 1 and 100. Will there be nine squares between 101 and 200?"

No.

"Why or why not?"

Because as the numbers being squared get larger, the difference between the squares also gets larger.

"What number is a good number to start with?"

We know that $30 \times 30 = 900$, so we choose to start with 30.

"What are the squares of counting numbers greater than 30?"

$31 \times 31 = 961$; $32 \times 32 = 1024$

"How many counting numbers have squares less than 1000?"

The first 31 counting numbers.

Check ***Look back.***

"Did we do what we were asked to do?"

Yes, we found that 31 counting numbers have squares less than 1000.

"Is our solution reasonable/expected?"

Yes. We knew it would be slightly more than 30.

LESSON 76

• Complex Fractions

Power Up — *Building Power*

facts Power Up P

mental math

a. **Positive/Negative:** $(+6) + (-18)$ -12

b. **Decimals/Exponents:** 6.25×10^{-2} 0.0625

c. **Algebra:** $9a - 4 = 32$ 4

d. **Fractional Parts:** 12 is $\frac{2}{3}$ of what number? 18

e. **Measurement:** 5 mm to cm 0.5 cm

f. **Fractional Parts:** What is $\frac{2}{3}$ of 12? 8

g. **Statistics:** Find the average of the set of numbers: 95, 95, 50. 80

h. **Calculation:** What is the total cost of a \$25 video game plus 6% sales tax? \$26.50

problem solving The squares of the first nine counting numbers are each less than 100. Altogether, how many counting numbers have squares that are less than 1000? 31

New Concept — *Increasing Knowledge*

A **complex fraction** is a fraction that contains one or more fractions in the numerator or denominator. Each of the following is a complex fraction:

$$\frac{\frac{3}{5}}{\frac{2}{3}} \qquad \frac{25\frac{2}{3}}{100} \qquad \frac{15}{7\frac{1}{3}} \qquad \frac{\frac{a}{b}}{\frac{b}{c}}$$

One way to simplify a complex fraction, is to multiply the complex fraction by a fraction name for 1 that makes the denominator 1.

Example 1

Simplify: $\frac{\frac{3}{5}}{\frac{2}{3}}$

Thinking Skill *Analyze*

What is the relationship between fraction pairs such as $\frac{2}{3}$ and $\frac{3}{2}$? What is their product? They are reciprocals. 1

Solution

We focus our attention on the denominator of the complex fraction. Our goal is to make the denominator 1. We multiply the denominator by the reciprocal of $\frac{2}{3}$, which is $\frac{3}{2}$, so that the new denominator is 1. We also multiply the numerator by $\frac{3}{2}$.

Facts Simplify.

$(-8) + (-2) = -10$	$(-8) - (-2) = -6$	$(-8)(-2) = 16$	$\frac{-8}{-2} = 4$
$(-9) + (+3) = -6$	$(-9) - (+3) = -12$	$(-9)(+3) = -27$	$\frac{-9}{+3} = -3$
$12 + (-2) = 10$	$12 - (-2) = 14$	$(12)(-2) = -24$	$\frac{12}{-2} = -6$
$(-4) + (-3) + (-2) = -9$	$(-4) - (-3) - (-2) = 1$	$(-4)(-3)(-2) = -24$	$\frac{(-4)(-3)}{(-2)} = -6$

1 Power Up

Facts

Distribute **Power Up P** to students. See answers below.

Mental Math

Encourage students to share different ways to mentally compute these exercises. Strategies for exercises **d** and **f** are listed below.

d. Solve Equation

$12 = \frac{2}{3} W_N$

$36 = 2\, W_N$

$18 = W_N$

Use Logical Reasoning

$\frac{2}{3}$ of what number equals 12?

$6 = \frac{1}{3}$ of that number

That number equals 3×6 and is 18.

f. Use a Unit Fraction

$\frac{1}{3}$ of 12 is 4.

$\frac{2}{3}$ of 12 is 8.

Multiply Fractions

$\frac{2}{3} \times \frac{12}{1} = \frac{2 \times 12}{3 \times 1} = 2 \times 4 = 8$

Problem Solving

Refer to **Power-Up Discussion,** p. 529B.

2 New Concepts

Instruction

Explain that although complex fractions may appear to be difficult, we can simplify them by using what we have learned about fractions, reciprocals, and operations with fractions.

Spend a few minutes reviewing reciprocals of fractions, whole numbers, and mixed numbers with students before beginning this lesson. Remind students what reciprocals are and how they are used.

Example 1

Instruction

Clarify that the expression is a fraction composed of a numerator, $\frac{3}{5}$, and a denominator, $\frac{2}{3}$. Explain that it means $\frac{3}{5} \div \frac{2}{3}$. The task is to simplify the fraction so that the numerator and the denominator are each whole numbers. Guide students to check whether the fraction is greater or less than 1.

"Is this fraction greater than or less than 1?" It is less than 1 because the numerator, $\frac{3}{5}$, is less than the denominator, $\frac{2}{3}$.

(continued)

2 New Concepts (Continued)

Example 1 (continued)

Instruction

Point out that the complex fractions in examples 1–3 are simplified by multiplying by a fraction equal to 1. Ask students to identify in example 1 the fraction equal to 1.

Example 2

Instruction

Be sure students know that they are to rewrite mixed numbers and whole numbers in the numerator and denominator as fractions when they simplify complex fractions. Explain that a whole number in the numerator or denominator should be written as a fraction with a denominator of 1.

Point out to students that the division bar between the fraction numerator and the fraction denominator is a little longer than the others. Tell them that they may emphasize that division bar by extending it even more when working these problems on paper.

(continued)

Visit www. SaxonPublishers. com/ActivitiesC2 for a graphing calculator activity.

$$\frac{\frac{3}{5}}{\frac{2}{3}} \times \frac{\frac{3}{2}}{\frac{3}{2}} = \frac{\frac{9}{10}}{1} \text{ or } \mathbf{\frac{9}{10}}$$

We multiplied the complex fraction by a complex name for 1 to change the denominator to 1. Since $\frac{9}{10}$ divided by 1 is $\frac{9}{10}$, the complex fraction simplifies to $\frac{9}{10}$.

An alternative method for simplifying some complex fractions is to treat the fraction as a division problem. We can change the format of the division problem to a more familiar form.

$$\begin{matrix}\text{divided} \\ \text{divisor}\end{matrix} \quad \frac{\frac{3}{5}}{\frac{2}{3}} \longrightarrow \frac{3}{5} \div \frac{2}{3}$$

Then we simplify the division using the method described in Lesson 25.

$$\frac{3}{5} \div \frac{2}{3} = \frac{3}{5} \cdot \frac{3}{2} = \mathbf{\frac{9}{10}}$$

Example 2

Simplify: $\dfrac{25\frac{2}{3}}{100}$

Solution

First we write both numerator and denominator as fractions.

$$\frac{\frac{77}{3}}{\frac{100}{1}}$$

Now we multiply the numerator and the denominator by $\frac{1}{100}$.

$$\frac{\frac{77}{3}}{\frac{100}{1}} \cdot \frac{\frac{1}{100}}{\frac{1}{100}} = \frac{\frac{77}{300}}{1} \text{ or } \mathbf{\frac{77}{300}}$$

Example 3

Simplify: $\dfrac{15}{7\frac{1}{3}}$

Solution

We begin by writing both numerator and denominator as improper fractions.

$$\frac{\frac{15}{1}}{\frac{22}{3}}$$

English Learners

In example 1, demonstrate the meaning of **alternative.** Say:

"An alternative is a another way to solve a problem and get the same result."

Have a student draw a right triangle on the board. Then have another student draw the same triangle in a different position. Then ask:

"How is the second triangle an alternative to the first?" Sample: The second triangle is drawn in a different way than the first but is the same triangle.

Math Background

Can a complex fraction be written as a fraction division problem?

Let's use the complex fraction in example 1 to explain this process: $\frac{\frac{3}{5}}{\frac{2}{3}}$

This division can be rewritten as $\frac{3}{5} \div \frac{2}{3}$. To solve the fraction division problem, we multiply $\frac{3}{5}$ by the reciprocal of the divisor, $\frac{3}{2}$. Notice that this is the same way the complex fraction in example 1 was simplified. The general form of a complex fraction demonstrates *why* we divide fractions by multiplying by the reciprocal of the divisor.

In general form,

$$\frac{\frac{a}{b}}{\frac{c}{d}} \cdot \frac{\frac{d}{c}}{\frac{d}{c}} = \frac{\frac{a}{b} \cdot \frac{d}{c}}{1} = \frac{a}{b} \cdot \frac{d}{c}$$

To make the denominator 1. The fraction $\frac{3}{22}$ was selected because it is the reciprocal of the denominator $\frac{22}{3}$.

Now we multiply the numerator and the denominator by $\frac{3}{22}$.

$$\frac{\frac{15}{1}}{\frac{22}{3}} \cdot \frac{\frac{3}{22}}{\frac{3}{22}} = \frac{\frac{45}{22}}{1} \text{ or } 2\frac{1}{22}$$

Discuss Why do you think $\frac{3}{22}$ was selected as the multiplier in this example?

Example 4

Change $83\frac{1}{3}\%$ to a fraction and simplify:

Solution

Thinking Skill
Generalize
Name three complex fractions equal to 1. See student answer.

A percent is a fraction that has a denominator of 100. Thus $83\frac{1}{3}\%$ is

$$\frac{83\frac{1}{3}}{100}$$

Next we write both numerator and denominator as fractions.

$$\frac{\frac{250}{3}}{\frac{100}{1}}$$

Now we multiply the numerator and the denominator by $\frac{1}{100}$.

$$\frac{\frac{250}{3}}{\frac{100}{1}} \cdot \frac{\frac{1}{100}}{\frac{1}{100}} = \frac{\frac{250}{300}}{1} = \frac{5}{6}$$

Practice Set ▶ **Generalize** Simplify each complex fraction:

a. $\frac{37\frac{1}{2}}{100}$ $\frac{3}{8}$ b. $\frac{12}{\frac{5}{6}}$ $14\frac{2}{5}$ c. $\frac{\frac{2}{5}}{\frac{2}{3}}$ $\frac{3}{5}$

Change each percent to a fraction and simplify:

d. $66\frac{2}{3}\%$ $\frac{2}{3}$ e. $8\frac{1}{3}\%$ $\frac{1}{12}$ f. $4\frac{1}{6}\%$ $\frac{1}{24}$

▶ g. **Justify** Which two properties of multiplication do we use to simplify complex fractions? Inverse Property; Identity Property

Written Practice *Strengthening Concepts*

1. (46) a. Nestor finished a 42-kilometer bicycle race in 1 hour 45 minutes ($1\frac{3}{4}$ hr). What was his average speed in kilometers per hour? 24 kilometers per hour
b. **Explain** How did we know that 1 hour and 45 minutes is $1\frac{3}{4}$ hours? 1 hour is 60 minutes, so 45 minutes is $\frac{45}{60}$ hour, which reduces to $\frac{3}{4}$.

▶ 2. (28) Akemi's scores in the diving competition were 7.9, 8.3, 8.1, 7.8, 8.4, 8.1, and 8.2. The highest and lowest scores were not counted. What was the average of the remaining scores? 8.12

3. (66) Use a ratio box to solve this problem. The school art club is having an exhibit. The ratio of oil paintings to acrylic paintings being displayed is 2 to 5. If there are 35 paintings displayed, how many of them are oil paintings? 10 oil paintings

▶ See Math Conversations in the sidebar.

2 New Concepts *(Continued)*

Example 3

Instruction

Be sure students understand that $\frac{3}{22}$ was selected as the multiplier because it is the reciprocal of $\frac{22}{3}$. The two fractions in the denominator will cancel each other, giving a denominator of 1.

Example 4

Instruction

Review if needed that a percent is a short way of writing a fraction with a denominator of 100. Point out that after the percent is rewritten as a fraction, simplify the fraction using the same method used as in example 2.

Practice Set

Problems a–c Generalize

Discuss the general approach to simplifying complex fractions. writing both numerator and denominator as fractions and then multiplying both by the reciprocal of the denominator

Then have students describe how they simplified each fraction.

Problem g Justify

Ask how each property is used and what it does to simplify the fraction. Sample: The Identity Property is used to multiply the whole fraction by 1, and it leaves a denominator of 1.

3 Written Practice

Math Conversations

Discussion opportunities are provided below.

Problem 2

Extend the Problem

Not counting the highest and lowest scores can affect the mean.

"What effect does not counting the highest and lowest scores have on the median?" none; the middle score remains in the middle

(continued)

Teacher Tip

For this lesson on simplifying complex fractions, students must understand these words: *simplify, complex fraction, reciprocal, numerator, denominator, improper fraction*, and *lowest terms*. Have students create a **class glossary** for the bulletin board. Students can work in small groups to write each word followed by examples of what the word means.

3 Written Practice (Continued)

Math Conversations

Discussion opportunities are provided below.

Problem 4 Connect

"What are some other ways to convert 3.5 grams to milligrams?" Samples: Move the decimal point 3 places to the right. Think: 1 gram is 1000 milligrams, so 3.5 grams is 3.5×1000 milligrams, or 3500 milligrams.

Problem 9 Generalize

"What pattern do you notice in these multiplication and division problems?" Samples: If there is one negative number, the answer is negative. When there are two negative numbers, you get a positive answer.

Problem 14 Analyze

Discuss how to translate this sentence into an equation. Sample: The word "of" means to use a multiplication sign.

Then ask students whether it is easier to translate these sentences into equations now than when they first learned how to do it.

Problem 15b Justify

Ask students to read their descriptions of how to check the answer. For each description, have another student carry out the procedure and ask a third student to explain why it works.

Errors and Misconceptions

Problem 6

To help students who have trouble with this problem, suggest that they act out the clockwise turn. Direct students to stand and face north. Suggest that they imagine their feet are positioned at the center of a large clock, facing 12 o'clock. Ask them to turn 90° ($\frac{1}{4}$ turn) in a clockwise direction, which is the direction that the hands of a clock move. They will be facing 3 o'clock, which represents east.

Problem 11

If some students are not able to count the faces, edges, and vertices using the picture, provide a manipulative of a square pyramid for them.

(continued)

▶ * **4.** (50) **Connect** Use a unit multiplier to convert 3.5 grams to milligrams.
3.5 grams $\cdot \frac{1000 \text{ milligrams}}{1 \text{ gram}} = 3500$ milligrams

* **5.** (76) Change $16\frac{2}{3}$ percent to a fraction and simplify. $\frac{1}{6}$

▶ **6.** (12, 28) Davie is facing north. If he turns 90° in a clockwise direction, what direction will he be facing? east

7. (60) One sixth of the rock's mass was quartz. If the mass of the rock was 144 grams, what was the mass of the quartz in the rock? 24 grams

8. (41, 57) For $a = 2$, evaluate

a. $\sqrt{2a^3}$ 4 **b.** $a^{-1} \cdot a^{-2}$ $\frac{1}{8}$

▶ * **9.** (73) **Generalize** Simplify each expression:

a. $\frac{-60}{-12}$ 5 **b.** $\left(-\frac{1}{2}\right)\left(\frac{1}{2}\right)$ $-\frac{1}{4}$

c. $\frac{40}{-8}$ −5 **d.** $\left(-\frac{1}{4}\right)\left(-\frac{1}{4}\right)$ $\frac{1}{16}$

10. (65) What is the circumference of the circle shown? 30π cm

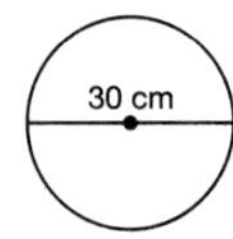

Leave π as π

▶ **11.** (67) The figure at right is a pyramid with a square base. Find the number of:

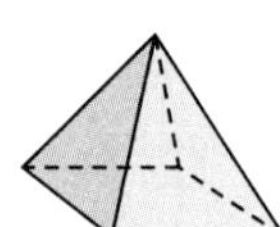

a. faces 5 faces

b. edges 8 edges

c. vertices 5 vertices

Write equations to solve problems **12–15.**

12. (60) What number is 10 percent of \$37.50? $W_N = 0.1 \times \$37.50$; \$3.75

13. (60) What number is $\frac{5}{8}$ of 72? $W_N = \frac{5}{8} \times 72$; 45

▶* **14.** (74) **Analyze** Twenty-five is what fraction of 60? $25 = W_F \times 60$; $\frac{5}{12}$

* **15.** (74) **a.** Sixty is what decimal part of 80? $60 = W_D \times 80$; 0.75

▶ **b.** **Justify** How can you check that your answer to **a** is correct? Sample: Multiply: $0.75 \times 80 = 60$

16. (62) In this figure $AC = AB$. Angles DCA and ACB are supplementary. Find the measure of

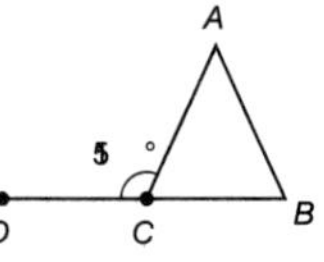

a. $\angle ACB$. 65°

b. $\angle ABC$. 65°

c. $\angle CAB$. 50°

▶ See Math Conversations in the sidebar.

17. (48) Complete the table.

Fraction	Decimal	Percent
$\frac{5}{6}$	**a.** $0.8\overline{3}$	**b.** $83\frac{1}{3}\%$
c. $\frac{1}{1000}$	**d.** 0.001	0.1%

18. c. Sample: Since the area of the original square was 81 square in.^{2}, I knew that the sides of the square were 9 in. Therefore the vertical side of the triangle of the cut off corner is 9 in. − 6 in. = 3 in., and the horizontal side is 9 in. − 5 in. = 4 in. Then I calculated the area of this triangle: $\frac{1}{2}$(3 in. × 4 in.) = 6 in.^{2}. So the area of the pentagon is 81 in.^{2} − 6 in.^{2} = 75 in.^{2}

▶* **18.** (75) **Analyze** A square sheet of paper with an area of 81 in.^{2} has a corner cut off, forming a pentagon as shown.

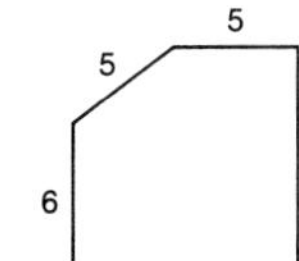

a. What is the perimeter of the pentagon? 34 in.

b. What is the area of the pentagon? 75 in.^{2}

c. **Explain** How did you find the area of the pentagon?

* **19.** (Inv. 6) **Conclude** What type of parallelogram has four congruent angles but not necessarily four congruent sides? rectangle

20. (12, 28) When water increases in temperature from its freezing point to its boiling point, the reading on a thermometer increases from 0°C to 100°C and from 32°F to 212°F. The temperature halfway between 0°C and 100°C is 50°C. What temperature is halfway between 32°F and 212°F? 122°F

▶ **Justify** For problems **21–24,** solve and check each equation. Show each step.

* **21.** (Inv. 7) $x - 25 = 96$ 121

* **22.** (Inv. 7) $\frac{2}{3}m = 12$ 18

* **23.** (Inv. 7) $2.5p = 6.25$ 2.5

* **24.** (Inv. 7) $10 = f + 3\frac{1}{3}$ $6\frac{2}{3}$

Simplify:

25. (20) $\sqrt{13^2 - 5^2}$ 12

26. (16) 1 ton − 400 lb 1600 lb

27. (26, 43) $3\frac{3}{4} \times 4\frac{1}{6} \times (0.4)^2$ (fraction answer) $2\frac{1}{2}$

28. (35, 43) $3\frac{1}{8} + 6.7 + 8\frac{1}{4}$ (decimal answer) 18.075

▶* **29.** (68) **Generalize** **a.** $(-3) + (-5) - (-3) - |+5|$ −10

b. $(-2.4) - (+1.2)$ −3.6

▶* **30.** (76) **Estimate** Before dividing, determine whether the quotient is greater than or less than 1 and state why. Then perform the calculation.

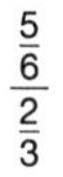

$$\frac{\frac{5}{6}}{\frac{2}{3}}$$

The quotient is a little more than 1 because the dividend is slightly greater than the divisor; $1\frac{1}{4}$

▶ See Math Conversations in the sidebar.

Looking Forward

Simplifying complex fractions prepares students for:

- **Lesson 77,** translating percent problems into equations with percents changed to fractional or decimal forms.
- **Lesson 110,** solving problems involving successive discounts.

3 Written Practice (Continued)

Math Conversations

Discussion opportunities are provided below.

Problem 18 Analyze

Have students analyze the given information. Ask questions like these:

"How does the information in the problem help you find the missing measurements?" Sample: You know the area of the square is 81 in.^{2}, so the length of the two unknown sides is 9 in.

"What other measurements are needed?" Sample: You need to draw the whole square and find the sides of the triangle you make at the top left.

"How do you find them?" Sample: Subtract the given side from 9 in.

Problem 18c Analyze

"Is subtracting the area of the triangle the only way to find the area of the figure? What other way could be used?" Sample: No, you can draw two lines to divide the figure into 3 rectangles and a triangle, and find the area of each of those.

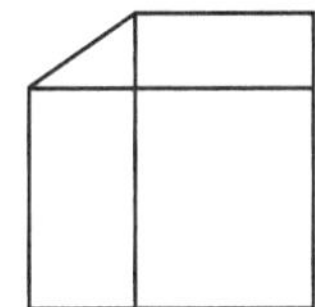

Problems 21–24 Justify

Discuss why checking the answer is an important part of solving a problem or working out an exercise.

"Why is checking the answer always important?" Sample: Sometimes one part of a question uses the answer to another one, so you want all the answers to be correct, and the only way to be sure is to check.

Problem 29a Generalize

Have students explain why the first step in simplifying expression a is to replace the absolute value of +5 with 5. Sample: The absolute value bars are like a grouping symbol, so you do that first.

Problem 30 Estimate

Ask a volunteer to explain how to determine whether the quotient will be greater than or less than 1. Then ask if anyone did it another way. See how many different ways students did this. Sample: I changed $\frac{2}{3}$ to $\frac{4}{6}$; since $\frac{5}{6}$ is greater than $\frac{4}{6}$, the answer will be more than 1.

• Percent of a Number, Part 2

Objectives

- Translate percent-of-a-number problems into equations and then solve the equations.

Lesson Preparation

Materials

- **Power Up P** (in *Instructional Masters)*

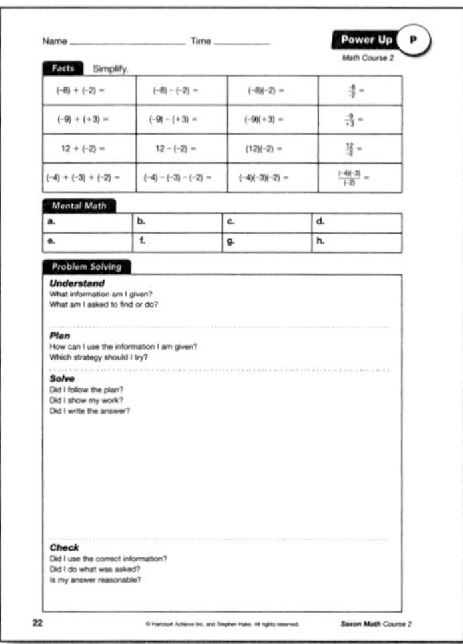

Name ________________ Time ________

Power Up P

Math Course 2

Facts Simplify.

$(-8) + (-2) =$	$(-8) - (-2) =$	$(-8)(-2) =$	$\frac{-8}{-2} =$
$(-9) + (+3) =$	$(-9) - (+3) =$	$(-9)(+3) =$	$\frac{-9}{+3} =$
$12 + (-2) =$	$12 - (-2) =$	$(12)(-2) =$	$\frac{12}{-2} =$
$(-4) + (-3) + (-2) =$	$(-4) - (-3) - (-2) =$	$(-4)(-3)(-2) =$	$\frac{(-4)(-3)}{(-2)} =$

Mental Math

a.	b.	c.	d.
e.	f.	g.	h.

Problem Solving

Understand
What information am I given?
What am I asked to find or do?

Plan
How can I use the information I am given?
Which strategy should I try?

Solve
Did I follow the plan?
Did I show my work?
Did I write the answer?

Check
Did I use the correct information?
Did I do what was asked?
Is my answer reasonable?

22 © Harcourt Achieve Inc. and Stephen Hake. All rights reserved. ***Saxon Math*** *Course 2*

Power Up P

Math Language

English Learners (ESL)

symmetrical

Technology Resources

Student eBook Complete student textbook in electronic format.

Resources and Planner CD Assessment, reteaching, and instructional masters, plus a pacing calendar with standards.

Test and Practice Generator CD Create additional practice sheets and custom-made tests.

www.SaxonPublishers.com Visit for more student activities and planning materials.

Inclusion

Adaptations CD Adapted lessons, investigations, practice and assessments.

Meeting Standards

National Council of Teachers of Mathematics (NCTM)

Numbers and Operations

NO.1a Work flexibly with fractions, decimals, and percents to solve problems

NO.1c Develop meaning for percents greater than 100 and less than 1

NO.3a Select appropriate methods and tools for computing with fractions and decimals from among mental computation, estimation, calculators or computers, and paper and pencil, depending on the situation, and apply the selected methods

NO.3c Develop and use strategies to estimate the results of rational-number computations and judge the reasonableness of the results

Power-Up Discussion *For use with Power Up, p. 534*

Problem-Solving Strategy: Write an Equation

On a balanced scale are a 25-g mass, a 100-g mass, and five identical blocks marked x, which are distributed as shown. What is the mass of each block marked x? Write an equation illustrated by this balanced scale.

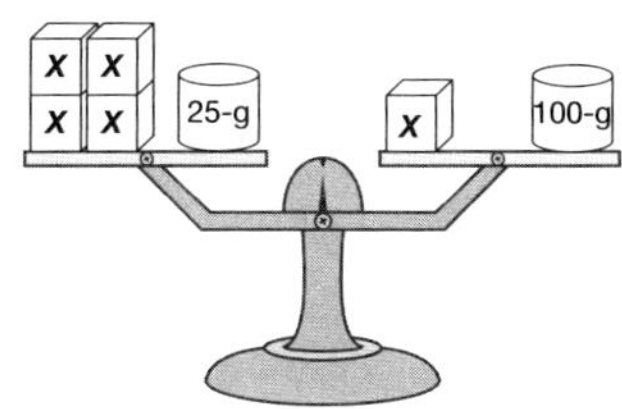

Understand ***Understand the problem.***

"What information are we given?"

A balanced scale has four blocks marked x and one 25-g mass on one side, and one block labeled x and one 100-g mass on the other.

"What are we asked to do?"

We are asked to write an equation that is illustrated by the balanced scale and to find the mass of each block marked x.

Plan ***Make a plan.***

"What problem-solving strategy will we use?"

We will *write an equation* to illustrate the balanced scale, then solve the equation to find the value of x.

Solve ***Carry out the plan.***

"What is the equation illustrated by the balanced scale?"

$4x + 25 \text{ g} = x + 100 \text{ g}$

"What equal masses can be removed from both sides of the scale to simplify the equation?"

One x block can be removed from each side.

"What is the simplified equation?"

$3x + 25 \text{ g} = 100 \text{ g}$

"What is the mass of each block marked x?"

25 g

Check ***Look back.***

"Did we do what we were asked to do?"

Yes, we wrote an equation to model the balanced scale, then found the value of each block marked x.

"How can we verify our solution is correct?"

We can substitute 25 g for x into our original equation:

$$4(25 \text{ g}) + 25 \text{ g} = (25 \text{ g}) + 100 \text{ g}$$
$$100 \text{ g} + 25 \text{ g} = 25 \text{ g} + 100 \text{ g}$$
$$125 \text{ g} = 125 \text{ g}$$

1 Power Up

Facts

Distribute **Power Up P** to students. See answers below.

Mental Math

Encourage students to share different ways to mentally compute these exercises. Strategies for exercises **c** and **d** are listed below.

c. Find an Equivalent Fraction

$\frac{100}{150} = \frac{300}{450}$

$\frac{30}{a} = \frac{300}{450} = \frac{30}{45}$

$a = 45$

Cross Multiply and Divide

$100a = 150 \times 30$

$a = \frac{150 \times 30}{100} =$

$a = 15 \times 3 = 45$

d. Find 1% and Multiply

$61 ~ $60

1% of $60 is 60¢.

15% of $60 = 15 × 60¢ = $9

Find 10% and 5%

10% of $60 is $6.

5% of $60 is $3.

15% of $60 = $6 + $3 = $9

Problem Solving

Refer to **Power-Up Discussion,** p. 534B.

2 New Concepts

Instruction

Remind students that they know how to answer questions such as: *What is 28% of 42?* Ask them to name real-world situations in which they might need to answer a percent-of-a-number question such as

"What percent of 80 is 52?"

Responses may include:

- Finding the percent of the discount when an item has been marked down.
- Determining the percent of students that are on a school team.
- Knowing the percent of students who ride a bus to school.

Example 1

Instruction

Students may have to be reminded that *is* indicates use of the equals sign and *of* indicates multiplication.

(continued)

LESSON 77

• Percent of a Number, Part 2

Power Up *Building Power*

facts Power Up P

mental math

a. **Positive/Negative:** (+12) − (−18) 30

b. **Exponents:** 4×10^6 4,000,000

c. **Ratio:** $\frac{100}{150} = \frac{30}{a}$ 45

d. **Estimation:** Estimate 15% of $61. $9

e. **Measurement:** 25 cm to m 0.25 m

f. **Fractional Parts:** 12 is $\frac{3}{4}$ of *n*. 16

g. **Statistics:** Find the average of the set of numbers: 100, 60, 90, 70. 80

h. **Calculation:** 10% of 50, × 6, + 2, ÷ 4, × 2, √‾, × 9, √‾, × 7, ÷ 2 21

problem solving

On a balanced scale are a 25-g mass, a 100-g mass, and five identical blocks marked *x*, which are distributed as shown. What is the mass of each block marked *x*? Write an equation illustrated by this balanced scale.

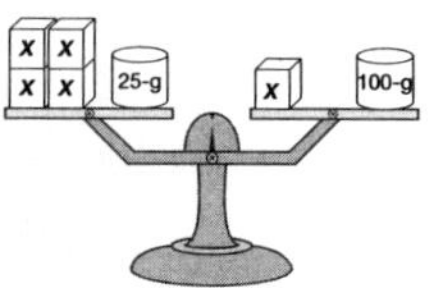

25 g; $4x + 25 = x + 100$

New Concept *Increasing Knowledge*

In Lesson 74 we practiced fractional-part problems involving fractions and decimals. In this lesson we will practice similar problems involving percents. First we translate the problem into an equation; then we solve the equation.

Example 1

What percent of 40 is 25?

Solution

We translate the question to an equation and solve.

What percent of 40 is 25? question

$W_P \times 40 = 25$ equation

To solve we divide both sides of the equation by 40.

$\frac{W_P \times \cancel{40}^1}{\cancel{40}_1} = \frac{25}{40}$ divided by 40

$W_P = \frac{5}{8}$ simplified

534 **Saxon** Math Course 2

Facts Simplify.

(−8) + (−2) = −10	(−8) − (−2) = −6	(−8)(−2) = 16	$\frac{-8}{-2} = 4$
(−9) + (+3) = −6	(−9) − (+3) = −12	(−9)(+3) = −27	$\frac{-9}{+3} = -3$
12 + (−2) = 10	12 − (−2) = 14	(12)(−2) = −24	$\frac{12}{-2} = -6$
(−4) + (−3) + (−2) = −9	(−4) − (−3) − (−2) = 1	(−4)(−3)(−2) = −24	$\frac{(-4)(-3)}{(-2)} = -6$

Since the question asked "what percent" and not "what fraction," we convert the fraction $\frac{5}{8}$ to a percent.

$$\frac{5}{8} \times 100\% = \mathbf{62\frac{1}{2}\%} \quad \text{converted to a percent}$$

Verify How can you decide if this answer is reasonable? Sample: Half, or 50%, of 40 is 20. Since 25 is slightly more than 20, 25 must be a little over 50% of 40.

Thinking Skills
Summarize

What steps did we follow to convert $\frac{5}{8}$ to a percent? Sample: We multiplied the fraction by 100%, then we simplified.

Example 2

What percent of \$3.50 is \$0.28?

Solution

We translate and solve.

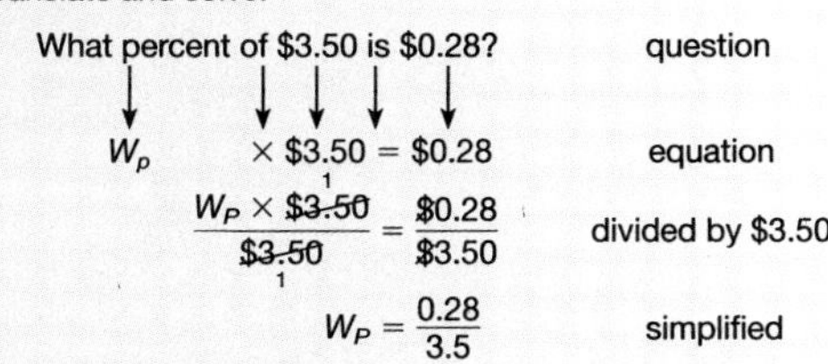

What percent of $3.50 is $0.28? question
W_P × $3.50 = $0.28 equation

$$\frac{W_P \times \cancel{\$3.50}^{1}}{\cancel{\$3.50}_{1}} = \frac{\$0.28}{\$3.50} \quad \text{divided by \$3.50}$$

$$W_P = \frac{0.28}{3.5} \quad \text{simplified}$$

We perform the decimal division.

$$W_P = \frac{0.28}{3.5} = \frac{2.8}{35} = 0.08 \quad \text{divided}$$

This is a decimal answer. The question asked for a percent answer so we convert the decimal 0.08 to 8%.

$$W_P = \mathbf{8\%} \quad \text{converted to a percent}$$

Thinking Skills
Summarize

How did we convert 0.08 to 8%? Sample: We multiplied 0.08 by 100 and inserted the percent symbol.

Example 3

Seventy-five percent of what number is 600?

Solution

We translate the question to an equation and solve. We can translate 75% to a fraction or to a decimal. We choose a fraction for this example.

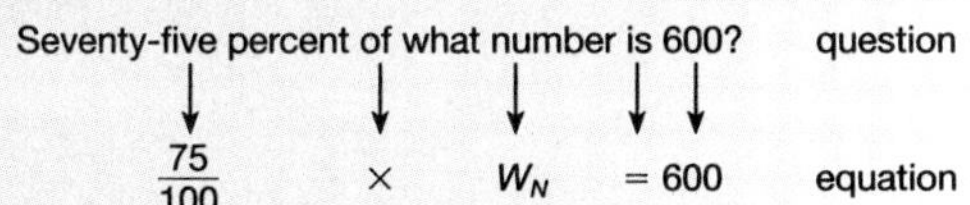

Seventy-five percent of what number is 600? question
75/100 × W_N = 600 equation

To solve, we multiply both sides by 100 over 75 as follows:

$$\frac{\cancel{100}^{1}}{\cancel{75}_{1}} \times \frac{\cancel{75}^{1}}{\cancel{100}_{1}} \times W_N = 600 \cdot \frac{100}{75} \quad \text{multiplied by } \frac{100}{75}$$

$$W_N = \mathbf{800} \quad \text{simplified}$$

2 New Concepts (Continued)

Example 1 (continued)

Instruction

Take some time to discuss and compare answers to the *Verify* question at the end of the example.

Example 2

Instruction

As students work through these examples be sure that they are able to identify what parts of the equation they are given and what they are to find. For example 2, ask:

"What are we given?" the total and the part of the total

"What are we to find?" the percent

Some students may stop when they find the fraction. Remind them that they need to rewrite the fraction as a percent.

Encourage students who may have difficulty with the decimal division to rewrite the problem in standard form. This will also help students place the decimal point in the correct place in their answer.

Example 3

Instruction

Ask students why using $\frac{3}{4}$ as the fraction rather than $\frac{75}{100}$ would result in the same answer. Because $\frac{3}{4}$ and $\frac{75}{100}$ are equivalent fractions.

(continued)

Math Background

How many variations of percent-of-a-number problems are there?

There are three variations of percent-of-a-number problems, but the questions can be asked in different ways. Percent-of-a-number problems follow the format *A* is *B*% of *C*. This can be written as the equation $A = B\% \times C$. In each variation, one of the variables is missing. Two questions and equations are given for each type listed below:

Find Part of the the Amount	What number is 10% of 50?	$A = 10\% \times 50$
	10% of 50 is what number?	$10\% \times 50 = A$
Find the Whole Amount	Five is 10% of what number?	$5 = 10\% \times C$
	10% of what number is 5?	$10\% \times C = 5$
Find the Percent	Five is what percent of 50?	$5 = B\% \times 50$
	What percent of 50 is 5?	$B\% \times 50 = 5$

Example 4

Instruction

Ask students why 50 is greater than 100% of 40. If they are not sure about that answer, point out that 40 is 100% of 40 and 50 is greater than 40.

Be sure that students understand the process of converting $\frac{5}{4}$ to a percent.

Example 5

Instruction

Work with students to predict whether the answer will be greater than or less than 60 before beginning the procedure for finding the answer.

Point out that in this example as in example 3, the unknown is a number, and not a percent. Students should read all percent-of-a-number problems carefully so that their answers will be given correctly.

Practice Set

Problems a–f Generalize

As students translate each statement into an equation, have them identify the given parts of each problem and explain which part they need to find—the percent, the total, or the part of the total.

Suggest that students predict a range for the answer to each question before solving. For example, since 24 is less than 40 but more than half of 40, the answer will be between 50% and 100%.

(continued)

Example 4

Fifty is what percent of 40?

Solution

Since 50 is more than 40, the answer will be greater than 100%. We translate to an equation and solve.

Fifty is what percent of 40?	question
$50 = W_P \times 40$	equation

We divide both sides by 40.

$$\frac{50}{40} = \frac{W_P \times \overset{1}{\cancel{40}}}{\underset{1}{\cancel{40}}} \quad \text{divided by 40}$$

$$\frac{5}{4} = W_P \quad \text{simplified}$$

We convert $\frac{5}{4}$ to a percent.

$$W_P = \frac{5}{4} \times 100\% = \mathbf{125\%} \quad \text{converted to a percent}$$

Example 5

Sixty is 150 percent of what number?

Solution

Predict Do you think the answer will be greater than or less than 60? Why?

Less than; Sample: If 60 were 100% of the number, the number would be 60. If 60 is 150% of the number, then the number must be less than 60.

We translate by writing 150% as either a decimal or a fraction. We will use the decimal form here.

Sixty is 150% of what number?	question
$60 = 1.5 \times W_N$	equation

We divide both sides of the equation by 1.5.

$$\frac{60}{1.5} = \frac{\overset{1}{\cancel{1.5}} \times W_N}{\underset{1}{\cancel{1.5}}} \quad \text{divided by 40}$$

$$\mathbf{40} = W_N \quad \text{simplified}$$

Practice Set ▸ Generalize Find each percent or quantity in **a–f.**

a. Twenty-four is what percent of 40? 60%

b. What percent of 6 is 2? $33\frac{1}{3}\%$

c. Fifteen percent of what number is 45? 300

▸ See Math Conversations in the sidebar.

Teacher Tip

For a **social studies connection,** tell students that in 2003 the population of China was 1,304,196,000. China was then the most populated country in the world, accounting for about 20.7% of the world's population. Have students use this information to answer this question:

"What was the approximate total world population in 2003?" about 6,300,000,000 or 6.3 billion; official approximation was 6,301,463,000

h. Sample: I could write an equation for the problem and substitute my answer into the equation. If my answer is correct, the equation will be true: $W_P \times 5.00 = 0.35$, $7\% \times 5 = 0.35$; $0.07 \times 5 = .35$, $0.35 = 0.35$.

d. What percent of 4 is 6? 150%

e. Twenty-four is 120% of what number? 20

f. What percent of $5.00 is $0.35? 7%

g. Rework example 5, writing 150% as a fraction instead of as a decimal. Fraction (when reduced) is $\frac{3}{2}$; answer is 40.

▸ h. **Justify** How can you show that your answer to problem **f** is correct?

Written Practice *Strengthening Concepts*

▸ 1. (65) Use a ratio box to solve this problem. Tammy saved nickels and pennies in a jar. The ratio of nickels to pennies was 2 to 5. If there were 70 nickels in the jar, how many coins were there in all? 245 coins

Refer to the line graph below to answer problems **2–4**.

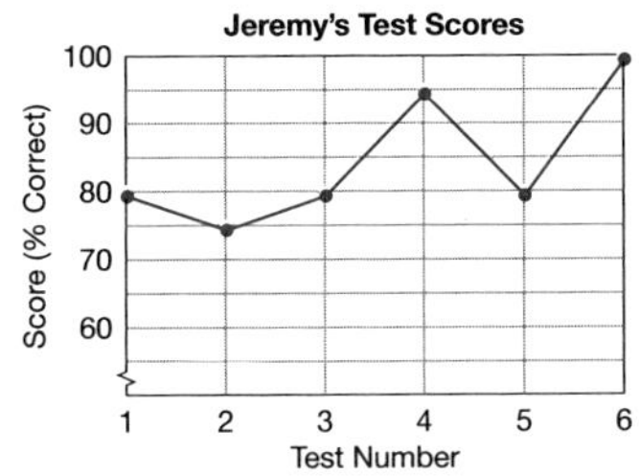

▸ 2. (38, 60) If there were 50 questions on Test 1, how many questions did Jeremy answer correctly? 40 questions

▸ 3. (28, 38) What was Jeremy's average score? (What was the mean of the scores?) 85%

▸ 4. (38, Inv. 5) a. Which score did Jeremy make most often? (What was the mode of the scores?) 80%

b. What was the difference between his highest score and his lowest score? (What was the range of the scores?) 25%

5. (67) Name the shape of each object:

a. a marble sphere

b. a length of pipe cylinder

c. a box of tissues rectangular prism

▸ * 6. (72) **Model** Use a Case 1/Case 2 ratio box to solve this problem. One hundred inches equals 254 centimeters. How many centimeters equals 250 inches? 635 centimeters

▸ See Math Conversations in the sidebar.

2 New Concepts (Continued)

Practice Set

Problem h Justify

Have volunteers read or write on the board reasons why their answers to exercise **f** are correct. Ask other students to think of questions to ask the volunteers so that they can defend their answers. Samples: Reason—I found that 10% of $5 is 50¢, and 35¢ is less than 50¢, so 7% is reasonable. Question—How can you be sure that the answer isn't 6% or 8%?

3 Written Practice

Math Conversations

Discussion opportunities are provided below.

Problems 2–4

Extend the Problem

Help students think about what the various statistics mean.

"Find Jeremy's median score. Why is it lower than his mean score?" Jeremy's median score is 80. The two higher scores raise the mean but do not change which scores are middle scores.

"Can you predict what his next score might be?" Samples: No, because there is no clear pattern. Yes, because he will get a score close to his average.

Be sure to point out that there is no way to predict what the next score will be.

Problem 6 Model

Take some time to review how to model ratio problems using the case 1-case 2 ratio boxes. Have a volunteer go to the board and draw and fill in his or her ratio box. Ask other students to tell how the box models the problem.

Errors and Misconceptions

Problem 1

Some students may record 175 as their answer. These students have found the number of pennies, not the total number of coins.

(continued)

3 Written Practice (Continued)

Math Conversations

Discussion opportunities are provided below.

Problem 7 Model

Guide students to see that the same diagram can be used even though the numbers change.

"What changes do you need to make to your diagram in order to represent the situation in problem 7e?" the total and the number in each box

"Why doesn't anything else change?" Sample: The diagram shows a ratio of 3 to 2 and that didn't change.

Problems 8–11 Formulate

After students have written the equations and solved these problems, discuss how these equations are like other equations.

"Are the equations you write for these problems different from other equations you have used?" no

"Do you work with them just like other equations?" yes

"Can you isolate the variable in these equations? How?" Sample: Yes, you can multiply or divide so that the coefficient of the variable is 1.

Problem 15 Generalize

Lead a discussion to compare parts a and b of this question.

"How are these two problems alike?" Sample: One part of each fraction is a whole number.

"How are they different?" Sample: In part **a**, the whole number is in the denominator, and in part **b**, the whole number is in the numerator.

Problem 16 Analyze

Discuss ways to analyze problems like this one. Ask questions like these:

"You can subdivide the figure in several ways. Why does the figure make sense to use the fewest parts?" Sample: The more parts you use, the more ways you can make a mistake.

"How does knowing the figure is symmetrical help?" Samples: It means that you can fill in measurements for unlabeled parts.

"Why should you start by figuring out all the unknown measurements?" Sample: It is easier to do it all at once, and then you have whatever you need when you are doing the calculations.

(continued)

---

7. 30 people: $\frac{3}{5}$ agreed: 6 people, 6 people, 6 people; $\frac{2}{5}$ disagreed: 6 people, 6 people

▶ * **7.** (36, 71) **Model** Diagram this statement. Then answer the questions that follow.
Three fifths of those present agreed, but the remaining 12 disagreed.

a. What fraction of those present disagreed? $\frac{2}{5}$

b. How many were present? 30

c. How many of those present agreed? 18

d. What was the ratio of those who agreed to those who disagreed? $\frac{3}{2}$

e. If there were 50 people present and 30 people agreed, would the ratio of those who agreed to those who disagreed change? Why or why not? No, because if 30 agreed and 20 disagreed, the ratio is still $\frac{30}{20} = \frac{3}{2}$.

▶ **Formulate** Write equations to solve problems **8–11.**

* **8.** (74) Forty is $\frac{4}{25}$ of what number? $40 = \frac{4}{25} \times W_N$; 250

9. (60) Twenty-four percent of 10,000 is what number? $0.24 \times 10{,}000 = W_N$; 2400

* **10.** (77) Twelve percent of what number is 240? $0.12 \times W_N = 240$; 2000

* **11.** (77) Twenty is what percent of 25? $20 = W_P \times 25$; 80%

* **12.** (73) Simplify:

a. $25(-5)$ −125

b. $-15(-5)$ 75

c. $\frac{-250}{-5}$ 50

d. $\frac{-225}{15}$ −15

13. (48) Complete the table.

Fraction	Decimal	Percent
a. $\frac{1}{5}$	0.2	**b.** 20%
c. $\frac{1}{50}$	**d.** 0.02	2%

14. $22.58; 1. Convert 7.5% to the decimal 0.075. 2. Multiply $21 × 0.075. 3. Add the product (1.575) to $21. 4. Round the sum to the nearest cent.

14. (46) A pair of pants costs $21 plus 7.5% sales tax. What is the total cost of the pants? Summarize how you found your answer.

▶* **15.** (76) **Generalize** Simplify:

a. $\frac{14\frac{2}{7}}{100}$ $\frac{1}{7}$

b. $\frac{60}{\frac{2}{3}}$ 90

▶* **16.** (75) **Analyze** Find the area of this symmetrical figure. Dimensions are in feet. Corners that look square are square. 96 ft²

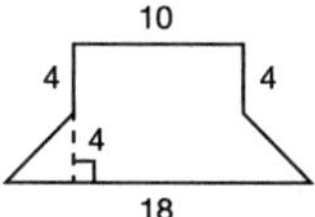

17. (cube: 2 cm, 2 cm, 2 cm)

b. One way to find the surface area of a cube is to find the area of one face of the cube and then multiply that area by 6.

17. (67, 70) Draw a cube with edges 2 cm long.

a. What is the volume of the cube? 8 cm³

b. Describe how to find the surface area of a cube.

▶ See Math Conversations in the sidebar.

English Learners

Demonstrate what **symmetrical** means in problem 16. Fold a piece of paper in half and say:

"If an object is symmetrical, it can be folded in half and both halves will match."

Cut from paper an equilateral triangle, square, rectangle, or regular pentagon. Then ask for volunteers to fold the shape so that there are two equal halves.

18. (51) According to the U.S. Census Bureau, in 2004 the total amount of sales on the Internet was about 69 billion dollars. Write 69 billion in scientific notation. 6.9×10^{10}

19. (65) Find the circumference of each circle:

a. 20π mm **b.** 62.8 mm

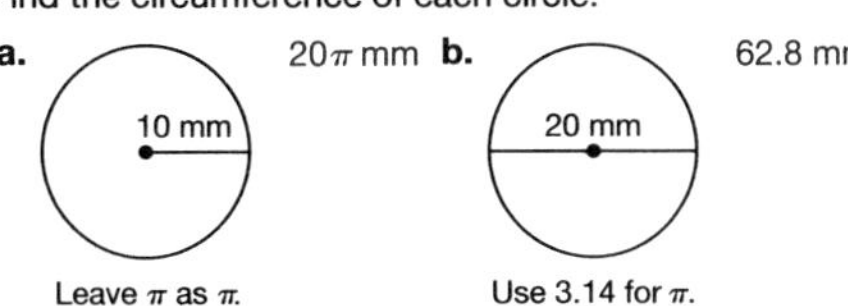

Justify For problems **20–22,** solve and check each equation. Show each step.

▸* **20.** (Inv. 7) $3x = 26.7$ 8.9 ▸ **21.** (Inv. 7) $y - 3\frac{1}{3} = 7$ $10\frac{1}{3}$

▸* **22.** (Inv. 7) $\frac{2}{3}x = 48$ 72

23. (56) Write the rule of the function with words and as an equation. Then find the missing numbers. To find *y*, multiply *x* by 4 and add 1. $y = 4x + 1$

x	*y*
3	13
1	5
2	9
4	17
0	1

Simplify:

▸* **24.** (63) **Generalize** $5^2 - \{2^3 + 3[4^2 - (4)(\sqrt{9})]\}$ 5

25. (49) 4 gal 3 qt 1 pt
+1 gal 2 qt 1 pt
6 gal 2 qt

▸ **26.** (50) $1\text{ ft}^2 \cdot \frac{12\text{ in.}}{1\text{ ft}} \cdot \frac{12\text{ in.}}{1\text{ ft}}$ 144 in.^{2}

27. (26) $5\frac{1}{3} \div \left(1\frac{1}{3} \div 3\right)$ 12

28. (30) $3\frac{1}{5} - 2\frac{1}{2} + 1\frac{1}{4}$ $1\frac{19}{20}$

29. (43) $3\frac{1}{3} \div 2.5$ (mixed-number answer) $1\frac{1}{3}$

30. (68) **a.** $(-3) + (-4) - (+5)$ −12

b. $(-6) - (-16) - (+30)$ −20

Early Finishers
Real-World Application

The Ortiz family had a large celebration dinner. The ages of the people at the dinner were:

1, 10, 10, 12, 16, 31, 35, 40, 65, 75, 90

Find the mean, median, mode, and range of the ages of the people at the dinner. Which best describes the ages of the people at the dinner? Justify your choice. mean: 35, median: 31, mode:10; range: 89; See student work. Sample: The range shows that the ages of the people at the dinner included young children, preteens, younger adults, middle-aged people, and senior citizens.

▸ See Math Conversations in the sidebar.

Looking Forward

Finding the percent of a number prepares students for:

- **Lesson 110,** solving problems involving successive discounts.

3 Written Practice *(Continued)*

Math Conversations

Discussion opportunities are provided below.

Problems 20–22 Justify

For each problem, give students an incorrect answer and ask how you can tell that the answer is wrong. Then have students tell what error may have been made.

Problem 24 Generalize

Have students work through this problem at the board, taking turns writing each step and telling what part of order of operations is used.

Errors and Misconceptions

Problem 20

If students get an answer of 80.1, they possibly multiplied 26.7 by 3 instead of dividing.

Problem 21

If students get an answer of $3\frac{2}{3}$, they possibly subtracted $3\frac{1}{3}$ from 7 instead of adding.

Problem 22

If students get an answer of 142, they possibly subtracted 2 instead of divided by 2 in the last step.

Problem 24

Remind students having difficulties to use the order of operations when simplifying the expression. They must simplify $\sqrt{9}$ before multiplying by 4.

Problem 26

For students who have trouble with canceling the units, point out that ft^2 can be rewritten as ft × ft to help with canceling.

Early Finishers

Ask questions to help students see that we infer different ideas depending on which measure we use to describe the ages of the guests.

"If I said the average age of the dinner guests was 35, what might you assume about the ages of most of the guests?" Sample: They were adults in their 30s and 40s.

"If I said the median age of the dinner guests was 31, what might you assume about the ages of most of the guests?" Sample: They were adults in their 20s, 30s, and 40s whose ages are half above 31 and half below 31.

"If I said the most common age of the dinner guests was 10, what might you assume about the ages of most of the guests?" Sample: They were children from 8 to 12 years old.

• Graphing Inequalities

Objectives

- Read and interpret the symbols ≥ and ≤.
- Graph an inequality on a number line.

Lesson Preparation

Materials

- **Power Up O** (in *Instructional Masters*)
- **Lesson Activity 15 Transparency** (in *Instructional Masters*)

Math Language

New

inequalities

Technology Resources

Student eBook Complete student textbook in electronic format.

Resources and Planner CD Blackline masters, plus a pacing calendar with standards.

Test and Practice Generator CD Create additional practice sheets and custom-made tests.

www.SaxonPublishers.com Visit for more student activities and planning materials.

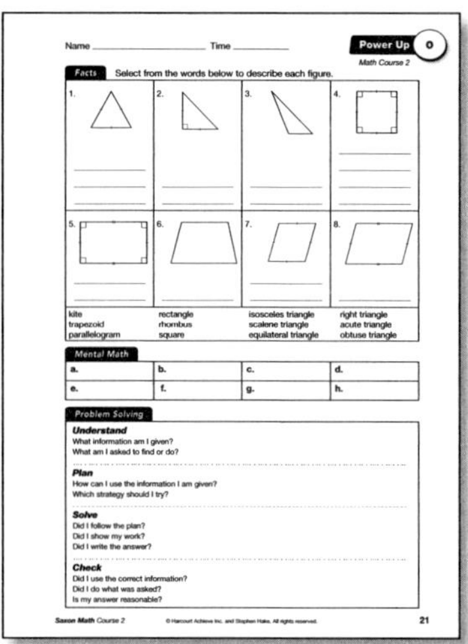

Power Up O

Lesson Activity 15

Inclusion

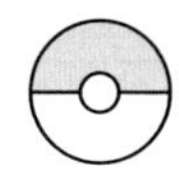

Adaptations CD Adapted lessons, investigations, practice and assessments.

Meeting Standards

National Council of Teachers of Mathematics (NCTM)

Numbers and Operations

NO.1b Compare and order fractions, decimals, and percents efficiently and find their approximate locations on a number line

Algebra

AL.3a Model and solve contextualized problems using various representations, such as graphs, tables, and equations

Communication

CM.3b Communicate their mathematical thinking coherently and clearly to peers, teachers, and others

Representation

RE.5a Create and use representations to organize, record, and communicate mathematical ideas

Power-Up Discussion *For use with Power Up, p. 540*

Problem-Solving Strategy: Make an Organized List

The uniform at WCMS consists of royal blue shirts with khaki pants. A light blue dress shirt and maroon tie is required for Mondays. Libosha has one dress shirt (with tie), three royal blue casual shirts, and three pairs of khaki pants. How many different combinations of the uniform can Libosha wear?

Understand — *Understand the problem.*

"What information are we given?"

Libosha has one light blue dress shirt (with maroon tie), three royal blue casual shirts, and three pairs of khaki pants.

"What are we asked to do?"

Determine how many different combinations of the uniform Libosha has.

Plan — *Make a plan.*

"What problem-solving strategy will we use?"

We will *make an organized list* of the possible combinations

"How can we abbreviate the items of clothing?"

Libosha has four shirts and three pairs of pants. If the shirts are designated A, B, C and D, and the pants 1, 2, and 3, one combination could be written A1.

Solve — *Carry out the plan.*

"What are the possible combinations?"

We begin with combinations containing A, then combinations containing B, and so on:

A1, A2, A3.   B1, B2, B3.   C1, C2, C3.   D1, D2, D3.

"How many different combinations of the uniform can Libosha wear?"

twelve

Check — *Look back.*

"Did we do what we were asked to do?"

Yes, we found that Libosha has twelve combinations of the uniform she can wear and we listed them in abbreviated form.

1 Power Up

Facts

Distribute **Power Up O** to students. See answers below.

Mental Math

Encourage students to share different ways to mentally compute these exercises. Strategies for exercises **d** and **g** are listed below.

d. Double and Halve

10% of \$640 = \$64

$\frac{1}{2}$ of \$64 = \$32

Double and Halve Another Way

5% of \$640 = 10% of \$320 = \$32

g. Average Pairs of Numbers

Average of 95 and 85 is 90

Average of 75 and 65 is 70

Average of 70 and 90 is 80

Find Pairs with Same Average

Average of 95 and 65 is 80

Average of 85 and 75 is 80

Average is 80

Problem Solving

Refer to **Power-Up Discussion,** p. 540B.

2 New Concepts

Instruction

Ask students to draw a number line from −10 to 10. Tell them to graph any number they choose that is equal to or greater than 5 by putting a solid dot at that number on the number line.

Then use a transparency of **Lesson Activity 15** Number Lines or draw on the board to make composite graph of numbers the students have graphed. If no mixed numbers or decimals are given, discuss the possibility of some of these numbers being equal to or greater than 5. Ask:

"How could you represent all the numbers that are equal to or greater than 5?" Put a solid dot at 5 and draw a ray extending to the right of that dot and ending with an arrowhead. On a second number line, repeat the activity for numbers equal to or less than 5.

Write $x \geq 5$ above the first number line and write $x \leq 5$ above the second number line to introduce these algebraic expressions.

(continued)

LESSON 78

• Graphing Inequalities

Power Up *Building Power*

facts Power Up O

mental math

a. **Positive/Negative:** $(-8) - (-16)$ 8

b. **Exponents:** $1^0 + 1^2$ 2

c. **Algebra:** $10p + 3 = 63$ 6

d. **Percent:** 5% of \$640.00 (double, halve) \$32.00

e. **Measurement:** 750 g to kg 0.75 kg

f. **Fractional Parts:** 12 is $\frac{1}{6}$ of m. 72

g. **Statistics:** Find the average of the set of numbers: 95, 85, 75, 65. 80

h. **Estimation:** Estimate a 15% tip on a \$31.49 bill. \$4.50 to \$4.80

problem solving

The uniform at WCMS consists of royal blue shirts with khaki pants. A light blue dress shirt and maroon tie is required for Mondays. Libosha has one dress shirt (with tie), three royal blue casual shirts, and three pairs of khaki pants. How many different combinations of the uniform can Libosha wear? 12

New Concept *Increasing Knowledge*

We have used the symbols >, <, and = to compare two numbers. In this lesson we will introduce the symbols ≥ and ≤. We will also practice graphing on the number line.

The symbols ≥ and ≤ combine the greater than/less than symbols with the equal sign. Thus, the symbol

$$\geq$$

is read, "greater than or equal to." The symbol

$$\leq$$

is read, "less than or equal to."

To graph a number on the number line, we draw a dot at the point that represents the number. Thus when we graph 4 on the number line, it looks like this:

−1 0 1 2 3 4 5 6 7 8 9

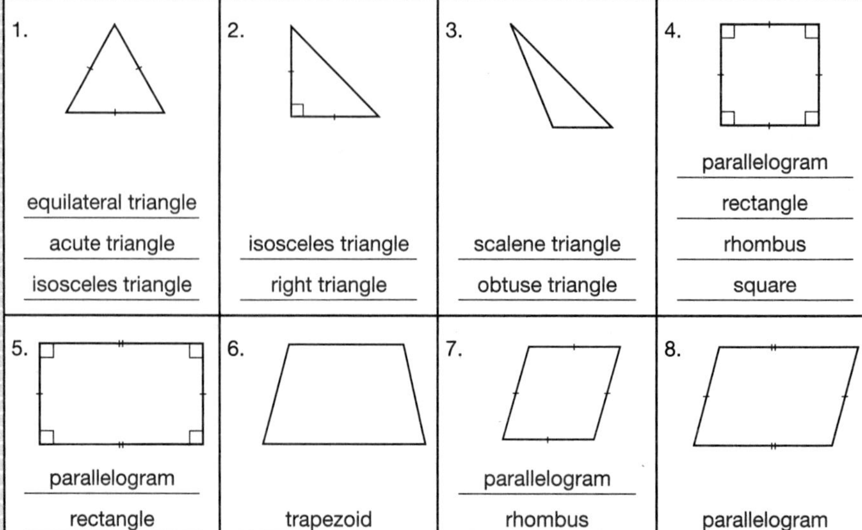

Facts Select from the words below to describe each figure.

1.	2.	3.	4.
equilateral triangle acute triangle isosceles triangle	isosceles triangle right triangle	scalene triangle obtuse triangle	parallelogram rectangle rhombus square
5.	**6.**	**7.**	**8.**
parallelogram rectangle	trapezoid	parallelogram rhombus	parallelogram
kite trapezoid parallelogram	rectangle rhombus square	isosceles triangle scalene triangle equilateral triangle	right triangle acute triangle obtuse triangle

540 *Saxon Math Course 2*

This time we will graph *all the numbers that are greater than or equal to 4.* We might think the graph should look like this:

−1 0 1 2 3 4 5 6 7 8 9

It is true that all the dots mark points that represent numbers greater than or equal to 4. However, we did not graph *all* the numbers that are greater than 4. For instance, we did not graph 10, 11, 12, and so on. Also, we did not graph numbers like $4\frac{1}{2}$, $5\frac{1}{3}$, $\sqrt{29}$, or 2π. If we were to graph all these numbers, the dots would be so close together that we would end up with a ray that goes on and on. Thus we graph all the numbers greater than or equal to 4 like this:

−1 0 1 2 3 4 5 6 7 8 9

The large dot marks the 4. The blue ray marks the numbers greater than 4. The blue arrowhead shows that this ray continues without end.

Expressions such as the following are called **inequalities:**

a $x \leq 4$ **b** $x > 4$

We read **a** as "x is less than or equal to 4." We read **b** as "x is greater than 4."

We can graph inequalities on the number line by graphing all the numbers that make the inequality a true statement.

Thinking Skill

Conclude

Would a graph of the inequality $x \geq 4$ include 3? Why or why not? no; The graph of x is greater than or equal to 4, and 3 is less than 4.

Example 1

Graph on a number line: $x \leq 4$

Solution

We are told to graph all numbers that are less than or equal to 4. We draw a dot at the point that represents 4, and then we shade all the points to the left of the dot. The red arrowhead shows that the shading continues without end.

−2 −1 0 1 2 3 4 5 6 7 8 9 10

Example 2

Graph on a number line: $x > 4$

Solution

We are told to graph all numbers greater than 4 *but not including* 4. We do not start the graph at 5, because we need to graph numbers like $4\frac{1}{2}$ and 4.001. To show that the graph does not include 4, *we draw an empty circle* at 4. Then we shade the portion of the number line to the right of the circle.

−2 −1 0 1 2 3 4 5 6 7 8 9 10

Discuss How would a graph of $x \geq 4$ differ from the graph of $x > 4$?

A graph of $x \geq 4$ would have a solid dot on the 4 to indicate that the graph includes 4.

2 New Concepts *(Continued)*

Instruction

Be sure that students understand the inequality symbols and the differences among them. In examples 1 and 2, they will learn how to differentiate the inequalities when they are graphing them on number lines.

Example 1

Instruction

Have students take turns graphing an inequality on the transparency of **Lesson Activity 15** Number Lines. Use the overhead projector to show the inequality to the class and ask students to identify it. Then ask a student to write the inequality near the graph.

Example 2

Instruction

Continue having students graph inequalities on the transparency of **Lesson Activity 15** Number Lines. After working through this example, take time to check understanding of the use of the dot or empty circle at the point that starts the graph. Also check that students know the difference between using dots to indicate integers and drawing a ray to indicate all numbers.

(continued)

Math Background

Why is knowing about inequalities important to other areas of mathematics?

Understanding inequalities is needed in answering questions where the answer is a range of possibilities, as opposed to a single correct answer. Many situations in the real world deal with inexact number comparisons. It becomes important to differentiate between possible solutions and those that are outside the range of possibility. An inequality is a way to show which numbers are included in the answer and which numbers are excluded. Inequalities can be shown on number lines and on the coordinate plane.

2 New Concepts (Continued)

Practice Set

Problems a–d (Error Alert)

If students have trouble sketching number lines, you may want to provide each student with a copy of the transparency for **Lesson Activity 15** Number Lines for these problems.

Problems c–d (Model)

After students have completed graphing the inequalities, have them compare graphing inequalities with plotting numbers on a number line.

Problem e (Explain)

Have volunteers explain why the empty circle is useful when graphing inequalities on a number line.

3 Written Practice

Math Conversations

Discussion opportunities are provided below.

Problem 1 (Explain)

Explain to students that a good explanation is made up of complete sentences and uses appropriate math language, that each step in the solution process is supported with facts, attributes, or formulas, and that if an answer is given, it is properly labeled.

Ask volunteers to read their explanations, and have other students point out a strength for each explanation.

Problems 9–12 (Formulate)

Check on whether students have mastered translating statements into equations. This example is for problem 9.

"How did you write an equation from this statement?" Sample: I wrote 42 in digits, then for "is" wrote an equals sign; on the other side of the equals sign, I wrote $\frac{7}{10}$ as a fraction, then a multiplication sign for "of" and W_N for "what number".

Repeat for problems 10–12. As students tell how they wrote their equations, encourage them to share their thinking about which words indicate specific math operations.

Errors and Misconceptions

Problem 2

Remind students whose answer is 44 inches that they must consider each month's snowfall amount.

(continued)

Practice Set

a. On a number line, graph all the numbers less than 2. –1 0 1 2 3

b. On a number line, graph all the numbers greater than or equal to 1. 0 1 2 3 4

Model Graph each inequality on a number line:

c. $x \le -1$ –4 –3 –2 –1 0 d. $x > -1$ –2 –1 0 1 2

e. **Explain** What is the difference in meaning between a dot and an empty circle on a number line graph?

e. A dot means the number is included in the graph. An empty circle means the number is excluded.

Written Practice *Strengthening Concepts*

* 1. (72) **Explain** If 4 cartons are needed to pack 30 paperback books, how many cartons are needed to pack 75 paperbacks? (Assume the books are the same size.) Explain how you found your answer. 10 cartons; See student work.

2. (55) In one northern city, the average snowfall after four months was 7 inches. What must the average snowfall be for the next two months in order to have a six-month average of 12 inches? 22 inches

3. (30) If the sum of $\frac{2}{3}$ and $\frac{3}{4}$ is divided by the product of $\frac{2}{3}$ and $\frac{3}{4}$, what is the quotient? $2\frac{5}{6}$

4. (54) Use a ratio box to solve this problem. Two seed types of flowering plants are monocotyledons and dicotyledons. Suppose the ratio of monocotyledons to dicotyledons in the nursery was 3 to 4. If there were 84 dicotyledons in the nursery, how many monocotyledons were there? 63 monocotyledons

5. (65) The diameter of a nickel is 21 millimeters. Find the circumference of a nickel to the nearest millimeter. 66 millimeters

* 6. (78) **Model** Graph each inequality on a separate number line:

a. $x > 2$ 1 2 3 4 5 b. $x \le 1$

6. b. –2 –1 0 1 2

7. (50) Use a unit multiplier to convert 1.5 kg to g. $1.5 \text{ kg} \cdot \frac{1000 \text{ g}}{1 \text{ kg}} = 1500 \text{ g}$

8. (65) Five sixths of the 30 people who participated in the taste test preferred Brand X. The rest preferred Brand Y.

a. How many more people preferred Brand X than preferred Brand Y? 20 more people

b. What was the ratio of the number of people who preferred Brand Y to the number who preferred Brand X? $\frac{1}{5}$

Formulate Write equations to solve problems **9–12**.

* 9. (74) Forty-two is seven tenths of what number? $42 = \frac{7}{10} \times W_N$; 60

* 10. (77) One hundred fifty percent of what number is 600? $1.5 \times W_N = 600$; 400

11. (60) Forty percent of 50 is what number? $0.4 \times 50 = W_N$; 20

▶ See Math Conversations in the sidebar.

Teacher Tip

In problem 4, make a **science connection** with the terms *monocotyledon* (mon-a-kot-l-eed-n) and *dicotyledon* (die-kot-l-eed-n). These are the names of the two major types of flowering plants. Palms, orchids, lilies, rice, corn, wheat, and sugar cane, are examples of monocotyledons. Apple, pear, cherry, peach trees, and roses are examples of dicotyledons.

* **12.** Forty is what percent of 50? $40 = W_P \times 50$; 80%
(77)

13. **a.** Write 1.5×10^{-3} in standard form. 0.0015
(57, 69)

b. Write 25×10^6 in scientific notation. 2.5×10^7

* **14.** Simplify:
(73)

a. $\frac{-4.5}{9}$ −0.5

▶ **b.** $\frac{-2.4}{-0.6}$ 4

c. 15(−20) −300

▶ **d.** −15(−12) 180

15. Complete the table.
(48)

Fraction	Decimal	Percent
a. $\frac{1}{2}$	**b.** 0.5	50%
$\frac{1}{12}$	**c.** $0.08\overline{3}$	**d.** $8\frac{1}{3}$%

* **16.** Simplify: $\frac{83\frac{1}{3}}{100}$ $\frac{5}{6}$
(76)

17.
$A = \frac{1}{2}(b_1 + b_2)h$
$A = \frac{1}{2}$(20 in. + 30 in.) 24 in.
$A = \frac{1}{2}$(50 in.) 24 in.
$A = 600$ in.^{2}

▶* **17.** Estimate On one wall of his room Kwan has a window shaped like a trapezoid with the dimensions shown. Estimate the area of the window in square inches. Show how you used the formula.
(75)

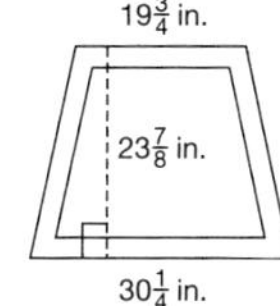

18.
10 cm
12 cm
24 cm

▶ **18.** A box of tissues is 24 cm long, 12 cm wide, and 10 cm tall. Draw the box and find its volume. 2880 cm^3
(70)

▶* **19.** Model Draw the box in problem **18** as if it were cut open and unfolded so that the six faces are lying flat.
(70)

19. one possibility
12
10
12
12
10
24 12

▶ **20.** Write the rule of this function with words and as an equation. Then find the missing number. To find y, multiply x by 5 and subtract 1. $y = 5x - 1$
(56)

Input x	Output y
2	9
3	14
4	19
5	24

21. A merchant sold an item for $18.50. If 30% of the selling price was profit, how much profit did the merchant make on the sale? $5.55
(60)

For problems **22–24,** solve and check each equation. Show each step.

22. $m + 8.7 = 10.25$ 1.55
(Inv. 7)

23. $\frac{4}{3}w = 36$ 27
(Inv. 7)

▶ **24.** $0.7y = 48.3$ 69
(Inv. 7)

▶ See Math Conversations in the sidebar.

3 Written Practice (Continued)

Math Conversations

Discussion opportunities are provided below.

Problem 17 Estimate

Discuss whether estimates varied and why. Ask how students rounded the given numbers. If some students have calculators, have them find the exact answer rounded to the nearest whole number, the difference from their estimate, and the percent difference. Sample: 597 in.^{2}, 3 in.^{2}, 0.5%

Ask volunteers to find the exact area using the fractions given in the drawing and the difference from the estimate of 600 in.^{2}.
$A = (\frac{1}{2})(19\frac{3}{4} + 30\frac{1}{4})(23\frac{7}{8}) = 596\frac{7}{8}$ in.^{2}, $3\frac{1}{8}$ in.^{2}

Problem 19 Model

Have students compare their drawings. Then ask:

"Why isn't there only one way to draw this model?" Sample: There are several ways to cut open and unfold the box.

Problem 20

Extend the Problem

"Will the graph of this function go through the origin?" no

"How do you know?" If you substitute 0 for x and then solve for y, you get $y = -1$. A function has one and only one value of y for each x value, so this function cannot go through (0, 0).

Errors and Misconceptions

Problems 14 b and d

Some students may need to be reminded that when multiplying or dividing two negative numbers, the product or quotient is positive.

Problem 18

If students are having difficulty because they want to draw features of the tissue box such as the dispensing hole, tell them to draw a simple rectangular prism. For the purposes of this problem, such details are unnecessary.

Problem 24

Watch for students who get 0.69 as their answer. This may mean they are confused about placing the decimal point. Review with students how to divide with decimals.

(continued)

3 Written Practice (Continued)

Math Conversations

Discussion opportunities are provided below.

Problem 25 Generalize

Have students explain where they began simplifying this expression. Sample: $\sqrt{4}$

Then ask whether the parentheses are grouping symbols or indicators of multiplication. multiplication

Emphasize the importance of understanding what the various symbols mean.

Errors and Misconceptions

Problem 26

Remind students who get 4 as an answer that the absolute value symbols are symbols of inclusion just like parentheses and braces.

Simplify:

▶* **25.** (63) Generalize $\{4^2 + 10[2^3 - (3)(\sqrt{4})]\} - \sqrt{36}$ 30

▶ **26.** (59) $|5 - 3| - |3 - 5|$ 0

27. (50) $1\text{ m}^2 \cdot \frac{100\text{ cm}}{1\text{ m}} \cdot \frac{100\text{ cm}}{1\text{ m}}$ 10,000 cm²

28. (26) $7\frac{1}{2} \cdot 3 \cdot \left(\frac{2}{3}\right)^2$ 10

29. (30) $3\frac{1}{5} - \left(2\frac{1}{2} - 1\frac{1}{4}\right)$ $1\frac{19}{20}$

30. (68) **a.** $(-10) - (-8) - (+6)$ −8

b. $\left(-\frac{1}{5}\right) + \left(-\frac{2}{5}\right) - \left(-\frac{3}{5}\right)$ 0

Early Finishers
Real-World Application

The Mendoza family needs to buy new carpet for their family room. The diagram below shows the dimensions of the family room.

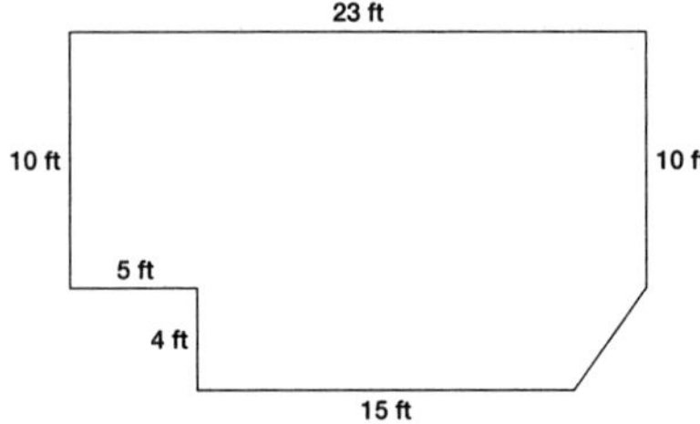

a. Calculate the area of this room. 296 ft²

b. If the Mendozas choose a carpet that costs $2.95 per square foot, how much will it cost them to carpet their family room? $873.20

▶ See Math Conversations in the sidebar.

Looking Forward

Graphing inequalities on a number line prepares students for:

- **Lesson 93,** graphing two-step equations and inequalities.

• Estimating Areas

Objectives

- Estimate areas using grid systems.

Lesson Preparation

Materials

- **Power Up P** (in *Instructional Masters*)
- **Investigation Activity 25** (in *Instructional Masters*) or **grid paper**

Optional

- **Teacher-provided material: centimeter and inch grid paper**

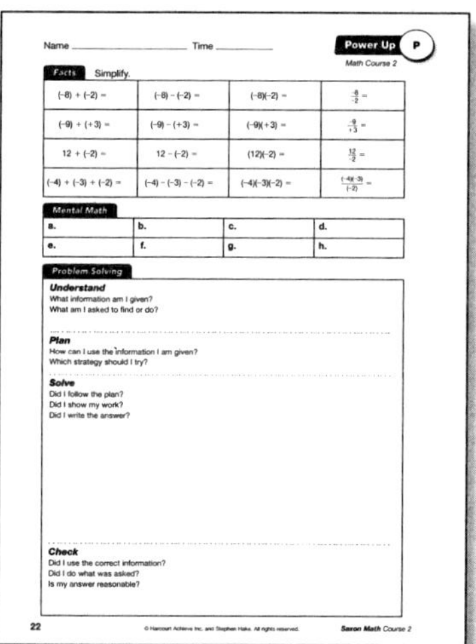
Power Up P
Facts Simplify.
Mental Math
Problem Solving
Understand
Plan
Solve
Check

Power Up P

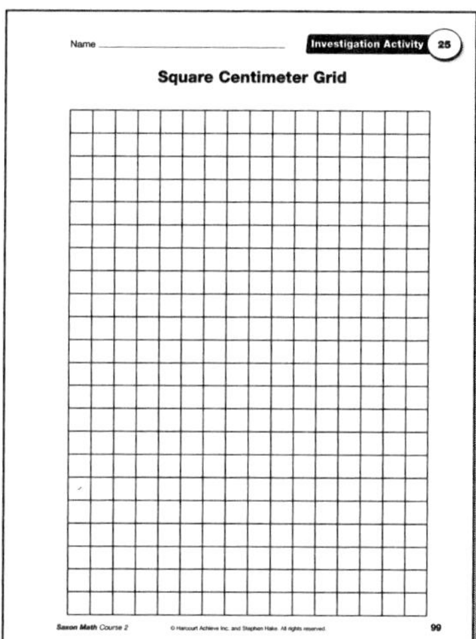
Investigation Activity 25
Square Centimeter Grid

Investigation Activity 25

Technology Resources

Student eBook Complete student textbook in electronic format.

Resources and Planner CD Blackline masters, plus a pacing calendar with standards.

Test and Practice Generator CD Create additional practice sheets and custom-made tests.

www.SaxonPublishers.com Visit for more student activities and planning materials.

Inclusion

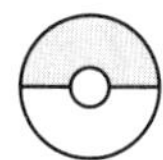

Adaptations CD Adapted lessons, investigations, practice and assessments.

Meeting Standards

National Council of Teachers of Mathematics (NCTM)

Numbers and Operations

NO.3c Develop and use strategies to estimate the results of rational-number computations and judge the reasonableness of the results

Measurement

ME.1c Understand, select, and use units of appropriate size and type to measure angles, perimeter, area, surface area, and volume

Problem Solving

PS.1b Solve problems that arise in mathematics and in other contexts

PS.1c Apply and adapt a variety of appropriate strategies to solve problems

Power-Up Discussion *For use with Power Up, p. 545*

Problem-Solving Strategy: Use Logical Reasoning/ Write an Equation

A 6-by-6 square of grid paper, ruled on the front and un-ruled on the back, is folded in half diagonally to form an isosceles right triangle. Then part of the paper is folded back as shown in the diagram. What is the area of the un-ruled part of the diagram?

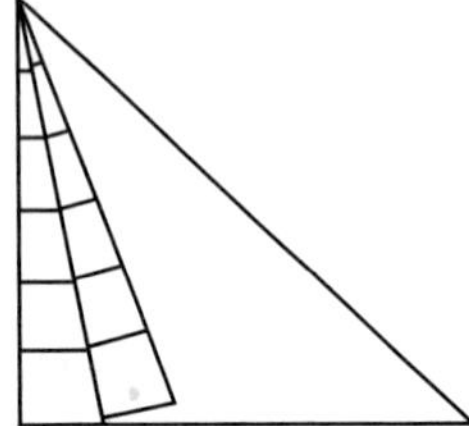

Understand ***Understand the problem.***

"What information are we given?"

We are given the illustration and description of an area formed from a folded 6-by-6 square grid.

"What are we asked to do?"

We are asked to find the area of the un-ruled portion of the illustration.

Plan ***Make a plan.***

"How should we approach the problem?"

If we *use logical reasoning,* we see that we can subtract from the area of the original triangle the area of the parts that are ruled.

"How can we find the area, if numbers or units are not given?"

We can count the squares on the grid and state the area in square units.

Solve ***Carry out the plan.***

"What is the area of the original triangle?"

The original triangle is a right triangle with a base and height of 6 units each, so the area of the triangle is $\frac{1}{2}(6 \times 6)$, which is 18 square units.

"What is the area of the folded-back triangle?"

The folded back triangle is a right triangle with a base and height of 1 unit and 6 units, so the area is $\frac{1}{2}(1 \times 6)$, which is 3 square units.

"How do we find the area of the un-ruled part of the figure?"

As we look at the figure we see two 1-by-6 triangles with grids. We should subtract both of these areas from the original triangle.

"What is the area of the un-ruled part of the figure?"

Area = area of original triangle − the area of two 1-by-6 triangles
$A = 18 - 2(3)$
$A = 12$
The un-ruled area is 12 square units.

Check ***Look back.***

"Did we do what we were asked to do?"

Yes, we found the area of the un-ruled part of the figure.

LESSON 79

Estimating Areas

Power Up

Building Power

facts Power Up P

mental math

a. **Positive/Negative:** $(-25) + (-15)$ −40

b. **Decimals/Exponents:** 3.75×10^3 3750

c. **Ratio:** $\frac{c}{100} = \frac{25}{10}$ 250

d. **Estimation:** Estimate 15% of $11.95. $1.80

e. **Measurement:** 1200 mL to L 1.2 L

f. **Fractional Parts:** 20 is $\frac{4}{5}$ of n. 25

g. **Statistics:** Find the average of the set of numbers: 60, 70, 80, 90, 100. 80

h. **Calculation:** Square 5, × 2, − 1, √, × 8, − 1, ÷ 5, × 3, − 1, ÷ 4, × 9, + 3, ÷ 3 25

problem solving A 6-by-6 square of grid paper, ruled on the front and un-ruled on the back, is folded in half diagonally to form an isosceles right triangle. Then part of the paper is folded back as shown in the diagram. What is the area of the un-ruled part of the diagram? 12 sq. units

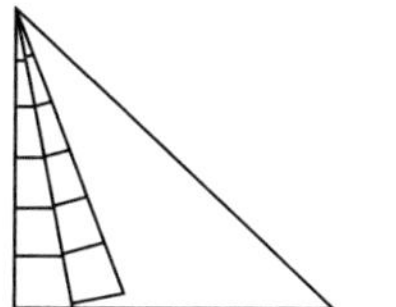

New Concept

Increasing Knowledge

Thinking Skill
Analyze
What do the dots on some of the squares mean? The squares are counted as "half" squares.

As Tucker balanced one foot on the scale he wondered how many pounds per square inch the scale was supporting. Tucker traced the outline of his shoe on a one-inch square grid and counted squares to estimate the area of his shoe. Here is a reduced image of the inch grid. Can you estimate the area of Tucker's shoe print?

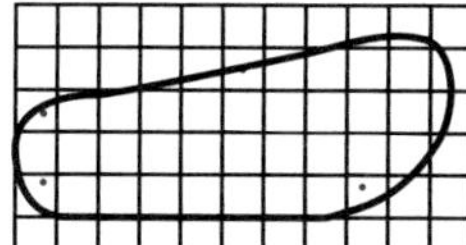

To estimate the area of the shoe print Tucker counted the complete or nearly complete squares within the shoe's outline as whole squares. Then he counted the squares that were about half within the outline as half squares. He counted 30 full or nearly full squares and four "half" squares.

Facts Simplify.

(−8) + (−2) = −10	(−8) − (−2) = −6	(−8)(−2) = 16	$\frac{-8}{-2} = 4$
(−9) + (+3) = −6	(−9) − (+3) = −12	(−9)(+3) = −27	$\frac{-9}{+3} = -3$
12 + (−2) = 10	12 − (−2) = 14	(12)(−2) = −24	$\frac{12}{-2} = -6$
(−4) + (−3) + (−2) = −9	(−4) − (−3) − (−2) = 1	(−4)(−3)(−2) = −24	$\frac{(-4)(-3)}{(-2)} = -6$

1 Power Up

Facts

Distribute **Power Up P** to students. See answers below.

Mental Math

Encourage students to share different ways to mentally compute these exercises. Strategies for exercises **c** and **d** are listed below.

c. Cross Multiply and Divide

$10c = 25 \times 100$

$c = 25 \times 10 = 250$

Find Equivalent Fraction

$\frac{25}{10} = \frac{250}{100}$

$c = 250$

d. 10% + 5%

$11.95 ~ $12

10% of $12 = $1.20

5% of $12 = $0.60

15% of $12 = $1.80

$\frac{1}{2}$ of 30%

$11.95 ~ $12

10% of $12 = $1.20

30% of $12 = $3.60

15% of $12 = $\frac{\$3.60}{2}$ = $1.80

Problem Solving

Refer to **Power-Up Discussion,** p. 545B.

2 New Concepts

Instruction

Draw a parallelogram on the board, labeling the base 10 cm and the height 8 cm. Ask a volunteer to review how to find the area of the parallelogram. Multiply the base by the height; 80 cm^2.

Then, draw a large handprint on the board. Ask students if we can find the area in the same way. Elicit that we can't, and that we must estimate it somehow. Explain that in this lesson, we will be learning a method for estimating area.

Explain to students that squares that are very nearly complete may be counted as whole squares, while squares that are almost entirely outside the shape may be left out of the estimate.

Ask students how to determine the area of 4 half squares. 4 groups of $\frac{1}{2}$ can be represented as $4 \times \frac{1}{2} = 2$, so they are equal to 2 wholes.

(continued)

2 New Concepts *(Continued)*

Instruction

Discuss whether Tucker's estimate is greater than or less than the actual area. Because there are several squares containing small parts of the figure that were not counted, it is likely that the estimate is low.

Ask whether using a smaller grid would give a better estimate. Yes, but it would take more time to count the squares, and keeping track of them would be more difficult.

Example

Instruction

Ask students if they can think of a way to use the symmetry of the circle to make counting the squares easier. Count the squares in a quarter-circle and multiply by 4.

If you want to provide a little more practice with this technique, ask students to use guess and check to find the size of castors needed so that the floor would be supporting 3 pounds per square inch. They would check by drawing a circle the size of their guess on a grid, counting the squares, and redoing the calculation. Castors with an 8-inch diameter are needed.

(continued)

Activity

Instruction

You may want to have some students use centimeter grid paper and others use inch grid paper. When students have finished the activity, have a class discussion to compare the areas of students' hands.

Tucker estimated that the area of his shoe print was 32 square inches. Tucker weighs 116 pounds, so he divided his weight by 32 in.^{2} and found that his weight was distributed to about $3\frac{1}{2}$ pounds per square inch.

$$\frac{116 \text{ lbs}}{33 \text{ in.}^2} \approx 3.52 \text{ lbs per in.}^2$$

Discuss Would the number of pounds per square inch on each foot be greater or less than 3.52 if Tucker stood on two feet? Explain. It would be less. The same weight would be distributed over a greater area.

Example

To prevent a 500 pound piano from damaging the floor, the owner put 6-inch diameter circular castors under the three legs of the piano. Use Tucker's method to estimate the area of each castor. Then find the pounds per square inch the floor supports.

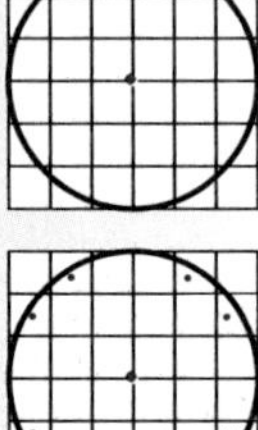

Solution

We count 24 whole or nearly whole squares. The "half squares" we mark with dots. There are 8 "half squares" that we count as 4 full squares. We estimate the total area of each castor as **28 square inches.**

There are three castors so their total area is about **84 in.^{2}.** The weight of the piano is distributed over the area of the three castors, so we divide the 500 lbs weight by 84 in.^{2} to find the pounds per square inch.

$$\frac{500 \text{ lbs}}{84 \text{ in.}^2} \approx \mathbf{6 \text{ lbs per in.}^2}$$

Infer The number of pounds per square inch may not be the same on each castor. Why is this true? The weight of the piano may not be evenly distributed over each of the three legs.

Activity

Estimating the Area of Your Handprint

Materials needed:

- Investigation Activity 25 or square centimeter grid paper

Step 1: Trace the outline of one hand with fingers together onto the grid paper.

Step 2: Then count squares to estimate the area of your handprint.

Math Background

What are some other techniques for finding the area of irregular figures?

The simplest way to find the area of an irregular figure is to use a grid system to break the irregular shape into simple squares. These squares are representative of the square units we use when measuring area. Unlike the calculations used to determine the area of a simple triangle or parallelogram, this method of estimation is a direct count of the square units in the shape.

Other techniques include breaking an irregular figure into various sized rectangles and finding the sum of the areas. For figures that are not easily divided into squares or rectangles, other shapes with easily determined areas, such as triangles, trapezoids, parallelograms, and hexagons, can be used in a similar manner. A weighing technique has also been used to determine area.

Practice Set ▶ **Estimate** Use figures A or B to estimate each area.

a. Figure A shows a map with a square kilometer grid and the outline of a lake. Estimate the area of the lake.
12 or 13 sq km

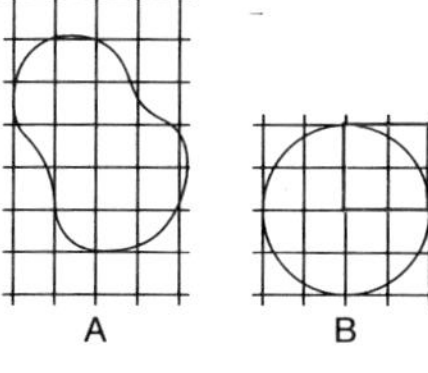

b. Figure B shows a square with sides 2 cm long and a circle with a radius of 2 cm. Estimate the area of the circle. The area of the circle is about how many times the area of the square? 13 cm^2, 3 times

Written Practice
Strengthening Concepts

1. (55) Students were grouped into 4 classrooms with an average of 33.5 students per classroom. If the students were regrouped into 5 classrooms, what would be the average number of students in each room? 26.8 students

2. (46) Nelda drove 315 kilometers and used 35 liters of gasoline. Her car averaged how many kilometers per liter of gas? $9\frac{\text{kilometers}}{\text{liter}}$

3. (66) The ratio of young people to adults at a contest was 7 to 5. If the total number of young people and adults was 1260, how many more young people were there than adults? 210 more young people

4. (69) Write each number in scientific notation:

a. 37.5×10^{-6} 3.75×10^{-5} **b.** 37.5×10^{6} 3.75×10^{7}

▶ *** 5.** (79) **Analyze** A circle with a radius of one inch has an area of about how many square inches? About 3 in.^{2}

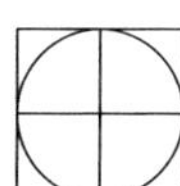

*** 6.** (78) **Model** Graph each inequality on a separate number line:

a. $x < 1$ −2 −1 0 1 2 **b.** $x \geq -1$ −2 −1 0 1 2

*** 7.** (72) Use a case 1–case 2 ratio box to solve this problem. Four inches of snow fell in 3 hours. At that rate, how long would it take for 1 foot of snow to fall? 9 hours

8. (71) Diagram this statement. Then answer the questions that follow.

Twelve students in the school play were dancers. This was $\frac{3}{8}$ of all the students in the play.

a. How many students did not dance in the play? 20 students

b. What percent of the students did not dance in the play? $62\frac{1}{2}\%$

8.
32 students
$\frac{3}{8}$ were dancers. — 4 students, 4 students, 4 students
$\frac{5}{8}$ did not dance. — 4 students, 4 students, 4 students, 4 students, 4 students

▶ See Math Conversations in the sidebar.

2 New Concepts (Continued)

Practice Set
Problems a and b Estimate

Encourage students to check their estimates by finding the area of the entire grid and subtracting the squares not contained in the outline.

3 Written Practice

Math Conversations

Discussion opportunities are provided below.

Problem 5 Analyze

After determining that the answer is about 3 in.^{2}, discuss with students whether the actual area is greater than or less than 3 in.^{2}. Have them refer to the diagram to support their answers. Sample: It is greater than 3 in.^{2}, because more than three-fourths of each of the 4 small squares is included in the circle.

(continued)

3 Written Practice (Continued)

Math Conversations

Discussion opportunities are provided below.

Problems 9–12 Formulate

Have some students read their equations. Then ask:

"Why does writing an equation make it easier to solve these problems?" Sample: It is easier to see what to do.

Continue by asking whether anyone solved any of the equations mentally, and if so, which one and how.

Problem 17 Analyze

Provide more experience in using geometric thinking to analyze problems. Have students work together to answer this question and then discuss what methods students used to find the answers.

"Suppose that a triangle of the same size was cut off the opposite corner. What would be the answers to parts a, b, and c?" a. hexagon, b. 36 in., c. 88 in.^{2}

Problem 18

Extend the Problem

"Suppose that this block was painted red on all six sides and then cut up into cubes with 1 centimeter edges." "How many cubes would there be?" 72

"How many cubes would have no paint on them?" 8

"How many cubes would have paint on only one side?" 28

You may also ask students to find the number of cubes with paint on 2 sides and the number of cubes with paint on 3 sides. 2 sides: 28, 3 sides: 8

Errors and Misconceptions

Problem 9

Suggest that students consider the range of reasonable answers for this problem. Since 35 is 100% of 35, a reasonable answer would be a number greater than 35.

Problem 17

If students were unable to start work on the problem because they did not know how to start, ask them how to find the length of one side of a square with an area of 100 square inches. They may also need help in recognizing that the cutoff corner is a right triangle with perpendicular sides of 3 inches and 4 inches.

(continued

▸ **Formulate** Write equations to solve problems **9–12**.

* **9.** (77) Thirty-five is 70% of what number? $35 = 0.7 \times W_N$; 50

* **10.** (77) What percent of 20 is 17? $W_P \times 20 = 17$; 85%

* **11.** (77) What percent of 20 is 25? $W_P \times 20 = 25$; 125%

* **12.** (77) Three hundred sixty is 75 percent of what number? $360 = \frac{3}{4} \times W_N$; 480

13. (73) Simplify:

a. $\frac{1.44}{-8}$ −0.18 **b.** $\frac{-14.4}{+6}$ −2.4

c. −12(1.2) −14.4 **d.** −1.6(−9) 14.4

14. (48) Complete the table.

Fraction	Decimal	Percent
$\frac{1}{25}$	**a.** 0.04	**b.** 4%
c. $\frac{2}{25}$	**d.** 0.08	8%

15. (60) At the Stanford Used Car Dealership, a salesperson is paid a commission of 5% of the sale price for every car he or she sells. If a salesperson sells a car for $13,500, how much would he or she be paid as a commission? $675.00

* **16.** (76) Simplify: $\frac{62\frac{1}{2}}{100}$ $\frac{5}{8}$

▸* **17.** (75) **Analyze** A square sheet of paper with an area of 100 in.^{2} has a corner cut off, as shown in the figure below.

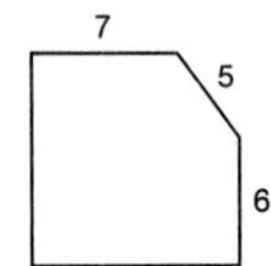

a. What is the name for this geometric figure? pentagon

b. What is the perimeter of the figure? 38 in.

c. What is the area of the figure? 94 in.^{2}

▸ **18.** (67, 70) In the figure at right, each small cube has a volume of 1 cubic centimeter.

a. What is the volume of this rectangular prism? 72 cm^3

b. What is the total surface area of the rectangular prism? 108 cm^2

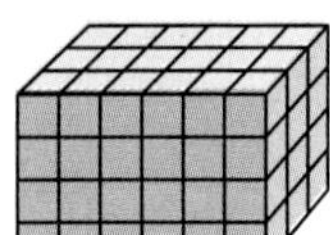

▸ See Math Conversations in the sidebar.

19. Find the circumference of each circle:
(65)

a. 3.14 m

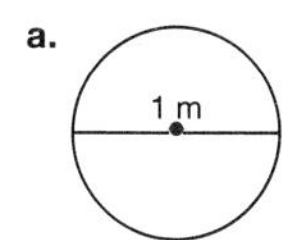

Use 3.14 for π.

b. π m

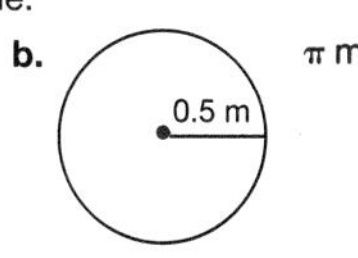

Leave π as π.

20. Classify each triangle as acute, right, or obtuse. Then classify each triangle as equilateral, isosceles, or scalene.
(62)

a. 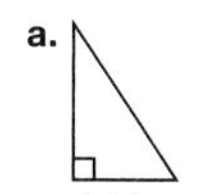 right; scalene

b. obtuse; isosceles

c. acute; equilateral

21. Which type of triangle has rotational symmetry? equilateral triangle
(58)

▶ *Justify* For problems **22–23**, solve and check each equation. Show each step.

* 22. $1.2x = 2.88$ 2.4
(Inv. 7)

* 23. $\frac{3}{2}w = \frac{9}{10}$ $\frac{3}{5}$
(Inv. 7)

Simplify:

▶* 24. **Generalize** $\frac{\sqrt{100} + 5[3^3 - 2(3^2 + 3)]}{5}$ 5
(63)

25. 3 hr 15 min 24 s − 2 hr 45 min 30 s = 29 min 54 s
(49)

26. $1 \text{ yd}^2 \cdot \frac{3 \text{ ft}}{1 \text{ yd}} \cdot \frac{3 \text{ ft}}{1 \text{ yd}}$ 9 ft²
(50)

27. $7\frac{1}{2} \cdot \left(3 \div \frac{5}{9}\right)$ $40\frac{1}{2}$
(26)

28. $4\frac{5}{6} + 3\frac{1}{3} + 7\frac{1}{4}$ $15\frac{5}{12}$
(30)

29. $3\frac{3}{4} \div 1.5$ (decimal answer) 2.5
(35, 43)

▶* 30. **Generalize**
(68)

a. $-0.1 - (-0.2) - (0.3)$ −0.2

b. $(-10) - |(-20) - (+30)|$ −60

Early Finishers
Real-World Application

Six houses in one community recently sold for these prices.

$130,000, $150,000, $120,000, $130,000, $210,000, $160,000

Use the mean, median, mode, and range to describe the selling prices. Which measure best describes the price of a typical house in this community? Justify your choice. mean $150,000; median $140,000; mode $130,000; range $90,000; Samples: The median gives the best description because half the houses sell for more and half sell for less. The median is closer to the price of most of the houses.

▶ See Math Conversations in the sidebar.

3 Written Practice (Continued)

Math Conversations

Discussion opportunities are provided below.

Problems 22 and 23 Justify

Ask volunteers to tell what steps they used to solve these equations and to give their answers. Ask other students to check those answers. Have the class agree on solutions to both equations.

Problem 24 Generalize

"Suppose you knew that the answer to problem 24 was 5. How could you find the value of the expression in the numerator without calculating it?" Sample: Multiply the denominator by 5.

"Suppose you knew the value of a simplified fraction was 10, and that its denominator was 6. How could you find the value of the expression in the numerator without calculating it?" Sample: Multiply the denominator by 10.

Problem 30 Generalize

Have students think about how grouping symbols affect the process of simplifying expressions.

"In the expression for part a, suppose that the parentheses were replaced by absolute value bars. What value would the simplified expression have?" −0.6

"To simplify the expression in part b, what term must be simplified first? Why?" Sample: You have to find the value of the expression inside the absolute value bars before finding the absolute value because if you find the absolute values of the two parts of the expression first, you get −10 instead of −50.

Errors and Misconceptions

Problem 24

To help students who struggled with this problem, remind them to pay close attention to the order of operations. Review *Please Excuse My Dear Aunt Sally* with them.

Looking Forward

Estimating area prepares students for:

- **Lesson 82,** finding the area of a circle.
- **Lesson 105,** finding the surface area of a right solid and a sphere.
- **Investigation 11,** using the scale factor in surface area and volume.
- **Lesson 113,** finding the volume of pyramids, cones, and spheres.

• Transformations

Objectives

- Draw a figure and its image reflected along a given line.
- Draw a figure and its image after a translation.
- Draw a figure and its image after a rotation.

Lesson Preparation

Materials

- **Power Up O** (in *Instructional Masters*)
- **Investigation Activity 13** (in *Instructional Masters*) or **graph paper**
- **Lesson Activity 19** (in *Instructional Masters*)
- **Teacher-provided material: cut-outs of triangle I** in the "New Concept" section of this lesson (which are easily made from index cards), **transparency film**

Optional

- **Teacher-provided material: mirrors or reflective devices**

Math Language

New	Maintain	English Learners (ESL)
reflection	coordinate plane	clockwise
rotation		counterclockwise
transformation		
translation		

Technology Resources

Student eBook Complete student textbook in electronic format.

Resources and Planner CD Blackline masters, plus a pacing calendar with standards.

Test and Practice Generator CD Create additional practice sheets and custom-made tests.

www.SaxonPublishers.com Visit for more student activities and planning materials.

Inclusion

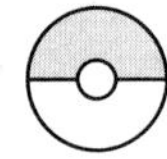

Adaptations CD Adapted lessons, investigations, practice and assessments.

Power Up O

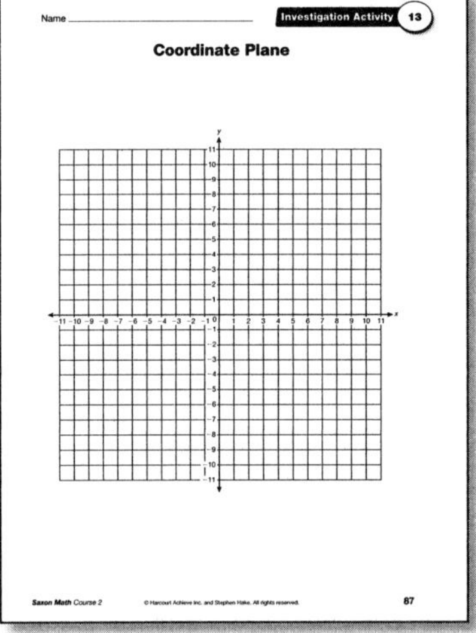

Name ____________ Investigation Activity 13

Coordinate Plane

Investigation Activity 13

Meeting Standards

National Council of Teachers of Mathematics (NCTM)

Geometry

GM.2a Use coordinate geometry to represent and examine the properties of geometric shapes

GM.3a Describe sizes, positions, and orientations of shapes under informal transformations such as flips, turns, slides, and scaling

GM.3b Examine the congruence, similarity, and line or rotational symmetry of objects using transformations

Power-Up Discussion *For use with Power Up, p. 550*

Problem-Solving Strategy: Use Logical Reasoning/ Draw a Diagram

Here are the front, top, and side views of an object. If this structure was constructed using 1-inch cubes, what would be the object's volume? Sketch a three-dimensional view of the structure.

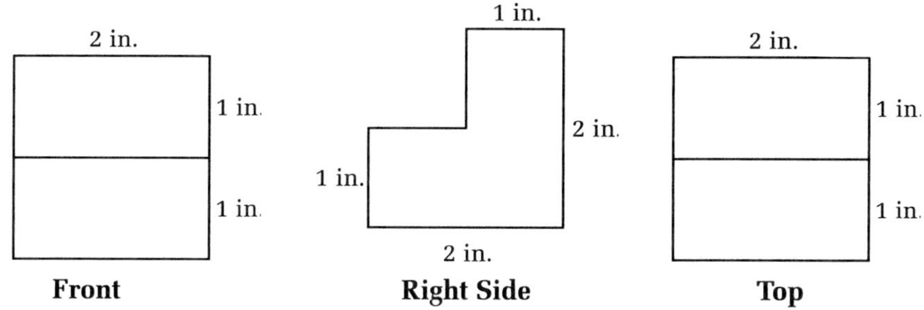

Understand ***Understand the problem.***

"What information are we given?"

We are shown the front, right side, and top views of an object.

"What are we asked to do?"

We are asked to sketch a three-dimensional view of the object, then find its volume.

Plan ***Make a plan.***

"What problem-solving strategy will we use?"

We will *use logical reasoning* to determine how many 1-inch cubes would be needed to build the structure and to *draw a diagram* of the object.

"What do we anticipate our answer to be in the range of?"

A solid cube measuring 2 in. × 2 in. × 2 in. has a volume of 8 cubic inches, so the volume of this structure should be less than that.

Solve ***Carry out the plan.***

"How many blocks would make up the bottom layer?"

four

"How many blocks would make up the top layer?"

two

"What is the volume of the structure?"

six cubic inches

"Can you describe and sketch the structure?"

It looks like a block 'L' shape that is as wide as it is tall.

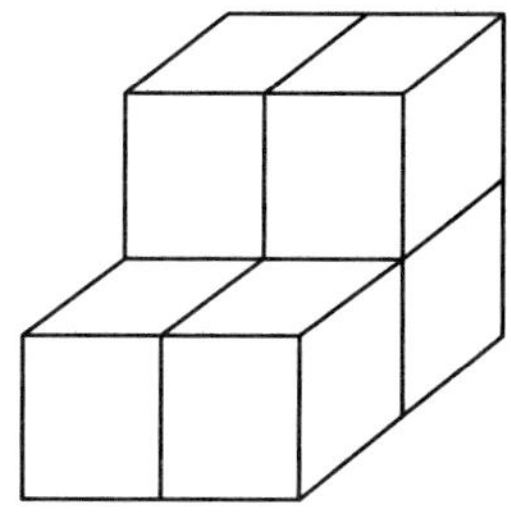

Check ***Look Back***

"Did we do what we were asked to do?"

Yes, we sketched a three-dimensional view of the object and found its volume in cubic inches.

1 Power Up

Facts

Distribute **Power Up O** to students. See answers below.

Mental Math

Encourage students to share different ways to mentally compute these exercises. Strategies for exercises **b** and **f** are listed below.

b. Decompose

$40^2 = (4 \times 10)^2 = 4^2 \times 10^2 =$
$16 \times 100 = 1600$

Use Factors

$40^2 = 40 \times 40 = 4 \times 10 \times 4 \times 10 =$
$4 \times 4 \times 10 \times 10 = 16 \times 100 = 1600$

f. Multiply Fractions

$\frac{3}{5} \times \frac{15}{1} = \frac{3}{1} \times \frac{3}{1} = 3 \times 3 = 9$

Use Unit Fractions

$\frac{1}{5}$ of $15 = 3$
$\frac{3}{5}$ of $15 = 9$

Problem Solving

Refer to **Power-Up Discussion,** p. 550B.

2 New Concepts

Instruction

Introduce this lesson by having students place their math book in position A, facedown on their desks, and then move it so it is face up in position B.

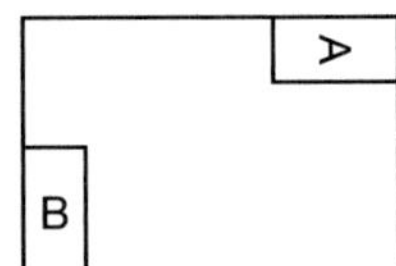

Ask students to repeat the movement slowly until they can identify three parts to the move: a *slide*, a *turn*, and a *flip*.

Provide each student with a cutout scalene right triangle congruent to the triangle shown on this page. An easy way to make them is to cut corners from index cards. Have students place their triangles on top of triangle I. Then ask them to move the triangle so that it fits exactly over triangle II, using as few moves as possible. Have volunteers describe the moves they made. Point out that the three moves can be made in any order.

(continued)

LESSON 80

• Transformations

Power Up *Building Power*

facts Power Up O

mental math

a. **Positive/Negative:** $(-30) - (+45)$ -75

b. **Exponents:** 40^2 1600

c. **Algebra:** $5q - 4 = 36$ 8

d. **Fractional Parts:** 15 is $\frac{3}{5}$ of n. 25

e. **Measurement:** 1500 m to km 1.5 km

f. **Fractional Parts:** What is $\frac{3}{5}$ of 15? 9

g. **Statistics:** Find the average of the set of numbers: 50, 60, 70. 60

h. **Geometry:** Find the perimeter and area of a square with sides 1.5 m long. 6 m; 2.25 m^2

problem solving

Here are the front, top, and side views of an object. If this structure was constructed using 1-inch cubes, what would be the object's volume? Sketch a three-dimensional view of the structure.

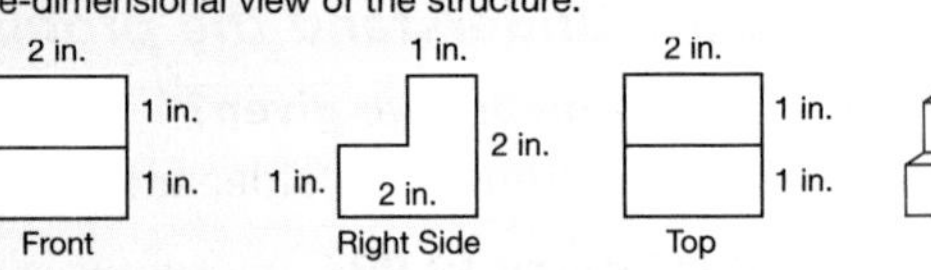

New Concept *Increasing Knowledge*

Recall that two figures are congruent if they are the same shape and size. Triangles I and II below are congruent, but they are not in the same position:

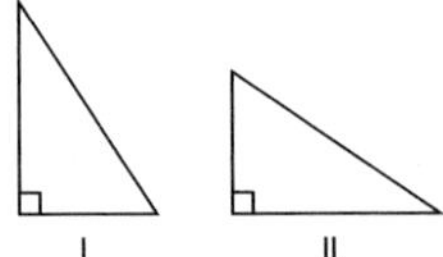

We can use three types of position change to move triangle I to the position of triangle II. One change of position is to "flip" triangle I over as though flipping a piece of paper, as shown on the following page.

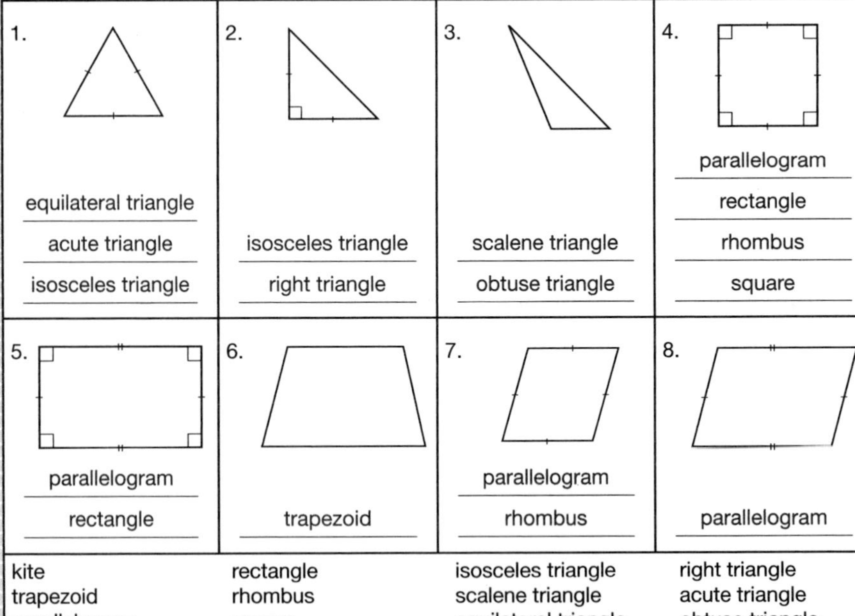

Facts Select from the words below to describe each figure.

1.	2.	3.	4.
equilateral triangle acute triangle isosceles triangle	isosceles triangle right triangle	scalene triangle obtuse triangle	parallelogram rectangle rhombus square
5.	**6.**	**7.**	**8.**
parallelogram rectangle	trapezoid	parallelogram rhombus	parallelogram
kite trapezoid parallelogram	rectangle rhombus square	isosceles triangle scalene triangle equilateral triangle	right triangle acute triangle obtuse triangle

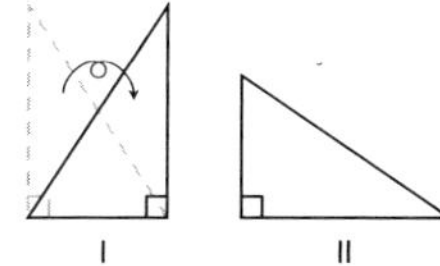

A second change of position is to "slide" triangle I to the right.

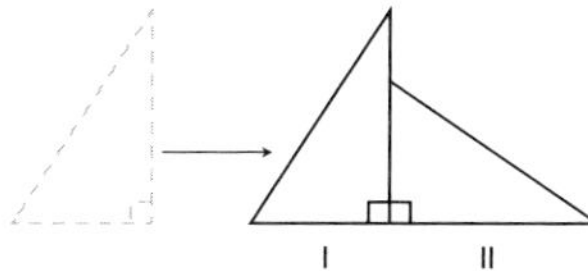

The third change of position is to "turn" triangle I 90° clockwise.

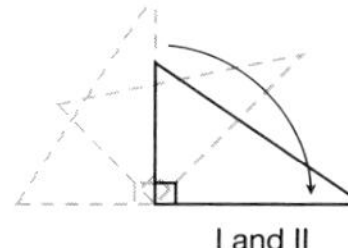

These "flips, slides, and turns" are called **transformations** and have special names, which are listed in this table.

Transformations

Movement	Name
flip	reflection
slide	transalation
turn	rotation

Math Language
A **coordinate plane** is a grid on which any point can be identified by an ordered pair of numbers.

A **reflection** of a figure in a line (a "flip") produces a mirror image of the figure that is reflected. On a coordinate plane we might reflect shapes in the lines represented by the *x*-axis or *y*-axis.

Example 1

The vertices of $\triangle RST$ are located at R (4, 3), S (4, 1), and T (1, 1). Draw $\triangle RST$ and its reflection in the *x*-axis.

Solution

We graph the vertices of $\triangle RST$ and draw the triangle. The triangle's reflection in the *x*-axis is where the triangle would appear if we flipped it across the *x*-axis. The reflection of each vertex is on the opposite side of the *x*-axis the same distance from the *x*-axis as the original vertex. So the reflection of R is at (4, −3). We call this vertex R', which we read as "R prime." The location of S' is (4, −1) and T' (1, −1). After we locate the vertices, we draw $\triangle R'S'T'$.

2 New Concepts *(Continued)*

Instruction

On an overhead projector, use the transparency of **Lesson Activity 19** Transformations to demonstrate the moves using *flip, slide,* and *turn* as you move the figure. Then repeat the demonstration using the terms *reflection, translation,* and *rotation* to help students learn the proper terminology.

Work through these transformations with the students. Be certain that students understand each change of position before continuing to the next change.

Have students who master the changes quickly do them in a different order so that they can see that the order of the moves does not affect the final position of the triangle. Connect this fact to the Fundamental Counting Principle by asking how many different combinations of the three moves there are. 6

Continue to help students develop fluency in the use of the more formal terms for these moves.

Example 1

Instruction

Before beginning this work with reflections, you may want to remind students that on a coordinate plane the *x*-axis is the horizontal line and the *y*-axis is the vertical line. If necessary, review plotting ordered pairs on a coordinate grid and explain that in an ordered pair, the first coordinate is the *x*-coordinate and the second coordinate is the *y*-coordinate.

Be sure students understand the use of prime and double prime symbols to indicate that the figure is a transformed image of the original figure.

(continued)

Math Background

Where do we see evidence of transformations in our everyday world?

People often use translations, rotations, and reflections, sometimes even simultaneously, as they move themselves and objects around. These movements are used when fitting pieces of jigsaw puzzles together, when putting parts of tools together, when flipping a pancake, and when catching a reflection in a mirror or window.

Translations are used when we click and drag objects on a computer screen or slide into home plate. Reflections are seen when we flip over pages in a book or arrange similar objects on a table. Our positions as we ride on merry-go-rounds go through a complete rotation. We can see dilations and reductions when photos are enlarged or in scale drawings.

English Learners

Explain the meaning of **clockwise** and **counterclockwise.** Say:

"Clockwise means to turn in the same direction as the hands on a clock."

Have students stand up and turn in a clockwise direction.

"Counterclockwise means to turn the opposite direction of the hands on a clock."

Have students stand up and turn in a counterclockwise direction.

2 New Concepts (Continued)

Example 1 (continued)

Instruction

Point out that to graph a reflection correctly, every point on the image must be exactly the same distance from the line of reflection as the corresponding points on the original figure. Any segment connecting corresponding points on the image and the original figure is perpendicular to the line of reflection.

Example 2

Instruction

Before beginning work on the example, provide practice with translating figures on coordinate grids by using the overhead projector and two sheets of transparency film. On one sheet, draw a pair of axes and then sketch a three- or four-sided figure with the vertices labeled.

Have students sketch the figure onto their own copies of the coordinate grid. Then give directions, such as *"move 3 units left and 2 units down."* Have students draw the image that is the result of following those directions. Use the second sheet to trace the original figure and perform the given translation so students can check their work.

As you work on the example, help students see the connection between the coordinates of the vertices of the original figure and the coordinates of the image. Write A (4, 3), B (4, 1), C (1, 1), and D (1, 3) on the chalkboard. Directly under those coordinates write A' (−1, −1), B' (−1, −3), C' (−4, −3), and D' (−4, −1). Then write the translation directions, "left 5 units and down 4 units." Point out that the "left 5 units" on the coordinate grid is 5 in the negative direction along the x-axis. "Down 4 units" is 4 in the negative direction along the y-axis.

(continued)

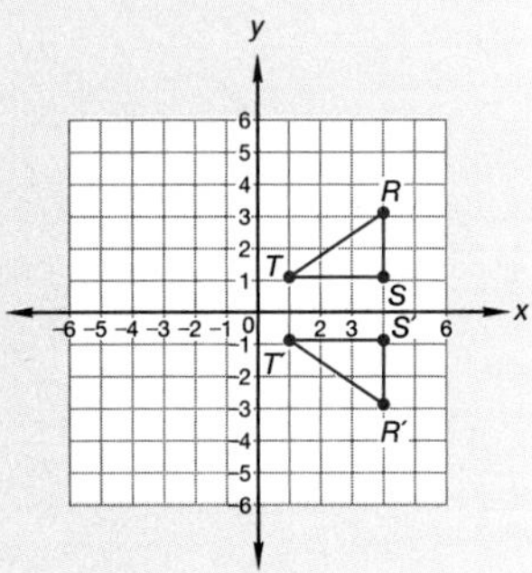

A **translation** "slides" a figure to a new position without turning or flipping the figure.

Example 2

Rectangle *ABCD* has vertices at *A* (4, 3), *B* (4, 1), *C* (1, 1), and *D* (1, 3). Draw ▭*ABCD* and its image, ▭*A′B′C′D′*, translated to the left 5 units and down 4 units.

Solution

We graph the vertices of ▭*ABCD* and draw the rectangle. Then we graph its image ▭*A′B′C′D′* by translating each vertex 5 units to the left and 4 units down. The translated vertices are ***A′* (−1, −1), *B′* (−1, −3), *C′* (−4, −3),** and ***D′* (− 4, −1).** We draw the sides of the rectangle to complete the image.

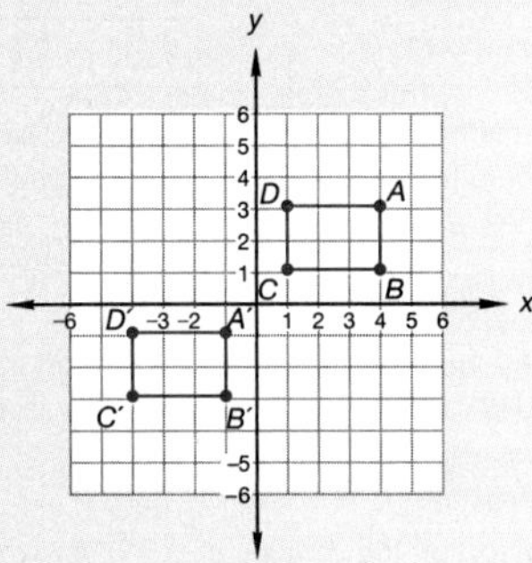

A **rotation** of a figure "turns" the figure about a specified point called the *center of rotation*. At the beginning of this lesson we rotated triangle I 90° clockwise. The center of rotation was the vertex of the right angle. In the illustration on the next page, triangle *ABC* is rotated 180° about the origin.

Manipulative Use

You may want to extend the experience with reflections in example 1. To help students explore **reflections** and how figures may look different when reflected, provide students with reflective devices such as **mirrors.** Then have students draw figures and explore how they change when they are reflected in a mirror.

Thinking Skill

Conclude

What happens if you rotate a figure 180° and then rotate it 180° again around the same point?
The figure returns to its original position.

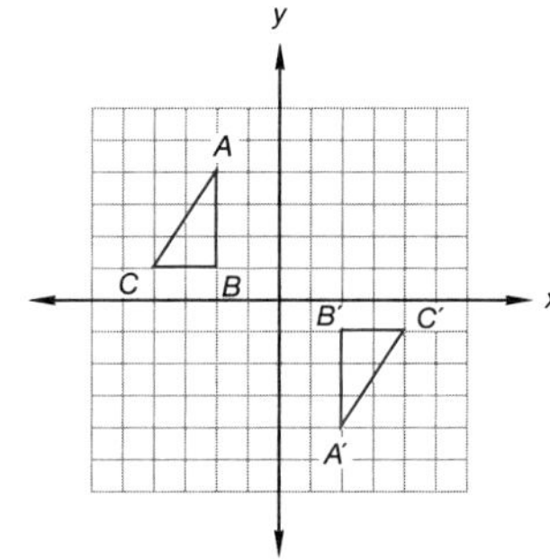

One way to view the effect of a rotation of a figure is to trace the figure on a piece of transparency film. Then place the point of a pencil on the center of rotation and turn the transparency film through the described rotation.

Example 3

The coordinates of the vertices of △*PQR* are *P* (3, 4), *Q* (3, 1), and *R* (1, 1). Draw △*PQR* and also draw its image, △*P′Q′R′*, after a counterclockwise rotation of 90° about the origin. What are the coordinates of the vertices of △*P′Q′R′*?

Solution

We graph the vertices of △*PQR* and draw the triangle.

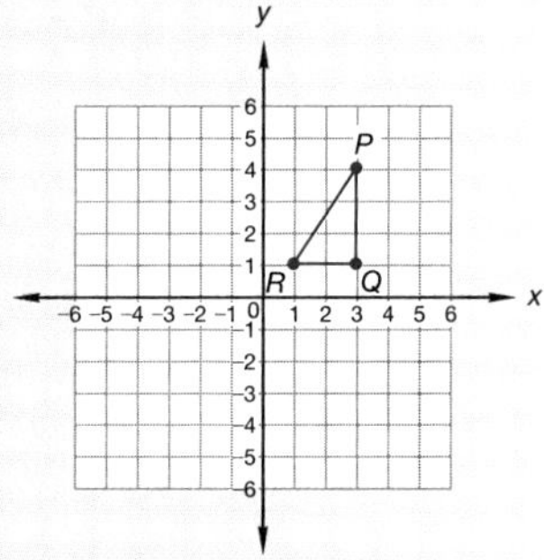

Then we place a piece of transparency film over the coordinate plane and trace the triangle. We also place a mark on the transparency aligned with the *x*-axis. This mark will align with the *y*-axis after the transparency is rotated 90°. After tracing the triangle on the transparency, we place the point of a pencil on the film over the origin, which is the center of rotation in this example. While keeping the graph paper still, we rotate the film 90° (one-quarter turn) counterclockwise. The image of the triangle rotates to the position shown, while the original triangle remains in place.

2 New Concepts (Continued)

Instruction

Make sure that students understand the *origin* is point (0, 0) on a coordinate plane. The origin is used as the *center of rotation* for problems in this lesson.

To help students understand why this transformation is a rotation and not a translation or reflection, demonstrate this rotation on an overhead projector.

Use two sheets of transparency film. On the first sheet, graph triangle *ABC*. Place the second sheet over the first, and trace triangle *ABC* onto it. Keeping the first sheet still, place a pencil at the origin and rotate the second sheet 180°.

Now give each student a small piece of transparency film. Have students trace triangle *ABC* from their book onto the film. Then have them place the point of their pencils on point (0, 0) and turn the film through the described rotation. Students can then see triangle *ABC* from their books and the desired image on the transparency film.

Example 3

Instruction

If students easily followed the introductory exercise, then just working through this example will provide enough experience with rotations. If students had problems, then use the technique with the two sheets of transparency film to go through this example as well.

(continued)

Teacher Tip

Make and keep copies of **Investigation Activity 13** Coordinate Plane in a convenient place. The students can use them as they work through this lesson, as well as lessons that follow where transformations may appear in practice exercises.

2 New Concepts (Continued)

Example 3 (continued)

Instruction

Point out that the prime symbols are used here to indicate that the new figure is a rotated image of the original figure.

Instruction

Have students explain why after a dilation the shapes are similar, but not congruent. Since we multiply the coordinates of each vertex by the same scale factor, the image is enlarged proportionately, so the shape remains the same and the figure and the image are similar. Because they are not the same size and shape, they are not congruent.

The *scale factor* of a dilation is the number by which we multiply the coordinates of the vertices. Students should note that multiplying by a scale factor of 1 does not change the figure.

(continued)

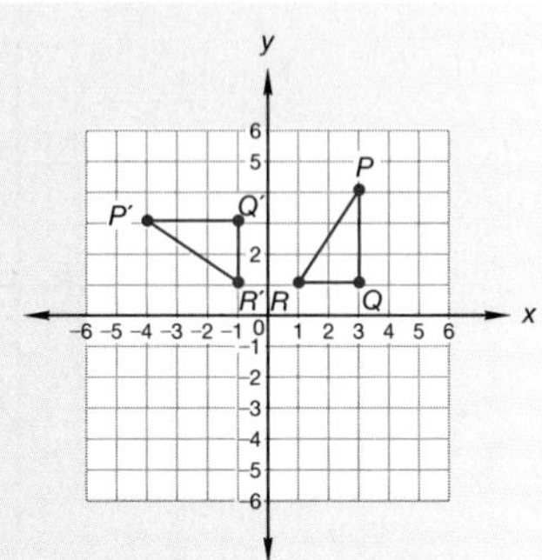

We name the rotated image $\triangle P'Q'R'$ and through the transparency see that the coordinates of the vertices are **P' (−4, 3), Q' (−1, 3),** and **R' (−1, 1).**

A **dilation** is a transformation that changes the size of a figure while preserving its shape. If we reduce or enlarge a figure, the resulting image is not congruent to the original figure, but the image is similar to the original figure because the shape is the same.

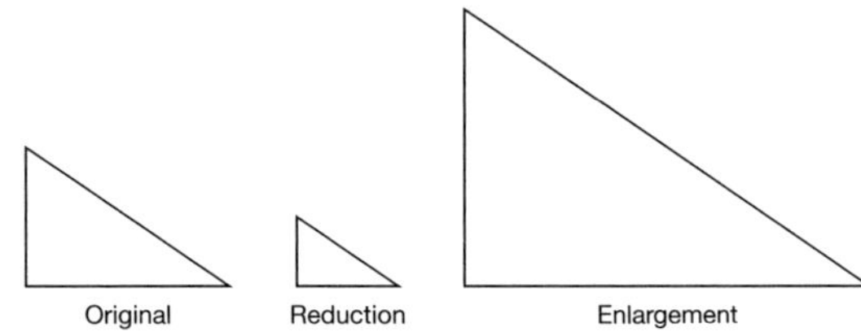

One way to change the size of a figure graphed on a coordinate plane is to multiply the coordinates of the figure's vertices by a constant number. Below we show the result of multiplying the coordinates of the vertices of a triangle by 2.

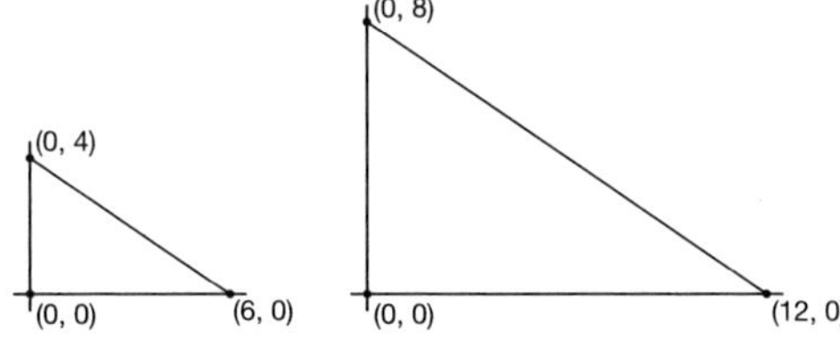

The number by which we multiply is the scale factor of the dilation. If we simply multiply the coordinates of the figure by the scale factor, then the center of the dilation is the origin.

Teacher Tip

To make a connection between this lesson and your art instruction, explain to students that **tessellations** are arrangements of closed figures that completely cover a plane so that there are no overlaps or gaps. These figures can be translated, rotated, or reflected so that they fit together to form a pattern. For a regular polygon to tessellate, the measure of the interior angle must be a factor of 360° as shown.

You may want students to experiment with tessellations as an art project. The Dutch artist M.C. Escher is famous for his tessellated art.

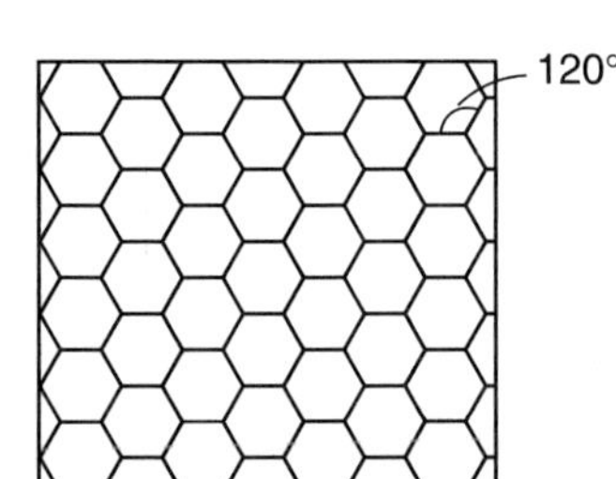

Example 4

Triangle *XYZ* has vertices at *X* (1, 1), *Y* (2, 1), and *Z* (1, 2). Draw △*XYZ* and the dilation image of △*XYZ* with the center of the dilation at the origin and with a scale factor of 3.

Solution

We draw △*XYZ*. To locate the vertices of its image, △*X′Y′Z′*, we multiply the coordinates of the vertices of △*XYZ* by 3.

△*XYZ*	*X* (1, 1)	*Y* (2, 1)	*Z* (1, 2)
△*X′Y′Z′*	*X′* (3, 3)	*Y′* (6, 3)	*Z′* (3, 6)

We graph the vertices of the dilation and complete the triangle.

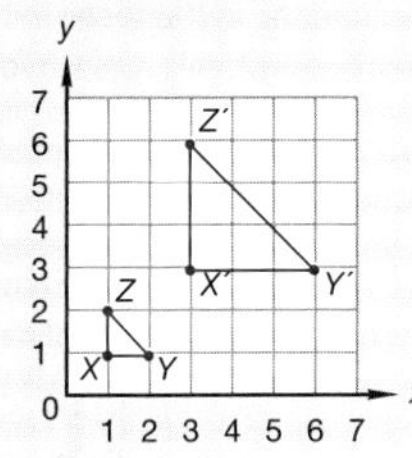

a.

Practice Set Perform each of the examples in this lesson before you do the Practice Set. Then draw each transformation and find the coordinates of its vertices.

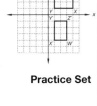

▸ **a.** Rectangle *WXYZ* has vertices at *W* (4, 3), *X* (4, 1), *Y* (1, 1), and *Z* (1, 3). Draw the rectangle and its image ▭*W′X′Y′Z′* after a 90° clockwise rotation about the origin. What are the coordinates of the vertices of ▭*W′X′Y′Z′*? *W′* (3, −4), *X′* (1, −4), *Y′* (1, −1), *Z′* (3, −1)

▸ **b.** The vertices of △*JKL* are *J* (1, −1), *K* (3, −2), and *L* (1, −3). Draw the triangle and its image after reflection in the y-axis, △*J′K′L′*. What are the coordinates of the vertices of △*J′K′L′*? *J′* (−1, −1), *K′* (−3, −2), *L′* (−1, −3)

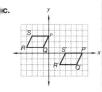

▸ **c.** Parallelogram *PQRS* has vertices at *P* (0, 3), *Q* (−1, 1), *R* (−4, 1), and *S* (−3, 3). Draw ▱*PQRS* and its image ▱*P′Q′R′S′* translated 6 units to the right and 3 units down. What are the coordinates of the vertices of ▱*P′Q′R′S′*? *P′* (6, 0), *Q′* (5, −2), *R′* (2, −2), *S′* (3, 0)

▸ **d.** Square *ABCD* has vertices at *A* (1, 1), *B* (1, −1), *C* (−1, −1), and *D* (−1, 1). Draw □*ABCD* and its dilated image □*A′B′C′D′* with the center of the dilation at the origin and with a scale factor of 2.

c.

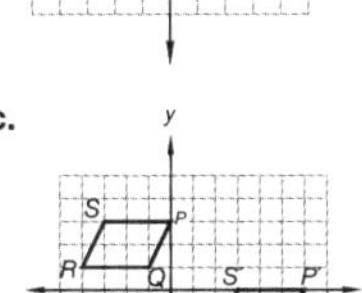

d.

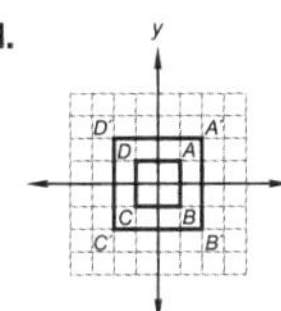

▸ See Math Conversations in the sidebar.

2 New Concepts (Continued)

Example 4

Instruction

Caution students to complete the boxes and coordinate grids neatly and accurately, remembering to use the prime symbols to designate the coordinates of the dilated image.

Practice Set

Problems a–d (Error Alert)

Check that students label the vertices of the original figures as well as those of the transformed images.

Problem b (Error Alert)

Some students may need a small piece of transparency film to work through this problem. If all students are having difficulty, then you may need to work through the problem using the overhead projector and two sheets of transparency film as in the demonstration of rotations that you did before working on example 2.

Check to see that students' answers are correct. Those who have the coordinates *J* (1, 1), *K* (3, 2), and *L* (1, 3) as their answer have reflected the triangle in the *x*-axis rather than in the *y*-axis.

3 Written Practice

Math Conversations

Discussion opportunities are provided below.

Problem 3 Explain

Tell students to think about a situation where the coin is tossed twice and the number cube is rolled once.

"Explain how you can use mental math to tell how many outcomes are in the sample space." Sample: $2 \times 2 \times 6$ is 24.

"Explain how you can use mental math to find the probability of tossing 2 heads and rolling a 1." Sample: You don't need to list the sample space to know that only one outcome is 2 heads and a 1, so the probability is 1 in 24.

Problem 7

Extend the Problem

Help students review their understanding of inequalities and how to represent them. Ask questions like these:

"For which inequality will the graph have an empty circle? Why?" Sample: For $x > -2$, because the -2 is not included.

"Which integers are solutions to both inequalities?" Sample: Both include 0 and -1.

Problem 9 Evaluate

Ask students to make up questions that can be answered using the information in this problem, mental math, and logical reasoning. Have them exchange papers and ask volunteers to read and answer the question they now have. Sample: Suppose that the 18 inches was $\frac{1}{3}$ of Nathan's height. Would he be taller or shorter than 6 feet? Answer: shorter

Errors and Misconceptions

Problem 5

If students have trouble solving this problem, have them identify the formula they use to find the circumference of the coin. $C = \pi d$

Problem 8

Students whose answer is 1600 people may have used 100 minutes to represent the whole amount of time. Make sure these students understand that they should not use 100%, but that they need to use the number of minutes in one hour, 60.

(continued)

Written Practice *Strengthening Concepts*

1. (55) Tina mowed lawns for 4 hours and earned \$7.00 per hour. Then she weeded flower beds for 3 hours and earned \$6.30 per hour. What was Tina's average hourly pay for the 7-hour period? \$6.70 per hour

2. (52) Evaluate: $x + (x^2 - xy) - y$ if $x = 4$ and $y = 3$ 5

▶ **3.** (36) **Explain** A coin is tossed and a number cube is rolled.

a. Write the sample space for the experiment.
{H1, H2, H3, H4, H5, H6, T1, T2, T3, T4, T5, T6}

b. Use the sample space to find the probability of getting tails and an odd number. $\frac{3}{12} = \frac{1}{4}$

4. (65) Use a ratio box to solve this problem. Nia found the ratio of trilobites to crustaceans in the fossil exhibit was 2 to 3. If there were 30 fossils in the exhibit, how many were trilobites? 12 trilobites

▶ **5.** (32, 66) The diameter of a half-dollar is 3 centimeters. What is the circumference of a half-dollar to the nearest millimeter? How do you know? 94 millimeters; Sample: $C = \pi d = 3.14 \times 3 \approx 9.42$; 9.42 cm = 94.2 mm, which rounds to 94 mm.

6. (50) Use a unit multiplier to convert $1\frac{1}{2}$ quarts to pints.

6. $1\frac{1}{2}$ quarts $\cdot \frac{2 \text{ pints}}{1 \text{ quart}}$ = 3 pints

▶ * **7.** (78) Graph each inequality on a separate number line: (See below.)

a. $x > -2$ **b.** $x \leq 0$

▶ * **8.** (72) Use a ratio box to solve this problem. In 25 minutes, 400 people entered the museum. At this rate, how many people would enter the museum in 1 hour? 960 people

▶ **9.** (71) **Evaluate** Diagram this statement. Then answer the questions that follow.

Nathan found that it was 18 inches from his knee joint to his hip joint. This was $\frac{1}{4}$ of his total height.

a. What was Nathan's total height in inches? 72 inches

b. What was Nathan's total height in feet? 6 feet

9.
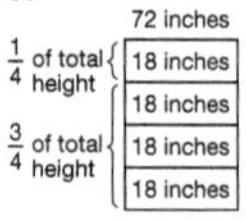

Write equations to solve problems **10–13.**

* **10.** (74) Six hundred is $\frac{5}{9}$ of what number? $600 = \frac{5}{9} \times W_N$; 1080

* **11.** (77) Two hundred eighty is what percent of 400? $280 = W_P \times 400$; 70%

12. (60) What number is 4 percent of 400? $W_N = 0.04 \times 400$; 16

* **13.** (77) Sixty is 60 percent of what number? $60 = 0.6 \times W_N$; 100

14. (73) Simplify:

a. $\frac{600}{-15}$ -40

b. $\frac{-600}{-12}$ 50

c. $20(-30)$ -600

d. $+15(40)$ 600

7. a.
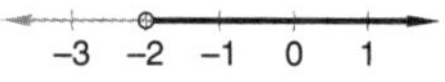

7. b.
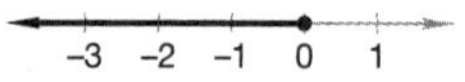

556 **Saxon** *Math Course 2*

▶ See Math Conversations in the sidebar.

▶ **15.** (60) Anil is paid a commission equal to 6% of the price of each appliance he sells. If Anil sells a refrigerator for \$850, what is Anil's commission on the sale? \$51

16. (48) Complete the table.

Fraction	Decimal	Percent
a. $\frac{3}{10}$	0.3	**b.** 30%
$\frac{5}{12}$	**c.** $0.41\overline{6}$	**d.** $41\frac{2}{3}$%

17. (69) Write each number in scientific notation:

a. 30×10^6 3×10^7 **b.** 30×10^{-6} 3×10^{-5}

▶* **18.** (75) Find the area of the trapezoid shown. Dimensions are in meters. 25 m²

19. (67, 70) Each edge of a cube measures 5 inches.

a. What is the volume of the cube? 125 in.³

b. What is the surface area of the cube? 150 in.²

▶ **20.** (14) In a bag are 100 marbles: 10 red, 20 white, 30 blue, and 40 green. If one marble is drawn from the bag, what is the probability that the marble will not be red, white, or blue? $\frac{2}{5}$

For problems **21–23**, solve and check each equation. Show each step.

* **21.** (Inv. 7) $17a = 408$ 24

* **22.** (Inv. 7) $\frac{3}{8}m = 48$ 128

* **23.** (Inv. 7) $1.4 = x - 0.41$ 1.81

Simplify:

24. (52) $\frac{2^3 + 4 \cdot 5 - 2 \cdot 3^2}{\sqrt{25} \cdot \sqrt{4}}$ 1

25. (43) $7\frac{1}{7} \times 1.4$ 10

26. (56) 10 lb 6 oz − 7 lb 11 oz = 2 lb 11 oz

27. (50) $1\text{ cm}^2 \cdot \frac{10\text{ mm}}{1\text{ cm}} \cdot \frac{10\text{ mm}}{1\text{ cm}}$ 100 mm²

28. (26) $7\frac{1}{2} \div \left(3 \cdot \frac{5}{9}\right)$ $4\frac{1}{2}$

29. (30, 57) $2^{-4} + 4^{-2}$ $\frac{1}{8}$

▶* **30.** (80) Triangle *ABC* with vertices at *A* (0, 2), *B* (2, 2), and *C* (2, 0) is reflected in the *x*-axis. Draw △*ABC* and its image △*A′B′C′*.

Lesson 80 557

▶ See Math Conversations in the sidebar.

Looking Forward

Performing transformations (reflections, translations, and rotations) prepares students for:

- **Lesson 89,** finding the measure of exterior angles of a triangle.

3 Written Practice (Continued)

Math Conversations

Discussion opportunities are provided below.

Problem 15

Extend the Problem

After students solve the following problem, have a discussion of how they found their answers.

"If Anil needs \$2100 a month for his living expenses, what amount does he need to sell to earn \$2100 in commission?" Sample: \$35,000; For every \$1000 of sales, Anil gets \$60. I divided \$2100 by \$60 and got 35, so he needs 35 × \$1000 in sales.

Problem 18

Extend the Problem

Connect this problem to this lesson. After students work through this problem, let them explain how they can transform the trapezoid and form a rectangle.

"Form a rectangle by combining a reflected, translated, or rotated image with the original trapezoid. The unlabeled sides of the two trapezoids should meet." Find the perimeter and area of the rectangle." perimeter: 30 m, area: 50 m²

Problem 20

Extend the Problem

Have students write, solve, and share two problems about this bag of marbles. You may want to suggest that the problems do not need to be probability problems. Sample: Find the ratio of green to white marbles. Ratio of green to white: 2 to 1. If 30 more green and white marbles are added in that same ratio, what is the ratio of green to red in the bag of 130 marbles? Ratio of green to red: 6 to 1.

Errors and Misconceptions

Problem 15

If students have answers greater than \$850, such as \$901, tell them to ask themselves whether the commission will be greater than or less than the amount of the sale.

Problem 30

To help students differentiate between the original figure and its reflection, suggest that they draw the reflection in a color different from the color of the original figure.

Assessment

30–40 minutes *For use after Lesson 80*

Distribute **Cumulative Test 15** to each student. Two versions of the test are available in *Saxon Math Course 2 Course Assessments Book*. Have students complete the **Power-Up Test** first. Allow 10 minutes. Then have students work the 20 numbered items on the **Cumulative Test.** Students may use copies of the answer sheet to record their work. Track individual and class progress with the **Test Analysis** forms.

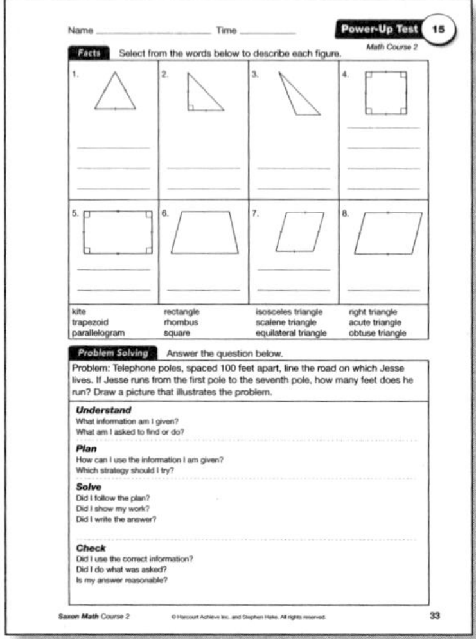

Power-Up Test 15

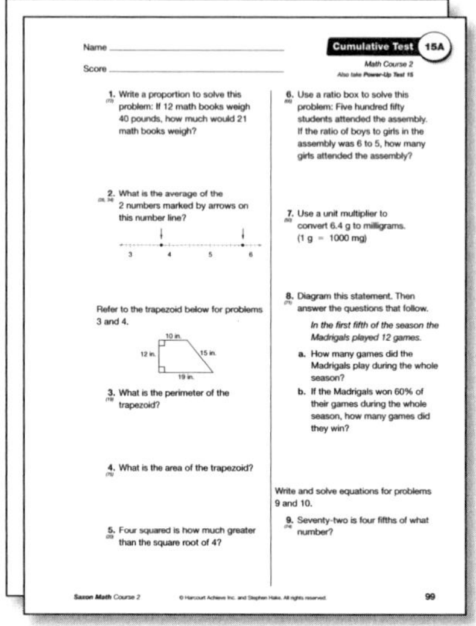

Cumulative Test 15A

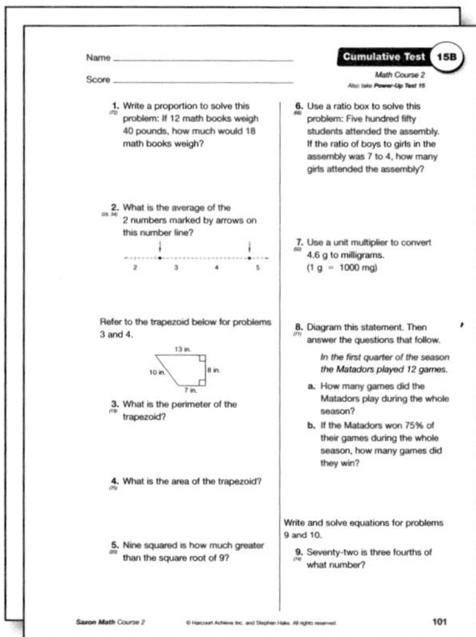

Alternative Cumulative Test 15B

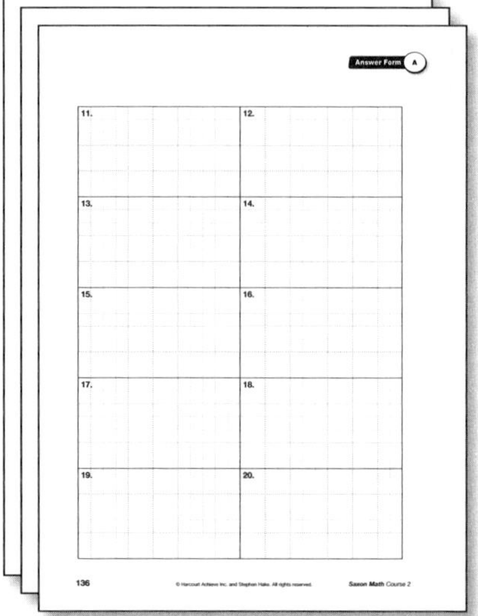

Optional Answer Forms

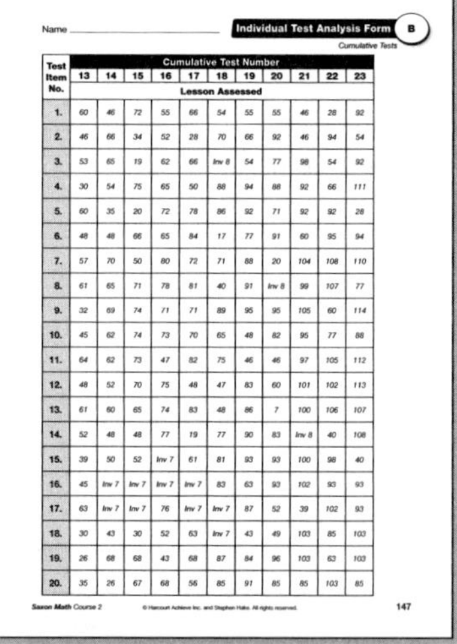

Individual Test Analysis Form

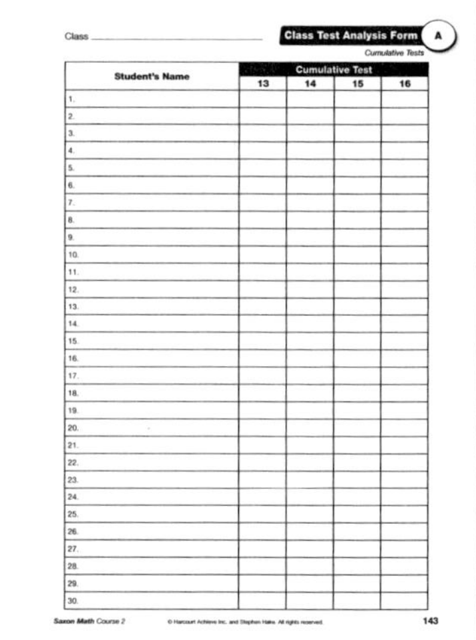

Class Test Analysis Form

Reteaching

Students who score below 80% on the assessment may be in need of reteaching. Look for the causes of student mistakes. If errors are conceptual, refer to the *Reteaching Masters* for reteaching.

Customized Benchmark Assessment

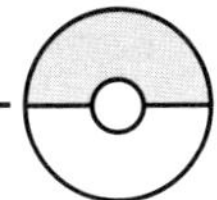

You can develop customized benchmark tests using the Test Generator located on the *Test and Practice Generator CD*.

This chart shows the lesson, the standard, and the test item question that can be found on the *Test and Practice Generator CD*.

LESSON	NEW CONCEPTS	LOCAL STANDARD	TEST ITEM ON CD
71	• Finding the Whole Group When a Fraction Is Known		8.71.1
72	• Implied Ratios		8.72.1
73	• Multiplying and Dividing Positive and Negative Numbers		8.73.1
74	• Fractional Part of a Number, Part 2		8.74.1
75	• Area of a Complex Figure		8.75.1
	• Area of a Trapezoid		8.75.2
76	• Complex Fractions		8.76.1
77	• Percent of a Number, Part 2		8.77.1
78	• Graphic Inequalities		8.78.1
79	• Estimating Areas		8.79.1
80	• Transformations		8.80.1

Using the Test Generator CD

- Develop tests in both English and Spanish.
- Choose from multiple-choice and free-response test items.
- Clone test items to create multiple versions of the same test.
- View and edit test items to make and save your own questions.
- Administer assessments through paper tests or over a school LAN.
- Monitor student progress through a variety of individual and class reports —for both diagnosing and assessing standards mastery.

Performance Task 15

Paint a Step Pyramid

Assign after Lesson 80 and Test 15

Objectives

- Draw views of a step pyramid showing the color of each section.
- Find the cost of paint needed to cover a surface area.
- Communicate their ideas through writing.

Materials

Performance Tasks 15A and **15B**

Preparation

Make copies of **Performance Tasks 15A** and **15B.** (One each per student.)

Time Requirement

30–60 minutes; Begin in class and complete at home.

Task

Explain to students that for this task they will be finding the cost to paint a step pyramid in a pattern of three different colors. They will be required to draw a side and top view of the step pyramid and to explain how they arrived at some of their answers. Point out that all of the information students need is on **Performance Tasks 15A** and **15B.**

Criteria for Evidence of Learning

- Draws correct views of the step pyramid that show the color of each section accurately.
- Accurately finds the area that needs to be covered by each paint color.
- Accurately finds the total cost of the paint.
- Communicates ideas clearly through writing.

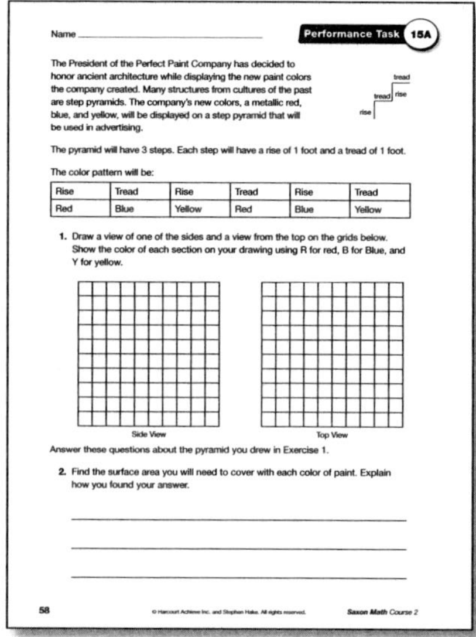

Name ______________________ **Performance Task 15A**

The President of the Perfect Paint Company has decided to honor ancient architecture while displaying the new paint colors the company created. Many structures from cultures of the past are step pyramids. The company's new colors, a metallic red, blue, and yellow, will be displayed on a step pyramid that will be used in advertising.

The pyramid will have 3 steps. Each step will have a rise of 1 foot and a tread of 1 foot.

The color pattern will be:

Rise	Tread	Rise	Tread	Rise	Tread
Red	Blue	Yellow	Red	Blue	Yellow

1. Draw a view of one of the sides and a view from the top on the grids below. Show the color of each section on your drawing using R for red, B for Blue, and Y for yellow.

Side View   Top View

Answer these questions about the pyramid you drew in Exercise 1.

2. Find the surface area you will need to cover with each color of paint. Explain how you found your answer.

58   © Harcourt Achieve Inc. and Stephen Hake. All rights reserved.   *Saxon Math Course 2*

Performance Task 15A

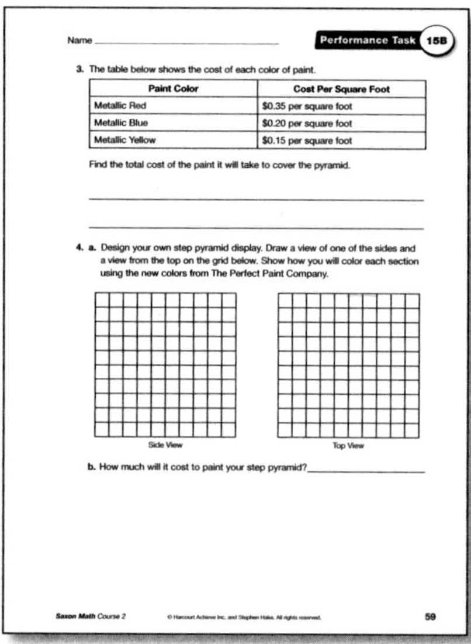

Name ______________________ **Performance Task 15B**

3. The table below shows the cost of each color of paint.

Paint Color	Cost Per Square Foot
Metallic Red	$0.35 per square foot
Metallic Blue	$0.20 per square foot
Metallic Yellow	$0.15 per square foot

Find the total cost of the paint it will take to cover the pyramid.

4. a. Design your own step pyramid display. Draw a view of one of the sides and a view from the top on the grid below. Show how you will color each section using the new colors from The Perfect Paint Company.

Side View   Top View

b. How much will it cost to paint your step pyramid? ______________

Saxon Math Course 2   © Harcourt Achieve Inc. and Stephen Hake. All rights reserved.   59

Performance Task 15B

Meeting Standards

National Council of Teachers of Mathematics (NCTM)

Geometry

GM.4a Draw geometric objects with specified properties, such as side lengths or angle measures

GM.4c Use visual tools such as networks to represent and solve problems

GM.4e Recognize and apply geometric ideas and relationships in areas outside the mathematics classroom, such as art, science, and everyday life

Communication

CM.3a Organize and consolidate their mathematical thinking through communication

Connections

CN.4a Recognize and use connections among mathematical ideas

Focus on

- **Probability and Odds**
- **Compound Events**
- **Experimental Probability**

Objectives

- Determine the chance of an event occurring.
- Determine the chance of an event's complement occurring.
- Determine the odds of an event occurring.
- Determine the probability of compound events.
- Distinguish between theoretical probability and experimental probability.

Lesson Preparation

Materials

- **Investigation Activity 13** (in *Instructional Masters*)
- **Investigation Activity 20** (in *Instructional Masters*)
- **Manipulative kit: 2 number cubes**

Optional

- **Teacher-provided material: coins**

Math Language

New

compound event	independent events	theoretical probability
experimental probability	odds	

Investigation Activity 13

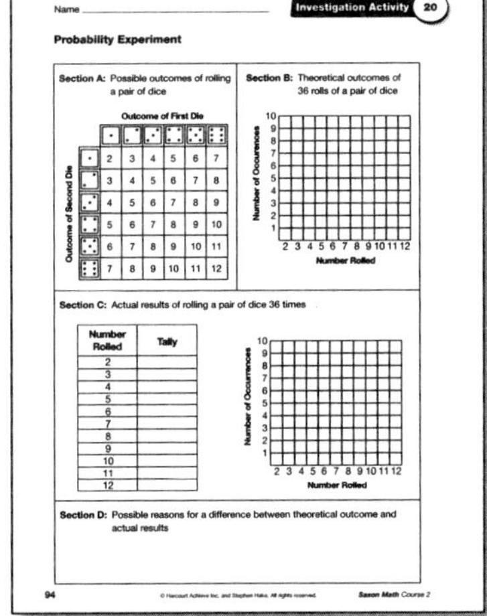

Investigation Activity 20

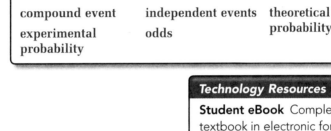

Technology Resources

Student eBook Complete student textbook in electronic format.

Resources and Planner CD Blackline masters, plus a pacing calendar with standards.

Test and Practice Generator CD Create additional practice sheets and custom-made tests.

www.SaxonPublishers.com Visit for more student activities and planning materials.

Inclusion

Adaptations CD Adapted lessons, investigations, practice and assessments.

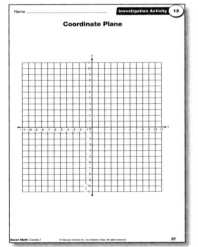

Meeting Standards

National Council of Teachers of Mathematics (NCTM)

Data Analysis and Probability

DP.4a Understand and use appropriate terminology to describe complementary and mutually exclusive events

DP.4b Use proportionality and a basic understanding of probability to make and test conjectures about the results of experiments and simulations

DP.4c Compute probabilities for simple compound events, using such methods as organized lists, tree diagrams, and area models

Reasoning and Proof

RP.2b Make and investigate mathematical conjectures

RP.2c Develop and evaluate mathematical arguments and proofs

INVESTIGATION 8

Begin the lesson by asking students to explain the definition of *probability* in their own words. Be sure it is discussed that probability is the likelihood that a particular event will occur.

Probability and Odds

Draw the following scale on the board

0	25%	50%	75%	100%
0	$\frac{1}{4}$	$\frac{1}{2}$	$\frac{3}{4}$	1

Remind students that probabilities range from 0 (not possible) to 1 (certain).

Point out that the sum of the chance that an event will occur and the chance that the event will not occur is always 100% or 1. These are called complementary events.

Math Conversations

Discussion opportunities are provided below.

Problems 1–4 Analyze

As students discuss the probability of each event occurring, ask a student to estimate the placement of the fraction on the number line.

(continued)

INVESTIGATION 8

Focus on

- **Probability and Odds**
- **Compound Events**
- **Experimental Probability**

probability and odds

We have defined the probability of an event as the ratio of favorable outcomes to the number of possible outcomes. The range of probability is from zero (impossible) to one (certain). We may express probability as a fraction, as a decimal, or as a percent (from 0% to 100%).

If we spin the spinner, the probability that the spinner will stop on 1 is $\frac{1}{4}$, 0.25, 25%. The **complement** of this event is the spinner not stopping on 1. The probability of the spinner not stopping on 1 is $\frac{3}{4}$, 0.75, 75%.

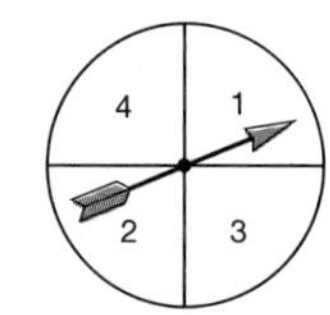

Thinking Skills

Conclude

If the chance of rain is 50%, what is the chance of "not rain?" 50%

Sometimes the word *chance* is used to refer to probability. On a weather report we might hear that the chance of rain is 60%, which means that the complement, the chance of "not rain," is 40%.

Another way to express the likelihood of an event is as **odds.** The odds of spinning 1 on the spinner above are 1 to 3 or 1:3. Odds show the ratio of favorable to unfavorable outcomes and are written with the word "to" or with a colon (:).

Odds
favorable to unfavorable
favorable : unfavorable

In other words, odds express the relationship between the probabilities of an event and its complement. Although we do not write odds as a fraction, we do reduce the numbers used to express odds.

Analyze Refer to the following statement to answer problems **1–7.**

One marble is drawn from a bag containing 3 red marbles, 4 white marbles, and 5 blue marbles.

▶ **1.** What is the probability of picking white? $\frac{1}{3}$

▶ **2.** What is the probability of not picking white? $\frac{2}{3}$

▶ **3.** What are the odds of picking white? 1 to 2

▶ **4.** What is the probability of picking red? Express the probability as a decimal. 0.25

▶ See Math Conversations in the sidebar.

5. What is the probability of not picking a red marble? Express the probability as a decimal. 0.75

6. What are the odds of picking a red marble? 1 to 3

7. What are the odds of picking a blue marble? 5 to 7

The meteorologist forecast the chance of rain as 20%.

8. According to the forecast, the chance it will not rain is what percent? 80%

▶ 9. **Analyze** According to the forecast, what are the odds of rain? 1:4

compound events

A **compound event** is composed of two or more simple events. For example, "getting heads twice" with two flips of a coin is a compound event.

To find the probability of two or more events occurring in a specific order, we multiply the probabilities of the events.

Example 1

A coin is tossed and a spinner is spun. What is the probability of getting heads and 4?

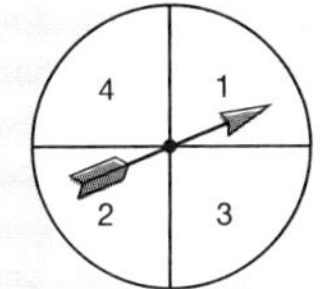

Solution

The probability of heads and 4, P (H and 4) is the probability of heads times the probability of 4.

$$P(\text{H and } 4) = P(\text{H}) \cdot P(4)$$
$$= \frac{1}{2} \cdot \frac{1}{4}$$
$$= \frac{1}{8}$$

Conclude What is the probability of getting tails and 4? $\frac{1}{8}$

Refer to the illustration in example 1 to answer problems 10–12.

Math Language
A sample space is a list of all the possible outcomes of an event.

▶ 10. **Represent** What is the sample space for one coin toss and one spin? {H1, H2, H3, H4, T1, T2, T3, T4}

11. Find the probability of heads and 2 by multiplying the probability of heads and the probability of 2. Check your answer by inspecting the sample space for the event. $\frac{1}{8}$

12. What are the odds of getting heads and 2? Check your answer by inspecting the sample space for the event. 1 to 7

▶ See Math Conversations in the sidebar.

Manipulative Use

Materials: 3 red, 4 white, and 5 blue marbles

Some students may need practice differentiating between the ratio used to express **probability** and that used to express **odds.** These students may need some hands-on experience. Have them simulate the activity for problems 1–7.

- Point out that when counting probability, they count the group that represents the favorable outcomes and the total number of marbles.
- When counting odds, however, they count the group that represents the favorable outcomes and the group that represents the unfavorable outcomes.

Probability and Odds (continued)

Math Conversations

Discussion opportunities are provided below.

Problem 9 **Analyze**

The probability of rain is 20%. This means that for every 100 days that had weather conditions similar to this day, it rained on 20 days. You can think of 20 out of 100 as 1 out of 5 or $\frac{1}{5}$. This means that for every 5 days that had weather conditions similar to this day, it rained on 1 out of those 5 days.

Since odds are based on complimentary events, we must look at the probability of it not raining, 80% or $\frac{4}{5}$. For every 5 days that had similar weather conditions, it did not rain on 4 out of 5 days.

The complimentary events are 1 day it did rain and 4 days it did not rain, so the odds of it raining are 1 to 4. The odds of it *not* raining are 4 to 1.

Compound Events

Instruction

Explain that a compound event is a combination of two or more events. As students proceed through example 1, ask:

"How many possible outcomes are there when flipping the coin?" 2

"What are they?" heads, tails

"Are they equally likely?" yes

"How many possible outcomes are there when spinning the spinner?" 4

"What are they?" 1, 2, 3, 4

"Are they equally likely?" yes

"What operation do you use to find the probability of a compound event?" multiplication

Math Conversations

Discussion opportunities are provided below.

Problem 10 **Represent**

Help students understand that the sample space is the arrangements of all possible outcomes for this event—one coin toss and one spin. There must be an outcome of heads or tails for each of the 4 outcomes on the spinner. It might help students to make a table.

Coin	H	T	H	T	H	T	H	T
Spinner	1	1	2	2	3	3	4	4

The sample space has 8 possible outcomes.

(continued)

Compound Events (continued)

Math Conversations

Discussion opportunities are provided below.

Problem 13 Explain

Students can inspect the table they made to analyze the sample space.

Coin	H	T	H	T	H	T	H	T
Spinner	1	1	2	2	3	3	4	4

The sample space has 8 possible outcomes.

They can see that the probability is 3 out of 8 or $\frac{3}{8}$.

They can also multiply $\frac{1}{2} \times \frac{3}{4} = \frac{3}{8}$.

Problem 15 Analyze

Emphasize that using multiplication to determine the probability of an event rather than writing out the entire sample space is a useful technique to complete many probability problems.

Prove this point by asking students to write the sample space for problem 15. {1 1, 1 2, 1 3, 1 4, 1 5, 1 6, 2 1, 2 2, 2 3, 2 4, 2 5, 2 6, 3 1, 3 2, 3 3, 3 4, 3 5, 3 6, 4 1, 4 2, 4 3, 4 4, 4 5, 4 6, 5 1, 5 2, 5 3, 5 4, 5 5, 5 6, 6 1, 6 2, 6 3, 6 4, 6 5, 6 6}

Point out that it is much easier to multiply the probabilities of tossing a 6 each time ($\frac{1}{6} \times \frac{1}{6}$) than writing out the entire sample space.

"Do we know with absolute certainty that the spinner looks like what is drawn? Explain." Sample: No, because the experiment could be different from what is actually there.

"What could have been done differently to get a more accurate drawing of the spinner? Explain." Sample: More experiments could have been because the law of averages says that the more experiments are done, the accurate the experimental probability is to the theoretical probability.

▸ **13.** Explain What is the probability of flipping heads and not spinning 2? Tell how you found the answer. Check your answer by inspecting the sample space. $\frac{3}{8}$, Multiply the probability of heads by the probability of not 2: $\frac{1}{2} \times \frac{3}{4} = \frac{3}{8}$.

14. If a coin is flipped three times, what is the probability of getting heads all three times? $\frac{1}{8}$

▸ **15.** If a number cube is rolled twice, what is the probability of getting 6 both times? $\frac{1}{36}$

16. Analyze If a number cube is rolled and a coin is tossed, what is the probability of getting 6 and heads? $\frac{1}{12}$

Events like tossing a coin, spinning a spinner, and rolling a number cube are **independent events.** One outcome does not affect the next outcome. If a tossed coin happens to land heads up three times in a row, then the probability of heads on the next toss is still just $\frac{1}{2}$. The so called "law of averages" does not apply to individual events. However, over a very large number of trials, we expect a coin will land heads up $\frac{1}{2}$ of the trials, and we expect a rolled number cube will end up 6 on $\frac{1}{6}$ of the trials. This leads us to the topic of experimental probability.

experimental probability

We can distinguish between **theoretical probability** and **experimental probability.** To determine the theoretical probability of an event, we analyze the relationship between favorable and possible outcomes. However, to find the experimental probability of an event we actually conduct many trials (experiments), and we count and compare the number of favorable outcomes to the number of trials.

$$\text{Experimental probability} = \frac{\text{number of favorable outcomes}}{\text{number of trials}}$$

Example 2

A baseball coach wants to select a player to be a pinch hitter. He knows that Cruz has 80 hits in 240 at-bats. What is the experimental probability of Cruz getting a hit if he is selected to pinch-hit?

Solution

The coach uses the batter's history to determine the probability of a hit. The favorable outcomes in this situation are hits, and the number of trials are at-bats.

$$\text{Probability} = \frac{\text{hits}}{\text{at-bats}} = \frac{80}{240} \text{ or } \frac{1}{3}$$

The experimental probability of a hit is $\frac{1}{3}$. (A baseball player's history of hits for at-bats is expressed as a decimal rounded to three decimal places without a leading zero. In this case, the player's batting average is .333.)

▸ See Math Conversations in the sidebar.

Manipulative Use

Emphasize that theoretical probability can be calculated without testing. Experimental probability, however, requires tests or trials.

Have students flip a coin 50 times and record what shows up, heads or tails, after each toss. Instruct them to calculate the **experimental probability** of flipping heads. Then have the students flip the coin 50 mores and record the results. Have them calculate the probability of flipping heads for all 100 experiments. Ask:

"What is the theoretical probability of flipping heads?" 0.50

"What was closer to the theoretical probability, flipping heads 50 or 100 times?" Sample: 100

"Why is it closer?" Sample: the law of averages

We can use probability experiments to find out information about a situation. Consider the spinner shown here. The spinner was spun 360 times. The results are recorded in the table.

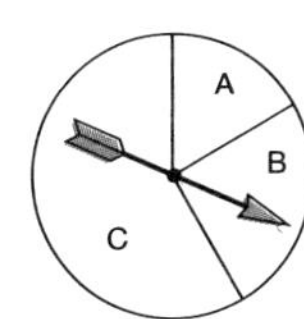

Math Language
In the table, the term *trial* means an *attempt* or *try*.

Analyze Refer to the table to answer questions 17–20.

Spinner Results	
Sector *A*	60
Sector *B*	90
Sector *C*	210
Total Trials	360

▶ **17.** What is the experimental probability of spinning *A*? $\frac{1}{6}$

▶ **18.** What is the experimental probability of spinning *B*? $\frac{1}{4}$

▶ **19.** What is the experimental probability of spinning *C*? $\frac{7}{12}$

▶ **20.** Based on the results of the experiment:

a. What fraction of the spinner's face is Sector *C*? $\frac{7}{12}$

b. About what percent of the spinner's face is Sector *B*? 25%

Activity

Experimental Probability

- Investigation Activity 20
- Two number cubes

Section A of **Investigation Activity 20** Probability Experiment displays the 36 equally likely outcomes of tossing a pair of number cubes. Section B is the outline of a bar graph. On the graph draw bars to indicate the theoretical outcome of tossing a pair of number cubes 36 times.

After completing Section B, take turns tossing the number cubes and recording the results for 36 tosses. Record and graph the results of the tosses in Section C.

If the results of the experiment differ from the theoretical outcome, discuss why you think the results differ and write your reasons in Section D.

extension

Create two classroom bar graphs to represent the results of all of the groups. First create a "Theoretical Outcomes" graph and then create an "Actual Results" graph by combining the results from every group. Does increasing the number of tosses (by counting all the tosses in the class) produce results closer to theoretical outcomes than were usually attained with just 36 rolls?

▶ See Math Conversations in the sidebar.

Experimental Probability

Math Conversations

Discussion opportunities are provided below.

Problems 17–20

Explain to students that the experimental probability of an event is often different from the theoretical probability of that event. However, the greater the number of trials, the more likely it is that the experimental probability will approach the theoretical probability.

Remind students that probabilities range from 0 (not possible) to 1 (certain).

Activity

Divide the class into groups of 2–4 students. Each group will need a copy of **Investigation Activity 20** Probability Experiment and two dot cubes. Review the Activity with students to be sure they are familiar with its contents.

For each group, as well as for the class as a whole, the graph for section B will be exactly the same. The bars should form an upside-down *v*-shape whose peak is at seven. The graphs for section C will vary.

Give students an opportunity to share their graphs and discuss the similarities and differences.

Ask students to compare the experimental probability of this activity to its theoretical probability.

Looking Forward

Theoretical and experimental probability prepares students for

- **Lesson 94,** the probability of dependent events.

Section 9 Overview

Lessons 81–90, Investigation 9

Lesson Planner

LESSON	NEW CONCEPTS	MATERIALS	RESOURCES
81	• Using Proportions to Solve Percent Problems		Power Up P Investigation Activity 13
82	• Area of a Circle	Overhead grid, scissors	Power Up Q Investigation Activity 13 Geometric Formulas poster
83	• Multiplying Numbers in Scientific Notation		Power Up R Investigation Activity 13
84	• Algebraic Terms		Power Up R Investigation Activity 13
85	• Order of Operations with Positive and Negative Numbers	Colored pencils	Power Up P Investigation Activity 13
86	• Number Families		Power Up S Investigation Activity 13
87	• Multiplying Algebraic Terms	Manipulative Kit: protractors	Power Up R Investigation Activity 13
88	• Multiple Unit Multipliers	Calculators	Power Up S Investigation Activity 13
89	• Diagonals • Interior Angles • Exterior Angles	Manipulative Kit: metric rulers, protractors 5 feet or more of string, chalk, 30 feet of masking tape, analog clock	Power Up R
90	• Mixed-Number Coefficients • Negative Coefficients		Power Up Q Investigation Activity 13
Inv. 9	• Graphing Functions		Investigation Activity 13

Lesson Highlights

Lessons 81–90, Investigation 9

Problem Solving

Strategies

- **Make an Organized List** Lesson 83
- **Use Logical Reasoning** Lessons 81, 82, 84, 85, 87, 90
- **Draw a Diagram** Lesson 90
- **Work Backwards** Lessons 84, 86
- **Write an Equation** Lessons 82, 87, 88, 89
- **Guess and Check** Lessons 81, 85, 86
- **Make a Model** Lesson 90
- **Find a Pattern** Lesson 88

Real-World Applications

pp. 562, 564–567, 569, 571–575, 577, 578, 580, 583, 584, 589, 590, 595, 600, 602, 603, 605–608, 610, 615, 616, 621–623, 625, 626, 629, 630

4-Step Process

Student Edition Lesson 84

Teacher Edition Lessons 81–90 (Power-Up Discussions)

Connections

Math and Other Subjects

Math and Geography p. 595

Math and History p. 562

Math and Science pp. 565, 583, 589, 600, 607

Math and Sports pp. 577, 595, 607, 615

Math and Social Studies p. 564

Math to Math

- **Problem Solving and Measurement** Lessons 81–90, Inv. 9
- **Algebra and Problem Solving** Lessons 81–90, Inv. 9
- **Fractions, Decimals, Percents, and Problem Solving** Lessons 81–90
- **Fractions and Measurement** Lessons 81, 89, 90
- **Measurement and Geometry** Lessons 81–90
- **Algebra, Measurement and Geometry** Inv. 9
- **Probability and Statistics** Lessons 82–86, 88, 90

Communication

Discuss

pp. 563, 581, 594, 599, 612

Summarize

p. 571

Explain

pp. 563, 565, 566, 570, 575, 598, 599, 605, 614, 625, 626, 630

Representation

Manipulatives/Hands On

pp. 605, 613

Model

pp. 573, 578, 584, 596, 602, 608, 616, 621

Represent

pp. 566, 577, 585, 589, 594, 595, 597, 601, 607, 615, 617, 625, 626, 629

Formulate an Equation

pp. 584, 596, 621, 630

Technology

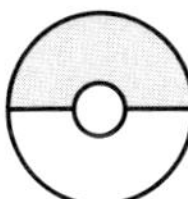

Student Resources

- **eBook**
- **Calculator** Lesson 88
- **Online Resources** at **www.SaxonPublishers.com/ActivitiesC2**
  - **Graphing Calculator Activity** Lesson 85 and Investigation 9
  - **Online Activities**
  - **Math Enrichment Problems**
  - **Math Stumpers**

Teacher Resources

- **Resources and Planner CD**
- **Adaptations CD** Lessons 81–90
- **Test & Practice Generator CD**
- **eGradebook**
- **Answer Key CD**

Content Highlights

Lessons 81–90, Investigation 9

Problem solving involving ratio and measurement continues throughout these lessons. Students calculate the area of circles and explore the interior and exterior of polygons. This section closes with students graphing functions to solve problems.

Problem Solving and Proportional Thinking

The graphic organizer is applicable to percent problems.

The graphic organizer used to solve ratio problems is also used for percent problems in Lesson 81 where students solve percent problems using proportions.

Geometry and Measurement

Circles, angles, and polygons are the focus of geometry in these lessons.

Students calculate the areas of circles in Lesson 82. They explore the relationship of interior and exterior angles and learn two ways to calculate the sum of the interior angles of a polygon in Lesson 89.

Equivalence

Students continue to convert measures.

Unit multipliers are used to convert measures, and using more than one unit multiplier makes it convenient to convert measures such as units of area from one unit to another, as students learn in Lesson 88. In Lesson 83 students multiply numbers in scientific notation.

Algebraic Thinking

Algebra topics are extended in these lessons.

Students identify algebraic terms, and they add like terms in Lesson 84. They also classify expressions as monomials, binomials, or trinomials. In Lesson 87 students multiply algebraic terms. In Lesson 85 they begin simplifying expressions with positive and negative numbers by following the order of operations. Students classify numbers in the real number system in Lesson 86. They solve equations with mixed number and negative coefficients in Lesson 90, and in Investigation 9 students graph functions to solve problems.

Assessment

A variety of weekly assessment tools are provided.

After Lesson 85:
- Power-Up Test 16
- Cumulative Test 16
- Performance Activity 16

After Lesson 90:
- Power-Up Test 17
- Cumulative Test 17
- Customized Benchmark Test
- Performance Task 17

Content Trace

Lessons 81–90, Investigation 9

LESSON	NEW CONCEPTS	PRACTICED	ASSESSED
81	• Using Proportions to Solve Percent Problems	Lessons 81, 82, 83, 84, 85, 86, 87, 88, 89, 90, 91, 101, 102	Tests 17, 18
82	• Area of a Circle	Lessons 82, 83, 84, 85, 86, 87, 88, 89, 90, 91, 93, 94, 96, 97, 98, 100, 101, 102, 103, 104	Tests 17, 20
83	• Multiplying Numbers in Scientific Notation	Lessons 83, 84, 85, 86, 87, 88, 89, 90, 91, 92, 93, 94, 95, 96, 97, 98, 99, 100, 101, 102, 104, 105, 106, 107, 108, 109, 110, 113, 114, 115, 116	Tests 17, 18, 19, 20
84	• Algebraic Terms	Lessons 84, 85, 86, 87, 88, 89, 90, 91, 92, 93, 94, 95, 96, 97, 98, 99, 102	Tests 17, 19
85	• Order of Operations with Positive and Negative Numbers	Lessons 85, 86, 87, 88, 89, 89, 90, 91, 92, 93, 94, 95, 96, 97, 98, 99, 100, 101, 111, 112, 113, 114, 115, 117	Tests 18, 20, 21, 22, 23
86	• Number Families	Lessons 86, 87, 88, 89, 90, 91, 95, 98, 100, 106, 114, 119	Tests 18, 19
87	• Multiplying Algebraic Terms	Lessons 87, 88, 89, 90, 91, 92, 93, 94, 95, 96, 98, 99, 102	Tests 18, 19, 21, 22, 23
88	• Multiple Unit Multipliers	Lessons 88, 89, 90, 91, 92, 93, 94, 95, 96, 101, 109, 113, 117, 119, 120	Tests 18, 19, 20, 23
89	• Diagonals	Lesson 117	Test 18
	• Interior Angles	Lessons 90, 96, 102, 111, 116, 117, 119	Tests 9, 18, 22, 23
	• Exterior Angles	Lessons 89, 90, 96, 102, 111, 116, 117	Test & Practice Generator
90	• Mixed-Number Coefficients	Lessons 90, 91, 92, 93, 94, 101, 103, 104, 112, 114, 120	Tests 19, 23
	• Negative Coefficients	Lessons 90, 91, 92, 93, 94	Test & Practice Generator
Inv. 9	• Graphing Functions	Lessons 81, 91, 92, 93, 94, 95, 96, 97, 98, 100, 101, 102, 103, 104, 105, 106, 107, 108, 109, 110, 111, 112, 113, 115	Test & Practice Generator

• Using Proportions to Solve Percent Problems

Objectives

- Use proportions to solve percent problems.

Lesson Preparation

Materials

- **Power Up P** (in *Instructional Masters*)
- **Investigation Activity 13** (in *Instructional Masters*) or **graph paper**

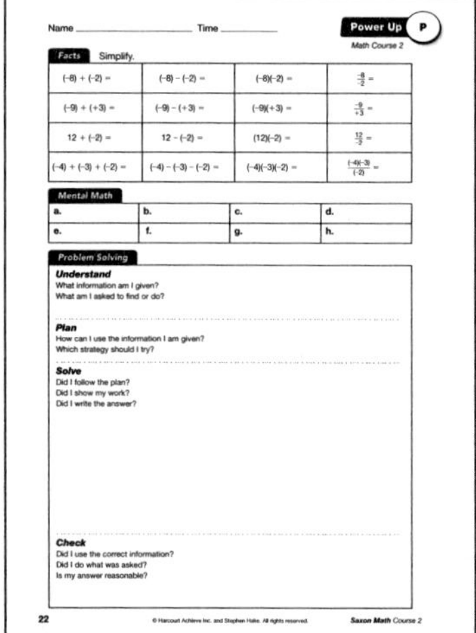

Power Up P

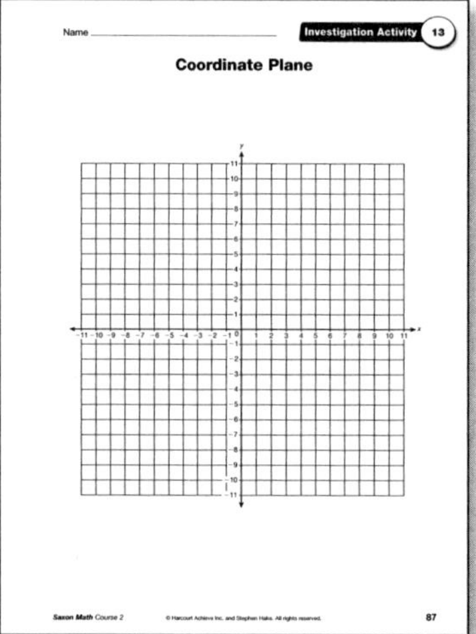

Investigation Activity 13

Math Language

English Learners (ESL)

reflect

Technology Resources

Student eBook Complete student textbook in electronic format.

Resources and Planner CD Blackline masters, plus a pacing calendar with standards.

Test and Practice Generator CD Create additional practice sheets and custom-made tests.

www.SaxonPublishers.com Visit for more student activities and planning materials.

Inclusion

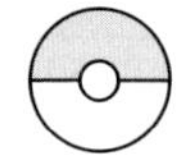

Adaptations CD Adapted lessons, investigations, practice and assessments.

Meeting Standards

National Council of Teachers of Mathematics (NCTM)

Numbers and Operations

NO.1a Work flexibly with fractions, decimals, and percents to solve problems

NO.2a Understand the meaning and effects of arithmetic operations with fractions, decimals, and integers

NO.3d Develop, analyze, and explain methods for solving problems involving proportions, such as scaling and finding equivalent ratios

Problem Solving

PS.1b Solve problems that arise in mathematics and in other contexts

Connections

CN.4c Recognize and apply mathematics in contexts outside of mathematics

Power-Up Discussion *For use with Power Up, p. 562*

Problem-Solving Strategy: Use Logical Reasoning/ Guess and Check

The Egyptians did not have symbols for numerators greater than 1, so they represented larger fractions as sums of unit fractions. For example, $\frac{6}{7}$ could be expressed as $\frac{1}{7} + \frac{1}{7} + \frac{1}{7} + \frac{1}{7} + \frac{1}{7} + \frac{1}{7}$, but it could also be expressed as $\frac{1}{2} + \frac{1}{3} + \frac{1}{42}$. Can you find three ways to write $\frac{7}{8}$ as a sum of unit fractions?

Understand — *Understand the problem.*

"What information are we given?"

We are told that fractions with numerators greater than 1 can be written as sums of unit fractions.

"What are we asked to do?"

We are asked to find three different ways to write $\frac{7}{8}$ as a sum of unit fractions.

Plan — *Make a plan.*

"What problem-solving strategy will we use?"

We will *use logical reasoning* to intelligently *guess and check.*

Solve — *Carry out the plan.*

"How can we write $\frac{7}{8}$ as the sum of $\frac{1}{8}$s?"

$\frac{1}{8} + \frac{1}{8} + \frac{1}{8} + \frac{1}{8} + \frac{1}{8} + \frac{1}{8} + \frac{1}{8} = \frac{7}{8}$

"We can use the Associative Property of Addition to group some of those $\frac{1}{8}$s into other unit fractions (for example, $\frac{1}{8} + \frac{1}{8} = \frac{1}{4}$). How can $\frac{1}{8}$s be combined to form other unit fractions that sum to $\frac{7}{8}$?"

$\frac{1}{4} + \frac{1}{4} + \frac{1}{4} + \frac{1}{8} = \frac{7}{8}$

$\frac{1}{2} + \frac{1}{4} + \frac{1}{8} = \frac{7}{8}$

"What do we notice about $\frac{1}{2} + \frac{1}{4} + \frac{1}{8} = \frac{7}{8}$?"

It is built of unit fractions in descending order.

Check — *Look back.*

"Did we do what we were asked to do?"

Yes, we found three different ways to write $\frac{7}{8}$ as the sum of unit fractions.

1 Power Up

Facts

Distribute **Power Up P** to students. See answers below.

Mental Math

Encourage students to share different ways to mentally compute these exercises. Strategies for exercises **c** and **d** are listed below.

c. Find an Equivalent Fraction

$\frac{6}{9} = \frac{2}{3} = \frac{40}{60}$

$t = 60$

Cross Multiply and Divide

$6t = 9 \times 40$

$t = (9 \times 40) \div 6 = (3 \times 40) \div 2$

$t = 60$

d. Find 1% and Multiply

1% of \$24 is 24¢

15 × 24¢ = (15 × 20)¢ + (15 × 4)¢ = (300 + 60)¢ = \$3.60

Add 10% and 5%

10% of \$24 is \$2.40

5% of \$24 is \$1.20

15% of \$24 is \$3.60

Problem Solving

Refer to **Power-Up Discussion,** p. 562F.

2 New Concepts

Instruction

Begin the lesson by reviewing how to set up a ratio box using information from the following word problem:

The ratio of red to yellow flowers in the vase is 5 to 4. If there are 18 flowers, how many are yellow?

	Ratio	Actual Count
Red	5	R
Yellow	4	Y
Total	9	18

There are 8 yellow flowers.

Tell students that in this lesson they will use ratio boxes to solve problems involving percents.

Point out that the order in which *salad* and *not salad* are listed in the ratio box is not important as long as the data for each row is correctly entered.

(continued)

LESSON 81

• Using Proportions to Solve Percent Problems

Power Up — *Building Power*

facts Power Up P

mental math

a. **Positive/Negative:** $(-10)(-10)$ +100

b. **Exponents:** 12×10^{-4} 0.0012

c. **Ratio:** $\frac{40}{t} = \frac{6}{9}$ 60

d. **Percent:** 15% of \$24.00 \$3.60

e. **Measurement:** 25 mm to cm 2.5 cm

f. **Fractional Parts:** 24 is $\frac{2}{3}$ of n. 36

g. **Geometry:** What do the interior angles of a triangle total? 180 degrees

h. **Calculation:** What is the total cost of a \$25 item plus 8% sales tax? \$27

problem solving

The Egyptians did not have symbols for numerators greater than 1, so they represented larger fractions as sums of unit fractions. For example, $\frac{6}{7}$ could be expressed $\frac{1}{7} + \frac{1}{7} + \frac{1}{7} + \frac{1}{7} + \frac{1}{7} + \frac{1}{7}$, but it could also be expressed as $\frac{1}{2} + \frac{1}{3} + \frac{1}{42}$. Can you find three ways to write $\frac{7}{8}$ as a sum of unit fractions?
$\frac{1}{8} + \frac{1}{8} + \frac{1}{8} + \frac{1}{8} + \frac{1}{8} + \frac{1}{8} + \frac{1}{8} = \frac{7}{8}$, $\frac{1}{4} + \frac{1}{4} + \frac{1}{4} + \frac{1}{8} = \frac{7}{8}$, $\frac{1}{2} + \frac{1}{4} + \frac{1}{8} = \frac{7}{8}$

New Concepts — *Increasing Knowledge*

A percent is a ratio in which 100 represents the total number in the group. Thus percent problems can be solved using the same method we use to solve ratio problems. Consider the following problem:

Math Language
Percents can be written using the symbol %. You can write thirty percent as 30%.

Thirty percent of the lunchtime customers ordered salad. If 21 customers did not order salad, how many lunchtime customers were there?

The problem is about two parts of a group. One part of the group ordered salad for lunch; the other part did not. The whole group is 100 percent. The part that ordered salad for lunch was 30 percent. Thus 70 percent did not order salad for lunch. We record these numbers in a ratio box just as we do with ratio problems.

	Percent	Actual Count
Salad	30	
Not salad	70	
Whole group	100	

Facts Simplify.

(−8) + (−2) = −10	(−8) − (−2) = −6	(−8)(−2) = 16	$\frac{-8}{-2} = 4$
(−9) + (+3) = −6	(−9) − (+3) = −12	(−9)(+3) = −27	$\frac{-9}{+3} = -3$
12 + (−2) = 10	12 − (−2) = 14	(12)(−2) = −24	$\frac{12}{-2} = -6$
(−4) + (−3) + (−2) = −9	(−4) − (−3) − (−2) = 1	(−4)(−3)(−2) = −24	$\frac{(-4)(-3)}{(-2)} = -6$

As we read the problem, we find an actual count as well. There were 21 customers who did not order salad. We record 21 in the appropriate place on the table and use letters in the remaining places.

	Percent	Actual Count
Salad	30	*S*
Not Salad	70	21
Whole Group	100	*W*

We use two of the rows in the table to write a proportion that we can use to solve the problem. **We always use the row in which both numbers are known.** Since the problem asks for the total number of lunchtime customers, we also use the third row.

	Percent	Actual Count
Salad	30	*S*
Not Salad	70	21
Whole Group	100	*W*

$$\frac{70}{100} = \frac{21}{W}$$

$$70W = 2100$$

$$W = 30$$

By solving the proportion, we find there were 30 lunchtime customers.

Conclude What other information can you find out about the lunchtime customers based on the solution to this problem? Sample: Nine customers ordered salad.

Example 1

Thinking Skill

Explain

How is the question in example 1 different from the previous question? Example 1 asks about a missing part. The previous question asks about the whole.

Forty percent of the students at Lincoln Middle School do not buy their lunch in the school cafeteria. If 480 students buy their lunch in the cafeteria, how many of the students do not buy their lunch in the cafeteria?

Solution

We solve this problem just as we solve a ratio problem. We use the percents to fill the percent column of the table. Together, all the students in the school are 100 percent. The part that does not buy lunch is 40 percent. Therefore, the part that buys lunch is 60 percent. The number 480 is the actual count of the students who buy their lunch. We write these numbers in the table.

	Percent	Actual Count
Do Not Buy Lunch	40	*N*
Buy Lunch	60	480
Total	100	*T*

Discuss How do you think we should decide which letters to use as variables in the table? Why?

Sample: We should use letters that help us remember what they stand for. In this case we can use *N* to stand for Not buy lunch, and *T* for Total.

Now we use the table to write a proportion. Since we know both numbers in the second row, we will use that row in the proportion. Since the problem asks us to find the actual count of students who do not buy their lunch in the cafeteria, we also use the first row of the table in the proportion.

2 New Concepts (Continued)

Instruction

Emphasize the importance of checking answers to the word problems presented in this lesson. Have students reread each word problem to make sure their answers make sense within the context of the problem. Suggest that they check by substituting the answer back into the original proportion. Have them simplify the fractions and compare. For example, in the problem about lunchtime customers, $\frac{70}{100} = \frac{21}{30}$ simplifies to $\frac{7}{10} = \frac{7}{10}$. The fractions in the proportion are equivalent so the proportion was solved correctly.

Have student volunteers demonstrate ways to use the solution, 30, to determine the number of lunchtime customers that ordered salad. Use subtraction: 30 (the number of lunchtime customers) − 21 (customers who did not order salad) = 9 (customers who ordered salad); or use a proportion: $\frac{30}{100} = \frac{s}{30}$

Example 1

Instruction

Have students notice that although only one percent is given in a problem, they can then fill in the total with 100 and the other percent with the difference between the given percent and 100. They are then ready to write either of two proportions since they will also have one of the numbers for the actual count.

(continued)

2 New Concepts *(Continued)*

Example 2

Instruction

Before starting to solve the problem in example 2, have students answer the thinking skill question in the student book margin. Then have them compare the answer, 13%, to their predictions. If their predictions were incorrect, have them use the ratio box to discuss why it makes sense that less than 50% of the people carpool.

Check that all students are able to set up the ratio box for percents and actual counts, and that they can then use the ratio box to write and solve the needed proportion.

You may want to conduct a class survey to find out how many students take a bus or public transit to school. Use a ratio box to find the percent of students who ride a bus or public transit to school. Then find the percent of students who get to school using other forms of transportation.

(continued)

	Percent	Actual Count
Do Not Buy Lunch	40	*N*
Buy Lunch	60	480
Total	100	*T*

$$\frac{40}{60} = \frac{N}{480}$$

$$60N = 19{,}200$$

$$N = 320$$

We find that **320 students** do not buy their lunch in the cafeteria.

Example 2

Thinking Skill

Predict

Will the answer to question **a.** be greater than or less than 50%? Why? Less than 50%; 261 is more than half of 300. Since more than half do not carpool, less than half do carpool.

In the town of Centerville, 261 of the 300 working people do not carpool.

a. What percent of the people carpool?

b. According to one national survey, approximately 13 percent of the working people in the United States carpool to work. Do the carpooling statistics in Centerville reflect the national carpooling statistics?

Solution

a. We make a ratio box and write in the numbers. The total number of working people in Centerville is 300, so 39 people carpool.

	Percent	Actual Count
Carpool	P_C	39
Do Not Carpool	P_N	261
Total	100	300

We use P_C to stand for the percent who carpool to work. We use the "carpool" row and the "total" row to write the proportion.

	Percent	Actual Count
Carpool	P_C	39
Do Not Carpool	P_N	261
Total	100	300

$$\frac{P_C}{100} = \frac{39}{300}$$

$$300P_C = 3900$$

$$P_C = 13$$

We find that **13 percent** of the people who work in Centerville carpool to work.

Conclude What percent of people do not carpool? How do you know? 87% do not carpool; 100% is the whole; 100 − 13 = 87

b. Since survey data show that approximately 13 percent of United States workers carpool to work, we find that Centerville's statistics **do reflect the national statistics.**

Example 3

The students had a spelling test with 40 words. Six of the words had four syllables. The rest had less than four syllables. What percent of the words had less than four syllables?

564 *Saxon Math Course 2*

English Learners

Explain the meaning of **reflect** in example 2. Say:

"What do you see when you look in a mirror?" yourself

"What you see in the mirror looks like you. If the Centerville statistics reflect the national statistics, it means the statistics look alike."

Solution

We notice that a little more than one tenth of the words had four syllables.

Predict From the given information, what percent can you estimate the answer will be? slightly less than 90%

We record the given information in a ratio box.

Explain How can we find out how many words had less than four syllables? Sample: Since 6 of the 40 words had four syllables, then 40 − 6 or 34 words had less than four syllables.

	Percent	Actual Count
Less Than Four Syllables	P_L	34
Four Syllables	P_F	6
Total	100	40

We want to know the percent of words with less than four syllables, so we use the "Less than four" row and the "Total" row to write the proportion.

$$\frac{P_L}{100} = \frac{34}{40}$$

$$40P_L = 3400$$

$$P_L = 85$$

On this test **85%** of the words had less than four syllables.

Practice Set

	Percent	A.C.
alfa	P_A	21
ot Alfalfa	P_N	49
tal	100	70

	Percent	A.C.
ead	40	120
ot Read	60	N
otal	100	T

	Percent	A.C.
rect	P_C	26
Correct	P_N	4
l	100	30

▶ **Generalize** Estimate each answer. Then use a ratio box to solve each problem.

a. Twenty-one of the 70 acres were planted with alfalfa. What percent of the acres was not planted in alfalfa? 70%

b. Lori still has 60% of the book to read. If she has read 120 pages, how many pages does she still have to read? 180 pages

c. Dewayne missed four of the 30 problems on the problem set. What percent of the problems did Dewayne answer correctly? $86\frac{2}{3}\%$

▶ **d.** **Classify** Tell whether you found a part, a whole, or a percent to solve each of problems **a** through **c.** **a.** a percent; **b.** a part; **c.** a percent.

Written Practice *Strengthening Concepts*

1.

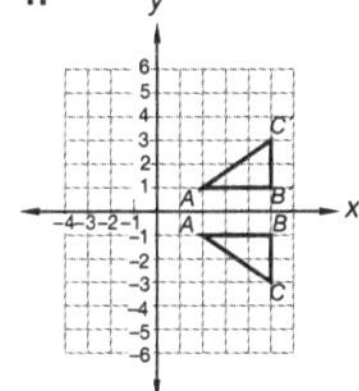

▶ * **1.** (80) **Evaluate** The coordinates of the vertices of $\triangle ABC$ are A (2, −1), B (5, −1), and C (5, −3). Draw the triangle and its image $\triangle A'B'C'$ reflected in the x-axis. What are the coordinates of the vertices of $\triangle A'B'C'$? A' (2, 1), B' (5, 1), C' (5, 3)

2. (66) Use a ratio box to solve this problem. Annuals are plants that complete their life cycle in one year. Perennials are plants that live for more than one year. In a botanical garden, the ratio of annuals to perennials was 9 to 5. If the total number of plants was 2800, how many annuals were there? 1800 annuals

▶ See Math Conversations in the sidebar.

2 New Concepts *(Continued)*

Example 3

Instruction

After you work through this example, go over the process of making and filling in a ratio box for a percent problem. This is the key skill of this lesson, and one that students should easily grasp.

You may want students to calculate the percent of correct answers they get on the Written Practice sections of each lesson for the next week or so. This provides practice in using percents that has an immediate interest for students.

Practice Set

Problems a–c Generalize

If students are not ready to work independently on these problems, guide them to estimate an answer for each one. Then lead the class in completing a ratio box and writing a proportion for each problem.

Problem d Classify

To emphasize that there are different ways to solve many problems, ask whether an equation could be written for problems **a–c.** Sample: Yes, but you can't use the information directly, because you need to make some calculations before you write the equation.

3 Written Practice

Math Conversations

Discussion opportunities are provided below.

Problem 1 Evaluate

Ask students what they notice about the coordinates of the reflected triangle. The absolute value of the corresponding coordinates is the same as those in the original triangle.

Then ask:

"Suppose the triangle was reflected in the y-axis instead of the x-axis. Predict what you would notice about the coordinates of that triangle and explain why this is so." Sample: The y-coordinates would be the same as the original, but the x-coordinates would be the opposite of the original. This is because the coordinates of a reflected image are the same distance from the line of reflection as in the original figure but on the opposite side of the y-axis.

(continued)

3 Written Practice (Continued)

Math Conversations

Discussion opportunities are provided below.

Problem 4a Explain

Discuss what type of graphical display would best represent this data and why it does. Sample: Box-and-whisker plot, because you can see how the data spreads out.

Problem 7 Represent

Have students gather information from the two number lines. Ask questions like these:

"What integers are on both graphs?" $-2, -1, 0, 1, 2, 3$

"Why isn't 4 on both graphs?" It is not included in $x < 4$, but it is in $x \geq -2$.

Problem 11 Analyze

Extend the Problem

"If the cube is rolled twice, what are the odds of rolling two 3s?" 1 to 35

"Suppose you roll a cube and get a 3. What are the odds of getting a 3 on the next roll?" 1 to 5

Point out that once the first cube has been rolled, the odds for rolling the second cube are the same as for a single roll.

(continued)

Use the information below to answer problems **3** and **4.**

Rory has been learning to type on his computer. On his last 15 typing practices he typed the following number of words per minute:
70, 85, 80, 85, 90, 80, 85, 80, 90, 95, 85, 90, 100, 85, 90.

3. (Inv. 4) **a.** What was the average (mean) number of words per minute Rory typed? 86

b. If the number of words typed per minute were arranged in order from greatest to least, which would be the middle number (median)? 85

▶ **4.** (Inv. 4) **a.** **Explain** How many words per minute did Rory type most often? How can you tell? Is this the mode, range, or mean of the number of words typed per minute?

4. a. 85; mode; Sample: I can look at the list of 15 numbers and see that he typed 85 words four times, which is more times than any other number.

b. What was the difference between the greatest and the least number of words per minute that Rory typed (range)? 30

5. (56) Danny is 6′1″ (6 ft 1 in.) tall. His sister is $5'6\frac{1}{2}''$ tall. Danny is how many inches taller than his sister? $6\frac{1}{2}$ inches

6. (72) Use a ratio box to solve this problem. Carmen bought 5 pencils for 75¢. At this rate, how much would she pay for a dozen pencils? $1.80

▶ *** 7.** (78) **Represent** Graph each inequality on a separate number line:
a. $x < 4$ **b.** $x \geq -2$

7. a.

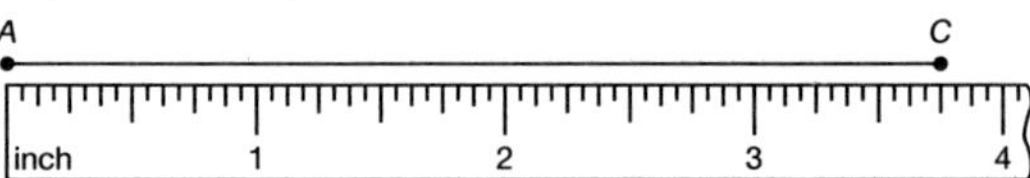

7. b.

8. (36, 71) Read this statement. Then answer the questions that follow.
So far Soon-Jin has sent out 48 invitations to her party. This is $\frac{4}{5}$ of all of the invitations she will send out.

a. How many invitations will Soon-Jin send out? 60 invitations

b. What is the ratio of invitations sent out already to those not sent out yet? $\frac{4}{1}$

9. (8) If point B is located halfway between points A and C, what is the length of segment AB? $1\frac{7}{8}$ inches

A C
inch 1 2 3 4

10. (41) If $x = 9$, what does $x^2 + \sqrt{x}$ equal? 84

▶* **11.** (Inv. 8) If a single number cube is rolled, what are the odds of getting a 3? 1 to 5

12. (48) Complete the table.

Fraction	Decimal	Percent
$2\frac{1}{4}$	**a.** 2.25	**b.** 225%
c. $\frac{9}{400}$	**d.** 0.0225	$2\frac{1}{4}\%$

▶ See Math Conversations in the sidebar.

Write equations to solve problems **13** and **14**.

13. (60) The store owner makes a profit of 40% of the selling price of an item. If an item sells for $12, how much profit does the store owner make? $p = 0.4 \times \$12$; $4.80

▶* **14.** (77) Analyze Fifty percent of what number is 0.4? $0.5 \times W_N = 0.4$; 0.8

* **15.** (76) Simplify: $\dfrac{16\frac{2}{3}}{100}$ $\frac{1}{6}$

Use ratio boxes to solve problems **16** and **17**.

16. 84%; Sample: I multiplied $\frac{21}{25} \times 100$ to find the percent: $\frac{21}{25} \times \frac{100}{1} = 84$ $= 84\%$

▶* **16.** (81) Justify In a restaurant, 21 of the 25 tables are round. What percent of the tables are round? Tell what you did to find out.

▶* **17.** (81) Twenty percent of the 4000 acres were plowed. How many acres were not plowed? 3200 acres

18. a. Sample: Angles *ABC* and *CBD* are supplementary (total 180°), so $m\angle CBD = 40°$.
b. Sample: Angles *CBD* and *DBE* are complementary (total 90°), so $m\angle DBE = 50°$.
c. Sample: Angles *DBE* and *EBA* are supplementary (total 180°), so $m\angle EBA = 130°$.

▶ **18.** (40) If the measure of ∠*ABC* is 140°, then

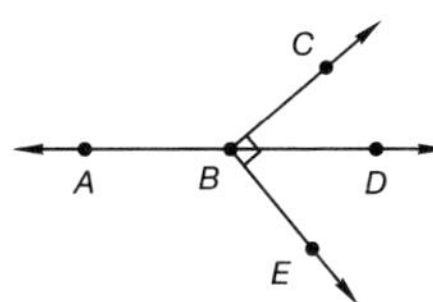

a. What is the measure of ∠*CBD*? How do you know? 40°

b. What is the measure of ∠*DBE*? How do you know? 50°

c. What is the measure of ∠*EBA*? How do you know? 130°

d. What is the sum of the measures of ∠*ABC*, ∠*CBD*, ∠*DBE*, and ∠*EBA*? 360°

19. (24) Write the prime factorization of the two terms of this fraction. Then reduce the fraction. $\frac{2 \cdot 2 \cdot 2 \cdot 3 \cdot 5 \cdot 5 \cdot 5}{2 \cdot 2 \cdot 3 \cdot 3 \cdot 5 \cdot 5 \cdot 7} = \frac{10}{21}$

$$\frac{3000}{6300}$$

* **20.** (58, 75) **a.** Find the area of this isosceles trapezoid. Dimensions are in inches. 180 in.^{2}

b. Trace the trapezoid on your paper. Then draw its line of symmetry.

10, 13, 12, 13, 20

20. b.

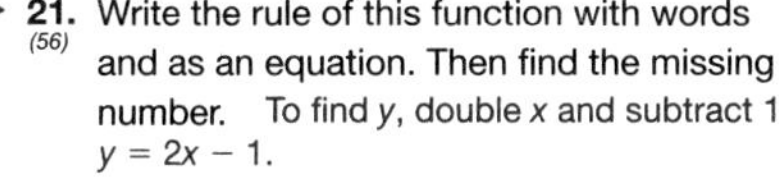

▶ **21.** (56) Write the rule of this function with words and as an equation. Then find the missing number. To find *y*, double *x* and subtract 1. $y = 2x - 1$.

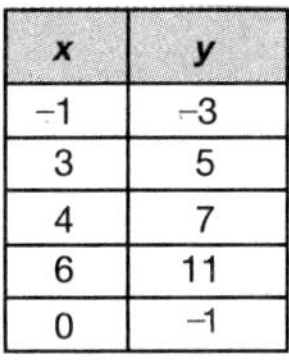

x	*y*
−1	−3
3	5
4	7
6	11
0	−1

▶ See Math Conversations in the sidebar.

3 Written Practice (Continued)

Math Conversations

Discussion opportunities are provided below.

Problem 14 Analyze

Have students use the answer to this question and mental math to answer questions like these:

"Fifty percent of what number is 0.2?" 0.4

"Fifty percent of what number is 0.8?" 1.6

"Twenty-five percent of what number is 0.2?" 0.8

Ask volunteers to make up percent problems and have others solve them.

Problem 16 Justify

Ask students to read their answers and to explain why they did each step. Sample: I multiplied $\frac{21}{25}$ by 100 to find the percent, because percent means per 100.

Errors and Misconceptions

Problem 17

Students may have difficulty setting up the ratio box. Have them read the problem carefully and list the important information. Have them identify what is known and what is unknown before drawing the ratio box. If necessary, help students set up the ratio box for this problem.

	Percent	Actual Count
Plowed	20	P
Not plowed	80	N
Total	100	4000

Remind them to solve for N, or not plowed.

Problem 18

Remind students to use what they know about supplementary and complementary angles to answer parts **a–d.**

Problem 21

If students are having difficulty completing this problem, focus their attention on the (3, 5), (4, 7), and (6, 11) pairs. Have them suggest a rule that works for these three pairs before testing the rule on the (−1, −3) pair.

(continued)

3 Written Practice (Continued)

Math Conversations

Discussion opportunities are provided below.

Problems 25–30 Generalize

Ask volunteers to tell whether any of these expressions can be simplified with mental math and then describe how. Sample: For problem 26, you can see that the square root of 2^2 is 2, the square root of 3^4 is 3^2, or 9, and the square root of 5^2 is 5. Then you calculate 5×2 is 10, 10×9 is 90.

The problems that students will most likely find easy to simplify mentally are 26, 29, and 30, but some students may be able to devise ways to do some of the others. You might ask why mental math is not appropriate or usable for those problems that are not mentioned.

Errors and Misconceptions

Problem 22

Remind students who do not write these numbers correctly in scientific notation that a number written in scientific notation has exactly one nonzero digit to the left of the decimal point.

▶ **22.** (69) Write each number in scientific notation:
a. 56×10^7 5.6×10^8 **b.** 56×10^{-7} 5.6×10^{-6}

For problems **23** and **24,** solve and check the equation. Show each step.

* **23.** (Inv. 7) $5x = 16.5$ 3.3 * **24.** (Inv. 7) $3\frac{1}{2} + a = 5\frac{3}{8}$ $1\frac{7}{8}$

▶ Generalize Simplify:

* **25.** (63) $3^2 + 5[6 - (10 - 2^3)]$ 29

26. (52) $\sqrt{2^2 \cdot 3^4 \cdot 5^2}$ 90

27. (43) $2\frac{2}{3} \times 4.5 \div 6$ (fraction answer) 2 or $\frac{2}{1}$

28. (26, 43) $\left(3\frac{1}{2}\right)^2 - (5 - 3.4)$ (decimal answer) 10.65

* **29.** (73) **a.** $(-1.2)(-9)$ 10.8 **b.** $(-3)(2.5)$ -7.5
c. $\left(\frac{1}{2}\right)\left(\frac{-1}{2}\right)$ $\frac{-1}{4}$ **d.** $\left(-\frac{1}{2}\right)\left(\frac{-1}{2}\right)$ $\frac{1}{4}$

30. (68) **a.** $(-3) + |-4| - (-5)$ 6
b. $(-18) - (+20) + (-7)$ -45
c. $\frac{1}{2} - \left(-\frac{1}{2}\right)$ 1

Early Finishers *Real-World Application*

The per barrel price of crude oil, in U.S. dollars per barrel, varies from day to day. Here are the closing prices rounded to the nearest tenth for a five-day period.

Mon.	Tues.	Wed.	Th.	Fri.
65.4	66.3	66.9	67.5	66.8

Which display—a line graph or a bar graph—is the most appropriate way to display this data if you want to emphasize the changes in the price of crude oil? Draw the display and justify your choice. line graph; Sample: While a bar graph can be used to display comparisons, a line graph would be better because it clearly displays a change over time. See student graphs.

▶ See Math Conversations in the sidebar.

Looking Forward

Using proportions to solve percent problems prepares students for:

- **Lesson 110,** finding successive discounts.

• Area of a Circle

Objectives

- Find the area of a circle.

Lesson Preparation

Materials

- **Power Up Q** (in *Instructional Masters*)

Optional

- **Investigation Activity 13** (in *Instructional Masters*) or **graph paper**
- **Teacher-provided material: overhead grid, scissors, grid paper**
- **Geometric Formulas poster**

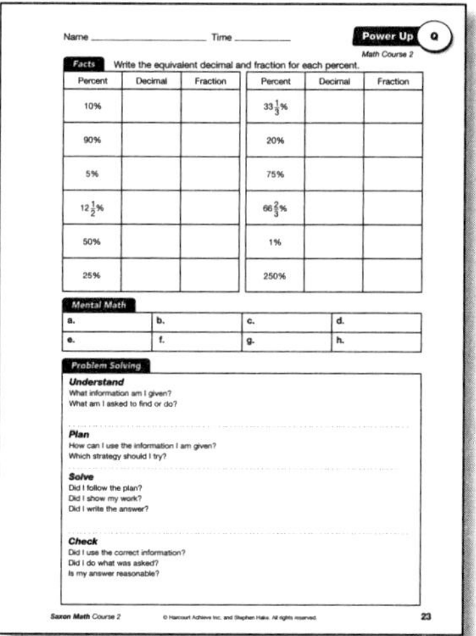

Name ______ Time ______ **Power Up Q** *Math Course 2*

Facts Write the equivalent decimal and fraction for each percent.

Percent	Decimal	Fraction	Percent	Decimal	Fraction
10%			$33\frac{1}{3}$%		
90%			20%		
5%			75%		
$12\frac{1}{2}$%			$66\frac{2}{3}$%		
50%			1%		
25%			250%		

Mental Math

a.	b.	c.	d.
e.	f.	g.	h.

Problem Solving

Understand
What information am I given?
What am I asked to find or do?

Plan
How can I use the information I am given?
Which strategy should I try?

Solve
Did I follow the plan?
Did I show my work?
Did I write the answer?

Check
Did I use the correct information?
Did I do what was asked?
Is my answer reasonable?

Saxon Math Course 2 23

Power Up Q

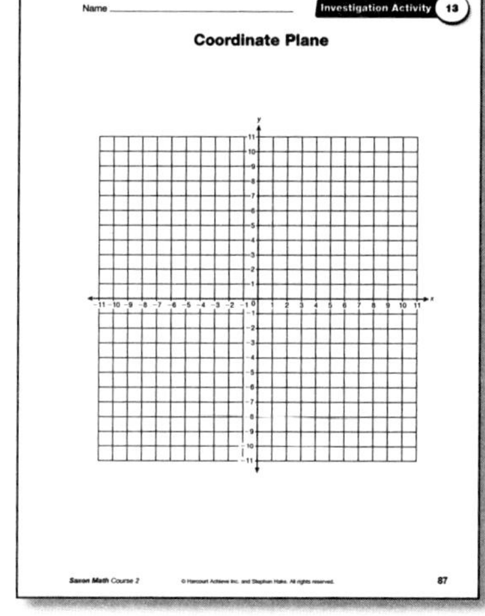

Name ______ **Investigation Activity 13**

Coordinate Plane

Saxon Math Course 2 87

Investigation Activity 13

Technology Resources

Student eBook Complete student textbook in electronic format.

Resources and Planner CD Blackline masters, plus a pacing calendar with standards.

Test and Practice Generator CD Create additional practice sheets and custom-made tests.

www.SaxonPublishers.com Visit for more student activities and planning materials.

Inclusion

Adaptations CD Adapted lessons, investigations, practice and assessments.

Meeting Standards

National Council of Teachers of Mathematics (NCTM)

Measurement

ME.2b Select and apply techniques and tools to accurately find length, area, volume, and angle measures to appropriate levels of precision

ME.2c Develop and use formulas to determine the circumference of circles and the area of triangles, parallelograms, trapezoids, and circles and develop strategies to find the area of more-complex shapes

Communication

CM.3b Communicate their mathematical thinking coherently and clearly to peers, teachers, and others

Power-Up Discussion *For use with Power Up, p. 569*

Problem-Solving Strategy: Use Logical Reasoning/ Write an Equation

A 60" × 104" rectangular tablecloth was draped over a rectangular table. Eight inches of cloth hung over the left edge of the table, 3 inches over the back, 4 inches over the right edge, and 7 inches over the front. In which directions (L, B, R, and F) and by how many inches should the tablecloth be shifted so that equal amounts of cloth hang over opposite edges of the table?

Understand **Understand the problem.**

"What information are we given?"

A rectangular tablecloth measuring 60 in. by 104 in. was draped over a rectangular table. Eight inches of cloth hung over the left edge of the table, 3 inches over the back, 4 inches over the right edge, and 7 inches over the front.

"What are we asked to do?"

We are asked to determine in which directions (L, B, R, and F) and by how many inches the tablecloth should be shifted so that equal amounts of cloth hang over opposite edges of the table.

Plan **Make a plan.**

"What problem-solving strategy will we use?"

We will *use logical reasoning* to determine in what directions and by how many inches the cloth should be shifted.

Solve **Carry out the plan.**

"How many inches total hang over the left and right sides?"

The tablecloth hangs 8 in. over the left side and 4 in. over the right side: 8 + 4 = 12 in.

"If an equal amount of cloth were hanging over the left and right sides, how many inches would be hanging over?"

6 in.

"How can we move the tablecloth so that 6 in. hangs over both the left and right sides?"

We can move it 2 in. to the right.

"How many inches total hang over the front and back of the table?"

The tablecloth hangs 3 inches over the back and 7 inches over the front: 3 + 7 = 10 in.

"If an equal amount of cloth were hanging over the front and back of the table, how many inches would be hanging over?"

5 in.

"How can we move the tablecloth so that 5 in. hangs over both the front and back of the table?"

We can move it 2 in. to the back.

Check **Look back.**

"Did we do what we were asked to do?"

Yes, we descibed how to center the tablecloth on the table by moving it 2 inches to the right and 2 inches back.

LESSON 82

• Area of a Circle

Power Up — *Building Power*

facts Power Up Q

mental math

a. **Positive/Negative:** $(-6) - (-24)$ 18

b. **Exponents:** 10^{-2} $\frac{1}{100}$ or 0.01

c. **Algebra:** $8n + 6 = 78$ 9

d. **Decimals/Measurement:** 3.14×10 ft 31.4 ft

e. **Measurement:** 150 cm to m 1.5 m

f. **Fractional Parts:** 24 is $\frac{3}{4}$ of n. 32

g. **Geometry:** What do you call two adjoining angles that total 180 degrees? supplementary angles

h. **Calculation:** 25% of 24, $\times$ 5, $-$ 2, $\div$ 2, $+$ 1, $\div$ 3, $\times$ 7, $+$ 1, $\sqrt{}$, $\times$ 10 60

problem solving A 60″ × 104″ rectangular tablecloth was draped over a rectangular table. Eight inches of cloth hung over the left edge of the table, 3 inches over the back, 4 inches over the right edge, and 7 inches over the front. In which directions (L, B, R, and F) and by how many inches should the tablecloth be shifted so that equal amounts of cloth hang over opposite edges of the table? 2″ to the back, and 2″ to the right.

New Concept — *Increasing Knowledge*

Math Language
Perpendicular segments meet to form a right angle.

We can find the areas of some polygons by multiplying two perpendicular segments.

- We find the area of a rectangle by multiplying the length by the width.

$$A = lw$$

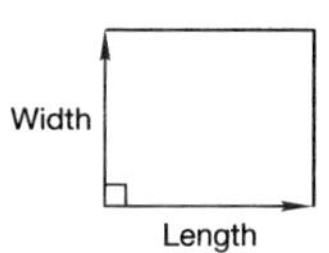

- We find the area of a parallelogram by multiplying the base by the height which gives us the area of a rectangle that equals the area of the parallelogram.

$$A = bh$$

Height
Base

- We find the area of a triangle by multiplying the base by the height (which gives us the area of a rectangle) and then dividing by 2.

$$A = \frac{bh}{2} \quad \text{or} \quad A = \frac{1}{2}bh$$

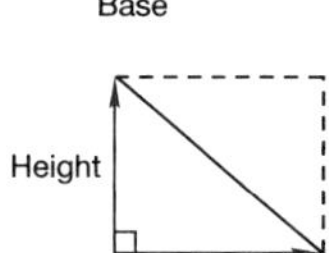

Facts Write the equivalent decimal and fraction for each percent.

Percent	Decimal	Fraction	Percent	Decimal	Fraction
10%	0.1	$\frac{1}{10}$	$33\frac{1}{3}$%	$0.\overline{3}$	$\frac{1}{3}$
90%	0.9	$\frac{9}{10}$	20%	0.2	$\frac{1}{5}$
5%	0.05	$\frac{1}{20}$	75%	0.75	$\frac{3}{4}$
$12\frac{1}{2}$%	0.125	$\frac{1}{8}$	$66\frac{2}{3}$%	$0.\overline{6}$	$\frac{2}{3}$
50%	0.5	$\frac{1}{2}$	1%	0.01	$\frac{1}{100}$
25%	0.25	$\frac{1}{4}$	250%	2.5	$2\frac{1}{2}$

1 Power Up

Facts

Distribute **Power Up Q** to students. See answers below.

Mental Math

Encourage students to share different ways to mentally compute these exercises. Strategies for exercises **e** and **f** are listed below.

e. Use a Unit Multiplier

$150 \text{ cm} \times \frac{1 \text{ m}}{100 \text{ cm}} = 1.5 \text{ m}$

Decompose and Add

100 cm = 1 m

50 cm = 0.5 m

150 cm = 1.5 m

f. Use a Unit Fraction

$24 = \frac{3}{4}n$

$8 = \frac{1}{4}n$

$n = 4 \times 8 = 32$

Use an Equation

$\frac{3}{4}n = 24$

$n = \frac{4}{3} \times 24$

$n = 4 \times 8 = 32$

Problem Solving

Refer to **Power-Up Discussion,** p. 569B.

2 New Concepts

Instruction

Remind students that they already know how to use a formula to find the area of rectangles, triangles, and parallelograms. Tell them that in this lesson they will learn to use a formula to find the area of a circle.

On the board, make a list of situations in which finding the area of a circle would be useful. Examples might include the area of:

- The part of a field watered by a circular sprinkler system.
- The space monitored by air traffic controllers at airports.
- A circular garden.
- A wrestling mat.

(continued)

2 New Concepts (Continued)

Instruction

On an overhead grid or the board, draw a circle and have students recall how they estimated the area of the circle by counting the unit squares and parts of unit squares. Then demonstrate the steps shown in this lesson.

You may choose to have students use grid paper and scissors to prove that the area of the circle is less than four squares with side lengths equal to the radius but more than three of these squares. Students can cut each square into its circular part and collect the remaining areas to demonstrate that the area of the circle is a little more than three squares.

Example

Instruction

In this example, three values for π are used: 3.14, $\frac{22}{7}$, and π. Remind students that 3.14, the decimal approximation of pi, should be used for calculations in this book unless otherwise directed.

(continued)

To find the area of a circle, we begin by multiplying the radius by the radius. This gives us the area of a square built on the radius.

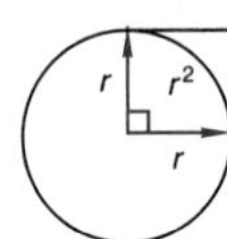

If the radius of the circle is 3, the area of the square is 3^2, which is 9. If the radius of the circle is r, the area of the square is r^2. We see that the area of the circle is less than the area of four of these squares.

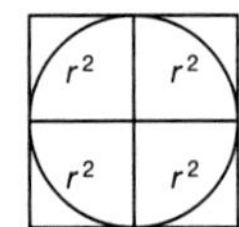

However, the area of the circle is more than the area of three squares.

The number of squares whose area exactly equals the area of the circle is between 3 and 4. The exact number is π. Thus, to find the area of the circle, we first find the area of the square built on the radius; then we multiply that area by π. This is summarized by the equation

$$A = \pi r^2$$

Example

Find the area of each circle:

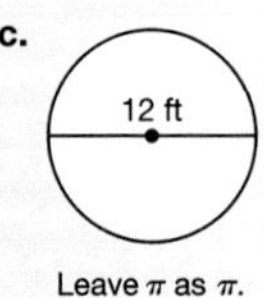

Solution

a. The area of a square built on the radius is 100 cm². We multiply this by π.

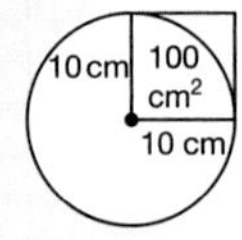

$A = \pi r^2$

$A \approx (3.14)(100 \text{ cm}^2)$

$A \approx \mathbf{314 \text{ cm}^2}$

Explain Why is the symbol ≈ used instead of = when 3.14 is substituted for π? Sample: 3.14 is an approximation of the value of π, and the symbol ≈ means "is approximately equal to."

Math Background

How can we explain why the formula for the area of a circle works?

Imagine cutting a circle into smaller and smaller sectors and alternating the slices to form a rectangular figure. Doing so will form a figure that approximates a rectangle.

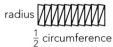

radius

$\frac{1}{2}$ circumference

As the slices become smaller, the length of the rectangle approaches half the circumference, and the height approaches the radius. The area of the rectangle can be expressed as:

$$\begin{aligned}\text{Area} &= \tfrac{1}{2}\text{ circumference} \cdot \text{radius}\\ &= \tfrac{1}{2}(2\pi r) \cdot (r)\\ &= \pi r^2\end{aligned}$$

Thinking Skill

Summarize

State the relationship between the diameter and the radius of a given circle. Sample: The diameter of a circle is two times the radius, or the radius is $\frac{1}{2}$ the diameter.

In **a** and **b** we substituted an approximate value for π. In **c** we used the symbol for pi. As no approximation was used, this answer is exact.

b. The area of a square built on the radius is 49 in.^{2}. We multiply this by π.

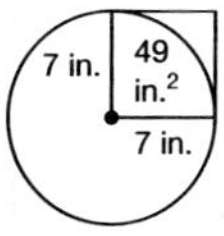

$$A = \pi r^2$$

$$A \approx \frac{22}{\cancel{7}_1} \cdot \cancel{49}^{7}\text{ in.}^2$$

$$A \approx \mathbf{154\ in.^2}$$

c. Since the diameter is 12 ft, the radius is 6 ft. The area of a square built on the radius is 36 ft^2. We multiply this by π.

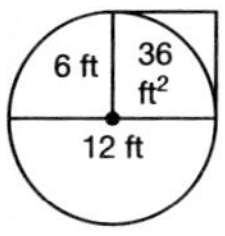

$$A = \pi r^2$$

$$A = \pi \cdot 36\text{ ft}^2$$

$$A = \mathbf{36\pi\ ft^2}$$

Infer In the answers for **a** and **b,** we used the $\approx$ symbol, while in **c** we used the = sign. Why did we not use $\approx$ in **c?**

Practice Set

a. Using 3.14 for π, calculate to the nearest square foot the area of circle c. in this lesson's example. 113 ft^2

▶ Find the area of each circle:

b.

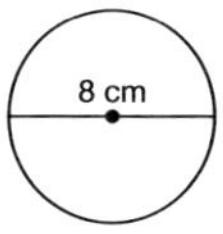

Use 3.14 for π.

c.

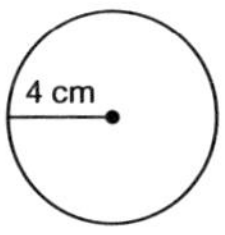

Leave π as π.

d.

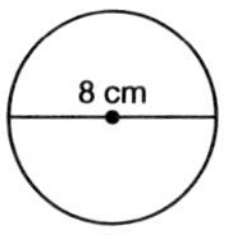

Use $\frac{22}{7}$ for π.

b. 50.24 cm^2 **c.** 16π cm^2 **d.** $50\frac{2}{7}$ cm^2

▶ **e.** *Estimate* Make a rough estimate of the area of a circle that has a diameter of 2 meters. Tell how you made your estimate.

e. about 3 m^2. Sample: The diameter of the circle is 2 m, so the radius is 1 m. Since $A = \pi r^2$, and $1^2 = 1$, $A \approx 3.14 \times 1 \approx 3$.

Written Practice *Strengthening Concepts*

1. (70) Find the volume of this rectangular prism. Dimensions are in feet. 20 ft^3

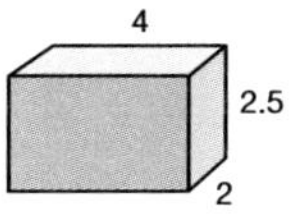

2. (28) The heights of five cherry trees are 6′3″, 6′5″, 5′11″, 6′2″, and 6′1″. Find the average height of the five trees. *Hint:* Change all measures to inches before dividing. 6′2″

3. (54) Use a ratio box to solve this problem. The student-teacher ratio at the high school was 20 to 1. If there were 48 high school teachers, how many students were there? 960 students

4. (50) An inch equals 2.54 centimeters. Use a unit multiplier to convert 2.54 centimeters to meters.

$$2.54\text{ centimeters} \cdot \frac{1\text{ meter}}{100\text{ centimeters}} = 0.0254\text{ meter}$$

▶ See Math Conversations in the sidebar.

2 New Concepts (Continued)

Example (continued)

Instruction

Explain to students that in parts **a, b,** and **c,** they were given the form of pi to use. Ask if they can think of another reason, in addition to gaining experience using these forms of pi, for why the particular form of pi was used with each problem. The forms are chosen to make the calculations as simple as possible. In part **a,** 3.14 is used because it is easy to calculate with multiples of 10. In part **b,** $\frac{22}{7}$ is used because the fraction can be reduced easily when dealing with multiples of 7. In part **c,** π is used because it offers an exact answer.

Practice Set

Problems b–d

Point out to students that each of these circles has the same diameter. Note that the only area that is exact is the answer given for problem **c.**

Problem e *Estimate*

Ask students whether they can give an exact value for the area of the circle in this problem. Sample: Yes; Because the radius is 1 meter, the area is exactly π square meters.

Math Background

You may want to tell students a bit more about π. In addition to $\frac{22}{7}$, other approximations for π have been derived, but most are very complex. A simple one that is accurate to 7 significant figures is $\frac{355}{113}$. An odd π fact is that in the late 1800's a bill attempting to define π was introduced in the Indiana legislature but it failed to pass into law. π can be an interesting and challenging topic for a research project.

3 Written Practice

Math Conversations

Discussion opportunities are provided below.

Problem 8

Extend the Problem

Have students compare the two expressions when $x = 8$ and $y = 4$. They are equal.

Tell students to choose any two numbers for x and y, and again compare the expressions. They will be equal.

Ask:

"Do you think that the two expressions are equal? Why?" Samples: Yes, we have used different pairs of numbers, and so far, the expressions are always equal. Maybe, they seem to be so far.

Problem 11

Extend the Problem

Discuss how the circumferences of the two circles differ. Point out that the answers to both parts are approximations of the exact circumference, 14π centimeters, which is a little more than the answer to part **a** and a little less than the answer to part **b**.

"What can we deduce from this information?" Sample: 3.14 is less than π, and $\frac{22}{7}$ is greater than π.

Problem 12

Extend the Problem

Continue along the lines of the previous discussion but for area. Again, both answers are approximations of the exact area, which is 49π cm^2.

"Compare the areas you found for parts a and b with the exact area. Which is greater? Which is less?" The area found in part **a** is less than the exact area and the area found in part **b** is greater than the exact area.

Errors and Misconceptions

Problem 14

Some students may get \$16 or \$0.16 as the answer. Suggest that they first assess what would be a reasonable answer. They may note that 10% of \$25 is \$2.50, and 5% of \$25 is \$1.25, so 6.4% of \$25 should be less than \$2.50 but more than and closer to \$1.25.

(continued)

* **5.** (78) Graph each inequality on a separate number line: (See below.)

a. $x < -2$ **b.** $x \geq 0$

6. (72) Use a case 1-case 2 ratio box to solve this problem. Don's heart beats 225 times in 3 minutes. At that rate, how many times will his heart beat in 5 minutes? 375 times

7. (36, 71) Read this statement. Then answer the questions that follow.

Two fifths of the performances were sold out. There were 15 performances that were not sold out.

a. How many performances were there? 25 performances

b. What was the ratio of sold out to not sold out performances? $\frac{2}{3}$

▶ **8.** (52) Compare: $x^2 - y^2 \; (=) \; (x + y)(x - y)$ if $x = 5$ and $y = 3$

9. (Inv. 1) What percent of this circle is shaded? 52%

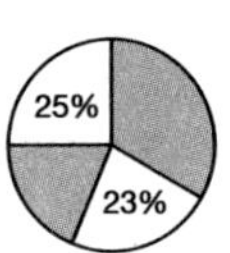

10. (Inv. 8) The meteorologist forecast the chance of rain to be 60%. Based on the forecast, what is the chance it will not rain? 40%

▶ **11.** (65) Find the circumference of each circle:

a. 43.96 cm

7 cm

Use 3.14 for π.

b. 44 cm

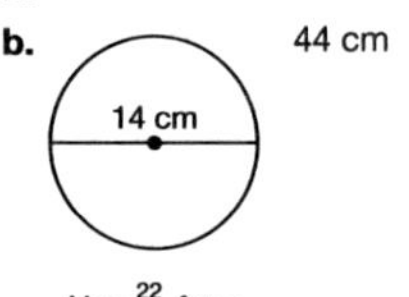

Use $\frac{22}{7}$ for π.

▶* **12.** (82) Find the area of each circle in problem **11.** **a.** 153.86 cm^2 **b.** 154 cm^2

13. (82) Complete the table.

Fraction	Decimal	Percent
a. $1\frac{3}{5}$	1.6	**b.** 160%
c. $\frac{2}{125}$	**d.** 0.016	1.6%

▶ **14.** (60) Write an equation to solve this problem: $M = 0.064 \times \$25$; \$1.60

How much money is 6.4% of \$25?

15. (69) Write each number in scientific notation:

a. 12×10^5 1.2×10^6 **b.** 12×10^{-5} 1.2×10^{-4}

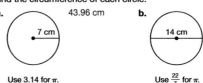

5. a. −5 −4 −3 −2 −1

b. −1 0 1 2 3

▶ See Math Conversations in the sidebar.

17. 120 pages, Sample: George has read 60% of the book, which is 180 pages. I wrote and solved an equation to find 60% of what number = 180: $0.6x = 180$, so $x = \frac{180}{0.6} = 300$. The book has 300 pages. Then I subtracted to find the number of pages George has left to read: $300 - 180 = 120$.

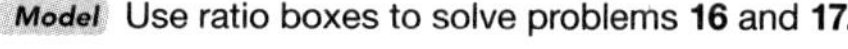

Model Use ratio boxes to solve problems **16** and **17.**

▶* **16.** *(81)* Sixty-four percent of the students correctly described the process of photosynthesis. If 63 students did not correctly describe the process of photosynthesis, how many students did correctly describe the process? 112 students

▶* **17.** *(81)* George still has 40 percent of his book to read. If George has read 180 pages, how many pages does he still have to read? How do you know?

▶* **18.** *(75)* Find the area of the figure shown. Dimensions are in inches. Corners that look square are square. 59 in.^{2}

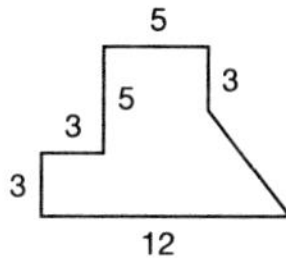

* **19.** *(80)* The coordinates of the vertices of $\triangle XYZ$ are X (4, 3), Y (4, 1), and Z (1, 1).

a. Draw $\triangle XYZ$ and its image $\triangle X'Y'Z'$ translated 5 units to the left and 3 units down.

b. What are the coordinates of the vertices of $\triangle X'Y'Z'$? **b.** X' (−1, 0), Y' (−1, −2), Z' (−4, −2)

a.

▶ **20.** *(24)* Write the prime factorization of the two terms of this fraction. Then reduce the fraction. $\frac{2 \cdot 2 \cdot 2 \cdot 2 \cdot 3 \cdot 5}{2 \cdot 2 \cdot 2 \cdot 2 \cdot 3 \cdot 17} = \frac{5}{17}$

$$\frac{240}{816}$$

▶ **21.** *(Inv. 2)* The figure below illustrates regular hexagon *ABCDEF* inscribed in a circle with center at point *M*.

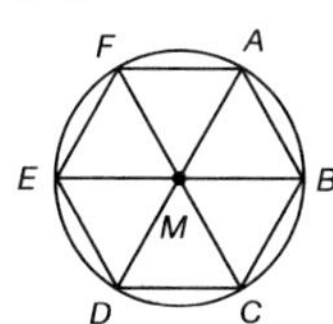

a. How many illustrated chords are diameters? 3 chords

b. How many illustrated chords are not diameters? 6 chords

c. What is the measure of central angle *AMB?* 60°

d. What is the measure of inscribed angle *ABC?* 120°

▶ **22.** *(51)* Write 100 million in scientific notation. 1×10^8

For problems **23** and **24,** solve and check the equation. Show each step.

23. *(Inv. 7)* $\frac{3}{4}x = 36$ 48

24. *(Inv. 7)* $3.2 + a = 3.46$ 0.26

▶ See Math Conversations in the sidebar.

3 Written Practice *(Continued)*

Math Conversations

Discussion opportunities are provided below.

Problems 16 and 17 Model

Explain that equations can also be used as models for these situations. Work with students to write an equation for one of the two problems.

Ask:

"Which method do you like better? Why?"

Sample: The ratio box, because it keeps everything in order and I don't make as many mistakes.

Problem 21

Extend the Problem

Have students continue to examine the geometric relationships in this figure. You may want to guide the discussion to cover topics for which students need review or refreshing. Possible topics include: vertical angles, supplementary angles, complementary angles, congruence, and symmetry.

Problem 22

Extend the Problem

Have students list as many ways as they can for representing 100 million. Samples: 10^8; 100,000,000; 50,000,000 + 50,000,000; 10,000 × 10,000; $2^8 \times 2^8$

Errors and Misconceptions

Problem 18

Students may have difficulty dividing this figure into parts. Have them draw the figure on paper and remind them that they can divide the figure into squares, rectangles, triangles, or trapezoids. Before they start finding the individual areas, they should label all lengths that they can.

Problem 20

Remind students whose answer is 48 that prime factorization is not the same as greatest common factor—that it is expressing a number as the product of only prime numbers.

Problem 21a

To help students who say that there are six chords that are diameters, remind them that $\overline{AD}$ is the same as $\overline{DA}$.

(continued)

3 Written Practice (Continued)

Math Conversations

Discussion opportunities are provided below.

Errors and Misconceptions

Problem 29

For students who have the wrong sign in the answer, suggest that they first determine what the sign of the answer is. Remind them to check whether the number of negative signs in an expression is odd or even.

Simplify:

25. (52) $\dfrac{\sqrt{3^2 + 4^2}}{5}$ 1

26. (52) $(8 - 3)^2 - (3 - 8)^2$ 0

27. (43, 45) $3\frac{1}{2} \div (7 \div 0.2)$ (decimal answer) 0.1

28. (43) $4.5 + 2\frac{2}{3} - 3$ (mixed-number answer) $4\frac{1}{6}$

▸ **29.** (73) **a.** $\dfrac{(-3)(-4)}{(-2)}$ −6 **b.** $\left(-\frac{2}{3}\right)\left(-\frac{3}{4}\right)$ $\frac{1}{2}$

30. (68) **a.** $(-0.3) + (-0.4) - (-0.2)$ −0.5

b. $(-20) + (+30) - |-40|$ −30

Early Finisher
Real-World Application

Henrietta recently completed a driver's safety course, which means that her insurance premiums will decrease. Before the course, Henrietta's insurance cost $172 per month. It now costs $127 per month.

a. How much was Henrietta paying for insurance per year? $2064

b. How much less is Henrietta now paying per year in premiums? $540

c. To the nearest whole number, what is the percent of decrease for her insurance premiums? 26%

▸ See Math Conversations in the sidebar.

Looking Forward

Finding the area of a circle prepares students for:

- **Lesson 95,** finding the volume of right circular cylinders.
- **Lesson 104,** finding the area of figures that contain semicircles and the area of sectors that are not semicircles.
- **Lesson 105,** finding the surface area of right circular cylinders and the surface area of spheres.
- **Lesson 113,** finding the volume of pyramids, cones, and spheres.

• Multiplying Numbers in Scientific Notation

Objectives

- Multiply numbers in scientific notation.

Lesson Preparation

Materials

- **Power Up R** (in *Instructional Masters*)

Optional

- **Investigation Activity 13** (in *Instructional Masters*) or **graph paper**

Math Language

Maintain

scientific notation

Technology Resources

Student eBook Complete student textbook in electronic format.

Resources and Planner CD Blackline masters, plus a pacing calendar with standards.

Test and Practice Generator CD Create additional practice sheets and custom-made tests.

www.SaxonPublishers.com Visit for more student activities and planning materials.

Power Up R

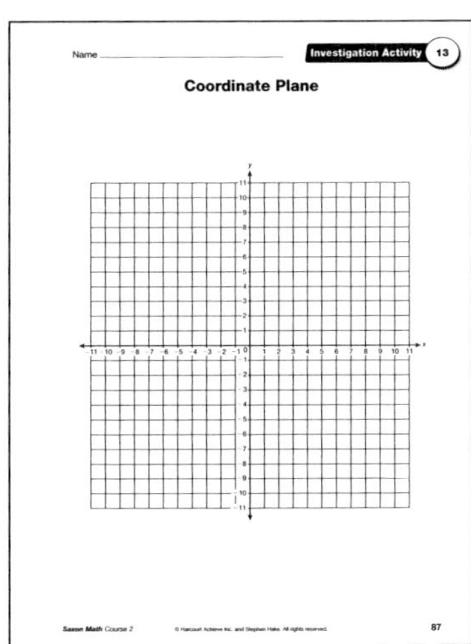
Name
Investigation Activity 13
Coordinate Plane

Investigation Activity 13

Inclusion

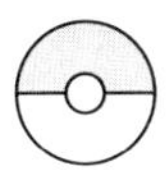

Adaptations CD Adapted lessons, investigations, practice and assessments.

Meeting Standards

National Council of Teachers of Mathematics (NCTM)

Numbers and Operations

NO.1e Develop an understanding of large numbers and recognize and appropriately use exponential, scientific, and calculator notation

NO.1g Develop meaning for integers and represent and compare quantities with them

NO.3b Develop and analyze algorithms for computing with fractions, decimals, and integers and develop fluency in their use

Problem Solving

PS.1b Solve problems that arise in mathematics and in other contexts

Connections

CN.4c Recognize and apply mathematics in contexts outside of mathematics

Power-Up Discussion *For use with Power Up, p. 575*

Problem-Solving Strategy: Make an Organized List

David and Lisa are in a chess tournament. The first player to win either two consecutive games, or a total of three games, wins the match. How many different sets of games are possible in the match?

Understand — Understand the problem.

"What information are we given?"

Two players are in a chess tournament. The first player to win either two games in a row or three games total wins the tournament.

"What are we asked to do?"

We are asked to find the number of sets of games that are possible in the match.

"What additional information are we going to have to find?"

We will need to find every possible outcome of the tournament (the *sample space* of the event).

Plan — Make a plan.

"What problem-solving strategy will we use?"

We will *make an organized list* of the possible outcomes.

Solve — Carry out the plan.

"What should we include in our list?"

The number of games played, how the games were won, and who won the match.

"The fewest number of games David and Lisa could play is two. What is the greatest number of games they could play?"

Five games, because after five games one person *must* have won 3 or more games.

"What are the possible outcomes resulting in a winner?"

2 games	DD	David	LL	Lisa
3 games	DLL	Lisa	LDD	David
4 games	DLDD	David	LDLL	Lisa
5 games	DLDLD	David	LDLDL	Lisa
	DLDLL	Lisa	LDLDD	David

"How many outcomes are possible?"

ten

Check — Look back.

"Did we do what we were asked to do?"

Yes, we found there are ten possible outcomes of the match.

LESSON 83

• Multiplying Numbers in Scientific Notation

Power Up — Building Power

facts Power Up R

mental math

a. **Positive/Negative:** $(-60) \div (+3)$ -20

b. **Decimals/Exponents:** 6.75×10^6 6,750,000

c. **Ratio:** $\frac{100}{150} = \frac{m}{30}$ 20

d. **Percent:** 15% of $120 $18

e. **Measurement:** 500 mg to g   0.5 g

f. **Fractional Parts:** 24 is $\frac{3}{8}$ of n.   64

g. **Geometry:** What do you call angles that share a common side and a common vertex?   adjacent angles

h. **Rate:** At 60 mph, how far will a car travel in $2\frac{1}{2}$ hours?   150 mi

problem solving David and Lisa are in a chess tournament. The first player to win either two consecutive games, or a total of three games, wins the match. How many different sets of games are possible in the match?   10

New Concept — Increasing Knowledge

From our earlier work with powers of 10, recall that

$$10^3 \text{ means } 10 \cdot 10 \cdot 10$$

and

$$10^4 \text{ means } 10 \cdot 10 \cdot 10 \cdot 10$$

Thus, $10^3 \cdot 10^4$ means 7 tens are multiplied.

$$10^3 \cdot 10^4 = 10^7$$

This multiplication illustrates an important rule of exponents learned in Lesson 47.

When we multiply powers of the same base, we add the exponents.

Explain How would you find the product of 10^5 and 10^5?

The bases are both 10, so the product has 10 as the base. Add the exponents: $5 + 5 = 10$, so the product is 10^{10}.

Math Language
A number expressed in **scientific notation** is written as the product of a decimal number and a power of 10.

We use this rule to multiply numbers expressed in scientific notation.

To multiply numbers written in scientific notation, we multiply the decimal numbers to find the decimal-number part of the product. Then we multiply the powers of 10 to find the power-of-10 part of the product. We remember that when we multiply powers of 10, we add the exponents.

Facts Find the area of each figure. Angles that look like right angles are right angles.

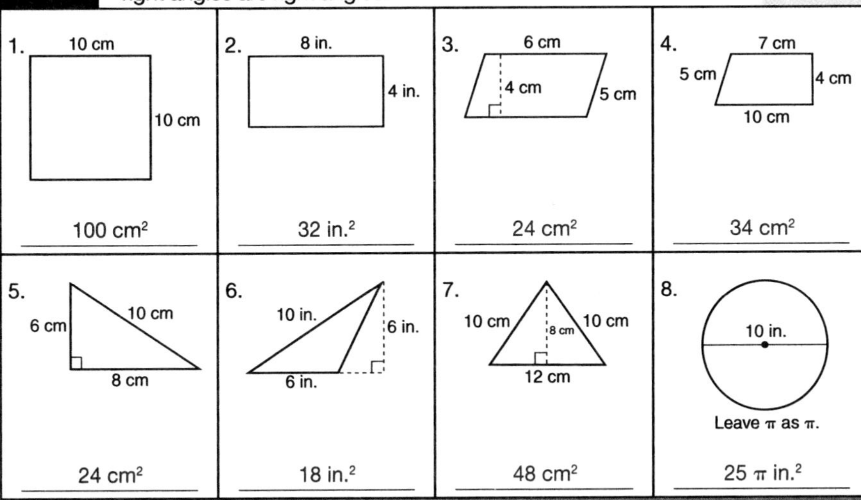

1 Power Up

Facts
Distribute **Power Up R** to students. See answers below.

Mental Math
Encourage students to share different ways to mentally compute these exercises. Strategies for exercises **c** and **e** are listed below.

c. Find Equivalent Fraction

$$\frac{100}{150} = \frac{100 \div 5}{150 \div 5} = \frac{20}{30}$$
$$m = 20$$

Cross Multiply and Divide

$$150m = 100 \times 30$$
$$m = \frac{100 \times 30}{150} = 10 \times 2$$
$$m = 20$$

e. Decompose

$$1000 \text{ mg} = 1 \text{ g}$$
$$500 \text{ mg} = 0.5 \text{ g}$$

Use a Unit Multiplier

$$500 \text{ mg} \times \frac{1 \text{ g}}{1000 \text{ mg}} = \frac{500}{1000 \text{ g}}$$
$$500 \text{ mg} = 0.5 \text{ g}$$

Problem Solving
Refer to **Power-Up Discussion,** p. 575B.

2 New Concepts

Instruction
Remind students that scientific notation is used to write very large or very small numbers. For example, two trillion can be written as 2×10^{12} and two hundred-thousandths can be written as 2×10^{-5}.

As you discuss the information on this page, point out that the rule in the box applies to both positive and negative exponents.

(continued)

2 New Concepts (Continued)

Example 1

Instruction

Explain that using the commutative and associative properties helps us group together numbers that are easy to multiply.

Example 2

Instruction

Remind students that 12×10^{11} is not in scientific notation. For an expression to be in scientific notation the number being multiplied by a power of ten must be greater than or equal to one and less than ten. First, rewrite 12 as 1.2×10^1, then multiply by 10^{11} to get 1.2×10^{12}.

Example 3

Instruction

After working through this example, you might ask students to write their answer 6×10^{-12} in standard form. Some students may write −6,000,000,000,000 as their answer. Remind them that a negative exponent does not indicate a negative number, but rather a decimal number.

Example 4

Instruction

Again emphasize the need to rewrite 35×10^{-5} in correct scientific notation form as a decimal number with only 1 nonzero digit to the left of the decimal point times a power of 10—in this case, 3.5×10^{-4}.

(continued)

Example 1

Multiply: $(1.2 \times 10^5)(3 \times 10^7)$

Solution

Notice that there are four factors.

$$1.2 \times 10^5 \times 3 \times 10^7$$

Using the Commutative Property, we reverse the order of two factors.

$$1.2 \times 3 \times 10^5 \times 10^7$$

Using the Associative Property, we group factors.

$$(1.2 \times 3) \times (10^5 \times 10^7)$$

Then we simplify each group.

$$\mathbf{3.6 \times 10^{12}}$$

Usually we do not show the commutative and associative steps; we simply multiply the powers of 10 separately.

Example 2

Multiply: $(4 \cdot 10^6)(3 \cdot 10^5)$

Solution

We multiply 4 by 3 and get 12. Then we multiply 10^6 by 10^5 and get 10^{11}. The product is

$$12 \times 10^{11}$$

We rewrite this expression in proper scientific notation.

$$(1.2 \times 10^1) \times 10^{11} = \mathbf{1.2 \times 10^{12}}$$

Example 3

Multiply: $(2 \cdot 10^{-5})(3 \cdot 10^{-7})$

Solution

We multiply 2 by 3 and get 6. To multiply 10^{-5} by 10^{-7}, we add the exponents and get 10^{-12}. Thus the product is

$$\mathbf{6 \times 10^{-12}}$$

Example 4

Multiply: $(5 \cdot 10^3)(7 \cdot 10^{-8})$

Solution

We multiply 5 by 7 and get 35. We multiply 10^3 by 10^{-8} and get 10^{-5}. The product is

$$35 \times 10^{-5}$$

Math Background

Can numbers written in scientific notation be added or subtracted?

Yes, numbers in scientific notation can be added or subtracted. To do this, both numbers must be rewritten so that each number has a power of 10 with the same exponent.

For example, $5.6 \times 10^5 + 2.8 \times 10^7$:

- Rewrite each number with the same exponent, 7: $(5.6 \times 10^5) + (2.8 \times 10^7) = (0.056 \times 10^7) + (2.8 \times 10^7)$
- Apply the Distributive Property: $(0.056 + 2.8) \times 10^7$
- Simplify inside the parentheses: 2.856×10^7

Subtraction can be done in a similar way.

We rewrite this expression in scientific notation.

$(3.5 \times 10^1) \times 10^{-5} = \mathbf{3.5 \times 10^{-4}}$

Practice Set

a. 5.88×10^9

b. 1.5×10^{13}

c. 8.4×10^{-10}

d. 4.2×10^{-6}

▶ **Generalize** Multiply. Write each product in scientific notation.

a. $(4.2 \times 10^6)(1.4 \times 10^3)$

b. $(5 \times 10^5)(3 \times 10^7)$

c. $(4 \times 10^{-3})(2.1 \times 10^{-7})$

d. $(6 \times 10^{-2})(7 \times 10^{-5})$

e.

$3 \times 10^3 \times 2 \times 10^4$	Given
$3 \times 2 \times 10^3 \times 10^4$	Commutative Property
$(3 \times 2) \times (10^3 \times 10^4)$	Associative Property
6×10^7	Simplified

▶ **e.** **Justify** Show the commutative and associative steps to multiply 3×10^3 and 2×10^4.

Written Practice

Strengthening Concepts

1. (46) The 16-ounce box costs \$3.36. The 24-ounce box costs \$3.96. The smaller box costs how much more per ounce than the larger box? \$0.045 more per ounce

2. (67, 70) The edges of a cube are 10 cm long.

a. What is the volume of the cube? 1000 cm^3

b. What is the surface area of the cube? 600 cm^2

3. (55) Jan read an average of 42 pages each day for 15 days. She read an average of 50 pages for the next five days. What was the average number of pages she read for all twenty days? 44 pages per day

4. (53) Hakim earns \$6 per hour at a part-time job. How much does he earn if he works for 2 hours 30 minutes? \$15

5. (50) Use a unit multiplier to convert 24 shillings to pence (1 shilling = 12 pence). $24 \text{ shillings} \cdot \frac{12 \text{ pence}}{1 \text{ shilling}} = 288 \text{ pence}$

▶ ***6.** (78) **Represent** Graph $x \le -1$ on a number line.

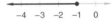

−4 −3 −2 −1 0

7. (72) Use a case 1–case 2 ratio box to solve this problem. Five is to 12 as 20 is to what number? 48

8. (41) If $a = 1.5$, what does $4a + 5$ equal? 11

9. (22) Four fifths of the football team's 30 points were scored on pass plays. How many points did the team score on pass plays? 24 points

▶ ***10.** (Inv. 8) **Generalize** A coin is tossed and the spinner is spun. What is the probability of heads and an even number? $\frac{1}{6}$

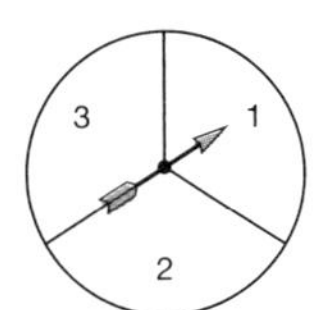

▶ See Math Conversations in the sidebar.

Teacher Tip

To vary how you present this or other lessons, try **teaching the lesson with student books closed.** Work the examples on the overhead and have students work along with you. Then go back to the student books, read the examples, and check whether students have any questions about the lesson before beginning the Practice Set and Written Practice.

2 New Concepts (Continued)

Practice Set

Problems a–d Generalize

Guide students through these problems. Although students can use mental math for most of these problems, explain that showing the steps is important and will be helpful if they need to look for an error. When all four are finished, ask:

"How many nonzero digits are to the left of the decimal point in all these answers? Why?" Sample: 1 digit, because that is correct scientific notation.

Problem e Justify

Ask students to tell what each property allows them to do and how it helps to make the computation simpler.

3 Written Practice

Math Conversations

Discussion opportunities are provided below.

Problem 6 Represent

Check understanding of the graph. Ask questions like:

"Is −4 part of the graph? Why?" Sample: Yes, the line passes through it.

"Is 10 part of the graph? Why?" Sample: No, the line doesn't pass through it.

"Is 0 part of the graph? Why?" Sample: No, only numbers less than or equal to −1 are on the graph.

"What does the dot at −1 mean?" Sample: −1 is part of the graph and is included in the inequality.

Problem 10 Generalize

"Suppose the spinner is spun 4 times. How many outcomes will be in the sample space?" 81

"What is the probability that the 3 will be spun all 4 times?" $\frac{1}{81}$

Errors and Misconceptions

Problem 10

To help those students who were not able to start on this problem, remind them to first find the probability of each event happening, and then multiply to find the probability of both happening.

(continued)

3 Written Practice (Continued)

Math Conversations

Discussion opportunities are provided below.

Problem 13

Extend the Problem

Ask students what the ratio of green apples to all the apples is. 2 to 7

Then have students name and give all other ratios for the apples in the basket. Make sure that students express ratios in lowest terms.

Problems 16 and 17 Model

Ask students to draw their ratio boxes on the board and explain how they solved the problems. Sample:

	Actual	%
Commercials (Minutes)	12	c
Total (Minutes)	60	100

After I made the ratio box, I wrote the proportion: $\frac{12}{60} = \frac{c}{100}$. I solved it by cross-multiplying: $60c = 12 \times 100$, and dividing to get $c = 20$. Commercials are shown for 20% of each hour.

Problem 19

Extend the Problem

"If all the dimensions are doubled, what is the area of the larger trapezoid?" 3600 m^2

"What do you notice about the areas of the two trapezoids?" Sample: The area of the larger one is 4 times that of the smaller one.

Errors and Misconceptions

Problem 19

Tell students who have forgotten the formula for a trapezoid that they can look up the formula and use it, or they can divide the trapezoid into two triangles, find the area for the two triangles, and add them to find the area of the trapezoid.

(continued)

11. (65) Find the circumference of each circle:

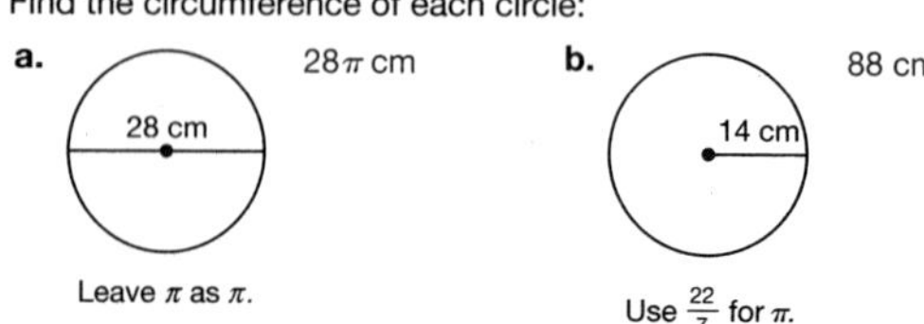

a. 28π cm b. 88 cm

12. (82) Find the area of each circle in problem 11 by using the indicated values for π. a. 196π cm^2 b. 616 cm^2

▶ **13.** (66) Use a ratio box to solve this problem. The ratio of red apples to green apples in the basket was 5 to 2. If there were 70 apples in the basket, how many of them were red? 50 apples were red

14. (48) Complete the table.

Fraction	Decimal	Percent
a. $2\frac{1}{2}$	**b.** 2.5	250%
$\frac{7}{12}$	**c.** $0.58\overline{3}$	**d.** $58\frac{1}{3}\%$

15. (46) What is the sales tax on an \$8.50 purchase if the sales-tax rate is $6\frac{1}{2}\%$? \$0.55

Model Use ratio boxes to solve problems **16** and **17.**

▶* **16.** (81) Monica found that 12 minutes of commercials aired during every hour of prime-time programming. Commercials were shown for what percent of each hour? 20%

▶* **17.** (81) Thirty percent of the boats that traveled up the river on Monday were steam-powered. If 42 of the boats that traveled up the river were not steam-powered, how many boats were there in all? 60 boats

Math Language
A **prime factorization** expresses a composite number as a product of its prime factors.

18. (24) Write the prime factorization of the numerator and denominator of this fraction. Then reduce the fraction. $\frac{2 \cdot 2 \cdot 3 \cdot 5 \cdot 7}{2 \cdot 3 \cdot 3 \cdot 5 \cdot 7} = \frac{2}{3}$

$$\frac{420}{630}$$

▶ **19.** (75) Find the area of the trapezoid at right. 900 m^2

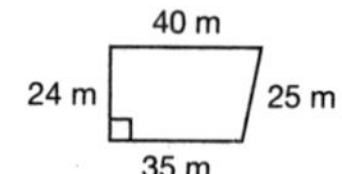

▶ See Math Conversations in the sidebar.

20. In this figure, $\angle A$ and $\angle B$ of $\triangle ABC$ are congruent. The measure of $\angle E$ is 54°. Find the measure of
(40)

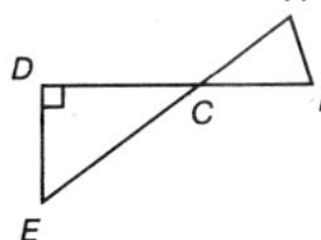

a. $\angle ECD$. 36° b. $\angle ECB$. 144°

c. $\angle ACB$. 36° d. $\angle BAC$. 72°

▶ 21. Write the rule of this function with words and as an equation. Then find the missing number.
(56)
To find y, multiply x by 2 and add 1. $y = 2x + 1$

x	y
2	5
5	11
7	15
10	21
−5	−9

▶*22. Generalize Multiply. Write each product in scientific notation.
(83)
a. $(3 \times 10^4)(6 \times 10^5)$ b. $(1.2 \times 10^{-3})(4 \times 10^{-6})$
1.8×10^{10} 4.8×10^{-9}

For problems **23** and **24,** solve and check the equation. Show each step.

23. $b - 1\frac{2}{3} = 4\frac{1}{2}$ $6\frac{1}{6}$
(Inv. 7)

24. $0.4y = 1.44$ 3.6
(Inv. 7)

Simplify:

▶ 25. $2^3 + 2^2 + 2^1 + 2^0 + 2^{-1}$ $15\frac{1}{2}$
(52, 57)

26. $0.6 \times 3\frac{1}{3} \div 2$ 1
(43)

27. a. $\frac{(-4)(-6)}{(-2)(-3)}$ 4
(73)
b. $(-3)(-4)(-5)$ −60

28. $\frac{5}{24} - \frac{7}{60}$ $\frac{11}{120}$
(30)

29. a. $(-3) + (-4) - (-5)$ −2
(68)
b. $(-1.5) - (+1.4) + (+1.0)$ −1.9

▶* 30. Analyze The coordinates of the vertices of $\triangle PQR$ are P (0, 1), Q (0, 0), and R (−2, 0). Draw the triangle and its image $\triangle P'Q'R'$ after a 180° clockwise rotation about the origin. What are the coordinates of the vertices of $\triangle P'Q'R'$? P' (0, −1), Q' (0, 0), R' (2, 0)
(80)

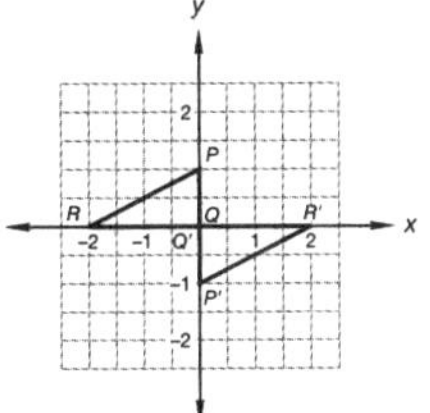

▶ See Math Conversations in the sidebar.

3 Written Practice (Continued)

Math Conversations

Discussion opportunities are provided below.

Problem 22 Generalize

Discuss how students solved these problems. Ask questions like the following:

"Do you rewrite all the steps? Why?"

"Do you eliminate some steps? Which ones?"

"Do you get the correct answers?"

"Are you checking your work? If so, how?"

Problem 30 Analyze

Ask how many students have started sketching their graphs without using graph paper. Let students who are successfully sketching explain how they do it, and have students who are still using graph paper tell what they need help with. Sample: For a rotation of 180°, I sketch the graph and then turn it half of a full turn. I renumber the axes and then find the new coordinates.

Errors and Misconceptions

Problem 21

Students who were unable to find the rule of the function need to learn some ways to uncover the rule. Suggest that they test 2 or 3 pairs using subtraction and division. If they get a common difference (d), the rule is *add the difference* and the equation is $y = x + d$. If they get a common quotient and remainder (qRn), the rule is *multiply by the quotient and add the remainder* and the equation is $y = qx + n$.

Problem 25

Watch for students who add the exponents. Even though the bases are all 2, the numbers are being added, not multiplied. Each term must be simplified before finding the total sum.

Looking Forward

Multiplying numbers in scientific notation prepares students for:

- **Lesson 111,** dividing in scientific notation.

• Algebraic Terms

Objectives

- Collect like terms in an algebraic expression.

Lesson Preparation

Materials

- **Power Up R** (in *Instructional Masters*)
- **Investigation Activity 13** (in *Instructional Masters*) or **graph paper**

Math Language

New

constant term	polynomials
like terms	term

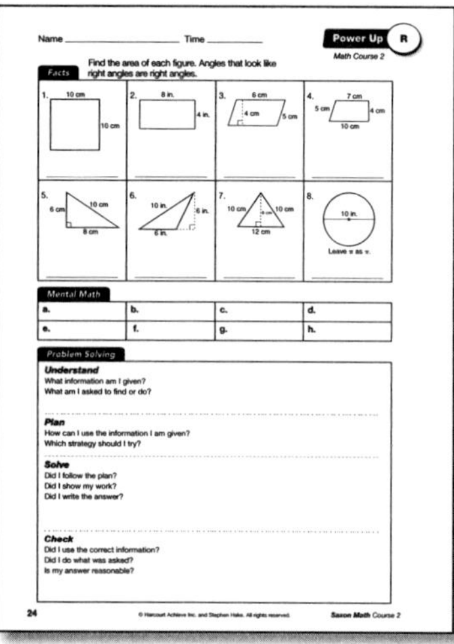

Power Up R

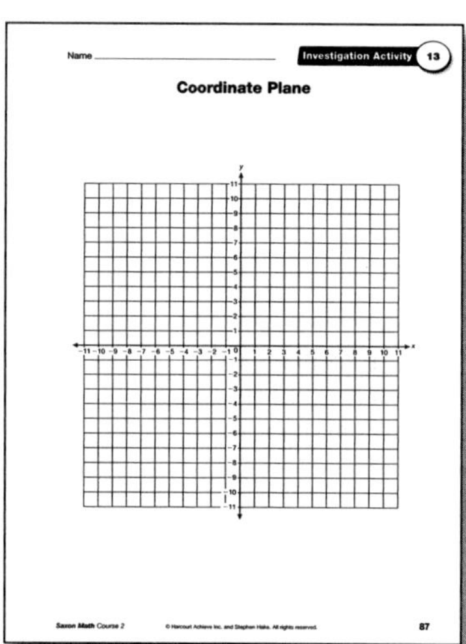

Coordinate Plane

Investigation Activity 13

Technology Resources

Student eBook Complete student textbook in electronic format.

Resources and Planner CD Blackline masters, plus a pacing calendar with standards.

Test and Practice Generator CD Create additional practice sheets and custom-made tests.

www.SaxonPublishers.com Visit for more student activities and planning materials.

Inclusion

Adaptations CD Adapted lessons, investigations, practice and assessments.

Meeting Standards

National Council of Teachers of Mathematics (NCTM)

Algebra

AL.1a Represent, analyze, and generalize a variety of patterns with tables, graphs, words, and, when possible, symbolic rules

AL.2a Develop an initial conceptual understanding of different uses of variables

AL.2d Recognize and generate equivalent forms for simple algebraic expressions and solve linear equations

Communication

CM.3b Communicate their mathematical thinking coherently and clearly to peers, teachers, and others

Power-Up Discussion *For use with Power Up, p. 580*

Problem-Solving Strategy: Work Backwards/ Use Logical Reasoning

Two hourglass sand timers, one of which runs for exactly 5 minutes and the other for exactly 3 minutes, were provided with a spelling game to time the players' turns. Show how to time a 7-minute turn using only the two provided timers.

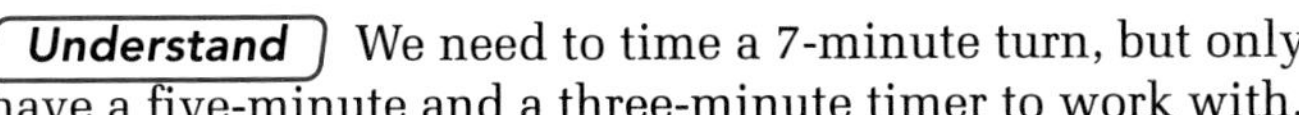

Understand We need to time a 7-minute turn, but only have a five-minute and a three-minute timer to work with.

Plan We will work backwards from what we know our result needs to be. We can use logical reasoning to find a way to measure 2 minutes with the three-minute and the five-minute timers.

Solve We will turn both timers over at the same time. When the three-minute timer is empty, the player will begin their turn. When the 2 minutes remaining in the five-minute timer runs out, we will immediately turn the five-minute timer back over.

Check We found a method for timing two minutes using a five-minute timer and a three-minute timer. The 2 minutes remaining in the five-minute timer + 5 minutes = a 7-minute turn.

1 Power Up

Facts

Distribute **Power Up R** to students. See answers below.

Mental Math

Encourage students to share different ways to mentally compute these exercises. Strategies for exercises **b** and **e** are listed below.

b. Decompose

$25^2 = 25 \times 25 = 25 \times (20 + 5) =$
$500 + 125 = 625$

Multiply Prime Factors

$25^2 = 5 \times 5 \times 5 \times 5 =$
$25 \times 5 \times 5 =$
$125 \times 5 = 625$

e. Decompose

$1.5 \text{ cm} = 1 \text{ cm} + 0.5 \text{ cm}$
$1 \text{ cm} = 10 \text{ mm}$
$0.5 \text{ cm} = 5 \text{ mm}$
$1.5 \text{ cm} = 15 \text{ mm}$

Use Unit Multiplier

$1.5 \text{ cm} \times \frac{10 \text{ mm}}{1 \text{ cm}} = 15 \text{ mm}$

Problem Solving

Refer to **Power-Up Discussion,** p. 580B.

2 New Concepts

Instruction

Tell students that in this lesson they will work with algebraic expressions. Algebraic expressions are made up of terms that are separated by plus or minus signs that are not inside symbols of inclusion. The terms can contain both numbers and letters.

(continued)

LESSON **84**

• Algebraic Terms

Power Up *Building Power*

facts Power Up R

mental math

a. **Positive/Negative:** $(-12) - (-12)$ 0

b. **Exponents:** 25^2 625

c. **Algebra:** $6m - 10 = 32$ 7

d. **Decimals/Measurement:** 3.14×30 cm 94.2 cm

e. **Measurement:** 1.5 cm to mm 15 mm

f. **Fractional Parts:** 30 is $\frac{5}{6}$ of n. 36

g. **Geometry:** What four-sided figure has only one set of parallel lines? trapezoid

h. **Calculation:** 12×12, -4, $\div 10$, $+1$, $\times 2$, $+3$, $\div 3$, $\times 5$, -1, $\div 6$, $\sqrt{\ }$ 3

problem solving Two hourglass sand timers, one of which runs for exactly 5 minutes and the other for exactly 3 minutes, were provided with a spelling game to time the players' turns. Show how to time a 7-minute turn using only the two provided timers.

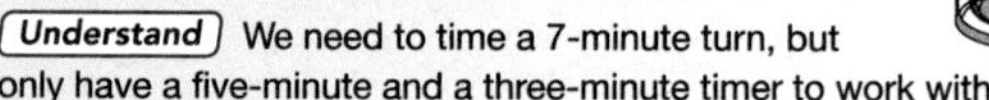

Understand We need to time a 7-minute turn, but only have a five-minute and a three-minute timer to work with.

Plan We will work backwards from what we know our result needs to be. We can use logical reasoning to find a way to measure 2 minutes with the three-minute and the five-minute timers.

Solve We will turn both timers over at the same time. When the three-minute timer is empty, the players will begin their turn. When the 2 minutes remaining in the five-minute timer runs out, we will immediately turn the five-minute timer back over.

Check We found a method for timing two minutes using a five-minute timer and a three-minute timer. The 2 minutes remaining in the five-minute timer + 5 minutes = a 7-minute turn.

New Concept *Increasing Knowledge*

We have used the word **term** in arithmetic to refer to the numerator or denominator of a fraction. For example, we reduce a fraction to its lowest terms. In algebra, *term* refers to a part of an algebraic expression or equation. **Polynomials** are algebraic expressions that contain one, two, three, or more terms.

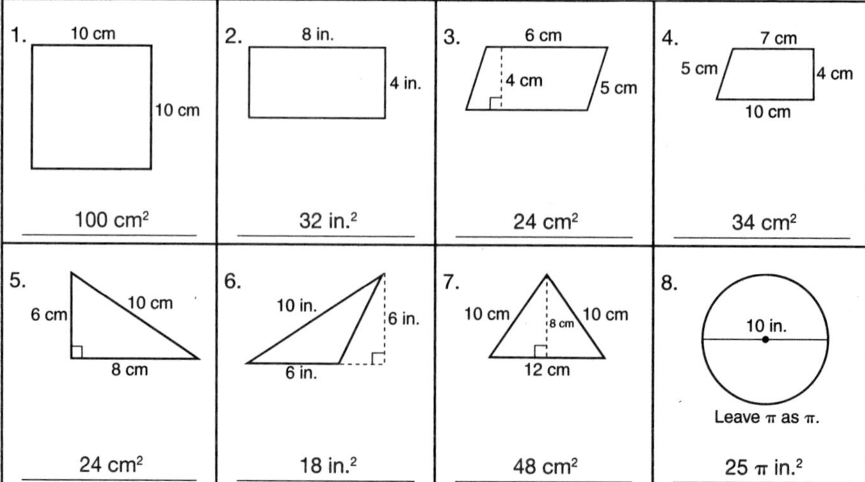

Facts Find the area of each figure. Angles that look like right angles are right angles.

1. 10 cm, 10 cm — 100 cm²	2. 8 in., 4 in. — 32 in.²	3. 6 cm, 4 cm, 5 cm — 24 cm²	4. 7 cm, 5 cm, 4 cm, 10 cm — 34 cm²
5. 6 cm, 10 cm, 8 cm — 24 cm²	6. 10 in., 6 in., 6 in. — 18 in.²	7. 10 cm, 8 cm, 10 cm, 12 cm — 48 cm²	8. 10 in. Leave π as π. — 25 π in.²

Some Polynomials

Type of Polynomials	Number of Terms	Example
monomial	1	$-2x$
binomial	2	$a^2 - 4b^2$
trinomial	3	$3x^2 - x - 4$

a binomial; It has two terms: m^2 and $5n^2$.

Discuss What type of polynomial is the term $m^2 + 5n^2$? Why?

Terms are separated from one another in an expression by plus or minus signs that are not within symbols of inclusion. To help us see the individual terms we have separated the terms of the binomial and trinomial examples with slashes:

$$a^2 \;/\; -4b^2 \qquad 3x^2 \;/\; -x \;/\; -4$$

Every term contains a positive or negative number and may contain one or more variables (letters). Sometimes the number is understood and not written. For instance, the understood number of a^2 is $+1$ since $a^2 = +1a^2$. **When a term is written without a number, it is understood that the number is 1. When a term is written without a sign, it is understood that the sign is positive.**

Term	$3x^2$	$-x$	-4
Number	$+3$	-1	-4
Variable	x^2	x	none

It is not necessary for a term to contain a variable. A term that does not contain a variable, like -4, is often called a **constant term,** because its value never changes.

Thinking Skill

Justify

Show how to use algebraic addition to combine the constant terms $+3$ and -1.

$+3 - 1 =$
$+3 + (-1) =$
$+2$

Constant terms can be combined by algebraic addition.

$$3x + 3 - 1 = 3x + 2 \qquad \text{added } +3 \text{ and } -1$$

Variable terms can also be combined by algebraic addition if they are **like terms.** Like terms have identical variable parts.

$$-3xy^2 + xy^2 \qquad \text{Like terms}$$

Like terms can be combined by algebraically adding the signed-number part of the terms.

$$-3xy^2 + xy^2 = -2xy^2$$

The signed number part of $+xy^2$ is $+1$. We get $-2xy^2$ by adding $-3xy^2$ and $+1xy^2$.

2 New Concepts *(Continued)*

Instruction

Ask students what the prefixes are in the names of these expressions. *poly-, mono-, bi-, tri-*

Challenge them to think of other words with these prefixes. *polygon, monotone, bifocals, triangle, and so on*

Use the table in the middle of the page to lead students to distinguish variable terms (terms with one or more letters) from constant terms (terms without letters). You may refer to the numerical part of a variable term as a *coefficient.* Every variable term has a numerical coefficient. The numerical coefficient of x^2 is 1. The numerical coefficient of $-x$ is -1.

Point out that expressions may have more than one constant term. When this happens, the constant terms may be combined. You may want to suggest that subtraction problems be changed to addition before combining like terms. For example, $3x + 3 - 1$ can be rewritten as $3x + 3 + (-1)$ and simplified to $3x + 2$.

Emphasize that *like terms* have identical variables raised to the same powers. For example, $4x^2y$ and $-2x^2y$ are like terms and can be combined to make $2x^2y$. Like terms are combined by adding the numerical coefficients. Point out that the variable does not change unless the result is zero. Also reinforce that terms such as $4x^2y$ and $4xy$ are not like terms and cannot be combined.

However, $4xy$ and $-3yx$ are like terms because the variables can be re-ordered using the Communicative Property.

(continued)

Math Background

How is the degree of a polynomial determined?

The degree of a polynomial is the highest degree of any term. The degree of a term with one variable equals the exponent of the variable. The degree of a term with more than one variable equals the sum of the exponents of the variables. Each of these terms are degree 4.

$$2x^4,\ -3x^2y^2,\ 7xy^3$$

The following polynomial is a second degree polynomial, called a quadratic.

$$3x^2 + x - 4$$

We often arrange the terms of a polynomial in descending order of degree.

2 New Concepts (Continued)

Example 1

Instruction

Ask students to write the polynomial on their papers, drawing slashes to separate the terms.

3x / + y / + x / − y

Then, have them code sets of like terms with distinct marking such as the following:

3x / + y / + x / − y

Finally, have them identify the numerical coefficients and collect like terms.

Help students understand how the properties are used to simplify the expression.

Example 2

Instruction

As in the first example, ask students to copy, separate, and code the terms of the expression.

After simplifying the expression, ask students to identify what kind of polynomial they have written. Is it a monomial, a binomial, or a trinomial? Have them explain their answers. The polynomial is a trinomial because it has three terms.

(continued)

Example 1

Use the commutative and associative properties to collect like terms in this algebraic expression.

$$3x + y + x - y$$

Solution

There are four terms in this expression. There are two x terms and two y terms. We can use the Commutative Property to rearrange the terms.

$3x + x + y - y$ Commutative Property

We use the Associative Property to group like terms.

$(3x + x) + (y - y)$ Associative Property

Adding $+3x$ and $+1x$ we get $+4x$. Then adding $+1y$ and $-1y$ we get $0y$, which is 0.

$4x + 0$ Simplified

$\mathbf{4x}$ Zero Property of Addition

Example 2

Collect like terms in this algebraic expression:

$$3x + 2x^2 + 4 + x^2 - x - 1$$

Solution

In this expression there are three kinds of terms: x^2 terms, x terms, and constant terms. Using the Commutative Property we arrange them to put like terms next to each other.

$2x^2 + x^2 + 3x - x + 4 - 1$ Commutative Property

Now we collect like terms.

$(2x^2 + x^2) + (3x - x) + (4 - 1)$ Associative Property

$\mathbf{3x^2 + 2x + 3}$ Simplified

Notice that x^2 terms and x terms are not like terms and cannot be combined by addition. There are other possible arrangements of the collected terms, such as the following:

$$2x + 3x^2 + 3$$

Customarily, however, we arrange terms in **descending order** of exponents so that the term with the largest exponent is on the left and the constant term is on the right. An expression written without a constant term is understood to have zero as a constant term.

Generalize Rewrite the expression $4 + 3x^2 + x$ in descending order.

$3x^2 + x + 4$

Thinking Skills

Conclude

Why are x^2 and x not like terms? While they have the same base, they have different exponents.

Teacher Tip

To help your students make a solid connection to this lesson's **abstract concepts of variables and constants,** have the class generate a list of real-world examples of variables and constants. Have students provide examples, such as,

- The number of eggs in one dozen is a constant, but the price of a dozen eggs is a variable.
- The number of months in a year is a constant, but the number of days in a month is a variable.

Ask students to think of a variety of situations in their examples.

Practice Set ▸ **Classify** Describe each of these expressions as a monomial, a binomial, or a trinomial:

a. $x^2 - y^2$ binomial

b. $3x^2 - 2x - 1$ trinomial

c. $-2x^3yz^2$ monomial

d. $-2x^2y - 4xy^2$ binomial

e. State the number of terms in the expressions in exercises **a–d.**
a. 2; **b.** 3; **c.** 1; **d.** 2

▸ **Justify** Collect like terms. Show your steps.

f. $3a + 2a^2 - a + a^2$
$3a^2 + 2a$

g. $5xy - x + xy - 2x$
$6xy - 3x$

h. $3 + x^2 + x - 5 + 2x^2$
$3x^2 + x - 2$

i. $3\pi + 1.4 - \pi + 2.8$
$2\pi + 4.2$

Written Practice *Strengthening Concepts*

1. (32) An increase in temperature of 10° on the Celsius scale corresponds to an increase of how many degrees on the Fahrenheit scale? 18°F

▸ * **2.** (84) **Generalize** Collect like terms: $2xy + xy - 3x + x$ $3xy - 2x$

3. (Inv. 4) Refer to the graph below to answer **a–c.**

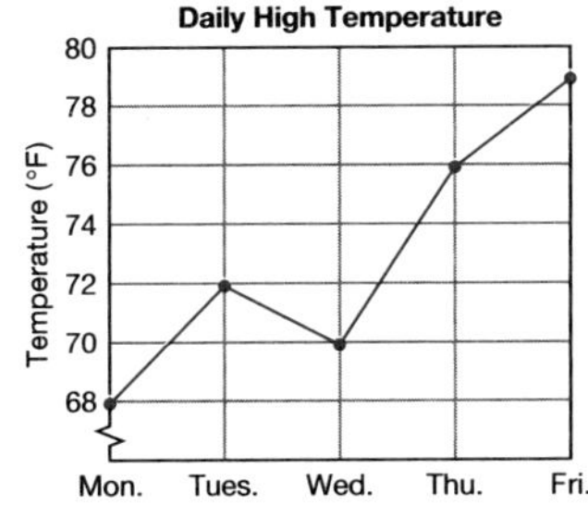

a. What was the range of the daily high temperatures from Monday to Friday? 11°F

b. Which day had the greatest increase in temperature from the previous day? Thursday

c. Wednesday's high temperature was how much lower than the average high temperature for these 5 days? 3°F

▸ **4.** (Inv. 4) Frank's points in ten games were as follows:

90, 90, 100, 95, 95, 85, 100, 100, 80, 100

For this set of points, find the **a** mean, **b** median, **c** mode, and **d** range. **a.** 93.5 **b.** 95 **c.** 100 **d.** 20

5. (66) Use a ratio box to solve this problem. The ratio of rowboats to sailboats in the bay was 3 to 7. If the total number of rowboats and sailboats in the bay was 210, how many sailboats were in the bay? 147 sailboats

▸ See Math Conversations in the sidebar.

2 New Concepts *(Continued)*

Practice Set

Problems a–d Classify

Have students explain why they classified each expression as they did. Discuss for each term what number and variable it contains, and whether the number or the sign is understood.

Problem c Error Alert

Watch for students who do not get *monomial* as the answer. Point out that there are no other addition or subtraction signs in the expression. The expression contains only one term, and so it is a monomial.

Problems f–i Justify

Discuss how students collected like terms. Emphasize the importance of using an organized approach. Go over the separate-and-code technique covered in the lesson.

3 Written Practice

Math Conversations

Discussion opportunities are provided below.

Problem 2 Generalize

Continue the discussion from the Practice Set. Ask volunteers to share the methods they used to collect like terms. Sample: I copied the expression using slashes to separate the terms, and then I put a line under the x terms and a double line under the xy terms. I decided that xy terms were higher in order than x terms, and I collected and combined the terms.

Errors and Misconceptions

Problem 2

Help students who have difficulty collecting like terms by reviewing the process of copying, separating, and coding the terms before collecting the like terms. Some students often cross out the like terms after they have been combined.

Problem 4

To help students who could not identify the range or the median of this data, suggest that they first arrange the numbers in order from least to greatest before calculating the statistics.

(continued)

3 Written Practice (Continued)

Math Conversations

Discussion opportunities are provided below.

Problem 6 Evaluate

Extend the Problem

Help students see how four reflections across the axes of a coordinate plane result in the return of the original figure. You may want to make a drawing on the board.

"In what quadrant was △ABC?" Quadrant II

"In what quadrant is its reflection in the x-axis, △A'B'C'?" Quadrant III

"If △A'B'C' is reflected in the y-axis, in what quadrant will that triangle lie?" Quadrant IV

"If it is then reflected in the x-axis, in what quadrant will that triangle lie?" Quadrant I

"If it is reflected once more in the y-axis, in what quadrant will its reflection be? Quadrant II

Problem 9 Evaluate

Extend the Problem

Ask students to use mental math to evaluate both expressions for $x = 4$ and for $x = 3$.

"What do you notice about the answers?" Samples: The values of both expressions are equal for the same value of x. The values are perfect squares.

"Do you think that what you notice will be true for all whole-number values of x?" Samples: It seems like they will always be equal. If x is 1, then the values are 0, and I am not sure if 0 is a perfect square.

Problems 17 and 18 Model

Point out that equations can also be used to model these situations. Have students work together to write equations for problems **17** and **18**. Then ask:

"How are these equations alike and different?" Sample: They are alike because they are percent-of-a-number problems, but they are different because you could write problem **17** directly from the given information, but for problem **18**, you had to find the percent of the saplings that were more than three feet tall.

Errors and Misconceptions

Problem 19

Some students may try to find the square root of 48. Help them understand that the side of a square is equal to the perimeter divided by 4 by reminding them that the perimeter is the distance around the square and then asking,

"What is the length of one side of a square with a perimeter of 48 inches?" 12

(continued)

6. 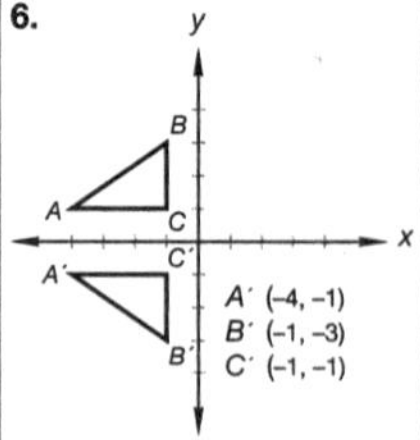

▶ * **6.** (80) Analyze Triangle ABC with vertices at $A(-4, 1)$, $B(-1, 3)$, and $C(-1, 1)$, is reflected in the x-axis. Draw $\triangle ABC$ and its reflection, $\triangle A'B'C'$. What are the coordinates of the vertices of $\triangle A'B'C'$?

7. (72) Write a proportion to solve this problem. If 4 cost $1.40, how much would 10 cost? $3.50

8. (71) Five-eighths of the members supported the treaty, whereas 36 opposed the treaty. How many members supported the treaty? 60 members

▶ **9.** (52) Evaluate Evaluate each expression for $x = 5$:

a. $x^2 - 2x + 1$ 16 **b.** $(x - 1)^2$ 16

10. (10) Compare: $f \ominus g$ if $\frac{f}{g} = 1$

11. (65, 82) **a.** Find the circumference of the circle shown. 18.84 in.

b. Find the area of the circle. 28.26 in.^{2}

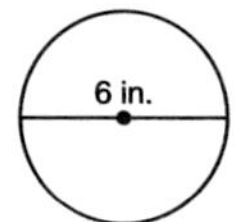

Use 3.14 for π.

12. (50) Use a unit multiplier to convert 4.8 meters to centimeters.
4.8 meters $\cdot \frac{100 \text{ centimeters}}{1 \text{ meter}}$ = 480 centimeters

13. (67) Draw a rectangular prism. A rectangular prism has how many faces?

13.  6 faces

14. (48) Complete the table.

Fraction	Decimal	Percent
$1\frac{4}{5}$	**a.** 1.8	**b.** 180%
c. $\frac{9}{500}$	**d.** 0.018	1.8%

15. (60) Write an equation to solve this problem. A merchant priced a product so that 30% of the selling price is profit. If the product sells for $18.00, how much is the merchant's profit? $p = 0.3 \times \$18.00$; $5.40

* **16.** (76) Simplify: $\frac{12\frac{1}{2}}{100}$ $\frac{1}{8}$

Model Use ratio boxes to solve problems **17** and **18**.

▶* **17.** (81) When the door was left open, 36 pigeons flew the coop. If this was 40 percent of all pigeons, how many pigeons were originally in the coop? 90 pigeons

▶* **18.** (81) Sixty percent of the saplings were 3 feet tall or less. If there were 300 saplings in all, how many were more than 3 feet tall? 120 saplings

▶ **19.** (19, 75) A square sheet of paper with a perimeter of 48 in. has a corner cut off, forming a pentagon as shown.

a. What is the perimeter of the pentagon? 44 in.

b. What is the area of the pentagon? 120 in.^{2}

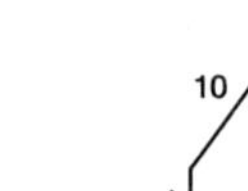

▶ See Math Conversations in the sidebar.

▶ **20.** (14, Inv. 5) **Analyze** The face of this spinner has been divided into seven sectors, the central angles of which have the following measures:

A 60°   *B* 90°   *C* 45°   *D* 30°

E 75°   *F* 40°   *G* 20°

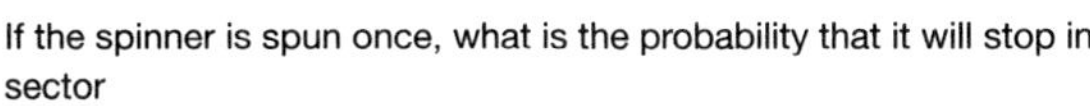

If the spinner is spun once, what is the probability that it will stop in sector

a. *A*? $\frac{1}{6}$ **b.** *C*? $\frac{1}{8}$ **c.** *E*? $\frac{5}{24}$

21. To find a term in the sequence, double the preceding term and add 1. *Note:* Other rule descriptions are possible, including "The value of the *n*th term is $2^n - 1$." Discuss various rules proposed by students.

21. (4) Describe the rule of this sequence. Then find the next three numbers of the sequence. 63, 127, 255

1, 3, 7, 15, 31, . . .

* **22.** (83) **Represent** Multiply. Write each product in scientific notation.

▶ **a.** $(1.5 \times 10^{-3})(3 \times 10^{6})$ 4.5×10^{3} **b.** $(3 \times 10^{4})(5 \times 10^{5})$ 1.5×10^{10}

Generalize Find each missing exponent:

▶* **23.** (47, 83) **a.** $10^2 \cdot 10^2 \cdot 10^2 = 10^{\square}$ 6   **b.** $\frac{10^2}{10^6} = 10^{\square}$ −4

For problems **24** and **25,** solve and check the equation. Show each step.

24. (Inv. 7) $b - 4.75 = 5.2$ 9.95   **25.** (Inv. 7) $\frac{2}{3}y = 36$ 54

Simplify:

26. (52) $\sqrt{5^2 - 4^2} + 2^3$ 11   **27.** (32) 1 m − 45 mm 955 mm

▶ **28.** (43) $\frac{9}{10} \div 2\frac{1}{4} \cdot 24$ (decimal answer) 9.6

29. (73) **a.** $\frac{(-8)(+6)}{(-3)(+4)}$ 4   **b.** $\left(\frac{1}{2}\right)\left(-\frac{1}{3}\right)\left(\frac{1}{4}\right)$ $-\frac{1}{24}$

30. (68) **a.** (+30) − (−50) − (+20) 60

b. (−0.3) − (−0.4) −(0.5) −0.4

Early Finishers
Real-World Application

Twenty students guessed the number of marbles in a glass container. The results are shown below.

28	20	15	19	37	40	22	42	30	36
25	28	25	33	45	20	50	32	21	30

Which type of display—a stem-and-leaf plot or a line graph—is the most appropriate way to display this data? Draw your display and justify your choice. stem-and-leaf plot; Sample: A stem-and-leaf plot is the most appropriate display because it can be used to display individual data points. A line graph usually displays a change over time. See student graphs.

▶ See Math Conversations in the sidebar.

3 Written Practice (Continued)

Math Conversations

Discussion opportunities are provided below.

Problem 20 Analyze

"What three sectors together have exactly 180°?" There are 2 sets that have exactly 180°: sectors A, B, and D; sectors A, C, and E

"What is the probability that the spinner will land in A, B, or D on one spin?" $\frac{1}{2}$

"What is the probability that the spinner will land in A, C, or E on one spin?" $\frac{1}{2}$

"What is the probability that the spinner will land in A, B, C, D, or E on one spin?" $\frac{5}{6}$

Problem 22a Represent

Point out that 4.5×10^3 is only one way to represent this number. Ask students to make a list of other representations of the number. Samples: 4500; 4000 + 500; $4 \times 10^3 + 5 \times 10^2$; $15 \times 3 \times 10^2$; $5 \times 5 \times 5 \times 3 \times 3 \times 2 \times 2$; four thousand, five hundred; 5000 − 500

Problem 23a and 23b Generalize

Have students tell what rules they used to find the missing exponents. Ask students to explain in their own words why these rules work.

Errors and Misconceptions

Problem 28

Point out to students whose answer is $9\frac{3}{5}$ that this problem called for a decimal answer and that there are two ways to get a decimal answer. All fractions can be changed to decimals before calculating or the calculations can be done with fractions and then converted to a decimal answer.

Looking Forward

Understanding algebraic terms prepares students for:

- **Lesson 87,** multiplying algebraic terms.
- **Lesson 96,** simplifying expressions using the Distributive Property with algebraic terms.
- **Lesson 102,** simplifying and solving equations.
- **Lesson 103,** simplifying expressions by dividing algebraic terms.
- **Lesson 115,** factoring algebraic expressions.

• Order of Operations with Positive and Negative Numbers

Objectives

- Simplify expressions that contain both positive and negative numbers.

Lesson Preparation

Materials

- **Power Up P** (in *Instructional Masters*)

Optional

- **Investigation Activity 13** (in *Instructional Masters*) or **graph paper**
- **Teacher-provided material: colored pencils**

Math Language

	English Learners (ESL)
	enclosed

Power Up P

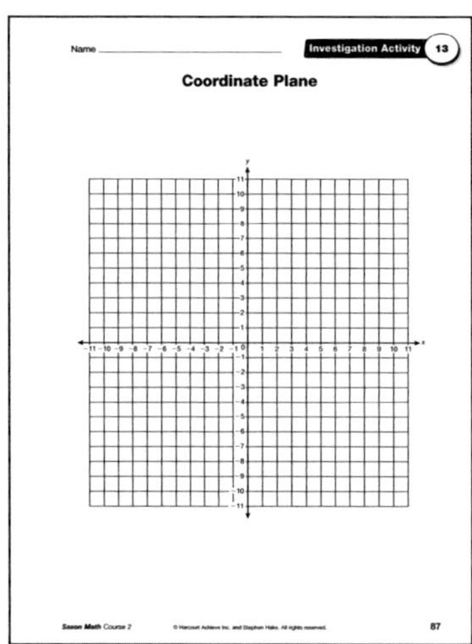
Name

Investigation Activity 13

Coordinate Plane

Investigation Activity 13

Technology Resources

Student eBook Complete student textbook in electronic format.

Resources and Planner CD Blackline masters, plus a pacing calendar with standards.

Test and Practice Generator CD Create additional practice sheets and custom-made tests.

www.SaxonPublishers.com Visit for more student activities and planning materials.

Inclusion

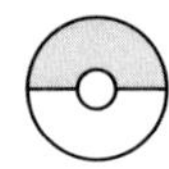

Adaptations CD Adapted lessons, investigations, practice and assessments.

Meeting Standards

National Council of Teachers of Mathematics (NCTM)

Numbers and Operations

NO.2a Understand the meaning and effects of arithmetic operations with fractions, decimals, and integers

NO.3b Develop and analyze algorithms for computing with fractions, decimals, and integers and develop fluency in their use

Communication

CM.3a Organize and consolidate their mathematical thinking through communication

Power-Up Discussion *For use with Power Up, p. 586*

Problem-Solving Strategy: Guess and Check/ Use Logical Reasoning

Copy this problem and fill in the missing digits:

$$\begin{array}{r} \_\,\_\,\_ \\ \times \quad \_ \\ \hline 1\,0\,0\,1 \end{array}$$

Understand ***Understand the problem.***

"What information are we given?"

We are shown a multiplication problem with two factors missing. The product is 1001.

"What are we asked to do?"

We are asked to find the missing factors.

Plan ***Make a plan.***

"What problem-solving strategy will we use?"

We will *guess and check* to find the two factors, and *use logical reasoning* to help us along the way.

Solve ***Carry out the plan.***

"The product ends in 1. What pairs of numbers have a product with a 1 in the ones place?"

$1 \times 1 = 1$, $3 \times 7 = 21$, $7 \times 3 = 21$, and $9 \times 9 = 81$

"Which of these numbers 1, 3, 7, and 9, cannot be the one-digit factor?"

The one-digit factor cannot be 1, because the product has four digits. The factor cannot be 3 or 9 because the product is not divisible by 3 or 9.

"What is the one-digit factor?"

7

"We know the product and one factor. How can we find the remaining factor?"

We can divide by 7.

"What is the three-digit factor?"

The factor is 143 because $1001 \div 7 = 143$.

"What is the solution?"

$$\begin{array}{r} 1\,4\,3 \\ \times \quad 7 \\ \hline 1\,0\,0\,1 \end{array}$$

Check ***Look back.***

"Did we do what we were asked to do?"

Yes, we found the missing products.

"How can we verify our solution is correct?"

Since we found the factors by division, we can use of multiplication to check our answer:

$143 \times 7 = 1001$

1 Power Up

Facts

Distribute **Power Up P** to students. See answers below.

Mental Math

Encourage students to share different ways to mentally compute these exercises. Strategies for exercises **c** and **e** are listed below.

c. Find Equivalent Fraction

$\frac{1}{1.5} = \frac{2}{3} = \frac{80}{120}$

$n = 120$

Cross Multiply and Divide

$n = 1.5 \times 80 = 1 \times 80 + \frac{1}{2} \times 80$

$n = 120$

e. Decompose

0.8 km = 8 × 0.1 km

1 km = 1000 m

0.1 km = 100 m

0.8 km = 800 m

Use a Unit Multiplier

$0.8 \text{ km} \times \frac{1000 \text{ m}}{1 \text{ km}} = 800 \text{ m}$

Problem Solving

Refer to **Power-Up Discussion,** p. 586B.

2 New Concepts

Instruction

Go over the mnemonic *Please Excuse My Dear Aunt Sally* if students need a quick review of order of operations.

Example 1

Instruction

Suggest that students copy this expression on their papers, draw slashes to separate the expression into its three terms, simplify each term, and finally combine like terms. Some students find that using colored pencils is helpful for this step.

(continued)

LESSON 85

• Order of Operations with Positive and Negative Numbers

Power Up — *Building Power*

facts Power Up P

mental math

a. **Positive/Negative:** (+12)(−6) −72

b. **Order of Operations/Exponents:** $(4 \times 10^3)(2 \times 10^6)$ 8×10^9

c. **Ratio:** $\frac{1}{1.5} = \frac{80}{n}$ 120

d. **Fractional Parts:** \$12 is $\frac{1}{4}$ of how much money (*m*)? \$48

e. **Measurement:** 0.8 km to m 800 m

f. **Fractional Parts:** What is $\frac{1}{4}$ of \$12? \$3

g. **Geometry:** What face on a pyramid designates its type? base

h. **Geometry:** Find the perimeter and area of a square with sides 2.5 m long. 10 m; 6.25 m^2

problem solving Copy this problem and fill in the missing digits:

$$\begin{array}{r} \_\,\_\,\_ \\ \times \quad \_ \\ \hline 1001 \end{array} \qquad \begin{array}{r} 143 \\ \times \quad 7 \\ \hline 1001 \end{array}$$

New Concept — *Increasing Knowledge*

Thinking Skill
Generalize
Use the sentence <u>P</u>lease <u>e</u>xcuse <u>m</u>y <u>d</u>ear <u>A</u>unt <u>S</u>ally to remember the correct order of operations.

To simplify expressions that involve several operations, we perform the operations in a prescribed order. We have practiced simplifying expressions with whole numbers. In this lesson we will begin simplifying expressions that contain negative integers as well.

Example 1

Simplify: $(-2) + (-2)(-2) - \frac{(-2)}{(+2)}$

Solution

First we multiply and divide in order from left to right.

$$(-2) + \underbrace{(-2)(-2)} - \underbrace{\frac{(-2)}{(+2)}}$$

$$(-2) + \quad (+4) \quad - (-1)$$

Facts Simplify.

(−8) + (−2) = −10	(−8) − (−2) = −6	(−8)(−2) = 16	$\frac{-8}{-2} = 4$
(−9) + (+3) = −6	(−9) − (+3) = −12	(−9)(+3) = −27	$\frac{-9}{+3} = -3$
12 + (−2) = 10	12 − (−2) = 14	(12)(−2) = −24	$\frac{12}{-2} = -6$
(−4) + (−3) + (−2) = −9	(−4) − (−3) − (−2) = 1	(−4)(−3)(−2) = −24	$\frac{(-4)(-3)}{(-2)} = -6$

Then we add and subtract in order from left to right.

$$\underbrace{\underbrace{(-2) + (+4)}_{(+2)} - (-1)}_{+3}$$

Mentally separating an expression into its terms can make an expression easier to simplify. Here is the same expression. This time we will use slashes to separate the terms.

$$(-2)\Big/ + (-2)(-2)\Big/ - \frac{(-2)}{(+2)}$$

First we simplify each term; then we combine the terms.

$$(-2)\Big/ + (-2)(-2)\Big/ - \frac{(-2)}{(+2)}$$

$$-2 \quad / \quad +4 \quad / \quad +1$$

$$+3$$

Example 2

Simplify each term. Then combine the terms.

$$-3(2 - 4) - 4(-2)(-3) + \frac{(-3)(-4)}{2}$$

Solution

We separate the individual terms with slashes. The slashes precede plus and minus signs that are not enclosed by parentheses or other symbols of inclusion.

$$-3(2 - 4)\Big/ - 4(-2)(-3)\Big/ + \frac{(-3)(-4)}{2}$$

Next we simplify each term.

$$-3(2 - 4)\Big/ - 4(-2)(-3)\Big/ + \frac{(-3)(-4)}{2}$$

$$-3(-2) \quad / \quad + 8(-3) \quad / \quad + \frac{12}{2}$$

$$+6 \quad / \quad -24 \quad / \quad +6$$

Now we combine the simplified terms.

$$+6 - 24 + 6$$

$$-18 + 6$$

$$\mathbf{-12}$$

2 New Concepts (Continued)

Example 1 (continued)

Instruction

You may need to review the following lessons with students who are having difficulty performing operations with positive and negative numbers:

Lesson 64, adding positive and negative numbers

Lesson 73, multiplying and dividing positive and negative numbers

Example 2

Instruction

Check that students are placing the slashes correctly on their papers. Most errors occur because students place them within parentheses or other symbols of inclusion.

To help students see how the grouping symbols affect answers, rewrite the problem on the board and ask:

"How does the answer change if we place brackets around $[4(-2)(-3) + \frac{(-3)(-4)}{2}]$***?"***
The answer changes to −24.

If students have difficulty simplifying this new expression, show them how to simplify the part of the equation that is now within brackets.

The expression within brackets simplifies to $4(6) + \frac{12}{2}$, then to $24 + 6$, and finally to 30. The complete expression with brackets simplifies to $6 - 30$, or -24.

(continued)

2 New Concepts *(Continued)*

Example 3

Instruction

Have volunteers explain how they identified where to place the slashes. Sample: I knew to place the slashes between terms. I identified the terms as the numbers separated by plus or minus signs.

Instruction

Ask students to explain why it is useful to use the commutative and associative properties to simplify expressions with positive and negative numbers. Guide them to see that the commutative and associative properties allow us to rearrange and regroup terms so terms with similar signs are placed together. This may make expressions easier to read and simplify.

Example 4

Instruction

After completing this example, review with students the method for simplifying expressions with signed numbers:

- Use slashes to separate terms.
- Use order of operations to simplify terms.
- Add the terms algebraically.

Discuss any questions that students may have.

(continued)

Example 3

Simplify: (−2) − [(−3) − (−4)(−5)]

Solution

There are only two terms, −2 and the bracketed quantity. By the order of operations, we simplify within brackets first, multiplying and dividing before adding and subtracting.

$$(-2) \;/\; -[(-3)-(-4)(-5)]$$

$$(-2) \;/\; -[(-3)-(+20)]$$

$$(-2) \;/\; -(-23)$$

$$(-2) \;/\; +23$$

$$\mathbf{+21}$$

Signed numbers are often written without parentheses. To simplify such expressions we simply add algebraically from left to right.

$$-3+4-5=-4$$

Another way to simplify this expression is to use the commutative and associative properties to rearrange and regroup the terms by their signs.

−3 + 4 − 5	Given
+4 − 3 − 5	Commutative Property
+4 + (−3 − 5)	Associative Property
+4 − 8	−3 − 5 = −8
−4	+4 − 8 = −4

Visit www.SaxonPublishers.com/ActivitiesC2 *for a graphing calculator activity.*

Example 4

Simplify: −2 + 3(−2) − 2(+4)

Solution

To emphasize the separate terms, we first draw a slash before each plus or minus sign that is not enclosed.

$$-2 \;/\; +3(-2) \;/\; -2(+4)$$

Next we simplify each term.

$$-2 \;/\; +3(-2) \;/\; -2(+4)$$

$$-2 \qquad -6 \qquad -8$$

Then we algebraically add the terms.

$$-2-6-8=\mathbf{-16}$$

English Learners

In example 4, explain the meaning of **enclosed.** Say:

"Enclosed means inside something. If a sign is enclosed, it is inside parentheses or brackets."

Write several numbers on the board. Invite students to come up and enclose a number in parentheses.

Practice Set ▶ **Justify** Simplify. Show steps and properties.

a. $(-3) + (-3)(-3) - \frac{(-3)}{(+3)}$ 7 **b.** $(-3) - [(-4) - (-5)(-6)]$ 31

c. $(-2)[(-3) - (-4)(-5)]$ 46 **d.** $(-5) - (-5)(-5) + |-5|$ −25

e. $-3 + 4 - 5 - 2$ −6 **f.** $-2 + 3(-4) - 5(-2)$ −4

g. $-3(-2) - 5(2) + 3(-4)$ −16 **h.** $-4(-3)(-2) - 6(-4)$ 0

Written Practice *Strengthening Concepts*

1. a. 84 b. 85 c. 90 d. 30

1. (Inv. 4) Find the **a** mean, **b** median, **c** mode, and **d** range of the following set of numbers:

70, 80, 90, 80, 70, 90, 75, 95, 100, 90

Use ratio boxes to solve problems **2–4:**

2. (66) The ratio of fiction to nonfiction books that Sarah read was 3 to 1. If she read 24 books, how many of the books were nonfiction? 6 books

3. (54) Mary weeded her flower garden. She found that the ratio of dandelions to marigolds in the garden was 11 to 4. If there were 44 marigolds in the garden, how many dandelions were there? 121 dandelions

4. (72) If sound travels 2 miles in 10 seconds, how far does sound travel in 1 minute? 12 miles

5. (50) Use a unit multiplier to convert 0.98 liter to milliliters.
0.98 liter $\cdot \frac{1000 \text{ milliliters}}{1 \text{ liter}}$ = 980 milliliters

▶ ***6.** (78) **Represent** Graph $x > 0$ on a number line.

−1 0 1 2 3

7.

$50,000
$5000
$5000
$5000
$5000
$5000
$5000
$5000
$5000
$5000
$5000

$\frac{7}{10}$ of the goal ($35,000); $\frac{3}{10}$ of the goal

7. (71) Diagram this statement. Then answer the questions that follow.

Thirty-five thousand dollars were raised in the charity drive. This was seven tenths of the goal.

a. The goal of the charity drive was to raise how much money? $50,000

b. The drive fell short of the goal by what percent? 30%

▶ ***8.** (66, 82) **Analyze** The radius of a circle is 4 meters. Use 3.14 for π to find the

a. circumference of the circle. 25.12 m

b. area of the circle. 50.24 m²

▶ ***9.** (Inv. 1) **Generalize** What fraction of this circle is shaded? $\frac{7}{20}$

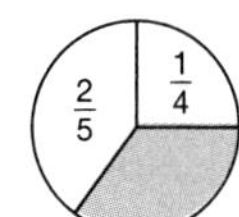

▶ See Math Conversations in the sidebar.

2 New Concepts (Continued)

Practice Set

Problems a–h Justify

After students finish simplifying these problems, discuss each problem by asking volunteers to take turns showing each step and explaining the reason for it. Sample: In problem **d,** the first thing to do is find the absolute value of −5.

3 Written Practice

Math Conversations

Discussion opportunities are provided below.

Problem 6 Represent

"Suppose we graph x < 0 on the same number line. What number is not represented?" 0

"What numbers are represented?" all the rational numbers except 0

Problem 8 Analyze

Discuss with students what formulas are needed to answer these questions. $C = 2\pi r$ and $A = \pi r^2$

After students find the answers, ask:

"What is the exact circumference? 8π m

"What is the exact area?" 16π m²

"Are the exact values greater than or less than the calculated values? Why?" Sample: The exact values are slightly greater than the calculated values because π is slightly greater than 3.14.

Clarify that "exact" means without rounding π. All measurement is approximate.

Problem 9 Generalize

Have students make statements about the information that is contained in this drawing.

"We see a circle and 2 fractions in the drawing, but more information is there for you to find. What statements can you make about this drawing?" Samples: The shaded part contains less than 180°. The angle of the $\frac{1}{4}$ sector is a right angle. There are 144 + 90 degrees in the two unshaded sectors. The $\frac{2}{5}$ sector is the largest sector.

(continued)

3 Written Practice (Continued)

Math Conversations

Discussion opportunities are provided below.

Problem 10 Analyze

Discuss other possibilities for two spins of the spinner. Ask questions like these:

"What is the probability of the spinner stopping twice in the $\frac{1}{4}$ sector?" $\frac{1}{16}$

"What is the probability of the spinner stopping twice in the $\frac{2}{5}$ sector?" $\frac{4}{25}$

"What is the probability of the spinner stopping once in the $\frac{1}{4}$ sector and once in the $\frac{2}{5}$ sector?" $\frac{1}{10}$

Have students explain how they determined each probability.

Problem 16 Generalize

"Let's see how many ways we can find to simplify this expression. Who will show us one way?" Sample: Make a complex fraction with $\frac{25}{3}$ in the numerator and $\frac{100}{1}$ in the denominator. Multiply the fraction by $\frac{3}{3}$ to get $\frac{25}{300}$ and that is $\frac{1}{12}$.

Continue until all methods that students have used have been described and explained.

Problem 17 Connect

Guide students to examine the relationships that are contained in the problem. Ask questions like these:

"How many seeds did not sprout?" 2

"What percent is that?" 5%

"What ratios can describe this information?" Samples: 19 to 1 (sprouted seeds to unsprouted seeds), 1 to 20 (unsprouted seeds to seeds planted)

Errors and Misconceptions

Problem 10

Watch out for students who get $\frac{14}{20}$ as their answer. These students have added the probability of the spinner landing on the shaded area to itself rather than multiplying the probability by itself.

Problem 17

If students were not able to solve this correctly, suggest that they use a ratio box to organize the information.

(continued)

▸* **10.** (Inv. 8) **Analyze** If the circle in problem **9** is the face of a spinner, and if the spinner is spun twice, what is the probability of the spinner stopping in the shaded area both times? $\frac{49}{400}$

11. (70) A certain rectangular box is 5 in. long, 4 in. wide, and 3 in. high. Draw the box and find its volume. 60 in.^{3}

11. 3 in. 4 in. 5 in.

12. (67) Suppose that the box described in problem **11** is cut open and unfolded. Draw the unfolded pattern and find the surface area. 94 in.^{2}

12. one possibility: 4 3 4 3 4 5 4

13. (48) Complete the table.

Fraction	Decimal	Percent
$\frac{1}{40}$	**a.** 0.025	**b.** $2\frac{1}{2}$%
c. $\frac{1}{400}$	**d.** 0.0025	0.25%

14. (60) When the Nelsons sold their house, they paid the realtor a fee of 6% of the selling price. If the house sold for $180,000, how much was the realtor's fee? $10,800

15. (21) **a.** Write the prime factorization of 17,640 using exponents. $2^3 \cdot 3^2 \cdot 5 \cdot 7^2$

b. How can you tell by looking at the answer to **a** that $\sqrt{17{,}640}$ is not a whole number? The exponents of the prime factors of 17,640 are not all even numbers.

▸* **16.** (76) **Generalize** Simplify: $\frac{8\frac{1}{3}}{100}$ $\frac{1}{12}$

Use ratio boxes to solve problems **17** and **18.**

▸* **17.** (81) **Connect** Max was delighted when he found that 38 of the 40 seeds he planted had sprouted. What percent of the seeds sprouted? 95%

* **18.** (81) Before the assembly began, only 35 percent of the students were seated. If 91 students were not seated, how many students were there in all? 140 students

19. (Inv. 6, 61) **a.** Classify the quadrilateral shown. 19. a. parallelogram

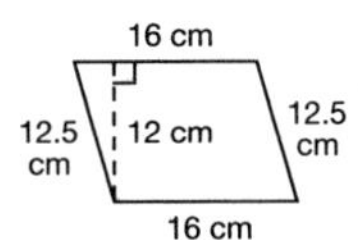

b. Find its perimeter. 57 cm

c. Find its area. 192 cm^2

d. This figure does not have line symmetry, but it does have point symmetry. Trace the figure on your paper, and locate its point of symmetry.

d. point of symmetry

20. (40) Find the missing numbers in the table by using the function rule. Then graph the x, y pairs on a coordinate plane and draw a line through the points and extending beyond the points.

$y = 2x - 1$

x	y
5	9
3	5
1	1

20. y x (5, 9) (3, 5) (1, 1)

▸ See Math Conversations in the sidebar.

21. Refer to the figure below to answer **a–d.**
(56)

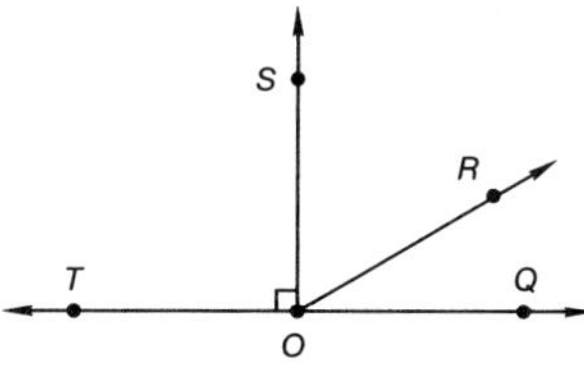

a. Find m∠*TOS*. 90°

b. Find m∠*QOT*. 180°

c. Angle *QOR* is one third of a right angle. Find m∠*QOR*. 30°

d. Find m∠*TOR*. 150°

▶* **22.** **Evaluate** Compare: $(5 \times 10^{-3})(6 \times 10^{8})$ ⊜ $(5 \times 10^{8})(6 \times 10^{-3})$
(51, 83)

For problems **23** and **24,** solve and check the equation. Show each step.

23. $13.2 = 1.2w$ 11
(Inv. 7)

24. $c + \frac{5}{6} = 1\frac{1}{4}$ $\frac{5}{12}$
(Inv. 7)

▶ **Generalize** Simplify:

25. $3\{20 - [6^2 - 3(10 - 4)]\}$ 6
(63)

26.
(49)

	3 hr 15 min 25 s
−	2 hr 45 min 30 s
	29 min 55 s

27. $2^0 + 0.2 + 2^{-2}$ (decimal answer) 1.45
(43, 57)

* **28.** **a.** $(-3) - \left[(-2) - (+2) - \frac{(-2)}{(-2)}\right]$ 2
(85)

b. $(-3) - [(-2) - (+4)(-5)]$ −21

▶* **29.** **Generalize** Collect like terms: $x^2 + 6x - 2x - 12$ $x^2 + 4x - 12$
(84)

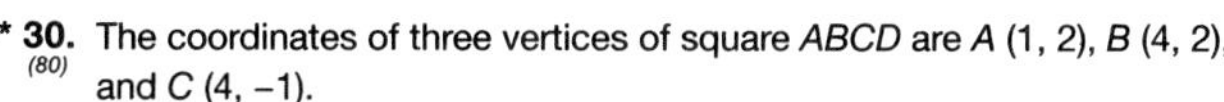

▶* **30.** The coordinates of three vertices of square *ABCD* are *A* (1, 2), *B* (4, 2), and *C* (4, −1).
(80)

a. Find the coordinates of *D* and draw the square. *D* (1, −1)

b. Reflect square *ABCD* in the *y*-axis, and draw its image, square *A′ B′ C′ D′*. What are the coordinates of the vertices of this reflection? *A′* (−1, 2), *B′* (−4, 2), *C′* (−4, −1), *D′* (−1, −1)

30.

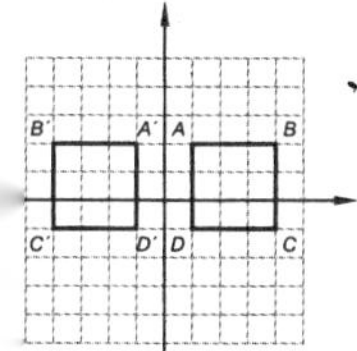

▶ See Math Conversations in the sidebar.

3 Written Practice (Continued)

Math Conversations

Discussion opportunities are provided below.

Problem 22 Evaluate

Ask students to explain how they can compare these two expressions without actually simplifying them. Sample: Since both expressions have exactly the same factors, they are equal.

Problems 25–28 Generalize

Discuss what mathematical relationships and facts students need to know in order to do these problems. Samples: order of operations, any number (except 0) to the 0 power is 1, 60 seconds in 1 minute, 60 minutes in 1 hour, how to work with brackets

Problem 29 Generalize

"What do we call this kind of expression?" polynomial

"How do we simplify an expression like this one?" Sample: Collect like terms and combine them.

"Why is it easy to collect like terms in this expression?" Sample: All the terms are already in descending order.

Errors and Misconceptions

Problem 30

If students have difficulty drawing the reflection, have them use a number 2 pencil to draw square *ABCD,* then fold the graph on the *y*-axis, and rub the area with the square with a fingernail or flat object so that the image transfers to its reflection. Each vertex has the same *y*-coordinate and opposite *x*-coordinate as the corresponding vertex in square *ABCD.*

Looking Forward

Simplifying expressions that contain both positive and negative numbers prepares students for:

- **Lesson 91,** evaluations with positive and negative numbers.
- **Lesson 103,** powers of negative numbers.

Assessment

30–40 minutes *For use after Lesson 85*

Distribute **Cumulative Test 16** to each student. Two versions of the test are available in *Saxon Math Course 2 Course Assessments Book.* Have students complete the **Power-Up Test** first. Allow 10 minutes. Then have students work the 20 numbered items on the **Cumulative Test.** Students may use copies of the answer sheet to record their work. Track individual and class progress with the **Test Analysis** forms.

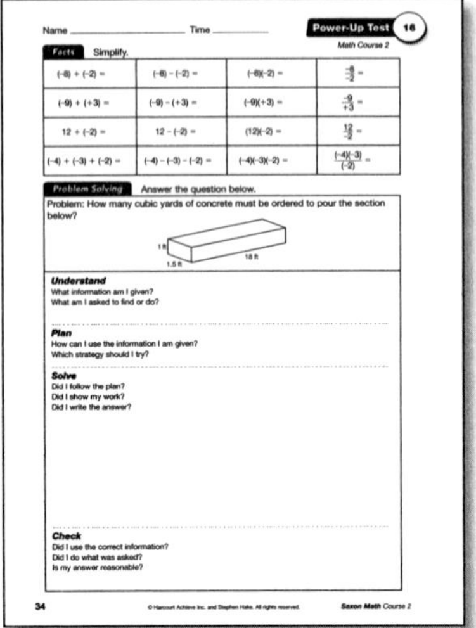
Power-Up Test 16

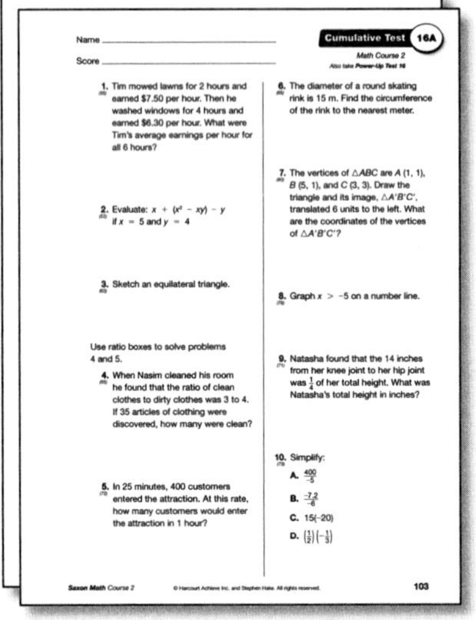
Name ____ Score ____ Cumulative Test 16A
Math Course 2

1. Tim mowed lawns for 2 hours and earned $7.50 per hour. Then he washed windows for 4 hours and earned $6.30 per hour. What were Tim's average earnings per hour for all 6 hours?

2. Evaluate: $x + (x^2 - xy) - y$ if $x = 5$ and $y = 4$

3. Sketch an equilateral triangle.

Use ratio boxes to solve problems 4 and 5.

4. When Nasim cleaned his room he found that the ratio of clean clothes to dirty clothes was 3 to 4. If 35 articles of clothing were discovered, how many were clean?

5. In 25 minutes, 400 customers entered the attraction. At this rate, how many customers would enter the attraction in 1 hour?

6. The diameter of a round skating rink is 15 m. Find the circumference of the rink to the nearest meter.

7. The vertices of $\triangle ABC$ are A (1, 1), B (5, 1), and C (3, 3). Draw the triangle and its image, $\triangle A'B'C'$, translated 6 units to the left. What are the coordinates of the vertices of $\triangle A'B'C'$?

8. Graph $x > -5$ on a number line.

9. Natasha found that the 14 inches from her knee joint to her hip joint was $\frac{1}{4}$ of her total height. What was Natasha's total height in inches?

10. Simplify:

Saxon Math Course 2 · © Harcourt Achieve Inc. and Stephen Hake. All rights reserved. · 103

Cumulative Test 16A

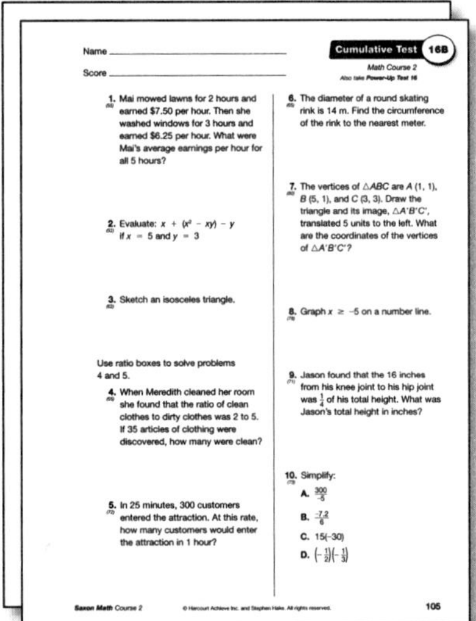
Name ____ Score ____ Cumulative Test 16B
Math Course 2

1. Mai mowed lawns for 2 hours and earned $7.50 per hour. Then she washed windows for 3 hours and earned $6.25 per hour. What were Mai's average earnings per hour for all 5 hours?

2. Evaluate: $x + (x^2 - xy) - y$ if $x = 5$ and $y = 3$

3. Sketch an isosceles triangle.

Use ratio boxes to solve problems 4 and 5.

4. When Meredith cleaned her room she found that the ratio of clean clothes to dirty clothes was 2 to 5. If 35 articles of clothing were discovered, how many were clean?

5. In 25 minutes, 300 customers entered the attraction. At this rate, how many customers would enter the attraction in 1 hour?

6. The diameter of a round skating rink is 14 m. Find the circumference of the rink to the nearest meter.

7. The vertices of $\triangle ABC$ are A (1, 1), B (5, 1), and C (3, 3). Draw the triangle and its image, $\triangle A'B'C'$, translated 5 units to the left. What are the coordinates of the vertices of $\triangle A'B'C'$?

8. Graph $x \geq -5$ on a number line.

9. Jason found that the 16 inches from his knee joint to his hip joint was $\frac{1}{4}$ of his total height. What was Jason's total height in inches?

10. Simplify:

Saxon Math Course 2 · © Harcourt Achieve Inc. and Stephen Hake. All rights reserved. · 105

Alternative Cumulative Test 16B

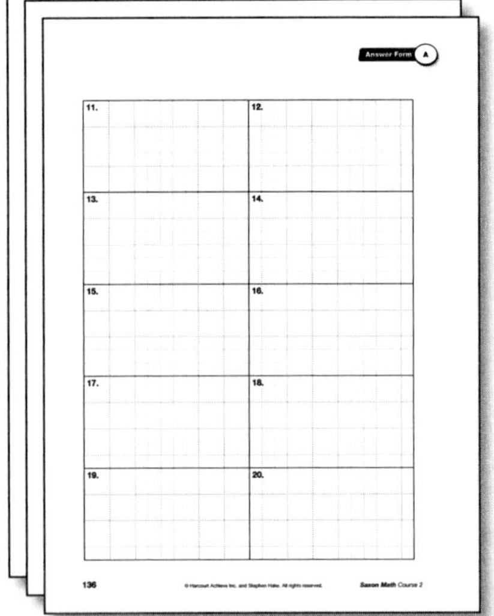
Optional Answer Forms

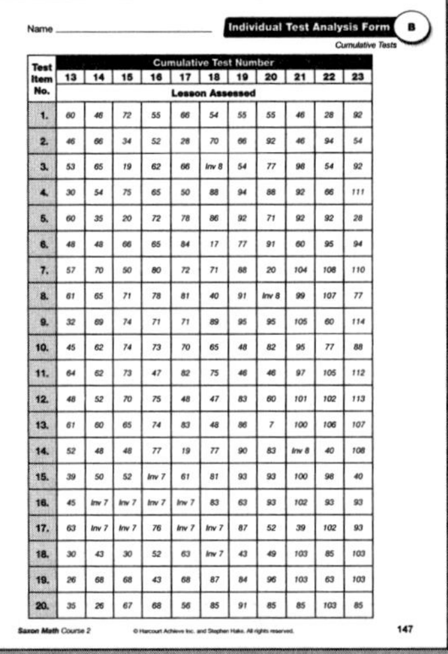
Name ____ Individual Test Analysis Form B
Cumulative Tests

Test Item No.	13	14	15	16	17	18	19	20	21	22	23
1.	60	46	72	55	66	54	55	55	46	28	92
2.	46	66	34	52	28	70	66	92	46	94	54
3.	53	65	19	62	66	Inv 8	54	77	98	54	92
4.	30	54	75	65	50	88	94	88	92	66	111
5.	60	35	20	72	78	86	92	71	92	92	28
6.	48	48	66	65	84	17	77	91	60	95	94
7.	57	70	50	80	72	71	88	20	104	108	110
8.	61	65	71	78	81	40	91	Inv 8	99	107	77
9.	32	69	74	71	71	89	95	95	105	60	114
10.	45	62	74	73	70	65	48	82	95	77	88
11.	64	62	73	47	82	75	46	46	97	105	112
12.	48	52	70	75	48	47	83	60	101	102	113
13.	61	60	65	74	83	48	86	7	100	106	107
14.	52	48	48	77	19	77	90	83	Inv 8	40	108
15.	39	50	52	Inv 7	61	81	93	93	100	98	40
16.	45	Inv 7	Inv 7	Inv 7	Inv 7	83	63	93	102	93	93
17.	63	Inv 7	Inv 7	76	Inv 7	Inv 7	87	52	39	102	93
18.	30	43	30	52	63	Inv 7	43	49	103	85	103
19.	26	68	68	43	68	87	84	96	103	63	103
20.	35	26	67	68	56	85	91	85	85	103	85

(Column header: Cumulative Test Number; Lesson Assessed)

Saxon Math Course 2 · © Harcourt Achieve Inc. and Stephen Hake. All rights reserved. · 147

Individual Test Analysis Form

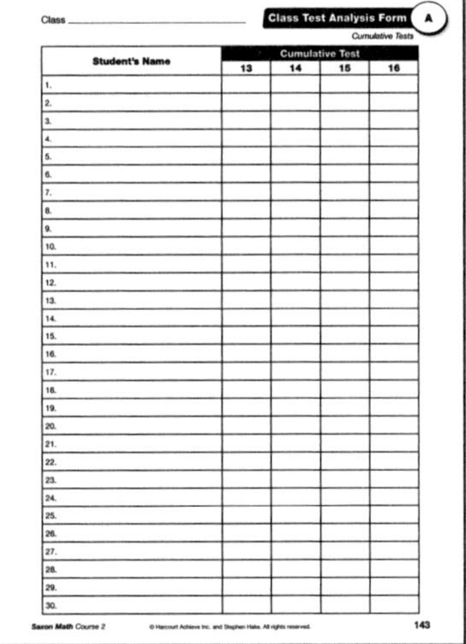
Class Test Analysis Form

Reteaching

Students who score below 80% on the assessment may be in need of reteaching. Look for the causes of student mistakes. If errors are conceptual, refer to the *Reteaching Masters* for reteaching.

Performance Activity 16

Order of Operations

Assign after Lesson 85 and Test 16

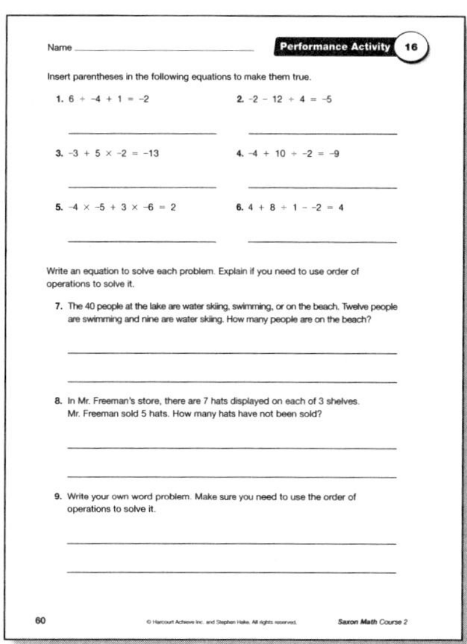

Name ______________________ **Performance Activity 16**

Insert parentheses in the following equations to make them true.

1. $6 \div -4 + 1 = -2$
2. $-2 - 12 \div 4 = -5$
3. $-3 + 5 \times -2 = -13$
4. $-4 + 10 \div -2 = -9$
5. $-4 \times -5 + 3 \times -6 = 2$
6. $4 + 8 \div 1 - -2 = 4$

Write an equation to solve each problem. Explain if you need to use order of operations to solve it.

7. The 40 people at the lake are water skiing, swimming, or on the beach. Twelve people are swimming and nine are water skiing. How many people are on the beach?
8. In Mr. Freeman's store, there are 7 hats displayed on each of 3 shelves. Mr. Freeman sold 5 hats. How many hats have not been sold?
9. Write your own word problem. Make sure you need to use the order of operations to solve it.

60 © Harcourt Achieve Inc. and Stephen Hake. All rights reserved. *Saxon Math Course 2*

Performance Activity 16

Objectives

- Insert parentheses in equations to make them true.
- Write an equation and explain how to use order of operations to solve it.
- Communicate ideas through writing.

Materials

Performance Activity 16

Preparation

Make copies of **Performance Activity 16.** (One per student.)

Time Requirement

15–30 minutes; Begin in class and complete at home.

Activity

Explain to students that for this activity they will be inserting parentheses in equations to make them true. They will also be writing equations for given situations and explaining if order of operations needs to be used to solve the equation. Explain that all of the information students need is on **Performance Activity 16.**

Criteria for Evidence of Learning

- Accurately inserts parentheses in equations to make them true.
- Accurately writes an equation for a situation and explains correctly if order of operations needs to be used in solving the equation.
- Communicates mathematical ideas clearly.

Meeting Standards

National Council of Teachers of Mathematics (NCTM)

Numbers and Operations

NO.2a Understand the meaning and effects of arithmetic operations with fractions, decimals, and integers

NO.3a Select appropriate methods and tools for computing with fractions and decimals from among mental computation, estimation, calculators or computers, and paper and pencil, depending on the situation, and apply the selected methods

Problem Solving

PS.1d Monitor and reflect on the process of mathematical problem solving

Communication

CM.3d Use the language of mathematics to express mathematical ideas precisely

Objectives

- Identify the counting numbers, whole numbers, integers, and rational numbers.
- Tell how the counting numbers, whole numbers, integers, and rational numbers are related.

Lesson Preparation

Materials

- **Power Up S** (in *Instructional Masters*)
- **Investigation Activity 13** (in *Instructional Masters*) or **graph paper**

Optional

- **Teacher-provided material: index cards**

Power Up S

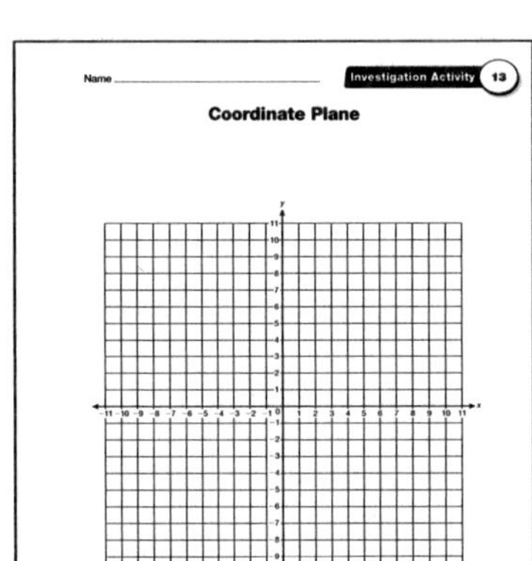

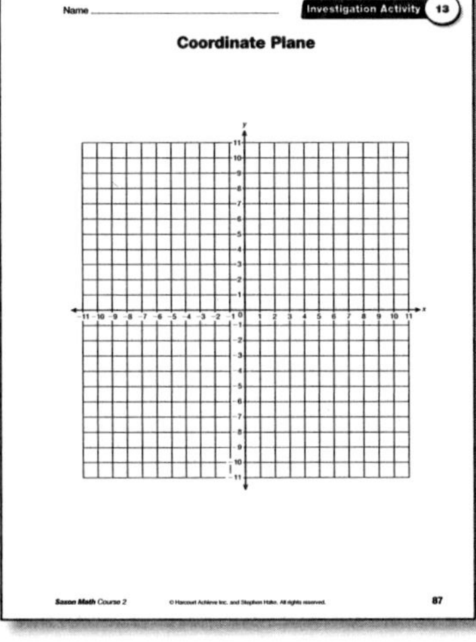

Investigation Activity 13

Math Language

New	English Learners (ESL)
rational numbers	ellipses

Technology Resources

Student eBook Complete student textbook in electronic format.

Resources and Planner CD Blackline masters, plus a pacing calendar with standards.

Test and Practice Generator CD Create additional practice sheets and custom-made tests.

www.SaxonPublishers.com Visit for more student activities and planning materials.

Inclusion

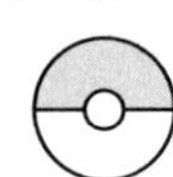

Adaptations CD Adapted lessons, investigations, practice and assessments.

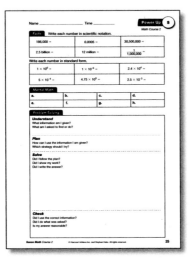

Meeting Standards

National Council of Teachers of Mathematics (NCTM)

Numbers and Operations

NO.1g Develop meaning for integers and represent and compare quantities with them

Reasoning and Proof

RP.2c Develop and evaluate mathematical arguments and proofs

Communication

CM.3a Organize and consolidate their mathematical thinking through communication

Representation

RE.5a Create and use representations to organize, record, and communicate mathematical ideas

Power-Up Discussion *For use with Power Up, p. 592*

Problem-Solving Strategy: Work Backwards/ Guess and Check

The expression $\sqrt[3]{8}$ means "the cube root of 8." The cube root notation, $\sqrt[3]{\ }$, is asking, "What number used as a factor three times equals the number under the symbol?" The cube root of 8 is 2 because $2 \times 2 \times 2 = 8$.
Find $\sqrt[3]{64}$. Find $\sqrt[3]{125}$. Find $\sqrt[3]{1{,}000{,}000}$.

Understand Understand the problem.

"What information are we given?"

A cube root of a number is a number that, when used as a factor three times, results in the original number. The symbol $\sqrt[3]{\ }$ indicates a cube root.

"What are we asked to do?"

We are asked to find three cube roots: $\sqrt[3]{64}$, $\sqrt[3]{125}$, and $\sqrt[3]{1{,}000{,}000}$.

Plan Make a plan.

"What problem-solving strategy will we use?"

We will *work backwards* by cubing numbers to see if we can find the numbers under the cube root symbol. For the largest cube root, we will *guess and check* to find the answer.

Solve Carry out the plan.

"What are the first five cubes?"

$$1^3 = 1 \times 1 \times 1 = 1$$
$$2^3 = 2 \times 2 \times 2 = 8$$
$$3^3 = 3 \times 3 \times 3 = 27$$
$$4^3 = 4 \times 4 \times 4 = 64$$
$$5^3 = 5 \times 5 \times 5 = 125$$

"According to our list, what is $\sqrt[3]{64}$?"

4

"What is $\sqrt[3]{125}$?"

5

"What is $\sqrt[3]{1{,}000{,}000}$?"

Because the 1,000,000 contains several zeros, we guess that the cube root of 1,000,000 is a power of 10. We try the first power of 10: $10 \times 10 \times 10 = 1000$.

"Does the second power of 10 work?"

The second power of 10 is 10^2, or 100. We know that $100 \times 100 \times 100 = 1{,}000{,}000$, so $\sqrt[3]{1{,}000{,}000} = 100$.

Check Look back.

"Did we do what we were asked to do?"

Yes, we found all three cube roots.

"How can we verify our answers are correct?"

We can cube the cube roots we found to ensure they match the numbers under the symbols.

1 Power Up

Facts

Distribute **Power Up S** to students. See answers below.

Mental Math

Encourage students to share different ways to mentally compute these exercises. Strategies for exercises **d** and **e** are listed below.

d. Find 1% and Multiply

$17.90 ≈ $18

1% of $18 = 18¢

15% of $18 = 15 × 18¢ =

15 × (10¢ + 8¢) =

150¢ + 120¢ = $2.70

Use 10% and 5%

$17.90 ≈ $18

10% of $18 = $1.80

5% of $18 = $0.90

15% of $18 = $2.70

e. Decompose

1 L = 1000 mL

$0.2\text{ L} = \frac{2}{10} \times 1000\text{ mL} = 200\text{ mL}$

Use a Unit Multiplier

$0.2\text{ L} \times \frac{1000\text{ mL}}{1\text{ L}} = 200\text{ mL}$

Problem Solving

Refer to **Power-Up Discussion,** p. 592B.

2 New Concepts

Instruction

Ask students to brainstorm ways they classify different things in real life. Examples might include classifying clothes according to style or color, classifying information into different subjects at school, or classifying food according to food groups. Lead the class in a discussion about classification. Elicit that classification involves grouping things according to shared characteristics. Tell students that numbers have characteristics, and that we can classify them into families depending upon their characteristics.

(continued)

LESSON 86

• Number Families

Power Up *Building Power*

facts Power Up S

mental math

a. **Positive/Negative:** $(-18) + (-40)$ −58

b. **Order of Operations/Exponents:** $(3 \times 10^{-3})(3 \times 10^{-3})$ 9×10^{-6}

c. **Algebra:** $7x + 4 = 60$ 8

d. **Percent/Estimation:** Estimate 15% of $17.90. $2.70

e. **Measurement:** 0.2 L to mL 200 mL

f. **Fractional Parts:** $30 is $\frac{1}{3}$ of m. $90

g. **Probability:** There are 5 red marbles, 2 green marbles, and 4 blue marbles in a bag. What is the probability of choosing a red marble? $\frac{5}{11}$

h. **Calculation:** What is the total cost of a $200 item plus 7% sales tax? $214

problem solving

The expression $\sqrt[3]{8}$ means "the cube root of 8." The cube root notation, $\sqrt[3]{\ }$, is asking, "What number used as a factor three times equals the number under the symbol?" The cube root of 8 is 2 because $2 \times 2 \times 2 = 8$. Find $\sqrt[3]{64}$. Find $\sqrt[3]{125}$. Find $\sqrt[3]{1{,}000{,}000}$. 4; 5; 100

New Concept *Increasing Knowledge*

Thinking Skill
Relate

If every counting number is a whole number, is every whole number a counting number? Explain. Sample: No. The whole-number family includes the counting numbers *and* the number zero. Because zero is a whole number but not a counting number, every whole number is not a counting number.

In mathematics we give special names to certain sets of numbers. Some of these sets are the counting numbers, the whole numbers, the integers, and the rational numbers. In this lesson we will review each of these **number families** and discuss how they are related.

- **The Counting Numbers.** Counting numbers are the numbers we say when we count. The first counting number is 1, the next is 2, then 3, and so on.

  Counting numbers: 1, 2, 3, 4, 5, ...

- **The Whole Numbers.** The members of the whole-number family are the counting numbers as well as the number zero.

  Whole numbers: 0, 1, 2, 3, 4, 5, ...

  If we use a dot to mark each of the whole numbers on the number line, the graph looks like this:

  −5 −4 −3 −2 −1 0 1 2 3 4 5

Facts Write each number in scientific notation.

$186{,}000 = 1.86 \times 10^5$	$0.0005 = 5 \times 10^{-4}$	$30{,}500{,}000 = 3.05 \times 10^7$
$2.5\text{ billion} = 2.5 \times 10^9$	$12\text{ million} = 1.2 \times 10^7$	$\frac{1}{1{,}000{,}000} = 1 \times 10^{-6}$

Write each number in standard form.

$1 \times 10^6 = 1{,}000{,}000$	$1 \times 10^{-6} = 0.000001$	$2.4 \times 10^4 = 24{,}000$
$5 \times 10^{-4} = 0.0005$	$4.75 \times 10^5 = 475{,}000$	$2.5 \times 10^{-3} = 0.0025$

Notice that there are no dots to the left of zero. This is because no whole number is a negative number. Also notice that there are no dots between consecutive whole numbers. Numbers between consecutive whole numbers are not "whole." The blue arrowhead on the right end of the number line indicates that the whole numbers increase without end.

- **The Integers.** The integer family includes all the whole numbers. It also includes the opposites (negatives) of the positive whole numbers. The list of integers goes on and on in both directions as indicated by the ellipses below.

  Integers: ..., − 4, −3, −2, −1, 0, 1, 2, 3, 4, ...

  A graph of the integers looks like this:

  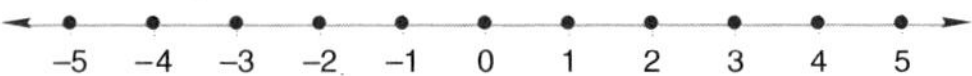

  The blue arrowheads on both ends of the number line indicate that the set of integers continues without end in both directions. Notice that integers do not include such numbers as $\frac{1}{2}$, $\frac{5}{3}$, and other fractions.

- **The Rational Numbers.** The family of **rational numbers** includes all numbers that can be written as a *ratio* (fraction) of two integers. Here are some examples of rational numbers:

  $$\frac{1}{2} \quad \frac{5}{3} \quad \frac{-3}{2} \quad \frac{-4}{1} \quad \frac{0}{2} \quad \frac{3}{1}$$

  Notice that the family of rational numbers includes all the integers, because every integer can be written as a fraction whose denominator is the number 1. For example, we can write −4 as a fraction by writing

  $$\frac{-4}{1}$$

  The set of rational numbers also includes all the positive and negative mixed numbers, because these numbers can be written as fractions. For example, we can write $4\frac{1}{5}$ as

  $$\frac{21}{5}$$

  Sometimes rational numbers are written in decimal form, in which case the decimal number will either terminate or repeat.

  $$\frac{1}{8} = 0.125 \qquad \frac{5}{6} = 0.8333\ldots = 0.8\overline{3}$$

  The diagram on the next page may be helpful in visualizing the relationships between these families of numbers. The diagram shows that the set of rational numbers includes all the other number families described in this lesson.

2 New Concepts (Continued)

Instruction

Help students understand that each new number family that is introduced contains all members of the previous number family. One way to do this is to construct the diagram on the next page on the board or overhead by drawing each box as you discuss the number family the box represents.

To encourage students to think more about the different types of number families, have them respond to the following statements with *true* or *false* and explain their answers.

- Between any two whole numbers there is another whole number. False; there is no whole number between consecutive whole numbers.
- All negative integers are rational numbers. True; all integers are also rational numbers.
- For any integer n, the absolute value of n is a counting number. False; 0 is an integer, but it is not a counting number.
- $\frac{4}{1}$ belongs to all four families, but $\frac{1}{4}$ belongs only to the family of rational numbers. True; $\frac{1}{4}$ is not a counting number, a whole number, or an integer.

(continued)

Math Background

What is a rational number?

A *rational number* is a number that can be expressed as a ratio of two integers: $\frac{p}{q}$, where p is any integer and q is any integer except 0. It may seem as if all decimals would be rational numbers, but not all decimals are rational numbers. All terminating and repeating decimals can be written as fractions, and therefore are rational numbers. But nonterminating, nonrepeating decimals, such as π, cannot be written as a ratio of integers and so are not rational. They are called *irrational numbers.*

A connection with early mathematics is that the ancient Egyptians expressed all their fractions as sums of unit fractions. They had no way to show a fraction like $\frac{7}{8}$—they would show it as $\frac{1}{2} + \frac{1}{4} + \frac{1}{8}$. A characteristic of rational numbers is that any positive rational number can be expressed as a sum of distinct reciprocals of positive integers, which are unit fractions.

English Learners

When discussing integers, demonstrate the meaning of **ellipses.** Write "−4, −3, −2, −1, 0, 1, 2, 3, 4," on the board. Draw ellipses to the left of −4 and to the right of 4. Say:

"The three dots beside −4 and 4 are called ellipses. They tell us that the numbers continue without end."

Write 10, 20, 30, 40, on the board, and have a volunteer draw ellipses to the right and left of the list of numbers.

2 New Concepts (Continued)

Instruction

If you have drawn the diagram on the board or overhead as you worked through the instruction, take a few minutes to have students express relationships between the families. Start with these examples and ask students to continue:

- All counting numbers are integers.
- Not all integers are whole numbers.

Example 1

Instruction

Ask students to explain why the number 4 is not included on the number line. Ask how the question could be rewritten to include the number 4. Graph the integers that are less than or equal to 4.

Example 2

Instruction

Point out that questions like these are often on standardized tests, so knowing these relationships will help students answer such questions quickly and will give them more time for other questions.

Practice Set

Problems a and b Represent

Discuss why the graphs consist of points and not rays. Sample: There are rational numbers between the integers that are not integers so we show the integers with points.

(continued)

The diagram shows four nested boxes, each of which represents a number family. The smallest box is the group of numbers called *Counting Numbers*. They are a subset of a larger group called *Whole Numbers*. The whole numbers in turn are a subset of a larger group called *Integers*. The integers in turn are a subset of the group called *Rational Numbers*.

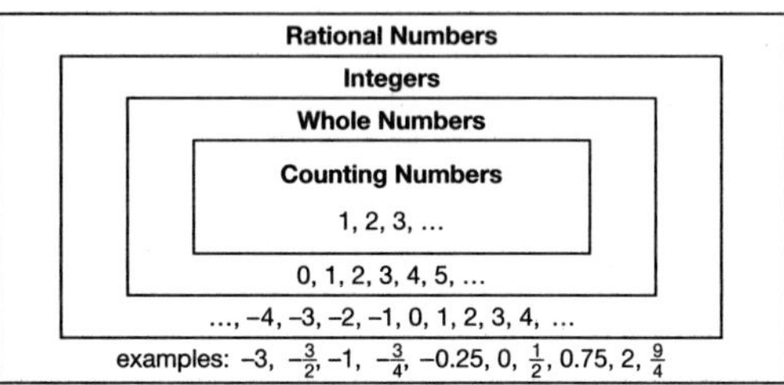

Discuss How does the diagram above visually represent the relationship between the different number families?

Example 1

Graph the integers that are less than 4.

Solution

We draw a number line and mark a dot at every integer that is less than 4. Since the set of integers includes whole numbers, we mark dots at 3, 2, 1, and 0. Since the integers also include the opposites of the positive whole numbers, we continue marking dots at −1, −2, −3, and so on. We then mark an arrowhead on the negative end of the line to indicate that the graph of integers that are less than 4 continues without end.

Verify Fractions such as $\frac{1}{2}$ are also less than 4. Why didn't we graph points for fractions such as $\frac{1}{2}$ on the number line above? The integer family includes only whole numbers and their opposites plus zero, as shown on the diagram.

Example 2

Answer true or false:

a. All whole numbers are integers.

b. All rational numbers are integers.

Solution

a. True. Every whole number is included in the family of integers.

b. False. Although every integer is a rational number, it is not true that every rational number is an integer. Rational numbers such as $\frac{1}{2}$ and $\frac{5}{3}$ are not integers.

Practice Set ▸ **Represent** Graph the integers that are:

a. greater than −4. (−4 −3 −2 −1 0)

b. less than 4. (−1 0 1 2 3 4)

▸ See Math Conversations in the sidebar.

Inclusion

Before the lesson, write 4 numbers from each different number set on index cards. Then, during the lesson draw on the board a diagram of the number sets similar to the one shown above. Shuffle the cards and distribute them to students in the class. Ask them to tape the card to the board in the section of the number set where their card belongs. For those cards that belong to more than one set, have the students place them in the inner most set.

c. false; The statement is false because the integer family includes all the whole numbers and their opposites.

▶ **Justify** Answer true or false. If the statement is false, explain why and give an example that proves it is false.

c. Every integer is a whole number.

d. Every integer is a rational number. true

Written Practice *Strengthening Concepts*

1. (46) Fragrant Scent was priced at $28.50 for 2 ounces, while Eau de Rue cost only $4.96 for 4 ounces. Fragrant Scent cost how much more per ounce than Eau de Rue? $13.01 more per ounce

2. (66) Use a ratio box to solve this problem. The ratio of rookies to veterans in the camp was 2 to 7. Altogether there were 252 rookies and veterans in the camp. How many of them were rookies? 56 rookies

3. (Inv. 4) Seven trunks were delivered to the costume department at the theater. The trunks weighed 197 lb, 213 lb, 246 lb, 205 lb, 238 lb, 213 lb, and 207 lb. Find the **a** mode, **b** median, **c** mean, and **d** range of this group of measures. **a.** 213 lb **b.** 213 lb **c.** 217 lb **d.** 49 lb

4. (50) Use a unit multiplier to convert 12 bushels to pecks (1 bushel = 4 pecks). 12 bushels $\cdot \frac{4 \text{ pecks}}{1 \text{ bushel}}$ = 48 pecks

5. (46) The Martins drove the 468 miles between Memphis, Tennessee and Cincinnati, Ohio in one day. If they left Memphis at 7 a.m. and arrived in Cincinnati at 4 p.m., what was the Martins' average speed? 52 miles per hour

▶ ***6.** (86) **Represent** Illustrate on a number line, the whole numbers that are less than or equal to 3.

7. (72) Use a ratio box to solve this problem. Nine is to 6 as what number is to 30? 45

8. (22) Nine tenths of the school's 1800 students attended the homecoming game.

a. How many of the school's students attended the homecoming game? 1620 students

b. What percent of the school's students did not attend the homecoming game? 10%

9. (52) Evaluate: $\sqrt{b^2 - 4ac}$ if $a = 1$, $b = 5$, and $c = 4$ 3

▶ ***10.** (Inv. 8) **Analyze** During basketball season Heidi has made 40 free throws and missed 20. What is the experimental probability that she will make her next free throw? $\frac{2}{3}$

▶ See Math Conversations in the sidebar.

2 New Concepts *(Continued)*

Practice Set

Problems c and d Justify

Have students give an example for any statement they find to be false. Sample: In **c**, the statement is false because −1 is an integer but it is not a whole number.

3 Written Practice

Math Conversations

Discussion opportunities are provided below.

Problem 6 Represent

Discuss what the points represent.

"Why are there only 4 points on the graph?" Sample: There are only 4 whole numbers less than or equal to 3.

"Are all 4 numbers also integers? Why or why not?" Sample: Yes, because all whole numbers are included in the integers.

"Are all 4 numbers also counting numbers? Why or why not?" Sample: No, because zero is not a counting number.

Problem 10 Analyze

Help students see that experimental probabilities can change as more data is accumulated.

"Suppose Heidi makes her next 2 free throws. What will the experimental probability be for her next free throw?" $\frac{42}{62}$ or $\frac{21}{31}$

"Is that greater than or less than the $\frac{2}{3}$ experimental probability after her 60 free throws? Why?" Sample: Greater than, because she did better in those 2 free throws than her average. Therefore, her new percent is almost 68%, so she gained one percent.

Errors and Misconceptions

Problem 10

Tell students whose answer is 2 to 1 that they need to compare the number of free throws made to the total number of throws, not the number of free throws missed.

(continued)

3 Written Practice (Continued)

Math Conversations

Discussion opportunities are provided below.

Problem 11 Connect

Ask how else the radius could be expressed. 1 ft

Have students use mental math to find the circumference and area of the circle using 1 foot as the radius. $C = 2\pi$ ft, $A = \pi$ ft^2

Discuss the need for labeling the answers with units if students do not use them.

Problems 16 and 17 Model

Point out that equations could also be used to model these situations. Discuss how using a ratio box or an equation is equally easy for problem 16. Then ask whether anyone can write just one equation to find the number of unsprouted seeds. This should not be easy for students to do, since they have not used equations for situations like this before. An equation using n for the unsprouted seeds is $48 = 0.75(48 + n)$. Emphasize that it is much easier to use a ratio box for this problem.

Problem 19 Classify

"To classify this figure, we have to know some mathematical definitions and notice things about the figure. What are the characteristics that make this a trapezoid?" Samples: It is a quadrilateral. It has only 2 parallel sides.

Make a class list of the characteristics of the figure that make it a trapezoid. Then have students explain how they know that these are present in the figure. Sample: It is a quadrilateral because it has four sides. It is a trapezoid because it has one pair of parallel sides. They are parallel because they are perpendicular to the same line.

(continued)

▶* **11.** (66, 82) **a.** Find the circumference of the circle shown. 24π in.

b. Find the area of the circle. 144π in.^{2}

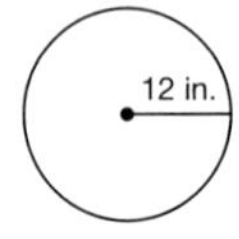

Leave π as π.

12. (47, 57) Find each missing exponent:

a. $10^8 \cdot 10^{-3} = 10^{\square}$ 5 **b.** $10^5 \div 10^8 = 10^{\square}$ −3

13. (67) The figure shown is a triangular prism. Copy the figure on your paper, and find the number of its

a. faces. 5 faces

b. edges. 9 edges

c. vertices. 6 vertices

14. (48) Complete the table.

Fraction	Decimal	Percent
a. $\frac{9}{10}$	0.9	**b.** 90%
$\frac{11}{12}$	**c.** $0.91\overline{6}$	**d.** $91\frac{2}{3}$%

15. (17) Obi is facing north. If he turns 360° in a clockwise direction, what direction will he be facing? Does the direction he turns affect the answer? Explain. north; Sample: Since 360° is a full circle, it does not matter if Obi turns right or left. Either way he will end up facing north again.

▶ Model Use ratio boxes to solve problems **16** and **17.**

* **16.** (81) The sale price of $24 was 60 percent of the regular price. What was the regular price? $40

* **17.** (81) Forty-eight corn seeds sprouted. This was 75 percent of the seeds that were planted. How many of the planted seeds did not sprout? 16 seeds

18. (77) Write an equation to solve this problem:

Thirty is what percent of 20?

$30 = W_P \times 20$; 150%

▶* **19.** (Inv. 6, 75) **a.** Classify What type of quadrilateral is shown? trapezoid

b. Find its perimeter. 90 mm

c. Find its area. 450 mm^2

15 mm, 25 mm, 20 mm, 30 mm

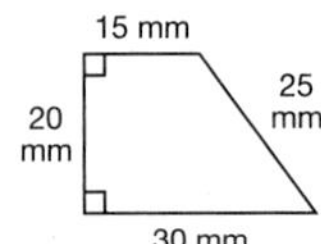

▶ See Math Conversations in the sidebar.

▶ **20.** Find the measure of each angle.
(17)

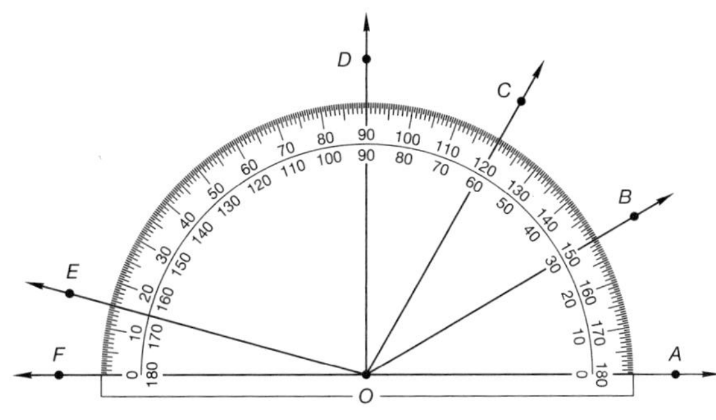

a. $\angle COF$ 120° **b.** $\angle AOE$ 165° **c.** $\angle BOE$ 135°

1.

(5, 6)
(3, 4)
(1, 2)

See student work.
Example: (0, 1)
$y = x + 1$
$(1) = (0) + 1$
$1 = 1$

21. Find the missing numbers in the table by using the function rule. Then graph the x, y pairs on a coordinate plane and extend a line through the points. Find another x, y pair on the line and test the numbers in the equation.
(56)

$y = x + 1$

x	y
3	4
5	6
1	2

▶* **22.** **Represent** Multiply. Write each product in scientific notation.
(83)

a. $(1.2 \times 10^5)(1.2 \times 10^{-8})$ 1.44×10^{-3}

b. $(6 \times 10^{-3})(7 \times 10^{-4})$ 4.2×10^{-6}

For problems **23** and **24,** solve and check the equation. Show each step.

▶ **23.** $56 = \frac{7}{8}w$ 64
(Inv. 7)

24. $4.8 + c = 7.34$ 2.54
(Inv. 7)

Simplify:

▶ **25.** $\sqrt{10^2 - 6^2} + \sqrt{10^2 - 8^2}$ 14
(52)

26. 5 lb 9 oz + 4 lb 7 oz = 10 lb
(49)

27. $1.4 \div 3\frac{1}{2} \times 10^3$ (decimal answer) 400
(43, 45)

▶* **28.** Simplify each expression.
(85)

a. $(-4)(-5) - (-4)(+3)$ 32 **b.** $(-2)[(-3) - (-4)(+5)]$ −34

* **29.** Collect like terms: $x^2 + 3xy + 2x^2 - xy$ $3x^2 + 2xy$
(84)

30. The factorization of $6x^2y$ is $2 \cdot 3 \cdot x \cdot x \cdot y$. Write the factorization of $9xy^2$. $3 \cdot 3 \cdot x \cdot y \cdot y$
(21)

▶ See Math Conversations in the sidebar.

3 Written Practice (Continued)

Math Conversations

Discussion opportunities are provided below.

Problem 22 Represent

Help students see how scientific notation makes it easy to compare numbers that are either very large or very small.

Problem 23 Generalize

"Is it necessary for the variable term to be on the left side of the equal sign to solve the equation?" Sample: No, we may solve for the variable on either side of the equal sign.

Problem 25

"Why is it necessary to treat the square root symbols in this problem as grouping symbols?" Sample: The expressions have different values. For example, $\sqrt{10^2} - \sqrt{6^2} = 4$, but $\sqrt{10^2 - 6^2} = 8$. Since the expressions have different values, it is necessary to simplify under the square root sign before finding the square root.

Errors and Misconceptions

Problem 20

If students use the wrong scale of the given protractor, ask them to decide first if the angle looks greater than a right angle, and if it does, then the measure should be greater than 90°.

Problem 22b

If students write 42×10^{-7} as the answer, remind them that they must write their answer in proper scientific notation so that there is only one non-zero digit to the left of the decimal point.

Problem 28

If students are having trouble with signs, remind them that subtracting a negative number is the same thing as adding a positive number.

Looking Forward

Identifying the counting numbers, whole numbers, integers, and rational numbers and telling how they are related prepares students for:

- **Lesson 100,** estimating the square roots of non-perfect square numbers and showing the approximate location of rational and irrational numbers on a number line.
- **Lesson 106,** learning more about square roots of numbers and cube roots of numbers.

• Multiplying Algebraic Terms

Objectives

- Multiply algebraic terms to simplify algebraic expressions.

Lesson Preparation

Materials

- **Power Up R** (in *Instructional Masters*)
- **Investigation Activity 13** (in *Instructional Masters*) or **graph paper**
- **Manipulative kit: protractors**

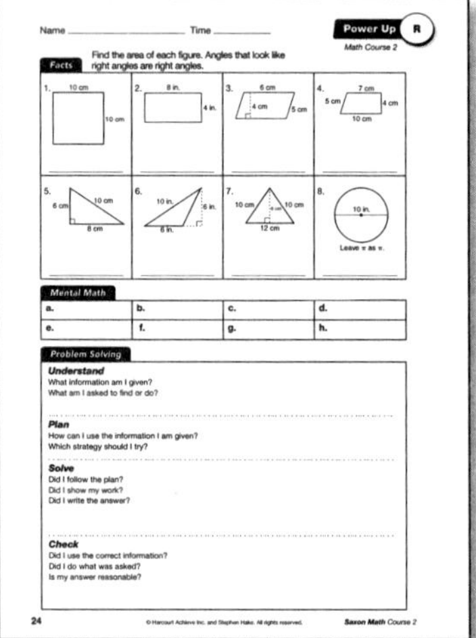

Power Up R

Coordinate Plane

Investigation Activity 13

Math Language

English Learners (ESL)
numerical parts

Technology Resources

Student eBook Complete student textbook in electronic format.

Resources and Planner CD Blackline masters, plus a pacing calendar with standards.

Test and Practice Generator CD Create additional practice sheets and custom-made tests.

www.SaxonPublishers.com Visit for more student activities and planning materials.

Inclusion

Adaptations CD Adapted lessons, investigations, practice and assessments.

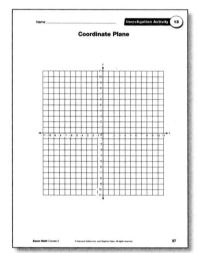

Meeting Standards

National Council of Teachers of Mathematics (NCTM)

Numbers and Operations

NO.1e Develop an understanding of large numbers and recognize and appropriately use exponential, scientific, and calculator notation

NO.2b Use the associative and commutative properties of addition and multiplication and the distributive property of multiplication over addition to simplify computations with integers, fractions, and decimals

Problem Solving

PS.1b Solve problems that arise in mathematics and in other contexts

PS.1c Apply and adapt a variety of appropriate strategies to solve problems

Power-Up Discussion *For use with Power Up, p. 598*

Problem-Solving Strategy: Write an Equation/ Use Logical Reasoning

On a balanced scale, four identical blocks marked m, a 250-g mass, and a 1000-g mass are distributed as shown. Find the mass of each block marked m. Write an equation illustrated by this balanced scale.

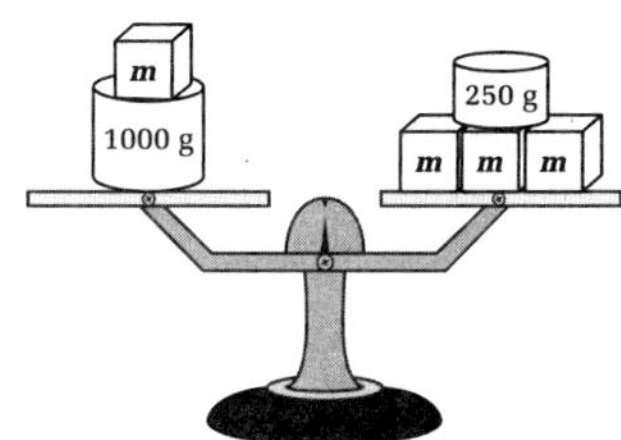

Understand ***Understand the problem.***

"What information are we given?"

On one side of a balanced scale is a block marked m and a 1000-g mass. On the other side of the balanced scale are three blocks marked m and a 250-g mass.

"What are we asked to do?"

We are asked to write the equation illustrated by the balanced scale and to find the mass of each block marked m.

Plan ***Make a plan.***

"What problem-solving strategy will we use?"

We have been asked to *write an equation,* but we will also *use logical reasoning.*

Solve ***Carry out the plan.***

"What equation illustrates the balanced scale?"

$1000 + m = 250 + 3m$

"How can we simplify the equation before we solve for m?"

We can take one m block off of each side.

"What is the resulting equation?"

$1000 = 250 + 2m$

"What is the mass of each block marked m?"

We solve to find that $m = 375$ g.

Check ***Look back.***

"Did we do what we were asked to do?"

Yes, we wrote an equation illustrated by the balanced scale and found the mass of each block marked m.

"How can we verify the solution is correct?"

We can substitute 375 g into our original equation:

$$(375) + 1000 = 3(375) + 250$$
$$1375 = 1125 + 250$$
$$1375 = 1375$$

1 Power Up

Facts
Distribute **Power Up R** to students. See answers below.

Mental Math
Encourage students to share different ways to mentally compute these exercises. Strategies for exercises **c** and **f** are listed below.

c. Multiply by Fraction Equal to 1

$\frac{10}{25} \times \frac{4}{4} = \frac{40}{100}$

$f = 40$

Use Logical Reasoning

$\frac{1}{25} = \frac{4}{100}$

$\frac{10}{25} = 10 \times \frac{4}{100} = \frac{40}{100}$

$f = 40$

f. Use Equivalent Equation

$\frac{2}{5}$ of $m = \$50$

$\frac{2}{5} \times m = 50$

$2m = 50 \times 5 = 250$

$m = 250 \div 2 = \$125$

Multiply by Reciprocal

$m = 50 \times \frac{5}{2} = \frac{250}{2}$

$m = \$125$

Problem Solving
Refer to **Power-Up Discussion,** p. 598B.

2 New Concepts

Instruction
Discuss with students whether order matters when multiplying factors.

"Does the order of the factors matter when you multiply?" no

"What property allows you to change the order of the factors?" the Commutative Property

If needed, review exponents with students. Be sure they understand that the exponent expresses how many times a number is used as a factor.

(continued)

LESSON 87

• Multiplying Algebraic Terms

Power Up — *Building Power*

facts Power Up R

mental math

a. **Positive/Negative:** $(-60) - (-30)$ -30

b. **Order of Operations/Exponents:** $(2 \times 10^5)(4 \times 10^{-3})$ 8×10^2

c. **Equivalent Fractions:** $\frac{f}{100} = \frac{10}{25}$ 40

d. **Decimals/Measurement:** 3.14 × 20 ft 62.8 ft

e. **Measurement:** 750 g to kg 0.75 kg

f. **Fractional Parts:** \$50 is $\frac{2}{5}$ of m. \$125

g. **Probability:** There are 9 blue marbles, 3 red marbles, and 8 purple marbles in a bag. Which color marble are you most likely to pick from the bag? blue

h. **Calculation:** $33\frac{1}{3}\%$ of 12, × 9, $\sqrt{\ }$, × 8, + 1, $\sqrt{\ }$, × 3, − 1, ÷ 2, ÷ 2, ÷ 2 $2\frac{1}{2}$

problem solving

On a balanced scale, four identical blocks marked m, a 250-g mass, and a 1000-g mass are distributed as shown. Find the mass of each block marked m. Write an equation illustrated by this balanced scale.

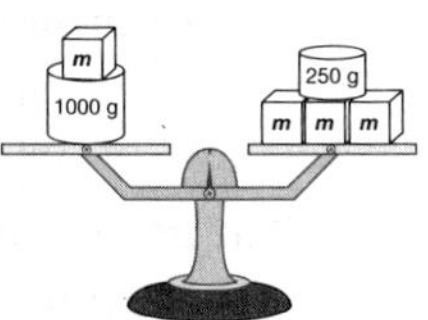

375 g; $m + 1000 = 3m + 250$

New Concept — *Increasing Knowledge*

Recall from Lesson 84 that like terms can be added and that adding like terms does not change the variable part of the term.

$$3x + 2x = 5x$$

However, if we multiply terms, all the factors in the multiplied terms appear in the product.

$(3x)(2x) = 3 \cdot x \cdot 2 \cdot x$	
$= 3 \cdot 2 \cdot x \cdot x$	Commutative Property
$= (3 \cdot 2)(x \cdot x)$	Associative Property
$= 6x^2$	Simplified

Explain What does the exponent 2 in x^2 mean? It means that x is used as a factor 2 times, so $6x^2$ means $6 \cdot x \cdot x$.

Facts Find the area of each figure. Angles that look like right angles are right angles.

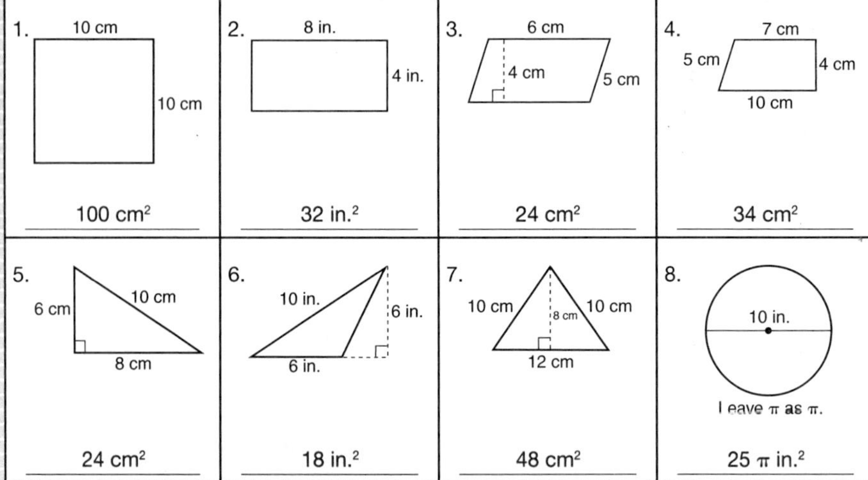

Briefly, we multiply the numerical parts of the terms and gather variable factors with exponents. Terms may be multiplied even if they are not like terms.

$$(-2x)(-3y) = 6xy$$

Example 1

Simplify: $(-3x^2y)(2x)(-4xy)$

Solution

The minus signs on these terms indicate negative numbers, not subtraction. We will multiply the three terms to make one term. First we list all the factors:

$$(-3) \cdot x \cdot x \cdot y \cdot (+2) \cdot x \cdot (-4) \cdot x \cdot y$$

Using the Commutative Property, we rearrange the factors as shown below.

$$(-3)(+2)(-4) \cdot x \cdot x \cdot x \cdot x \cdot y \cdot y$$

Using the Associative Property, we then group the factors by multiplying the numerical factors and gathering the variable factors with exponents.

$$\mathbf{24x^4y^2}$$

Discuss How can you determine that the product will be negative or positive? Count the negative signs. An odd number of negative signs gives a negative product, an even number of negative signs gives a positive product.

Example 2

Simplify: $(-2ab)(a^2b)(3b^3)$

Solution

Thinking Skill

Explain

What happens to the exponents when a and a^2 are multiplied? The exponents are added: $a^1 \cdot a^2 = a^{1+2} = a^3$.

The numerical factors are −2, 1, and 3, and their product is −6. The product of a and a^2 is a^3. The product of b, b, and b^3 is b^5.

$$(-2ab)(a^2b)(3b^3) = \mathbf{-6a^3b^5}$$

Recall that we can multiply exponents to find a power of a power.

$$(x^a)^b = x^{ab}$$

If a term with multiple factors is raised to a power, then the exponent applies to each of the factors.

$$(3xy)^2 = (3xy)(3xy)$$

$$\text{So, } (3xy)^2 = 3^2x^2y^2 = 9x^2y^2$$

If a term that includes exponents is raised to a power, then we can multiply the exponents in the term by the power.

$$(3x^2y^3)^2 = 3^2(x^2)^2(y^3)^2 = 9x^4y^6$$

2 New Concepts (Continued)

Example 1 and 2

Instruction

You may need to remind some students that $x \cdot x \cdot x \cdot x$ is equal to x^4, not $4x$, and $y \cdot y$ is equal to y^2, not $2y$.

Suggest that the first thing to do with these expressions is to decide whether the product will be negative or positive. If needed, remind students that when multiplying positive and negative numbers, the sign of the product can be determined by counting the number of negative signs in the problem.

(continued)

Math Background

How is algebra different from arithmetic?

Only numbers and operations are involved in arithmetic, the most fundamental and simplest branch of mathematics, and algorithms for the operations and an order of operations are taught. In algebra, the use of symbols is added to the use of numbers and operations.

Algebra expands the scope of mathematics to include:

- Working with unknown values and writing and solving equations about them.
- Describing functional relationships and using variables to write and solve equations for them.
- Generalizing the laws of arithmetic and beginning to explore number systems.

English Learners

Students may need help with the term **numerical parts.** Say:

"The numerical parts of a problem are the numbers in the problem."

On the board, write:

$(-2x)(-3y)$ and $5a + (-6b) + (-4c)$

Circle −2 and −3. Say:

"These are the numerical parts of this problem."

Ask volunteers to circle the numerical parts of the other problem.

2 New Concepts (Continued)

Example 3

Instruction

Go over the two methods with the class. Point out that one method can be used to check an answer found with the other method. Another method for checking problems like these is to choose small values for the variables and substitute them into both the original and simplified expressions. If the values are the same, then it is reasonable to assume that the answer is correct.

Practice Set

Problems a–d Justify

Discuss whether a sequence of steps can be used for problems like these. Lead students to see that these three steps can be used to find any product.

1. Determine the sign of the product.
2. Multiply the numerical coefficients.
3. Multiply each letter factor by others of the same letter and use an exponent to show how many times the letter is used as a factor. Do this one letter at a time, in any order of the letters.

Problems e–i Generalize

Have students explain the rules for working with powers. Ask when the exponents are added and when they are multiplied. added when multiplying factors; multiplied when raising a term to a power

3 Written Practice

Errors and Misconceptions

Problem 3

If students do not get the correct answer, suggest that they read the question carefully. Help them understand that they can use the total number of students and the number of girls to find the number of boys, and then they can find the ratio.

(continued)

Example 3

Simplify: $(-3a^2b^3)^2$

Solution

We show two methods.

Method 1: Show factors.

$$(-3a^2b^3)^2 = (-3a^2b^3)(-3a^2b^3)$$
$$= (-3)aabbb(-3)aabbb$$
$$= (-3)(-3)aaaabbbbbb$$
$$= \mathbf{9a^4b^6}$$

Method 2: Apply exponent rules.

$$(-3a^2b^3)^2 = (-3)^2(a^2)^2(b^3)^2$$
$$= \mathbf{9a^4b^6}$$

Practice Set ▶ Justify Find the following products. Show and justify each step.

a. $(-3x)(-2xy)$ $6x^2y$

b. $3x^2(xy^3)$ $3x^3y^3$

c. $(2a^2)(-3ab^3)$ $-6a^3b^3$

d. $(-4x)(-5x^2y)$ $20x^3y$

▶ Generalize Find each product by multiplying the numerical factors and gathering variable factors with exponents.

e. $(-xy^2)(xy)(2y)$ $-2x^2y^4$

f. $(-3m)(-2mn)(m^2n)$ $6m^4n^2$

g. $(4wy)(3wx)(-w^2)(x^2y)$ $-12w^4x^3y^2$

h. $5d(-2df)(-3d^2fg)$ $30d^4f^2g$

i. Simplify (show two methods): $(3xy^3)^2$ $9x^2y^6$; See student work.

Written Practice *Strengthening Concepts*

1. (53) How far will a jet travel in 2 hours 30 minutes if its average speed is 450 miles per hour? 1125 miles

2. (50) Use a unit multiplier to convert 12.5 centimeters to meters. 12.5 centimeters $\cdot \frac{1 \text{ meter}}{100 \text{ centimeters}}$ = 0.125 meter

▶ **3.** (54) Use a ratio box to solve this problem. If 240 of the 420 students in the auditorium were girls, what was the ratio of boys to girls in the auditorium? $\frac{3}{4}$

4. (28) Giraffes are the tallest of all land mammals. One giraffe is 18′3″ tall. Another giraffe is 17′10″ tall and a third giraffe is 17′11″ tall. What is the average height of these 3 giraffes? 18′

▶ See Math Conversations in the sidebar.

1. a.

5. (46) The Xiong family traveled by car 468 miles on 18 gallons of gas. Their car averaged how many miles per gallon? 26 miles per gallon

▶ ***6.** (86) **Represent** On a number line, graph the whole numbers that are less than or equal to 5.

7. (72) Use a ratio box to solve this problem. The road was steep. Every 100 yards the elevation increased 36 feet. How many feet did the elevation increase in 1500 yards? 540 feet

8. (61) The quadrilateral in this figure is a parallelogram. Find the measure of

a. $\angle a$. 75° **b.** $\angle b$. 105°

c. $\angle c$. 75° **d.** $\angle d$. 75°

e. $\angle e$. 105°

9. (41) If $x = -4$ and $y = 3x - 1$, then y equals what number? -13

▶ ***10.** (65, 82) **Analyze** Find each measure for this circle. Use $\frac{22}{7}$ for π.

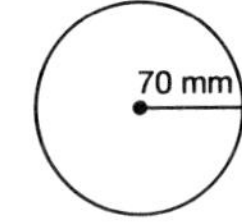

a. circumference 440 mm

b. area 15,400 mm^2

11. (Inv. 3, 61) The coordinates of the vertices of parallelogram $ABCD$ are A (5, 5), B (10, 5), C (5, 0), and D (0, 0).

a. On graph paper, graph the vertices. Then draw the parallelogram.

b. Find the area of the parallelogram. 25 units^2

c. Find the measure of each angle of the parallelogram. $m\angle A = 135°$; $m\angle B = 45°$; $m\angle C = 135°$; $m\angle D = 45°$

12. (70) The shape shown was built of 1-inch cubes. What is the volume of the shape? 48 in.^{3}

▶ **13.** (48) Complete the table.

Fraction	Decimal	Percent
a. $\frac{1}{8}$	**b.** 0.125	$12\frac{1}{2}\%$
$\frac{7}{8}$	**c.** 0.875	**d.** $87\frac{1}{2}\%$

14. (60) Write an equation to solve this problem and find the answer.

What number is 25 percent of 4? $W_N = \frac{1}{4} \times 4$; 1

▶ See Math Conversations in the sidebar.

3 Written Practice (Continued)

Math Conversations

Discussion opportunities are provided below.

Problem 6 Represent

Discuss the representation of whole numbers less than or equal to 5.

"Why are dots used?" Sample: We are only plotting whole numbers.

"Why is 0 included?" Sample: It is a whole number less than 5.

"Why is 5 included?" Sample: It is equal to 5.

"Why is −5 not included?" Sample: It is not a whole number.

Problem 10 Analyze

Discuss how thinking about the value of the radius might make calculating easier.

"Suppose the radius is 7 mm. How will the answers change from the original problem?" Sample: You drop one zero from the circumference and drop 2 zeros from the area.

"Suppose the radius is 700 mm. How will the answers change from the original problem?" Sample: You attach one zero to the circumference and attach 4 zeros to the area.

"How could we change the units from 70 mm to make the calculations easier?" Sample: You could change 70 mm to 7 centimeters and express the circumference in cm and in area in cm^2.

Problem 13 Analyze

Extend the Problem

Have students use mental math and the numbers in the table to find fraction-decimal-percent equivalents for $\frac{2}{8}$, $\frac{3}{8}$, $\frac{4}{8}$, $\frac{5}{8}$, and $\frac{6}{8}$. $\frac{2}{8}$ or $\frac{1}{4}$, 0.25, 25%; $\frac{3}{8}$, 0.375, $37\frac{1}{2}\%$; $\frac{4}{8}$ or $\frac{1}{2}$, 0.5, 50%; $\frac{5}{8}$, 0.625, $62\frac{1}{2}\%$; $\frac{6}{8}$ or $\frac{3}{4}$, 0.75, 75%

(continued)

3 Written Practice (Continued)

Math Conversations

Discussion opportunities are provided below.

Problems 15 and 16 Model

Have students compare using ratio boxes and equations for modeling these problem situations.

"Which method do you prefer? Explain why." Sample: Ratio boxes, because they are easy to set up.

"Which do you prefer?" Sample: Equations sometimes, because they can be faster.

"With which one are you less likely to make an error?" Sample: Ratio boxes, because they organize the information.

Problem 18 Analyze

Discuss ways to divide or change this figure so that its area can be calculated. Sample:

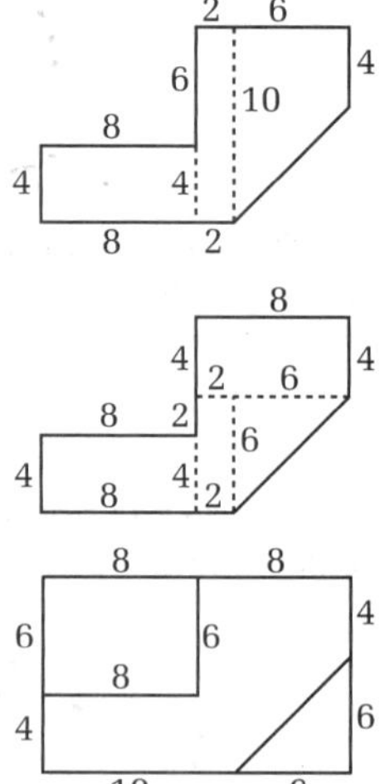

Problem 21 Generalize

After students finish working on this problem, ask volunteers to tell what points they chose to check and why. Sample: I chose (1, –1) because the numbers are easy to work with.

Errors and Misconceptions

Problem 16

To help students whose answer is 3333 feet, make sure they understand that the 60% given represents the distance traveled, while the 2000 meters given represents the distance remaining. The 2000 meters therefore represents 100% − 60% = 40% of the race.

Problems 23 and 24

If students write only the answers, remind them that the problem asked them to show all the steps.

(continued)

Model Use ratio boxes to solve problems **15** and **16**.

▶* **15.** *(81)* The sale price of $24 for a board game was 80 percent of the regular price. What was the regular price? $30

▶* **16.** *(81)* David had finished 60 percent of the race, but he still had 2000 meters to run. How long was his race? 5000 meters

17. *(77)* Write an equation to solve this problem and find the answer.

One hundred is what percent of 80? $100 = W_P \times 80$; 125%

▶* **18.** *(75)* **Analyze** Find the area of this figure. Dimensions are in centimeters. Corners that look square are square. 94 cm²

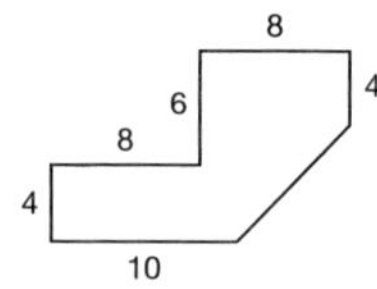

Math Reading
The small square marks a right angle. ∠*EOD* is a right angle.

19. *(40)* In the figure below, angle *AOE* is a straight angle and m∠*AOB* = m∠*BOC* = m∠*COD*.

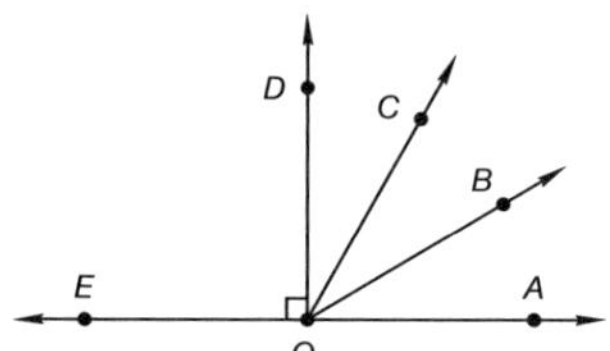

a. Find m∠*AOB*. 30°

b. Find m∠*AOC*. 60°

c. Find m∠*EOC*. 120°

d. Which angle is the supplement of ∠*EOC*? ∠*COA* or ∠*AOC*

* **20.** *(76)* Simplify: $\frac{66\frac{2}{3}}{100}$ $\frac{2}{3}$

21. See student work. Sample: (4, 5)
$y = 2x - 3$
$(5) = 2(4) - 3$
$5 = 8 - 3$
$5 = 5$

▶* **21.** *(56)* **Generalize** Find the missing numbers in the table using the function rule. Then graph the *x*, *y* pairs on a coordinate plane and extend a line through the points. Find another *x*, *y* pair on the line and check the numbers in the equation.

$y = 2x - 3$

x	y
1	−1
2	1
3	3

* **22.** *(83)* Multiply. Write each product in scientific notation.

a. $(4 \times 10^{-5})(2.1 \times 10^{-7})$ 8.4×10^{-12}

b. $(4 \times 10^{5})(6 \times 10^{7})$ 2.4×10^{13}

▶ For problems **23** and **24**, solve and check the equation. Show each step.

23. *(Inv. 7)* $d - 8.47 = 9.1$ 17.57

24. *(Inv. 7)* $0.25m = 3.6$ 14.4

▶ See Math Conversations in the sidebar.

Generalize Simplify:

▶ **25.** (52) $\frac{3 + 5.2 - 1}{4 - 3 + 2}$ 2.4

▶ **26.** (32) 1 kg − 75 g 925 g

▶ **27.** (43) $3.7 + 2\frac{5}{8} + 15$ (decimal answer) 21.325

▶* **28.** (85) **a.** $(-5) - (-2)[(-3) - (+4)]$ −19

b. $\frac{(-3) + (-3)(+4)}{(+3) + (-4)}$ 15

▶* **29.** (87) **a.** $(3x)(4y)$ $12xy$

b. $(6m)(-4m^2n)(-mnp)$ $24m^4n^2p$

c. $(3x^3)^2$ $9x^6$

▶* **30.** (84) **Generalize** Collect like terms:

$$3ab + a - ab - 2ab + a \quad 2a$$

Early Finishers
Real-World Application

While on vacation, Sanjay and Aditi decide to spend an afternoon biking. They can rent the bikes from one of two companies in town. Beau's Bikes charges $10 per hour per bike. Celine's Cycles charges $4 per hour per bike plus an initial fixed fee of $15 per bike.

a. Let t represent the time one bike is rented (in hours) and y represent the total cost of renting one bike. Represent the cost from each company with an algebraic expression. Beau's Bikes: $y = 10t$; Celine's Cycles: $y = 4t + 15$.

b. If Sanjay and Aditi expect to bike for 2 hours, from which bike shop should they rent? Support your answer. Beau's Bikes; Sample: It costs $3 less per bike.

c. If they want to bike for 4 hours, from which bike shop should they rent? Support your answer. Celine's Cycles; Sample: It costs $9 less per bike.

▶ See Math Conversations in the sidebar.

3 Written Practice *(Continued)*

Math Conversations

Discussion opportunities are provided below.

Problems 25–29 Generalize

Have students generate a list of all the mathematical tools and ideas they use to simplify expressions. Sample: order of operations, properties, exponent rules, collecting like terms, rules for signed numbers

Discuss how confident students are in using them, and go over any for students who may need help.

Problem 30 Generalize

"Since there are no exponents on these terms, how do you arrange them in descending order?" Sample: I think the ab terms have a higher order than the a terms, so I put them first.

Errors and Misconceptions

Problem 26

Watch for students whose answers indicate that they did not rewrite the measurements using the same unit before subtracting. Remind them that both measurements need to be expressed with the same unit. The answer can be written as either 925 g or 0.925 kg.

Looking Forward

Understanding how to multiply algebraic terms prepares students for:

- **Lesson 96,** simplifying expressions by using the Distributive Property with algebraic terms.
- **Lesson 103,** simplifying expressions by dividing algebraic terms.
- **Lesson 109,** solving equations with exponents.
- **Lesson 115,** factoring algebraic expressions.

• Multiple Unit Multipliers

Objectives

- Use more than one unit multiplier to convert from one unit to another.

Lesson Preparation

Materials

- **Power Up S** (in *Instructional Masters*)
- **Investigation Activity 13** (in *Instructional Masters*) or **graph paper**
- **Teacher-provided material: calculators**

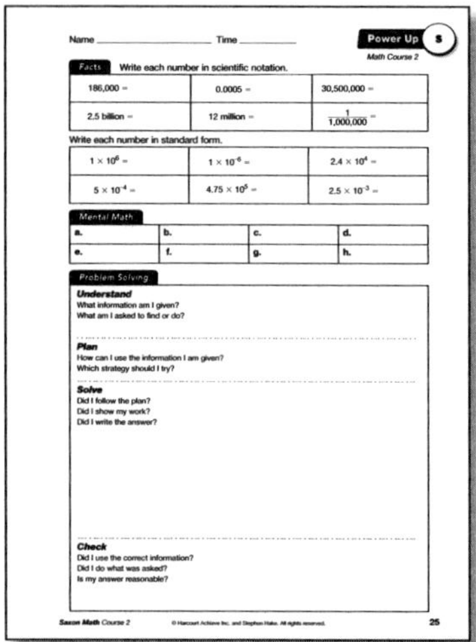

Name ______ Time ______ **Power Up S** *Math Course 2*

Facts Write each number in scientific notation.

186,000 =	0.0005 =	30,500,000 =
2.5 billion =	12 million =	$\frac{1}{1,000,000}$ =

Write each number in standard form.

1×10^6 =	1×10^{-6} =	2.4×10^4 =
5×10^{-4} =	4.75×10^5 =	2.5×10^{-3} =

Mental Math

a.	b.	c.	d.
e.	f.	g.	h.

Problem Solving

Understand
What information am I given?
What am I asked to find or do?

Plan
How can I use the information I am given?
Which strategy should I try?

Solve
Did I follow the plan?
Did I show my work?
Did I write the answer?

Check
Did I use the correct information?
Did I do what was asked?
Is my answer reasonable?

Saxon Math Course 2 © Harcourt Achieve Inc. and Stephen Hake. All rights reserved. 25

Power Up S

Investigation Activity 13

Math Language

English Learners (ESL)
regions

Technology Resources

Student eBook Complete student textbook in electronic format.

Resources and Planner CD Blackline masters, plus a pacing calendar with standards.

Test and Practice Generator CD Create additional practice sheets and custom-made tests.

www.SaxonPublishers.com Visit for more student activities and planning materials.

Inclusion

Adaptations CD Adapted lessons, investigations, practice and assessments.

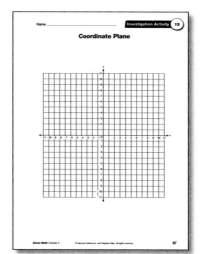

Meeting Standards

National Council of Teachers of Mathematics (NCTM)

Measurement

ME.1b Understand relationships among units and convert from one unit to another within the same system

ME.2f Solve simple problems involving rates and derived measurements for such attributes as velocity and density

Problem Solving

PS.1b Solve problems that arise in mathematics and in other contexts

Representation

RE.5b Select, apply, and translate among mathematical representations to solve problems

Power-Up Discussion *For use with Power Up, p. 604*

Problem-Solving Strategy: Find a Pattern/ Write an Equation

Some auto license plates take the form of one letter, followed by three numbers, followed by three letters. How many different license plates are possible?

Understand ***Understand the problem.***

"What information are we given?"

Some license plates take the form of one letter, followed by three numbers, followed by three letters.

"What are we asked to do?"

We are asked to determine how many different license plates are possible.

Plan ***Make a plan.***

"What problem-solving strategy will we use?"

We will try to *find a pattern* or *write an equation* to determine the number of possible plates.

Solve ***Carry out the plan.***

"We will use the Fundamental Counting Principle to help us find the number of plates that are possible. How many different letters can we choose from in each of the four instances?"

26

Teacher Note: Take a few minutes to review the Fundamental Counting Principle if students have trouble remembering how it works.

"How many different numbers can we choose from in each of the three instances?"

10

"We can multiply to find the total number of plates possible. How many plates are possible?"

$$26 \times 10 \times 10 \times 10 \times 26 \times 26 \times 26 = 456{,}976{,}000$$

Check ***Look back.***

"Did we do what we were asked to do?"

Yes, we found the total number of possible license plates.

1 Power Up

Facts

Distribute **Power Up S** to students. See answers below.

Mental Math

Encourage students to share different ways to mentally compute these exercises. Strategies for exercises **d, e,** and **h** are listed below.

d. Double, then Halve

$15\% \times \$100 = 0.15 \times \$100 = \$15$

e. Use Unit Multiplier

$2.54 \text{ cm} \times \frac{10 \text{ mm}}{1 \text{ cm}} = 25.4 \text{ mm}$

Use Logical Reasoning

1 cm = 10 mm
2 cm = 20 mm
0.54 cm = 5.4 mm
2.54 cm = 25.4 mm

h. Double, then Halve

$2\frac{1}{2} \text{ h} \times 2 = 5 \text{ h}$

$\frac{500 \text{ mi}}{\text{h}}$ for 5 h = 2500 mi

$\frac{1}{2} \times 2500 \text{ mi} = 1250 \text{ mi}$

Use Logical Reasoning

1 h → 500 mi
$\frac{1}{2}$ h → 250 mi
$2\frac{1}{2}$ h → 500 + 500 + 250 mi = 1250 mi

Problem Solving

Refer to **Power-Up Discussion,** p. 604B.

2 New Concepts

Instruction

Have students brainstorm situations in which it would be useful to convert measurements. Sample suggestions may include:

- changing from miles per hour to kilometers per hour
- changing from kilograms to pounds for a recipe
- changing lengths to different unit measurements, such as feet to inches

Tell students that in this lesson, they will learn to convert measurements using multiple unit multipliers.

Spending most of the instructional time teaching how to set up conversion problems will reduce student error. Use what students already know about unit multipliers as a basis for instruction.

(continued)

LESSON **88**

• Multiple Unit Multipliers

Power Up *Building Power*

facts Power Up S

mental math

a. **Positive/Negative:** $(-15)(+5)$ -75

b. **Order of Operations/Exponents:** $(1.5 \times 10^4)(2 \times 10^5)$ 3×10^9

c. **Algebra:** $3t + 4 = 40$ 12

d. **Percent/Mental Math:** $7\frac{1}{2}\% \times \$200$ \$15

e. **Measurement:** 2.54 cm to mm 25.4 mm

f. **Fractional Parts:** \$1.50 is $\frac{3}{5}$ of m. \$2.50

g. **Geometry:** When looking at a geometric shape and its mirror image what is this called? reflection

h. **Rate:** At 500 mph, how far will an airplane fly in $2\frac{1}{2}$ hours? 1250 mi

problem solving Some auto license plates take the form of one letter, followed by three numbers, followed by three letters. How many different license plates are possible? 456,976,000 license plates

New Concept *Increasing Knowledge*

We can repeatedly multiply a number by 1 without changing the number.

$$5 \cdot 1 = 5$$
$$5 \cdot 1 \cdot 1 = 5$$
$$5 \cdot 1 \cdot 1 \cdot 1 = 5$$

Since unit multipliers are forms of 1, we can also multiply a measure by several unit multipliers without changing the measure.

Example 1

Use two unit multipliers to convert 5 hours to seconds.

Solution

We are changing units from hours to seconds.

hours ⟶ seconds

We will perform the conversion in two steps. We will change from hours to minutes with one unit multiplier and from minutes to seconds with a second unit multiplier. For each step we write a unit multiplier.

Facts Write each number in scientific notation.

$186{,}000 = 1.86 \times 10^5$	$0.0005 = 5 \times 10^{-4}$	$30{,}500{,}000 = 3.05 \times 10^7$
$2.5 \text{ billion} = 2.5 \times 10^9$	$12 \text{ million} = 1.2 \times 10^7$	$\frac{1}{1{,}000{,}000} = 1 \times 10^{-6}$

Write each number in standard form.

$1 \times 10^6 = 1{,}000{,}000$	$1 \times 10^{-6} = 0.000001$	$2.4 \times 10^4 = 24{,}000$
$5 \times 10^{-4} = 0.0005$	$4.75 \times 10^5 = 475{,}000$	$2.5 \times 10^{-3} = 0.0025$

hours ⟶ minutes ⟶ seconds

$$5\ \text{hr} \cdot \frac{60\ \text{min}}{1\ \text{hr}} \cdot \frac{60\ \text{s}}{1\ \text{min}} = \mathbf{18{,}000\ s}$$

Discuss What is the difference between the 60 in the first unit multiplier and the 60 in the second unit multiplier? The first is the number of minutes in one hour, the second is the number of seconds in one minute.

To convert from one unit of area to another, it is helpful to use two unit multipliers.

Example 2

Diego wants to carpet a 16 ft by 9 ft room that has an area of 144 ft². Carpet is sold by the square yard. How many square yards of carpet does Diego need?

Solution

Thinking Skill

Explain

Diego could have converted 16 ft and 9 ft to yards. Which method would you use? Explain. Sample: Using a unit multiplier that relates feet and yards: 1 yd = 3 feet. 16 ft = $\frac{16}{3}$ yd and 9 ft = 3 yd; $\frac{16}{3}$ yd × 3 yd = 16 yd²

Recall that ft² means ft · ft. Thus, to convert from square feet to square yards, we convert from feet to yards twice. To perform the conversion we will use two unit multipliers. (1 yd = 3 ft)

$$144\ \text{ft} \cdot \text{ft} \cdot \frac{1\ \text{yd}}{3\ \text{ft}} \cdot \frac{1\ \text{yd}}{3\ \text{ft}} = \frac{144\ \text{yd}^2}{9} = 16\ \text{yd}^2$$

Diego needs **16 yd²** of carpet

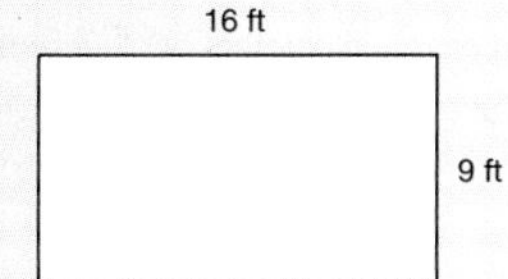

To convert units of volume we may use three unit multipliers.

Example 3

A masonry contractor needs to pour a concrete foundation for a block wall. The foundation is one foot deep, one foot wide, and 100 feet long. A cement truck will deliver the concrete. How many cubic yards of concrete should the contractor order?

Solution

The foundation is a rectangular prism. Its volume is 100 ft³ (1 ft · 1 ft · 100 ft). We will use three unit multipliers to convert cubic feet to cubic yards.

$$100\ \text{ft}^3 \cdot \frac{1\ \text{yd}}{3\ \text{ft}} \cdot \frac{1\ \text{yd}}{3\ \text{ft}} \cdot \frac{1\ \text{yd}}{3\ \text{ft}} = \frac{100\ \text{yd}^3}{27} \approx 3.7\ \text{yd}^3$$

We find that 100 ft³ is about 3.7 yd³. The contractor wants to be sure there is enough concrete, so the contractor should order **4 cubic yards.**

We use two or more unit multipliers to convert rates if both units are changing.

Teacher Tip

To **connect the topic** of this lesson to the students' surroundings, let students work in groups of two or three to measure the dimensions of nearby locations, such as the length and width of the classroom, the width of hallways, or the length of windowpanes. Have them measure the dimensions using whatever measuring tools you have available in either customary or metric units.

Then have students convert their measurements to the other system using what they have learned in this lesson. To check their work, have them measure the dimensions of the locations again using the other system.

2 New Concepts (Continued)

Example 1

Instruction

In this example, the conversion is from hours to seconds, which uses two unit multipliers.

$$1\ \text{hr} = 60\ \text{min and}\ 1\ \text{min} = 60\ \text{sec}$$

Show students how to create a pattern for converting with two unit multipliers.

$$5\ \text{hr} \cdot \text{—} \cdot \text{—} = ?\ \text{sec}$$

Use the unit multipliers to fill in both fractions.

$$5\ \text{hr} \cdot \frac{60\ \text{min}}{1\ \text{hr}} \cdot \frac{60\ \text{sec}}{1\ \text{min}} = ?\ \text{sec}$$

Tell students that they can use this pattern whenever they use two unit multipliers.

Examples 2 and 3

Instruction

If needed, use the conversion technique described above, to work through examples 2 and 3. Help students to notice that conversions of lengths require only one unit multiplier, conversions of area require 2 unit multipliers, and conversions of volume require 3 unit multipliers.

For example 3, some students may benefit from sketching the concrete foundation first. As a class, create a sketch of the foundation.

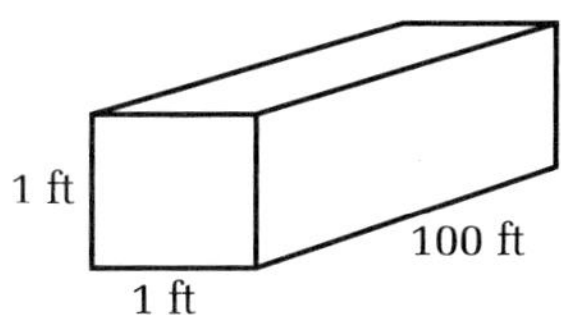

(continued)

2 New Concepts (Continued)

Example 4

Instruction

If students are having difficulty understanding how to cancel measurement units, remind them that they cancel a pair of units one at a time, and that one unit of the pair must be in a numerator and the other one in a denominator.

Help students understand that when there is more than one unit multiplier, the order in which they are converted does not matter. The Commutative Property of Multiplication allows factors to change order without changing the answer.

Example 5

Instruction

Explain to students that when they convert within a measurement system, either the customary system or the metric system, the conversions are exact, not approximations. When they convert from the customary system to the metric system, or vice versa, the conversions are usually approximations.

Point out that in this example, the measures in the unit multipliers are rounded to the nearest hundredth and that the answer is rounded to the nearest whole number. Remind students that when they are converting across measurement systems, they should round consistently.

Practice Set

Problems a–c Connect

Discuss why it is important to write all the units when working with unit multipliers. Sample: You have to be sure that all the units you don't need cancel out.

Problem b Error Alert

Allow students to use either $\frac{3}{2}$ or 1.5 for this conversion. You may want to demonstrate that the answer is the same for both.

Example 4

As Tina approached the traffic light she slowed to 36 kilometers per hour. Convert 36 kilometers per hour to meters per minute.

Solution

We convert from kilometers per hour to meters per minute $\left(\frac{\text{km}}{\text{hr}} \rightarrow \frac{\text{m}}{\text{min}}\right)$. We use one unit multiplier to convert the distance, kilometers to meters (1 km = 1,000 m). We use another unit multiplier to convert the time, hours to minutes (1 hr = 60 min).

km ⟶ m   hr ⟶ min

$$\frac{36\ \cancel{\text{km}}}{1\ \cancel{\text{hr}}} \cdot \frac{1000\ \text{m}}{1\ \cancel{\text{km}}} \cdot \frac{1\ \cancel{\text{hr}}}{60\ \text{min}} = \frac{36000\ \text{m}}{60\ \text{min}} = \mathbf{\frac{600\ m}{min}}$$

When using multiple unit multipliers it is often helpful to use a calculator for the arithmetic.

Example 5

Claude's car averages 12 kilometers per liter of fuel. Claude's car averages about how many miles per gallon?

Solution

We convert kilometers per liter to miles per gallon $\left(\frac{\text{km}}{\text{L}} \rightarrow \frac{\text{mi}}{\text{gal}}\right)$. We use one unit multiplier to convert kilometers to miles (1 km ≈ 0.62 mi) and another unit multiplier to convert liters to gallons (1 gal ≈ 3.781 L).

km ⟶ mi   L ⟶ gal

$$\frac{12\ \cancel{\text{km}}}{1\ \cancel{\text{L}}} \cdot \frac{0.62\ \text{mi}}{1\ \cancel{\text{km}}} \cdot \frac{3.78\ \cancel{\text{L}}}{1\ \text{gal}} = \frac{(12)(0.62)(3.78)\ \text{mi}}{1\ \text{gal}}$$

Using a calculator we find the product is 28.1232 mpg, which we round to the nearest whole number. Claude's car averages about **28 miles per gallon.**

Practice Set

Connect Use two or more unit multipliers to perform each conversion:

▶ **a.** 5 yards to inches $5\ \cancel{\text{yd}} \cdot \frac{3\ \cancel{\text{ft}}}{1\ \cancel{\text{yd}}} \cdot \frac{12\ \text{in.}}{1\ \cancel{\text{ft}}} = 180\ \text{in.}$

▶ **b.** $1\frac{1}{2}$ hours to seconds $1\frac{1}{2}\ \cancel{\text{hr}} \cdot \frac{60\ \cancel{\text{min}}}{1\ \cancel{\text{hr}}} \cdot \frac{60\ \text{s}}{1\ \cancel{\text{min}}} = 5400\ \text{s}$

▶ **c.** 15 yd^2 to square feet $15\ \cancel{\text{yd}^2} \cdot \frac{3\ \text{ft}}{1\ \cancel{\text{yd}}} \cdot \frac{3\ \text{ft}}{1\ \cancel{\text{yd}}} = 135\ \text{ft}^2$

d. 270 ft^3 to cubic yards $270\ \cancel{\text{ft}^3} \cdot \frac{1\ \text{yd}}{3\ \cancel{\text{ft}}} \cdot \frac{1\ \text{yd}}{3\ \cancel{\text{ft}}} \cdot \frac{1\ \text{yd}}{3\ \cancel{\text{ft}}} = 10\ \text{yd}^3$

e. Robert ran 800 meters in two minutes. His average speed was how many kilometers per hour? $\frac{800\ \cancel{\text{m}}}{2\ \cancel{\text{min}}} \cdot \frac{1\ \text{km}}{1000\ \cancel{\text{m}}} \cdot \frac{60\ \cancel{\text{min}}}{1\ \text{hr}} = 24\frac{\text{km}}{\text{hr}}$

f. One cubic inch is about how many cubic centimeters? (1 in. ≈ 2.54 cm) You may use a calculator to multiply. Round your answer to the nearest cubic centimeter. $1\ \cancel{\text{in.}^3} \cdot \frac{2.54\ \text{cm}}{1\ \cancel{\text{in.}}} \cdot \frac{2.54\ \text{cm}}{1\ \cancel{\text{in.}}} \cdot \frac{2.54\ \text{cm}}{1\ \cancel{\text{in.}}} = 16.387064\ \text{cm}^3$; One cubic inch is about 16 cubic cm.

606 Saxon Math Course 2

▶ See Math Conversations in the sidebar.

Written Practice *Strengthening Concepts*

3. a. 36 ft^2
b. 108 ft^3

7.

	27 lights
$\frac{2}{3}$ were on (18).	9 lights
	9 lights
$\frac{1}{3}$ were off.	9 lights

1. (53) Janis earns $8 per hour at a part-time job. How much does she earn working 3 hours 15 minutes? $26.00

2. (55) During a 10-day period an athlete's average resting heart rate after exercising was 58. The athlete's average heart rate during the first 4 days was 61. What was the average heart rate during the last 6 days? 56

▶ *** 3.** (88) **Connect** Use unit multipliers to perform each conversion:
a. 4 yd^2 to square feet **b.** 4 yd^3 to cubic feet

4. (54) Use a ratio box to solve this problem. The ratio of woodwinds to brass instruments in the orchestra was 3 to 2. If there were 15 woodwinds, how many brass instruments were there? 10 brass instruments

▶ *** 5.** (86) **Represent** On a number line, graph the counting numbers that are less than 4.

0 1 2 3 4

6. (72) Use a ratio box to solve this problem. Oranges were on sale 8 for $3. At that price, how much would 3 dozen oranges cost? $13.50

7. (71) Diagram this statement. Then answer the questions that follow.
When Sandra walked through the house, she saw that 18 lights were on and only $\frac{1}{3}$ of the lights were off.
a. How many lights were off? 9 lights
b. What percent of the lights were on? $66\frac{2}{3}\%$

8. (63) Evaluate: $a - [b - (a - b)]$ if $a = 5$ and $b = 3$ 4

▶ *** 9.** (Inv. 8) A spinner is divided into two regions as shown. The spinner was spun 60 times and stopped in region B 42 times. Based on the experiment, what is the probability of the spinner stopping in region A on the next spin? Write the probability as a decimal. 0.3

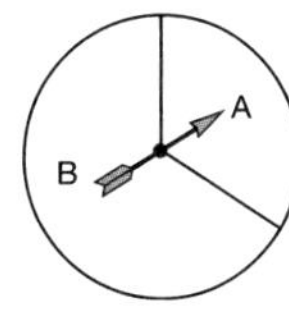

▶ **10.** (66, 82) To make a large circle on the field, Nathan tied a 30-foot rope to a pole. Then he walked around the stake with the rope extended as he scraped the ground with another stake. Use 3.14 for π to find the
a. circumference of the circle. 188.4 ft
b. area of the circle. 2826 ft^2
c. What measure of a circle does the rope represent? radius

▶ See Math Conversations in the sidebar.

3 Written Practice

Math Conversations

Discussion opportunities are provided below.

Problem 3 Connect

Discuss why two unit multipliers are needed for part **a** and three unit multipliers are needed for part **b.** Then ask:

"How many unit multipliers are needed to change 4 yards to feet?" Sample: only one, 3 feet to 1 yard

Problem 5 Represent

Ask why 0 is not on the graph. Sample: It is not a counting number.

Problem 9

Extend the Problem

"Use the results of this experiment to estimate the size in degrees of regions A and B." Sample: I found that the spinner stopped in region A 18 times, so I made ratios for both and multiplied them by 360°. I found that region A is about 108° and region B is about 252°.

"Does your estimate make sense? Why?" Samples: Yes, because region A looks like a little more than a 90° angle and the two angles total 360°. Perhaps—it is hard to tell, because the drawing doesn't show that much difference, so I think that more data would give a better answer.

Errors and Misconceptions

Problem 10

If students give answers without units, remind them the answer must include units and have them check that their answers are written with the correct unit of measurement.

(continued)

English Learners

In problem 9 explain the meaning of **regions.** Say:

"A region is an area. In problem 9, region A is smaller than region B."

Draw a circle on the board. Ask a volunteer to divide the circle into 4 regions.

3 Written Practice (Continued)

Math Conversations

Discussion opportunities are provided below.

Problem 11 Analyze

Have students use mental math to find the probability that a spinner spun 3 times would land in the shaded area all 3 times. $\frac{1}{64}$

You may want to ask more probability questions about this circle as a spinner or ask students to make up some.

Problems 17 and 18 Model

Ask volunteers to draw their ratio boxes on the board. Discuss whether the data was entered correctly and have other students write a proportion for each ratio box and solve the problem. Finally have other students check the answers and tell whether they are correct.

Problem 20c Analyze

Discuss an alternative way to solve this problem.

"Suppose you did not remember the formula for the area of a trapezoid. How could you find the area of this trapezoid?" Sample: I could divide the figure into a rectangle and a triangle, find their areas, and add them.

Errors and Misconceptions

Problem 17

Guide students who give 25% as the answer to understand the question asks for the percent the sale price, \$18, is of the regular price of the shirt, \$24, not the percent of the reduction in price.

Problem 18

If students give an answer of 113, they may have thought that 375 corresponds to 100%, because the full capacity of the auditorium is 375. Tell them to read the problem carefully to see exactly what the problem is asking. Point out that since there are more people who wanted a seat than actual seats, the answer must be greater than 375.

(continued)

▶ **11.** (Inv. 1) What percent of this circle is shaded? 25%

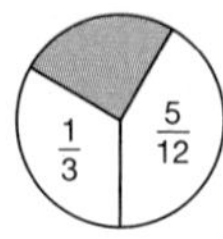

12. (67, 70) Draw a cube with edges 3 cm long.

a. What is the volume of the cube? 27 cm^3

b. What is the surface area of the cube? 54 cm^2

12. 3 cm, 3 cm, 3 cm

Collect like terms:

13. (84) $2x + 3y - 5 + x - y - 1$ $\quad 3x + 2y - 6$

14. (84) $x^2 + 2x - x - 2$ $\quad x^2 + x - 2$

15. (48) Complete the table.

Fraction	Decimal	Percent
a. $\frac{1}{8}$	0.125	b. $12\frac{1}{2}\%$
$\frac{3}{8}$	c. 0.375	d. $37\frac{1}{2}\%$

16. (76) Simplify: $\dfrac{60}{1\frac{1}{4}}$ $\quad$ 48

▶ **Model** Use ratio boxes to solve problems **17** and **18.**

* **17.** (81) The regular price of a shirt is \$24. The sale price is \$18. The sale price is what percent of the regular price? 75%

* **18.** (81) The auditorium seated 375, but this was enough for only 30 percent of those who wanted a seat. How many wanted a seat but could not get one? 875

19. (77) Write an equation to solve this problem: $24 = \frac{1}{4} \times W_N$; 96

Twenty-four is 25 percent of what number? Find the answer.

* **20.** (Inv. 6, 75) **a.** Classify this quadrilateral. trapezoid

b. Find its perimeter. 140 mm

▶ **c.** **Analyze** Find its area. 900 mm^2

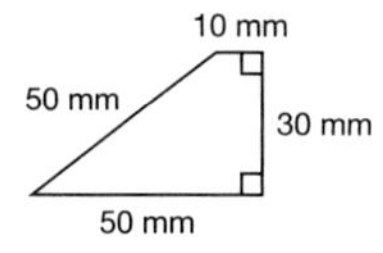

21. (56) Find the missing numbers in the table by using the function rule. Then graph the x, y pairs and a line through those points that shows all x, y pairs that satisfy the equation. Select the x, y pair where the line crosses the y-axis and check the numbers in the equation.

$y = x - 5$

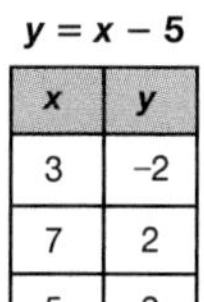

x	y
3	-2
7	2
5	0

21.

$y = x - 5$
$(-5) = (0) - 5$
$-5 = -5$

▶ See Math Conversations in the sidebar.

5.

Math Language
The symbol $\square JKLM$ means rectangle $JKLM$.

* **22.** (83) Multiply. Write each product in scientific notation.

a. $(9 \times 10^{-6})(4 \times 10^{-8})$ 3.6×10^{-13}

b. $(9 \times 10^{6})(4 \times 10^{8})$ 3.6×10^{15}

For problems **23** and **24,** solve and check the equation. Show each step.

23. (Inv. 7) $8\frac{5}{6} = d - 5\frac{1}{2}$ $14\frac{1}{3}$ **24.** (Inv. 7) $\frac{5}{6}m = 90$ 108

▶* **25.** (80) Evaluate Three vertices of rectangle $JKLM$ are J (−4, 2), K (0, 2), and L (0, 0).

a. Find the coordinates of M and draw the rectangle. M (−4, 0)

b. Translate $\square JKLM$ 4 units right, 2 down. Draw the translated image $\square J'K'L'M'$, and write the coordinates of its vertices. J' (0, 0), K' (4, 0), L' (4, −2), M' (0, −2)

▶ **26.** (20, 52) Which of the following does not equal 4^3? **d.** $4^2 + 4$

a. 2^6 **b.** $4 \cdot 4^2$ **c.** $\frac{4^4}{4}$ **d.** $4^2 + 4$

▶ **27.** (43) **a.** Find 50% of $\frac{2}{3}$ of 0.12. Write the answer as a decimal. 0.04

b. Is $\frac{2}{3}$ of 50% of 0.12 the same as 50% of $\frac{2}{3}$ of 0.12? Explain. Yes; because of the Commutative Property of Multiplication

▶ Generalize Simplify:

28. (63) $6\{5 \cdot 4 - 3[6 - (3 - 1)]\}$ 48

* **29.** (85) **a.** $\frac{(-3)(-4) - (-3)}{(-3) - (+4)(+3)}$ −1

b. $(+5) + (-2)[(+3) - (-4)]$ −9

* **30.** (87) **a.** $(-2x)(-3x)$ $6x^2$

b. $(ab)(2a^2b)(-3a)$ $-6a^4b^2$

c. $(-3x)^2$ $9x^2$

Early Finishers
Real-World Application

A group of 200 volunteers were shown television commercials A, B, C, and D. Then the volunteers were asked to identify their favorite commercial. The results are shown below.

A	B	C	D
78	35	45	42

a. Which type of display—a circle graph or a histogram—is the most appropriate way to display this data? Draw your display and justify your choice. circle graph; Sample: This data represents parts of a whole, which are well displayed on a circle graph. A histogram is a type of bar graph used to show data displayed in ranges of data. See student graphs.

▶ See Math Conversations in the sidebar.

3 Written Practice (Continued)

Math Conversations

Discussion opportunities are provided below.

Problem 25 Evaluate

Help students see that even though a transformed figure may look like another transformed figure, the two images may not be the same.

"If rectangle JKLM had been rotated 180° to the translated position of rectangle J'K'L'M', would it be the same image?" Sample: No, because the corresponding vertices would not be the same even though the shapes are the same and in the same position.

Problem 26 Analyze

Discuss with students how using a process of elimination can help them determine the choice for the correct answer.

"Do any of the choices obviously appear to equal 4^3?" Sample: Choice b does because you can add the exponents and 2 + 1 is 3. Choice c does because you can subtract the exponents, and 4 − 1 is 3. Choice a does because 4 equals 2^2, so 2^6 is the same as 4^3.

Point out that choices **a, b,** and **c** can be eliminated so the answer is **d.**

Problems 28–30 Generalize

Have students explain what steps they used to simplify these expressions. Lead students to see that using a systematic approach helps to prevent errors.

Errors and Misconceptions

Problem 27

Encourage students who did not get the correct answers to write each statement as an expression. Remind them in these statements, the word *of* can be written as a multiplication symbol.

Looking Forward

Understanding how to convert from one unit to another using more than one unit multiplier prepares students for:

- **Lesson 98,** using a scale to find either the model measurements or the actual measurements of an object and converting from one unit to another.
- **Lesson 114,** finding volume, capacity, and mass in the metric system.

• Diagonals
• Interior Angles
• Exterior Angles

Objectives

- Draw the diagonals of a polygon.
- Find the sum of the measures of the interior angles of a polygon.
- Find the measure of each interior angle of a regular polygon.
- Find the sum of the measures of the exterior angles of a polygon.
- Find the measure of each exterior angle of a regular polygon.

Lesson Preparation

Materials

- **Power Up R** (in *Instructional Masters*)
- **Lesson Activity 21** (in *Instructional Masters*)
- **Manipulative kit: metric rulers, protractors**
- **Teacher-provided material: 5 feet or more of string, chalk, 30 feet of masking tape, analog clock, narrow strips of paper or straws**

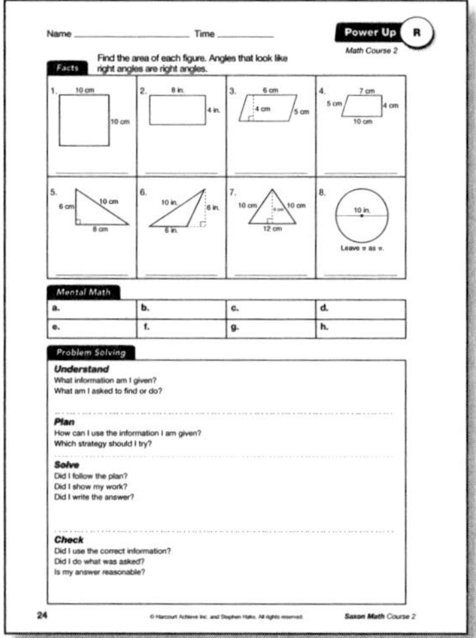

Power Up R

Math Language

New	Maintain	English Learners (ESL)
exterior angles	polygon	perspective
interior angles	regular polygon	

Technology Resources

Student eBook Complete student textbook in electronic format.

Resources and Planner CD Assessment, reteaching, and instructional masters, plus a pacing calendar with standards.

Test and Practice Generator CD Create additional practice sheets and custom-made tests.

www.SaxonPublishers.com Visit for more student activities and planning materials.

Inclusion

Adaptations CD Adapted lessons, investigations, practice and assessments.

Meeting Standards

National Council of Teachers of Mathematics (NCTM)

Geometry

GM.1c Create and critique inductive and deductive arguments concerning geometric ideas and relationships, such as congruence, similarity, and the Pythagorean relationship

GM.2b Use coordinate geometry to examine special geometric shapes, such as regular polygons or those with pairs of parallel or perpendicular sides

GM.4a Draw geometric objects with specified properties, such as side lengths or angle measures

GM.4d Use geometric models to represent and explain numerical and algebraic relationships

GM.4e Recognize and apply geometric ideas and relationships in areas outside the mathematics classroom, such as art, science, and everyday life

Connections

CN.4a Recognize and use connections among mathematical ideas

Power-Up Discussion *For use with Power Up, p. 610*

Problem-Solving Strategy: Write an Equation

Sarita rode the G-Force Ride at the fair. The cylindrical chamber spins, forcing riders against the wall while the floor drops away. If the chamber is 30 feet in diameter and if it spins around 30 times during a ride, how far do the riders travel? Do riders travel more or less than $\frac{1}{2}$ mile?

Understand ***Understand the problem.***

"Which information is important to us in solving this problem?"

The chamber of the ride is 30 feet in diameter, and it spins around 30 times during a ride.

"What are we asked to do?"

We are asked to determine how far a rider travels in feet, then compare the distance in feet to $\frac{1}{2}$ mile.

Plan ***Make a plan.***

"What problem-solving strategy will we use?"

We will *write an equation* to find the total distance traveled.

"How will the information we know fit into the strategy we have chosen?"

The circumference of the G-Force Ride multiplied by the number of spins in one ride will equal the distance the riders travel.

Teacher's Note: Encourage students to guess whether the riders will travel more or less than $\frac{1}{2}$ mile. Students may not expect the riders to travel so far since the chamber is only 30 feet in diameter.

Solve ***Carry out the plan.***

"What distance do the riders travel in one spin?"

They travel the circumference of the ride: 30 ft $\times\ \pi = C$.

"What is the distance the riders travel in 30 spins?"

They travel 30 times as far: 30 $\times$ 30 ft $\times\ \pi = D$.

"Using 3.14 for pi, what is the approximate distance the riders travel?"

$30 \times 30 \times 3.14 = 2826$ ft

"Is 2826 ft more or less than $\frac{1}{2}$ mile?"

One mile is equal to 5280 ft, so $\frac{1}{2}$ mile is 2640 ft. The riders travel more than one half mile.

Check ***Look back.***

"Did we do what we were asked to do?"

Yes, we found that the riders travel 2826 ft, more than one half mile.

"Is our solution expected?"

Answers will vary according to what students anticipated.

Power Up

Facts

Distribute **Power Up R** to students. See answers below.

Mental Math

Encourage students to share different ways to mentally compute these exercises. Strategies for exercises **c** and **e** are listed below.

c. Multiply by Fraction Equivalent to 1

$\frac{2}{2.5} \times \frac{4}{4} = \frac{8}{10}$

$g = 10$

Cross Multiply and Divide

$2g = 2.5 \times 8$

$g = \frac{2.5 \times 8}{2} = 2.5 \times 4$

$g = 10$

e. Use Logical Reasoning

$1 \text{ m} = 100 \text{ cm}$

$1.87 \text{ m} = 1.87 \times 100 \text{ cm} = 187 \text{ cm}$

Use a Unit Multiplier

$1.87 \text{ m} \times \frac{100 \text{ cm}}{1 \text{ m}} = 187 \text{ cm}$

Problem Solving

Refer to **Power-Up Discussion,** p. 610B.

2 New Concepts

Instruction

To check that students recall correctly what a *diagonal* is, ask them to name any other diagonals in this quadrilateral. There is only one other diagonal, segment *DB*.

Math Language

Point out that line segments that connect two vertices of a polygon are either **sides** or **diagonals,** depending upon whether the vertices are adjacent or nonadjacent, respectively.

(continued)

LESSON 89

• Diagonals
• Interior Angles
• Exterior Angles

Power Up — *Building Power*

facts Power Up R

mental math

a. Positive/Negative: $(-80) \div (-4)$ + 20

b. Order of Operations/Exponents: $(2.5 \times 10^{-4})(3 \times 10^{8})$ 7.5×10^{4}

c. Ratio: $\frac{8}{g} = \frac{2}{2.5}$ 10

d. Percent/Estimation: Estimate $7\frac{3}{4}\%$ of \$8.29. \$0.64

e. Measurement: 1.87 m to cm 187 cm

f. Fractional Parts: \$1.00 is $\frac{2}{5}$ of *m*. \$2.50

g. Geometry: What do you call an angle that measures 90 degrees? right angle

h. Calculation: 10% of 80, × 3, + 1, $\sqrt{\ }$, × 7, + 1, ÷ 2, ÷ 2, $\sqrt{\ }$, × 10, + 2, ÷ 4 8

problem solving

Sarita rode the G-Force Ride at the fair. The cylindrical chamber spins, forcing riders against the wall while the floor drops away. If the chamber is 30 feet in diameter and if it spins around 30 times during a ride, how far do the riders travel? Do riders travel more or less than $\frac{1}{2}$ mile? 2826 feet; more than $\frac{1}{2}$ mile

New Concepts — *Increasing Knowledge*

diagonals

Recall that a **diagonal** of a polygon is a line segment that passes through the polygon between two nonadjacent vertices. In the figure below, segment *AC* is a diagonal of quadrilateral *ABCD*.

Math Language

A **polygon** is a closed flat figure with straight sides. In a **regular polygon,** all sides and angles are equal in measure.

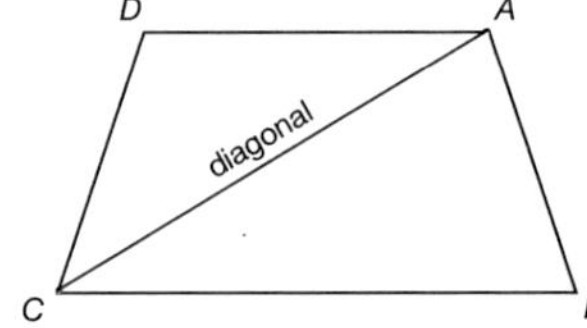

Facts Find the area of each figure. Angles that look like right angles are right angles.

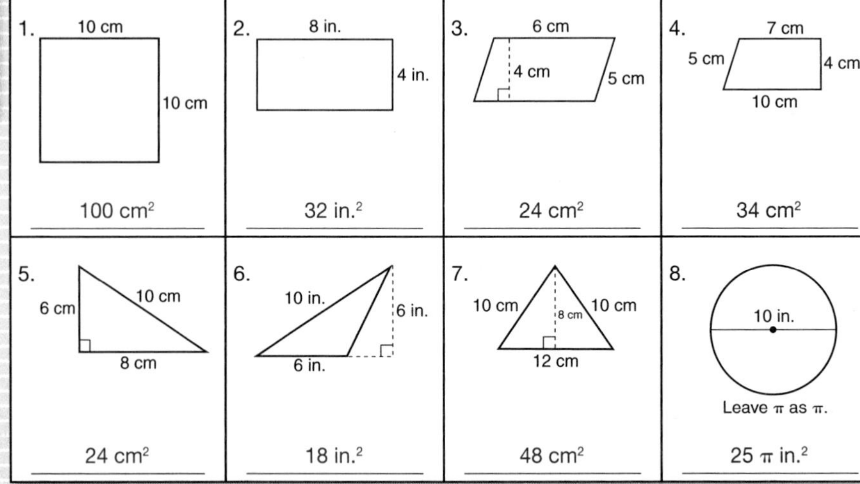

Example 1

From one vertex of regular hexagon *ABCDEF*, how many diagonals can be drawn? (Trace the hexagon and illustrate your answer.)

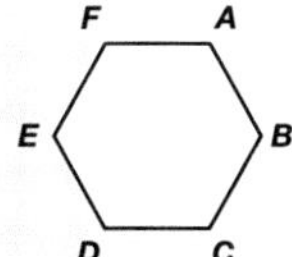

Solution

We can select any vertex from which to draw the diagonals. We choose vertex *A*. Segments *AB* and *AF* are sides of the hexagon and are not diagonals. Segments drawn from *A* to *C*, *D*, and *E* are diagonals. So **3 diagonals** can be drawn.

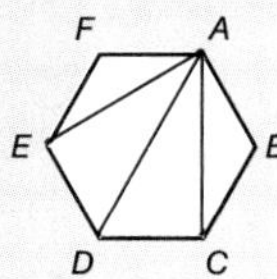

interior angles

Notice in example 1 that the three diagonals from vertex *A* divide the hexagon into four triangles. We will draw arcs to emphasize each angle of the four triangles.

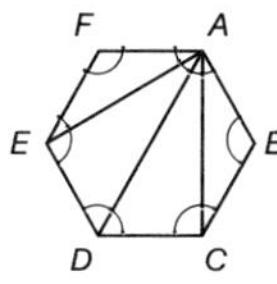

Angles that open to the interior of a polygon are called **interior angles.** We see that $\angle B$ of the hexagon is also $\angle B$ of $\triangle ABC$. Angle *C* of the hexagon includes $\angle BCA$ of $\triangle ABC$ and $\angle ACD$ of $\triangle ACD$.

No. All the angles of the triangles can be accounted for in the angles of the hexagon.

Analyze Are there any angles of the four triangles that are not included in the angles of the hexagon?

Although we may not know the measure of each angle of each triangle, we nevertheless can conclude that the measures of the six angles of a hexagon have the same total as the measures of the angles of four triangles, which is $4 \times 180° = 720°$.

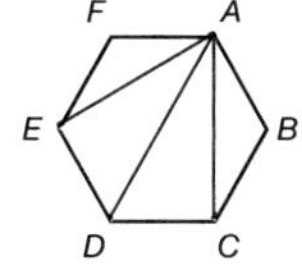

The sum of the measures of the six interior angles of a hexagon is 720°.
$4 \times 180° = 720°$

Since hexagon *ABCDEF* is a regular hexagon, we can also calculate the measure of each angle of the hexagon.

2 New Concepts *(Continued)*

Example 1

Instruction

Have students who chose a vertex other than *A* in example 1 draw their hexagons with diagonals on the board. As a class, discuss the similarities and differences between the drawings.

Instruction

Make a class list of what students know about the angles of triangles. Some examples might include:

- Triangles have three angles.
- The angles of an equilateral triangle all have the same measure.
- The sum of the measures of the angles of any triangle is 180°.

You may want students to explore whether the sum of the measures of the interior angles of any hexagon is always 720°. Have students draw a few hexagons of different sizes and shapes. Then ask them to draw all the diagonals from one vertex. Have them identify how many triangles they divided each hexagon into. They will all have 4 triangles.

Since the sum of the measures of the interior angles of a triangle is 180°, just as for a regular hexagon, the sum of the interior angles of all their hexagons is 720°.

(continued)

2 New Concepts (Continued)

Example 2

Instruction

After completing example 2, provide each student with a copy of **Lesson Activity 21** Polygons.

Regular Polygon	Number of sides	Number of triangles formed	Sum of interior angles	Measure of each interior angle
△	3	1	180	60
□	4	2	360	90
⬠	5	3	540	108
⬡	6	4	720	120
	7	5	900	$128\frac{4}{7}$
	8	6	1080	135
Pattern	n	$n - 2$	$180(n - 2)$	$\frac{180(n-2)}{n}$

Ask students to draw as many diagonals as possible from one of the interior angles of each regular polygon. Then have students complete the table. Guide students through the activity step-by-step, one polygon at a time.

To complete the last row of the transparency, have students look for the patterns and explain them in words. Then have them write algebraic expressions to describe the patterns, providing guidance as needed.

Example 3

Instruction

Ask students if they can determine the measure of each interior angle of the quadrilateral by dividing the sum of the measures of the interior angles by 4. Have them explain their answers. no; The quadrilateral is not a regular polygon, so the interior angles are not all the same measure.

(continued)

Example 2

Maura inscribed a regular hexagon in a circle. Find the measure of each angle of the regular hexagon *ABCDEF*.

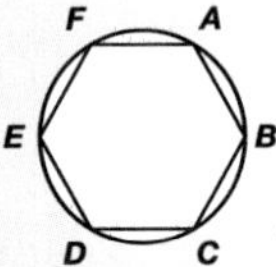

Solution

From the explanation above we know that the hexagon can be divided into four triangles. So the sum of the measures of the angles of the hexagon is $4 \times 180°$, which is 720°. Since the hexagon is regular, the six angles equally share the available 720°. So we divide 720° by 6 to find the measure of each angle.

$$720° \div 6 = 120°$$

We find that each angle of the hexagon measures **120°**.

Example 3

Draw a quadrilateral and one of its diagonals. What is the sum of the measures of the interior angles of the quadrilateral?

Solution

We draw a four-sided polygon and a diagonal.

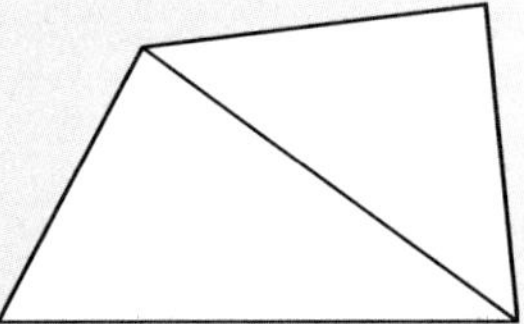

Although we do not know the measure of each angle, we can find the sum of their measures. The sum of the measures of the angles of a triangle is 180°. From the drawing above, we see that the total measure of the angles of the quadrilateral equals the total measure of the angles of two triangles. So the sum of the measures of the interior angles of the quadrilateral is

$$2 \times 180° = \mathbf{360°}$$

Discuss Will the sum of the measures of the interior angles of *all* quadrilaterals be 360°? Explain.

Yes; The measure of the interior angles of all quadrilaterals is 360° because for any quadrilateral we can draw one diagonal that divides it into two triangles.

exterior angles

In example 2 we found that each interior angle of a regular hexagon measures 120°. By performing the following activity, we can get another perspective on the angles of a polygon.

English Learners

When discussing exterior angles, explain the meaning of **perspective.** Say:

"When you get another perspective, it means you see, think or do things in a different way. For example, if you learn to play an instrument, you will listen to music in a new and different way."

Ask volunteers to give an example of an activity that changed their perspective. Sample: playing a new sport

Activity

Exterior Angles

Materials needed:

- A length of string (5 feet or more)
- Chalk
- Masking tape (optional)

Before performing this activity, lay out a regular hexagon in the classroom or on the playground. This can be done by inscribing a hexagon inside a circle as described in Investigation 2. Use the string and chalk to sweep out the circle and to mark the vertices and sides of the hexagon. If desired, mark the sides of the hexagon with masking tape.

After the hexagon has been prepared, walk the perimeter of the hexagon while making these observations:

1. Notice the direction you were facing when you started around the hexagon as well as when you finished going around the hexagon after six turns.
2. Notice how much you turned at each "corner" of the hexagon. Did you turn more than, less than, or the same as you would have turned at the corner of a square?

Each student should have the opportunity to walk the perimeter of the hexagon.

Going around the hexagon, we turned at every corner. If we did not turn, we would continue going straight.

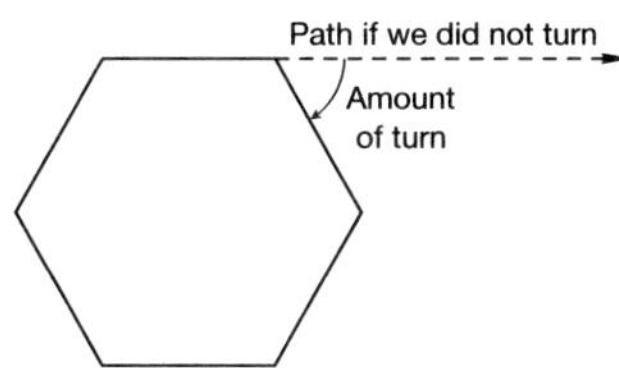

The amount we turned at the corner in order to stay on the hexagon equals the measure of the **exterior angle** of the hexagon at that vertex.

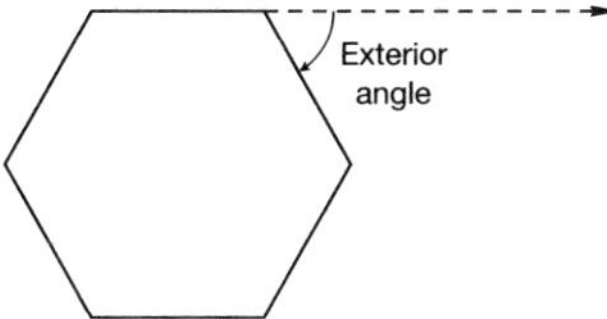

Activity

Instruction

Before class, have volunteers help you construct a regular hexagon on the playground or on the gym or classroom floor, by following the instructions given on the student page.

It may be helpful to use masking tape to show the path people would take if they did not turn at the corner as they walked the perimeter of the hexagon.

Before each student takes a turn walking the perimeter of the hexagon, carefully go over the two observations that need to be made. Have a few students demonstrate. The remaining students may take turns walking the perimeter as time permits now or while the class is working on the Practice Set and Written Practice.

Relate making a full turn around the hexagon to the number of degrees in a complete turn around a circle. Guide students to see that the sum of the measures of the exterior angles of any polygon is 360°.

(continued)

Teacher Tip

To help students see that the sum of the measures of the **exterior angles of any convex polygon** is 360°, have them draw several different polygons. Ask them to number each exterior angle, cut the angles apart, and fasten them to a sheet of paper so that the sides of one angle align with the sides of the next angle. Then have students compare the constructed figures.

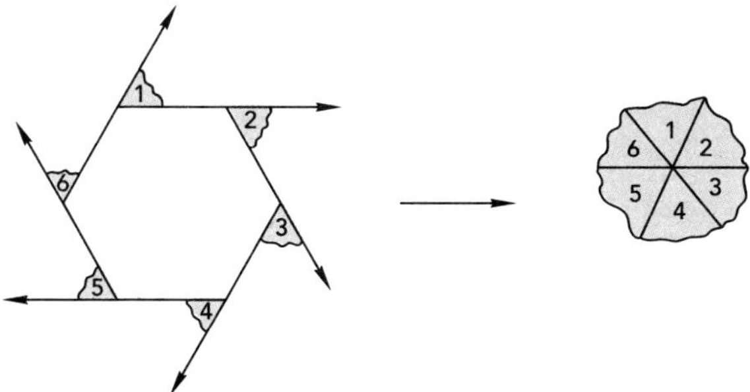

2 New Concepts (Continued)

Example 4

Instruction

Go over the two ways to determine the measure of an exterior angle of a regular polygon—dividing the sum of the exterior angles (360°) by the number of angles in the polygon or using the definition of a supplementary angle. Students may use whichever method they prefer.

After students have calculated that each exterior angle measures 60°, ask them to confirm their findings by measuring the exterior angles of a hexagon with a protractor.

Practice Set

Problems a–f Analyze

You may want to create a worksheet with the figures and questions from examples 1–4 so that students can work through them again without the aid of the solutions. Students can then refer to the solutions in the book only when necessary.

For more practice, students can repeat parts **a**–**f** for regular hexagons, heptagons, and octagons. If they do this, ask what they notice about the answers to part **f.** They are all 180°.

Problem c Explain

Ask students to explain why an n-gon can be divided into $(n - 2)$ triangles. Sample: When you start at a vertex, there are 2 adjacent sides that each one needs one more side to make a triangle with a diagonal; after that each new side makes a new triangle, so the number of triangles is equal to the number of sides minus 2.

We can calculate the measure of each exterior angle of a regular hexagon by remembering how many turns were required in order to face the same direction as when we started. We remember that we made six small turns. In other words, after six turns we had completed one full turn of 360°.

If all the turns are in the same direction, the sum of the exterior angles of any polygon is 360°.

Example 4

What is the measure of each exterior angle of a regular hexagon?

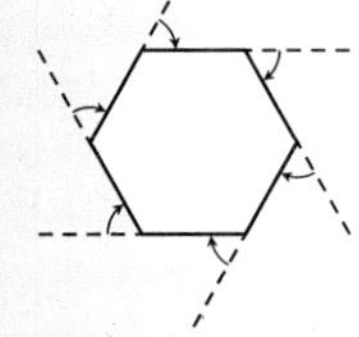

Solution

Traveling all the way around the hexagon completes one full turn of 360°. Each exterior angle of a regular hexagon has the same measure, so we can find the measure by dividing 360° by 6.

$$360° \div 6 = 60°$$

We find that each exterior angle of a regular hexagon measures **60°.**

Notice that an interior angle of a polygon and its exterior angle are supplementary, so their combined measures total 180°.

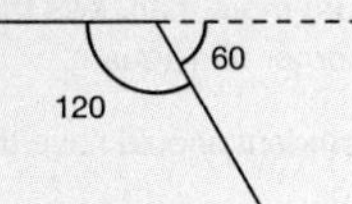

Analyze How can you determine the measure of an exterior angle if you know the measure of the interior angle?

Sample: The interior and exterior angles are supplementary. By subtracting the interior angle from 180°, you would have the measure of the exterior angle. For example, 180° − 120° = 60°.

Practice Set ▶ Analyze Work examples 1–4. Then solve **a–f.**

a. Trace this regular pentagon. How many diagonals can be drawn from one vertex? Show your work. 2 diagonals

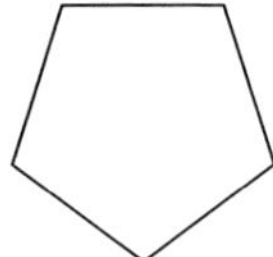

a. one possibility:

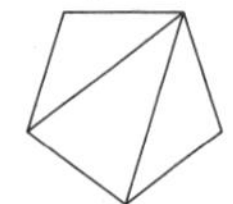

b. The diagonals drawn in problem **a** divide the pentagon into how many triangles? 3 triangles

c. Explain What is the sum of the measures of the five interior angles of a pentagon? How do you know?

c. 540°; In a pentagon you can draw 2 diagonals from any vertex to form three triangles. The sum of the measures of the angles of each triangle is 180°. So the sum of the measures of the interior angles of a pentagon is 3 × 180° = 540°.

d. What is the measure of each interior angle of a regular pentagon? $\frac{540°}{5} = 108°$

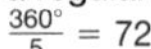

e. What is the measure of each exterior angle of a regular pentagon? $\frac{360°}{5} = 72°$

▶ See Math Conversations in the sidebar.

f. What is the sum of the measures of an interior and exterior angle of a regular pentagon? $108° + 72° = 180°$

Written Practice *Strengthening Concepts*

1. (72) Use a ratio box to solve this problem. Jason's remote-control car traveled 440 feet in 10 seconds. At that rate, how long would it take the car to travel a mile? 120 seconds or 2 minutes

2. (54) Use a ratio box to help you solve this problem. There are novels, biographies, and field guides in one bookcase of the class library. The ratio of novels to biographies is 3 to 2. The ratio of biographies to field guides is 3 to 4. If there are 18 novels, how many field guides are there? Tell how you found the answer.

2. 16 field guides. Sample: Use a ratio box to find how many biographies there are. Then use another ratio box to find the number of field guides.

3. (70) Kwame measured the shoe box and found that it was 30 cm long, 15 cm wide, and 12 cm tall. What was the volume of the shoe box? 5400 cm^3

▸ * 4. (44, Inv. 8) **Generalize** A baseball player's batting average is a ratio found by dividing the number of hits by the number of at-bats and writing the result as a decimal number rounded to the nearest thousandth. If Erika had 24 hits in 61 at-bats, what was her batting average? 0.393

▸ * 5. (88) **Connect** Christina ran 3,000 meters in 10 minutes. Use two unit multipliers to convert her average speed to kilometers per hour. 18 km per hr

▸ * 6. (86) **Represent** On a number line, graph the integers greater than −4.

6. 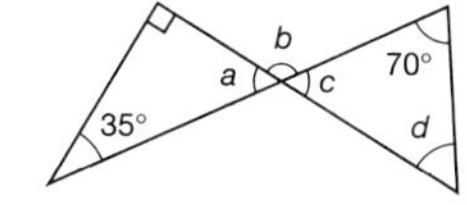

7. (71) Draw a diagram of this statement. Then answer the questions that follow.

Jimmy bought the astronomy book for \$12. This was $\frac{3}{4}$ of the regular price.

a. What was the regular price of the astronomy book? \$16

b. Jimmy bought the astronomy book for what percent of the regular price? 75%

7. 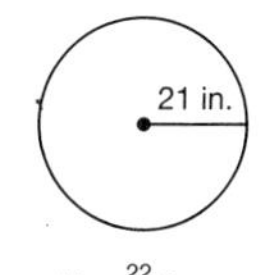

8. (40) Use the figure below to find the measure of each angle.

a. $\angle a$ 55° b. $\angle b$ 125° c. $\angle c$ 55° d. $\angle d$ 55°

9. (65, 82) a. What is the circumference of this circle? 132 in.

b. What is the area of this circle? 1386 in.^2

21 in.

Use $\frac{22}{7}$ for π.

▸ See Math Conversations in the sidebar.

3 Written Practice

Math Conversations

Discussion opportunities are provided below.

Problem 4 Generalize

This problem allows students to see a real-world use of ratios that may be of interest to many of them.

"Why do batting averages make it easy to compare how well players are hitting?" Sample: Not every player gets to bat the same number of times, so just seeing how many hits a player gets doesn't give as much information as seeing the ratio of hits to at-bats. That is like knowing what the probability of getting a hit is for a given player.

Problem 5 Connect

Ask students to tell how they decided on the unit multipliers they used. After some different approaches have been described, ask why it is necessary to be careful in setting up the unit multipliers. Sample: If you mix up the units in the numerator and denominator, they won't cancel and you will get the wrong answer.

Problem 6 Represent

"Why isn't an open circle used for −4?" Sample: We aren't plotting all numbers, just integers, so we don't have to show that −4 is not included because we don't plot it at all.

Errors and Misconceptions

Problem 5

This problem requires using two unit multipliers because meters must be converted to kilometers and minutes to hours. Watch that students write the unit multipliers in such a way that meters and minutes cancel.

(continued)

3 Written Practice (Continued)

Math Conversations

Discussion opportunities are provided below.

Problems 15 and 16 Model

Remind students that they can also write equations directly to model these problem situations. Work as a class to write and solve equations for the two problems. Samples:

15. $0.45 \times 300 = m$, $m = 135$

16. $0.75(24 + d) = 24$, $d = 8$

The equation for problem 16 is not as easy to write as the one for problem 15. Point out that using a ratio box for problem 16 may be easier than writing an equation.

Problem 19 Analyze

Discuss what else students know about regular triangles. Samples: all angles are equal and equal 60°; all sides are equal; you can put 6 together to make a hexagon

Then ask:

"How do the interior and exterior angles of a regular triangle compare to the interior and exterior angles of a regular hexagon?" Sample: They are just the opposite of each other: the interior angles of a regular triangle are equal to the exterior angles of a regular hexagon, and the interior angles of a regular hexagon are equal to the exterior angles of a regular triangle.

Problem 20

Extend the Problem

"The graph of this equation passes through the origin (0, 0). Suppose the equation was $y = \frac{1}{4}x$. Would the graph pass through the origin?" yes

"Suppose the equation was $y = 2x$. Would the graph pass through the origin?" yes

"Suppose the equation was $y = -4x$. Would the graph pass through the origin?" yes

"Do you think that the graph will pass through the origin for any value of the coefficient of x? Why?" Sample: yes, because if x is 0, y has to be 0 too.

Errors and Misconceptions

Problem 14

Some students may benefit from using an actual or paper clock to act out this problem. If a clock is not available, have them draw pictures of clock faces with the minute hand pointing at 12. Then have them draw the hour hand in different positions to form angles equal to $\frac{1}{3}$ of a circle.

(continued)

---

10. (76) Simplify: $\dfrac{91\frac{2}{3}}{100}$ $\frac{11}{12}$

11. (52) Evaluate: $\dfrac{ab + a}{a + b}$ if $a = 10$ and $b = 5$ 4

12. (20, 35) Compare: $a^2 \bigcirc a$ if $a = 0.5$ (answer: <)

13. (48) Complete the table.

Fraction	Decimal	Percent
$\frac{7}{8}$	**a.** 0.875	**b.** $87\frac{1}{2}$%
c. $8\frac{3}{4}$	**d.** 8.75	875%

▸ **14.** (17) At three o'clock and at nine o'clock, the hands of a clock form angles equal to $\frac{1}{4}$ of a circle.

a. At which two hours do the hands of a clock form angles equal to $\frac{1}{3}$ of a circle? 4:00, 8:00

b. The angle described in part **a** measures how many degrees? 120°

▸ Model Use ratio boxes to solve problems **15** and **16.**

* **15.** (81) Forty-five percent of the 300 shoppers in a supermarket bought milk. How many of the shoppers in a supermarket bought milk? 135 shoppers

* **16.** (81) The sale price of $24 was 75% of the regular price. The sale price was how many dollars less than the regular price? $8

17. (77) Write an equation to solve this problem:

Twenty is what percent of 200? $20 = W_P \times 200$; 10%

18. a.

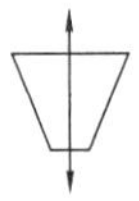

18. (58, 75) **a.** Trace this isosceles trapezoid and draw its line of symmetry.

b. Find the area of the trapezoid. 480 mm^2

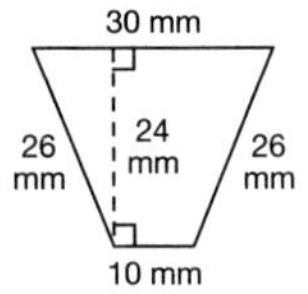

▸* **19.** (89) Analyze What is the measure of each exterior angle of a regular triangle? 120°

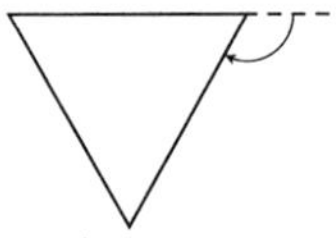

20.

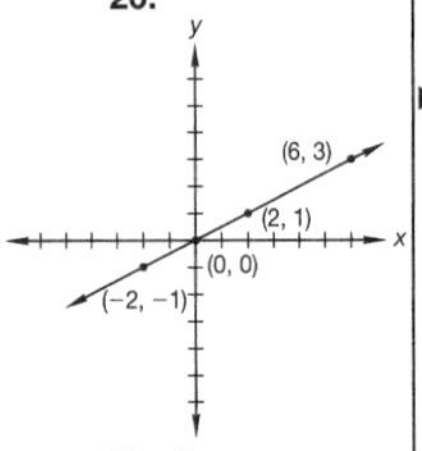

The line intercepts the y-axis at (0, 0)

▸* **20.** (56) Find the missing numbers in the table by using the function rule. Then graph the x, y pairs and extend a line through the points. At what x, y pair does the graph of the equation intercept (cross) the y-axis?

$y = \frac{1}{2}x$

x	y
6	3
2	1
−2	−1

▸ See Math Conversations in the sidebar.

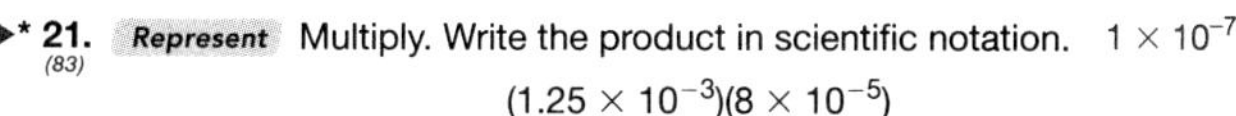

*** 21.** (83) **Represent** Multiply. Write the product in scientific notation. 1×10^{-7}

$$(1.25 \times 10^{-3})(8 \times 10^{-5})$$

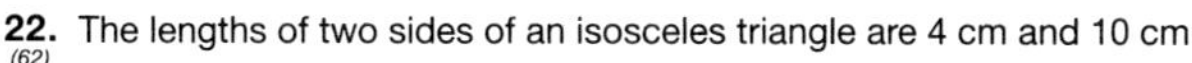

22. (62) The lengths of two sides of an isosceles triangle are 4 cm and 10 cm.

a. Draw the triangle and find its perimeter. 24 cm

b. Can there be more than one answer? Why or why not?

22. a. (triangle with sides 10 cm, 10 cm, 4 cm)

b. There can only be one answer. A triangle with side lengths of 4 cm, 4 cm, and 10 cm cannot exist.

For problems **23** and **24,** solve and check the equation. Show each step.

23. (Inv. 7) $\frac{4}{9}p = 72$ 162

24. (Inv. 7) $12.3 = 4.56 + f$ 7.74

*** 25.** (84) **Generalize** Collect like terms:

$$2x + 3y - 4 + x - 3y - 1 \quad 3x - 5$$

Generalize Simplify:

26. (63) $\frac{9 \cdot 8 - 7 \cdot 6}{6 \cdot 5}$ 1

27. (43, 57) $3.2 \times 4^{-2} \times 10^2$ 20

28. (43) $13\frac{1}{3} - \left(4.75 + \frac{3}{4}\right)$ (mixed-number answer) $7\frac{5}{6}$

*** 29.** (85) **a.** $\frac{(+3) + (-4)(-6)}{(-3) + (-4) - (-6)}$ -27

b. $(-5) - (+6)(-2) + (-2)(-3)(-1)$ 1

*** 30.** (87) **a.** $(3x^2)(2x)$ $6x^3$

b. $(-2ab)(-3b^2)(-a)$ $-6a^2b^3$

c. $(-4ab^3)^2$ $16a^2b^6$

Early Finishers
Math Applications

Write *True or False* for each statement.

Some prisms have a curved surface. false
No pyramids have a circular base. true
All prisms are constructed from polygons. true
All three-dimensional figures have at least one vertex. false
Some three-dimensional figures have no edges. true
All faces of a triangular prism are triangles. false
One face of a pyramid can be a rectangle. true

▶ See Math Conversations in the sidebar.

3 Written Practice (Continued)

Math Conversations

Discussion opportunities are provided below.

Problem 21 Represent

Challenge students to find as many other ways as possible to represent the product. Samples: one ten millionth, 0.0000001, 10^{-7}

Problems 26–30 Generalize

Have students explain how they simplified these expressions. Discuss what mathematical rules or properties helped in simplifying them. Sample: For problem 30b, I determined that the product was negative; I calculated the coefficient to be 6, I added 1 plus 1 to get the exponent for the *a* factor, and I added 1 plus 2 to get the *b* exponent. The exponent rules helped to simplify the expression.

Errors and Misconceptions

Problem 22

Students will need a ruler to solve this problem. If they have difficulty answering part b, suggest that they try to draw all possible isosceles triangles with sides of 4 cm and 10 cm. Some students may find it helpful to work with narrow strips of paper or straws cut to lengths of 4 cm and 10 cm.

Problems 26–30

If students are not able to simplify these expressions correctly, review order of operations with them before having students redo these problems. Remind students who had difficulty with the expressions in problem 30 that the exponents are added when multiplying exponential terms with the same base.

Looking Forward

Finding the sum of the measures of the interior angles of a polygon and finding the measure of each interior angle prepares students for:

- **Lesson 97,** understanding why triangles are similar.

• Mixed-Number Coefficients
• Negative Coefficients

Objectives

- Solve an equation that has a mixed-number coefficient.
- Solve an equation that has a negative coefficient.

Lesson Preparation

Materials

- **Power Up Q** (in *Instructional Masters*)
- **Investigation Activity 13** (in *Instructional Masters*) or **graph paper**

Math Language

Maintain
coefficient

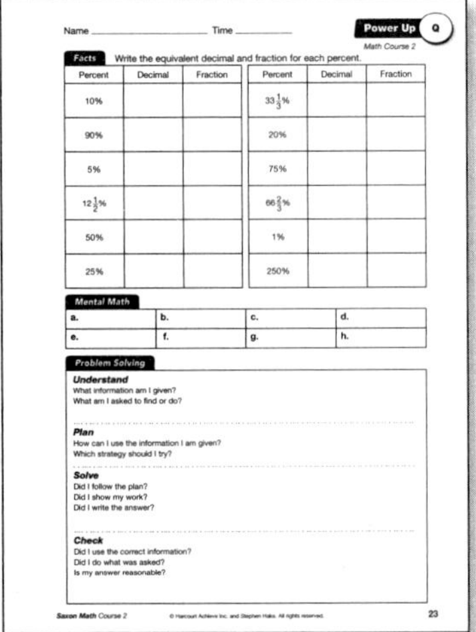

Power Up Q

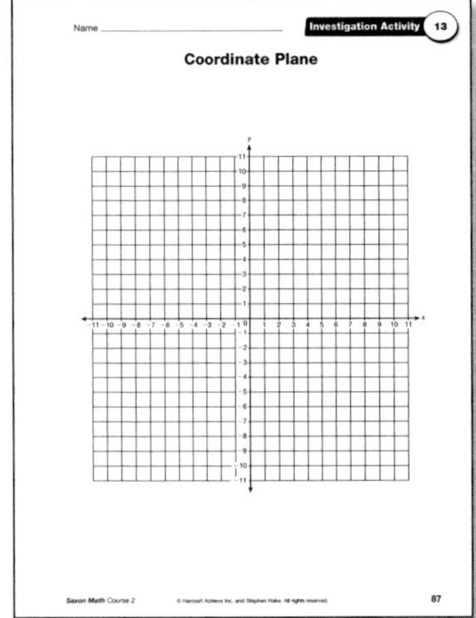

Investigation Activity 13

Technology Resources

Student eBook Complete student textbook in electronic format.

Resources and Planner CD Blackline masters, plus a pacing calendar with standards.

Test and Practice Generator CD Create additional practice sheets and custom-made tests.

www.SaxonPublishers.com Visit for more student activities and planning materials.

Inclusion

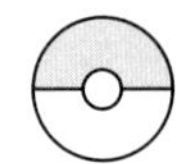

Adaptations CD Adapted lessons, investigations, practice and assessments.

Meeting Standards

National Council of Teachers of Mathematics (NCTM)

Numbers and Operations

NO.1a Work flexibly with fractions, decimals, and percents to solve problems

Algebra

AL.2d Recognize and generate equivalent forms for simple algebraic expressions and solve linear equations

Problem Solving

PS.1c Apply and adapt a variety of appropriate strategies to solve problems

Connections

CN.4b Understand how mathematical ideas interconnect and build on one another to produce a coherent whole

Power-Up Discussion *For use with Power Up, p. 618*

Problem-Solving Strategy: Make a Model/Use Logical Reasoning/Draw a Diagram

Here are the front, side, and top views of a structure. Construct this object using 1-inch cubes, and find the volume of the object. Then draw a three-dimensional view of the structure.

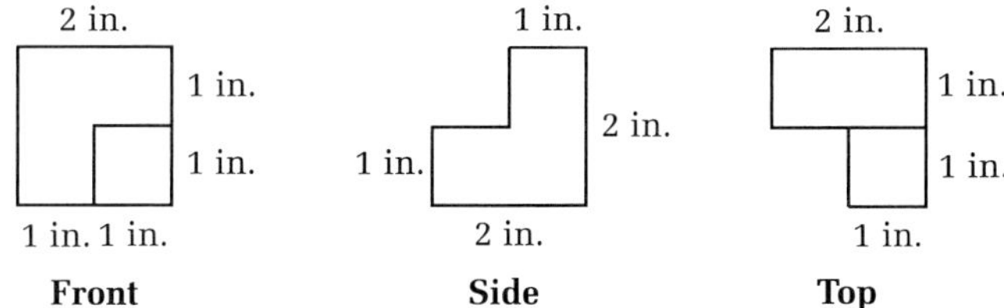

Understand **Understand the problem.**

"What information are we given?"

We are shown the front, side, and top views of a structure.

"What are we asked to do?"

We are asked to construct the object using 1-inch cubes and find its volume, then draw a three-dimensional view of the object.

Teacher's Note: If cubes are unavailable, guide students through the visualization process making sure each student understands why the volume is 5 cubic inches.

Plan **Make a plan.**

"What problem-solving strategy will we use?"

We have been asked to *make a model* and to *draw a diagram.* We will *use logical reasoning* to help us visualize the placement of the cubes.

Solve **Carry out the plan.**

"What does the structure look like in three dimensions?"

It looks like a 4-cube square with one cube in front of the bottom-right cube.

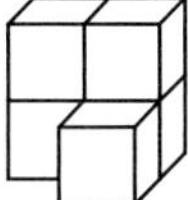

"What is the volume of the structure?"

5 cubic inches

"Sketch the object in three dimensions."

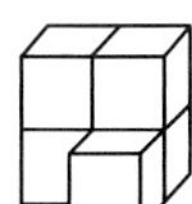

Check **Look back.**

"Did we do what we were asked to do?"

Yes, we found the volume of the object and sketched it in three dimensions.

1 Power Up

Facts

Distribute **Power Up Q** to students. See answers below.

Mental Math

Encourage students to share different ways to mentally compute these exercises. Strategies for exercises **c** and **d** are listed below.

c. Divide First

$4w - 8 = 36$
$w - 2 = 9$
$w = 9 + 2 = 11$

Isolate the Variable

$4w - 8 = 36$
$4w = 44$
$w = 11$

d. Use 10% and 5%

$\$23.89 \approx \$24$
10% of \$24 is \$2.40
5% of \$24 is \$1.20
15% of \$24 is \$3.60

Decompose

$\$23.89 \approx \$24$
$\$24 \times 0.15 =$
$(\$20 \times 0.15) + (\$4 \times 0.15) =$
$\$3.00 + \$0.60 = \$3.60$

Problem Solving

Refer to **Power-Up Discussion,** p. 618B.

2 New Concepts

Instruction

Begin this lesson by reviewing with students how to solve equations with fractional coefficients. Explain that they are going to build on this skill to solve equations that have mixed-number and negative coefficients.

Explain to students that *multiplying by the reciprocal of the coefficient* uses the inverse property of multiplication to make the coefficient of the variable 1.

(continued)

LESSON 90

• Mixed-Number Coefficients
• Negative Coefficients

Power Up *Building Power*

facts Power Up Q

mental math

a. **Positive/Negative:** $(-50) - (-30)$ -20

b. **Order of Operations/Exponents:** $(4.2 \times 10^{-6})(2 \times 10^{-4})$ 8.4×10^{-10}

c. **Algebra:** $4w - 8 = 36$ 11

d. **Percent/Estimation:** Estimate 15% of \$23.89. \$3.60

e. **Measurement:** 800 g to kg 0.8 kg

f. **Fractional Parts:** \$1.00 is $\frac{4}{5}$ of m. \$1.25

g. **Geometry:** What do you call an angle that is greater than 90 degrees? obtuse

h. **Geometry:** A cube with edges 10 inches long has a volume of how many cubic inches? 1000 in.^{3}

problem solving

Here are the front, side, and top views of a structure. Construct this object using 1-inch cubes, and find the volume of the object. Then draw a three-dimensional view of the structure.

; 5 in.^{3}

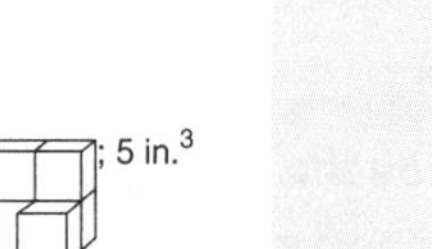

Front

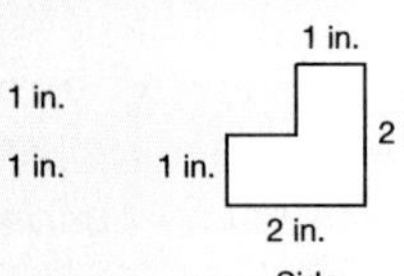

Side

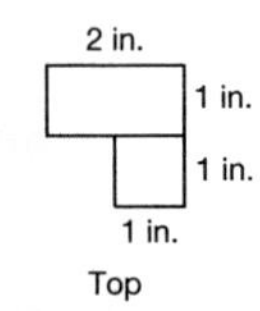

Top

New Concepts *Increasing Knowledge*

mixed-number coefficients

We have solved equations that have fractional coefficients by multiplying by the reciprocal of the coefficient.

$$\frac{4}{5}x = 7$$

Math Language
A **coefficient** is the number that is multiplied by a variable in an algebraic term.

Here the coefficient of x is $\frac{4}{5}$, so we multiply both sides by the reciprocal of $\frac{4}{5}$, which is $\frac{5}{4}$.

$$\frac{\cancel{5}}{\cancel{4}} \cdot \frac{\cancel{4}}{\cancel{5}}x = \frac{5}{4} \cdot 7 \quad \text{multiplied both sides by } \frac{5}{4}$$

$$x = \frac{35}{4} \quad \text{simplified}$$

Facts Write the equivalent decimal and fraction for each percent.

Percent	Decimal	Fraction	Percent	Decimal	Fraction
10%	0.1	$\frac{1}{10}$	$33\frac{1}{3}\%$	$0.\overline{3}$	$\frac{1}{3}$
90%	0.9	$\frac{9}{10}$	20%	0.2	$\frac{1}{5}$
5%	0.05	$\frac{1}{20}$	75%	0.75	$\frac{3}{4}$
$12\frac{1}{2}\%$	0.125	$\frac{1}{8}$	$66\frac{2}{3}\%$	$0.\overline{6}$	$\frac{2}{3}$
50%	0.5	$\frac{1}{2}$	1%	0.01	$\frac{1}{100}$
25%	0.25	$\frac{1}{4}$	250%	2.5	$2\frac{1}{2}$

To solve an equation that has a mixed-number coefficient, we convert the mixed number to an improper fraction as the first step. Then we multiply both sides by the reciprocal of the improper fraction.

Example 1

Solve: $3\frac{1}{3}x = 5$

Solution

First we write $3\frac{1}{3}$ as an improper fraction.

$$\frac{10}{3}x = 5 \quad \text{fraction form}$$

Then we multiply both sides of the equation by $\frac{3}{10}$, which is the reciprocal of $\frac{10}{3}$.

$$\frac{\overset{1}{\cancel{3}}}{\underset{1}{\cancel{10}}} \cdot \frac{\overset{1}{\cancel{10}}}{\underset{1}{\cancel{3}}}x = \frac{3}{\underset{2}{\cancel{10}}} \cdot \frac{\overset{1}{\cancel{5}}}{1} \quad \text{multiplied both sides by } \frac{3}{10}$$

$$x = \frac{3}{2} \quad \text{simplified}$$

In arithmetic we usually convert an improper fraction such as $\frac{3}{2}$ to a mixed number. Recall that in algebra we usually leave improper fractions in fraction form.

Example 2

Solve: $2\frac{1}{2}y = 1\frac{7}{8}$

Solution

Since we will be multiplying both sides of the equation by a fraction, we first convert both mixed numbers to improper fractions.

$$\frac{5}{2}y = \frac{15}{8} \quad \text{fraction form}$$

Then we multiply both sides by $\frac{2}{5}$, which is the reciprocal of $\frac{5}{2}$.

$$\frac{\overset{1}{\cancel{2}}}{\underset{1}{\cancel{5}}} \cdot \frac{\overset{1}{\cancel{5}}}{\underset{1}{\cancel{2}}}y = \frac{\overset{1}{\cancel{2}}}{\underset{1}{\cancel{5}}} \cdot \frac{\overset{3}{\cancel{15}}}{\underset{4}{\cancel{8}}} \quad \text{multiplied both sides by } \frac{2}{5}$$

$$y = \frac{3}{4} \quad \text{simplified}$$

negative coefficients

To solve an equation with a negative coefficient, we multiply (or divide) both sides of the equation by a negative number. The coefficient of x in this equation is negative.

$$-3x = 126$$

To solve this equation, we can either divide both sides by -3 or multiply both sides by $-\frac{1}{3}$. The effect of either method is to make $+1$ the coefficient of x. We show both ways on the following page.

Thinking Skill

Identify

What is the coefficient of x in the equation: $-x + 2 = 17$? -1

2 New Concepts (Continued)

Example 1

Instruction

Review with students how to rewrite a mixed number as an improper fraction.

$$3\frac{1}{3} = 3\frac{1}{3} = \frac{10}{3}$$

As students work through examples 1 and 2 on the page, remind them of the four-step process for solving these equations:

- Write each mixed number as an improper fraction.
- Identify the reciprocal of the coefficient.
- Multiply both sides of the equation by the reciprocal of the coefficient.
- Simplify the equation as necessary.

Explain to students that they can check their answers by replacing the variable in the original equation with the value they have found for the variable. Point out that leaving the answer as an improper fraction makes it easier to check the answer.

$$\frac{10}{3}\left(\frac{3}{2}\right) = 5$$

$$\frac{\overset{5}{\cancel{10}}}{\underset{1}{\cancel{3}}} \cdot \frac{\overset{1}{\cancel{3}}}{\underset{1}{\cancel{2}}} = 5$$

$$5 = 5$$

Example 2

Instruction

Ask students to explain why they multiply both sides of the equation by $\frac{2}{5}$. Sample: In order to make the coefficient of the variable one.

Instruction

As you discuss negative coefficients, ask students to explain how -3 and $-\frac{1}{3}$ are related. Elicit that since $-3 = -\frac{3}{1}$ and $-\frac{1}{3}$ is the reciprocal of $-\frac{3}{1}$, -3 and $-\frac{1}{3}$ are reciprocals of each other.

(continued)

Teacher Tip

In this lesson there are many ways for students to make errors, especially when rewriting fractions, canceling numbers, and multiplying with negatives. Encourage students to **check their answers.** Replacing the variable in the original equation with the solution is a good technique for students to practice and become comfortable performing on a regular basis.

2 New Concepts (Continued)

Example 3

Instruction

To reinforce the main concepts of this lesson, ask students why we multiply by the reciprocal of the coefficient in this example. Sample: We want to isolate the variable.

Example 4

Instruction

You may want to have students solve the equation by multiplying by $-\frac{1}{5}$. Ask them to show each step.

$$-5x = 0.24$$
$$-5\left(-\tfrac{1}{5}\right)x = 0.24\left(-\tfrac{1}{5}\right)$$
$$x = \tfrac{24}{100}\left(-\tfrac{1}{5}\right)$$
$$x = -\frac{24}{500}$$
$$x = -\frac{6}{125}$$
$$x = -0.048$$

Practice Set

Problems a–h Generalize

Discuss what it means to isolate the variable, and have students tell how they did that for each problem. Sample: For problem a, I multiplied both sides of the equation by $\frac{8}{9}$.

Problem i Conclude

Have volunteers read their explanations. Then ask how many others checked their answers that way. For each one, discuss why the method is a good one or why it might not work. Continue until all different methods have been described. Sample: I do the problem a second time without looking at what I did the first time. Discussion: You might make the same error both times.

Method 1	**Method 2**
$-3x = 126$	$-3x = 126$
$\frac{-3x}{-3} = \frac{126}{-3}$	$\left(-\frac{1}{3}\right)(-3x) = \left(-\frac{1}{3}\right)(126)$
$x = -42$	$x = -42$

Example 3

Solve: $-\frac{2}{3}x = \frac{4}{5}$

Solution

We multiply both sides of the equation by the reciprocal of $-\frac{2}{3}$, which is $-\frac{3}{2}$.

$-\frac{2}{3}x = \frac{4}{5}$ — equation

$\left(-\frac{3}{2}\right)\left(-\frac{2}{3}x\right) = \left(-\frac{3}{2}\right)\left(\frac{4}{5}\right)$ — multiplied by $-\frac{3}{2}$

$x = \mathbf{-\frac{6}{5}}$ — simplified

Example 4

Solve: $-5x = 0.24$

Solution

We may either multiply both sides by $-\frac{1}{5}$ or divide both sides by -5. Since the right side of the equation is a decimal number, it appears that dividing by -5 will be easier.

$-5x = 0.24$ — equation

$\frac{-5x}{-5} = \frac{0.24}{-5}$ — divided by -5

$x = \mathbf{-0.048}$ — simplified

Practice Set ▶ Generalize Solve:

a. $1\frac{1}{8}x = 36$ 32

b. $3\frac{1}{2}a = 490$ 140

c. $2\frac{3}{4}w = 6\frac{3}{5}$ $\frac{12}{5}$

d. $2\frac{2}{3}y = 1\frac{4}{5}$ $\frac{27}{40}$

e. $-3x = 0.45$ -0.15

f. $-\frac{3}{4}m = \frac{2}{3}$ $-\frac{8}{9}$

g. $-10y = -1.6$ 0.16

h. $-2\frac{1}{2}w = 3\frac{1}{3}$ $-\frac{4}{3}$

▶ **i.** Conclude When solving an equation, how can you show that your answer is correct? Sample: Substitute your answer for the value for the variable in the original equation and solve.

▶ See Math Conversations in the sidebar.

Written Practice *Strengthening Concepts*

1. The sum of 0.8 and 0.9 is how much greater than the product of 0.8 and 0.9? Use words to write the answer. *(31, 35)* ninety-eight hundredths

▶ 2. For this set of scores, find the: *(Inv. 4)*

a. mean 8.5 **b.** median 8.5

c. mode 8 **d.** range 4

8, 6, 9, 10, 8, 7, 9, 10, 8, 10, 9, 8

3. A 24-ounce jar of applesauce costs $1.68. A 58-ounce jar costs $2.88. Which costs more per ounce? How much more? *(46)* The 24-ounce jar costs more; $0.02 more per ounce.

▶ * 4. **Analyze** The figure at right is a regular decagon. One of the exterior angles is labeled *a*, and one of the interior angles is labeled *b*. *(89)*

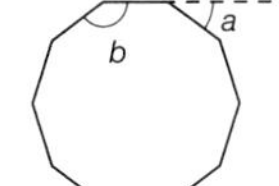

a. What is the measure of each exterior angle of the decagon? 36°

b. What is the measure of each interior angle? 144°

▶ * 5. **Generalize** Collect like terms: $x^2 + 2xy + y^2 + x^2 - y^2$ *(84)* $2x^2 + 2xy$

Model Use ratio boxes to solve problems **6** and **7.**

▶ * 6. A pair of binoculars were on sale for $36. This was 90% of the regular price. What was the regular price? *(81)* $40

▶ * 7. Seventy-five percent of the citizens voted for Graham. If there were 800 citizens, how many of them did not vote for Graham? *(81)* 200 citizens

▶ 8. **Model** Write equations to solve **a** and **b.** *(77)*

a. Twenty-four is what percent of 30? $24 = W_P \times 30$; 80%

b. Thirty is what percent of 24? $30 = W_P \times 24$; 125%

▶ * 9. **Connect** Use unit multipliers to perform these conversions: *(88)*

a. 2 ft^2 to square inches 288 sq. in.

b. 1 m^3 to cubic centimeters 1,000,000 cm^3

10.

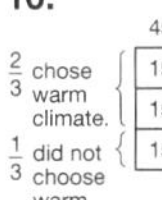

10. Three hundred people said they prefer a vacation in a warm climate. This was $\frac{2}{3}$ of the people surveyed. *(71)*

a. How many people were surveyed? 450

b. How many people surveyed did not choose a warm climate? 150

11. If $x = 4.5$ and $y = 2x + 1$, then y equals what number? *(41)* 10

▶ See Math Conversations in the sidebar.

3 Written Practice

Math Conversations

Discussion opportunities are provided below.

Problem 4 Analyze

"We have examined the interior and exterior angles of several different regular polygons. What pattern do you notice?" Sample: As the number of sides increases, the interior angles become greater and the exterior angles become smaller.

Problem 5 Generalize

"How many different kinds of like terms are in the original expression?" three: x^2, y^2, and xy terms

"How many different kinds of like terms are in the simplified expression?" two: x^2 and xy terms

"Why are there fewer like terms in the simplified expression?" Sample: The y^2 terms added to 0.

Problems 6–8 Model

Work together as a class to resolve problems 6 and 7 using equations, and problem 8 with a ratio box. Then compare the two methods:

"Is one way faster than the other?" Sample: Sometimes I can write an equation very quickly, but other times it takes a lot of thinking.

"Is one way easier than the other?" Sample: Ratio boxes take longer but they are easier to make and fill in.

"Is one way more accurate than the other?" Sample: If you work carefully, both ways are about the same.

"Do you always get the same answer?" Sample: You have to, unless you make a mistake.

Problem 9 Connect

Discuss the need for knowing the equivalents for common measures. Make a list of the ones that seem to be used often in textbook problems. Samples: yards, feet, and inches; meters, centimeters, and millimeters; hours, minutes, and seconds

Errors and Misconceptions

Problem 2

If students were not able to organize the data to find these answers, suggest that they first put the numbers in order from least to greatest.

(continued)

3 Written Practice (Continued)

Math Conversations

Discussion opportunities are provided below.

Problem 19 Classify

Continue with questions about classification. Use the following and then ask students if they can make up some for the class to answer.

"What integers are not whole numbers?" negative integers

"Are counting numbers rational numbers?" yes

Problem 20 Analyze

Guide students to analyze the information and extend the problem.

"Why can you draw the rectangle with only 3 coordinates?" Sample: Once you connect those three points with segments, you can see where the last one goes.

"Suppose you rotate rectangle WXYZ 90° counterclockwise about the origin three more times, where will it be?" Sample: Back in its original position.

"How many degrees will it have moved around?" 360°

"What kind of turn would it have made?" Sample: A full turn.

Errors and Misconceptions

Problem 13

Watch for students who have 144 square inches as their answer. These students have used 1 foot rather than 3 inches as the length of each side.

Problem 20

Some students may need a copy of **Investigation Activity 13** Coordinate Plane or graph paper to answer this problem. Continue to encourage sketching graphs without graph paper.

(continued)

---

12. (36) A coin is tossed three times. One possible outcome is HHH.

a. Write the sample space for the experiment. {HHH, HHT, HTH, HTT, THH, THT, TTH, TTT}

b. What is the probability of getting heads at least twice? $\frac{1}{2}$

▸ **13.** (20) If the perimeter of a square is 1 foot, what is the area of the square in square inches? 9 square inches

14. (48) Complete the table.

Fraction	Decimal	Percent
a. $1\frac{3}{4}$	1.75	**b.** 175%

15. (46) If the sales-tax rate is 6%, what is the total price of a $325 printer including sales tax? $344.50

16. (83) Multiply. Write the product in scientific notation. 4.8×10^{-2}

$$(6 \times 10^4)(8 \times 10^{-7})$$

17. (67, 70) A cereal box 8 inches long, 3 inches wide, and 12 inches tall is shown.

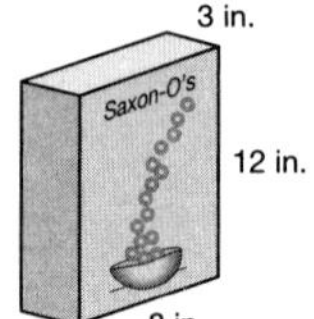

a. What is the volume of the box? 288 in.^{3}

b. What is the surface area of the box? 312 in.^{2}

18. (65, 82) **a.** Find the circumference of the circle at right. 314 mm

b. Find the area of the circle. 7850 mm^2

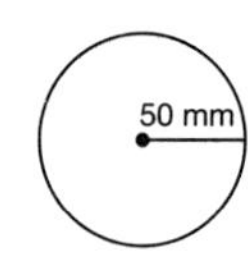

Use 3.14 for π.

▸* **19.** (86) Classify Make a list of the whole numbers that are not counting numbers. 0

20.

▸* **20.** (80) Analyze The coordinates of three vertices of ▭WXYZ are $W(0, 3)$, $X(5, 3)$, and $Y(5, 0)$.

a. Find the coordinates of Z and draw the rectangle. $Z(0, 0)$

b. Rotate ▭WXYZ 90° counterclockwise about the origin, and draw its image ▭W′X′Y′Z′. Write the coordinates of the vertices. $W'(-3, 0)$, $X'(-3, 5)$, $Y'(0, 5)$, $Z'(0, 0)$

21. (60) What mixed number is $\frac{2}{3}$ of 20? $13\frac{1}{3}$

22. (78) On a number line graph $x \le 4$.

−1 0 1 2 3 4 5

For problems **23–25,** solve the equation. Show each step.

23. (Inv. 7) $x + 3.5 = 4.28$ 0.78

24. (90) $2\frac{2}{3}w = 24$ 9

25. (90) $-4y = 1.4$ −0.35

▸ See Math Conversations in the sidebar.

▶ **Generalize** Simplify:

26. $10^1 + 10^0 + 10^{-1}$ (decimal answer) 11.1
(57)

*** 27.** **a.** $(-2x^2)(-3xy)(-y)$ $-6x^3y^2$
(87)
b. $(3x^2y^3)^2$ $9x^4y^6$

28. $\frac{8}{75} - \frac{9}{100}$ $\frac{1}{60}$
(30)

*** 29.** **a.** $(-3) + (-4)(-5) - (-6)$ 23
(85)
b. $\frac{(-2)(-4)}{(-4) - (-2)}$ -4

30. Compare for $x = 10$ and $y = 5$:
(52)

$$x^2 - y^2 \ (=) \ (x + y)(x - y)$$

Early Finishers
Real-World Application

The Fernandez family is creating a semicircle driveway. In order to buy the right amount of concrete and grass, they need to calculate the area of the semicircle below. Use 3.14 for π.

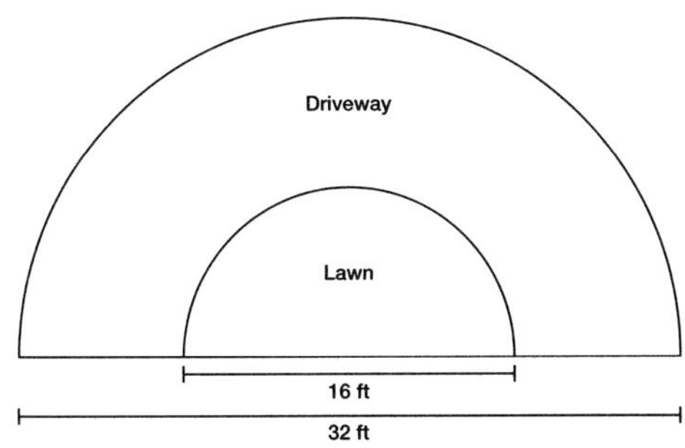

a. What is the area of the driveway? 301.44 ft²

b. Approximately how many tons of asphalt does the Fernandez family need to purchase if one ton covers 22.5 ft². sample: 13.4 tons

c. If each ton of asphalt costs $33, how much will is cost the Fernandez family to pave the driveway? sample: $442.20

▶ See Math Conversations in the sidebar.

3 Written Practice (Continued)

Math Conversations

Discussion opportunities are provided below.

Problems 26–30 Generalize

Have students tell what they simplified first in each expression and explain why they did that. Sample: In 29b, I simplified the numerator first, because it is easier to simplify than the denominator.

Errors and Misconceptions

Problem 29b

Remind students who did not get the correct answer that both the numerator and denominator must be simplified before the ratio can be simplified. They should also note that in the numerator −2 and −4 are factors, but in the denominator they are terms. Therefore, −2 and −4 cannot be canceled.

Looking Forward

Solving equations that have negative coefficients prepares students for:

- **Lesson 93,** solving two-step equations and inequalities.
- **Lesson 101,** translating expressions into equations and solving the equations.
- **Lesson 102,** simplifying and solving equations.
- **Lesson 109,** solving equations with exponents.

Assessment

30–40 minutes *For use after Lesson 90*

Distribute **Cumulative Test 17** to each student. Two versions of the test are available in *Saxon Math Course 2 Course Assessments Book.* Have students complete the **Power-Up Test** first. Allow 10 minutes. Then have students work the 20 numbered items on the **Cumulative Test.** Students may use copies of the answer sheet to record their work. Track individual and class progress with the **Test Analysis** forms.

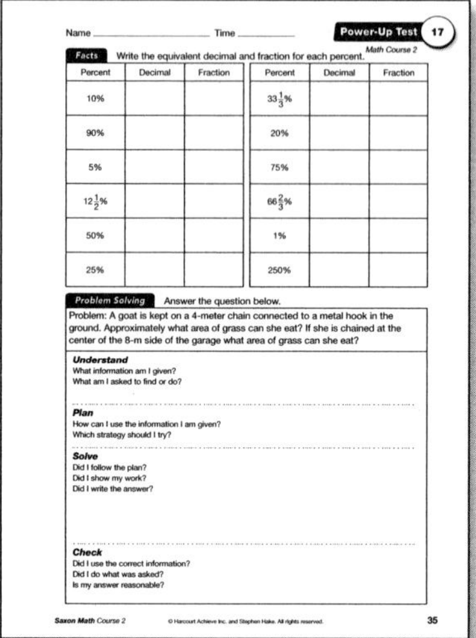
Name ________ Time ________ **Power-Up Test 17**

Math Course 2

Facts Write the equivalent decimal and fraction for each percent.

Percent	Decimal	Fraction	Percent	Decimal	Fraction
10%			$33\frac{1}{3}\%$		
90%			20%		
5%			75%		
$12\frac{1}{2}\%$			$66\frac{2}{3}\%$		
50%			1%		
25%			250%		

Problem Solving Answer the question below.

Problem: A goat is kept on a 4-meter chain connected to a metal hook in the ground. Approximately what area of grass can she eat? If she is chained at the center of the 8-m side of the garage what area of grass can she eat?

Understand
What information am I given?
What am I asked to find or do?

Plan
How can I use the information I am given?
Which strategy should I try?

Solve
Did I follow the plan?
Did I show my work?
Did I write the answer?

Check
Did I use the correct information?
Did I do what was asked?
Is my answer reasonable?

***Saxon Math** Course 2* © Harcourt Achieve Inc. and Stephen Hake. All rights reserved. 35

Power-Up Test 17

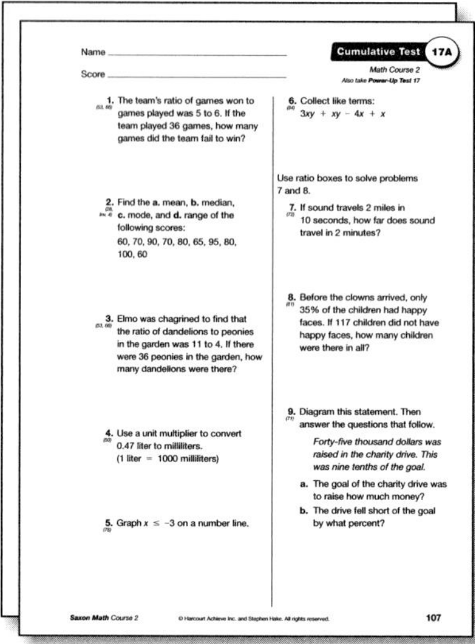
Name ________ **Cumulative Test 17A**

Score ________ *Math Course 2*

*Also take **Power-Up Test 17***

1. The team's ratio of games won to games played was 5 to 6. If the team played 36 games, how many games did the team fail to win?
2. Find the **a.** mean, **b.** median, **c.** mode, and **d.** range of the following scores:
   60, 70, 90, 70, 80, 65, 95, 80, 100, 60
3. Elmo was chagrined to find that the ratio of dandelions to peonies in the garden was 11 to 4. If there were 36 peonies in the garden, how many dandelions were there?
4. Use a unit multiplier to convert 0.47 liter to milliliters. (1 liter = 1000 milliliters)
5. Graph $x \leq -3$ on a number line.
6. Collect like terms:
   $3xy + xy - 4x + x$

Use ratio boxes to solve problems 7 and 8.

7. If sound travels 2 miles in 10 seconds, how far does sound travel in 2 minutes?
8. Before the clowns arrived, only 35% of the children had happy faces. If 117 children did not have happy faces, how many children were there in all?
9. Diagram this statement. Then answer the questions that follow.
   Forty-five thousand dollars was raised in the charity drive. This was nine tenths of the goal.
   a. The goal of the charity drive was to raise how much money?
   b. The drive fell short of the goal by what percent?

***Saxon Math** Course 2* © Harcourt Achieve Inc. and Stephen Hake. All rights reserved. 107

Cumulative Test 17A

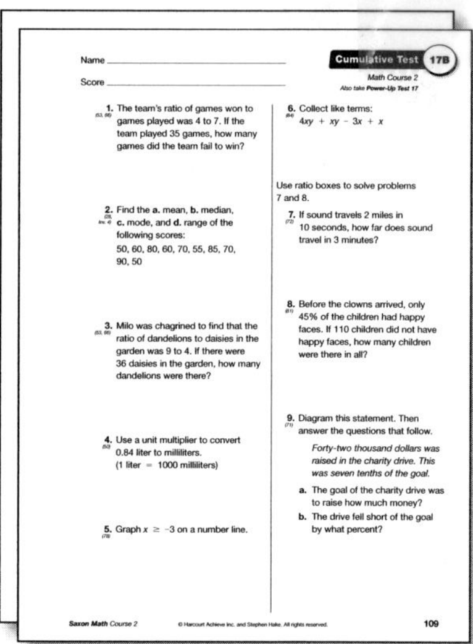
Name ________ **Cumulative Test 17B**

Score ________ *Math Course 2*

*Also take **Power-Up Test 17***

1. The team's ratio of games won to games played was 4 to 7. If the team played 35 games, how many games did the team fail to win?
2. Find the **a.** mean, **b.** median, **c.** mode, and **d.** range of the following scores:
   50, 60, 80, 60, 70, 55, 85, 70, 90, 50
3. Milo was chagrined to find that the ratio of dandelions to daisies in the garden was 9 to 4. If there were 36 daisies in the garden, how many dandelions were there?
4. Use a unit multiplier to convert 0.84 liter to milliliters. (1 liter = 1000 milliliters)
5. Graph $x \geq -3$ on a number line.
6. Collect like terms:
   $4xy + xy - 3x + x$

Use ratio boxes to solve problems 7 and 8.

7. If sound travels 2 miles in 10 seconds, how far does sound travel in 3 minutes?
8. Before the clowns arrived, only 45% of the children had happy faces. If 110 children did not have happy faces, how many children were there in all?
9. Diagram this statement. Then answer the questions that follow.
   Forty-two thousand dollars was raised in the charity drive. This was seven tenths of the goal.
   a. The goal of the charity drive was to raise how much money?
   b. The drive fell short of the goal by what percent?

***Saxon Math** Course 2* © Harcourt Achieve Inc. and Stephen Hake. All rights reserved. 109

Alternative Cumulative Test 17B

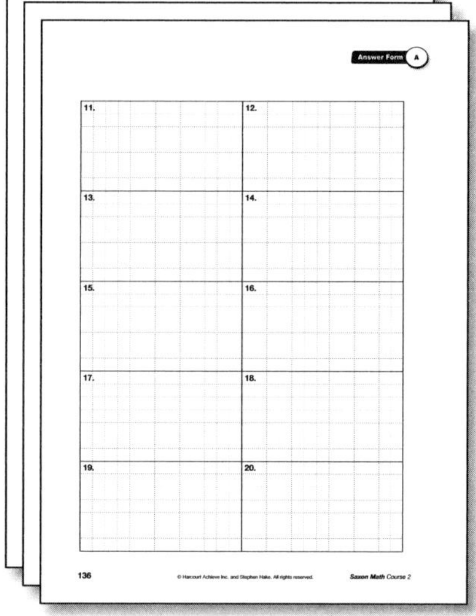
Answer Form A

11. 12. 13. 14. 15. 16. 17. 18. 19. 20.

136 © Harcourt Achieve Inc. and Stephen Hake. All rights reserved. ***Saxon Math** Course 2*

Optional Answer Forms

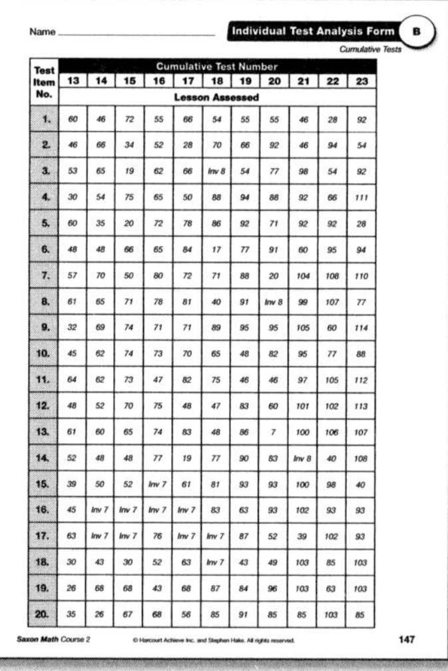
Name ________ **Individual Test Analysis Form B**

Cumulative Tests

Test Item No.	13	14	15	16	17	18	19	20	21	22	23
	Lesson Assessed										
1.	60	46	72	55	66	54	55	55	46	28	92
2.	46	66	34	52	28	70	66	92	46	94	54
3.	53	65	19	62	66	Inv 8	54	77	98	54	92
4.	30	54	75	65	50	88	94	88	92	66	111
5.	60	35	20	72	78	86	92	71	92	92	28
6.	48	48	66	65	84	17	77	91	60	95	94
7.	57	70	50	80	72	71	88	20	104	108	110
8.	61	65	71	78	81	40	91	Inv 8	99	107	77
9.	32	69	74	71	71	89	95	95	105	60	114
10.	45	62	74	73	70	65	48	82	95	77	88
11.	64	62	73	47	82	75	46	46	97	105	112
12.	48	52	70	75	48	47	83	60	101	102	113
13.	61	60	65	74	83	48	86	7	100	106	107
14.	52	48	48	77	19	77	90	83	Inv 8	40	108
15.	39	50	52	Inv 7	61	81	93	93	100	98	40
16.	45	Inv 7	Inv 7	Inv 7	Inv 7	83	63	93	102	93	93
17.	63	Inv 7	Inv 7	76	Inv 7	Inv 7	87	52	39	102	93
18.	30	43	30	52	63	Inv 7	43	49	103	85	103
19.	26	68	68	43	68	87	84	96	103	63	103
20.	35	26	67	68	56	85	91	85	85	103	85

***Saxon Math** Course 2* © Harcourt Achieve Inc. and Stephen Hake. All rights reserved. 147

Individual Test Analysis Form

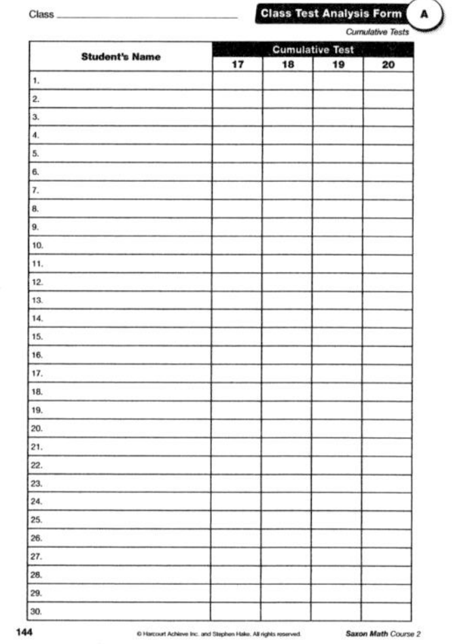
Class ________ **Class Test Analysis Form A**

Cumulative Tests

Student's Name	17	18	19	20
1.				
2.				
3.				
4.				
5.				
6.				
7.				
8.				
9.				
10.				
11.				
12.				
13.				
14.				
15.				
16.				
17.				
18.				
19.				
20.				
21.				
22.				
23.				
24.				
25.				
26.				
27.				
28.				
29.				
30.				

144 © Harcourt Achieve Inc. and Stephen Hake. All rights reserved. ***Saxon Math** Course 2*

Class Test Analysis Form

Reteaching

Students who score below 80% on the assessment may be in need of reteaching. Look for the causes of student mistakes. If errors are conceptual, refer to the *Reteaching Masters* for reteaching.

Customized Benchmark Assessment

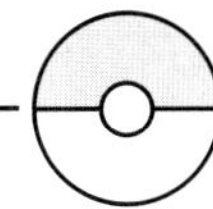

You can develop customized benchmark tests using the Test Generator located on the *Test and Practice Generator CD.*

This chart shows the lesson, the standard, and the test item question that can be found on the *Test and Practice Generator CD.*

LESSON	NEW CONCEPTS	LOCAL STANDARD	TEST ITEM ON CD
81	• Using Proportions to Solve Percent Problems		9.81.1
82	• Area of a Circle		9.82.1
83	• Multiplying Numbers in Scientific Notation		9.83.1
84	• Algebraic Terms		9.84.1
85	• Order of Operations with Positive and Negative Numbers		9.85.1
86	• Number Families		9.86.1
87	• Multiplying Algebraic Terms		9.87.1
88	• Multiple Unit Multipliers		9.88.1
89	• Diagonals		9.89.1
	• Interior Angles		9.89.2
	• Exterior Angles		9.89.3
90	• Mixed-Number Coefficients		9.90.1
	• Negative Coefficients		9.90.2

Using the Test Generator CD

- Develop tests in both English and Spanish.
- Choose from multiple-choice and free-response test items.
- Clone test items to create multiple versions of the same test.
- View and edit test items to make and save your own questions.
- Administer assessments through paper tests or over a school LAN.
- Monitor student progress through a variety of individual and class reports —for both diagnosing and assessing standards mastery.

Performance Task 17

Set Up a Sale

Assign after Lesson 90 and Test 17

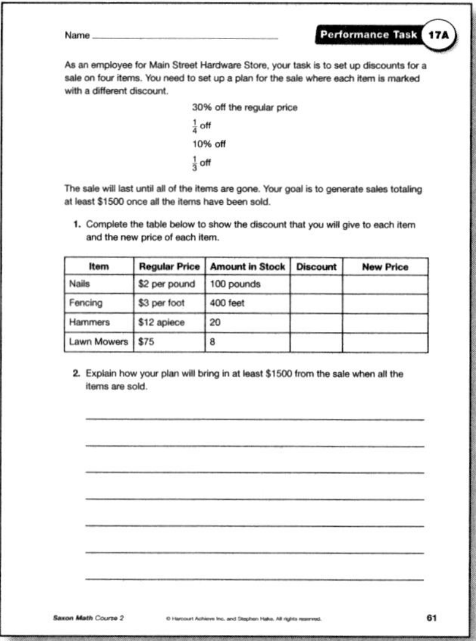

Name ____________ **Performance Task 17A**

As an employee for Main Street Hardware Store, your task is to set up discounts for a sale on four items. You need to set up a plan for the sale where each item is marked with a different discount.

30% off the regular price

$\frac{1}{4}$ off

10% off

$\frac{1}{3}$ off

The sale will last until all of the items are gone. Your goal is to generate sales totaling at least $1500 once all the items have been sold.

1. Complete the table below to show the discount that you will give to each item and the new price of each item.

Item	Regular Price	Amount in Stock	Discount	New Price
Nails	$2 per pound	100 pounds		
Fencing	$3 per foot	400 feet		
Hammers	$12 apiece	20		
Lawn Mowers	$75	8		

2. Explain how your plan will bring in at least $1500 from the sale when all the items are sold.

Saxon Math Course 2 © Harcourt Achieve Inc. and Stephen Hake. All rights reserved. 61

Performance Task 17A

Objectives

- Compute with fractions and percents
- Write equations and ratios to show relationships
- Communicate their ideas through writing

Materials

Performance Tasks 17A and **17B**

Preparation

Make copies of **Performance Tasks 17A** and **17B.** (One each per student.)

Time Requirement

about 30 minutes; Begin in class and finish at home.

Task

Explain to students that for this task they will be employees of the Main Street Hardware Store. They will set up a plan where they establish the sale price of several items. The sale prices must result in $1500 in sales when all the items are sold. They will be required to explain their plan and answer questions about it. Point out that all of the information students need is on **Performance Tasks 17A** and **17B.**

Criteria for Evidence of Learning

- Develops a realistic plan with sale prices that result in a sale income of $1500.
- Completes the table with all necessary information.
- Communicates ideas clearly through writing.

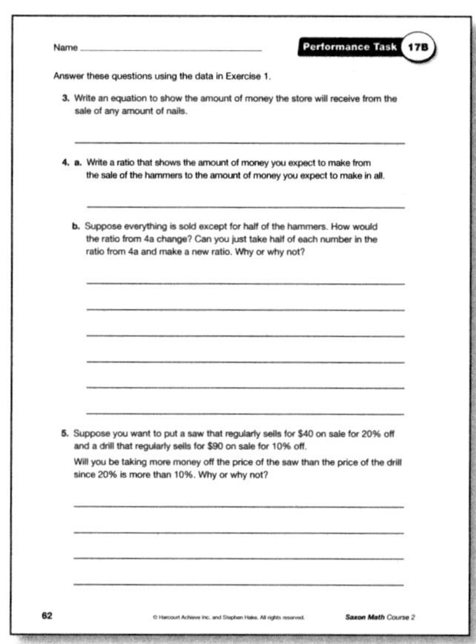

Name ____________ **Performance Task 17B**

Answer these questions using the data in Exercise 1.

3. Write an equation to show the amount of money the store will receive from the sale of any amount of nails.

4. a. Write a ratio that shows the amount of money you expect to make from the sale of the hammers to the amount of money you expect to make in all.

   b. Suppose everything is sold except for half of the hammers. How would the ratio from 4a change? Can you just take half of each number in the ratio from 4a and make a new ratio. Why or why not?

5. Suppose you want to put a saw that regularly sells for $40 on sale for 20% off and a drill that regularly sells for $90 on sale for 10% off.
   Will you be taking more money off the price of the saw than the price of the drill since 20% is more than 10%. Why or why not?

62 © Harcourt Achieve Inc. and Stephen Hake. All rights reserved. Saxon Math Course 2

Performance Task 17B

Meeting Standards

National Council of Teachers of Mathematics (NCTM)

Numbers and Operations

NO.1a Work flexibly with fractions, decimals, and percents to solve problems

NO.1d Understand and use ratios and proportions to represent quantitative relationships

NO.3a Select appropriate methods and tools for computing with fractions and decimals from among mental computation, estimation, calculators or computers, and paper and pencil, depending on the situation, and apply the selected methods

Problem Solving

PS.1b Solve problems that arise in mathematics and in other contexts

PS.1c Apply and adapt a variety of appropriate strategies to solve problems

Communication

CM.3a Organize and consolidate their mathematical thinking through communication

CM.3d Use the language of mathematics to express mathematical ideas precisely

Focus on
• Graphing Functions

Objectives
- Write an equation for a direct variation function.
- Create a function table for a direct variation function and graph it on a coordinate plane.
- Identify real-world situations that can be described by a direct variation function.
- Write an equation for an inverse variation function.
- Create a function table for an inverse variation function and graph it on a coordinate plane.

Lesson Preparation

Materials
- **Investigation Activity 13** (in *Instructional Masters*)

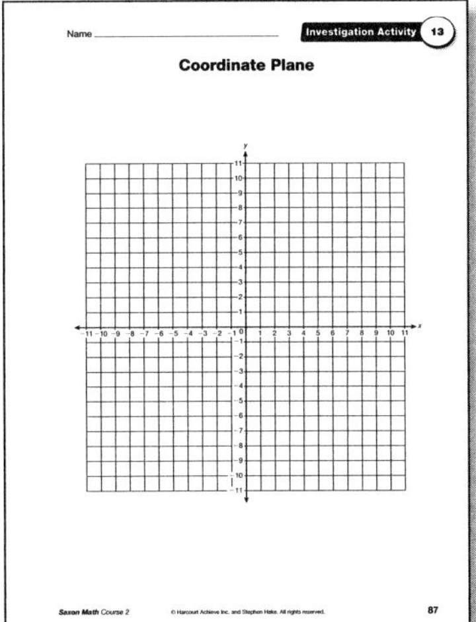
Investigation Activity 13

Math Language

New	Maintain	
direct variation	constant	independent variable
direct proportion	dependent variable	variable
inverse variation		

Technology Resources

Student eBook Complete student textbook in electronic format.

Resources and Planner CD Assessment, reteaching, and instructional masters, plus a pacing calendar with standards.

Test and Practice Generator CD Create additional practice sheets and custom-made tests.

www.SaxonPublishers.com Visit for more student activities and planning materials.

Inclusion

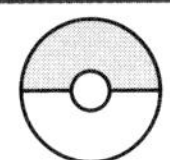

Adaptations CD Adapted lessons, investigations, practice and assessments.

Meeting Standards

National Council of Teachers of Mathematics (NCTM)

Numbers and Operations

NO.1d Understand and use ratios and proportions to represent quantitative relationships

Algebra

AL.1a Represent, analyze, and generalize a variety of patterns with tables, graphs, words, and, when possible, symbolic rules

AL.1c Identify functions as linear or nonlinear and contrast their properties from tables, graphs, or equations

AL.3a Model and solve contextualized problems using various representations, such as graphs, tables, and equations

Geometry

GM.1b Understand relationships among the angles, side lengths, perimeters, areas, and volumes of similar objects

Representation

RE.5a Create and use representations to organize, record, and communicate mathematical ideas

INVESTIGATION 9

Begin this lesson by describing, or encouraging students to describe, a variety of real-world situations that contain functions. Ask students to tell the rule for each situation.

For example:

- A worker is paid $200 for 20 hours of work.
  Pay = $10 per hour
- A cyclist travels 24 miles in 3 hours.
  Rate = 8 miles per hour
- A customer paid $2.60 for 4 apples.
  Price = $0.65 per apple.

Explain to students that in this lesson they will learn to graph functions like these. They will use their graphs to compare two quantities and show a variety of values for the function.

Instruction

Provide students with several copies of **Investigation Activity 13** Coordinate Plane or sheets of graph paper to complete this activity.

As you graph the function $y = 2x$ on an overhead projector,

- Have students follow along on their own grids.
- Point out that the coordinates listed in the table are values for x and y that make the function rule a true statement (satisfy the equation).
- Explain that the first number in the coordinates is always the x value; the second is always the y value.

(continued)

INVESTIGATION 9

Focus on

• Graphing Functions

As we have seen, functions can be displayed as graphs on a coordinate plane. Let's review what we learned. To graph a function, we use each (x, y) pair of numbers as coordinates of a point on the plane.

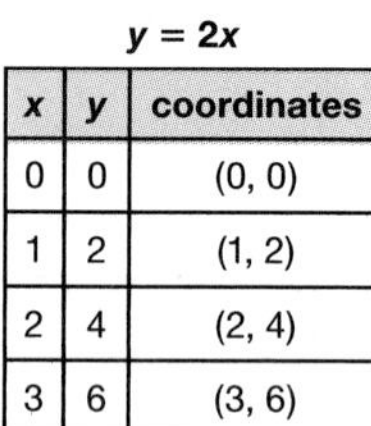

y = 2x

x	y	coordinates
0	0	(0, 0)
1	2	(1, 2)
2	4	(2, 4)
3	6	(3, 6)

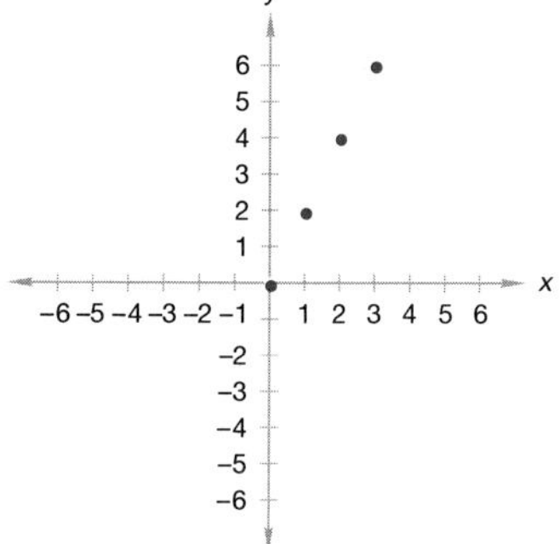

Visit www.SaxonPublishers.com/ActivitiesC2 *for a graphing calculator activity.*

On the coordinate plane above, we graphed four pairs of numbers that satisfy the equation of the function. Although the table lists only four pairs of numbers for the function, the graph of the function includes many other pairs of numbers that satisfy the equation. By extending a line through and beyond the graphed points, we graph all possible pairs of numbers that satisfy the equation. Each point on the graphed line below represents a pair of numbers that satisfies the equation of the function $y = 2x$.

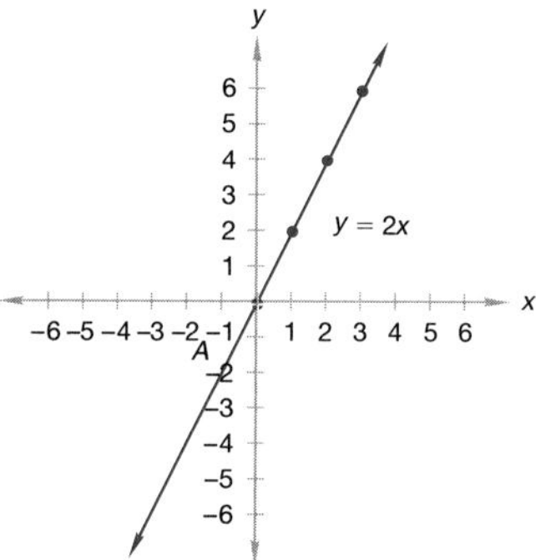

Math Background

"What information is needed in order to graph a linear function?"

A linear function requires only two coordinate pairs in order to be graphed. Consider the equation $y = x + 1$. By substituting two different values for x, preferably ones that are not too close, the function can be graphed.

If $x = 0$, $y = 1$

If $x = 3$, $y = 4$

Alternately, if all we are given two coordinate points, we can graph the function and find its rule.

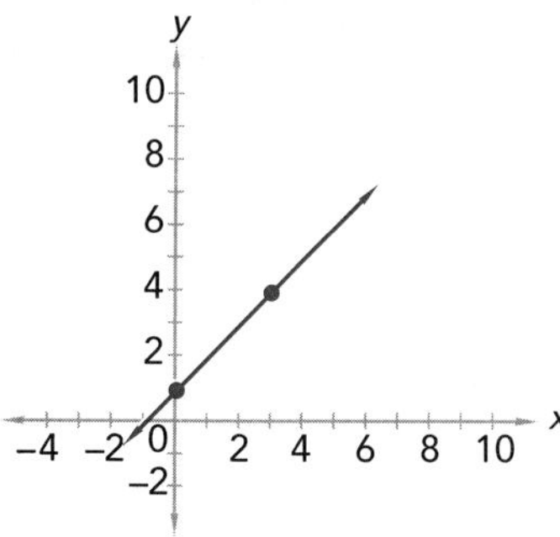

Thinking Skill

Explain

Why doesn't the graph need to indicate units? Sample: Regardless of the units, this same formula is used to find the perimeter of a square.

1. The endpoint of the ray is (0, 0). If the graph were a line, there would be negative numbers for the length of the side and for the perimeter. Lengths cannot be negative, so the graph cannot be a line.

2. Doubling the side lengths doubles the perimeter.

Note: This is true of any polygon.

3. $p = 3s$

s	p
1	3
2	6
3	9

p = perimeter of triangle
s = length of side

Perimeter of an Equilateral Triangle

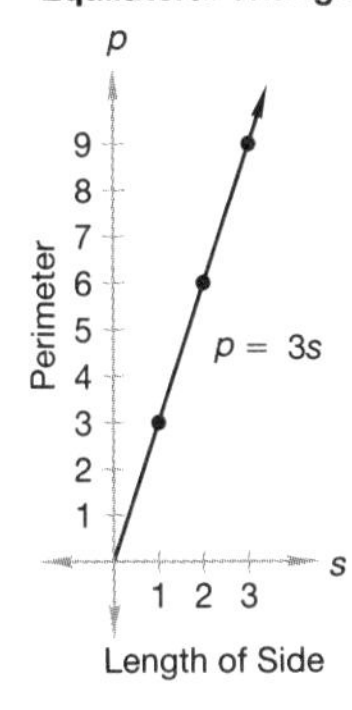

Below we graph the relationship between the side-length and perimeter of a square. In the equation we use s for the length of a side and p for the perimeter. We only graph the numerical relationship of the measures, so we do not designate units. It is assumed that the unit used to measure the length of the side is also used to measure the perimeter.

$p = 4s$

s	p
1	4
2	8
3	12

Perimeter (*p*) of a Square with Side Length *s*

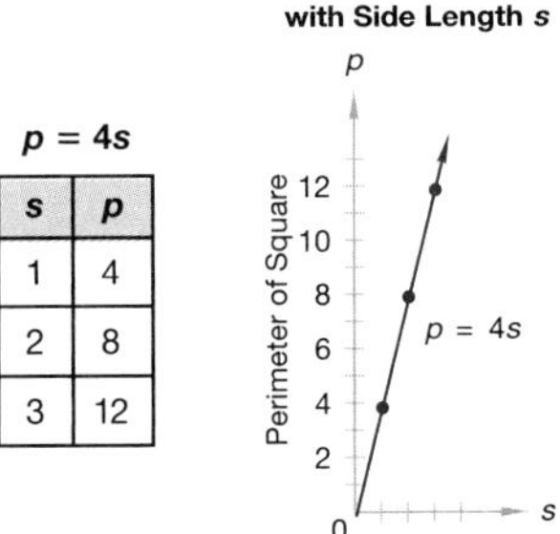

Notice that the x- and y-axes are renamed s and p for this function.

1. The graph of this function is a ray. What are the coordinates of the endpoint of the ray? Why is the graph of this function a ray and not a line?

▸ 2. *Analyze* Notice that the graph of the function $p = 4s$ is straight and not curved. Imagine two squares in which the side lengths of the larger square are twice the side lengths of the smaller square. Draw the two squares and find the perimeter of each. What effect does doubling the side length of a square have on the perimeter?

▸ 3. *Represent* The relationship between the length of a side of an equilateral triangle and the perimeter of the triangle is a function that can be graphed. Write an equation for the function using s for the length of a side and p for the perimeter. Next make a table of (s, p) pairs for side lengths 1, 2, and 3. Then draw a rectangular coordinate system with an s-axis and a p-axis, and graph the function.

Rates are functions that can be graphed. Many rates involve time as one of the variables. Speed, for example, is a function of distance and time. Suppose Sam enters a walk-a-thon and walks at a steady rate of 3 miles per hour. The distance (d) in miles that Sam travels is a function of the number of hours (h) that Sam walks. This relationship is expressed in the following equation:

$$d = 3h$$

▸ See Math Conversations in the sidebar.

Instruction

Ask students the following question.

"Why is the graph shown in the first quadrant only?" Both values, the perimeter and side length, must be positive to be in quadrant I. The first quadrant is the only quadrant in which both coordinates are positive.

Explain that the x- and y-axes can be renamed with any letters. However, it is important to assign the renamed variables to the correct axes:

- the x-axis is considered the "input" axis, or the independent variable of the function. It is always a horizontal axis.
- the y-axis is considered the "output" axis, or the dependent variable of the function. It is always the vertical axis.

"Why is the length of the sides of the square, s, assigned to the x-axis and the perimeter, p, assigned to the y-axis?" The perimeter of the square depends upon the length of the side. So, the perimeter is assigned to the vertical axis and the side length is assigned to the horizontal axis.

Math Conversations

Discussion opportunities are provided below.

Problem 2 Analyze

Once students have answered the question, ask them whether there is a generalization they can make for how multiplying the side lengths affects the measure of the perimeter. The perimeter of a square is multiplied by the same factor by which the side lengths are multiplied.

Problem 3 Represent

Students will need graph paper or a copy of **Investigation Activity 13** Coordinate Plane to complete this problem. You might wish to have a student work at the overhead with grid paper and explain how to set up the graph.

(continued)

Instruction

Explain to students that a *rate* is a ratio that compares two measures.

"In the table, which is the independent variable and which is the dependent variable?" The independent variable is time, and the dependent variable is distance.

Math Conversations

Discussion opportunities are provided below.

Problem 4 Represent

Remind students to put time on the *x*-axis and distance on the *y*-axis. Ask students if they need to write all the numbers on the axes. no; but you must leave spaces for all the numbers so the line has the appropriate points on it.

Problem 7 Explain

Have students explain why the graph is only in the first quadrant. because Sam could not have jogged a negative distance or time

(continued)

The table below shows how far Sam walks in 1, 2, and 3 hours.

d* = 3*h

h	*d*
1	3
2	6
3	9

d = distance in miles
h = time in hours

A graph of the function shows how far Sam walks in any number of hours, including fractions of hours.

Thinking Skill
Explain
Could you have divided each hour into sixths? Why or why not? Sample: Yes. Each division would represent 10 minutes. Any factor of 60 could be used to evenly divide the spaces between the hours.

Distance Sam Walks at 3 mph

d
Distance in Miles
9 8 7 6 5 4 3 2 1 0
d = 3h
1 2 3 4 h
Time in Hours

Notice that we labeled both axes of the graph. Also notice that we adjusted the scale of the graph so that each tick mark on the horizontal scale represents one fourth of an hour (15 minutes).

▶ 4. *Represent* Suppose Sam entered a jog-a-thon and was able to jog at a steady pace of 6 miles per hour for 2 hours. Following the pattern described for the walk-a-thon, write an equation for a 6-mile-per-hour rate, and make a table that shows how far Sam had jogged after 1 hour and how far he had jogged after 2 hours. Then draw a graph of the function and label each axis. Let every tick mark on the time axis represent 10 minutes.

4. ***d* = 6*h***

h	*d*
1	6
2	12

d = distance in miles
h = time in hours

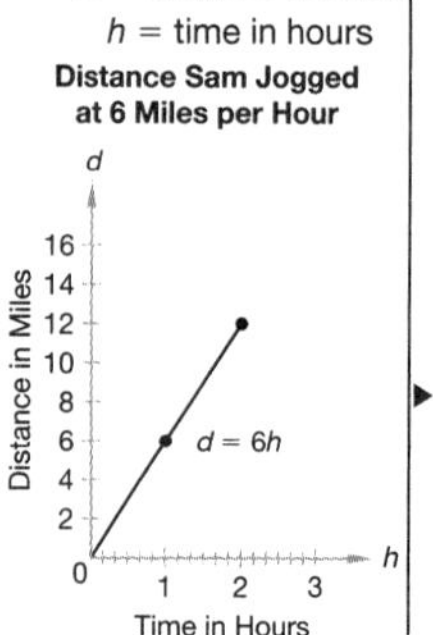

5. Refer to the graph drawn in problem 4 to find the distance Sam had jogged in 40 minutes. 4 miles

6. Refer to the graph drawn in problem 4 to find how long it took Sam to jog 9 miles. $1\frac{1}{2}$ hours

▶ 7. *Explain* Why is the graph of the distance Sam jogged a segment and not a ray? Sam did not continue jogging forever. He stopped after 2 hours.

626 ***Saxon*** *Math Course 2*

▶ See Math Conversations in the sidebar.

The functions we have considered in this investigation so far are examples of direct variation. **Direct variation** is a relationship between two variables in which a change in one variable results in a proportional change in the other variable. In most real-world applications, if one variable increases, the other increases, or if one variable decreases the other decreases. For example, if Gina is paid by the hour, then the more hours she works, the more she is paid. If she works fewer hours, her total pay decreases. We say that Gina's total pay is **directly proportional** to the number of hours she works.

This means we can form a proportion with two pairs of numbers that follow the rule of the function. A square with a side length of 3 has a perimeter of 12. A square with a side length of 5 has a perimeter of 20. These pairs of numbers form a proportion because the ratios are equal to each other.

Side length:	3	5
Perimeter:	12	20

8. See student work. Sample: $\frac{2}{10} = \frac{3}{15}$, $2 \cdot 15 = 3 \cdot 10$, $30 = 30$. Yes, the cross products are equal.

▶ **8.** *Verify* This table shows the number of dollars Gina earns working a given number of hours. Select two pairs of numbers from the table and use them to write a proportion. Are the cross products of the proportion equal?

Hours	Dollars
1	5
2	10
3	15
4	20

An equation with variables that are directly proportional often has this form.

$$y = kx$$

The letter k refers to a constant, meaning a number that does not change. For example, the perimeter and side length of a square are directly proportional and the formula that relates them has this form.

$$p = 4s \text{ (The constant is 4.)}$$

Here are some more examples of direct variation and their equations. Notice that as one variable increases, the other also increases.

- The number of pounds (p) of apples purchased and the cost (c) ($c = kp$)
- The time (t) spent walking and the distance (d) walked ($d = kt$)

9. Three of the choices can be written in the form $y = kx$. However, choice **C** would be $k = xy$. Thus, **C** is not an example of direct variation.

▶ **9.** *Classify* Which of the following is not an example of direct variation?

A The length of the side of a regular hexagon and the perimeter of the hexagon.

B The number of books in a stack and the height of the stack.

C The speed at which you travel to school and the time it takes to get to school.

D The length of a segment in inches and its length in centimeters.

▶ See Math Conversations in the sidebar.

Instruction

When discussing direct proportions, it may be helpful to compare equal ratios with equivalent fractions. For example, when the ratios $\frac{3}{12}$ and $\frac{5}{20}$ are simplified, both ratios are equal to $\frac{1}{4}$.

Math Conversations

Discussion opportunities are provided below.

Problem 8 Verify

Help the students notice that they can work across the table or they can work down.

$$\frac{\text{hours}}{\text{hours}}\ \frac{1}{2} = \frac{5}{10}\ \frac{\text{dollars}}{\text{dollars}}$$

$$\frac{\text{hours}}{\text{dollars}}\ \frac{2}{10} = \frac{4}{20}\ \frac{\text{hours}}{\text{dollars}}$$

If necessary, review with students how to calculate cross products.

For $\frac{2}{10}$ and $\frac{4}{20}$:

$$\frac{2}{10} \times \frac{4}{20}$$
$$2 \cdot 20 = 40$$
$$10 \cdot 4 = 40$$
$$\frac{2}{10} = \frac{4}{20}$$

Problem 9 Classify

Point out that a constant is the opposite of a variable in that it never changes. Make sure students understand that "k" is a symbol often used to mean *constant.*

This diagram might help students visualize the relationships of the variables.

constant

dependent variable → $y = kx$ ← independent variable

(continued)

Math Conversations

Discussion opportunities are provided below.

Problem 10 Classify

Some students may have to be reminded that the origin is the point (0, 0).

Ask students to explain why graphs B, C, and D are not examples of direct variation. Graph B does not go through the origin. Graph C is not a straight line. Graph D has a negative slope.

Problem 11 Connect

"What is the independent variable? The dependent variable?" The number of minutes is the independent variable. The number of revolutions is the dependent variable.

"Why is the graph a line segment?" The ride only goes from 0 to 4 minutes.

Instruction

Provide students with the following example for inverse variation to help introduce this portion of the lesson. Draw the following table on the board and ask:

"What are some possible widths of a rectangle with an area of 24 square units?"

l	1	2	3	4	6	8	12	24
w	24	12	8	6	4	3	2	1

"What do you notice about the relationship between the width and length?" As the length increases, the width decreases.

"What about the area?" The area remains constant.

(continued)

The graph of a function with direct variation is a straight line (or ray or segment or aligned points) that includes the origin.

10. Graph **A** is an example of direct variation because the graph of the function is a straight line and includes the origin.

▶ **10.** Classify Which graphed function below is an example of direct variation? Explain your choice.

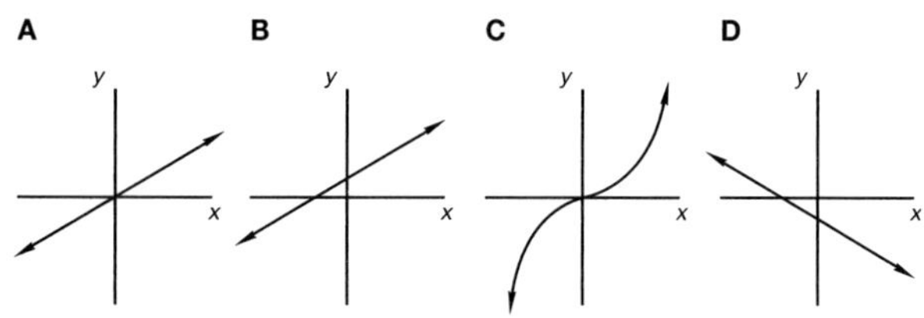

11. $r = 3m$

m	*r*
1	3
2	6
3	9
4	12

▶ **11.** The large carousel at the fair makes three revolutions per minute and operates for four minutes at a time. Write an equation and create a function table that relates the input, minutes (*m*), to the output, revolutions (*r*). Then plot the numbers on a coordinate plane and draw a segment for the length of a ride.

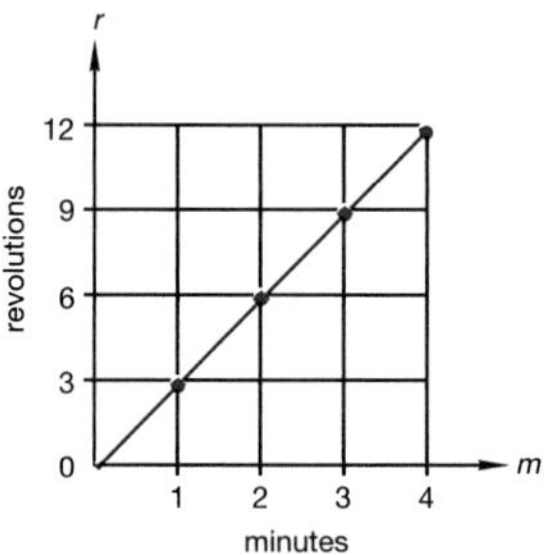

In summary, there are two requirements for a function to be a direct proportion.

- The pair (0, 0) satisfies the function. (The graph of the function includes the origin.)
- The number pairs that satisfy the function, other than (0, 0), form a constant ratio, so any two pairs form a proportion. (The graph of the function is a line or aligned points.)

Now we will consider inverse variation. **Inverse variation** is a relationship between two variables in which a change in one variable results in an inversely proportional change in the other variable. For instance, if one variable doubles (is multiplied by 2), then the other variable is halved (multiplied by the reciprocal of 2).

628 **Saxon** *Math Course 2*

▶ See Math Conversations in the sidebar.

Choice C in problem 9 is an example of inverse variation. The variables are the speed or rate (r) of the trip and the time (t) for the trip. The product of the two variables is the distance (d) to school, which does not change. So as the speed increases, the time required to complete the trip decreases proportionately. We can express this relationship with this equation.

$$rt = d$$

In this inverse variation equation, the variables are multiplied and the product is constant. Here is another example. If a trip takes Adam 2 hours traveling at 60 miles per hour, then the trip would take Adam twice as long, 4 hours, if he traveled at half the speed, 30 miles per hour. Notice that the products of these two descriptions are equal to each other. Both equal 120 miles.

$$2 \text{ hr} \times 60 \text{ mph} = 4 \text{ hr} \times 30 \text{ mph}$$

Since the products are equal for any two pairs of numbers that satisfy the relationship, we can solve inverse proportion problems by writing an equation with two products equal to each other. Thus, to find how long it would take Adam to make the trip at 40 mph, we can write and solve this equation.

$$2 \text{ hr} \times 60 \text{ mph} = t \times 40 \text{ mph}$$

13.

120 mile trip

Rate (mph)	Time (hr)
60	2
40	3
30	4
20	6

12. What is the solution to the equation? 3 hr

▸ **13.** Represent Make a function table that shows Adam's rate in miles per hour and his time in hours to make the 120 mile trip at these speeds: 60 mph, 40 mph, 30 mph, and 20 mph.

14. Multiply each pair of numbers in the table. What do you find about the products? The products are equal.

15.

60, 50, 40, 30, 20, 10
1 2 3 4 5 6
Time (hr)
y
$xy = 6$
x

▸ **15.** Represent Graph the pairs of numbers in the table from problem **13.** Notice that the points are not aligned and that 0, 0 is not a solution pair for the function.

The graph of an inverse proportion is a curve and not a line. The graph does not include the origin and does not intercept an axis. The graph may include points in the third quadrant as we see in the graph of $xy = 6$.

"Work" problems also provide examples of functions that involve measures that are products. Consider the following "work" problem.

Rafi and one friend can roof the whole house in 24 hours. How many hours would it take Rafi and two friends to roof the whole house?

"Work" problems often involve the measures "person-hours" or "person-days." A person-hour is one person working one hour. Projects can be estimated to require a certain number of person-hours of labor. To find the number of person-hours it takes to complete a job, we multiply the number of people working times the number of hours they work.

▸ See Math Conversations in the sidebar.

Math Conversations

Discussion opportunities are provided below.

Instruction

Continue the discussion of the inverse variation model of rectangle dimensions from the previous page. Graph the coordinate pairs listed in the table.

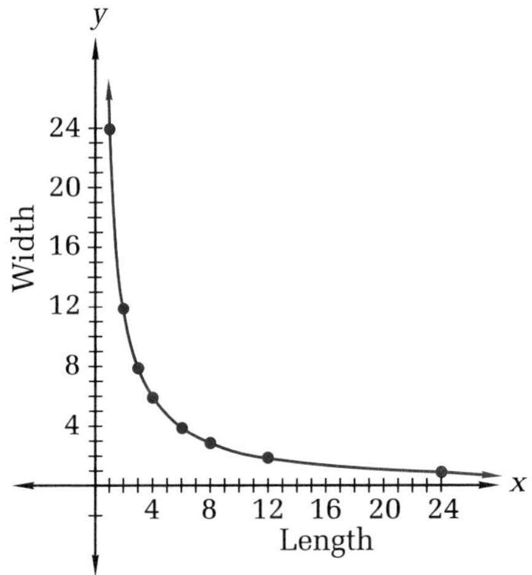

Discuss with students the shape of the graph and contrast it with the direct variation graph.

Problem 13 Represent

Ask a student volunteer to draw the function table on the board.

Problem 15 Represent

First ask students why the graph in problem **15** does not include the coordinates (0, 0). (0, 0) would indicate no time and no rate, which does not fit with the situation described in the problem.

Then suggest that students think about the rules of multiplication with positive and negative numbers to help answer the question.

(continued)

Teacher Tip

The **inverse variation** situations described in the lesson can be complex and difficult for many students to understand. Place students in pairs, or small groups, to discuss some of the situations presented in the lesson. Help students understand why the graph of an inverse proportion is a curve, and how the first and third quadrants relate.

Instruction

Ask students what the constant is in a "work" problem. the number of person-hours required to do the job

Ask students to explain how they can check their work. Replace the t in the equation with 16. The equation should remain balanced.

Math Conversations

Discussion opportunities are provided below.

Problem 17 Formulate

Extend the Problem

Have students make a table to show how many workers are needed to harvest the field in 2, 4, 6, and 8 days.

Days	2	4	6	8
Workers	12	6	4	3

Problem 18 Explain

The goal in process is to come up with a pair of numbers easily multiplied, perhaps including a multiple of 10. Suggest that students study the numbers to look for one that can be doubled or halved to result in a multiple of 10.

In the example on the previous page, the job is "to roof the whole house." The labor required to do the job is 2 people for 24 hours which is 48 person-hours. With three people working, the job is still 48 person-hours, but because more people are working, less time is needed. To solve the problem we can begin by writing an equation that shows the two products are equal.

person-hours = person-hours

(2 people) (24 hours) = (3 people) (t hours)

16. What is the solution to the equation? 16 hours

▶ **17.** Formulate Solve the following "work" problem by writing and solving an equation that shows two products are equal.

If three people can harvest the field in 8 days, how many people are needed to harvest the field in two days?
(3 people) (8 days) = (n people) (2 days); 12 people

We can use inverse variation to help us multiply numbers mentally. If we need to find the product of two numbers, we can decrease one factor and increase the other factor proportionately.

$$24 \times 15 = p$$

Instead of multiplying 24 and 15, we can first mentally halve 24 and double 15. This gives us 12 and 30 as factors which we can mentally multiply to find the product, 360.

▶ **18.** Explain Mentally find the product of 25 and 18 and explain how you found the product. double 25 and halve 18. The result is 50 and 9, the product of which is 450.

Here we summarize the characteristics of inverse variation.

- As one variable changes, the other variable changes inversely.
- Zero is not a solution for either variable of the function. (The graph does not include the origin or points on either axis.)
- The products of the number pairs that satisfy the function are equal to each other.

▶ See Math Conversations in the sidebar.

Looking Forward

Graphing functions on the coordinate plane prepares students for:

- **Lesson 107,** finding the slope of a line using the graph of a function.
- **Lesson 116,** transforming an equation to slope-intercept form and graphing equations using the slope and the y-intercept.
- **Lesson 120,** graphing nonlinear equations on the coordinate plane.

Section 10 Overview

Lessons 91–100, Investigation 10

Lesson Planner

LESSON	NEW CONCEPTS	MATERIALS	RESOURCES
91	• Evaluations with Positive and Negative Numbers		Power Up S Investigation Activity 13
92	• Percent of Change	Newspapers, magazines	Power Up T Investigation Activity 13
93	• Two-Step Equations and Inequalities	Graph paper, sticky notes	Power Up T Investigation Activity 13
94	• Probability of Dependent Events	Graph paper, calculators, color tiles, bag, playing cards or index cards	Power Up S Investigation Activity 13
95	• Volume of a Right Solid	Graph paper	Power Up T Investigation Activity 13
96	• Estimating Angle Measures • Distributive Property with Algebraic Terms	Protractors, color tiles, oak tag, paper fasteners	Power Up U Lesson Activity 22 Transparency
97	• Similar Triangles • Indirect Measure	Metersticks, rulers and/or tape measures, protractors, string	Power Up T
98	• Scale • Scale Factor	Graph paper, protractors, yardstick, color cubes, maps, string, index cards	Power Up U Investigation Activity 13
99	• Pythagorean Theorem	Inch and metric rulers, color tiles	Power Up T
100	• Estimating Square Roots • Irrational Numbers	Metric rulers, calculators, index cards	Power Up U Investigation Activity 13
Inv. 10	• Using a Compass and a Straightedge, Part 2	Metric rulers, compasses, protractors, tagboard, string, chalk	

Lesson Highlights

Lessons 91–100, Investigation 10

Problem Solving

Strategies

- **Find a Pattern** Lesson 91
- **Make It Simpler** Lesson 99
- **Make an Organized List** Lesson 94
- **Use Logical Reasoning** Lessons 93, 95, 96, 97, 100
- **Draw a Diagram** Lessons 98, 100
- **Write an Equation** Lessons 92, 96, 97, 99
- **Guess and Check** Lesson 94
- **Work Backwards** Lesson 95

Real-World Applications

pp. 632, 633, 635, 637–641, 645, 646, 648–651, 655–660, 664, 665, 667, 670–675, 677, 679, 682, 683, 685, 686, 690, 691, 696

4-Step Process

Teacher Edition Lessons 91–100 (Power-Up Discussions)

Communication

Discuss

pp. 632, 643, 671–673, 678, 686, 702

Explain

pp. 632, 644, 648, 649, 658, 664, 669, 671, 678, 682, 690, 691, 694, 696, 700

Connections

Math and Other Subjects

Math and Art pp. 648, 679, 682, 697
Math and Science pp. 674, 690, 696
Math and Sports pp. 635, 639
Math and Social Studies p. 639

Math to Math

- **Problem Solving and Measurement** Lessons 91–100, Inv. 10
- **Algebra and Problem Solving** Lessons 91–100
- **Fractions, Decimals, Percents, and Problem Solving** Lessons 91–100
- **Fractions and Measurement** Lessons 96, 98, 100
- **Measurement and Geometry** Lessons 91–100, Inv. 10
- **Algebra, Measurement, and Geometry** Lessons 98–100
- **Probability and Statistics** Lessons 92–100

Representation

Manipulatives/Hands On

pp. 636, 640, 649, 650, 658, 661, 662, 664, 670, 673, 679–684, 687, 688, 694, 695, 699, 700–703

Model

pp. 638, 673, 675, 676, 682, 690, 691, 696, 698

Represent

pp. 634, 640, 645, 647, 652, 658, 666, 684

Formulate an Equation

pp. 633, 647, 655, 674

Technology

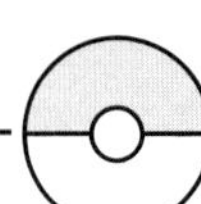

Student Resources

- **eBook**
- **Calculator** Lessons 91, 94, 96, 100
- **Online Resources** at **www.SaxonPublishers.com/ActivitiesC2**
  - **Graphing Calculator Activity** Lesson 100
  - **Real-World Investigation 5** after Lesson 98
  - **Online Activities**
  - **Math Enrichment Problems**
  - **Math Stumpers**

Teacher Resources

- **Resources and Planner CD**
- **Adaptations CD** Lessons 91–100
- **Test & Practice Generator CD**
- **eGradebook**
- **Answer Key CD**

Students continue to use the ratio box to solve ratio applications. They begin to evaluate expressions with rational numbers. This section closes as students learn about the Pythagorean Theorem and draw constructions using a compass and straightedge.

Problem Solving and Proportional Thinking

The graphic organizer is used for probability, similarity, and scale problems.

Students learn to use proportions to solve percent of change problems in Lesson 92. Students use the probability ratio in Lesson 94 to calculate compound probabilities of events that are not independent. Similar triangles have side lengths that are proportional, and in Lesson 97 students learn to use similar triangles to perform indirect measures. Students use proportions to solve problems related to scale models in Lesson 98.

Problem Solving and Algebraic Thinking

Evaluating expressions is extended to both positive and negative rational numbers.

In algebra students evaluate algebraic expressions with positive and negative numbers in Lesson 91. They solve two-step equations and inequalities in Lesson 93 and apply the Distributive Property to algebraic expressions in Lesson 96.

Geometry and Measurement

Estimation is a key topic in geometry and measurement.

Geometry is emphasized in Lessons 95–97 as students calculate volumes, estimate angle measures, and work with similar triangles. In Lesson 99 students are introduced to the Pythagorean Theorem, which leads naturally to the topics of Lesson 100, irrational numbers and estimating square roots. In Investigation 10 students pick up the compass and straight edge again for the second investigation on geometric construction.

Assessment

A variety of weekly assessment tools are provided.

After Lesson 95:
- Power-Up Test 18
- Cumulative Test 18
- Performance Activity 18

After Lesson 100:
- Power-Up Test 19
- Cumulative Test 19
- Customized Benchmark Test
- Performance Task 19

Content Trace

Lessons 91–100, Investigation 10

LESSON	NEW CONCEPTS	PRACTICED	ASSESSED
91	• Evaluations with Positive and Negative Numbers	Lessons 91, 92, 93, 94, 95, 96, 99, 101, 102, 105, 109, 118, 120	Tests 19, 20
92	• Percent of Change	Lessons 92, 93, 94, 95, 96, 97, 98, 99, 100, 101, 102, 103, 105, 106, 107, 108, 109, 110, 111, 112, 113, 114, 115, 116, 117, 118, 119, 120	Tests 19, 20, 21, 22, 23
93	• Two-Step Equations and Inequalities	Lessons 93, 94, 95, 96, 97, 98, 99, 100, 101, 103, 104, 106, 110, 112, 113, 114, 115, 117, 118, 119, 120	Tests 19, 20, 22, 23
94	• Probability of Dependent Events	Lessons 94, 95, 96, 97, 98, 100, 101, 104, 105, 107, 108, 109, 111, 113	Tests 19, 20, 22, 23
95	• Volume of a Right Solid	Lessons 95, 96, 97, 99, 100, 103, 105, 106, 107, 108, 109, 110, 111, 114, 115, 116	Tests 19, 20, 21, 22
96	• Estimating Angle Measures	Lessons 96, 98, 103, 104, 118, 119	Test 20
	• Distributive Property with Algebraic Terms	Lessons 96, 97, 99, 100, 101, 105, 106, 107, 110, 111, 116, 117, 118, 119, 120	Test 20
97	• Similar Triangles	Lessons 97, 98, 99, 103, 104, 105, 108, 110, 111, 112, 113, 115, 116, 117, 118, 119, 120	Tests 21, 22
	• Indirect Measure	Lessons 97, 118	
98	• Scale	Lessons 99, 100, 103, 105, 110, 118	Test 21
	• Scale Factor	Lessons 98, 99, 100, 101, 103, 104, 105, 107, 108, 110, 111, 112, 113, 115, 120	Tests 21, 22
99	• Pythagorean Theorem	Lessons 99, 100, 101, 103, 104, 105, 106, 107, 108, 109, 110, 111, 112, 114, 115, 118, 120	Test 21
100	• Estimating Square Roots	Lessons 100, 101, 103, 107	Test 21
	• Irrational Numbers	Lessons 100, 102, 106, 110, 118	Test 21
Inv. 10	• Using a Compass and a Straightedge, Part 2	Investigation 10, Lesson 103	Test & Practice Generator

• Evaluations with Positive and Negative Numbers

Objective

- Evaluate expressions with negative numbers in place of variables.

Lesson Preparation

Materials

- **Power Up S** (in *Instructional Masters*)
- **Teacher-provided material: graph paper**

Optional

- **Investigation Activity 13** (in *Instructional Masters*)

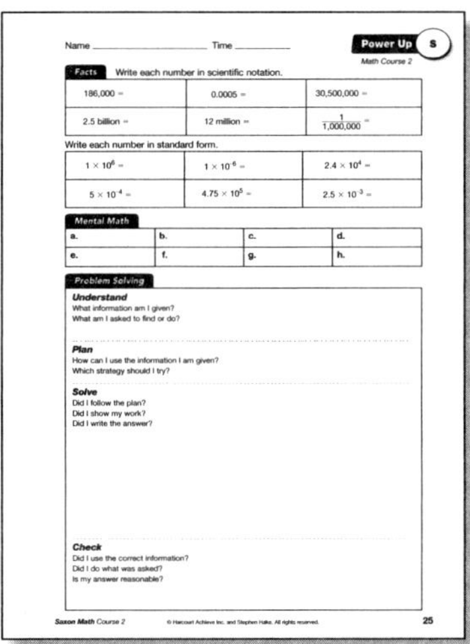
Name ________ Time ________ Power Up S
Math Course 2

Facts Write each number in scientific notation.

186,000 =	0.0005 =	30,500,000 =
2.5 billion =	12 million =	$\frac{1}{1,000,000}$ =

Write each number in standard form.

1×10^6 =	1×10^{-6} =	2.4×10^4 =
5×10^{-4} =	4.75×10^5 =	2.5×10^{-3} =

Mental Math

a.	b.	c.	d.
e.	f.	g.	h.

Problem Solving

Understand
What information am I given?
What am I asked to find or do?

Plan
How can I use the information I am given?
Which strategy should I try?

Solve
Did I follow the plan?
Did I show my work?
Did I write the answer?

Check
Did I use the correct information?
Did I do what was asked?
Is my answer reasonable?

Saxon Math Course 2 © Harcourt Achieve Inc. and Stephen Hake. All rights reserved. 25

Power Up S

Technology Resources

Student eBook Complete student textbook in electronic format.

Resources and Planner CD Assessment, reteaching, and instructional masters, plus a pacing calendar with standards.

Test and Practice Generator CD Create additional practice sheets and custom-made tests.

www.SaxonPublishers.com Visit for more student activities and planning materials.

Inclusion

Adaptations CD Adapted lessons, investigations, practice and assessments.

Meeting Standards

National Council of Teachers of Mathematics (NCTM)

Numbers and Operations

NO.2c Understand and use the inverse relationships of addition and subtraction, multiplication and division, and squaring and finding square roots to simplify computations and solve problems

Algebra

AL.1b Relate and compare different forms of representation for a relationship

AL.3a Model and solve contextualized problems using various representations, such as graphs, tables, and equations

Communication

CM.3d Use the language of mathematics to express mathematical ideas precisely

Power-Up Discussion *For use with Power Up, p. 631*

Problem-Solving Strategy: Find a Pattern

Simplify the first three terms of the following sequence. Then write and simplify the next two terms.

$$\sqrt{1^3}, \sqrt{1^3 + 2^3}, \sqrt{1^3 + 2^3 + 3^3}, \ldots$$

Understand Understand the problem.

"What information are we given?"

We are shown the first three terms of a pattern.

"What are we asked to do?"

We are asked to simplify the first three terms, then extend (and simplify) the pattern for two more terms.

Plan Make a plan.

"What problem-solving strategy will we use?"

We will try to *find a pattern* and use the pattern's rule to find the value of the next two terms.

Solve Carry out the plan.

"What are the first three terms simplified?"

1, 3, and 6

"What are the next two terms?"

$\sqrt{1^3 + 2^2 + 3^3 + 4^3}, \sqrt{1^3 + 2^3 + 3^3 + 4^3 + 5^3}$

"What are the next two terms simplified?"

10 and 15

Teacher Note: Point out that the sequence is a sequence of triangular numbers. Ask students to find the next 3 terms in the sequence without writing them out as radical expressions and simplifying.

Check Look back.

"Did we do what we were asked to do?"

Yes, we simplified the first three terms of the sequence, then found and simplified the next two.

"How can we verify the simplifications are correct?"

We see that the pattern of numbers formed by the simplification is another important sequence of numbers (triangular numbers). The pattern encourages us to think that our simplifications are correct, because they are predictable.

LESSON 91

• Evaluations with Positive and Negative Numbers

Power Up *Building Power*

facts Power Up S

mental math

a. **Positive/Negative:** (−84) + (−50) −134

b. **Order of Operations/Exponents:** $(1.2 \times 10^3)(1.2 \times 10^3)$ 1.44×10^6

c. **Ratio:** $\frac{w}{90} = \frac{80}{120}$ 60

d. **Mental Math:** $6 \times 2\frac{1}{2}$ (*Think:* $6 \times 2 + 6 \times \frac{1}{2}$) 15

e. **Measurement:** 1.5 L to mL 1500 mL

f. **Fractional Parts:** \$20 is $\frac{1}{10}$ of *m*. \$200

g. **Geometry:** What type of angle measures less than 90 degrees? acute

h. **Calculation:** 50% of 40, + 1, ÷ 3, × 7, + 1, × 2, $\sqrt{\ }$, × 5, − 1, $\sqrt{\ }$, × 4, + 2, ÷ 2 15

problem solving Simplify the first three terms of the following sequence. Then write and simplify the next two terms.

$$\sqrt{1^3}, \sqrt{1^3 + 2^3}, \sqrt{1^3 + 2^3 + 3^3}, \ldots$$

1; 3; 6; $\sqrt{1^3 + 2^3 + 3^3 + 4^3} = 10$; $\sqrt{1^3 + 2^3 + 3^3 + 4^3 + 5^3} = 15$

New Concept *Increasing Knowledge*

We have practiced evaluating expressions such as

$$x - xy - y$$

with positive numbers in place of *x* and *y*. In this lesson we will practice evaluating such expressions with negative numbers as well. When evaluating expressions with signed numbers, it is helpful to first replace each variable with parentheses. This will help prevent making mistakes in signs.

Example 1

Thinking Skill
Analyze
What are the terms in this expression? *x*, *xy*, and *y*

Evaluate: $x - xy - y$ if $x = -2$ and $y = -3$

Solution

We write parentheses for each variable.

( ) − ( )( ) − ( ) parentheses

Now we write the proper numbers within the parentheses.

(−2) − (−2)(−3) − (−3) insert numbers

Facts Write each number in scientific notation.

$186{,}000 = 1.86 \times 10^5$	$0.0005 = 5 \times 10^{-4}$	$30{,}500{,}000 = 3.05 \times 10^7$
$2.5 \text{ billion} = 2.5 \times 10^9$	$12 \text{ million} = 1.2 \times 10^7$	$\frac{1}{1{,}000{,}000} = 1 \times 10^{-6}$

Write each number in standard form.

$1 \times 10^6 = 1{,}000{,}000$	$1 \times 10^{-6} = 0.000001$	$2.4 \times 10^4 = 24{,}000$
$5 \times 10^{-4} = 0.0005$	$4.75 \times 10^5 = 475{,}000$	$2.5 \times 10^{-3} = 0.0025$

1 Power Up

Facts

Distribute **Power Up S** to students. See answers below.

Mental Math

Encourage students to share different ways to mentally compute these exercises. Strategies for exercises **c** and **f** are listed below.

c. Cross Multiply

$120w = 7200$
$6 \times 12 = 72$, so
$60 \times 120 = 7200$
$w = 60$

Equivalent Fractions

$\frac{80}{120} \div \frac{40}{40} = \frac{2}{3}$
$\frac{2}{3} \times \frac{30}{30} = \frac{60}{90}$
$w = 60$

f. Multiply by 10

$20 \div \frac{1}{10} = 20 \times \frac{10}{1} = 200$
$m = 200$

Reasoning

10 is $\frac{1}{10}$ of 100, so
20 is $\frac{1}{10}$ of 200
$m = 200$

Problem Solving

Refer to **Power-Up Discussion,** p. 631F.

2 New Concepts

Instruction

Introduce this lesson by reviewing with students how to substitute positive numbers into algebraic expressions.

- Start by writing $x - xy - y$ on the board.
- Have students evaluate the expression using $x = 2$ and $y = 3$. $2 - (2)(3) - 3 = -7$

Example 1

Instruction

Some students may confuse the concepts of *terms* and *variables* in algebraic expressions. Review that a term is a number, a variable, the product of a number and variable(s), or the quotient of a number and variable(s). Terms are separated by plus or minus signs in an expression.

(continued)

2 New Concepts (Continued)

Example 2

Instruction

Tell students to suppose Nikki found $x = -1$ to be the solution to the equation. Have them use substitution to check this answer. Ask them to explain why Nikki's solution is incorrect. Students should find that when substituting -1 for x, the equation simplifies to $2 = -1$. Therefore, Nikki's answer must be incorrect.

Practice Set

Problem d Verify

Ask students to solve for x and show that their answer is correct. $x = \frac{1}{3}$

Problems e and f Justify

Ask student volunteers to work at the board and explain how to check each equation.

3 Written Practice

Math Conversations

Discussion opportunities are provided below.

Problem 2

Extend the Problem

"Which measure of central tendency best describes this data, mean or median?"

Sample: Since the numbers have a broad range of 25, the median, 8, is best since it indicates that half the data are above and half the data are below.

(continued)

Sample: $x = 2$ and $y = -3$:
$x - xy - y =$
$(2) - (2)(-3) - (-3) =$
$(2) - (-6) - (-3) =$
$(8) - (-3) =$
$8 + 3 = 11$

By the order of operations, we multiply before adding.

$(-2) - (+6) - (-3)$ multiplied

Then we add algebraically from left to right.

$(-8) - (-3)$ added -2 and -6

-5 added -8 and $+3$

Discuss What are some values for x and y that will result in a positive solution?

Example 2

Nikki says the solution of the equation $3x + 5 = -1$ is -2. Show how Nikki can check her answer.

Solution

Nikki can replace x in the original equation with -2 and simplify.

$3x + 5 = -1$

$3(-2) + 5 = -1$ Substituted -2

$-6 + 5 = -1$ Multiplied $3(-2)$

$-1 = -1$ Added -6 and $+5$

The two sides of the equation are equal. Nikki's solution is checked.

Practice Set

c. $4(-4) + 25 = 9$
$-16 + 25 = 9$
$9 = 9\surd$

d. $3(-5) + 7 = 8$
$-15 + 7 = 8$
$-8 \neq 8$
-5 is not a solution

e. $4x = -20$
$x = \frac{-20}{4}$
$x = -5$
Check:
$4x = -20$
$(4)(-5) = -20$
$-20 = -20$

Generalize Evaluate each expression. Write parentheses as the first step.

a. $x + xy - y$ if $x = 3$ and $y = -2$ -1

b. $-m + n - mn$ if $m = -2$ and $n = -5$ -13

Verify Check each solution for the original equations.

c. $4x + 25 = 9$, solution: $x = -4$

▶ **d.** $3x + 7 = 8$, solution: $x = -5$

Justify Solve and check these equations.

▶ **e.** $4x = -20$ ▶ **f.** $-2x = 16$

g. **Explain** How did you check your solutions for **e** and **f?** (See below.)

Written Practice *Strengthening Concepts*

f. $-2x = 16$
$\frac{-2x}{-2} = \frac{16}{-2}$
$x = -8$
Check:
$-2x = 16$
$-2(-8) = 16$
$16 = 16$

1. (55) In a museum gallery, the average height of the six paintings on one wall is 86 cm. The average height of the four paintings on another wall is 94 cm. What is the average height of all ten of the paintings? 89.2 cm

▶ **2.** (Inv. 4) The mean of these numbers is how much greater than the median? 3

3, 12, 7, 5, 18, 6, 9, 28

g. Sample: I substituted the value I found for the variable into the original equation. Then I evaluated the equation. If the two sides of the equation were equal, I knew my solution was correct.

▶ See Math Conversations in the sidebar.

3. (46) The Singhs completed a 130-mile trip in $2\frac{1}{2}$ hours. What was their average speed in miles per hour? 52 miles per hour

Use ratio boxes to solve problems **4–7.**

4. (66) The ratio of workers to supervisors at the job site was 3 to 5. Of the 120 workers and supervisors at the job site, how many were workers? 45 workers

5. (72) Vera bought 3 notebooks for $8.55. At this rate, how much would 5 notebooks cost? $14.25

6. (60) A software program for guitar lessons is on sale for 80% of the original price of $54. What is the sale price? $43.20

▶ 7. (81) Forty people came to the party. This was 80 percent of those who were invited. How many were invited? 50 people

8. (77) Write equations to solve **a** and **b**.
   a. Twenty is 40 percent of what number? $20 = 0.4 \times W_N$; 50
   b. Twenty is what percent of 40? $20 = W_P \times 40$; 50%

9. (88) Use two unit multipliers to convert 3600 in.^{2} to square feet. 25 square feet

10. (71) Read this statement. Then answer the questions that follow:
   Three fourths of the exhibits at the science fair were about physical science. There were 60 physical science exhibits.
   a. How many exhibits were at the science fair? 80 exhibits
   b. What percent of the exhibits were not about physical science? 25%

▶* 11. (91) **Generalize** Evaluate: $x - y - xy$ if $x = -3$ and $y = -2$ −7

▶* 12. (Inv. 9) **Analyze** If three painters can paint the house in 12 hours, how long would it take four painters to paint the house? 9 hours

13. (Inv. 6, 75)
   a. Classify this quadrilateral. trapezoid
   b. Find the perimeter of the figure. 60 mm
   c. Find the area of the figure. 210 mm^2

15 mm
13 mm
12 mm
20 mm

   d. The sum of the measures of the interior angles of a quadrilateral is 360°. If the acute interior angle of the figure measures 75°, what does the obtuse interior angle measure? 105°

14. (2, 41) Which property is illustrated by each equation?
   a. $a + (b + c) = (a + b) + c$ Associative Property of Addition
   b. $ab = ba$ Commutative Property of Multiplication
   c. $a(b + c) = ab + ac$ Distributive Property

15. (62) The lengths of two sides of an isosceles triangle are 5 inches and 1 foot. Draw the triangle and find its perimeter in inches. 29 in.

15.
12 in. 12 in.
5 in.

▶ See Math Conversations in the sidebar.

3 Written Practice (Continued)

Math Conversations

Discussion opportunities are provided below.

Problem 7

Extend the Problem

Give students an opportunity to solve this problem using different strategies. Ask students to share their strategies with the class. Some strategies might include the following.

Draw a Diagram

$80\% = \frac{4}{5}$ Draw fifths.

10	10	10	10	

Since $\frac{4}{5} = 40$, $\frac{1}{5} = 10$

50 people were invited.

Write an Equation

$$W_N \times 80\% = 40$$
$$\frac{4}{5}n = 40$$
$$\frac{4}{5}n \times \frac{5}{4} = 40 \times \frac{5}{4}$$
$$n = 50$$

Problem 11 Generalize

Suggest that students draw parentheses for each variable first, then substitute the negative numbers for the variables in the expression.

$$(\ ) - (\ ) - (\ )(\ )$$

Ask a student to explain how to simplify this expression.

Problem 12 Analyze

Explain to students that with work problems, the key is to remember that with either condition, the house will be completed. So, set the conditions equal to each other.

3 painters in 12 hours = 4 painters in x hours. Now, students can set up and solve an equation.

$$3 \cdot 12 = 4x$$
$$9 = x$$

(continued)

3 Written Practice (Continued)

Math Conversations

Discussion opportunities are provided below.

Problem 19 Analyze

Have a student name three other points on the line. Sample: (4, 12), (5, 15), (6, 18)

Problem 20

Extend the Problem

"What is the measure of ∠DCA? Explain how you know." 120°; $\angle x$ and $\angle DCA$ form a straight angle; the sum of both angle measures = 180°; 180° − 60° = 120°

Problem 22 Represent

Extend the Problem

Ask students if the following numbers are a part of the solution. Have them explain why.

$14 \qquad -10 \qquad \frac{1}{2} \qquad -\frac{1}{2} \qquad 0 \qquad 10\frac{1}{2}$

The problem asks for integers, and $\frac{1}{2}$, $-\frac{1}{2}$, and $10\frac{1}{2}$ are not integers. −10 is not greater than −3. 0 and 14 are integers greater than −3 and are part of the solution.

Errors and Misconceptions

Problem 16

If students are having difficulty with this problem, remind them that when we multiply numbers in scientific notation we multiply the decimal numbers first and then we multiply the powers of 10. Also review that when multiplying powers of 10, we add the exponents.

Problem 21

If students don't know how to begin simplifying this expression, remind them to write parentheses and then place the terms of the expression in the parentheses. Then they can combine like terms.

$$-3x - 3 - x - 1$$

There are 4 terms in this expression.

$$(\ ) - (\ ) - (\ ) - (\ )$$
$$(-3x) - (3) - (1x) - (1)$$

Combine like algebraic terms.

$$-3x - (1x) = -4x$$

Combine like numerical terms.

$$-3 - 1 = -4$$

Solution: $-4x - 4$

(continued)

▶* **16.** Multiply. Write the product in scientific notation. 1.2×10^{-10}
(83)

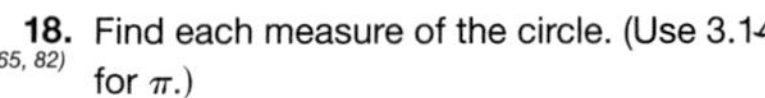

$(2.4 \times 10^{-4})(5 \times 10^{-7})$

17. A pyramid with a square base has how many
(67)

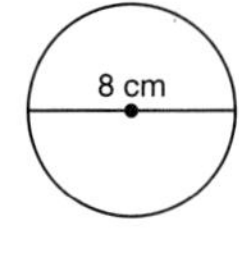

a. faces? 5 faces

b. edges? 8 edges

c. vertices? 5 vertices

18. Find each measure of the circle. (Use 3.14 for π.)
(65, 82)

8 cm

a. circumference 25.12 cm

b. area 50.24 cm^2

▶* **19.** Analyze One yard equals three feet. The table at right shows three pairs of equivalent measures.
(Inv. 9)

yd	ft
1	3
2	6
3	9

a. Plot these points on a coordinate graph, using yards for the horizontal axis and feet for the vertical axis. Then draw a ray through the points to show all pairs of equivalent measures.

b. Does the graph show direct variation? Explain your answer.

19. a

feet: 0, 3, 6, 9, 12; yards: 0, 1, 2, 3, 4

b. Yes, the graph shows direct variation. The points are aligned. The pair 0,0 is a solution, and the other solution pairs have the same proportion.

▶ **20.** Refer to the figure below to answer **a–d.**
(40)

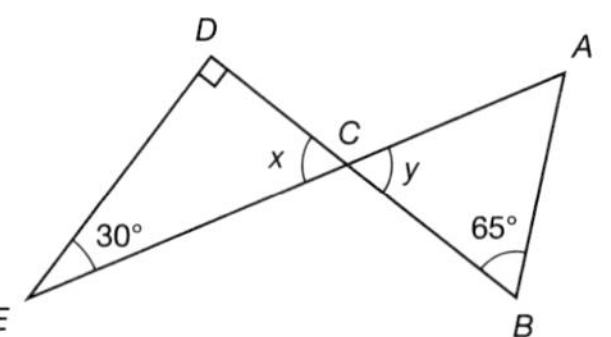

a. What is m∠x? 60°

b. What is m∠y? 60°

c. What is m∠A? 55°

d. Are the two triangles similar? Why or why not?

20. d. No; Corresponding angles of similar triangles have the same measure. The angles in these two triangles have different measures.

▶* **21.** **a.** Add algebraically: $-3x - 3 - x - 1$ $\quad -4x - 4$
(84, 87)

b. Multiply: $(-3x)(-3)(-x)(-1)$ $\quad 9x^2$

▶* **22.** Represent On a number line, graph all integers greater than or equal to −3.
(86)

−4 −3 −2 −1 0

▶ See Math Conversations in the sidebar.

23. (32) Segment *AB* is how many millimeters longer than segment *BC*? 20 mm

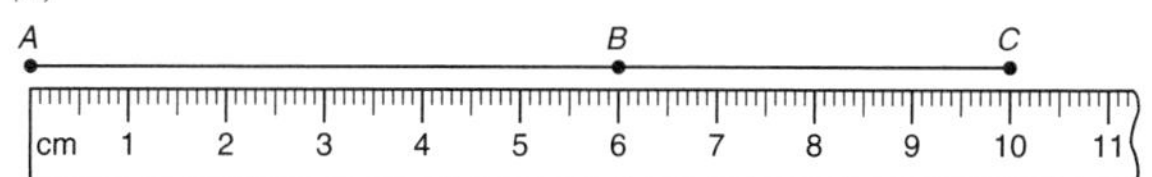

▶ **Justify** For problems **24–26**, solve and check. Show each step.

24. (Inv. 7) $5 = y - 4.75$ 9.75

*** 25.** (90) $3\frac{1}{3}y = 7\frac{1}{2}$ $\frac{9}{4}$

*** 26.** (90) $-9x = 414$ −46

Simplify:

27. (50) $\frac{32 \text{ ft}}{1 \text{ s}} \cdot \frac{60 \text{ s}}{1 \text{ min}}$ $1920\frac{\text{ft}}{\text{min}}$

28. (43) $5\frac{1}{3} + 2.5 + \frac{1}{6}$ (mixed-number answer) 8

▶ **29.** (43, 45) $\dfrac{2\frac{3}{4} + 3.5}{2\frac{1}{2}}$ (decimal answer) 2.5

*** 30.** (85, 91) **a.** $\dfrac{(-3) - (-4)(+5)}{(-2)}$ $-8\frac{1}{2}$

b. $-3(+4) - 5(+6) - 7$ −49

Early Finishers
Real-World Application

Tobey is using a step counter as part of a fitness program. During lunch, he walks 441 steps. Each step averages 30 inches in length.

a. Use unit multipliers to calculate Tobey's total distance during lunch (in feet). 441 steps $\times \frac{30 \text{ inches}}{1 \text{ step}} \times \frac{1 \text{ foot}}{12 \text{ inches}}$; 1102.5 feet

b. Use a unit multiplier and a calculator to find his total distance during lunch (in miles). Round to the nearest hundredth of a mile.

b. 1102.5 feet $\times \frac{1 \text{ mile}}{5280 \text{ feet}}$; 0.21 mile

c. In a week, will Tobey's lunchtime activity total a mile? Explain.
If 0.21 miles is the typical distance Tobey travels during lunchtime, then in 5 days Tobey will walk about a mile. 5 × 0.21 mi = 1.05 mi

▶ See Math Conversations in the sidebar.

3 Written Practice (Continued)

Math Conversations

Discussion opportunities are provided below.

Problems 24–26

Ask volunteers to work at the board and explain each step of the solution and then check. Answers will vary.

Problem 29 Analyze

Extend the Problem

Discuss different ways to simplify the expression. Change the fractions to decimals: $2\frac{1}{2} = 2.5$ and $2\frac{3}{4} = 2.75$, so the expression becomes $\frac{2.75 + 3.5}{2.5} = \frac{6.25}{2.5} \times \frac{10}{10} = \frac{62.5}{25}$ or 2.5

Change the decimal to a fraction:

$$\frac{2\frac{3}{4} + 3\frac{1}{2}}{2\frac{1}{2}} = \frac{6\frac{1}{4}}{2\frac{1}{2}}$$

$$\frac{25}{4} \cdot \frac{2}{5} = \frac{5}{2} = 2\frac{1}{2} = 2.5$$

Looking Forward

Understanding how to evaluate expressions with positive and negative numbers in place of variables prepares students for:

- **Lesson 93,** solving two-step equations and inequalities and checking their solutions.
- **Lesson 108,** solving a formula for a variable by substituting given values for other variables.
- **Lesson 109,** solving equations with exponents and checking solutions.

• Percent of Change

Objectives

- Identify problems that use a percent to describe an amount of change.
- Use a ratio box to solve percent of change problems.

Lesson Preparation

Materials

- **Power Up T** (in *Instructional Masters*)
- **Teacher-provided material: graph paper**

Optional

- **Teacher-provided material: newspapers, magazines**
- **Investigation Activity 13** (in *Instructional Masters*)

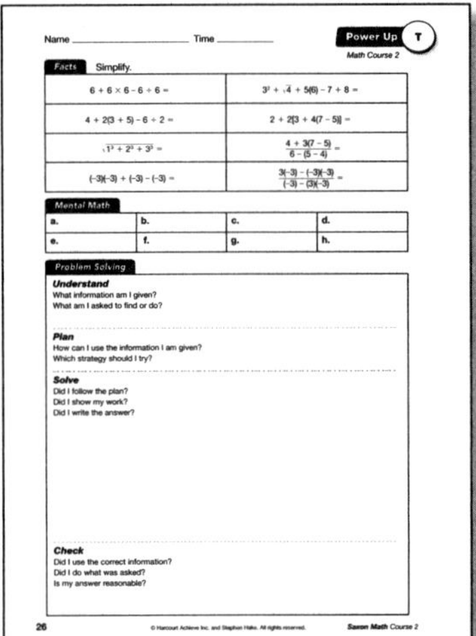

Name ________ Time ______ **Power Up T** *Math Course 2*

Facts Simplify.

$6 + 6 \times 6 - 6 \div 6 =$	$3^2 + \sqrt{4} + 5(6) - 7 + 8 =$
$4 + 2(3 + 5) - 6 \div 2 =$	$2 + 2[3 + 4(7 - 5)] =$
$\sqrt{1^3 + 2^3 + 3^3} =$	$\frac{4 + 3(7 - 5)}{6 - (5 - 4)} =$
$(-3)(-3) + (-3) - (-3) =$	$\frac{3(-3) - (-3)(-3)}{(-3) - (3)(-3)} =$

Mental Math

a.	b.	c.	d.
e.	f.	g.	h.

Problem Solving

Understand
What information am I given?
What am I asked to find or do?

Plan
How can I use the information I am given?
Which strategy should I try?

Solve
Did I follow the plan?
Did I show my work?
Did I write the answer?

Check
Did I use the correct information?
Did I do what was asked?
Is my answer reasonable?

26 © Harcourt Achieve Inc. and Stephen Hake. All rights reserved. *Saxon Math Course 2*

Power Up T

Math Language

English Learners (ESL)
decrease
increase

Technology Resources

Student eBook Complete student textbook in electronic format.

Resources and Planner CD Assessment, reteaching, and instructional masters, plus a pacing calendar with standards.

Test and Practice Generator CD Create additional practice sheets and custom-made tests.

www.SaxonPublishers.com Visit for more student activities and planning materials.

Inclusion

Adaptations CD Adapted lessons, investigations, practice and assessments.

Meeting Standards

National Council of Teachers of Mathematics (NCTM)

Numbers and Operations

NO.1a Work flexibly with fractions, decimals, and percents to solve problems

NO.1c Develop meaning for percents greater than 100 and less than 1

Problem Solving

PS.1b Solve problems that arise in mathematics and in other contexts

Power-Up Discussion *For use with Power Up, p. 636*

Problem-Solving Strategy: Write an Equation

What is the average of these fractions?

$$\frac{1}{12}, \frac{1}{6}, \frac{1}{4}, \frac{1}{3}, \frac{5}{12}$$

Understand **Understand the problem.**

"What information are we given?

We are given a list of five fractions.

"What are we asked to do?"

We are asked to find the average of the five fractions.

Plan **Make a plan.**

"What problem-solving strategy will we use?"

We will *write an equation* to find the average.

Solve **Carry out the plan.**

"How do we find the average of a group of numbers?"

We add the numbers, then divide the sum by the number of addends.

"How should we begin finding the average of these fractions?"

We will need to rewrite the fractions with a common denominator.

"What is the lowest common denominator of the listed fractions?"

12

"What is the list of fractions rewritten with denominators of 12?"

$\frac{1}{12}, \frac{2}{12}, \frac{3}{12}, \frac{4}{12}, \frac{5}{12}$

"What is the sum of the fractions?"

$\frac{1}{12} + \frac{2}{12} + \frac{3}{12} + \frac{4}{12} + \frac{5}{12} = \frac{15}{12}$

"What is the average?"

$\frac{15}{12} \div 5 = \frac{3}{12} = \frac{1}{4}$

Check **Look back.**

"Did we do what we were asked to do?"

Yes, we found the average of the list of fractions.

Teacher Note: Extend this problem-solving problem by having students find the averages of other groups of fractions.

"Is there a shortcut to finding the average?"

Yes, if a set of numbers is equally spaced like this set is, then the average (mean) equals the median. From the list above we see that the median is $\frac{3}{12}$ which equals $\frac{1}{4}$.

1 Power Up

Facts

Distribute **Power Up T** to students. See answers below.

Mental Math

Encourage students to share different ways to mentally compute these exercises. Strategies for exercises **a** and **h** are listed below.

a. Subtract Absolute Values

$75 - 50 = 25$

Keep the sign. -25

Add the Opposite

$(-75) - (-50) = (-75) + (+50)$

$-75 + 50 = -25$

h. Decompose and Multiply

$\$8 \times 4 = \$32$

$\$8 \times \frac{1}{2} = \$4$

$\$32 + \$4 = \$36$

Equivalent Expression

$\$4 \times 9 = \$36$

Problem Solving

Refer to **Power-Up Discussion,** p. 636B.

2 New Concepts

Instruction

Newspapers and magazines are filled with percent of change situations.

- Bring in some examples of advertisements or articles that involve percent of change.
- Distribute them among the students.
- Have each student read one example to the class and explain if the change is an increase or a decrease.

(continued)

LESSON **92**

Percent of Change

Power Up *Building Power*

facts Power Up T

mental math

a. Positive/Negative: $(-75) - (-50)$ -25

b. Order of Operations/Exponents: $(1.5 \times 10^{-5})(1.5 \times 10^{-5})$ 2.25×10^{-10}

c. Algebra: $50 = 3m + 2$ 16

d. Mental Math: $6 \times 3\frac{1}{3}$ (*Think:* $6 \times 3 + 6 \times \frac{1}{3}$) 20

e. Measurement: 0.3 m to cm 30 cm

f. Percent: \$6 is 10% of *m*. \$60

g. Geometry: What type of angle measures 180 degrees? straight angle

h. Rate: At \$8.00 per hour, how much money will Kenji earn working $4\frac{1}{2}$ hours? \$36.00

problem solving What is the average of these fractions? $\frac{1}{12}, \frac{1}{6}, \frac{1}{4}, \frac{1}{3}, \frac{5}{12}$ $\frac{1}{4}$

New Concept *Increasing Knowledge*

The percent problems that we have considered before now have used a percent to describe part of a whole. In this lesson we will consider percent problems that use a percent to describe an amount of change. The change may be an increase or a decrease. Adding sales tax to a purchase is an example of an increase. Marking down the price of an item for a sale is an example of a decrease.

Increase

original number + amount of change = new number

Decrease

original number − amount of change = new number

We can use a ratio box to help us with "increase-decrease" problems. However, there is a difference in the way we set up the ratio box. When we make a table for a "parts of a whole" problem, the bottom number in the percent column is 100 percent.

	Percent	Actual Count
Part		
Part		
Whole	100	

Facts Simplify.

$6 + 6 \times 6 - 6 \div 6 = 41$	$3^2 + \sqrt{4} + 5(6) - 7 + 8 = 42$
$4 + 2(3 + 5) - 6 \div 2 = 17$	$2 + 2[3 + 4(7 - 5)] = 24$
$\sqrt{1^3 + 2^3 + 3^3} = 6$	$\frac{4 + 3(7 - 5)}{6 - (5 - 4)} = 2$
$(-3)(-3) + (-3) - (-3) = 9$	$\frac{3(-3) - (-3)(-3)}{(-3) - (3)(-3)} = -3$

When we set up a ratio box for an "increase-decrease" problem, we also have three rows. The three rows represent the original number, the amount of change, and the new number. We will use the words ***original, change,*** and ***new*** on the left side of the ratio box. The difference in the setup is where we put 100 percent. Most "increase-decrease" problems consider the original amount to be 100 percent. So the top number in the percent column will be 100 percent.

	Percent	Actual Count
Original	100	
Change		
New		

If the change is an **increase,** we **add** it to the original amount to get the new amount. If the change is a **decrease,** we **subtract** it from the original amount to get the new amount.

Example 1

The county's population increased 15 percent from 1980 to 1990. If the population in 1980 was 120,000, what was the population in 1990?

Solution

First we identify the type of problem. The percent describes an amount of change. This is an increase problem. We make a ratio box and write the words "original," "change," and "new" down the side. Since the change was an increase, we write a plus sign in front of "change."

In the "percent" column we write 100 percent for the original (1980 population) and 15 percent for the change. We add to get 115 percent for the new (1990 population).

In the "actual count" column we write 120,000 for the original population and use the letters C for "change" and N for "new."

	Percent	Actual Count
Original	100	120,000
+ Change	15	C
New	115	N

$$\frac{100}{115} = \frac{120{,}000}{N}$$

We are asked for the new population. Since we know both numbers in the first row, we use the first and third rows to write the proportion.

$$\frac{100}{115} = \frac{120{,}000}{N}$$

$$100N = 13{,}800{,}000$$

$$N = 138{,}000$$

The county's population in 1990 was **138,000.**

2 New Concepts (Continued)

Instruction

Tell students that percents can describe parts of a whole and that percents can describe changes. When students consider how to solve a percent problem, they need to decide whether the percent is describing part of a whole or a change.

If students have trouble deciding which kind of ratio box to use to solve a problem, have them compare the words in the box to the words in the problem. If the words *part* or *whole* are in the problem, they should probably use the parts of a whole ratio box. If the words *original, change,* or *new* are in the problem, they should probably use the percent of change ratio box.

Example 1

Instruction

Demonstrate how to set up the ratio box. Point out that if the box is set up correctly, the numbers will be in order to write the proportion. Remind students to draw neat boxes so that they will not confuse numbers or write numbers in the wrong place.

(continued)

Math Background

Finding the percent of change is used in any real world situation where there is an increase or decrease that needs to be determined.

- Population increases or decreases
- Enrollment increases or decreases
- Profit and loss
- Sales and discounts
- Wholesale and markup
- Income and expenses

The percent of increase or decrease can be computed using the following formula.

$$\frac{\text{Change in Quantity}}{\text{Original Quantity}} \times 100\% = \text{Percent of Change}$$

In this lesson, students will use a ratio box to set up a proportion.

English Learners

Before example 1, explain the difference between **increase** and **decrease.** Say:

"Increase means growing or getting larger. Decrease means becoming less or smaller. Would a discount increase or decrease the price?" decrease

"If the price is marked up, will it increase or decrease?" increase

2 New Concepts *(Continued)*

Example 2

Instruction

When students see the words sale price and original price, they should expect the problem to be a percent of decrease problem.

"What does R represent?" original price

"What does C represent?" the change; amount decreased

"How can you find the amount of the decrease?" set up a proportion to solve for C

Ask a student volunteer to solve the problem at the board and use the result to check the solution.

Set up the proportion

$$\frac{100}{30} = \frac{35}{C}$$

$$100C = 35 \times 30;\ C = \$10.50$$

Check: $24.50 + $10.50 = $35

Example 3

Instruction

Ask a student to set up the proportion at the board.

$$\frac{100}{175} = \frac{20}{R}$$

Ask students how they could check the answer.

Subtract: $35 − $20 = $15.

Solve an Equation: $15 = W_P \times 20$.

Draw a Diagram: 75% suggests fourths

25% $5	25% $5	25% $5	25% $5

$15 is 75% of $20.

Practice Set

Problems a–d Model

Have students work at the board to show how to set up the proportion and explain how to solve the problem.

(continued)

Example 2

The price was reduced 30 percent. If the sale price was $24.50, what was the original price?

Solution

First we identify the problem. This is a decrease problem. We make a ratio box and write "original," "change," and "new" down the side, with a minus sign in front of "change." In the percent column we write 100 percent for original, 30 percent for change, and 70 percent for new. The sale price is the new actual count. We are asked to find the original price.

	Percent	Actual Count
Original	100	R
− Change	30	C
New	70	24.50

$$\frac{100}{70} = \frac{R}{24.50}$$

$$70R = 2450$$

$$R = 35$$

The original price was **$35.00.**

Example 3

A merchant bought an item at wholesale for $20 and marked the price up 75% to sell the item at retail. What was the merchant's retail price for the item?

Solution

This is an increase problem. We make a table and record the given information.

	Percent	Actual Count
Original (Wholesale)	100	20
+ Change (Markup)	75	M
New (Retail)	175	R

$$\frac{100}{175} = \frac{20}{R}$$

$$100R = 3500$$

$$R = 35$$

The merchant's retail price for the item was **$35.**

Thinking Skill

Formulate

We can use a ratio box to solve *part-of-a-whole* and *increase-decrease* word problems. How are the problems different?

Sample: A part-of-a-whole problem tells us two parts or one part and the whole. We find the whole or the missing part. An increase-decrease problem asks us to find a percent of a whole, which we either add to or subtract from the whole.

Practice Set

▶ *Model* Use a ratio box to solve each problem.

a. The regular price was $24.50, but the item was on sale for 30 percent off. What was the sale price? $17.15

b. The number of students taking algebra increased 20% in one year. If 60 students are taking algebra this year, how many took algebra last year? 50 students

Teacher Tip

Explain that to buy an item at **wholesale prices** means to buy a large quantity of the item for a low price. Stores buy wholesale and sell smaller quantities at a higher price, known as the **retail price.** Explain that when students are asked to find a retail price, they are dealing with a percent increase over the wholesale price. This change is called the *markup.*

c. Bikes were on sale for 20 percent off. Tomas bought one for $120. How much money did he save by buying the bike at the sale price instead of at the regular price? $30

d. The clothing store bought shirts for $15 each and marked up the price 80% to sell the shirts at retail. What was the retail price of each shirt? $27

▶ e. *Classify* In which of the problems above is the change an increase? b and d

Written Practice *Strengthening Concepts*

1. (21) The product of the first three prime numbers is how much less than the sum of the next three prime numbers? 1

2. (55) Dara scored an average of 88 points per game in five crossword games. What score must she average on the next two games to have a seven-game average of 90? 95

3. (46) Jenna finished a 2-mile race in 15 minutes. What was her average speed in miles per hour? 8 miles per hour

Use ratio boxes to solve problems **4–7.**

4. (66) Forty-five of the 80 students walk to school. What is the ratio of students who walk to school to students who do not walk to school? $\frac{9}{7}$

▶ 5. (72) Two dozen pencils cost $3.60. At that rate, how much would 60 pencils cost? $9.00

▶ * 6. (92) *Generalize* The population of Houston, TX increased about 25 percent from 1990 to 2000. If the population of Houston was about 1,600,000 people in 1990, what was the population in 2000? about 2 million people

* 7. (92) Because of an unexpected cold snap, the price of oranges increased 50% in one month. If the price after the increase was 75¢ each, what was the price before the increase? 50¢ each

8. (77) Write equations to solve **a** and **b**.

a. Sixty is what percent of 75? $60 = W_p \times 75$; 80%

b. Seventy-five is what percent of 60? $75 = W_p \times 60$; 125%

▶ * 9. (88) *Connect* The snail moved one foot in 2 minutes. Use two unit multipliers to find its average speed in yards per hour. 10 yd per hr

10. (71) Diagram this statement. Then answer the questions that follow.

Five eighths of the trees in the grove were deciduous. There were 160 deciduous trees in the grove.

a. How many trees were in the grove? 256 trees

b. How many of the trees in the grove were not deciduous? 96 trees

10.
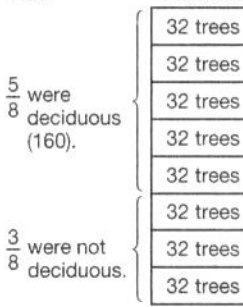

▶ See Math Conversations in the sidebar.

2 New Concepts (Continued)

Practice Set

Problem e *Classify*

Ask students to explain how to recognize percent of change problems. Answers will vary.

3 Written Practice

Math Conversations

Discussion opportunities are provided below.

Problem 5

Extend the Problem

Ask students to develop a formula based on the unit price for a pencil. Then, they should use their formula to determine the price of 100 pencils.

Sample: $3.60 ÷ 24 = 0.15 = 15¢ per pencil; the formula is $n \times 0.15 = c$, where n = the number of pencils and c = the total cost; 100 × 0.15 = $15.00, the cost of 100 pencils

Problem 6 *Generalize*

One student said "If the population increased at the same rate over the next 10 years, it would be 2,400,000."

"What did the student do wrong? What is the correct answer?" The student assumed that 400,000 is the constant rate. The constant rate is 25%. 25% of 2,000,000 is 2.5 million people.

Problem 9 *Connect*

Have a volunteer work at the board to solve this problem.

$$\frac{1 \cancel{\text{ft}}}{2 \cancel{\text{min}}} \times \frac{1 \text{ yd}}{3 \cancel{\text{ft}}} \times \frac{60 \cancel{\text{min}}}{1 \text{ hr}} = \frac{60 \text{ yd}}{2 \cdot 3 \cdot 1 \text{ hr}}$$

$$= \frac{60 \text{ yd}}{6 \text{ hr}} = \frac{10 \text{ yd}}{1 \text{ hr}}$$

(continued)

3 Written Practice (Continued)

Math Conversations

Discussion opportunities are provided below.

Problem 11 Analyze

Have a student volunteer work this problem at the board. Lead the students through a discussion about the solution.

$$y = 3x - 1$$
$$y = (3)(-5) - (1)$$
$$y = -15 + (-1)$$
$$y = -16$$

Problem 14b Generalize

Extend the Problem

Ask students to write one equation that will give them the total price. Sample: $157.50 × 1.06 = $166.95

If students cannot develop this equation on their own, write it on the board and ask why it works. Sample: multiplying by 1.06 is the same as multiplying by 100% or 1 ($157.50) and multiplying by 0.06 gives the sale tax (6%)

Problem 19

Extend the Problem

"If you were to make a vertical cut through the center of this triangular prism, what plane shape would you see?"

vertical cut

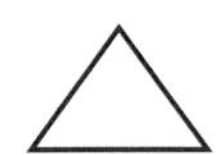

Problem 21b Represent

Ask students how they can show all the ordered pairs. Draw a line through the given 3 points and put an arrow at each end of the line.

Problem 21c Analyze

Ask students to identify the "clue" in the equation that tells us that x and y are not directly proportional. The "+1" in the equation, because addition and subtraction do not indicate proportion

(continued)

▸* **11.** (91) **Analyze** If $x = -5$ and $y = 3x - 1$, then y equals what number? −16

12. (60) Compare: 30% of 20 ⊜ 20% of 30

13. (58, 75) **a.** Find the area of this isosceles trapezoid. 45 cm²

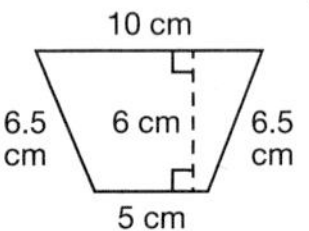

b. Trace the figure and draw its line of symmetry.

13. b.

* **14.** (46, 92) **Generalize** A merchant bought a stereo at wholesale for $90.00 and marked up the price 75% to sell the stereo at retail.

a. What was the retail price of the stereo? $157.50

▸ **b.** If the stereo sells at the retail price, and the sales-tax rate is 6%, what is the total price including sales tax? $166.95

15. (83) Multiply. Write the product in scientific notation. 2.4×10^8

$$(8 \times 10^{-5})(3 \times 10^{12})$$

16. (48) Complete the table.

Fraction	Decimal	Percent
$2\frac{1}{3}$	**a.** $2.\overline{3}$	**b.** $233\frac{1}{3}\%$
c. $\frac{1}{30}$	**d.** $0.0\overline{3}$	$3\frac{1}{3}\%$

* **17.** (36) One ace is missing from an otherwise normal deck of cards. How many aces are still in the deck? How many cards are still in the deck? If a card is selected at random, what is the probability that the selected card will be an ace? 3 aces, 51 cards, $\frac{3}{51} = \frac{1}{17}$

18. (60) What number is 250 percent of 60? 150

▸ **19.** (67) A triangular prism has how many

a. triangular faces? 2

b. rectangular faces? 3

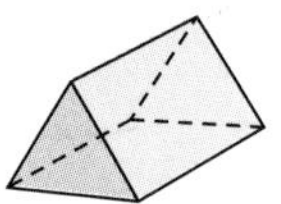

20. (66) John measured the diameter of his bicycle tire and found that it was 24 inches. What is the distance around the tire to the nearest inch? (Use 3.14 for π.) 75 inches

▸* **21.** (56, Inv. 9) **a.** Find the missing numbers in the table by using the function rule.

$y = 2x + 1$

x	y
0	1
3	7
−2	−3

b. **Represent** Plot the (x, y) pairs on a coordinate plane, and then draw a line showing all (x, y) pairs that satisfy the function.

21. b.

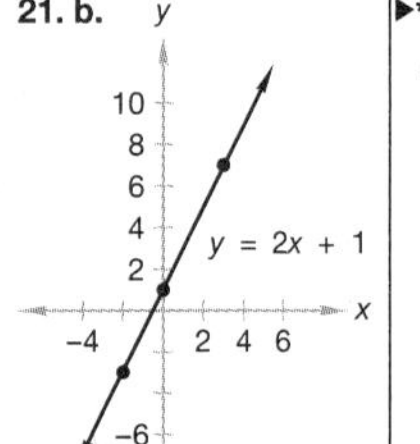

c. **Analyze** In this function are x and y directly proportional? Explain your answer. No, x and y are not directly proportional because the x, y pair 0, 0 is not a solution.

▸ See Math Conversations in the sidebar.

▶ **22.** (66) The ratio of the measures of two angles was 4 to 5. If the sum of their measures was 180°, what was the measure of the smaller angle? 80°

▶* **23.** (84, 87) **Generalize** Simplify:

a. $x + y + 3 + x - y - 1$ $2x + 2$

b. $(3x)(2x) + (3x)(2)$ $6x^2 + 6x$

c. $(x^3y)^2$ x^6y^2

24. parallelogram; Sample:

24. (Inv. 6) Draw a pair of parallel lines. Draw a second pair of parallel lines that intersect but are not perpendicular to the first pair. What kind of quadrilateral is formed?

▶ **Justify** For problems **25–27,** solve and check. Show each step.

* **25.** (90) $3\frac{1}{7}x = 66$ 21

26. (Inv. 7) $w - 0.15 = 4.9$ 5.05

* **27.** (90, 91) $-8y = 600$ −75

Simplify:

28. (52) $(2 \cdot 3)^2 - 2(3^2)$ 18

29. (43) $5 - \left(3\frac{1}{3} - 1.5\right)$ $3\frac{1}{6}$

▶* **30.** (85, 91) **a.** $\frac{(-8)(-6)(-5)}{(-4)(-3)(-2)}$ 10

b. $-6 - 5(-4) - 3(-2)(-1)$ 8

Early Finishers *Real-World Application*

A toy manufacturer has 45 workers and releases 3,600 dolls a week. The manufacturer plans on increasing the number of workers by 70%, which will increase the number of dolls a week proportionally.

a. On average, how many dolls are created by each worker weekly? 80 dolls

b. If the manufacturer increases the workforce by 70%, how many dolls will be released weekly? 6,120 dolls

▶ See Math Conversations in the sidebar.

3 Written Practice (Continued)

Math Conversations

Discussion opportunities are provided below.

Problem 23 Generalize

Ask students how they could use mental math to solve each problem.

Sample:

Problem a	Problem b	Problem c
$y + (-y) = 0$	$3 \cdot 2 \cdot x \cdot x = 6x^2$	$x^{3 \cdot 2} = x^6$
$x + x = 2x$	$3 \cdot 2 \cdot x = 6x$	$y^{1 \cdot 2} = y^2$
$3 - 1 = 2$		x^6y^2
$2x + 2$	$6x^2 + 6x$	

Problems 25–27 Justify

Ask student volunteers to work at the board to solve these equations and explain how to check the solutions.

Errors and Misconceptions

Problem 22

If students are unsure how to proceed, point out that they can draw a ratio box. Make sure that students draw a ratio box with three rows, including one for the total. Once students realize that the sum of the measures, 180, pairs with the sum of the parts in the ratio, 9, they will be able to solve by cross multiplying.

Problem 30

If students are slowed down by the negative signs, explain that it is often easier to solve multiplication and division problems first and then figure out whether the answer should have a positive or negative sign. They can simply count the negative signs. If the number is even, the answer is positive.

Looking Forward

Solving percent of change problems using ratio boxes and equations prepares students for:

- **Lesson 110,** finding successive discounts.

• Two-Step Equations and Inequalities

Objectives

- Solve two-step equations.
- Solve two-step inequalities.

Lesson Preparation

Materials

- **Power Up T** (in *Instructional Masters*)
- **Teacher-provided material: graph paper**

Optional

- **Teacher-provided material: sticky notes**
- **Investigation Activity 13** (in *Instructional Masters*)

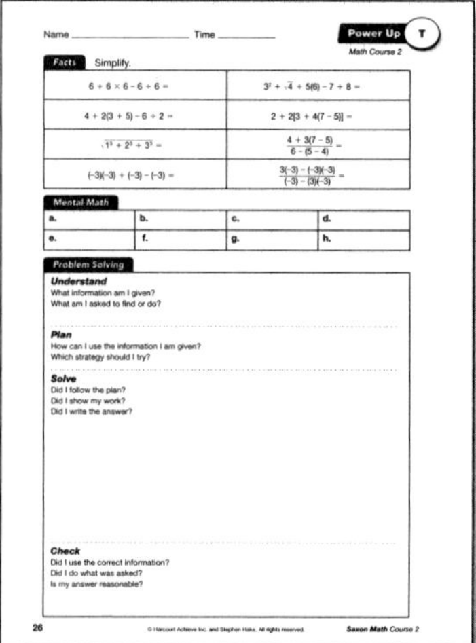

Power Up T

Math Language

English Learners (ESL)
interchange

Technology Resources

Student eBook Complete student textbook in electronic format.

Resources and Planner CD Assessment, reteaching, and instructional masters, plus a pacing calendar with standards.

Test and Practice Generator CD Create additional practice sheets and custom-made tests.

www.SaxonPublishers.com Visit for more student activities and planning materials.

Inclusion

Adaptations CD Adapted lessons, investigations, practice and assessments.

Meeting Standards

National Council of Teachers of Mathematics (NCTM)

Algebra

AL.2a Develop an initial conceptual understanding of different uses of variables

AL.2d Recognize and generate equivalent forms for simple algebraic expressions and solve linear equations

Problem Solving

PS.1c Apply and adapt a variety of appropriate strategies to solve problems

Power-Up Discussion *For use with Power Up, p. 642*

Problem-Solving Strategy: Use Logical Reasoning

Luke put 2 red pens, 7 blue pens, and 1 black pen in a bag, closed it, and shook it up. If the pens are the same size, weight, and texture, what is the probability of choosing a red pen? A red *or* black pen? What is the probability of *not* choosing a blue pen? If Luke does choose a blue pen, but gives it away, what is the probability he will choose *another* blue pen?

Understand — Understand the problem.

"What information are we given?"

Luke put 2 red pens, 7 blue pens, and 1 black pen in a bag. He chooses pens from the bag at random.

"What are we asked to do?"

We are asked to determine the probabilities of several different events.

Plan — Make a plan.

"What problem-solving strategy will we use?"

We will *use logical reasoning* to determine the probability of each event.

"How many pens does Luke have in total?"

2 red + 7 blue + 1 black = 10 pens

Solve — Carry out the plan.

"What is the probability of choosing a red pen?"

Two of the ten pens are red: $\frac{2}{10} = \frac{1}{5}$

"What is the probability of choosing a red or black pen?"

Two of the 10 pens are red and one is black: $\frac{(2 + 1)}{10} = \frac{3}{10}$

"What is the probability of not choosing a blue pen?"

Three of the ten pens are not blue: $\frac{3}{10}$

"If we do not choose a blue pen, what color pen must we choose?"

We must choose a red or or black pen. The probability is the same for not choosing a blue pen as it is for choosing a red or black pen.

"If Luke choose a blue pen and gives it away, how many pens are left in his bag?"

nine

"If Luke chooses a blue pen and gives it away, what is the probability that he will select another blue pen with his next draw?"

Six of the nine remaining pens are blue: $\frac{6}{9} = \frac{2}{3}$.

Check — Look back.

"Did we do what we were asked to do?"

Yes, we found the probability of each event described in the problem.

1 Power Up

Facts

Distribute **Power Up T** to students. See answers below.

Mental Math

Encourage students to share different ways to mentally compute these exercises. Strategies for exercises **d** and **e** are listed below.

d. Convert to Inches

$1\text{ ft}^2 + 1\text{ ft}^2 = 2\text{ ft}^2$

$12\text{ in.}^2 + 12\text{ in.}^2 = 2\text{ ft}^2$

$144\text{ in.}^2 + 144\text{ in.}^2 = 288\text{ in.}^2$

Think Area

1 square foot has 12 in. on each side

$12 \times 12 = 144$

$1\text{ square foot} = 144\text{ in.}^2$

$144\text{ in.}^2 + 144\text{ in.}^2 = 288\text{ in.}^2$

e. Equivalent Expressions

$8 \times \frac{9}{4} = 8 \times 9 \div 4$

$72 \div 4 = 36 \div 2 = 18 \div 1$ or 18

Decompose and Multiply

$(8 \times 2) + (8 \times \frac{1}{4})$

$16 + 2 = 18$

Problem Solving

Refer to **Power-Up Discussion,** p. 642B.

2 New Concepts

Instruction

Tell students that many problems involve more than one step, and in this lesson, they will solve problems by using two steps to isolate the variable.

To solve two-step equations, we employ two properties of equalities to create simplified equations.

(continued)

LESSON 93

• Two-Step Equations and Inequalities

Power Up *Building Power*

facts Power Up T

mental math

a. **Positive/Negative:** $(-25)(-8)$ 200

b. **Order of Operations/Exponents:** $(2.5 \times 10^8)(3 \times 10^{-4})$ 7.5×10^4

c. **Ratio:** $\frac{100}{x} = \frac{22}{55}$ 250

d. **Measurement:** 2 ft^2 equals how many square inches? 288 in.^2

e. **Calculation:** $8 \times 2\frac{1}{4}$ 18

f. **Percent:** 10% less than 60 54

g. **Geometry:** A slide moves triangle *ABC* to form triangle *A′B′C′*. What is the proper name of the transformation that formed $\triangle A'B'C'$? translation

h. **Estimation:** Estimate the product of 3.14 and 4.9 cm. 15 cm

problem solving Luke put 2 red pens, 7 blue pens, and 1 black pen in a bag, closed it, and shook it up. If the pens are the same size, weight, and texture, what is the probability of choosing a red pen? A red *or* black pen? What is the probability of *not* choosing a blue pen? If Luke does choose a blue pen, but gives it away, what is the probability he will choose *another* blue pen? $\frac{1}{5}, \frac{3}{10}, \frac{3}{10}, \frac{2}{3}$

New Concept *Increasing Knowledge*

Since Investigation 7 we have practiced solving one-step balanced equations. In this lesson we will practice solving two-step equations.

This balance scale illustrates a two-step equation.

$2x + 5 = 35$

On the left side of the equation are two terms, $2x$ and 5. To solve the equation, we first isolate the variable term by subtracting 5 from (or adding -5 to) both sides of the equation.

$2x + 5 - 5 = 35 - 5$ subtracted 5 from both sides

$2x = 30$
simplified

Facts Simplify.

$6 + 6 \times 6 - 6 \div 6 = 41$	$3^2 + \sqrt{4} + 5(6) - 7 + 8 = 42$
$4 + 2(3 + 5) - 6 \div 2 = 17$	$2 + 2[3 + 4(7 - 5)] = 24$
$\sqrt{1^3 + 2^3 + 3^3} = 6$	$\frac{4 + 3(7 - 5)}{6 - (5 - 4)} = 2$
$(\ 3)(-3) + (-3) - (-3) = 9$	$\frac{3(-3) - (-3)(-3)}{(-3) - (3)(-3)} = -3$

Thinking Skill

Discuss

Demonstrate that you can multiply by $\frac{1}{2}$ in order to isolate the variable. Why does this work?

$\frac{1}{2} \cdot \frac{2x}{1} = \frac{1}{2} \cdot \frac{30}{1}$; Sample: Multiplying 2 by its reciprocal, $\frac{1}{2}$, results in 1.

We see that $2x = 30$, so we divide by 2 (or multiply by $\frac{1}{2}$) to find $1x$.

$\frac{2x}{2} = \frac{30}{2}$	divided both sides by 2
$x = 15$	simplified

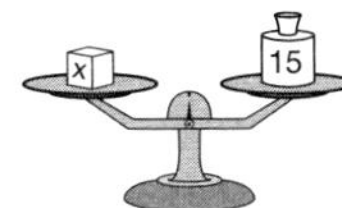

Example 1

Solve this equation. Show all steps.

$$\mathbf{0.4x + 1.2 = 6}$$

Solution

First we isolate the variable term by subtracting 1.2 from both sides of the equation. Then we divide both sides by 0.4.

$0.4x + 1.2 = 6$	equation
$0.4x + 1.2 - 1.2 = 6 - 1.2$	subtracted 1.2 from both sides
$0.4x = 4.8$	simplified
$\frac{0.4x}{0.4} = \frac{4.8}{0.4}$	divided both sides by 0.4
$x = \mathbf{12}$	simplified

Justify Show how to check the solution. Describe your process.

$0.4x + 1.2 = 6$, $0.4(12) + 1.6 = 6$, $4.8 + 1.2 = 6$, $6 = 6$; I substituted the value of x, 12, in place of x in the original equation. Then I simplified the equation and found that the two sides are equal.

Example 2

Solve this equation. Show all steps.

$$-\frac{2}{3}x - \frac{1}{2} = \frac{1}{3}$$

Solution

First, we isolate the variable term by adding $\frac{1}{2}$ to both sides of the equation. Then we find $1x$ by multiplying both sides of the equation by $-\frac{3}{2}$.

$-\frac{2}{3}x - \frac{1}{2} = \frac{1}{3}$	equation
$-\frac{2}{3}x - \frac{1}{2} + \frac{1}{2} = \frac{1}{3} + \frac{1}{2}$	added $\frac{1}{2}$ to both sides
$-\frac{2}{3}x = \frac{5}{6}$	simplified
$\left(-\frac{3}{2}\right)\left(-\frac{2}{3}x\right) = \left(-\frac{3}{2}\right)\left(\frac{5}{6}\right)$	multiplied both sides by $-\frac{3}{2}$
$x = -\frac{5}{4}$	simplified

Math Background

Does $4x - 2 = 6$ mean the same as $6 = 4x - 2$?

Yes. When an equation is reversed, the equals sign does not change and the quantities remain equal.

Does $3 < 2x + 1$ mean the same as $2x + 1 > 3$?

Yes. When an inequality is reversed, the inequality sign is also reversed. Mathematically speaking, $a < b$ implies that $b > a$.

2 New Concepts (Continued)

Instruction

Ask students questions about the balance scale.

"What changed on the left side of the scale?" The 5 weight was removed.

"What changed on the right side of the scale?" The 35 weight was reduced to a 30 weight.

"Why were both sides changed?" Both sides were changed by the same amount to keep the scale balanced.

Example 1

Instruction

Remind students of the order of operations: first multiply/divide, then add/subtract. Tell students that solving two-step equations requires working backward: first undo addition/subtraction, then undo multiplication/division.

Example 2

Instruction

If students have difficulty understanding why $-\frac{3}{2}$ was chosen as the multiplier, remind them that the variable can be isolated when its coefficient is 1. The result is 1 when a coefficient is multiplied by its reciprocal. The reciprocal has the same sign as the original coefficient.

Demonstrate how to check the solution.

$$-\frac{2}{3}\left(-\frac{5}{4}\right) - \frac{1}{2} = \frac{1}{3}$$

$$\frac{10}{12} - \frac{1}{2} = \frac{1}{3}$$

$$\frac{5}{6} - \frac{3}{6} = \frac{1}{3}$$

$$\frac{2}{6} = \frac{1}{3}$$

$$\frac{1}{3} = \frac{1}{3}$$

(continued)

2 New Concepts (Continued)

Example 3

Instruction

Interchanging the two sides of an equation employs the Symmetric Property of Equality, which is symbolized this way:

If $a = b$, then $b = a$.

Ask a student volunteer to check the solution at the board.

$$-15 = 3(-7) + 6$$
$$-15 = -21 + 6$$
$$-15 = -15$$

Example 4

Instruction

Review the inequality symbols and their meanings.

$>$ is greater than
$\geq$ is greater than or equal to
$<$ is less than
$\leq$ is less than or equal to

(continued)

Example 3

Solve: $-15 = 3x + 6$

Solution

Thinking Skill
Explain
Interchange the sides of the equation. Why will the solution remain the same?
$3x + 6 = -15$; Sample: The solution is the same because the relationship of the constants and the variable did not change.
$-15 = 3(-7) + 6$
$-15 = -21 + 6$
$-15 = -15$

The variable term is on the right side of the equal sign. We may interchange the entire right side of the equation with the entire left side if we wish (just as we may interchange the contents of one pan of a balance scale with the contents of the other pan). However, we will solve this equation without interchanging the sides of the equation.

$-15 = 3x + 6$	equation
$-15 - 6 = 3x + 6 - 6$	subtracted 6 from both sides
$-21 = 3x$	simplified
$\frac{-21}{3} = \frac{3x}{3}$	divided both sides by 3
$\mathbf{-7 = x}$	simplified

Justify Show how to check the solution.

In this lesson we have practiced procedures for solving equations. We may follow similar procedures for solving inequalities in which the variable term is positive.[1] To solve an inequality, we isolate the variable while maintaining the inequality.

Example 4

Solve this inequality and graph its solution: $2x - 5 \geq 1$

Solution

We see that the variable term ($2x$) is positive. We begin by adding 5 to both sides of the inequality. Then we divide both sides of the inequality by 2.

$2x - 5 \geq 1$	inequality
$2x - 5 + 5 \geq 1 + 5$	added 5 to both sides
$2x \geq 6$	simplified
$\frac{2x}{2} \geq \frac{6}{2}$	divided both sides by 2
$\mathbf{x \geq 3}$	simplified

[1] Procedures for solving inequalities with a negative variable term will be taught in a later course.

English Learners

In example 3, explain what it means to **interchange** things. Say:

"To interchange means to trade or have two things switch places."

Have two students interchange seats. Ask the class what happened after they moved. They switched seats.

Inclusion

Students may have difficulty understanding the algorithm for solving a two-step equation. An alternative method where parts of the equation are covered up and solved separately may help. For example 3, instead of first subtracting 6 and then dividing by 3, have the students do the following steps.

$-15 = 3x + 6$	write down the equation
$-15 = ? + 6$	cover up 3x with a sticky note
$? = -21$	find the missing value using mental math

Now have the students uncover the 3x do the final steps.

$3x = -21$	write down the equation
$3? = -21$	cover up x with a sticky note
$? = -7$	find the missing value using mental math

Connect the separated steps with the algorithm used for example 3.

We check the solution by replacing x in the original inequality with numbers equal to and greater than 3. We try 3 and 4 below.

$2x - 5 \geq 1$	original inequality
$2(3) - 5 \geq 1$	replaced x with 3
$1 \geq 1$	simplified and checked
$2(4) - 5 \geq 1$	replaced x with 4
$3 \geq 1$	simplified and checked

No; Sample: The solution to the equation is $x \geq 3$, and $2 < 3$. Replacing x with 2 results in the untrue statement $-1 \geq 1$.

Predict Would the number 2 satisfy the inequality? Why or why not?

Now we graph the solution $x \geq 3$.

−2 −1 0 1 2 3 4 5 6 7 8

This graph indicates that all numbers greater than or equal to 3 satisfy the original inequality.

Discuss Why is the dot at 3 solid? The solid dot indicates that the solution includes 3.

Practice Set

Justify Solve each equation. Show and justify all steps. Check each solution.

a. $8x - 15 = 185$ 25 **b.** $0.2y + 1.5 = 3.7$ 11

▸ **c.** $\frac{3}{4}m - \frac{1}{3} = \frac{1}{2}$ $\frac{10}{9}$ **d.** $1\frac{1}{2}n + 3\frac{1}{2} = 14$ 7

e. $-6p + 36 = 12$ 4 **f.** $38 = 4w - 26$ 16

Represent Solve these inequalities and graph their solutions:

g. $x \geq -2$ (−3 −2 −1 0 1)

h. $x < 3$ (0 1 2 3 4)

▸ **g.** $2x + 5 \geq 1$ ▸ **h.** $2x - 5 < 1$

Written Practice *Strengthening Concepts*

1. (46) From Sim's house to the lake is 30 kilometers. If he completed the round trip on his bike in 2 hours 30 minutes, what was his average speed in kilometers per hour? 24 kilometers per hour

2. (Inv. 4) Find the **a** mean and **b** range for this set of numbers: **a.** 9 **b.** 37

3, 9, 7, 5, 10, 4, 5, 8, 5, 4, 8, 40

Use ratio boxes to solve problems **3–5.**

3. (36, 66) The ratio of red marbles to blue marbles in a bag of 600 red and blue marbles was 7 to 5.

a. How many marbles were blue? 250 marbles

b. If one marble is drawn from the bag, what is the probability that the marble will be blue? $\frac{5}{12}$

▸ See Math Conversations in the sidebar.

2 New Concepts (Continued)

Example 4 (continued)

Instruction

Point out that an infinite number of solutions exist for this inequality. Every point shown on the number line is included in the solution. Emphasize that any number greater than or equal to 3 is included, and all fractional numbers greater than 3 are part of the solution set.

Suggest that students pick a point that is not on the graph and test it in the original inequality after they have graphed the solution to an inequality. This value should make the inequality a false statement.

Practice Set

Problem c Justify

Remind students that in algebra, they shouldn't change improper fractions to mixed numbers.

Problems g and h Error Alert

If students are not using the correct dot, remind students to use a solid dot when they graph inequalities with $\geq$ or $\leq$ symbols.

When graphing inequalities that use a $>$ or $<$ symbol, they should use an empty circle.

3 Written Practice

Math Conversations

Discussion opportunities are provided below.

Problem 6 Generalize

Ask students to list the steps for simplifying this expression. It may help students to list $-x$ as $-1x$

Step 1: Determine the sign.
The answer is positive since there is an even number of negative signs.
Step 2: List the factors.
$(-3) \cdot x \cdot x \cdot (2) \cdot x \cdot y \cdot (-1) \cdot (x) \cdot (3) \cdot y \cdot y$
Step 3: Use the Commutative Property.
$(-3) \cdot (2) \cdot (3) \cdot (-1) \cdot x \cdot x \cdot x \cdot x \cdot y \cdot y \cdot y$
Step 4: Use the Associative Property and simplify.

$$18x^4y^3$$

Problem 13

Extend the Problem

"What shape is the part that was cut off?" a right triangle

"What are the dimensions of this shape? What is its area?" The dimensions of the square are 12 in. on a side, so the dimensions of the right triangle are 6 in. by 8 in. by 10 in. is Area = 24 in.^{2}.

Problem 15 Generalize

Ask a volunteer to draw a ratio box on the board and explain how to setup the proportion.

	Percent	Actual
Original (Wholesale)	100	\$3.60
+ Change (Markup)	120	M
New (Retail)	220	R

$$\frac{100}{220} = \frac{\$3.60}{R}$$

Errors and Misconceptions

Problem 5

Some students may think that parts **a** and **b** ask the same question. Lead students to see that **b** is the opposite of **a**.

(continued)

4. (72) The machine could punch out 500 plastic pterodactyls in 20 minutes. At that rate, how many could it punch out in $1\frac{1}{2}$ hours? 2250 plastic pterodactyls

▶ *** 5.** (92) **a.** The price of a T-shirt was reduced by 25%. If the original price was \$24, what was the sale price? \$18

b. The price of a backpack was reduced by 25%. If the sale price was \$24, what was the original price? \$32

▶ *** 6.** (87) **Generalize** Multiply: $(-3x^2)(2xy)(-x)(3y^2)$ $18x^4y^3$

7. (36) A bag normally contains a dozen marbles, 4 of which are blue. However, 2 blue marbles are missing. If a marble is selected at random from the bag, what is the probability that the selected marble will be blue? $\frac{2}{10} = \frac{1}{5}$

*** 8.** (88) Use two unit multipliers to convert 7 days to minutes. 10,080 minutes

9. (22) Diagram this statement. Then answer the questions that follow.

Five ninths of the 45 cars pulled by the locomotive were not tanker cars.

a. How many tanker cars were pulled by the locomotive? 20 tanker cars

b. What percent of the cars pulled by the locomotive were not tanker cars? $55\frac{5}{9}\%$

9. 45 cars

$\frac{5}{9}$ were not tanker cars.	5 cars
	5 cars
	5 cars
	5 cars
	5 cars
$\frac{4}{9}$ were tanker cars.	5 cars
	5 cars
	5 cars
	5 cars

10. (33, 48) Compare: $\frac{1}{3}$ ⊘> 33%

*** 11.** (91) Evaluate: $ab - a - b$ if $a = -3$ and $b = -1$ 7

12. (46) Find the total price, including 5% tax, for a meal that includes a \$7.95 dish, a 90¢ beverage, and a \$2.35 dessert. \$11.76

▶ **13.** (9, 75) A corner was cut from a square sheet of paper to form this pentagon. Dimensions are in inches.

6, 10, 12, 4

a. What is the perimeter of the pentagon? 44 in.

b. What is the area of the pentagon? 120 in.^{2}

14. (48) Complete the table.

Fraction	Decimal	Percent
a. $\frac{2}{25}$	0.08	**b.** 8%
c. $\frac{1}{12}$	**d.** $0.08\overline{3}$	$8\frac{1}{3}\%$

▶*** 15.** (92) **Generalize** A retailer buys a toy for \$3.60 and marks up the price 120%. What is the retail price of the toy? \$7.92

16. (83) Multiply. Write the product in scientific notation. 4.8×10^5

$$(8 \times 10^{-3})(6 \times 10^7)$$

17. (67, 70) Each edge of a cube is 10 cm long.

a. What is the volume of the cube? 1000 cm^3

b. What is the surface area of the cube? 600 cm^2

▶ See Math Conversations in the sidebar.

18. (65, 82) **a.** What is the area of the circle shown? 314 cm^2

b. What is the circumference of the circle? 62.8 cm

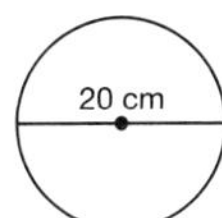

Use 3.14 for π.

19. (84) Collect like terms: $-x + 2x^2 - 1 + x - x^2$ $x^2 - 1$

20. (56, Inv. 9) **a.** Find the missing numbers in the table by using the function rule.

b. Represent Plot the points and draw a line.

c. Analyze Are x and y directly proportional? Why or why not?

$y = 2x + 3$

x	y
1	5
0	3
−2	−1

21. (74) Write an equation to solve this problem:

$60 = \frac{3}{8} \times W_N$; 160 Sixty is $\frac{3}{8}$ of what number?

* **22.** (93) Represent Solve this inequality and graph its solution: $2x - 5 > -1$

23. (40) Refer to the figure below to answer **a** and **b**.

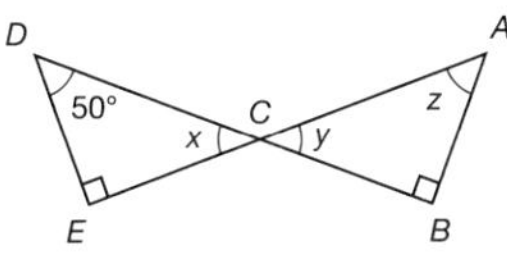

a. Find the measures of $\angle x$, $\angle y$, and $\angle z$.
$m\angle x = 40°$; $m\angle y = 40°$; $m\angle z = 50°$

b. Are the two triangles similar? Why or why not?

24. (34) Connect What is the sum of the numbers labeled A and B on the number line below? 0.87

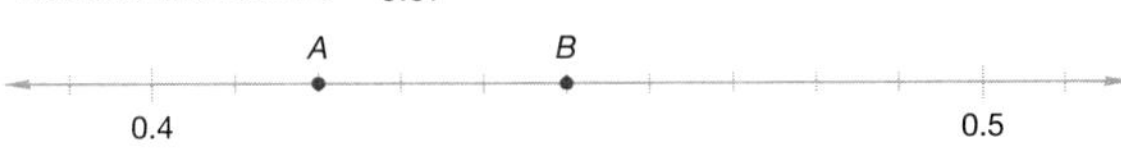

Generalize For problems **25–28,** solve and check. Show each step.

* **25.** (93) $3x + 2 = 9$ $\frac{7}{3}$

* **26.** (93) $\frac{2}{3}w + 4 = 14$ 15

* **27.** (93) $0.2y - 1 = 7$ 40

* **28.** (90) $-\frac{2}{3}m = 6$ −9

Simplify:

29. (57, 63) $3(2^3 + \sqrt{16}) - 4^0 - 8 \cdot 2^{-3}$ 34

* **30.** (85, 91) **a.** $\dfrac{(-9)(+6)(-5)}{(-4) - (-1)}$ −90

b. $-3(4) + 2(3) - 1$ −7

20. b.

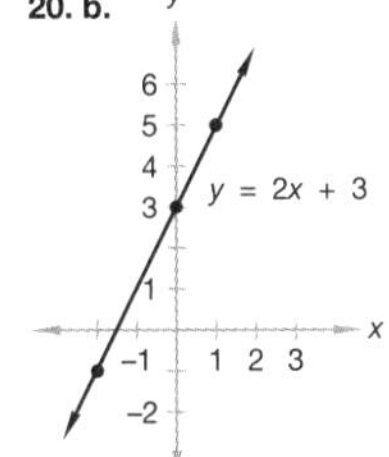

20. c. No, x and y are not directly proportional. Although the graph is a line the x, y pair 0, 0 is not a solution.

22. $x > 2$

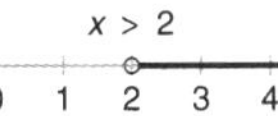

23. b. Yes. The triangles have the same shape. Their corresponding angles are congruent.

▶ See Math Conversations in the sidebar.

3 Written Practice (Continued)

Math Conversations

Discussion opportunities are provided below.

Problem 20 Represent

"Is the point $(\frac{1}{2}, 4)$ a solution of the graph? Explain." When you plot the point $(\frac{1}{2}, 4)$ it is on the line. In the equation $y = 2x + 3$, $2(\frac{1}{2}) + 3 = 1 + 3$ or 4, so $(\frac{1}{2}, 4)$ is a solution of the equation.

Problem 22 Represent

"How would the graph change if the inequality was $2x - 5 \geq -1$?" the dot would be filled in

Problem 24 Connect

"What is the mean of the numbers represented by A and B?" 0.435

"What number is halfway between points A and B?" 0.435

Looking Forward

Solving two-step equations and inequalities prepares students for:

- **Lesson 101,** translating expressions into equations and solving the equations.
- **Lesson 102,** simplifying and solving equations.
- **Lesson 106,** solving literal equations and transforming formulas.
- **Lesson 108,** substituting into formulas and solving for a desired variable.
- **Lesson 109,** solving equations with exponents.

• Probability of Dependent Events

Objectives

- Find the probability of dependent events occurring in a specified order.
- Use a calculator to calculate probabilities.

Lesson Preparation

Materials

- **Power Up S** (in *Instructional Masters*)
- **Teacher-provided material: calculators, graph paper**

Optional

- **Investigation Activity 13** (in *Instructional Masters*)
- **Manipulative kit: color tiles, bag**
- **Teacher-provided material: playing cards, index cards, or slips of paper**

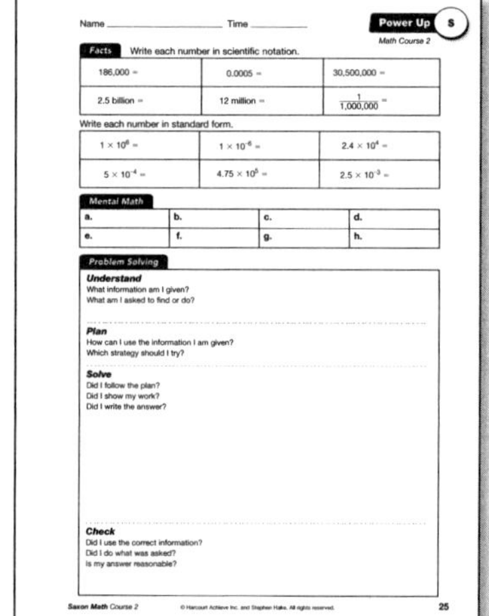

Name ____________ Time ________

Power Up S
Math Course 2

Facts Write each number in scientific notation.

186,000 =	0.0005 =	30,500,000 =
2.5 billion =	12 million =	$\frac{1}{1,000,000}$ =

Write each number in standard form.

1×10^6 =	1×10^{-6} =	2.4×10^4 =
5×10^{-4} =	4.75×10^5 =	2.5×10^{-3} =

Mental Math

a.	b.	c.	d.
e.	f.	g.	h.

Problem Solving

Understand
What information am I given?
What am I asked to find or do?

Plan
How can I use the information I am given?
Which strategy should I try?

Solve
Did I follow the plan?
Did I show my work?
Did I write the answer?

Check
Did I use the correct information?
Did I do what was asked?
Is my answer reasonable?

Saxon Math Course 2 © Harcourt Achieve Inc. and Stephen Hake. All rights reserved. 25

Power Up S

Math Language

New	Maintain	English Learners (ESL)
dependent event	independent event	shuffle

Technology Resources

Student eBook Complete student textbook in electronic format.

Resources and Planner CD Assessment, reteaching, and instructional masters, plus a pacing calendar with standards.

Test and Practice Generator CD Create additional practice sheets and custom-made tests.

www.SaxonPublishers.com Visit for more student activities and planning materials.

Inclusion

Adaptations CD Adapted lessons, investigations, practice and assessments.

Meeting Standards

National Council of Teachers of Mathematics (NCTM)

Data Analysis and Probability

DP.4b Use proportionality and a basic understanding of probability to make and test conjectures about the results of experiments and simulations

DP.4c Compute probabilities for simple compound events, using such methods as organized lists, tree diagrams, and area models

Problem Solving

PS.1b Solve problems that arise in mathematics and in other contexts

Power-Up Discussion *For use with Power Up, p. 648*

Problem-Solving Strategy: Guess and Check/ Make an Organized List

Darla designed a stained glass window that incorporates 20 squares, triangles, and circles altogether. The window has 2 more triangles than twice the number of squares. The number of circles in the window is a multiple of three. How many of each shape appears in Darla's window if there are at least two of each shape?

Understand — *Understand the problem.*

"What information are we given?"

Darla designed a stained glass window incorporating 20 shapes: squares, triangles, and circles. The window has 2 more triangles than twice the number of squares, and the number of circles in the window is a multiple of three.

"What are we asked to do?"

We are asked to determine how many of each shape appear in Darla's window if there are at least two of each shape.

Plan — *Make a plan.*

"What problem-solving strategy will we use?"

We will *guess and check* to help us find the answer. We will *make an organized list* to help us keep track of our guesses.

Solve — *Carry out the plan.*

"How do we begin?"

We begin by choosing choosing 2 as the number of squares (because there are fewer squares than triangles, and we know there are at least two of each shape). Then we calculate the number of triangles by multiplying the number of squares by two and adding two. Then we look for a number of circles that is a multiple of three and that, along with the numbers of squares and triangles, adds to 20:

Squares (s)	**Triangles** ($t = 2s + 2$)	**Circles** ($c = 20 - t$; c **must be a multiple of 3**)	**Total**
2	6	12	20
3	8	9	20
4	10	6	20
5	12	3	20

"Can we stop listing combinations of shapes here?"

Yes, because there are at least two of each shape, and there is no smaller multiple of three that is greater than two.

"How many different combinations of shapes could be in Darla's window?"

four different combinations

Check — *Look back.*

"Did we do what we were asked to do?"

Yes, we found four different combinations of shapes that could be in Darla's window using the information given in the problem.

1 Power Up

Facts

Distribute **Power Up S** to students. See answers below.

Mental Math

Encourage students to share different ways to mentally compute these exercises. Strategies for exercises **a** and **c** are listed below.

a. Decompose

Even number of negative signs, so the answer is positive.

$\frac{12 \times 12}{6} = \frac{12}{1} \times \frac{12}{6} = 12 \times 2$ or 24

Equivalent Expression

Even number of negative signs, so the answer is positive.

$(144 \div 12) \div (6 \div 12) = 12 \div \frac{1}{2}$

$12 \div \frac{1}{2} = 12 \times \frac{2}{1}$ or 24

c. Use Decimals

$5w = 4.5 - 1.5$, or 3

$w = \frac{3}{5}$

Since $\frac{1}{5} = 0.20$, $\frac{3}{5} = 0.60$

Equivalent Expression

$50w = 45 - 15$ or 30

$50w = 30$

$w = \frac{30}{50} = \frac{3}{5} = 0.60$

Problem Solving

Refer to **Power-Up Discussion,** p. 648B.

2 New Concepts

Instruction

Remind students that if an event is certain to happen, the probability is 1. If the event is certain not to happen, the probability is 0. All other probabilities can be stated as fractions, between 0 and 1, which should be simplified, if possible.

(continued)

LESSON 94

• Probability of Dependent Events

Power Up

Building Power

facts Power Up S

mental math

a. **Positive/Negative:** $(-144) \div (-6)$ 24

b. **Order of Operations/Exponents:** $(1.5 \times 10^{-8})(4 \times 10^{3})$ 6×10^{-5}

c. **Algebra:** $5w + 1.5 = 4.5$ 0.6

d. **Measurement:** Convert 30°C to degrees Fahrenheit. 86°F

e. **Calculation:** $6 \times 2\frac{2}{3}$ 16

f. **Percent:** 10% more than 50 55

g. **Geometry:** Name the transformation that turns a figure around a point? rotation

h. **Calculation:** 25% of 40, × 4, + 2, ÷ 6, × 9, + 1, $\sqrt{\ }$, × 3, + 1, $\sqrt{\ }$ 5

problem solving

Darla designed a stained glass window that incorporates 20 squares, triangles, and circles altogether. The window has 2 more triangles than twice the number of squares. The number of circles in the window is a multiple of three. How many of each shape appears in Darla's window if there are at least two of each shape? See Power-Up Discussion.

New Concept

Increasing Knowledge

Thinking Skills

Explain

In your own words explain the difference between independent and dependent events?

Sample: An independent event is not affected by any other event. A dependent event depends on something that has already happened.

The probability experiments we have studied so far involve **independent events** which means that the probability of an event occurring is not affected by the other events. The outcome of the toss of a coin, the roll of a number cube, or the spin of a spinner does not affect future outcomes.

An event is a **dependent event** if its probability is influenced by a prior event. For example, if a marble is drawn from a bag of mixed marbles and is not replaced, then the probability for the next draw differs from the probability of the first draw because the number and mix of marbles remaining in the bag has changed.

The probability of dependent events occurring in a specified order is a product of the first event and the recalculated probabilities of each subsequent event.

Example 1

Two red marbles, three white marbles, and four blue marbles are in a bag. If one marble is drawn and not replaced, and a second marble is drawn, what is the probability that both marbles will be red?

Facts Write each number in scientific notation.

$186{,}000 = 1.86 \times 10^5$	$0.0005 = 5 \times 10^{-4}$	$30{,}500{,}000 = 3.05 \times 10^7$
2.5 billion $= 2.5 \times 10^9$	12 million $= 1.2 \times 10^7$	$\frac{1}{1{,}000{,}000} = 1 \times 10^{-6}$

Write each number in standard form.

$1 \times 10^6 = 1{,}000{,}000$	$1 \times 10^{-6} = 0.000001$	$2.4 \times 10^4 = 24{,}000$
$5 \times 10^{-4} = 0.0005$	$4.75 \times 10^5 = 475{,}000$	$2.5 \times 10^{-3} = 0.0025$

Solution

Two of the nine marbles are red, so the probability of red on the first draw is $\frac{2}{9}$.

$$\text{1st Draw: } P(\text{Red}) = \frac{2}{9}$$

If a red marble is removed from the bag on the first draw, then only one of the remaining eight marbles is red. Thus, the probability of red on the second draw is $\frac{1}{8}$.

$$\text{2nd Draw: } P(\text{Red}) = \frac{1}{8}$$

To find the probability of red on both the first and second draw, we multiply the probabilities of the two events.

$$P(\text{Red, Red}) = \frac{2}{9} \cdot \frac{1}{8} = \mathbf{\frac{1}{36}}$$

Explain Why is the product of $\frac{2}{9} \cdot \frac{1}{8}$ shown as $\frac{1}{36}$? Sample: $\frac{2}{9} \cdot \frac{1}{8} = \frac{2}{72}$ which simplifies to $\frac{1}{36}$.

Example 2

Two cards are drawn from a regular shuffled deck. What is the probability of drawing two aces?

Solution

Although two cards are drawn simultaneously we calculate the probability of each card separately and in sequence. Four of the 52 cards are aces, so the probability of the first card being an ace is $\frac{4}{52}$ which reduces to $\frac{1}{13}$.

$$\text{First card: } P(\text{Ace}) = \frac{4}{52} = \frac{1}{13}$$

Since the first card must be an ace in order for both cases to be aces, only three of the remaining 51 cards are aces. Thus the probability of the second card being an ace is $\frac{3}{51}$ which reduces to $\frac{1}{17}$.

$$\text{Second card: } P(\text{Ace}) = \frac{3}{51} = \frac{1}{17}$$

The probability that both cards drawn are aces is the product of the probabilities of each event.

$$P(Ace, Ace) = \frac{1}{13} \cdot \frac{1}{17} = \mathbf{\frac{1}{221}}$$

Many calculators have an **exponent key** such as y^x or x^y that can be used to calculate probabilities.

Suppose you were going to take a ten-question true-false test. Instead of reading the questions, you decide to guess every answer. What is the probability of guessing the correct answer to all ten questions?

The probability of correctly guessing the first answer is $\frac{1}{2}$. The probability of correctly guessing the first two answers is $\frac{1}{2} \cdot \frac{1}{2}$, or $(\frac{1}{2})^2$. (Since $\frac{1}{2} \cdot \frac{1}{2} = \frac{1}{4}$, we may also write $(\frac{1}{2})^2$ as $\frac{1}{2^2}$.) The probability of correctly guessing the first three answers is $(\frac{1}{2})^3$, or $\frac{1}{2^3}$. Thus, the probability of guessing the correct answer to all ten questions is $(\frac{1}{2})^{10}$, or $\frac{1}{2^{10}}$. To find 2^{10} on a calculator with a y^x or x^y key, we use these keystrokes:

2 New Concepts (Continued)

Example 1

Instruction

Point out that the symbol P(event) is used to represent all of the events that occur. Draw student attention to how P(Red, Red) is used to show that you are to find the probabilities of two events.

After completing the example ask students to find the probability of both draws being a red marble if the first marble is replaced. $\frac{4}{81}$; each draw is the same $\frac{2}{9}$

Example 2

Instruction

Once students see the probability of drawing two aces, have them calculate the probability of drawing three aces from a regular deck of cards.

$$P(\text{Ace, Ace, Ace}) = \frac{1}{13} \times \frac{1}{17} \times \frac{1}{25} = \frac{1}{5525}$$

Instruction

Have students check whether their calculators have an exponent key. If so, have them complete the exercise as you read through it.

(continued)

Math Background

How are independent and dependent events different?

Events are *independent* when the outcome of one event has no influence on the outcome of another event. Consider tossing a coin and spinning a spinner with 2 equal parts labeled 1 and 2. What is the probability of tossing heads and spinning 2?

$$P(\text{H}, 2) = \frac{1}{2} \times \frac{1}{2} \text{ or}$$

The outcome of the toss *does not* affect the outcome of the spinner.

Events are *not independent* when the outcome of one event does influence the outcome of another event. Consider a bag of 4 blue and 4 yellow tiles. The probability of drawing a blue tile is 4 out of 8 or $\frac{1}{2}$. If you don't replace the blue tile, the probability of drawing another blue tile is 3 out of 7 or $\frac{3}{7}$. The probability of drawing two blue tiles in a row is $\frac{1}{2} \times \frac{3}{7}$ or $\frac{3}{14}$.

The outcome of the first draw *does* affect the outcome of the second draw.

English Learners

In example 2, explain the term **shuffle.** Say:

"When you shuffle cards, you mix them up or change the order of the cards."

Demonstrate shuffling cards using playing cards, index cards, or slips of paper.

2 New Concepts *(Continued)*

Instruction

For the multiple choice-test solution, some students may see $1.099511628 \times 10^{12}$ or an alternate form of scientific notation on the display when using a calculator to compute 4^{20}. Explain to them that 1×10^{12} is a rounded form of 4^{20} as indicated by the ≈ symbol.

Practice Set

Problem a Analyze

Have students explain how they know their answers are correct.

3 Written Practice

Math Conversations

Discussion opportunities are provided below.

Problem 7 Generalize

Have students explain their reasoning.

Sample: 360 is the whole so it is 100%. 20% less than 100% is 80%. The number that is 80% of 360 is 20% less than 360.

Ask students to find the number.

$\frac{4}{5} \times 360 = 72 \times 4$ or 288

Problem 8 Generalize

Ask a student volunteer to draw a ratio box on the board and explain the solution.

	Percent	Actual
Original	100	R
− Change	20	C
New	80	$20

$$\frac{100}{80} = \frac{R}{\$20}$$

$$100 \cdot \$20 = 80R$$
$$\$2000 = 80R$$
$$\$25 = R$$

Errors and Misconceptions

Problem 2

If students write 74 as an answer, explain that they have only found the average of 2 hours when there is data for each of 6 hours. Students should list the data and then add and divide.

$$68, 68, 80, 80, 80, 80 = 456$$
$$456 \div 6 = 76 \text{ miles per hour}$$

Problem 5

If students write 8 as an answer, explain that 8 is the number of losses. They need to perform one more step to find the number of games. Add the number of wins to the number of losses.

(continued)

The number displayed is 1024. Therefore, the probability of correctly guessing all ten true-false answers is

$$\frac{1}{1024}$$

Correctly guessing all ten answers has the same likelihood as tossing heads with a coin ten times in a row. The chance of being successful by guessing is very small.

Probabilities that are extremely unlikely may be displayed by a calculator in scientific notation.

$\frac{1}{4^{20}} \approx \frac{1}{1 \times 10^{12}}$ This is less than one chance in a trillion.

Analyze Find the probability of correctly guessing the correct answer to every question on a twenty-question, four-option multiple-choice test.

Practice Set

▸ **a.** **Analyze** In a bag are two red marbles, three white marbles, and four blue marbles. If one marble is drawn from the bag and not replaced and then a second marble is drawn from the bag, what is the probability of drawing two blue marbles? $\frac{1}{6}$

b. If two cards are drawn from a regular shuffled deck, what is the probability that both cards will be diamonds? $\frac{1}{17}$

Written Practice *Strengthening Concepts*

1. (51) Twenty-one billion is how much more than 9.8 billion? Write the answer in scientific notation. 1.12×10^{10}

▸ **2.** (53, 55) The train traveled at an average speed of 68 miles per hour for the first 2 hours and at an average speed of 80 miles per hour for the next 4 hours. What was the train's average speed for the 6-hour trip? 76 miles per hour

3. (46) A 10-pound box of laundry detergent costs $15.45. A 15-pound box costs $20.50. Which box costs the most per pound? How much more per pound does it cost? 10-pound box; $0.18 per pound more

4. (36, 67) In a rectangular prism, what is the ratio of faces to edges? $\frac{1}{2}$

Use ratio boxes to solve problems **5–8.**

▸ **5.** (66) The team's win-loss ratio was 3 to 2. If the team won 12 games and did not tie any games, how many games did the team play? 20 games

6. (72) Twenty-four is to 36 as 42 is to what number? 63

▸ ***7.** (92) **Generalize** The number that is 20% less than 360 is what percent of 360? 80%

▸ ***8.** (92) **Generalize** During the sale shirts were marked down 20 percent to $20. What was the regular price of the shirts (the price before the sale)? $25

***9.** (88) Use two unit multipliers to perform each conversion:

a. 144 ft^2 to square yards $16\ yd^2$

b. 1 kilometer to millimeters 1,000,000 millimeters

▸ See Math Conversations in the sidebar.

Manipulative Use

Materials: color tiles, 4 each of blue, red, and yellow; bag

Acting out the situation can help students understand why the probability of simultaneous events, such as two tiles being drawn from a bag, are calculated separately. Have students work in groups to draw 2 tiles from a bag and calculate the probability of drawing 2 blue tiles when the tiles are:

- drawn and replaced,
- drawn without being replaced,
- drawn simultaneously.

10. Read this statement. Then answer the questions that follow.
(71)
An author wrote $\frac{2}{5}$ of her new book. She has written a total of 120 pages.

a. How many pages will her book have when it is finished? 300 pages

b. How many more pages does she need to write? 180 pages

11. If a pair of 1–6 number generators is tossed once, what is the probability that the total number rolled will be
(36)

a. 1? 0 **b.** 2? $\frac{1}{36}$ **c.** 3? $\frac{2}{36} = \frac{1}{18}$

▶* 12. **Analyze** If $y = 4x - 3$ and $x = -2$, then y equals what number? -11
(91)

▶ 13. The perimeter of a certain square is 4 yards. Find the area of the square in square feet. 9 square feet
(16, 20)

14. The sale price of the new car was $18,500. The sales-tax rate was 6.5 percent.
(46, 60)

a. What was the sales tax on the car? $1202.50

b. What was the total price including tax? $19,702.50

c. If the commission paid to a salesperson is 2 percent of the sale price, how much is the commission on a $18,500 sale? $370

15. Complete the table.
(48)

Fraction	Decimal	Percent
a. $\frac{2}{3}$	**b.** $0.\overline{6}$	$66\frac{2}{3}\%$
$1\frac{3}{4}$	**c.** 1.75	**d.** 175%

* 16. **a.** What is 200 percent of $7.50? $15.00
(60, 92)

▶ **b.** **Analyze** What is 200 percent more than $7.50? $22.50

17. Multiply. Write the product in scientific notation. 1.6×10^{11}
(83)

$$(2 \times 10^8)(8 \times 10^2)$$

18. Roberto puts 1-inch cubes in a box with inside dimensions as shown. How many cubes will fit in this box? 96 cubes
(70)

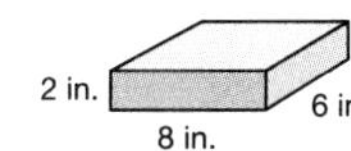

19. The length of each side of the square equals the diameter of the circle. The area of the square is how much greater than the area of the circle? 42 in.^{2}
(82)

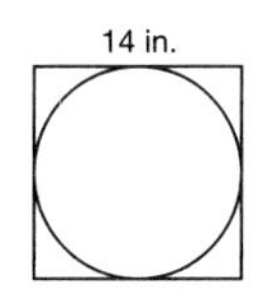

Use $\frac{22}{7}$ for π.

▶ See Math Conversations in the sidebar.

3 Written Practice (Continued)

Math Conversations

Discussion opportunities are provided below.

Problem 12 Analyze

Ask a student to work at the board to substitute the values and solve for y.

"If x = 2, would y be positive or negative? Explain how you know?" positive because $4x$ is greater than 3

$$y = 4(2) - 3$$
$$y = 8 - 3$$
$$y = 5$$

Problem 13

Extend the Problem

"How many one-foot square tiles would you need to carpet a closet that is 6 ft by 8 ft?" $6 \times 8 = 48$ ft^2; 48 foot-square tiles

Have a student draw a diagram to show the answer.

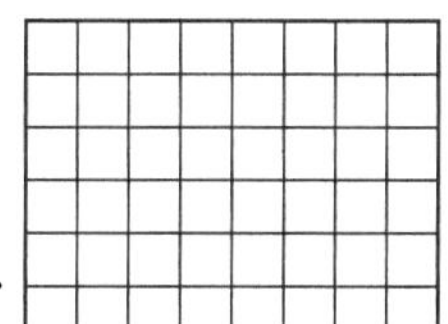

"To find the number of two-foot square tiles needed to carpet a 6 ft by 8 ft closet, can you divide 48 by 2? Explain." no; the tiles are 2 feet on each side, you need to divide by 2×2 or 4; $48 \div 4 = 12$

Have a student draw a diagram to show the answer.

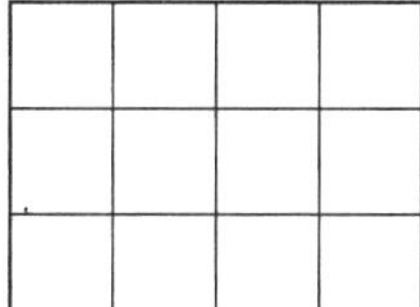

Problem 16b Analyze

Have students explain their reasoning.
Sample: $7.50 is the whole, or 100%.
$7.50 + 200% more is
100% + 100% + 100%, therefore,
$7.50 + $7.50 + $7.50 = $22.50.

(continued)

3 Written Practice (Continued)

Math Conversations

Discussion opportunities are provided below.

Problem 21b Represent

Extend the Problem

"How would the graph of y = 6x be the same as y = 3x and how would it be different?" Sample: same: the line would include 0, 0 as a solution; different: the graph of $y = 6x$ would be steeper.

Problem 22 Represent

"How would you change the inequality to include all numbers 2 or greater in the solution set?" $2x - 5 \geq -1$

Problem 26 Justify

"How can you predict whether you will need to find a common denominator before you solve the equation?" Sample: $-6\frac{2}{3}m$ means multiplication so you do not need common denominators.

Problem 30 Analyze

"Is it fair to say that there is about a 50% chance of drawing a white or a red marble from the bag?" Sample: yes; $\frac{2}{9} + \frac{3}{9} = \frac{5}{9}$ which is close to $\frac{4.5}{9}$

---

21. b.

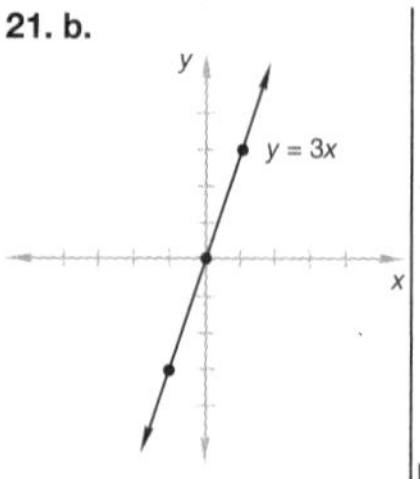

c. Yes, x and y are directly proportional. The graph is a line, and 0,0 is a solution.

22.

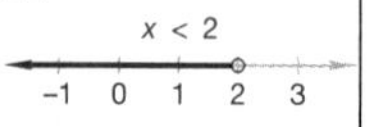

20. (42, 45) Divide 7.2 by 0.11 and write the quotient with a bar over the repetend. $65.\overline{45}$

*** 21.** (56, Inv. 9) **a.** Find the missing numbers in the table by using the function rule.

$y = 3x$

x	y
1	3
0	0
−1	−3

▶ **b.** Represent Graph the function.

c. Are x and y directly proportional? Why or why not?

▶* **22.** (93) Represent Solve this inequality and graph its solution: $2x - 5 < -1$

23. (40) In the figure at right, the measure of $\angle AOC$ is half the measure of $\angle AOD$. The measure of $\angle AOB$ is one third the measure of $\angle AOD$.

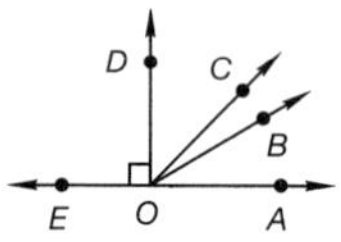

a. Find m$\angle AOB$. 30°

b. Find m$\angle EOC$. 135°

24. (8) The length of segment BC is how much less than the length of segment AB? $\frac{1}{4}$ in.

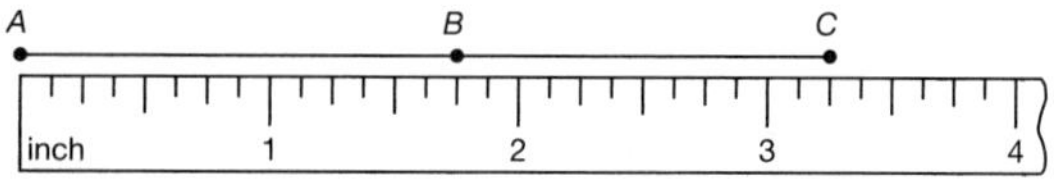

Justify For problems **25** and **26,** solve the equation. Show each step.

*** 25.** (93) $1.2p + 4 = 28$ 20

▶* **26.** (90) $-6\frac{2}{3}m = 1\frac{1}{9}$ $-\frac{1}{6}$

Simplify:

27. (84, 87) **a.** $6x^2 + 3x - 2x - 1$ $6x^2 + x - 1$

b. $(5x)(3x) - (5x)(-4)$ $15x^2 + 20x$

*** 28.** (85, 91) **a.** $\frac{(-8) - (-6) - (4)}{-3}$ 2

b. $-5(-4) - 3(-2) - 1$ 25

*** 29.** (91) Evaluate: $b^2 - 4ac$ if $a = -1$, $b = -2$, and $c = 3$ 16

▶* **30.** (94) Analyze In a bag are two red marbles, three white marbles, and four blue marbles.

a. One marble is drawn and put back in the bag. Then a marble is drawn again. What is the probability of drawing a white marble on both draws? Are the events dependent or independent? $\frac{1}{9}$; independent

b. One marble is drawn and not replaced. Then a second marble is drawn. What is the probability of drawing a white marble on both draws? Are the events independent or dependent? $\frac{1}{12}$; dependent

▶ See Math Conversations in the sidebar.

• Volume of a Right Solid

Objective

- Find the volume of a right solid.

Lesson Preparation

Materials

- **Power Up T** (in *Instructional Masters*)
- **Teacher-pvovided material: graph paper**

Optional

- **Investigation Activity 13** (in *Instructional Masters*)

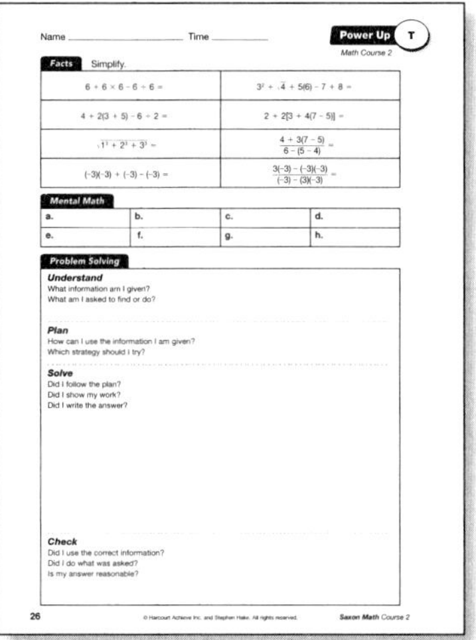

Power Up T

Math Language

New	Maintain	English Learners (ESL)
right solid	prism	abbreviated
	volume	

Technology Resources

Student eBook Complete student textbook in electronic format.

Resources and Planner CD Assessment, reteaching, and instructional masters, plus a pacing calendar with standards.

Test and Practice Generator CD Create additional practice sheets and custom-made tests.

www.SaxonPublishers.com Visit for more student activities and planning materials.

Inclusion

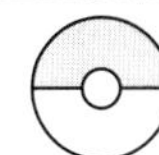

Adaptations CD Adapted lessons, investigations, practice and assessments.

Meeting Standards

National Council of Teachers of Mathematics (NCTM)

Geometry

GM.4b Use two-dimensional representations of three-dimensional objects to visualize and solve problems such as those involving surface area and volume

GM.4e Recognize and apply geometric ideas and relationships in areas outside the mathematics classroom, such as art, science, and everyday life

Measurement

ME.1c Understand, select, and use units of appropriate size and type to measure angles, perimeter, area, surface area, and volume

ME.2b Select and apply techniques and tools to accurately find length, area, volume, and angle measures to appropriate levels of precision

ME.2d Develop strategies to determine the surface area and volume of selected prisms, pyramids, and cylinders

Power-Up Discussion *For use with Power Up, p. 653*

Problem-Solving Strategy: Work Backwards/ Use Logical Reasoning

Copy this problem and fill in the missing digits:

$$\begin{array}{r} \_\,\_\,\_ \\ \times \quad \_ \\ \hline 1101 \end{array}$$

Understand ***Understand the problem.***

"What information are we given?"

We are shown a multiplication problem with both factors missing.

"What are we asked to do?"

We are asked to find both missing factors.

Plan ***Make a plan.***

"What problem-solving strategy will we use?"

We will *use logical reasoning* to look for a single-digit factor of 1101, then *work backwards* to find the other factor.

Solve ***Carry out the plan.***

"Since the product ends with 1, what single-digit factors can we rule out?"

We can rule out 2, 4, 6, and 8 because the product is odd. We can rule out 5 because the last digit is not 5 or 0. We can also rule out 1 because the product has four digits, and we can rule out 9 because the product is not divisible by 9.

"Is 1101 divisible by 3?"

Yes, $1 + 1 + 0 + 1 = 3$. We make our first guess and write 3 as the single-digit factor. We divide 1101 by 3 and work backwards to find that the top factor is 367:

$$\begin{array}{r} 367 \\ \times \quad 3 \\ \hline 1101 \end{array}$$

Check ***Look back.***

"Did we do what we were asked to do?"

Yes, we found the missing factors to complete the given multiplication problem.

"How can we verify the solution is correct?"

We can use the inverse operation (division) to check our answer:
$1101 \div 3 = 367$.

LESSON 95

• Volume of a Right Solid

Power Up — Building Power

facts Power Up T

mental math

a. **Positive/Negative:** (72) + (−100) −28

b. **Order of Operations/Exponents:** $(2.5 \times 10^6)(2.5 \times 10^6)$ 6.25×10^{12}

c. **Ratio:** $\frac{60}{100} = \frac{y}{1.5}$ 0.9

d. **Measurement:** Convert 25°C to degrees Fahrenheit. 77°F

e. **Calculation:** $8 \times 2\frac{3}{4}$ 22

f. **Percent:** 50% more than 60 90

g. **Probability:** There are 6 pairs of black socks, 3 pairs of white socks, and 2 pairs of brown socks. What is the probability of selecting a pair of white socks? $\frac{3}{11}$

h. **Calculation/Percent:** 10% of 300 is how much more than 20% of 100? 10

problem solving

Copy this problem and fill in the missing digits: 3 is the only single-digit number greater than 1 by which 1101 is divisible.

$$\begin{array}{r} \_\_\_ \\ \times \quad \_ \\ \hline 1101 \end{array} \qquad \begin{array}{r} 367 \\ \times \quad 3 \\ \hline 1101 \end{array}$$

New Concept — Increasing Knowledge

Math Language
Volume (*V*) is the measure of cubic units of space occupied by a solid figure.

A **right solid** is a geometric solid whose sides are perpendicular to the base. **The volume of a right solid equals the area of the base times the height.** This rectangular solid is a right solid. It is 5 m long and 2 m wide, so the area of the base is 10 m^2.

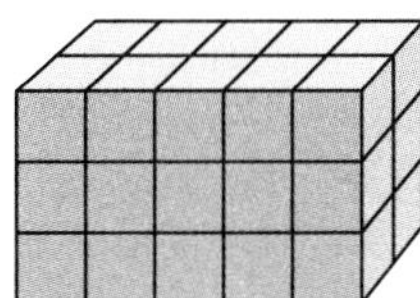

One cube will fit on each square meter of the base, and the cubes are stacked 3 m high, so

$$\begin{aligned} \text{Volume} &= \text{area of the base} \times \text{height} \\ &= 10 \text{ m}^2 \times 3 \text{ m} \\ &= 30 \text{ m}^3 \end{aligned}$$

Facts Simplify.

$6 + 6 \times 6 - 6 \div 6 = 41$	$3^2 + \sqrt{4} + 5(6) - 7 + 8 = 42$
$4 + 2(3 + 5) - 6 \div 2 = 17$	$2 + 2[3 + 4(7 - 5)] = 24$
$\sqrt{1^3 + 2^3 + 3^3} = 6$	$\frac{4 + 3(7 - 5)}{6 - (5 - 4)} = 2$
$(-3)(-3) + (-3) - (-3) = 9$	$\frac{3(-3) - (-3)(-3)}{(-3) - (3)(-3)} = -3$

1 Power Up

Facts

Distribute **Power Up T** to students. See answers below.

Mental Math

Encourage students to share different ways to mentally compute these exercises. Strategies for exercises **e** and **f** are listed below.

e. Decompose

$(8 \times 2) + (8 \times \frac{3}{4})$
$(16) + (8 \times 3) \div 4$
$16 + (24 \div 4) = 16 + 6$ or 22

Multiply Then Divide

$8 \times \frac{11}{4} = 88 \div 4$
$88 \div 4 = 22$

f. Use a Fraction

$\frac{1}{2} \cdot 60 = 30$
$60 + 30 = 90$

Use a Mixed Number

$60 \times 1\frac{1}{2} = 60 \times \frac{3}{2}$
$(60 \times 3) \div 2 = 180 \div 2$ or 90

Problem Solving

Refer to **Power-Up Discussion,** p. 653B.

2 New Concepts

Instruction

Most students will be familiar with the formula $V = lwh$. You may need to review the formula $V = Ah$ where A = the area of the base.

"What dimensions do we use to find the area of the base?" length and width

"What do we multiply the area of the base by to find the volume of a rectangular prism?" height

"What is the formula for finding the volume of a rectangular prism?" *Volume = area of base × height*

(continued)

2 New Concepts (Continued)

Instruction

Point out that each right solid introduced has two congruent, parallel bases. If a base is not specified, students should choose one of these congruent shapes and use it as the base.

Example 1

Instruction

Some students may have difficulty understanding why the triangle is the base of this right triangular prism when looking at the first diagram. Explain that although the rectangular face appears to be the base, it does not have a congruent and parallel face and therefore cannot be the base.

Example 2

Instruction

Once students find the volume using π, have them estimate the volume using 3.14 for π. Remind students that since their answer is an approximation, they must use the $\approx$ sign which means is approximately equal to. $\approx 7850 \text{ cm}^3$

(continued)

If the base of the solid is a polygon, the solid is called a **prism.** If the base of a right solid is a circle, the solid is called a **right circular cylinder.**

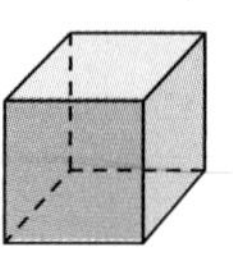
Right square prism

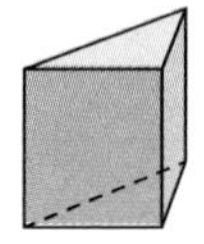
Right triangular prism

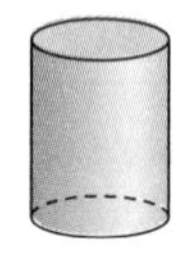
Right circular cylinder

Identify What is another name for a right square prism? What is the shape of the base of each figure shown? cube; square, triangle, circle

Example 1

Find the volume of the right triangular prism below. Dimensions are in centimeters. We show two views of the prism.

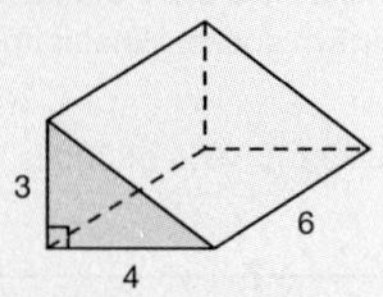

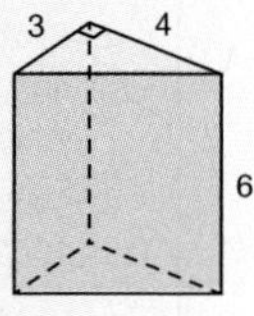

Solution

The area of the base is the area of the triangle.

$$\text{Area of base} = \frac{(4 \text{ cm})(3 \text{ cm})}{2} = 6 \text{ cm}^2$$

The volume equals the area of the base times the height.

$$\text{Volume} = (6 \text{ cm}^2)(6 \text{ cm}) = \mathbf{36 \text{ cm}^3}$$

Example 2

The diameter of this right circular cylinder is 20 cm. Its height is 25 cm. What is its volume? Leave π as π.

Solution

First we find the area of the base. The diameter of the circular base is 20 cm, so the radius is 10 cm.

$$\text{Area of base} = \pi r^2 = \pi(10 \text{ cm})^2 = 100\pi \text{ cm}^2$$

The volume equals the area of the base times the height.

$$\text{Volume} = (100\pi \text{ cm}^2)(25 \text{ cm}) = \mathbf{2500\pi \text{ cm}^3}$$

Math Background

Can you find the volume of a prism whose edges are not perpendicular to the base?

A right prism is a geometric solid whose edges are perpendicular to its base. When a prism has edges that are *not* perpendicular to the bases, the height of the prism is the perpendicular distance between the bases.

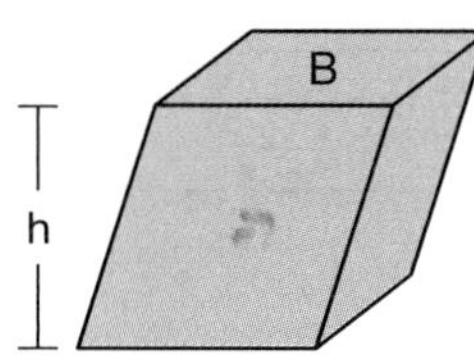

The formula for the volume remains equal to the area of one base times the height, even though the prism is not a right prism.

Since $A = \pi r^2$, replace *B* with πr^2 and get $V = \pi r^2 h$.
To create a formula for a triangular prism, we replace B with the formula for the area of the triangular base.
To avoid the confusion of the height of the triangle and the height of the prism, we can substitute *a* for altitude in place of *h* for height of the triangle.

Recall the formula for the volume of a rectangular solid.

$$V = \text{Area of base} \times \text{height } (V = Bh)$$

We can apply this formula to cylinders and prisms as well.

Formulate The base of a cylinder is a circle. Create a specific formula for the volume of a cylinder by replacing B in the formula with the formula for the area of a circle.

Formulate Create a specific formula for the volume of a triangular prism.
$V = \frac{1}{2}abh$
Many objects in the real world are composed of combinations of basic shapes like the solids in this lesson. We can calculate the volumes of such objects by dividing them into parts, finding the volume of each part, and then adding the volumes.

Example 3

Eric stores gardening tools in a shed with the dimensions shown. Find the approximate volume of the shed.

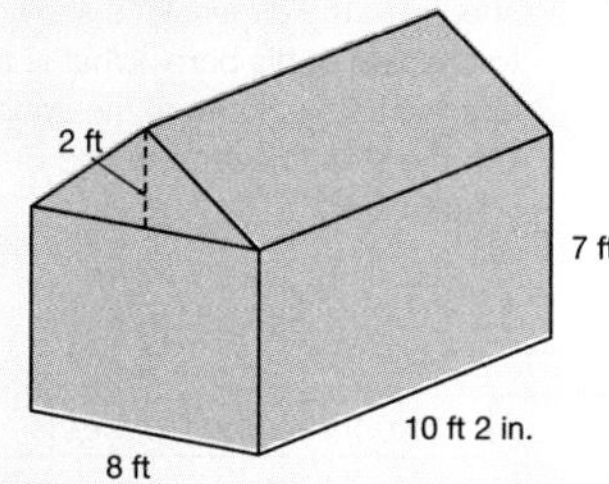

Solution

We separate the structure into a triangular prism and a rectangular prism. We round the dimensions. For example, the notation 10′2″ means 10 feet, 2 inches, which we round to 10 ft.

The volume of the triangular prism is about

$$V = \frac{1}{2}abh$$

$$V = \frac{1}{2}(2 \text{ ft})(8 \text{ ft})(10 \text{ ft}) = 80 \text{ ft}^3$$

The volume of the rectangular prism is about

$$V = lwh$$

$$V = (10 \text{ ft})(8 \text{ ft})(7 \text{ ft}) = 560 \text{ ft}^3$$

The volume of the shed is about

$$80 \text{ ft}^3 + 560 \text{ ft}^3 = \mathbf{640 \text{ ft}^3}$$

2 New Concepts (Continued)

Instruction

The formula for the area of a circle is $A = \pi r^2$. Be sure that students substitute πr^2 for A in $V = Ah$, making the formula $V = \pi r^2 h$.

Have students use this formula for the area of a triangle, $A = \frac{1}{2}ab$. Be sure that they substitute $\frac{1}{2}ab$ for A in $V = Ah$, making the formula $V = \frac{1}{2}abh$.

Example 3

Instruction

Before beginning any calculations, discuss with students the dimensions of this figure, making sure that they understand where to separate the figure. Ask them to identify the length, width, and height of each figure.

The volume formula used for the rectangular prism is *lwh*. Discuss with students how to combine this formula with the formula for the area of the triangular prism.

(continued)

Teacher Tip

Some students may have trouble using the **volume formula** that has the formula for the area of the base imbedded within it. Suggest that these students find the volume of a solid figure in two parts:

- first finding the area of the base
- then multiplying by the height.

English Learners

Before example 3, explain the meaning of **abbreviated**. Say:

"When you abbreviate, you make a word or phrase shorter. Usually, formulas are abbreviated, using letters instead of whole words."

Have a student write their first and last name and then abbreviate their name by writing their initials.

2 New Concepts (Continued)

Practice Set

Problem d (Error Alert)

If students try to compute the volume as one solid, point out that they can separate the solid into two rectangular prisms (with measures of $4 \times 10 \times 2$ and $3 \times 10 \times 5$ or $7 \times 10 \times 2$ and $3 \times 10 \times 3$).

Problem f

Remind students that the ultimate goal of this example is to find the volume of the entire shed, not just of the individual shapes. This is why both volumes must be added to answer the question.

3 Written Practice

Math Conversations

Discussion opportunities are provided below.

Problem 1 Analyze

Extend the Problem

Most students will solve this as a multi-step problem. Ask students to write one expression that could be used to represent and solve the problem. $[(\$0.35 \cdot 40) + \$1.40] \div 4 = \$3.85$

"Why do you multiply $0.35 × 40?" there are 40 tenths in 4 miles

(continued)

Practice Set

Analyze Find the volume of each right solid shown. Dimensions are in centimeters.

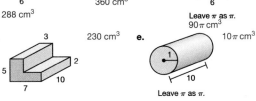

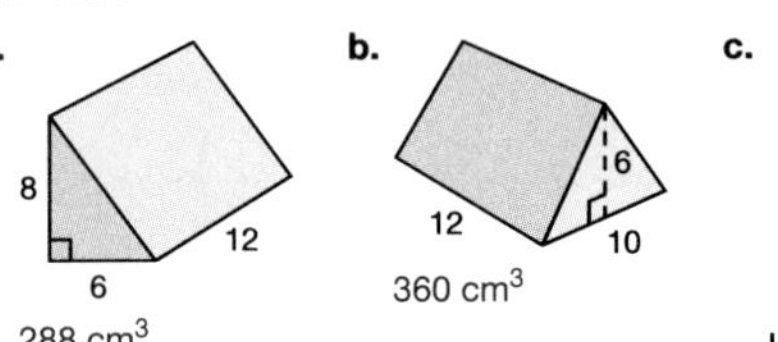

a. 288 cm³

b. 360 cm³

c. (10, 6) Leave π as π. 90π cm³

▶ d. (3, 5, 2, 7, 10) 230 cm³

e. (1, 10) Leave π as π. 10π cm³

▶ f. List A farmer added an attached shed with the dimensions shown to the side of his barn. What is the approximate volume of the addition? List the steps needed to find the volume.

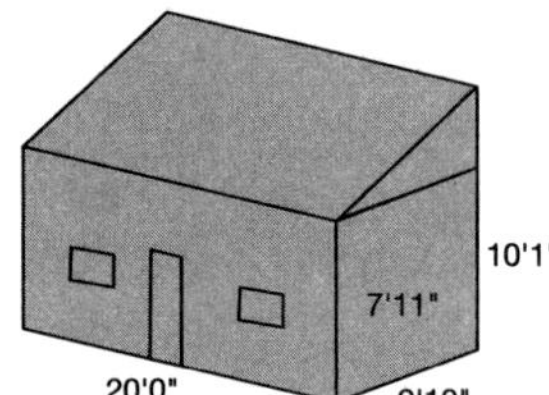

f. about 1800 ft³; Sample: 1. Round the measurement to whole numbers. 2. Divide the shed into two sections, a rectangular prism and triangular prism. 3. Find the volume of each section. 4. Add the two volumes.

Written Practice *Strengthening Concepts*

▶ 1. (55) The taxi ride cost \$1.40 plus 35¢ for each tenth of a mile. What was the average cost per mile for a 4-mile taxi ride? \$3.85 per mile

2. (Inv. 4) The table at right shows student responses to a survey. The students were asked to rate a television special on a scale from 1.0 to 10.0. Create a box-and-whisker plot for these ratings.

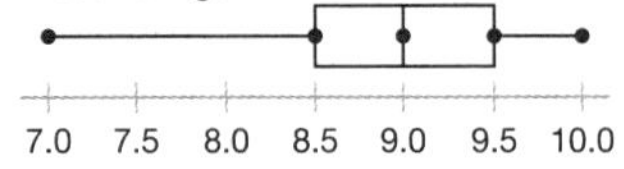

Ratings of Television Special

Rating	Number of Students
10.0	IIII
9.5	𝍸 I
9.0	𝍸 III
8.5	𝍸 II
8.0	III
7.5	I
7.0	I

▶ See Math Conversations in the sidebar.

3\. a.

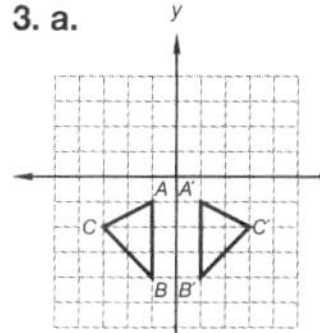

5\. $\frac{1}{3}$; The area of the rectangle is $12 \cdot 8 =$ 96 square units. The area of the triangle is $A = \frac{1}{2}bh = \frac{1}{2}(6)8 =$ 24 square units. So the area of the unshaded portion of the rectangle is 72 square units. The ratio is 24 to 72, or $\frac{24}{72}$, which reduces to $\frac{1}{3}$.

3. (80) The coordinates of the vertices of $\triangle ABC$ are A $(-1, -1)$, B $(-1, -4)$, and C $(-3, -2)$. The reflection of $\triangle ABC$ in the y-axis is its image $\triangle A'B'C'$.

a. Draw both triangles.

b. Write the coordinates of the vertices of $\triangle A'B'C'$.
A' $(1, -1)$, B' $(1, -4)$, C' $(3, -2)$

4. (53) If Gabriela is paid $12 per hour, how much will she earn in 4 hours 20 minutes? $52

▸ **5.** (36, 75) In this rectangle, what is the ratio of the shaded area to the unshaded area? How do you know?

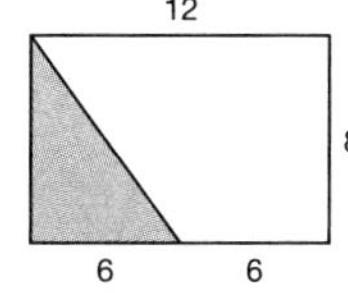

6. (72) If 600 pounds of sand costs $7.20, what would be the cost of 1 ton of sand at the same price per pound? $24.00

▸ *** 7.** (92) **Generalize** The cost of production rose 30%. If the new cost is $3.90 per unit, what was the old cost per unit? $3.00 per unit

▸ *** 8.** (92) **Generalize** If a grocery store marks up cereal 30%, what is the retail price of a large box of cereal that costs the store $3.90? $5.07

*** 9.** (88) Use two unit multipliers to convert 1000 mm^2 to square centimeters.
10 cm^2

10. (71) Read this statement. Then answer the questions that follow.

Three fifths of the middle school students do not play a musical instrument. The other 60 students do play an instrument.

a. How many middle school students are there?
150 middle school students

b. How many middle school students do not play an instrument?
90 middle school students

*** 11.** (Inv. 9) If Jim jogs to school at 6 miles per hour the trip takes 10 minutes. If he rides his bike to school at 12 miles per hour, how long does the trip take? 5 minutes

*** 12.** (91) Evaluate: $m(m + n)$ if $m = -2$ and $n = -3$ 10

13. (36) If two number cubes are tossed once, what is the probability that the total number rolled will be

a. 7? $\frac{6}{36} = \frac{1}{6}$

b. a number less than 7? $\frac{15}{36} = \frac{5}{12}$

▸ *** 14.** (95) The diameter of a soup can is 6 cm. Its height is 10 cm. What is the volume of the soup can? (Use 3.14 for π.) 282.6 cm^3

▸ See Math Conversations in the sidebar.

3 Written Practice (Continued)

Math Conversations

Discussion opportunities are provided below.

Problem 7 Generalize

"What percent can we use to represent the original price?" 100%

"What percent can we use to represent the original price plus the 30% increase?" 130%

"What proportion can we use to find the original price?" $\frac{100}{130} = \frac{R}{\$3.90}$

If necessary, ask a volunteer to write a ratio box on the board to show how to set up the proportion.

Problem 8 Generalize

Help students compare and contrast this problem with problem 7.

"What percent can we use to represent the wholesale price?" 100%

"What percent can we use to represent the retail price (wholesale + markup)?" 130%

"Do we need to find the original price or the retail price?" retail price

"What proportion can we use to find the retail price?" $\frac{100}{130} = \frac{\$3.90}{N}$

If necessary, ask a volunteer to write a ratio box on the board to show how to set up the proportion.

Errors and Misconceptions

Problem 5

Some students may answer $\frac{1}{4}$ because they can visualize that 4 congruent triangles are equal to the area of the rectangle. Explain that if they drew in the lines to make the 4 triangles, they would see that there is one triangle shaded and 3 triangles are unshaded so the ratio of shaded triangles to unshaded triangles is 1 to 3 or $\frac{1}{3}$.

Problem 14

Watch for students who use $\pi 6^2$ to find the area of the base. Remind them that they must use the radius of the circle, not the diameter. Since the radius is $\frac{1}{2}$ the diameter, the radius of the circular base is 3 cm.

(continued)

3 Written Practice (Continued)

Math Conversations

Discussion opportunities are provided below.

Problem 15

Extend the Problem

Ask students to sketch the top view and bottom view of this figure.

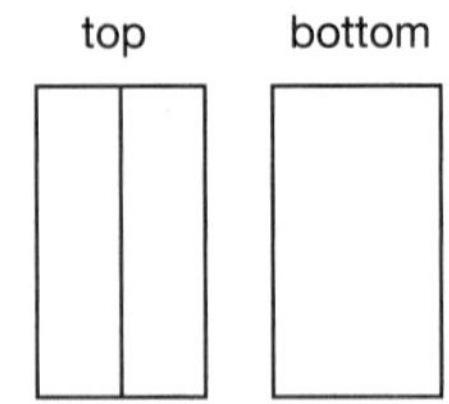

Then ask students to draw the shape they would see if they view the front and view the right side.

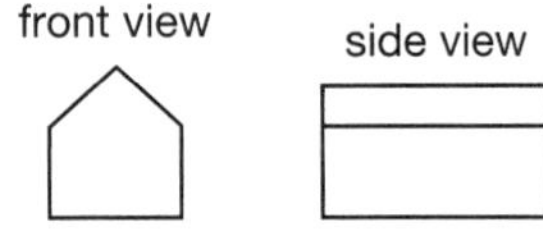

Problem 17a Analyze

Ask students to explain how they know their answers are correct.

First Draw	Second Draw
$\frac{\text{3 white}}{\text{9 marbles}}$	$\frac{\text{4 blue}}{\text{8 marbles}}$

$$\frac{3}{9} \times \frac{4}{8} = \frac{12}{72} \text{ or } \frac{1}{6}$$

Problem 20c Analyze

Ask students if they would be able to answer this question without graphing the function. Have them explain their answer. Yes, x must be 0 to intersect the y-axis; you could solve for y using the function rule.

Problem 22 Represent

"Why is there an empty circle at both ends of the graph?" the solution set is greater than −2; 0 is not a negative number

Errors and Misconceptions

Problem 15

Some students may need help realizing that to find the height of the triangle, they must subtract the height of the rectangle from the total height of the figure.

(continued)

▶* **15.** *(95)* The sketch shows the outline of a building. The peak of the roof is 16 feet above the ground. What is the volume of the building? (Hint: Divide the figure into a rectangular prism and a triangular prism.) 15,600 ft^3

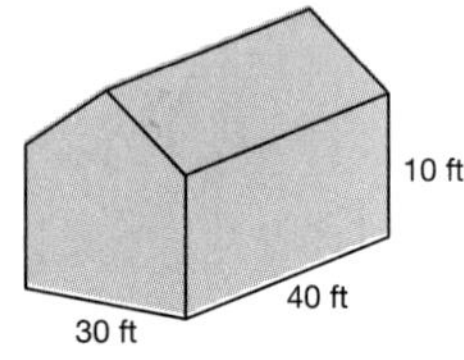

16. *(46)* Find the total cost, including 6 percent sales tax, of 2 tacos at \$2.25 each, 2 fruit drinks at \$1.20 each, and a salad at \$1.30. \$8.69

▶* **17.** *(94)* **a.** Analyze There are two red, three white, and four blue marbles in a bag. If Chad pulls two marbles from the bag, what is the probability that one will be white and the other blue? $\frac{1}{6}$

b. Explain Will the order of the draws affect the probability. Support your answer.

17. b. No; The probability is the same no matter which color Chad pulls out first. Sample: White first: $\frac{3}{9}$. Blue second: $\frac{4}{8}$. $\frac{3}{9} \cdot \frac{4}{8} = \frac{12}{72}$, or $\frac{1}{6}$. Blue first: $\frac{4}{9}$. White second: $\frac{3}{8}$. $\frac{4}{9} \cdot \frac{3}{8} = \frac{12}{72}$, or $\frac{1}{6}$. As the probabilities are both $\frac{1}{6}$ order doesn't matter.

18. *(84, 87)* Simplify:

a. $(-2xy)(-2x)(x^2y)$ $4x^4y^2$

b. $6x - 4y + 3 - 6x - 5y - 8$ $-9y - 5$

19. *(83)* Multiply. Write the product in scientific notation. 3.2×10^{-1}

$$(8 \times 10^{-6})(4 \times 10^4)$$

* **20.** *(56, Inv. 9)* **a.** Use the function rule to complete the table.

b. Graph the function.

▶ **c.** Analyze At what point does the graph of the function intersect the y axis? (0, 1)

$y = \frac{1}{2}x + 1$

x	y
6	4
4	3
−2	0

20. b. $y = \frac{1}{2}x + 1$

21. *(40)* Find the measures of the following angles.

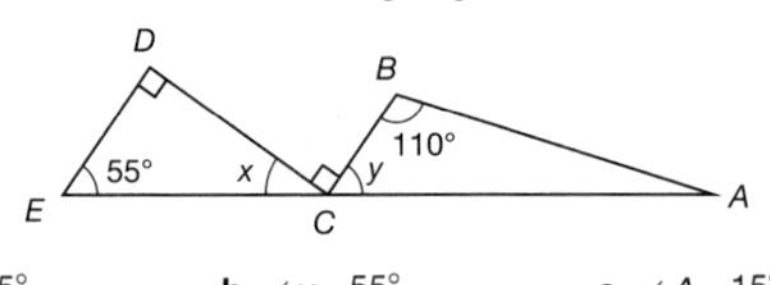

a. $\angle x$ 35° **b.** $\angle y$ 55° **c.** $\angle A$ 15°

▶ **22.** *(78)* Represent On a number line, graph all the negative numbers that are greater than −2.

−3 −2 −1 0 1

23. *(34)* What is the average of the numbers labeled A and B on the number line below? 1.54

▶ See Math Conversations in the sidebar.

26.

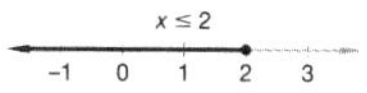

▶ **Justify** For problems 24 and 25, solve and check. Show each step.

* **24.** (93) $-5w + 11 = 51$ -8

* **25.** (93) $\frac{4}{3}x - 2 = 14$ 12

* **26.** (93) Solve this inequality and graph its solution:

$$0.9x + 1.2 \le 3$$

▶ **Generalize** Simplify:

27. (57) $\frac{10^3 \cdot 10^2}{10^5} - 10^{-1}$ $\frac{9}{10}$ or 0.9

28. (63) $\sqrt{1^3 + 2^3} + (1 + 2)^3$ 30

29. (23, 26) $5 - 2\frac{2}{3}\left(1\frac{3}{4}\right)$ $\frac{1}{3}$

30. (85, 91) **a.** $\frac{(-10) + (-8) - (-6)}{(-2)(+3)}$ 2

b. $-8 + 3(-2) - 6$ -20

Early Finishers
Real-World Application

The Li family has four children born in different years.

a. List all possible orders of boy and/or girl children that the Li family could have. Use B for boy and G for girl.

b. Find the probability that a family with four children has exactly two boys and two girls in any order. Sample: $\frac{3}{8}$

a. There are 16: BBBB, BBBG, BBGB, BGBB, GBBB, BBGG, BGBG, BGGB, GBBG, GBGB, GGBB, GGGB, GGBG, GBGG, BGGG, GGGG.

▶ See Math Conversations in the sidebar.

3 Written Practice (Continued)

Math Conversations

Discussion opportunities are provided below.

Problems 24 and 25 Justify

Ask students to explain how they could solve each problem using mental math. Answers will vary.

Problem 27

Extend the Problem

Ask students to make one change in the problem so the answer will be 0.99 instead of 0.9. Sample: subtract 10^{-2} instead of 10^{-1}

Problems 27–30 Generalize

Ask students to decide whether they would use mental math or paper and pencil to solve each problem. Have them explain their choice. Answers will vary.

Looking Forward

Finding the volume of a right solid prepares students for:

- **Lesson 105,** finding the surface area of right solids.
- **Lesson 113,** finding the volume of pyramids, cones, and spheres.

Assessment

30–40 minutes *For use after Lesson 95*

Distribute **Cumulative Test 18** to each student. Two versions of the test are available in *Saxon Math Course 2 Course Assessments Book.* Have students complete the **Power-Up Test** first. Allow 10 minutes. Then have students work the 20 numbered items on the **Cumulative Test**. Students may use copies of the answer sheet to record their work. Track individual and class progress with the **Test Analysis** forms.

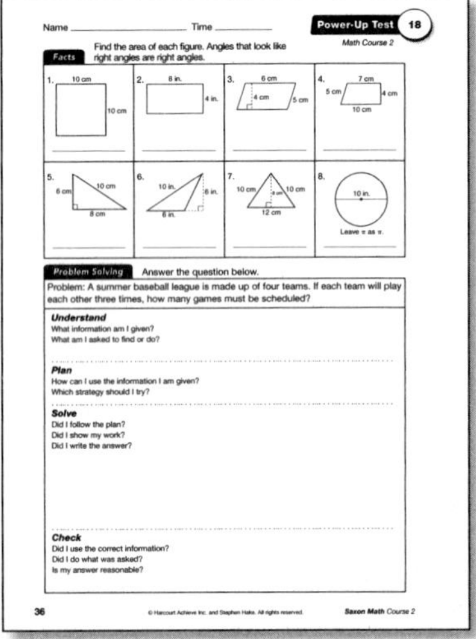

Name ______ Time ______ **Power-Up Test 18**
Math Course 2

Facts Find the area of each figure. Angles that look like right angles are right angles.

Problem Solving Answer the question below.

Problem: A summer baseball league is made up of four teams. If each team will play each other three times, how many games must be scheduled?

Understand
What information am I given?
What am I asked to find or do?

Plan
How can I use the information I am given?
Which strategy should I try?

Solve
Did I follow the plan?
Did I show my work?
Did I write the answer?

Check
Did I use the correct information?
Did I do what was asked?
Is my answer reasonable?

36 © Harcourt Achieve Inc. and Stephen Hake. All rights reserved. **Saxon Math** Course 2

Power-Up Test 18

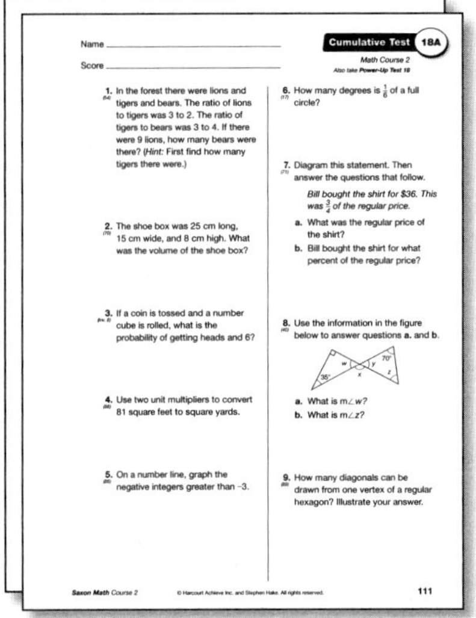

Name ______ **Cumulative Test 18A**
Score ______ *Math Course 2*
Also take ***Power-Up Test 18***

1. In the forest there were lions and tigers and bears. The ratio of lions to tigers was 3 to 2. The ratio of tigers to bears was 3 to 4. If there were 9 lions, how many bears were there? (*Hint:* First find how many tigers there were.)

2. The shoe box was 25 cm long, 15 cm wide, and 8 cm high. What was the volume of the shoe box?

3. If a coin is tossed and a number cube is rolled, what is the probability of getting heads and 6?

4. Use two unit multipliers to convert 81 square feet to square yards.

5. On a number line, graph the negative integers greater than −3.

6. How many degrees is $\frac{1}{6}$ of a full circle?

7. Diagram this statement. Then answer the questions that follow.

   Bill bought the shirt for $36. This was $\frac{3}{4}$ of the regular price.

   a. What was the regular price of the shirt?

   b. Bill bought the shirt for what percent of the regular price?

8. Use the information in the figure below to answer questions **a.** and **b.**

   a. What is m∠*w*?

   b. What is m∠*z*?

9. How many diagonals can be drawn from one vertex of a regular hexagon? Illustrate your answer.

Saxon Math Course 2 © Harcourt Achieve Inc. and Stephen Hake. All rights reserved. 111

Cumulative Test 18A

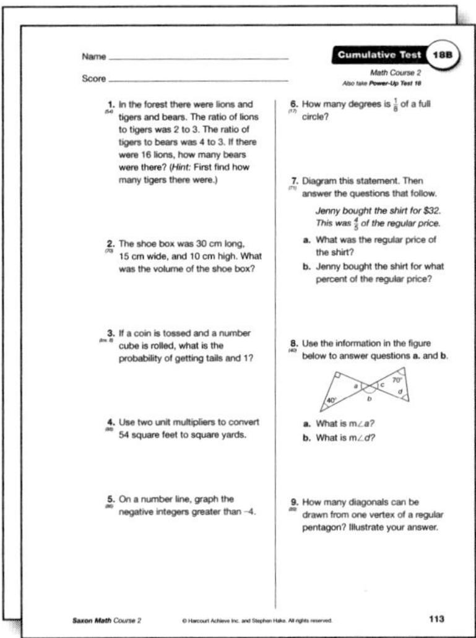

Name ______ **Cumulative Test 18B**
Score ______ *Math Course 2*
Also take ***Power-Up Test 18***

1. In the forest there were lions and tigers and bears. The ratio of lions to tigers was 2 to 3. The ratio of tigers to bears was 4 to 3. If there were 16 lions, how many bears were there? (*Hint:* First find how many tigers there were.)

2. The shoe box was 30 cm long, 15 cm wide, and 10 cm high. What was the volume of the shoe box?

3. If a coin is tossed and a number cube is rolled, what is the probability of getting tails and 1?

4. Use two unit multipliers to convert 54 square feet to square yards.

5. On a number line, graph the negative integers greater than −4.

6. How many degrees is $\frac{1}{8}$ of a full circle?

7. Diagram this statement. Then answer the questions that follow.

   Jenny bought the shirt for $32. This was $\frac{4}{5}$ of the regular price.

   a. What was the regular price of the shirt?

   b. Jenny bought the shirt for what percent of the regular price?

8. Use the information in the figure below to answer questions **a.** and **b.**

   a. What is m∠*a*?

   b. What is m∠*d*?

9. How many diagonals can be drawn from one vertex of a regular pentagon? Illustrate your answer.

Saxon Math Course 2 © Harcourt Achieve Inc. and Stephen Hake. All rights reserved. 113

Alternative Cumulative Test 18B

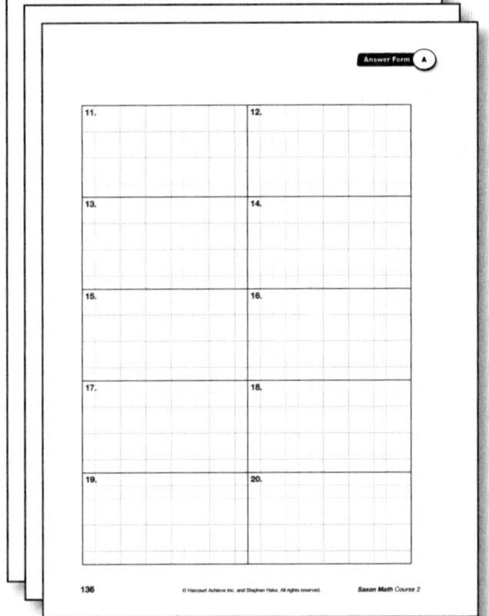

Answer Form A

11.	12.
13.	14.
15.	16.
17.	18.
19.	20.

136 © Harcourt Achieve Inc. and Stephen Hake. All rights reserved. **Saxon Math** Course 2

Optional Answer Forms

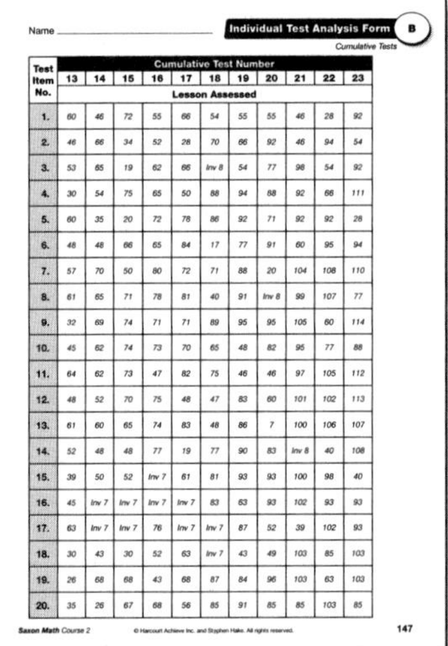

Name ______ **Individual Test Analysis Form B**
Cumulative Tests

Test Item No.	13	14	15	16	17	18	19	20	21	22	23
	Lesson Assessed										
1.	60	46	72	55	66	54	55	55	46	28	92
2.	46	66	34	52	28	70	66	92	46	94	54
3.	53	65	19	62	66	Inv 8	54	77	98	54	92
4.	30	54	75	65	50	88	94	88	92	66	111
5.	60	35	20	72	78	86	92	71	92	92	28
6.	48	48	66	65	84	17	77	91	60	95	94
7.	57	70	50	80	72	71	88	20	104	108	110
8.	61	65	71	78	81	40	91	Inv 8	99	107	77
9.	32	69	74	71	71	89	95	95	105	60	114
10.	45	62	74	73	70	65	48	82	95	77	88
11.	64	62	73	47	82	75	46	46	97	105	112
12.	48	52	70	75	48	47	83	60	101	102	113
13.	61	60	65	74	83	48	86	7	100	106	107
14.	52	48	48	77	19	77	90	83	Inv 8	40	108
15.	39	50	52	Inv 7	61	81	93	93	100	98	40
16.	45	Inv 7	Inv 7	Inv 7	Inv 7	83	63	93	102	93	93
17.	63	Inv 7	Inv 7	76	Inv 7	Inv 7	87	52	39	102	93
18.	30	43	30	52	63	Inv 7	43	49	103	85	103
19.	26	68	68	43	68	87	84	96	103	63	103
20.	35	26	67	68	56	85	91	85	85	103	85

(Column headers 13–23: Cumulative Test Number)

Saxon Math Course 2 © Harcourt Achieve Inc. and Stephen Hake. All rights reserved. 147

Individual Test Analysis Form

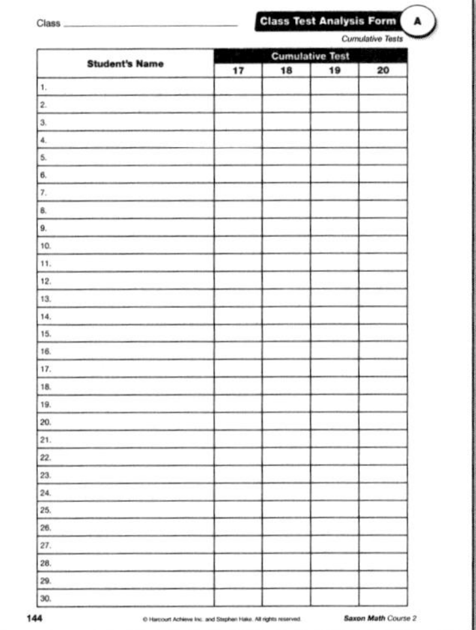

Class ______ **Class Test Analysis Form A**
Cumulative Tests

	Student's Name	Cumulative Test 17	18	19	20
1.					
2.					
3.					
4.					
5.					
6.					
7.					
8.					
9.					
10.					
11.					
12.					
13.					
14.					
15.					
16.					
17.					
18.					
19.					
20.					
21.					
22.					
23.					
24.					
25.					
26.					
27.					
28.					
29.					
30.					

144 © Harcourt Achieve Inc. and Stephen Hake. All rights reserved. **Saxon Math** Course 2

Class Test Analysis Form

Reteaching

Students who score below 80% on the assessment may be in need of reteaching. Look for the causes of student mistakes. If errors are conceptual, refer to the *Reteaching Masters* for reteaching.

Performance Activity 18

Selecting Tools and Techniques

Assign after Lesson 95 and Test 18

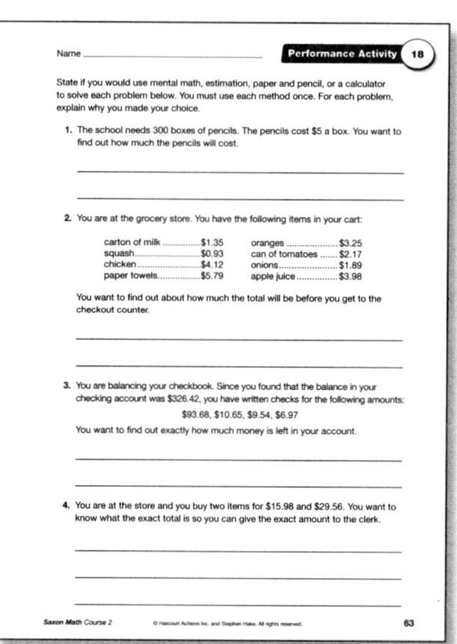

Name ______________________ **Performance Activity 18**

State if you would use mental math, estimation, paper and pencil, or a calculator to solve each problem below. You must use each method once. For each problem, explain why you made your choice.

1. The school needs 300 boxes of pencils. The pencils cost $5 a box. You want to find out how much the pencils will cost.

2. You are at the grocery store. You have the following items in your cart:

carton of milk	$1.35	oranges	$3.25
squash	$0.93	can of tomatoes	$2.17
chicken	$4.12	onions	$1.89
paper towels	$5.79	apple juice	$3.98

You want to find out about how much the total will be before you get to the checkout counter.

3. You are balancing your checkbook. Since you found that the balance in your checking account was $326.42, you have written checks for the following amounts:

$93.68, $10.65, $9.54, $6.97

You want to find out exactly how much money is left in your account.

4. You are at the store and you buy two items for $15.98 and $29.56. You want to know what the exact total is so you can give the exact amount to the clerk.

Saxon Math Course 2 63

Performance Activity 18

Objectives

- Choose mental math, estimation, paper and pencil, or a calculator to solve a problem.
- Communicate their ideas through writing.

Materials

Performance Activity 18

Preparation

Make copies of **Performance Activity 18.** (One each per student.)

Time Requirement

15–30 minutes; Begin in class and complete at home.

Activity

Explain to students that for this activity they will be choosing mental math, estimation, paper and pencil, or a calculator to solve a problem. They will be required to explain their choice. Explain that all of the information students need is on **Performance Activity 18.**

Criteria for Evidence of Learning

- Makes a reasonable choice for a tool or technique to solve a problem.
- Communicates mathematical ideas clearly.

Meeting Standards

National Council of Teachers of Mathematics (NCTM)

Numbers and Operations

NO.1d Understand and use ratios and proportions to represent quantitative relationships

NO.2a Understand the meaning and effects of arithmetic operations with fractions, decimals, and integers

NO.3a Select appropriate methods and tools for computing with fractions and decimals from among mental computation, estimation, calculators or computers, and paper and pencil, depending on the situation, and apply the selected methods

NO.3c Develop and use strategies to estimate the results of rational-number computations and judge the reasonableness of the results

Problem Solving

PS.1c Apply and adapt a variety of appropriate strategies to solve problems

Communication

CM.3a Organize and consolidate their mathematical thinking through communication

• Estimating Angle Measures
• Distributive Property with Algebraic Terms

Objectives

- Estimate angle measures by relating angle measures to the hands of a clock.
- Use the Distributive Property to simplify expressions with algebraic terms.

Lesson Preparation

Materials

- **Power Up U** (in *Instructional Masters*)
- **Lesson Activity 22 Transparency** (in *Instructional Masters*)
- **Manipulative kit: protractors**

Optional

- **Teacher-provided material: oak tag, paper fasteners**
- **Manipulative kit: color tiles**

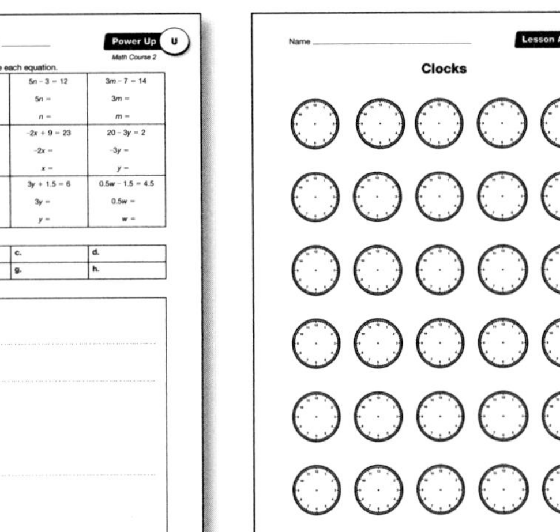
Name ______ Time ______ Power Up U

Math Course 2

Facts Complete each step to solve each equation.

Mental Math

Problem Solving

Understand

Plan

Solve

Check

Power Up U

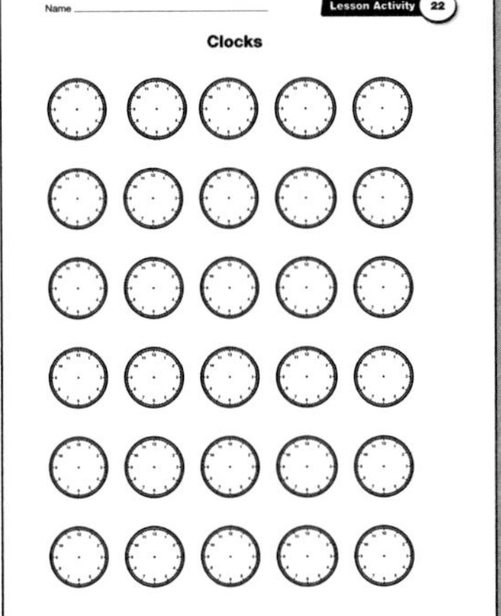
Name ______ Lesson Activity 22

Clocks

Lesson Activity 22

Math Language

English Learners (ESL)
clear parentheses

Technology Resources

Student eBook Complete student textbook in electronic format.

Resources and Planner CD Blackline masters, plus a pacing calendar with standards.

Test and Practice Generator CD Create additional practice sheets and custom-made tests.

www.SaxonPublishers.com Visit for more student activities and planning materials.

Inclusion

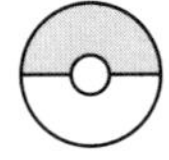

Adaptations CD Adapted lessons, investigations, practice and assessments.

Meeting Standards

National Council of Teachers of Mathematics (NCTM)

Numbers and Operations

NO.2b Use the associative and commutative properties of addition and multiplication and the distributive property of multiplication over addition to simplify computations with integers, fractions, and decimals

Algebra

AL.2c Use symbolic algebra to represent situations and to solve problems, especially those that involve linear relationships

Measurement

ME.1c Understand, select, and use units of appropriate size and type to measure angles, perimeter, area, surface area, and volume

ME.2a Use common benchmarks to select appropriate methods for estimating measurements

Power-Up Discussion *For use with Power Up, p. 660*

Problem-Solving Strategy: Use Logical Reasoning/ Write an Equation

At a recent banquet, every two guests shared a dish of chicken, every three guests shared a dish of rice, and every four guests shared a dish of vegetables. If there were a total of 65 dishes in all, how many guests were at the banquet?

Understand ***Understand the problem.***

"What information are we given?"

We are told the number and type of dishes shared among guests at the banquet and that there are 65 dishes in all.

"What are we asked to do?"

We are asked to determine how many guests were at the banquet.

Plan ***Make a plan.***

"What problem-solving strategy will we use?"

We will *use logical reasoning* to help us *write an equation* to find the answer.

Solve ***Carry out the plan.***

"We will use g to represent the number of guests. Can we write an expression representing the number of dishes of chicken using this variable?"

$\frac{1}{2}g$

"Can we write a similar expression for the number of dishes of rice?"

$\frac{1}{3}g$

"The number of dishes of vegetables?"

$\frac{1}{4}g$

"If we add these three expressions, what should the total be?"

65

"Can we write an equation to show that relationship?"

$\frac{1}{2}g + \frac{1}{3}g + \frac{1}{4}g = 65$

"How can we solve this equation?"

We need to add all the terms containing the variable g. To do this we must first write the fractions $\frac{1}{2}$, $\frac{1}{3}$, and $\frac{1}{4}$ with common denominators: $\frac{6}{12}g + \frac{4}{12}g + \frac{3}{12}g = 65$

"What do we do next?"

We add the terms and solve the equation for g:

$$\frac{13}{12}g = 65$$

$$\frac{12}{13} \times \frac{13}{12}g = 65 \times \frac{12}{13}$$

$$g = 60$$

"How many guests were at the banquet?"

60 guests

Check ***Look back.***

"Did we do what we were asked to do?"

Yes, we found the number of guests at the banquet.

"How can we verify our solution?"

We can substitute 60 into the equation we found for the number of dishes at the party: $\frac{1}{2}(60) + \frac{1}{3}(60) + \frac{1}{4}(60) = 30 + 20 + 15 = 65$

1 Power Up

Facts

Distribute **Power Up U** to students. See answers below.

Mental Math

Encourage students to share different ways to mentally compute these exercises. Strategies for exercises **f** and **h** are listed below.

f. Use a Fraction

$\frac{1}{4} \cdot 80 = 20$

$80 + 20 = 100$

Use a Mixed Number

$80 \times 1\frac{1}{4} = 80 \cdot \frac{5}{4}$

$(80 \times 5) \div 4 = 400 \div 4$ or 100

h. Use 10%

10% of \$50 = \$5

Half of \$5 is \$2.50

\$5 + \$2.50 = \$7.50

Use 5%

5% × \$50 = 10% × \$25 or \$2.50

\$2.50 × 3 = \$7.50

Problem Solving

Refer to **Power-Up Discussion**, p. 660B.

2 New Concepts

Instruction

Review that a clock is a circle broken into 12 equal hour divisions and 60 equal minute divisions. Tell students that they will be learning how to estimate angles using the divisions on a clock face as a mental image.

(continued)

LESSON **96**

• Estimating Angle Measures
• Distributive Property with Algebraic Terms

Power Up *Building Power*

facts Power Up U

mental math

a. **Positive/Negative:** $(-27) - (-50)$ 23

b. **Order of Operations/Exponents:** $(5 \times 10^5)(2 \times 10^7)$ 1×10^{13}

c. **Algebra:** $160 = 80 + 4y$ 20

d. **Measurement:** Convert 15°C to degrees Fahrenheit. 59°F

e. **Calculation:** $9 \times 1\frac{2}{3}$ 15

f. **Percent:** 25% more than \$80 \$100

g. **Geometry:** A rectangular solid measures 5 in. × 3 in. × 2 in. What is the volume of the solid? 30 cubic inches

h. **Percent/Estimation:** Estimate 15% of \$49.75. \$7.50

problem solving At a recent banquet, every two guests shared a dish of chicken, every three guests shared a dish of rice, and every four guests shared a dish of vegetables. If there were a total of 65 dishes in all, how many guests were at the banquet? 60 guests

New Concepts *Increasing Knowledge*

estimating angle measures

In this lesson we will learn a technique for estimating the measure of an angle. To estimate angle measures, we need a mental image of a degree scale—a mental protractor. We can "build" a mental image of a protractor from a mental image we already have—the face of a clock.

The face of a clock is a full circle, which is 360°, and is divided into 12 numbered divisions that mark the hours. From one numbered division to the next is $\frac{1}{12}$ of a full circle. One twelfth of 360° is 30°. Thus the measure of the angle formed by the hands of a clock at 1 o'clock is 30°, at 2 o'clock is 60°, and at 3 o'clock is 90°.

Facts Complete each step to solve each equation.

$2x + 5 = 45$ $2x = 40$ $x = 20$	$3y + 4 = 22$ $3y = 18$ $y = 6$	$5n - 3 = 12$ $5n = 15$ $n = 3$	$3m - 7 = 14$ $3m = 21$ $m = 7$
$15 = 3a - 6$ $21 = 3a$ $7 = a$	$24 = 2w + 6$ $18 = 2w$ $9 = w$	$-2x + 9 = 23$ $-2x = 14$ $x = -7$	$20 - 3y = 2$ $-3y = -18$ $y = 6$
$\frac{1}{2}m + 6 = 18$ $\frac{1}{2}m = 12$ $m = 24$	$\frac{3}{4}n - 12 = 12$ $\frac{3}{4}n = 24$ $n = 32$	$3y + 1.5 = 6$ $3y = 4.5$ $y = 1.5$	$0.5w - 1.5 = 4.5$ $0.5w = 6$ $w = 12$

A clock face is further divided into 60 smaller divisions that mark the minutes. From one small division to the next is $\frac{1}{60}$ of a circle, and $\frac{1}{60}$ of 360° is 6°.

Thus, **from one minute mark to the next on the face of a clock is 6°.**

Here we have drawn an angle on the face of a clock. The vertex of the angle is at the center of the clock. One side of the angle is set at 12, and the other side of the angle is at "8 minutes after."

Since each minute of separation represents 6°, the measure of this angle is 8 × 6°, which is 48°. With some practice we can usually estimate the measure of an angle to within 5° of its actual measure.

Example 1

a. Estimate the measure of $\angle BOC$ in the figure below.

b. Use a protractor to find the measure of $\angle BOC$.

c. By how many degrees did your estimate differ from your measurement?

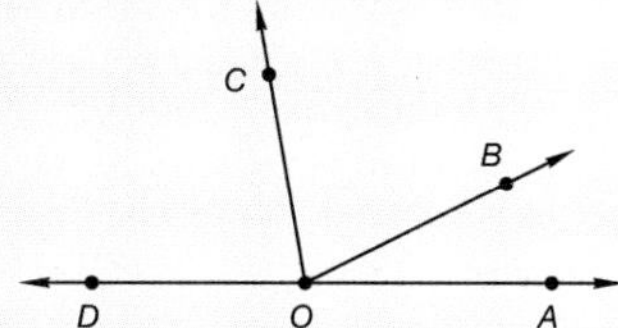

Solution

a. We use a mental image of a clock face on $\angle BOC$ with $\overrightarrow{OC}$ set at 12. Mentally we see that $\overrightarrow{OB}$ falls more than 10 minutes "after." Perhaps it is 12 minutes after. Since 12 × 6° = 72°, we estimate that m$\angle BOC$ is **72°.**

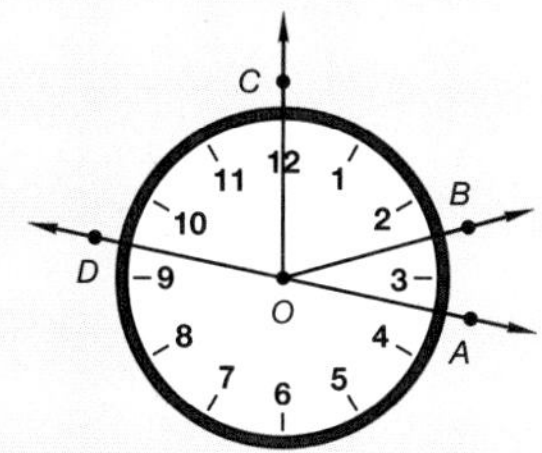

Math Background

Is using a clock face the only technique for estimating angle measures?

No. Another technique for estimating angle measure is to visualize a right angle that has been divided into six 15° sections. To construct a representation of this mental tool, begin by dividing a right angle in half to form two 45° angles. Then divide each of these two angles into three equal parts. The figure provides estimates of these angles:

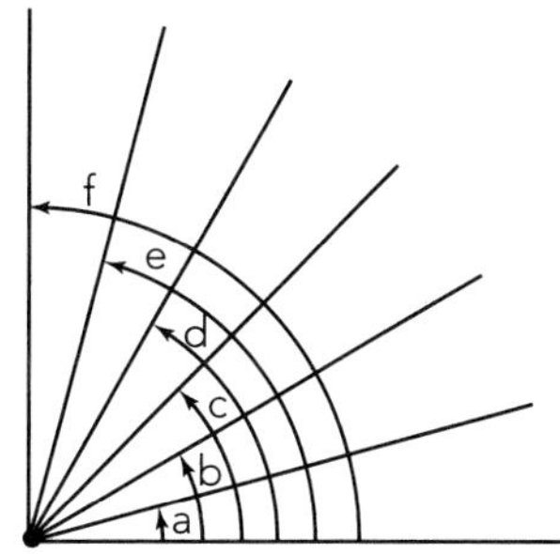

$\angle a \approx 15°$ $\angle b \approx 30°$ $\angle c \approx 45°$

$\angle d \approx 60°$ $\angle e \approx 75°$ $\angle f \approx 90°$

If students have a difficult time visualizing the clock face, have them use this figure as an additional tool to estimate angle measures.

2 New Concepts (Continued)

Instruction

Demonstrate how to use a clock as a measuring tool.

- Use the transparency of **Lesson Activity 22** Clocks.
- Draw lines that divide the clock into halves, then into quarters, and finally into twelfths.
- Ask volunteers to measure the angle of each new division.
- Use a protractor to verify the angles measures.

Demonstrate how to estimate angles.

- Draw several angles and place on the overhead projector.
- Encourage students to estimate the measure of each angle. Write their estimate next to each angle.
- Then place the transparency of **Lesson Activity 22** Clocks over each angle and ask students to find the measure. As a class, compare the mental estimates and the measures found using the clock face.

Example 1

Instruction

If students are having difficulty estimating the measure of $\angle BOC$, suggest that they first decide if the angle's measure is greater than or less than 90°. Students should estimate that the angle is about 10° to 15° less than 90°.

(continued)

2 New Concepts (Continued)

Example 1 (continued)

Ask students to estimate the measure of $\angle DOC$ and then measure it with a protractor. Have them discuss the difference between their estimate and the measured value of $\angle DOC$. Estimates will vary; the measured value of $\angle DOC$ is approximately 78°.

Instruction

Quickly review the Distributive Property. Find the area of a 22 ft by 7 ft patio.

$$7(22) = 7(20 + 2) = (7 \times 20) + (7 \times 2)$$

Tell students that, in this lesson, they will use the Distributive Property to simplify expressions that involve distributing both positive and negative numbers.

Example 2

Instruction

Ask students what sign a product will have if the numbers being multiplied are both positive, negative, or opposite.
same sign: the product will be positive
opposite signs: the product will be negative

(continued)

---

b. We trace $\angle BOC$ on our paper and extend the sides so that we can use a protractor. We find that $m\angle BOC$ is **75°**.

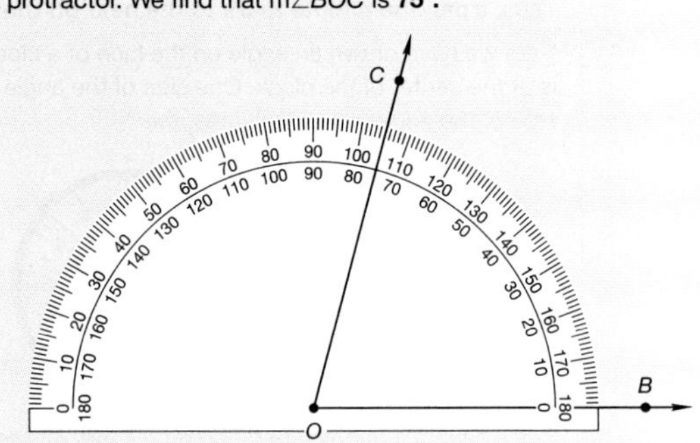

c. Our estimate of 72° differs from our measurement of 75° by **3°**.

Discuss A student estimated that $m\angle DOC$ was about 36°. Without measuring this angle, do you think that this estimate is close to the actual measure? Explain.

No; Sample: If each minute on a mental clock represents 6°, 36° would be the angle formed by clock hands at 6 minutes after 12 o'clock. $m\angle DOC$ is much larger, in fact it is closer to the measure of a right angle, 90°.

distributive property with algebraic terms

Recall from Lesson 41 that the Distributive Property "spreads" multiplication over terms that are algebraically added. We illustrated the Distributive Property with this equation:

$$a(b + c) = ab + ac$$

The Distributive Property is frequently used in algebra to simplify expressions and solve equations.

Example 2

Simplify:

a. $2(x - 3)$ **b.** $-2(x + 3)$

c. $-2(x - 3)$ **d.** $x(x - 3)$

Solution

a. We multiply 2 by x, and we multiply 2 by -3.

$$2(x - 3) = \mathbf{2x - 6}$$

b. We multiply -2 by x, and we multiply -2 by 3.

$$-2(x + 3) = \mathbf{-2x - 6}$$

c. We multiply -2 by x, and we multiply -2 by -3.

$$-2(x - 3) = \mathbf{-2x + 6}$$

d. We multiply x by x, and we multiply x by -3.

$$x(x - 3) = \mathbf{x^2 - 3x}$$

Thinking Skills

Analyze

Why is the simplified expression in **b** $-2x - 6$ and not $-2x + 6$? Because a negative number (-2) multiplied by a positive number $(+3)$ will always produce a negative number.

Manipulative Use

Materials: oak tag, paper fasteners

Some students may benefit from a **hands-on experience** working with a **clock face** before they can mentally visualize an angle on it.

Have students make a large, oak tag clock face with two, equal length strips of oak tag fastened to the center with a paper fastener.

They can construct different angles, such as a 120° angle or a 75° angle, by moving the hands on the paper clock.

Ask them to describe how different angle measures appear on the face.

Example 3

Simplify: $x^2 + 2x + 3(x - 2)$

Solution

Math Language
Like terms have identical variables.

We first use the Distributive Property to clear parentheses. Then we add like terms.

$x^2 + 2x + 3(x - 2)$	expression
$x^2 + 2x + 3x - 6$	Distributive Property
$x^2 + (2x + 3x) - 6$	Associative Property
$\mathbf{x^2 + 5x - 6}$	added $2x$ and $3x$

Example 4

Simplify: $x^2 + 2x - 3(x - 2)$

Solution

In this example multiply $x - 2$ by -3.

$x^2 + 2x - 3(x - 2)$	Given
$x^2 + 2x - 3x + 6$	Distributive Property
$x^2 + (2x - 3x) + 6$	Associative Property
$\mathbf{x^2 - x + 6}$	$2x - 3x = -x$

Practice Set

▶ *Analyze* By counting minute marks on the clock face below, find the measure of each angle:

a. $\angle AOB$ 24° **b.** $\angle AOC$ 120° **c.** $\angle AOD$ 42°

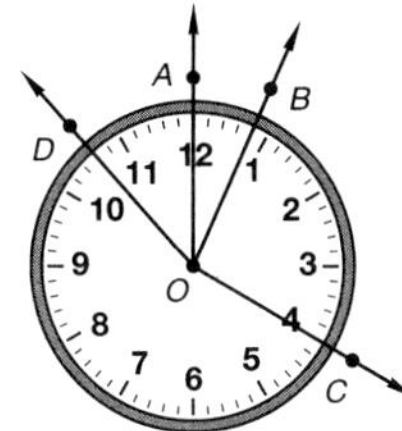

▶ Simplify:

d. $x(x - y)$ $x^2 - xy$ **e.** $-3(2x - 1)$ $-6x + 3$

f. $-x(x - 2)$ $-x^2 + 2x$ **g.** $-2(4 - 3x)$ $-8 + 6x$

▶ *Justify* Simplify. Show and justify each step.

h. $x^2 + 2x - 3(x + 2)$ $x^2 - x - 6$ **i.** $x^2 - 2x - 3(x - 2)$ $x^2 - 5x + 6$

▶ See Math Conversations in the sidebar.

2 New Concepts (Continued)

Examples 3 and 4

Instruction

Remind students that for a like term to have identical variable parts, both the letter and the power have to be the same.

Encourage students to simplify the expressions in examples 3 and 4 by assigning a value for x. For example, assign 4 as the value for x. Have students compare the answers. 30; 18

Practice Set

Problems a and c *Analyze*

Make sure students are counting spaces between tick marks and not the tick marks themselves.

"How many minutes are there between the first and second tick mark?" 1

"How many degrees does each minute represent?" 6

Problems d–i *Justify*

Extend the Problem

Provide these students with more complex expressions that involve distributing algebraic terms.

$-xy(3x - 2)$ $-3x^2y + 2xy$

$x^2(2x^2 + 4x - 2)$ $2x^4 + 4x^3 - 2x^2$

$-4y(3xy + 2y)$ $-12xy^2 - 8y^2$

(continued)

Teacher Tip

Tell students that the hour intervals on a clock are also commonly used to **indicate the direction** an object is positioned in relation to another.

For example, an object at 2 o'clock is approximately 60° to the right of the original object.

Ask students to describe the direction of an object's position in relation to themselves using hour intervals as indicators of direction.

English Learners

In the solution for example 3, explain what it means to **clear parentheses.** Tell students:

"To clear parentheses means to simplify the problem by removing the parentheses."

Write the following expression on the board:

$$6 + (7 - 4)$$

Ask a volunteer to clear the parentheses.

2 New Concepts (Continued)

Practice Set (continued)

Problems j–m Estimate

Encourage students to use 90° as their benchmark for estimates. Students will need a protractor to check their estimates.

3 Written Practice

Math Conversations

Discussion opportunities are provided below.

Problem 4 Explain

Ask students why the ratio 2 to 3 represents the triangular prism when there are 6 edges and 9 vertices. "For every 2 edges there are 3 vertices" is the same ratio as "for every 6 edges there are 9 vertices."

Errors and Misconceptions

Problem 3

If students write the answer as 80 gallons, point out that they need to find how many tanks of gas, not how many gallons of gas are needed. Students should divide 80 by 16 for an answer of 5 tanks.

Problem 7

If students have 30 as an answer they have set up a proportion to find the number of additional people rather than the new total number. Help them draw a ratio box to set up the proportion

$$\frac{100}{125} = \frac{120}{x}$$

(continued)

▶ **Estimate** In practice problems **j–m,** estimate the measure of each angle. Then use a protractor to measure each angle. By how many degrees did your estimate differ from your measurement?

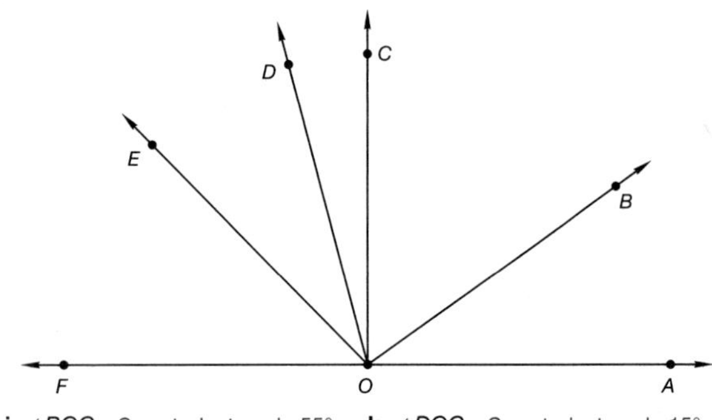

j. $\angle BOC$ See student work; 55°
k. $\angle DOC$ See student work; 15°
l. $\angle FOE$ See student work; 45°
m. $\angle FOB$ See student work; 145°

Written Practice *Strengthening Concepts*

1. (55) In May the merchant bought 3 bikes for an average price of \$280 per bike. In June the merchant bought 5 bikes at an average price of \$240 per bike. What was the average price of all the bikes the merchant bought in May and June? \$255 per bike

2. (20) What is the quotient when 9 squared is divided by the square root of 9? 27

▶ 3. (28) The Adams' car has a 16-gallon gas tank. How many tanks of gas will the car use on a 2000-mile trip if the car averages 25 miles per gallon? 5 tanks

▶ 4. (28) **Explain** In a triangular prism, what is the ratio of the number of vertices to the number of edges? Tell how you found your answer.

4. $\frac{2}{3}$; Sample: I found the number of vertices (6) and the number of edges (9). Then I wrote this information as the ratio 6 to 9 or $\frac{6}{9}$, which reduces to $\frac{2}{3}$.

Use ratio boxes to solve problems **5–7.**

5. (72) If 12 dollars can be exchanged for 100 yuan, what is the cost in dollars of an item that sells for 475 yuan? 57 dollars

* 6. (92) Sixty is 20 percent less than what number? 75

▶ * 7. (92) The average number of customers per day increased 25 percent during the sale. If the average number of customers per day before the sale was 120, what was the average number of customers per day during the sale? 150 customers per day

8. (77) Write equations to solve these problems:
   a. Sixty is what percent of 50? $60 = W_P \times 50$; 120%
   b. Fifty is what percent of 60? $50 = W_P \times 60$; $83\frac{1}{3}\%$

▶ See Math Conversations in the sidebar.

10. a. angles: $\angle A$ and $\angle E$, $\angle B$ and $\angle D$, $\angle ACB$ and $\angle ECD$ (or $\angle BCA$ and $\angle DCE$); sides: $\overline{AB}$ and $\overline{ED}$ (or $\overline{BA}$ and $\overline{DE}$), $\overline{BC}$ and $\overline{DC}$ (or $\overline{CB}$ and $\overline{CD}$), $\overline{AC}$ and $\overline{EC}$ (or $\overline{CA}$ and $\overline{CE}$)

9. (88, Inv. 9) **a.** A college student earns 12 dollars per hour at a part-time job. Use two unit multipliers to convert this pay rate into cents per min. 20¢ per minute

b. Is the student's pay directly proportional or inversely proportional to the number of hours worked? directly proportional

10. (18, 40) Triangle *ABC* is similar to triangle *EDC*.

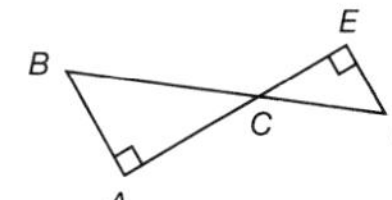

a. List three pairs of corresponding angles and three pairs of corresponding sides.

b. If $m\angle ABC = 53°$, what is $m\angle ECD$? 37°

▸* **11.** (Inv. 9) Analyze Ralph has 48 square floor tiles which he wants to arrange into a rectangle. Here is one arrangement that has 3 rows of 16 tiles.

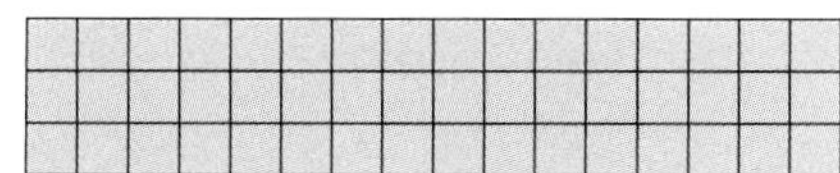

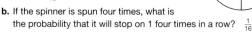

Describe the arrangement of 48 tiles that makes a rectangle with the smallest perimeter. a 6 by 8 rectangle

12. (91) Evaluate: $c(a + b)$ if $a = -4$, $b = -3$, and $c = -2$ 14

13. (16, 20) The perimeter of a certain square is 1 yard. Find the area of the square in square inches. 81 square inches

14. (Inv. 8) The face of this spinner is divided into one half and two fourths.

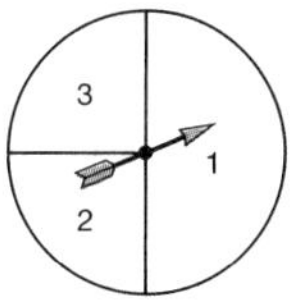

a. If the spinner is spun two times, what is the probability that it will stop on 3 both times? $\frac{1}{16}$

b. If the spinner is spun four times, what is the probability that it will stop on 1 four times in a row? $\frac{1}{16}$

* **15.** (95) Generalize Find the volume of each solid. Dimensions are in centimeters.

a. 27 cm³

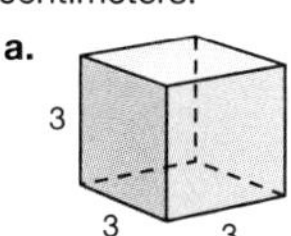

▸ **b.** 60 cm³

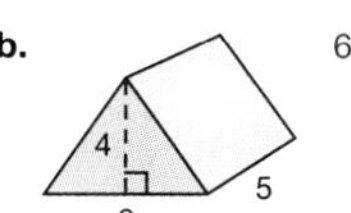

16. (46) Find the total price, including 7 percent sales tax, of 20 square yards of carpeting priced at \$14.50 per square yard. \$310.30

17. (48) Complete the table.

Fraction	Decimal	Percent
a. $\frac{3}{80}$	**b.** 0.0375	$3\frac{3}{4}$%

* **18.** (60, 92) Raincoats regularly priced at \$24 were on sale for $33\frac{1}{3}$% off.

a. What is $33\frac{1}{3}$% of \$24? \$8

b. What is $33\frac{1}{3}$% less than \$24? \$16

▸ See Math Conversations in the sidebar.

3 Written Practice (Continued)

Math Conversations

Discussion opportunities are provided below.

Problem 11 Analyze

If students are not able to generalize that the closer the figure is to a square the lesser the perimeter, help them work the following problem with 9 tiles.

Form all the different ways you can make a rectangle with 9 tiles. Find the perimeter of each.

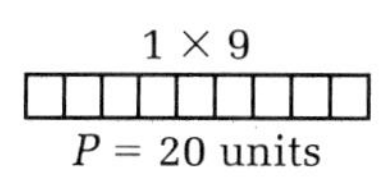

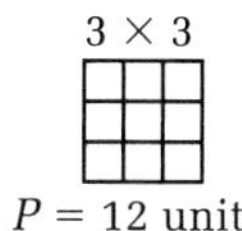

Help students see that the more sides of a square that touch other sides, the lesser the perimeter.

Problem 15b Generalize

"How many triangular prisms would you need to put together to make a rectangular prism? Explain." 2; Just as two congruent triangles can be joined by cutting and fitting together to form a rectangle, so two congruent triangular prisms can be joined to form a rectangular prism. One of the prisms will need to be cut and joined to the other, as shown below.

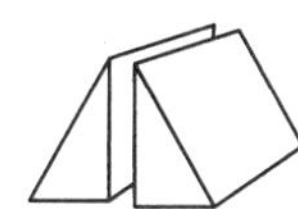

=

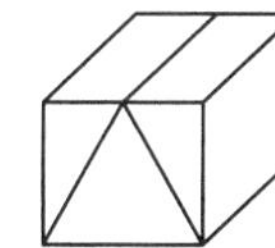

(continued)

3 Written Practice (Continued)

Math Conversations

Discussion opportunities are provided below.

Problem 21 Estimate

"At which numbers would the hands of a clock be pointing to show an angle measurement of 270°?" Sample: 9:00

Problem 22 Conclude

Remind students that an **interior angle** of a polygon opens to the inside of the polygon, and an **exterior angle** is the supplementary angle of an interior angle.

"What is the total sum of the interior angle measures of a regular octagon?" 8×135 or 1080°

Problem 23

Extend the Problem

"Are the x-axis and y-axis lines of symmetry of the original figure? Explain."
Yes, each axis bisects the original figure.

"Are they lines of symmetry of the translated figure? Explain."
No, each axis intersects at one point on the figure.

Problem 24 Analyze

Ask students how the graph of this solution would change if the less than sign (<) was changed to a less than or equal to sign (≤). The dot at 4 on the number line would be closed rather than open.

(continued)

19. (83) Multiply. Write the product in scientific notation. 2.4×10^{-4}

$(3 \times 10^3)(8 \times 10^{-8})$

20. (65, 82) **a.** Find the circumference of the circle at right. 12π m

b. Find the area of the circle. 36π m^2

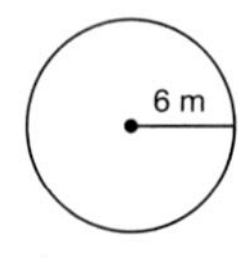

Leave π as π.

▶* **21.** (96) Estimate Use the clock face to estimate the measure of each angle:

a. $\angle BOC$ 90°

b. $\angle COA$ 150°

c. $\angle DOA$ 48°

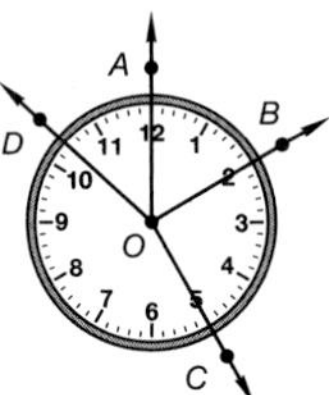

▶* **22.** (89) **a.** Conclude What is the measure of each exterior angle of a regular octagon? 45°

b. What is the measure of each interior angle of a regular octagon? 135°

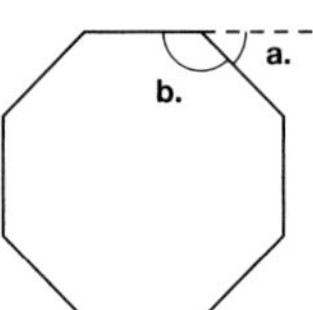

▶ **23.** (80) Find the coordinates of the vertices of □ $Q'R'S'T'$, which is the image of □ $QRST$, translated 4 units right and 4 units down. Q' (8, −4), R' (4, 0), S' (0, −4), T' (4, −8)

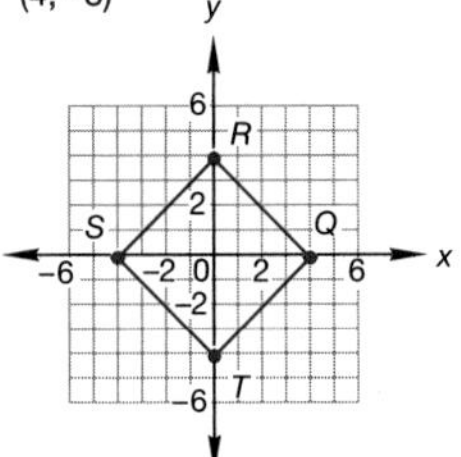

▶* **24.** (93) Represent Solve this inequality and graph its solution:

$0.8x + 1.5 < 4.7$

$x < 4$

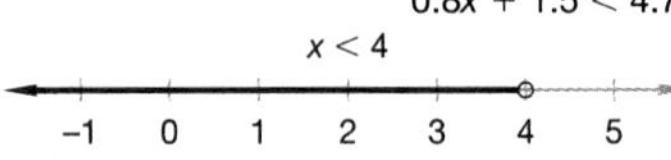

▶ See Math Conversations in the sidebar.

Justify For problems **25** and **26,** solve and check. Show each step.

* **25.** (93) $2\frac{1}{2}x - 7 = 13$ 8

* **26.** (93) $-3x + 8 = 14$ -2

▶ Generalize Simplify:

* **27.** (96) **a.** $-3(x - 4)$ $-3x + 12$

b. $x(x + y)$ $x^2 + xy$

28. (85) **a.** $\frac{(-4) - (-8)(-3)(-2)}{-2}$ -22

b. $(-3)^2 + 3^2$ 18

29. (28) **a.** $(-4ab^2)(-3b^2c)(5a)$ $60a^2b^4c$

b. $a^2 + ab - ab - b^2$ $a^2 - b^2$

▶* **30.** (94) Analyze Gloria had two sets of alphabet cards (A–Z). She mixed the two sets together to form a single stack of cards. Then Gloria drew three cards from the stack without replacing them. What is the probability that she drew either a card with an L or a card with an R all three times? $\frac{1}{5525}$

Early Finishers
Real-World Application

A fuel plant has 2 cylindrical fuel tanks that are 85 ft tall, with a diameter of 32 ft. You may use a calculator for the following questions.

a. How many cubic feet can both tanks hold? Use $\pi = 3.14$. $136{,}652.8\text{ ft}^3$

b. To the nearest whole gallon, how many gallons can both tanks hold? Note: one cubic foot is approximately 7.48 gallons. 1,022,163 gallons

▶ See Math Conversations in the sidebar.

3 Written Practice *(Continued)*

Math Conversations

Discussion opportunities are provided below.

Problems 27–29 Generalize

Ask students to decide whether they would use mental math or paper and pencil to solve each problem. Have them explain their choice. Answers will vary.

Problem 30 Analyze

"Write the fractions you would need to multiply to determine the probability of drawing the letters TALLY if you don't replace the card each time."

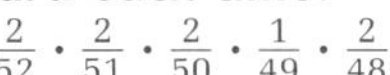

$\frac{2}{52} \cdot \frac{2}{51} \cdot \frac{2}{50} \cdot \frac{1}{49} \cdot \frac{2}{48}$

Errors and Misconceptions

Problem 27

If students are not distributing the negative sign correctly, have them circle the number and sign they are distributing. This will force them to take notice of the sign of every number they are to distribute. Then have them draw lines from the sign to show how they will distribute the number.

Looking Forward

Using the Distributive Property with Algebraic Terms prepares students for:

- **Lesson 102,** simplifying and solving equations by using the Distributive Property.
- **Lesson 115,** factoring algebraic expressions.

• Similar Triangles
• Indirect Measure

Objectives

- Identify the corresponding angles and corresponding sides of similar triangles.
- Use proportions to find the lengths of unknown sides of similar triangles.
- Use proportions to measure the height of an object indirectly.

Lesson Preparation

Materials

- **Power Up T** (in *Instructional Masters*)
- **Manipulative kit: metersticks, rulers, and/or tape measures**

Optional

- **Manipulative kit: protractors**
- **Teacher-provided material: string**

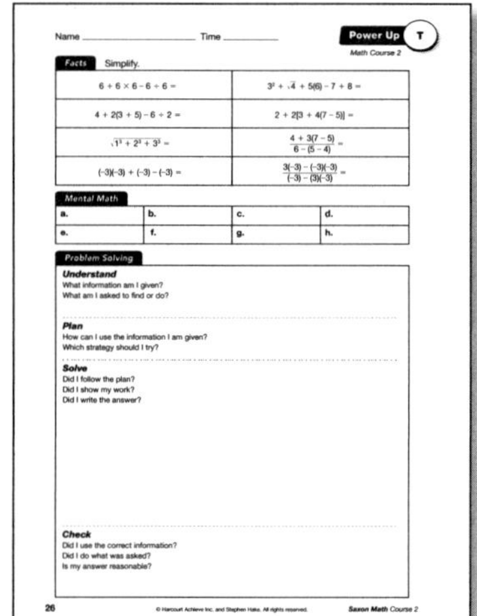

Name ____________ Time ________ **Power Up T** *Math Course 2*

Facts Simplify.

$6 + 6 \times 6 - 6 \div 6 =$	$3^2 + \sqrt{4} + 5(6) - 7 + 8 =$
$4 + 2(3 + 5) - 6 \div 2 =$	$2 + 2[3 + 4(7 - 5)] =$
$\sqrt{1^3 + 2^3 + 3^3} =$	$\frac{4 + 3(7 - 5)}{6 - (5 - 4)} =$
$(-3)(-3) + (-3) - (-3) =$	$\frac{3(-3) - (-3)(-3)}{(-3) - (3)(-3)} =$

Mental Math

a.	b.	c.	d.
e.	f.	g.	h.

Problem Solving

Understand
What information am I given?
What am I asked to find or do?

Plan
How can I use the information I am given?
Which strategy should I try?

Solve
Did I follow the plan?
Did I show my work?
Did I write the answer?

Check
Did I use the correct information?
Did I do what was asked?
Is my answer reasonable?

26 © Harcourt Achieve Inc. and Stephen Hake. All rights reserved. *Saxon Math Course 2*

Power Up T

Math Language

English Learners (ESL)
directly measure
indirectly estimate

Technology Resources

Student eBook Complete student textbook in electronic format.

Resources and Planner CD Assessment, reteaching, and instructional masters, plus a pacing calendar with standards.

Test and Practice Generator CD Create additional practice sheets and custom-made tests.

www.SaxonPublishers.com Visit for more student activities and planning materials.

Inclusion

Adaptations CD Adapted lessons, investigations, practice and assessments.

Meeting Standards

National Council of Teachers of Mathematics (NCTM)

Geometry

GM.1b Understand relationships among the angles, side lengths, perimeters, areas, and volumes of similar objects

GM.1c Create and critique inductive and deductive arguments concerning geometric ideas and relationships, such as congruence, similarity, and the Pythagorean relationship

GM.4d Use geometric models to represent and explain numerical and algebraic relationships

Measurement

ME.2a Use common benchmarks to select appropriate methods for estimating measurements

ME.2e Solve problems involving scale factors, using ratio and proportion

Power-Up Discussion — *For use with Power Up, p. 668*

Problem-Solving Strategy: Write an Equation/ Use Logical Reasoning

Six identical blocks marked x, a 1.7-lb weight, and a 4.3-lb weight were balanced on a scale as shown. Write an equation to represent this balanced scale and find the weight of each block marked x.

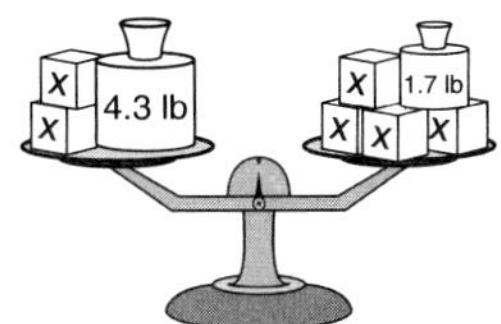

Understand — *Understand the problem.*

"What information are we given?"

We are told how some blocks and weights are distributed on a balanced scale.

"What are we asked to do?"

We are asked to write an equation representing the balanced scale, then find the value of each block marked x.

Plan — *Make a plan.*

"What problem-solving strategy will we use?"

We will *write an equation* to represent the scale, then *use logical reasoning* to solve the equation and find the weight of each block marked x.

Solve — *Carry out the plan.*

"What equation represents the balanced scale?"

$2x + 4.3 = 4x + 1.7$

"What can we mentally remove from both sides of the scale so that the scale remains balanced?"

We can remove two of the blocks marked x.

"What is the simplified equation?"

$4.3 = 2x + 1.7$

"What is the first step in solving the equation?"

We subtract 1.7 from both sides: $2.6 = 2x$.

"What is the weight of each block marked x?"

$x = 1.3$ lb

Check — *Look back.*

"Did we do what we were asked to do?"

Yes, we wrote an equation representing the balanced scale and found the weight of each block marked x.

"How can we verify our solution is correct?"

We can substitute 1.3 for x in the original equation and simplify:

$$2(1.3) + 4.3 = 4(1.3) + 1.7$$
$$2.6 + 4.3 = 5.2 + 1.7$$
$$6.9 = 6.9$$

1 Power Up

Facts
Distribute **Power Up T** to students. See answers below.

Mental Math
Encourage students to share different ways to mentally compute these exercises. Strategies for exercises **c** and **f** are listed below.

c. Cross Multiply

$3m = 0.6 \times 4.5$

$3m = 0.3 \times 9$

$3m = 2.7$

$m = 0.9$

Equivalent Fractions

$\frac{0.6}{3} \div \frac{3}{3} = \frac{0.2}{1}$

$\frac{0.2}{1} \cdot \frac{4.5}{4.5} = \frac{0.90}{4.5}$

$m = 0.9$

f. Use One-fourth

$\frac{1}{4} \cdot \$80 = \$20$

$\$80 - \$20 = \$60$

Use three-fourths

$\frac{3}{4} \cdot \$80 = (\$80 \div 4)3$

$\$20 \cdot 3 = \$60$

Problem Solving
Refer to **Power-Up Discussion,** p. 668B.

2 New Concepts

Instruction
Have students recall the characteristics of similar figures. Answers may include:
- figures have the same shape
- figures may be the same size or different sizes
- corresponding angles are congruent.

Explain that students can use what they know about similar triangles and proportions to find the length of a side of a triangle.

(continued)

LESSON **97**

• Similar Triangles
• Indirect Measure

Power Up *Building Power*

facts Power Up T

mental math

a. **Positive/Negative:** $(-5)(-5)(-5)$ -125

b. **Order of Operations/Exponents:** $(5 \times 10^6)(6 \times 10^5)$ 3×10^{12}

c. **Ratio:** $\frac{m}{4.5} = \frac{0.6}{3}$ 0.9

d. **Measurement:** Convert 5°C to degrees Fahrenheit. 41°F

e. **Calculation:** $10 \times 6\frac{1}{2}$ 65

f. **Percent:** 25% less than \$80 \$60

g. **Measurement:** One cup is what fraction of a pint? $\frac{1}{2}$

h. **Calculation:** $\sqrt{100}$, × 7, + 2, ÷ 8, × 4, $\sqrt{\ }$, × 5, − 2, ÷ 2, ÷ 2, ÷ 2 $3\frac{1}{2}$

problem solving

Six identical blocks marked x, a 1.7-lb weight, and a 4.3-lb weight were balanced on a scale as shown. Write an equation to represent this balanced scale and find the weight of each block marked x. $x = 1.3$ lb

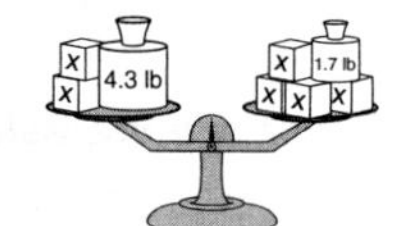

New Concepts *Increasing Knowledge*

similar triangles

We often use tick marks to indicate congruent angles.

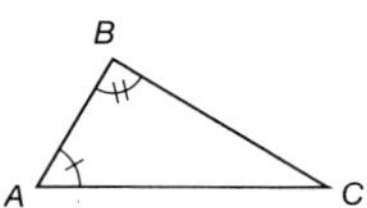

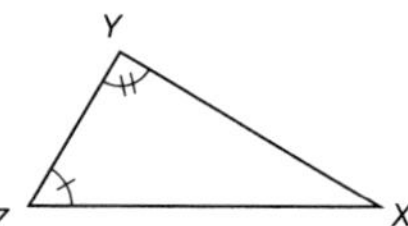

In the triangles above, the single tick marks indicate that angles A and Z have equal measures. The double tick marks indicate that angles B and Y have equal measures. Can we conclude that angles C and X also have equal measures?

Yes. Since the sum of the angle measures of each triangle is 180° the remaining angles, C and X, must have equal measures.

Recall from Lesson 18 that corresponding angles of similar figures have the same measure. The converse is also true. If three angles in one triangle have the same measures as three angles in another triangle, the triangles are *similar triangles*. So triangles ABC and ZYX are similar. Also recall that similar triangles have three pairs of corresponding angles and three pairs of corresponding sides. On the following page, we show the corresponding angles and sides for the triangles above:

Facts Simplify.

$6 + 6 \times 6 - 6 \div 6 = 41$	$3^2 + \sqrt{4} + 5(6) - 7 + 8 = 42$
$4 + 2(3 + 5) - 6 \div 2 = 17$	$2 + 2[3 + 4(7 - 5)] = 24$
$\sqrt{1^3 + 2^3 + 3^3} = 6$	$\frac{4 + 3(7 - 5)}{6 - (5 - 4)} = 2$
$(-3)(-3) + (-3) - (-3) = 9$	$\frac{3(-3) - (-3)(-3)}{(-3) - (3)(-3)} = -3$

Corresponding Angles	Corresponding Sides
$\angle A$ and $\angle Z$	$\overline{AB}$ and $\overline{ZY}$
$\angle B$ and $\angle Y$	$\overline{BC}$ and $\overline{YX}$
$\angle C$ and $\angle X$	$\overline{CA}$ and $\overline{XZ}$

In this lesson we will focus our attention on the following characteristic of similar triangles:

> **The lengths of corresponding sides of similar triangles are proportional.**

This means that ratios formed by corresponding sides are equal, as we illustrate with the two triangles below.

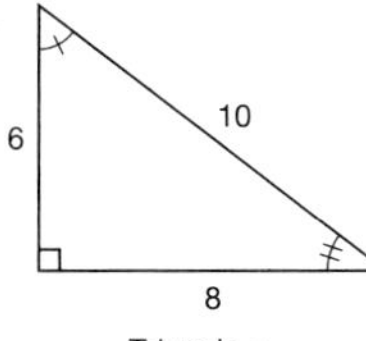

Triangle *a*

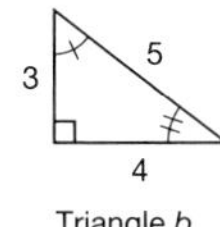

Triangle *b*

The lengths of the corresponding sides of triangles *a* and *b* are 6 and 3, 8 and 4, and 10 and 5. These pairs of lengths can be written as equal ratios.

$$\frac{\text{triangle } a}{\text{triangle } b} \quad \frac{6}{3} = \frac{8}{4} = \frac{10}{5}$$

Notice that each of these ratios equals 2. If we choose to put the lengths of the sides of triangle *b* on top, we get three ratios, each equal to $\frac{1}{2}$.

$$\frac{\text{triangle } b}{\text{triangle } a} \quad \frac{3}{6} = \frac{4}{8} = \frac{5}{10}$$

We can write proportions using equal ratios in order to find the lengths of unknown sides of similar triangles.

Thinking Skills

Explain

Do triangles have to be the same size to be similar? No. The corresponding sides of similar triangles must be proportional but they do not have to be equal.

Example 1

Estimate the length *a*. Then use a proportion to find *a*.

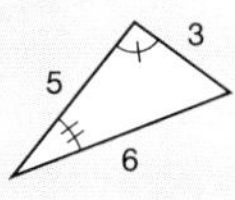

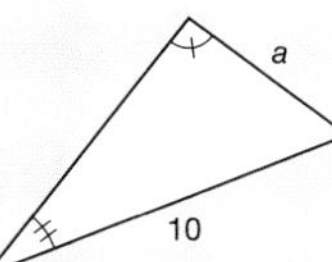

Solution

The tick marks indicate two pairs of congruent angles in the triangles. Because the sum of the interior angles of every triangle is 180°, we know that the unmarked angles are also congruent. Thus the two triangles are similar, and the lengths of the corresponding sides are proportional.

2 New Concepts *(Continued)*

Instruction

Have students look at the columns of corresponding angles and sides and the triangles they refer to. Ask students:

"Is there a correct order in which you write the letters for the corresponding sides?" Yes, the letters used to name the corresponding angles are listed in the same order. For example, since $\triangle ABC$ is similar to $\triangle ZYX$, we write that $\overline{AB}$ corresponds to $\overline{ZY}$ rather than $\overline{YZ}$.

"Do triangles have to have the same orientation in order to be similar?" No. Similar triangles can also be shown with different orientations. Only their angle measures or corresponding sides determine whether they are similar.

(continued)

Math Background

Are the side lengths of similar triangles always proportional?

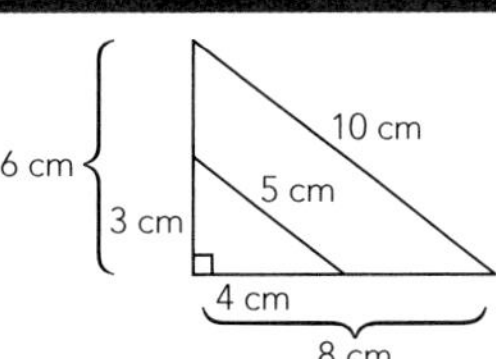

Yes. The corresponding sides of similar triangles always maintain the same proportion. This diagram shows that when two sides of a triangle are doubled in length, the third side also is doubled. The idea is particularly helpful when using indirect measurement. If we know that two triangles are similar, and we know the lengths of the sides of one triangle and at least one side length of the second triangle, we can find the other side lengths using proportions.

2 New Concepts (Continued)

Example 1

Instruction

Emphasize that the proportion relates corresponding sides of the two triangles.

If students are having difficulty setting up the proportions, have them use a ratio box to solve.

	Length of Side 1	Length of Side 2
Triangle 1	6	3
Triangle 2	10	a

Instruction

Begin a discussion on indirect measurement by asking:

"What are some situations in which it might be difficult to physically measure something?" the height of a building; the distance across a lake

Point out that the examples in this lesson about indirect measure deal with right triangles. However, it is not necessary that the triangles formed be right triangles. It is only necessary for them to be similar.

The triangles formed by vertical figures and their shadows are similar since vertical figures make right angles with the ground, and the angles formed when the sun casts their shadows are congruent.

(continued)

The side of length 6 in the smaller triangle corresponds to the side of length 10 in the larger triangle. Thus the side lengths of the larger triangle are not quite double the side lengths of the smaller triangle. Since the side of length a in the larger triangle corresponds to the side of length 3 in the smaller triangle, a should be a little less than 6. We estimate a to be 5.

We now use corresponding sides to write a proportion and solve for a. We decide to write the ratios so that the sides from the smaller triangle are on top.

$$\frac{6}{10} = \frac{3}{a} \quad \text{equal ratios}$$

$$6a = 30 \quad \text{cross multiplied}$$

$$a = \mathbf{5} \quad \text{solved}$$

indirect measure

Sarah looked up and said, "I wonder how tall that tree is." Beth looked down and said, "It's about 25 feet tall." Beth did not *directly* measure the height of the tree. Instead she used her knowledge of proportions to *indirectly* estimate the height of the tree.

The lengths of the shadows cast by two objects are proportional to the heights of the two objects (assuming the objects are in the same general location).

We can separate the objects and their shadows into two "triangles."

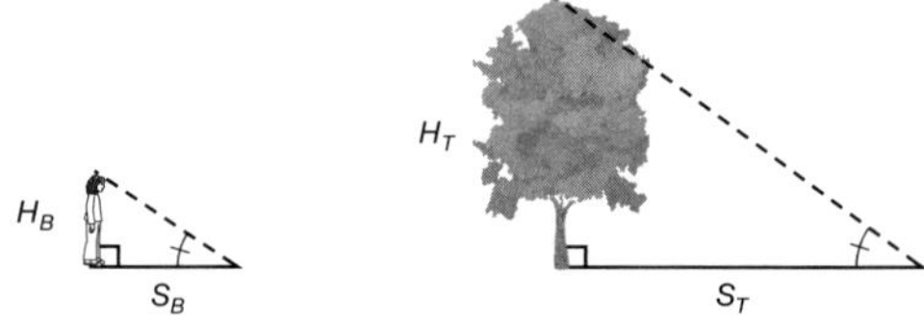

We assume that the ground is flat and level, and that both the tree and Beth are perpendicular to the ground. We also assume that the angle of the Sun's light is the same for both Beth and the tree. Thus the triangles are similar.

Manipulative Use

Materials: string, protractors, meter sticks or rulers

Have students use string and protractors to create **similar triangles.** After confirming that the triangles have equal corresponding angles, have students use meter sticks or rulers to confirm that the sides are proportional.

English Learners

Explain the meaning of the words **directly measure** and **indirectly estimate.** Ask students:

"How many feet long is my desk?" Collect feedback

Tell students their guesses are examples of an indirect estimate. Next, take a ruler and precisely measure your desk. Tell the students the result and inform them this actual measurement is known as a direct measure. Compare and discuss the indirect estimates to the actual direct measure.

Thinking Skill
Explain

In indirect measurement, why must the light strike the objects at the same angle? If the light does not strike the objects at approximately the same angle, the lengths of the shadows will not be proportional.

Discuss Why do we have to make these assumptions? (See below.)

The height of Beth (H_B) and the length of Beth's shadow (S_B) are proportional to the height of the tree (H_T) and the length of the tree's shadow (S_T). We can record the relationship in a ratio box.

	Height of Object	Length of Shadow
Beth	H_B	S_B
Tree	H_T	S_T

How did Beth perform the calculation? We suggest two ways. Knowing her own height (5 ft), she may have estimated the length of her shadow (6 ft) and the length of the shadow of the tree (30 ft). She then could have solved this proportion in which the dimensions are feet:

$$\frac{5}{H_T} = \frac{6}{30}$$

$$6H_T = 5 \cdot 30$$

$$H_T = 25$$

Another way Beth may have estimated the height of the tree is by estimating that the tree's shadow was five times as long as her own shadow. If the tree's shadow was five times as long as her shadow, then the tree's height must have been five times her height.

$$5 \text{ ft} \times 5 = 25 \text{ ft}$$

Example 2

To indirectly measure the height of a telephone pole on the playground, some students measured the length of the shadow cast by the pole. The shadow measured 24 ft and the length of the shadow cast by a vertical meterstick was 40 cm. About how tall was the telephone pole?

Solution

We sketch the objects and their shadows using the given information.

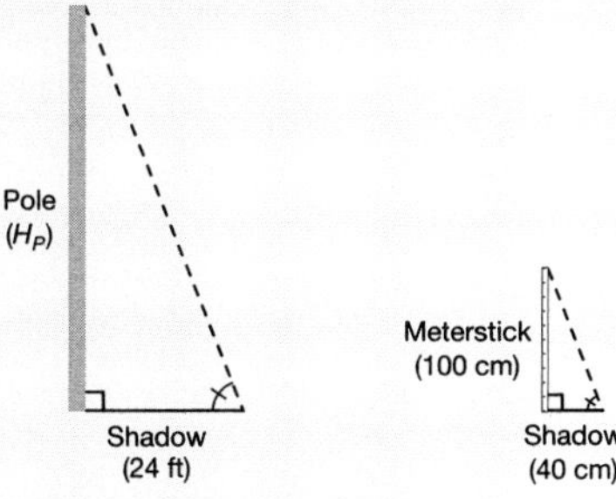

Note: Figures not drawn to scale.

If the ground were not level or if the tree were not perpendicular, the triangles would not be similar. Also, if the angle of the Sun's light were not the same, the triangles would not be similar.

2 New Concepts (Continued)

Instruction

Explain to students that the assumptions for a given problem must be made and also stated. The assumptions assure that the angles of the triangles are congruent, and should be clearly stated for anyone who reads the problem.

Example 2

Instruction

Encourage students to sketch a picture of the objects, labeling the known measurements. Doing so will help them when they set up their ratio boxes and proportions.

(continued)

2 New Concepts (Continued)

Example 2 (continued)

Instruction

Explain that although students can change different units of length to the same unit, as long as the units are consistent within a specific triangle, changing them is not required.

Make sure that students understand why their answer is written in feet. Encourage them to look through the example to ensure they know where the centimeters were cancelled.

Example 3

Instruction

Ask a student to sketch and label a picture of the objects in this problem.

(continued)

We use a ratio box to record the given information. Then we write and solve a proportion.

	Height of Object	Length of Shadow
Meterstick	100 cm	40 cm
Pole	H_P	24 ft

$$\frac{100}{H_P} = \frac{40}{24}$$

$$40\,H_P = 24 \cdot 100$$

$$H_P = 60$$

We find that the height of the telephone pole was about **60 feet.** Note that the two objects were measured using different units. Exercise caution whenever mixing units in proportions to ensure the solution is expressed in the desired units. You may choose to include units in your calculation, as we have done below.

$$\frac{100\text{ cm}}{H_P} = \frac{40\text{ cm}}{24\text{ ft}}$$

$$40\text{ cm} \cdot H_P = 24\text{ ft} \cdot 100\text{ cm}$$

$$H_P = \frac{\overset{6}{\cancel{24}}\text{ ft} \cdot \overset{10}{\cancel{100}}\,\cancel{\text{cm}}}{\underset{1}{\cancel{\overset{\cancel{4}}{40}}}\,\cancel{\text{cm}}}$$

$$H_P = 60\text{ ft}$$

Example 3

Brad saw that his shadow was the length of about one big step (3 ft). He then walked along the shadow of a nearby flagpole and found that it was eight big steps long. Brad is about 5 ft tall. Which is the best choice for the height of the flagpole?

A 15 ft **B** 24 ft **C** 40 ft **D** 60 ft

Solution

We can estimate the heights of objects by the lengths of their shadows. In this example, Brad, who is about 5 ft tall, cast a shadow about 3 ft long. So Brad is nearly twice as tall as the length of the shadow he cast. The shadow of the flagpole was the length of about eight big steps, or about 24 ft. So the height of the pole is about, but not quite, twice the length of its shadow. Thus, the best choice for the height of the pole is **C 40 ft.**

Discuss Is there a quicker way to estimate that the pole is about 40 feet tall? If so, describe it. Sample: Yes. We do not have to use the measure of 3 ft. We know that Brad's height (5 ft) casts a shadow that is 1 step in length. We know that the flagpole casts a shadow that is 8 steps in length. If 1 step equals 5 ft, then 8 steps equal 8 · 5 ft, or 40 ft.

672 Saxon Math Course 2

Activity

Indirect Measure

Materials: metersticks, rulers and/or tape measures.

Have small groups of students indirectly measure the height of a tree, building, pole, or other tall object as described in example 2.

Discuss If different groups measure the same object, discuss why and how answers differ.

The meterstick might not be held vertically or the ground might not be level. Also, groups might round their measurements differently.

Practice Set

a. corresponding angles: $\angle W$ and $\angle R$; $\angle Y$ and $\angle Q$; $\angle X$ and $\angle P$; corresponding sides: $\overline{YW}$ and $\overline{QR}$; $\overline{WX}$ and $\overline{RP}$; $\overline{XY}$ and $\overline{PQ}$

▸ **a.** **Analyze** Identify each pair of corresponding angles and each pair of corresponding sides in these two triangles:

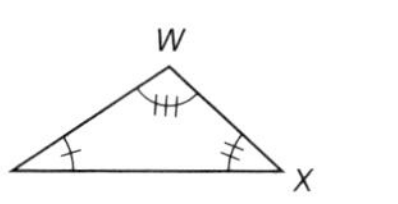

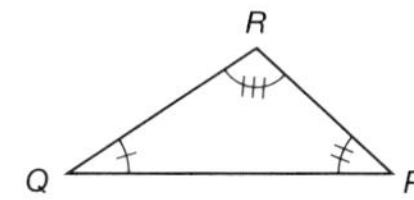

Refer to the figures shown to answer problems **b–e.**

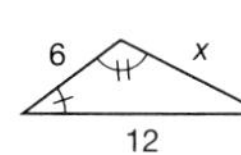

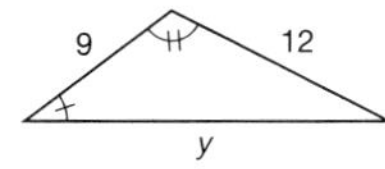

b. Estimate the length x. See student work.

c. Find the length x. 8

d. Estimate the length y. See student work.

e. Find the length y. 18

▸ **f.** **Model** A tree casts a shadow 18 feet long, while a 6-foot pole casts a shadow 9 feet long. How tall is the tree? Draw a diagram to illustrate the problem. 12 feet; See student work.

▸ **g.** **Estimate** As Donald stood next to a pole supporting a basketball hoop, he noticed that the shadow of the pole was about twice the length of his own shadow. If Donald is 5 ft 6 in. tall, what is a reasonable estimate of the height of the pole? about 11 ft

Written Practice

Strengthening Concepts

1. (46) Marta gave the clerk \$10 for a CD that was on sale for \$8.95 plus 6 percent tax. How much money should she get back? \$0.51

2. (51) Three hundred billion is how much less than two trillion? Write the answer in scientific notation. 1.7×10^{12}

▸ See Math Conversations in the sidebar.

Activity

Instruction

Students will need meter sticks, rulers, and/or tape measures for this activity.

Have students discuss why their measurements may differ. Then have them discuss the role that human error and instrument error play in measurement.

2 New Concepts (Continued)

Practice Set

Problem a Analyze

Encourage students to use the correct order for corresponding sides. Developing this work habit now will help them in future geometry classes.

Problem f Model

Ask a volunteer to sketch the diagram for this problem at the board. Use the diagram for a class discussion of the solution.

Problem g Estimate

"How do you know that your estimate is reasonable?" 5 ft 6 in. is $5\frac{1}{2}$ ft; $5\frac{1}{2}$ ft $+ 5\frac{1}{2}$ ft $= 11$ ft

3 Written Practice

Math Conversations

Discussion opportunities are provided below.

Problem 6 Analyze

"What are the ordered pairs for △ABC?"

$A(-1, 4)$, $B(-1, 1)$, $C(-3, 1)$

"What are the ordered pairs for △A′B′C′?"

$A'(4, 4)$, $B'(4, 1)$, $C'(2, 1)$

"How do the ordered pairs show that the figure was translated 5 units to the right?"

x for A becomes $-1 + 5 = 4$ A'
x for B becomes $-1 + 5 = 4$ B'
x for C becomes $-3 + 5 = 2$ C'

Problems 9–11 Represent

Extend the Problem

Have volunteers write a proportion and the equation for each problem at the board. Discuss which representation is easier to solve.

Problem 9: $\frac{250}{100} = \frac{40}{x}$

Problem 10: $\frac{40}{60} = \frac{x}{100}$

Problem 11: $\frac{40}{100} = \frac{x}{6}$

Errors and Misconceptions

Problem 8

If students answer 588 leeks, they set up the proportion incorrectly. Ask them if the ratio of radishes to leeks is 5 leeks for every 7 radishes, are there more radishes or leeks in the garden? Then have them compare 588 and 420 to see that the number of leeks cannot be greater than the number of radishes.

(continued)

3. (Inv. 4) The table shows how much protein is in one serving of different foods made from grain.

Food	Protein (grams)
Oatmeal	6
Shredded Wheat	3
Bagel (plain)	7
White Bread	2
Whole-wheat Bread	3
Bran Flakes	4
Corn Flakes	2
Pasta	7
Bran Muffin	3

a. Find the median, mode, and range of the data.
median: 3; mode: 3; range: 5

b. Which combination would give you more protein, one serving of white bread and one serving of pasta, or one bran muffin and one bagel? 1 bran muffin and 1 bagel

Use ratio boxes to solve problems **4** and **5.**

4. (72) Coming down a long hill on their bikes, members of a cycling club averaged 18 miles per hour. If it took them 2 minutes to come down the hill, how long was the hill? 0.6 miles

5. (72) If Nelson biked 2640 yards in 5 minutes, how far could he bike in 8 minutes at the same rate? 4224 yards

▶ *** 6.** (80) Analyze Describe the transformation that moves $\triangle ABC$ to its image $\triangle A'B'C'$. translation of 5 units to the right

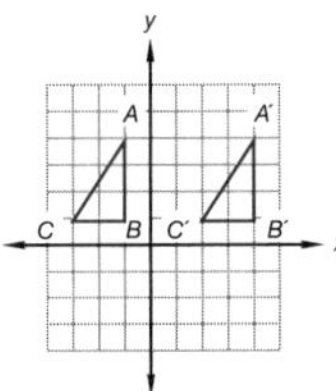

7. (16, 60) Three fourths of a yard is how many inches? 27 inches

▶ **8.** (54) Use a ratio box to solve this problem. The ratio of leeks to radishes growing in a garden was 5 to 7. If 420 radishes were growing in the garden, how many leeks were there? 300 leeks

▶ Write equations to solve problems **9–11.**

9. (77) Forty is 250 percent of what number? $40 = 2.5 \times W_N$; 16

10. (77) Forty is what percent of 60? $40 = W_P \times 60$; $66\frac{2}{3}\%$

11. (60) What decimal number is 40 percent of 6? $W_D = 0.4 \times 6$; 2.4

▶ See Math Conversations in the sidebar.

▸* **12.** (92) **Model** Use a ratio box to solve this problem. The price of one model of car increased 10 percent in one year. If the price this year is \$17,600, what was the price last year? \$16,000

13. (28, 34) What is the average of the two numbers marked by arrows on the number line below? 1.91

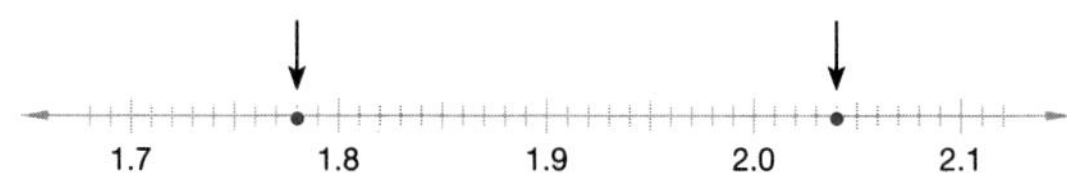

▸ **14.** (48) Complete the table.

Fraction	Decimal	Percent
a. $3\frac{1}{4}$	3.25	**b.** 325%
$\frac{1}{6}$	**c.** $0.1\overline{6}$	**d.** $16\frac{2}{3}$%

15. (Inv. 9) If Betty walks to school at 3 miles per hour the trip takes 15 minutes. How long does the trip take if she jogs to school at 5 miles per hour? 9 minutes

16. (83) Multiply. Write the product in scientific notation. 3.24×10^5

$$(5.4 \times 10^8)(6 \times 10^{-4})$$

▸ **17.** (62, 82) **Connect** Find the **a** circumference and **b** area of a circle with a radius of 10 millimeters. (Use 3.14 for π.) **a.** 62.8 mm **b.** 314 mm^2

18. (75) Find the area of the trapezoid shown. Dimensions are in feet. 80 ft^2

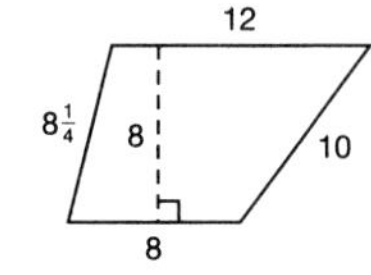

▸* **19.** (95) Find the volume of each of these right solids. Dimensions are in meters. (Leave π as π.)

a. 2 m^3

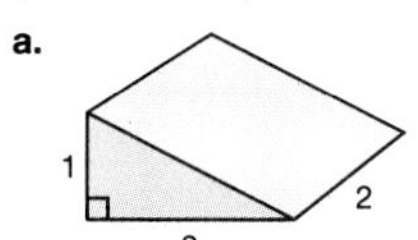

b. π m^3

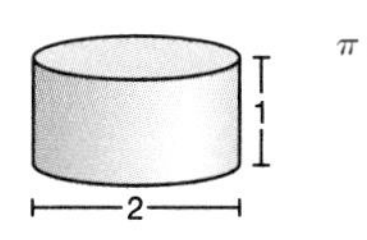
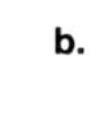

20. (40) Refer to the figure below. What are the measures of the following angles?

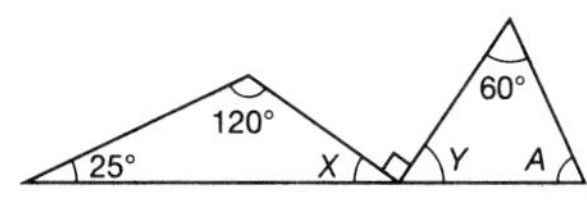

a. $\angle X$ 35° **b.** $\angle Y$ 55° **c.** $\angle A$ 65°

▸ See Math Conversations in the sidebar.

3 Written Practice (Continued)

Math Conversations

Discussion opportunities are provided below.

Problem 12 Model

Ask a student to draw a ratio box at the board and explain the solution.

	Percent	Actual
Last Year	100	L
+ Change	10	C
This Year	110	\$17,600

$$\frac{100}{110} = \frac{L}{\$17{,}600}$$

$$100 \cdot \$17{,}600 = 110L$$
$$\$1{,}760{,}000 = 110L$$
$$\$16{,}000 = L$$

Problem 17 Connect

Have students explain how they can solve each part of the problem using mental math.

Sample:

For circumference

$(10 \cdot 3.14) + (10 \cdot 3.14) = 31.4 + 31.4$ or 62.8 mm

For area

$(100 \cdot 3.14) = 314$ mm

Problem 19 Generalize

Extend the Problem

Draw the top and front views of these figures.

a. Triangular Prism

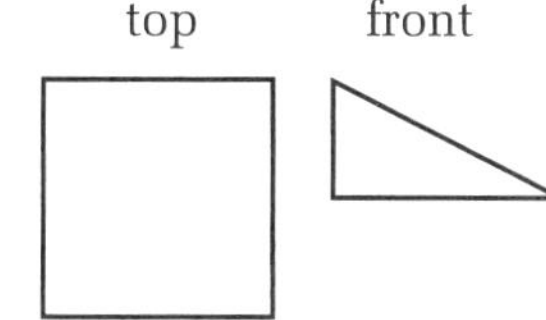

b. Cylinder

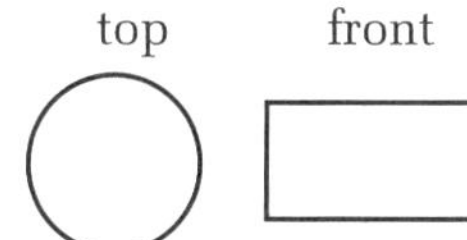

Errors and Misconceptions

Problem 14

If students write 3.25 as $3\frac{1}{4}$%, ask them what percent 0.03 is? If 0.03 is 3%, then $3\frac{1}{4}$% is 0.0325. Have students look at 3.25 as compared to 0.0325.

(continued)

3 Written Practice (Continued)

Math Conversations

Discussion opportunities are provided below.

Problem 21 Generalize

After students find the length of x, ask them to find the length of y. 9 cm

Problem 22 Model

Ask a volunteer to sketch the diagram for this problem on the board. Use the diagram for a class discussion of the solution.

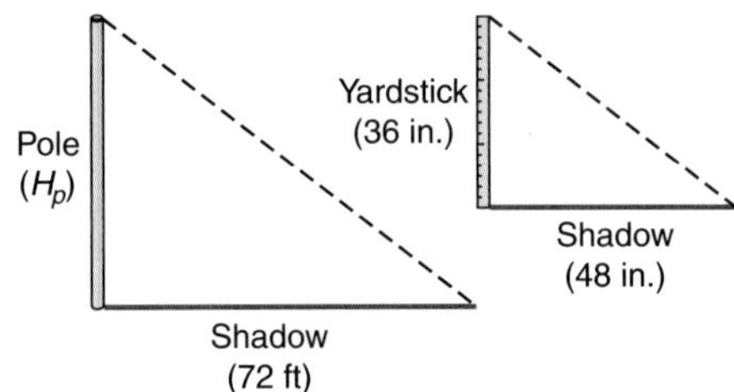

Problems 26–29 Generalize

Ask students to decide whether they would use mental math or paper and pencil to solve each problem. Have them explain their choice. Answers will vary.

Problem 30 Analyze

Have students list the sample space.

AB, AC, AD, AE
BA, BC, BD, BE
CA, CB, CD, CE
DA, DB, DC, DE
EA, EB, EC, ED

▸* 21. (97) Generalize The triangles below are similar. Find the length of x. Dimensions are in centimeters. 8 cm

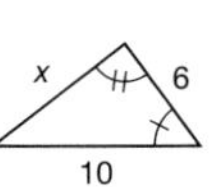

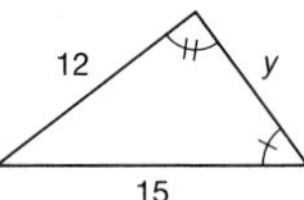

▸* 22. (97) Model How tall is a power pole that casts a 72-foot shadow if a nearby vertical yardstick casts a 48-inch shadow? Draw a diagram to illustrate the problem. 54 feet; See student diagrams.

23. (29) Estimate: $\frac{(38{,}470)(607)}{79}$ 300,000

Generalize For problems **24** and **25**, solve and check. Show each step.

* 24. (93) $1.2m + 0.12 = 12$

* 25. (93) $1\frac{3}{4}y - 2 = 12$

24. $m = 9.9$
$1.2m + 0.12 = 12$
$1.2m = 11.88$
$m = \frac{11.88}{1.2}$
$m = 9.9$

25. $y = 8$
$1\frac{3}{4}y - 2 = 12$
$1\frac{3}{4}y = 14$
$y = 14 \div \frac{4}{7}$
$y = 8$

▸ Generalize Simplify:

26. (84) $3x - y + 8 + x + y - 2$ $4x + 6$

* 27. (96) **a.** $3(x - y)$ $3x - 3y$

b. $x(y - 3)$ $xy - 3x$

28. (43) $3\frac{1}{3} \div \left(4.5 \div 1\frac{1}{8}\right)$ $\frac{5}{6}$

29. (85) $\frac{(-2) - (+3) + (-4)(-3)}{(-2) + (+3) - (+4)}$ $-2\frac{1}{3}$

▸* 30. (94) Analyze Sam placed five alphabet cards face down on a table. Then he asked students to pick up two cards.

A B C
D E

a. What is the probability that a student will pick up two vowels? $\frac{1}{10}$

b. What is the probability the student will pick up two consonants? $\frac{3}{10}$

Early Finishers
Math Applications

Draw a 0 to 4 number line and divide each unit into fourths. Then, estimate the position of each number on the number line.

$\frac{1}{2}$ $\quad 2.25 \quad 3.\overline{3} \quad 0.125 \quad 3\frac{3}{4} \quad 2.8\overline{3}$

See student work. Order of number on the number line is: 0.125, $\frac{1}{2}$, 2.25, $2.8\overline{3}$, $3.\overline{3}$, $3\frac{3}{4}$.

▸ See Math Conversations in the sidebar.

Looking Forward

Working with similar triangles and proportions prepares students for:

- **Lesson 98,** determining the scale factor in a proportion.

• Scale
• Scale Factor

Objectives

- Use a scale to write a proportion to find a measurement on either a model of an object or the actual object.
- Determine the scale factor in a proportion.
- Use the scale factor to solve a proportion.

Lesson Preparation

Materials

- **Power Up U** (in *Instructional Masters*)
- **Investigation Activity 13** (in *Instructional Masters*) or **graph paper**
- **Manipulative kit: protractors**

Optional

- **Manipulative kit: yardstick, color cubes**
- **Teacher-provided material: maps, string, index cards**

Power Up U

Investigation Activity 13

Math Language

New

scale

scale factor

Technology Resources

Student eBook Complete student textbook in electronic format.

Resources and Planner CD Blackline masters, plus a pacing calendar with standards.

Test and Practice Generator CD Create additional practice sheets and custom-made tests.

www.SaxonPublishers.com Visit for more student activities and planning materials.

Inclusion

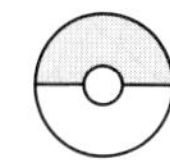

Adaptations CD Adapted lessons, investigations, practice and assessments.

Meeting Standards

National Council of Teachers of Mathematics (NCTM)

Numbers and Operations

NO.3d Develop, analyze, and explain methods for solving problems involving proportions, such as scaling and finding equivalent ratios

Geometry

GM.4c Use visual tools such as networks to represent and solve problems

GM.4d Use geometric models to represent and explain numerical and algebraic relationships

GM.4e Recognize and apply geometric ideas and relationships in areas outside the mathematics classroom, such as art, science, and everyday life

Measurement

ME.2e Solve problems involving scale factors, using ratio and proportion

Power-Up Discussion *For use with Power Up, p. 677*

Problem-Solving Strategy: Draw a Diagram

If two people shake hands, one handshake takes place. If three people all shake hands with one another, three handshakes take place. If four people all shake hands with one another, we can determine how many handshakes take place by drawing four dots (for people) and connecting the dots with segments (for handshakes). Then we count the segments (six). Use this method to count the number of handshakes that would take place between five people.

Understand — Understand the problem.

"What information are we given?"

We are told how to count the number of handshakes that take place between a number of people.

"What are we asked to do?"

We are asked to determine how many handshakes take place between five people if they all shake hands with one another.

Plan — Make a plan.

"What problem-solving strategy will we use?"

We will *draw a diagram* to find the number of handshakes.

Teacher Note: Encourage students to estimate the number of handshakes that will take place. Often students jump to the conclusion that six people shaking everyone else's hand results in 6 x 6 = 36 or 6 x 5 = 30 handshakes.

Solve — Carry out the plan.

"What should our diagram look like?"

We should draw five dots and connect every dot to every other dot with a line segment:

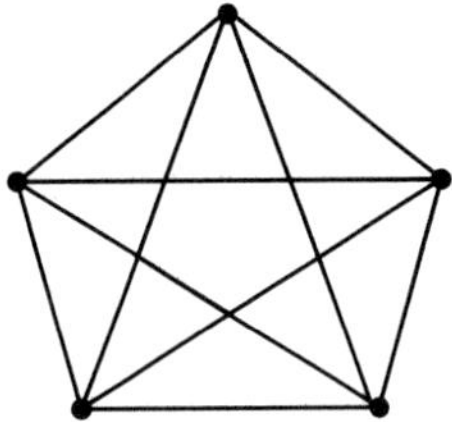

"How many handshakes take place?"

There are 10 segments in our diagrams, so 10 handshakes would take place between five different people.

Check — Look back.

"Did we do what we were asked to do?"

Yes, we drew a diagram to find that 10 handshakes would take place between five people.

"How can we verify our solution?"

We can choose five students to act out the situation and count the number of handshakes that take place.

Teacher Note: Encourage students to compare their estimates to the solution. Some students may have recognized the number of handshakes as a sequence of triangular numbers.

LESSON 98

• Scale
• Scale Factor

Power Up — *Building Power*

facts Power Up U

mental math

a. **Positive/Negative:** $(-360) \div (8)$ -45

b. **Order of Operations/Exponents:** $(2.5 \times 10^7)(4 \times 10^{-2})$ 1×10^6

c. **Algebra:** $2c + 1\frac{1}{2} = 6\frac{1}{2}$ $2\frac{1}{2}$

d. **Measurement:** Convert 0.02 kg to g. 20 g

e. **Calculation:** $4 \times 3\frac{3}{4}$ 15

f. **Percent:** $33\frac{1}{3}\%$ more than $60 $80

g. **Measurement:** A centimeter is what fraction of a meter? $\frac{1}{100}$

h. **Rate:** At 12 mph, how far can Toby ride a bike in 1 hour and 45 minutes? 21 mi

problem solving

If two people shake hands, one handshake takes place. If three people all shake hands with one another, three handshakes take place. If four people all shake hands with one another, we can determine how many handshakes take place by drawing four dots (for people) and connecting the dots with segments (for handshakes). Then we count the segments (six). Use this method to count the number of handshakes that would take place between five people. 10 handshakes

New Concepts — *Increasing Knowledge*

scale

In the preceding lesson we discussed similar triangles. Scale models and scale drawings are other examples of similar shapes. Scale models and scale drawings are reduced (or enlarged) renderings of actual objects. As is true of similar triangles, the lengths of corresponding parts of scale models and the objects they represent are proportional.

The **scale** of a model is stated as a ratio. For instance, if a model airplane is $\frac{1}{24}$ the size of the actual airplane, the scale is stated as $\frac{1}{24}$ or 1:24. We can use the given scale to write a proportion to find a measurement on either the model or the actual object. A ratio box helps us put the numbers in the proper places.

Example 1

A model airplane is built with a scale of 1:24. If the wingspan of the model is 18 inches, the wingspan of the actual airplane is how many feet?

Facts Complete each step to solve each equation.

$2x + 5 = 45$ $2x = 40$ $x = 20$	$3y + 4 = 22$ $3y = 18$ $y = 6$	$5n - 3 = 12$ $5n = 15$ $n = 3$	$3m - 7 = 14$ $3m = 21$ $m = 7$
$15 = 3a - 6$ $21 = 3a$ $7 = a$	$24 = 2w + 6$ $18 = 2w$ $9 = w$	$-2x + 9 = 23$ $-2x = 14$ $x = -7$	$20 - 3y = 2$ $-3y = -18$ $y = 6$
$\frac{1}{2}m + 6 = 18$ $\frac{1}{2}m = 12$ $m = 24$	$\frac{3}{4}n - 12 = 12$ $\frac{3}{4}n = 24$ $n = 32$	$3y + 1.5 = 6$ $3y = 4.5$ $y = 1.5$	$0.5w - 1.5 = 4.5$ $0.5w = 6$ $w = 12$

1 Power Up

Facts

Distribute **Power Up U** to students. See answers below.

Mental Math

Encourage students to share different ways to mentally compute these exercises. Strategies for exercises **c** and **h** are listed below.

c. Use Fractions

$6\frac{1}{2} - 1\frac{1}{2} = 5$

$5 \div 2 = 2\frac{1}{2}$

Equivalent Expression

$4c + 3 = 13$

$4c = 10$

$c = 10 \div 4$ or $2\frac{1}{2}$

h. Multiply

$12 \cdot 1\frac{3}{4} = 12 \cdot \frac{7}{4}$

$(12 \cdot 7) \div 4 = 84 \div 4$ or 21 mi

Reasoning

12 miles in 1 hour

3 (15 min intervals) $\times$ 3 (mi per 15 min) = 9

12 + 9 = 21 mi

Problem Solving

Refer to **Power-Up Discussion,** p. 677B.

2 New Concepts

Instruction

Encourage students to share examples of occasions when a scale model or drawing might be necessary. Examples might include:

- designing buildings, vehicles, maps, or toys
- floor plans
- advertisements
- sample products

Elicit from students that the model is a small representation of the actual item and that the parts of the model and the item are proportional.

In this lesson students will learn about scale, or the proportion between similar objects.

(continued)

2 New Concepts (Continued)

Example 1

Instruction

Emphasize that units must be the same for both the model and the actual item when determining scale. For example, if 1 inch on a model represents 3 feet on the actual object, the scale is not 1:3. The scale is 1:36, because 3 feet = 36 inches.

This concept is also used when finding distances on a road map. The scale of the map tells you how a distance on the map relates to real distance. Ask students why a map with a scale of 1:1 would be ineffective. A map with a scale of 1:1 would be as big as the actual distance it represented.

(continued)

Solution

Thinking Skill

Explain

If you made a model with a scale of 3:1, would the model be larger or smaller than the original object? How do you know? Larger; a scale of 3:1 means that 3 units on the model equal 1 unit on the original.

The scale indicates that the dimensions of the actual airplane are 24 times the dimensions of the model, so the wingspan is 24 times 18 inches. Note that the model is measured in inches, but the question asks for the wingspan in feet. Thus we will divide the product of 18 and 24 by 12. This is the calculation:

$$\frac{18 \cdot 24}{12} = 36$$

The wingspan is 36 feet.

Another way to approach this problem is to construct a ratio box as we have done with ratio problems. In one column we write the ratio numbers, which are the scale numbers. In the other column we write the measures. The first number of the scale refers to the model. The second number refers to the object. We can use the entries in the ratio box to write a proportion.

	Scale	Measure
Model	1	18
Object	24	w

$$\frac{1}{24} = \frac{18}{w}$$

$$w = 432$$

The wingspan of the model was given in inches. Solving the proportion, we find that the full-size wingspan is 432 inches. We are asked for the wingspan in feet, so we convert units from inches to feet.

$$432 \text{ in.} \cdot \frac{1 \text{ ft}}{12 \text{ in.}} = 36 \text{ ft}$$

We find that the wingspan of the airplane is **36 feet**.

Discuss Could you find the actual length of the airplane if you were given the length of the model plane? Why or why not?

Yes. The model is built to scale of 1:24. This means that every part of the actual plane is 24 times every part of the model if you are using the same units.

We can graphically portray the relationship between the measures of an object and a scale model. Below we show a graph of the measures of the airplane and its model. Notice that the scale of the model is inches while the scale of the actual airplane is feet. Since the scale is 1:24, one inch on the model corresponds to 24 inches, which is 2 feet, on the actual airplane.

Scale of Airplane Model

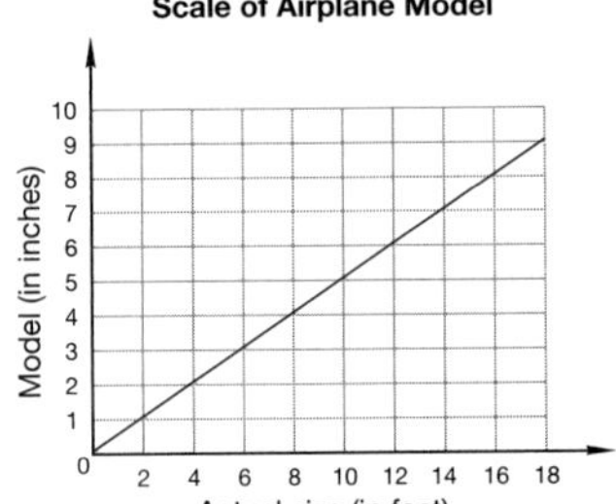

Every point on the graphed line represents a length on the airplane and its corresponding measure on the model.

Math Background

What is the difference between a scale and a scale factor?

Scale is a ratio that compares a linear measurement on an object to a linear measurement on a similar object. For example, if the scale of a toy car is 1:8, every unit on the model represents eight units on the actual object.

A scale factor tells how many times larger or smaller one object is than another. In the above example, the scale factor of the toy car to the actual car is 8 because the actual car is 8 times the length of the toy car.

If the model is built to scale, the relationship between the measures of the scale model and the measure of the original are the same for every point on the graph.

Summarize Why is a graph of the relationship between the measures of a scale model and an original always a straight line?

Example 2

Sofia is molding a model of a car from clay. The scale of the model is 1:36. If the height of the car is 4 feet 6 inches, what should be the height of the model in inches?

Solution

First we convert 4 feet 6 inches to inches:

$$4 \text{ feet } 6 \text{ inches} = 4(12) + 6 = 54 \text{ inches}$$

Then we construct a ratio box using 1 and 36 as the ratio numbers, write the proportion, and solve.

	Scale	Measure
Model	1	m
Object	36	54

$$\frac{1}{36} = \frac{m}{54}$$

$$36m = 54$$

$$m = \frac{54}{36} = 1\frac{1}{2}$$

The height of the model car should be **$1\frac{1}{2}$ inches.**

scale factor

We have solved proportions by using cross products. Sometimes a proportion can be solved more quickly by noting the **scale factor.** The scale factor is the number of times larger (or smaller) the terms of one ratio are when compared with the terms of the other ratio. The scale factor in the proportion below is 6 because the terms of the second ratio are 6 times the terms of the first ratio.

$$\frac{3}{4} = \frac{18}{24}$$

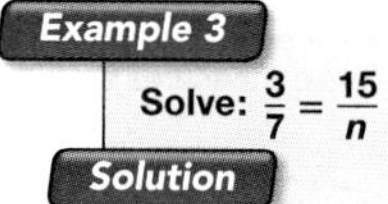

Example 3

Solve: $\frac{3}{7} = \frac{15}{n}$

Solution

Instead of finding cross products, we note that multiplying the numerator 3 by 5 gives us the other numerator, 15. Thus the scale factor is 5. We use this scale factor to find n.

$$\frac{3}{7} \times \frac{5}{5} = \frac{15}{35}$$

We find that n is **35.**

2 New Concepts (Continued)

Example 2

Instruction

After explaining scale factor to students, have them use the height of the model car and the actual car to determine the scale factor.

$54 \div 1.5 = 36$

The scale factor can be determined by dividing the scale as well as by dividing the measurements of the figures.

Instruction

Point out that both scale and scale factor can usually be used in calculations, but frequently one will be more convenient than the other.

On a road map the scale is usually given as the number of actual miles that are equivalent to one inch on the map. It is easy to measure a number of inches on the map and multiply by the number of miles on the scale.

Using the scale factor would be awkward, because it would give you an actual distance in inches. To be useful, this measure would then be changed to miles, adding a step to your calculations.

Example 3

Instruction

Remind students that $\frac{3}{7}$ can be multiplied by $\frac{5}{5}$ because $\frac{5}{5}$ is equal to 1. The Identity Property of Multiplication states that multiplying by 1 does not change the value of a number.

(continued)

Manipulative Use

Throughout this lesson, provide manipulatives so students can use them to **illustrate determining scale and scale factors.** Cubes, maps, and string are examples of manipulatives that can be useful to students.

2 New Concepts (Continued)

Example 4

Instruction

Point out that the corresponding sides of the triangles must be identified before the scale factor can be calculated.

Have students examine the two similar triangles. A 20-cm side on one triangle corresponds to a 25-cm side on the other triangle. Tell students that when calculating the scale factor, you must state which triangle is the starting point. The scale factor from the smaller triangle to the larger triangle is $\frac{25}{20}$, or 1.25. The scale factor from the larger triangle to the smaller triangle is $\frac{20}{25}$, or 0.8.

Instruction

- Have students use the **Color Cubes** from the Manipulative Kit to model the cubes shown here.
- One cube can be used to represent cube A.
- Two layers of four cubes can represent cube B.

Using cubes to represent units can help students determine linear, area, and volume relationships.

(continued)

Example 4

These two triangles are similar. Calculate the scale factor from the smaller triangle to the larger triangle.

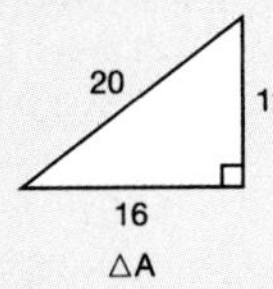

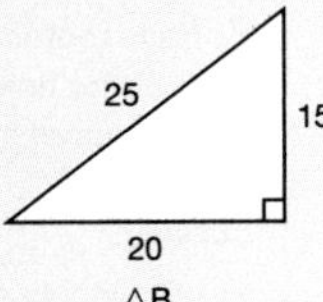

Solution

Math Language
The term *dimension* refers to the length of any side of △A or △B.

If we multiply the length of one side of the smaller triangle by the scale factor, we get the length of the corresponding side of the larger triangle.

$$\text{Dimension of } \triangle A \times \text{scale factor} = \text{dimension of } \triangle B$$

We may select any pair of corresponding sides to calculate the scale factor. Here, we will select the longest sides. We write an equation using *f* for the scale factor and then solve for *f*.

$$20f = 25$$

$$f = \frac{25}{20}$$

$$f = \frac{\mathbf{5}}{\mathbf{4}} \text{ or } \mathbf{1.25}$$

Generalize Find the scale factor of △A to △B using a different pair of corresponding sides. Sample: $16f = 20$; $f = \frac{20}{16}$; $f = \frac{5}{4}$ or 1.25

In this book we will express the scale factor in decimal form unless otherwise directed.

Math Language
The term *linear measures* refers to measures of lengths of lines.

Note that the scale factor refers to the *linear measures* of two similar figures and not to the area or volume measures of the figures. The scale factor from cube A to cube B below is 2 because the linear measures of cube B are twice the corresponding measures of cube A.

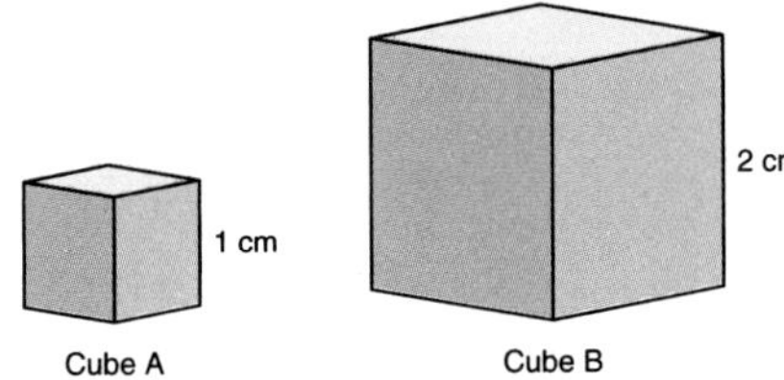

However, the surface area of cube B is 4 times the surface area of cube A, and the volume of cube B is 8 times the volume of cube A. Since we multiply two dimensions of a figure to calculate the area of the figure, the relationship between the areas of two figures is the scale factor times the scale factor; in other words, the scale factor squared. Likewise, the relationship between the volumes of two similar figures is the scale factor cubed.

Manipulative Use

Help students see how scaling can be used to **create floor plans** by having students draw a scale plan of the classroom.

- Have volunteers use a yardstick to measure the walls of the room.
- Write the measurements on the board or overhead.
- Choose a scale, such as 1:24 (1 half of an inch to 1 foot), and have students draw individual plans on graph paper.
- Be sure to measure doors and windows and allow students to draw furniture in the room.

Example 5

The smaller of two similar rectangular prisms has dimensions of 2 cm by 3 cm by 4 cm. The larger rectangular prism has dimensions of 6 cm by 9 cm by 12 cm.

a. What is the scale factor from the smaller to the larger rectangular prism?

b. The area of any face of the larger prism is how many times the area of the corresponding face of the smaller prism?

c. The volume of the larger solid is how many times the volume of the smaller solid?

Solution

Before answering the questions, we draw the two figures.

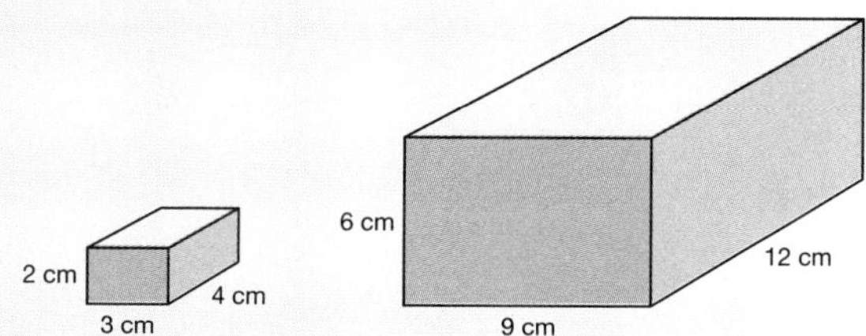

a. We select any two corresponding linear measures to calculate the scale factor. We choose the 2-cm and the 6-cm measures.

Dimension of smaller × scale factor = dimension of larger

$$2f = 6$$

$$f = 3$$

We find that the scale factor is **3.**

b. Since the scale factor from the smaller to the larger figure is 3, the area of any face of the larger figure should be $3^2 = 9$ times the area of the corresponding face of the smaller figure. We confirm this relationship by comparing the area of a 6-by-9-cm face of the larger prism with the corresponding 2-by-3-cm face of the smaller prism.

Area of 6-by-9-cm face = 54 cm^2

Area of 2-by-3-cm face = 6 cm^2

We see that the area of the selected face of the larger prism is indeed **9 times** the area of the corresponding face of the smaller prism.

c. Since the scale factor of the linear dimensions of the two figures is 3, the volume of the larger prism should be $3^3 = 27$ times the volume of the smaller prism. We confirm this relationship by performing the calculations.

Volume of 6-by-9-by-12-cm prism = 648 cm^3

Volume of 2-by-3-by-4-cm prism = 24 cm^3

Inclusion

Students may need a physical model to understand scale factors in multi-dimensions. Have the students build a 1 by 2 by 3 and a 2 by 4 by 6 rectangular prism using the **color cubes** from the Manipulative Kit. Then instruct the students to count the length of one side on the smaller prism and then the length of its corresponding side on the larger prism. Ask the students:

"How many times greater is the larger side than the smaller side?" 2

Instruct the students to count the number of squares that cover the top of the smaller prism and then the same for the larger prism. Ask:

"How many times greater is the larger area than the smaller area?" 4

Instruct the students to count the number of cubes used to build each prism. Some may need to disassemble the models to do this. Ask:

"How many times greater is the larger volume than the smaller volume?" 8

2 New Concepts *(Continued)*

Example 5

Instruction

After studying example 5 and its solution, have students write a solution to parts **a–c** using the scale factor from the larger to the smaller rectangular prism. scale factor = $\frac{1}{3}$; area is $\frac{1}{9}$ of the larger area; volume is $\frac{1}{27}$ the larger volume

Ask students:

"Does the shape of the object affect the relationship between the scale factor of two objects?" No, it does not. The factor is squared when it is applied in two dimensions and cubed when applied in three, regardless of the shape of the objects.

(continued)

2 New Concepts (Continued)

Practice Set

Problem a Analyze

Point out that the length will initially be found in inches. The unit factor $\frac{1 \text{ ft}}{12 \text{ in.}}$ is used to change inches to feet.

Problem e Generalize

Have students calculate the scale factor from the larger rectangle to the smaller rectangle. $\frac{4}{10} = 0.40 = \frac{2}{5}$

Ask students, what is the relationship between the two scale factors? Each scale factor is the reciprocal of the other.

Problem f Explain

"The area of the smaller rectangle is what part of the area of the larger rectangle?"

Sample: $\frac{2}{5}$; $2.5 = 2\frac{5}{10} = 2\frac{1}{2} = \frac{5}{2}$; $\frac{2}{5}$ is the reciprocal of $\frac{5}{2}$

Problem g Model

Students will need **Investigation Activity 13** Coordinate Plane or graph paper to complete this problem. The units of the horizontal axis should be in feet, and the units of the vertical axis should be in inches.

Problem h Estimate

Discuss each answer choice and ask students to give reasons why the choice is reasonable or not reasonable.

Dividing 648 cm^3 by 24 cm^3, we find that the larger volume is indeed **27 times** the smaller volume.

$$\frac{648 \text{ cm}^3}{24 \text{ cm}^3} = 27$$

Showing this calculation another way demonstrates more clearly why the larger volume is 3^3 times the smaller volume.

$$\frac{\text{Volume of larger prism}}{\text{Volume of smaller prism}} = \frac{\overset{3}{\cancel{6 \text{ cm}}} \cdot \overset{3}{\cancel{9 \text{ cm}}} \cdot \overset{3}{\cancel{12 \text{ cm}}}}{\underset{1}{\cancel{2 \text{ cm}}} \cdot \underset{1}{\cancel{3 \text{ cm}}} \cdot \underset{1}{\cancel{4 \text{ cm}}}} = 3^3$$

It is important to note that the measurements used to calculate scale factor must have the same units. If the measurements have different units, we should convert before calculating scale factor.

Practice Set

▶ **a.** Analyze The blueprints were drawn to a scale of 1:24. If a length of a wall on the blueprint was 6 in., what was the length in feet of the wall in the house? $\frac{6 \cdot \overset{2}{\cancel{24}}}{\underset{1}{\cancel{12}}} = 12$ feet

b. Bret is carving a model ship from balsa wood using a scale of 1:36. If the ship is 54 feet long, the model ship should be how many inches long? $\frac{\overset{54}{}}{\underset{3}{\cancel{36}}} \cdot \cancel{12} = 18$ inches

Generalize Solve by using the scale factor:

c. $\frac{5}{7} = \frac{15}{w}$ 21

d. $\frac{x}{3} = \frac{42}{21}$ 6

▶ **e.** Generalize These two rectangles are similar. Calculate the scale factor from the smaller rectangle to the larger rectangle. 2.5

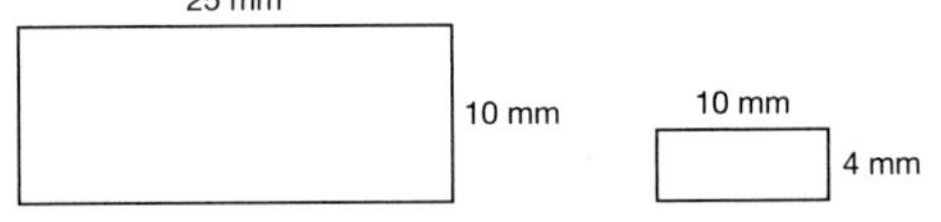

f. 6.25 times. We can divide the area of the larger rectangle by the area of the smaller rectangle: $\frac{250}{40} = 6.25$. We can square the scale factor: $(2.5)^2 = 6.25$.

▶ **f.** Explain The area of the larger rectangle above is how many times the area of the smaller rectangle? Show two ways to find the answer.

▶ **g.** Model The scale of the car model in example 2 is 1:36. This means 1 inch on the model corresponds to 36 inches (that is, 3 feet) on the actual car. On grid paper make a graph that shows this relationship. Make the units of the horizontal axis feet to represent the car. On the vertical axis use inches for the model. Use the graph following example 1 as a pattern.

g.

Scale of Car Model

Model (in inches): 0, 1, 2, 3, 4, 5

Actual Size (in feet): 3, 6, 9, 12

▶ **h.** Estimate The statue of the standing World War II general was $1\frac{1}{2}$ times life-size. Which is the most reasonable estimate for the height of the statue? C

A 4 ft **B** 6 ft **C** 9 ft **D** 15 ft

▶ See Math Conversations in the sidebar.

Written Practice *Strengthening Concepts*

1. $\frac{2}{5}$; Sample: There are 6 cards and 3 of them have an A on them. After the first pick, there are 5 cards, 2 of which are As. So the probability that the next card is an A is $\frac{2}{5}$.

* **1.** (94) **Explain** Ariana writes the letters of her first name on index cards, one letter per card. She turns the cards over and mixes them up. Then she chooses a card. If this card is an A, what is the probability that the next card will also be an A? Tell how you found your answer.

Use ratio boxes to solve problems **2–4.**

* **2.** (92) The regular price of the shoes was \$45, but they were on sale for 20 percent off. What was the sale price? \$36

3. (72) In 2002, \$5.00 was equal to about 40 Norwegian kroner. At that time, what was the cost in dollars of an item that cost 100 kroner? \$12.50

▶ * **4.** (92) **Formulate** The number of students in chorus increased 25 percent this year. If there are 20 more students in chorus this year than there were last year, how many students are in chorus this year? 100 students

5. (84, 87) Simplify: $(3x)(x) - (x)(2x)$ x^2

6. (55) In her first 6 basketball games Ann averaged 10 points per game. In her next 9 games she averaged 15 points per game. How many points per game did Ann average during her first 15 games? 13 points per game

▶ **7.** (46) Ingrid started her trip at 8:30 a.m. with a full tank of gas and an odometer reading of 43,764 miles. When she stopped for gas at 1:30 p.m., the odometer read 44,010 miles.

a. If it took 12 gallons to fill the tank, her car averaged how many miles per gallon? 20.5 miles per gallon

b. Ingrid traveled at an average speed of how many miles per hour? 49.2 miles per hour

8. (74) Write an equation to solve this problem. Three fifths of Tyrone's favorite number is 60. What is Tyrone's favorite number? $\frac{3}{5} \times W_N = 60$; 100

9.

9. (Inv. 3, 80) On a coordinate plane, graph the points $(-3, 2)$, $(3, 2)$, and $(-3, -2)$.

a. If these points designate three of the vertices of a rectangle, what are the coordinates of the fourth vertex of the rectangle? Draw the rectangle. $(3, -2)$

b. Draw the image of the rectangle in **a** after a 90° clockwise rotation about the origin. What are the coordinates of the vertices of the rotated image? $(2, 3)$, $(2, -3)$, $(-2, -3)$, $(-2, 3)$

▶ **10.** (36, 86) What is the ratio of counting numbers to integers in this set of numbers? $\frac{1}{3}$

$$\{-3, -2, -1, 0, 1, 2\}$$

11. (20, 41) Find a^2 if $\sqrt{a} = 3$. 81

▶* **12.** (92) **Generalize** An antique dealer bought a chair for \$40 and sold the chair for 60% more. What was the selling price? \$64

▶ See Math Conversations in the sidebar.

Math Conversations

Discussion opportunities are provided below.

Problem 4 Formulate

Have students write the proportions that could be set up to find the number of students in chorus last year. Start with a ratio box.

	Percent	Actual
Last Year	100	L
+ Change	25	20
This Year	125	T

$$\frac{100}{25} = \frac{L}{20}$$

Problem 12 Generalize

Have volunteers use both an equation and a proportion to solve the problem. Ask students which representation is easier to use.

Errors and Misconceptions

Problem 7

If students have a wrong answer for this multi-step problem, help them list the steps of the problem, so they can find their own error.

Step 1: 8:30 to 1:30 is 5 hours
Step 2: 44,010 − 43,764 = 246
Step 3: 246 ÷ 12 = 20.5 miles per gallon
Step 4: 246 ÷ 5 = 49.2 miles per hour

Problem 10

If students have $\frac{3}{3}$ as an answer, they have included 0 as a counting number. Remind them that counting numbers begin with 1. If students have $\frac{2}{5}$ as an answer, they did not include 0 as an integer. Remind students that integers is the set of all positive numbers and their opposites and 0.

(continued)

3 Written Practice (Continued)

Math Conversations

Discussion opportunities are provided below.

Problem 16 Represent

Extend the Problem

Write these rational numbers on the board.

$$\frac{7}{-25} \quad \frac{-7}{50} \quad -\frac{7}{100}$$

If necessary, lead a class discussion about the placement of the negative signs. Use $\frac{4}{2}$ so students can use mental math.

$$\frac{4}{-2} = 4 \div -2 \text{ or } -2 \qquad \frac{-4}{2} = -4 \div 2 \text{ or } -2$$

$$-\frac{4}{2} = (-1)\left(\frac{4}{2}\right) = -1 \cdot 2 \text{ or } -2$$

It does not matter where the negative sign is placed; it is the same negative number.

Ask a volunteer to draw a number line on the board and estimate the placement of the fractions on the number line.

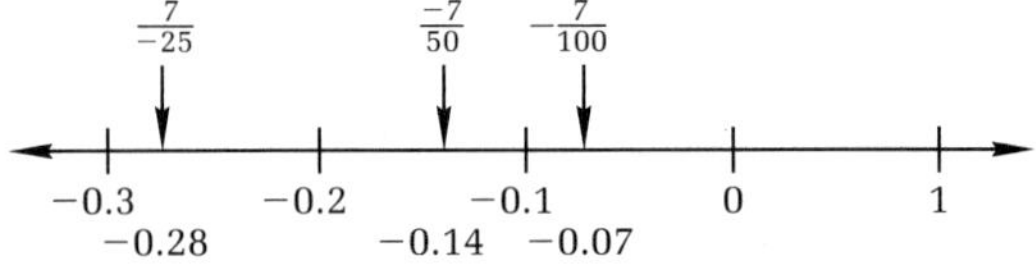

Discuss with students which representation is easier for placing the numbers on the number line, fractions or decimals.

Problem 18 Represent

"How can you change the function so that x and y are directly proportional?" $y = 2x$

Problem 21 Generalize

Extend the Problem

"John said, 'You can multiply 96 in.² by 2.5 to get the area of the larger triangle.' Is John right? Explain." No; Since area has 2 dimensions, you need to multiply $2.5 \times 2.5 \times 96$ which gives 600 in.². Students can check this answer using the formula for area of a triangle.

(continued)

Write equations to solve problems **13** and **14**.

13. (77) Forty is what percent of 250? $40 = W_P \times 250$; 16%

14. (77) Forty percent of what number is 60? $0.4 \times W_N = 60$; 150

15. (8, 85) **a.** Segment *BC* is how much longer than segment *AB*? **a.** $\frac{3}{4}$ inch

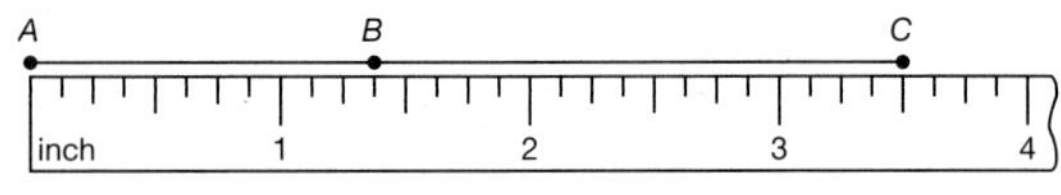

b. Convert the length of segment *AC* to centimeters. 8.89 cm

▶ **16.** (78) Graph on a number line: $x \le 3$ 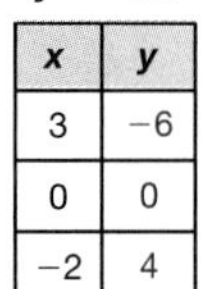

17. (48) Complete the table.

Fraction	Decimal	Percent
a. $\frac{7}{500}$	**b.** 0.014	1.4%

▶* **18.** (56, Inv. 9) Represent Find the missing numbers in the table by using the function rule. Then graph the function.

$y = -2x$

x	y
3	−6
0	0
−2	4

a. Where does the graph of the function intersect the *y*-axis? (0, 0)

b. Analyze Are *x* and *y* directly proportional? Explain your answer.

18.

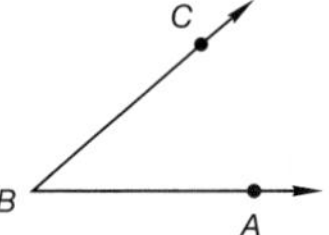

b. Yes, *x* and *y* are directly proportional. The graph is a line and (0, 0) is included.

19. (66, 82) Find each measure of a circle that has a diameter of 2 feet. (Use 3.14 for π.)

a. circumference 6.28 ft

b. area 3.14 ft²

* **20.** (96) Estimate the measure of $\angle ABC$. Then trace the angle, extend the sides, and measure the angle with a protractor. See student work; 40°

Generalize Refer to the figures below to answer problems **21** and **22**.

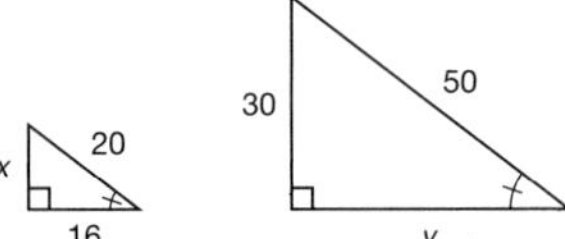

▶* **21.** (97) Find *x* and *y*. Then find the area of the smaller triangle. Dimensions are in inches. $x = 12$ in.; $y = 40$ in.; area $= 96$ in.²

* **22.** (98) Calculate the scale factor from the smaller triangle to the larger triangle. 2.5

▶ See Math Conversations in the sidebar.

23. Multiply. Write the product in scientific notation. 7×10^{-2}
(83)

$$(1.4 \times 10^{-6})(5 \times 10^{4})$$

▸ *Justify* For problems **24** and **25,** solve and check. Show each step.

24. $m = -20$
$-\frac{3}{5}m + 8 = 20$
$-\frac{3}{5}m = 12$
$m = \frac{12}{-\frac{3}{5}}$
$m = -20$

25. $x = 39$
$0.3x - 2.7 = 9$
$0.3x = 11.7$
$x = 39$

* **24.** $-\frac{3}{5}m + 8 = 20$
(93)

* **25.** $0.3x - 2.7 = 9$
(93)

▸ *Generalize* Simplify:

26. $\sqrt{5^3 - 5^2}$ 10
(52)

27. 1 gal 1 qt − 1 qt 1 pt = 3 qt 1 pt
(49)

28. $(0.25)\left(1\frac{1}{4} - 1.2\right)$ 0.0125
(43)

29. $7\frac{1}{3} - \left(1\frac{3}{4} \div 3.5\right)$ $6\frac{5}{6}$
(43)

30. $\frac{(-2)(3) - (3)(-4)}{(-2)(-3) - (4)}$ 3
(85)

Early Finishers
Real-World Application

A local farmer wishes to fertilize one of his fields, but he must first find its area. The field is in the shape of right triangle *ABC* shown below. After making some measurements, the farmer knows the following information:

Segment *DE* is 18 feet long and parallel to segment *BC*. *AD* is 15 feet long. The total length of *AB* is 900 feet. (Note: $\triangle ABC$ is not to scale)

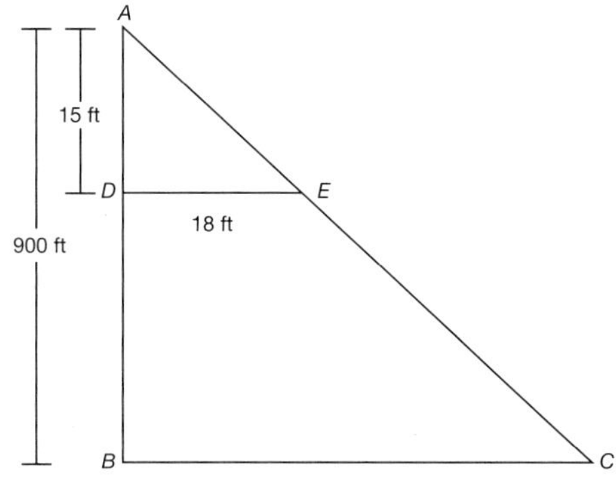

a. Use a proportion to find the length of $\overline{BC}$. Sample: $\frac{18}{15} = \frac{BC}{900}$; 1080 ft

b. What is the total area of the field in square feet? 486,000 ft^2

▸ See Math Conversations in the sidebar.

3 Written Practice (Continued)

Math Conversations

Discussion opportunities are provided below.

Problems 24 and 25 Justify

Have volunteers work at the board as they solve each problem.

Problems 26–30 Generalize

Ask students to decide whether they would use mental math or paper and pencil to solve each problem. Have them explain their choice.

Looking Forward

Translating mathematical phrases and geometric relationships into algebraic equations and solving the equations prepares students for:

- **Lesson 102,** simplifying and then solving equations.
- **Lesson 109,** translating and solving equations with exponents.

Pythagorean Theorem

Objective

- Use the Pythagorean Theorem to find the unknown length of a side of a right triangle.

Lesson Preparation

Materials

- **Power Up T** (in *Instructional Masters*)

Optional

- **Manipulative kit: inch and metric rulers, color tiles**

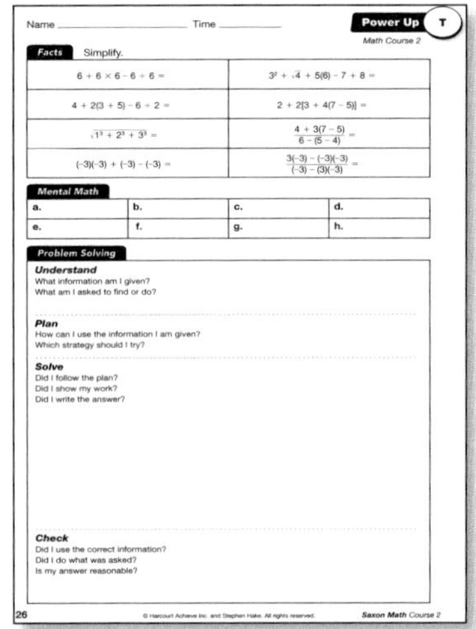

Name ____________ Time ________ **Power Up T** *Math Course 2*

Facts Simplify.

$6 + 6 \times 6 - 6 \div 6 =$	$3^2 + \sqrt{4} + 5(6) - 7 + 8 =$
$4 + 2(3 + 5) - 6 \div 2 =$	$2 + 2[3 + 4(7 - 5)] =$
$\sqrt{1^3 + 2^3 + 3^3} =$	$\frac{4 + 3(7 - 5)}{6 - (5 - 4)} =$
$(-3)(-3) + (-3) - (-3) =$	$\frac{3(-3) - (-3)(-3)}{(-3) - (3)(-3)} =$

Mental Math

a.	b.	c.	d.
e.	f.	g.	h.

Problem Solving

Understand
What information am I given?
What am I asked to find or do?

Plan
How can I use the information I am given?
Which strategy should I try?

Solve
Did I follow the plan?
Did I show my work?
Did I write the answer?

Check
Did I use the correct information?
Did I do what was asked?
Is my answer reasonable?

26 © Harcourt Achieve Inc. and Stephen Hake. All rights reserved. *Saxon Math Course 2*

Power Up T

Math Language

New	English Learners (ESL)
hypotenuse	tip
legs	
Pythagorean Theorem	

Technology Resources

Student eBook Complete student textbook in electronic format.

Resources and Planner CD Assessment, reteaching, and instructional masters, plus a pacing calendar with standards.

Test and Practice Generator CD Create additional practice sheets and custom-made tests.

www.SaxonPublishers.com Visit for more student activities and planning materials.

Inclusion

Adaptations CD Adapted lessons, investigations, practice and assessments.

Meeting Standards

National Council of Teachers of Mathematics (NCTM)

Algebra

AL.3a Model and solve contextualized problems using various representations, such as graphs, tables, and equations

Geometry

GM.1c Create and critique inductive and deductive arguments concerning geometric ideas and relationships, such as congruence, similarity, and the Pythagorean relationship

GM.4d Use geometric models to represent and explain numerical and algebraic relationships

Problem Solving

PS.1b Solve problems that arise in mathematics and in other contexts

Power-Up Discussion *For use with Power Up, p. 686*

Problem-Solving Strategy: Write an Equation/ Make It Simpler

Carpeting is sold by the square yard. If carpet is priced at $25 per square yard (including tax and installation), how much will it cost to carpet a classroom that is 36 feet long and 36 feet wide?

Understand **Understand the problem.**

"What information are we given?"

We are told that a particular type of carpeting is priced at $25 per square yard (including tax and installation).

"What are we asked to do?"

We are asked to determine how much it will cost to carpet a classroom that is 36 feet long and 36 feet wide.

Plan **Make a plan.**

"What problem-solving strategy will we use?"

We will *make the problem simpler,* then *write an equation* to find the total cost.

Solve **Carry out the Plan.**

"Carpeting is sold by the square yard. How can we adapt the dimensions of the room so we can calculate the area in square yards?"

We can change the length and width to yards: $36 \text{ ft} \div 3 = 12 \text{ yd}$

"How many square yards of carpeting are needed to carpet the room?"

$12 \text{ yd} \times 12 \text{ yd} = 144 \text{ sq. yards}$

"Can we write an equation to find the total cost (c) of carpeting the room?"

$c = \$25/\text{yard} \times 144 \text{ yards}$

"What is the total cost?"

$3600

Check **Look back.**

"Did we do what we were asked to do?"

Yes, we found the cost of carpeting the classroom.

1 Power Up

Facts

Distribute **Power Up T** to students. See answers below.

Mental Math

Encourage students to share different ways to mentally compute these exercises. Strategies for exercises **e** and **f** are listed below.

e. Decompose

$12 \cdot 2 = 24$

$12 \cdot \frac{1}{3} = 4$

$24 + 4 = 28$

Equivalent Expression

$(12 \div 3)(2\frac{1}{3} \cdot 3)$

$4(\frac{7}{3} \cdot \frac{3}{1}) = 4 \cdot 7$ or 28

f. Multiply by $\frac{1}{3}$

$\frac{1}{3} \cdot 60 = 20$

$60 - 20 = 40$

Multiply by $\frac{2}{3}$

$\frac{2}{3} \cdot 60 = (60 \div 3) \cdot 2$

$20 \cdot 2 = 40$

Problem Solving

Refer to **Power-Up Discussion,** p. 686B.

2 New Concepts

Instruction

Ask students to explain why the right angle is always the largest angle in a right triangle. Since a triangle's interior angle measures total 180° and 90° is half of 180°, each of the other two angles must be less than 90°.

Explain to students that the properties of a right angle make it possible to determine the length of one of its sides if the other two are known. Tell them that in this lesson they will study right angles.

(continued)

LESSON **99**

• Pythagorean Theorem

Power Up *Building Power*

facts Power Up T

mental math

a. **Positive/Negative:** $(-1.5) + (4.5)$ 3

b. **Order of Operations/Exponents:** $(8 \times 10^6)(4 \times 10^4)$ 3.2×10^{11}

c. **Ratio:** $\frac{0.15}{30} = \frac{0.005}{n}$ 1

d. **Measurement:** Convert −15°C to degrees Fahrenheit. 5°F

e. **Calculation:** $12 \times 2\frac{1}{3}$ 28

f. **Percent:** $33\frac{1}{3}\%$ less than \$60 \$40

g. **Geometry:** What shape(s) has 6 faces and 8 vertices? rectangular prism

h. **Power/Roots:** What is the square root of the sum of 6^2 and 8^2? 10

problem solving Carpeting is sold by the square yard. If carpet is priced at \$25 per square yard (including tax and installation), how much would it cost to carpet a classroom that is 36 feet long and 36 feet wide? \$3600

New Concept *Increasing Knowledge*

Thinking Skill
Explain

Why is the hypotenuse of a right triangle always opposite the right angle? The longest side of any triangle is opposite the largest angle. In a right triangle, the right angle is always the largest angle. Therefore, the hypotenuse is opposite the right angle.

The longest side of a right triangle is called the **hypotenuse.** The other two sides are called **legs.** Every right triangle has a property that makes right triangles very important in mathematics. **The area of the square drawn on the hypotenuse of a right triangle equals the sum of the areas of the squares drawn on the legs.**

Discuss Identify by their measure the hypotenuse and legs of the triangle shown. The hypotenuse is the longest side (5). The legs are the other two sides (3) and (4).

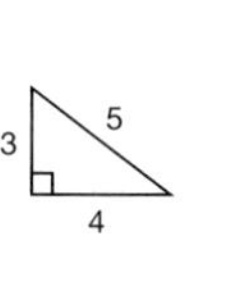

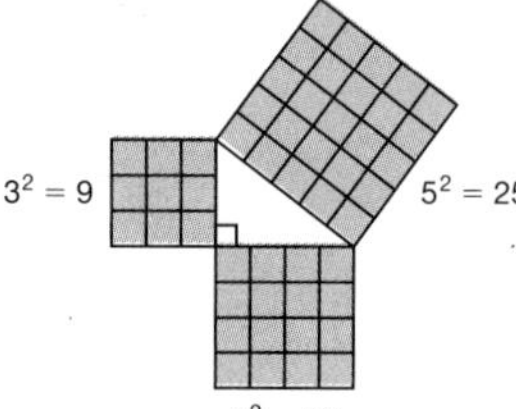

The triangle on the left is a right triangle. On the right we have drawn and shaded a square on each side of the triangle. We have divided the squares into units and can see that their areas are 9, 16, and 25. Notice that the area of the largest square equals the sum of the areas of the other two squares.

$$25 = 16 + 9$$

Facts Simplify.

$6 + 6 \times 6 - 6 \div 6 = 41$	$3^2 + \sqrt{4} + 5(6) - 7 + 8 = 42$
$4 + 2(3 + 5) - 6 \div 2 = 17$	$2 + 2[3 + 4(7 - 5)] = 24$
$\sqrt{1^3 + 2^3 + 3^3} = 6$	$\frac{4 + 3(7 - 5)}{6 - (5 - 4)} = 2$
$(-3)(-3) + (-3) - (-3) = 9$	$\frac{3(-3) - (-3)(-3)}{(-3) - (3)(-3)} = -3$

To solve right-triangle problems using the Pythagorean theorem, we will draw the right triangle, as well as squares on each side of the triangle.

Example 1

Copy this triangle. Draw a square on each side. Find the area of each square. Then find *c*.

Solution

We copy the triangle and draw a square on each side of the triangle as shown.

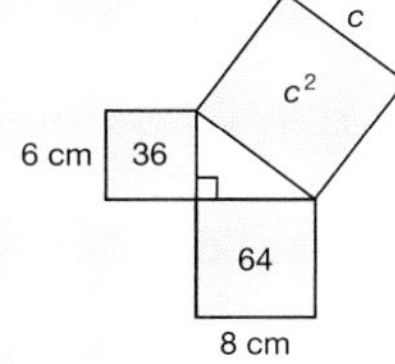

We were given the lengths of the two shorter sides. The areas of the squares on these sides are **36 cm²** and **64 cm²**. The Pythagorean theorem says that the sum of the areas of the smaller squares equals the area of the largest square.

$$36 \text{ cm}^2 + 64 \text{ cm}^2 = \mathbf{100 \text{ cm}^2}$$

This means that each side of the largest square must be 10 cm long because $(10 \text{ cm})^2$ equals 100 cm^2. Thus

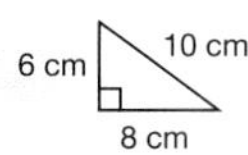

$$c = \mathbf{10 \text{ cm}}$$

Explain How is the formula for the area of a square, $A = s^2$, used when finding the lengths of the sides of a right triangle?

Math Language

Remember that $\sqrt{100} = 10$, or the square root of 100 is 10.

The formula is used to find the areas of the squares of each leg and again when finding the length of the hypotenuse by taking the square root of the area of its square.

Example 2

In this triangle, find *a*. Dimensions are in inches.

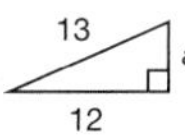

Solution

We copy the triangle and draw a square on each side. The area of the largest square is 169 in.². The areas of the smaller squares are 144 in.² and a^2. By the Pythagorean theorem, a^2 plus 144 in.² must equal 169 in.².

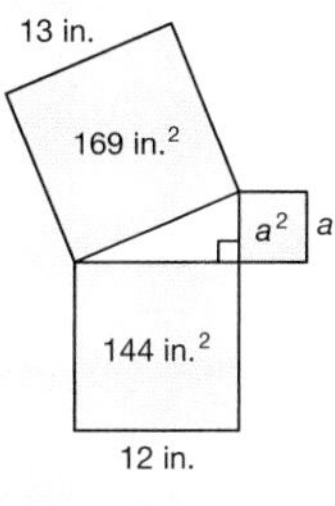

$$a^2 + 144 \text{ in.}^2 = 169 \text{ in.}^2$$

Subtracting 144 in.² from both sides, we see that

$$a^2 = 25 \text{ in.}^2$$

This means that a equals **5 in.**, because $(5 \text{ in.})^2$ is 25 in².

2 New Concepts (Continued)

Example 1

Instruction

Point out that the 3–4–5 triangle is similar to the 6–8–10 triangle in this example. The scale factor is 2. All triangles similar to the 3–4–5 triangle are right triangles. However, not all right triangles are similar. The two angles that are not right angles can differ, and its sides might not be in proportion with each other.

Example 2

Instruction

When the lengths of the sides of a right triangle are integers, the integers form what is known as a Pythagorean triplet. There are infinitely many Pythagorean triplets. Some common ones are the 3–4–5 triplet, the 5–12–13 triplet, the 8–15–17 triplet, and the 7–24–25 triplet. Pythagorean triplets are used frequently in problems because having all sides being integers makes calculations easier.

(continued)

Math Background

If the square of the length of one side of a triangle is equal to the sum of the squares of the lengths of the other two sides, is the triangle always a right triangle?

Yes. This concept is known as the converse of the Pythagorean theorem. The converse helps when classifying triangles. In a triangle with the longest side c:

- if $c^2 = a^2 + b^2$, the triangle is a right triangle.
- if $c^2 > a^2 + b^2$, the triangle is obtuse.
- if $c^2 < a^2 + b^2$, the triangle is acute.

Inclusion

Have students use the **color tiles** from the Manipulative Kit to see the proof of the *Pythagorean theorem.* For instance, have them create the 3 by 3, 4 by 4, and 5 by 5 squares off the 3 by 4 by 5 right triangle. Then ask:

"Does $3^2 + 4^2 = 5^2$? Explain."

Sample: Yes, because the 9 tiles and 16 tiles equal the 25 tiles off the right triangle.

Have the students use the color tiles in the same manner to solve the missing side length in example 1.

2 New Concepts (Continued)

Example 3

Instruction

- Have students use a ruler to draw the triangle in this example to scale.
- Ask students to draw the legs of the triangle first and then draw the hypotenuse to connect the legs.
- Then have them measure the hypotenuse to check their answer.

Example 4

Instruction

- Explain that the converse is the reverse of a statement. For example, if a conditional statement is in the form *If A, then B,* the converse of the statement is *If B, then A.*
- Be sure that students understand that not all converse statements hold true. For example, the statement *All squares are rectangles* is true. However, its converse *All rectangles are squares* is not true.

Ask students the following:

"What about the Pythagorean theorem indicates that the converse of it must be true?" The Pythagorean theorem applies *only* to right triangles. If this were not true, the converse of the theorem would not be true.

(continued)

Example 3

Find the perimeter of this triangle. Dimensions are in centimeters.

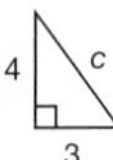

Solution

We can draw a square on each side and use the Pythagorean theorem to find c. The areas of the two smaller squares are 16 cm^2 and 9 cm^2. The sum of these areas is 25 cm^2, so the area of the largest square is 25 cm^2. Thus the length c is 5 cm. Now we add the lengths of the sides to find the perimeter.

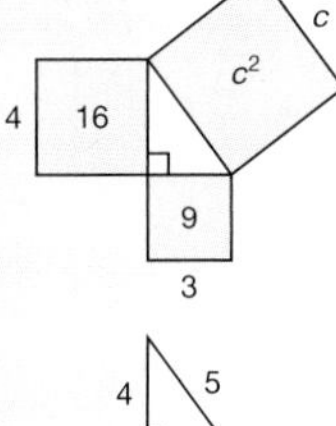

$$\text{Perimeter} = 4 \text{ cm} + 3 \text{ cm} + 5 \text{ cm}$$
$$= \mathbf{12\ cm}$$

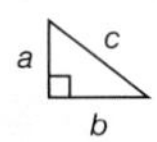

Example 4

Copy this right triangle and draw squares on the sides. Then write an equation that shows the relationship between the areas of the squares.

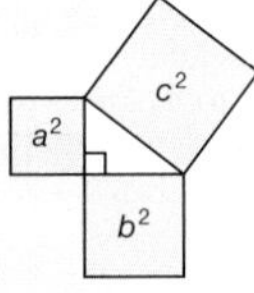

Solution

We copy the triangle and draw a square on each side. Squaring the lengths of the sides of the triangle gives us the areas of the squares: a^2, b^2, and c^2. By the Pythagorean theorem, the sum of the areas of the smaller two squares is equal to the area of the largest square.

$$\mathbf{a^2 + b^2 = c^2}$$

This equation is commonly used to algebraically express the Pythagorean theorem: The sum of the squares of the legs equals the square of the hypotenuse. **The Pythagorean theorem applies to all right triangles and it applies only to right triangles.**

The converse of the Pythagorean theorem is true. If the sum of the squares of two sides of a triangle equals the square of the third side, then the triangle is a right triangle.

This property of right triangles was known to the Egyptians as early as 2000 b.c., but it is named for a Greek mathematician who lived about 550 b.c. The Greek's name was Pythagoras, and the property is called the **Pythagorean theorem.** The Greeks are so proud of Pythagoras that they have issued a postage stamp that illustrates the theorem. Here we show a reproduction of the stamp:

Example 5

The side lengths of three triangles are given. Which triangle is a right triangle?

A 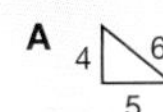

B 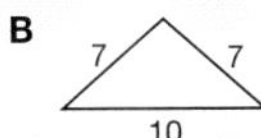

C 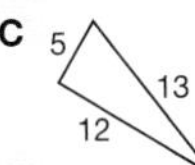

Solution

We square the lengths of the sides looking for a Pythagorean relationship.

A 4^2 5^2 6^2
$16 + 25 \neq 36$

B 7^2 7^2 10^2
$49 + 49 \neq 100$

C 5^2 12^2 13^2
$25 + 144 = 169$

Only triangle **C** is a right triangle because it is the only triangle in which the sum of the squares of two sides equals the square of the third side.

Practice Set

Analyze Copy the triangles and draw the squares on the sides of the triangles as you work problems **a–c.**

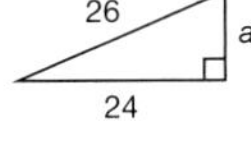

▸ **a.** Use the Pythagorean theorem to find the length *a*. 10

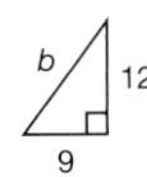

b. Use the Pythagorean theorem to find the length *b*. 15

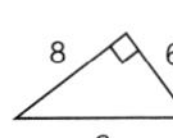

c. Find the perimeter of this triangle. Dimensions are in feet. 24 feet

▸ **d.** *Justify* Which triangle below is a right triangle? Show your work and defend your answer.

A 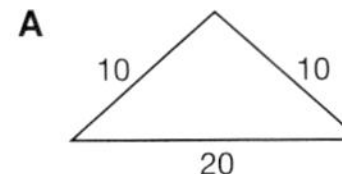

B 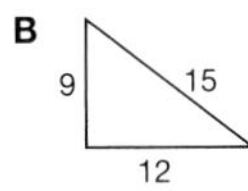

C 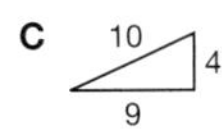

d. Triangle B; For triangle B: $9^2 + 12^2 = 15^2$, $81 + 144 = 225$. For triangle A: $10^2 + 10^2 \neq 20^2$, $100 + 100 \neq 400$. For triangle C: $4^2 + 9^2 \neq 10^2$, $16 + 81 \neq 100$. Only the dimensions of triangle B satisfy the Pythagorean theorem.

▸ See Math Conversations in the sidebar.

2 New Concepts (Continued)

Example 5

Instruction

Remind students that they should not make assumptions based on how the figure looks. A triangle may look like a right triangle because it has one angle that is 89°. But it is not a right triangle.

Practice Set

Problem a (Error Alert)

Some students may be confused because their answers are not integers (such as 35.384). These students have mistakenly solved an equation that uses side *a* as the hypotenuse. Have students reread the question and look at the diagram again to try and find their mistake.

Problem d Justify

Before they solve, have students identify the hypotenuse. Ask students to explain why each of the other triangles is not a right triangle.

3 Written Practice

Math Conversations

Discussion opportunities are provided below.

Problem 1 Explain

Ask students to explain how they can use mental math to solve this problem. 10% of 15 is \$1.50, half of \$1.50 is 75¢, \$1.50 + 75¢ = \$2.25

Problem 9

Extend the Problem

"If you drew a reflection of this triangle across diameter AB, would the two triangles together form a rectangle? Explain why or why not." no; It would form a quadrilateral but not a rectangle because the angles of the quadrilateral at A and B would not be right angles. However, a rotation would form a rectangle.

Problem 10 Model

Ask a student to draw the ratio box at the board.

	Percent	Actual
Before	100	\$3.40
−Change	20	C
After	80	A

$$\frac{100}{80} = \frac{\$3.40}{A}$$

$$100A = 80 \cdot \$3.40$$
$$100A = 272$$
$$A = \$2.72$$

Problem 11 Explain

"If an item is increased by 20%, the new price is what percent of the original price?" 120%; 100% + 20% = 120%

Errors and Misconceptions

Problem 4

If students write \$1.28 or \$1.29 as an answer, they divided by 2 instead of 32. Point out that 2 pounds must be changed to ounces before dividing.

(continued)

Written Practice *Strengthening Concepts*

▶ **1.** (46) Explain The meal cost \$15. Christie left a tip that was 15 percent of the cost of the meal. How much money did Christie leave for a tip? \$2.25

2. (57) Twenty-five ten-thousandths is how much greater than twenty millionths? Write the answer in scientific notation. 2.48×10^{-3}

3. (Inv. 4) Find these measures for the number of days in the months of a leap year.

a. mean 30.5 days **b.** median 31 days

c. mode 31 days **d.** range 2 days

▶ **4.** (46) The 2-pound box costs \$2.72. The 48-ounce box costs \$3.60. The smaller box costs how much more per ounce than the larger box? 1¢ more per ounce

Use ratio boxes to solve problems **5** and **6.**

5. (72) If 80 pounds of seed costs \$96, what would be the cost of 300 pounds of seed? \$360

6. (66) The ratio of stalactites to stalagmites in the cavern was 9 to 5. If the total number of stalactites and stalagmites was 1260, how many stalagmites were in the cavern? 450 stalagmites

7. (16, 60) Five eighths of a pound is how many ounces? 10 ounces

8. (77) Write equations to solve **a** and **b.**

a. Ten percent of what number is 20? $0.1 \times W_N = 20$; 200

b. Twenty is what percent of 60? $20 = W_P \times 60$; $33\frac{1}{3}\%$

▶ **9.** (62) In this figure, central angle BDC measures 60°, and inscribed angle BAC measures 30°. Angles ACD and BCD are complementary.

a. Classify $\triangle ABC$ by angles. right triangle

b. Classify $\triangle BCD$ by sides. equilateral triangle

c. Classify $\triangle ADC$ by sides. isosceles triangle

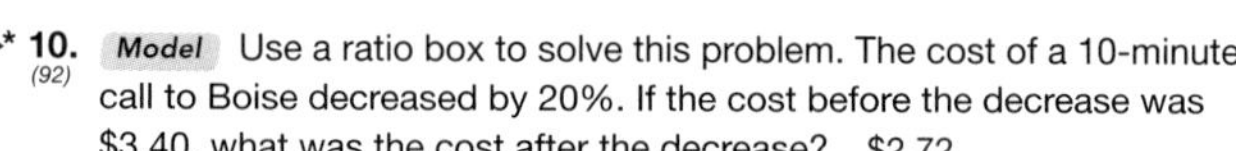

▶* **10.** (92) Model Use a ratio box to solve this problem. The cost of a 10-minute call to Boise decreased by 20%. If the cost before the decrease was \$3.40, what was the cost after the decrease? \$2.72

▶* **11.** (92) Explain An item is on sale for 20% off the regular price. The sale price is what percent of the regular price? How do you know? 80%; Sample: 100% − 20% = 80%

▶ See Math Conversations in the sidebar.

English Learners

In problem 1, explain the meaning of **tip.** Say:

"When you go to a restaurant, you should leave extra money for the waiter or waitress. This is called a tip."

Ask students why you might want to leave a large tip. To recognize good service from the waiter/waitress

12. (37) What is the area of the shaded region of this rectangle? 9 units^2

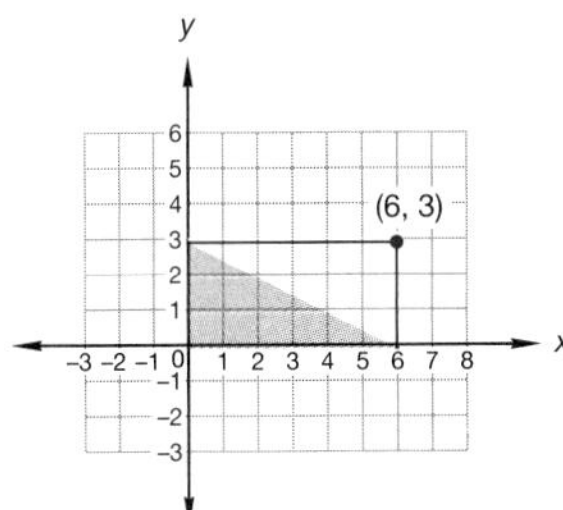

▶* **13.** (98) **Model** Use a ratio box to solve this problem. On a 1:60 scale-model airplane, the wingspan is 8 inches. The wingspan of the actual airplane is how many inches? What is the wingspan of the actual airplane in feet? 480 inches; 40 feet

14. (48) Complete the table.

Fraction	Decimal	Percent
$1\frac{1}{3}$	**a.** $1.\overline{3}$	**b.** $133\frac{1}{3}\%$
c. $\frac{1}{75}$	**d.** $0.01\overline{3}$	$1\frac{1}{3}\%$

15. (84, 87) Simplify:

a. $(ax^2)(-2ax)(-a^2)$ $2a^4x^3$

b. $\frac{1}{2}\pi + \frac{2}{3}\pi - \pi$ $\frac{1}{6}\pi$

16. (83) Multiply. Write the product in scientific notation. 7.29×10^5

$(8.1 \times 10^{-6})(9 \times 10^{10})$

17. (20, 52) Evaluate: $\sqrt{c^2 - b^2}$ if $c = 15$ and $b = 12$ 9

▶* **18.** (99) **Analyze** Use the Pythagorean theorem to find c. 12

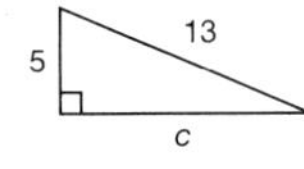

19. Sample: Find the area of the circular base and multiply it by the height of right solid; $V = 3140$ cm^3.

▶* **19.** (95) **Explain** How would you would find the volume of this right solid? Then find the volume. Dimensions are in centimeters. (Use 3.14 for π.)

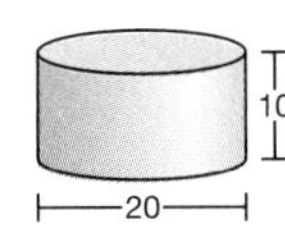

20. (40) Refer to the figure below to find the measures of the following angles.

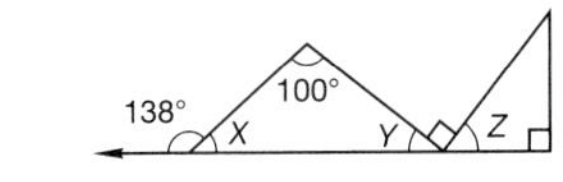

a. $\angle X$ 42° **b.** $\angle Y$ 38° **c.** $\angle Z$ 52°

▶ See Math Conversations in the sidebar.

3 Written Practice (Continued)

Math Conversations

Discussion opportunities are provided below.

Problem 13 Model

Ask a student to draw the ratio box at the board.

	Scale	Measure
Model	1	8 in.
Actual	60	A

$$\frac{1}{60} = \frac{8}{A}$$
$$1A = 8 \cdot 60$$
$$A = 480$$
$$480 \div 12 = 40 \text{ ft}$$

Problem 18 Analyze

Have a volunteer show the solution on the board.

$$5^2 + b^2 = 13^2$$
$$-25 + 25 + b^2 = 169 - 25$$
$$b^2 = 144$$
$$b = 12$$

Problem 19 Explain

Extend the Problem

"If you double the diameter and the height of the cylinder, will the volume quadruple? Explain why or why not." No; volume has 3 dimensions, multiply 2^3 times the volume; $2 \cdot 2 \cdot 2 = 8$; the volume would be 8 times the original volume.

Errors and Misconceptions

Problem 18

Students may not notice that one leg in this triangle is labeled c. Remind them that the sum of the squares of the legs equals the hypotenuse, regardless of the variables used for the legs. Encourage students to draw squares on the side of the right triangle and calculate the areas of the squares.

(continued)

3 Written Practice (Continued)

Math Conversations

Discussion opportunities are provided below.

Problem 21b Analyze

"What is the scale factor from the larger triangle to the smaller triangle? Explain why." $\frac{2}{3}$; $1.5 = 1\frac{1}{2} = \frac{3}{2}$; the reciprocal of $\frac{3}{2}$ is $\frac{2}{3}$; the scale factor from the larger triangle to the smaller triangle is $\frac{2}{3}$.

Problem 23 Generalize

Ask a volunteer to solve and check these problems at the board.

Problem 30 Generalize

Have students use the Distributive Property to multiply the following.

$-(x - 4)$ $-(x - 2)$

$-x + 4$ $-x + 2$

* **21.** (97, 98) Analyze These triangles are similar. Dimensions are in inches.

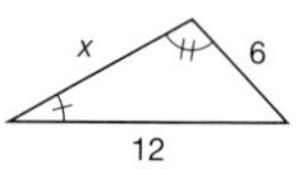

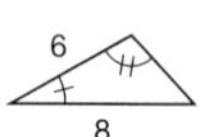

a. Find x. 9 inches

▶ **b.** What is the scale factor from the smaller triangle to the larger triangle? 1.5

c. The area of the larger triangle is how many times the area of the smaller triangle? *Hint:* Use the scale factor found in **b.** 2.25 times

22. (29) Estimate: $\frac{(41{,}392)(395)}{81}$ 200,000

Generalize For problems **23** and **24,** solve and check. Show each step.

▶* **23.** (93) $4n + 1.64 = 2$ 0.09

* **24.** (93) $3\frac{1}{3}x - 1 = 49$ 15

25. (98) $\frac{17}{25} = \frac{m}{75}$ 51

Simplify:

26. (20, 52) $3^3 + 4^2 - \sqrt{225}$ 28

27. (52, 57) $\sqrt{225} - 15^0 + 10^{-1}$ $14\frac{1}{10}$ or 14.1

28. (43) $\left(3\frac{1}{3}\right)(0.75)(40)$ 100

29. (85, 91) $\frac{-12 - (6)(-3)}{(-12) - (-6) + (3)}$ −2

▶* **30.** (96) Generalize Using the Distributive Property, we know that $2(x - 4)$ equals $2x - 8$. Use the Distributive Property to multiply $3(x - 2)$.
$3x - 6$

Early Finishers
Math Applications

Which type of display—a bar graph or a Venn diagram—is the most appropriate way to display the factors and common factors of the numbers 12 and 36? Draw your display and justify your choice. Venn diagram; Sample: The data for the factors and common factors of the numbers 12 and 36 represents sets that overlap. A Venn diagram is a good choice for this type of data. See student displays.

▶ See Math Conversations in the sidebar.

Looking Forward

Finding the unknown length of a side of a right triangle using the Pythagorean theorem prepares students for:

- **Lesson 112,** applying the Pythagorean theorem to real situations to determine missing measurements.

• Estimating Square Roots
• Irrational Numbers

Objectives

- Determine which consecutive integers the square root of a non-perfect square falls between.
- Estimate a decimal value for the square root of a non-perfect square.
- Use a calculator to find a value close to the square root of a non-perfect square.
- Show approximate locations of points representing rational and irrational numbers on a number line.

Lesson Preparation

Materials

- **Power Up U** (in *Instructional Masters*)
- **Manipulative kit: metric rulers**
- **Teacher-provided material: calculators**

Optional

- **Investigation Activity 13** (in *Instructional Masters*) or **graph paper**
- **Teacher-provided material: index cards**

Power Up U

Math Language

New	English Learners (ESL)
irrational number	consecutive whole numbers
real number	

Technology Resources

Student eBook CD Complete student textbook in electronic format.

Resources and Planner CD Blackline masters, plus a pacing calendar with standards.

Test and Practice Generator CD Create additional practice sheets and custom-made tests.

www.SaxonPublishers.com Visit for more student activities and planning materials.

Inclusion

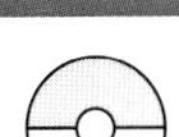

Adaptations CD Adapted lessons, investigations, practice and assessments.

Meeting Standards

National Council of Teachers of Mathematics (NCTM)

Numbers and Operations

NO.2c Understand and use the inverse relationships of addition and subtraction, multiplication and division, and squaring and finding square roots to simplify computations and solve problems

NO.3a Select appropriate methods and tools for computing with fractions and decimals from among mental computation, estimation, calculators or computers, and paper and pencil, depending on the situation, and apply the selected methods

NO.3c Develop and use strategies to estimate the results of rational-number computations and judge the reasonableness of the results

Power-Up Discussion *For use with Power Up, p. 693*

Problem-Solving Strategy: Use Logical Reasoning/ Draw a Diagram

The figure represents a three-dimensional solid. Draw the top, front, back, left, and right views of the solid.

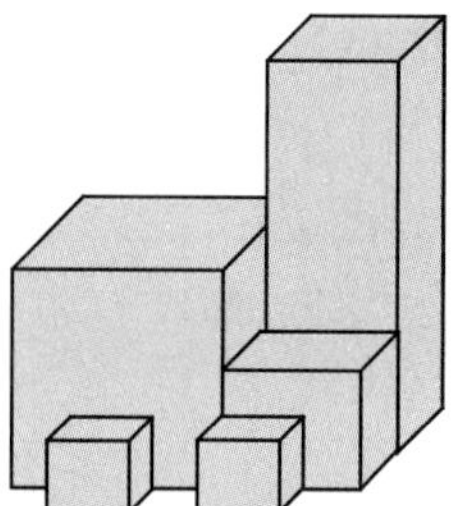

Understand ***Understand the problem.***

"What information are we given?"

We are shown a three-dimensional sketch of a structure.

"What are we asked to do?"

We are asked to draw the top, front, back, left, and right views of the solid.

Plan ***Make a plan.***

"What problem-solving strategy will we use?"

We will *use logical reasoning* to *draw a diagram* of each view specified in the problem.

"What 2-dimensional geometric shapes will we use to draw the views?"

We will use various sized squares and rectangles.

Solve ***Carry out the plan.***

"How can we draw the top?"

There are two congruent squares on the right, one large square on the left, and two small squares in front.

Teacher Note: Continue walking students through the drawing of each view in a similar fashion. Ensure students are able to visualize each orientation of the object.

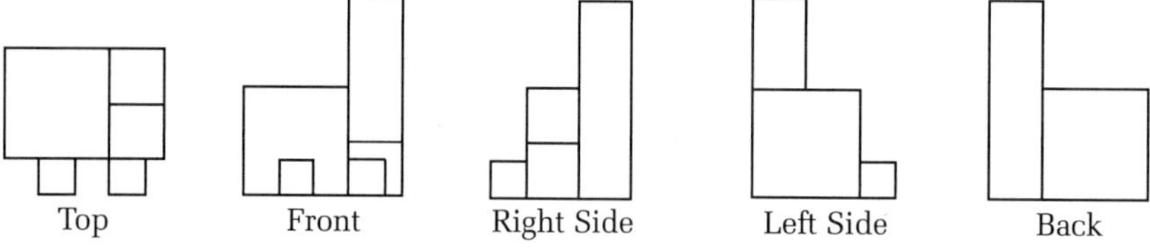

Check ***Look back.***

"Did we do what we were asked to do?"

Yes, we drew each two-dimensional view of the three-dimensional object we were shown.

LESSON 100

• Estimating Square Roots
• Irrational Numbers

Power Up *Building Power*

facts Power Up U

mental math

a. **Positive/Negative:** (−1.5) − (−7.5) 6

b. **Order of Operations/Exponents:** $(5 \times 10^{-5})(5 \times 10^{-5})$ 2.5×10^{-9}

c. **Algebra:** 100 = 5*w* − 20 24

d. **Measurement:** Convert −20°C to degrees Fahrenheit. −4°F

e. **Calculation:** $20 \times 3\frac{3}{4}$ 75

f. **Percent:** $33\frac{1}{3}$% less than \$24 \$16

g. **Geometry:** Which shape(s) has no vertices? sphere

h. **Calculation:** 25% of 44, × 3, − 1, ÷ 4, × 7, − 1, ÷ 5, × 9, + 1, $\sqrt{\ }$, − 1, $\sqrt{\ }$ 3

problem solving The figure represents a three-dimensional solid. Draw the top, front, back, left, and right views of the solid.

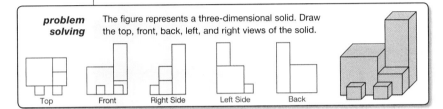

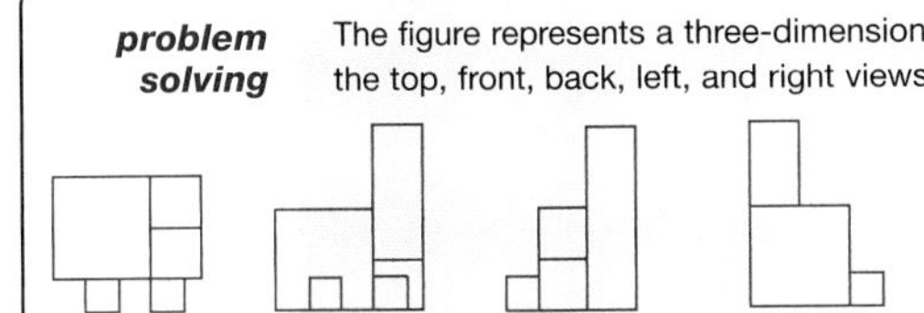

New Concepts *Increasing Knowledge*

estimating square roots

Reading Math
Read $\sqrt{25}$ as "the square root of 25."

These counting numbers are perfect squares:

1, 4, 9, 16, 25, 36, 49, 64, . . .

Recall that the square root of a perfect square is an integer.

$\sqrt{25} = 5$ $\sqrt{36} = 6$

The square root of a number that is between two perfect squares is not an integer but can be estimated.

$\sqrt{29} = ?$

Since 29 is between the perfect squares 25 and 36, we can conclude that $\sqrt{29}$ is between $\sqrt{25}$ and $\sqrt{36}$.

$\sqrt{25} = 5$ $\sqrt{29} = ?$ $\sqrt{36} = 6$

Facts Complete each step to solve each equation.

2*x* + 5 = 45 2*x* = 40 *x* = 20	3*y* + 4 = 22 3*y* = 18 *y* = 6	5*n* − 3 = 12 5*n* = 15 *n* = 3	3*m* − 7 = 14 3*m* = 21 *m* = 7
15 = 3*a* − 6 21 = 3*a* 7 = *a*	24 = 2*w* + 6 18 = 2*w* 9 = *w*	−2*x* + 9 = 23 −2*x* = 14 *x* = −7	20 − 3*y* = 2 −3*y* = −18 *y* = 6
$\frac{1}{2}m + 6 = 18$ $\frac{1}{2}m = 12$ *m* = 24	$\frac{3}{4}n - 12 = 12$ $\frac{3}{4}n = 24$ *n* = 32	3*y* + 1.5 = 6 3*y* = 4.5 *y* = 1.5	0.5*w* − 1.5 = 4.5 0.5*w* = 6 *w* = 12

1 Power Up

Facts

Distribute **Power Up U** to students. See answers below.

Mental Math

Encourage students to share different ways to mentally compute these exercises. Strategies for exercises **a** and **e** are listed below.

a. Use Decimals

−1.5 − (−7.5) =
−1.5 + (7.5) = 6

Equivalent Expression

(−1.5 + 1.5) − (−7.5 + 1.5) =
(0) − (−6) = 6

e. Use Fractions

$(20 \cdot 3) + (20 \cdot \frac{3}{4}) =$
$60 + [(20 \cdot 3) \div 4] =$
$60 + (60 \div 4) =$
$60 + 15 = 75$

Use Decimals

3.75(10 + 10)
37.5 + 37.5 = 75

Problem Solving

Refer to **Power-Up Discussion**, p. 693B.

2 New Concepts

Instruction

To help students identify the integers associated with each perfect square, point out that the sequence shown can also be thought of as $1^2, 2^2, 3^2, 4^2, 5^2, 6^2, 7^2, 8^2, \ldots$

"What does the phrase 'square root of 29' mean?" Students should recognize that this means "a number multiplied by itself has a product of 29".

(continued)

2 New Concepts (Continued)

Instruction

Point out to students that since 29 is closer to 25 than 36, $\sqrt{29}$ is closer to 5 than 6.

Example 1

Instruction

Provide students with additional examples by writing several problems on the board. Discuss how to find the consecutive whole numbers between which the square root lies. For example, $\sqrt{61}$ is greater than $\sqrt{49}$ and less than $\sqrt{64}$. So, $\sqrt{61}$ is between 7 and 8.

Ask a volunteer to draw a number line on the chalkboard to estimate whether $\sqrt{200}$ would be closer to 14 or 15. As the class observes the solution process, encourage class discussion by letting them know that they can ask questions or challenge the answer.

(continued)

We see that $\sqrt{29}$ is between 5 and 6. On this number line we see that $\sqrt{29}$ is between 5 and 6 but not exactly halfway between.

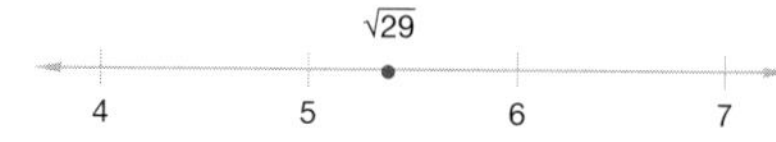

Example 1

Between which two consecutive whole numbers is $\sqrt{200}$?

Solution

We remember that $\sqrt{100}$ is 10, so $\sqrt{200}$ is more than 10. We might guess that $\sqrt{200}$ is 20. We check our guess.

$20 \times 20 = 400$ too large

Our guess is much too large. Next we guess 15.

$15 \times 15 = 225$ too large

Since 15 is still too large, we try 14.

$14 \times 14 = 196$ too small

We see that 14 is less than $\sqrt{200}$ and 15 is more than $\sqrt{200}$. So $\sqrt{200}$ is between the consecutive whole numbers **14** and **15.**

Generalize Using the same method, we find that $\sqrt{10}$ is between which two consecutive whole numbers? $\sqrt{9} = 3$ and $\sqrt{16} = 4$, so $\sqrt{10}$ is between 3 and 4.

irrational numbers

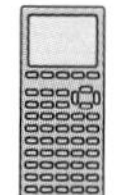

Visit www.SaxonPublishers.com/ActivitiesC2 *for a graphing calculator activity.*

At the beginning of this lesson we found that $\sqrt{29}$ is between 5 and 6. We can refine our estimate by finding a decimal (or fraction) that is closer to $\sqrt{29}$. We try 5.4.

$5.4 \times 5.4 = 29.16$ too large

Since 5.4 is too large, we try 5.3.

$5.3 \times 5.3 = 28.09$ too small

We see that $\sqrt{29}$ is between 5.3 and 5.4. We may continue refining our estimate by finding numbers closer to $\sqrt{29}$. However, no matter how many numbers we try, we will not find a decimal (or fraction) that equals $\sqrt{29}$.

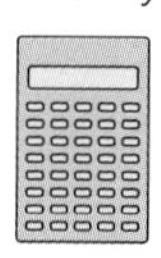

If we use a calculator, we can quickly find a number close to $\sqrt{29}$. If we enter these keystrokes

√ 2 9 = or 2 9 √
(depending on the type of calculator)

the number displayed on an 8-digit calculator is

5.3851648

This number is close to $\sqrt{29}$ but does not equal $\sqrt{29}$, as we see in the first step of checking the answer:

$$\begin{array}{r} \overset{6}{} \\ 5.3851648 \\ \times\ 5.3851648 \\ \hline 4 \end{array}$$

Thinking Skill

Explain

How many decimal places will be in the product of these two factors? How do you know?

fourteen; the product will have as many decimal places as are in both factors combined.

694 **Saxon** Math Course 2

English Learners

In example 1, explain the meaning of **consecutive whole numbers.** Say:

"Consecutive whole numbers are two whole numbers that lie next to each other on a number line."

Draw a number line showing 0 to 6. Say:

"One and two are consecutive whole numbers. Name two consecutive whole numbers shown on this number line." Sample: 2 and 3

Math Background

Can we use the square root of a number to help find the factors of a number?

Yes. The diagram shows the factor pairs of 100. If 100 is divided by a factor, the quotient is the other factor in the pair.

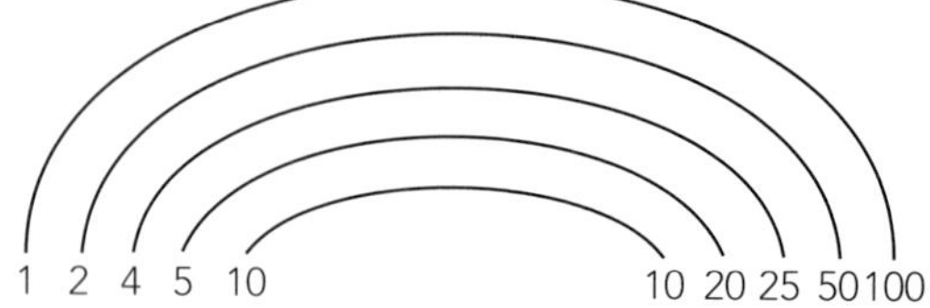

Notice that the central pair of factors is the square root of 100. To find the factors of 100, it is only necessary to test numbers equal to or less than $\sqrt{100}$.

The remaining factors in each pair can be found by dividing the original number by each factor below its square root.

We see immediately that the product is not 29.00000000000000 because the digit in the last decimal place is 4.

Actually $\sqrt{29}$ is a number that cannot be exactly expressed as a decimal or fraction and therefore is *not a rational number*. Rather $\sqrt{29}$ is an **irrational number**—a number that cannot be expressed as a ratio of two integers.

Nevertheless, $\sqrt{29}$ is a number that has an exact value. For instance, if the legs of this right triangle are exactly 2 cm and 5 cm, we find by the Pythagorean theorem that the length of the hypotenuse is $\sqrt{29}$ cm.

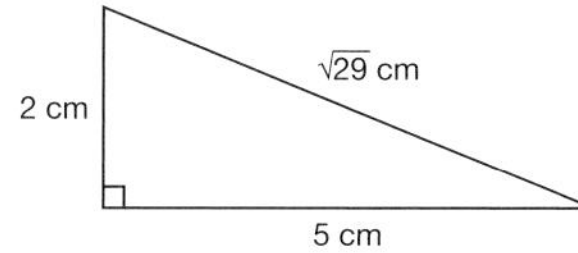

If we measure the hypotenuse with a centimeter ruler, we find that the length is about 5.4 cm, which is an approximation of $\sqrt{29}$ cm.

Other examples of irrational numbers include π (the circumference of a circle with a diameter of 1), $\sqrt{2}$ (the length of the diagonal of a square with sides of 1), and the square roots of counting numbers that are not perfect squares. The irrational numbers, together with the rational numbers, make up the set of **real numbers.**

Real Numbers

Rational Numbers	Irrational Numbers

All of the numbers represented by points on the number line are real numbers and are either rational or irrational.

Example 2

Draw a number line and show the approximate location of the points representing the following real numbers. Then describe each number as rational or irrational.

$$\pi \quad \sqrt{2} \quad 2.\overline{3} \quad -\tfrac{1}{2}$$

Solution

We draw a number line and mark the location of the integers from -1 through 4. We position π ($\approx$ 3.14) between 3 and 4 but closer to 3. Since $\sqrt{2}$ is between $\sqrt{1}$ (= 1) and $\sqrt{4}$ (= 2), we position $\sqrt{2}$ between 1 and 2 but closer to 1. The repeating decimal $2.\overline{3}$ $(= 2\frac{1}{3})$ is closer to 2 than to 3. The negative fraction $-\frac{1}{2}$ is halfway between 0 and -1.

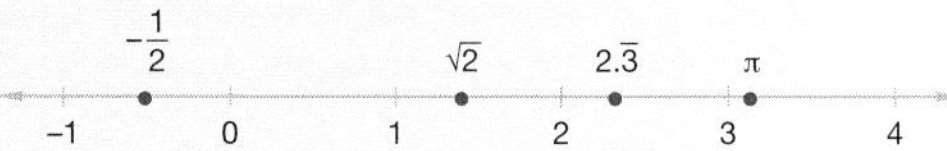

Repeating decimal numbers are rational. Thus, both $-\frac{1}{2}$ **and** $2.\overline{3}$ **are rational, while** $\sqrt{2}$ **and** π **are irrational.**

2 New Concepts (Continued)

Instruction

Remind students that calculators truncate (clip off) answers that exceed their displays. Most calculators also truncate any 0s at the end of an answer.

You may wish to go back to the Venn diagram that students studied in Lesson 86 and add irrational and real numbers as shown.

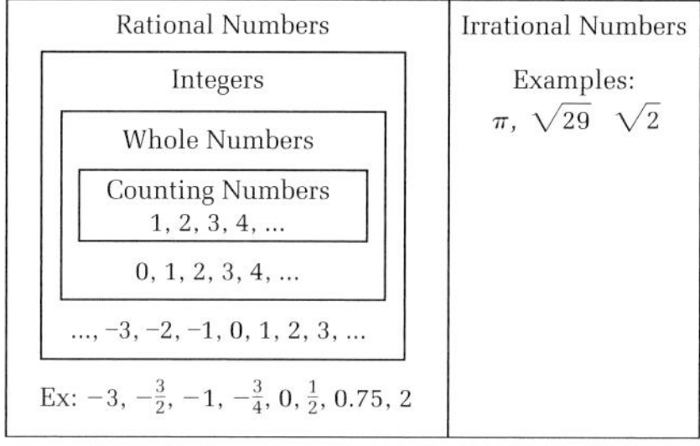

"Of which group is −2 a member?" integers, rationals, and reals

"Of which group is $\frac{1}{2}$ a member?" rationals and reals

"Of which group is $\sqrt{3}$ a member?" irrationals and reals

Example 2

Instruction

Be sure students understand these terms:

- A *repeating decimal* has one or more digits that repeat infinitely (0.8181... or $0.\overline{81}$).
- A *terminating decimal* has a finite number of digits (0.125).
- A non-repeating, non-terminating decimal is one that neither terminates nor repeats (3.1428571... the value of pi).

(continued)

Teacher Tip

Some students may have difficulty **approximating square roots.**

- Review the idea of square roots and perfect squares.
- Use the number line to illustrate familiar perfect squares, then label the approximate location for $\sqrt{29}$.

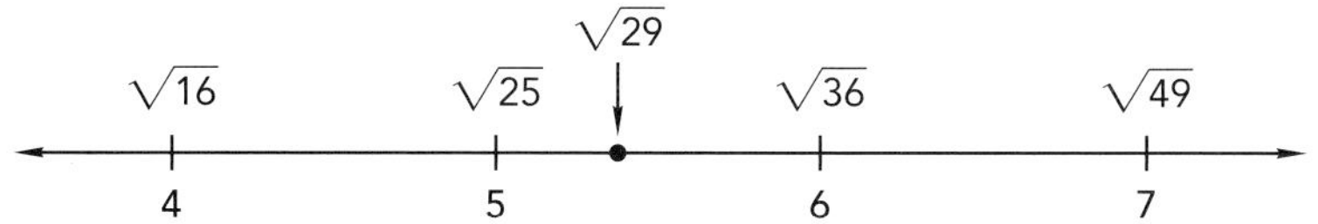

- Use a number line to locate the position of $\sqrt{200}$. Again label the locations of the perfect squares first.
- Have students continue working with number lines until they are successful working through the problems without them.

Inclusion

Before the lesson, write four numbers from each different number set on index cards. Then during the lesson draw on the board a Venn diagram of the number sets similar to the one above. Shuffle the cards and distribute them to students in the class. Ask them to tape the card to the board in the section of the number set where their cards belong. For those cards that belong to more than one set, have the students place them in the innermost set.

2 New Concepts (Continued)

Practice Set

Problem e *Error Alert*

If students have an answer of $y^2 = 3$, explain that they need to solve for y not y^2. They should write the answer using a square root symbol.

$$\begin{aligned} 2^2 &= 1^2 + y^2 \\ 4 &= 1 + y^2 \\ 4 - 1 &= y^2 \\ 3 &= y^2 \\ \sqrt{3} &= y \end{aligned}$$

Problem f *Model*

"How can you estimate the number that is halfway between 2 and π?" add 2 and 3.14 and divide by 2

"What is the number?" 2.57

3 Written Practice

Math Conversations

Discussion opportunities are provided below.

Problem 2b *Analyze*

"Is it fair to say that there is an 80% chance that the spinner will stop on a number greater than 3?" yes; a 4 out of 5 chance is an 80% chance

Problem 8

Extend the Problem

Ask a volunteer to draw a diagram to represent this problem.

Sample:

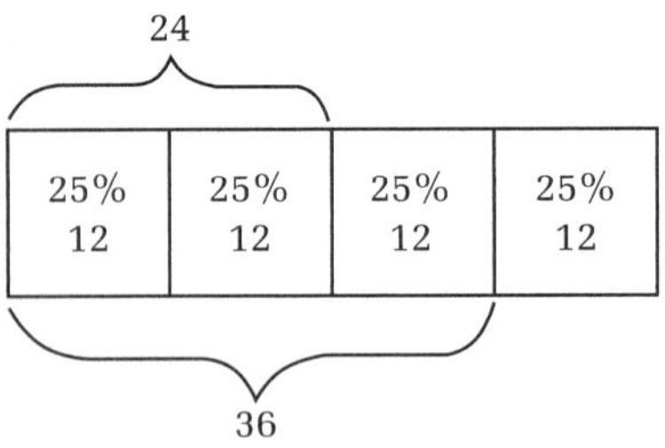

(continued)

Practice Set

Classify Which of these types of decimal numbers are irrational?

repeating/terminating   non-repeating/non-terminating

non-repeating/non-terminating

Each square root below is between which two consecutive whole numbers?

a. $\sqrt{7}$ 2 and 3   **b.** $\sqrt{70}$ 8 and 9   **c.** $\sqrt{700}$ 26 and 27

d. Find x:

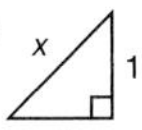

$\sqrt{2}$

▶ **e.** Find y:

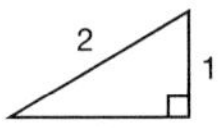

$\sqrt{3}$

f.

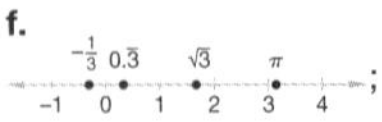

; $\sqrt{3}$, π

▶ **f.** ***Model*** Draw a number line and show the approximate location of the points representing these real numbers. Which of them are irrational?

$\sqrt{3}$ $0.\overline{3}$ π $-\frac{1}{3}$

Written Practice *Strengthening Concepts*

1. (28) Alberto paid \$30.00 for $2\frac{1}{2}$ pounds of cheese that cost \$6.60 per pound and 2 boxes of crackers that cost \$1.79 each. How much money should he get back? \$9.92

*** 2.** (21, Inv. 8) The face of this spinner is divided into fifths.

a. What is the probability that the spinner will not stop on a prime number on one spin? $\frac{2}{5}$

▶ **b.** ***Explain*** If the spinner is spun twice, what is the probability that it will stop on a prime number both times? Explain how you found the answer.

2. b. $\frac{9}{25}$; The two spins are independent events. The probability of the spinner stopping on a prime number twice is the product of the probability of each event: $\frac{3}{5} \times \frac{3}{5}$.

3. (28, 86) What is the average of the first 10 counting numbers? 5.5

4. (53) At an average speed of 50 miles per hour, how long would it take to complete a 375-mile trip? $7\frac{1}{2}$ hours

Use ratio boxes to solve problems **5–7.**

5. (72) The Johnsons traveled 300 kilometers in 4 hours. At that rate, how long will it take them to travel 500 kilometers? Write the answer in hours and minutes. 6 hours 40 minutes

6. (66) The ratio of children to adults at the museum was 1 to 15. If there were 800 visitors at the museum, how many children were there? 50 children

7. (92) The population of a colony of birds decreased 30 percent over one winter. If the population the next spring was 350, what was the population before winter came? 500

▶ **8.** (60, 74) Three fourths of Genevieve's favorite number is 36. What number is one half of Genevieve's favorite number? 24

▶ See Math Conversations in the sidebar.

Manipulative Use

- You may wish to give students time to explore how to find **square roots using calculators.**
- Suggest they key in perfect squares, such as 4, 9, or 16, where the square roots are already known.
- Then invite them to find $\sqrt{29}$ as described in the text.
- Ask,

"Why doesn't the calculator return an exact result? Is an exact result possible?" The calculator has a limited display, and the number is infinitely long; no, the decimal does not terminate.

9. (77) Write equations to solve **a** and **b**.

a. Three hundred is 6 percent of what number? $300 = 0.06 \times W_N$; 5000

b. Twenty is what percent of 10? $20 = W_P \times 10$; 200%

10. (46) What is the total price of a $40 item including 6.5% sales tax? $42.60

▶* **11.** (96) Generalize Using the Distributive Property, we know that $3(x + 3)$ equals $3x + 9$. Use the Distributive Property to multiply $x(x + 3)$. $x^2 + 3x$

▶ **12.** (Inv. 9) The ordered pairs (0, 0), (−2, −4), and (2, 4) designate points that lie on the graph of the equation $y = 2x$. Graph the equation on a coordinate plane, and name another (x, y) pair from the 3rd quadrant that satisfies the equation.

12. (0, 0), (2, 4), (−2, −4), $y=2x$

{Another point from the 3rd quadrant could be (−1, −2) or (−3, −6)}

* **13.** (Inv. 9, 98) Nathan used the data in the graph below to mold a scale model of a car from clay. The car is 4 feet tall, and he used the graph to find that the model should be 2 inches tall.

a. The length of the car's bumper is 5 feet. Use the graph to find the proper length of the model's bumper. $2\frac{1}{2}$ inches

b. What is the scale factor from the car to the model? Write the scale factor as a fraction. $\frac{1}{24}$

▶ **c.** Estimate Nathan's completed model was 7 inches long. Estimate the length of the car. 14 feet

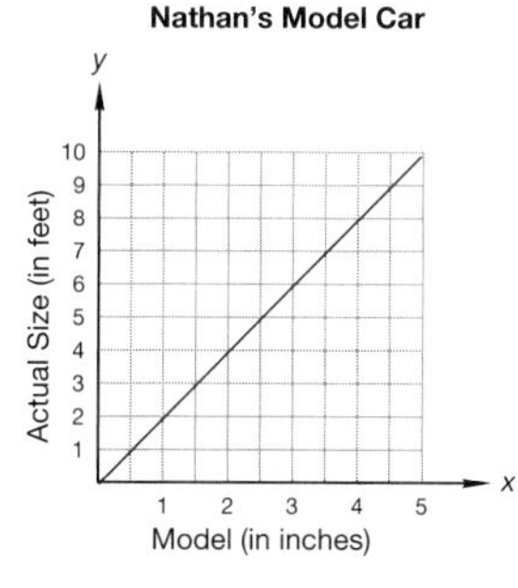

▶* **14.** (98) Analyze The edge of one cube measures 2 cm. The edge of a larger cube measures 6 cm.

a. What is the scale factor from the smaller cube to the larger cube? 3

b. The area of each face of the larger cube is how many times the area of a face of the smaller cube? 9 times

c. The volume of the larger cube is how many times the volume of the smaller cube? 27 times

15. (36) If the spinner is spun twice, two of the possible outcomes are C, A and A, C. Write the sample space for this experiment.

15. {AA, AB, AC, BA, BB, BC, CA, CB, CC}

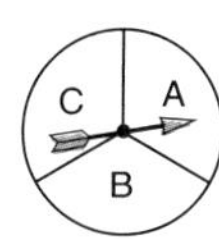

▶ See Math Conversations in the sidebar.

3 Written Practice (Continued)

Math Conversations

Discussion opportunities are provided below.

Problem 11 Generalize

Ask students to use the Distributive Property to multiply the following.

$-x(x + 3)$ $(-x^2) + (-3x)$

Problem 12

Extend the Problem

What would the ordered pairs be if the line is translated 4 units to the right.

(2, −4), (4, 0), (6, 4)

Problem 13c Estimate

Discuss the different ways to estimate the answer.

Sample: Extend the graph.

Solve a proportion: $\frac{1}{2} = \frac{7}{x}$; $x = 14$

Set up a function table:

in.	1	2	3	4	5	6	7
ft	2	4	6	8	10	12	14

Problem 14 Analyze

Have students explain their thinking for each part of this problem.

Sample:

a: the scale factor is 3 since 3 times 2 is 6

b: 9 times because area has 2 dimensions and $3 \cdot 3 = 9$

c: 27 times because volume has 3 dimensions and $3 \cdot 3 \cdot 3 = 27$

(continued)

3 Written Practice (Continued)

Math Conversations

Discussion opportunities are provided below.

Problem 18 Analyze

Extend the Problem

Ask students to write the next 3 terms in this sequence. $\sqrt{100}$, $\sqrt{81}$, $\sqrt{64}$, $\sqrt{49}$

$\sqrt{36}$, $\sqrt{25}$, $\sqrt{16}$

Problem 22 Analyze

"How would you change the dimensions of the cylinder so that the volume becomes half as much?" Sample: change the height to 5 cm

Problems 24 and 25 Justify

Ask students to work on these solutions at the board. Have them explain why their answers are correct.

Problem 30 Model

"Estimate the number that is halfway between 1.5 and $\sqrt{5}$. Explain how you found your answer." Sample: 1.87; estimate the square root of 5 as 2.24 and add it to 1.5; divide the sum by 2

Errors and Misconceptions

Problem 16

If students divide 18 by 25 and make a computational error, ask them,

"25 times what number equals 100?" When students answer 4, show them that they can multiply 4 × 18 to get 72.

Problem 24

If students write $12\frac{4}{9}$ as the answer, they simplified 8^0 to 8 instead of 1. Remind them that any number raised to 1 is that number and any number raised to 0 is 1.

▶ **16.** (48) Complete the table.

Fraction	Decimal	Percent
a. $\frac{18}{25}$	**b.** 0.72	72%

17. (83) Multiply. Write the product in scientific notation. 2.7×10^{10}

$(4.5 \times 10^6)(6 \times 10^3)$

▶* **18.** (100) Analyze Each square root is between which two consecutive whole numbers?

a. $\sqrt{40}$ 6 and 7 **b.** $\sqrt{20}$ 4 and 5

19. (65, 82) Find the **a** circumference and **b** area of a circle that has a radius of 7 inches. (Use $\frac{22}{7}$ for π.) **a.** 44 in.; **b.** 154 in.^{2}

* **20.** (99) Analyze Use the Pythagorean theorem to find a. Dimensions are in centimeters. 8 cm

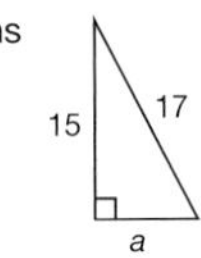

Analyze For problems **21** and **22,** find the volume of each right solid. Dimensions are in centimeters. (Use 3.14 for π.)

* **21.** (95)

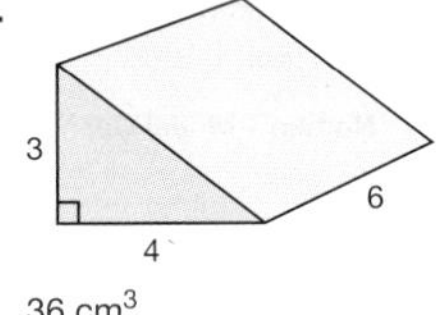

36 cm^3

▶* **22.** (95) 125.6 cm^3

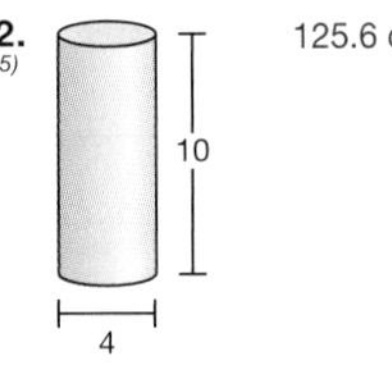

23. (40) In the figure at right, find the measures of angles a, b, and c. m∠a = 132°; m∠b = 48°; m∠c = 42°

c 48° b a

Justify For problems **24** and **25,** solve the equation. Show each step.

▶* **24.** (57, 93) $-4\frac{1}{2}x + 8^0 = 4^3$ −14

▶* **25.** (98) $\frac{15}{w} = \frac{45}{3.3}$ 1.1

Simplify:

26. (52) $\sqrt{6^2 + 8^2}$ 10

27. (43) $3\frac{1}{3}\left(7.2 \div \frac{3}{5}\right)$ 40

28. (43) $8\frac{5}{6} - 2.5 - 1\frac{1}{3}$ 5

29. (85) $\frac{|-18| - (2)(-3)}{(-3) + (-2) - (-4)}$ −24

▶* **30.** (100) Model Draw a number line and show the approximate locations of 1.5, −0.5, and $\sqrt{5}$.

−0.5 1.5 $\sqrt{5}$
−1 0 1 2 3

▶ See Math Conversations in the sidebar.

Looking Forward

Investigating irrational numbers by estimating square roots prepares students for:

- **Lesson 112,** applying the Pythagorean theorem to real situations to determine missing measurements.

698 **Saxon** Math Course 2

Assessment

30–40 minutes *For use after Lesson 100*

Distribute **Cumulative Test 19** to each student. Two versions of the test are available in *Saxon Math Course 2 Course Assessments Book.* Have students complete the **Power-Up Test** first. Allow 10 minutes. Then have students work the 20 numbered items on the **Cumulative Test.** Students may use copies of the answer sheet to record their work. Track individual and class progress with the **Test Analysis** forms.

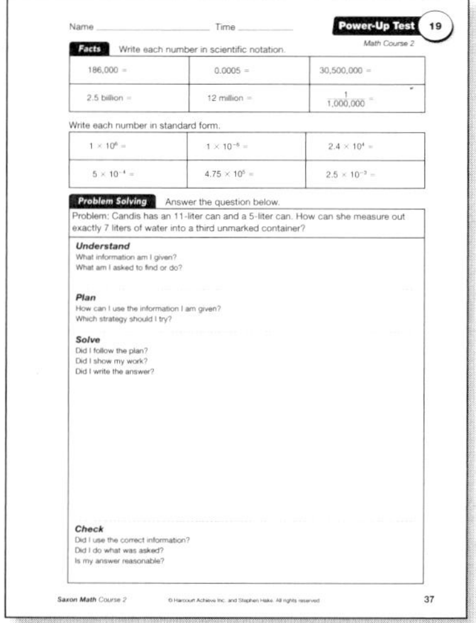

Power-Up Test 19

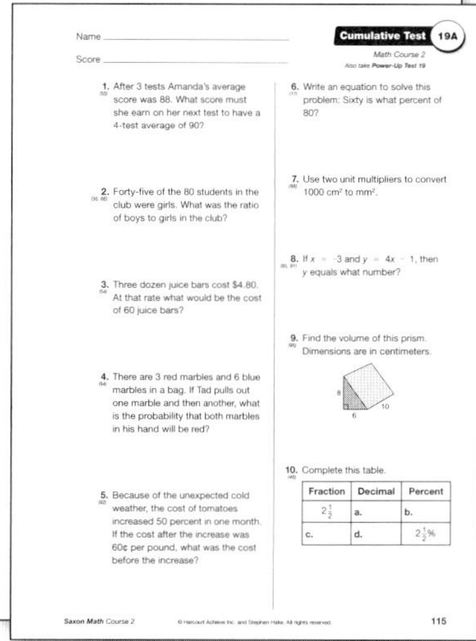

Cumulative Test 19A

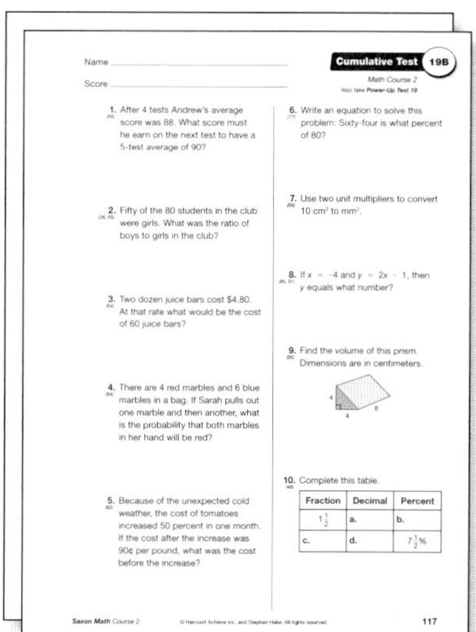

Alternative Cumulative Test 19B

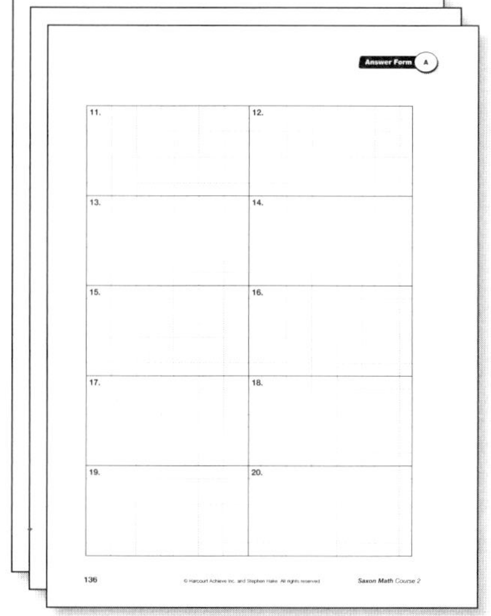

Optional Answer Forms

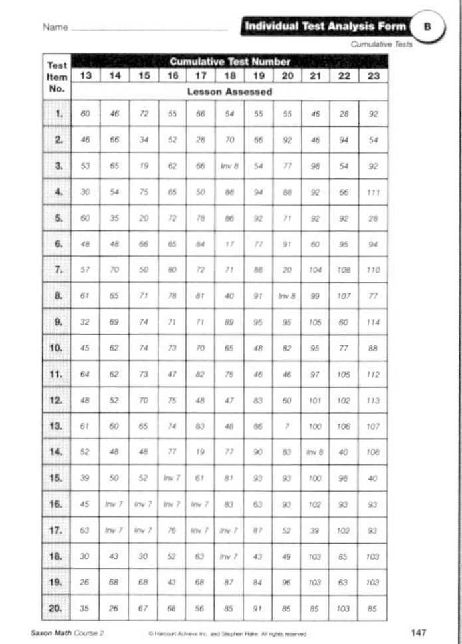

Individual Test Analysis Form

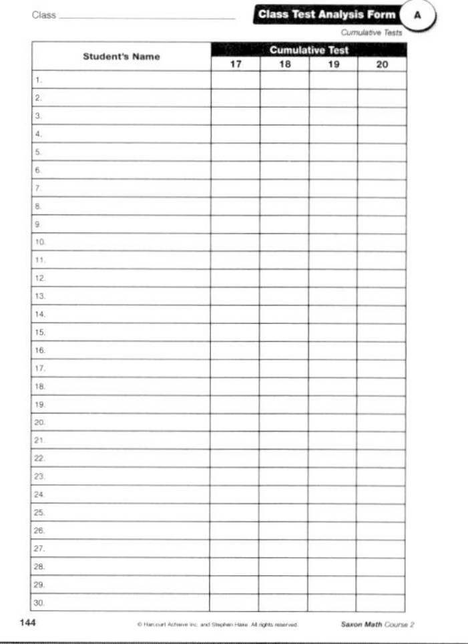

Class Test Analysis Form

Reteaching

Students who score below 80% on the assessment may be in need of reteaching. Look for the causes of student mistakes. If errors are conceptual, refer to the *Reteaching Masters* for reteaching.

Customized Benchmark Assessment

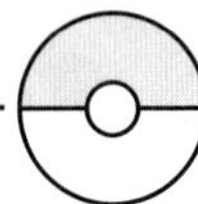

You can develop customized benchmark tests using the Test Generator located on the *Test and Practice Generator CD.*

This chart shows the lesson, the standard, and the test item question that can be found on the *Test and Practice Generator CD.*

LESSON	NEW CONCEPTS	LOCAL STANDARD	TEST ITEM ON CD
91	• Evaluations with Positive and Negative Numbers		10.91.1
92	• Percent of Change		10.92.1
93	• Two-Step Equations and Inequalities		10.93.1
94	• Probability of Dependent Events		10.94.1
95	• Volume of a Right Solid		10.95.1
96	• Estimating Angle Measures		10.96.1
	• Distributive Property with Algebraic Terms		10.96.2
97	• Similar Triangles		10.97.1
	• Indirect Measure		10.97.2
98	• Scale		10.98.1
	• Scale Factor		10.98.2
99	• Pythagorean Theorem		10.99.1
100	• Estimating Square Roots		10.100.1
	• Irrational Numbers		10.100.2

Using the Test Generator CD

- Develop tests in both English and Spanish.
- Choose from multiple-choice and free-response test items.
- Clone test items to create multiple versions of the same test.
- View and edit test items to make and save your own questions.
- Administer assessments through paper tests or over a school LAN.
- Monitor student progress through a variety of individual and class reports —for both diagnosing and assessing standards mastery.

Performance Task 19

Probability Experiment

Assign after Lesson 100 and Test 19

Objectives

- Construct the sample space for a probability experiment.
- Find the probability of an event.
- Communicate their ideas through writing.

Materials

Performance Tasks 19A and **19B**

Preparation

Make copies of **Performance Tasks 19A** and **19B.** (One each per student.)

Time Requirement

30–60 minutes; Begin in class and complete at home.

Task

Explain to students that for this task they will be finding the sample space for a probability experiment. They will find the probability of different events in the experiment. They will be required to explain how they found the sample space and how they found the probability of each of the events. Point out that all of the information students need is on **Performance Tasks 19A** and **19B.**

Criteria for Evidence of Learning

- Constructs the correct sample space for the probability experiment.
- Finds the probability of each event correctly.
- Communicates ideas clearly through writing.

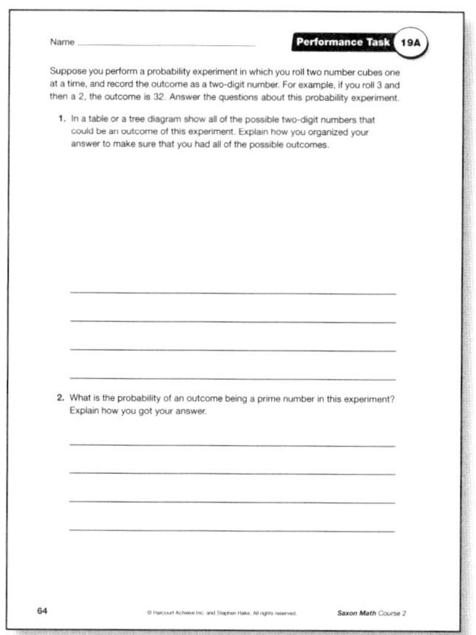

Name ______________ **Performance Task 19A**

Suppose you perform a probability experiment in which you roll two number cubes one at a time, and record the outcome as a two-digit number. For example, if you roll 3 and then a 2, the outcome is 32. Answer the questions about this probability experiment.

1. In a table or a tree diagram show all of the possible two-digit numbers that could be an outcome of this experiment. Explain how you organized your answer to make sure that you had all of the possible outcomes.

2. What is the probability of an outcome being a prime number in this experiment? Explain how you got your answer.

64 © Harcourt Achieve Inc. and Stephen Hake. All rights reserved. *Saxon Math Course 2*

Performance Task 19A

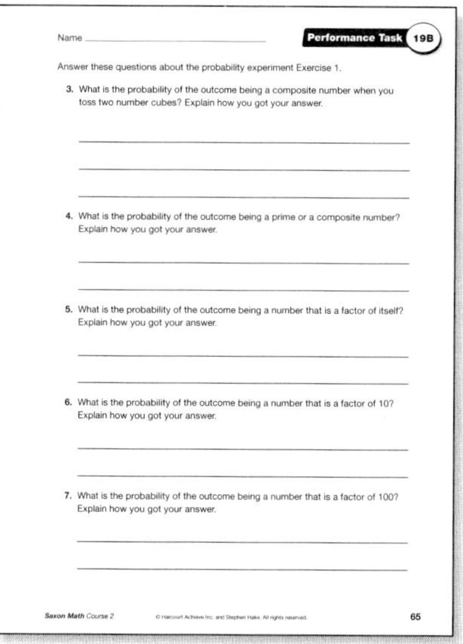

Name ______________ **Performance Task 19B**

Answer these questions about the probability experiment Exercise 1.

3. What is the probability of the outcome being a composite number when you toss two number cubes? Explain how you got your answer.

4. What is the probability of the outcome being a prime or a composite number? Explain how you got your answer.

5. What is the probability of the outcome being a number that is a factor of itself? Explain how you got your answer.

6. What is the probability of the outcome being a number that is a factor of 10? Explain how you got your answer.

7. What is the probability of the outcome being a number that is a factor of 100? Explain how you got your answer.

Saxon Math Course 2 © Harcourt Achieve Inc. and Stephen Hake. All rights reserved. 65

Performance Task 19B

Meeting Standards

National Council of Teachers of Mathematics (NCTM)

Data Analysis and Probability

DP.4a Understand and use appropriate terminology to describe complementary and mutually exclusive events

DP.4b Use proportionality and a basic understanding of probability to make and test conjectures about the results of experiments and simulations

DP.4c Compute probabilities for simple compound events, using such methods as organized lists, tree diagrams, and area models

Problem Solving

PS.1b Solve problems that arise in mathematics and in other contexts

Reasoning and Proof

RP.2b Make and investigate mathematical conjectures

Communication

CM.3a Organize and consolidate their mathematical thinking through communication

Focus on

• Using a Compass and a Straightedge, Part 2

Objectives

- Use a compass and a straightedge to bisect a line segment and an angle.
- Use a compass and a straightedge to inscribe a square and a regular octagon in a circle.

Lesson Preparation

Materials

- **Manipulative kit: metric rulers, compasses, protractors**

Optional

- **Teacher-provided material: tag board, foam board, or extra notebook paper, string and chalk**

Math Language

New	Maintain
angle bisector	inscribe
bisect	
perpendicular bisector	

Technology Resources

Student eBook Complete student textbook in electronic format.

Resources and Planner CD Assessment, reteaching, and instructional masters, plus a pacing calendar with standards.

Test and Practice Generator CD Create additional practice sheets and custom-made tests.

www.SaxonPublishers.com Visit for more student activities and planning materials.

Inclusion

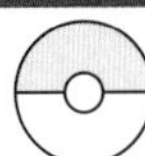

Adaptations CD Adapted lessons, investigations, practice and assessments.

Meeting Standards

National Council of Teachers of Mathematics (NCTM)

Geometry

GM.4a Draw geometric objects with specified properties, such as side lengths or angle measures

Measurement

ME.2b Select and apply techniques and tools to accurately find length, area, volume, and angle measures to appropriate levels of precision

Problem Solving

PS.1c Apply and adapt a variety of appropriate strategies to solve problems

INVESTIGATION 10

Focus on

• Using a Compass and Straightedge, Part 2

In Investigation 2 we used a compass to draw circles, and we used a compass and straightedge to inscribe a regular hexagon and a regular triangle in a circle. In this investigation we will use a compass and straightedge to **bisect** (divide in half) a line segment and an angle. We will also inscribe a square and a regular octagon in a circle.

Materials needed:

- Compass
- Ruler or straightedge
- Protractor

Use a metric ruler to draw a segment 6 cm long. Label the endpoints *A* and *C*.

Next open a compass so that the distance between the pivot point and pencil point is more than half the length of the segment to be bisected (in this case, more than 3 cm). You will swing arcs from both endpoints of the segment, so do not change the compass radius once you have it set. Place the pivot point of the compass on one endpoint of the segment, and make a curve by swinging an arc on both sides of the segment as shown.

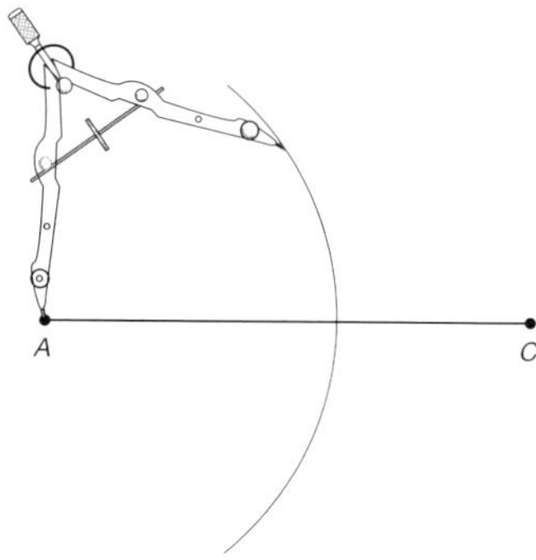

INVESTIGATION 10

Introduce this investigation by having students recall what they have already learned about:

- drawing circles
- inscribing regular polygons in circles
- finding the measure of inscribed and central angles

Explain to students that they will now use the same tools to bisect line segments and angles and inscribe a square and a regular octagon in circles.

Preparing the Materials

- Use an overhead compass and ruler to demonstrate the steps in each construction as students perform them.
- Students will need a ruler, compass, and protractor for this activity and throughout the lesson.

Instruction

Suggest that students put a solid dot at each end of their line segment to give them a place to put the pivot point of their compass.

Encourage students to draw a relatively large arc above and below the segment. If the arc is too small, the second arc will not cross. Students will need to return to this point in the directions to draw a larger arc.

(continued)

Teacher Tip

When **using a compass,** some students may struggle because their compasses slip. Putting a piece of tagboard, foam board, or several sheets of notebook paper under students' papers may help. Remind students that a "light touch" is needed. If a student still struggles, suggest trying another compass or working with a partner.

Instruction

- Tell students that point *B* is called the *midpoint* of the segment, the point that divides the segment into two equal parts.
- Point out that the horizontal *line segment* has two distinct endpoints, whereas the vertical line extends in opposite directions without end indicated by the arrowheads at both ends.

Math Conversations

Discussion opportunities are provided below.

Problem 3 Explain

"Suppose you constructed a perpendicular bisector of segment AB, how would that line compare with the perpendicular bisector at point B?" They would be parallel lines.

Have a volunteer work at the overhead to construct the perpendicular bisector as students work at their desks. Label the new point R.

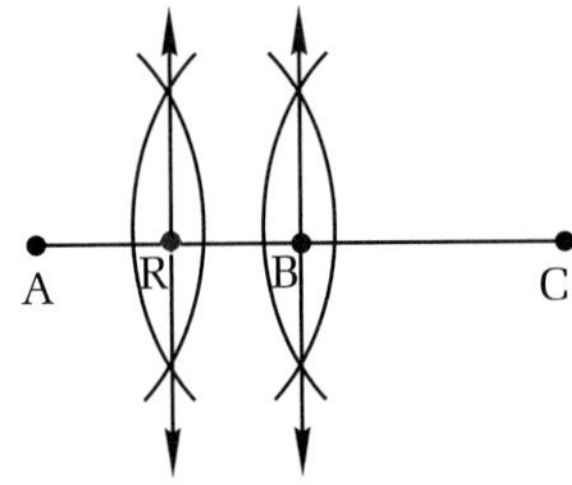

Ask students if they have other suggestions for constructing parallel lines.

Then move the pivot point of the compass to the other endpoint of the segment, and, without resetting the compass, swing an arc that intersects the other arc on both sides of the segment. Now draw a line through the two points where the arcs intersect to divide the original segment into two parts. Label the point where the line intersects the segment point *B*.

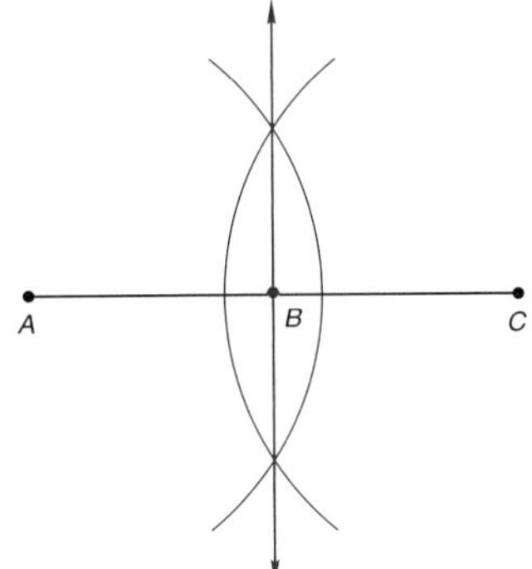

Thinking Skill
Predict

Can we predict the measures of *AB* and *BC*? Explain.
Yes. When we *bisect* something we divide it in half. Therefore point *B* divides $\overline{AC}$ into two equal parts. Since $\overline{AC}$ measures 6 cm, each part must measure 3 cm.

1. Use a metric ruler to find *AB* and *BC*. 3 cm; 3 cm
2. Where the line and segment intersect, four angles are formed. What is the measure of each angle? 90°

Using a compass and straightedge to create geometric figures is called **construction.** You just constructed the **perpendicular bisector** of a segment.

▶ 3. Explain Why is the line you constructed called the perpendicular bisector of the segment? The line is perpendicular to the segment and divides the segment in half.

We can use a perpendicular bisector to help us **inscribe** a square in a circle. Draw a dot on your paper to be the center of a circle. Set the distance between the points of your compass to 2 cm. Then place the pivot point of the compass on the dot and draw a circle. Use a straightedge to draw a diameter of the circle.

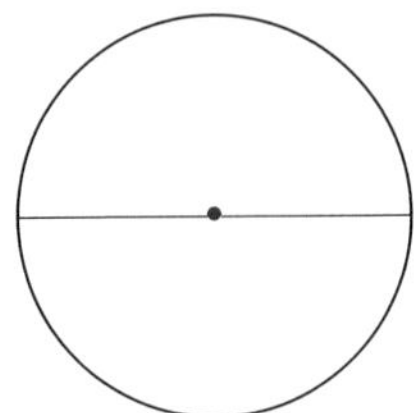

▶ See Math Conversations in the sidebar.

Math Background

What are the differences between drawing, sketching, and constructing?

- If you are asked to draw a geometric figure, you may use a ruler and a protractor to measure lengths of sides and angles.
- If you are asked to sketch a geometric figure, you are not required to use a straightedge to ensure your lines are straight or a ruler or protractor to ensure your sides and angles are properly measured.
- Constructing, or construction, is a mathematical drawing that requires exactness. Straightedges and compasses are the only instruments permitted. Constructions do not involve rulers or protractors to measure the figure as it is being constructed.

The two points where the diameter intersects the circle are the endpoints of the diameter. Open the compass a little more than the radius of the circle, and construct the perpendicular bisector of the diameter you drew.

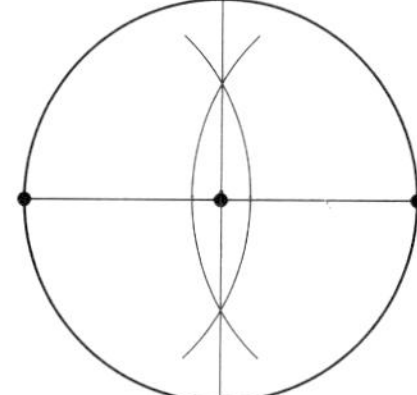

The perpendicular bisector is another diameter of the circle. The two diameters divide the circle into quarters. Draw chords between the points on the circle that are the endpoints of the two diameters.

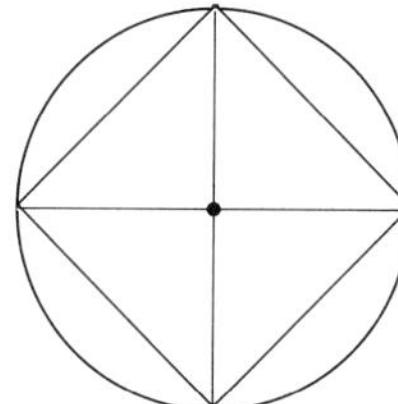

You have inscribed a square in a circle.

4. Each angle of the square is an inscribed angle of the circle. What is the measure of each angle of the square? 90°

5. **Conclude** Notice that within the square are four small right triangles. Two sides of each small triangle are radii of the circle. If the radius of the circle is 2 cm, then

▸ **a.** what is the area of each small right triangle? 2 cm²

▸ **b.** how can we find the area of the inscribed square? Add the areas of the four small right triangles. The area of the square is 8 cm².

Use a straightedge to draw an angle. With the pivot point of the compass on the vertex of the angle, draw an arc that intersects the sides of the angle. For reference call these points *R* and *S*, and label the vertex *V*.

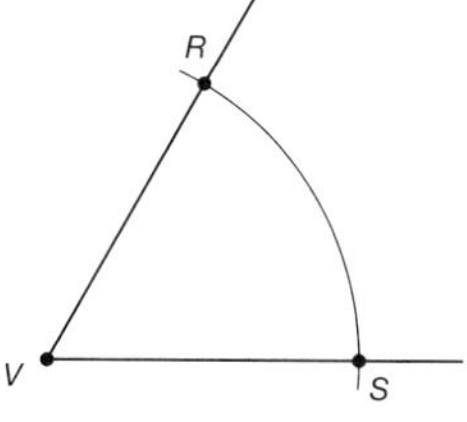

▸ See Math Conversations in the sidebar.

Instruction

Have students put a dot at each point where the diameter intersects the circle. Then ask:

"Do you think a perpendicular bisector can be drawn if the arcs are inside the circle? Outside the circle?" A perpendicular bisector can be drawn using any arcs which radii exceed the radius of the circle.

Display a square inscribed in a circle on an overhead projector, and ask:

"Can anyone label the center, diameter, chords, inscribed angles, and radii?"

Invite a volunteer to label the diagram.

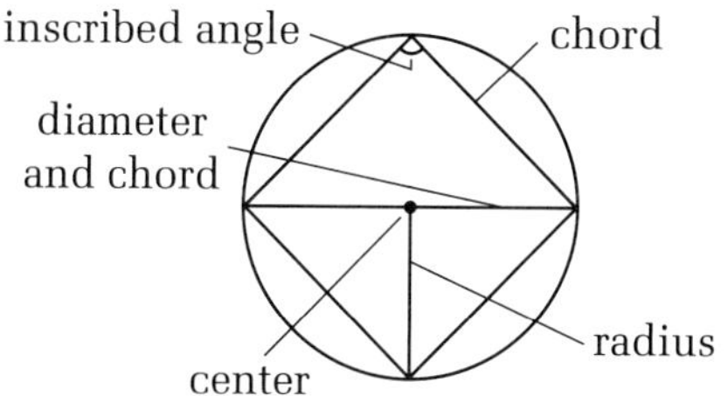

Math Conversations

Discussion opportunities are provided below.

Problem 5a Conclude

Ask students to explain how they found their answers. Sample: the radii are the legs of the right triangle. $(2 \cdot 2) \div 2 = 2 \text{ cm}^2$

Problem 5b Conclude

"How could you find the perimeter of the square?" the perimeter is about 6.8 cm

$$2^2 + 2^2 = c^2$$
$$4 + 4 = c^2$$
$$\sqrt{8} = c$$
$$2.8 \approx c$$
$$2 + 2 + 2.8 = 6.8$$

Teacher Tip

Stress the need for students to include **appropriate math language** in their explanations and comments. Below is a list of terms to be reviewed for this lesson.

arcs	*concentric circles*
chord	*diameter*
circumference	*inscribed*
center	*inscribed angle*
central angle	*radius*
circle	*sector*
compass	*semicircles*

Math Conversations

Discussion opportunities are provided below.

Problem 7 Discuss

Some students may refer to the ray as a bisector. Although it would not be incorrect, emphasize that there are different types of bisectors such as segment bisectors and angle bisectors.

Encourage students to be as precise as possible when using math language. Since angle bisector is more precise than bisector, they should use the term angle bisector.

Instruction

Use an overhead projector or the board to demonstrate the construction step-by-step for the class. A string and a piece of chalk can be used for a compass.

(continued)

Set the compass so that it is open more than half the distance between *R* and *S*. With the pivot point on *R*, swing an arc. Then, with the pivot point on *S*, swing another arc that intersects the one centered at *R*. Label the point of intersection *T*.

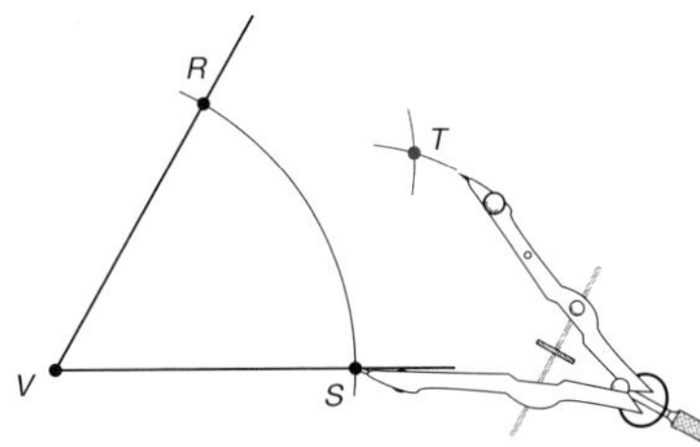

Using a straightedge, draw a ray from the vertex *V* through point *T*. Ray *VT* divides ∠*RVS* into two congruent angles.

6. Use a protractor to measure the original angle you drew and the two smaller angles formed when you constructed the ray. Record all three angle measures for your answer. What did you notice?

6. Each of the smaller angles should be half the measure of the larger angle.

In this activity you constructed an **angle bisector.**

▶ **7.** Discuss Why is the ray called an angle bisector?

7. The ray divides the original angle into two congruent angles. That is, the ray divides the angle in half.

Draw a circle and a diameter of the circle. Then construct a diameter that is a perpendicular bisector of the first diameter. Your work should look like the circle shown below. We have labeled points *M*, *X*, *Y*, and *Z* for reference.

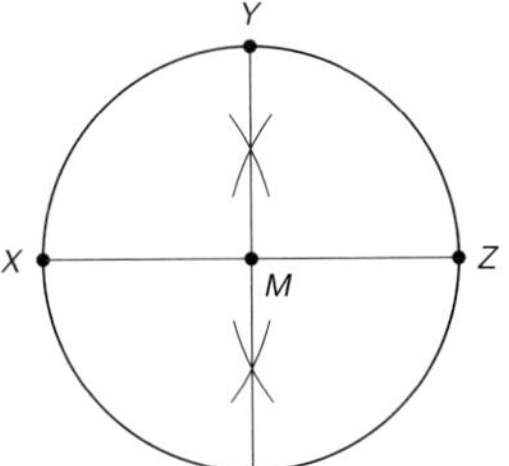

Swing intersecting arcs from points *Y* and *Z* to locate the angle bisector of ∠*YMZ*. Also swing intersecting arcs from points *X* and *Y* to locate the angle bisector of ∠*XMY*.

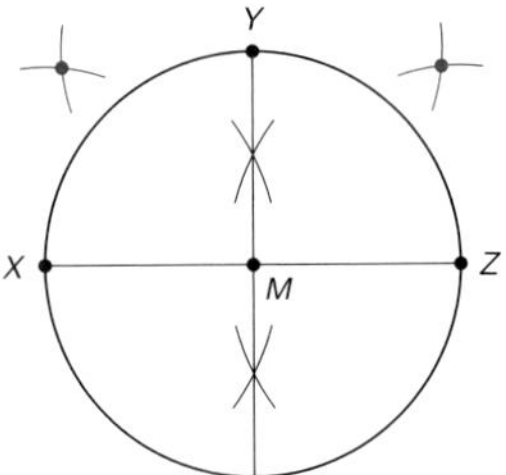

▶ See Math Conversations in the sidebar.

Draw two lines through the center of the circle that passes through the points where the arcs intersect. These two lines together with the two diameters divide the circle into eighths.

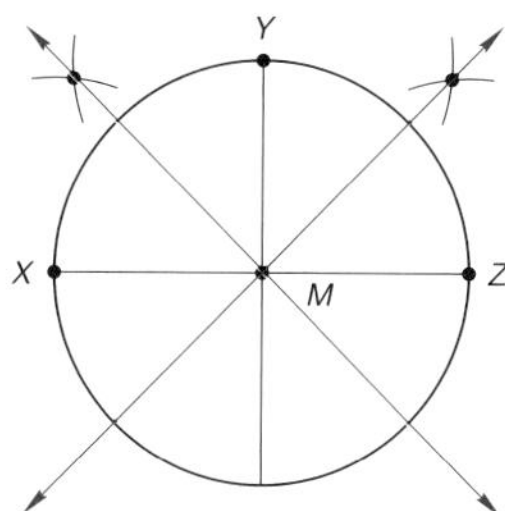

▸ 8. **Conclude** What is the measure of each small central angle that is formed? 45°

There are 8 points of intersection around the circle. Draw chords from point to point around the circle to inscribe a regular octagon in the circle.

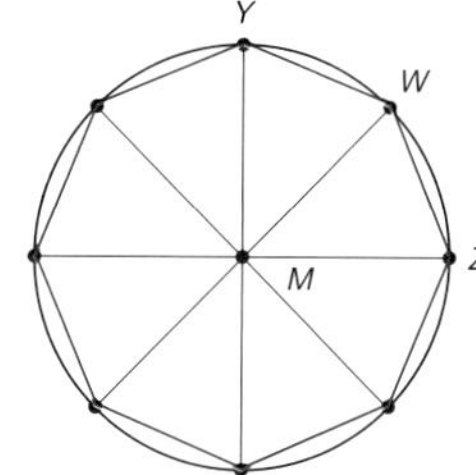

9. The octagon is divided into how many congruent triangles? 8

Analyze Refer to the inscribed octagon to answer problems **10–14.**

▸ 10. Segments *MW*, and *MZ* are radii of the same circle. Classify $\triangle WMZ$ by sides. isosceles

▸ 11. What is the measure of $\angle WMZ$? How do you know?

▸ 12. What are the measures of $\angle MWZ$ and $\angle MZW$? How do you know?

▸ 13. What is the measure of $\angle YWZ$? How do you know?

▸ 14. What is the measure of each inscribed angle formed by the sides of the octagon? 135°

11. The measure of $\angle WMZ$ is 45° which can be found by calculating $\frac{1}{8}$ of 360° or by measuring with a protractor.

12. Each angle measures $67\frac{1}{2}°$. The measures of the three angles of $\triangle WMZ$ total 180°. The angle at *M* is 45°, so the angles at *W* and *Z* equally share the remaining 135°.

13. $\angle YWZ$ measures 135°. $\angle YWZ$ is the sum of $\angle MWY$ and $\angle MWZ$, each of which measures $67\frac{1}{2}°$.

▸ See Math Conversations in the sidebar.

Instruction

Ask students to discuss this question:

"Why was it unnecessary to swing intersecting arcs below the two bottom sectors of the circle?" Drawing a line from the intersecting arc through point *M* forms a straight line that will also bisect the angle of the lower sector through which it extends. There is no need to draw the extra arcs.

Math Conversations

Discussion opportunities are provided below.

Problem 8 Conclude

"How do you know that each small central angle has a measure of 45°?" A circle measures 360°. The perpendicular diameters created four 90° angles, which were then all bisected. Half of 90° is 45°.

Problem 10 Analyze

Some students may have difficulty when starting to answer this question. Point out that the sum of the angle measures formed at the center must equal 360°. Each angle has a measure of 360° ÷ 8, or 45°. The triangles cannot be equilateral; they are isosceles.

"Why do you think only an inscribed hexagon results in equilateral triangles?" The central angle is 60° (360° ÷ 60° = 6). Two congruent sides (radii) have opposite angles equal. 180° − 60° = 120°; 120° ÷ 2 = 60°

Problems 11–14 Analyze

Encourage students to use what they have already learned to prove their statements. All the angles about point *M* measure 45° and the sum of the angles of a triangle is 180°.

Looking Forward

Using a compass and straightedge to bisect line segments and angles and to inscribe squares and regular octagons in circles prepares students for:

- **Lesson 117,** copying geometric figures.

Section 11 Overview

Lessons 101–110, Investigation 11

Lesson Planner

LESSON	NEW CONCEPTS	MATERIALS	RESOURCES
101	• Translating Expressions Into Equations		Power Up Q Investigation Activity 13
102	• Transversals • Simplifying Equations	Masking tape, graph paper	Power Up U Investigation Activity 13
103	• Powers of Negative Numbers • Dividing Terms • Square Roots of Monomials	Graph paper, protractors, inch rulers	Power Up U Investigation Activity 13
104	• Semicircles, Arcs, and Sectors	Graph paper	Power Up V Investigation Activity 13
105	• Surface Area of a Right Solid • Surface Area of a Sphere	Manipulative Kit: tape measures, Relational Geosolids Boxes, cans, label from a can, ball, scissors, grapefruit, sponges, safety scissors, rulers	Power Up Q Investigation Activity 13
106	• Solving Literal Equations • Transforming Formulas • More on Roots	Graph paper	Power Up V Investigation Activity 13
107	• Slope	Graph paper	Power Up Q Lesson Activity 23 Transparency Investigation Activity 13
108	• Formulas and Substitutions	Graph paper	Power Up V Investigation Activity 13
109	• Equations with Exponents	Graph paper	Power Up V Investigation Activity 13
110	• Simple Interest and Compound Interest • Successive Discounts	Calculators, pictures, magazines, computer spreadsheets	Power Up Q Investigation Activity 13
Inv. 11	Scale Factor in Surface Area and Volume	Manipulative Kit: inch rulers Scissors, tape, tagboard	Investigation Activity 25

Lesson Highlights
Lessons 101–110, Investigation 11

Problem Solving
Strategies
- **Make an Organized List** Lesson 104
- **Use Logical Reasoning** Lessons 103, 104, 105, 107, 109
- **Draw a Diagram** Lessons 106, 109, 110
- **Work Backwards** Lesson 105
- **Write an Equation** Lessons 101, 102, 106, 107, 108

Real-World Applications
pp. 704, 706, 707, 710, 714, 715, 721, 723, 727, 728, 736–738, 742, 744, 751, 752, 754–756, 758, 759, 762, 763, 765, 768–772, 776, 777

4-Step Process
Teacher Edition Lessons 101–110 (Power-Up Discussions)

Connections
Math and Other Subjects
- **Math and Art** pp. 736, 771
- **Math and Architecture** pp. 744, 752, 758, 776
- **Math and History** p. 758
- **Math and Science** pp. 751, 755, 770, 777
- **Math and Sports** pp. 707
- **Math and Social Studies** p. 756

Math to Math
- **Problem Solving and Measurement** Lessons 101–110, Inv. 11
- **Algebra and Problem Solving** Lessons 101–110
- **Fractions, Decimals, Percents, and Problem Solving** Lessons 101–110
- **Fractions and Measurement** Lessons 101, 103, 108
- **Measurement and Geometry** Lessons 101–110, Inv. 11
- **Proportional Relationships and Geometry** Lessons 101, 103–110, Inv. 11
- **Algebra, Measurement, and Geometry** Lessons 102–106, 108–110
- **Probability and Statistics** Lessons 101–109

Communication
Discuss
pp. 706, 732, 741, 747, 749, 755

Summarize
p. 719

Explain
pp. 718, 727, 735, 736, 743, 745, 752, 760, 763, 768

Formulate a Problem
pp. 770

Representation
Manipulatives/Hands On
pp. 711, 722, 723, 734, 735, 764, 766, 767

Model
pp. 709, 711, 716, 742, 773, 777

Represent
pp. 775, 777

Formulate an Equation
pp. 705, 707, 708, 714, 722, 736, 742, 756, 762

Technology

Student Resources
- **eBook**
- **Calculator** Lesson 110
- **Online Resources** at **www.SaxonPublishers.com/ActivitiesC2**
  - **Real-World Investigation 3** after Lesson 113
  - **Online Activities**
  - **Math Enrichment Problems**
  - **Math Stumpers**

Teacher Resources
- **Resources and Planner CD**
- **Adaptations CD** Lessons 101–110
- **Test & Practice Generator CD**
- **eGradebook**
- **Answer Key CD**

Content Highlights

Lessons 101–110, Investigation 11

Problem solving is emphasized in this section as students formally solve algebraic problems. They also solve percent problems. This section closes with surface area and volume.

Problem Solving and Algebraic Thinking

Translating expressions into equations is core to solving algebraic problems.

Students translate expressions into equations in Lesson 101. They add to their skills of simplifying equations in Lesson 102. Students divide terms and find the square roots of terms in Lessons 103, and they transform formulas and solve literal equations in Lesson 106. We refer to the slope of the graph of linear equations, and in Lesson 107 students learn to calculate the slope of a line. Students again practice substitution and evaluation with formulas in Lesson 108, and in Lesson 109 they solve equations with exponents.

Problem Solving and Proportional Thinking

Many consumer applications involve percent.

Students demonstrate the difference between simple interest and compound interest in Lesson 110. They also solve problems involving successive discounts. Investigation 11 gives students the opportunity to extend their proportional thinking to the relationship between the scale factor of similar figures and the ratios of their surface areas and volumes.

Geometry and Measurement

Concepts involving circles and angles are extended with arcs and sectors.

In Lesson 102 students relate the angles that are formed where a transversal intersects parallel lines. They calculate the lengths of arcs and the areas of sectors of circles in Lesson 104. Students find surface areas in Lesson 105, and continue working with scale factors, surface area, and volume in Investigation 11.

Assessment

A variety of weekly assessment tools are provided.

After Lesson 105:
- Power-Up Test 20
- Cumulative Test 20
- Performance Activity 20

After Lesson 110:
- Power-Up Test 21
- Cumulative Test 21
- Customized Benchmark Test
- Performance Task 21

Content Trace

Lessons 101–110, Investigation 11

LESSON	NEW CONCEPTS	PRACTICED	ASSESSED
101	• Translating Expressions Into Equations	Lessons 101, 102, 103, 105, 106, 107, 108, 109, 111, 116, 117, 118, 119	Test 21
102	• Transversals	Lessons 102, 105, 109, 111, 118	Test 22
	• Simplifying Equations	Lessons 102, 103, 104, 105, 106, 107, 108, 109, 111, 116, 117, 119, 120	Tests 21, 22
103	• Powers of Negative Numbers	Lessons 103, 104, 105, 106, 108, 110, 111, 116, 117	Tests 21, 22, 23
	• Dividing Terms	Lessons 103, 104, 105, 106, 107, 110, 111, 116, 117, 118, 119, 120	Tests 21, 22, 23
	• Square Roots of Monomials	Lessons 105, 106, 107, 108, 110, 111, 116	Square Roots of Monomials
104	• Semicircles, Arcs, and Sectors	Lessons 104, 105, 106, 107, 108, 110, 111, 112, 114, 115, 116, 118	Tests 21, 22
105	• Surface Area of a Right Solid	Lessons 105, 106, 107, 108, 109, 110, 111, 112, 114, 115, 116, 119, 120	Test 21
	• Surface Area of a Sphere	Lessons 105, 108, 112, 118, 120	Test & Practice Generator
106	• Solving Literal Equations	Lessons 106, 107, 110, 111, 112, 116, 117	Test 22
	• Transforming Formulas	Lessons 117, 119, 120	Test 22
	• More on Roots	Lessons 106, 107, 108, 109, 116, 117	Test 21
107	• Slope	Lessons 107, 108, 109, 110, 111, 113, 115, 116, 119, 120	Tests 22, 23
108	• Formulas and Substitutions	Lessons 108, 111, 113, 114, 115, 116, 119	Tests 22, 23
109	• Equations with Exponents	Lessons 109, 110, 111, 116, 118, 119, 120	Test & Practice Generator
110	• Simple Interest and Compound Interest	Lessons 110, 111, 112, 113, 114, 115, 117, 119, 120	Test 23
	• Successive Discounts	Lessons 110, 112, 113, 115	Test & Practice Generator
Inv. 11	• Scale Factor in Surface Area and Volume	Investigation 11	Test & Practice Generator

• Translating Expressions into Equations

Objectives

- Translate mathematical phrases into algebraic form.
- Translate geometric relationships into algebraic equations and solve.

Lesson Preparation

Materials

- **Power Up Q** (in *Instructional Masters*)
- **Investigation Activity 13** (in *Instructional Masters*) or **graph paper**

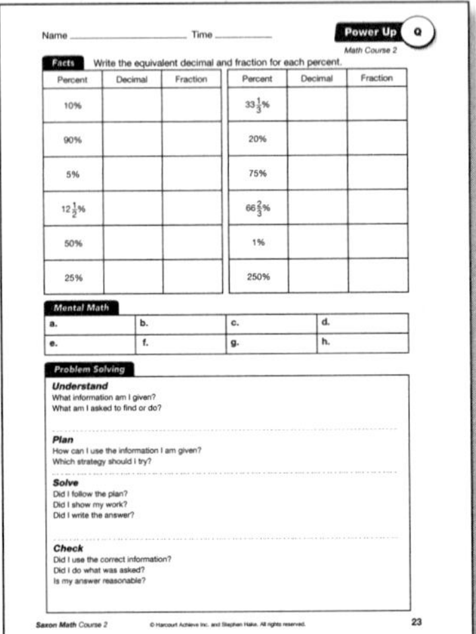

Power Up Q

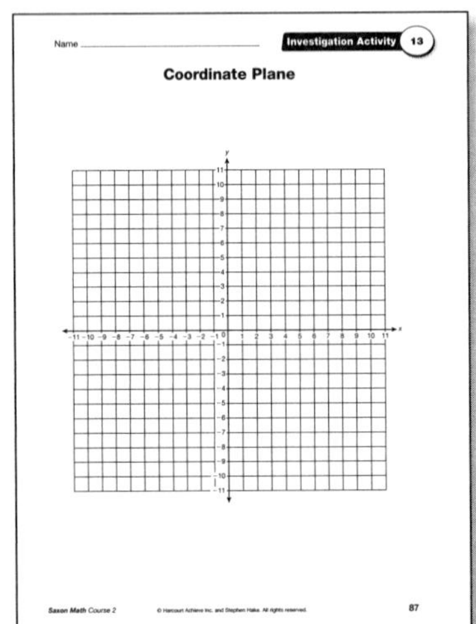

Investigation Activity 13

Math Language

English Learners (ESL)
unstated number

Technology Resources

Student eBook Complete student textbook in electronic format.

Resources and Planner CD Blackline masters, plus a pacing calendar with standards.

Test and Practice Generator CD Create additional practice sheets and custom-made tests.

www.SaxonPublishers.com Visit for more student activities and planning materials.

Inclusion

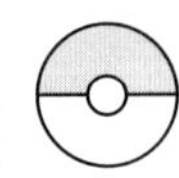

Adaptations CD Adapted lessons, investigations, practice and assessments.

Meeting Standards

National Council of Teachers of Mathematics (NCTM)

Algebra

AL.1a Represent, analyze, and generalize a variety of patterns with tables, graphs, words, and, when possible, symbolic rules

AL.1b Relate and compare different forms of representation for a relationship

AL.2d Recognize and generate equivalent forms for simple algebraic expressions and solve linear equations

AL.3a Model and solve contextualized problems using various representations, such as graphs, tables, and equations

Problem Solving

PS.1b Solve problems that arise in mathematics and in other contexts

Power-Up Discussion For use with Power Up, p. 704

Problem-Solving Strategy: Write an Equation

Jess works at an electronics store that is having a 30% off sale. In addition to the sale, he gets an employee discount on all purchases. The original prices of the items he buys are \$22.50, \$37.85, and \$19.23. If the total price after the sale and employee discounts are applied is \$49.02, what percentage is Jess's employee discount?

Understand ***Understand the problem.***

"What information are we given?"

We are told the prices of the items bought, the percentage that is taken off because of the sale, and the final amount paid.

"What are we asked to do?"

We are asked to find the employee discount.

Plan ***Make a plan.***

"What problem-solving strategy will we use?"

We will *write several equations.*

Solve ***Carry out the plan.***

"What is the total price before any discounts?"

$\$22.50 + \$37.85 + \$19.23 = \$79.58$

"What is the sale price?"

$\$79.58 - 0.30(\$79.58) = \$55.71$

"How much money did Jess save with his discount?"

$\$55.71 - \$49.02 = \$6.69$

"What percentage of the sale price was discounted?"

$W_P \times \$55.71 = \$6.69$

$$W_P = \frac{\$6.69}{\$55.71}$$

$W_P = 0.120$ or 12%

Check ***Look back.***

"Did we find the answer to the question that was asked?"

Yes. The employee discount is 12%.

"How can we check that our solution is correct?"

We can work backwards substituting our answer for the employee discount.

1 Power Up

Facts

Distribute **Power Up Q** to students. See answers below.

Mental Math

Encourage students to share different ways to mentally compute these exercises. Strategies for exercises **c** and **e** are listed below.

c. Use Division

$0.4 \div 2 = 0.2$

$0.12 \div 2 = 0.06$

$w = 0.06$

Equivalent Fractions

$\frac{0.4}{0.12} \div \frac{0.4}{0.4} = \frac{1}{0.3}$

$\frac{1}{0.3} \cdot \frac{0.2}{0.2} = \frac{0.2}{0.06}$

$w = 0.06$

e. Multiply First

$(3 \cdot 80) \div 4$

$240 \div 4 = 60$

Divide First

$(80 \div 4)3$

$20 \cdot 3 = 60$

Problem Solving

Refer to **Power-Up Discussion,** p. 704F.

2 New Concepts

Instruction

Write this sentence on the board:

Lucy said Ben went swimming.

"Who went swimming, Lucy or Ben?"

Help students see that without punctuation there is no way of knowing.

"Lucy,"said Ben, "went swimming."

Lucy said, "Ben went swimming."

Help students make the connection between the elements of grammar and the elements of mathematics.

Grammar	**Mathematics**
phrases	expressions
sentences	equations
punctuation	order of operations

Tell students that in this lesson, they will be translating phrases into expressions and sentences into equations.

(continued)

LESSON **101**

• Translating Expressions into Equations

Power Up *Building Power*

facts Power Up Q

mental math[1]

a. Positive/Negative: $(-2)(-2)(-2)(-2)$ 16

b. Order of Operations/Exponents: $(5 \times 10^{-5})(6 \times 10^{-6})$ 3×10^{-10}

c. Ratio: $\frac{0.2}{w} = \frac{0.4}{0.12}$ 0.06

d. Measurement: Convert −25°C to degrees Fahrenheit. −13°F

e. Fractional Parts: $\frac{3}{4}$ of $80 $60

f. Percent: 25% less than $80 $60

g. Probability: A spinner has 4 equal sections with blue, red, orange, and purple. What is the probability that the spinner will land on orange? $\frac{1}{4}$

h. Percent/Estimation: Estimate a 15% tip on a $29.78 bill. $4.50

problem solving

Jess works at an electronics store that is having a 30% off sale. In addition to the sale, he gets an employee discount on all purchases. The original prices of the items he buys are $22.50, $37.85, and $19.23. If the total price after the sale and employee discounts are applied is $49.02, what percentage is Jess's employee discount? 12%

New Concept *Increasing Knowledge*

An essential skill in mathematics is the ability to translate language, situations, and relationships into mathematical form. Since the earliest lessons of this book we have practiced translating word problems into equations that we then solved. In this lesson we will practice translating other common patterns of language into algebraic form. We will also use our knowledge of geometric relationships to write equations to solve geometry problems.

The table on the next page shows examples of mathematical language translated into algebraic form. Notice that the word *number* is represented by a letter in italic form. We can use any letter to represent an unknown number.

Facts Write the equivalent decimal and fraction for each percent.

Percent	Decimal	Fraction	Percent	Decimal	Fraction
10%	0.1	$\frac{1}{10}$	$33\frac{1}{3}\%$	$0.\overline{3}$	$\frac{1}{3}$
90%	0.9	$\frac{9}{10}$	20%	0.2	$\frac{1}{5}$
5%	0.05	$\frac{1}{20}$	75%	0.75	$\frac{3}{4}$
$12\frac{1}{2}\%$	0.125	$\frac{1}{8}$	$66\frac{2}{3}\%$	$0.\overline{6}$	$\frac{2}{3}$
50%	0.5	$\frac{1}{2}$	1%	0.01	$\frac{1}{100}$
25%	0.25	$\frac{1}{4}$	250%	2.5	$2\frac{1}{2}$

Examples of Translations

English	Symbols
twice a number	$2n$
five more than a number	$x + 5$
three less than a number	$a - 3$
half of a number	$\frac{1}{2}h$ or $\frac{h}{2}$
the product of a number and seven	$7b$
Seventeen is five more than twice a number.	$17 = 2n + 5$

The last translation in the examples above resulted in an equation that can be solved to find the unstated number. We will solve a similar equation in the next example.

Example 1

If five less than twice a number is seventeen, what is the number?

Solution

We will use the letter x to represent the unknown as we translate the sentence into an equation.

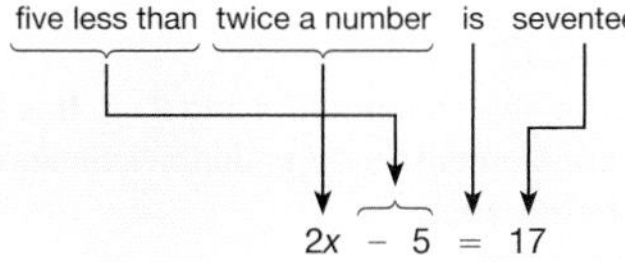

Now we solve the equation.

$2x - 5 = 17$	equation
$2x - 5 + 5 = 17 + 5$	added 5 to both sides
$2x = 22$	simplified
$\frac{2x}{2} = \frac{22}{2}$	divided both sides by 2
$x = 11$	simplified

We find that the number described is **11.** Five less than twice eleven is seventeen.

Formulate Write and simplify an equation that can be used to verify that 11 is the correct number. $2(11) - 5 = 17$; $22 - 5 = 17$; $17 = 17$

In example 2 on the next page, we will translate a situation involving variables into an equation. Then we will use the equation to solve the problem.

2 New Concepts (Continued)

Instruction

Tell students that a mathematical phrase contains at least one operation. The last translation in the table is actually a complete sentence that translates into an equation.

Example 1

Instruction

Write this on the board.

5 less than twice a number is seventeen.

- Point out that *is* means 'is equal to' and is expressed as an equals sign.
- Explain that phrases such as 'five less than twice a number' may be incorrectly translated when taken out of context.
- Distinguish between 'five less than twice a number' ($2n - 5$) and 'five is less than twice a number' ($5 < 2n$).

Many students will try to write the translation sequentially from left to right as they do language sentences. Point out that they should read the entire statement before translating it. Sometimes the first part of a phrase is not the first number in the translation.

(continued)

Teacher Tip

Some students may need additional practice. Write these sentences on the board and ask students to **translate** them **into equations.**

Three times a number is 30. $3n = 30$
Six more than twice a number is 30. $2n + 6 = 30$
Six less than three times a number is 30. $3n - 6 = 30$
12 is half of what number? $12 = \frac{1}{2}n$
Five less than two thirds of a number is seven. $\frac{2}{3}n - 5 = 7$

English Learners

Underneath the chart of translations, explain the meaning of **unstated number.** Write $17 = n + 5$ on the board. Tell students:

"An unstated number is an unknown number. A letter is often used in place of the unknown or unstated number."

Ask students:

"What is the value of the unstated number in this equation?" $n = 12$

2 New Concepts (Continued)

Example 2

Instruction

Give students an opportunity to discuss the problem-solving process in conjunction with writing an equation.

Understand

"What information are we given?"

- \$1.50 for each ride
- \$3.00 per mile
- ride is 6.4 mi

"What are we asked to do?"

- Write an equation and use it to solve the problem.
- Use f for the total fare and m for the number of miles.
- Find the total fare for a 6.4 mi ride.

Plan

"How can we set up an equation?"

- \$3.00 per mile translates to $3m$.
- \$1.50 for each ride translates to $3m + \$1.50$.
- Use f for the total fare. The equation is $3m + \$1.50 = f$

Solve

"How do we solve the equation?"

- Substitute the numbers that we know into the equation. $3(6.4) + \$1.50 = f$

Read through the solution in the text with the students. Then have students verify their math.

- Substitute the numbers into the original equation.

$$3(6.4) + \$1.50 = \$20.70$$
$$\$20.70 = \$20.70 \text{ Check}$$

Check

"How can we determine if the answer is reasonable?"

We know that \$3.00 per mile times 6 miles would be \$18, and that \$18 + \$1.50 = \$19.50. Since 6.4 miles is a little over 6 miles, it is reasonable that the answer is a little over \$19.50.

Example 3

Instruction

Tell students that a diagram can be used instead of words to provide information for writing an equation and solving a problem.

(continued)

Example 2

A taxi company charges \$1.50 plus \$3.00 per mile metered at tenths of a mile. Write an equation that relates the total fare (f) in dollars to the number of miles (m) of a taxi ride. Then use the equation to find the fare for a 6.4 mile taxi ride.

Solution

To find the fare (the price of the ride), we multiply the distance in miles (to the tenth of a mile) by \$3.00. Then we add \$1.50. Without the dollar signs the formula is:

$$f = 3m + 1.5$$

To find the fare for a 6.4 mile ride we substitute 6.4 in place of m and simplify to find f.

$f = 3(6.4) + 1.5$	Substituted 6.4
$f = 19.2 + 1.5$	Multiplied 3 and 6.4
$f = 20.7$	Added 19.2 and 1.5

Now we express the answer in dollar form. The fare for the ride is **\$20.70.**

Generalize Find the fare for a 10-mile ride. \$31.50

We can also translate geometric relationships into algebraic expressions.

Example 3

The angles marked x and $2x$ in this figure are supplementary. What is the measure of the larger angle?

2x
x

Solution

The sum of the angle measures is 180°. We write this relationship as an equation.

$$2x + x = 180°$$

Since $2x + x = 3x$, we may simplify then solve the equation.

$2x + x = 180°$	equation
$3x = 180°$	simplified
$\frac{3x}{3} = \frac{180°}{3}$	divided both sides by 3
$x = 60°$	simplified

The solution of the equation is 60°, but 60° is not the answer to the question. We were asked to find the measure of the larger angle, which in the diagram is marked $2x$. Since x is 60°, we find that the larger angle measures $2(60°) =$ **120°.**

Discuss How are angles x and 2x related in size? The measure of angle 2x is twice the measure of angle x.

Teacher Tip

Once students are comfortable translating words into expressions, have them work in reverse to **translate the expressions** into words:

3x three times a number
x + 4 four more than a number
n − 5 five less than a number
6x − 1 one less than six times a number
3w − 2 = 7 two less than three times a number is seven

Practice Set Formulate Write and solve an equation for each of these problems:

a. Six more than the product of a number and three is 30. What is the number? $3x + 6 = 30$; 8

b. Ten less than half of what number is 30? $\frac{1}{2}x - 10 = 30$; 80

▶ **c.** What is the measure of the smallest angle in this figure? $3x + 2x = 90°$; 36°

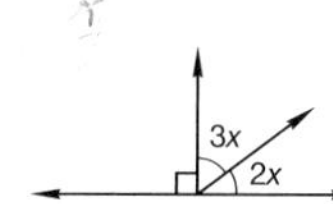

▶ **d.** Find the measure of each angle of this triangle. $x + 2x + 3x = 180°$; $x = 30°$; $2x = 60°$; $3x = 90°$

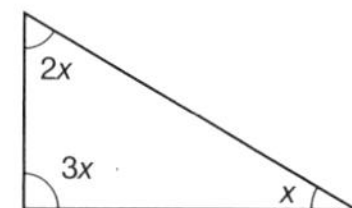

e. An online movie ticket service charges $8 per ticket plus a $2 transaction fee. Write an equation that relates the price (p) of buying tickets (t) through this service. Then use the equation to find the cost of 5 tickets. $p = 8t + 2$; $42

Written Practice *Strengthening Concepts*

1. (Inv. 4) The following numbers are Katie's 100-meter dash times, in seconds, during track season. Find the **a** median, **b** mode, and **c** range of these times.

12.3, 11.8, 11.9, 11.7, 12.0, 11.9, 12.1, 11.6, 11.8

a. 11.9 **b.** 11.8 and 11.9 **c.** 0.7

▶ **2.** (53) Jackson earns $10 per hour at his part-time job. How much money does he earn for working 3 hours and 45 minutes? $37.50

Use ratio boxes to solve problems **3–6.**

3. (72) The recipe called for 3 cups of flour and 2 eggs to make 6 servings. If 15 cups of flour were used to make more servings, how many eggs should be used? 10 eggs

4. (72) Lester can type 48 words per minute. At that rate, how many words can he type in 90 seconds? 72 words

5. (81) Ten students were wearing athletic shoes. This was 40 percent of the class. How many students were in the class? 25 students

6. (92) The dress was on sale for 40 percent off the regular price. If the regular price was $45, what was the sale price? $27.00

▶ *** 7.** (96) Generalize Use the Distributive Property to clear parentheses. Then simplify by adding like terms. $2x - 12$

$$3(x - 4) - x$$

▶ **8.** (88) Use two unit multipliers to convert 3 gallons to pints. 24 pints

▶ See Math Conversations in the sidebar.

2 New Concepts (Continued)

Practice Set

Problems c and d Formulate

Ask students to describe the geometric information shown in each diagram. In problem **c,** there is a right angle marked, so we know that the sum of the two acute angles is 90°. In problem **d,** the sum of the angles in a triangle is 180°.

3 Written Practice

Math Conversations

Discussion opportunities are provided below.

Problem 2

Extend the Problem

Ask students to share the different strategies they used to solve this problem. Possible strategies may include:

Draw a Diagram

15 min $2.50	15 min $2.50	15 min $2.50	15 min $2.50

$10 per hour

Use Reasoning

$10 per hour	3 × $10	= $30
$5 per half hour	3 × $2.50	= $7.50
$2.50 per 15 min	$30 + $7.50	= $37.50

Write an Equation

$$\frac{\$10}{60 \text{ min}} = \frac{x}{225 \text{ min}}$$

$$60x = 2250$$

$$x = \$37.50$$

Problem 7 Generalize

"How would the answer change if the 3 were negative? Explain your reasoning."

$-3(x - 4) - x$ $-4x + 12$

Errors and Misconceptions

Problem 8

If students have difficulty setting up the expression, explain that they should start with the largest unit of measure and work toward the smallest unit of measure.

$$\frac{3 \text{ gal}}{1} \cdot \frac{4 \text{ qt}}{1 \text{ gal}} \cdot \frac{2 \text{ pt}}{1 \text{ qt}}$$

(continued)

3 Written Practice *(Continued)*

Math Conversations

Discussion opportunities are provided below.

Problem 10 Generalize

"What perfect square is close to 200?" Some students may suggest $15 \times 15 = 225$

"Since 225 is greater than 200, what number should we try?" $14 \times 14 = 196$

Ask students to estimate the square root. Students should estimate 14.1 or 14.2.

Problem 11 Analyze

Ask students to explain why w is less than m. $w = 0.5$ and $m = 1 \div 0.5$ or 2

Problem 13 Formulate

Have students translate this statement. *Twenty is greater than three less than the product of 4 and a number.* $20 > 4n - 3$

Problem 14

Extend the Problem

Write these expressions on the board.

$0.05 \times 10^2 \quad 0.5 \times 10^3 \quad 50 \times 10^{-1} \quad 500 \times 10^{-2}$

Tell students that these expressions all share the same characteristic except for one.

"Which one does not belong? Explain why." All have the same value except for 0.5×10^3

Errors and Misconceptions

Problem 11

If students think $w > m$, they may have written the reciprocal of 0.5 as $\frac{1}{0.5}$ and seeing a fraction assumed that $m < w$. Have students write the reciprocal as $1 \div 0.5$ and find the quotient.

(continued)

9.

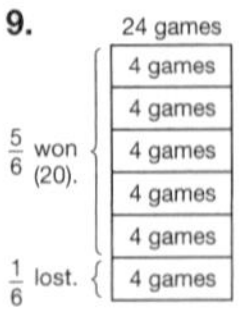

9. Diagram this statement. Then answer the questions that follow. *(36, 71)*

The Trotters won $\frac{5}{6}$ of their games. They won 20 games and lost the rest.

a. How many games did they play? 24 games

b. What was the Trotters' win-loss ratio? $\frac{5}{1}$

▶* **10.** Generalize Between which two consecutive whole numbers is $\sqrt{200}$? 14 and 15 *(100)*

▶* **11.** Analyze Compare: $w \bigcirc\!\!\!\!< \; m$ if w is 0.5 and m is the reciprocal of w. *(9)*

12. Find the area of the hexagon shown at right. Dimensions are in centimeters. Corners that look square are square. 84 cm^2 *(75)*

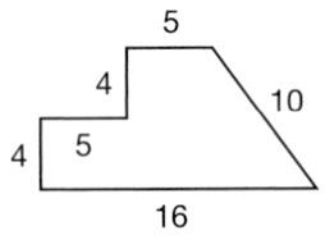

▶* **13.** Formulate Write an equation to solve this problem: *(101)*

Three less than the product of six and what number is 45? $6n - 3 = 45$; 8

▶ **14.** Multiply. Write the product in scientific notation. 3.2×10^7 *(83)*

$(8 \times 10^8)(4 \times 10^{-2})$

15. Complete the table. *(48)*

Fraction	Decimal	Percent
a. $\frac{1}{50}$	0.02	**b.** 2%
c. $\frac{1}{500}$	**d.** 0.002	0.2%

16.

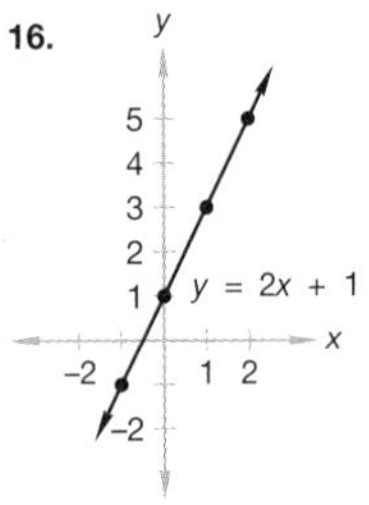

16. Find the missing numbers in the table by using the function rule. Then graph the function on a coordinate plane. *(56, Inv. 9)*

y = 2x + 1

x	y
−1	−1
0	1
1	3
2	5

17. Find the volume of this solid. Dimensions are in inches. 80 $in.^3$ *(95)*

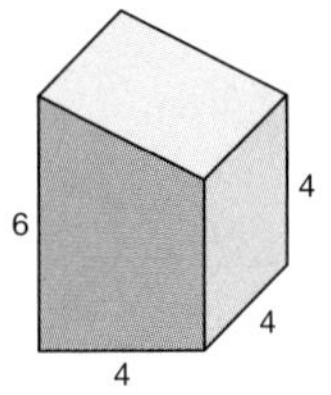

▶ See Math Conversations in the sidebar.

18. (65, 82) Find each measure of the circle at right. (Leave π as π.)

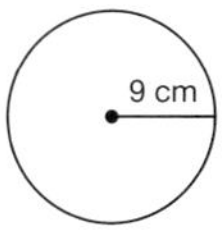

a. circumference 18π cm

b. area 81π cm^2

* **19.** (Inv. 9) If a number cube is rolled what are the odds of not getting 6? 5 to 1

▶* **20.** (101) **Conclude** The two acute angles in this figure are complementary. What are the measures of the two angles? $x = 30°$; $2x = 60°$

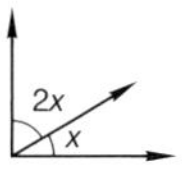

21. (44) Divide 1.23 by 9 and write the quotient

a. with a bar over the repetend. $0.1\overline{36}$

b. rounded to three decimal places. 0.137

▶* **22.** (99) **Analyze** If BC is 9 cm and AC is 12 cm, then what is AB? 15 cm

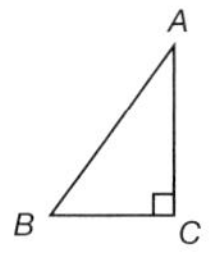

23.

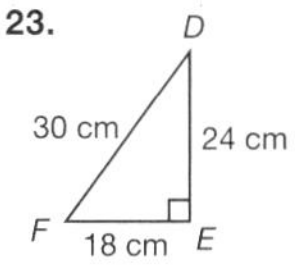

▶* **23.** (98) **Model** The scale factor from $\triangle ABC$ in problem 22 to $\triangle DEF$ is 2. Draw $\triangle DEF$, then find

a. the perimeter of $\triangle DEF$. 72 cm

b. the area of $\triangle DEF$. 216 cm^2

* **24.** (94) In a bag were 6 red marbles and 4 blue marbles. If Lily pulls a marble out of the bag with her left hand and then pulls a marble out with her right hand, what is the probability that the marble in each hand will be blue? $\frac{4}{10} \cdot \frac{3}{9} = \frac{2}{15}$

25. (90) Solve: $3\frac{1}{7}d = 88$ 28

▶* **26.** (93) **Model** Solve this inequality and graph its solution:

$3x + 20 \geq 14$

$x \geq -2$

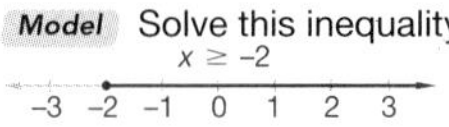

Simplify:

27. (52) $5^2 + (3^3 - \sqrt{81})$ 43

* **28.** (96) $3x + 2(x - 1)$ $5x - 2$

29. (43) $\left(4\frac{4}{9}\right)(2.7)\left(1\frac{1}{3}\right)$ 16

30. (85) $(-2)(-3) - (-4)(-5)$ −14

▶ See Math Conversations in the sidebar.

3 Written Practice (Continued)

Math Conversations

Discussion opportunities are provided below.

Problem 20 Conclude

Ask a student to write the solution on the board and explain each step.

Problem 22 Analyze

Extend the Problem

"What is the perimeter?" 36 cm

"What is the area?" 54 cm^2

Problem 23 Model

Ask a volunteer to sketch the diagrams of both triangles on the board.

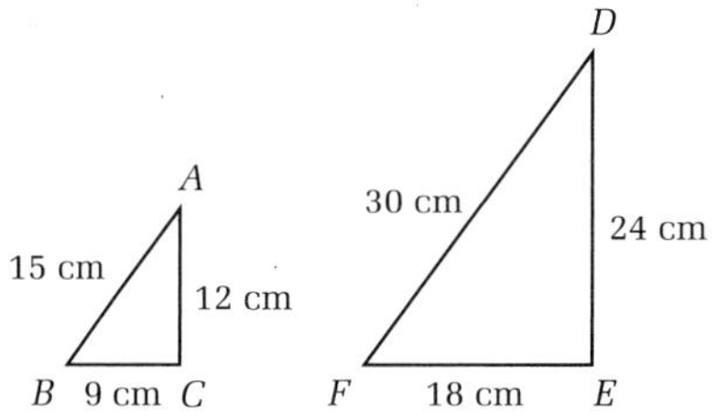

Lead a discussion about how to find the lengths of each side of the larger triangle.

Problem 26 Model

"Are any rational numbers included in the solution?" Yes; Accept any rational number that satisfies the criteria of the inequality, for example, $\frac{1}{2}$ and 0.63.

Looking Forward

Translating mathematical phrases and geometric relationships into algebraic equations prepares students for:

- **Lesson 102,** simplifying and then solving equations.
- **Lesson 109,** translating and solving equations with exponents.

• Transversals
• Simplifying Equations

Objectives

- Find the measures of the eight angles formed when a transversal intersects a pair of parallel lines.
- Identify the special pairs of angles formed when a transversal intersects a pair of lines.
- Simplify an equation as the first step of the solution.

Lesson Preparation

Materials

- **Power Up U** (in *Instructional Masters*)
- **Investigation Activity 13** (in *Instructional Masters*) or **graph paper**

Optional

- **Teacher-provided material: masking tape**

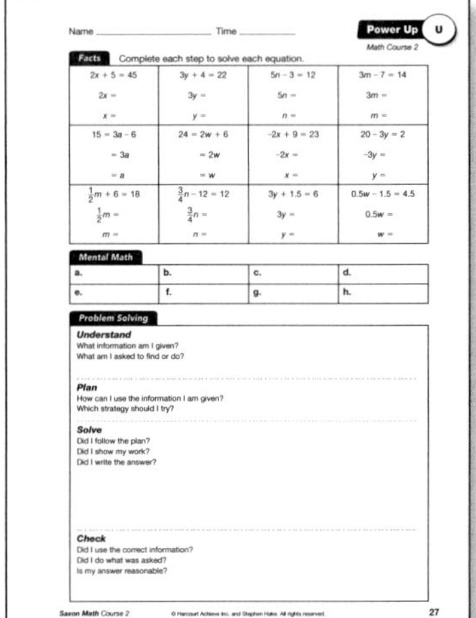

Name ______________ Time ________ **Power Up U** *Math Course 2*

Facts Complete each step to solve each equation.

$2x + 5 = 45$ $2x =$ $x =$	$3y + 4 = 22$ $3y =$ $y =$	$5n - 3 = 12$ $5n =$ $n =$	$3m - 7 = 14$ $3m =$ $m =$
$15 = 3a - 6$ $= 3a$ $= a$	$24 = 2w + 6$ $= 2w$ $= w$	$-2x + 9 = 23$ $-2x =$ $x =$	$20 - 3y = 2$ $-3y =$ $y =$
$\frac{1}{2}m + 6 = 18$ $\frac{1}{2}m =$ $m =$	$\frac{3}{4}n - 12 = 12$ $\frac{3}{4}n =$ $n =$	$3y + 1.5 = 6$ $3y =$ $y =$	$0.5w - 1.5 = 4.5$ $0.5w =$ $w =$

Mental Math

a.	b.	c.	d.
e.	f.	g.	h.

Problem Solving

Understand
What information am I given?
What am I asked to find or do?

Plan
How can I use the information I am given?
Which strategy should I try?

Solve
Did I follow the plan?
Did I show my work?
Did I write the answer?

Check
Did I use the correct information?
Did I do what was asked?
Is my answer reasonable?

Saxon Math Course 2 © Harcourt Achieve Inc. and Stephen Hake. All rights reserved. 27

Power Up U

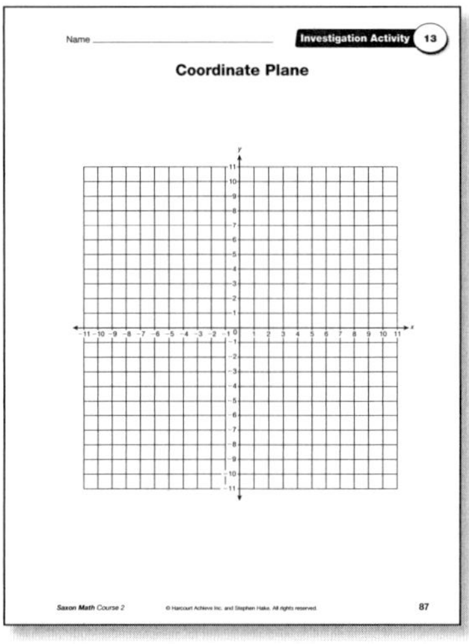

Name ______________ **Investigation Activity 13**

Coordinate Plane

Investigation Activity 13

Math Language

New		English Learners (ESL)
alternate exterior angles	corresponding angles	exterior
alternate interior angles	transversal	interior

Technology Resources

Student eBook Complete student textbook in electronic format.

Resources and Planner CD Blackline masters, plus a pacing calendar with standards.

Test and Practice Generator CD Create additional practice sheets and custom-made tests.

www.SaxonPublishers.com Visit for more student activities and planning materials.

Inclusion

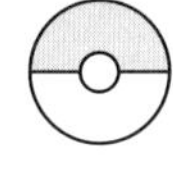

Adaptations CD Adapted lessons, investigations, practice and assessments.

Meeting Standards

National Council of Teachers of Mathematics (NCTM)

Numbers and Operations

NO.2c Understand and use the inverse relationships of addition and subtraction, multiplication and division, and squaring and finding square roots to simplify computations and solve problems

Algebra

AL.2d Recognize and generate equivalent forms for simple algebraic expressions and solve linear equations

Geometry

GM.1a Precisely describe, classify, and understand relationships among types of two- and three-dimensional objects using their defining properties

Power-Up Discussion *For use with Power Up, p. 710*

Problem-Solving Strategy: Write an Equation

The first computer can complete a payroll for 720 employees in 8 hours. The second computer can complete the same payroll in 12 hours. Working together, how long will it take the two computers to complete a payroll for 720 employees?

Understand — *Understand the problem.*

"What information are we given?"

We are told that one computer can process paychecks for 720 employees in 8 hours, and another can complete the same payroll in 12 hours.

"What are we asked to do?"

We are asked to determine how long the two computers would take to complete a payroll for 720 employees if they were working together.

Plan — *Make a plan.*

"What problem-solving strategy will we use?"

We will *write an equation* to find the time required.

Teacher's Note: Encourage students to estimate the total time it will take to process the payroll. Students often jump to the conclusion that the average of 8 hours and 12 hours is 10 hours (the faster computer helps the slower computer, but the slower computer slows down the faster computer), so it will take 10 hours.

Solve — *Carry out the plan.*

"How many paychecks can the first computer process in 1 hour?"

$720 \text{ checks} \div 8 \text{ hours} = 90\frac{\text{checks}}{\text{hour}}$

"How many paychecks can the second computer process in 1 hour?"

$720 \text{ checks} \div 12 \text{ hours} = 60\frac{\text{checks}}{\text{hour}}$

"How many paychecks can the two computers process together in 1 hour?"

$90 + 60 = 150\frac{\text{checks}}{\text{hour}}$

"How long will it take the computers to process the payroll at a rate of 150 checks/hour?"

$720 \text{ checks} \div 150\frac{\text{checks}}{\text{hour}} = \frac{72}{15} = 4\frac{12}{15} = 4\frac{4}{5}$ hours, or 4 hours and 48 minutes

Check — *Look back.*

Teacher Note: Encourage students to compare their estimates to their calculated answers. Point out that two computers working together nearly halve the faster computer's processing time.

"Did we do what we were asked to do?"

Yes, we found the time it would take the two computers working together to process the payroll.

"How can we verify the solution is correct?"

We can calculate the number of checks each computer would compute in 4 hours and 48 minutes, then add them to ensure they total 720:

$$90 \cdot (4\tfrac{4}{5}) = 432 \text{ checks for computer 1}$$
$$60 \cdot (4\tfrac{4}{5}) = 288 \text{ checks for computer 2}$$
$$432 + 288 = 720 \text{ checks total}$$

Power Up

Facts

Distribute **Power Up U** to students. See answers below.

Mental Math

Encourage students to share different ways to mentally compute these exercises. Strategies for exercises **d** and **f** are listed below.

d. Reasoning

1000 mL = 1 L, so
500 mL = 0.5 L

Move the Decimal Point

1000 mL = 1 L
500 ÷ 1000 = 0.5
500 mL = 0.5 L

f. Reasoning

100% + 100% + 50%
40 + 40 + 20 = 100

Multiply

250% = 2.5
2.5 × 40 = 100

Problem Solving

Refer to **Power-Up Discussion,** p. 710B.

2 New Concepts

Instruction

Begin by drawing a line on the board. Then have a volunteer draw a line that intersects the line you drew.

"At how many points do the lines intersect?" one

"How many angles are formed?" four

"What kind of angles are they?" acute and obtuse (If the volunteer drew a perpendicular line, the angles are right angles.)

Tell students that in this lesson they will learn about the special pairs of angles formed when a third line intersects two parallel lines.

(continued)

LESSON **102**

• Transversals
• Simplifying Equations

Power Up *Building Power*

facts Power Up U

mental math

a. **Positive/Negative:** $(-0.25) + (-0.75)$ −1

b. **Order of Operations/Exponents:** $(3 \times 10^{10})(2 \times 10^{-2})$ 6×10^8

c. **Algebra:** $3x + 2\frac{1}{2} = 10$ $2\frac{1}{2}$

d. **Measurement:** Convert 500 mL to L. 0.5 L

e. **Percent:** 150% of \$40 \$60

f. **Percent:** 150% more than \$40 \$100

g. **Probability:** A spinner has 3 sections with red, blue, and red. What is the probability that the spinner will land on red? $\frac{2}{3}$

h. **Calculation:** Start with a score, − 5, × 2, + 2, ÷ 4, + 1, $\sqrt{\ }$, × 7, − 1, ÷ 10. 2

problem solving The first computer can complete a payroll for 720 employees in 8 hours. The second computer can complete the same payroll in 12 hours. Working together, how long will it take the two computers to complete a payroll for 720 employees? 4 hours and 48 minutes

New Concepts *Increasing Knowledge*

transversals

A **transversal** is a line that intersects one or more other lines in a plane. In this lesson we will pay particular attention to the angles formed when a transversal intersects a pair of parallel lines. Notice the eight angles that are formed.

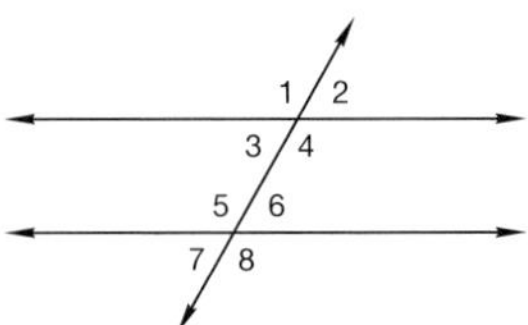

In this figure there are four acute angles numbered 2, 3, 6, and 7, and there are four obtuse angles numbered 1, 4, 5, and 8. All of the acute angles have the same measure, and all of the obtuse angles have the same measure.

Facts Complete each step to solve each equation.

$2x + 5 = 45$ $2x = 40$ $x = 20$	$3y + 4 = 22$ $3y = 18$ $y = 6$	$5n - 3 = 12$ $5n = 15$ $n = 3$	$3m - 7 = 14$ $3m = 21$ $m = 7$
$15 = 3a - 6$ $21 = 3a$ $7 = a$	$24 = 2w + 6$ $18 = 2w$ $9 = w$	$-2x + 9 = 23$ $-2x = 14$ $x = -7$	$20 - 3y = 2$ $-3y = -18$ $y = 6$
$\frac{1}{2}m + 6 = 18$ $\frac{1}{2}m = 12$ $m = 24$	$\frac{3}{4}n - 12 = 12$ $\frac{3}{4}n = 24$ $n = 32$	$3y + 1.5 = 6$ $3y = 4.5$ $y = 1.5$	$0.5w - 1.5 = 4.5$ $0.5w = 6$ $w = 12$

Example 1

Thinking Skill
Conclude
When would all eight angles formed by a transversal intersecting two parallel lines be equal? When the transversal is perpendicular to the two parallel lines, the angles formed are right angles.

Transversal *t* intersects parallel lines *l* and *m* so that the measure of $\angle a$ is 105°. Find the measure of angles *b–h*.

Solution

All the obtuse angles have the same measure, so **$\angle a$, $\angle d$, $\angle e$, and $\angle h$ each measure 105°.** Each of the acute angles is a supplement of an obtuse angle, so each acute angle measures

$$180° - 105° = 75°$$

Thus, **$\angle b$, $\angle c$, $\angle f$, and $\angle g$ each measure 75°.**

When a transversal intersects a pair of lines, special pairs of angles are formed. In example 1, $\angle a$ and $\angle e$ are **corresponding angles** because the position of $\angle e$ corresponds to the position of $\angle a$ (to the left of the transversal and above lines *m* and *l*). Name three more pairs of corresponding angles in example 1. $\angle b$ and $\angle f$, $\angle c$ and $\angle g$, $\angle d$ and $\angle h$

Angle *a* and $\angle h$ in example 1 also form a special pair of angles. They are on alternate sides of the transversal and are outside of (not between) the parallel lines. So $\angle a$ and $\angle h$ are called **alternate exterior angles.** Name another pair of alternate exterior angles in example 1. $\angle b$ and $\angle g$

Angles *d* and *e* in example 1 are **alternate interior angles** because they are on alternate sides of the transversal and in the interior of (between) the parallel lines. Name another pair of alternate interior angles in example 1. $\angle c$ and $\angle f$

Model Draw 2 vertical parallel lines with a transversal intersecting them. Label the angles formed 1–8. List the angles that have the same measure. See student work.

Example 2

Transversal *r* intersects parallel lines *p* and *q* to form angles 1–8.

a. Name four pairs of corresponding angles.

b. Name two pairs of alternate exterior angles.

c. Name two pairs of alternate interior angles.

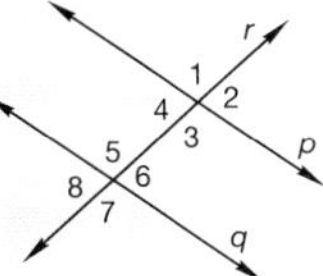

2 New Concepts *(Continued)*

Example 1

Instruction

Once students have finished this example, ask them:

"If lines l and m were not parallel to one another, would all of the obtuse angles still have the same measure?" No, if the lines were not parallel the angles would have different measures.

Instruction

- Point out to students that the names of the special pairs of angles actually help one to locate them.
- Discuss the words *alternate, exterior,* and *interior* and how these words apply to transversals and pairs of parallel lines.

Have students point and label the special pairs of angles in their drawings as they explain how they identified them.

Example 2

Instruction

Tell students that it is important that they pay close attention to the labels of the angles.

- The labels may sometimes be numbers and sometimes letters.
- They may not follow the same order around the figure.
- The figure may not always have the same orientation.

(continued)

Math Background

Is there a case when all the angles formed by a transversal intersecting two parallel lines are equal?

Yes, when a transversal is perpendicular to the pair of parallel lines, all the angles formed are right angles.

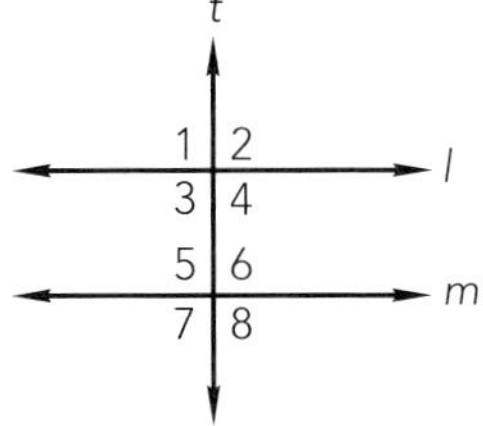

English Learners

Before example 2, explain the meaning of **interior** and **exterior.** Draw a large circle on the board. Write the number one inside the circle and 2 outside the circle. Say:

"The number one is in the interior of the circle. The number 2 is located on the exterior of the circle."

Ask volunteers to write their name on the interior or exterior of the circle.

Inclusion

Students may benefit from a physical activity demonstrating transversals. Tape different sets of two parallel lines and a transversal on the floor. The student starts with the right foot on the first angle to the right and hops with the left to the closest congruent angle. Moving in a forward direction, the student hops to the closest congruent angle. Students continue until all angles congruent to the first angle on the right have been hopped upon. Switch to the left.

2 New Concepts (Continued)

Instruction

"How many variable terms are there?" two

"How many constant terms?" two

Emphasize that we can combine any like terms. Once like terms have been identified, they can be added or subtracted by focusing on the signed-number part of the terms.

Remind students that if a term is written without a coefficient, it is understood that the coefficient is 1.

Example 3

Instruction

Emphasize that the goal in solving these equations is to simplify until the variable is isolated on one side of the equation.

Ask a student to explain each step for simplifying. Ask a different student to explain each step of the solution.

Once students explain that like terms must have the same exponent, ask students to identify the exponent of x. 1

(continued)

Solution

a. $\angle 1$ **and** $\angle 5$, $\angle 2$ **and** $\angle 6$, $\angle 3$ **and** $\angle 7$, $\angle 4$ **and** $\angle 8$

b. $\angle 1$ **and** $\angle 7$, $\angle 2$ **and** $\angle 8$

c. $\angle 4$ **and** $\angle 6$, $\angle 3$ **and** $\angle 5$

simplifying equations

One step to solving some equations is to collect like terms. In this equation we can collect variable terms and constant terms as the first step of the solution.

$$3x - x - 5 + 8 = 17$$
$$(3x - x) + (-5 + 8) = 17$$
$$2x + 3 = 17$$

Math Language
Here we use the term *collect* to mean "to bring together in one place."

Example 3

Simplify and then solve this equation.

$$3x + 5 - x = 17 + x - x$$

Solution

We collect like terms on each side of the equal sign. On the left side, combining $3x$ and $-x$ gives us $2x$. On the right side, combining $+x$ and $-x$ gives us zero.

$3x + 5 - x = 17 + x - x$	equation
$3x - x + 5 = 17 + x - x$	Commutative Property
$(3x - x) + 5 = 17 + (x - x)$	Associative Property
$2x + 5 = 17$	simplified

Now we solve the simplified equation.

$2x + 5 = 17$	equation
$2x + 5 - 5 = 17 - 5$	subtracted 5 from both sides
$2x = 12$	simplified
$\frac{2x}{2} = \frac{12}{2}$	divided both sides by 2
$x = \mathbf{6}$	simplified

Predict If the example included the term x^2, would x^2 be collected as a like term with $3x$ and $-x$? Support your reasoning. No. The three terms have the same variable, x, but the term x^2 has a different exponent.

Example 4

Simplify this equation by removing the variable term from one side of the equation. Then solve the equation.

$$5x - 17 = 2x - 5$$

Teacher Tip

Some may benefit from listing the **steps for simplifying equations.** The sequence of simplifying steps generally follows this order:

1. Clear parentheses, if any.
2. Collect like terms on each side.
3. Remove the variable terms from one side, if variable terms appear on both sides.
4. Remove the constant term from the variable side by adding or subtracting.
5. Make the coefficient of the variable 1 by multiplying or dividing.

Solution

We see an x-term on both sides of the equal sign. We may remove the x-term from either side. We choose to remove the variable term from the right side. We do this by subtracting $2x$ from both sides of the equation.

$5x - 17 = 2x - 5$	equation
$5x - 17 - 2x = 2x - 5 - 2x$	subtracted $2x$ from both sides
$3x - 17 = -5$	simplified

Now we solve the simplified equation.

$3x - 17 = -5$	equation
$3x - 17 + 17 = -5 + 17$	added 17 to both sides
$3x = 12$	simplified
$\frac{3x}{3} = \frac{12}{3}$	divided both sides by 3
$x = \mathbf{4}$	simplified

Example 5

Solve: $3x + 2(x - 4) = 32$

Solution

We first apply the Distributive Property to clear parentheses.

$3x + 2(x - 4) = 32$	equation
$3x + 2x - 8 = 32$	Distributive Property
$5x - 8 = 32$	added $3x$ and $2x$
$5x = 40$	added 8 to both sides
$x = \mathbf{8}$	multiplied both sides by $\frac{1}{5}$

Practice Set

Refer to this figure to answer problems **a–d.**

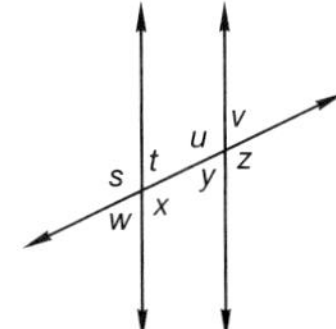

a. Name four pairs of corresponding angles.
$\angle s$ and $\angle u$, $\angle t$ and $\angle v$, $\angle w$ and $\angle y$, $\angle x$ and $\angle z$

b. Name two pairs of alternate interior angles. $\angle t$ and $\angle y$, $\angle x$ and $\angle u$

c. Name two pairs of alternate exterior angles. $\angle s$ and $\angle z$, $\angle w$ and $\angle v$

▶ **d.** Conclude If the measure of $\angle w$ is 80°, what is the measure of each of the other angles? $m\angle t = m\angle v = m\angle y = 80°$; $m\angle s = m\angle u = m\angle x = m\angle z = 100°$

▶ See Math Conversations in the sidebar.

2 New Concepts (Continued)

Example 4

Instruction

"Why do you think we chose to remove the variable from the right side rather than the left side?" to make solving for x easier by keeping the terms positive

Ask a volunteer to remove the variable term from the left side and solve.

$$5x - 17 = 2x - 5$$
$$5x - 17 - 5x = 2x - 5 - 5x$$
$$-17 = -3x - 5$$
$$-17 + 5 = -3x - 5 + 5$$
$$-12 = -3x$$
$$\frac{-12}{-3} = \frac{-3x}{-3}$$
$$4 = x$$

Example 5

Instruction

Encourage students to check their solutions.

"How can we check that our answer is correct?" Replace the variable in the original equation with the solution.

Practice Set

Problem d Conclude

Have students explain how they determined the angle measures. Angle w measures 80° and is acute, so each acute angle measures 80°. Each obtuse angle is a supplement of an acute angle, so each obtuse angle measures 100° since 180° − 80° = 100°.

(continued)

2 New Concepts (Continued)

Practice Set (continued)

Problem i (Error Alert)

Some students may have difficulty using the Distributive Property to simplify $-2(x - 4)$. Work through these steps with the student.

$$3x - 2(x - 4) = 32$$
$$3x - 2x + 8 = 32$$
$$x + 8 = 32$$
$$x = 24$$

3 Written Practice

Math Conversations

Discussion opportunities are provided below.

Problem 2 Formulate

Write this sentence on the board.

Three times a number minus twelve is 36.

"Is this a better way to say the same mathematical sentence? Why or why not?" no; the sentence is ambiguous. It can be translated $3(n - 12) = 36$.

Problem 3b

Extend the Problem

Challenge students to write a formula for determining the sum of the angle measures of any regular polygon. Accept any formula that works for every regular polygon. Some students may start with $n - 2$ as the formula for determining the number of triangles in a polygon; $S = (n - 2) \times 180$ is a formula that will give the sum of the angle measures.

Problem 9 Justify

Ask a volunteer to work the solution at the board and explain why the answer is correct.

Errors and Misconceptions

Problem 2

If students have written +3 in their equations, explain that "the product of what number and three" is a phrase that designates two factors. The word *and* does not imply addition in this situation.

(continued)

Solve the following equations. Show and justify each step.

e. $3w - 10 + w = 90$ 25

f. $x + x + 10 + 2x - 10 = 180$ 45

g. $3y + 5 = y - 25$ −15

h. $4n - 5 = 2n + 3$ 4

▶ **i.** $3x - 2(x - 4) = 32$ 24

j. $3x = 2(x - 4)$ −8

Written Practice — *Strengthening Concepts*

* **1.** (36, Inv. 8) Jorge is playing a board game and hopes to roll a sum of 5. He tosses a pair of number cubes.

a. What is the probability that the sum of the numbers tossed will be 5? $\frac{4}{36} = \frac{1}{9}$

b. What are the odds that the sum of the numbers tossed will not be 5? 8 to 1

▶ * **2.** (101) Formulate Write an equation to solve this problem:

Twelve less than the product of what number and three is 36?

$3x - 12 = 36$; 16

* **3.** (89) The figure shows three sides of a regular decagon.

a. What is the measure of each exterior angle? 36°

▶ **b.** What is the measure of each interior angle? 144°

Use ratio boxes to solve problems **4–7.**

4. (66) The ratio of youths to adults in the stadium was 3 to 7. If 4500 people were in the stadium, how many adults were present? 3150 adults

5. (72) Every time the knight moved over 2, he moved up 1. If the knight moved over 8, how far did he move up? 4

6. (81) Eighty percent of those who were invited came to the party. If 40 people were invited to the party, how many did not come? 8 people

7. (81) The dress was on sale for 60 percent of the regular price. If the sale price was $24, what was the regular price? $40

* **8.** (101) Formulate Write an equation to solve this problem:

Three more than twice a number is −13.

$2n + 3 = -13$; −8

▶ * **9.** (101) Justify The obtuse and acute angles in the figure at the right are supplementary. Find the measure of each angle. Show your work.

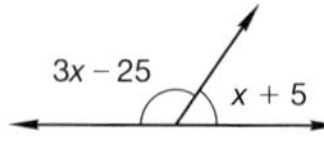

9. obtuse angle = 125°, acute angle = 55°; The sum of supplementary angles is 180°. Set the two angles equal to 180° and solve for *x*. Then use the value of *x* to find the value of each expression.

$(3x - 25) + (x + 5) = 180$
$4x - 20 = 180$
$x = 50$

obtuse:
$3(50) - 25 = 125$
acute:
$50 + 5 = 55$

▶ See Math Conversations in the sidebar.

10. (71) Read this statement. Then answer the questions that follow.

Exit polls showed that 7 out of 10 voters cast their ballots for the incumbent. The incumbent received 1400 votes.

a. How many people were surveyed? 2000 people

b. What percent of people did not vote for the incumbent? 30%

▶* **11.** (91) **Evaluate** $x + xy - xy$ if $x = 3$ and $y = -2$ 3

12. (99) **Verify** Is this triangle a right triangle? Explain how you know. No, the triangle is not a right triangle because the sum of the squares of the two shorter sides does not equal the square of the longest side.

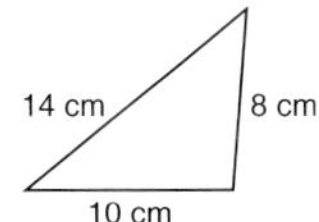

13. (32) If the perimeter of a square is 1 meter, what is the area of the square in square centimeters? 625 cm^2

14. (46) Find the total price, including tax, of a $12.95 bat, a $7.85 baseball, and a $49.50 glove. The tax rate is 7 percent. $75.22

15. (83) Multiply. Write the product in scientific notation. 1.05×10^{12}

$$(3.5 \times 10^5)(3 \times 10^6)$$

▶* **16.** (102) **Conclude** Lines l and m are parallel and are intersected by transversal q.

a. Which angle corresponds to $\angle c$? $\angle g$

b. Which angle is the alternate interior angle of $\angle e$? $\angle d$

c. Which angle is the alternate exterior angle of $\angle h$? $\angle a$

d. If $m\angle a$ is 110°, what is $m\angle f$? 70°

17. (60, 92) **a.** What number is 125% of 84? 105

b. What number is 25% more than 84? 105

▶ **18.** (Inv. 8) If the chance of rain is 40%, what are the odds that it will not rain? 3 to 2

19. (70) What is the volume of this rectangular prism? Dimensions are in feet. 72 ft^3

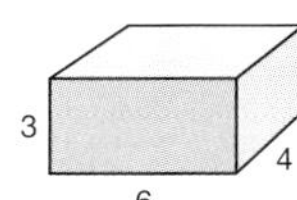

20. (65, 82) Find both measures of the circle at right. (Use $\frac{22}{7}$ for π.)

a. circumference 44 m

b. area 154 m^2

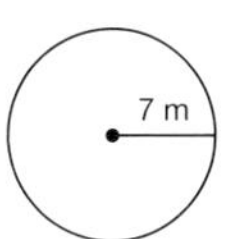

▶ See Math Conversations in the sidebar.

3 Written Practice (Continued)

Math Conversations

Discussion opportunities are provided below.

Problem 11 Evaluate

"One student said that the value of x will always be the value of this expression for any values of x and y. Is the student correct? Explain." Yes; when xy is subtracted from xy, only x remains, therefore, the value of x will always be the value of the expression.

Problem 16

"If the transversal was perpendicular to these parallel lines, what would the angle measures be?" all angles would be 90°

Problem 18

Extend the Problem

Draw this diagram on the board. Ask students if they think it represents both a 40% chance of rain and the 3 to 2 odds of no rain.

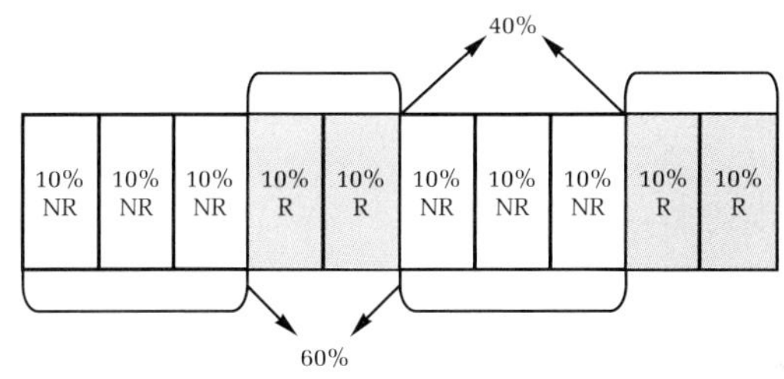

(continued)

Lesson 102 715

3 Written Practice (Continued)

Math Conversations

Discussion opportunities are provided below.

Problem 24 Model

Have students include these numbers on their number lines.

$\sqrt{1}$	$\sqrt{2}$	$\sqrt{3}$
at 1	about 1.4	about 1.7

Problems 25 and 26 Generalize

Ask volunteers to work at the board and explain each step of the solutions.

Errors and Misconceptions

Problem 22

If students have difficulty with this problem, point out that segments WZ and XY are intersected by transversal XZ.

"What two angles are equal in measure?"

Angles b and ZXY are equal in measure since they are alternate interior angles.

21.

x	y
−1	−3
0	0
2	6

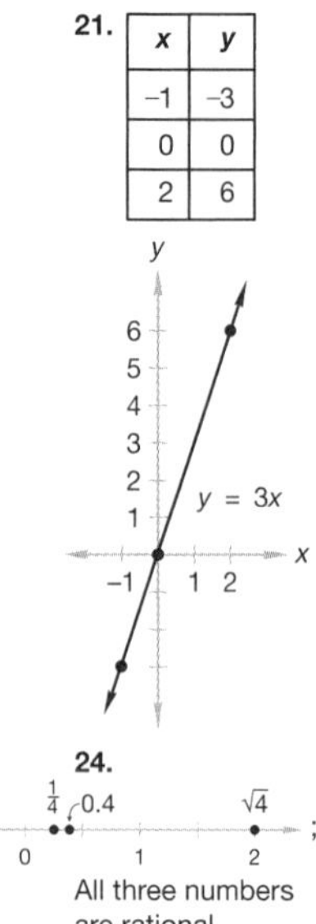

24.

All three numbers are rational.

21. (56, Inv. 9) Create a table using the function rule $y = 3x$. In the table choose −1, 0, and 2 for x and find the value of y. Then graph the function on a coordinate plane.

▸ **22.** (40) Polygon $ZWXY$ is a rectangle. Find the measures of the following angles:

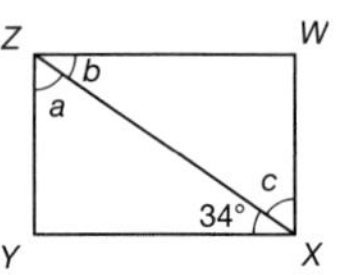

a. $\angle a$ 56° **b.** $\angle b$ 34° **c.** $\angle c$ 56°

23. (78) Graph on a number line: $x \geq -2$

−3 −2 −1 0 1

▸* **24.** (100) Model Draw a number line and show the locations of these numbers. Which are rational?

$$0.4, \frac{1}{4}, \sqrt{4}$$

▸ Generalize Solve:

* **25.** (57, 102) $3x + x + 3^0 = 49$ 12

* **26.** (102) $3y + 2 = y + 32$ 15

* **27.** (102) $x + 2(x + 3) = 36$ 10

Simplify:

28. (84, 87) **a.** $(3x^2y)(-2x)(xy^2)$ $-6x^4y^3$

b. $-3x + 2y - x - y$ $-4x + y$

c. $(-2xy^2)^2$ $4x^2y^4$

29. (43) $\left(4\frac{1}{2}\right)(0.2)(10^2)$ 90

30. (85) $\frac{(-4)(+3)}{(-2)} - (-1)$ 7

Early Finishers
Choose A Strategy

The figure below is made up of a regular octagon and eight isosceles triangles. The height of each triangle is equal to the distance from the center of the octagon to the midpoint of the base of the triangle. Explain how you can determine the fractional part of the entire figure that one triangle represents.

Sample: Since the height of each triangle is equal to the distance from the center of its base to the center of the octagon, you could fold the triangles over to cover the octagon. Since the area of the octagon is equal to the area of the 8 triangles, the area of the octagon is $\frac{1}{2}$ the area of the figure and the area of the 8 triangles is $\frac{1}{2}$ the area of the figure. $\frac{1}{2} \div 8 = \frac{1}{16}$, so one triangle is $\frac{1}{16}$ the area of the entire figure.

▸ See Math Conversations in the sidebar.

Looking Forward

Simplifying and then solving an equation prepares students for:

- **Lesson 109,** solving equations with exponents.

• Powers of Negative Numbers
• Dividing Terms
• Square Roots of Monomials

Objectives

- Determine whether the sign of the product of three or more factors is positive or negative.
- Raise a negative number to a power.
- Divide terms by removing pairs of factors that equal 1.
- Use two methods to find the square root of a monomial.

Lesson Preparation

Materials

- **Power Up U** (in *Instructional Masters*)
- **Investigation Activity 13** (in *Instructional Masters*) or **graph paper**
- **Manipulative kit: protractors, inch rulers**

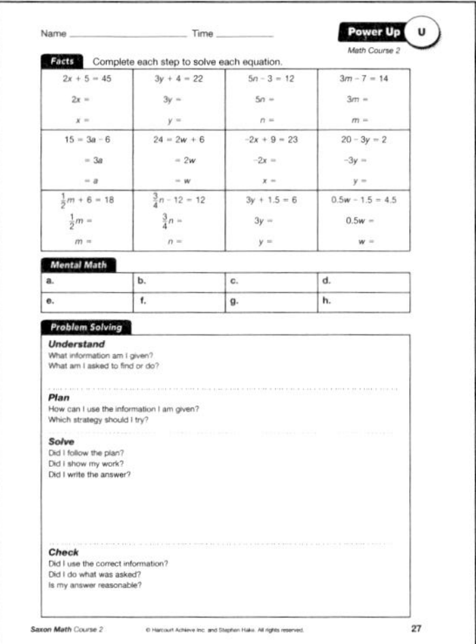
Power Up U

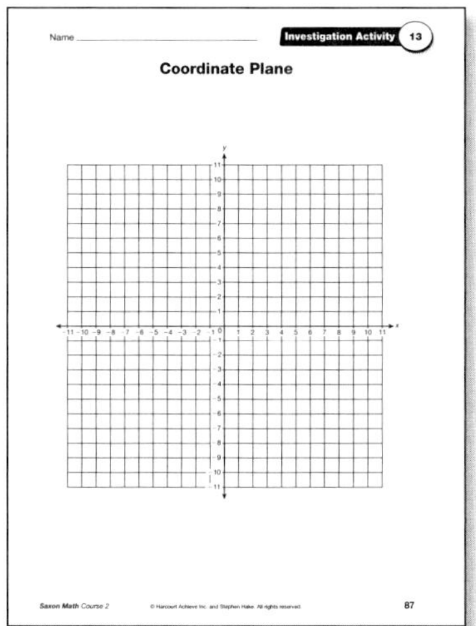
Investigation Activity 13

Technology Resources

Student eBook Complete student textbook in electronic format.

Resources and Planner CD Blackline masters, plus a pacing calendar with standards.

Test and Practice Generator CD Create additional practice sheets and custom-made tests.

www.SaxonPublishers.com Visit for more student activities and planning materials.

Inclusion

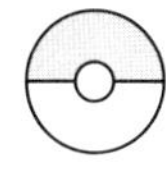
Adaptations CD Adapted lessons, investigations, practice and assessments.

Meeting Standards

National Council of Teachers of Mathematics (NCTM)

Numbers and Operations

NO.2a Understand the meaning and effects of arithmetic operations with fractions, decimals, and integers

NO.2c Understand and use the inverse relationships of addition and subtraction, multiplication and division, and squaring and finding square roots to simplify computations and solve problems

NO.3b Develop and analyze algorithms for computing with fractions, decimals, and integers and develop fluency in their use

Algebra

AL.2d Recognize and generate equivalent forms for simple algebraic expressions and solve linear equations

Power-Up Discussion *For use with Power Up, p. 717*

Problem-Solving Strategy: Use Logical Reasoning

Sheena's younger sister quickly calculated several products on a piece of scrap paper. In her hurry, she misplaced the product of 0.203 and 4.16. She determined from her notes that the product was 0.84448, 8.21218, 0.88444, or 0.04848. Without calculating, Sheena told her sister the correct answer. What is the correct answer, and how did Sheena know?

Understand ***Understand the problem.***

"What information are we given?"

We are told that Sheena's sister has misplaced the product of 0.203 and 4.16.

"What are we asked to do?"

We are asked to explain how Sheena was able to pick the correct product from a list without calculating.

Plan ***Make a plan.***

"What problem-solving strategy will we use?"

We will *use logical reasoning* to eliminate the listed products one-by-one until we figure out how Sheena was able to pinpiont the correct product.

Solve ***Carry out the plan.***

"We may first estimate the product to eliminate any that are too big or too small. Approximately what is the product of Sheena's sister's two factors?"

$0.2 \times 4 = 0.8$

"What products on the list can we eliminate?"

We can eliminate 8.21218 and 0.04848.

"What do we notice about the two remaining products?"

0.84448 and 0.88444: One product ends with an 8 and the other product ends with a 4.

"What digit would be at the end of the product of 0.203 and 4.16?"

The product of the end numbers, 3 and 6 = 18, so 8 should be at the end of the product of 0.203 and 4.16.

"Which is the correct product?"

0.84448

"How did Sheena know?"

She knew the approximate value of the product (0.8) and the digit that the product should end with (8), so she was able to quickly identify it on the list.

Check ***Look back.***

"Did we do what we were asked to do?"

Yes, we determined how Sheena was able to pick the product from a list without calculating.

LESSON

103

- **Powers of Negative Numbers**
- **Dividing Terms**
- **Square Roots of Monomials**

Power Up

Building Power

facts Power Up U

mental math

a. **Positive/Negative:** $(-2.5) \div (-5)$ 0.5

b. **Order of Operations/Exponents:** $(3 \times 10^{-4})(4 \times 10^{-3})$ 1.2×10^{-6}

c. **Algebra:** $2y + y = 45$ 15

d. **Measurement:** Convert $-30°$C to degrees Fahrenheit. $-22°$F

e. **Percent:** $33\frac{1}{3}\%$ of \$600 \$200

f. **Percent:** $33\frac{1}{3}\%$ less than \$600 \$400

g. **Geometry:** If you are buying sod for your yard, what will you need to find to determine how much sod you need to cover your yard? the area of the yard

h. **Scientific Notation:** The expression $(3 \times 10^3)^2$ means $(3 \times 10^3)(3 \times 10^3)$. Write the product in scientific notation. 9×10^6

problem solving

Sheena's younger sister quickly calculated several products on a piece of scrap paper. In her hurry, she misplaced the product of 0.203 and 4.16. She determined from her notes that the product was 0.84448, 8.21218, 0.88444, or 0.04848. Without calculating, Sheena told her sister the correct answer. What is the correct answer, and how did Sheena know? 0.84448; See script for explanation.

New Concepts

Increasing Knowledge

powers of negative numbers

One way to multiply three or more signed numbers is to multiply the factors in order from left to right, keeping track of the signs with each step, as we show here:

$(-3)(-4)(+5)(-2)(+3)$	problem
$(+12)(+5)(-2)(+3)$	multiplied $(-3)(-4)$
$(+60)(-2)(+3)$	multiplied $(+12)(+5)$
$(-120)(+3)$	multiplied $(+60)(-2)$
-360	multiplied $(-120)(+3)$

Another way to keep track of signs when multiplying signed numbers is to count the number of negative factors. Notice the pattern in the multiplications on the following page.

Facts Complete each step to solve each equation.

$2x + 5 = 45$ $2x = 40$ $x = 20$	$3y + 4 = 22$ $3y = 18$ $y = 6$	$5n - 3 = 12$ $5n = 15$ $n = 3$	$3m - 7 = 14$ $3m = 21$ $m = 7$
$15 = 3a - 6$ $21 = 3a$ $7 = a$	$24 = 2w + 6$ $18 = 2w$ $9 = w$	$-2x + 9 = 23$ $-2x = 14$ $x = -7$	$20 - 3y = 2$ $-3y = -18$ $y = 6$
$\frac{1}{2}m + 6 = 18$ $\frac{1}{2}m = 12$ $m = 24$	$\frac{3}{4}n - 12 = 12$ $\frac{3}{4}n = 24$ $n = 32$	$3y + 1.5 = 6$ $3y = 4.5$ $y = 1.5$	$0.5w - 1.5 = 4.5$ $0.5w = 6$ $w = 12$

1 Power Up

Facts

Distribute **Power Up U** to students. See answers below.

Mental Math

Encourage students to share different ways to mentally compute these exercises. Strategies for exercises **d** and **e** are listed below.

d. Use an Equivalent Measure

Every 10°C is 18°F.

When C is 0, F is 32.

$-30°$C is the same as $(3 \times (-18) + 32)$F

$-54 + 32 = -54 + 30 + 2 = -22$

$-30°\text{C} = -22°\text{F}$

Use the Formula

$F = \frac{9}{5}C + 32$

$F = \frac{9}{5} \times (-30) + 32$

$F = 9 \times (-6) + 32$

$F = -54 + 32 = -54 + 30 + 2 = -22$

$-30°\text{C} = -22°\text{F}$

e. Triple, Divide by 3

$33\frac{1}{3}\%$ of \$600 =

100% of \$200 = \$200

Use a Fraction

$33\frac{1}{3}\% = \frac{1}{3}$

$\frac{1}{3} \times \$600 = \$200$

Problem Solving

Refer to **Power-Up Discussion,** p. 717B.

2 New Concepts

Instruction

Discuss with students what they recall about multiplying positive and negative numbers. Be sure that these points are covered:

- The product of two positive integers is positive.
- The product of two negative integers is positive.
- The product of a positive integer and a negative integer is negative.

(continued)

2 New Concepts *(Continued)*

Instruction

Once you have discussed these two methods, apply the second method to the first problem. First write $(-3)(-4)(+5)(-2)(+3)$ on the board or overhead. Ask:

> ***"Without doing all the multiplication, how can you determine whether the answer will be positive or negative?"*** There is an odd number of negative factors, so the answer will be negative.

As you discuss the *thinking skill*, point out the importance of reading the entire problem before solving. Finding a factor of 0 before multiplying will save time on homework and tests.

Example 1

Instruction

Ask a volunteer to name a set of three factors that has a positive product, using both positive and negative signs. Ask another volunteer to name a set of three factors that has a negative product. Call on enough volunteers to be sure that the class understands this concept.

Instruction

Ask a student to identify which number is the exponent and which is the base in $(-3)^4$. The exponent is 4; the base is -3. Without the parentheses the base would be 3, not -3.

Example 2

Instruction

Point out that when a negative integer is raised to a power, the product will be negative if the power is an odd number, and will be positive if the power is an even number.

Instruction

To introduce dividing terms, ask students how they would simplify the fraction $\frac{420}{36}$. Students should recall how to write the prime factorizations of the numerator and denominator and use canceling to reduce.

(continued)

$-1 = -1$	odd
$(-1)(-1) = +1$	even
$(-1)(-1)(-1) = -1$	odd
$(-1)(-1)(-1)(-1) = +1$	even
$(-1)(-1)(-1)(-1)(-1) = -1$	odd

If the number of negative factors is even, the product is positive. If the number of negative factors is odd, the product is negative.

Thinking Skill
Explain
Tell how to find the following product without multiplying: (–2)(4)(–5)(0)(5). The product is 0 because one of the multiplied factors is 0. The product of 0 and any other factor is 0.

Note: If any of the multiplied factors are zero, their product is also zero (which has no sign).

Example 1

Find the product: $(+3)(+4)(-5)(-2)(-3)$

Solution

There are three negative factors (an odd number), so the product will be a negative number. We multiply and get

$$(+3)(+4)(-5)(-2)(-3) = \mathbf{-360}$$

We did not need to count the number of positive factors, because positive factors do not change the sign of a product.

We remember that an exponent can indicate how many times the base is used as a factor.

$$(-3)^4 \text{ means } (-3)(-3)(-3)(-3)$$

Example 2

Simplify:

a. $(-2)^4$ **b.** $(-2)^5$

Solution

a. The expression $(-2)^4$ means $(-2)(-2)(-2)(-2)$. There is an even number of negative factors, so the product is a positive number. Since 2^4 is 16, we find that $(-2)^4$ is **+16.**

b. The expression $(-2)^5$ means $(-2)(-2)(-2)(-2)(-2)$. This time there is an odd number of negative factors, so the product is a negative number. Since $2^5 = 32$, we find that $(-2)^5 =$ **–32.**

dividing terms

We divide terms by removing pairs of factors that equal 1.

$$\frac{4a^3b^2}{ab} = \frac{2\cdot 2\cdot \overset{1}{\cancel{a}}\cdot a\cdot a\cdot \overset{1}{\cancel{b}}\cdot b}{\underset{1}{\cancel{a}}\cdot \underset{1}{\cancel{b}}}$$
$$= 4a^2b$$

718 *Saxon Math Course 2*

Example 3

Simplify: $\frac{12x^3yz^2}{3x^2y}$

Solution

We factor the two terms and remove pairs of factors that equal 1. Then we regroup the remaining factors.

$$\frac{12x^3yz^2}{3x^2y} = \frac{2 \cdot 2 \cdot \overset{1}{\cancel{3}} \cdot \overset{1}{\cancel{x}} \cdot \overset{1}{\cancel{x}} \cdot x \cdot \overset{1}{\cancel{y}} \cdot z \cdot z}{\underset{1}{\cancel{3}} \cdot \underset{1}{\cancel{x}} \cdot \underset{1}{\cancel{x}} \cdot \underset{1}{\cancel{y}}}$$

$$= \mathbf{4xz^2}$$

Summarize In $4xz^2$, what exponent do you understand x to have? When a number has no exponent, the exponent is understood to be 1.

Example 4

Simplify: $\frac{10a^3bc^2}{8ab^2c}$

Solution

We factor the terms and remove common factors. Then we regroup the remaining factors.

$$\frac{10a^3bc^2}{8ab^2c} = \frac{\overset{1}{\cancel{2}} \cdot 5 \cdot \overset{1}{\cancel{a}} \cdot a \cdot a \cdot \overset{1}{\cancel{b}} \cdot \overset{1}{\cancel{c}} \cdot c}{\underset{1}{\cancel{2}} \cdot 2 \cdot 2 \cdot \underset{1}{\cancel{a}} \cdot \underset{1}{\cancel{b}} \cdot b \cdot \underset{1}{\cancel{c}}}$$

$$= \mathbf{\frac{5a^2c}{4b}}$$

square roots of monomials

A monomial is a perfect square if its prime factorization can be separated into two identical groups of factors.

$$25x^2 = 5 \cdot 5 \cdot x \cdot x$$
$$= 5x \cdot 5x$$

Since the factors of $25x^2$ can be separated into $5x \cdot 5x$, we know that $25x^2$ is a perfect square and that $5x$ is a square root of $25x^2$.

Example 5

Which monomial is a perfect square?

A $8x^2y^4$ **B** $4x^2y$ **C** $36x^2y^4$

Solution

A monomial is a perfect square if the coefficient is a perfect square (like 4 or 36) and if the exponents of the variables are all even (like x^2y^4). Thus $8x^2y^4$ is not a perfect square because 8 is not a perfect square, and $4x^2y$ is not a perfect square because the exponent of $y(1)$ is odd. The perfect square is choice **C** $\mathbf{36x^2y^4}$.

2 New Concepts *(Continued)*

Example 3

Instruction

Caution students that they need to check that both the numerator and the denominator are one-term expressions (monomials) before they cancel the same factor from both the numerator and the denominator.

Example 4

Instruction

Have students compare the answers to examples 3 and 4. Ask why the solution to example 4 still contains a division bar. The denominator in example 4 contains factors that can't be cancelled by factors in the numerator.

Explain that this is an acceptable form for the answer because it has been simplified as much as possible.

Instruction

To introduce square roots of monomials, have students recall how to find the square roots of perfect squares and of numbers expressed as exponents.

Example 5

Instruction

Ask volunteers to give examples of monomials that are perfect squares and those that are not. For those that aren't, have other students explain why not.

(continued)

Teacher Tip

This lesson focuses on **new applications of skills** students have learned throughout the year. To divide monomials, they will use prime factorization and cancellation, as they did when simplifying fractions. To find the square roots of perfect square monomials, they will look for the perfect squares and work with powers of variables.

The ability to decompose expressions is needed for future work in algebra. Spend plenty of time demonstrating how to rewrite expressions with variables and exponents so that the factors are clear.

2 New Concepts (Continued)

Example 6

Instruction

As you demonstrate both methods, explain why we can find the square root of the variable terms in method 2 by taking half of their exponents.

Have students describe what they see as advantages and disadvantages of both methods of finding the square root of a perfect square monomial. Tell them that they may use whichever method they like.

Practice Set

Problems a–i Generalize

Discuss how students simplified these expressions. Ask what they did first, and whether they saw anything they could do to make their work simpler. Sample: For problem **b,** I noticed that the digits were the same as in problem **a.** The only difference was the sign of the product.

Problems g–i Error Alert

Some students may find it helpful to write the exponent 1 with those variables in which the exponent is not written but is understood.

Problems j–m Classify

Have several volunteers explain how they decide whether a monomial is a perfect square. Encourage questions from other students to help clarify this concept. Sample: First I look at the number part. If it is not a perfect square, I can stop because the monomial can't be a perfect square if the number is not. If it is, then I look at all the exponents. If one of them is odd or if a variable has no exponent, then the monomial can't be a perfect square. But if both parts check out, the monomial is a perfect square.

Example 6

Simplify: $\sqrt{36x^2y^4}$

Solution

We show two methods.

Method 1: Separate the factors of $36x^2y^4$ into two identical groups.

$$36x^2y^4 = 2 \cdot 2 \cdot 3 \cdot 3 \cdot x \cdot x \cdot y \cdot y \cdot y \cdot y$$
$$= (2 \cdot 3 \cdot x \cdot y \cdot y)(2 \cdot 3 \cdot x \cdot y \cdot y)$$
$$= (6xy^2)(6xy^2)$$

We see that a square root of $36x^2y^4$ is $\mathbf{6xy^2}$.

Method 2: Find the square root of 36 and half of each exponent.

$$\sqrt{36x^2y^4} = \mathbf{6xy^2}$$

Practice Set ▶ Generalize Simplify:

a. $(-5)(-4)(-3)(-2)(-1)$ -120

b. $(+5)(-4)(+3)(-2)(+1)$ 120

c. $(-2)^3$ -8

d. $(-3)^4$ 81

e. $(-9)^2$ 81

f. $(-1)^5$ -1

g. $\frac{6a^2b^3c}{3ab}$ $2ab^2c$

h. $\frac{8xy^3z^2}{6x^2y}$ $\frac{4y^2z^2}{3x}$

i. $\frac{15mn^2p}{25m^2n^2}$ $\frac{3p}{5m}$

▶ Classify For **j–m** state whether the monomial is a perfect square. If it is a perfect square, find a square root of the monomial.

j. $12x^2y^4$ not a perfect square

k. $49a^2b^6c^4$ perfect square; $7ab^3c^2$

l. x^6y^2 perfect square; x^3y

m. $16a^2b^3$ not a perfect square

Written Practice *Strengthening Concepts*

1. (Inv. 4) The table below shows a tally of the scores earned by students on a class test. Find the **a** mode and **b** median of the 29 scores. a 85 b 90

Class Test Scores

Score	Number of Students
100	|||
95	𝍸 |
90	𝍸 |
85	𝍸 ||||
80	||||
70	|

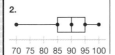

2. (Inv. 4) Draw a box-and-whisker plot for the data presented in problem **1.**

2.

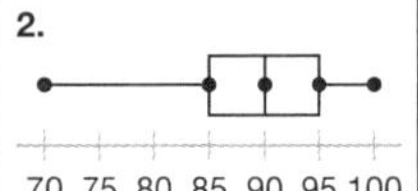

▶ See Math Conversations in the sidebar.

3. (46) The dinner bill totaled $25. Mike left a 15% tip. How much money did Mike leave for a tip? $3.75

4. (46) The plane completed the flight in $2\frac{1}{2}$ hours. If the flight covered 1280 kilometers, what was the plane's average speed in kilometers per hour? 512 kilometers per hour

Use ratio boxes to solve problems **5–9.**

5. (72) Jeremy earned $33 for 4 hours of work. How much would he earn for 7 hours of work at the same rate? $57.75

6. (54) If 40 percent of the lights were on, what was the ratio of lights on to lights off ? $\frac{2}{3}$

7. (92) Lesley saved $25 buying a coat at a sale that offered 20 percent off. What was the regular price of the coat? $125

8. (92) A shopkeeper bought the item for $30 and sold it for 60 percent more. How much profit did the shopkeeper make on the item? $18

*** 9.** (50, 98) **a.** The $\frac{1}{20}$ scale model of the rocket stood 54 inches high. What was the height of the actual rocket? 1080 inches

b. Find the height of the actual rocket in feet. 90 feet

▶*** 10.** (98) Analyze The volume of the rocket in problem 9 is how many times the volume of the model? $20^3 = 8000$ times

▶ **11.** (60) A mile is about eight fifths kilometers. Eight fifths kilometers is how many meters? 1600 meters

▶*** 12.** (99) Analyze Use the Pythagorean theorem to find the length of the longest side of a right triangle whose vertices are (3, 1), (3, −2), and (−1, −2). 5 units

▶ **13.** (Inv. 8) Alina has made 35 out of 50 free throws. What is the statistical chance that Alina will make her next free throw? 70%

14. (17) What percent of 25 is 20? 80%

▶*** 15.** (Inv. 10) **a.** Generalize The shaded sector is what fraction of the whole circle? $\frac{1}{3}$

b. The unshaded sector is what percent of the circle? $66\frac{2}{3}\%$

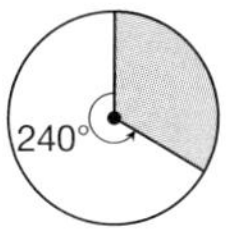

16. (56, Inv. 9) Find the missing numbers in the table by using the function rule. Then graph the function on a coordinate plane. Are *x* and *y* directly proportional? Explain your answer. Yes, *x* and *y* are directly proportional because the graph is a line and (0, 0) is included.

$y = -x$

x	y
2	−2
0	0
−1	1

16.

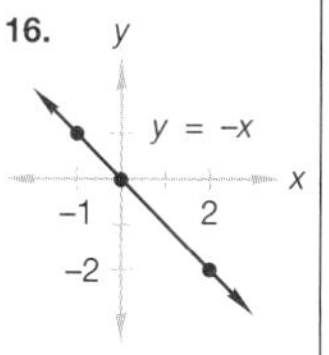

▶ See Math Conversations in the sidebar.

3 Written Practice

Math Conversations

Discussion opportunities are provided below.

Problem 10 Analyze

"What information in problem 9 helps you solve this problem?" the scale

"Why don't you need the dimensions of the rocket and the model to solve this problem?" Sample: The question asks how many times greater the volume of the real rocket is than the model. The scale tells how much the dimensions have been reduced, so you can use the scale to find the change in volume.

Problem 12 Analyze

"What are the perimeter and area of this triangle?" perimeter: 12 units; area: 6 units^2

"Will these be the perimeter and area of all 3-4-5 right triangles?" yes

"What are the perimeter and area of a 6-8-10 right triangle?" perimeter: 24 units; area: 24 units^2

"What happened to the perimeter when the lengths doubled?" It doubled.

"What happened to the area when the lengths doubled?" It quadrupled.

Problem 15 Generalize

Ask what happens to both sectors if the shading is removed from half of the shaded part. Sample: The shaded part loses 60° and the unshaded part gains 60°. The shaded part is 50% less than what it was; the unshaded part is 25% greater than what it was.

Errors and Misconceptions

Problem 11

For students whose answer is 625 meters, point out that $\frac{8}{5}$ is greater than one because it is an improper fraction. Explain that they should expect the answer to be greater than 1000 meters.

Problem 13

Some students may have answered 50% since there are only two possible outcomes each time a player has a free throw. Point out that Alina's statistical history of making 35 out of 50 free throws indicates that the two outcomes (making or not making the shot) are not equally likely. Help students understand that when statistical information is available, it is used to determine the chance of an event.

(continued)

3 Written Practice (Continued)

Math Conversations

Discussion opportunities are provided below.

Problem 17 Formulate

Discuss why it is important to pay attention to the words used and the order of the words when translating statements into equations. Point out that a careless reader might write the equation for this problem as $3 - 2x = -7$ or as $3 - 2x = x - 7$.

Problem 19 Generalize

Extend the Problem

"What are the lengths of the hypotenuses?" In the larger triangle, 25, and in the smaller, 20.

"Do the sides of both triangles form Pythagorean triplets?" yes

Problem 20 Estimate

Ask students to describe how they estimated the measure of $\angle AOB$. Sample: 55°, because it looks like it is close to a 45° angle, but larger, and it looks like it is almost a 60° angle.

Problem 23a Justify

Have volunteers put their solutions on the board and give the reason for each step they made. Encourage discussion of each procedure. Sample: Volume = Area of base × height—this is the formula; $V = \frac{1}{2}bh \times h$—this is the rewritten formula; $V = \frac{1}{2} \times 6 \times 3 \times 6$—this is the formula with the values; $V = 54$—this is the solution; the volume is 54 ft³—this is the answer.

Errors and Misconceptions

Problem 19

If students estimate that x is 8, they may have thought incorrectly that the difference between the heights is 4 and the difference between the bases is 4. The word *factor* in the term *scale factor* should remind students that similar figures are related by multiplication, not by addition or subtraction. The scale factor is $\frac{12}{16}$, or $\frac{3}{4}$, and $\frac{3}{4}$ of 12 is 9.

(continued)

▶* **17.** (101) **Formulate** Write an equation to solve this problem: $2x - 3 = -7$; -2

Three less than twice what number is -7?

18. (40) Quadrilateral *ABCD* is a rectangle. The measure of $\angle ACB$ is 36°. Find the measures of the following angles:

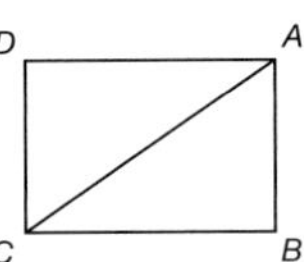

a. $\angle CAB$ 54° **b.** $\angle CAD$ 36° **c.** $\angle ACD$ 54°

▶* **19.** (97, 98) **Generalize** The two triangles below are similar.

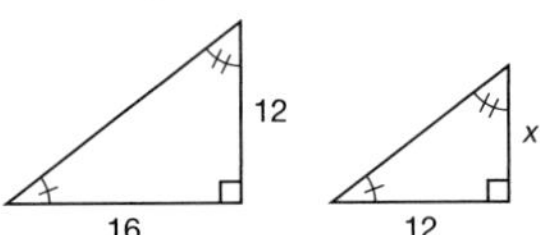

a. Estimate, then calculate, the length x. See student work; 9

b. Find the scale factor from the larger triangle to the smaller triangle. 0.75

▶* **20.** (96) **Estimate** What is the approximate measure of $\angle AOB$. Use a protractor to verify your answer. See student work; 50°

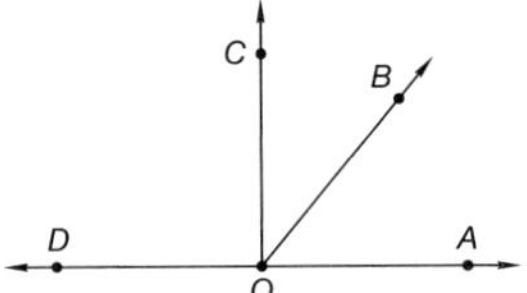

21. (66, 82) Find the **a** circumference and **b** area of a circle with a diameter of 2 feet. (Use 3.14 for π.) **a.** 6.28 ft **b.** 3.14 ft²

* **22.** (100) Which of these numbers is between 12 and 13? C

A $\sqrt{13}$ **B** $\sqrt{130}$ **C** $\sqrt{150}$

* **23.** (88, 95) ▶ **a.** **Justify** Find the volume of this right prism. Units are feet. Show each step of your solution. 54 ft³; See student work.

b. Convert the volume to cubic yards. 2 yd³

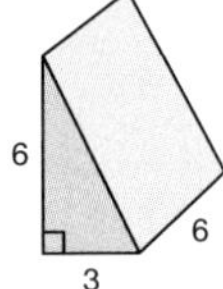

▶ See Math Conversations in the sidebar.

* **24.** Find the volume of this right circular cylinder. (95) (Use 3.14 for π.) 84.78 units^3

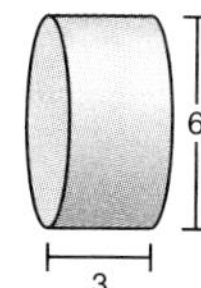

Solve:

▶* **25.** (102) Generalize $3x + x - 5 = 2(x - 2)$ $\frac{1}{2}$

26. (90, 93) $6\frac{2}{3}f - 5 = 5$ $\frac{3}{2}$

Simplify:

27. (26, 57) $10\frac{1}{2} \cdot 1\frac{3}{7} \cdot 5^{-2}$ $\frac{3}{5}$

28. (43) $12.5 - 8\frac{1}{3} + 1\frac{1}{6}$ $5\frac{1}{3}$

▶* **29.** (85, 103) **a.** $\dfrac{(-3)(-2)(-1)}{-|(-3)(+2)|}$ 1

b. $3^2 - (-3)^2$ 0

* **30.** (103) **a.** $\dfrac{6a^3b^2c}{2abc}$ $3a^2b$

b. $\sqrt{9x^2y^4}$ $3xy^2$

Early Finishers
Real-World Application

India is creating a map of her neighborhood as shown below. She draws a right triangle with a base of 8 cm and a height of 6 cm.

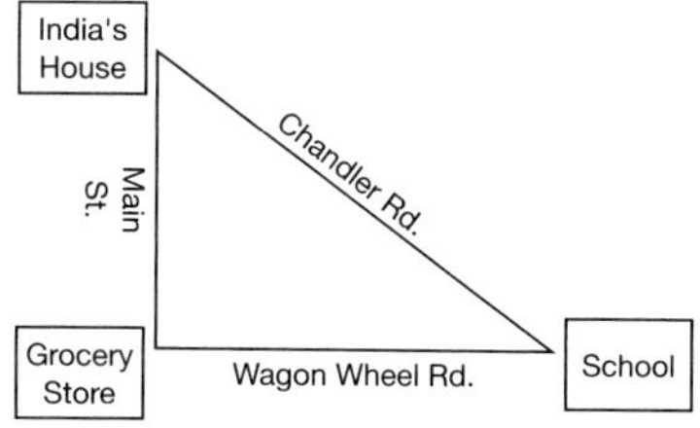

a. Redraw India's triangle on graph paper with a ruler. Measure the length of the hypotenuse. 10 cm

b. Using the Pythagorean Theorem, solve for the length of the hypotenuse ($a^2 + b^2 = c^2$). Did you get the same answer as your measurement? $6^2 + 8^2 = c^2$; $64 + 36 = c^2$; $\sqrt{100} = c$; $10 = c$; yes

c. If India's scale for the map is 1 cm = 0.6 mi., how many miles is it from her house to school using Main St. then Wagon Wheel Rd.? 8.4 miles

▶ See Math Conversations in the sidebar.

3 Written Practice (Continued)

Math Conversations

Discussion opportunities are provided below.

Problem 25 Generalize

Ask students why we solve equations but simplify expressions. Sample: When you solve an equation, you get an answer that is a value that satisfies the equation; when you simplify an expression, you just make it easier to work with.

Errors and Misconceptions

Problem 29a

Watch for students who give the incorrect answer -1. They have probably assumed that since there are two negative signs in the denominator, it has a positive value. Point out that they need to simplify the absolute value first.

Looking Forward

Simplifying algebraic expressions prepares students for:

- **Lesson 106,** transforming literal equations to solve for a specific variable and changing a formula to solve for a specific variable.
- **Lesson 115,** factoring algebraic expressions by dividing by the GCF.

Semicircles, Arcs, and Sectors

Objectives

- Find the lengths of semicircles and the areas they enclose.
- Find the lengths of arcs that are not semicircles.
- Find the areas of sectors that are not semicircles.

Lesson Preparation

Materials

- **Power Up V** (in *Instructional Masters*)
- **Investigation Activity 13** (in *Instructional Masters*) or **graph paper**

Math Language

New	Maintain
major arc	arcs
minor arc	
sectors	
semicircle	

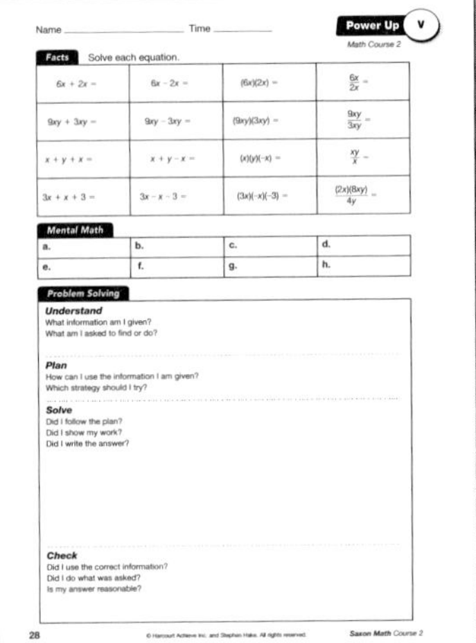

Power Up V

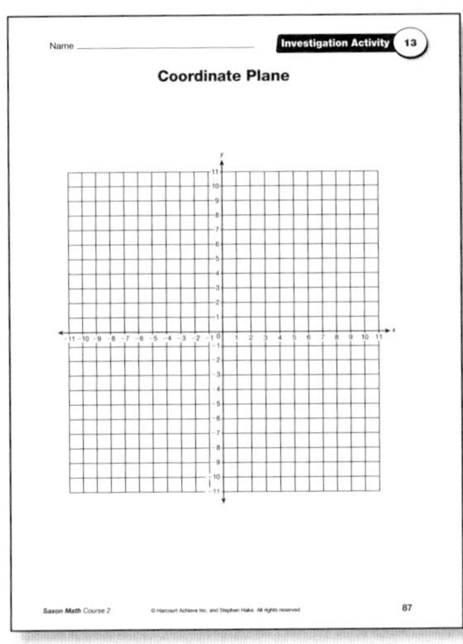

Investigation Activity 13

Technology Resources

Student eBook Complete student textbook in electronic format.

Resources and Planner CD Blackline masters, plus a pacing calendar with standards.

Test and Practice Generator CD Create additional practice sheets and custom-made tests.

www.SaxonPublishers.com Visit for more student activities and planning materials.

Inclusion

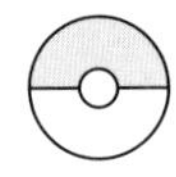

Adaptations CD Adapted lessons, investigations, practice and assessments.

Meeting Standards

National Council of Teachers of Mathematics (NCTM)

Geometry

GM.1a Precisely describe, classify, and understand relationships among types of two- and three-dimensional objects using their defining properties

GM.3a Describe sizes, positions, and orientations of shapes under informal transformations such as flips, turns, slides, and scaling

GM.4e Recognize and apply geometric ideas and relationships in areas outside the mathematics classroom, such as art, science, and everyday life

Measurement

ME.1c Understand, select, and use units of appropriate size and type to measure angles, perimeter, area, surface area, and volume

Power-Up Discussion *For use with Power Up, p. 724*

Problem-Solving Strategy: Use Logical Reasoning/ Make an Organized List

If three standard number cubes are tossed simultaneously, what is the probability that the sum of the three number cubes will be less than or equal to 5?

Understand ***Understand the problem.***

"What information are we given?"

Three number cubes are tossed simultaneously.

"What are we asked to do?"

We are asked to find the probability that the sum of the three number cubes will be five or less.

Plan ***Make a plan.***

"What problem-solving strategy will we use?"

We will *use logical reasoning* to *make an organized list* of the ways to roll five or less. Then we will compare that to the total number of possible outcomes to determine the probability.

Solve ***Carry out the plan.***

"What sums less than or equal to five can we roll with three number cubes?"

3, 4, 5

"How should we structure our list?"

We should write the totals, then write each possible way to achieve that total below:

3	4	5
1, 1, 1	1, 1, 2	1, 1, 3
	1, 2, 1	1, 3, 1
	2, 1, 1	3, 1, 1
		1, 2, 2
		2, 1, 2
		2, 2, 1

"How many different ways are there to roll a number 5 or less?"

10

"How many different possible outcomes are there for tossing three number cubes simultaneously?"

We use the Fundamental Counting Principle to determine that there are $6 \times 6 \times 6$, or 216 possible outcomes.

Teacher Note: You may need to remind students what the Fundamental Counting Principle is and how it can be applied.

"What is the probability of rolling a number 5 or less?"

$\frac{10}{216}$, or $\frac{5}{108}$

Check ***Look back.***

"Did we do what we were asked to do?"

Yes, we determined the probability of rolling a number 5 or less with one toss of three number cubes.

1 Power Up

Facts

Distribute **Power Up V** to students. See answers below.

Mental Math

Encourage students to share different ways to mentally compute these exercises. Strategies for exercises **d** and **f** are listed below.

d. Visualize Area

One square yard has 3 feet on each side

$3 \times 3 = 9 \text{ ft}^2$

Use Reasoning

1 yard has 3 ft

1 square yard has two dimensions

$3 \times 3 = 9 \text{ ft}^2$

f. Move the Decimal Point

$300\% = 3$

$3 \times \$25 = \$75$

Reasoning

$100\% + 200\% = 300\%$

$\$25 + \$50 = \$75$

Problem Solving

Refer to **Power-Up Discussion** p. 724B.

2 New Concepts

Instruction

Be sure students understand that the length of a semicircle referred to here is the distance halfway around a circle on its circumference and does not include the length of the diameter.

semicircle

half a circle

Example 1

Instruction

"How do we know that the diameter is 10 meters?" The radius is 5 meters, so the diameter is twice that, or 10 meters.

"How can we determine the length of the rectangular part of this figure?" The length of the rectangle is equal to the measure of the diameter, 10 meters.

(continued)

LESSON 104

• Semicircles, Arcs, and Sectors

Power Up *Building Power*

facts Power Up V

mental math

a. **Positive/Negative:** $(-0.25) - (-0.75)$ 0.5

b. **Scientific Notation:** $(5 \times 10^5)^2$ 2.5×10^{11}

c. **Algebra:** $80 = 4m - 20$ 25

d. **Measurement:** Convert 1 sq. yd to sq. ft. 9 sq. ft

e. **Percent:** 200% 0f $25 $50

f. **Percent:** 200% more than $25 $75

g. **Geometry:** A yard is shaped like an octagon and each side measures 4 ft. What is the perimeter of the yard? 32 ft

h. **Rate:** At 12 mph, how far can Sherry skate in 45 minutes? 9 miles

problem solving If three standard number cubes are tossed simultaneously, what is the probability that the sum of the three number cubes will be less than or equal to 5? $\frac{5}{108}$

New Concept *Increasing Knowledge*

A **semicircle** is half of a circle. Thus the length of a semicircle is half the circumference of a circle with the same radius. The area enclosed by a semicircle and its diameter is half the area of the full circle.

Example 1

Find the perimeter of this figure. Dimensions are in meters.

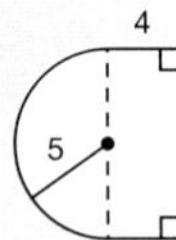

Solution

The length of the semicircle is half the circumference of a circle whose diameter is 10.

$$\text{Length of semicircle} = \frac{\pi d}{2} \approx \frac{(3.14)(10 \text{ m})}{2} \approx 15.7 \text{ m}$$

Facts Solve each equation.

$6x + 2x = 8x$	$6x - 2x = 4x$	$(6x)(2x) = 12x^2$	$\frac{6x}{2x} = 3$
$9xy + 3xy = 12xy$	$9xy - 3xy = 6xy$	$(9xy)(3xy) = 27x^2y^2$	$\frac{9xy}{3xy} = 3$
$x + y + x = 2x + y$	$x + y - x = y$	$(x)(y)(-x) = -x^2y$	$\frac{xy}{x} = y$
$3x + x + 3 = 4x + 3$	$3x - x - 3 = 2x - 3$	$(3x)(-x)(-3) = 9x^2$	$\frac{(2x)(8xy)}{4y} = 4x^2$

Now we can label all the dimensions on the figure and add them to find the perimeter.

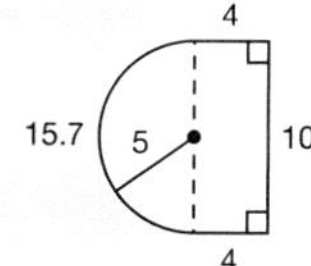

Perimeter ≈ 10 m + 4 m + 15.7 m + 4 m

≈ **33.7 m**

Thinking Skill

Analyze

How do we know that the height of the rectangle is 10 meters? Sample: The height of the rectangle is equal to the diameter of the circle. Since the radius of the circle is 5 meters, the diameter is 10 meters.

Example 2

Find the area of this figure. Dimensions are in meters.

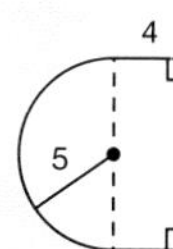

Solution

We divide the figure into two parts. Then we find the area of each part.

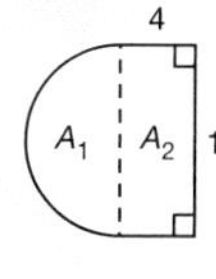

$$A_1 = \frac{\pi r^2}{2} \approx \frac{3.14(25 \text{ m}^2)}{2} \approx 39.25 \text{ m}^2$$

$$A_2 = l \times w = 4 \text{ m} \times 10 \text{ m} = 40 \text{ m}^2$$

The total area of the figure equals $A_1 + A_2$.

$$\text{Total area} = A_1 + A_2 \approx 39.25 \text{ m}^2 + 40 \text{ m}^2 \approx \mathbf{79.25 \text{ m}^2}$$

Math Language

A **sector** is a portion of a circle bound by two radii and an arc.

We can calculate the lengths of **arcs** and the areas of **sectors** by determining the fraction of a circle represented by the arc or sector.

Example 3

Find the area of the shaded sector of this circle.

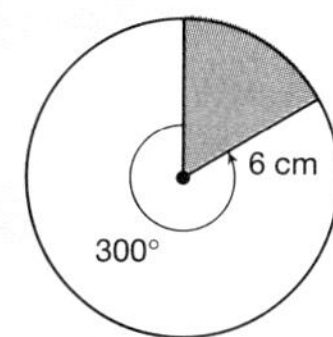

2 New Concepts (Continued)

Example 1 (continued)

Instruction

Students should understand that ≈33.7 m means *about* 33.7 m.

"Why is this answer an approximation?" Any calculation that involves pi is an approximation.

Example 2

Instruction

Make sure students understand the formulas used to find the area of the semicircle and the rectangle.

"Why do we divide the formula for the area of a circle by 2?" to find the area of a semicircle, which is half of a circle

Example 3

Instruction

- Draw a circle on the chalkboard and shade a quarter of it.
- Point out that the shaded portion is a sector of the circle, and that the part of the circumference containing it is an arc.
- Tell them that the central angle of this sector has a measure of 90°, a quarter of the degrees in a circle. Therefore, the area of the sector is $\frac{90}{360}$ or $\frac{1}{4}$ the area of the circle. The area of a 90° sector is $\frac{\pi r^2}{4}$.

Lead students to apply the same reasoning to this example.

(continued)

Math Background

Is a sector of a circle the same as an arc of a circle?

No. An arc is part of the circumference. It has length but no area. A sector is the region that is bordered by an arc and two radii of a circle. A sector occupies area. Both an arc and a sector can be described by the degree measure of the central angle that includes the arc or the sector. The figures show a 60° arc and a 60° sector.

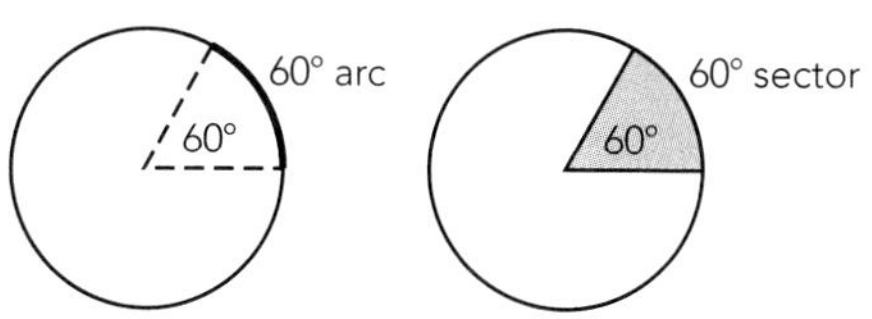

2 New Concepts (Continued)

Example 3 (continued)

Instruction

Once students find the area of a sector, ask them to write a general formula for the area of any sector. $A = \frac{\pi r^2}{n}$, where n is equal to the fractional part of the circle that the sector represents.

Instruction

Make sure students understand that:

- It is the size of an arc in relation to a semicircle that determines whether it is minor or major.
- Minor and major arcs are conventionally named differently—two-letter and three-letter names. However, an arc's name does not determine whether it is minor or major.
- It is not incorrect to name a minor arc with three letters.

Example 4

Instruction

Some students may find it interesting to know that an angle, such as that found by major arc *ADC,* whose measure is greater than 180° but less than 360° is called *a reflex angle*. The two angle measures in this circle have a sum of 70° + 290° = 360°.

(continued)

Solution

The central angle of the shaded sector measures 60° (the full circle, 360°, minus the given angle, 300°). Since 60° is $\frac{1}{6}$ of a circle ($\frac{60}{360} = \frac{1}{6}$), the area of the sector is $\frac{1}{6}$ of the area of the circle.

$$\text{Area of 60° sector} = \frac{\pi r^2}{6}$$

$$\approx \frac{3.14(\overset{1}{\cancel{6}}\text{ cm})(6\text{ cm})}{\underset{1}{\cancel{6}}}$$

$$\approx \mathbf{18.84\ cm^2}$$

As we discussed in Investigation 2, an arc is part of the circumference of a circle. In the following figure we see two arcs between point *A* and point *B*.

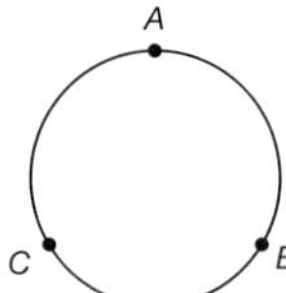

The arc from *A* clockwise to *B* is called a **minor arc** because it is less than a semicircle. We may refer to this arc as arc *AB* (abbreviated $\overset{\frown}{AB}$). The arc from *A* counterclockwise to *B* is called a **major arc** because it is greater than a semicircle. Major arcs are named with three letters. The major arc between point *A* and point *B* may be named arc *ACB*.

Analyze Name all the minor arcs found in the figure above. Then name all the major arcs. minor arcs: $\overset{\frown}{AB}$, $\overset{\frown}{BC}$, and $\overset{\frown}{CA}$; major arcs: $\overset{\frown}{ABC}$, $\overset{\frown}{BCA}$, and $\overset{\frown}{CAB}$.

We can measure an arc in degrees. The number of degrees in an arc equals the measure of the central angle of the arc. If minor arc *AB* in the figure above measures 120°, then the measure of major arc *ACB* is 240° because the sum of the measures of the major arc and minor arc must be 360°.

Example 4

In this figure, central angle *AOC* measures 70°. What is the measure of major arc *ADC*?

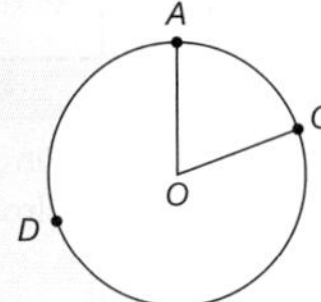

Solution

An arc may be described by the measure of its central angle. The arc in the interior of the 70° angle *AOC* is a 70° arc. However, the larger arc from point *A* counterclockwise through point *D* to point *C* measures 360° minus 70°, which is **290°.**

Teacher Tip

Tying the idea of **arcs and sectors** with something students are familiar with can help them understand both the topic and its uses. Relate clock faces—the sector created by the arc on the clock and the hour and minute hands—and circle graphs to arcs and sectors to give students a better real-world understanding.

Example 5

A minor arc with a radius of 2, centered at the origin, is drawn from the positive *x*-axis to the positive *y*-axis. What is the length of the arc?

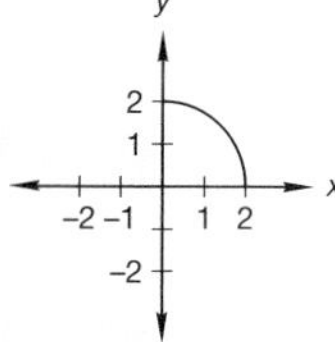

Solution

A minor arc is less than 180°. We see that the arc is $\frac{1}{4}$ of a circle, which is 90°. The length of the arc is $\frac{1}{4}$ of the circumference of a circle with a radius of 2 (and a diameter of 4).

$$\text{Length of } 90° \text{ arc} = \frac{\pi d}{4}$$

$$\approx \frac{3.14(\overset{1}{\cancel{4}} \text{ units})}{\underset{1}{\cancel{4}}}$$

$$\approx \mathbf{3.14 \text{ units}}$$

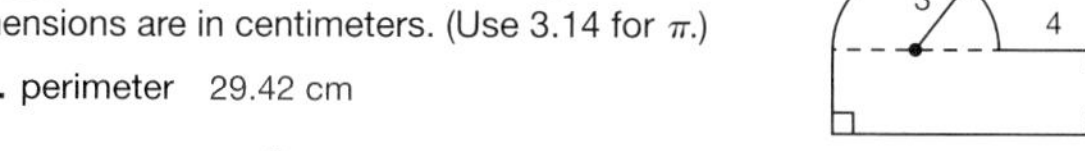

Practice Set

c. Sample: The segment is one eighth of the area of a circle because $\frac{45}{360} = \frac{1}{8}$. To find the area of the sector, find the area of the entire circle and divide it by 8: $A = \frac{\pi r^2}{8} = \frac{\pi 16}{8} = 2\pi \text{ cm}^2$.

Analyze Find each measure of this figure. Dimensions are in centimeters. (Use 3.14 for π.)

▶ **a.** perimeter 29.42 cm

▶ **b.** area 44.13 cm^2

▶ **c.** Explain Describe how to find the area of this 45° sector. (Leave π as π.) Then find the area.

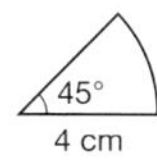

d. Find the perimeter of the figure in problem **c.** (Include the arc and two segments. Use 3.14 for π.) 11.14 cm

Written Practice *Strengthening Concepts*

1. (60) The merchant sold the item for \$12.50. If 40 percent of the selling price was profit, how much money did the merchant earn in profit? \$5.00

▶ ***2.** (94) Analyze If two marbles are pulled from a bag containing eight blue marbles, seven green marbles, and six yellow marbles, what is the probability that both marbles will be green? Express the probability as a decimal number. 0.10

3. (55) In 10 jump-rope trials, Kiesha's average number of jumps per minute is 88. If her least number of jumps, 70, is not counted, what is her average for the remaining 9 trials? 90 jumps

4. (46) The 36-ounce container cost \$3.42. The 3-pound container cost \$3.84. The smaller container cost how much more per ounce than the larger container? 1.5¢ more per ounce

▶ See Math Conversations in the sidebar.

2 New Concepts (Continued)

Example 5

Instruction

Ask these questions as students look at the diagram for this example.

"What information about the arc is given to us by the figure?" The arc is part of the circumference of a circle that has a radius of 2 units. The central angle of the arc is 90°.

"How can we use this information to find the length of the arc?" Use the radius to find the circumference of the circle. Use the measure of the central angle to find the fractional part of the circumference the arc is.

Practice Set

Problems a–c Analyze

Some students will find it helpful to copy the figure on paper and label the dimensions they must add to find the perimeter.

"What is the length of the radius? The diameter? The rectangle?" 3 cm, 6 cm, 10 cm by 3 cm

Problem c Explain

Ask a student to write the equation for finding the area on the board. Identify how each part of the equation relates to the problem.

3 Written Practice

Math Conversations

Discussion opportunities are provided below.

Problem 2 Analyze

Have students explain why their answer is correct. Sample:

First draw: $\frac{7 \text{ green marbles}}{21 \text{ total marbles}} = \frac{1}{3}$

Second draw: $\frac{6 \text{ green marbles}}{20 \text{ total marbles}} = \frac{3}{10}$

$$\frac{3}{10} \cdot \frac{1}{3} = 0.10$$

(continued)

3 Written Practice (Continued)

Math Conversations

Discussion opportunities are provided below.

Problem 5

Extend the Problem

"Do you think this equation can be used to solve the problem? Why or why not?"

$$h = \frac{(308 - 128) \div 18}{2}$$

yes; 308 − 128 gives the number of pages left to read; ÷ 18 gives the number of half hours needed to finish the book; divided by 2 converts the number of half hours to hours

Problem 8 Generalize

Ask students to explain how they can use mental math to solve this problem.

$\frac{45}{60} = \frac{3}{4}$ or 75%

5% of \$60 = \$3; 45 ÷ 5 = 9; \$3 × 9 = \$27

(continued)

▶ **5.** (72) Sean read 18 pages in 30 minutes. If he has finished page 128, how many hours will it take him to finish his 308-page book if he continues reading at the same rate? 5 hours

6. (74) Matthew was thinking of a certain number. If $\frac{5}{6}$ of the number was 75, what was $\frac{3}{5}$ of the number? 54

7. (54) A naturalist collected and released 12 crayfish and 180 tadpoles from a creek. Based on this sample, what was the ratio of crayfish to tadpoles in the creek? $\frac{1}{15}$

▶ **8.** (60, 77) Generalize Write equations to solve **a** and **b**.

a. What percent of \$60 is \$45? $W_P \times \$60 = \$45$; 75%

b. How much money is 45 percent of \$60? $M = 0.45 \times \$60$; \$27

In the figure below, $\overline{AD}$ is a diameter and $\overline{CB}$ is a radius of 12 units. Central angle ACB measures 60°. Refer to the figure to answer problems **9–11.** (Leave π as π.)

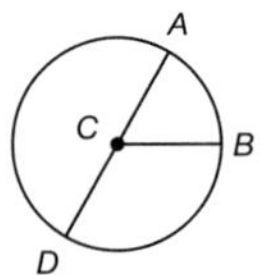

9. (65, 82) **a.** What is the area of the circle? 144π units^2

b. What is the circumference of the circle? 24π units

* **10.** (104) What is the area of sector BCD? 48π units^2

* **11.** (104) **a.** How many degrees is the major arc from B through A to D (arc BAD)? 240°

b. How long is arc BAD? 16π units

12. (Inv. 9) Make a table of ordered pairs for the function $y = 2x - 1$. Use −1, 0, and 1 as x values in the table. Then graph the function on a coordinate plane.

12. $y = 2x - 1$

x	y
−1	−3
0	−1
1	1

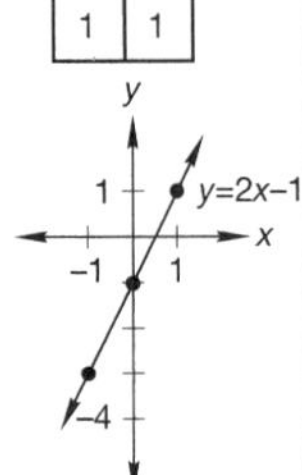

13. (48) Complete the table on the right.

Fraction	Decimal	Percent
a. $\frac{11}{500}$	**b.** 0.022	2.2%

* **14.** (Inv. 9) Analyze The graph on the next page shows the distance a car traveled at a certain constant speed.

a. According to this graph, how far did the car travel in 1 hour 15 minutes? 75 miles

▶ See Math Conversations in the sidebar.

728 Saxon Math Course 2

▶ **b.** Analyze Estimate the speed of the car in miles per hour as indicated by the graph. The car traveled about 60 miles in 1 hour, so its speed was about 60 miles per hour.

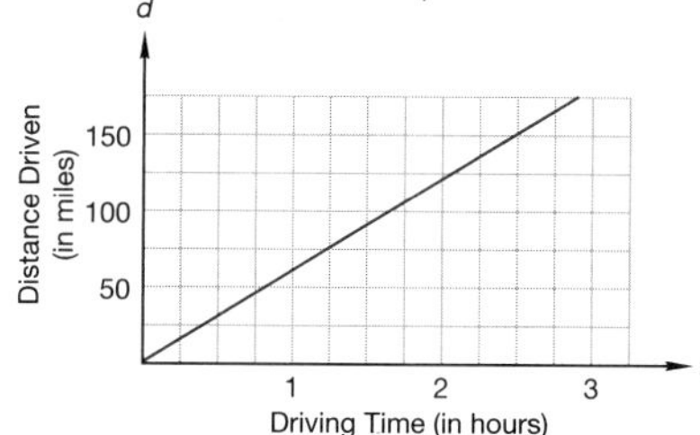

* **15.** (91) Compare: $ab \bigcirc a - b$ if a is positive and b is negative. <

16. (83) Multiply. Write the product in scientific notation. 3.24×10^5

$$(3.6 \times 10^{-4})(9 \times 10^8)$$

▶* **17.** (104) Analyze Find the area of the figure at right. Dimensions are in centimeters. (Use 3.14 for π.) 32.13 cm²

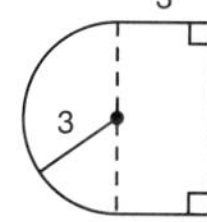

* **18.** (104) Find the perimeter of the figure in problem **17.** 21.42 cm

19. (67, 70) **a.** Find the volume of this solid in cubic inches. Dimensions are in feet. 1728 in.³

b. Find the surface area of this cube in square feet. 6 ft²

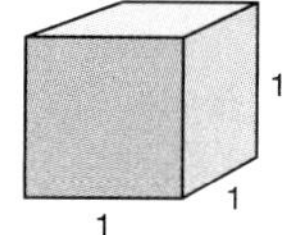

▶* **20.** (96) Predict What angle is formed by the hands of a clock at 5:00? 150°

21. (40) Find $m\angle x$ in the figure at right. 49°

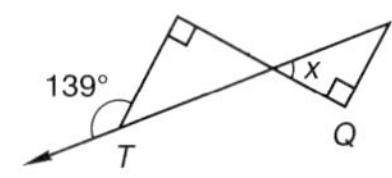

▶* **22.** (97, 98) Analyze The triangles below are similar.

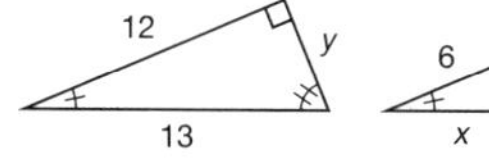

a. Find x. $6\frac{1}{2}$

b. Find the scale factor from the smaller triangle to the larger triangle. 2

c. The area of the larger triangle is how many times the area of the smaller triangle? 4 times

▶ See Math Conversations in the sidebar.

3 Written Practice (Continued)

Math Conversations

Discussion opportunities are provided below.

Problem 14b Analyze

"How could you write a proportion to determine the speed in 1 hour?" 1 hr and 15 min = 1.25 hours; 75 mi in 1.25 hr $\frac{1.25}{75} = \frac{1}{x}$; $1.25x = 75$; $x = 60$ mi in 1 hr

Problem 17 Analyze

Ask a student to write the steps of the solution on the board. $(3.14 \cdot 9) \div 2 = 14.13$; $18 + 14.13 = 32.13$ cm²

"Why did you multiply 3.14 x 9?" 9 is the radius squared

"Why did you divide by 2?" it is a semicircle

"Why did you add 18?" it is the area of the rectangle

Problem 20 Predict

"Each minute on a clock is how many degrees?" 6°

"How many degrees is it from one number to the next number?" 30°

"How many degrees is it from the 12 to the 5?" 5 × 30° or 150°

Problem 22 Analyze

Have students explain their reasoning for each part of the problem.

a. $\frac{12}{13} = \frac{6}{x}$; $78 \div 12x = 6.5$

b. $2 \times 6 = 12$; $2 \times 6.5 = 13$; the scale factor is 2

c. The length of each side of the larger triangle is 2 times the length of the corresponding sides of the smaller triangle. Area has two dimensions, so $2 \times 2 = 4$. The area of the larger triangle is 4 times the length of the smaller triangle.

Errors and Misconceptions

Problem 22

If students find that $x = 7$, they may think that the differences between the hypotenuses is 6 because the difference between the heights is 6. Remind them that similar figures are related by multiplication not by addition or subtraction. The scale factor is $12 \div 6$ or 2, $2 \times 6.5 = 13$.

(continued)

3 Written Practice (Continued)

Math Conversations

Discussion opportunities are provided below.

Problem 23 Justify

"What is the length of side of the smaller triangle that corresponds to side y in the larger triangle? Explain how you know." The scale factor from the smaller triangle to the larger triangle is 2, so the scale factor from the larger triangle to the smaller triangle is the reciprocal or $\frac{1}{2}$. Side $y = 5$ units, so the corresponding side in the smaller triangle is $\frac{1}{2} \cdot y$ or 2.5 units.

Problems 24 and 25 Generalize

Ask students to work at the board to show and explain each step of the solution.

Problem 30 Generalize

Ask students how they can solve these problems using mental math. Answers will vary.

Errors and Misconceptions

Problem 30a

If students have 0 as an answer, they subtracted $6 - 6$. Lead them through the steps of the problem and point out that they should have subtracted $6 - (-6)$, which simplifies to $6 + 6$ or 12.

23. Since y is one leg of a right triangle, we can use the Pythagorean theorem.
$y^2 + 12^2 = 13^2$
$y^2 + 144 = 169$
$y^2 = 25$
$y = 5$

▶* **23.** (99) Justify Find the value of y in the triangle in problem **22.** Justify your answer.

▶ Generalize Solve and check:

24. (90, 93) $2\frac{3}{4}w + 4 = 48$ 16

* **25.** (102) $2.4n + 1.2n - 0.12 = 7.08$ 2

Simplify:

26. (20) $\sqrt{(3^2)(10^2)}$ 30

27. (102, 103) **a.** $\frac{24x^2y}{8x^3y^2}$ $\frac{3}{xy}$ **b.** $2x(x - 1) - \sqrt{4x^4}$ $-2x$

28. (43) $12.5 - \left(8\frac{1}{3} + 1\frac{1}{6}\right)$ 3

29. (43) $4\frac{1}{6} \div 3\frac{3}{4} \div 2.5$ $\frac{4}{9}$

▶* **30.** (85, 103) Generalize

a. $\frac{(-3)(4)}{-2} - \frac{(-3)(-4)}{-2}$ 12 **b.** $\frac{(-2)^3}{(-2)^2}$ -2

Early Finishers
Real-World Application

Salim wants to create a triangular-shaped garden to grow prize roses. He plans to lay brick around the perimeter. With a tape measure Salim measured the length of the sides of the triangle to be 5 yards and 9 yards as shown below.

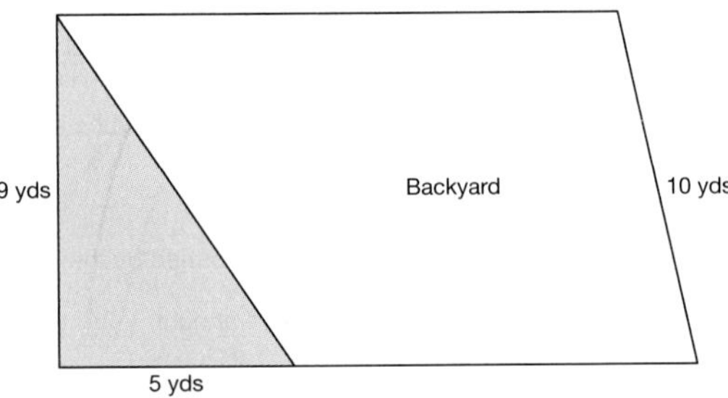

a. What is the approximate length of the third side of Salim's garden? Sample: 10.3 yards

b. What is the approximate perimeter of the rose garden (in feet)? Sample: 72.9 ft

c. If each brick is 7 inches long, approximately how many will he need to buy for the perimeter of the garden? Sample: 125 bricks

▶ See Math Conversations in the sidebar.

• Surface Area of a Right Solid
• Surface Area of a Sphere

Objectives

- Calculate the surface area of a right solid.
- Calculate the surface area of a sphere.

Lesson Preparation

Materials

- **Power Up Q** (in *Instructional Masters*)
- **Investigation Activity 13** (in *Instructional Masters*) or **graph paper**

Optional

- **Manipulative kit: tape measures, Relational GeoSolids triangular prism**
- **Teacher-provided material: examples of right prisms and cylinders (boxes, cans, etc.), label from can of soup, ball, scissors, grapefruit, rectangular sponges, safety scissors, inch and metric rulers**

Math Language

Maintain	English Learners (ESL)
surface area	lateral faces
right solid	

Technology Resources

Student eBook Complete student textbook in electronic format.

Resources and Planner CD Blackline masters, plus a pacing calendar with standards.

Test and Practice Generator CD Create additional practice sheets and custom-made tests.

www.SaxonPublishers.com Visit for more student activities and planning materials.

Inclusion

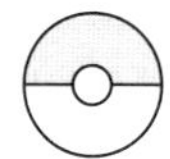

Adaptations CD Adapted lessons, investigations, practice and assessments.

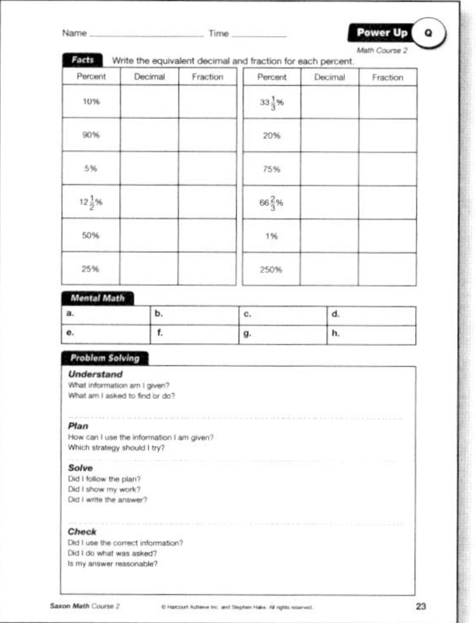

Name ______ Time ______ **Power Up Q** *Math Course 2*

Facts Write the equivalent decimal and fraction for each percent.

Percent	Decimal	Fraction	Percent	Decimal	Fraction
10%			$33\frac{1}{3}\%$		
90%			20%		
5%			75%		
$12\frac{1}{2}\%$			$66\frac{2}{3}\%$		
50%			1%		
25%			250%		

Mental Math

a.	b.	c.	d.
e.	f.	g.	h.

Problem Solving

Understand
What information am I given?
What am I asked to find or do?

Plan
How can I use the information I am given?
Which strategy should I try?

Solve
Did I follow the plan?
Did I show my work?
Did I write the answer?

Check
Did I use the correct information?
Did I do what was asked?
Is my answer reasonable?

Saxon Math Course 2 © Harcourt Achieve Inc. and Stephen Hake. All rights reserved. 23

Power Up Q

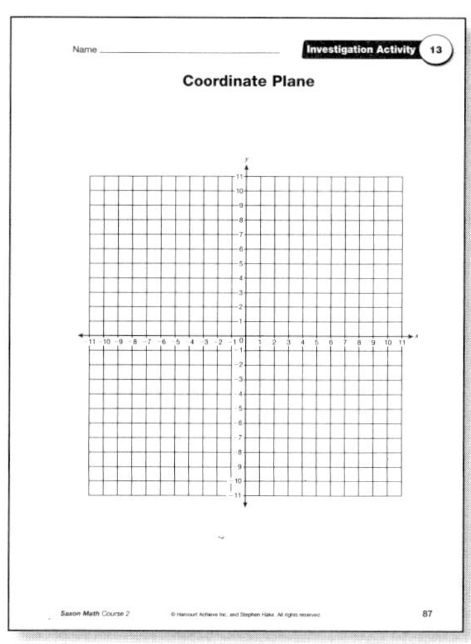

Name ______ **Investigation Activity 13**

Coordinate Plane

Saxon Math Course 2 © Harcourt Achieve Inc. and Stephen Hake. All rights reserved. 87

Investigation Activity 13

Meeting Standards

National Council of Teachers of Mathematics (NCTM)

Geometry

GM.4b Use two-dimensional representations of three-dimensional objects to visualize and solve problems such as those involving surface area and volume

GM.4d Use geometric models to represent and explain numerical and algebraic relationships

Measurement

ME.1c Understand, select, and use units of appropriate size and type to measure angles, perimeter, area, surface area, and volume

ME.2d Develop strategies to determine the surface area and volume of selected prisms, pyramids, and cylinders

Power-Up Discussion *For use with Power Up, p. 731*

Problem-Solving Strategy: Use Logical Reasoning/ Work Backwards

Copy this problem and fill in the missing digits.

```
          91½
     __)___
        __
         __
         __
          _
```

Understand ***Understand the problem.***

"What information are we given?"

We are shown a division problem with a quotient of $91\frac{1}{2}$, a missing 2-digit divisor, and a missing 3-digit dividend.

"What are we asked to do?"

We are asked to find the missing digits.

Plan ***Make a plan.***

"What problem-solving strategy will we use?"

We will *use logical reasoning* and *work backwards* to find the missing digits.

Solve ***Carry out the plan.***

"What does a remainder of $\frac{1}{2}$ tell us?"

The remainder is one-half of the divisor. The remainder will have be 5, 6, 7, 8, or 9, and the divisor will be 10, 12, 14, 16, or 18.

"Will we need to guess and check with each of the five possible divisors?"

No. The digit 9 is in the tens place of the quotient, and according to our problem, 9 times the divisor is a two-digit product. We know that $10 \times 9 = 90$, but $12 \times 9 = 108$, which is a 3-digit number. Twelve is too large, and 14, 16, and 18 also going to be too large for the divisor. We write 10 as the divisor and continue filling in missing digits, checking our arithmetic as we go.

```
       91½              91½
  10)___           10)915
     90                90
     __                 15
     10                 10
      5                  5
```

Check ***Look back.***

"Did we do what we were asked to do?"

Yes, we found all the missing digits.

"How can we verify our solution is correct?"

We can use the inverse operation of division to check our answer: $91\frac{1}{2} \times 10 = 910 + 5 = 915$.

LESSON 105

• Surface Area of a Right Solid
• Surface Area of a Sphere

Power Up

Building Power

facts Power Up Q

mental math

a. **Positive/Negative:** $(-2)^4$ 16

b. **Scientific Notation:** $(4 \times 10^{-4})^2$ 1.6×10^{-7}

c. **Algebra:** $2w + 3w = 60$ 12

d. **Measurement:** Convert −35°C to degrees Fahrenheit. −31°F

e. **Percent:** 200% of \$50 \$100

f. **Percent:** 100% more than \$50 \$100

g. **Geometry:** Two triangles are similar if their corresponding sides are proportional.

h. **Calculation:** Square 10, − 1, ÷ 9, × 4, + 1, ÷ 9, × 10, − 1, √ , × 5, + 1, √ , ÷ 3. 2

problem solving Copy this problem and fill in the missing digits:

$$\begin{array}{r} 91\frac{1}{2} \\ \_\_\overline{)\_\_\_} \\ \underline{\_\_} \\ \_\_ \\ \underline{\_\_} \\ \_ \end{array} \qquad \begin{array}{r} 91\frac{1}{2} \\ 10\overline{)915} \\ \underline{90} \\ 15 \\ \underline{10} \\ 5 \end{array}$$

New Concepts

Increasing Knowledge

surface area of a right solid

Recall that the total area of the surface of a geometric solid is called the **surface area** of the solid.

The block shown has six rectangular faces. We add the areas of these six faces to find the total surface area.

Area of top	= 5 cm × 6 cm =	30 cm²
Area of bottom	= 5 cm × 6 cm =	30 cm²
Area of front	= 3 cm × 6 cm =	18 cm²
Area of back	= 3 cm × 6 cm =	18 cm²
Area of side	= 3 cm × 5 cm =	15 cm²
+ Area of side	= 3 cm × 5 cm =	15 cm²
Total surface area		= 126 cm²

Facts Write the equivalent decimal and fraction for each percent.

Percent	Decimal	Fraction	Percent	Decimal	Fraction
10%	0.1	$\frac{1}{10}$	$33\frac{1}{3}\%$	$0.\overline{3}$	$\frac{1}{3}$
90%	0.9	$\frac{9}{10}$	20%	0.2	$\frac{1}{5}$
5%	0.05	$\frac{1}{20}$	75%	0.75	$\frac{3}{4}$
$12\frac{1}{2}\%$	0.125	$\frac{1}{8}$	$66\frac{2}{3}\%$	$0.\overline{6}$	$\frac{2}{3}$
50%	0.5	$\frac{1}{2}$	1%	0.01	$\frac{1}{100}$
25%	0.25	$\frac{1}{4}$	250%	2.5	$2\frac{1}{2}$

1 Power Up

Facts

Distribute **Power Up Q** to students. See answers below.

Mental Math

Encourage students to share different ways to mentally compute these exercises. Strategies for exercises **a** and **d** are listed below.

a. Evaluate Signs Separately

An even number of negative signs equals a positive product.

$2 \cdot 2 \cdot 2 \cdot 2 = 16$

Evaluate Signs While Computing

$-2 \cdot -2 = 4$

$4 \cdot -2 = -8$

$-8 \cdot -2 = 16$

d. Use 10%

Double the Celsius: $-35 + -35 = -70$

Subtract 10%: $-70 - (-7) = -63$

Subtract 32: $-63 - (+32) = -31$°F

Use $\frac{9}{5}$

Multiply by $\frac{9}{5}$: $-35 \cdot \frac{9}{5} = -63$

Subtract 32: $-63 - 32 = -31$°F

Problem Solving

Refer to **Power-Up Discussion**, p. 731B.

2 New Concepts

Instruction

The surface area of a solid is the sum of the areas of all its surfaces. The lateral surface area of right prisms and cylinders is the sum of the areas of the non-base surfaces. Bring into class examples of boxes and cans. Divide the class into groups, give each group a tape measure, and have students find the total surface area of these objects.

(continued)

2 New Concepts (Continued)

Example 1

Instruction

Use the triangular prism **Relational GeoSolids** from the Manipulative Kit to help explain the concept in this example. Provide a display of the figure's net and record the area of each section in its corresponding section.

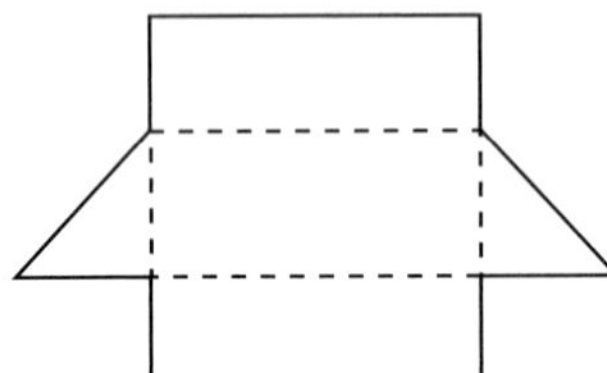

Instruction

"Why is the lateral surface area of a prism equal to the perimeter of its base times the height?" The height of each rectangular face is the same (6 cm). The length of the other side of each rectangular face is included in the perimeter of the base of the prism.

(continued)

Example 1

Math Language
This triangular prism is a **right solid** because its sides are perpendicular to its base(s).

Find the surface area of this triangular prism. Dimensions are in centimeters.

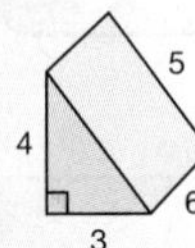

Solution

There are two triangular faces and three rectangular faces.

$$\begin{aligned}
\text{Area of triangle} &= \frac{3\text{ cm} \cdot 4\text{ cm}}{2} = 6\text{ cm}^2\\
\text{Area of triangle} &= \frac{3\text{ cm} \cdot 4\text{ cm}}{2} = 6\text{ cm}^2\\
\text{Area of rectangle} &= 6\text{ cm} \cdot 3\text{ cm} = 18\text{ cm}^2\\
\text{Area of rectangle} &= 6\text{ cm} \cdot 4\text{ cm} = 24\text{ cm}^2\\
+\ \text{Area of rectangle} &= 6\text{ cm} \cdot 5\text{ cm} = 30\text{ cm}^2\\
\text{Total surface area} &= \mathbf{84\text{ cm}^2}
\end{aligned}$$

Discuss Would seeing every face of a right solid be helpful in finding its surface area? Is there a way that we could see every face?

Seeing every face would help us understand the dimensions of each of the faces. We could make a sketch of each face and label the dimensions.

The triangular prism in example 1 has two bases that are triangles and three lateral faces that are rectangles.

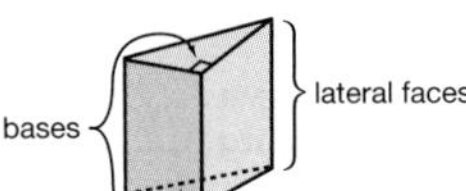

The total area of the lateral faces is called the **lateral surface area.** A quick way to find the lateral surface area of a prism is to multiply the perimeter of the base by the height (the distance between the bases).

Perimeter of base: 3 cm + 4 cm + 5 cm = 12 cm

Height: 6 cm

Lateral surface area: 12 cm · 6 cm = 72 cm^2

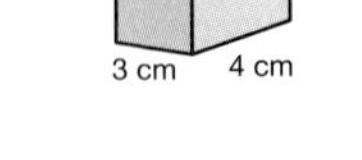

Explain When finding the perimeter of the base, how did we know which face to use?

A prism has two bases that are parallel and congruent. Only the triangular faces are both congruent and parallel so they are the bases.

We use the concept of lateral surface area to find the surface area of a circular cylinder.

Example 2

a. What is the area of the label on a soup can with dimensions as shown?

b. What is the total surface area of the soup can?

Use $\frac{22}{7}$ for π.

English Learners

Demonstrate the meaning of **lateral faces.**

Hold up a geometric solid of a triangular prism (from the math manipulative kit). Point out the lateral faces and bases of the prism to students.

Then, use a different geometric figure (from the math manipulative kit) and ask students to identify the lateral faces and bases.

Solution

a. If we remove the label from a soup can, we see that it is a rectangle. One dimension of the rectangle is the circumference of the can, and the other dimension is the height of the can. The area of the label equals the *lateral surface area* of the soup can.

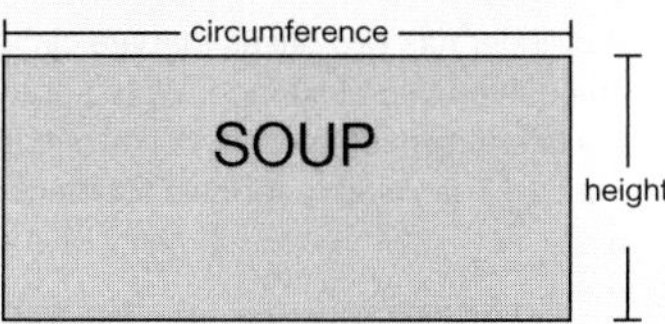

To find the area of the label, we multiply these two dimensions.

$$\text{Lateral area} = \text{circumference} \cdot \text{height}$$
$$= \pi d \cdot \text{height}$$
$$= \frac{22}{7} \cdot 7 \text{ cm} \cdot 10 \text{ cm}$$
$$= \mathbf{220\ cm^2}$$

b. The total surface area of the can consists of the lateral surface area plus the circular top and bottom of the can. Recall that the area of a circle is found by multiplying the square of the radius by π.

$$A = \pi r^2$$

We use $\frac{22}{7}$ for π and $\frac{7}{2}$ cm (or 3.5 cm) for the radius.

$$A = \frac{22}{7}\left(\frac{7}{2}\text{ cm}\right)^2$$
$$A \approx \frac{22}{7} \cdot \frac{7}{2} \cdot \frac{7}{2}\text{ cm}^2$$
$$A = \frac{77}{2}\text{ cm}^2 \text{ (or } 38.5 \text{ cm}^2)$$

We have found the area of one circular surface. However, the can has both a top and a bottom, so we add the areas of the top, bottom, and lateral surface.

Area of top	= 38.5 cm²
Area of bottom	= 38.5 cm²
+ Area of lateral surface	= 220.0 cm²
Total surface area	= 297.0 cm²

The total surface area of the soup can is **297 cm²**.

We can use the concepts in this lesson to create formulas for surface area.

A cube has six congruent faces. If we let s stand for the length of each edge, then what is the area of each face? Write a formula for the total surface area (A_s) for the cube. s^2; $A_s = 6s^2$

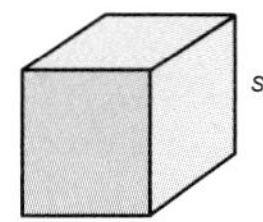

2 New Concepts (Continued)

Example 2

Instruction

Demonstrate the lateral surface area of a cylinder by removing the label of a soup can or similar product. (You may want to do this ahead of class.) Tape the label in place or wrap the can with paper to unwrap for the class. Ask students what measures of the cylinder the length and width of the label represent. the circumference and height of the cylinder

Instruction

Cube: Guide students to see that the area of each face is s^2. Since there are 6 faces, the formula for the total surface area is $A_s = 6s^2$.

(continued)

Manipulative Use

Materials: cereal boxes, cylindrical oatmeal boxes

As a **homework assignment** have students make a **net for a cylindrical container and a rectangular box.** They can cut the containers apart or measure them and draw a net.

They should measure the dimensions of the rectangles and the diameters of the circles to calculate the areas of the regions of their net. Then they use the areas of the regions to find the total surface area of each object.

2 New Concepts (Continued)

Instruction

Rectangular Prism: Guide students to see that the area of the top and bottom are each lw. The area of the front and back are each lh. The area of the left and right sides are each wh. Adding these areas we get $A_s = 2lw + 2lh + 2wh$.

Cylinder: The area of the lateral surface is the circumference of the base times the height of the cylinder: $A_L = 2\pi rh$. The area of each base is $A_B = \pi r^2$. Adding these areas we get: $A_s = 2\pi rh + 2\pi r^2$.

You may wish to demonstrate the surface area of a sphere using an actual grapefruit in class. Slicing through the widest part of the grapefruit results in the largest circle, which is called the great circle. The area of the outer peel of the grapefruit is 4 times the area of the cross section circle.

Example 3

Instruction

Remind students that when computing with pi, it is often necessary to round the answer to a specific place value. For this example, the answer is rounded to the nearest whole number.

(continued)

A rectangular prism has six faces. The top and bottom are congruent. The front and back are congruent. The left face and right face are congruent. Write a formula for the total surface area (A_s) for a rectangular prism that uses l, w, and h. $A_s = 2lw + 2lh + 2wh$

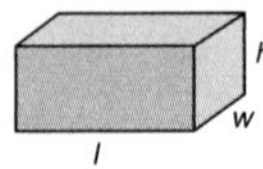

A cylinder has two bases that are circles and one curved lateral surface. Write a formula for the lateral surface area (A_L) of a cylinder using r and h. Then write a formula for the total surface area. $A_L = 2\pi rh + 2\pi r^2$

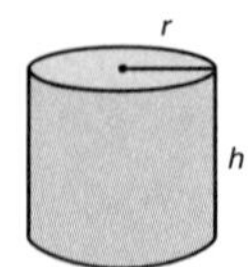

surface area of a sphere

To calculate the surface area of a sphere, we may first calculate the area of the largest cross section of the sphere. Slicing a grapefruit in half provides a visual representation of a cross section of a sphere.

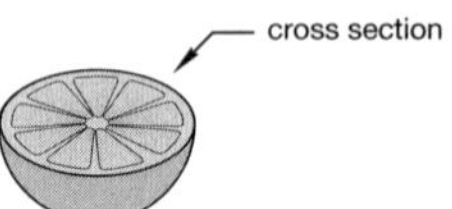

The circle formed by cutting the grapefruit in half is the cross section of the spherical grapefruit. The surface area of the entire sphere is four times the area of this circle. To find the surface area of the sphere, we calculate the area of its largest cross section ($A = \pi r^2$); then we multiply the cross sectional area by four.

Surface area of a sphere = $4\pi r^2$

Example 3

A tennis ball has a diameter of about 6 cm. Find the surface area of the tennis ball to the nearest square centimeter.

Use 3.14 for π.

Solution

A tennis ball is spherical. If its diameter is 6 cm, then its radius is 3 cm.

$$\begin{aligned}\text{Surface area} &= 4\pi r^2 \\ &\approx 4(3.14)(3\text{ cm})^2 \\ &\approx 4(3.14)(9\text{ cm}^2) \\ &\approx 113.04\text{ cm}^2\end{aligned}$$

We round the answer to **113 cm^2**.

Math Background

You can demonstrate that the surface area of the sphere is equal to the lateral surface area of the cylinder. The lateral surface of a solid is any face or surface that is not a base. Use a ball and paper cut to equal the circumference and diameter of the ball. Roll the ball in the paper and fold up the top and bottom.

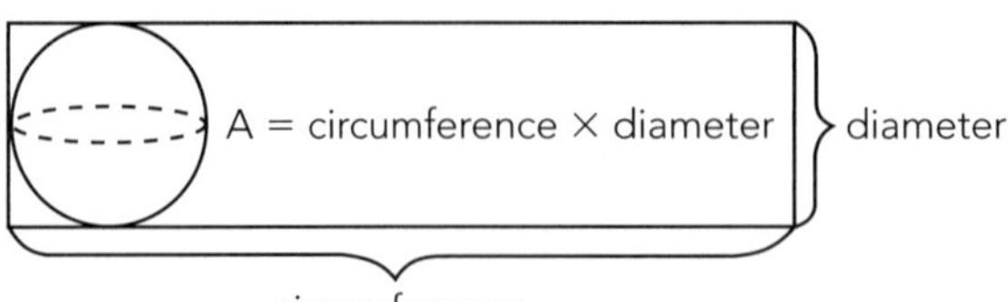

There will be gaps but it is easy to picture that folded over parts would fill in on the gaps. Now derive the formula.

Area = circumference · diameter (length × width)

Area = $\pi \cdot 2 \cdot r \quad \cdot \quad 2 \cdot r$ Substitute what we know.

Area = $2 \cdot 2 \cdot \pi \cdot r \cdot r$ Use the Associative Property.

Surface Area of a Sphere = $4\pi r^2$

Example 4

Find the total surface area of this figure. (Units are centimeters.)

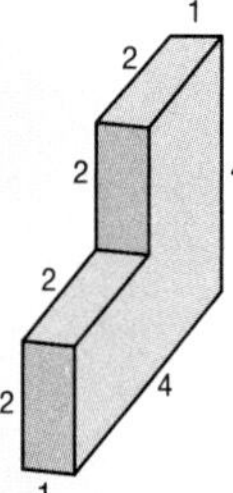

Solution

The figure has eight surfaces:

Two congruent L-shapes (each 12 cm^2)

One 1×4 back rectangle (4 cm^2)

One 1×4 bottom rectangle (4 cm^2)

Four 1×2 stairstep rectangles (each 2 cm^2)

Adding these areas we find the total surface area is **40 cm^2**.

Practice Set

a. Find the surface area of this rectangular solid. Dimensions are in inches. 248 in.^{2}

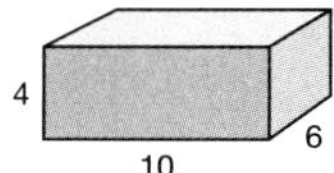

▸ **b.** Analyze Find the surface area of this triangular prism. Dimensions are in inches. 288 in.^{2}

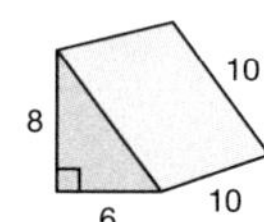

▸ **c.** Analyze Find the area of the label on this can of tuna. 125.6 cm^2

d. Find the total surface area of the can. 282.6 cm^2

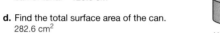

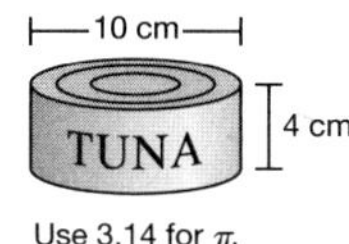

Use 3.14 for π.

e. The diameter of a golf ball is about 4 cm. Find the surface area of a golf ball to the nearest square centimeter. (Use 3.14 for π.) 50 cm^2

▸ **f.** Analyze If the figure in problem **b** is attached to the figure in problem **a** as shown, what is the total surface area of the combined figures? 416 in.^{2}

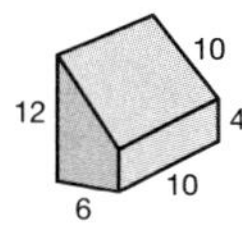

▸ **g.** Explain Is the surface area of **f** equal to the sum of the surface areas of **a** and **b?** Why or why not?

g. No. The top of the rectangular prism and the bottom of the triangular prism are not part of the surface area of the combined shape.

▸ See Math Conversations in the sidebar.

2 New Concepts (Continued)

Example 4

Instruction

Students should discuss different ways to break apart this figure. Point out that they can use strategies similar to ones they used when they needed to break apart plane figures.

Practice Set

Problem b Analyze

"Are the dimensions of each rectangular face the same? If not what are the dimensions?" no; 6 in. by 10 in., 8 in. by 10 in., 10 in. by 10 in.

Problem c Error Alert

Some students may include the bases in their computation. Remind them that the label only covers the lateral (curved) surface not the circular bases.

Problem f Analyze

"How did you compute the surface area of the combined figures?" Sample: Use the measurements of the new figure and compute the surface area; use the combined area from problems a and b and subtract the area of two 60-in.^{2} rectangular faces or 120 in.^{2}

Problem g Explain

If students have difficulty visualizing this problem, sketch the solid on the board and draw lines to show where the two figures meet.

Manipulative Use

Materials: thick rectangular sponges, safety scissors, and rulers

You can help students visualize how to **break a compound solid** apart.

- Cut sections out of the sponges to make compound figures.
- Students can use safety scissors to cut the compound shape apart.
- If you prefer, they could draw on the sponge to show how to cut the figure apart.
- Then they measure the dimensions and find the surface area of the total figure.

3 Written Practice

Math Conversations

Discussion opportunities are provided below.

Problem 3

Extend the Problem

"A student said that to evaluate this expression, you can just subtract the value of b from a because the square root symbol cancels the exponents. Is the student right? Why or why not?" no; you have to subtract the squared numbers before you apply the square root symbol, so the answer is not 2, it is 6

Problem 9 Generalize

Ask a student to draw the ratio box at the board.

	Scale	Measure
Model	1	M
Actual	36	60 ft = 720 in.

$$\frac{1}{36} = \frac{M}{720}$$

$$36M = 720$$

$$M = 20 \text{ in.}$$

Problem 10 Explain

"How can you check your answer?"
$80 + 100 = 180°$; each pair of acute and obtuse angles form a straight angle

Problems 11 and 12 Formulate

Ask students to write a proportion that could be used to solve each problem.

11. $\frac{\$3}{\$60} = \frac{x}{100}$ $\quad 60x = 300 \quad x = 5\%$

12. $\frac{10}{100} = \frac{x}{4}$ $\quad 100x = 40 \quad x = \frac{2}{5}$

Ask students which representation they find easier to use, an equation or a proportion. Have them explain why.

Errors and Misconceptions

Problem 2

If students did not correctly put these numbers in order, or correctly compute them, have them insert zeros so all the numbers have the same number of places.

(continued)

Written Practice *Strengthening Concepts*

1. (51) Twenty billion is how much greater than nine hundred million? Write the answer in scientific notation. 1.91×10^{10}

▸ 2. (Inv. 4) The mean of the following numbers is how much less than the median? 0.51

3.2, 4.28, 1.2, 3.1, 1.17

▸ 3. (52) Evaluate: $\sqrt{a^2 - b^2}$ if $a = 10$ and $b = 8$ 6

4. (53) If Tyra is paid at a rate of \$8.50 per hour, how much will she earn if she works $6\frac{1}{2}$ hours? \$55.25

Use ratio boxes to solve problems **5–9.**

5. (72) A 5-pound bag of flour costs \$1.24. What is the cost of 75 pounds of flour? \$18.60

6. (92) The regular price of the dress was \$30. The dress was on sale for 25% off.

   a. What was the sale price? \$22.50

   b. What percent of the regular price was the sale price? 75%

7. (66) The ratio of students to parents at the assembly was 7 to 3. If the total number of students and parents assembled was 210, how many parents were at the assembly? 63 parents

8. (92) The original price of a hockey helmet and mask was \$60. Brandon bought one on sale for 30% off. What did he pay for the mask? \$42

▸ * 9. (102) **Generalize** Chen and his sister are making a model plane at a 1:36 scale. If the length of the actual plane is 60 feet, how many inches long should they make the model? Begin by converting 60 feet to inches. 20 inches

▸* 10. (102) **Explain** Transversal r intersects parallel lines s and t. If the measure of each acute angle is $4x$ and the measure of each obtuse angle is $5x$, then what is the measure of each acute and each obtuse angle?

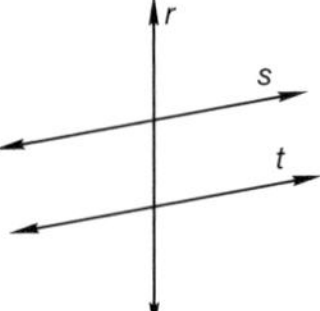

10. 80°, 100°; Sample: The acute angles and the obtuse angles are supplementary, so the sum of an acute and an obtuse angle is 180°. I set the sum of the two measures equal to 180° and solved for x. $4x + 5x = 180°$, $9x = 180°$, $x = 20°$. Thus, each acute angle measures $4(20) = 80°$, and each obtuse angle measures $5(20) = 100°$.

Formulate Write equations to solve problems **11–13.**

▸ 11. (77) What percent of \$60 is \$3? $W_P \cdot \$60 = \$3$; 5%

▸ 12. (60) What fraction is 10 percent of 4? $W_P = \frac{1}{10} \times 4$; $\frac{2}{5}$

* 13. (101) Twelve less than twice what number is 86? $2x - 12 = 86$; 49

* 14. (99) The coordinates of the vertices of a right triangle are $(-2, -2)$, $(-2, 2)$, and $(1, -2)$. Find the length of the hypotenuse of this triangle. 5 units

▸ See Math Conversations in the sidebar.

736 **Saxon** *Math Course 2*

20.

* **15.** Compare: a^3 ⓢ a^2 if a is negative
(103)

▶* **16.** Carmela has a deck of 26 alphabet cards. She mixes the cards, places them face down on the table, and turns them over one at a time. What is the probability that the first two cards she turns over are vowel cards (a, e, i, o, u)? $\frac{5}{26} \times \frac{4}{25} = \frac{20}{650}, \frac{2}{65}$
(94)

* **17.** Alejandro bounced a big ball with a diameter of 20 inches. Using 3.14 for π, find the surface area of the ball. 1256 in.^{2}
(105)

18. Multiply. Write the product in scientific notation. 2.56×10^{-13}
(83)

$$(8 \times 10^{-4})(3.2 \times 10^{-10})$$

▶* **19.** Analyze Find the perimeter of the figure at right. Dimensions are in meters. (Use 3.14 for π.) 81.4 m
(104)

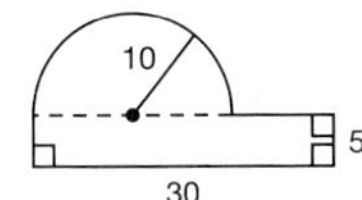

20. Find the missing numbers in the table by using the function rule. Then graph the function on a coordinate plane.
(56, Inv. 9)

$y = -2x - 1$

x	y
3	−7
−2	3
0	−1

21. Find the **a** volume and **b** surface area of this cube. Dimensions are in millimeters. **a.** 125 mm^3 **b.** 150 mm^2
(67, 70)

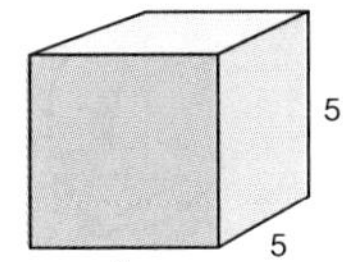

▶* **22.** Analyze Find the volume of this right circular cylinder. Dimensions are in centimeters. (Use 3.14 for π.) 3140 cm^3
(95)

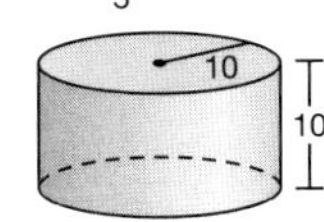

▶* **23.** Analyze The total surface area of the cylinder in problem **22** includes the areas of two circles and the curved side. What is the total surface area of the cylinder? 1256 cm^2
(105)

▶ **24.** Find m∠b in the figure at right. Explain how you found your answer. 30°; Sample: First find m∠a: 90° + 30° + m∠a = 180°; m∠a = 60°. m∠a = m∠y because they are vertical angles. Therefore, m∠y + m∠b + 90° = 180°; m∠b = 30°.
(40)

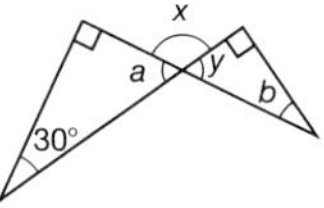

▶ See Math Conversations in the sidebar.

3 Written Practice (Continued)

Math Conversations

Discussion opportunities are provided below.

Problem 19 Analyze

"Why can you use 2πr to find the circumference?" $2r$ = the diameter; the Associative Property lets us regroup the numbers.

Problem 22 Analyze

Ask a student to work at the board and explain the steps for finding the volume. Ask students how they can check the answer.

Problem 23 Analyze

Ask a student to work at the board and explain the steps for finding the surface area. Ask students how they can check the answer.

Problem 24

Extend the Problem

Ask students to find the measure of ∠x. Have them explain their reasoning. ∠x + ∠y = 180°; ∠y = 60°, so ∠x = 180° − 60° or 120°

Errors and Misconceptions

Problem 17

If students have 5024 as an answer, they squared the diameter, 20 in., instead of taking half, 10 in. and squaring with a result of 100. Point out the formula requires the radius squared and ask them to recalculate the answer.

(continued)

3 Written Practice (Continued)

Math Conversations

Discussion opportunities are provided below.

Problem 25a Generalize

Some students may need assistance estimating. Point out that the triangles have the same orientation, therefore, 6 is to x as 12 is to 8.

Explain that since 8 is more than half of 12, x is more than half of 6. The triangle on the right is smaller than the triangle on the left by a factor of $\frac{8}{12}$ or $\frac{2}{3}$. So, x is $\frac{2}{3}$ of 6.

Problems 26 and 27 Generalize

Explain how to use mental math to solve this problem. Answers will vary.

Problems 28–30 Generalize

Ask volunteers to write these solutions at the board. Discuss the steps and the order in which the steps should be done.

Errors and Misconceptions

Problem 30a

Watch for students who incorrectly cancel what they believe to be common factors. Point out that both the numerator and the denominator need to be completely simplified before common factors can be canceled.

* **25.** (97, 98) **Generalize** The triangles shown are similar.

▶ **a.** Estimate, then calculate, the length x. See student work; 4

b. Find the scale factor from the smaller triangle to the larger triangle. 1.5

c. The area of the larger triangle is how many times the area of the smaller triangle? 2.25 times

6 12 x 8

Generalize Solve:

▶* **26.** (102) $4\frac{1}{2}x + 4 = 48 - x$ 8

▶ **27.** (98) $\frac{3.9}{75} = \frac{c}{25}$ 1.3

▶ **Generalize** Simplify:

28. (43) $3.2 \div \left(2\frac{1}{2} \div \frac{5}{8}\right)$ $\frac{4}{5}$ or 0.8

* **29.** (96, 103) **a.** $\frac{(2xy)(4x^2y)}{8x^2y}$ xy

b. $3(x+3) - \sqrt{9x^2}$ 9

▶ **30.** (57, 85) **a.** $\frac{(-10)(-4) - (3)(-2)(-1)}{(-4) - (-2)}$ −17

b. $(-2)^4 - (-2)^2 + 2^0$ 13

Early Finishers
Real-World Application

Whitney's family is moving across the state. The moving company will move the family's 4000 lbs. of boxes for $1800. Forty-five pounds can be safely moved in a small moving box and 65 lbs. in a large moving box.

a. If Whitney's father filled 21 small boxes to the weight limit, how many large boxes can he fill? 47 large boxes

b. Approximately how much is it costing Whitney's family to have the large boxes moved? accept $1300 to $1400

▶ See Math Conversations in the sidebar.

Looking Forward

Finding the surface area of right solids and spheres prepares students for:

- **Lesson 113,** finding the volume of pyramids, cones, and spheres.

Assessment

30–40 minutes | *For use after Lesson 105*

Distribute **Cumulative Test 20** to each student. Two versions of the test are available in *Saxon Math Course 2 Course Assessments Book.* Have students complete the **Power-Up Test** first. Allow 10 minutes. Then have students work the 20 numbered items on the **Cumulative Test.** Students may use copies of the answer sheet to record their work. Track individual and class progress with the **Test Analysis** forms.

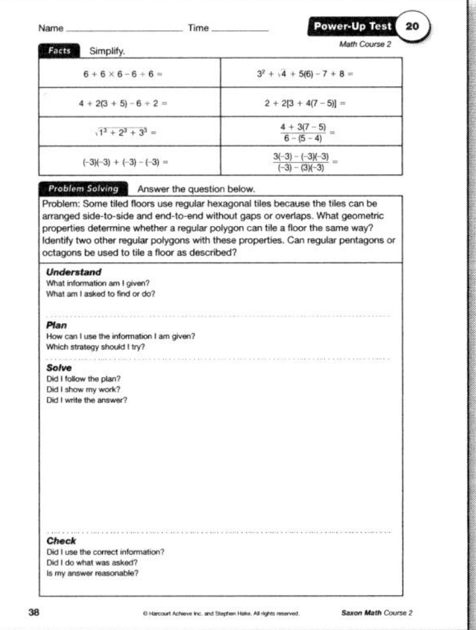

Name ______ Time ______ **Power-Up Test 20** *Math Course 2*

Facts Simplify.

6 + 6 × 6 − 6 ÷ 6 =	$3^2 + -4 + 5(6) - 7 + 8 =$
4 + 2(3 + 5) − 6 ÷ 2 =	2 + 2[3 + 4(7 − 5)] =
$\sqrt{1^3 + 2^3 + 3^3} =$	$\frac{4 + 3(7 - 5)}{6 - (5 - 4)} =$
(−3)(−3) + (−3) − (−3) =	$\frac{3(-3) - (-3)(-3)}{(-3) - (3)(-3)} =$

Problem Solving Answer the question below.

Problem: Some tiled floors use regular hexagonal tiles because the tiles can be arranged side-to-side and end-to-end without gaps or overlaps. What geometric properties determine whether a regular polygon can tile a floor the same way? Identify two other regular polygons with these properties. Can regular pentagons or octagons be used to tile a floor as described?

Understand
What information am I given?
What am I asked to find or do?

Plan
How can I use the information I am given?
Which strategy should I try?

Solve
Did I follow the plan?
Did I show my work?
Did I write the answer?

Check
Did I use the correct information?
Did I do what was asked?
Is my answer reasonable?

38 © Harcourt Achieve Inc. and Stephen Hake. All rights reserved. *Saxon Math Course 2*

Power-Up Test 20

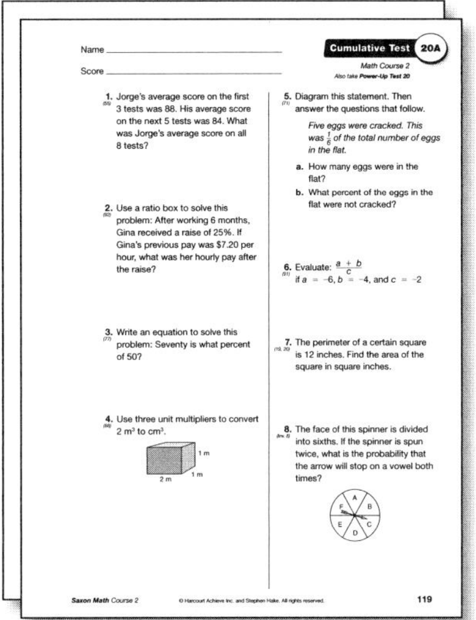

Name ______ Score ______ **Cumulative Test 20A** *Math Course 2* *Also take Power-Up Test 20*

1. Jorge's average score on the first 3 tests was 88. His average score on the next 5 tests was 84. What was Jorge's average score on all 8 tests?

2. Use a ratio box to solve this problem: After working 6 months, Gina received a raise of 25%. If Gina's previous pay was $7.20 per hour, what was her hourly pay after the raise?

3. Write an equation to solve this problem: Seventy is what percent of 50?

4. Use three unit multipliers to convert 2 m³ to cm³.

5. Diagram this statement. Then answer the questions that follow. *Five eggs were cracked. This was $\frac{1}{6}$ of the total number of eggs in the flat.*
a. How many eggs were in the flat?
b. What percent of the eggs in the flat were not cracked?

6. Evaluate: $\frac{a + b}{c}$ if a = −6, b = −4, and c = −2

7. The perimeter of a certain square is 12 inches. Find the area of the square in square inches.

8. The face of this spinner is divided into sixths. If the spinner is spun twice, what is the probability that the arrow will stop on a vowel both times?

Saxon Math Course 2 © Harcourt Achieve Inc. and Stephen Hake. All rights reserved. 119

Cumulative Test 20A

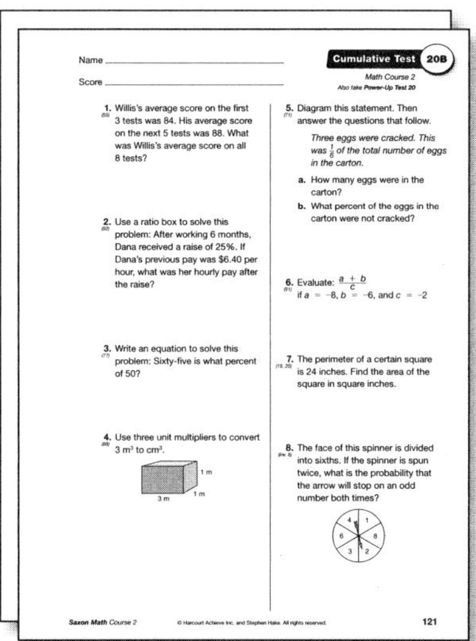

Name ______ Score ______ **Cumulative Test 20B** *Math Course 2* *Also take Power-Up Test 20*

1. Willis's average score on the first 3 tests was 84. His average score on the next 5 tests was 88. What was Willis's average score on all 8 tests?

2. Use a ratio box to solve this problem: After working 6 months, Dana received a raise of 25%. If Dana's previous pay was $6.40 per hour, what was her hourly pay after the raise?

3. Write an equation to solve this problem: Sixty-five is what percent of 50?

4. Use three unit multipliers to convert 3 m³ to cm³.

5. Diagram this statement. Then answer the questions that follow. *Three eggs were cracked. This was $\frac{1}{4}$ of the total number of eggs in the carton.*
a. How many eggs were in the carton?
b. What percent of the eggs in the carton were not cracked?

6. Evaluate: $\frac{a + b}{c}$ if a = −8, b = −6, and c = −2

7. The perimeter of a certain square is 24 inches. Find the area of the square in square inches.

8. The face of this spinner is divided into sixths. If the spinner is spun twice, what is the probability that the arrow will stop on an odd number both times?

Saxon Math Course 2 © Harcourt Achieve Inc. and Stephen Hake. All rights reserved. 121

Alternative Cumulative Test 20B

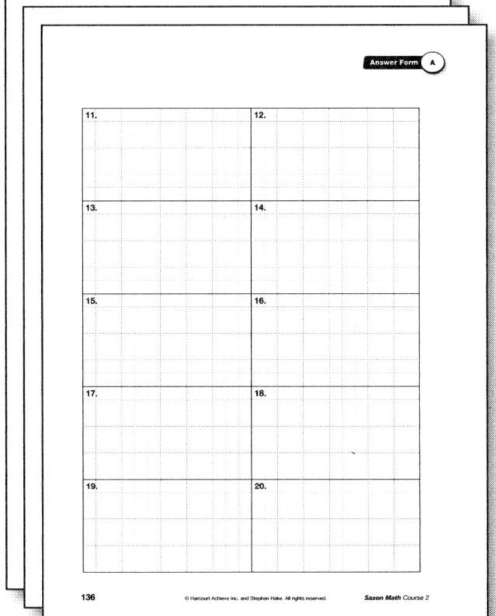

Answer Form A

11. 12. 13. 14. 15. 16. 17. 18. 19. 20.

136 © Harcourt Achieve Inc. and Stephen Hake. All rights reserved. *Saxon Math Course 2*

Optional Answer Forms

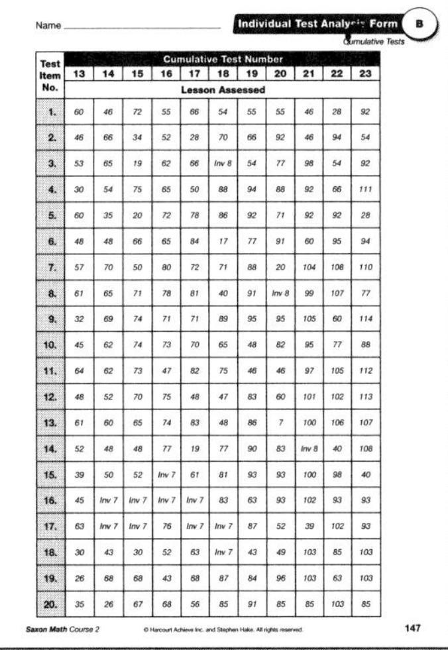

Name ______ **Individual Test Analysis Form B** *Cumulative Tests*

Test Item No.	13	14	15	16	17	18	19	20	21	22	23
	Lesson Assessed										
1.	60	46	72	55	66	54	55	55	46	28	92
2.	46	66	34	52	28	70	66	92	46	94	54
3.	53	65	19	62	66	Inv 8	54	77	98	54	92
4.	30	54	75	65	50	88	94	88	92	66	111
5.	60	35	20	72	78	86	92	71	92	92	28
6.	48	48	66	65	84	17	77	91	60	95	94
7.	57	70	50	80	72	71	88	20	104	108	110
8.	61	65	71	78	81	40	91	Inv 8	99	107	77
9.	32	69	74	71	71	89	95	95	105	60	114
10.	45	62	74	73	70	65	48	82	95	77	88
11.	64	62	73	47	82	75	46	46	97	105	112
12.	48	52	70	75	48	47	83	60	101	102	113
13.	61	60	65	74	83	48	86	7	100	106	107
14.	52	48	48	77	19	77	90	83	Inv 8	40	108
15.	39	50	52	Inv 7	61	81	93	93	100	98	40
16.	45	Inv 7	Inv 7	Inv 7	Inv 7	83	63	93	102	93	93
17.	63	Inv 7	Inv 7	76	Inv 7	Inv 7	87	52	39	102	93
18.	30	43	30	52	63	Inv 7	43	49	103	85	103
19.	26	68	68	43	68	87	84	96	103	63	103
20.	35	26	67	68	56	85	91	85	85	103	85

Saxon Math Course 2 © Harcourt Achieve Inc. and Stephen Hake. All rights reserved. 147

Individual Test Analysis Form

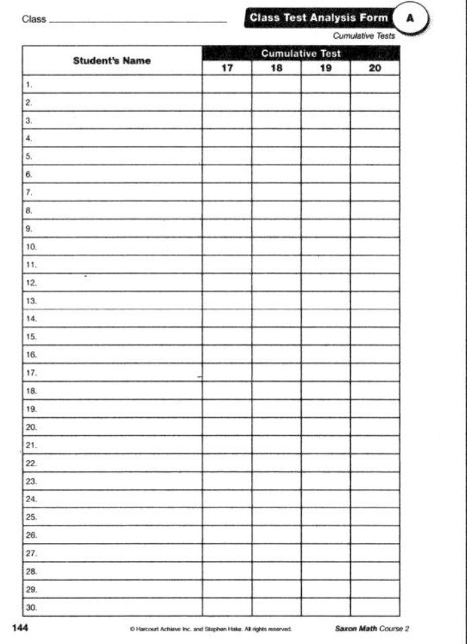

Class ______ **Class Test Analysis Form A** *Cumulative Tests*

	Student's Name	17	18	19	20
1.					
2.					
3.					
4.					
5.					
6.					
7.					
8.					
9.					
10.					
11.					
12.					
13.					
14.					
15.					
16.					
17.					
18.					
19.					
20.					
21.					
22.					
23.					
24.					
25.					
26.					
27.					
28.					
29.					
30.					

144 © Harcourt Achieve Inc. and Stephen Hake. All rights reserved. *Saxon Math Course 2*

Class Test Analysis Form

Reteaching

Students who score below 80% on the assessment may be in need of reteaching. Look for the causes of student mistakes. If errors are conceptual, refer to the *Reteaching Masters* for reteaching.

Performance Activity 20

Read a Map

Assign after Lesson 105 and Test 20

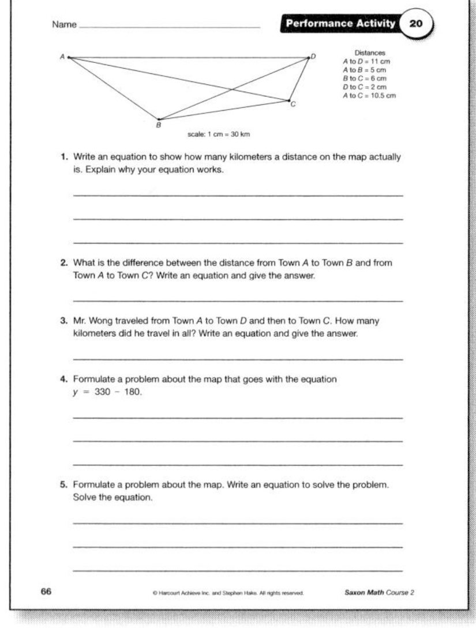

Name ____________ **Performance Activity 20**

1. Write an equation to show how many kilometers a distance on the map actually is. Explain why your equation works.

2. What is the difference between the distance from Town *A* to Town *B* and from Town *A* to Town *C*? Write an equation and give the answer.

3. Mr. Wong traveled from Town *A* to Town *D* and then to Town *C*. How many kilometers did he travel in all? Write an equation and give the answer.

4. Formulate a problem about the map that goes with the equation $y = 330 - 180$.

5. Formulate a problem about the map. Write an equation to solve the problem. Solve the equation.

66 *Saxon Math Course 2*

Performance Activity 20

Objectives

- Use a scale to find distances on a map.
- Write and solve equations for problems that involve a map.
- Formulate problems about a map.
- Communicate their ideas through writing.

Materials

Performance Activity 20

Preparation

Make copies of **Performance Activity 20.** (One each per student.)

Time Requirement

15–30 minutes; Begin in class and complete at home.

Activity

Explain to students that for this activity they will be using a scale to find distances on a map. They will write equations to solve problems and they will formulate problems. They will be required to explain why one of the equations they wrote works. Explain that all of the information students need is on **Performance Activity 20.**

Criteria for Evidence of Learning

- Uses the scale of the map accurately to determine distances.
- Writes equations that accurately represent situations involving the map.
- Formulates a problem about the map and writes an equation that accurately represents the problem.
- Communicates mathematical ideas clearly.

Meeting Standards

National Council of Teachers of Mathematics (NCTM)

Geometry

GM.4c Use visual tools such as networks to represent and solve problems

GM.4e Recognize and apply geometric ideas and relationships in areas outside the mathematics classroom, such as art, science, and everyday life

Measurement

ME.1b Understand relationships among units and convert from one unit to another within the same system

ME.2b Select and apply techniques and tools to accurately find length, area, volume, and angle measures to appropriate levels of precision

Connections

CN.4c Recognize and apply mathematics in contexts outside of mathematics

• Solving Literal Equations
• Transforming Formulas
• More on Roots

Objectives

- Transform literal equations.
- Transform formulas.
- Find the two square roots of a positive number.
- Find the cube root of a number.

Lesson Preparation

Materials

- **Power Up V** (in *Instructional Masters*)
- **graph paper**

Optional

- **Investigation Activity 13** (in *Instructional Masters*)

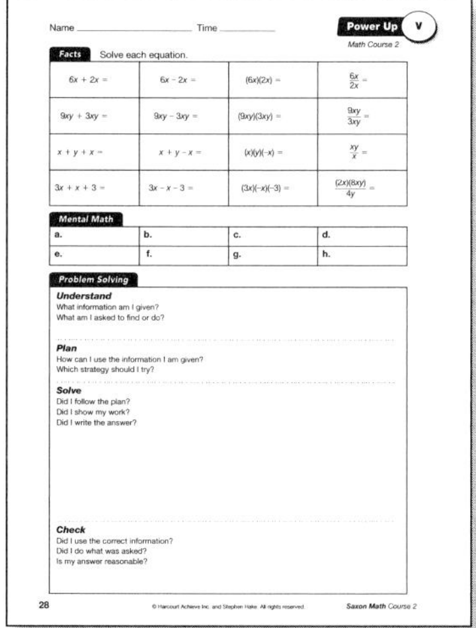

Power Up V

Math Language

English Learners (ESL)
designate

Technology Resources

Student eBook Complete student textbook in electronic format.

Resources and Planner CD Assessment, reteaching, and instructional masters, plus a pacing calendar with standards.

Test and Practice Generator CD Create additional practice sheets and custom-made tests.

www.SaxonPublishers.com Visit for more student activities and planning materials.

Inclusion

Adaptations CD Adapted lessons, investigations, practice and assessments.

Meeting Standards

National Council of Teachers of Mathematics (NCTM)

Numbers and Operations

NO.2c Understand and use the inverse relationships of addition and subtraction, multiplication and division, and squaring and finding square roots to simplify computations and solve problems

NO.3b Develop and analyze algorithms for computing with fractions, decimals, and integers and develop fluency in their use

Algebra

AL.1b Relate and compare different forms of representation for a relationship

AL.2d Recognize and generate equivalent forms for simple algebraic expressions and solve linear equations

Power-Up Discussion *For use with Power Up, p. 739*

Problem-Solving Strategy: Draw a Diagram/ Write an Equation

Every whole number can be expressed as the sum of, at most, four squares. In the diagram we can see that 12 is made up of one 3×3 square and three 1×1 squares. The number sentence that represents the diagram is $12 = 9 + 1 + 1 + 1$.

Diagram how 15, 18, and 20 are composed of—at most—four smaller squares. Write a number sentence to represent each diagram. (*Hint*: You may reposition the smaller squares if necessary.)

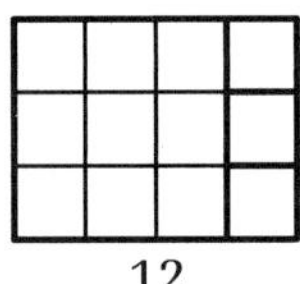

12

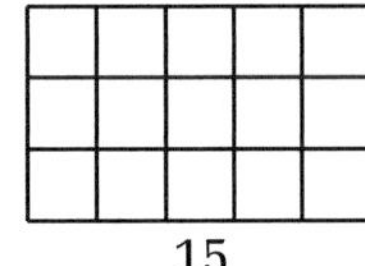

15

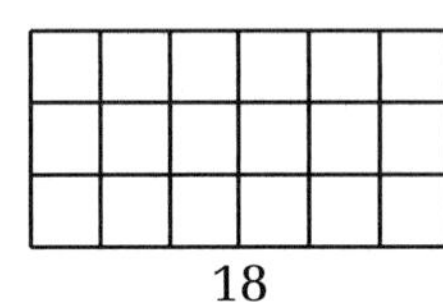

18

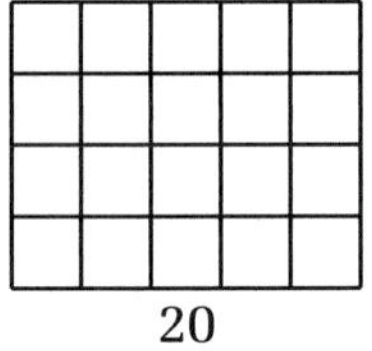

20

Understand ***Understand the problem.***

"What information are we given?"

Every whole number can be expressed as the sum of, at most, four squares.

"What are we asked to do?"

We are asked to diagram how 15, 18, and 20 can be composed of one, two, three, or four smaller squares, and to write a number sentence for each diagram.

Plan ***Make a plan.***

"What problem-solving strategy will we use?"

We have been asked to *draw a diagram* and *write a number sentence.*

Solve ***Carry out the plan.***

"How can we represent the three numbers shown as a sum of four or fewer squares?"

We can divide 15 into one large 3-by-3 square, one 2-by-2 square, and two 1-by-1 squares. We can split 18 into two equal 3-by-3 squares. We create one 4-by-4 square and one 2-by-2 square from 20 smaller squares:

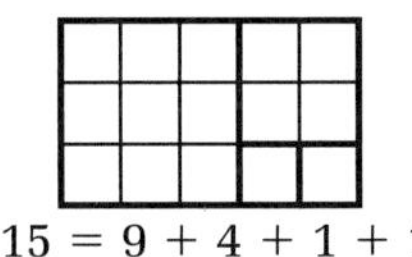

$15 = 9 + 4 + 1 + 1$

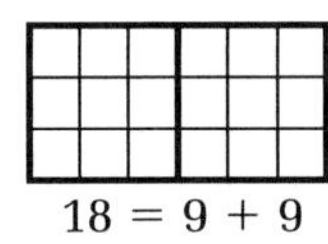

$18 = 9 + 9$

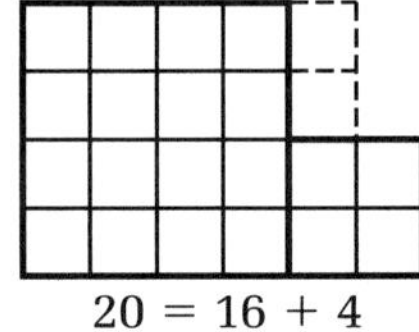

$20 = 16 + 4$

Check ***Look back.***

"Did we do what we were asked to do?

Yes, we drew diagrams and wrote number sentences for each of the three numbers.

"How does drawing a diagram help us verify our solution is valid?"

We can see the solution, so we can visually verify that our methods were correct.

LESSON 106

• Solving Literal Equations
• Transforming Formulas
• More on Roots

Power Up — *Building Power*

facts Power Up V

mental math

a. **Positive/Negative:** $(-5)^3$ -125

b. **Scientific Notation:** $(8 \times 10^3)(5 \times 10^{-5})$ 4×10^{-1}

c. **Ratio:** $\frac{a}{3.6} = \frac{0.9}{1.8}$ 1.8

d. **Measurement:** Convert 2 sq. yd to sq. ft. 18 sq. ft

e. **Percent:** $66\frac{2}{3}$% of $45 $30

f. **Percent:** $33\frac{1}{3}$% less than $45 $30

g. **Geometry:** When plotting an ordered pair on a coordinate grid, which axis do you start with? the *x*-axis

h. **Percent/Estimation:** Estimate a 15% tip on a $39.67 bill. $6.00

problem solving

Every whole number can be expressed as the sum of, *at most,* four squares. In the diagram we can see that 12 is made up of one 3 × 3 square and three 1 × 1 squares. The number sentence that represents the diagram is 12 = 9 + 1 + 1 + 1.

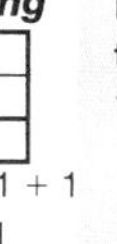

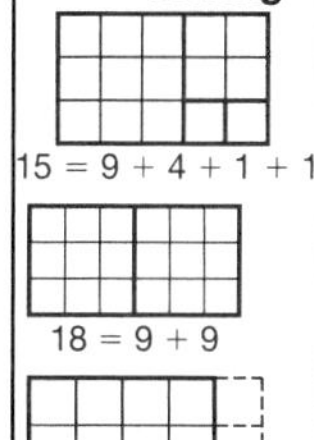

15 = 9 + 4 + 1 + 1

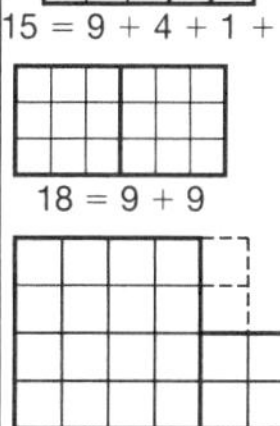

18 = 9 + 9

20 = 16 + 4

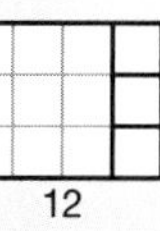

12

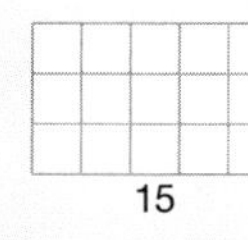

15

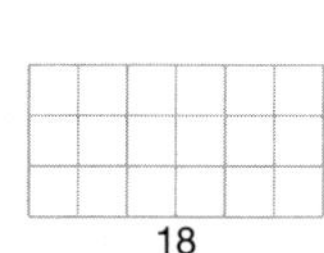

18

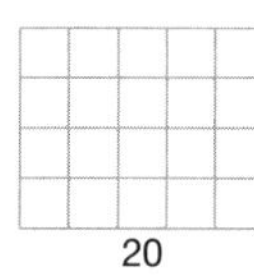

20

Diagram how 15, 18, and 20 are composed of—at most—four smaller squares. Write a number sentence to represent each diagram. (*Hint:* You may reposition the smaller squares if necessary.)

New Concepts — *Increasing Knowledge*

solving literal equations

A **literal equation** is an equation that contains letters instead of numbers. We can rearrange (transform) literal equations by using the rules we have learned.

Lesson 106 739

Facts Solve each equation.

$6x + 2x = 8x$	$6x - 2x = 4x$	$(6x)(2x) = 12x^2$	$\frac{6x}{2x} = 3$
$9xy + 3xy = 12xy$	$9xy - 3xy = 6xy$	$(9xy)(3xy) = 27x^2y^2$	$\frac{9xy}{3xy} = 3$
$x + y + x = 2x + y$	$x + y - x = y$	$(x)(y)(-x) = -x^2y$	$\frac{xy}{x} = y$
$3x + x + 3 = 4x + 3$	$3x - x - 3 = 2x - 3$	$(3x)(-x)(-3) = 9x^2$	$\frac{(2x)(8xy)}{4y} = 4x^2$

1 Power Up

Facts

Distribute **Power Up V** to students. See answers below.

Mental Math

Encourage students to share different ways to mentally compute these exercises. Strategies for exercises **c** and **d** are listed below.

c. Cross Multiply and Divide

$1.8a = 3.6 \times 0.9$

$a = (3.6 \times 0.9) \div 1.8$

$a = 2 \times 0.9$

$a = 1.8$

Find an Equivalent Fraction

$\frac{0.9}{1.8} \times \frac{2}{2} = \frac{1.8}{3.6}$

$a = 1.8$

d. Find 1 Unit and Multiply

$1\text{ yd}^2 = \frac{3\text{ ft}}{\text{yd}} \times \frac{3\text{ ft}}{\text{yd}} = 9\text{ ft}^2$

$2\text{ yd}^2 = 18\text{ ft}^2$

Use Unit Multipliers

$2\text{ yd}^2 \times \frac{3\text{ ft}}{\text{yd}} \times \frac{3\text{ ft}}{\text{yd}} = 18\text{ ft}^2$

Problem Solving

Refer to **Power-Up Discussion,** p. 739B.

2 New Concepts

Instruction

Provide a quick review by solving for *x* in the equation: $x + 5 = 7$. Point out to students that they have been solving for variables in many previous lessons. Write the equation and the steps of its solution on the board.

$$x + 5 = 7$$
$$x + 5 - 5 = 7 - 5$$
$$x = 2$$

(continued)

2 New Concepts (Continued)

Example 1

Instruction

As you work through this example, write the equation and the steps of its solution to the right of the solution of $x + 5 = 7$.

$x + 5 = 7$	$x + a = b$
$x + 5 - 5 = 7 - 5$	$x + a - a = b - a$
$x = 2$	$x = b - a$

Explain to students that solving for a variable in a literal equation focuses on the *process* of solving an equation, rather than on finding the numerical answer to the equation.

Example 2

Instruction

Now that students have an understanding of literal equations, ask them to solve the following equation for x: $\frac{x}{a} = b$.

$$\frac{x}{a} = b$$
$$\frac{x}{a}(a) = b(a)$$
$$x = ab$$

Instruction

Tell students that they should show or describe all of their steps when transforming literal equations and formulas, especially when they are changing the way a formula is written.

Example 3

Instruction

Have students solve the equation for w using the values $l = 4$, $A = 8$; the values $l = 6$, $A = 24$; and the values $l = 5$, $A = 15$. This should help students understand that the formula can be solved for any reasonable values for the rectangle.

Instruction

Remind students that a perfect square is the product when a whole number is multiplied by itself. Emphasize that the symbol $\sqrt{\ }$ implies *only* the principal square root.

(continued)

Example 1

Solve for x: $x + a = b$

Solution

We solve for x by isolating x on one side of the equation. We do this by adding $-a$ to both sides of the equation.

$x + a = b$	equation
$x + a - a = b - a$	added $-a$ to both sides
$\mathbf{x = b - a}$	simplified

Example 2

Solve for x: $ax = b$

Solution

To solve for x, we divide both sides of the equation by a.

$ax = b$	equation
$\frac{\overset{1}{\cancel{a}}x}{\underset{1}{\cancel{a}}} = \frac{b}{a}$	divided by a
$x = \mathbf{\frac{b}{a}}$	simplified

transforming formulas

Formulas are literal equations that we can use to solve certain kinds of problems. Often it is necessary to change the way a formula is written.

Example 3

Solve for w: $A = lw$

Solution

This is a formula for finding the area of a rectangle. We see that w is to the right of the equal sign and is multiplied by l. To undo the multiplication by l, we can divide both sides of the equation by l.

$A = lw$	equation
$\frac{A}{l} = \frac{\overset{1}{\cancel{l}}w}{\underset{1}{\cancel{l}}}$	divided by l
$w = \mathbf{\frac{A}{l}}$	simplified

Thinking Skill

Verify

How can we verify that the changed formula is true?

Substitute any value for l and w into both formulas and solve for A. If the value of A is the same, the changed formula is true.

more on roots

The perfect square 25 has both positive and negative square roots, 5 and −5.

$$5 \cdot 5 = 25 \qquad (-5)(-5) = 25$$

Thus the equation $x^2 = 25$ has two solutions, 5 and −5.

Math Background

"Can you approximate a square root on a calculator without the square root key?"

Yes, you can use a guess and average method. Guess what the square root of the number might be. Divide the number by this first guess. If the quotient and the divisor are about the same, the first guess is a good approximation of the square root. If not, use the average of the quotient and the guess as the second guess. Divide and see how close this quotient is to the new divisor. If they are about the same, then the second guess is a good approximation of the square root. If not, continue averaging and dividing until the guess and quotient are about the same. For example: Find the square root of 117.

First guess:	10.5; 117 ÷ 10.5 = 11.14
Second guess:	(10.5 + 11.14) ÷ 2 = 10.82; 117 ÷ 10.82 = 10.81
Third guess:	(10.81 + 10.82) ÷ 2 = 10.815; 117 ÷ 10.815 = 10.818

So the square root of 117 is about 10.82 (10.815 × 10.815 = 117.0724).

The positive square root of a number is sometimes called the *principal* square root. So the principal square root of 25 is 5. The radical symbol $\sqrt{\ }$ implies the principal root. So $\sqrt{25}$ is 5 only and does not include −5.

Example 4

What are the two square roots of 5?

Solution

The two square roots of 5 are $\boldsymbol{\sqrt{5}}$ and the opposite of $\sqrt{5}$, which is $\boldsymbol{-\sqrt{5}}$.

A radical symbol may be used to indicate other roots besides square roots. The expression below means **cube root** of 64. The small 3 is called the **index** of the root. The cube root of 64 is the number that, when used as a factor three times, yields a product of 64.

$$\sqrt[3]{64}$$

$$(?)(?)(?) = 64$$

Thus the cube root of 64 is 4 because

$$4 \cdot 4 \cdot 4 = 64$$

Discuss Is −4 a cube root of 64? Why or why not? No; The cube of −4 is a negative number: (−4)(−4)(−4) = −64

Example 5

Simplify:

a. $\boldsymbol{\sqrt[3]{1000}}$ **b.** $\boldsymbol{\sqrt[3]{-27}}$

Solution

a. The cube root of 1000 is **10** because $10 \cdot 10 \cdot 10 = 1000$. Notice that −10 is not a cube root of 1000, because $(-10)(-10)(-10) = -1000$.

b. The cube root of −27 is **−3** because $(-3)(-3)(-3) = -27$.

Predict Which will be a negative number, the cube root of 8 or the cube root of −8? cube root of −8

Practice Set

a. Solve for a: $a + b = c$ $a = c - b$

▶ **b.** **Analyze** Solve for w: $wx = y$ $w = \frac{y}{x}$

c. Solve for y: $y - b = mx$ $y = mx + b$

d. Solve the formula for the area of a parallelogram for b.

$A = bh$ $b = \frac{A}{h}$

▶ **e.** **Predict** What are the two square roots of 16? 4, −4

▶ **Generalize** Simplify:

f. $\sqrt[3]{125}$ 5 **g.** $\sqrt[3]{-8}$ −2

▶ See Math Conversations in the sidebar.

Teacher Tip

For this lesson and for future work, provide support for the development of good work habits by requesting that when solving for an unknown, students consistently **write each step on a separate line.** This is a simple way to help students avoid mistakes when solving equations.

2 New Concepts (Continued)

Example 4

Instruction

Point out that we don't need to find a numerical value for the square root of 5. The symbolic representation is enough for this problem and others like it.

Instruction

Help students understand that because the root is used as a factor three times they can find the cube root of both positive and negative numbers. The cube root of a positive number is positive, and the cube root of a negative number is negative.

Example 5

Instruction

Provide a concrete example for the concept of cubes and cube roots connecting them with the volume of a cube and the length of its edges. Point out that volume is expressed in cubic units.

Check understanding by asking:

"Can the answer to part b be (−3)(3)(3)? Why or why not?" No, because the factors must be the same number with the same sign.

Practice Set

Problem b Analyze

Discuss what methods students used to solve for w. Samples: divide by x; multiply by $\frac{1}{x}$

Problem e Predict

Help students understand that all positive numbers have two square roots, one that is positive and one that is negative. The positive square root is sometimes called the principal square root.

Problems f and g Generalize

Ask students to explain why the cube root for problem **f** is positive while the cube root for problem **g** is negative. Sample: The cube root has to be a factor 3 times, so it has to be positive for a positive number, and negative for a negative number. A positive can be a factor any number of times and still be positive, but a negative factor times a negative factor is positive and it becomes negative again only by multiplying again by a negative factor.

3 Written Practice

Math Conversations

Discussion opportunities are provided below.

Problem 1 Estimate

"What mental computation could Marcos have used before he went to the checkout to be sure that $20 was enough to pay for his purchases?" Sample: $1.85 rounds to $2 and $12.95 rounds to $13. $2 + $2 + $13 is $17, and even if the tax was 10%, that would be $1.70, and $17 and $1.70 is $18.70, so $20 is enough.

Problem 5 Analyze

Have students imagine that the triangle is translated so that the base is on the x-axis. Discuss what would change and what would remain the same. Use the following questions to start the discussion and ask students to explain their answers.

"Will the coordinates change?" yes

"Is the length of the hypotenuse the same?" yes

"Does the length of the base change?" no

Errors and Misconceptions

Problem 2

There are a couple of ways that students can make errors in this problem. Some students may not remember that 1 is not prime, and some students may have included 11, which is prime but has 2 digits. Help students see that there are 4 one-digit prime numbers on the spinner.

(continued)

Written Practice *Strengthening Concepts*

▶ **1.** (46) **Estimate** Marcos bought 2 pairs of socks priced at $1.85 per pair and a T-shirt priced at $12.95. The sales tax was 6%. If Marcos paid with a $20 bill, what was his change? (round to the nearest cent) $2.35

▶ * **2.** (Inv. 8) The face of this spinner is divided into twelfths.

a. If the spinner is spun once, what are the odds that the spinner will land on a one-digit prime number? 1 to 2

b. If the spinner is spun twice, what is the chance that it will land on an even number both times? 25%

3. (46) At $5.60 per pound, the cheddar cheese costs how many cents per ounce? 35¢ per ounce

4. (55) After 6 days at her new job, Katelyn had wrapped an average number of 90 gifts per day. She wrapped 75 of the gifts on her first day. If the first day is not counted, what is the average number of gifts Katelyn wrapped per day during the next 5 days? 93

▶ * **5.** (99) **Analyze** The ordered pairs (2, 4), (2, −1), and (0, −1) designate the vertices of a right triangle. What is the length of the hypotenuse of the triangle? $\sqrt{29}$ units

Use ratio boxes to solve problems **6–8.**

6. (72) Justin finished 3 problems in 4 minutes. At that rate, how long will it take him to finish the remaining 27 problems? 36 minutes

7. (66) The ratio of members to visitors in the pool was 2 to 3. If there were 60 people in the pool, how many were visitors? 36 visitors

8. (92) The number of students enrolled in chemistry increased 25 percent this year. If there are 80 students enrolled in chemistry this year, how many were enrolled in chemistry last year? 64 students

9. (106) **a.** What are the two square roots of 64? 8 and −8

b. What is the cube root of −64? −4

10. (60) Write an equation to solve this problem: $W_N = 2.25 \times 40$; 90

What number is 225 percent of 40?

* **11.** (100) **a.** **Model** Draw a number line and show the locations of these numbers:

$$|-2|, \frac{2}{2}, \sqrt{2}, 2^2$$

b. Which of these numbers are rational numbers? $|-2|, \frac{2}{2}, 2^2$

11. a.

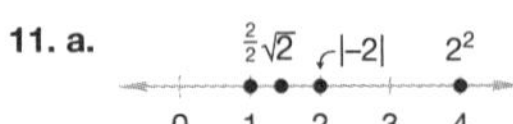

▶ See Math Conversations in the sidebar.

English Learners

Explain the meaning of **designate** in problem 5. Say:

"Designate means to show or point out. If ordered pairs designate a point, that means that the pairs show where the point is located (on the coordinate plane)."

Ask students to designate a location to put student jackets and caps in the classroom. Have students explain why they designated that area.

Write equations to solve problems **12** and **13**.

▶ **12.** Sixty-six is $66\frac{2}{3}$ percent of what number? $66 = \frac{2}{3} \times W_N$; 99
(77)

13. Seventy-five percent of what number is 2.4? $0.75 \times W_N = 2.4$; 3.2
(77)

14. Complete the table.
(48)

Fraction	Decimal	Percent
a. $1\frac{1}{20}$	**b.** 1.05	105%

15. Make a table of ordered pairs for the function $y = x - 2$. Then graph the function on a coordinate plane. See student work.
(Inv. 9)

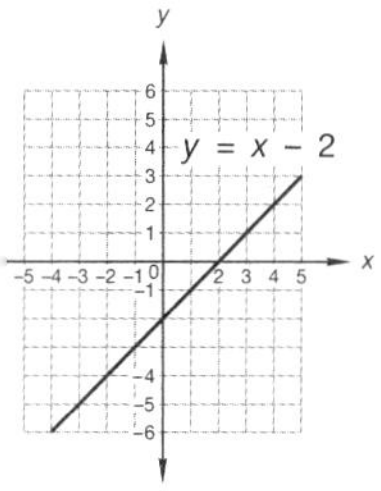

16. Divide 6.75 by 81 and write the quotient rounded to three decimal places. 0.083
(42)

17. Multiply. Write the product in scientific notation. 2.88×10^{-15}
(83)

$$(4.8 \times 10^{-10})(6 \times 10^{-6})$$

18. Evaluate: $x^2 + bx + c$ if $x = -3$, $b = -5$, and $c = 6$ 30
(91)

▶* **19.** **Explain** Find the area of this figure. Dimensions are in millimeters. Corners that look square are square. (Use 3.14 for π.) Show your work and explain how you found your answer.
(104)

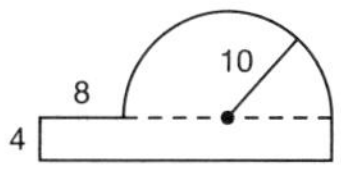

19. 269 mm^2; Sample: The dimensions of the rectangle are 4 mm by 28 mm (10 + 10 + 8). Its area is 112 mm^2. The area of the semicircle is $\frac{\pi r^2}{2} = \frac{3.14(100)}{2} =$ 157 mm^2. 112 + 157 = 269 mm^2, the area of the entire figure.

* **20.** **a.** Find the surface area of this right triangular prism. Dimensions are in centimeters. 132 cm^2
(88, 105)

b. Convert the surface area to square millimeters. 13,200 mm^2

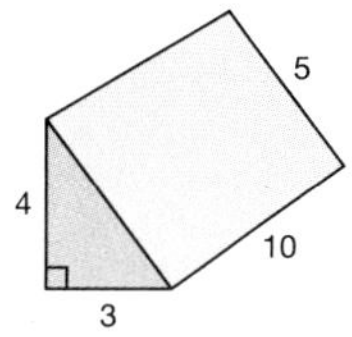

▶* **21.** **Analyze** Find the volume of this right circular cylinder. Dimensions are in inches. (Use 3.14 for π.) 31.4 in.^{3}
(95)

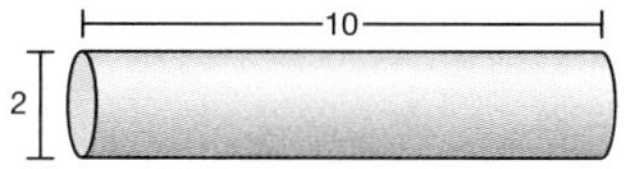

22. Find $m\angle b$ in the figure below. 40°
(40)

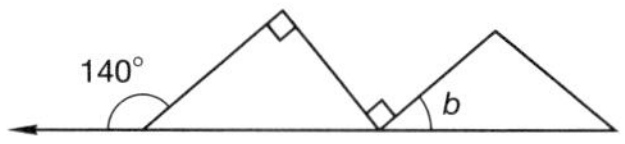

* **23.** **a.** Solve for x: $x + c = d$ $x = d - c$
(106)

b. Solve for n: $an = b$ $n = \frac{b}{a}$

▶* **24.** **Generalize** Solve: $6w - 2(4 + w) = w + 7$ 5
(102)

▶ See Math Conversations in the sidebar.

3 Written Practice *(Continued)*

Math Conversations

Discussion opportunities are provided below.

Problem 19 Explain

Ask students to explain how they subdivided the figure and what formulas they used. There really is only one way for students to subdivide this figure (unless they subdivide the rectangle), and you may want to use this opportunity to explain that sometimes there are several ways to solve a problem, but often, as in this problem, there is only one way. The figure is subdivided into a 4 mm by 28 mm rectangle and a semicircle with a radius of 10 mm.

Problem 21 Analyze

"Suppose the dimensions are in feet or some other unit. How would the answer change?" Sample: Only the units would change.

Problem 24 Generalize

Have volunteers describe how they solved the equation. Ask them to include an explanation of how they isolated the variable. Sample: First I simplified the left side of the equation, next I isolated the w terms on the left side by subtracting w from both sides, then I added 8 to both sides, and finally I divided both sides by 3.

Errors and Misconceptions

Problem 12

To help students whose answer is 44, have them check how they wrote the equation. It should be $66 = \frac{2}{3} \times W_N$, not $\frac{2}{3} \times 66 = W_N$.

Problem 19

Students whose answer is 426 mm^2 forgot to divide the area of the circle by 2. Have them go back over their steps to be sure that they used $\frac{\pi r^2}{2}$ and not just πr^2.

(continued)

3 Written Practice (Continued)

Math Conversations

Discussion opportunities are provided below.

Errors and Misconceptions

Problem 26

If students give an answer of 39, then they did not read the problem carefully enough to notice the word *product*. Have them reread the problem again.

25. (93) Solve this inequality and graph its solution:

$$6x + 8 < 14$$

$x < 1$

−2 −1 0 1 2

▶* **26.** (101) Thirty-seven is five less than the product of what number and three? 14

Generalize Simplify:

27. (63) $25 - [3^2 + 2(5 - 3)]$ 12

* **28.** (103) $\dfrac{6x^2 + (5x)(2x)}{4x}$ $4x$

29. (57) $4^0 + 3^{-1} + 2^{-2}$ $1\frac{7}{12}$

* **30.** (103, 105) $(-3)(-2)(+4)(-1) + (-3)^2 + \sqrt[3]{-64} - (-2)^3$ −11

Early Finishers
Real-World Application

The illustration below represents a semicircular window with a stained glass circle in the middle.

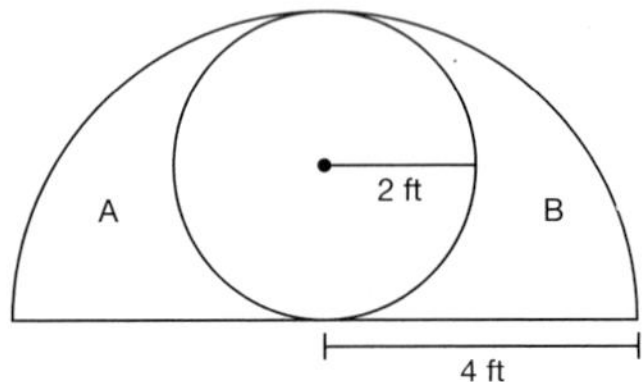

a. What is the area of the entire window? 25.12 ft^2

b. What is the area of the circular stained glass window? 12.56 ft^2

c. What is the combined area of sections A and B of the window? Use 3.14 for π. 12.56 ft^2

d. What portion of the whole window is the stained glass? Sample: The stained glass is $\frac{1}{2}$ the size of the semicircle.

▶ See Math Conversations in the sidebar.

Looking Forward

Transforming a formula by solving for a specific variable prepares students for:

- **Lesson 108,** substituting values into formulas.

• Slope

Objectives

- Determine whether the slope of a line is positive, negative, zero or cannot be determined.
- Find the slope of a line from its graph.

Lesson Preparation

Materials

- **Power Up Q** (in *Instructional Masters*)
- **Lesson Activity 23 Transparency** (in *Instructional Masters*) or **graph paper**
- **Lesson Activity 24** (in *Instructional Masters*)

Optional

- **Investigation Activity 13** (in *Instructional Masters;* several per student)

Math Language

New	English Learners (ESL)
slope	leg of a triangle

Technology Resources

Student eBook Complete student textbook in electronic format.

Resources and Planner CD Blackline masters, plus a pacing calendar with standards.

Test and Practice Generator CD Create additional practice sheets and custom-made tests.

www.SaxonPublishers.com Visit for more student activities and planning materials.

Inclusion

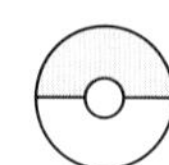

Adaptations CD Adapted lessons, investigations, practice and assessments.

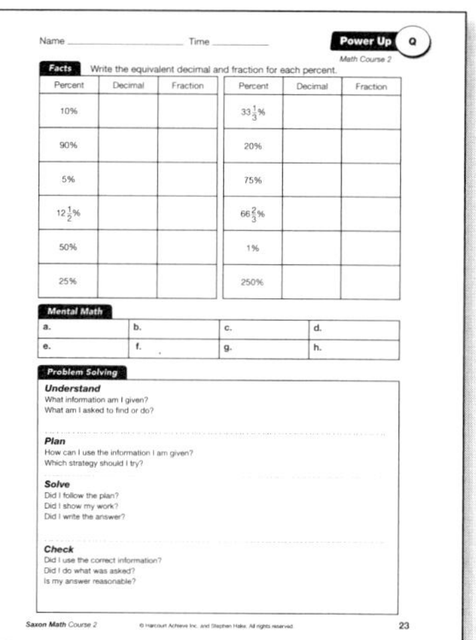

Name ________ Time ________ **Power Up Q** *Math Course 2*

Facts Write the equivalent decimal and fraction for each percent.

Percent	Decimal	Fraction	Percent	Decimal	Fraction
10%			$33\frac{1}{3}\%$		
90%			20%		
5%			75%		
$12\frac{1}{2}\%$			$66\frac{2}{3}\%$		
50%			1%		
25%			250%		

Mental Math

a.	b.	c.	d.
e.	f.	g.	h.

Problem Solving

Understand
What information am I given?
What am I asked to find or do?

Plan
How can I use the information I am given?
Which strategy should I try?

Solve
Did I follow the plan?
Did I show my work?
Did I write the answer?

Check
Did I use the correct information?
Did I do what was asked?
Is my answer reasonable?

Saxon Math Course 2 © Harcourt Achieve Inc. and Stephen Hake. All rights reserved. 23

Power Up Q

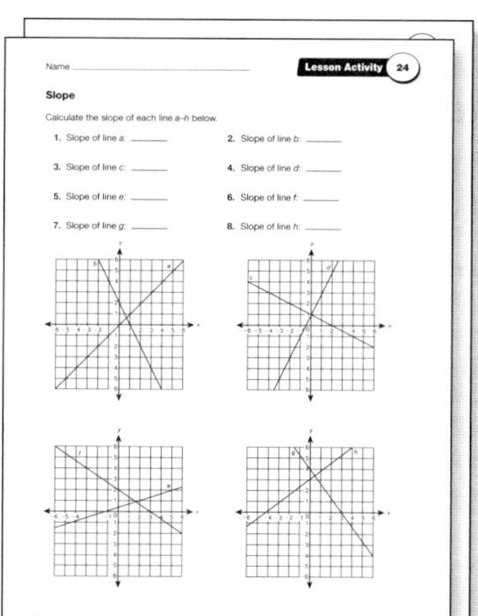

Name ________ **Lesson Activity 24**

Slope

Calculate the slope of each line *a–h* below.

1. Slope of line *a*: ______
2. Slope of line *b*: ______
3. Slope of line *c*: ______
4. Slope of line *d*: ______
5. Slope of line *e*: ______
6. Slope of line *f*: ______
7. Slope of line *g*: ______
8. Slope of line *h*: ______

98 © Harcourt Achieve Inc. and Stephen Hake. All rights reserved. *Saxon Math* Course 2

Lesson Activity 24

Meeting Standards

National Council of Teachers of Mathematics (NCTM)

Algebra

AL.2b Explore relationships between symbolic expressions and graphs of lines, paying particular attention to the meaning of intercept and slope

AL.4a Use graphs to analyze the nature of changes in quantities in linear relationships

Geometry

GM.4d Use geometric models to represent and explain numerical and algebraic relationships

Power-Up Discussion For use with Power Up, p. 745

Problem-Solving Strategy: Use Logical Reasoning/ Write an Equation

Four identical blocks marked x, a 250-g mass, and a 500-g mass were balanced on a scale as shown. Write an equation to represent this balanced scale, and find the mass of each block.

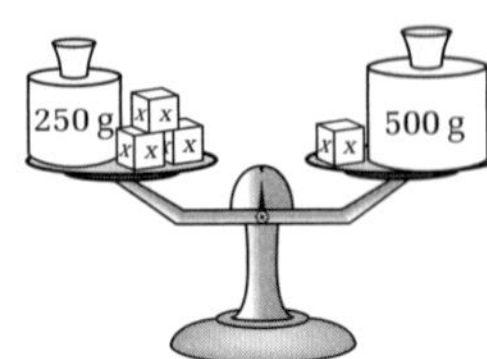

Understand Understand the problem.

"What information are we given?"

Some blocks marked x and some weights are distributed on a balanced scale.

"What are we asked to do?"

We are asked to write an equation to represent the balanced scale, and to find the mass of each block marked x.

Plan Make a plan.

"What problem-solving strategy will we use?"

We will *write an equation* to represent the scale, then *use logical reasoning* to simplify and solve the equation to solve for x.

Solve Carry out the plan.

"What is the equataion that is depicted by the balanced scale?"

$3x + 250 = x + 500$

"What can we mentally remove from each side of the scale?"

One block marked x.

"If we remove one block from each side of the scale, what will be the simplified equation be?

$2x + 250 = 500$

"What is the mass of each of the blocks?"

125 g

Check Look back.

"Did we do what we were asked to do?"

Yes, we wrote an equation illustrating the balanced scale and found the mass of each block marked x.

"How can we verify our solution is correct?"

We can substitute the value for x into the original equation:

$$3(125) + 250 = (125) + 500$$
$$375 + 250 = 125 + 500$$
$$625 = 625$$

LESSON
107

• Slope

Power Up — *Building Power*

facts Power Up Q

mental math

a. **Positive/Negative:** $(-2.5)(-4)$ 10

b. **Scientific Notation:** $(2.5 \times 10^6)^2$ 6.25×10^{12}

c. **Algebra:** $2x - 1\frac{1}{2} = 4\frac{1}{2}$ 3

d. **Measurement:** Convert −50°C to degrees Fahrenheit. −58°F

e. **Percent:** 75% of \$60 \$45

f. **Percent:** 75% more than \$60 \$105

g. **Measurement:** 32 oz. is what fraction of a gallon? $\frac{1}{4}$

h. **Calculation:** 7×8, -1, $\div 5$, $\times 3$, $+2$, $\div 5$, $\times 7$, $+1$, $\times 2$, -1, $\div 3$, $+3$, $\sqrt{\ }$ 6

problem solving

Four identical blocks marked *x*, a 250-g mass, and a 500-g mass were balanced on a scale as shown. Write an equation to represent this balanced scale, and find the mass of each block. $x = 125$ g

New Concept — *Increasing Knowledge*

Below are the graphs of two functions. The graph of the function on the left indicates the number of feet that equal a given number of yards. Changing the number of yards by one changes the number of feet by three. The graph of the function on the right shows the inverse relationship, the number of yards that equal a given number of feet. Changing the number of feet by one changes the number of yards by one third.

Thinking Skill
Explain

Why does changing the number of feet by 1 change the number of yards by $\frac{1}{3}$? The relationship of yards to feet is: 1 yd = 3 ft, or 1 to 3 or $\frac{1}{3}$.

Yards to Feet

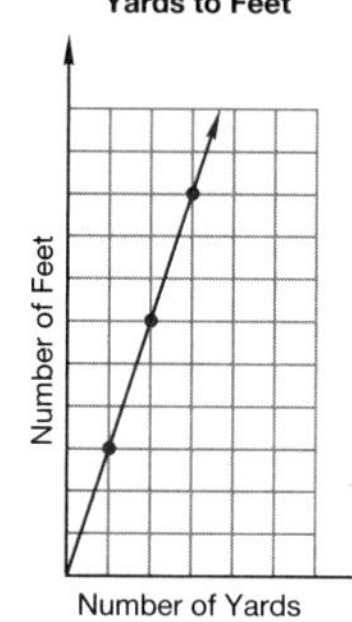

Feet to Yards

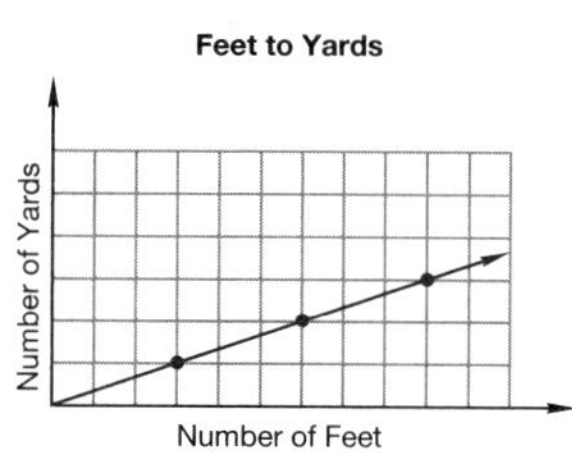

Facts Write the equivalent decimal and fraction for each percent.

Percent	Decimal	Fraction	Percent	Decimal	Fraction
10%	0.1	$\frac{1}{10}$	$33\frac{1}{3}\%$	$0.\overline{3}$	$\frac{1}{3}$
90%	0.9	$\frac{9}{10}$	20%	0.2	$\frac{1}{5}$
5%	0.05	$\frac{1}{20}$	75%	0.75	$\frac{3}{4}$
$12\frac{1}{2}\%$	0.125	$\frac{1}{8}$	$66\frac{2}{3}\%$	$0.\overline{6}$	$\frac{2}{3}$
50%	0.5	$\frac{1}{2}$	1%	0.01	$\frac{1}{100}$
25%	0.25	$\frac{1}{4}$	250%	2.5	$2\frac{1}{2}$

1 Power Up

Facts

Distribute **Power Up Q** to students. See answers below.

Mental Math

Encourage students to share different ways to mentally compute these exercises. Strategies for exercises **d**, **e**, and **g** are listed below.

d. Use Known Information

I know that −40°C is the same as −40°F.
10°C = 18°F, so −50°C = −40°F − 18°F.
−50°C = − 58°F

e. Use Logical Reasoning

$75\% = \frac{3}{4}$
$\frac{1}{4}$ of 60 = 15
$\frac{3}{4}$ of 60 = 45

Multiply by a Fraction

$75\% = \frac{3}{4}$
$\frac{3}{4} \times 60 = 3 \times 15 = 45$

g. Convert Units

32 oz = 1 qt
4 qt = 1 gal
32 oz = $\frac{1}{4}$ gal

Make a Fraction

1 gal = 128 oz
$\frac{32 \text{ oz}}{128 \text{ oz}} = \frac{1}{4}$
32 oz = $\frac{1}{4}$ gal

Problem Solving

Refer to **Power-Up Discussion,** p. 745B.

2 New Concepts

Instruction

Have students describe what they know about graphed lines. Elicit that graphed lines show how a change in one variable will affect another variable. Explain to students that finding the slope of a graphed line gives us a number to describe this relationship.

Students may not recognize the term *inverse relationship.* Explain that the graph on the left shows $\frac{\text{feet}}{\text{yards}}$, $\frac{3}{1}$, while the graph on the right shows $\frac{\text{yards}}{\text{feet}}$, $\frac{1}{3}$. The fraction $\frac{1}{3}$ is the inverse of $\frac{3}{1}$. Relationships between variables are inverse if one variable increases as the other decreases.

(continued)

2 New Concepts (Continued)

Instruction

Guide students to understand that when we say that the slope is upward or downward, we are referring to its direction from left to right.

Example 1

Instruction

Ask students to visualize what it would be like if they could walk along the line of each graph in this example from left to right. Suggest that students can use this technique to determine if the slope of a line is positive, negative, zero, or undefined.

Sample answers may include:

- Walking on this line is like walking uphill. The slope is positive.
- Walking on this line is like walking on a flat surface. The slope is zero.
- Walking on this line is like walking downhill. The slope is negative.
- Walking on this line would be impossible because it is vertical. The slope cannot be determined.

Tell students that sometimes the term *undefined* is used to refer to graphs for which the slope cannot be determined.

(continued)

Notice that the graph of the function on the left has a steep upward slant going from left to right, while the graph of the function on the right also has an upward slant but is not as steep. The "slant" of the graph of a function is called its **slope.** We assign a number to a slope to indicate how steep the slope is and whether the slope is upward or downward. If the slope is upward, the number is positive. If the slope is downward, the number is negative. If the graph is horizontal, the slope is neither positive nor negative; it is zero. If the graph is vertical, the slope cannot be determined.

Example 1

State whether the slope of each line is positive, negative, zero, or cannot be determined.

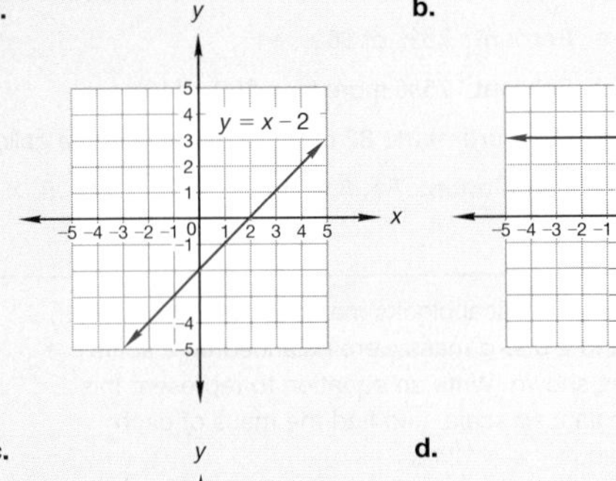

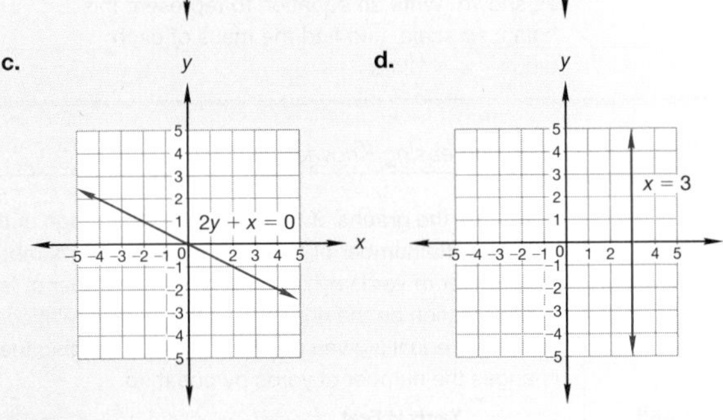

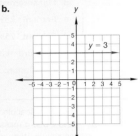

Solution

To determine the sign of the slope, follow the graph of the function with your eyes *from left to right* as though you were reading.

a. From left to right, the graphed line rises, so the slope is **positive.**

b. From left to right, the graphed line does not rise or fall, so the slope is **zero.**

c. From left to right, the graphed line slopes downward, so the slope is **negative.**

Teacher Tip

Emphasize that there are many ways to **find the slope of a line.** But there is only one slope for any one line. Encourage students to share their work to see the different ways of finding slope.

Math Background

Why are the slope of a horizontal line zero and the slope of a vertical line undefined?

Slope is a ratio of two numbers representing the rise and the run of a line. One of the two numbers is zero if a line is horizontal or vertical. A line that is horizontal has no rise, so whatever number is chosen for the run, the rise is zero. A line that is vertical has no run, so whatever number is chosen for the rise, the run is zero.

So for a horizontal line, the slope $\frac{0}{n}$ equals 0. For a vertical line, the slope $\frac{n}{0}$ is undefined because division by zero is undefined.

d. There is no left to right component of the graphed line, so we cannot determine if the line is rising or falling. The slope is not positive, not negative, and not zero. The slope of a vertical line **cannot be determined.**

To determine the numerical value of the slope of a line, it is helpful to draw a right triangle using the background grid of the coordinate plane and a portion of the graphed line. First we look for points where the graphed line crosses intersections of the grid. We have circled some of these points on the graphs below.

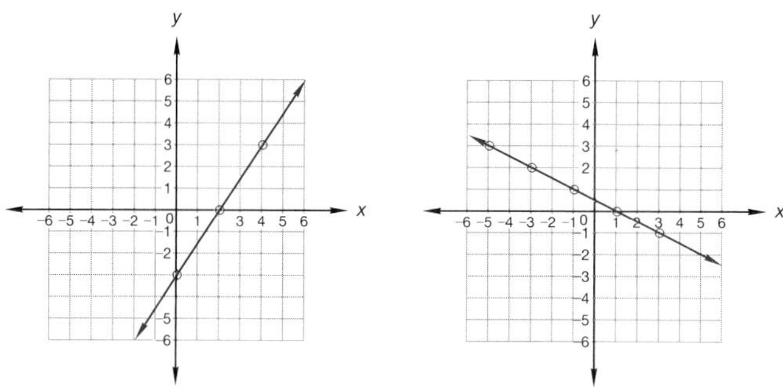

Next we select two points from the graphed line and, following the background grid, sketch the legs of a right triangle so that the legs intersect the chosen points. (It is a helpful practice to first select the point to the left and draw the horizontal leg to the right. Then draw the vertical leg to meet the line.)

Discuss Why do you think we look for points where the graphed line crosses intersections of the grid?

If we didn't use those points, we would have to use estimated fractional values to determine the rise and run.

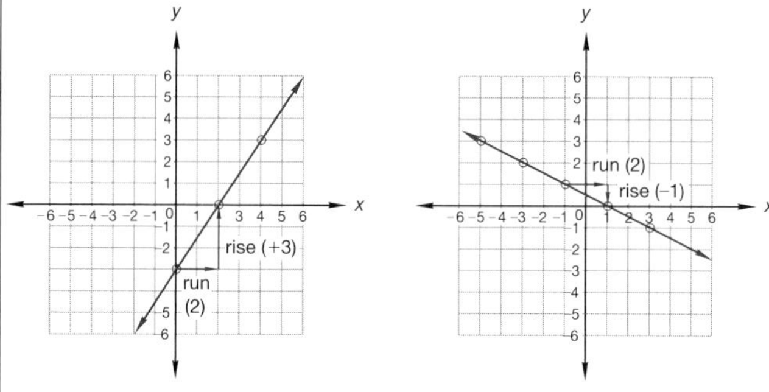

We use the words **run** and **rise** to describe the two legs of the right triangle. The *run* is the length of the horizontal leg, and the *rise* is the length of the vertical leg. We assign a positive sign to the rise if it goes up to meet the graphed line and a negative sign if it goes down to meet the graphed line. In

2 New Concepts *(Continued)*

Instruction

Use the transparency of **Lesson Activity 23** Slope to demonstrate how to use the *rise* and *run* to determine the slope of a line. Emphasize that it is wise to avoid fractional values for the rise and run. To do this, students can use any two points on the line that are at the intersections of the lines on the grid.

Point out to students that they can use any set of points to find the slope of these lines.

- They may find a rise or run based on any two points on the graph, not necessarily points that are nearest to each other.
- A negative run is possible if students do not select a first point that is to the left of the second point being used. Tell students that if both the rise and run are negative, the slope will be a positive number.

For the *Discuss* question, point out that finding a rise and run using estimated fractional values is inexact and may make finding the slope more difficult. Using two whole number points close together on the line will usually result in finding a simple fraction that represents the slope in one step.

(continued)

English Learners

Draw a right triangle on the board. Point to the two legs and say:

"The leg of a triangle is one of the two shorter sides. A right triangle has two legs."

Draw 3 triangles on the board and ask students to identify the legs of each triangle.

2 New Concepts (Continued)

Instruction

Remind students that for a positive slope, both rise and run can be stated as positive values. For a negative slope, either the rise or the run must be stated as a negative. We generally write the run as a positive number and the rise as a negative or positive number depending on whether the slope is negative or positive.

Emphasize the phrase "rise over run" to students. Suggest the following mnemonic device: *You must rise before you can run.* Students may adapt their own mnemonic device, but they should know that the rise is the numerator of the ratio and the run is the denominator.

Example 2

Instruction

Before beginning the work on this example, have students look at the graph and tell you what they know about the slope just by looking at the line. Sample: the slope is positive, the slope is less than 1

(continued)

the graph on the left, the run is 2 and the rise is +3. In the graph on the right, the run is 2 and the rise is −1. We use these numbers to write the slope of each graphed line.

So the slopes of the graphed lines are these ratios:

$$\frac{\text{rise}}{\text{run}} = \frac{+3}{2} = \frac{3}{2} \qquad \frac{\text{rise}}{\text{run}} = \frac{-1}{2} = -\frac{1}{2}$$

The slope of a line is the ratio of its rise to its run ("rise over run").

$$\textbf{slope} = \frac{\textbf{rise}}{\textbf{run}}$$

A line whose rise and run have equal values has a slope of 1. A line whose rise has the opposite value of its run has a slope of −1.

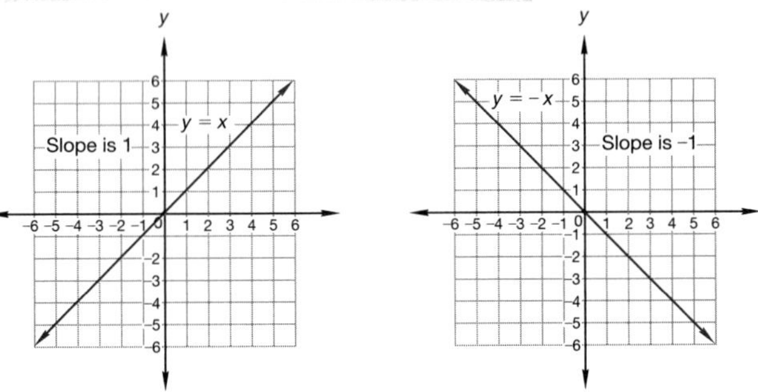

A line that is steeper than the lines above has a slope either greater than 1 or less than −1. A line that is less steep than the lines above has a slope that is between −1 and 1.

Example 2

Find the slope of the graphed line below.

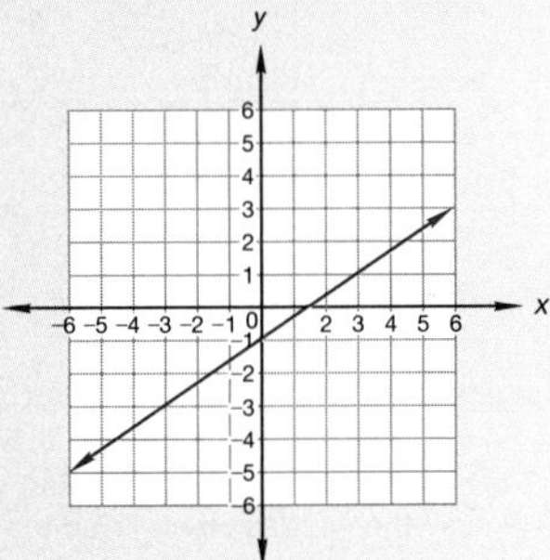

Solution

We note that the slope is positive. We locate and select two points where the graphed line passes through intersections of the grid. We choose the points (0, −1) and (3, 1). Starting from the point to the left, (0, −1), we draw the horizontal leg to the right. Then we draw the vertical leg up to (3, 1).

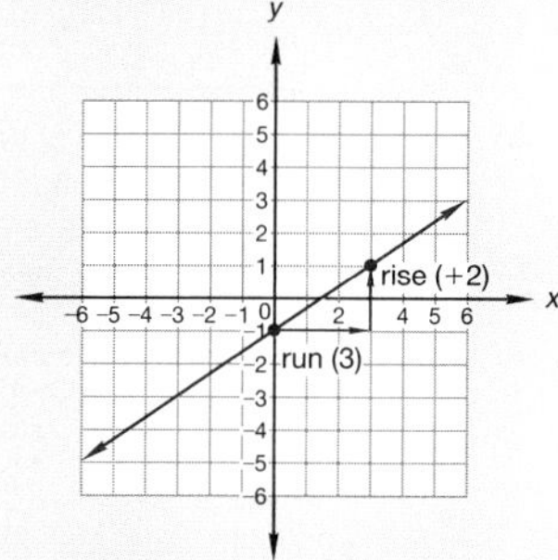

We see that the run is 3 and the rise is positive 2. We write the slope as "rise over run."

$$\text{slope} = \frac{2}{3}$$

Analyze If we had chosen the points (−3, −3) and (3, 1), the run would be 6 and the rise 4. However, the slope would be the same. Why is this true?

$\frac{4}{6}$ reduces to $\frac{2}{3}$. No matter what points we choose on the line, the slope will always be the same.

One way to check the calculation of a slope is to "zoom in" on the graph. When the horizontal change is one unit to the right, the vertical change will equal the slope. To illustrate this, we will zoom in on the square just below and to the right of the origin of the graph above.

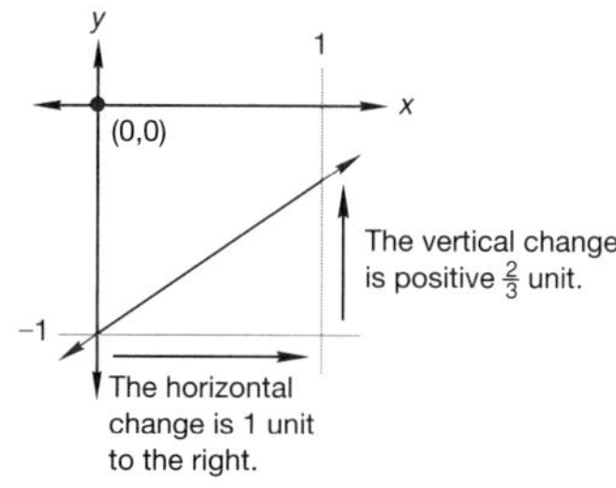

Discuss Summarize how we can *zoom in* to see if a calculated slope is reasonable. **1.** Locate a point of the graph where the graph of the equation passes through the intersection of two grid lines. **2.** Zoom in on this one-unit wide section. **3.** Estimate where the line of the graph intersects the next vertical grid line to the right. **4.** This estimate is the approximate slope and should be close to the calculated slope. For example, in the example shown, the graph of the equation passes through the vertical grid line at about $\frac{2}{3}$ of its height, so the slope is $\frac{2}{3}$.

Inclusion

Many students can benefit from seeing how *slope* is used in the real world. For instance, the *pitch* of a roof is an example of slope. Ask a student to draw on the board a roof with a pitch used in snowy weather. Ask another student to draw a roof with a pitch used to collect the most sunlight on solar panels.

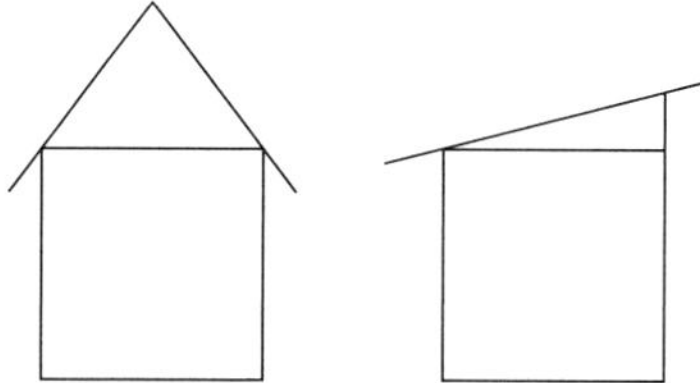

"Why would you use a high-pitched roof in snowy weather?" Sample: snow can easily fall off

"Why would you use a low-pitched roof for solar panels?" Sample: so that the panels can have the most exposure

2 New Concepts (Continued)

Example 2 (continued)

Instruction

Write the two chosen points on the board or overhead. Circle (0, −1).

"This point on the line contains one positive and one negative value. What does this tell us about the rise or run or the slope of the line?" nothing

Emphasize to students that a negative value in one of the points on the line does not make the rise, the run, or the slope negative. It is only the distance between two points that determines these values.

As you discuss the *Analyze* question, you may want to demonstrate quickly how the rise-over-run procedure would work for the points (−3, −3) and (3, 1). Emphasize that both points have integer values and are located at an intersection on the grid.

Instruction

When reviewing the illustration that "zooms in" on one square on the graph, remind students that the *origin* of a graph is where the *x*-axis and *y*-axis intersect. Its coordinates are (0, 0).

Be certain that students understand that the square shown is just to the right and just below the origin.

After completing the *Discuss* question, ask students to describe what they think a single square would look like when they "zoom in" on the graph of a line with a slope greater than 1. The line would intersect the top of the square rather than the right side. The line would move less than one unit right for a full unit up.

(continued)

Activity

Instruction

Provide each student with a copy of **Lesson Activity 24** Slope. Encourage students to draw the rise and run arrows on each graph. You may also provide students with extra copies of **Investigation Activity 13** Coordinate Plane or graph paper to help them complete the activity.

2 New Concepts (Continued)

Practice Set

Problem a Generalize

To see how well students are generalizing the concept of slope, have them look at the two graphs on the first page of this lesson before starting to work on this problem. Ask:

"The slope of one of these graphs is greater than 1, and the slope of the other is less than 1. Which one has a slope greater than 1? Which one has a slope less than 1?" The slope of "Yards to Feet" is greater than 1. The slope of "Feet to Yards" is less than 1.

Problem c Generalize

Discuss how best to find the slope mentally. Many find it easier to calculate the slope first and then decide whether it is positive or negative. Let volunteers describe the procedure they used.

Problem d Analyze

Guide students to notice that their answers equal the slopes they found in problem **c.** By examining this idea, students can gain a deeper understanding of what slope is and why it is an important tool used in graphs.

Activity

Slope

Materials needed:

- **Lesson Activity 24**

Calculate the slope (rise over run) of each graphed line on the activity by drawing right triangles.

Practice Set

▶ **a.** Generalize Find the slopes of the "Yards to Feet" and the "Feet to Yards" graphs on the first page of this lesson. "Yards to Feet": 3; "Feet to Yards": $\frac{1}{3}$

b. Find the slopes of graphs **a** and **c** in example 1. 1; $-\frac{1}{2}$

▶ **c.** Generalize Mentally calculate the slope of each graphed line below by counting the run and rise rather than by drawing right triangles.

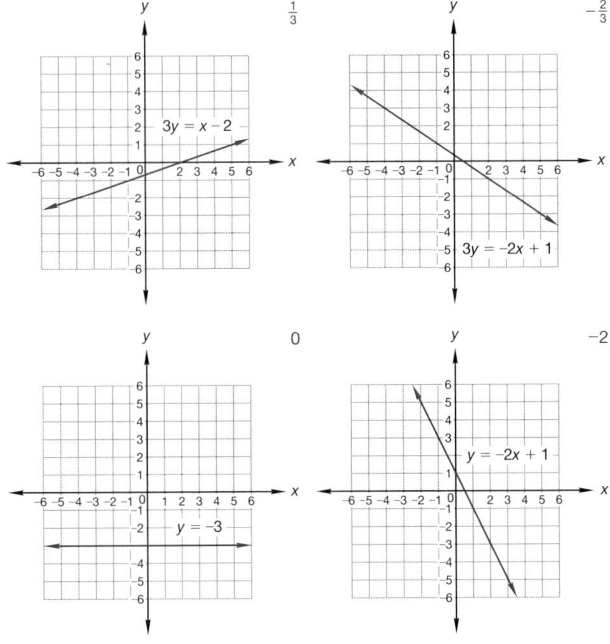

▶ **d.** Analyze For each unit of horizontal change to the right on the graphed lines above, what is the vertical change? $\frac{1}{3}$; $-\frac{2}{3}$; 0; −2

▶ See Math Conversations in the sidebar.

Written Practice *Strengthening Concepts*

1. (92) The shirt regularly priced at \$27 was on sale for $\frac{1}{3}$ off. What was the sale price? \$18

2. (51) Nine hundred seventy-five billion is how much less than one trillion? Write the answer in scientific notation. 2.5×10^{10}

3. (Inv. 4) What is the **a** range and **b** mode of this set of numbers? **a.** 11 **b.** 16

16, 6, 8, 17, 14, 16, 12

Use ratio boxes to solve problems **4–6.**

4. (72) Sonia rode her bike from home to the lake. Her average speed was 12 miles per hour. If it took her 40 minutes to reach the lake, what was the distance from her home to the lake? Explain how you solved the problem. 8 miles; See student work.

5. (66) The ratio of swallowtail butterflies to skipper butterflies in the butterfly conservatory was 5 to 2. If there were 140 butterflies in the conservatory, how many of the butterflies were swallowtails? 100

6. (92) The average cost of a new car increased 8 percent in one year. Before the increase the average cost of a new car was \$16,550. What was the average cost of a new car after the increase? \$17,874

▶ ***7.** (99) **Analyze** The points (3, −2), (−3, −2), and (−3, 6) are the vertices of a right triangle. Find the perimeter of the triangle. 24 units

8. (40) In this figure, $\angle ABC$ is a right angle.

a. Find $m\angle ABD$. 40°

b. Find $m\angle DBC$. 50°

c. Find $m\angle BCD$. 40°

▶ **d.** Which triangles in this figure are similar? All three triangles are similar.

Write equations to solve problems **9–11.**

9. (77) Sixty is 125 percent of what number? $60 = 1.25 \times W_N$; 48

10. (77) Sixty is what percent of 25? $60 = W_P \times 25$; 240%

***11.** (101) Sixty is four more than twice what number? $60 = 2n + 4$; 28

▶ **12.** (14, 94) In a can are 100 marbles: 10 yellow, 20 red, 30 green, and 40 blue.

a. If a marble is drawn from the can, what is the chance that the marble will not be red? $\frac{80}{100} = 80\%$

b. If the first marble is not replaced and a second marble is drawn from the can, what is the probability that both marbles will be yellow? $\frac{10}{100} \cdot \frac{9}{99} = \frac{1}{110}$

▶ See Math Conversations in the sidebar.

3 Written Practice

Math Conversations

Discussion opportunities are provided below.

Problem 7 Analyze

Help students to see that this triangle has sides with whole-number lengths that satisfy the Pythagorean theorem. Ask them what they notice about the lengths of the sides. Discuss how when two non-hypotenuse sides of a right triangle are in the ratio 3 to 4, the hypotenuse will have a value of 5 if used to form another ratio with either side.

Problem 8d

Extend the Problem

"Name the three similar triangles and explain why they are similar." $\triangle ABC$, $\triangle ABD$, and $\triangle BDC$; they all have a right angle, a 40° angle, and a 50° angle

"Are any of the triangles congruent? Explain why or why not." No, none of the corresponding sides are equal.

Problem 12

Extend the Problem

Have students make up questions about the bag of marbles that can be solved using mental math. Sample: What percent of the marbles are red or green? 50% What is the probability that a marble drawn from the can will be blue or red? $\frac{3}{5}$ Suppose 10 blue marbles are removed from the can. What is the probability then that 2 marbles drawn from the can with the first one returned to the can will both be blue? $\frac{1}{9}$

(continued)

3 Written Practice (Continued)

Math Conversations

Discussion opportunities are provided below.

Problem 14 Analyze

Ask questions that provide models for understanding and analyzing the information provided in problems.

"What unit should you use for the answer?" Sample: The information is given in feet, so I would use feet.

"What information is not needed to find the answer to the problem?" the height of the Washington Monument

Problem 17 Analyze

Extend the Problem

Have the students answer the three questions for the functions $y = x$ and $y = x - 1$. Then discuss how all three graphs are alike and how they are different. Sample: Their slopes are all the same.

Problem 21 Explain

Use this problem to check on students' understanding of surface area. Ask questions like:

"What does total surface area mean?"

"How do you find the total surface area of any cylinder?"

"How would you find the total surface area of any solid figure?"

Errors and Misconceptions

Problem 16a

Encourage students to square numbers like 10, 20, 30, and 40 to help them close in on the two numbers. When they find that 20^2 is 400 and 30^2 is 900, they will realize that the numbers can be found between 20 and 30.

Problem 18

Students whose answer is 36π cm² found the area of the entire circle. Help them see that they can find the number of degrees in the shaded part, then make a fraction of the shaded part and the whole, and then multiply the total area by the fraction.

Problem 22

Show students who were not able to find the measure of $\angle x$ how to work through the problem in three steps. The first step is to work out that $\angle ACB$ is 30°. The next step is to work out that $\angle DCA$ is 60°. The last step is to work out that $\angle x$ (or CDE) is 30°. All of these determinations are based on knowing that the sum of the angles of a triangle is 180° and that a right angle is 90°.

(continued)

---

13. Complete the table. (48)

Fraction	Decimal	Percent
$\frac{5}{6}$	**a.** $0.8\overline{3}$	**b.** $83\frac{1}{3}\%$

▶* **14.** Analyze The Washington Monument is a little more than 555 ft tall. It has a square base that measures 55 ft, $1\frac{1}{2}$ in. on each side. What is the perimeter of the base of the monument? 220 ft, 6 in., or $220\frac{1}{2}$ ft (48)

15. Multiply. Write the product in scientific notation. 1.62×10^5 (83)

$$(1.8 \times 10^{10})(9 \times 10^{-6})$$

* **16.** ▶**a.** Between which two consecutive whole numbers is $\sqrt{600}$? 24 and 25 (100, 106)

b. What are the two square roots of 10? $\sqrt{10}$ and $-\sqrt{10}$

▶* **17.** Analyze Use the function $y = x + 1$ to answer **a–c.** (Inv. 9, 107)

a. Find three x, y pairs for the function. See student work

b. Graph these number pairs on a coordinate plane and draw a line through the points.

c. What is the slope of the graphed line? 1

17. b.

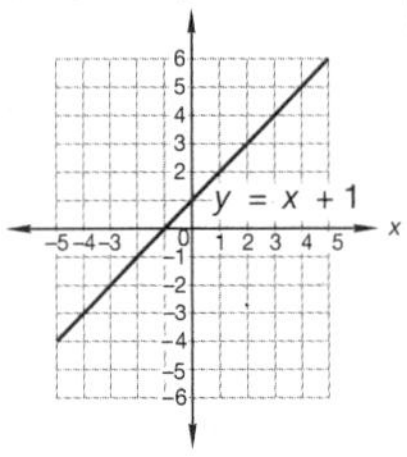

▶ **18.** If the radius of this circle is 6 cm, what is the area of the shaded region? 24π cm² (104)

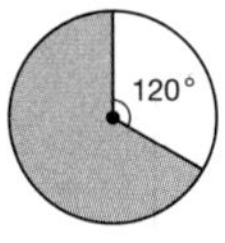

Leave π as π.

* **19.** Find the surface area of this rectangular solid. Dimensions are in inches. 160 in.² (105)

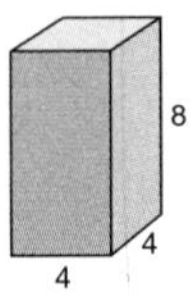

20. Find the volume of this right circular cylinder. Dimensions are in centimeters. (Use 3.14 for π.) 502.4 cm³ (95)

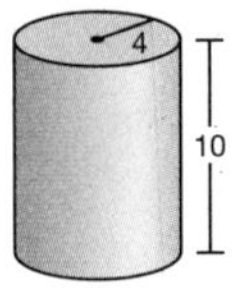

21. 351.68 cm²; Sample: I found the area of one circular face and multiplied it by 2. Then I found the area of the cylinder's rectangular lateral surface and added it to the area of the two bases.

▶* **21.** Explain Find the total surface area of the cylinder in problem **20.** Explain how you got your answer. (105)

▶ **22.** The polygon $ABCD$ is a rectangle. Find $m\angle x$. 30° (40)

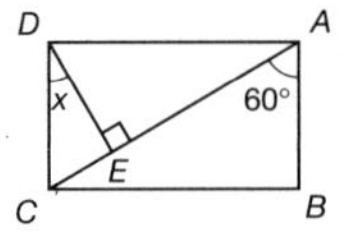

▶ See Math Conversations in the sidebar.

▶* **23.** (107) **Analyze** Find the slope of the graphed line: 2

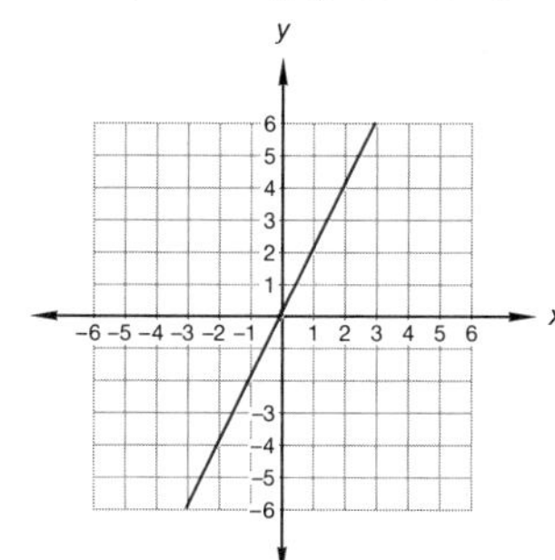

▶ ***24.** (106) **Generalize** Solve for x in each literal equation:

a. $x - y = z$ $\quad x = z + y$

b. $w = xy$ $\quad x = \frac{w}{y}$

Solve:

25. (98) $\frac{a}{21} = \frac{1.5}{7}$ $\quad$ 4.5

▶* **26.** (102) $6x + 5 = 7 + 2x$ $\quad \frac{1}{2}$

▶ **Generalize** Simplify:

27. (63) $62 + 5\{20 - [4^2 + 3(2 - 1)]\}$ $\quad$ 67

* **28.** (103) $\frac{(6x^2y)(2xy)}{4xy^2}$ $\quad 3x^2$

29. (43) $5\frac{1}{6} + 3.5 - \frac{1}{3}$ $\quad 8\frac{1}{3}$

30. (85) $\frac{(5)(-3)(2)(-4) + (-2)(-3)}{|-6|}$ $\quad$ 21

Early Finishers
Real-World Application

Mrs. Cohen took a survey of 10 students in her class. She asked them how many school sporting events they attended last year. These are the results of the survey.

Two students attended 7 games.
Three students attended 8 games.
One student attended 9 games.
Two students attended 10 games.
One student attended 11 games.
One student attended 17 games.

a. Choose a line plot, line graph, or a Venn diagram to display this data. Justify your choice. See student work. Sample: This data shows frequency so use a line plot.

b. Draw your display and then find the mean, median, mode, and range. Identify any outliers. mean: 9.5; median: 8.5; mode: 8; range: is 10; outlier: 17

c. Formulate questions to conduct a similar survey of 30 students in your school. Write three conclusions that can be made based on your collected data. See student work.

▶ See Math Conversations in the sidebar.

Looking Forward

Understanding slope prepares students for:

- **Lesson 116,** using the slope-intercept form of a line to identify the slope and y-intercept of the line and using these to graph the equation.

3 Written Practice (Continued)

Math Conversations

Discussion opportunities are provided below.

Problem 23 Analyze

Discuss how students analyzed the graph to find its slope. Ask questions like these:

"How did you find the slope?" Sample: I marked the rise and the run using points (−6, −3) and (2, 4), and then calculated the rise, 12, over the run, 6, and so the slope is 2.

"Did anyone find the slope mentally?" Sample: Yes, I counted 1 over from the origin and up 2—that means the slope is 2.

"Why is the slope positive?" Sample: Because the rise and the run are both positive.

Problem 24 Generalize

Have students explain how they solved these equations. Then ask how these answers could be checked. Sample: You can check them the same way as you check any other equation—substitute the values back into the original equation and see if both sides are equal.

Problems 27–30 Generalize

Lead a discussion of ways to think about what is needed to simplify these problems. Ask questions like these:

"For which of these problems is order of operations not needed? Why?" Sample: problem 29, because you can simply work left to right

"For which one do you use all of the order of operations rules? Why?" Sample: problem 27, because it has parentheses, brackets, exponents, multiplication, addition, and subtraction

"For which one do you need the exponent rules? Why?" Sample: problem 28, because there are variables with powers to multiply

Errors and Misconceptions

Problem 26

Watch for students whose answer is $x = 1\frac{1}{2}$. They simply moved terms from one side of the equation to the other. Help them see that they must do the same thing to both sides of the equation—that, for example, to collect the x terms on the left side of the equation, they need to subtract $2x$ from both sides of the equation.

• Formulas and Substitution

Objective

- Use formulas to describe numerical relationships.
- Understand the use of variables in formulas to represent unknowns.
- Use substitution to solve equations or to transform formulas.

Lesson Preparation

Materials

- **Power Up V** (in *Instructional Masters*)

Optional

- **Investigation Activity 13** (in Instructional Masters) or **graph paper**

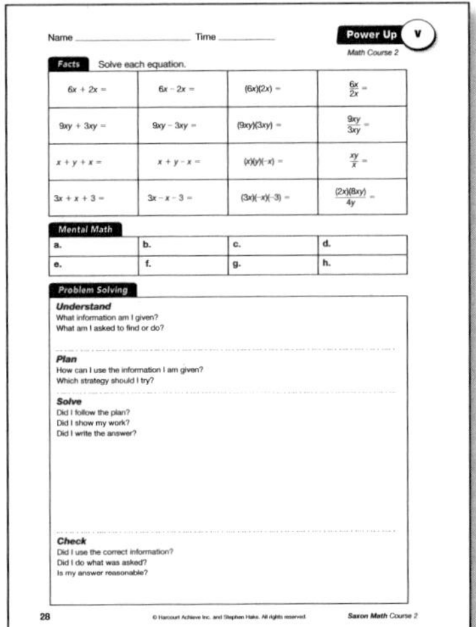

Name ____________ Time ________ **Power Up V** *Math Course 2*

Facts Solve each equation.

$6x + 2x =$	$6x - 2x =$	$(6x)(2x) =$	$\frac{6x}{2x} =$
$9xy + 3xy =$	$9xy - 3xy =$	$(9xy)(3xy) =$	$\frac{9xy}{3xy} =$
$x + y + x =$	$x + y - x =$	$(x)(y)(-x) =$	$\frac{xy}{x} =$
$3x + x + 3 =$	$3x - x - 3 =$	$(3x)(-x)(-3) =$	$\frac{(2x)(8xy)}{4y} =$

Mental Math

a.	b.	c.	d.
e.	f.	g.	h.

Problem Solving

Understand
What information am I given?
What am I asked to find or do?

Plan
How can I use the information I am given?
Which strategy should I try?

Solve
Did I follow the plan?
Did I show my work?
Did I write the answer?

Check
Did I use the correct information?
Did I do what was asked?
Is my answer reasonable?

28 © Harcourt Achieve Inc. and Stephen Hake. All rights reserved. *Saxon Math Course 2*

Power Up V

Technology Resources

Student eBook Complete student textbook in electronic format.

Resources and Planner CD Assessment, reteaching, and instructional masters, plus a pacing calendar with standards.

Test and Practice Generator CD Create additional practice sheets and custom-made tests.

www.SaxonPublishers.com Visit for more student activities and planning materials.

Inclusion

Adaptations CD Adapted lessons, investigations, practice and assessments.

Meeting Standards

National Council of Teachers of Mathematics (NCTM)

Algebra

AL.1b Relate and compare different forms of representation for a relationship

AL.2a Develop an initial conceptual understanding of different uses of variables

AL.2d Recognize and generate equivalent forms for simple algebraic expressions and solve linear equations

Problem Solving

PS.1c Apply and adapt a variety of appropriate strategies to solve problems

Power-Up Discussion *For use with Power Up, p. 754*

Problem-Solving Strategy: Write an Equation

Some auto license plates take the form of two letters, followed by three numbers, followed by two letters. How many different license plates are possible?

Understand ***Understand the problem.***

"What information are we given?"

Some license plates take the form of two letters, followed by three numbers, followed by two letters: XX###XX

"What are we asked to do?"

We are asked to determine how many different license plates are possible.

Plan ***Make a plan.***

"What problem-solving strategy will we use?"

We will *write an equation* to find the number of possible license plates.

Solve ***Carry out the plan.***

"We will use the Fundamental Counting Principle to help us find the number of plates that are possible. How many different letters can we choose from in each of the four instances?"

26

Teacher Note: Take a few minutes to review the Fundamental Counting Principle if students have trouble remembering how it works.

"How many different numbers can we choose from in each of the three instances?"

10

"We can multiply to find the total number of plates possible. How many plates are possible?"

$26 \times 26 \times 10 \times 10 \times 10 \times 26 \times 26 = 456{,}976{,}000$

Check ***Look back.***

"Did we do what we were asked to do?"

Yes, we found the total number of possible license plates.

Teacher Note: Point out that the number of license plates possible for the type of plate described in Lesson 88 is the same. Help students see that the Commutative Property of Multiplication is the reason the two products are equal. We are multiplying the same factors in both cases, just in different orders.

1 Power Up

Facts

Distribute **Power Up V** to students. See answers below.

Mental Math

Encourage students to share different ways to mentally compute these exercises. Strategies for exercises **d** and **e** are listed below.

d. Use an Equivalent Measure

$1 \text{ yd}^2 = \frac{3 \text{ ft}}{1 \text{ yd}} \times \frac{3 \text{ ft}}{1 \text{ yd}} = 9 \text{ ft}^2$

$3 \text{ yd}^2 = 3 \times 9 \text{ ft}^2 = 27 \text{ ft}^2$

Use Unit Multipliers

$3 \text{ yd}^2 \times \frac{3 \text{ ft}}{1 \text{ yd}} \times \frac{3 \text{ ft}}{1 \text{ yd}} = 27 \text{ ft}^2$

e. Use an Equivalent Fraction

$150\% = \frac{3}{2}$

$\frac{3}{2} \times \$120 = \frac{\$360}{2} = \$180$

Use Logical Reasoning

100% of \$120 = \$120

50% of \$120 = \$60

150% of \$120 = \$180

Problem Solving

Refer to **Power-Up Discussion,** p. 754B.

2 New Concepts

Instruction

Ask students to name real-world situations in which they or someone in their family has used a formula. Students might suggest:

- Figuring out how much fertilizer to buy for a lawn or garden.
- Determining the volume of a storage container when the measures are known.
- Finding the average speed traveled on a trip if the distance and time are known.
- Changing a Celsius temperature to a Fahrenheit temperature when visiting a foreign country.

Example 1

Instruction

This formula relates distance to rate and time.

distance traveled = rate (or speed) × time

It could be describing a bike ride of 36 miles (d) at a speed of 9 mi/h (r). Solving the equation shows that the time for the bike ride, t, would be 4 hours.

(continued)

LESSON 108

• Formulas and Substitution

Power Up — *Building Power*

facts Power Up V

mental math

a. **Positive/Negative:** $(-1)^5 + (-1)^6$ 0

b. **Scientific Notation:** $(2.5 \times 10^{-5})(4 \times 10^{-3})$ 1×10^{-7}

c. **Algebra:** $5y - 2y = 24$ 8

d. **Measurement:** Convert 3 sq. yd to sq. ft. 27 sq. ft

e. **Percent:** 150% of \$120 \$180

f. **Percent:** \$120 increased 50% \$180

g. **Algebra:** Complete the table by using the function rule. $y = 4x + 4$ 36

y	20	24	28	
x	4	5	6	8

h. **Rate:** At 60 mph, how far can Freddy drive in $3\frac{1}{2}$ hours? 210 mi

problem solving Some auto license plates take the form of two letters, followed by three numbers, followed by two letters. How many different license plates are possible? 456,976,000 license plates

New Concept — *Increasing Knowledge*

A formula is a literal equation that describes a relationship between two or more variables. Formulas are used in mathematics, science, economics, the construction industry, food preparation—anywhere that measurement is used.

To use a formula, we replace the letters in the formula with measures that are known. Then we solve the equation for the measure we wish to find.

Thinking Skill — Analyze

What measures do you know? What unknown measure do you need to find? distance (d) and the rate (r); time (t).

Example 1

Use the formula $d = rt$ to find t when d is 36 and r is 9.

Solution

This formula describes the relationship between distance (d), rate (r), and time (t). We replace d with 36 and r with 9. Then we solve the equation for t.

$d = rt$ formula

$36 = 9t$ substituted

$\mathbf{t = 4}$ divided by 9

Facts Solve each equation.

$6x + 2x = 8x$	$6x - 2x = 4x$	$(6x)(2x) = 12x^2$	$\frac{6x}{2x} = 3$
$9xy + 3xy = 12xy$	$9xy - 3xy = 6xy$	$(9xy)(3xy) = 27x^2y^2$	$\frac{9xy}{3xy} = 3$
$x + y + x = 2x + y$	$x + y - x = y$	$(x)(y)(-x) = -x^2y$	$\frac{xy}{x} = y$
$3x + x + 3 = 4x + 3$	$3x - x - 3 = 2x - 3$	$(3x)(-x)(-3) = 9x^2$	$\frac{(2x)(8xy)}{4y} = 4x^2$

Another way to find t is to first solve the formula for t.

$d = rt$ formula

$t = \frac{d}{r}$ divided by r

Then replace d and r with 36 and 9 and simplify.

$t = \frac{36}{9}$ substituted

$t = \mathbf{4}$ divided

Connect If a bike ride is 36 miles, and the rate is 9 miles per hour, how long will the trip take? 4 hours

Example 2

Use the formula $F = 1.8C + 32$ to find F when C is 37.

Solution

This formula is used to convert measurements of temperature from degrees Celsius to degrees Fahrenheit. We replace C with 37 and simplify.

$F = 1.8C + 32$ formula

$F = 1.8(37) + 32$ substituted

$F = 66.6 + 32$ multiplied

$F = \mathbf{98.6}$ added

Thus, 37 degrees Celsius equals 98.6 degrees Fahrenheit.

Discuss How could we use the formula to convert from degrees Fahrenheit to degrees Celsius? Replace F with the number of degrees Fahrenheit and solve for C.

Practice Set

▸ **a.** Use the formula $A = bh$ to find b when A is 20 and h is 4. 5

▸ **b.** Use the formula $A = \frac{1}{2}bh$ to find b when A is 20 and h is 4. 10

▸ **c.** Use the formula $F = 1.8C + 32$ to find F when C is -40. -40

▸ **d.** **Connect** The formula for converting from Fahrenheit to Celsius is often given as $F = \frac{9}{5}C + 32$. How are $\frac{9}{5}$ and 1.8 related? 1.8 is the decimal equivalent of $\frac{9}{5}$

Written Practice *Strengthening Concepts*

1. (46) The main course cost \$8.35. The beverage cost \$1.25. Dessert cost \$2.40. Alexi left a tip that was 15 percent of the total price of the meal. How much money did Alexi leave for a tip? \$1.80

▸ **2.** (57) Twelve hundred-thousandths is how much greater than twenty millionths? Write the answer in scientific notation. 1×10^{-4}

3. (Inv. 4) Arrange the following numbers in order from least to greatest. Then find the median and the mode of the set of numbers.
4, 7, 8, 8, 8, 9, 9, 10, 12, 15; median = 8.5; mode = 8

8, 12, 9, 15, 8, 10, 9, 8, 7, 4

▸ See Math Conversations in the sidebar.

Math Background

Why are there two temperature scales?

Actually three temperature scales, the Fahrenheit, the Celsius, and the Kelvin scales, are in use across the world today, and two others, the Rankine and the Réaumur, are used occasionally for scientific experiments.

In the United States and a few other places, the Fahrenheit scale, developed by Daniel Gabriel Fahrenheit, a German physicist, is used for ordinary temperature measurement. Its scale is based on 32 for the freezing point of water and 212 for the boiling point of water, with 180° between the two.

In most of the rest of the world and for much scientific research, the Celsius scale is used. This scale, based on 0 for the freezing point of water and 100 for the boiling point of water, was invented by the Swedish astronomer Anders Celsius. It is sometimes called the centigrade scale because there is 100° between the two points that define the scale.

2 New Concepts (Continued)

Example 1 (continued)

Instruction

Once students have answered the *Connect* question, ask:

"How did you know that the answer is given in hours?" Sample: The two units of miles cancel and you are left with hours as the only unit. Since the rate was given in miles per hour, and the distance traveled was 36 miles, the answer had to be given in units of time.

Example 2

Instruction

Suggest to students that they use parentheses, as is done in this example, when substituting a value for a measure that is a factor.

Practice Set

Problems a and b (Error Alert)

Help students decide which of the two methods for solving formulas presented in example 1 they like better. Since they can solve for b either by substituting the values of the variables first and then transforming, or by transforming first and then substituting, encourage them to use one method for problem **a** and the other for problem **b.**

Problems c and d (Connect)

First connect these problems to science by telling students that $-40°$ is the only temperature at which the Celsius temperature is equal to the Fahrenheit temperature. Then discuss with students why it is useful to have two variations of a formula. You can choose the fraction or the decimal form depending on which is easier to use with the numbers you are working with.

3 Written Practice

Math Conversations

Discussion opportunities are provided below.

Problem 2 (Justify)

Point out that another way to represent 20 millionths is 2 hundred-thousandths. Ask whether knowing that would make it easy to find the difference mentally. Sample: Yes, I can just think 12 – 2 is 10, and 10 hundred-thousandths is 1 ten-thousandth, so I just have to write it out to change it into scientific notation.

(continued)

3 Written Practice (Continued)

Math Conversations

Discussion opportunities are provided below.

Problem 12 Analyze

After students have finished working on this problem, go over it with them. You might draw a coordinate grid with the line on the board. Choose (−6, 5) and (0, 1) as the points to use. Have volunteers demonstrate how to find the rise, the run, and the slope. $-4, 6, -\frac{2}{3}$

Then have students tell what points they chose and whether they found a different slope. Everyone should have found the same slope regardless of the points chosen.

Problem 13 Analyze

"If Liz is using a sheet of paper that is $8\frac{1}{2}$ inches by 11 inches, and she wants a quarter-inch margin all around, what is the greatest amount of floor area she can draw?" 16 feet by 21 feet

"What size paper would she need if her house is 60 feet long and 38 feet wide?" at least $30\frac{1}{2}$ inches long and $19\frac{1}{2}$ inches wide

Problem 14 Formulate

Ask students to tell what kind of triangle this is and have them support their answers. It is an isosceles right triangle because it has 2 equal angles and a right angle. Then present this question:

"Suppose the length of the two congruent sides is s. What formula can you write for the area of the triangle?" Sample: $A = \frac{s^2}{2}$

Errors and Misconceptions

Problem 4

Students whose answer is $\frac{1}{9}$ did not notice that the two events are dependent events. Remind them that the probability for taking the second marker is not the same as for the first since one marker has been removed from the box.

Problem 11

If students give an answer of −24, they have written the equation as $56 = 8 - 2x$. Help them to see that it should be $56 = 2x - 8$, because 8 should be subtracted from $2x$.

(continued)

▶ **4.** (94) There are 12 markers in a box: 4 blue, 4 red, and 4 yellow. Without looking, Lee gives one marker to Lily and takes one for himself. What is the probability that both markers will be blue? $\frac{4}{12} \cdot \frac{3}{11} = \frac{1}{11}$

Use ratio boxes to solve problems **5–7.**

5. (72) If Milton can exchange $200 for 300 Swiss francs, how many dollars would a 240-franc Swiss watch cost? $160

6. (66) The jar was filled with red beans and brown beans in the ratio of 5 to 7. If there were 175 red beans in the jar, what was the total number of beans in the jar? 420 beans

7. (92) During the off-season the room rates at the resort were reduced by 35 percent. If the usual rates were $90 per day, what would be the cost of a 2-day stay during the off-season? $117

8. (60) Three eighths of a ton is how many pounds? 750 pounds

Write equations to solve problems **9–11.**

9. (60) What number is 2.5 percent of 800? $W_N = 0.025 \times 800$; 20

10. (77) Ten percent of what number is $2500? $0.1 \times W_N = \$2500$; $25,000

▶* **11.** (101) Fifty-six is eight less than twice what number? $56 = 2x - 8$; 32

▶* **12.** (107) Analyze Find the slope of the graphed line: $-\frac{2}{3}$

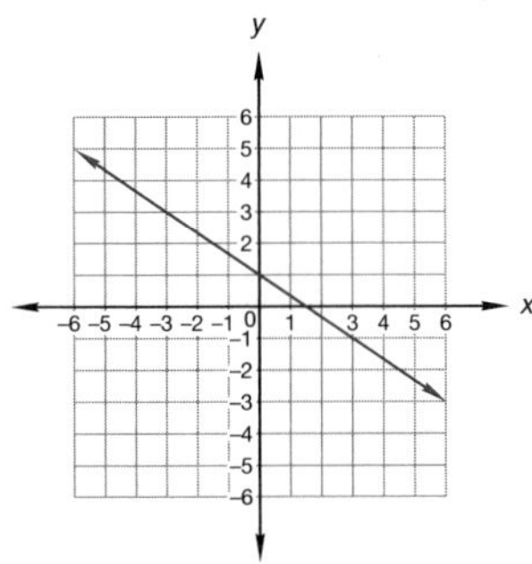

▶* **13.** (98) Analyze Liz is drawing a floor plan of her house. On the plan, 1 inch equals 2 feet.

a. What is the floor area of a room that measures 6 inches by $7\frac{1}{2}$ inches on the plan? Use a ratio box to solve the problem. 180 ft²

b. One of the walls in Liz's house is 17 feet $9\frac{1}{2}$ inches long. Estimate how long this wall would appear in Liz's floor plan, and explain how you arrived at your estimate.

13. b. 9 in.; We round 17 ft $9\frac{1}{2}$ in. to 18 ft. Since every 2 ft is 1 in. in the floor plan, we estimate by dividing 18 by 2.

▶* **14.** (101) Formulate Find the measure of each angle of this triangle by writing and solving an equation. $4x = 180°$; $x = 45°$; $2x = 90°$

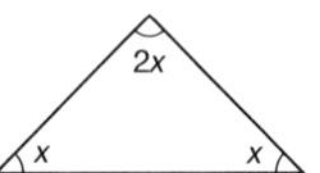

▶ See Math Conversations in the sidebar.

15. Multiply. Write the product in scientific notation. 2.24×10^{-2}
(83)

$$(2.8 \times 10^5)(8 \times 10^{-8})$$

▶* 16. The formula $c = 2.54n$ is used to convert inches (n) to centimeters (c). Find c when n is 12. 30.48 cm
(108)

17. a. Make a table that shows three pairs of numbers that satisfy the function $y = 2x$.
(Inv. 9)

b. Graph the number pairs on a coordinate plane, and draw a line through the points.

c. Find the slope of the line. 2

17. a. Sample:

x	y
1	2
2	4
3	6

17. b. $y = 2x$

18. Find the perimeter of this figure. Dimensions are in inches. (Use 3.14 for π.) 20.28 in.
(104)

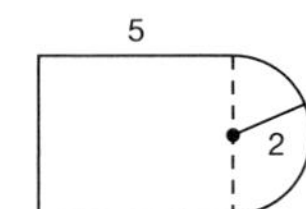

▶* 19. Analyze Find the surface area of this cube. Dimensions are in inches. 600 in.^{2}
(105)

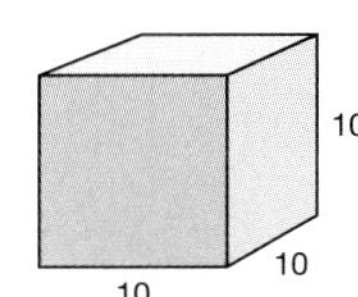

▶ 20. Find the volume of this right circular cylinder. Dimensions are in centimeters. (Use 3.14 for π.) 392.5 cm^3
(95)

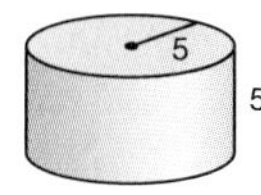

21. Find m$\angle x$ in the figure below. 30°
(40)

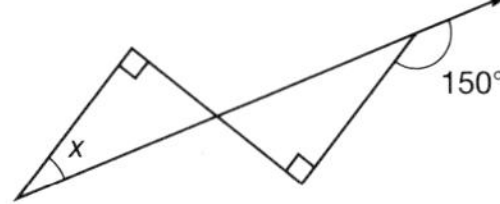

22. These triangles are similar. Dimensions are in centimeters.
(97, 98)

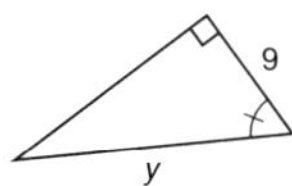

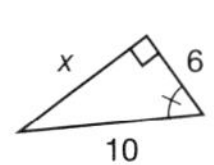

a. Find y. 15 cm

b. Find the scale factor from the smaller to the larger triangle. 1.5

c. The area of the larger triangle is how many times the area of the smaller triangle? 2.25 times

▶ 23. Use the Pythagorean theorem to find x in the smaller triangle from problem **22.** 8 cm
(99)

▶ See Math Conversations in the sidebar.

3 Written Practice (Continued)

Math Conversations

Discussion opportunities are provided below.

Problem 16

Extend the Problem

"What can you say about the relationship between centimeters and feet from the answer to this problem?" Sample: Since 12 inches is 1 foot, a foot is about 30 cm.

"How about the relationship between millimeters and inches?" Sample: Since 30 cm is 300 mm, 12 inches is about 300 mm.

Problem 19 Analyze

Have students define surface area in their own terms and explain how to find the surface area of a figure. Then ask how many students used mental math to solve the problem. Have one student explain how he or she did it. Sample: The side is 10 in.^{2} so the area of a side is 100 in.^{2}, and there are 6 sides so the surface area is 600 in.^{2}.

Problem 23 Analyze

"Remember that some right triangles have sides in the ratio of 3 to 4 to 5. Explain how to use that relationship to find x in the smaller triangle." Sample: Look at the two given sides; think 6 is twice 3, and 10 is twice 5, so the other side must be twice 4, or 8 cm.

Errors and Misconceptions

Problem 20

Some students may get an answer of 157 cm^3. They multiplied the formula for the circumference of a circle, rather than the area, by the height of the cylinder. Explain that to get volume they must multiply an area by a height.

(continued)

3 Written Practice (Continued)

Math Conversations

Discussion opportunities are provided below.

Problem 25 Generalize

Point out that the first step in solving this equation would be to change the mixed number to an improper fraction. Then ask whether multiplying both sides of the equation by 3 or adding x to both sides should be done next. Lead students to see that it doesn't matter which step is done next.

Problem 30b Generalize

Ask students what happens to the sum if the fifth term in the pattern is added. The sum becomes −1. Then ask for the sum if the sixth term is added. The sum becomes 0. Finally ask:

"What happens if the expression is extended indefinitely?" Sample: The sum will be −1 or 0 depending on whether there is an odd number of terms or an even number of terms.

Errors and Misconceptions

Problem 25

Have students whose answer is 9.6 go back and check their work. They probably multiplied $\frac{5}{3}$ by $2x$ instead of by x. Tell them to write each step on a separate line so that their work is done in order.

---

* **24.** (105) Find the surface area of a globe that has a diameter of 10 inches. (Use 3.14 for π.) 314 in.^{2}

▸* **25.** (102) Generalize Solve: $1\frac{2}{3}x = 32 - x$ 12

Generalize Simplify:

* **26.** (96, 103) $2x(2y + 1) - \sqrt{16x^2y^2}$ 2x

* **27.** (103) $\frac{(-4ax)(3xy)}{-6x^2}$ 2ay

28. (63) $1.1\{1.1[1.1(1000)]\}$ 1331

29. (26) $3\frac{3}{4} \cdot 2\frac{2}{3} \div 10$ 1

* **30.** (103, 106) **a.** $(-6) - (7)(-4) + \sqrt[3]{125} + \frac{(-8)(-9)}{(-3)(-2)}$ 39

▸ **b.** $(-1) + (-1)^2 + (-1)^3 + (-1)^4$ 0

Early Finishers
Math and Architecture

The Pantheon was built in 125 A.D. in ancient Rome. The structure is in the shape of a cylinder with a dome on the top. The diameter and height of the cylinder is about 43 meters. The diameter of the dome (half sphere) is also about 43 meters.

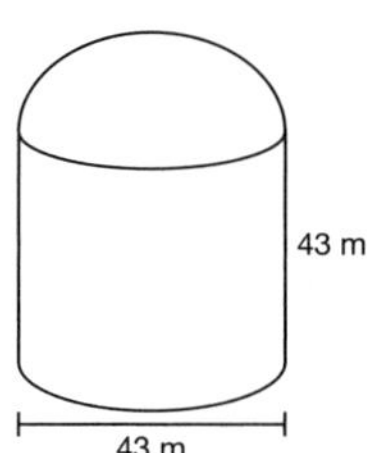

a. What is the lateral surface area of the cylindrical portion of the Pantheon? Use 3.14 for π. 5805.86 m^2

b. What is the surface area of the dome? Use 3.14 for π. 2902.93 m^2

c. What is the surface area of the floor? 1451.46 m^2

d. What is the total interior surface area of the Pantheon? 10,160.25 m^2

▸ See Math Conversations in the sidebar.

Looking Forward

Working with formulas and substitution prepares students for:

- **Lesson 112,** using the Pythagorean theorem to solve real world problems.
- **Lesson 113,** using formulas to find the volume of pyramids, cones, and spheres.
- **Lesson 114,** using formulas to find volume, capacity, and mass in the metric system.

• Equations with Exponents

Objective

- Solve equations that have variables with exponents of 2.

Lesson Preparation

Materials

- **Power Up V** (in *Instructional Masters*)
- **Teacher-provided material: graph paper**

Optional

- **Investigation Activity 13** (in *Instructional Masters*)

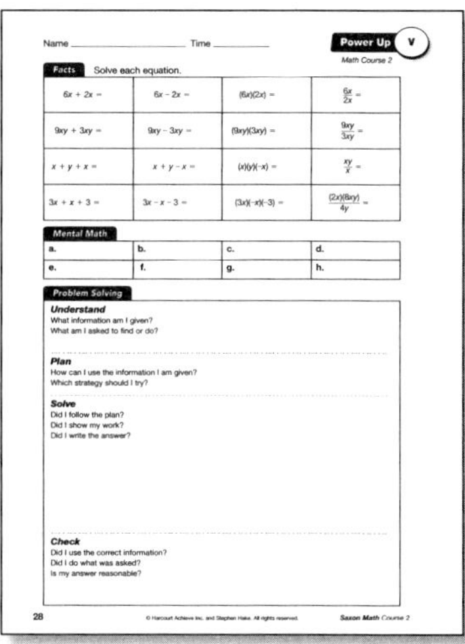
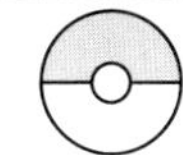

Power Up V

Math Language

	Maintain	English Learners (ESL)
	proportion	true-false game

Technology Resources

Student eBook Complete student textbook in electronic format.

Resources and Planner CD Assessment, reteaching, and instructional masters, plus a pacing calendar with standards.

Test and Practice Generator CD Create additional practice sheets and custom-made tests.

www.SaxonPublishers.com Visit for more student activities and planning materials.

Inclusion

Adaptations CD Adapted lessons, investigations, practice and assessments.

Meeting Standards

National Council of Teachers of Mathematics (NCTM)

Algebra

AL.2a Develop an initial conceptual understanding of different uses of variables

AL.3a Model and solve contextualized problems using various representations, such as graphs, tables, and equations

Connections

CN.4a Recognize and use connections among mathematical ideas

Power-Up Discussion *For use with Power Up, p. 759*

Problem-Solving Strategy: Use Logical Reasoning/ Draw a Diagram

When you purchase hardwood, each board is sawn to specified widths and lengths. Hardwoods have their own unit of measure called "board foot" (bf). A board that is 1 in. thick, 12 in. wide, and 12 in. long measures 1 board foot (1 bf). Each of the following boards also measures 1 bf:

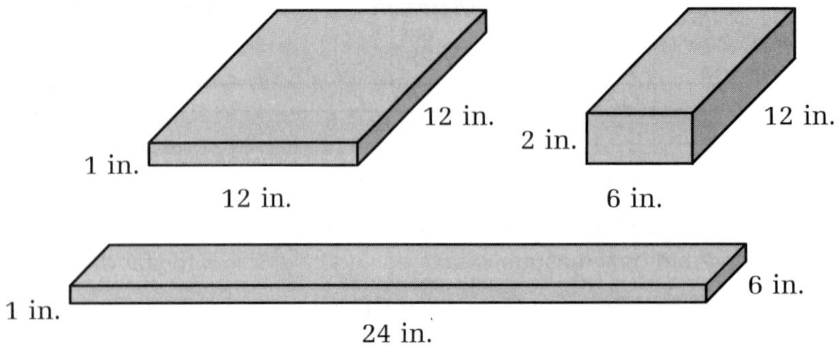

Can you find a formula for determining bf? Draw three more examples of 1 board foot.

Understand — *Understand the problem.*

"What information are we given?"

A board measuring 1 in. by 12 in. by 12 in. is equal to one board foot. We are also shown two other boards equal to one board foot.

"What are we asked to do?"

We are asked to find a formula for calculating a board's measure in board feet.

Plan — *Make a plan.*

"What problem-solving strategy will we use?"

We will *use logical reasoning* to analyze the three examples of a board foot, and then *draw a diagram* to illustrate our conclusion.

Solve — *Carry out the plan.*

"How do the boards differ from each other?"

Their heights, lengths, and widths vary, usually by a factor of 2.

"The length, widths, and heigths differ, but do the boards have something in common?"

Each of the three board foots have a volume of 144 cubic inches.

"What is a formula for finding bf?"

bf = Volume/144

"What are some other possible boards that would measure 1 board foot?"

A 3 in.-by-4 in.-by-12 in. board, a 4 in.-by-6-in.-by-6 in. board, and a 2 in.-by-2 in.-by-36 in. board. There are several other combinations of dimensions that would work as well. The product of the 3 dimensions should be 144 in.^3.

Check — *Look back.*

"Did we do what we were asked to do?"

Yes, we determined a formula for board foot and found the dimensions of three other boards that measure 1 board foot.

LESSON **109**

• Equations with Exponents

Power Up — *Building Power*

facts Power Up V

mental math

a. **Positive/Negative:** $(-\frac{1}{2})(-\frac{1}{2})$ $\frac{1}{4}$

b. **Scientific Notation:** $(1.2 \times 10^{12})^2$ 1.44×10^{24}

c. **Ratio:** $\frac{20}{40} = \frac{c}{2}$ 1

d. **Measurement:** Convert 150 cm to m. 1.5 m

e. **Percent:** $12\frac{1}{2}\%$ of \$80 \$10

f. **Percent:** $12\frac{1}{2}\%$ less than \$80 \$70

g. **Number Sense:** Change $\frac{1}{3}$ to a decimal and percent. .33 and $33\frac{1}{3}\%$

h. **Calculation:** Find $\frac{1}{3}$ of 60, + 5, × 2, − 1, $\sqrt{\ }$, × 4, − 1, ÷ 3, square that number, − 1, ÷ 2. 40

problem solving When you purchase hardwood, each board is sawn to specified widths and lengths. Hardwoods have their own unit of measure called "board foot" (bf). A board that is 1 in. thick, 12 in. wide, and 12 in. long measures 1 board foot (1 bf). Each of the following boards also measures 1 bf:

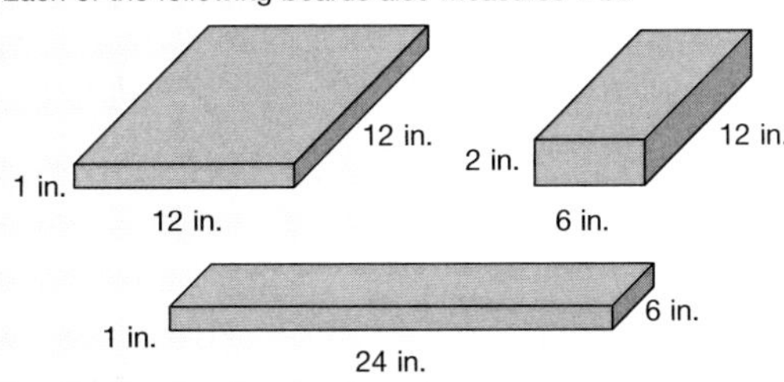

Can you find a formula for determining bf? Draw three more examples of 1 board foot. (Draw a diagram, use logical reasoning) $bf = \frac{l \times w \times h}{144}$. Other possible board feet: 3″ × 4″ × 12″, 4″ × 6″ × 6″, 2″ × 2″ × 36″

New Concept — *Increasing Knowledge*

In the equations we have solved thus far, the variables have had an exponent of 1. You have not seen the exponent, because we usually do not write the exponent when it is 1. In this lesson we will consider equations that have variables with exponents of 2, such as the following equation:

$$3x^2 + 1 = 28$$

1 Power Up

Facts

Distribute **Power Up V** to students. See answers below.

Mental Math

Encourage students to share different ways to mentally compute these exercises. Strategies for exercises **e** and **f** are listed below.

e. Double, Halve

$12\frac{1}{2}\%$ of 80 = 25% of 40 =

$\frac{1}{4} \times 40 = 10$

Use a Fraction

$12\frac{1}{2}\% = \frac{1}{8}$

$\frac{1}{8} \times 80 = 10$

f. Use a Fraction

$80 - (\frac{1}{8} \times 80) =$

$80 - 10 = 70$

Use an Equivalent Expression

$12\frac{1}{2}\%$ less than 80 = $87\frac{1}{2}\%$ of 80 =

$\frac{7}{8} \times 80 = 70$

Problem Solving

Refer to **Power-Up Discussion**, p. 759B.

2 New Concepts

Instruction

Ask students whether they remember working with any equations that had variables with an exponent of 2. Some examples might include:

- Area of a square: $A = s^2$
- Pythagorean theorem: $a^2 + b^2 = c^2$
- Area of a circle: $A = \pi r^2$

(continued)

Facts Solve each equation.

$6x + 2x = 8x$	$6x - 2x = 4x$	$(6x)(2x) = 12x^2$	$\frac{6x}{2x} = 3$
$9xy + 3xy = 12xy$	$9xy - 3xy = 6xy$	$(9xy)(3xy) = 27x^2y^2$	$\frac{9xy}{3xy} = 3$
$x + y + x = 2x + y$	$x + y - x = y$	$(x)(y)(-x) = -x^2y$	$\frac{xy}{x} = y$
$3x + x + 3 = 4x + 3$	$3x - x - 3 = 2x - 3$	$(3x)(-x)(-3) = 9x^2$	$\frac{(2x)(8xy)}{4y} = 4x^2$

2 New Concepts (Continued)

Instruction

Point out that the same rules are used with working with terms like x^2 as with terms like x. Explain that the phrase *both solutions satisfy the equation* means that both answers will work to make the equation true.

Example 1

Instruction

Help students see that the steps in solving equations like this one are to isolate the term with the variable, then remove the coefficient of the variable, and finally find the square root.

Example 2

Instruction

Remind students that $-\sqrt{5}$ and $\sqrt{-5}$ are not the same. The first expression is the *negative square root of five*. The second expression is *the square root of negative five*. The negative square root of a number is a real number, the square root of a negative number is not a real number.

(continued)

Thinking Skill

Explain

Why do we subtract 1 from both sides of the equation first? to isolate the variable

Isolating the variable in this equation takes three steps: first we subtract 1 from both sides; next we divide both sides by 3; then we find the square root of both sides. We show the results of each step below.

$3x^2 + 1 = 28$	equation
$3x^2 = 27$	subtracted 1 from both sides
$x^2 = 9$	divided both sides by 3
$x = 3, -3$	found the square root of both sides

Notice that there are two solutions, 3 and −3. Both solutions satisfy the equation, as we show below.

$3(3)^2 + 1 = 28$	$3(-3)^2 + 1 = 28$
$3(9) + 1 = 28$	$3(9) + 1 = 28$
$27 + 1 = 28$	$27 + 1 = 28$
$28 = 28$	$28 = 28$

When the variable of an equation has an exponent of 2, we remember to look for two solutions.

Example 1

Solve: $3x^2 - 1 = 47$

Solution

There are three steps. We show the results of each step.

$3x^2 - 1 = 47$	equation
$3x^2 = 48$	added 1 to both sides
$x^2 = 16$	divided both sides by 3
$x = \mathbf{4, -4}$	found the square root of both sides

Verify Check both solutions. See student work.

Example 2

Solve: $2x^2 = 10$

Solution

We divide both sides by 2. Then we find the square root of both sides.

$2x^2 = 10$	equation
$x^2 = 5$	divided both sides by 2
$x = \mathbf{\sqrt{5}, -\sqrt{5}}$	found the square root of both sides

Since $\sqrt{5}$ is an irrational number, we leave it in radical form. The negative of $\sqrt{5}$ is $-\sqrt{5}$ and not $\sqrt{-5}$.

Verify Check both solutions. See student work.

Math Background

What is the difference between the arithmetic mean and the geometric mean?

The arithmetic mean of two numbers, a and b, is half the sum of the two numbers. It can be found by solving this equation for m.

$$m = \frac{1}{2}(a + b)$$

The geometric mean of two numbers, a and b, is the square root of the product of the numbers. It can be found by solving this proportion for M.

$$\frac{a}{M} = \frac{M}{b}$$

$$M^2 = ab$$

$$M = \sqrt{ab}$$

Example 3

Five less than what number squared is 20?

Solution

We translate the question into an equation.

$$n^2 - 5 = 20$$

We solve the equation in two steps.

$n^2 - 5 = 20$	equation
$n^2 = 25$	added 5 to both sides
$n = 5, -5$	found the square root of both sides

There are two numbers that answer the question, **5** and **−5.**

Example 4

In this figure the area of the larger square is 4 square units, which is twice the area of the smaller square. What is the length of each side of the smaller square?

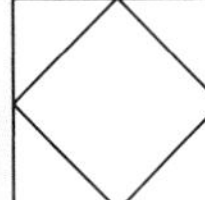

Solution

We will use the letter s to stand for the length of each side of the smaller square. So its area is s^2. Since the area of the large square (4) is twice the area of the small square, the area of the small square is 2.

$$s^2 = 2$$

We solve this equation in two steps by finding the square root of each side.

$s^2 = 2$	equation
$s = \sqrt{2}, -\sqrt{2}$	found the square root of both sides

Although there are two solutions there is only one answer because lengths are positive, not negative. Thus, each side of the smaller square is $\sqrt{2}$ **units.**

Example 5

Solve: $\frac{x}{3} = \frac{12}{x}$

Solution

Math Language

A **proportion** is a statement that shows two ratios are equal.

First we cross multiply. Then we find the square root of both sides.

$\frac{x}{3} = \frac{12}{x}$	proportion
$x^2 = 36$	cross multiplied
$x = 6, -6$	found the square root of both sides

There are two solutions to the proportion, **6** and **−6.**

2 New Concepts (Continued)

Example 3

Instruction

Caution students that it is important always to check both answers even though it may seem to be extra work. Sometimes one of the roots will not work when put back into the original equation.

Example 4

Instruction

Some students may want to use the equation $s^2 = \frac{1}{2}(4)$ and may get a value for s of $2\sqrt{\frac{1}{2}}$. This expression is equivalent to $\sqrt{2}$.

Remind students that they should always refer back to the original problem to determine if all values for the variable satisfy the equation and make sense in the context of the problem. In this case, both $\sqrt{2}$ and $-\sqrt{2}$ satisfy the equation, but since the answer represents a length, a negative number makes no sense.

Example 5

Instruction

It is necessary to solve equations like the one in this example when finding the geometric mean of two numbers. In general, the geometric mean of two numbers is the square root of their product.

(continued)

2 New Concepts (Continued)

Practice Set

Problems a and b Generalize

Have students tell what steps they used to solve these equations. Make sure that the last step is checking the answers in the original equation.

Problem d Error Alert

Point out that only the positive root makes sense as an answer for this problem.

3 Written Practice

Math Conversations

Discussion opportunities are provided below.

Problem 2 Conclude

Continue to examine the relationships present in this figure. As students answer the questions, ask them to explain their thinking. Ask questions such as:

"Name two sets of 4 equal angles." Sample: angles b, c, x, y

"Which angles are supplementary angles?" Sample: angles w and x

"Using the information in part d, are there any complementary angles in this figure?" Sample: angles z and w

Problem 4 Justify

"If Santiago has $10 in quarters and $10 in dimes, does the ratio of the number of quarters to the number of dimes change?" no

"Why not?" Sample: He has twice as many of both kinds, so the ratio stays the same.

Errors and Misconceptions

Problem 4

Tell students who did not know how many quarters or dimes are in $5 to think of the number of quarters or dimes in $1 and then multiply by 5. There are 20 quarters or 50 dimes in $5.

(continued)

Practice Set Generalize Solve and check each equation:

▶ **a.** $3x^2 - 8 = 100$ 6, −6 ▶ **b.** $x^2 + x^2 = 12$ $\sqrt{6}, -\sqrt{6}$

c. Five less than twice what negative number squared is 157? −9

▶ **d.** The area of a square is 3 square units. What is the length of each side? $\sqrt{3}$ units

e. $\frac{w}{4} = \frac{9}{w}$ 6, −6

Written Practice *Strengthening Concepts*

1. (45) What is the quotient when the product of 0.2 and 0.05 is divided by the sum of 0.2 and 0.05? 0.04

▶ **2.** (102) Conclude In the figure at right, a transversal intersects two parallel lines.

a. Which angle corresponds to $\angle d$? $\angle z$

b. Which angle is the alternate interior angle to $\angle d$? $\angle w$

c. Which angle is the alternate exterior angle to $\angle b$? $\angle y$

d. If the measure of $\angle a$ is m and the measure of $\angle b$ is $3m$, then each obtuse angle measures how many degrees? 135°

3. (101) Twenty is five more than the product of ten and what decimal number? 1.5

▶ **4.** (36) Justify Santiago has $5 in quarters and $5 in dimes.

a. What is the ratio of the number of quarters to the number of dimes? $\frac{2}{5}$;

b. Explain how you found your answer. Sample: I found that $5 = 20 quarters and $5 = 50 dimes. So the ratio of quarters to dimes is $\frac{20}{50} = \frac{2}{5}$.

Use ratio boxes to solve problems **5–7.**

5. (92) Sixty is 20 percent more than what number? 50

6. (92) The City-Wide Department Store is having a 25% off sale. What is the sale price of an item that originally cost $36? $27

7. (72) Jaime ran the first 3000 meters in 9 minutes. At that rate, how long will it take Jaime to run the entire 5000 meters race? 15 minutes

8. (88) Use unit multipliers to convert Jaime's average speed in problem 7 to kilometers per hour. 20 km per hour

9. (77) Write an equation to solve this problem: $60 = 1.5 \times W_N$; 40

Sixty is 150 percent of what number?

762 **Saxon** Math Course 2

▶ See Math Conversations in the sidebar.

10.

	702 cards
$\frac{2}{3}$ kept	234 cards
	234 cards
$\frac{1}{3}$ given away (234)	234 cards

12. $(\frac{1}{2})^5 = \frac{1}{32}$

10. Diagram this statement. Then answer the questions that follow. (71)

Diane kept $\frac{2}{3}$ of her baseball cards and gave the remaining 234 cards to her brother.

a. How many cards did Diane have before she gave some to her brother? 702 cards

b. How many baseball cards did Diane keep? 468 cards

11. (Inv. 9) **Explain** In the formula for the circumference of a circle, $C = \pi d$, are C and d directly or inversely proportional? Why? directly proportional; Sample: $C = \pi d$ is in the form $y = kx$ where π is the constant.

12. (94) Yasmine is playing a true-false geography game. She has answered 15 of her 20 questions correctly. What is the probability that she will answer the five remaining questions correctly?

13. (75) Find the area of this trapezoid. Dimensions are in centimeters. 36 cm^2

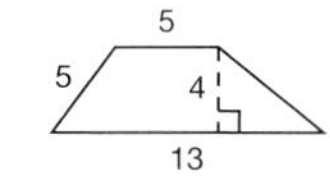

▸* **14.** (95) **Analyze** Find the volume of this solid. Dimensions are in inches. 162 in.^{3}

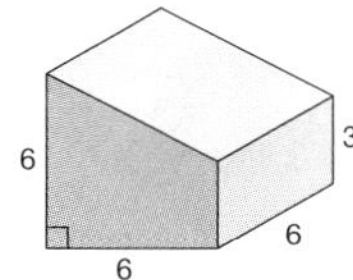

▸* **15.** (105) **Analyze** A rectangular label is wrapped around a can with the dimensions shown. The label has an area of how many square inches? (Use 3.14 for π.) 56.52 in.^{2}

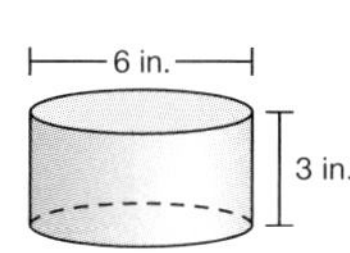

16. (46) The skateboard costs $36. The tax rate is 6.5 percent.

a. What is the tax on the skateboard? $2.34

b. What is the total price, including tax? $38.34

17. (48) Complete the table.

Fraction	Decimal	Percent
a. $\frac{1}{200}$	**b.** 0.005	$\frac{1}{2}$%

18. (92) What number is $66\frac{2}{3}$ percent more than 48? 80

19. (83) Multiply. Write the product in scientific notation. 4.8×10^{-3}

$$(6 \times 10^{-8})(8 \times 10^4)$$

▸ See Math Conversations in the sidebar.

3 Written Practice (Continued)

Math Conversations

Discussion opportunities are provided below.

Problem 14 Analyze

Have students share the methods that they used to find the volume of the solid. Ask how many students noticed that they could use the trapezoidal face as a base and have one student explain how to find the volume that way. Have others tell what they did—some may have subdivided the solid into two prisms.

Problem 15 Analyze

"The question asks you to find the area of a label wrapped around the can. What do you have to assume about the label in order to answer the question?" Sample: It doesn't go on the top or bottom, and it doesn't overlap but it covers the entire side of the can.

Errors and Misconceptions

Problem 15

If students find the surface area of the can, have them reread the problem and note that the label would cover only the surface of the side of the can, not the top and bottom surfaces.

(continued)

English Learners

Explain how to play a **true-false game** like the one in problem 12. Say:

"In a true-false game, you must decide if a statement is true or false."

Write, "Eight is an even number." on the board. Read the statement and ask a volunteer to tell if the statement is true or false. Give students a chance to make up statements for a true-false game.

3 Written Practice (Continued)

Math Conversations

Discussion opportunities are provided below.

Problem 22 Conclude

Extend the Problem

Tell students that the circle is the base for a spinner. Have them make up problems for partners to solve. Sample: What is the probability of the spinner stopping 4 times in a row in section 3x? $\frac{81}{10{,}000}$

Problem 23 Analyze

Extend the Problem

"One way to draw a line 10 units long on a coordinate grid without a ruler is to count 10 units on one of the gridlines. How can you draw a line 10 units long without a ruler and without using a gridline?" Sample: Draw two legs of a right triangle that are 6 units and 8 units long, then connect the ends. The line will be 10 units long.

Errors and Misconceptions

Problem 20

If some students need grid paper, supply them with copies of **Investigation Activity 13** Coordinate Plane. Encourage them to make sketches of coordinate grids without graph paper.

Problem 24

Some students may give only the positive root as the answer. Point out to them that there are two answers to this problem: 4 and −4.

---

20. b. $y = \frac{2}{3}x - 1$

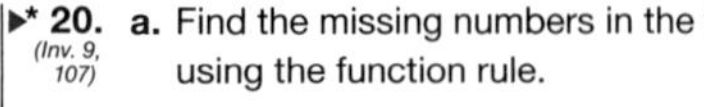

▶* **20.** (Inv. 9, 107) **a.** Find the missing numbers in the table by using the function rule.

b. Then graph the function on a coordinate plane.

c. What is the slope of the graphed line? $\frac{2}{3}$

$y = \frac{2}{3}x - 1$

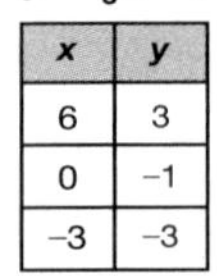

x	y
6	3
0	−1
−3	−3

21. (66) Use a ratio box to solve this problem. The ratio of the measures of the two acute angles of the right triangle is 7 to 8. What is the measure of the smallest angle of the triangle? 42°

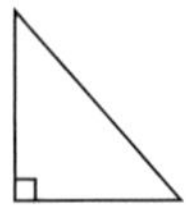

▶* **22.** (101) Conclude The relationship between the measures of four central angles of a circle is shown in this figure. What is the measure of the smallest central angle shown? 36°

▶* **23.** (99) Analyze We can use the Pythagorean theorem to find the distance between two points on a coordinate plane. To find the distance from point *M* to point *P*, we draw a right triangle and use the lengths of the legs to find the length of the hypotenuse. What is the distance from point *M* to point *P*? $\sqrt{29}$ units

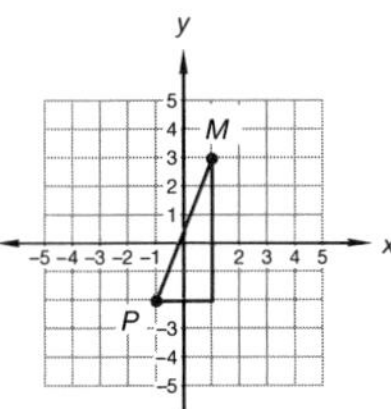

Solve and check.

▶ **24.** (109) $3m^2 + 2 = 50$ 4, −4

* **25.** (102) $7(y - 2) = 4 - 2y$ 2

Simplify:

26. (20) $\sqrt{144} - (\sqrt{36})(\sqrt{4})$ 0

27. (96) $x^2y + xy^2 + x(xy - y^2)$ $2x^2y$

28. (43) $\left(1\frac{5}{9}\right)(1.5) \div 2\frac{2}{3}$ $\frac{7}{8}$

29. (43) $9.5 - \left(4\frac{1}{5} - 3.4\right)$ 8.7

30. (57, 91, 106) **a.** $\frac{(-18) + (-12) - (-6)(3)}{-3}$ 4

b. $\sqrt[3]{1000} - \sqrt[3]{125}$ 5

c. $2^2 + 2^1 + 2^0 + 2^{-1}$ $7\frac{1}{2}$ or 7.5

764 **Saxon** Math Course 2

▶ See Math Conversations in the sidebar.

Looking Forward

Working with equations with exponents prepares students for:

- **Lesson 112,** applications of the Pythagorean theorem.

• Simple Interest and Compound Interest
• Successive Discounts

Objectives

- Calculate simple interest.
- Calculate compound interest.
- Use a calculator to calculate compound interest.
- Calculate successive discounts.

Lesson Preparation

Materials

- **Power Up Q** (in *Instructional Masters*)
- **Teacher-provided material: calculators, graph paper,** 3 per student

Optional

- **pictures, magazines, computer spreadsheets**
- **Investigation Activity 13** (in *Instructional Masters*)

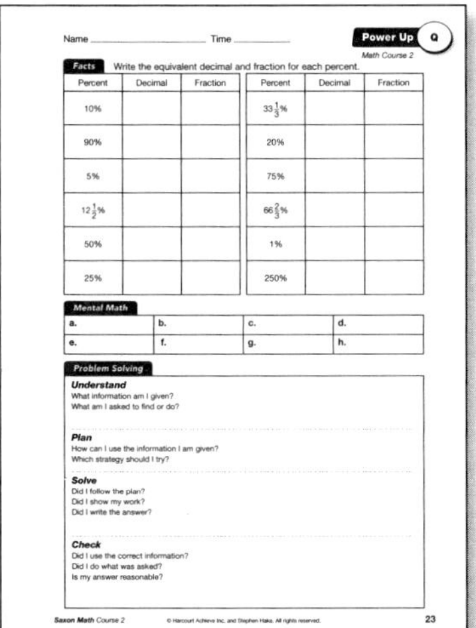

Power Up Q

Math Language

New

compound interest	**simple interest**
interest	**successive discount**
principal	

Technology Resources

Student eBook Complete student textbook in electronic format.

Resources and Planner CD Assessment, reteaching, and instructional masters, plus a pacing calendar with standards.

Test and Practice Generator CD Create additional practice sheets and custom-made tests.

www.SaxonPublishers.com Visit for more student activities and planning materials.

Inclusion

Adaptations CD Adapted lessons, investigations, practice and assessments.

Meeting Standards

National Council of Teachers of Mathematics (NCTM)

Numbers and Operations

NO.1c Develop meaning for percents greater than 100 and less than 1

Algebra

AL.3a Model and solve contextualized problems using various representations, such as graphs, tables, and equations

Problem Solving

PS.1b Solve problems that arise in mathematics and in other contexts

Connections

CN.4c Recognize and apply mathematics in contexts outside of mathematics

Power-Up Discussion *For use with Power Up, p. 765*

Problem-Solving Strategy: Draw a Diagram

Sonya, Sid, and Sinead met at the gym on Tuesday. Sonya goes to the gym every two days. The next day she will be at the gym is Thursday. Sid goes to the gym every three days. The next day Sid will be at the gym is Friday. Sinead goes to the gym every four days. She will next be at the gym on Saturday. What will be the next day that Sonya, Sid, and Sinead are at the gym on the same day?

Understand ***Understand the problem.***

"What information are we given?"

We are told how often three people work out, and that they were all at the gym on a certain day.

"What are we asked to do?"

We are asked to find the next day the three people will meet at the gym.

Plan ***Make a plan.***

"What problem-solving strategy will we use?"

We will *draw a diagram* to help us track the three workout schedules and determine when they will intersect once again.

Solve ***Carry out the plan.***

"How do we construct our diagram?"

We begin by listing several days of the week in order, beginning with the Tuesday all three were there. Then we use curved lines to mark of each workout schedule. The next day where all three lines meet will be the next day all three are at the gym:

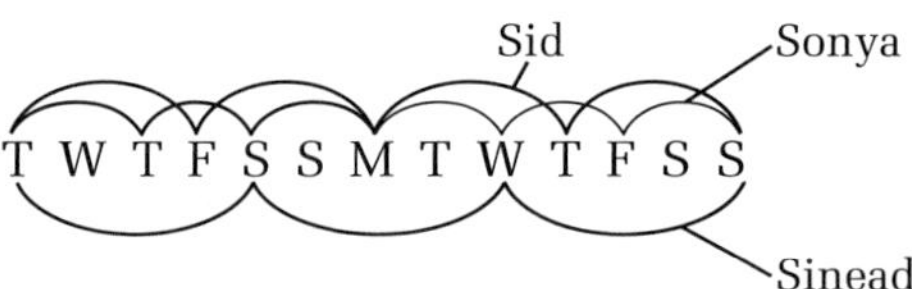

"On what day do Sonya, Sid, and Sinead next meet at the gym?"

Sunday

Check ***Look back.***

"Did we do what we were asked to do?"

Yes, we found the next day that all three will be at the gym.

LESSON 110

• Simple Interest and Compound Interest
• Successive Discounts

Power Up — *Building Power*

facts Power Up Q

mental math

a. **Exponents:** $(-\frac{1}{2})^2$ $\frac{1}{4}$

b. **Scientific Notation:** $(9 \times 10^6)(6 \times 10^9)$ 5.4×10^{16}

c. **Algebra:** $4w - 1 = 9$ $\frac{5}{2}$

d. **Measurement:** 1.5 L to mL. 1500 mL

e. **Percent:** 150% of \$60 \$90

f. **Percent:** \$60 increased 50% \$90

g. **Number Sense:** Change $\frac{1}{5}$ to a decimal and percent. .2 and 20%

h. **Measurement:** Start with the number of minutes in half an hour. Multiply by the number of feet in a yard; add the number of years in a decade; then find the square root of that number. What is the answer? 10

problem solving Sonya, Sid, and Sinead met at the gym on Monday. Sonya goes to the gym every two days. The next day she will be at the gym is Wednesday. Sid goes to the gym every three days. The next day Sid will be at the gym is Thursday. Sinead goes to the gym every four days. She will next be at the gym on Friday. What will be the next day that Sonya, Sid, and Sinead are at the gym on the same day? Saturday

New Concepts — *Increasing Knowledge*

simple interest and compound interest

When you deposit money in a bank, the bank does not simply hold your money for safekeeping. Instead, it spends your money in other places to make more money. For this opportunity the bank pays you a percentage of the money deposited. The amount of money you deposit is called the **principal.** The amount of money the bank pays you is called **interest.**

There is a difference between **simple interest** and **compound interest.** Simple interest is paid on the principal only and not paid on any accumulated interest. For instance, if you deposited \$100 in an account that pays 6% simple interest, you would be paid 6% of \$100 (\$6) each year your \$100 was on deposit. If you take your money out after three years, you would have a total of \$118.

Facts Write the equivalent decimal and fraction for each percent.

Percent	Decimal	Fraction	Percent	Decimal	Fraction
10%	0.1	$\frac{1}{10}$	$33\frac{1}{3}\%$	$0.\bar{3}$	$\frac{1}{3}$
90%	0.9	$\frac{9}{10}$	20%	0.2	$\frac{1}{5}$
5%	0.05	$\frac{1}{20}$	75%	0.75	$\frac{3}{4}$
$12\frac{1}{2}\%$	0.125	$\frac{1}{8}$	$66\frac{2}{3}\%$	$0.\bar{6}$	$\frac{2}{3}$
50%	0.5	$\frac{1}{2}$	1%	0.01	$\frac{1}{100}$
25%	0.25	$\frac{1}{4}$	250%	2.5	$2\frac{1}{2}$

1 Power Up

Facts

Distribute **Power Up Q** to students. See answers below.

Mental Math

Encourage students to share different ways to mentally compute these exercises. Strategies for exercises **d** and **e** are listed below.

d. Use a Unit Multiplier

$1.5 \text{ L} \times \frac{1000 \text{ mL}}{1 \text{ L}} = 1500 \text{ mL}$

Use Logical Reasoning

1 L = 1000 mL
0.5 L = 500 mL
1.5 L = 1500 mL

e. Use a Fraction

$150\% = \frac{3}{2}$

$\frac{3}{2} \times \$60 = \frac{\$180}{2} = \$90$

Use Logical Reasoning

100% of \$60 = \$60
50% of \$60 = \$30
150% of \$60 = \$90

Problem Solving

Refer to **Power-Up Discussion,** p. 765B.

2 New Concepts

Instruction

Ask students why they think many people put money in banks instead of just keeping it at home. Answers might include convenience and safety.

Point out that many bank accounts also pay customers for the use of their money. The banks use the money that people deposit to make loans to other people who then pay interest on the loan as they repay it. Ask whether any students have bank accounts that earn interest. Explain that knowing the interest rate for an account is a consideration when choosing where to open a savings account.

You may want to invite a representative from a local bank to visit your class and discuss the types of interest-earning accounts offered by the bank as well as the benefits of each type.

(continued)

2 New Concepts (Continued)

Instruction

As a class, calculate the simple interest on $100 using an overhead projector or the board. Discuss how the $100 generates interest each year.

Continue working as a class to calculate the compound interest on $100. Discuss how the $100 earns money in the first year and then how both the principal and the interest generates additional interest in successive years. If the rate remains the same, the amount of interest paid each year increases because interest is paid on the accumulated interest as well as on the principal.

As you work on the *Thinking Skill* question, students may use calculators or estimation to find the differences between simple and compound interest over the time spans. The important point for them to see is how much more an account grows with compound interest than with simple interest.

Example 1

Instruction

Tell students that interest compounded annually is used in this lesson. However, most banks compound interest on their accounts more frequently. Some are compounded monthly, and others are compounded daily. Explain that when interest rates are equal, the more often interest is compounded, the more interest is earned.

(continued)

Simple Interest

$100.00	principal
$6.00	first-year interest
$6.00	second-year interest
+ $6.00	third-year interest
$118.00	total

Most interest-bearing accounts, however, are compound-interest accounts, not simple-interest accounts. In a compound-interest account, interest is paid on accumulated interest as well as on the principal. If you deposited $100 in an account with 6% annual percentage rate, the amount of interest you would be paid each year increases if the earned interest is left in the account. After three years you would have a total of $119.10.

Compound Interest

$100.00	principal
$6.00	first-year interest (6% of $100.00)
$106.00	total after one year
$6.36	second-year interest (6% of $106.00)
$112.36	total after two years
$6.74	third-year interest (6% of $112.36)
$119.10	total after three years

Notice that in three years, $100.00 grows to $118.00 at 6% simple interest, while it grows to $119.10 at 6% compound interest. The difference is not very large in three years, but as this table shows, the difference can become large over time.

Thinking Skill
Analyze
After 10 years, what is the difference in the interest earned through simple and compound interest? After 30 years? After 50 years?
$19.08; $294.35; $1442.02

Total Value of $100 at 6% Interest

Number of Years	Simple Interest	Compound Interest
3	$118.00	$119.10
10	$160.00	$179.08
20	$220.00	$320.71
30	$280.00	$574.35
40	$340.00	$1028.57
50	$400.00	$1842.02

Example 1

Make a table that shows the value of a $1000 investment growing at 10% compounded annually after 1, 2, 3, 4, and 5 years.

Teacher Tip

In this lesson the vocabulary and concept load may be overwhelming for some students. Creating a class **vocabulary bulletin board** with the words, definitions, and examples can help students develop the understanding needed to work with interest problems successfully. Assign words to pairs or small groups of students and have them define the word and create an example. If you have any pictures that will help build understanding, add them to the display.

Math Background

Is interest money earned or money paid?

Interest can be either earned or paid. When money is deposited in an interest-bearing account, interest is paid to the depositor. When money is borrowed, the borrower pays interest to the person or bank that loaned the money. Businesses such as banks, where people can both deposit and borrow money, charge interest to customers who borrow money and pay interest to depositors whose money they use to lend.

Solution

After the first year, $1000 grows 10% to $1100. After the second year, the value increases 10% of $1100 ($110) to a total of $1210. We continue the pattern for five years in the table below.

Total Value of $1000 at 10% Interest

Number of Years	Compound Interest
1	$1100.00
2	$1210.00
3	$1331.00
4	$1464.10
5	$1610.51

Notice that the amount of money in the account after one year is 110% of the original deposit of $1000. This 110% is composed of the starting amount, 100%, plus 10%, which is the interest earned in one year. Likewise, the amount of money in the account the second year is 110% of the amount in the account after one year. To find the amount of money in the account each year, we multiply the previous year's balance by 110% (or the decimal equivalent, which is 1.1).

Even with a simple calculator we can calculate compound interest. To perform the calculation in example 1, we could follow this sequence:

$$1000 \times 1.1 \times 1.1 \times 1.1 \times 1.1 \times 1.1 =$$

The circuitry of some calculators permits repeating a calculation by pressing the [=] key repeatedly.[1] To make the calculations in example 1, we try this keystroke sequence:

[1] [.] [1] [×] [1] [0] [0] [0] [=]

This keystroke sequence first enters 1.1, which is the decimal form of 110% (100% principal plus 10% interest), then the times sign, then 1000 for the $1000 investment. Pressing the [=] key once displays

1100.

which is the value ($1100) after one year. Pressing the [=] key a second time multiplies the displayed number by 1.1, the first number we entered. The new number displayed is

1210.

10 yr, $2593.74; 20 yr, $6727.50

representing $1210, the value after two years. Each time the [=] key is pressed, the calculator displays the account value after a successive year. Using this method, find the value of the account after 10 years and after 20 years.

[1] This calculator function varies with make and model of calculator. See instructions for your calculator if the keystroke sequence described in this lesson does not work for you.

2 New Concepts (Continued)

Example 1 (continued)

Instruction

Tell students that banks use computer programs to calculate the interest both on savings and on loans. Suggest that anyone who has an interest-bearing savings account take a look at the account and see how his or her savings have grown.

Instruction

Check with students to confirm that the keystroke sequence described works with their calculators. If not, work with students to develop step-by-step procedures that they can use.

Explain that many interest rates involve fractions. Have students work through the solution for example 1 again with their calculators using $9\frac{3}{4}\%$. Have them find the decimal equivalent (0.0975) before multiplying the principal by the percent. $1097.50, $1204.51, $1321.95, $1450.84, $1592.30

(continued)

Teacher Tip

For this lesson, be sure that each student can use his or her **calculator** to solve interest problems. If you have computers in your classroom or access to a computer lab, show students how a **computer spreadsheet** program can be used to find interest amounts. Encourage students to learn more about using spreadsheets.

Inclusion

Many students can benefit from seeing the process of interest calculation in a comparison of the two different types. Write the following table on the board, discuss the calculations, and then ask students to help fill in the rest of the table. Ask:

	Simple Interest		Compound Interest	
	$100 Balance	**10% Interest**	**$100 Balance**	**10% Interest**
Year 1	$100	$10	$100	$10
Year 2	$100	$10	$110	$11
Year 3	$100	$10	$121	$12.10
Year 4	$100	$10	$133.10	$13.13
Year 5	$100	$10	$146.41	$14.64

"Does the interest rate remain constant throughout the five years of investment?" yes

"Does the interest earned remain constant?" no

"Why does the interest earned change when the rate stays the same?" Sample: The investor is earning interest on interest.

2 New Concepts (Continued)

Instruction

Discuss the response to the *Explain* question as a class. Allow for alternate explanations based on the calculator used by each student.

Example 2

Instruction

Have students use their calculators to compute the answer to this example as you guide them in the process.

Example 3

Instruction

Point out that time expressed in months is written as a fractional part of a year. *Annual interest* is the same as interest over one year.

Example 4

Instruction

Present the two methods for finding successive discounts, step by step, on an overhead projector or on the board.

(continued)

No. This keystroke sequence multiplies the displayed number by 1000, the first number entered, not by 1.1.

Try entering the factors in the reverse order.

1 0 0 0 × 1 . 1 =

Explain Are the same amounts displayed as were displayed with the prior entry when the = key is repeatedly pressed? Why or why not?

Example 2

Use a calculator to find the value after 12 years of a $2000 investment that earns $7\frac{1}{2}$% interest compounded annually.

Solution

The interest rate is $7\frac{1}{2}$%, which is 0.075 in decimal form. We want to find the total value, including the principal. So we multiply the $2000 investment by $107\frac{1}{2}$%, which we enter as 1.075. The keystroke sequence is

1 . 0 7 5 × 2 0 0 0 =

We then press the = key 11 more times to find the value after 12 years. We round the final display to the nearest cent, **$4763.56.**

Example 3

Calculate the interest earned on an $8000 deposit in 9 months if the annual interest rate is 6%.

Solution

The deposit earns 6% interest in one year, which is

$$0.06 \times \$8000 = \$480$$

In 9 months the deposit earns just $\frac{9}{12}$ of this amount.

$$\frac{9}{12} \times \$480 = \mathbf{\$360}$$

successive discounts

Related to compound interest is **successive discount.** To calculate successive discount, we find a percent of a percent. In the following example we show two methods for finding successive discounts.

Thinking Skill

Connect

How is calculating compound interest related to calculating successive discounts? Both require us to perform an operation, then perform a similar operation on the result of the first operation.

Example 4

An appliance store reduced the price of a $400 washing machine 25%. When the washing machine did not sell at the sale price, the store reduced the sale price 20% to its clearance price. What was the clearance price of the washing machine?

Solution

One way to find the answer is to first find the sale price and then find the clearance price. We will use a ratio box to find the sale price.

	Percent	Actual Count
Original	100	400
– Change	25	D
New (Sale)	75	S

$$\frac{100}{75} = \frac{400}{S}$$
$$100S = 30{,}000$$
$$S = 300$$

We find that the sale price was $300. The second discount, 20%, was applied to the sale price, not to the original price. So for the next calculation we consider the sale price to be 100% and the clearance price to be what remains after the discount.

	Percent	Actual Count
Original	100	300
– Change	20	D
New (Clearance)	80	C

$$\frac{100}{80} = \frac{300}{C}$$
$$100C = 24{,}000$$
$$C = 240$$

We find that the clearance price of the washing machine was **$240.**

Another way to look at this problem is to consider what percent of the original price is represented by the sale price. Since the original price was discounted 25%, the sale price represents 75% of the original price.

Sale price = 75% of the original price

Furthermore, since the sale price was discounted 20%, the clearance price was 80% of the sale price.

Clearance price = 80% of the sale price

So the clearance price was 80% of the sale price, which was 75% of the original price.

Clearance price = 80% of 75% of $400
= $0.8 \times 0.75 \times$ $400
= $0.6 \times$ $400
= **$240**

See student work. Students may prefer the second method, because it allows us to set up the problem mentally without ratio boxes and solve it in fewer steps.

Evaluate Which method, the first or the second, is a more efficient way to find a clearance price after a successive discount?

Practice Set ▸

a. **Generalize** When Mai turned 21, she invested $2000 in an Individual Retirement Account (IRA) that has grown at a rate of 10% compounded annually. If the account continues to grow at that rate, what will be its value when Mai turns 65? (Use the calculator method taught in this lesson.) $132,528.15

b. Mrs. Rojas deposited $6000 into an account paying 4% interest annually. After 8 months Mrs. Rojas withdrew the $6000 plus interest. Altogether, how much money did Mrs. Rojas withdraw? What fraction of a year's interest was earned? $6160; $\frac{8}{12}$ or $\frac{2}{3}$

▸ See Math Conversations in the sidebar.

2 New Concepts (Continued)

Example 4 (continued)

Instruction

If you notice that some students are adding the percents for successive discounts instead of multiplying them, work through the following example with them. Tell them that a $120 coat is reduced 50 percent and then reduced 60 percent.

"How does this example show you that you cannot add the percents in successive discounts?" The total would be greater than 100 percent.

Ask students to use successive discounts to find the final cost of the coat and then explain their work. The coat is $60 after the first discount of $60, and $24 after the second discount of $36.

As you discuss the *Evaluate* question, advise students to be familiar with both methods, even if they prefer to use one of them most of the time.

Practice Set

Problem a Generalize

Have students work with partners to do this problem. When students finish, ask volunteers to explain how they solved the problem.

You may want to explain that an IRA is an account in which people can invest money to use after they retire.

(continued)

2 New Concepts (Continued)

Practice Set

Problem d Formulate

Have students read their problems aloud for the class to solve or let students exchange problems.

3 Written Practice

Math Conversations

Discussion opportunities are provided below.

Problem 2 Generalize

Ask students to describe how they decided to set up the problem. Have them tell which method they used and why they used it.

Problem 6 Analyze

Have students explain how they analyzed the given information to decide what they needed to do to solve the problem. You may want to extend this problem by asking students to find the area of the figure. $29\frac{3}{4}$ in.^{2}

Errors and Misconceptions

Problem 7

If students give an answer of 4, they averaged the three given numbers. Help them to see that if the average of four numbers is 8, and three of the four numbers are less than 8, then the fourth number must be greater than 8.

(continued)

c. A television regularly priced at $300 was placed on sale for 20% off. When the television still did not sell, the sale price was reduced 20% for clearance. What was the clearance price of the television? $192

▶ **d.** Formulate Write and solve an original word problem that involves compound or simple interest. See student work.

Written Practice *Strengthening Concepts*

1. (46) Rosita bought 3 paperback books for $5.95 each. The sales-tax rate was 6 percent. If she paid for the purchase with a $20 bill, how much money did she get back? $1.08

▶ * **2.** (110) Generalize Hector has a coupon for 10% off the price of any item in the store. He decides to buy a shirt regularly priced at $24 that is on sale for 25% off. If he uses his coupon, how much will Hector pay for the shirt before sales tax is applied? $16.20

3. (80) Triangle *ABC* with vertices *A* (3, 0), *B* (3, 4), and *C* (0, 0) is rotated 90° clockwise about the origin to its image $\triangle A'B'C'$. Graph both triangles. What are the coordinates of the vertices of $\triangle A'B'C'$?
A' (0, −3), B' (4, −3), C' (0, 0)

4. (72) Jorge burned 370 calories by hiking for one hour.

a. How many calories would Jorge burn if he hiked for 2 hours 30 minutes? 925 calories

b. Suppose Jorge's dinner consisted of a 6 oz steak (480 calories), a baked potato (145 calories), 4 spears of asparagus (15 calories), and one cup of strawberries (45 calories). How many hours would Jorge need to hike to burn the calories he ate at dinner? Round your answer to the nearest minute. 685 calories $\times \frac{1\text{ h}}{370\text{ calories}}$ = 1.85 hours = 111 minutes = 1 hour and 51 minutes

5. (72) If a dozen roses costs $20.90, what is the cost of 30 roses? $52.25

▶ * **6.** (104) Analyze A semicircle was cut out of a square. What is the perimeter of the resulting figure shown? (Use $\frac{22}{7}$ for π.) 32 in.

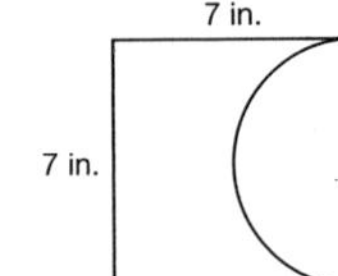

▶ **7.** (55) The average of four numbers is 8. Three of the numbers are 2, 4, and 6. What is the fourth number? 20

Write equations to solve problems **8–10.**

8. (77) One hundred fifty is what percent of 60?
$150 = W_P \times 60$; 250%

9. (77) Sixty percent of what number is 150? $0.6 \times W_N = 150$; 250

* **10.** (109) Generalize Six more than the square of what negative number is 150?
$(-x)^2 + 6 = 150$; −12

▶ See Math Conversations in the sidebar.

11. Graph the points (3, 1) and (–1, –2) on a coordinate plane. Then draw a right triangle, and use the Pythagorean theorem to find the distance between the points. 5 units
(99)

Use ratio boxes to solve problems **12** and **13.**

12. The price of the dress was reduced by 40 percent. If the sale price was \$48, what was the regular price? \$80
(92)

Reading Math

Read the term *1:36* as "one to thirty-six."

▶* **13.** **Generalize** The car model was built on a 1:36 scale. If the length of the car is 180 inches, how many inches long is the model? 5 inches
(98)

14. The positive square root of 80 is between which two consecutive whole numbers? 8 and 9
(100)

11.

▶* **15.** **Analyze** Make a table of ordered pairs for the function $y = -x + 1$. Then graph the function. What is the slope of the graphed line? See student work; –1
(Inv. 9, 107)

16. Solve this inequality and graph its solution: $x \geq -2$
(93)

$$5x + 12 \geq 2$$

17. Multiply. Write the product in scientific notation. 5.67×10^5
(83)

$$(6.3 \times 10^7)(9 \times 10^{-3})$$

15.

$y = -x + 1$

▶* **18.** **Generalize** Solve for y: $\frac{1}{2}y = x + 2$ $y = 2x + 4$
(96, 106)

▶* **19.** **Generalize** What is the total account value after 3 years on a deposit of \$4000 at 9% interest compounded annually? \$5180.12
(110)

20. The triangles below are similar. Dimensions are in inches.
(97, 98)

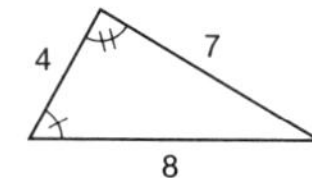

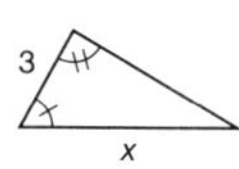

▶ **a.** Estimate, then calculate, the length x.
See student work; 6 in.

b. Find the scale factor from the larger to the smaller triangle. 0.75

21. Find the volume of this triangular prism. Dimensions are in inches. 960 in.^{3}
(95)

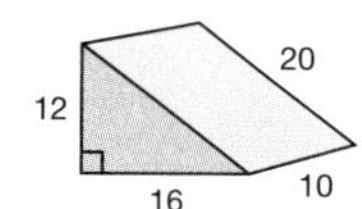

▶* **22.** **Generalize** Find the total surface area of the triangular prism in problem **21.** 672 in.^{2}
(105)

23. Find m∠x in the figure at right. 110°
(40)

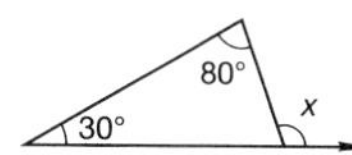

▶ See Math Conversations in the sidebar.

3 Written Practice *(Continued)*

Math Conversations

Discussion opportunities are provided below.

Problem 13 Generalize

Ask students to explain why it makes sense to use a proportion or a ratio box to solve this problem.

Problem 15 Analyze

Discuss what quadrants the line passes through. quadrants I, II, and IV Ask whether the line will ever pass through quadrant III. no Then discuss how the equation might be changed so that the line would pass through quadrant III. Samples: $y = -x - 1$, $y = x - 1$

Problem 18 Generalize

Have students tell what the first step in their solutions was and why they did it that way. Sample: I multiplied both sides by 2 so that y would be by itself on the left side.

Problem 19 Generalize

Have students predict whether the compound interest or simple interest would pay more. compound interest Then have them calculate the simple interest and compare the two. \$1080, the compound interest is greater

Problem 22 Generalize

Guide students to think about the information needed to solve this problem.

"How many faces are on this solid?" 5

"How many different surface areas do you need to calculate?" Sample: four, because two are the same

Errors and Misconceptions

Problem 18

Students whose answer is $y = x + 1$ did not multiply both terms on the right side of the equation by 2. Remind them that when multiplying or dividing both sides of an equation by a number, all terms must be multiplied or divided by that number.

Problem 20a

If students were not able to estimate and calculate the length x, help them first to see that since 3 is less than 4, x will be less than 8. Good estimates would be 6 or 7. Then guide them to see that 8 is to x as 4 is to 3, or they could also see that 8 is twice 4, so x has to be twice 3, or 6.

(continued)

3 Written Practice (Continued)

Math Conversations

Discussion opportunities are provided below.

Problems 24 and 25 Generalize

"How can you tell by looking at these equations that they will both have two solutions?" Sample: You can see that you will have to find the square root.

Problems 26–30 Generalize

"For which of these problems would you expect to use canceling to help simplify the problem?" problems 27 and 29

Errors and Misconceptions

Problem 24

Some students may get 36 as the answer. They used w, not $w \times w$, in writing the equation for the proportion. Help them see that w must be used as a factor twice and should be expressed as w^2.

▶ **Generalize** Solve:

* **24.** (109) $\frac{w}{2} = \frac{18}{w}$ 6, −6

* **25.** (109) $3\frac{1}{3}w^2 - 4 = 26$ 3, −3

▶ **Generalize** Simplify:

26. (63) $16 - \{27 - 3[8 - (3^2 - 2^3)]\}$ 10

* **27.** (103) $\frac{(6ab^2)(8ab)}{12a^2b^2}$ $4b$

28. (43) $3\frac{1}{3} + 1.5 + 4\frac{5}{6}$ $9\frac{2}{3}$

29. (26) $20 \div \left(3\frac{1}{3} \div 1\frac{1}{5}\right)$ $7\frac{1}{5}$

* **30.** (103) $(-3)^2 + (-2)^3$ 1

Early Finishers
Real-World Application

A local town wants to paint the entire surface of its water tank. The tank is in the shape of a cylinder. Because it is elevated, the bottom surface needs to be painted. The diameter of the tank is 30 feet and the height is 20 feet.

a. What is the surface area of the tank? Use 3.14 for π. 3297 square feet

b. Paint costs $22 per gallon and is only sold in whole gallons. The tank only needs one coat of paint. If one gallon covers approximately 250 square feet, how many gallons of paint should the town purchase? 14 gallons

772 **Saxon** Math Course 2

▶ See Math Conversations in the sidebar.

Assessment

30–40 minutes *For use after Lesson 110*

Distribute **Cumulative Test 21** to each student. Two versions of the test are available in *Saxon Math Course 2 Course Assessments Book.* Have students complete the **Power-Up Test** first. Allow 10 minutes. Then have students work the 20 numbered items on the **Cumulative Test.** Students may use copies of the answer sheet to record their work. Track individual and class progress with the **Test Analysis** forms.

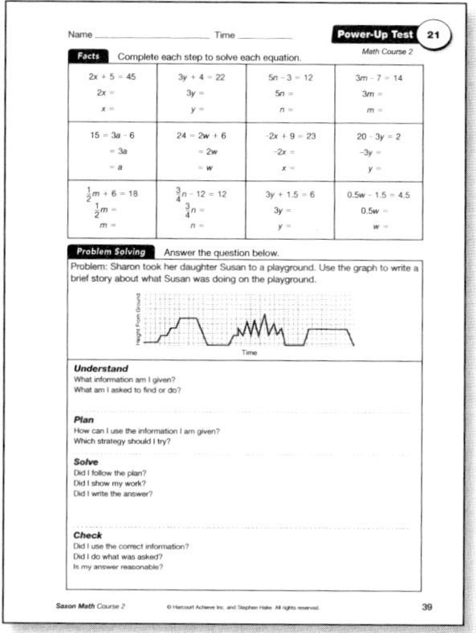

Power-Up Test 21

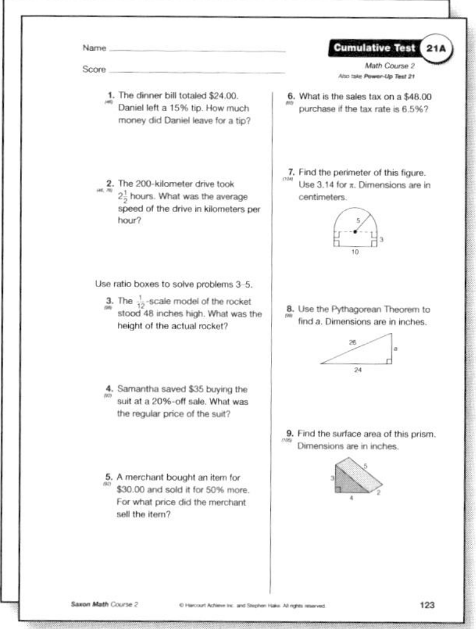

Cumulative Test 21A

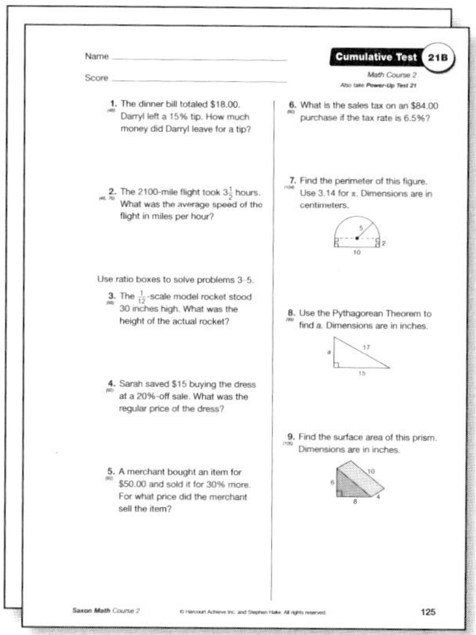

Alternative Cumulative Test 21B

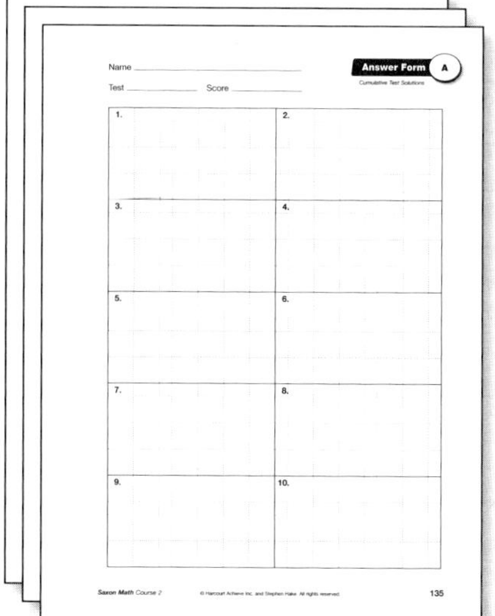

Optional Answer Forms

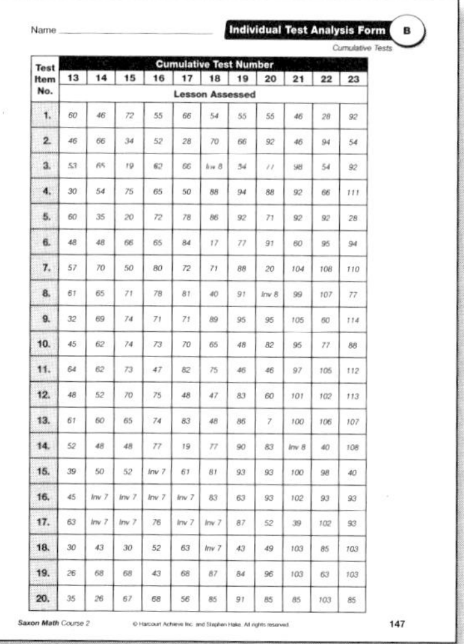

Individual Test Analysis Form

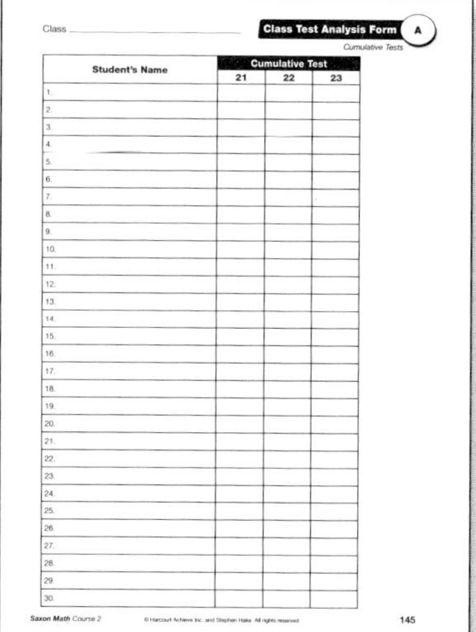

Class Test Analysis Form

Reteaching

Students who score below 80% on the assessment may be in need of reteaching. Look for the causes of student mistakes. If errors are conceptual, refer to the *Reteaching Masters* for reteaching.

Customized Benchmark Assessment

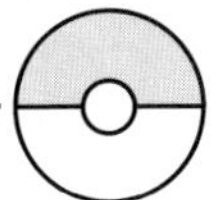

You can develop customized benchmark tests using the Test Generator located on the *Test and Practice Generator CD.*

This chart shows the lesson, the standard, and the test item question that can be found on the *Test and Practice Generator CD.*

LESSON	NEW CONCEPTS	LOCAL STANDARD	TEST ITEM ON CD
101	• Translating Expressions Into Equations		11.101.1
102	• Transversals		11.102.1
	• Simplifying Equations		11.102.2
103	• Powers of Negative Numbers		11.103.1
	• Dividing Terms		11.103.2
	• Square Roots of Monomials		11.103.3
104	• Semicircles, Arcs, and Sectors		11.104.1
105	• Surface Area of a Right Solid		11.105.1
	• Surface Area of a Sphere		11.105.2
106	• Solving Literal Equations		11.106.1
	• Transforming Formulas		11.106.2
	• More on Roots		11.106.3
107	• Slope		11.107.1
108	• Formulas and Substitutions		11.108.1
109	• Equations with Exponents		11.109.1
110	• Simple Interest and Compound Interest		11.110.1
	• Successive Discounts		11.110.2

Using the Test Generator CD

- Develop tests in both English and Spanish.
- Choose from multiple-choice and free-response test items.
- Clone test items to create multiple versions of the same test.
- View and edit test items to make and save your own questions.
- Administer assessments through paper tests or over a school LAN.
- Monitor student progress through a variety of individual and class reports —for both diagnosing and assessing standards mastery.

Performance Task 21

Make Inferences from Graphs

Assign after Lesson 110 and Test 21

Objectives

- Make inferences from data in graphs.
- Make convincing arguments to support inferences.
- Communicate their ideas through writing.

Materials

Performance Tasks 21A and **21B.**

Preparation

Make copies of **Performance Tasks 21A** and **21B.** (One each per student.)

Time Requirement

30–60 minutes; Begin in class and complete at home.

Task

Explain to students that for this task they will be drawing conclusions from the 2000 United States census for a Web site about the United States. They will make inferences from a graph of the population in the United States from 1960 to 2000 and a graph that shows the age distribution of the population in the United States in 2000. They will make convincing arguments to support those inferences. Point out that all of the information students need is on **Performance Tasks 21A** and **21B.**

Criteria for Evidence of Learning

- Makes reasonable inferences from data in graphs.
- Makes convincing arguments to support inferences.
- Communicates ideas clearly through writing.

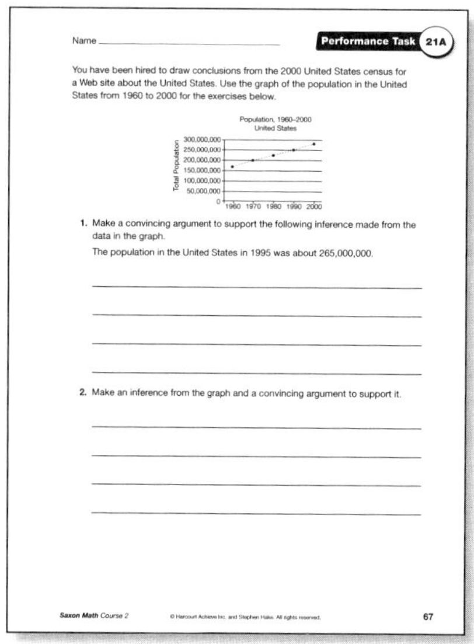

Name ________________ **Performance Task 21A**

You have been hired to draw conclusions from the 2000 United States census for a Web site about the United States. Use the graph of the population in the United States from 1960 to 2000 for the exercises below.

1. Make a convincing argument to support the following inference made from the data in the graph.

   The population in the United States in 1995 was about 265,000,000.

2. Make an inference from the graph and a convincing argument to support it.

Saxon Math Course 2 © Harcourt Achieve Inc. and Stephen Hake. All rights reserved. 67

Performance Task 21A

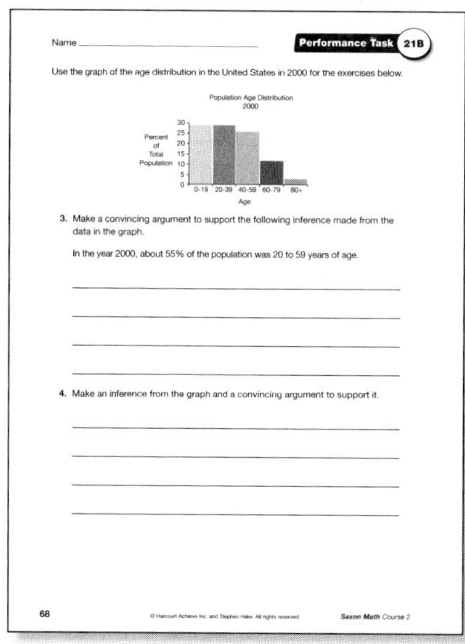

Name ________________ **Performance Task 21B**

Use the graph of the age distribution in the United States in 2000 for the exercises below.

3. Make a convincing argument to support the following inference made from the data in the graph.

   In the year 2000, about 55% of the population was 20 to 59 years of age.

4. Make an inference from the graph and a convincing argument to support it.

68 © Harcourt Achieve Inc. and Stephen Hake. All rights reserved. *Saxon Math* Course 2

Performance Task 21B

Meeting Standards

National Council of Teachers of Mathematics (NCTM)

Data Analysis and Probability

DP.2b Discuss and understand the correspondence between data sets and their graphical representations, especially histograms, stem-and-leaf plots, box plots, and scatterplots

Reasoning and Proof

RP.2b Make and investigate mathematical conjectures

Communication

CM.3a Organize and consolidate their mathematical thinking through communication

Focus on

• Scale Factor in Surface Area and Volume

Objectives
- Learn the relationships between length, surface area and volume in three-dimensional shapes.
- Examine how the scale factor between objects changes with edge length, surface area and volume.
- Examine how the ratio of surface area to volume decreases as the size of the object increases.
- Understand that a scale increase in one dimension results in a squared scale increase in two dimensions and a cubed scale increase in three dimensions.

Lesson Preparation

Materials

- **Investigation Activity 25 or 1-cm grid paper,** 4 copies per student
- **Manipulative kit:** inch rulers
- **Teacher-provided material: scissors, tape**

Optional
- **Teacher-provided material: card stock or tagboard**

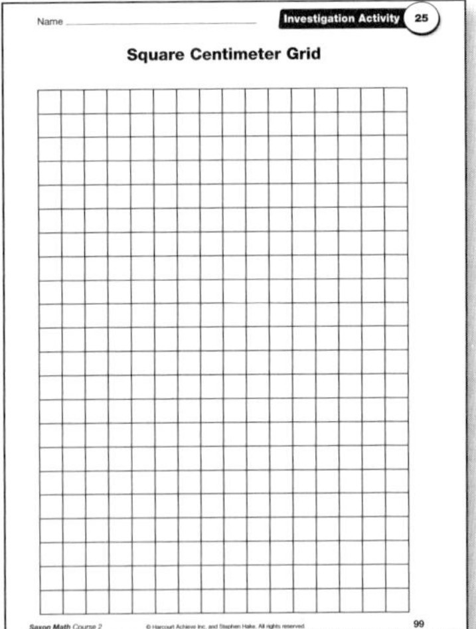

Investigation Activity 25

Technology Resources

Student eBook Complete student textbook in electronic format.

Resources and Planner CD Assessment, reteaching, and instructional masters, plus a pacing calendar with standards.

Test and Practice Generator CD Create additional practice sheets and custom-made tests.

www.SaxonPublishers.com Visit for more student activities and planning materials.

Inclusion

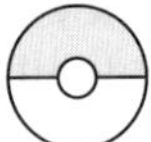

Adaptations CD Adapted lessons, investigations, practice and assessments.

Meeting Standards

National Council of Teachers of Mathematics (NCTM)

Numbers and Operations

NO.3a Select appropriate methods and tools for computing with fractions and decimals from among mental computation, estimation, calculators or computers, and paper and pencil, depending on the situation, and apply the selected methods

Geometry

GM.1b Understand relationships among the angles, side lengths, perimeters, areas, and volumes of similar objects

GM.4b Use two-dimensional representations of three-dimensional objects to visualize and solve problems such as those involving surface area and volume

Measurement

ME.2e Solve problems involving scale factors, using ratio and proportion

Problem Solving

PS.1b Solve problems that arise in mathematics and in other contexts

INVESTIGATION 11

Focus on

• Scale Factor in Surface Area and Volume

In this investigation we will study the relationship between length, surface area, and volume of three-dimensional shapes. We begin by comparing the measures of cubes of different sizes.

Activity

Scale Factor in Surface Area and Volume

Materials needed:

- 3 photocopies of **Investigation Activity 25** Square Centimeter Grid or 3 sheets of 1-cm grid paper
- Scissors
- Tape

Use the provided materials to build models of four cubes with edges 1 cm, 2 cm, 3 cm, and 4 cm long. Mark, cut, fold, and tape the grid paper so that the *grid is visible* when each model is finished.

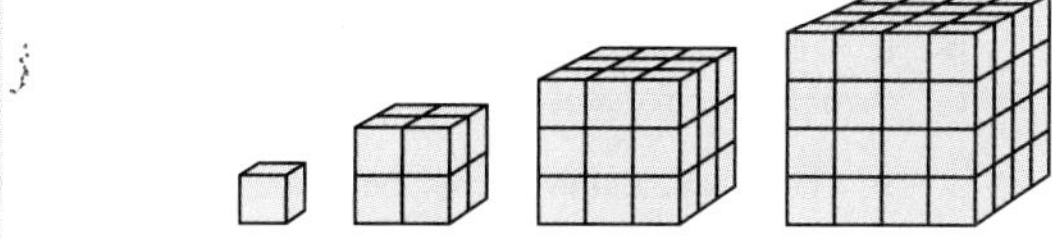

One pattern that folds to form a model of a cube is shown below. Several other patterns also work.

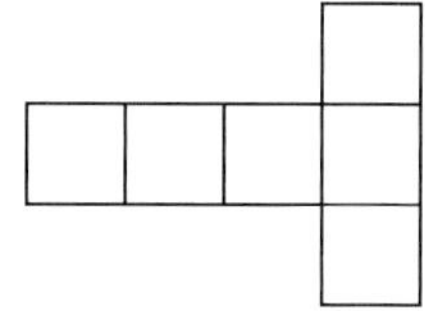

Copy this table on your paper and record the measures for each cube.

Thinking Skill
Model
Draw a different pattern with 6 squares that folds to form a cube. See student work.

Measures of Four Cubes

	1-cm cube	2-cm cube	3-cm cube	4-cm cube
Edge length (cm)	1	2	3	4
Surface area (cm^2)	6	24	54	96
Volume (cm^3)	1	8	27	64

INVESTIGATION 11

In this investigation, students will examine how the size comparison, or scale factor, between objects changes when we measure edge length, surface area, and volume.

Preparing the Materials

This activity requires students to design their own patterns for cubes. This can be time consuming and may be assigned as out-of-class work prior to addressing the questions in this investigation. Building demonstration models of each cube on the student page ahead of time will provide helpful visuals for students.

Activity

Patterns that will fold into a cube are sometimes called *nets* of a cube. There are 11 different nets that will fold into a cube.

Some students will be able to fill in the table without building the models. However, it is important for students to build the models in order to see the relationships between lengths, surface areas, and volumes.

Make sure that the students' tables contain the correct measurement information before they answer the first nine problems on the next page. Without correct measures, students will not be able to develop the pattern.

Math Background

Which net for a cube allows for the greatest number of cubes to be made from one sheet of grid paper?

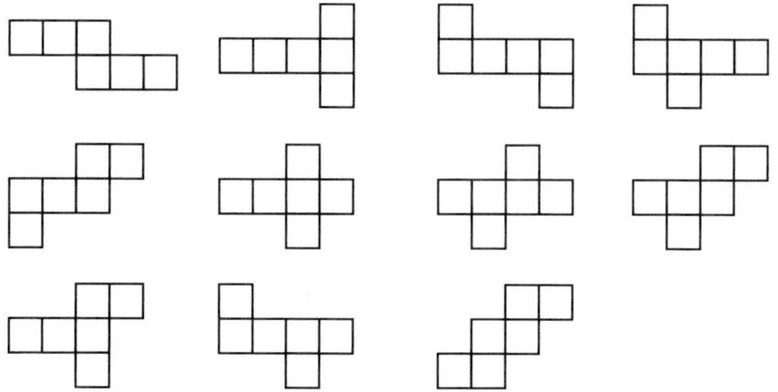

There are 11 different nets that can be folded to make a cube. The last one pictured can be repeated on the same grid over and over with little or no waste.

Math Conversations

Discussion opportunities are provided below.

Problems 7–9 Analyze

Lead students in a discussion about what we mean when we say "larger."

- one dimension: having a greater edge length
- two dimensions: having a greater area
- three dimensions: having a greater volume

Problems 10–15 Predict

If students are having difficulty seeing the pattern, have them construct a chart displaying the comparisons next to one another.

You may wish to provide graph paper to students so they can construct nets of a 6-cm cube and then discuss these problems.

Refer to the table on the previous page to answer the following questions:

Compare the 2-cm cube to the 1-cm cube.

1. The edge length of the 2-cm cube is how many times the edge length of the 1-cm cube? 2 times
2. The surface area of the 2-cm cube is how many times the surface area of the 1-cm cube? 4 times
3. The volume of the 2-cm cube is how many times the volume of the 1-cm cube? 8 times

Compare the 4-cm cube to the 2-cm cube.

4. The edge length of the 4-cm cube is how many times the edge length of the 2-cm cube? 2 times
5. The surface area of the 4-cm cube is how many times the surface area of the 2-cm cube? 4 times
6. The volume of the 4-cm cube is how many times the volume of the 2-cm cube? 8 times

Analyze Compare the 3-cm cube to the 1-cm cube.

7. ▶ The edge length of the 3-cm cube is how many times the edge length of the 1-cm cube? 3 times
8. ▶ The surface area of the 3-cm cube is how many times the surface area of the 1-cm cube? 9 times
9. ▶ The volume of the 3-cm cube is how many times the volume of the 1-cm cube? 27 times

Predict Use the patterns that can be found in answers 1–9 to predict the comparison of a 6-cm cube to a 2-cm cube.

10. ▶ The edge length of a 6-cm cube is how many times the edge length of a 2-cm cube? 3 times
11. ▶ The surface area of a 6-cm cube is how many times the surface area of a 2-cm cube? 9 times
12. ▶ The volume of a 6-cm cube is how many times the volume of a 2-cm cube? 27 times
13. ▶ Calculate **a** the surface area and **b** the volume of a 6-cm cube. **a.** 216 cm^2 **b.** 216 cm^3
14. ▶ The calculated surface area of a 6-cm cube is how many times the surface area of a 2-cm cube? 9 times
15. ▶ The calculated volume of a 6-cm cube is how many times the volume of a 2-cm cube? 27 times

▶ See Math Conversations in the sidebar.

Teacher Tip

When **making nets,** you might want to duplicate grid paper on heavy paper such as tagboard or card stock.

In problems 1–6 we compared the measures of a 2-cm cube to a 1-cm cube and the measures of a 4-cm cube to a 2-cm cube. In both sets of comparisons, the scale factors from the smaller cube to the larger cube were calculated. The dimensions of the larger square were twice the dimensions of the smaller square. That means that the scale factor from the smaller square to the larger square was 2. If we know the scale factor we can find the multiplier for area and volume as we see in this table.

Length, Area, and Volume Multipliers for Scale Factor 2

Measurement	Multiplier
Edge Length	2
Surface Area	$2^2 = 4$
Volume	$2^3 = 8$

Likewise, in problems **7–15** we compared the measures of a 3-cm cube to a 1-cm cube and a 6-cm cube to a 2-cm cube. We calculated the following multipliers for scale factor 3:

Length, Area, and Volume Multipliers for Scale Factor 3

Measurement	Multiplier
Edge Length	3
Surface Area	$3^2 = 9$
Volume	$3^3 = 27$

Represent Make a table similar to the one above where the edge length scale factor is 4. The scale factors for the surface area and volume are $4^2 = 16$ and $4^3 = 64$.

asurement	Multiplier
ge Length	4
rface Area	$4^2 = 16$
Volume	$4^3 = 64$

Generalize Refer to the above description of scale factors to answer problems **16–20.**

16. Mia calculated the scale factors from a 6-cm cube to a 30-cm cube.

a. From the smaller cube to the larger cube, what is the scale factor? 5

▶ **b.** **Conclude** Make a table like the two above, identifying the multiplier for the edge length, surface area, and volume of a figure with this scale factor.

asurement	Multiplier
ge Length	5
rface Area	$5^2 = 25$
Volume	$5^3 = 125$

▶ **17.** **Generalize** Bethany noticed that the scale factor relationships for cubes also applies to spheres. She found the approximate diameters of a table tennis ball ($1\frac{1}{2}$ in.), a baseball (3 in.), and a playground ball (9 in.). Find the multiplier for:

a. the volume of the table tennis ball to the volume of the baseball. $2^3 = 8$

b. the surface area of the baseball to the surface area of the playground ball. $3^2 = 9$

Investigation 11 **775**

▶ See Math Conversations in the sidebar.

Instruction

After examining the second table, students should be able to describe the pattern in the table. Make sure that students understand that if the scale factor for the edge length is $\frac{a}{b}$, the scale factor for the surface area is $\frac{a^2}{b^2}$, and the scale factor for the volume is $\frac{a^3}{b^3}$.

Math Conversations

Discussion opportunities are provided below.

Problem 16b Conclude

After completing the table, have students write a description summarizing the relationships shown in the three tables.

Problem 17 Generalize

Students should not need the formulas for the volume and surface area of a sphere to answer this question.

If you choose to have them check their work through calculation, point out that the formula for the volume of a sphere is $v = \frac{4}{3}\pi r^3$, where r is the radius of the sphere, and the formula for the surface area of a sphere is $A = 4\pi r^2$.

(continued)

Math Conversations

Discussion opportunities are provided below.

Problems 18 and 19 Generalize

Discuss the fact that similar plane shapes have area relationships such as the surface area relationships of solid objects. Point out that there are no volume relationships for plane figures such as rectangles and circles because plane figures have only two dimensions. Volume requires three dimensions.

Problem 20 Generalize

The pattern students have found for the relationship of edge length, surface area, and volume holds true for cubes, spheres, pyramids, and other geometric figures. Have them discuss whether they would also hold true for complex and irregular shapes, such as a house, a tree, or even a person. Yes; discussion should reflect an understanding that a scale increase in one dimension will always indicate a squared scale increase in two dimensions and a cubed scale increase in three dimensions.

Problem 21 Analyze

Extend the Problem

"Can two different shapes with the same volume have different surface areas?" yes

You can support this discussion by having students find the surface area and volume of a cube with an 8 cm edge, then the surface area and volume of a rectangular prism with length 16, width 8, and height 4.

(continued)

▶ **18.** Generalize The photo lab makes 5-by-7-in. enlargements from $2\frac{1}{2}$-by-$3\frac{1}{2}$-in. wallet-size photos.

a. Find the scale factor from the smaller photo to the enlargement. 2

b. The picture area of the larger photo is what multiple of the picture area of the smaller photo? $2^2 = 4$

19. Scale factor: $1.5^2 = 2.25$
Price: \$10.00 × 2.25 = \$22.50

▶ **19.** Generalize Rommy wanted to charge the same price per square inch of cheese pizza regardless of the size of the pizza. Since all of Rommy's pizzas were the same thickness, he based his prices on the scale factor for area. If he sells a 10-inch diameter cheese pizza for \$10.00, how much should he charge for a 15-inch diameter cheese pizza?

▶ **20.** Generalize The Egyptian archaeologist knew that the scale-factor relationships for cubes also applies to similar pyramids. The archaeologist built a $\frac{1}{100}$ scale model of the Great Pyramid. Each edge of the base of the model was 2.3 meters, while each edge of the base of the Great Pyramid measured 230 meters.

a. From the smaller model to the Great Pyramid, what was the scale factor for the length of corresponding edges? 100

b. The area of the Great Pyramid is what multiple of the area of the model? $100^2 = 10{,}000$

c. The volume of the Great Pyramid is what multiple of the volume of the model? $100^3 = 1{,}000{,}000$

Notice from the chart that you completed near the beginning of this investigation that as the size of the cube becomes greater, the surface area and volume become much greater. Also notice that the volume increases at a faster rate than the surface area. The ratio of surface area to volume changes as the size of an object changes.

Ratio of Surface Area to Volume of Four Cubes

	1-cm cube	2-cm cube	3-cm cube	4-cm cube
Surface Area to Volume	6 to 1	3 to 1	2 to 1	1.5 to 1

The ratio of surface area to volume affects the size and shape of containers used to package products. The ratio of surface area to volume also affects the world of nature.

Analyze Consider the relationship between surface area and volume as you answer problems **21–25.**

▶ **21.** Sixty-four 1-cm cubes were arranged to form one large cube. Austin wrapped the large cube with paper and sent the package to Betsy. The volume of the package was 64 cm³. What was the surface area of the exposed wrapping paper? 96 cm²

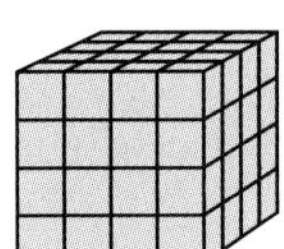

▶ See Math Conversations in the sidebar.

22. When Betsy received the package she divided the contents into eight smaller cubes each composed of eight 2-cm cubes. Betsy wrapped the eight cubes with paper and sent them on to Charlie. The total volume of the eight packages was still 64 cm^3. What was the total surface area of the exposed wrapping paper of the eight packages?
$8 \times 24\ cm^2 = 192\ cm^2$

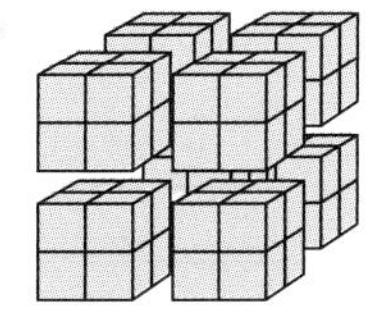

23. Charlie opened each of the eight packages and individually wrapped each 1-cm cube. Since there were 64 cubes, the total volume was still 64 cm^3. What was the total surface area of exposed wrapping paper for all 64 packages? $64 \times 6\ cm^2 = 384\ cm^2$

24. Although the volumes are the same, the small cubes will melt sooner than the large block because a much greater surface area is exposed to the warmer surroundings.

▸ 24. **Predict** After a summer picnic, the ice in two large insulated containers was emptied on the ground to melt. A large block of ice in the form of a 6-inch cube fell out of one container. An equal quantity of ice, but in the form of 1-inch cubes, fell scattered out of the other container. Which, if either, do you think will melt sooner, the large block of ice or the small scattered cubes? Explain your answer.

25. If someone does not eat very much, we might say that he or she "eats like a bird." However, birds must eat large amounts, relative to their body weights, in order to maintain their body temperature. Since mammals and birds regulate their own body temperature, there is a limit to how small a mammal or bird may be. Comparing a hawk and a sparrow in the same environment, which of the two might eat a greater percentage of its weight in food every day? Explain your answer.

extensions

▸ a. Investigate how the weight of a bird and its wingspan are related.

▸ b. Investigate reasons why the largest sea mammals are so much larger than the largest land mammals.

▸ c. Brad's dad is 25% taller than Brad and weighs twice as much. Explain why you think this height-weight relationship may or may not be reasonable.

25. Because the surface area of a smaller animal is greater relative to its volume than the surface area for a larger animal, smaller animals work harder to regulate body temperature than larger animals in the same environment. So smaller animals, like sparrows, need to eat a greater percentage of their weight in food than do larger animals, like hawks.

▸ See Math Conversations in the sidebar.

Math Conversations

Discussion opportunities are provided below.

Problem 24 Predict

"If the 1-inch cubes were stacked together so they formed a cube the same size as the solid block of ice, which do you think would melt first?" Sample: the melting time would be about the same.

Looking Forward

Comparing the relationships between lengths, surface areas, and volumes of three-dimensional shapes prepares students for:

- **Lesson 114,** finding volume, capacity, and mass in the metric system.

Extensions

a. **Model** Students should research data about birds and their wingspans. They should make a scale drawing of the wingspans. Wingspans should be labeled with the name of the bird and its weight. Students can draw line segments to represent the wingspans.

b. **Represent** Students can research data about the size of land and sea mammals. They choose an appropriate way to display the data and make a short report to the class about their conclusions.

c. **Conclude** Consider two objects that are similar. If the height, width, and depth of the larger object are 25 percent greater than the smaller object, then the scale factor from the smaller object to the larger is $\frac{125}{100}$ or $\frac{5}{4}$. Therefore, the volume of the larger object is $(\frac{5}{4})^3$ times the volume of the smaller object. $(\frac{5}{4})^3$ equals $\frac{125}{64}$, which is nearly 2. The volume of the larger object is about twice the volume of the smaller object. Assuming a constant weight, it is reasonable to think the larger object weighs about twice as much.

Section 12 Overview

Lessons 111–120, Investigation 12

Lesson Planner

LESSON	NEW CONCEPTS	MATERIALS	RESOURCES
111	• Dividing in Scientific Notation	Graph paper	**Power Up V** **Investigation Activity 13**
112	• Applications of the Pythagorean Theorem	Manipulative Kit: inch rulers Pencils; graph paper; calculators	**Power Up W** **Investigation Activity 13**
113	• Volumes of Pyramids, Cones, and Spheres	Manipulative Kit: Relational GeoSolids Sand, salt or rice; water	**Power Up V** **Investigation Activity 13**
114	• Volume, Capacity, and Mass in the Metric System	Two 1-liter bottles (1 filled with water)	**Power Up W**
115	• Factoring Algebraic Expressions	Graph paper	**Power Up V** **Investigation Activity 13**
116	• Slope-Intercept Form of Linear Equations	Graph paper, calculators	**Power Up W** **Investigation Activity 13**
117	• Copying Geometric Figures	Manipulative Kit: compasses, protractors Straightedges Calculators, colored pencils	**Power Up V**
118	• Division by Zero	Manipulative Kit: inch rulers, protractors, straightedges Calculators	**Power Up W** **Investigation Activity 13**
119	• Graphing Area and Volume Formulas	Manipulative Kit: metric rulers, protractors, compasses, straightedges	**Power Up V** **Investigation Activity 13**
120	• Graphing Nonlinear Equations	Manipulative Kit: metric rulers Calculators	**Power Up W** **Investigation Activity 13**
Inv. 12	Platonic Solids	Manipulative Kit: rulers Scissors, tape or glue	**Investigation Activities 26–28**

Lesson Highlights

Lessons 111–120, Investigation 12

Problem Solving

Strategies

- **Find a Pattern** Lesson 111, 118
- **Use Logical Reasoning** Lessons 113, 116, 119, 120
- **Draw a Diagram** Lessons 117, 118
- **Work Backwards** Lessons 112, 115
- **Write an Equation** Lessons 114, 117
- **Guess and Check** Lessons 114, 115

Real-World Applications

pp. 780–783, 786–791, 796, 797, 800, 801, 806, 807, 812–814, 816, 821, 828, 829, 841, 842

4-Step Process

Teacher Edition Lessons 111–120 (Power-Up Discussions)

Connections

Math and Other Subjects

- **Math and Art** p. 796
- **Math and Architecture** pp. 796, 824
- **Math and Geography** p. 821
- **Math and History** pp. 780, 824
- **Math and Science** pp. 779, 781, 801, 807
- **Math and Sports** pp. 788, 821

Math to Math

- **Problem Solving and Measurement** Lessons 111–115, 117–120
- **Algebra and Problem Solving** Lessons 111–120
- **Fractions, Decimals, Percents, and Problem Solving** Lessons 111–120
- **Fractions and Measurement** Lessons 117, 120
- **Measurement and Geometry** Lessons 111–120
- **Proportional Relationships and Geometry** Lessons 111–113, 115–120
- **Algebra, Measurement, and Geometry** Lessons 112, 113, 115–120
- **Probability and Statistics** Lessons 111–120

Communication

Discuss

pp. 792, 805, 819, 826, 828, 838

Summarize

p. 820

Explain

pp. 791, 806, 813, 815, 828, 829, 839

Representation

Manipulatives/Hands On

pp. 785, 787, 791–794, 799, 801, 817–821, 823

Model

pp. 819, 831

Represent

pp. 810, 813, 814, 830

Technology

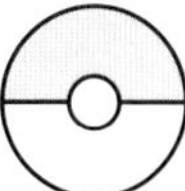

Student Resources

- **eBook**
- **Calculator** Lessons 116–118, 120
- **Online Resources** at **www.SaxonPublishers.com/ActivitiesC2**
  - **Graphing Calculator Activities** Lessons 116, 120
  - **Real-World Investigation 6** after Lesson 113
  - **Online Activities**
  - **Math Enrichment Problems**
  - **Math Stumpers**

Teacher Resources

- **Resources and Planner CD**
- **Adaptations CD** Lessons 111–120
- **Test & Practice Generator CD**
- **eGradebook**
- **Answer Key CD**

Content Highlights

Algebraic ideas are extended in this section as students learn about the slope-intercept form of equations and graph area and volume functions. Geometry and measurement includes students building and analyzing platonic solids.

Algebraic Thinking

Expressions and equations continue to be a key topic.

Algebra topics in these lessons include factoring algebraic expressions in Lesson 115, recognizing the slope-intercept form of a linear equation in Lesson 116, and exploring the reasons for the prohibition of dividing by zero in Lesson 118.

Geometry and Measurement

Geometric solids are explored and analyzed.

Students apply the Pythagorean theorem to solve problems in Lesson 112. They calculate the volumes of pyramids, cones, and spheres in Lesson 113. There is a connection in the metric system between the measures of volume, capacity, and mass, and students explore that relationship in Lesson 114. Using a compass and straightedge, students copy geometric figures in Lesson 117, and they wrap up the course by building models of Platonic solids in Investigation 12.

Algebra and Geometry

Students connect algebra and geometry as they graph area and volume functions.

Students combine algebra and geometry in Lesson 119 by graphing area and volume functions. In Lesson 120 students graph other nonlinear functions after making a table of ordered pairs.

Assessment

A variety of weekly assessment tools are provided.

After Lesson 115:
- Power-Up Test 22
- Cumulative Test 22
- Performance Activity 22

After Lesson 120:
- Power-Up Test 23
- Cumulative Assessment 23
- Customized Benchmark Test
- Performance Task 23

Content Trace

Lessons 111–120, Investigation 12

LESSON	NEW CONCEPTS	PRACTICED	ASSESSED
111	• Dividing in Scientific Notation	Lessons 111, 112, 114, 115, 116, 117, 118, 119, 120	Test 23
112	• Applications of the Pythagorean Theorem	Lessons 112, 113, 117, 118, 119, 120	Test 23
113	• Volume of Pyramids, Cones, and Spheres	Lessons 113, 114, 115, 116, 117, 118, 119, 120	Test 23
114	• Volume, Capacity, and Mass in the Metric System	Lessons 114, 115, 116, 117, 120	Test 23
115	• Factoring Algebraic Expressions	Lessons 115, 116, 117, 118, 119, 120	Test & Practice Generator
116	• Slope-Intercept Form of Linear Equations	Lessons 116, 117, 118, 119, 120	Test & Practice Generator
117	• Copying Geometric Figures	Lessons 117, 118, 119	Test & Practice Generator
118	• Division by Zero	Lessons 118, 119, 120	Test & Practice Generator
119	• Graphing Area and Volume Formulas	Lesson 119	Test & Practice Generator
120	• Graphing Nonlinear Equations	Lesson 120	Test & Practice Generator
Inv. 12	• Platonic Solids	Investigation 12	Test & Practice Generator

• Dividing in Scientific Notation

Objective

- Divide numbers in scientific notation.

Lesson Preparation

Materials

- **Power Up V** (in *Instructional Masters*)
- **graph paper,** 2 per student

Optional

- **Investigation Activity 13** (in *Instructional Masters*)

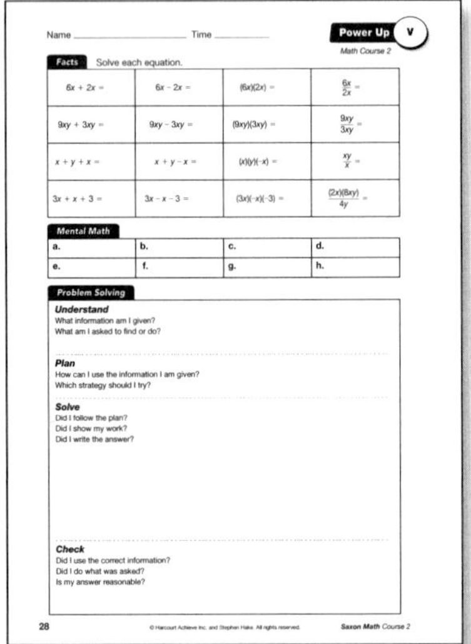

Name ____________ Time ________

Power Up V
Math Course 2

Facts Solve each equation.

$6x + 2x =$	$6x - 2x =$	$(6x)(2x) =$	$\frac{6x}{2x} =$
$9xy + 3xy =$	$9xy - 3xy =$	$(9xy)(3xy) =$	$\frac{9xy}{3xy} =$
$x + y + x =$	$x + y - x =$	$(x)(y)(-x) =$	$\frac{xy}{x} =$
$3x + x + 3 =$	$3x - x - 3 =$	$(3x)(-x)(-3) =$	$\frac{(2x)(8xy)}{4y} =$

Mental Math

a.	b.	c.	d.
e.	f.	g.	h.

Problem Solving

Understand
What information am I given?
What am I asked to find or do?

Plan
How can I use the information I am given?
Which strategy should I try?

Solve
Did I follow the plan?
Did I show my work?
Did I write the answer?

Check
Did I use the correct information?
Did I do what was asked?
Is my answer reasonable?

28 © Harcourt Achieve Inc. and Stephen Hake. All rights reserved. *Saxon Math Course 2*

Power Up V

Math Language

English Learners (ESL)
minted

Technology Resources

Student eBook CD Complete student textbook in electronic format.

Resources and Planner CD Assessment, reteaching, and instructional masters, plus a pacing calendar with standards.

Test and Practice Generator CD Create additional practice sheets and custom-made tests.

www.SaxonPublishers.com Visit for more student activities and planning materials.

Inclusion

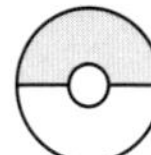

Adaptations CD Adapted lessons, investigations, practice and assessments.

Meeting Standards

Power-Up Discussion *For use with Power Up, p. 778*

Problem-Solving Strategy: Find a Pattern

Find the next three numbers in this sequence: 1, 1, 2, 3, 5, 8, 13, ...

Understand ***Understand the problem.***

"What information are we given?"

We are shown the first seven terms of a sequence: 1, 1, 2, 3, 5, 8, and 13.

"What are we asked to do?"

We are asked to determine the next three terms of the sequence.

Plan ***Make a plan.***

"What problem-solving strategy will we use?"

We will *find the pattern,* then use the pattern's rule to find the next several terms.

Solve ***Carry out the plan.***

"Does the pattern increase evenly?"

No. It increases different amounts each time: +0, +1, +1, +2, +3, +5, ...

"What do we notice about the sequence of differences?"

It is equal to the given sequence with each term shifted one position to the right.

"How do we find each term?"

Each term is the sum of the two terms before it.

"What will the next three terms be?"

21, 34, 55

Check ***Look back.***

"Did we do what we were asked to do?"

Yes, we found the next three numbers in the given sequence.

Teacher's Note: You may wish to tell students that this is a special sequence associated with a mathematician named Fibonacci. Encourage students to research Fibonacci on line or in your school's library.

1 Power Up

Facts

Distribute **Power Up V** to students. See answers below.

Mental Math

Encourage students to share different ways to mentally compute these exercises. Strategies for exercises **e** and **h** are listed below.

e. Divide by the Reciprocal

$33\frac{1}{3}\% = \frac{1}{3}$

Think: multiplying by $\frac{1}{3}$ is the same as dividing by 3.

$\$150 \div 3 = \$50$

Use a Fraction

$33\frac{1}{3}\% = \frac{1}{3}$

$\frac{1}{3} \times \$150 = \$50$

h. Multiply by a Fraction

$\$198.75 \approx \$200$

$8\% = \frac{8}{100}$

$\frac{8}{100} \times \$200 = 8 \times \$2 = \$16$

Use Logical Reasoning

8% of \$100 is \$8.

8% of \$200 is \$16.

Problem Solving

Refer to **Power-Up Discussion,** p. 778B.

2 New Concepts

Instruction

Tell students that astronomical units, AU, are used when describing extremely large distances, such as interplanetary distances, because conventional units of measure are not convenient. Miles are too small and light years are too large to permit easy comparisons of numbers.

As you discuss the Thinking Skill question, help students understand that comparing the distances is easier with astronomical units than with kilometers.

(continued)

LESSON 111

• Dividing in Scientific Notation

Power Up *Building Power*

facts Power Up V

mental math

a. **Positive/Negative:** $(-0.25) \div (-5)$ 0.05

b. **Scientific Notation:** $(8 \times 10^{-4})^2$ 6.4×10^{-7}

c. **Algebra:** $3m + 7m = 600$ 60

d. **Measurement:** Convert 1 ft^2 to square inches. 144 $in.^2$

e. **Percent:** $33\frac{1}{3}\%$ of \$150 \$50

f. **Percent:** \$150 reduced by $33\frac{1}{3}\%$ \$100

g. **Probability:** A spinner is in 6 sections with red, blue, yellow, red, purple, and pink. What is the probability of the spinner landing on red? $\frac{1}{3}$

h. **Percent/Estimation:** Estimate 8% tax on a \$198.75 purchase. \$16.00

problem solving Find the next three numbers in this sequence: 1, 1, 2, 3, 5, 8, 13, ... 21, 34, 55

New Concept *Increasing Knowledge*

One unit astronomers use to measure distances within our solar system is the **astronomical unit** (AU). An astronomical unit is the average distance between Earth and the Sun, which is roughly 150,000,000 km (or 93,000,000 mi).

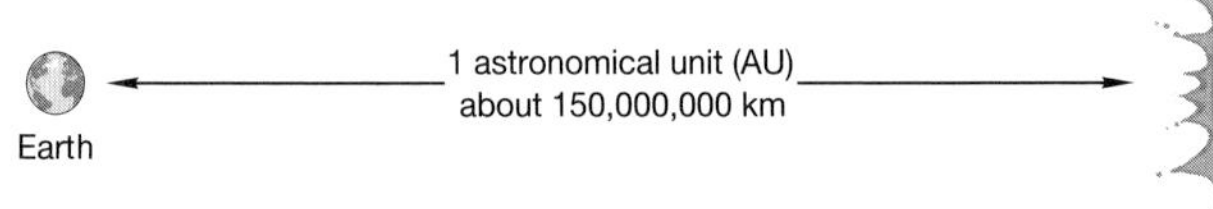

For instance, at a point in Saturn's orbit when it is 1.5 billion kilometers from the Sun, its distance from the Sun is 10 AU.

$$1{,}500{,}000{,}000 \text{ km} \cdot \frac{1 \text{ AU}}{150{,}000{,}000 \text{ km}} = 10 \text{ AU}$$

This means that the distance from Saturn to the Sun is about 10 times the average distance between Earth and the Sun.

When dividing very large or very small numbers, it is helpful to use scientific notation. Here we show the same calculation in scientific notation:

$$\frac{1.5 \times 10^9 \text{ km}}{1.5 \times 10^8 \text{ km/AU}} = 10 \text{ AU}$$

In this lesson we will practice dividing numbers in scientific notation.

Thinking Skill
Generalize

How many times smaller is the distance from the Sun to Earth compared to the distance from the Sun to Saturn? 10 times smaller

Facts Solve each equation.

$6x + 2x = 8x$	$6x - 2x = 4x$	$(6x)(2x) = 12x^2$	$\frac{6x}{2x} = 3$
$9xy + 3xy = 12xy$	$9xy - 3xy = 6xy$	$(9xy)(3xy) = 27x^2y^2$	$\frac{9xy}{3xy} = 3$
$x + y + x = 2x + y$	$x + y - x = y$	$(x)(y)(-x) = -x^2y$	$\frac{xy}{x} = y$
$3x + x + 3 = 4x + 3$	$3x - x - 3 = 2x - 3$	$(3x)(-x)(-3) = 9x^2$	$\frac{(2x)(8xy)}{4y} = 4x^2$

Recall that when we multiply numbers in scientific notation, we multiply the powers of 10 by adding their exponents.

$$(6 \times 10^6)(1.5 \times 10^2) = 9 \times 10^8$$

Furthermore, we have this important rule:

When we divide numbers written in scientific notation, we divide the powers of 10 by subtracting their exponents.

$$\frac{6 \times 10^6}{1.5 \times 10^2} = 4 \times 10^4 \longleftarrow (6-2=4)$$

Example 1

Write each quotient in scientific notation:

a. $\frac{6 \times 10^8}{1.2 \times 10^6}$ **b.** $\frac{3 \times 10^3}{6 \times 10^6}$ **c.** $\frac{2 \times 10^{-2}}{8 \times 10^{-8}}$

Solution

a. To find the quotient, we divide 6 by 1.2 and 10^8 by 10^6.

$$12.\overline{)60.} = 5. \qquad 10^8 \div 10^6 = 10^2 \longleftarrow (8-6=2)$$

The quotient is $\mathbf{5 \times 10^2}$.

b. We divide 3 by 6 and 10^3 by 10^6.

$$6\overline{)3.0} = 0.5 \qquad 10^3 \div 10^6 = 10^{-3} \longleftarrow (3-6=-3)$$

The quotient is 0.5×10^{-3}. We write the quotient in scientific notation.

$$\mathbf{5 \times 10^{-4}}$$

c. We divide 2 by 8 and 10^{-2} by 10^{-8}.

$$8\overline{)2.00} = 0.25 \qquad 10^{-2} \div 10^{-8} = 10^6 \longleftarrow [-2-(-8)=6]$$

The quotient is 0.25×10^6. We write the quotient in scientific notation.

$$\mathbf{2.5 \times 10^5}$$

Example 2

The distance from the Sun to Earth is about 1.5×10^8 km. Light travels at a speed of about 3×10^5 km per second. About how many seconds does it take light to travel from the Sun to Earth?

Solution

We divide 1.5×10^8 km by 3×10^5 km/s.

$$\frac{1.5 \times 10^8 \text{ km}}{3 \times 10^5 \text{ km/s}} = 0.5 \times 10^3 \text{ s}$$

We may write the quotient in proper scientific notation, $\mathbf{5 \times 10^2}$ **s** or in standard form, **500 s.** It takes about 500 seconds.

2 New Concepts (Continued)

Instruction

Discuss with students what they remember about multiplying with scientific notation.

Demonstrate why for division of powers of 10 the exponents are subtracted. Write 10^6 and 10^2 in expanded form on the board or on an overhead projector. Show students that common factors in the numerator and the denominator can be canceled and that the result is the same as if the exponents had been subtracted.

$$\frac{6 \times 10^6}{1.5 \times 10^2} = \frac{6 \times 10 \times 10 \times 10 \times 10 \times \cancel{10} \times \cancel{10}}{1.5 \times \cancel{10} \times \cancel{10}}$$

Example 1

Instruction

Point out that besides subtracting the exponents when dividing the powers of 10, the decimal numbers must also be divided and the answer should be written in scientific notation.

Some students may have a tendency to subtract the smaller exponent from the larger exponent. Make sure that students understand that they are to subtract the exponent of the divisor from the exponent of the dividend.

Example 2

Instruction

When students have worked through the first part of the solution, ask why the answer is not in correct scientific notation. Then discuss the various ways to express the answer.

(continued)

Math Background

You can't divide 3^2 by 4^5 by dividing 3 by 4, and then subtracting exponents. Why can 3×10^2 be divided by 4×10^5 by dividing 3 by 4, and then subtracting exponents?

To divide numbers with exponents by subtracting those exponents, the bases must be the same. The numbers 3 and 4 are the bases in 3^2 and 4^5. Because the bases are not the same, the numbers cannot be divided using subtraction of exponents. Since the base in both 3×10^2 and 4×10^5 is 10, these numbers can be divided using subtraction of exponents and their coefficients, 3 and 4, are divided in the same way as any whole numbers.

2 New Concepts (Continued)

Practice Set

Problems a–h Generalize

Ask volunteers to explain how they did each of these problems.

Problem i Justify

Have students explain why the rule works.

Problems e–h Error Alert

These problems require students to rewrite the quotients so that they are in correct scientific notation. Remind students that the coefficient must be equal to or greater than 1 but less than 10.

3 Written Practice

Math Conversations

Discussion opportunities are provided below.

Problem 2 Analyze

Extend the Problem

"What is the difference of y and 15?" Note that there are two answers: 25 and –25.

"What is the quotient of 600 divided by y?" 15

"What is the quotient of 600 divided by 25?" Note that there are two possible answers that students may give: 15 and y.

"Why do you not need to divide to answer the last two questions?" Sample: Because I already know that the product of 15 and 40 is 600, and division is the inverse of multiplication.

Errors and Misconceptions

Problem 6b

If students are not able to find this answer, remind them that the sum of the exterior angles of any polygon is 180° and suggest that they can use that information and the answer to 6a to find the answer.

(continued)

Practice Set ▸ Generalize Write each quotient in scientific notation:

a. $\frac{3.6 \times 10^9}{2 \times 10^3}$ 1.8×10^6

b. $\frac{7.5 \times 10^3}{2.5 \times 10^9}$ 3×10^{-6}

c. $\frac{4.5 \times 10^{-8}}{3 \times 10^{-4}}$ 1.5×10^{-4}

d. $\frac{6 \times 10^{-4}}{1.5 \times 10^{-8}}$ 4×10^4

e. $\frac{4 \times 10^{12}}{8 \times 10^4}$ 5×10^7

f. $\frac{1.5 \times 10^4}{3 \times 10^{12}}$ 5×10^{-9}

g. $\frac{3.6 \times 10^{-8}}{6 \times 10^{-2}}$ 6×10^{-7}

h. $\frac{1.8 \times 10^{-2}}{9 \times 10^{-8}}$ 2×10^5

i. Justify Which rule for working with exponents did you use to complete the divisions in **a–h**?

i. Sample: When we divide numbers written in scientific notation, we divide the powers of 10 by subtracting their exponents.

Written Practice *Strengthening Concepts*

1. (12) The first Indian-head penny was minted in 1859. The last Indian-head penny was minted in 1909. For how many years were Indian-head pennies minted? 51 years (The year 1859 should be counted.)

▸ 2. (28) Analyze The product of y and 15 is 600. What is the sum of y and 15? 55

3. (36, 54) Thirty percent of the class wanted to go to the Museum of Natural History. The rest of the class wanted to go to the Planetarium.
   a. What fraction of the class wanted to go to the Planetarium? $\frac{7}{10}$
   b. What was the ratio of those who wanted to go to the Museum of Natural History to those who wanted to go to the Planetarium? $\frac{3}{7}$

4. (80) Triangle ABC with vertices A (0, 3), B (0, 0), and C (4, 0) is translated one unit left, one unit down to make the image $\triangle A'B'C'$. What are the coordinates of the vertices of $\triangle A'B'C'$? A' (−1, 2), B' (−1, −1), C' (3, −1)

5. (21) a. Write the prime factorization of 1024 using exponents. 2^{10}
   b. Find $\sqrt{1024}$. 32

6. (89) A portion of a regular polygon is shown at right. Each interior angle measures 150°.
   a. What is the measure of each exterior angle? 30°
   ▸ b. The polygon has how many sides? 12 sides
   c. What is the name for a polygon with this number of sides? dodecagon

150°

7. (92) The Science Store advertised a 40% discount on all equipment. A rock tumbler's sale price was $48.00. What was the original price? $80

▸ See Math Conversations in the sidebar.

English Learners

In problem 1, explain the term **minted.** Say:

"Minted means stamped or printed. The United States Mint stamps the coins and prints the bills we use."

Ask students to describe the images minted on the front and back of a quarter.

8. (94) In a bag are 12 marbles: 3 red, 4 white, and 5 blue. One marble is drawn from the bag and not replaced. A second marble is drawn and not replaced. Then a third marble is drawn.

a. What is the probability of drawing a red, a white, and a blue marble in that order? $\frac{3}{12} \cdot \frac{4}{11} \cdot \frac{5}{10} = \frac{1}{22}$

b. What is the probability of drawing a blue, a white, and a red marble in that order? $\frac{5}{12} \cdot \frac{4}{11} \cdot \frac{3}{10} = \frac{1}{22}$

*** 9.** (101) Write an equation to solve this problem: $2x + 6 = 36$; 15

Six more than twice what number is 36?

▶*** 10.** (101) **a.** **Conclude** What is the measure of each acute angle of this triangle? 45°

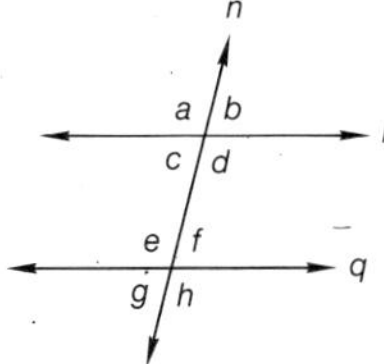

b. **Explain** What did you need to know about the measures of the angles of a triangle to solve this problem? Sample: The sum of the measures of a triangle is 180°.

▶*** 11.** (106) Solve for c^2: $c^2 - b^2 = a^2$ $c^2 = a^2 + b^2$

Math Language
The symbol ∥ means *is parallel to*. $l \parallel q$ means line l is parallel to line q.

▶*** 12.** (102) **Conclude** In the figure below, if $l \parallel q$ and $m\angle h = 105°$, what is the measure of

n
a b c d — l
e f g h — q

a. $\angle a$? 105° **b.** $\angle b$? 75°

c. $\angle c$? 75° **d.** $\angle d$? 105°

*** 13.** (108) The formula below may be used to convert temperature measurements from degrees Celsius (*C*) to degrees Fahrenheit (*F*). Find *F* to the nearest degree when *C* is 17. 63°F

$$F = 1.8C + 32$$

4.
y
x + y = 1
x

▶ **14.** (Inv. 5) Make a table of ordered pairs showing three or four solutions for the equation $x + y = 1$. Then graph all possible solutions. See student work.

▶*** 15.** (Inv. 9, 107) **Analyze** Refer to the graph you made in problem 14 to answer **a** and **b**.

a. What is the slope of the graph of $x + y = 1$? -1

b. Where does the graph of $x + y = 1$ intersect the y-axis? (0, 1)

▶ See Math Conversations in the sidebar.

3 Written Practice *(Continued)*

Math Conversations

Discussion opportunities are provided below.

Problem 10a Conclude

Explain that there is no need to use a protractor for this problem. Have students tell how they thought about the problem in order to solve it. Ask what the answer would be if the angle labeled $2x$ were labeled $4x$. 30°

Problem 10b Explain

Have volunteers read their answers to this question. Ask each student why the information they describe is needed to solve the problem.

Problem 12 Conclude

Review some angle relationships by having students further analyze the figure, using the given information. Ask questions such as:

"Which angles are equal?" Sample: angles *b*, *c*, *f*, *g*

"Which angles are vertical angles?" Sample: angles *a* and *d*

"Which angles are supplementary angles?" Sample: angles *a* and *b*, angles *a* and *f*

"Which angles are complementary angles?" There are no complementary angles.

Problem 15 Analyze

Ask students to tell what method they used to find the slope of the graph. If any found it by inspection of the graph, ask them to describe what they did. Sample: I could see that the slope would be negative because the line went down from left to right. Then I saw that the run was 1 and the rise was –1, so the slope was –1.

Errors and Misconceptions

Problem 11

Students who give the answer $c = \sqrt{a^2 + b}$ did not read the problem carefully. Have them reread the problem and note what the problem asked.

Problem 14

If students can't tell whether they have chosen points that satisfy the equation, tell them that all the points they find should be on the same straight line.

(continued)

3 Written Practice (Continued)

Math Conversations

Discussion opportunities are provided below.

Problem 16 Analyze

Have students determine what fraction of the circle the 45° sector is. Then have them express that fraction as a decimal and as a percent. $\frac{1}{8}$, 0.125, $12\frac{1}{2}\%$

Problem 17 Connect

"Suppose that the students discover that they do not have enough paper. About how much paper would they need to wrap a poster around the top third of the can?" Sample: a little more than 6 ft^2 of paper

Problem 21 Connect

"Sal can choose among CDs that compound interest weekly, monthly, or annually at the same rate. Which way would give the greatest total value after 60 months?" Sample: weekly, because the more often they compound the interest, the more there is

Problem 22 Conclude

Have students find the two lengths that are still unknown, *BD* and *AD*. Then ask what they notice about the values of lengths *AB, BD,* and *AD*. Sample: They are perfect squares.

(continued)

▸* **16.** (104) **Analyze** What is the area of a 45° sector of a circle with a radius of 12 in.? Use 3.14 for π and round the answer to the nearest square inch. 57 $in.^2$

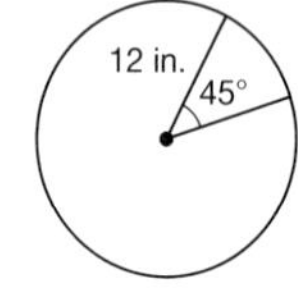

Refer to the illustration of the trash can to answer problems **17** and **18**.

▸* **17.** (105) **Connect** The students in Room 8 decided to wrap posters around school trash cans to encourage others to properly dispose of trash. The illustration shows the dimensions of the trash can. Converting the dimensions to feet and using 3.14 for π, find the number of square feet of paper needed to wrap around each trash can. 18.84 ft^2

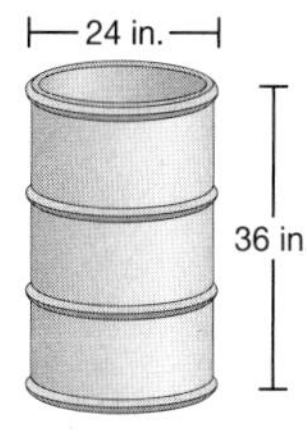

18. (95) The trash can illustrated has the capacity to hold how many cubic feet of trash? 9.42 ft^3

* **19.** (109) Find two solutions to each of these equations:

a. $2x^2 + 1 = 19$ 3, −3

b. $2x^2 - 1 = 19$ $\sqrt{10}, -\sqrt{10}$

20. (99) What is the perimeter of a triangle with vertices (−1, 2), (−1, −1), and (3, −1)? 12 units

▸* **21.** (110) **Connect** Sal deposited $5000 in a 60-month CD that paid 5% interest compounded annually. What was the total value of the CD after 5 years? $6381.41

▸* **22.** (97, 99) **Conclude** The figure at right shows three similar triangles. If *AC* is 15 cm and *BC* is 20 cm,

a. what is *AB*? 25 cm

b. what is *CD*? 12 cm

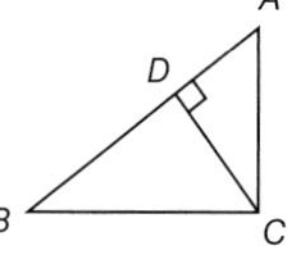

* **23.** (111) Express each quotient in scientific notation:

a. $\frac{3.6 \times 10^8}{6 \times 10^6}$ 6×10^1

b. $\frac{3.6 \times 10^{-8}}{1.2 \times 10^{-6}}$ 3×10^{-2}

24. (40) In the figure below, if the measure of $\angle x$ is 140°, what is the measure of $\angle y$? 130°

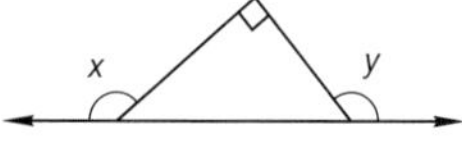

Solve:

25. (102) $5x + 3x = 18 + 2x$ 3

26. (98) $\frac{3.6}{x} = \frac{4.5}{0.06}$ 0.048

▸ See Math Conversations in the sidebar.

Generalize Simplify:

▶* **27.** (103) **a.** $(-1)^6 + (-1)^5$ 0 **b.** $(-10)^6 \div (-10)^5$ -10

* **28.** (96, 103) ▶**a.** $\frac{(4a^2b)(9ab^2c)}{6abc}$ $6a^2b^2$ **b.** $x(x - c) + \sqrt{c^2x^2}$ x^2

29. (85) $(-3) + (+2)(-4) - (-6)(-2) - (-8)$ -15

30. (43, 45) $\frac{3\frac{1}{3} \cdot 1\frac{4}{5} + 1.5}{0.03}$ 250

Early Finishers
Real-World Application

You open a savings account with an initial deposit of \$1500. The bank offers an annual interest rate of 4% compounded annually on its savings accounts.

a. What will your balance be after two years, if no additional deposits or withdrawals are made? \$1622.40

b. Three years after your initial deposit, you decide to use the money in your account to buy a \$2000 car. How much more money will you need to buy the car? \$312.70

▶ See Math Conversations in the sidebar.

3 Written Practice (Continued)

Math Conversations

Discussion opportunities are provided below.

Problems 27a–b Generalize

Point out that there are two negative signs in these problems and ask why the answers are not positive. Sample: In problem 27a, the values are −1 and 1 after they are simplified and they add to 0. In problem 27b, there really are 11 negative signs, so the answer is negative.

Errors and Misconceptions

Problem 28a

Students whose answer is $6ab$ are trying to cancel a variable in each factor of the numerator with a variable in the denominator. Explain that they should write the numerator as one term and that each variable can cancel with only one other variable, and that one is in the numerator and the other is in the denominator.

• Applications of the Pythagorean Theorem

Objectives

- Use the Pythagorean Theorem to solve real-word problems.
- Identify Pythagorean triplets.

Lesson Preparation

Materials

- **Power Up W** (in *Instructional Masters*)
- **Manipulative kit: inch rulers, protractors**
- **Teacher-provided material: full-length, unsharpened pencils, graph paper**

Optional

- **Teacher-provided material: calculators**
- **Investigation Activity 13** (in *Instructional Masters*)

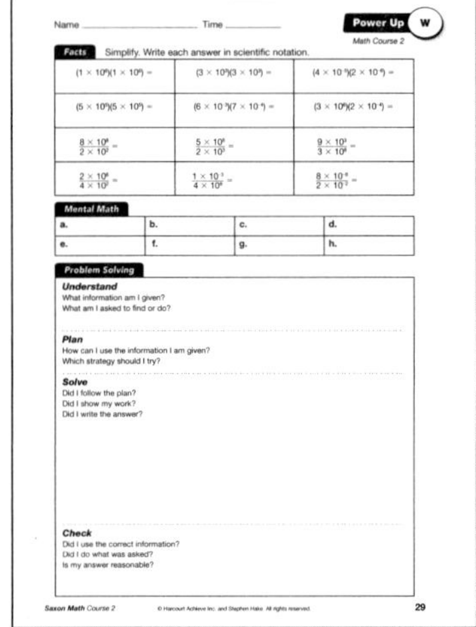

Name ______ Time ______ **Power Up W** *Math Course 2*

Facts Simplify. Write each answer in scientific notation.

(1 × 10[illegible])(1 × 10[illegible]) =	(3 × 10[illegible])(3 × 10[illegible]) =	(4 × 10[illegible])(2 × 10[illegible]) =
(5 × 10[illegible])(5 × 10[illegible]) =	(6 × 10[illegible])(7 × 10[illegible]) =	(3 × 10[illegible])(2 × 10[illegible]) =
8 × 10[illegible] / 2 × 10[illegible] =	5 × 10[illegible] / 2 × 10[illegible] =	9 × 10[illegible] / 3 × 10[illegible] =
2 × 10[illegible] / 4 × 10[illegible] =	1 × 10[illegible] / 4 × 10[illegible] =	8 × 10[illegible] / 2 × 10[illegible] =

Mental Math

a.	b.	c.	d.
e.	f.	g.	h.

Problem Solving

Understand
What information am I given?
What am I asked to find or do?

Plan
How can I use the information I am given?
Which strategy should I try?

Solve
Did I follow the plan?
Did I show my work?
Did I write the answer?

Check
Did I use the correct information?
Did I do what was asked?
Is my answer reasonable?

Saxon Math Course 2 © Harcourt Achieve Inc. and Stephen Hake. All rights reserved. 29

Power Up W

Math Language

Maintain	English Learners (ESL)
Pythagorean triplet	level
hypotenuse	

Technology Resources

Student eBook Complete student textbook in electronic format.

Resources and Planner CD Assessment, reteaching, and instructional masters, plus a pacing calendar with standards.

Test and Practice Generator CD Create additional practice sheets and custom-made tests.

www.SaxonPublishers.com Visit for more student activities and planning materials.

Inclusion

Adaptations CD Adapted lessons, investigations, practice and assessments.

Meeting Standards

National Council of Teachers of Mathematics (NCTM)

Algebra

AL.3a Model and solve contextualized problems using various representations, such as graphs, tables, and equations

Geometry

GM.1c Create and critique inductive and deductive arguments concerning geometric ideas and relationships, such as congruence, similarity, and the Pythagorean relationship

GM.4d Use geometric models to represent and explain numerical and algebraic relationships

GM.4e Recognize and apply geometric ideas and relationships in areas outside the mathematics classroom, such as art, science, and everyday life

Power-Up Discussion *For use with Power Up, p. 784*

Problem-Solving Strategy: Work Backwards

When all the cards from a 52-card deck are dealt to three players, each player receives 17 cards, and there is one extra card. Sharla invented a new deck of cards so that any number of players up to 6 can play and there will be no extra cards. How many cards are in Sharla's deck if the number is less than 100?

Understand — *Understand the problem.*

"What information are we given?"

Sharla invented a new deck that can be divided evenly 1, 2, 3, 4, 5, or 6 ways.

"What are we asked to do?"

We are asked to determine how many cards are in her deck if the number is less than 100.

Plan — *Make a plan.*

"What problem-solving strategy will we use?"

We will use number sense and *work backwards* from the largest factor to find the number of cards in Sharla's deck.

Solve — *Carry out the plan.*

"What are the multiples of 6 descending from 100 to 52?"

96, 90, 84, 78, 72, 66, 60, 54

"Which multiples of 6 are also multiples of 5?"

90 and 60

"Are 90 and 60 multiples of 4?"

No. Only 60 is a multiple of 4.

"Is 60 a multiple of 3?"

Yes.

"A multiple of 2?"

Yes.

"How many cards are in Sharla's deck of cards?"

There are 60 cards in her deck.

Check — *Look back.*

"Did we do what we were asked to do?"

Yes, we found that Sharla's deck has 60 cards.

Teacher's Note: Extend this problem by asking students to predict how many cards would be in a deck that could be dealt evenly to up to 7 players. They may be surprised to learn that the number is 420!

1 Power Up

Facts

Distribute **Power Up W** to students. See answers below.

Mental Math

Encourage students to share different ways to mentally compute these exercises. Strategies for exercises **d** and **e** are listed below.

d. Use the Formula

$F = \frac{9}{5}C + 32$

$F = \frac{9}{5} \times 50 + 32$

$F = 9 \times 10 + 32$

$F = 90 + 32 = 122$

$50°C = 122°F$

Use Logical Reasoning

Every $10°C = 18°F$

$0°C$ is the same as $32°F$

$50°C = (5 \times 18 + 32)°F$

$50°C = 122°F$

e. Double, Halve

25% of \$2000 =

50% of \$1000 =

100% of \$500 = \$500

Use a Fraction

$25\% = \frac{1}{4}$

$\frac{1}{4} \times \$2000 = \$500$

Problem Solving

Refer to **Power-Up Discussion**, p. 784B.

2 New Concepts

Instruction

Students have used the Pythagorean theorem to find one side of a right triangle when the other two sides were known and may have briefly been introduced to *Pythagorean triplets.* In this lesson, students learn practical uses for this theorem.

The Pythagorean triplets, and multiples of them, are helpful because the relationships among them can be determined by using a ratio instead of more complicated calculations.

Point out that 6, 8, and 10 are multiples of 3, 4, and 5. Have students tell why this is so. Continue with the other multiples in this list, and then ask students to name two or more other multiples of 3, 4, and 5. Sample: 15, 20, and 25; 18, 24, and 30; 30, 40, and 50

(continued)

LESSON **112**

• Applications of the Pythagorean Theorem

Power Up *Building Power*

facts Power Up W

mental math

a. **Positive/Negative:** $(-10)^2 + (-10)^3$ -900

b. **Scientific Notation:** $(8 \times 10^6) \div (4 \times 10^3)$ 2×10^3

c. **Algebra:** $m^2 = 100$ 10, −10

d. **Measurement:** Convert 50°C to degrees Fahrenheit. 122°F

e. **Percent:** 25% of \$2000 \$500

f. **Percent:** \$2000 increased 25% \$2500

g. **Geometry:** Which pyramid has 5 faces and 5 vertices? square

h. **Calculation:** Start with 2 dozen, + 1, × 4, + 20, ÷ 3, + 2, ÷ 6, × 4, − 3, $\sqrt{\ }$, ÷ 2. $2\frac{1}{2}$

problem solving When all the cards from a 52-card deck are dealt to three players, each player receives 17 cards, and there is one extra card. Sharla invented a new deck of cards so that any number of players up to 6 can play and there will be no extra cards. How many cards are in Sharla's deck if the number is less than 100? 60 cards

New Concept *Increasing Knowledge*

Workers who construct buildings need to be sure that the structures have square corners. If the corner of a 40-foot-long building is 89° or 91° instead of 90°, the other end of the building will be about 8 inches out of position.

One way construction workers can check whether a building under construction is square is by using a **Pythagorean triplet.** The numbers 3, 4, and 5 satisfy the Pythagorean theorem and are an example of a Pythagorean triplet.

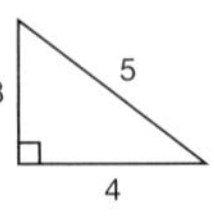

$3^2 + 4^2 = 5^2$

Sample: 15-20-25 and 300-400-500

Thinking Skill

Analyze

Name two more Pythagorean triplets.

Multiples of 3-4-5 are also Pythagorean triplets.

3-4-5

6-8-10

9-12-15

12-16-20

Facts Simplify. Write each answer in scientific notation.

$(1 \times 10^6)(1 \times 10^6) =$ 1×10^{12}	$(3 \times 10^3)(3 \times 10^3) =$ 9×10^6	$(4 \times 10^{-5})(2 \times 10^{-6}) =$ 8×10^{-11}
$(5 \times 10^5)(5 \times 10^5) =$ 2.5×10^{11}	$(6 \times 10^{-3})(7 \times 10^{-4}) =$ 4.2×10^{-6}	$(3 \times 10^6)(2 \times 10^{-4}) =$ 6×10^2
$\frac{8 \times 10^8}{2 \times 10^2} = 4 \times 10^6$	$\frac{5 \times 10^6}{2 \times 10^3} = 2.5 \times 10^3$	$\frac{9 \times 10^3}{3 \times 10^8} = 3 \times 10^{-5}$
$\frac{2 \times 10^6}{4 \times 10^2} = 5 \times 10^3$	$\frac{1 \times 10^{-3}}{4 \times 10^8} = 2.5 \times 10^{-12}$	$\frac{8 \times 10^{-8}}{2 \times 10^{-2}} = 4 \times 10^{-6}$

Before pouring a concrete foundation for a building, construction workers build wooden forms to hold the concrete. Then a worker or building inspector may use a Pythagorean triplet to check that the forms make a right angle. First the perpendicular sides are marked at selected lengths. Then the diagonal distance between the marks is checked to be sure the three measures are a Pythagorean triplet.

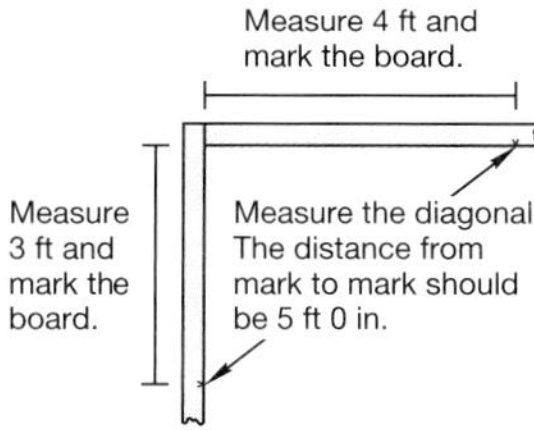
Measure 4 ft and
mark the board.
Measure
3 ft and
mark the
board.
Measure the diagonal.
The distance from
mark to mark should
be 5 ft 0 in.

If the three measures form a Pythagorean triplet, what can the worker conclude? The corner forms a 90° angle.

Activity

Application of the Pythagorean Theorem

Materials needed by each group of 2 or 3 students:

- Two full-length, unsharpened pencils (or other straightedges)
- Ruler
- Protractor

Position two pencils (or straightedges) so that they appear to form a right angle. Mark one pencil 3 inches from the vertex of the angle and the other pencil 4 inches from the vertex. Then measure from mark to mark to see whether the distance between the marks is 5 inches. Adjust the pencils if necessary.

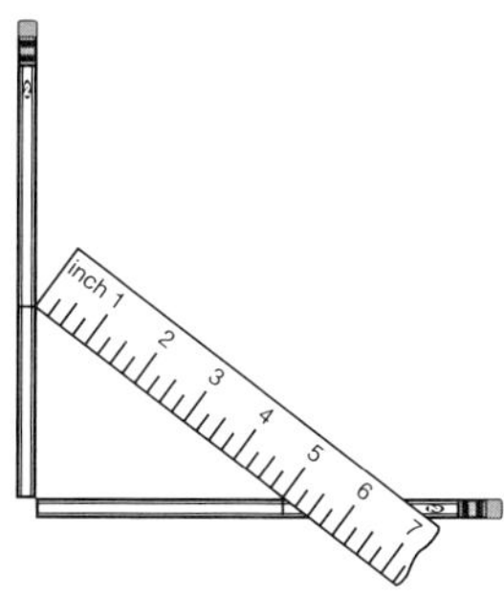

Trace the angle formed. Then use a protractor to confirm that the angle formed by the pencils measures 90°.

Conclude Keep the pencils at a right angle. If you mark the pencils at 6 cm and 8 cm, what will be the distance between the marks? 10 cm

2 New Concepts (Continued)

Instruction

Be sure students understand that the construction example uses a Pythagorean triplet because it makes the calculations easier. The worker could obtain an exact right angle using a right triangle that is not a Pythagorean triplet. The important part of the example is that comparing the sides of a triangle and using the Pythagorean Theorem assure that the angle is a right angle.

Sometimes a Pythagorean triplet is called a *Pythagorean triple*. Tell students that these two terms are synonymous.

Activity

Instruction

For the activity, each pair or small group of students will need two full-length, unsharpened pencils or other straightedges. Each group will also need a ruler and a protractor. While one person holds the pencils steady, another person measures, marks, and traces.

Be sure students make the marks on the sides of the pencils that form the inside of the right angle. If the marks are made on the top or outer side of the pencil, the measurement of 5 inches, as shown in the diagram, may not be accurate, and the resulting angle may not measure 90°.

When students trace the angle, caution them to hold the pencil they use to trace perpendicular to the paper. If the tracing pencil is not held at a consistent angle, the drawing may not be accurate.

As you discuss the answer to the *Conclude* question, point out that students can confirm this measurement by recognizing that the triangle is a multiple of a 3-4-5 Pythagorean triplet.

Math Background

Is there a formula for generating Pythagorean triplets?

Yes. Select two positive integers L and S so that L is larger than S. Use the selected integers in these formulas to find an *a-b-c* Pythagorean triplet. The example below used L = 3 and S = 2.

Formula	Example
$a = 2LS$	$a = 2 \cdot 3 \cdot 2 = 12$
$b = L^2 - S^2$	$b = 3^2 - 2^2 = 5$
$c = L^2 + S^2$	$c = 3^2 + 2^2 = 13$

Because $5^2 + 12^2 = 13^2$, the numbers 5, 12, and 13, are a Pythagorean triplet.

2 New Concepts (Continued)

Example 1

Instruction

Discuss the multiples of the 5-12-13 Pythagorean triplet, and have students tell how each triplet was found. Ask students to name one or two more triplets. Samples: 25-60-65; 50-120-130

Example 2

Instruction

Explain that a vertical segment drawn down from the peak of the roof divides the isosceles triangle into two congruent right triangles each with a base of 12 feet. The slope "4 in 12" means that in 12 horizontal units, the roof rises or falls 4 vertical units. Since the horizontal base is 12 feet, the height of the triangle is 4 feet.

You may want to ask an architect or a carpenter to speak to the class about the importance of triangles and right angles in construction projects.

A right triangle is sometimes defined as a triangle with a right angle formed by the legs of the triangle and a hypotenuse that is the side opposite the right angle.

(continued)

Example 1

The numbers 5, 12, and 13 are a Pythagorean triplet because $5^2 + 12^2 = 13^2$. What are the next three multiples of this Pythagorean triplet?

Solution

To find the next three multiples of 5-12-13, we multiply each number by 2, by 3, and by 4.

10-24-26

15-36-39

20-48-52

Example 2

A roof is being built over a 24-ft-wide room. The slope of the roof is 4 in 12. Calculate the length of the rafters needed for the roof. (Include 2 ft for the rafter tail.)

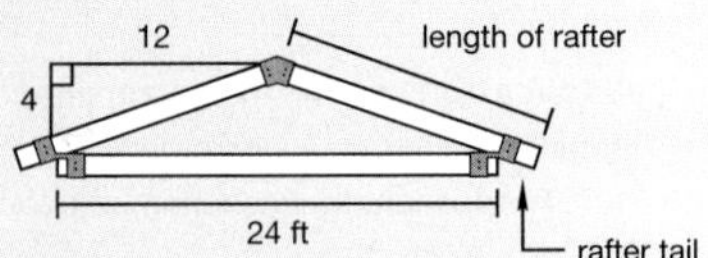

Solution

Math Language
The longest side of a right triangle is called the *hypotenuse*. The other two sides are called *legs*.

We consider the length of a rafter to be the hypotenuse of a right triangle. The width of the room is 24 ft, but a rafter spans only half the width of the room. So the base of the right triangle is 12 ft. The slope of the roof, 4 in 12, means that for every 12 horizontal units, the roof rises (or falls) 4 vertical units. Thus, since the base of the triangle is 12 ft, its height is 4 ft, as shown above.

We use the Pythagorean theorem to calculate the hypotenuse.

$$a^2 + b^2 = c^2$$
$$(4\text{ ft})^2 + (12\text{ ft})^2 = c^2$$
$$16\text{ ft}^2 + 144\text{ ft}^2 = c^2$$
$$160\text{ ft}^2 = c^2$$
$$\sqrt{160}\text{ ft} = c$$
$$12.65\text{ ft} \approx c$$

Using a calculator we find that the hypotenuse is about 12.65 feet. We add 2 feet for the rafter tail.

$$12.65\text{ ft} + 2\text{ ft} = 14.65\text{ ft}$$

To convert 0.65 ft to inches, we multiply.

$$0.65\text{ ft} \times \frac{12\text{ in.}}{1\text{ ft}} = 7.8\text{ in.}$$

We round this up to 8 inches. So the length of each rafter is about **14 ft 8 in.**

786 **Saxon** Math Course 2

Example 3

Serena went to a level field to fly a kite. She let out all 200 ft of string and tied it to a stake. Then she walked out on the field until she was directly under the kite, 150 feet from the stake. About how high was the kite?

Solution

We begin by sketching the problem. The length of the kite string is the hypotenuse of a right triangle, and the distance between Serena and the stake is one leg of the triangle. We use the Pythagorean theorem to find the remaining leg, which is the height of the kite.

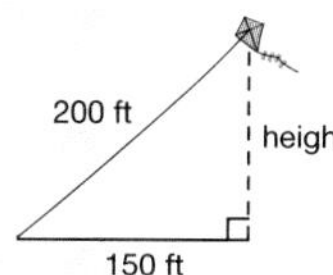

$$a^2 + b^2 = c^2$$
$$a^2 + (150\text{ ft})^2 = (200\text{ ft})^2$$
$$a^2 + 22{,}500\text{ ft}^2 = 40{,}000\text{ ft}^2$$
$$a^2 = 17{,}500\text{ ft}^2$$
$$a = \sqrt{17{,}500}\text{ ft}$$
$$a \approx 132\text{ ft}$$

Using a calculator, we find that the height of the kite was about **132 ft.**

Discuss How do we know we can use the Pythagorean theorem to solve this problem?

Because Serena stood on a level field directly under the kite, Serena's feet, the kite, and the stake create the vertices of a right triangle. Since we have the measurements of the hypotenuse and one of the legs, we can find the length of the other leg by using the Pythagorean theorem.

Practice Set

▸ **a.** A 12-foot ladder was leaning against a building. The base of the ladder was 5 feet from the building. How high up the side of the building did the ladder reach? Write the answer in feet and inches rounded to the nearest inch. 10 feet 11 inches

▸ **b.** Figure *ABCD* illustrates a rectangular field 400 feet long and 300 feet wide. The path from *A* to *C* is how much shorter than the path from *A* to *B* to *C*? 200 feet

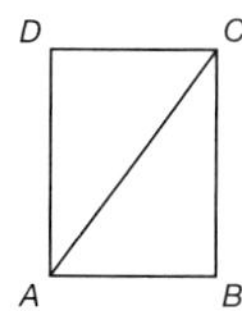

▸ **c.** A contractor checks the forms for a concrete slab. He marks the forms at 8 ft and at 6 ft. Then he measures between the marks and finds that the distance is 10 feet 2 inches. Is the corner a right angle? How do you know?

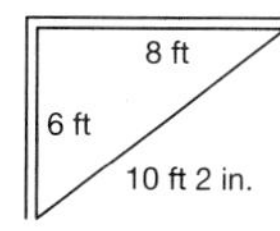

c. The corner is not a right angle. If the corner were a right angle, then the distance between the marks would be 10 feet even, because 6-8-10 is a Pythagorean triplet. (Since the distance between the marks is a little more than 10 feet, the angle is a little more than 90°.)

▸ See Math Conversations in the sidebar.

2 New Concepts *(Continued)*

Example 3

Instruction

Encourage students to sketch the triangle as you work through this example. Knowing how to sketch a problem situation accurately will help students correctly write an equation for the situation.

Explain that a calculator is helpful in solving this problem, but that students must use the Pythagorean Theorem first to set up the problem. A calculator is used only to do the computation after the equation is written.

For the *Discuss* question, help students see that knowing all three parts of a Pythagorean triplet or recognizing that two sides of a triangle are in a ratio that connects to a Pythagorean triplet will make solving these problems very easy.

Practice Set

Problems a–c Analyze

Discuss whether any of the problems can be solved using a Pythagorean triplet. b and c Let students use calculators for problem a.

Problem a Error Alert

Help students recognize that the length of the ladder is the hypotenuse by suggesting that they sketch this problem.

Students will need to use calculators. They will find that the top of the ladder is $\sqrt{119}$ feet, which is approximately 10.9087 feet up the wall. Remind students that this number is not 10 ft 9 in. It is 10 ft plus 0.9087 ft. To find the number of inches in 0.9087 ft, have students multiply 12 in. by 0.9087 and round to the nearest whole inch.

English Learners

In example 3, explain the meaning of **level.** Tell students:

"A level field is smooth and flat. It is straight across, not bumpy."

Ask students what they think it means to level a driveway. It means to make the concrete on the driveway flat or even.

3 Written Practice

Math Conversations

Discussion opportunities are provided below.

Problem 2 Connect

Ask students if they notice that this problem is related to the Pythagorean theorem.

Problem 8 Analyze

"Suppose the item still did not sell, and it is marked down again, but now it is reduced 60%. What is the new price?" 10¢

Errors and Misconceptions

Problem 3

If students find the median and the mode of the numbers in the second column (4.5, 3 and 6), point out that these numbers tell them how many students received the corresponding score in the first column. The sum of the second column shows that the scores are for 27 students. If necessary, have students list the 27 scores and then find the median and the mode.

Problem 6

If students give an answer of $36, they misread the problem or had trouble writing the equation for the situation. Point out that the regular price of the jacket must be greater than the sale price.

(continued)

Written Practice *Strengthening Concepts*

* **1.** (110) Mrs. Garcia deposited $3000 in an account paying 8 percent interest compounded annually. She withdrew her money with interest 3 years later. How much did she withdraw? $3779.14

▸ * **2.** (20, 28) Connect What is the square root of the sum of 3 squared and 4 squared? 5

▸ **3.** (Inv. 4) Find the **a** median and **b** mode of the following quiz scores:
a. 90 **b.** 95

Class Quiz Scores

Score	Number of Students
100	2
95	7
90	6
85	6
80	3
70	3

4. (46) The driver completed the 840-kilometer trip in 10 hours 30 minutes. What was the driver's average speed in kilometers per hour?
80 kilometers per hour

Use ratio boxes to solve problems **5–7:**

5. (72) Barbara earned $48 for 6 hours of work. At that rate, how much would she earn for 8 hours of work? $64

▸ **6.** (92) José paid $48 for a jacket at 25 percent off of the regular price. What was the regular price of the jacket? $64

7. (92) Troy bought a baseball card for $6 and sold it for 25 percent more than he paid for it. How much profit did he make on the sale? $1.50

▸ * **8.** (110) Analyze At a yard sale an item marked $1.00 was reduced 50%. When the item still did not sell, the sale price was reduced 50%. What was the price of the item after the second discount? $0.25

9. (36) A test was made up of multiple-choice questions and short-answer questions. If 60% of the questions were multiple-choice, what was the ratio of multiple-choice to short-answer questions? $\frac{3}{2}$

10. (99) The points (3, 11), (−2, −1), and (−2, 11) are the vertices of a right triangle. Use the Pythagorean theorem to find the length of the hypotenuse of this triangle. 13 units

11. (88) The final stage of the 2004 Tour de France was 163 km long. Bicyclist Tom Boonen covered that distance in about 4 hours. Find his approximate average speed in miles per hour.
One km ≈ 0.6 mile. About 24 miles per hour

▸ See Math Conversations in the sidebar.

12. (77) What percent of 2.5 is 2? Explain how you can determine if your answer is reasonable. 80%; Sample: 2 is less than 2.5 but more than half of 2.5, so the percent should be less than 100% but greater than 50%.

▶ **13.** (Inv. 8) What are the odds of having a coin land tails up on 4 consecutive tosses of a coin? 1 to 15

▶* **14.** (110) **Generalize** How much interest is earned in 6 months on $4000 deposited at 9 percent annual simple interest? $180

15. (48) Complete the table.

Fraction	Decimal	Percent
$\frac{5}{8}$	**a.** 0.625	**b.** 62.5%

* **16.** (111) Divide. Write each quotient in scientific notation:

a. $\frac{5 \times 10^8}{2 \times 10^4}$ 2.5×10^4 **b.** $\frac{1.2 \times 10^4}{4 \times 10^8}$ 3×10^{-5}

▶* **17.** (112) **Connect** The frame of this kite is formed by two perpendicular pieces of wood whose lengths are shown in inches. A loop of string connects the four ends of the sticks. How long is the string? 70 inches

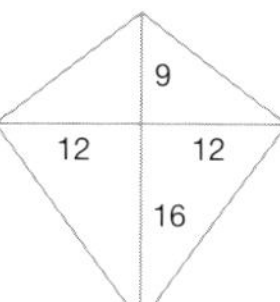

▶* **18.** (106) **Analyze** Solve for t: $d = rt$ $t = \frac{d}{r}$

19. (Inv. 9) Make a table that shows three pairs of numbers for the function $y = -x$. Then graph the number pairs on a coordinate plane, and draw a line through the points. See student work.

▶* **20.** (104) Find the perimeter of this figure. The arc in the figure is a semicircle. Dimensions are in centimeters. (Use 3.14 for π.) 91.4 cm

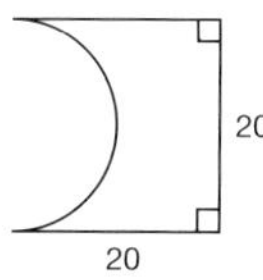

21. (97, 98) The triangles below are similar. Dimensions are in centimeters.

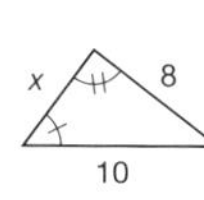

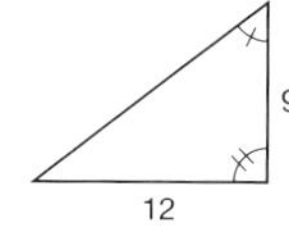

a. Find x. 6 cm

b. Find the scale factor from the smaller to the larger triangle. 1.5

22. (21) **a.** Write the prime factorization of 1 trillion using exponents. $2^{12} \cdot 5^{12}$

b. Find the positive square root of 1 trillion. 1,000,000

▶ See Math Conversations in the sidebar.

3 Written Practice (Continued)

Math Conversations

Discussion opportunities are provided below.

Problem 14 Generalize

"If $180 simple interest is earned in 6 months, how much will be earned in 5 years?" Sample: 5 years equals 60 months, so it would be 10 times $180 or $1800.

Problem 17 Connect

Have students explain why the area of the kite can be represented as $12(9 + 16)$ in.^{2} Sample: The two triangles at the top have a combined area of 12×9, and the two at the bottom have a combined area of 12×16. Then ask students to describe how that value can be computed mentally. Sample: $12(9 + 16) = 12 \times 25 = 6 \times 50 = 3 \times 100 = 300$

Problem 18 Analyze

Have students solve the equation for r. $r = \frac{d}{t}$ Then ask:

"Is d directly proportional to r? Why?" Sample: yes, because if r increases d increases

"Is d directly proportional to t? Why?" Sample: yes, because if t increases d increases

"If d doesn't change, how are r and t related? Why?" Sample: They are inversely proportional because if one of them increases, the other has to decrease.

Problem 20

Extend the Problem

Ask students to find the area of the figure. They should use 3.14 for π and not use calculators. 243 cm^2

Errors and Misconceptions

Problem 13

Students whose answer is 1 to 16 have determined the probability, not the odds. Review the difference between odds and probability with them.

(continued)

3 Written Practice (Continued)

Math Conversations

Discussion opportunities are provided below.

Problem 23 Connect

Have students find the volume of the prism using mental math. 540 ft^3 Then ask:

"What size rectangular prism would have twice that volume?" Sample: a prism that is 9 ft × 12 ft × 10 ft

"What size rectangular prism would have the same volume as the triangular prism?" Sample: a prism that is 9 ft × 12 ft × 5 ft

"What size rectangular prism would have half the volume of the triangular prism?" Sample: a prism that is 9 ft × 6 ft × 5 ft

Problem 30 Model

"Suppose that the grapefruit had a radius of 14 centimeters. How many times greater would its surface area be than for this grapefruit?" 4 times greater

Errors and Misconceptions

Problem 23

It is likely that students whose answer is 576 square feet neglected to use the formula for a triangle when finding the area of the base, and instead simply multiplied 9 by 12. Have them redo the problem using the formula for a triangle to find the area of the base. Remind them to write each step of their solutions on a separate line so that they can easily check their work.

Problem 29

If students have an answer of 110, then they most likely cancelled the negative in the denominator with both negatives in the numerator. Tell them that they do not cancel negative signs, but rather count them to find the sign of the product or quotient. In this case there are 3, or an odd number, in the fraction, so the fraction will simplify to a negative number.

▶* **23.** (105) Connect Find the surface area of this right triangular prism. Dimensions are in feet. 468 ft^2

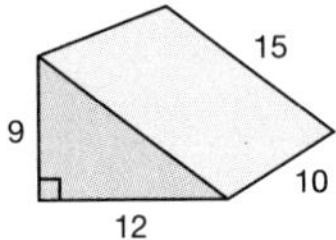

Solve:

24. (98) $\frac{16}{2.5} = \frac{48}{f}$ 7.5

25. (93) $2\frac{2}{3}x - 3 = 21$ 9

Simplify:

26. (57, 63) $10^2 - [10 - 10(10^0 - 10^{-1})]$ 99

27. (43) $2\frac{3}{4} - \left(1.5 - \frac{1}{6}\right)$ $1\frac{5}{12}$

28. (43) $3.5 \div 1\frac{2}{5} \div 3$ $\frac{5}{6}$

▶ **29.** (85) $|-4| - (-3)(-2)(-1) + \frac{(-5)(4)(-3)(2)}{-1}$ −110

▶* **30.** (105) The large grapefruit was nearly spherical and had a diameter of 14 cm. Using $\frac{22}{7}$ for π, find the approximate surface area of the grapefruit to the nearest hundred square centimeters. 600 square centimeters

Early Finishers
Real-World Application

A student surveyed 8 friends asking the type of pets they have. Here are the results.

Mark and Janet have both a cat and a parakeet.
Lisa has a dog and myna bird.
James has a cat.
Loretta and Jorge have a dog and a cat.
Rosa has a dog.
Rodney has a parrot.

a. Choose a line plot, line graph, or a Venn diagram to display this data. Draw your display and justify your choice.

b. Formulate questions to conduct a similar survey of 30 students in your school. Write three conclusions that can be made based on your collected data. See student work.

a. Venn diagram; Sample: A Venn diagram shows all the pets and all the people who have them. A line plot could only show one type of pet.

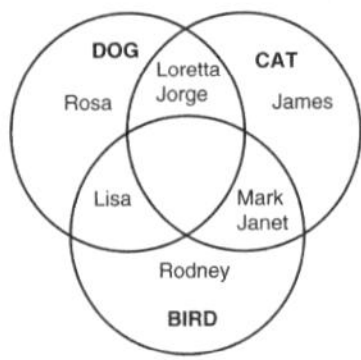

790 Saxon Math Course 2

▶ See Math Conversations in the sidebar.

• Volume of Pyramids, Cones, and Spheres

Objectives

- Use a formula to find the volume of a pyramid.
- Use a formula to find the volume of a cone.
- Use a formula to find the volume of a sphere.

Lesson Preparation

Materials

- **Power Up V** (in *Instructional Masters*)
- **Teacher-provided material: graph paper; sand, salt, or rice**
- **Manipulative kit: Relational GeoSolids**

Optional

- **Teacher-provided material: water**
- **Investigation Activity 13** (in *Instructional Masters*)

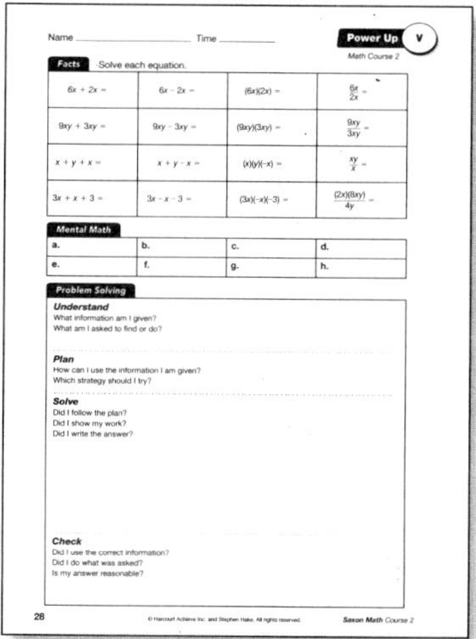

Name ________ Time ________ Power Up V

Math Course 2

Facts Solve each equation.

$6x + 2x =$	$6x - 2x =$	$(6x)(2x) =$	$\frac{6x}{2x} =$
$9xy + 3xy =$	$9xy - 3xy =$	$(9xy)(3xy) =$	$\frac{9xy}{3xy} =$
$x + y + x =$	$x + y - x =$	$(x)(y)(-x) =$	$\frac{xy}{x} =$
$3x + x + 3 =$	$3x - x - 3 =$	$(3x)(-x)(-3) =$	$\frac{(2x)(8xy)}{4y} =$

Mental Math

a.	b.	c.	d.
e.	f.	g.	h.

Problem Solving

Understand
What information am I given?
What am I asked to find or do?

Plan
How can I use the information I am given?
Which strategy should I try?

Solve
Did I follow the plan?
Did I show my work?
Did I write the answer?

Check
Did I use the correct information?
Did I do what was asked?
Is my answer reasonable?

28 *Saxon Math* Course 2

Power Up V

Math Language

Maintain	English Learners (ESL)
pyramid	voids

Technology Resources

Student eBook Complete student textbook in electronic format.

Resources and Planner CD Assessment, reteaching, and instructional masters, plus a pacing calendar with standards.

Test and Practice Generator CD Create additional practice sheets and custom-made tests.

www.SaxonPublishers.com Visit for more student activities and planning materials.

Inclusion

Adaptations CD Adapted lessons, investigations, practice and assessments.

Meeting Standards

National Council of Teachers of Mathematics (NCTM)

Geometry

GM.4b Use two-dimensional representations of three-dimensional objects to visualize and solve problems such as those involving surface area and volume

GM.4d Use geometric models to represent and explain numerical and algebraic relationships

GM.4e Recognize and apply geometric ideas and relationships in areas outside the mathematics classroom, such as art, science, and everyday life

Measurement

ME.1c Understand, select, and use units of appropriate size and type to measure angles, perimeter, area, surface area, and volume

ME.2d Develop strategies to determine the surface area and volume of selected prisms, pyramids, and cylinders

Power-Up Discussion For use with Power Up, p. 791

Problem-Solving Strategy: Use Logical Reasoning

Sylvia wants to pack a 9-by-14 in. rectangular picture frame that is $\frac{1}{2}$ in. thick into a rectangular box. The box has inside dimensions of 12-by-9-by-10 in. Describe why you think the frame will or will not fit into the box.

Understand Understand the problem.

"What information are we given?"

A 9-by-14 in. rectangular picture frame that is $\frac{1}{2}$ in. thick needs to fit into a rectangular box that has inside dimensions of 12 in. by 9 in. by 10 in.

"What are we asked to do?"

We are asked to describe why the frame will or will not fit into the box.

Plan Make a plan.

"What problem-solving strategy will we use?"

We will *use logical reasoning* to determine whether the frame can fit inside the box.

"What additional geometric principles might we need to apply to solve this problem?"

the Pythogorean Theorem

Solve Carry out the plan.

"Is the box of adequate dimensions for the frame to rest on its side?"

Yes. The box is 10 inches high, and the frame is only 9 inches wide.

"How does it appear we should try to place the frame in the box?"

Resting on its side and positioned diagonally across the box.

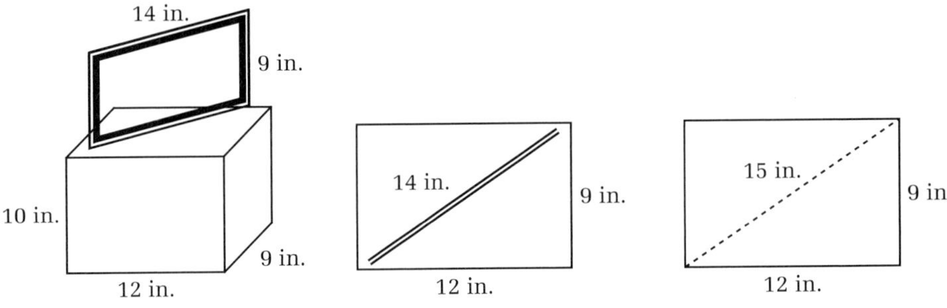

"How can we find the diagonal of the box?"

We can use the Pythagorean Theorem: $9^2 + 12^2 = c^2$; $81 + 144 = c^2$; $225 = c^2$, so $c = 15$. The diagonal on the box is 15 inches.

"Will the picture frame fit in the box?"

The diagonal of the box is 15 inches, and the frame is only 14 inches long. That leaves 1 inch to accommodate for the $\frac{1}{2}$ inch thickness of the frame.

Check Look back.

"Did we do what we were asked to do?"

Yes, we described how Sylvia can position the frame in the box, and we explained how it will fit.

LESSON

113

Volume of Pyramids, Cones, and Spheres

Power Up *Building Power*

facts Power Up V

mental math

a. **Positive/Negative:** $0.75 \div (-3)$ -0.25

b. **Scientific Notation:** $(6 \times 10^6) \div (3 \times 10^{10})$ 2×10^{-4}

c. **Algebra:** $10m + 1.5 = 7.5$ 0.6

d. **Measurement:** Convert 2 ft^2 to square inches. 288 in.^{2}

e. **Percent:** $66\frac{2}{3}\%$ of \$2400 \$1600

f. **Percent:** \$2400 reduced by $66\frac{2}{3}\%$ \$800

g. **Geometry:** Which pyramid has 6 faces and 6 vertices? pentagonal

h. **Rate:** At 500 mph, how long will it take a plane to travel 1250 miles? $2\frac{1}{2}$ hr

problem solving

Sylvia wants to pack a 9-by-14 in. rectangular picture frame that is $\frac{1}{2}$ in. thick into a rectangular box. The box has inside dimensions of 12-by-9-by-10 in. Describe why you think the frame will or will not fit into the box. See script for explanation.

New Concept *Increasing Knowledge*

A **pyramid** is a geometric solid that has three or more triangular faces and a base that is a polygon. Each of these figures is a pyramid:

 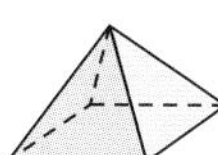 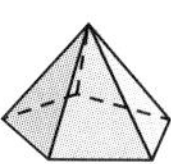

Thinking Skill
Explain
Both pyramids and triangular prisms have surfaces that are triangles. How are the two different?

The volume of a pyramid is $\frac{1}{3}$ the volume of a prism that has the same base and height. Recall that the volume of a prism is equal to the area of its base times its height.

Volume of a prism = area of base · height

To find the volume of a pyramid, we first find the volume of a prism that has the same base and height. Then we divide the result by 3 (or multiply by $\frac{1}{3}$).

Volume of pyramid = $\frac{1}{3}$ · area of base · height

A pyramid has triangular faces. Its single base is a polygon that may, or may not, be triangular. A triangular prism has faces that are quadrilaterals. Its two bases are triangular.

Facts Solve each equation.

$6x + 2x = 8x$	$6x - 2x = 4x$	$(6x)(2x) = 12x^2$	$\frac{6x}{2x} = 3$
$9xy + 3xy = 12xy$	$9xy - 3xy = 6xy$	$(9xy)(3xy) = 27x^2y^2$	$\frac{9xy}{3xy} = 3$
$x + y + x = 2x + y$	$x + y - x = y$	$(x)(y)(-x) = -x^2y$	$\frac{xy}{x} = y$
$3x + x + 3 = 4x + 3$	$3x - x - 3 = 2x - 3$	$(3x)(-x)(-3) = 9x^2$	$\frac{(2x)(8xy)}{4y} = 4x^2$

1 Power Up

Facts

Distribute **Power Up V** to students. See answers below.

Mental Math

Encourage students to share different ways to mentally compute these exercises. Strategies for exercises **d** and **e** are listed below.

d. Use Logical Reasoning

$1 \text{ ft}^2 = 144 \text{ in.}^2$

$2 \text{ ft}^2 = 2 \times 144 \text{ in.}^2 = 288 \text{ in.}^2$

Use Unit Multipliers

$2 \text{ ft}^2 \times \frac{12 \text{ in.}}{1 \text{ ft}} \times \frac{12 \text{ in.}}{1 \text{ ft}} = 288 \text{ in.}^2$

e. Find a Fraction for the Percent

$66\frac{2}{3}\% = \frac{2}{3}$

$\frac{2}{3} \times \$2400 = 2 \times \$800 = \$1600$

Use a Unit Fraction

$\frac{1}{3} \times \$2400 = \$800$

$\frac{2}{3} \times \$2400 = \$1600$

Problem Solving

Refer to **Power-Up Discussion,** p. 791B.

2 New Concepts

Instruction

Begin by discussing the types of figures for which students can already find the volume. Explain that knowing how to find the volume of solids such as prisms, cubes, and cylinders is the first step toward finding the volume of solids such as pyramids, spheres, and cones.

Use **Relational GeoSolids** from the Manipulative Kit to illustrate and demonstrate the concepts in this lesson. You will need the large cube, the square pyramid, the large cylinder, the cone, and the sphere, along with some sand, salt, or rice for filling them.

Fill the square pyramid and ask students to predict how many times you can pour the contents into the cube. Then demonstrate that the cube will hold three times the contents of the pyramid.

(continued)

2 New Concepts (Continued)

Example 1

Instruction

"How do we know the height of the pyramid?" The height of the cube is the same as its sides, so its height is 6 cm. Since the height of the pyramid is the same as that of the cube, its height is 6 cm.

Example 2

Instruction

Use the **Relational GeoSolids** from the Manipulative Kit to show the relationship between the height of the cone and the height of the cylinder as well as the diameter of the base of each.

You may need to remind students that the formula for the area of a circle is $A = \pi r^2$.

Use a cone to show students that the *slant height* is measured on the outside surface from the vertex to the base while the *height* is the perpendicular distance inside the cone from the vertex to the base. Suggest that students think of the height as a pole holding up the cone at its peak.

(continued)

Example 1

The pyramid at right has the same base and height as the cube that contains it. Each edge of the cube is 6 centimeters.

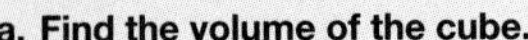

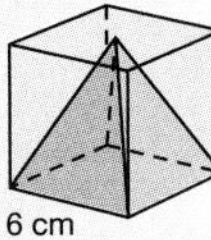

a. Find the volume of the cube.

b. Find the volume of the pyramid.

Solution

a. The volume of the cube equals the area of the base times the height.

$$\text{Area of base} = 6\text{ cm} \times 6\text{ cm} = 36\text{ cm}^2$$

$$\text{Volume of cube} = \text{area of base} \cdot \text{height}$$
$$= (36\text{ cm}^2)(6\text{ cm})$$
$$= \mathbf{216\ cm^3}$$

b. The volume of the pyramid is $\frac{1}{3}$ the volume of the cube, so we divide the volume of the cube by 3 (or multiply by $\frac{1}{3}$).

$$\text{Volume of pyramid} = \frac{1}{3}(\text{volume of prism})$$
$$= \frac{1}{3}(216\text{ cm}^3)$$
$$= \mathbf{72\ cm^3}$$

Discuss In this example, if all we were given was the volume of the pyramid, could we find the length of the edge of the cube? Explain your answer.

Yes; The volume of the pyramid is $\frac{1}{3}$ the volume of the cube. So we could multiply the volume of the pyramid by 3 to get the cube's volume. Then, since a cube's edges all have the same length, we could find the cube root of the cube's volume to find the length of each edge.

The volume of a cone is $\frac{1}{3}$ the volume of a cylinder with the same base and height.

Volume of cone $= \frac{1}{3} \cdot$ **area of base · height**

Math Language

The *height* of a cone is the perpendicular distance from the vertex to the base.

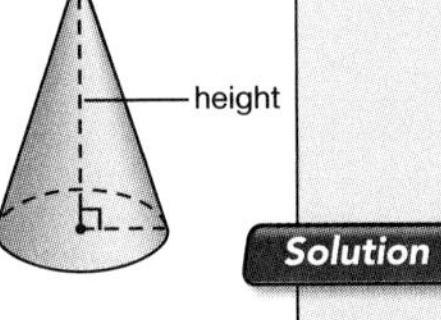

Example 2

Find the volume of this circular cone. Dimensions are in centimeters. (Use 3.14 for π.)

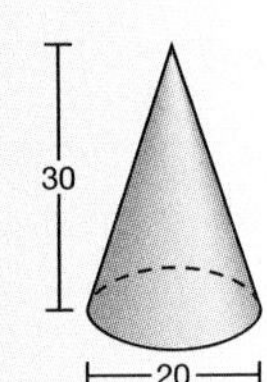

Solution

We first find the volume of a cylinder with the same base and height as the cone.

$$\text{Volume of cylinder} = \text{area of circle} \cdot \text{height}$$
$$\approx (3.14)(10\text{ cm})^2 \cdot 30\text{ cm}$$
$$\approx 9420\text{ cm}^3$$

Math Background

What is the difference between triangular prisms and pyramids?

Both have faces that are triangles, so sometimes it may not be easy to tell them apart. Informally speaking, a pyramid comes to a point, and a prism does not. To be more precise, look at the definitions:

- A triangular prism has two congruent triangular bases that are parallel. The other faces are quadrilaterals.
- A pyramid has a single base that is a polygon. Its remaining faces are triangles. The triangular faces meet at a point called the vertex.

Then we find $\frac{1}{3}$ of this volume.

$$\text{Volume of cone} = \frac{1}{3}\text{ (volume of cylinder)}$$

$$\approx \frac{1}{3} \cdot 9420 \text{ cm}^3$$

$$\approx \mathbf{3140\ cm^3}$$

We have used the general formula for the volume of a pyramid and cone. Using an uppercase A for the area of the base, the general formula is

$$V = \frac{1}{3}Ah$$

We can develop a specific formula for various pyramids and cones by replacing A in the general formula with the formula for the area of the base.

Write a formula for the volume of a pyramid with a square base. $V = \frac{1}{3}s^2h$

Write a formula for the volume of a cone with a circular base. $V = \frac{1}{3}\pi r^2h$

There is a special relationship between the volume of a cylinder, the volume of a cone, and the volume of a sphere. Picture two identical cylinders whose heights are equal to their diameters. In one cylinder is a cone with the same diameter and height as the cylinder. In the other cylinder is a sphere with the same diameter as the cylinder.

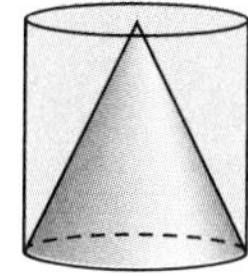

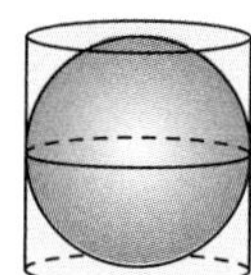

We have learned that the volume of the cone is $\frac{1}{3}$ the volume of the cylinder. Remarkably, the volume of the sphere is twice the volume of the cone, that is, $\frac{2}{3}$ the volume of the cylinder. Here we use a balance scale to provide another view of this relationship.

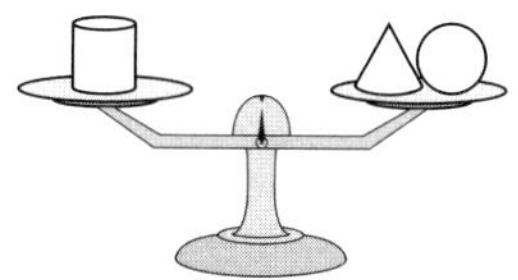

Imagine that the objects on the balance scale are solid and composed of the same material. The diameters of all three solids are equal. The heights of the cylinder and cone equal their diameters. The balance scale shows that the combined masses of the cone and sphere equal the mass of the cylinder. The cone's mass is $\frac{1}{3}$ of the cylinder's mass, and the sphere's mass is $\frac{2}{3}$ of the cylinder's mass.

The formula for the volume of a sphere can be derived from our knowledge of cylinders and their relationship to spheres. First consider the volume of any cylinder whose height is equal to its diameter. In this diagram we have labeled the diameter, d; the radius, r; and the height, h.

2 New Concepts (Continued)

Example 2 (continued)

Instruction

You may want to explain how to find the formulas for the volume of a pyramid with a square base and the volume of a cone with a circular base.

Volume of a pyramid with a square base:

The formula for the area of a square is $A = s^2$. When students use the formula $V = \frac{1}{3}Ah$ to find the volume of a square pyramid, they can replace the A in the formula with s^2, creating the formula $V = \frac{1}{3}s^2h$.

Volume of a cone with a circular base:

The formula for the area of a circle is $A = \pi r^2$. When students use the formula $V = \frac{1}{3}Ah$ to find the volume of a cone, they can replace the A in the formula with πr^2, creating the formula $V = \frac{1}{3}\pi r^2h$.

Instruction

As you explain the special relationship between the volume of the cylinder, cone, and sphere, you may assign specific values for the volumes to give the picture more meaning.

Explain how it is important that the objects on the scale are made of the same substance. Objects with the same volume but made of different materials may have different masses. If the masses are not the same, the scales will not balance.

(continued)

Inclusion

For the student who needs a physical demonstration, use the cylinder, cone, and sphere from the Manipulative Kit. Have the student measure the heights and radii of the objects in centimeters to confirm that their volumes are comparable. 5 cm; 2.5 cm Instruct the student to fill the cone with water and transfer it to the cylinder. Ask him/her:

"How much space does the cone's contents take up in the cylinder?" $\frac{1}{3}$

Instruct the student to fill the sphere with water and transfer it to the cylinder. Ask the student:

"How much space do the sphere's contents take up in the cylinder?" the remaining $\frac{2}{3}$

Discuss how the demonstration connects to the volume formulas.

2 New Concepts (Continued)

Instruction

Point out the difference between the height notations on the left and right sides of the cylinder. This is a special case in which the height (h) of the cylinder is equal to its diameter (d). These dimensions would correspond to the height (diameter) of a sphere completely contained in the cylinder.

Use the cylinder, cone, and sphere geometric solids to demonstrate the relative volume of these figures. Use a cone to fill a sphere twice and a cylinder three times. Point out that the diameters of all three objects are equal in measure and the heights of the cylinder and cone are equal in length to their diameters.

Example 3

Instruction

After working through this example, you can review the volume concepts in this lesson by asking students to find the volume of a cylinder and a cone whose diameters and heights are the same as the diameter of the ball in this example. Have students round their answers to the nearest hundred cubic centimeters. volume of cylinder is about 6300 cm^3; volume of cone is about 2100 cm^3

Have students compare the volumes of the cone, cylinder, and sphere. Ask whether

- the rounded volume of the cone is equal to $\frac{1}{3}$ the rounded volume of the cylinder. yes
- the rounded volume of the sphere is equal to $\frac{2}{3}$ the rounded volume of the cylinder. yes

(continued)

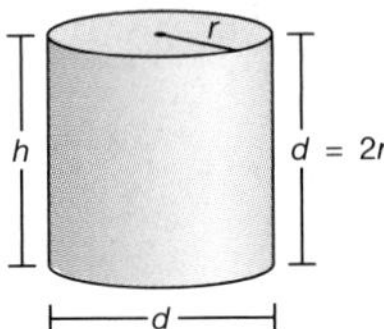

Recall that we can calculate the volume of a cylinder by multiplying the area of its circular base times its height.

$$\text{Volume of cylinder} = \text{area of circle} \cdot \text{height}$$

$$V = \pi r^2 \cdot h$$

For a cylinder whose height is equal to its diameter, we can replace h in the formula with d or with $2r$, since two radii equal the diameter.

$V = \pi r^2 \cdot h$	formula for volume of a cylinder
$V = \pi r^2 \cdot 2r$	replaced h with $2r$, which equals the height of the cylinder
$V = 2\pi r^3$	rearranged factors

This formula, $V = 2\pi r^3$, gives the volume of a cylinder whose height is equal to its diameter. The volume of a sphere is $\frac{2}{3}$ of the volume of a cylinder with the same diameter and height.

$$\text{Volume of sphere} = \frac{2}{3} \cdot \text{volume of cylinder}$$

$$= \frac{2}{3} \cdot 2\pi r^3 \quad \text{substituted}$$

$$= \frac{4}{3}\pi r^3 \quad \text{multiplied } \tfrac{2}{3} \text{ by 2}$$

We have found the formula for the volume of a sphere.

Volume of a sphere = $\frac{4}{3}\pi r^3$

Example 3

A ball with a diameter of 20 cm has a volume of how many cubic centimeters? (Round the answer to the nearest hundred cubic centimeters.)

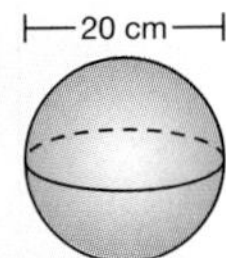

Use 3.14 for π.

Solution

The diameter of the sphere is 20 cm, so its radius is 10 cm. We use the formula for the volume of a sphere, substituting 3.14 for π and 10 cm for r.

$V = \frac{4}{3}\pi r^3$ formula

$\approx \frac{4}{3}(3.14)(10\text{ cm})^3$ substituted 3.14 for π and 10 cm for r

$\approx \frac{4}{3}(3.14)(1000\text{ cm}^3)$ cubed 10 cm

$\approx \frac{4}{3}(3140\text{ cm}^3)$ multiplied 3.14 by 1000 cm^3

$\approx 4186\frac{2}{3}\text{ cm}^3$ multiplied $\frac{4}{3}$ by 3140 cm^3

$\approx$ **4200 cm^3** rounded to nearest hundred cubic centimeters

Practice Set Pictured are two identical cylinders whose heights are equal to their diameters. In one cylinder is the largest cone it can contain. In the other cylinder is the largest sphere it can contain. Packing material is used to fill all the voids in the cylinders not occupied by the cone or sphere. Use this information to answer problems **a–e.**

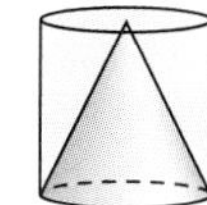

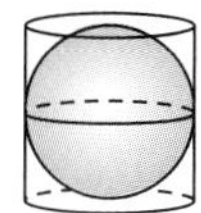

▶ **a.** What fraction of the cylinder containing the cone is occupied by the cone? $\frac{1}{3}$

▶ **b.** What fraction of the cylinder containing the cone is occupied by the packing material? $\frac{2}{3}$

▶ **c.** What fraction of the cylinder containing the sphere is occupied by the sphere? $\frac{2}{3}$

▶ **d.** What fraction of the cylinder containing the sphere is occupied by the packing material? $\frac{1}{3}$

▶ **e.** *Conclude* If the cone and sphere were removed from their boxes and all the packing material from both boxes was put into one box, what portion of the box would be filled with packing material? All of the box would be filled. $(\frac{1}{3} + \frac{2}{3} = 1)$

f. A pyramid with a height of 12 inches and a base 12 inches square is packed in the smallest cubical box that can contain it. What is the volume of the box? What is the volume of the pyramid? 1728 in.^{3}; 576 in.^{3}

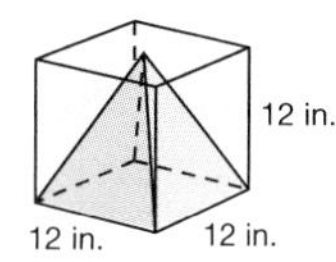

▶ *Analyze* Find the volume of each figure below. For both calculations, leave π as π.

g. 6 in. 18π in.^{3}

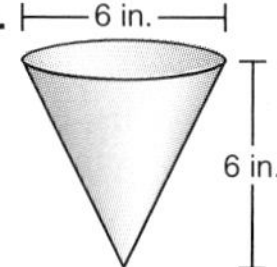

6 in.

h. 6 in. 36π in.^{3}

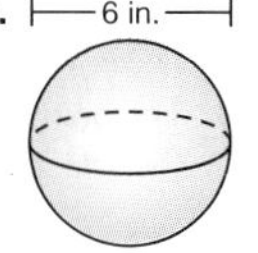

▶ See Math Conversations sidebar.

2 New Concepts *(Continued)*

Practice Set

Problems a–e

Extend the Problem

You may assign a value for the height and diameter of the cylinders. Have students calculate the volumes of the cylinder, cone, and sphere, and use these volumes to answer these questions.

Problem e Conclude

Ask students to explain the reasons for their answers. Sample: $\frac{2}{3}$ of the box holding the cone is filled with packing material and $\frac{1}{3}$ of the box holding the sphere is filled with packing material, so when they are both put in an empty box they will fill it.

Problems g and h Analyze

Have students describe how they found the volume of these figures. Ask whether they used a specific formula or found a fraction of the volume of the cylinder that would contain the figures.

English Learners

Explain the meaning of **voids.** Say:

"If an area is void, it means it doesn't have anything in it. It is empty. Voids are empty spaces or holes in something."

Ask students to give an example of an object with voids in it. Sample: swiss cheese

3 Written Practice

Math Conversations

Discussion opportunities are provided below.

Problem 1 Generalize

Have students explain why the two discounts can't be added and then applied once to the original price. Sample: That can't be done because the amount taken off would be greater than what it should be. You can have three successive 50% discounts, but if you added them, you can't have a 150% discount.

Problem 8

Extend the Problem

Ask students to resolve the problem using a ratio box. Then ask volunteers to show their work at the board. Sample:

	Actual	Percent
Part	\$1.50	W_P
Total	\$30	100

$$\$30 \times W_P = 100 \times \$1.50$$
$$W_P = \frac{100 \times \$1.50}{\$30} = 5\%$$

Problem 10 Generalize

Have students examine the difference between the interest earned with compound interest and what it would be with simple interest. First ask how they would calculate the simple interest earned in 3 years. Then have them find the difference. Ask why the compound interest is greater. Sample: The simple interest is \$200 a year, so for three years, it is \$600. The difference is \$24.32. Compound interest is greater because the interest earns interest.

Errors and Misconceptions

Problem 9

Students who give an answer of $1\frac{1}{4}$ found fifty percent of $2\frac{1}{2}$ instead of finding the number that $2\frac{1}{2}$ is 50% of. Have these students reread the problem and help them write the needed equation: $50\% \times W_N = 2\frac{1}{2}$ and then suggest that they change 50% to $\frac{1}{2}$.

Problem 12

If students say that the model will be 456 feet tall, they have reversed the ratio. Point out that the model should be smaller than the statue, which is 19 feet tall.

(continued)

Written Practice *Strengthening Concepts*

▶ * **1.** (110) Generalize Find the sale price of a \$24 item after successive discounts of 25% and 25%. \$13.50

2. (51) Ten billion is how much greater than nine hundred eighty million? Write the answer in scientific notation. 9.02×10^9

3. (Inv. 4) The median of the following numbers is how much less than the mean? 0.94

1.4, 0.5, 0.6, 0.75, 5.2

4. (46) Nelda worked 5 hours and earned \$34. Christy worked 6 hours and earned \$45.

a. How much did Nelda earn per hour? \$6.80 per hour

b. How much did Christy earn per hour? \$7.50 per hour

c. Christy earned how much more per hour than Nelda? \$0.70 more per hour

5. (72) Use a ratio box to solve this problem. If 24 kilograms of seed costs \$31, what is the cost of 42 kilograms of seed? \$54.25

6. (60) A kilometer is about $\frac{5}{8}$ of a mile. A mile is 1760 yards. A kilometer is about how many yards? about 1100 yards

7. (94) **a.** A card is drawn from a deck of 52 playing cards and replaced. Then another card is drawn. What is the probability of drawing a heart both times? $\frac{1}{16}$

b. What is the probability of drawing two hearts if the first card is not replaced? $\frac{1}{17}$

Write equations to solve problems **8** and **9.**

▶ **8.** (77) What percent of \$30 is \$1.50? $W_P \times \$30 = \$1.50$; 5%

▶ **9.** (77) Fifty percent of what number is $2\frac{1}{2}$? $\frac{1}{2} \times W_N = 2\frac{1}{2}$; 5

▶* **10.** (110) Generalize Mr. Rodrigo put \$5000 he had saved from his salary in an account that paid 4 percent interest compounded annually. How much interest was earned in 3 years? \$624.32

Use ratio boxes to solve problems **11** and **12.**

11. (92) A merchant sold an item at a 20 percent discount from the regular price. If the regular price was \$12, what was the sale price of the item? \$9.60

▶ **12.** (98) After visiting the Abraham Lincoln Memorial in Washington D.C., Jessica decided to sculpt a replica of Lincoln in his chair. The statue is 19 feet tall, and Jessica will sculpt it at $\frac{1}{24}$ of its actual height. How many inches tall will her version be? 9.5 inches tall

13. (37, 62) The points (0, 4), (−3, 2), and (3, 2) are the vertices of an isosceles triangle. Find the area of the triangle. 6 units^2

▶ See Math Conversations sidebar.

* **14.** Use the Pythagorean theorem to find the length of one of the two congruent sides of the triangle in problem 13. (*Hint:* First draw an altitude to form two right triangles.) $\sqrt{13}$ units
(112)

▸* **15.** **Estimate** Roughly estimate the volume of a tennis ball in cubic centimeters by using 6 cm for the diameter and 3 for π. Round the answer to the nearest ten cubic centimeters. 110 cm^3
(113)

16. Multiply. Write the product in scientific notation. 4.41×10^4
(83)

$$(6.3 \times 10^6)(7 \times 10^{-3})$$

▸* **17.** **Analyze** Tim can get from point *A* to point *B* by staying on the sidewalk and turning left at the corner *C*, or he can take the shortcut and walk straight from point *A* to point *B*. How many yards can Tim save by taking the shortcut? Begin by using the Pythagorean theorem to find the length of the shortcut. 20 yards
(112)

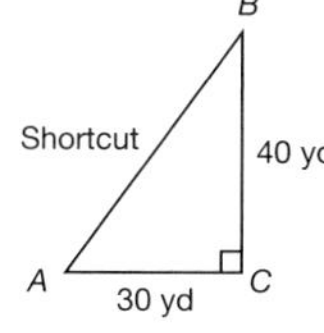

* **18.** **a.** Solve for *h*: $A = \frac{1}{2}bh$ $\quad h = \frac{2A}{b}$
(108)

▸ **b.** **Analyze** Use the formula $A = \frac{1}{2}bh$ to find *h* when $A = 16$ and $b = 8$. 4

19. $y = -2x + 1$

▸* **19.** **Evaluate** Make a table that shows three pairs of numbers for the function $y = -2x + 1$. Then graph the number pairs on a coordinate plane, and draw a line through the points to show other number pairs that satisfy the function. What is the slope of the graphed line? See student work; -2
(Inv. 9, 107)

* **20.** Find the volume of the pyramid shown. Dimensions are in meters. 16,000 m^3
(113)

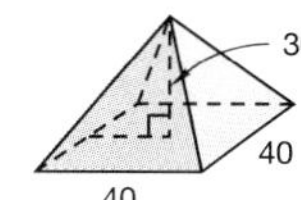

▸* **21.** Find the volume of the cone at right. Dimensions are in centimeters. 6280 cm^3
(113)

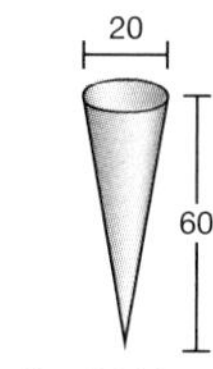

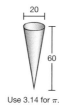

Use 3.14 for π.

▸ See Math Conversations in the sidebar.

3 Written Practice (Continued)

Math Conversations

Discussion opportunities are provided below.

Problem 15 Estimate

Ask how the volume changes when the radius is doubled. It increases by a factor of 8, or 8 times.

Problem 17 Analyze

Have students tell how they examined the information in the problem and how this led to the way they solved the problem. After two or three descriptions, ask:

"How many of you recognized that you could use a Pythagorean triplet to solve this problem? What helped you to recognize the triplet?" Sample: I saw that the two legs were 30 and 40, and they are 3×10 and 4×10, so I knew that the hypotenuse would be 5×10.

Problem 18b Analyze

"Suppose that A = 16 and b = 4. What is h?" 8

"How are b and h related when A remains the same?" Sample: They are inversely proportional to each other.

Problem 19 Evaluate

Have students compare the equation and the slope of the graph. Ask what they notice about them. Sample: The coefficient of *x* is the same as the slope.

Errors and Misconceptions

Problem 21

For students who get answers that are too large, such as 62,800 cm^3, have them check the arithmetic. They most likely did not correctly multiply the value for π by 100.

(continued)

3 Written Practice (Continued)

Math Conversations

Discussion opportunities are provided below.

Problem 22 Evaluate

Have students name the corresponding angles in both triangles and tell why they are corresponding angles. Sample: angle A corresponds to angle C because they are both 30°.

Problem 30 Generalize

"If a cube-shaped box was made that would exactly hold the Great Pyramid, about what would its volume be? Explain your reasoning." Sample: It would be about 270 million cubic feet because it would be 3 times the volume of the Great Pyramid.

Errors and Misconceptions

Problem 25

Students who do not get a correct answer may have had trouble simplifying the expressions contained within the parentheses and brackets. Have them simplify one part at a time, and write each step on a separate line.

▸* **22.** (40) **Evaluate** Refer to the figure below to find the measures of the following angles. Dimensions are in centimeters.

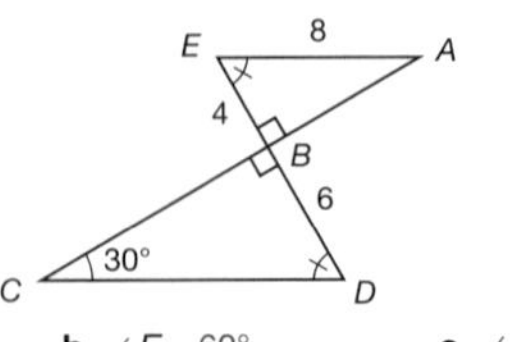

a. $\angle D$ 60° **b.** $\angle E$ 60° **c.** $\angle A$ 30°

23. (97) In the figure in problem **22,** what is the length of $\overline{CD}$? 12 cm

Solve:

24. (98) $\frac{7.5}{d} = \frac{25}{16}$ 4.8

▸ **25.** (93) $1\frac{3}{5}w + 17 = 49$ 20

Simplify:

26. (63) $5^2 - \{4^2 - [3^2 - (2^2 - 1^2)]\}$ 15

27. (30) $1\frac{3}{4} + 2\frac{2}{3} - 3\frac{5}{6}$ $\frac{7}{12}$

28. (26) $\left(1\frac{3}{4}\right)\left(2\frac{2}{3}\right) \div 3\frac{5}{6}$ $1\frac{5}{23}$

29. (85) $(-7) + |-3| - (2)(-3) + (-4) - (-3)(-2)(-1)$ 4

▸* **30.** **Generalize** The Great Pyramid of Khufu in Egypt, is a giant pyramid with a square base. The length of each side of the square base is about 750 feet and its height is about 480 feet. About what is the volume of the Great Pyramid of Khufu? 90,000,000 ft^3

Early Finishers
Math Applications

Use grid paper to sketch three-dimensional figures that would match all three views shown below. See student work.

a. TOP FRONT SIDE

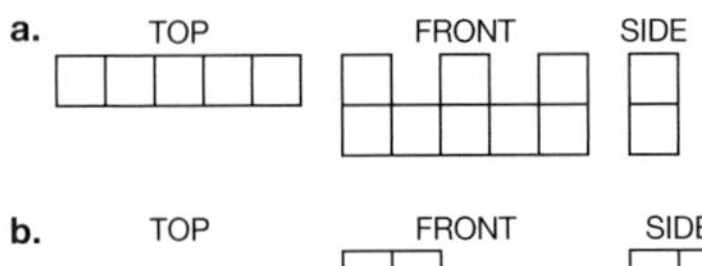

b. TOP FRONT SIDE

▸ See Math Conversations sidebar.

Looking Forward

Understanding volume of pyramids, cones, and spheres prepares students for:

- **Lesson 114,** using volume, capacity, and mass in the metric system.

• Volume, Capacity, and Mass in the Metric System

Objective

- Use the relationships among the units of volume, capacity, and mass in the metric system to solve problems.

Lesson Preparation

Materials

- **Power Up W** (in *Instructional Masters*)

Optional

- **Teacher-provided material: Two 1-liter bottles (1 filled with water)**

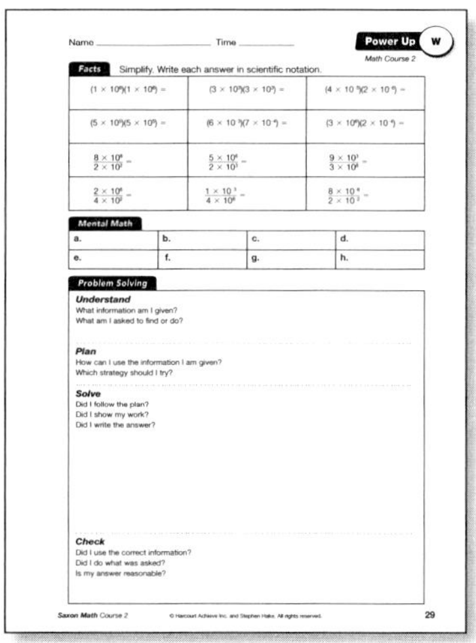
Name ______ Time ______ **Power Up W**

Math Course 2

Facts Simplify. Write each answer in scientific notation.

Mental Math

a.	b.	c.	d.
e.	f.	g.	h.

Problem Solving

Understand
What information am I given?
What am I asked to find or do?

Plan
How can I use the information I am given?
Which strategy should I try?

Solve
Did I follow the plan?
Did I show my work?
Did I write the answer?

Check
Did I use the correct information?
Did I do what was asked?
Is my answer reasonable?

Saxon Math Course 2 29

Power Up W

Technology Resources

Student eBook Complete student textbook in electronic format.

Resources and Planner CD Assessment, reteaching, and instructional masters, plus a pacing calendar with standards.

Test and Practice Generator CD Create additional practice sheets and custom-made tests.

www.SaxonPublishers.com Visit for more student activities and planning materials.

Inclusion

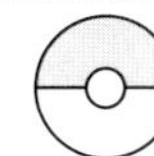

Adaptations CD Adapted lessons, investigations, practice and assessments.

Meeting Standards

National Council of Teachers of Mathematics (NCTM)

Measurement

ME.1a Understand both metric and customary systems of measurement

ME.1b Understand relationships among units and convert from one unit to another within the same system

ME.1c Understand, select, and use units of appropriate size and type to measure angles, perimeter, area, surface area, and volume

Connections

CN.4c Recognize and apply mathematics in contexts outside of mathematics

Power-Up Discussion *For use with Power Up, p. 799*

Problem-Solving Strategy: Write an Equation/ Guess and Check

There are three types of balls, each a different size and color, placed against a 7-foot long wall. They are orange, red, and green with surface areas of 201 in.^{2}, 314 in.^{2}, and 706.5 in.^{2}, respectively. If they take up the full length of the wall with no space left over, how many balls of each color are there?

Understand ***Understand the problem.***

"What information are we given?"

We are given the surface area of each type of ball and the length of space that all of the balls take up.

"What are we asked to do?"

We are asked to find how many of each type of ball there is.

Plan ***Make a plan.***

"What problem-solving strategy will we use?"

We will *write an equation* and use our answers to help us *guess and check* until we find the correct answers.

Solve ***Carry out the plan.***

"How can we find the length of space that each ball takes up?"

We can use the surface area to find the diameter.

$$SA = 4\pi r^2 \quad \frac{SA}{4\pi} = r^2 \quad \sqrt{\frac{SA}{4\pi}} = r \quad d = 2r = 2\sqrt{\frac{SA}{4\pi}}$$

$$d_O = 2\sqrt{\frac{201}{4\pi}} = 2\sqrt{16} = 8 \text{ in.}$$

$$d_R = 2\sqrt{\frac{314}{4\pi}} = 2\sqrt{25} = 10 \text{ in.}$$

$$d_G = 2\sqrt{\frac{706.5}{4\pi}} = 2\sqrt{56.25} = 15 \text{ in.}$$

"What is the greatest number of green balls we can have?"

There is at least one ball of each color, so we can subtract the diameters of the orange and red balls from the length of the wall in inches to find the most space that green balls can take up: 84 in. − 10 in. − 8 in. = 66 in.
Since 66 in. ÷ 15 in. = 4 R6, so there can be at most 4 green balls.

"If there are 4 green balls, how much space is left for orange and red balls?"

84 − (4 × 15) = 24 in.

"Does any combination of 8- and 10-inch balls equal 24 inches?" no

"If there are 3 green balls, how much space is left for orange and red balls?"

84 − (3 × 15) = 39 in.

"Does any combination of 8- and 10-inch balls equal 39 inches?" no

"If there are 2 green balls, how much space is left for orange and red balls?"

84 − (2 × 15) = 54 in.

"Does any combination of 8- and 10-inch balls equal 54 inches?"

yes, (3 × 8) + (3 × 10) = 54

"If there is 1 green ball, how much space is left for orange and red balls?"

84 − 15 = 69 in.

"Does any combination of 8- and 10-inch balls equal 69 inches?" no

"How many balls of each size are there?"

2 15-inch balls + 3 8-inch balls + 3 10-inch balls = 84 inches

Check ***Look back.***

"Did we find the answer to the question that was asked?"

Yes. There are 2 green balls, 3 red balls, and 3 orange balls.

LESSON

114

• Volume, Capacity, and Mass in the Metric System

Power Up

Building Power

facts

Power Up W

mental math

a. **Positive/Negative:** $(-3)^3 + (-3)^2$ -18

b. **Scientific Notation:** $(4 \times 10^8)^2$ 1.6×10^{17}

c. **Algebra:** $10m - m = 9^2$ 9

d. **Measurement:** Convert 60°C to degrees Fahrenheit. 140°F

e. **Percent:** 150% of \$3000 \$4500

f. **Percent:** 150% more than \$3000 \$7500

g. **Geometry:** Which figure has unlimited lines of symmetry? circle

h. **Calculation:** Find 25% of 40, − 1, × 5, − 1, ÷ 2, − 1, ÷ 3, × 10, + 2, ÷ 9, ÷ 2, $\sqrt{\ }$. 2

problem solving

There are three types of balls, each a different size and color, placed against a 7-foot long wall. They are orange, red, and green with surface areas of 201 in.^{2}, 314 in.^{2}, and 706.5 in.^{2}, respectively. If they take up the full length of the wall with no space left over, how many balls of each color are there? 2 green balls, 3 red balls, and 3 orange balls

New Concept

Increasing Knowledge

Thinking Skill

Summarize

What is the difference between volume, capacity, and mass? Volume is the amount of space an object occupies. Capacity is the amount of liquid a container can hold. Mass is the amount of matter in an object.

Units of volume, capacity, and mass are closely related in the metric system. The relationships between these units are based on the physical characteristics of water under certain standard conditions. We state two commonly used relationships.

One milliliter of water has a volume of 1 cubic centimeter and a mass of 1 gram.

One cubic centimeter can contain 1 milliliter of water, which has a mass of 1 gram.

One liter of water has a volume of 1000 cubic centimeters and a mass of 1 kilogram.

Lesson 114 799

Facts Simplify. Write each answer in scientific notation.

$(1 \times 10^6)(1 \times 10^6) =$ 1×10^{12}	$(3 \times 10^3)(3 \times 10^3) =$ 9×10^6	$(4 \times 10^{-5})(2 \times 10^{-6}) =$ 8×10^{-11}
$(5 \times 10^5)(5 \times 10^5) =$ 2.5×10^{11}	$(6 \times 10^{-3})(7 \times 10^{-4}) =$ 4.2×10^{-6}	$(3 \times 10^6)(2 \times 10^{-4}) =$ 6×10^2
$\frac{8 \times 10^8}{2 \times 10^2} = 4 \times 10^6$	$\frac{5 \times 10^6}{2 \times 10^3} = 2.5 \times 10^3$	$\frac{9 \times 10^3}{3 \times 10^8} = 3 \times 10^{-5}$
$\frac{2 \times 10^6}{4 \times 10^2} = 5 \times 10^3$	$\frac{1 \times 10^{-3}}{4 \times 10^8} = 2.5 \times 10^{-12}$	$\frac{8 \times 10^{-8}}{2 \times 10^{-2}} = 4 \times 10^{-6}$

1 Power Up

Facts

Distribute **Power Up W** to students. See answers below.

Mental Math

Encourage students to share different ways to mentally compute these exercises. Strategies for exercises **e** and **f** are listed below.

e. Multiply by a Fraction

$150\% = \frac{3}{2}$

$\frac{3}{2} \times \$3000 = 3 \times \$1500 = \$4500$

Use Logical Reasoning

100% of \$3000 is \$3000

50% of \$3000 is \$1500

150% of \$3000 is \$4500

f. Use the Previous Answer

150% of \$3000 is \$4500

\$3000 + 150% of \$3000 =

\$3000 + \$4500 = \$7500

Use an Equivalent Expression

150% more than \$3000 is 250% of \$3000

$250\% = \frac{5}{2}$

$\frac{5}{2} \times \$3000 = 5 \times \$1500 = \$7500$

Problem Solving

Refer to **Power-Up Discussion,** p. 799B.

2 New Concepts

Instruction

Show students a full 1-liter bottle of water and ask what the volume of the water in the bottle is. Explain that the volume of the liquid is the same as the capacity of the bottle. Review the differences of volume, capacity, and mass.

- *Volume* is the amount of space matter occupies and is measured in units such as cubic centimeters.
- *Capacity* is the amount of matter that a container can hold and is measured in units such as milliliters.
- *Mass* is the amount of matter in an object and is measured in units such as grams.

To demonstrate the relationships between these units for water at certain standard conditions, draw this chart on the board:

Capacity	Volume	Mass
1 mL	1 cm^3	1 g
1 L	1000 cm^3	1 kg

(continued)

2 New Concepts (Continued)

Instruction

Students should easily distinguish between mass and the other two measures. Spend enough time on these examples so that students can distinguish between volume and capacity.

Example 1

Instruction

As you work through the solution, you may demonstrate why both 30,000 cm³ and 30,000 milliliters are equal to 30 liters by using unit multipliers.

$$30{,}000 \text{ cm}^3 \times \frac{1 \text{ L}}{1000 \text{ cm}^3} = 30 \text{ L}$$

$$30{,}000 \text{ mL} \times \frac{1 \text{ L}}{1000 \text{ mL}} = 30 \text{ L}$$

To help students understand the difference between mass and weight, you can explain that a 1-kilogram mass weighs about 2.2 pounds on Earth due to the force of gravity, but that on the Moon, the same mass would weigh about one-sixth of its weight on Earth, or about 0.37 pounds.

Example 2

Instruction

Mention to students that the method used by Malaika in this example for measuring the capacity of the vase is commonly used to find the capacity (or volume) of irregularly shaped objects.

(continued)

One thousand cubic centimeters can contain 1 liter of water, which has a mass of 1 kilogram.

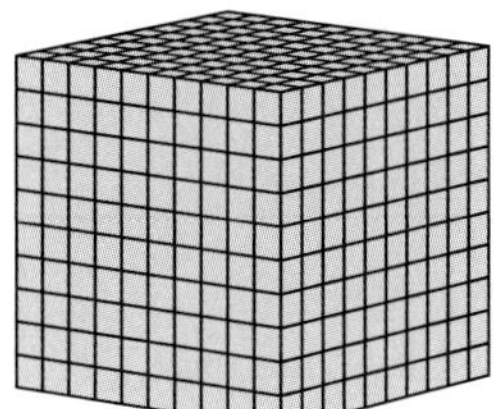

Explain How many cubic centimeters can a 2.5 liter container of water hold? Explain how you determined your answer.

2500 cubic centimeters; Sample: Since 1000 cubic centimeters can hold 1 liter of water, multiply 1000 by 2.5 to find how many cubic centimeters a 2.5 liter container can hold.

Example 1

Ray has a fish aquarium that is 50 cm long and 20 cm wide. If the aquarium is filled with water to a depth of 30 cm,

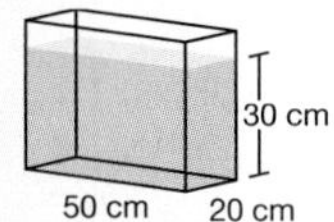

a. how many liters of water would be in the aquarium?

b. what would be the mass of the water in the aquarium?

Solution

First we find the volume of the water in the aquarium.

$$(50 \text{ cm})(20 \text{ cm})(30 \text{ cm}) = 30{,}000 \text{ cm}^3$$

a. Each cubic centimeter of water is 1 milliliter. Thirty thousand milliliters is **30 liters.**

b. Each liter of water has a mass of 1 kilogram, so the mass of the water in the aquarium is **30 kilograms.** (Since a 1-kilogram mass weighs about 2.2 pounds on Earth, the water in the aquarium weighs about 66 pounds.)

Conclude Ray put an aquarium rock in the tank. The water level increased from 30 cm to 30.2 cm. What is the volume of the rock?
$50 \times 20 \times 0.2 = 200 \text{ cm}^3$

Example 2

Malaika wanted to find the volume of a vase. She filled a 1-liter beaker with water and then used all but 240 milliliters to fill the vase.

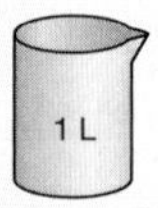

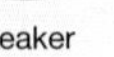

beaker vase

a. What is the volume of the vase?

b. If the mass of the vase is 640 grams, what is the mass of the vase filled with water?

Math Background

How does the metric system relate capacity, volume, and mass?

In the metric system 1 cubic centimeter (cm³), a measure of volume, is equivalent to 1 milliliter (mL), a measure of fluid volume or capacity. For example, a container with a volume of 1 cm³ will hold 1 mL of water.

In the metric system mass is related to the volume of water, under certain standard conditions of temperature and pressure, and so also to capacity, because the metric system defines 1 gram (g) as equal to 1 cm³ (or 1 mL) of water at the temperature of its maximum density. So, for water under certain conditions, 1 mL = 1 cm³ = 1 g.

Solution

a. The 1-liter beaker contains 1000 mL of water. Since Malaika used 760 mL, (1000 mL − 240 mL), the volume of the inside of the vase is **760 cm^3.**

b. The mass of the water (760 g) plus the mass of the vase (640 g) is **1400 g.**

Practice Set

a. What is the mass of 2 liters of water? 2 kg or 2000 g

b. What is the volume of 3 liters of water? 3000 cm^3

▸ **c.** *Analyze* When the bottle was filled with water, the mass increased by 1 kilogram. How many milliliters of water were added? 1000 milliliters

▸ **d.** *Analyze* A tank that is 25 cm long, 10 cm wide, and 8 cm deep can hold how many liters of water? 2 liters

Written Practice

Strengthening Concepts

1. (46, 92) The regular price of a bowling ball was \$72.50, but it was on sale for 20% off. What was the total sale price including 7% sales tax? Use a ratio box to find the sale price. Then find the sales tax and total price. \$62.06

2. (55) A zoologist tagged 4 tortoises in a conservation area. The average weight of the 4 tortoises was 87 pounds. The zoologist then tagged 2 more tortoises. The average weight of all 6 tortoises was 90 pounds. What was the average weight of the last 2 tortoises? 96 pounds

3. (Inv. 8) There are 27 marbles in a bag: 6 red, 9 green, and 12 blue. If one marble is drawn from the bag,

a. what is the probability that the marble will be blue? $\frac{4}{9}$

b. what is the chance that the marble will be green? $33\frac{1}{3}\%$

c. what are the odds that the marble will not be red? 7 to 2

Math Language
The **odds** of an event occurring is the ratio of the favorable outcomes to unfavorable outcomes.

▸ **4.** (46) If a box of 12 dozen pencils costs \$10.80, what is the cost per pencil? $7\frac{1}{2}$¢ per pencil

▸ *** 5.** (110) *Generalize* How much interest is earned in 6 months on \$5000 at 8% annual simple interest? \$200

6. (Inv. 5) One fourth of the students on a bus were listening to music. One third of the students were talking. The rest were reading.

a. Draw a circle graph that displays this information.

b. If six students were listening to music, how many students were reading? 10 students

6. a. Class Test Scores

R L T

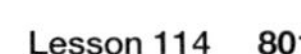

▸ See Math Conversations in the sidebar.

Teacher Tip

For this lesson you may want to provide a **hands-on experience** with capacity, volume, and mass. Prepare a one-liter container filled with water. Show it to the class and explain that the container holds 1000 cm^3 of water and that, under certain conditions, the water has a mass of 1000 grams.

Pass the container around so students can hold the container and see the volume, or space, that the water takes up. To give them a sense of the mass of the water, have the students compare the full container and an identical empty container.

2 New Concepts *(Continued)*

Practice Set

Problem c *Analyze*

Ask students how the mass of the water added to the bottle tells us what the capacity of the bottle is. Sample: The bottle was filled and a kilogram of water is 1000 mL or 1 liter of water, so the capacity of the bottle is 1 liter.

Problem d *Analyze*

Ask how the volume of the tank is related to its capacity. Sample: The volume is 2000 cm^3, so it can hold 2000 mL of water. Volume is the space enclosed, capacity is how much you can put in the space.

Problem d *Error Alert*

Watch for students who do not see that first they need to multiply the dimensions to find the volume of the tank and then they need to use the unit multiplier $\frac{1 \text{ L}}{1000 \text{ cm}^3}$ to find the capacity of the tank in liters.

3 Written Practice

Math Conversations

Discussion opportunities are provided below.

Problem 5 *Generalize*

"How do you calculate simple interest for periods of time less than a year?" Sample: You make a fraction of the period of a time and a year. This is easier if it is months, and not days. Then you multiply the simple interest for a year by the fraction.

"Are simple interest and compound interest the same for the first year?" Sample: Maybe. If the interest is compounded annually, they are. If it is compounded more often, such as weekly or monthly, then they are not.

Errors and Misconceptions

Problem 4

Students whose answer is 90¢ per pencil did not notice the word *dozen* or they did not multiply 12 by 12 to get the number of pencils in 12 dozen. Have these students reread the problem and do the calculation again.

(continued)

3 Written Practice (Continued)

Math Conversations

Discussion opportunities are provided below.

Problem 8 Estimate

Point out that the formula has to be used to find the answer. Then ask why the answer is an estimate. Sample: It is an estimate because we don't know the exact diameter of the snowball and we are using a rough approximation of π.

Problem 11 Analyze

See whether students agree that it seems as if there are two fairly simple questions to answer for this problem. Then ask them to list all the mathematics they need to answer the questions. Samples: plotting points on a coordinate grid, finding lengths on a grid, knowing Pythagorean triplets, knowing the formula for the area of a trapezoid, computing with fractions, knowing how to add and multiply

Problem 14 Generalize

"What do you notice about the two fractions?" Sample: They are reciprocals.

"What do you notice about the two answers?" Sample: It is not as easy to see but they are reciprocals.

If students do not believe that the answers are reciprocals, multiply them to show the answer is 1 and the expressions are reciprocals. $2.5 \times 10^{-3} \times 4 \times 10^{2} = 2.5 \times 4 \times 10^{-3} \times 10^{2} = 10 \times 10^{-1} = 1$

Problem 17a Analyze

Have students solve the equation for π. Then ask how this formula relates to the meaning of π. Sample: $\pi = \frac{C}{d}$; π is the ratio of the circumference of a circle to its diameter.

Errors and Misconceptions

Problem 19

For students who give 36.84 cm as the answer, check whether they used 6 cm as the radius or forgot to divide the circumference of the circle by 2. Then have them rewrite the problem, putting each step on a separate line and explaining what each step does.

(continued)

7. (66) The ratio of students who ride a bus to students who walk to school is 5 to 2. If there are 1400 students in the school, how many students ride a bus? 1000 students

▸ * **8.** (113) Estimate The snowball grew in size as it rolled down the hill. By the time it came to a stop, its diameter was about four feet. Using 3 for π, estimate the number of cubic feet of snow in the snowball. 32 ft^3

Write equations to solve problems **9** and **10.**

9. (60) What is 120% of \$240? $W_N = 1.2 \times \$240$; \$288

10. (77) Sixty is what percent of 150? $60 = W_P \times 150$; 40%

▸* **11.** (75, 99) Analyze The points (3, 2), (6, −2), (−2, −2), and (−2, 2) are the vertices of a trapezoid.

a. Find the area of the trapezoid. 26 units^2

b. Find the perimeter of the trapezoid. 22 units

12. (100) **a.** Arrange these numbers in order from least to greatest: $-6, 0.6, \sqrt{6}, 6^2$ $\sqrt{6}, 6^2, -6, 0.6$

b. Which of the numbers in **a** are rational numbers? Why? 6^2, −6, 0.6; They can be written as the ratio of two integers.

13. (48) Complete the table.

Fraction	Decimal	Percent
$1\frac{4}{5}$	**a.** 1.8	**b.** 180%

▸* **14.** (111) Generalize Divide. Write each quotient in scientific notation:

a. $\frac{5 \times 10^{-9}}{2 \times 10^{-6}}$ 2.5×10^{-3} **b.** $\frac{2 \times 10^{-6}}{5 \times 10^{-9}}$ 4×10^{2}

15. (83) What is the product of answers **a** and **b** in problem 14? 1

16. (88) Use unit multipliers to convert one square kilometer to square meters. 1,000,000 m^2

* **17.** (108) ▸**a.** Analyze Solve for *d:* $C = \pi d$ $d = \frac{C}{\pi}$

b. Use the formula $C = \pi d$ to find d when C is 62.8. (Use 3.14 for π.) 20

18. (94) With one toss of a pair of number cubes, what is the probability that the total rolled will be a prime number? (Add the probabilities for each prime-number total.) $\frac{15}{36} = \frac{5}{12}$

▸* **19.** (104) Find the perimeter of the figure at right. Dimensions are in centimeters. (Use 3.14 for π.) 27.42 cm

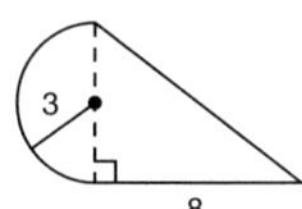

▸ See Math Conversations in the sidebar.

* **20.** (105, 113) **a.** Find the surface area of the cube shown. Dimensions are in feet. 54 ft^2

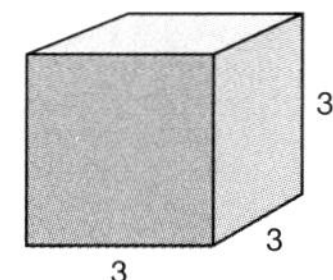

b. Analyze If the cube contains the largest pyramid it can hold, what is the volume of the pyramid? 9 ft^3

21. (95) Find the volume of this right circular cylinder. Dimensions are in meters. (Use 3.14 for π.) 235.5 m^3

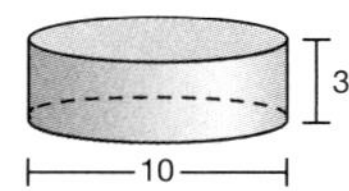

22. (40) Find the measures of the following angles:

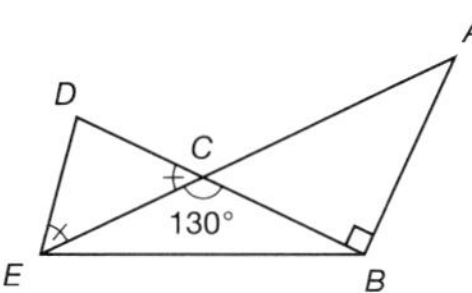

a. $\angle ACB$ 50° **b.** $\angle CAB$ 40° **c.** $\angle CDE$ 80°

23. (70) An aquarium that is 40 cm long, 10 cm wide, and 20 cm deep is filled with water. Find the volume of the water in the aquarium. 8000 cm^3

24. (93) Solve: $0.8m - 1.2 = 6$ 9

▶ **25.** (93) Model Solve this inequality and graph its solution: (See below.)

$$3(x - 4) < x - 8$$

Simplify:

26. (57) $4^2 \cdot 2^{-3} \cdot 2^{-1}$ 1

27. (32) 1 kilogram − 50 grams 950 grams

28. (43) $(1.2)\left(3\frac{3}{4}\right) \div 4\frac{1}{2}$ 1

29. (43) $2\frac{3}{4} - 1.5 - \frac{1}{6}$ $1\frac{1}{12}$

30. (85) $(-3)(-2) - (2)(-3) - (-8) + (-2)(-3) + |-5|$ 31

Early Finishers
Math Applications

Use graph paper to show Triangle ABC with these coordinates:

A (1, 4), B (4, 4) and C (1, 1).

a. Reflect Triangle ABC over the horizontal axis and label its image $A'B'C'$. What are the coordinates of $A'B'C'$? A' (1, −4), B' (4, −4), C' (1, −1)

b. Now reflect Triangle ABC over the vertical axis. What are the coordinates of the triangle formed? (−1, 4), (−4, 4), (−1, 1)

25.

$x < 2$

−2 −1 0 1 2 3

▶ See Math Conversations in the sidebar.

3 Written Practice (Continued)

Math Conversations

Discussion opportunities are provided below.

Problem 25 Model

Ask students why the empty circle is placed on the 2. Sample: 2 is not one of the values that is included in the inequality.

Errors and Misconceptions

Problem 25

Some students may solve and plot the inequality as $x < -2$. They probably neglected to multiply $(x - 4)$ by 3 and rewrote the inequality in the first step as $3x - 4 < x - 8$. Have them check and redo their work.

Lesson 114 803

• Factoring Algebraic Expressions

Objectives

- Factor a monomial.
- Factor a polynomial by finding the greatest common factor of the terms of the polynomial.

Lesson Preparation

Materials

- **Power Up V** (in *Instructional Masters*)
- **Teacher-provided material: graph paper,** 2 per student

Optional

- **Investigation Activity 13** (in *Instructional Masters*)

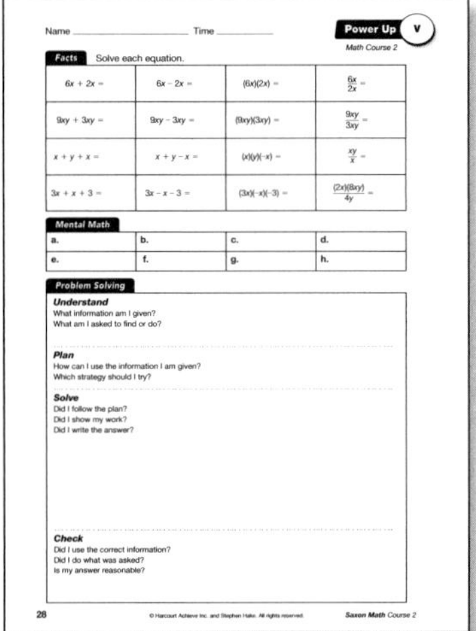

Name ________ Time ________ **Power Up V** *Math Course 2*

Facts Solve each equation.

$6x + 2x =$	$6x - 2x =$	$(6x)(2x) =$	$\frac{6x}{2x} =$
$9xy + 3xy =$	$9xy - 3xy =$	$(9xy)(3xy) =$	$\frac{9xy}{3xy} =$
$x + y + x =$	$x + y - x =$	$(x)(y)(-x) =$	$\frac{xy}{x} =$
$3x + x + 3 =$	$3x - x - 3 =$	$(3x)(-x)(-3) =$	$\frac{(2x)(8xy)}{4y} =$

Mental Math

a.	b.	c.	d.
e.	f.	g.	h.

Problem Solving

Understand
What information am I given?
What am I asked to find or do?

Plan
How can I use the information I am given?
Which strategy should I try?

Solve
Did I follow the plan?
Did I show my work?
Did I write the answer?

Check
Did I use the correct information?
Did I do what was asked?
Is my answer reasonable?

28 © Harcourt Achieve Inc. and Stephen Hake. All rights reserved. *Saxon Math* Course 2

Power Up V

Math Language

New	Maintain
monomial	polynomial

Technology Resources

Student eBook Complete student textbook in electronic format.

Resources and Planner Assessment, reteaching, and instructional masters, plus a pacing calendar with standards.

Test and Practice Generator CD Create additional practice sheets and custom-made tests.

www.SaxonPublishers.com Visit for more student activities and planning materials.

Inclusion

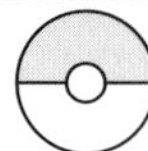

Adaptations CD Adapted lessons, investigations, practice and assessments.

Meeting Standards

National Council of Teachers of Mathematics (NCTM)

Numbers and Operations

NO.1f Use factors, multiples, prime factorization, and relatively prime numbers to solve problems

NO.2b Use the associative and commutative properties of addition and multiplication and the distributive property of multiplication over addition to simplify computations with integers, fractions, and decimals

Algebra

AL.2d Recognize and generate equivalent forms for simple algebraic expressions and solve linear equations

Power-Up Discussion *For use with Power Up, p. 804*

Problem-Solving Strategy: Guess and Check/ Work Backwards

In the following three problems, each letter represents the same missing digit in each of the problems. Work as a team to determine the digit each letter represents.

$$\begin{array}{r} \text{A B C D E F} \\ \times\ \text{B} \\ \hline 248{,}712 \end{array} \qquad \begin{array}{r} \text{B C G H A B} \\ \times\ \text{D} \\ \hline 746{,}136 \end{array} \qquad \begin{array}{r} \text{H C F A D F} \\ \times\ \text{C} \\ \hline 2{,}984{,}544 \end{array}$$

Understand ***Understand the problem.***

"What information are we given?"

We are shown three separate multiplication problems with missing digits. We are told that each letter represents the same missing digit in each of the three problems.

"What are we asked to do?"

We are asked to determine which letter (A, B, C, D, E, F, G, H) represents which of the digits 0–9. (Note that there are only eight letters, so two digits will not be used.)

Plan ***Make a plan.***

"What problem-solving strategies will we use?"

We will *guess and check* and *work backwards* to find the digits.

"How could we most efficiently guess and check?"

If we work as separate teams on each of the three problems simultaneously, we will be able to verify our conclusions against one another's and will complete the challenge more quickly.

Solve ***Carry out the plan.***

"What is indicated by each product that results from a 6-digit factor and a 1-digit factor?"

In the first problem, A × B must be 2, so A will be 1 and B will be 2.
In the second problem, B × D must be 7 or less. B can be 2 and D can be 3.
In the third problem, H × C must be 29 or less.

"What is the value of each letter?"

A = 1, B = 2, C = 4, D = 3, E = 5, F = 6, G = 8, and H = 7.

Check ***Look back.***

"Did we do what we were asked to do?"

Yes, we found which digit is represented by each letter.

"How can we verify our solution is correct?"

We can substitute the values we found back into the original equations to verify our findings.

1 Power Up

Facts

Distribute **Power Up V** to students. See answers below.

Mental Math

Encourage students to share different ways to mentally compute these exercises. Strategies for exercises **b** and **g** are listed below.

b. Multiply by the Reciprocal

$(4 \times 10^8) \div (4 \times 10^8) = 1$

$\frac{(4 \times 10^8) \times 1}{(4 \times 10^8)} = 1$

Use Logical Reasoning

The two expressions are the same. Anything divided by itself equals 1.

g. Compare to Primes

First few primes: 2, 3, 5, 7, 11, 13, 17, 19, 23

Only 19 is a prime, so 19 doesn't belong.

Use Elimination

12, 15, and 21 have factors other than themselves and 1, so they are composite. 19 has only 19 and 1 as factors, so it is prime and doesn't belong.

Problem Solving

Refer to **Power-Up Discussion,** p. 804B.

2 New Concepts

Instruction

Help students relate the prefixes *mono, bi-,* and *tri-* to the number of terms in a polynomial. Ask:

"What other words begin with mono-, bi-, or tri-?" Answers may include monopoly, monotone, bicycle, bicentennial, triangle, and tripod.

"Do the prefixes in these words mean the same as in monomial, binomial, and trinomial?" Yes; in each case, *mono-* means one, *bi-* means two, and *tri-* means three.

(continued)

LESSON 115

• Factoring Algebraic Expressions

Power Up *Building Power*

facts Power Up V

mental math

a. **Positive/Negative:** 10^{-2} $\frac{1}{100}$

b. **Scientific Notation:** $(4 \times 10^8) \div (4 \times 10^8)$ 1

c. **Ratio:** $\frac{1.44}{1.2} = \frac{1.2}{g}$ 1

d. **Measurement:** Convert 250 cm to m. 2.5 m

e. **Fractional Parts:** $\frac{2}{3}$ of \$1200 \$800

f. **Fractional Parts:** \$1200 reduced $\frac{1}{3}$ \$800

g. **Primes/Composites:** Which does not belong in the list 12, 15, 19, 21? 19

h. **Money:** A nickel is how many cents less than 3 dimes and 3 quarters? 100¢

problem solving

In the following three problems, each letter represents the same missing digit in each of the problems. Work as a team to determine the digit each letter represents.

ABCDEF	BCGHAB	HCFADF
× B	× D	× C
248,712	746,136	2,984,544

A = 1, B = 2, C = 4, D = 3, E = 5, F = 6, G = 8, and H = 7

New Concept *Increasing Knowledge*

Algebraic expressions are classified as either **monomials** or **polynomials.** Monomials are single-term expressions such as the following three examples:

$$6x^2y^3 \qquad \frac{5xy}{2w} \qquad -6$$

Polynomials are composed of two or more terms. All of the following algebraic expressions are polynomials:

$$3x^2y + 6xy^2 \qquad x^2 + 2x + 1 \qquad 3a + 4b + 5c + d$$

Polynomials may be further classified by the number of terms they contain. For example, expressions with two terms are called binomials, and expressions with three terms are called trinomials. So $3x^2y + 6xy^2$ is a binomial, and $x^2 + 2x + 1$ is a trinomial.

Facts Solve each equation.

$6x + 2x = 8x$	$6x - 2x = 4x$	$(6x)(2x) = 12x^2$	$\frac{6x}{2x} = 3$
$9xy + 3xy = 12xy$	$9xy - 3xy = 6xy$	$(9xy)(3xy) = 27x^2y^2$	$\frac{9xy}{3xy} = 3$
$x + y + x = 2x + y$	$x + y - x = y$	$(x)(y)(-x) = -x^2y$	$\frac{xy}{x} = y$
$3x + x + 3 = 4x + 3$	$3x - x - 3 = 2x - 3$	$(3x)(-x)(-3) = 9x^2$	$\frac{(2x)(8xy)}{4y} = 4x^2$

Recall that to factor a monomial, we express the numerical part of the term as a product of prime factors, and we express the literal (letter) part of the term as a product of factors (instead of using exponents). Here we factor $6x^2y^3$:

$$6x^2y^3 \quad \text{original form}$$

$$(2)(3)xxyyy \quad \text{factored form}$$

Thinking Skill

Analyze

Some polynomials have a GCF of 1. What is the only factor common to all terms in $6a^2 + 4b^2 + 3ab$? 1

Some polynomials can also be factored. To factor a polynomial we first find the greatest common factor (GCF) of the terms of the polynomial. Then we use the Distributive Property to write the expression as a product of the GCF and the remaining polynomial.

To factor $3x^2y + 6xy^2$, we first find the GCF of $3x^2y$ and $6xy^2$. With practice we may find the GCF visually. This time we will factor both terms and circle the common factors.

$$3x^2y \quad + \quad 6xy^2$$

$$\textcircled{3} \cdot \textcircled{x} \cdot x \cdot \textcircled{y} + 2 \cdot \textcircled{3} \cdot \textcircled{x} \cdot y \cdot \textcircled{y}$$

We find that the GCF of $3x^2y$ and $6xy^2$ is $3xy$. Notice that removing $3xy$ from $3x^2y$ by division leaves x. Removing $3xy$ from $6xy^2$ by division leaves $2y$.

$$\frac{3x^2y}{3xy} + \frac{6xy^2}{3xy} \quad 3xy \text{ removed by division}$$

$$x + 2y \quad \text{remaining binomial}$$

We write the factored form of $3x^2y + 6xy^2$ this way:

$$3xy(x + 2y) \quad \text{factored form}$$

Notice that we began with a binomial and ended with the GCF of its terms times a binomial.

Conclude What property can you use to mentally check that you have factored correctly? Distributive Property

Discuss What might indicate that you have not found the greatest common factor?

Sample: If every term within the parentheses contains the same variable, then that variable is another common factor and should be included in the GCF.

Example 1

Factor the monomial $12a^2b^3c$.

Solution

We factor 12 as (2)(2)(3), and we factor a^2b^3c as *aabbbc*.

$$12a^2b^3c = \mathbf{(2)(2)(3)aabbbc}$$

Example 2

Factor the trinomial $6a^2b + 4ab^2 + 2ab$.

2 New Concepts (Continued)

Instruction

Remind students that GCF stands for *greatest common factor*. Explain that the terms in a polynomial may contain common factors that are not the GCF. The factors 3, x, y, xy, $3x$, and $3y$ are all common factors of $3x^2y + 6xy^2$, but none of them is the GCF.

Point out that after factoring out the GCF, the remaining polynomial will always have the same number of terms as the original polynomial.

As you discuss the *Conclude* question, suggest that students use the Distributive Property to check that they have factored correctly.

Example 1

Instruction

It is important for students to realize that the GCF must be factored out of each of the terms in the polynomial. Note that some polynomials will have no common factors other than 1, and the GCF will be 1. An example of such a polynomial is $6a^2 + 4b^2 + 3ab$.

Show students how to check the answer by multiplying the factors together. The product should be the original monomial.

Example 2

Instruction

Point out that all numerical and variable common factors must be included in the GCF.

(continued)

Math Background

Does every polynomial have a greatest common factor?

Yes, except for monomials, which have only one term. A monomial can be factored, but it cannot have a common factor.

The greatest common factor (GCF) is the greatest factor that divides evenly into each term of a polynomial. The GCF can contain numbers or variables, or both. The number 1 is always a factor of any term in a polynomial. If there is no other common factor, 1 is the GCF of a polynomial.

2 New Concepts (Continued)

Example 2 (Continued)

Instruction

Show students how to check this answer by using the Distributive Property. Multiplying the three terms by the GCF should give a product that is the original trinomial. When multiplying the GCF times a polynomial, emphasize that students must multiply the GCF times every term in the polynomial.

Practice Set

Problem g Classify

Ask why the expression in problem **f** is a trinomial. It has 3 terms.

Continue by asking what type of polynomial the expressions in problems **d** and **c** are.
d: binomial; c: monomial

3 Written Practice

Math Conversations

Discussion opportunities are provided below.

Problem 1 Explain

Have students explain how they can check their answers. Samples: Go over each step; make an estimate.

Problem 2 Verify

Point out that the answers to parts **a, b,** and **c** all look different. Then ask:

"Do these answers represent the same or different likelihoods?" Sample: They represent the same likelihood and are all different ways of showing that likelihood.

Errors and Misconceptions

Problem 3

Help students whose answer is 405 mi/day to see that they must not just average the two given numbers, but instead they need first to find the 5-day sum by multiplying 310 mi by 4 and adding the 500 mi driven on the fifth day, and then divide that sum by 5.

(continued)

Solution

First we find the greatest common factor of the three terms. Often we can do this visually. Notice that each term has 2 as a factor, *a* as a factor, and *b* as a factor. So the GCF is $2ab$. Next we divide each term of the trinomial by $2ab$ to find what remains of each term after $2ab$ is factored out of the expression.

$$\frac{6a^2b}{2ab} + \frac{4ab^2}{2ab} + \frac{2ab}{2ab} \quad 2ab \text{ removed by division}$$

$$3a + 2b + 1 \quad \text{remaining trinomial}$$

Notice that the third term is 1, not zero. This is because we divided $2ab$ by $2ab$; we did not subtract.

Now we write the factored expression in this form:

GCF(remaining polynomial)

The GCF is $2ab$ and the remaining trinomial is $3a + 2b + 1$.

$$\mathbf{2ab(3a + 2b + 1)}$$

Practice Set

Factor each algebraic expression:

a. $8m^2n$ $(2)(2)(2)mmn$

b. $12mn^2$ $(2)(2)(3)mnn$

c. $18x^3y^2$ $(2)(3)(3)xxxyy$

d. $8m^2n + 12mn^2$ $4mn(2m + 3n)$

e. $8xy^2 - 4xy$ $4xy(2y - 1)$

f. $6a^2b^3 + 9a^3b^2 + 3a^2b^2$ $3a^2b^2(2b + 3a + 1)$

▶ **g.** Classify What type of polynomial is the expression in problem **f?** trinomial

Written Practice *Strengthening Concepts*

▶ * **1.** (110) Explain How much interest is earned in 9 months on a deposit of \$7,000 at 4% simple interest? How did you find your answer?

1. \$210; Sample: The deposit earns \$280 in one year, so in 9 months, the deposit earns $\frac{3}{4}$ of \$280, or \$210

▶ **2.** (Inv. 8) With two tosses of a coin,

a. what is the probability of getting two heads? $\frac{1}{4}$

b. what is the chance of getting two tails? 25%

c. what are the odds of getting heads, then tails? 1 to 3

▶ **3.** (55) On the first 4 days of their trip, the Schmidts averaged 310 miles per day. On the fifth day they traveled 500 miles. How many miles per day did they average for the first 5 days of their trip? 348 $\frac{\text{mi}}{\text{day}}$

4. (46) An 18-ounce bottle of strawberry-melon juice costs \$2.16. The 1-quart container costs \$3.36. Which costs more per ounce, the bottle or container? How much more per ounce? bottle costs more; $1\frac{1}{2}$ cents per ounce more

Use ratio boxes to solve problems **5** and **6.**

5. (72) The school's new laser printer printed 160 pages in 5 minutes. At this rate, how long would it take to print 800 pages? 25 minutes

▶ See Math Conversations in the sidebar.

Teacher Tip

For this lesson, the best way you can support students as they are learning to **factor polynomials** is to provide plenty of practice. You may want to find additional examples for students who need more practice with this skill.

Answers like $3a^2b^2(2b + 3a + 1)$ may look more like problems than answers for many students. Help students understand that one of the main differences between algebra and arithmetic is that work becomes more abstract and complex.

6. (66) Volunteers for the local birding group located a roost of robins and starlings. They were able to determine that the ratio of robins to starlings was 7 to 5 in a hemlock tree that had 120 robins and starlings. How many robins were in the tree? 70 robins

7. (74) Kenny was thinking of a certain number. If $\frac{3}{4}$ of the number was 48, what was $\frac{5}{8}$ of the number? 40

8. (92) A used car dealer bought a car for $5500 and sold the car at a 40% markup. If the purchaser paid a sales tax of 8%, what was the total price of the car including tax? $8316

* 9. (110) **Generalize** What is the sale price of an $80 skateboard after successive discounts of 25% and 20%? $48

10. (99) The points (−3, 4), (5, −2), and (−3, −2) are the vertices of a triangle.
   a. Find the area of the triangle. 24 units^2
   b. Find the perimeter of the triangle. 24 units

* 11. (114) A glass aquarium with the dimensions shown has a mass of 5 kg when empty. What is the mass of the aquarium when it is half full of water? 10 kg

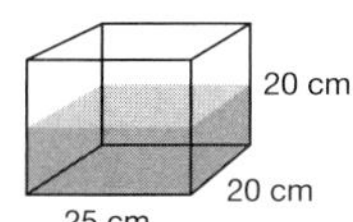

12. (48) Complete the table.

Fraction	Decimal	Percent
a. $\frac{7}{8}$	0.875	**b.** $87\frac{1}{2}$%

13. (54, 72) The nurse measured Latisha's resting heart rate by counting the number of times her heart beat over a 15 second interval. If the nurse counted 17 beats, what is Latisha's heart rate in beats per minute?
68 beats per minute

* 14. (83, 111) Simplify and express each answer in scientific notation:
   a. $(6.4 \times 10^6)(8 \times 10^{-8})$ 5.12×10^{-1}
   b. $\frac{6.4 \times 10^6}{8 \times 10^{-8}}$ 8×10^{13}

15. (88) Use a unit multiplier to convert three feet to centimeters.
91.44 centimeters

16. a. $b = \frac{2A}{h}$

* 16. (108) **a.** Solve for b: $A = \frac{1}{2}bh$
   b. Use the formula $A = \frac{1}{2}bh$ to find b when A is 24 and h is 6. 8
   c. **Extend** Solve for h: $A = \frac{1}{2}bh$. $h = \frac{2A}{b}$

17.

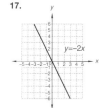

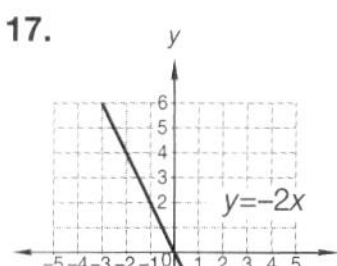

* 17. (Inv. 9, 107) **Analyze** Find three pairs of numbers that satisfy the function $y = -2x$. Then graph the number pairs on a coordinate plane, and draw a line through the points to show other number pairs that satisfy the function. What is the slope of the graphed line? See student work; −2

▶ See Math Conversations in the sidebar.

3 Written Practice (Continued)

Math Conversations

Discussion opportunities are provided below.

Problem 9 Generalize

Have students explain how to find the total cost of the skateboard with the two discounts and a sales tax of 5%. Sample: After you find and subtract the amount for the two discounts, you multiply by 1.05 to get the total.

Problem 16c Extend

Ask students to use this formula to write an expression for $\frac{1}{2}$. $\frac{1}{2} = \frac{A}{bh}$ Then discuss whether this equation could be used to find the value of one of the letters if the other two are known. Sample: It represents the same relationship, so it could be used. Help students see that since the area is usually what is determined, the usual form of the formula is most useful.

Problem 17 Analyze

Discuss with students various aspects of the graph of $y = -2x$. Ask about what pairs of numbers were found that satisfy the function, whether it passes through the origin, what quadrants the line passes through, why it passes through only two quadrants, and so on.

Errors and Misconceptions

Problem 6

Students who have answers of 8.4 or 84 robins have probably confused using ratio boxes for percent with ratio boxes for actual counts. Help them to see that they can use 12 as the total in the ratio column and 120 in the actual count column and then write a proportion to find the number of robins.

Problem 13

If students give an answer less than 68 beats per minute, they did not set up the proportion correctly. Suggest that they use a case 1-case 2 ratio box with "time in seconds" and "beats" as the labels.

(continued)

3 Written Practice (Continued)

Math Conversations

Discussion opportunities are provided below.

Problem 18 Analyze

First ask whether enough information is included in the problem to find the perimeter. yes Then have students find the perimeter. 26.28 mm Finally ask how to convert the perimeter to centimeters. Sample: Move the decimal point one place to the left.

Problem 20b Analyze

"Suppose the sphere is pulverized and the largest cone the cylinder can hold is placed base down in it. If the pulverized sphere is then poured into the cylinder, what happens?" Sample: It exactly fills the cylinder.

Problem 23 Analyze

Discuss what information is given in the problem. the dimensions of the cube

Then ask:

"What dimensions are needed to find the volume of the pyramid?" the sides of its base and its height

"Which of these is not shown on the drawing?" the height

"What can you assume about the height from the drawing?" that the height is the same as the height of the cube

Errors and Misconceptions

Problem 26

Students whose answer is 3 did not simplify the expressions under the radicals correctly. They probably dropped the exponents and combined the bases. Help them see, for example, that they needed to find the square of 3 and subtract that from the square of 5, which is 25 − 9, or 16, and then find the square root of 16.

▸* **18.** (104) Analyze Find the area of this figure. Dimensions are in millimeters. Corners that look square are square. (Use 3.14 for π.) 29.72 mm^2

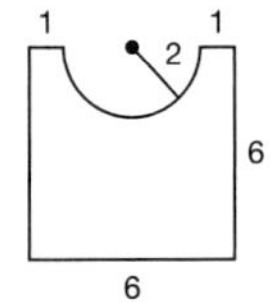

* **19.** (95, 105) **a.** Find the surface area of the cube. 60,000 cm^2

b. Find the volume of the cube. 1,000,000 cm^3

c. How many meters long is each edge of the cube? 1 m

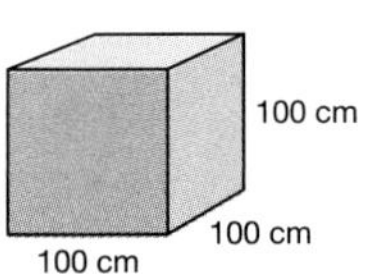

* **20.** (95, 113) **a.** Find the volume of the right circular cylinder. Dimensions are in inches. 6750π in.^{3}

▸ **b.** Analyze If within the cylinder is the largest sphere it can contain, what is the volume of the sphere? 4500π in.^{3}

30

30

Leave π as π.

21. (40) Find the measures of the following angles:

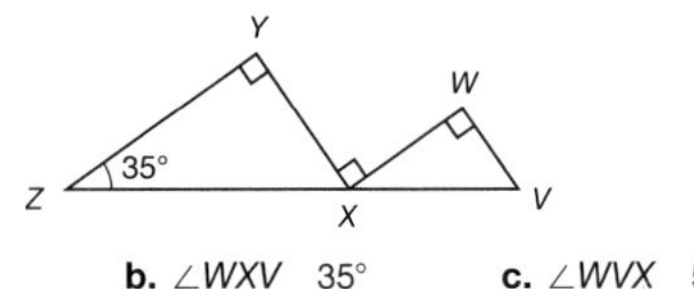

a. $\angle YXZ$ 55° **b.** $\angle WXV$ 35° **c.** $\angle WVX$ 55°

22. (97) In the figure in problem **21,** ZX is 21 cm, YX is 12 cm, and XV is 14 cm. Write a proportion to find WV. 8 cm

▸* **23.** (113) Analyze A pyramid is cut out of a plastic cube with dimensions as shown. What is the volume of the pyramid? 72 in.^{3}

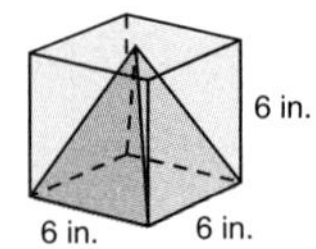

Solve:

24. (93) $0.4n + 5.2 = 12$ 17

25. (98) $\frac{18}{y} = \frac{36}{28}$ 14

Simplify:

▸ **26.** (20) $\sqrt{5^2 - 3^2} + \sqrt{5^2 - 4^2}$ 7

27. (56) 3 yd − 2 ft 1 in. 2 yd 11 in.

28. (43) $3.5 \div \left(1\frac{2}{5} \div 3\right)$ $7\frac{1}{2}$ or 7.5

29. (57) $3.5 + 2^{-2} - 2^{-3}$ $3\frac{5}{8}$ or 3.625

30. (85) $\frac{(3)(-2)(4)}{(-6)(2)} + (-8) + (-4)(+5) - (2)(-3)$ −20

▸ See Math Conversations in the sidebar.

Assessment

30–40 minutes *For use after Lesson 115*

Distribute **Cumulative Test 22** to each student. Two versions of the test are available in *Saxon Math Course 2 Course Assessments Book.* Have students complete the **Power-Up Test** first. Allow 10 minutes. Then have students work the 20 numbered items on the **Cumulative Test.** Students may use copies of the answer sheet to record their work. Track individual and class progress with the **Test Analysis** forms.

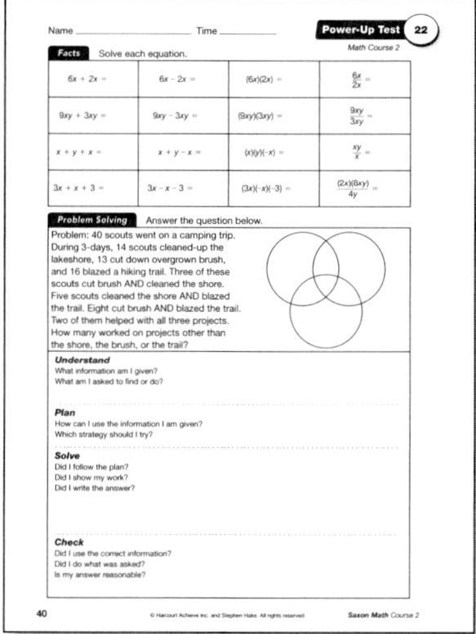

Name ______ Time ______ **Power-Up Test 22** *Math Course 2*

Facts Solve each equation.

$6x + 2x =$	$6x - 2x =$	$(6x)(2x) =$	$\frac{6x}{2x} =$
$9xy + 3xy =$	$9xy - 3xy =$	$(9xy)(3xy) =$	$\frac{9xy}{3xy} =$
$x + y + x =$	$x + y - x =$	$(x)(y)(-x) =$	$\frac{xy}{x} =$
$3x + x + 3 =$	$3x - x - 3 =$	$(3x)(-x)(-3) =$	$\frac{(2x)(8xy)}{4y} =$

Problem Solving Answer the question below.

Problem: 40 scouts went on a camping trip. During 3-days, 14 scouts cleaned-up the lakeshore, 13 cut down overgrown brush, and 16 blazed a hiking trail. Three of these scouts cut brush AND cleaned the shore. Five scouts cleaned the shore AND blazed the trail. Eight cut brush AND blazed the trail. Two of them helped with all three projects. How many worked on projects other than the shore, the brush, or the trail?

Understand
What information am I given?
What am I asked to find or do?

Plan
How can I use the information I am given?
Which strategy should I try?

Solve
Did I follow the plan?
Did I show my work?
Did I write the answer?

Check
Did I use the correct information?
Did I do what was asked?
Is my answer reasonable?

40 © Harcourt Achieve Inc. and Stephen Hake. All rights reserved. *Saxon Math Course 2*

Power-Up Test 22

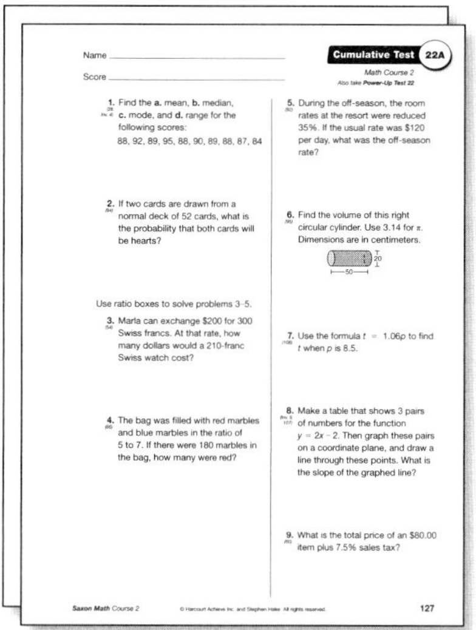

Name ______ Score ______ **Cumulative Test 22A** *Math Course 2* Also take **Power-Up Test 22**

1. Find the **a.** mean, **b.** median, **c.** mode, and **d.** range for the following scores:
88, 92, 89, 95, 88, 90, 89, 88, 87, 84

2. If two cards are drawn from a normal deck of 52 cards, what is the probability that both cards will be hearts?

Use ratio boxes to solve problems 3–5.

3. Marla can exchange \$200 for 300 Swiss francs. At that rate, how many dollars would a 210-franc Swiss watch cost?

4. The bag was filled with red marbles and blue marbles in the ratio of 5 to 7. If there were 180 marbles in the bag, how many were red?

5. During the off-season, the room rates at the resort were reduced 35%. If the usual rate was \$120 per day, what was the off-season rate?

6. Find the volume of this right circular cylinder. Use 3.14 for π. Dimensions are in centimeters.

7. Use the formula $t = 1.06p$ to find t when p is 8.5.

8. Make a table that shows 3 pairs of numbers for the function $y = 2x - 2$. Then graph these pairs on a coordinate plane, and draw a line through these points. What is the slope of the graphed line?

9. What is the total price of an \$80.00 item plus 7.5% sales tax?

Saxon Math Course 2 © Harcourt Achieve Inc. and Stephen Hake. All rights reserved. 127

Cumulative Test 22A

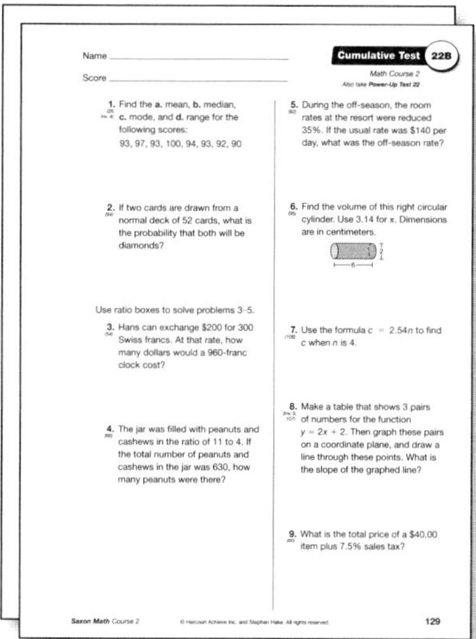

Name ______ Score ______ **Cumulative Test 22B** *Math Course 2* Also take **Power-Up Test 22**

1. Find the **a.** mean, **b.** median, **c.** mode, and **d.** range for the following scores:
93, 97, 93, 100, 94, 93, 92, 90

2. If two cards are drawn from a normal deck of 52 cards, what is the probability that both will be diamonds?

Use ratio boxes to solve problems 3–5.

3. Hans can exchange \$200 for 300 Swiss francs. At that rate, how many dollars would a 960-franc clock cost?

4. The jar was filled with peanuts and cashews in the ratio of 11 to 4. If the total number of peanuts and cashews in the jar was 630, how many peanuts were there?

5. During the off-season, the room rates at the resort were reduced 35%. If the usual rate was \$140 per day, what was the off-season rate?

6. Find the volume of this right circular cylinder. Use 3.14 for π. Dimensions are in centimeters.

7. Use the formula $c = 2.54n$ to find c when n is 4.

8. Make a table that shows 3 pairs of numbers for the function $y = 2x + 2$. Then graph these pairs on a coordinate plane, and draw a line through these points. What is the slope of the graphed line?

9. What is the total price of a \$40.00 item plus 7.5% sales tax?

Saxon Math Course 2 © Harcourt Achieve Inc. and Stephen Hake. All rights reserved. 129

Alternative Cumulative Test 22B

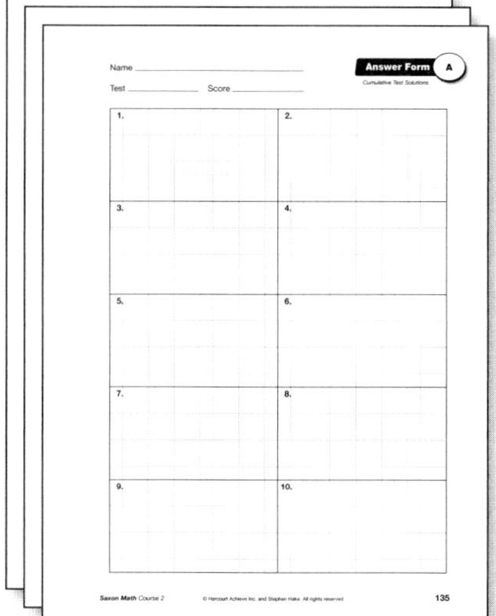

Name ______ Test ______ Score ______ **Answer Form A** Cumulative Test Solutions

1. 2. 3. 4. 5. 6. 7. 8. 9. 10.

Saxon Math Course 2 © Harcourt Achieve Inc. and Stephen Hake. All rights reserved. 135

Optional Answer Forms

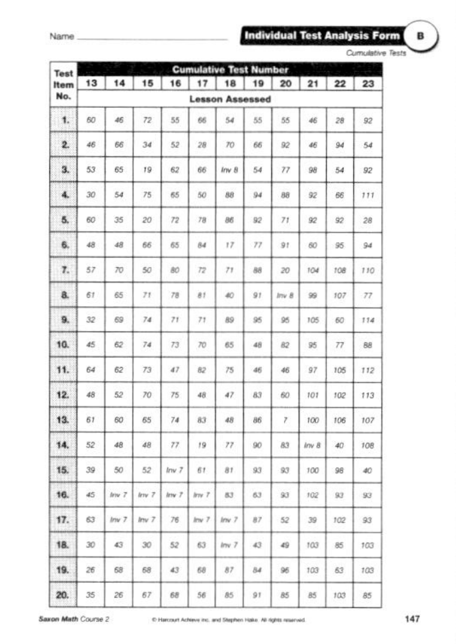

Name ______ **Individual Test Analysis Form B** *Cumulative Tests*

Test Item No.	Cumulative Test Number 13	14	15	16	17	18	19	20	21	22	23
	Lesson Assessed										
1.	60	46	72	55	66	54	55	55	46	28	92
2.	46	66	34	52	28	70	66	92	46	94	54
3.	53	65	19	62	66	Inv 8	54	77	98	54	92
4.	30	54	75	65	50	88	94	88	92	66	111
5.	60	35	20	72	78	86	92	71	92	92	28
6.	48	48	66	65	84	17	77	91	60	95	94
7.	57	70	50	80	72	71	88	20	104	108	110
8.	61	65	71	78	81	40	91	Inv 8	99	107	77
9.	32	69	74	71	71	89	95	95	105	60	114
10.	45	62	74	73	70	65	48	82	95	77	88
11.	64	62	73	47	82	75	46	46	97	105	112
12.	48	52	70	75	48	47	83	60	101	102	113
13.	61	60	65	74	83	48	86	7	100	106	107
14.	52	48	48	77	19	77	90	83	Inv 8	40	108
15.	39	50	52	Inv 7	61	81	93	93	100	98	40
16.	45	Inv 7	Inv 7	Inv 7	Inv 7	83	63	93	102	93	93
17.	63	Inv 7	Inv 7	76	Inv 7	Inv 7	87	52	39	102	93
18.	30	43	30	52	63	Inv 7	43	49	103	85	103
19.	26	68	68	43	68	87	84	96	103	63	103
20.	35	26	67	68	56	85	91	85	85	103	85

Saxon Math Course 2 © Harcourt Achieve Inc. and Stephen Hake. All rights reserved. 147

Individual Test Analysis Form

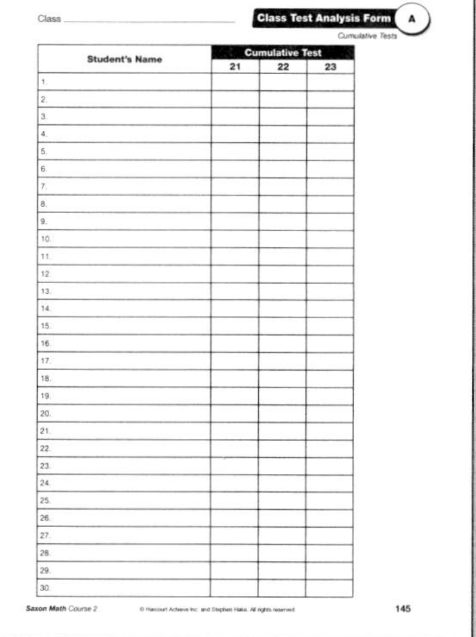

Class ______ **Class Test Analysis Form A** Cumulative Tests

	Student's Name	Cumulative Test 21	22	23
1.				
2.				
3.				
4.				
5.				
6.				
7.				
8.				
9.				
10.				
11.				
12.				
13.				
14.				
15.				
16.				
17.				
18.				
19.				
20.				
21.				
22.				
23.				
24.				
25.				
26.				
27.				
28.				
29.				
30.				

Saxon Math Course 2 © Harcourt Achieve Inc. and Stephen Hake. All rights reserved. 145

Class Test Analysis Form

Reteaching

Students who score below 80% on the assessment may be in need of reteaching. Look for the causes of student mistakes. If errors are conceptual, refer to the *Reteaching Masters* for reteaching.

Performance Activity 22

Pyramids

Assign after Lesson 115 and Test 22

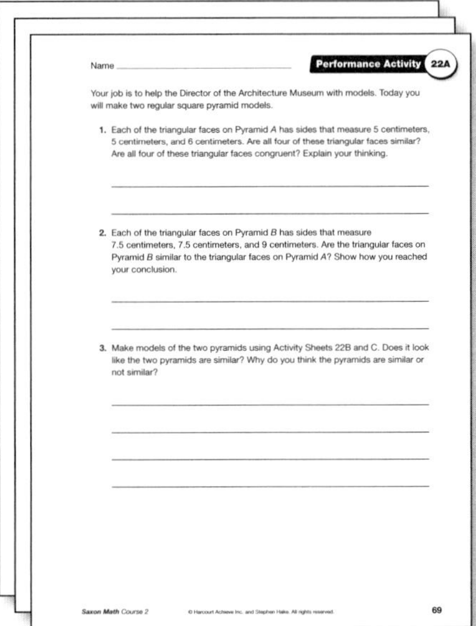

Name ____________ **Performance Activity 22A**

Your job is to help the Director of the Architecture Museum with models. Today you will make two regular square pyramid models.

1. Each of the triangular faces on Pyramid *A* has sides that measure 5 centimeters, 5 centimeters, and 6 centimeters. Are all four of these triangular faces similar? Are all four of these triangular faces congruent? Explain your thinking.

2. Each of the triangular faces on Pyramid *B* has sides that measure 7.5 centimeters, 7.5 centimeters, and 9 centimeters. Are the triangular faces on Pyramid *B* similar to the triangular faces on Pyramid *A*? Show how you reached your conclusion.

3. Make models of the two pyramids using Activity Sheets 22B and C. Does it look like the two pyramids are similar? Why do you think the pyramids are similar or not similar?

Saxon Math *Course 2* 69

Performance Activity 22A, 22B, and 22C

Objectives

- Identify geometric figures that are similar.
- Identify geometric figures that are congruent.
- Construct models of solid figures (pyramids).
- Communicate their ideas through writing.

Materials

Performance Activities 22A, 22B, and **22C**

Tape

Scissors

Preparation

Make copies of **Performance Activities 22A, 22B,** and **22C.** (One each per student.)

Time Requirement

15–30 minutes; Begin in class and complete at home.

Activity

Explain to students that for this activity they will be helping the Director of the Architecture Museum by constructing models of pyramids. They will look at the faces of one pyramid to see if they are both similar and congruent. They will compare both pyramids to see if their faces and the pyramids themselves are similar. They will justify their conclusions. Explain that all of the information students need is on **Performance Activities 22A, 22B,** and **22C.**

Criteria for Evidence of Learning

- Constructs accurate models of two regular square pyramids.
- Concludes that the triangular faces on Pyramid *A* are similar and congruent.
- Concludes that the triangular faces on Pyramid *B* are similar to the triangular faces on Pyramid *A*.
- Concludes that Pyramid *A* is similar to Pyramid *B*.
- Communicates mathematical ideas clearly.

Meeting Standards

National Council of Teachers of Mathematics (NCTM)

Geometry

GM.1a Precisely describe, classify, and understand relationships among types of two- and three-dimensional objects using their defining properties

GM.1b Understand relationships among the angles, side lengths, perimeters, areas, and volumes of similar objects

GM.1c Create and critique inductive and deductive arguments concerning geometric ideas and relationships, such as congruence, similarity, and the Pythagorean relationship

Communication

CM.3a Organize and consolidate their mathematical thinking through communication

Connections

CN.4b Understand how mathematical ideas interconnect and build on one another to produce a coherent whole

Slope-Intercept Form of Linear Equations

Objectives

- Write a linear equation in slope-intercept form.
- Determine the slope and the y-intercept from an equation written in slope-intercept form.
- Graph a linear equation using only the slope and y-intercept.

Lesson Preparation

Materials

- **Power Up W** (in *Instructional Masters*)
- **Teacher-provided material: graph paper,** 5 per student

Optional

- **Investigation Activity 13** (in *Instructional Masters*)
- **Teacher-provided material: calculators**

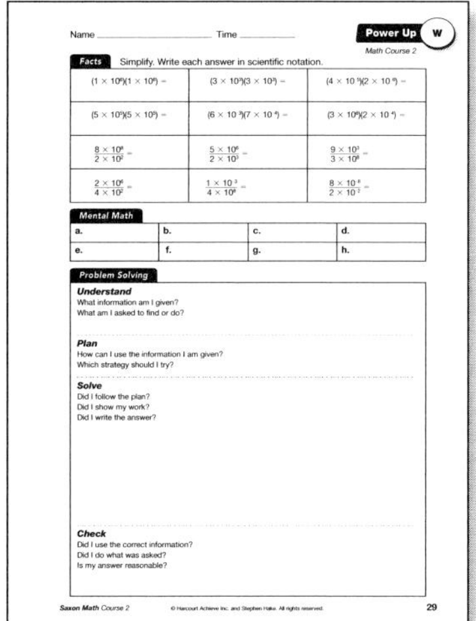

Name ______ Time ______

Power Up W
Math Course 2

Facts Simplify. Write each answer in scientific notation.

(1 × 10[illegible])(1 × 10[illegible]) =	(3 × 10[illegible])(3 × 10[illegible]) =	(4 × 10[illegible])(2 × 10[illegible]) =
(5 × 10[illegible])(5 × 10[illegible]) =	(6 × 10[illegible])(7 × 10[illegible]) =	(3 × 10[illegible])(2 × 10[illegible]) =
8 × 10[illegible] / 2 × 10[illegible] =	5 × 10[illegible] / 2 × 10[illegible] =	9 × 10[illegible] / 3 × 10[illegible] =
2 × 10[illegible] / 4 × 10[illegible] =	1 × 10[illegible] / 4 × 10[illegible] =	8 × 10[illegible] / 2 × 10[illegible] =

Mental Math

a.	b.	c.	d.
e.	f.	g.	h.

Problem Solving

Understand
What information am I given?
What am I asked to find or do?

Plan
How can I use the information I am given?
Which strategy should I try?

Solve
Did I follow the plan?
Did I show my work?
Did I write the answer?

Check
Did I use the correct information?
Did I do what was asked?
Is my answer reasonable?

Saxon Math Course 2 © Harcourt Achieve Inc. and Stephen Hake. All rights reserved. 29

Power Up W

Math Language

New	English Learners (ESL)
slope-intercept form	transform
y-intercept	

Technology Resources

Student eBook Complete student textbook in electronic format.

Resources and Planner CD Assessment, reteaching, and instructional masters, plus a pacing calendar with standards.

Test and Practice Generator CD Create additional practice sheets and custom-made tests.

www.SaxonPublishers.com Visit for more student activities and planning materials.

Inclusion

Adaptations CD Adapted lessons, investigations, practice and assessments.

Meeting Standards

National Council of Teachers of Mathematics (NCTM)

Algebra

AL.2b Explore relationships between symbolic expressions and graphs of lines, paying particular attention to the meaning of intercept and slope

AL.2c Use symbolic algebra to represent situations and to solve problems, especially those that involve linear relationships

AL.2d Recognize and generate equivalent forms for simple algebraic expressions and solve linear equations

AL.4a Use graphs to analyze the nature of changes in quantities in linear relationships

Power-Up Discussion *For use with Power Up, p. 809*

Problem-Solving Strategy: Use Logical Reasoning

Three tennis balls just fit into a cylindrical container. What fraction of the volume of the container is occupied by the tennis balls?

Understand Understand the problem.

"What information are we given?"

Three tennis balls just fit into a cylindrical container.

"What are we asked to do?"

We are asked to determine what fraction of the volume of the container is occupied by the tennis balls.

Plan Make a plan.

"What problem-solving strategy will we use?"

We will *use logical reasoning* to find the fraction occupied by the tennis balls.

"What do we know about the volume of a sphere as related to the volume of a cylinder with the same diameter?"

If the cylinder's height is equal to its diameter, the sphere's volume will be $\frac{2}{3}$ the volume of the cylinder.

Solve Carry out the plan.

"If the three tennis balls "just fit" into the container, what can we deduce about the dimensions of the container?"

Its diameter is equal to the diameter of the tennis balls, and its height is equal to three times its diameter.

"If we mentally "cut" the container into three equal pieces, each containing one ball, what fraction of each piece is occupied by one tennis ball?"

$\frac{2}{3}$

"What fraction of the whole container is occupied by tennis balls?"

$\frac{2}{3}$

Check Look back.

"Did we do what we were asked to do?"

Yes, we found that $\frac{2}{3}$ of the container's volume is occupied by the tennis balls.

LESSON 116

• Slope-Intercept Form of Linear Equations

Power Up — *Building Power*

facts Power Up W

mental math

a. **Positive/Negative:** $(-2)^2 + 2^{-2}$ $4\frac{1}{4}$

b. **Scientific Notation:** $(5 \times 10^5) \div (2 \times 10^2)$ 2.5×10^3

c. **Algebra:** $3x + 1.2 = 2.4$ 0.4

d. **Measurement:** Convert 1 m^2 to cm^2. 10,000 cm^2

e. **Percent:** 125% of \$400 \$500

f. **Percent:** \$400 increased 25% \$500

g. **Primes/Composites:** Which does not belong in the list 2, 23, 41, 48? 48

h. **Percent/Estimation:** Estimate $8\frac{3}{4}$% sales tax on a \$41.19 purchase. \$3.60

problem solving Three tennis balls just fit into a cylindrical container. What fraction of the volume of the container is occupied by the tennis balls? $\frac{2}{3}$

New Concept — *Increasing Knowledge*

The three equations below are equivalent equations. Each equation has the same graph as shown.

a. $2x + y - 4 = 0$

b. $2x + y = 4$

c. $y = -2x + 4$

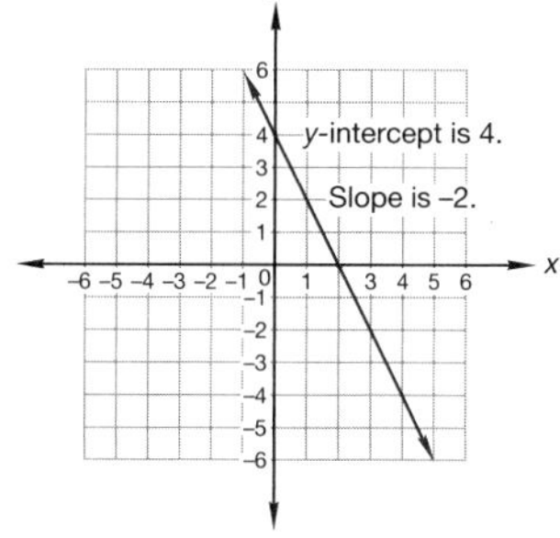

Thinking Skill
Verify

Solve equations **a** and **b** for y to prove the equations are equivalent. Show your work.
a. $2x + y - 4 + 4 = 0 + 4$; $2x - 2x + y = 4 - 2x$; $y = -2x + 4$;
b. $2x - 2x + y = 4 - 2x$; $y = -2x + 4$

Facts Simplify. Write each answer in scientific notation.

$(1 \times 10^6)(1 \times 10^6) = 1 \times 10^{12}$	$(3 \times 10^3)(3 \times 10^3) = 9 \times 10^6$	$(4 \times 10^{-5})(2 \times 10^{-6}) = 8 \times 10^{-11}$
$(5 \times 10^5)(5 \times 10^5) = 2.5 \times 10^{11}$	$(6 \times 10^{-3})(7 \times 10^{-4}) = 4.2 \times 10^{-6}$	$(3 \times 10^6)(2 \times 10^{-4}) = 6 \times 10^2$
$\frac{8 \times 10^8}{2 \times 10^2} = 4 \times 10^6$	$\frac{5 \times 10^6}{2 \times 10^3} = 2.5 \times 10^3$	$\frac{9 \times 10^3}{3 \times 10^8} = 3 \times 10^{-5}$
$\frac{2 \times 10^6}{4 \times 10^2} = 5 \times 10^3$	$\frac{1 \times 10^{-3}}{4 \times 10^8} = 2.5 \times 10^{-12}$	$\frac{8 \times 10^{-8}}{2 \times 10^{-2}} = 4 \times 10^{-6}$

1 Power Up

Facts

Distribute **Power Up W** to students. See answers below.

Mental Math

Encourage students to share different ways to mentally compute these exercises. Strategies for exercises **e** and **g** are listed below.

e. Use a Fraction

$125\% = \frac{5}{4}$

$\frac{5}{4} \times \$400 = 5 \times \$100 = \$500$

Use Logical Reasoning

100% of \$400 is \$400.

25% of \$400 is \$100.

125% of \$400 is \$500.

g. Look for Even Numbers

Even numbers > 2 are not prime.

48 is an even number > 2.

48 is not prime and does not belong.

Look for More than 2 Factors

Prime numbers have only 2 factors.

48 has more than 2 factors.

48 is not prime and does not belong.

Problem Solving

Refer to **Power-Up Discussion,** p. 809B.

2 New Concepts

Instruction

Students know how to graph equations by finding and plotting ordered pairs that satisfy the equations. Explain that the slope-intercept form of an equation can be graphed without finding values that satisfy the equation.

As a class, make a table of values for the first equation shown on this page on an overhead projector or on the board.

- Ask a volunteer to graph the line for this equation.
- Use a colored dot to indicate the y-intercept, and use the terms *rise* and *run* to remind students how to find the slope of a line.
- Repeat this process for the second equation. Students should quickly see that the graph is the same line.
- Repeat the same procedure for the last equation. Students should again see that the graph is the same line.

Explain that these equations are equivalent and that their graphs are the same line.

(continued)

2 New Concepts (Continued)

Instruction

Help students remember the slope-intercept form by pointing out that the slope and the y-intercept are given in the same order that the name of the form states—slope, then intercept.

When students respond to the *Represent* question, in addition to naming the equation, have them identify the slope and the y-intercept of the graph of the equation.

Example 1

Instruction

Point out that in order for the equation to be in slope-intercept form, the terms on the right side of the equation may need to be rearranged as in this example. Note that the sign of a term moves with the term when you use the Commutative Property.

After discussing the solution, you may provide students with additional equations to rewrite in slope-intercept form. Two equations you might use are $5x + 2y = 14$ and $3y - 15 = 21x$. $y = -\frac{5}{2}x + 7$; $y = 7x + 5$ Ask students to give the slope and the y-intercept for each of these equations.

(continued)

Equation **c** is in a special form called **slope-intercept form.** When an equation is in slope-intercept form, the coefficient of x is the slope of the graph of the equation, and the constant is the **y-intercept** (where the graph of the equation intercepts the y-axis).

slope

$$y = (-2)x \ (+4)$$

y-intercept

Notice the order of the terms in this equation. The equation is solved for y, and y is to the left of the equal sign. To the right of the equal sign is the x-term and then the constant term. The model for slope-intercept form is written this way:

Slope-Intercept Form
$\boldsymbol{y = mx + b}$

In this model, m stands for the slope and b for the y-intercept.

Represent What is the equation, in slope-intercept form, for a line whose slope is 4 and whose y-intercept is -2? $y = 4x - 2$

Example 1

Transform this equation so that it is in slope-intercept form.

$$3x + y = 6$$

Solution

We solve the equation for y by subtracting $3x$ from both sides of the equation.

$3x + y = 6$	equation
$3x + y - 3x = 6 - 3x$	subtracted $3x$ from both sides
$y = 6 - 3x$	simplified

Next, using the Commutative Property, we rearrange the terms on the right side of the equal sign so that the x-term precedes the constant term.

$y = 6 - 3x$	equation
$\boldsymbol{y = -3x + 6}$	Commutative Property

Discuss What happens to the signs when you use the Commutative Property. Sample: They move with the terms.

Math Background

If you know the slope and y-intercept of a graph, can you find the equation of the line?

Yes. Because you know the slope, m, and the y-intercept, b, of the graph, you can substitute these values into the slope-intercept form $y = mx + b$. For example, if the slope of a line is 5 and the y-intercept is -2, you know $m = 5$ and $b = -2$. The equation of the line is $y = 5x - 2$.

English Learners

In example 1, explain the meaning of the word **transform.** Tell students:

"To transform something means to change the form or the look of it. In math, transforming an equation only changes the look not the value."

Ask students to transform the following expression so that it does not contain parentheses.

$2(x + y)$

$2x + 2y$

Example 2

Graph $y = -3x + 6$ using the slope and y-intercept.

Solution

The slope of the graph is the coefficient of x, which is -3, and the y-intercept is $+6$, which is located at $+6$ on the y-axis. From this point we move to the right 1 unit and down 3 units because the slope is -3. This gives us another point on the line. Continuing this pattern, we identify a series of points through which we draw the graph of the equation.

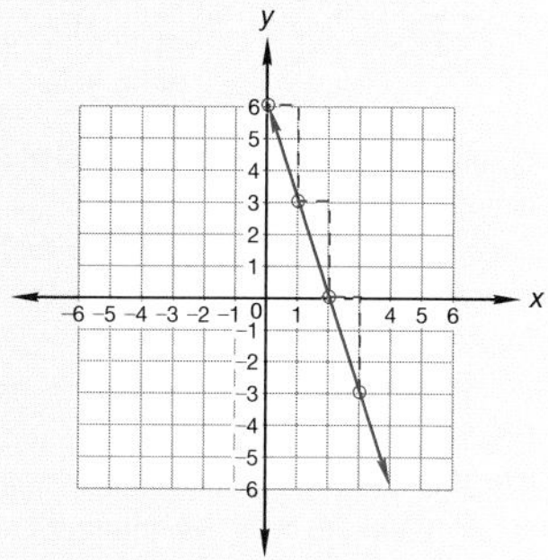

Example 3

Using only slope and y-intercept, graph $y = x - 2$.

Solution

Visit www.SaxonPublishers.com/ActivitiesC2 *for a graphing calculator activity.*

The slope is the coefficient of x, which is $+1$. The y-intercept is -2. We begin at -2 on the y-axis and sketch a line that has a slope of $+1$.

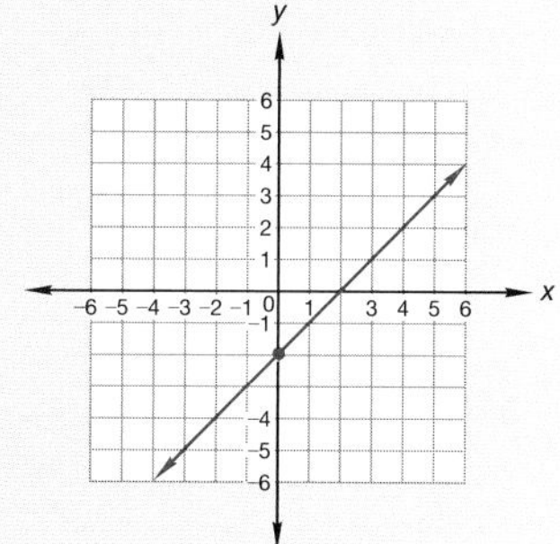

2 New Concepts (Continued)

Example 2

Instruction

Demonstrate the process of graphing the equations in this and the next example on an overhead projector or on the board. Emphasize that students do not need to make a table of ordered pairs to graph these equations.

Example 3

Instruction

This example is similar to that in example 2 except that the slope is positive and the y-intercept is negative. You may want to ask students how many points they need to find to be sure that they are drawing the correct line. Although two points determine a line, many students will want to use more than two points. It is not necessary to go into this concept now.

(continued)

2 New Concepts *(Continued)*

Example 4

Instruction

Point out that the graph of an equation can be extended and used to find values for the function that are outside the range of known values. This is called *extrapolation.*

In this example, students will extrapolate from known values to determine an unknown value, using both the slope-intercept form of an equation and the graph of that equation. Emphasize that whether a slope-intercept equation or its graph is used to solve a problem, the answer will be the same.

Explain that an equation in slope-intercept form can be used to find a value of x if the y value is known. To demonstrate this, show how the equation in this example can be used to find the distance from below the edge of the roof for any given height.

"If the height is 18 feet, what is the distance from below the edge of the roof?" $18 = \frac{4}{12}x + 8$. The distance is 30 feet.

(continued)

Example 4

Robert noticed a bird's nest in line with the slope of his roof. He knew that the slope of the roof was 4 in 12. He also knew that the edge of the roof was 8 feet high.

He measured 48 feet from the edge of the roof to a spot directly under the nest. Then he calculated the height of the nest. How high was the nest?

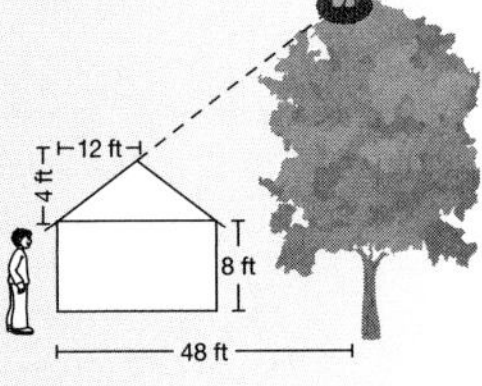

Solution

To find the answer, we can make a table, write an equation or make a graph. The slope of the roof is 4 in 12. So for every 12 horizontal feet the roof rises 4 feet. The edge of the roof is 8 feet high. As Robert walks 12 feet toward the tree the line of the roof is 4 feet higher, which is 12 feet. We begin the pattern with 0 and 8, and then we continue the pattern.

Run	Height
0	8
12	12
24	16
36	20
48	24

We also can write an equation in slope-intercept form. The slope of the roof is 4 in 12 which is $\frac{4}{12}$. The intercept is 8 feet, where the roof begins.

$$y = \frac{4}{12}x + 8$$

In this equation, y equals the height of the roof slope x feet from the edge. So the height of the roof slope 48 feet from the edge is 24 feet.

$$y = \frac{4}{12}(48) + 8$$

$$y = 24$$

We also can graph the equation $y = \frac{4}{12}x + 8$ in the first quadrant and find the height where x is 48.

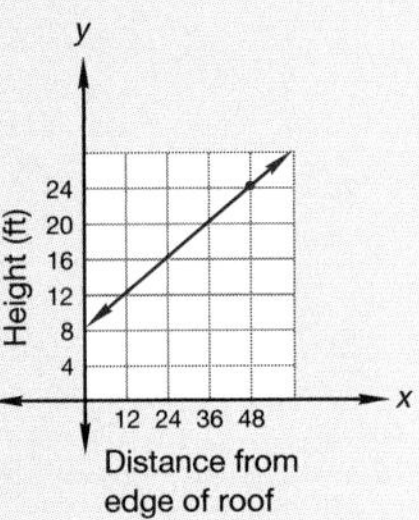

The table, the equation and the graph show that the height of the nest is **24 feet.**

Practice Set ▶ *Represent* Write each equation below in slope-intercept form:

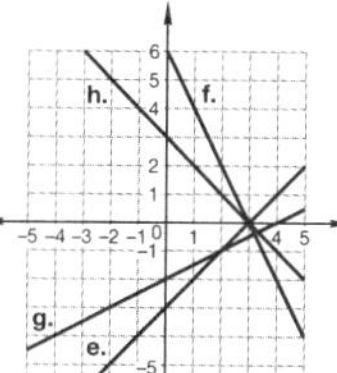

a. $2x + y = 3$
$y = -2x + 3$

b. $y - 3 = x$
$y = x + 3$

c. $2x + y - 3 = 0$
$y = -2x + 3$

d. $x + y = 4 - x$
$y = -2x + 4$

▶ *Connect* Using only slope and y-intercept, graph each of these equations:

e. $y = x - 3$

f. $y = -2x + 6$

g. $y = \frac{1}{2}x - 2$

h. $y = -x + 3$

▶ **i.** *Explain* How did you graph the equation in **h?**

i. Sample: The slope is -1; the y-intercept is 3; From (0, 3), I moved right 1 unit and down 1 unit because the slope is -1. This gives us another point on the line.

Written Practice

Strengthening Concepts

1. (Inv. 8) A pair of number cubes is rolled once.

a. What is the probability of rolling a total of 5 (expressed as a decimal rounded to two decimal places)? 0.11

b. What is the chance of rolling a total of either 4 or 7? 25%

c. What are the odds of rolling a total of 12? 1 to 35

▶ *** 2.** (20) A kilobyte of memory is 2^{10} bytes. Express the number of bytes in a kilobyte in standard form. 1024 bytes

3. (92) Which sign seems to advertise the better sale? Explain your choice.

Sale! 40% off the regular price!	Sale! 40% of the regular price!

3. The better sale seems to be the "40% of" sale, which is 60% off the regular price. Sixty percent off is better than 40% off.

▶ **4.** (48) Complete the table.

Fraction	Decimal	Percent
a. $1\frac{3}{4}$	**b.** 1.75	175%
$\frac{1}{12}$	**c.** $0.08\overline{3}$	**d.** $8\frac{1}{3}\%$

▶ **5.** (80) Triangle ABC with vertices A (0, 3), B (0, 0), and C (4, 0) is rotated 180° about the origin to $\triangle A'B'C'$. What are the coordinates of the vertices of $\triangle A'B'C'$? A' (0, −3), B' (0, 0), C' (−4, 0)

6. (89) What is the measure of each exterior angle and each interior angle of a regular 20-gon? 18°; 162°

7. (92) At a 30%-off sale Melba bought a jacket for $42. How much money did Melba save by buying the jacket on sale instead of paying the regular price? $18

▶ See Math Conversations in the sidebar.

2 New Concepts *(Continued)*

Practice Set

Problems a–d *Represent*

Have students explain how all the equations they wrote are alike. Sample: They are all in the form $y = mx + b$.

Problems e–h *Connect*

Suggest that students divide their graph paper into four sections and draw a pair of axes in each section. They can then graph one equation in each section.

Ask volunteers to tell how they graphed each of these equations. Then discuss why each one started with finding the y-intercept. Sample: You need that point to start using the slope to find the line.

Problem i *Explain*

Let one student read his or her explanation. Then ask students how they can check that their graphs represent the equation. Sample: Choose ordered pairs from the graph and substitute them into the equation. Have students choose one of the four graphs they made for problems **e–h** and check their work.

3 Written Practice

Math Conversations

Discussion opportunities are provided below.

Problem 2

Extend the Problem

Tell students that the prefix *kilo-* means 1000, and a kilobyte is about 1000 bytes. As a class, use your calculators to write the following in standard form.

$$1 \text{ megabyte} = 2^{20}$$

$$1 \text{ gigabyte} = 2^{30}$$

Ask students what the prefixes *mega-* and *giga-* mean. million and billion

Problem 4 *Connect*

Ask students to give examples for which the sale price can be calculated both ways using mental math. Sample: a $50 sweater would be $30 at 40% off and $20 at 40% of the regular price

Errors and Misconceptions

Problem 5

Students whose answer is (3, 0), (0, −4) and (0, 0) rotated the figure only 90°. Explain that a 180° turn will move the figure across two quadrants.

(continued)

3 Written Practice (Continued)

Math Conversations

Discussion opportunities are provided below.

Problem 11 Represent

"Which angle is congruent to one of the angles in an equilateral triangle? Explain why." Sample: The $6x + 12$, or 60°, angle. The reason is that the angles in an equilateral triangle are all equal and they measure 60° because $180° \div 3 = 60°$.

Problem 13 Analyze

Extend the Problem

Help students see how the mathematics they are learning can be used for practical purposes.

"The wallpaper strip costs \$19.95 a yard, and is sold only in whole yards. How much wallpaper should be ordered?" Sample: I divided 195 inches by 36. 195 inches is about 5.4 yards. So 6 yards must be ordered.

"How much will the wallpaper strip cost?" Samples: $\$19.95 \times 6 = \$20 \times 6 - 5¢ \times 6$, or \$119.70. I used a calculator to get \$119.70.

Problem 16 Analyze

Ask students to tell which dimension is not needed to solve the problem and explain why. Sample: 9 cm, because I only need the lengths of the parallel sides and the height to find the area.

Errors and Misconceptions

Problem 11

For students who do not get the correct answer, tell them that they first need to solve for x in an equation that has the sum of the angles of the triangle equal to 180°. After they find the value of x, they use it to determine the values of the three angles and then compare them.

Problem 15

If students give 6000 cm² as their answer, they simply multiplied the three given dimensions. Point out that they need to find the area of the triangular face of the prism and multiply that by the height of the prism. Suggest that they think of the prism as standing on one of the triangular faces.

(continued)

---

* **8.** (114) The figure illustrates an aquarium with interior dimensions as shown.

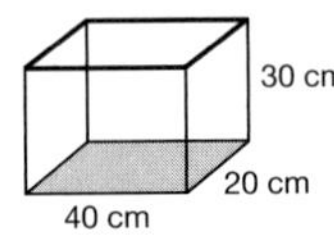

a. The aquarium has a maximum capacity of how many liters? 24 liters

b. If the aquarium is filled with water, what would be the mass of the water in the aquarium? 24 kg

9. (50) Use a unit multiplier to convert 24 kg to lb. (Use the approximation 1 kg ≈ 2.2 lb.) $24 \text{ kg} \cdot \frac{2.2 \text{ lb}}{1 \text{ kg}} = 52.8 \text{ lb}$

10. (101) Write an equation to solve this problem: $2x - 6 = 48$; 27

Six less than twice what number is 48?

▸* **11.** (101) Represent Find the measure of the largest angle of the triangle shown. What equation could you write to help solve this problem? 64°; $8x - 8 + 7x + 8 + 6x + 12 = 180$

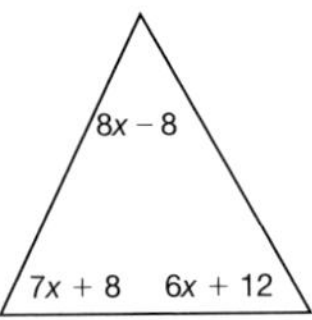

* **12.** (106) Solve for C: $F = 1.8C + 32$ $\quad C = \frac{F - 32}{1.8}$

▸* **13.** (104) Analyze The inside surface of this archway will be covered with a strip of wallpaper. How long must the strip of wallpaper be in order to reach from the floor on one side of the archway around to the floor on the other side of the archway? Round the answer to the nearest inch. (Use 3.14 for π.) 195 in.

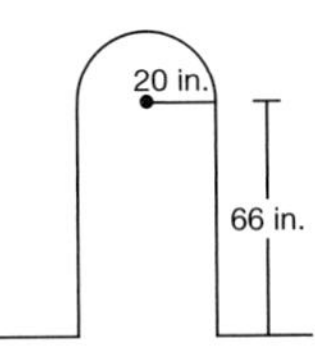

* **14.** (105) What is the total surface area of the right triangular prism below? 1500 cm²

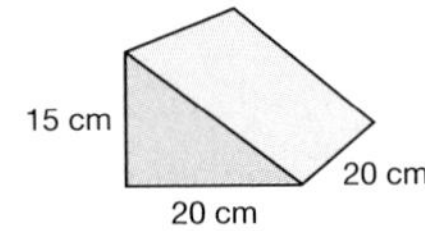

▸ **15.** (95) What is the volume of the right triangular prism in problem 14? 3000 cm³

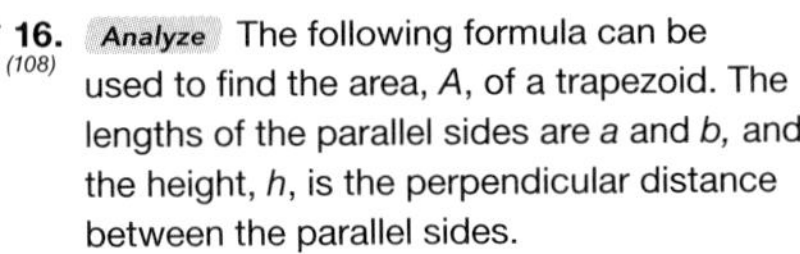

Thinking Skill
Identify

If $a = 12$, what values will be substituted in the formula for b and h? $b = 18$; $h = 8$

▸* **16.** (108) Analyze The following formula can be used to find the area, A, of a trapezoid. The lengths of the parallel sides are a and b, and the height, h, is the perpendicular distance between the parallel sides.

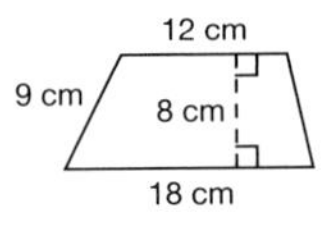

$$A = \frac{1}{2}(a + b)h$$

Use this formula to find the area of the trapezoid shown above. 120 cm²

▸ See Math Conversations in the sidebar.

* 17. (107) **Analyze** Find the slope of each line and the point where each line intersects the y-axis: **a.** 1; (0, −2) **b.** −2; (0, 4)

a.

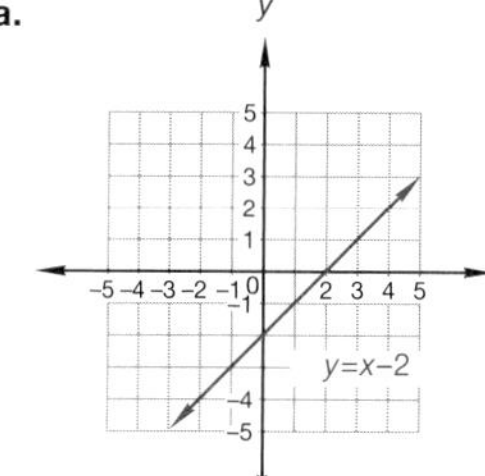

b.

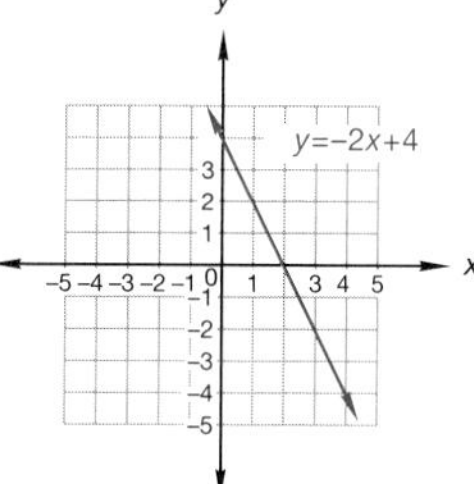

* 18. (109) Find two solutions for $3x^2 - 5 = 40$. $\sqrt{15}, -\sqrt{15}$

* 19. (111) **Generalize** Express each quotient in scientific notation:

a. $\dfrac{8 \times 10^{-4}}{4 \times 10^{8}}$ 2×10^{-12} **b.** $\dfrac{4 \times 10^{8}}{8 \times 10^{-4}}$ 5×10^{11}

20. (83) **Explain** What is the product of the two quotients in Exercise 19? Explain how you found your answer. 1; The two quotients are reciprocals, and the product of a pair of reciprocals is 1.

* 21. (116) **Generalize** Factor each algebraic expression:

a. $9x^2y$ $(3)(3)xxy$

b. $10a^2b + 15a^2b^2 + 20abc$ $5ab(2a + 3ab + 4c)$

* 22. (113) **Analyze** A playground ball just fits inside a cylinder with an interior diameter of 12 in. What is the volume of the ball? Round the answer to the nearest cubic inch. (Use 3.14 for π.) 904 in.^{3}

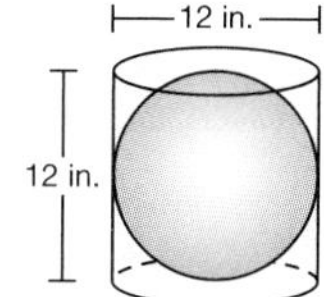

* 23. (40) **a.** In the figure, what is m∠BCD? 65°

b. In the figure, what is m∠BAC? 65°

c. In the figure, what is m∠ACD? 25°

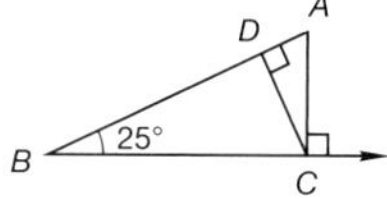

d. **Conclude** What can you conclude about the three triangles in the figure? The three triangles are similar.

24. (97) Refer to the figure in problem **23** to complete this proportion: CD

$$\frac{BD}{BC} = \frac{?}{CA}$$

Solve:

25. (102) $x - 15 = x + 2x + 1$ −8

26. (102) $0.12(m - 5) = 0.96$ 13

▸ See Math Conversations in the sidebar.

3 Written Practice (Continued)

Math Conversations

Discussion opportunities are provided below.

Problem 17 Analyze

Have students explain how they found the slope and the intercept. Sample: For **a,** I looked at the graph and it was going up 1 unit for every unit it was going over. So the slope is positive 1. The line goes across the y-axis at −2, so −2 is the y-intercept.

Problem 19 Generalize

Lead students to examine the two quotients and tell what they notice about them. Samples: Only the numbers 4, 8, and 10 are used in the expressions. The numerator of **a** is the same as the denominator of **b,** and the numerator of **b** is the same as the denominator of **a,** so they are reciprocals.

Problem 21 Generalize

Have students tell how each of these expressions is classified as a polynomial. Samples: **a** has only one term, so it is a monomial; **b** is a trinomial because it has three terms.

Problem 22 Analyze

Extend the Problem

After you ask the question below, have students predict an answer. Then work together as a class to find the answer.

"Is the lateral area of the cylinder greater than the surface area of the sphere?" They are the same. The lateral area of the cylinder is $4\pi r^2$ because the formula is LA $= 2\pi rh$ and $h = 2r$, so LA $= 2\pi r \times 2r$, or $4\pi r^2$. The surface area of a sphere is $4\pi r^2$.

Problem 23d Conclude

Ask students to explain why the three triangles are similar. Sample: Their angle measures are all the same.

(continued)

3 Written Practice (Continued)

Math Conversations

Discussion opportunities are provided below.

Problems 27–30 Analyze

Choose one problem and have students take turns doing each step at the board. On each turn, ask the student to explain the reason for what was done. If time permits, go through all four problems this way.

Errors and Misconceptions

Problem 27

Students whose answer is $ab - ac + bc - ba$ did not recognize that ab and ba are like terms. Help them to see that the order of factors does not matter when looking for like terms.

▶ **Analyze** Simplify:

27. (96) $a(b - c) + b(c - a)$ $bc - ac$ or $-ac + bc$

*** 28.** (103) $\sqrt{\dfrac{(8x^2y)(12x^3y^2)}{(4xy)(6y^2)}}$ $2x^2$

*** 29.** (103, 105) **a.** $(-3)^2 + (-2)(-3) - (-2)^3$ 23

b. $\sqrt[3]{-8} + \sqrt[3]{8}$ 0

30. (7, 35) If $\overline{AB}$ is 1.2 units long and $\overline{BD}$ is 0.75 unit long, what is the length of $\overline{AD}$? 0.45 unit

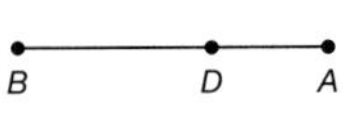

Early Finishers *Real-World Application*

Hugh owns the triangular plot of land △XYZ. He hopes to buy the adjacent plot △WXY, seen in the figure below.

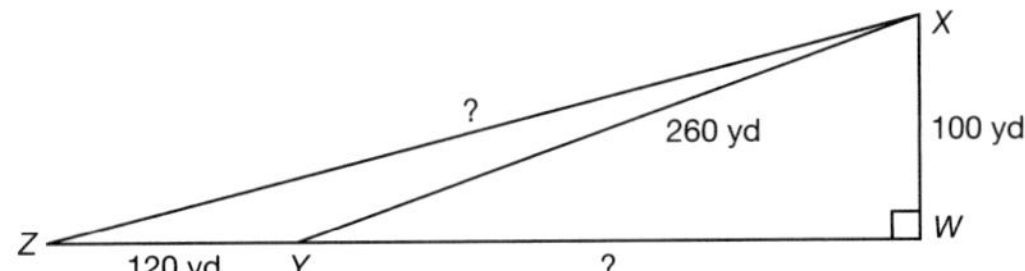

a. Find the new southern length of his land, segment WZ, if he buys the adjacent plot. 360 yd

b. Find the new diagonal length of his land, segment XZ, to the nearest yard. 374 yd

c. Once Hugh buys all of this land, he wants to fence the outer perimeter, △WXZ, uniformly with a white, wooden fence. If the fence costs \$8 per linear foot, about how much will it cost for Hugh to fence in this land? \$20,016

816 *Saxon Math Course 2*

▶ See Math Conversations in the sidebar.

Looking Forward

Writing equations in slope-intercept form and using the slope and y-intercept to graph an equation prepares students for:

- **Lesson 120,** graphing nonlinear equations.

Copying Geometric Figures

Objectives

- Copy a segment.
- Construct parallel lines.
- Copy an angle.
- Copy a triangle.

Lesson Preparation

Materials

- **Power Up V** (in *Instructional Masters*)
- **Manipulative kit: compasses, protractors, straightedges**
- **Teacher-provided material: calculators**

Optional

- **Teacher-provided material: colored pencils**

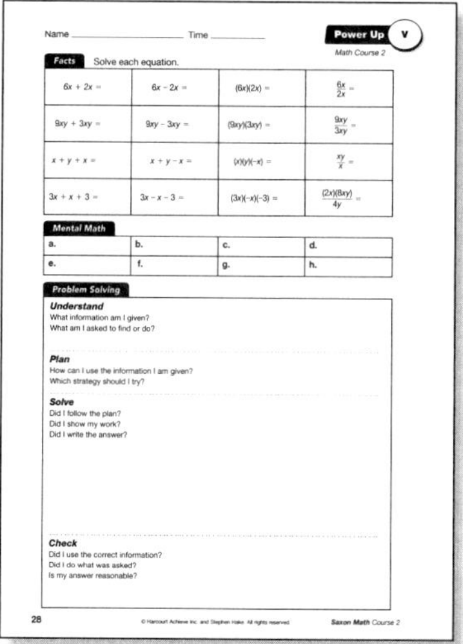

Name ______ Time ______ **Power Up V**

Math Course 2

Facts Solve each equation.

$6x + 2x =$	$6x - 2x =$	$(6x)(2x) =$	$\frac{6x}{2x} =$
$9xy + 3xy =$	$9xy - 3xy =$	$(9xy)(3xy) =$	$\frac{9xy}{3xy} =$
$x + y + x =$	$x + y - x =$	$(x)(y)(-x) =$	$\frac{xy}{x} =$
$3x + x + 3 =$	$3x - x - 3 =$	$(3x)(-x)(-3) =$	$\frac{(2x)(8xy)}{4y} =$

Mental Math

a.	b.	c.	d.
e.	f.	g.	h.

Problem Solving

Understand
What information am I given?
What am I asked to find or do?

Plan
How can I use the information I am given?
Which strategy should I try?

Solve
Did I follow the plan?
Did I show my work?
Did I write the answer?

Check
Did I use the correct information?
Did I do what was asked?
Is my answer reasonable?

28 © Harcourt Achieve Inc. and Stephen Hake. All rights reserved. *Saxon Math Course 2*

Power Up V

Math Language

English Learners (ESL)
at-bats

Technology Resources

Student eBook Complete student textbook in electronic format.

Resources and Planner CD Assessment, reteaching, and instructional masters, plus a pacing calendar with standards.

Test and Practice Generator CD Create additional practice sheets and custom-made tests.

www.SaxonPublishers.com Visit for more student activities and planning materials.

Inclusion

Adaptations CD Adapted lessons, investigations, practice and assessments.

Meeting Standards

National Council of Teachers of Mathematics (NCTM)

Geometry

GM.1a Precisely describe, classify, and understand relationships among types of two- and three-dimensional objects using their defining properties

GM.4a Draw geometric objects with specified properties, such as side lengths or angle measures

Communication

CM.3b Communicate their mathematical thinking coherently and clearly to peers, teachers, and others

Power-Up Discussion For use with Power Up, p. 817

Problem-Solving Strategy: Draw a Diagram/ Write an Equation

There are three numbers whose sum is 180. The second number is twice the first number, and the third number is three times the first number. Create a visual representation of the equation, and then find the three numbers.

Understand Understand the problem.

"What information are we given?"

There are three numbers whose sum is 180. The second number is twice the first number, and the third number is three times the first number

"What are we asked to do?"

We are asked to create a visual representation of the equation, then find the three numbers.

Plan Make a plan.

"What problem-solving strategy will we use?"

We will *draw a diagram* and then *write an equation* to find the value of the three numbers.

Solve Carry out the plan.

"If we use a rectangular prism to represent the first number, what would the three numbers look like?"

= 180

"How should we proceed?"

If six prisms together total 180, then each prism has a value of 30. The three numbers are 30, 60, and 90.

Check Look back.

"Did we do what we were asked to do?"

Yes, we created a visual representation of the equation illustrated by the problem and found the value of each of the three numbers.

"How can we verify the solution is correct?"

We can add the three numbers we found to verify they total 180:
$30 + 60 + 90 = 180$.

LESSON

117

• Copying Geometric Figures

Power Up *Building Power*

facts Power Up V

mental math

a. **Positive/Negative:** $\frac{(-90)(-4)}{-6}$ -60

b. **Scientific Notation:** $(7 \times 10^{-4}) \div (2 \times 10^{-6})$ 3.5×10^2

c. **Algebra:** $2a^2 = 50$ 5, −5

d. **Measurement:** Convert 100°C to Fahrenheit. 212°F

e. **Percent:** $12\frac{1}{2}\%$ of $4000 $500

f. **Percent:** $12\frac{1}{2}\%$ less than $4000 $3500

g. **Geometry:** Angles *A* and *B* are

A. complementary A

B. supplementary

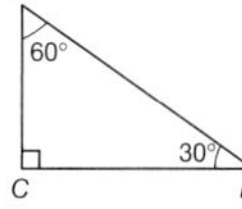

h. **Calculation:** Find 10% of 60, + 4, × 8, + 1, $\sqrt{\ }$, × 3, + 1, ÷ 4, × 5, + 1, $\sqrt{\ }$, − 7. −1

problem solving There are three numbers whose sum is 180. The second number is twice the first number, and the third number is three times the first number. Create a visual representation of the equation, and then find the three numbers.

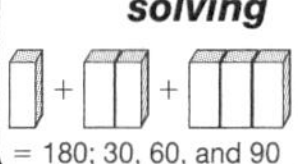

= 180; 30, 60, and 90

New Concept *Increasing Knowledge*

Recall from Investigations 2 and 10 that we used a compass and straightedge to construct circles, regular polygons, angle bisectors, and perpendicular bisectors of segments. We may also use a compass and straightedge to copy figures.

Copying a Segment

We set the radius of the compass to match the length of the segment. Then we draw a dot to represent one endpoint of the new segment and swing an arc from that dot with the compass with the same setting.

Original segment

Set the radius of the compass to match the length of the segment. Then draw a dot and swing an arc from the dot using the compass setting.

Facts Solve each equation.

$6x + 2x = 8x$	$6x - 2x = 4x$	$(6x)(2x) = 12x^2$	$\frac{6x}{2x} = 3$
$9xy + 3xy = 12xy$	$9xy - 3xy = 6xy$	$(9xy)(3xy) = 27x^2y^2$	$\frac{9xy}{3xy} = 3$
$x + y + x = 2x + y$	$x + y - x = y$	$(x)(y)(-x) = -x^2y$	$\frac{xy}{x} = y$
$3x + x + 3 = 4x + 3$	$3x - x - 3 = 2x - 3$	$(3x)(-x)(-3) = 9x^2$	$\frac{(2x)(8xy)}{4y} = 4x^2$

1 Power Up

Facts

Distribute **Power Up V** to students. See answers below.

Mental Math

Encourage students to share different ways to mentally compute these exercises. Strategies for exercises **d** and **e** are listed below.

d. Remember the Equivalent

100°C is the boiling point of water.
212°F is the boiling point of water.
100°C = 212°F

Use the Formula

$F = 1.8C + 32$
$F = 1.8 \times 100 + 32$
$F = 212$
100°C = 212°F

e. Double, Halve

$12\frac{1}{2}\%$ of $4000 =
25% of $2000 =
50% of $1000 =
100% of $500 = $500

Use a Fraction

$12\frac{1}{2}\% = \frac{1}{8}$
$\frac{1}{8} \times \$4000 = \$500$

Problem Solving

Refer to **Power-Up Discussion,** p. 817B.

2 New Concepts

Instruction

Investigations 2 and 10 should have given students some proficiency with using a compass and a straightedge. If you know that some students have difficulty manipulating a compass, have them practice drawing circles and arcs before beginning the lesson.

Have students brainstorm professions in which it may be necessary to draw many geometric figures. Students may suggest some or all of the following:

- Art
- Engineering
- Architecture
- Design

Provide each student with a compass and ruler or other straightedge. Demonstrate the steps for copying a segment on the board or overhead while students follow along.

(continued)

2 New Concepts (Continued)

Instruction

Ask why, when copying a line segment, a line can be drawn from the dot to any point on the arc. The radius of the compass is equal to the length of the original segment. Therefore, connecting the dot with any point on the arc will result in a copy of the original segment.

For copying the pair of parallel lines, have students notice that the length of the line segments is not something that has to be copied exactly, rather it is the distance between the lines that must be the same at all points. This is accomplished by using the compass to locate two points that are the same distance from a drawn line as the distance between the two original parallel lines.

As you work through the section on copying angles, ask students to use a protractor to draw a 45° angle and then set the protractor aside. Have them follow along with you as you demonstrate the steps for copying an angle on an overhead projector or on the board if you have a board compass. Caution students to draw their beginning rays where they will have enough room for the copied angle.

Have students put a solid dot on one end of the ray and label the intersections A, B, A', and B' as they follow along with your demonstration.

(continued)

Draw a segment from the dot to any point on the arc to match the length of the original segment.

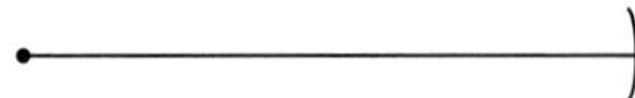

Now suppose we are asked to construct two parallel lines that are the same distance apart as another pair of parallel lines. We use the compass to find the distance between the lines and set the radius of the compass at that distance. We use that setting to mark the distance between the copied lines.

Set the compass to match the distance between the original parallel lines.

Draw a line. Then, using a compass, swing arcs from any two points on the line.

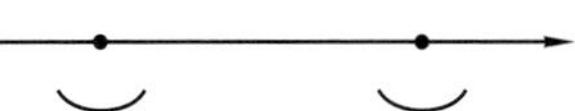

Now draw a second line that just touches the two arcs.

Copying an Angle

Suppose we are given this angle to copy:

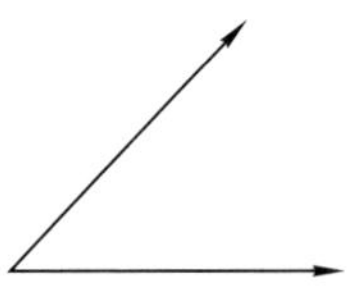

We begin by drawing a ray to form one side of the angle.

Now we need to find a point through which to draw the second ray. We find this point in two steps. First we set the compass and draw an arc across both rays of the original angle from the vertex of the angle. Without resetting the compass, we then draw an arc of the same size from the endpoint of the ray, as we show here.

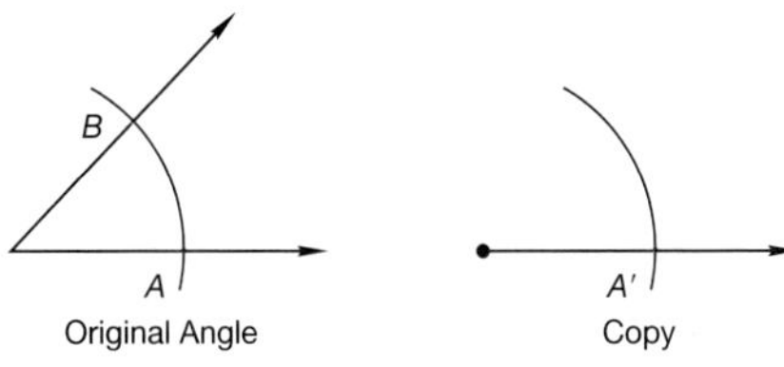

For the second step, we reset the compass to equal the distance from A to B on the original angle. To verify the correct setting, we swing a small arc through point B while the pivot point is on point A. With the compass at this setting, we move the pivot point to point A' of the copy and draw an arc that intersects the first arc we drew on the copy.

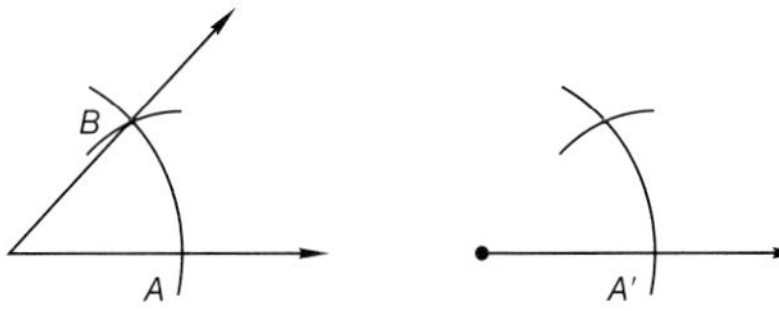

As a final step, we draw the second ray of the copied angle through the point at which the arcs intersect.

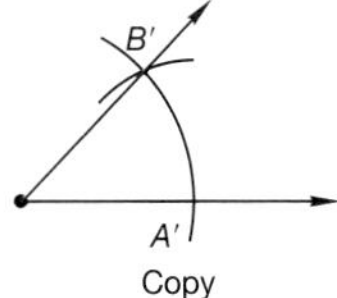

Copy

a protractor, to check that the measures of both angles are equal

Discuss What tool can we use to check our work?

Model Using a straightedge, draw an obtuse angle. Using a compass, copy the angle. See student work.

Copying a Triangle

We use a similar method to copy a triangle. Suppose we are asked to copy $\triangle XYZ$.

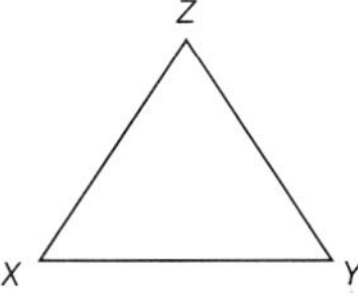

Math Language

We use an apostrophe or the word *prime* to indicate that an endpoint or vertex is related to another endpoint or vertex in a different figure.

We begin by drawing a segment equal in length to segment XY. We do this by setting the compass so that the pivot point is on X and the drawing point is on Y. We verify the setting by drawing a small arc through point Y. To copy this segment, we first sketch a ray with endpoint X'. Then we locate Y' by swinging an arc with the preset compass from point X'.

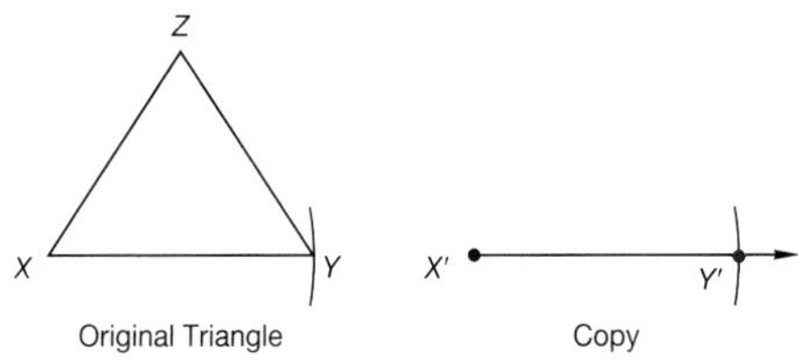

2 New Concepts (Continued)

Instruction

Continue with your demonstration, checking that students are following along without difficulty.

When you finish the construction, use the *Discuss* question to have students check the measures of the two angles using a protractor.

Have students practice this skill by drawing an obtuse angle and copying it.

When "Copying a Triangle," have students draw a triangle on their paper, and as with the angle copying, follow along as you demonstrate the process. Again have students draw a solid dot on one end of the ray and label the figures as they work along with you. You may want to discuss this question:

"When copying a triangle, does it matter which side is copied first? Why or why not?" No. A triangle is formed by connecting three points. Any segment provides two of those points, and any two points can be used to find the third.

(continued)

2 New Concepts *(Continued)*

Instruction

Point out the importance of keeping the compass setting the same after setting it to the length of each segment. The arc drawn to create the copy must be exactly the same as the arc drawn from the original. The setting will likely change from step to step, unless the sides of the triangle are all equal.

You may want to ask students if they think the technique for copying a triangle could be applied to figures with four or more sides. Why or why not? Sample: Yes, any polygon can be divided into a series of triangles.

(continued)

Activity

Instruction

Have students use a straightedge to draw the original angle and triangle. Suggest that they draw the original figures large enough that their partners can easily manipulate their compasses as they copy the figure.

2 New Concepts *(Continued)*

Practice Set

Problem c Summarize

Have pairs of students explain and demonstrate how to copy parallel lines with a compass and straightedge. Suggest that one student does the explanation while the other does the demonstration.

To further test students' understanding of the concepts in this lesson, have them explain and demonstrate how to copy segments, angles, and triangles using a compass and straightedge.

To locate Z' on the copy, we will need to draw two different arcs, one from point X' and one from point Y'. We set the compass on the original triangle so that the distance between its points equals XZ. With the compass at this setting, we draw an arc from X' on the copy.

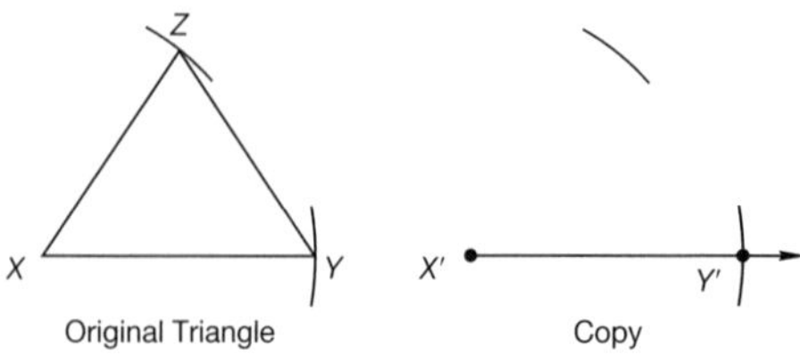

Original Triangle   Copy

Now we change the setting of the compass to equal YZ on the original. With this setting we draw an arc from Y' that intersects the other arc.

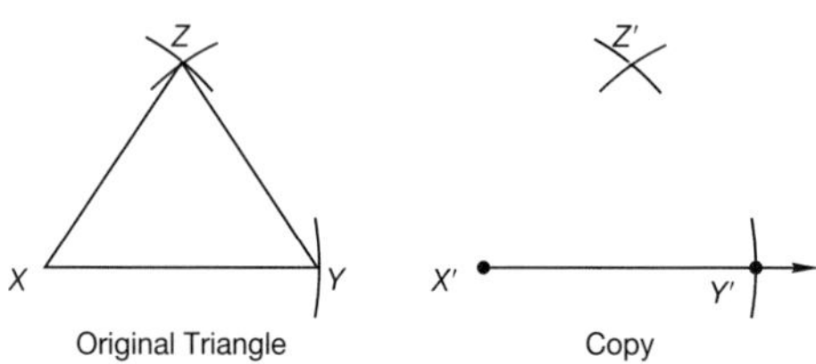

Original Triangle   Copy

The point where the arcs intersect, which we have labeled Z', corresponds to point Z on the original triangle. To complete the copy, we draw segments $X'Z'$ and $Y'Z'$.

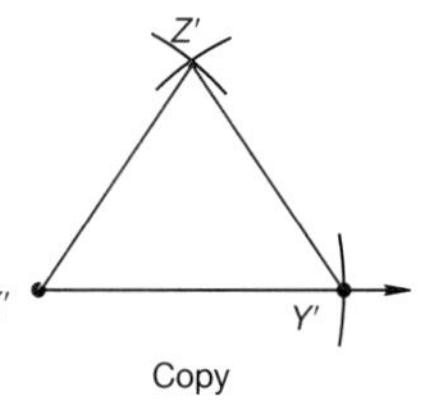

Copy

Activity

Copying Angles and Triangles

For this activity work with a partner. One partner draws an angle that the partner copies. Then switch roles. After each partner has drawn and copied an angle, repeat the process with triangles.

Set the compass to match the distance between the original parallel lines. Draw a line using the straightedge. From any two points on the line, swing arcs using the compass. Then draw a second line that just touches the two arcs.

Practice Set

a. Use a protractor to draw an 80° angle. Then use a compass and straightedge to copy the angle. See student work.

b. With a protractor, draw a triangle with angles of 30°, 60°, and 90°. Then use a compass and straightedge to copy the triangle. See student work.

▸ **c.** Summarize Without looking back at the lesson, explain how to copy a pair of parallel lines using a compass and a straight edge.

▸ See Math Conversations in the sidebar.

Teacher Tip

In this lesson, you can foster success by **encouraging students to share their work** with one another. Students can look over or check one another's work.

Sharing work can help students who are struggling by allowing them to see how other students constructed the figures in this lesson. You may even want to have some students work together so that a student experiencing some difficulty can watch a more skilled student carry out the process.

Written Practice *Strengthening Concepts*

▶ * **1.** (110) Generalize How much interest is earned in four years on a deposit of \$10,000 if it is allowed to accumulate in an account paying 7% interest compounded annually? \$3107.96

2. (Inv. 8) In 240 at-bats Taneisha has 60 hits.

a. What is the statistical probability that Taneisha will get a hit in her next at-bat? $\frac{1}{4}$

b. What are the odds of Taneisha getting a hit in her next at-bat? 1 to 3

3. (55) The average attendance at the first four meetings of the drama club was 75%. At the next six meetings, the average attendance was 85%. What was the average attendance at all ten meetings? 81%

▶ **4.** (48) Justify Complete the table.

Fraction	Decimal	Percent
a. $1\frac{2}{5}$	1.4	**b.** 140%
$\frac{11}{12}$	**c.** $0.91\overline{6}$	**d.** $91\frac{2}{3}$%

5. (80) The image of $\triangle ABC$ reflected in the y-axis is $\triangle A'B'C'$. If the coordinates of vertices A, B, and C are $(-1, 3)$, $(-3, 0)$, and $(0, -2)$, respectively, then what are the coordinates of vertices A', B', and C'? A' (1, 3), B' (3, 0), C' (0, −2)

6. (89) The figure at right shows regular octagon $ABCDEFGH$.

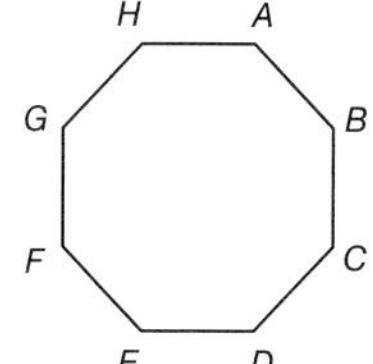

a. What is the measure of each exterior angle? 45°

b. What is the measure of each interior angle? 135°

c. How many diagonals can be drawn from vertex A? 5 diagonals

7. (92) From 1990 to 2000, the population of Phoenix, Arizona increased from about 980,000 people to about 1,321,000 people. The population increased by what percent? Round your answer to the nearest one percent. about 35%

8. (114) A beaker is filled with water to the 500 mL level.

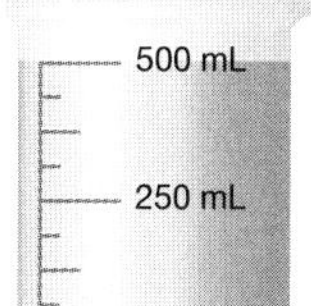

a. What is the volume of the water in cubic centimeters? 500 cubic centimeters

b. What is the mass of the water in kilograms? 0.5 kilogram

▶ See Math Conversations in the sidebar.

English Learners

Refer students to problem 2. Explain the meaning of the term **at-bats.** Tell students:

"At-bat is a player's official turn to bat. Taneisha had 240 at-bats (turns to hit the ball) and out of 240 at-bats she hit the ball 60 times."

Ask:

"If a player has 200 at-bats, or turns to bat, and hits the ball 100 times, what is his percentage of hits at-bat?" 50%

3 Written Practice

Math Conversations

Discussion opportunities are provided below.

Problem 1 Generalize

Students will need calculators for this question. You may want to extend the question to doubling and tripling the principal.

"How many years would it take for the accumulated interest to be greater than the principal?" Sample: The interest is almost as great as the principal at the end of 10 years, and much greater at the end of 11 years.

Problem 4 Justify

Ask students to work together to make a fraction-decimal-percent chart for the twelfths at the board. Then have students look for patterns in the chart and discuss any ways that can help them remember these equivalents.

Fraction	Decimal	Percent
$\frac{1}{12}$	$0.08\overline{3}$	$8\frac{1}{3}$%
$\frac{2}{12}$ or $\frac{1}{6}$	$0.16\overline{6}$	$16\frac{2}{3}$%
$\frac{3}{12}$ or $\frac{1}{4}$	0.25	25%
$\frac{4}{12}$ or $\frac{1}{3}$	$0.33\overline{3}$	$33\frac{1}{3}$%
$\frac{5}{12}$	$0.41\overline{6}$	$41\frac{2}{3}$%
$\frac{6}{12}$ or $\frac{1}{2}$	0.5	50%
$\frac{7}{12}$	$0.58\overline{3}$	$58\frac{1}{3}$%
$\frac{8}{12}$ or $\frac{2}{3}$	$0.66\overline{6}$	$66\frac{2}{3}$%
$\frac{9}{12}$ or $\frac{3}{4}$	0.75	75%
$\frac{10}{12}$ or $\frac{5}{6}$	$0.83\overline{3}$	$83\frac{1}{3}$%
$\frac{11}{12}$	$0.91\overline{6}$	$91\frac{2}{3}$%
$\frac{12}{12}$	1	100%

(continued)

3 Written Practice (Continued)

Math Conversations

Discussion opportunities are provided below.

Problem 12 Generalize

When students have solved the equation, ask:

"Where have you seen this equation before?" the Pythagorean theorem

"What are some sets of three whole numbers that satisfy this equation?" Samples: 3-4-5; 5-12-13; 8-15-17; 7-24-25; and multiples of these

"What are these numbers called?" Pythagorean triplets or Pythagorean triples

Problem 14 Analyze

After students find the answers to parts **a–c,** discuss what might happen if the triangle is moved in the coordinate plane.

"Suppose the triangle is translated 4 units to the right and 4 units down. In what quadrant will the translated triangle be?" Quadrant IV

"Will its perimeter or area change?" no

"How has the triangle changed?" Sample: The coordinates of corresponding points are different.

Problem 15 Analyze

Extend the Problem

Have students analyze what happens when dimensions are transposed.

"Suppose the diameter is 8 inches and the height is 6 inches. Do the two volumes change? If so, how?" Sample: Yes; the cylinder is 96π in.^{3} and the cone is 32π in.^{3} and both of those volumes are $\frac{1}{3}$ greater than the volumes of first cylinder and cone.

"Which dimension has more effect on the volume—diameter or height?" Sample: The diameter because changing the diameter changes the radius, which is a factor twice in a volume calculation.

Errors and Misconceptions

Problem 13

For students who think there is an equal likelihood of landing in any one of the four sectors, tell them that the likelihoods depend on the size of the sector. Have them calculate what fraction of the circle each sector is before attempting to answer the questions.

(continued)

9. (88) Use two unit multipliers to convert 540 ft^2 to yd^2. 60 yd^2

10. (101) Write an equation to solve this problem:

Six more than three times what number squared is 81?
$3x^2 + 6 = 81$; 5, −5

11. (93) Solve this inequality and graph its solution:

$$\frac{3}{4}x + 12 < 15$$

$x < 4$

▶ ***12.** (106) Generalize Solve for c^2: $c^2 - a^2 = b^2$ $c^2 = b^2 + a^2$ or $c^2 = a^2 + b^2$

▶ **13.** (Inv. 8) The face of this spinner is divided into four sectors. Sectors *B* and *D* are 90° sectors, and sector *C* is a 120° sector. If the arrow is spun once,

a. what is the probability (expressed as a decimal) that it will stop in sector *B*? 0.25

b. what is the chance that it will stop in sector *C*? $33\frac{1}{3}\%$

c. what are the odds that it will stop in sector *A*? 1 to 5

▶ ***14.** (112) Analyze The coordinates of the vertices of a square are (0, 4), (3, 0), (−1, −3), and (−4, 1).

a. What is the length of each side of the square? 5 units

b. What is the perimeter of the square? 20 units

c. What is the area of the square? 25 units^2

▶ ***15.** (113) Analyze A right circular cylinder and a cone have an equal height and an equal diameter as shown.

a. What is the volume of the cylinder? 72π in.^{3}

b. What is the volume of the cone? 24π in.^{3}

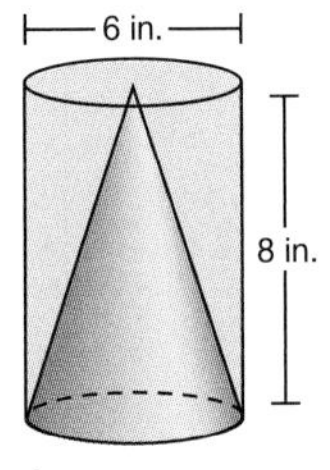

Leave π as π.

***16.** (106) The formula for the volume of a rectangular prism is

$$V = lwh$$

a. Transform this formula to solve for *h*. $h = \frac{V}{lw}$

b. Find *h* when *V* is 6000 cm^3, *l* is 20 cm, and *w* is 30 cm. 10 cm

822 **Saxon** Math Course 2

▶ See Math Conversations in the sidebar.

* **17.** Refer to the graph shown below to answer **a–c.**
(116)

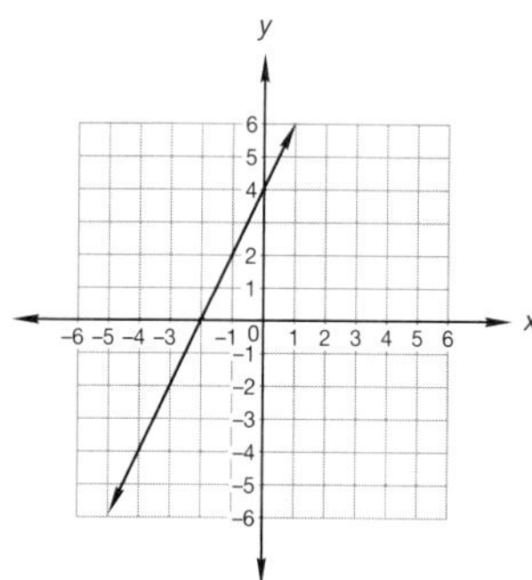

a. Analyze What is the slope of the line? 2

b. At what point does the line intersect the y-axis? (0, 4)

c. What is the equation of the line in slope-intercept form? $y = 2x + 4$

* **18.** Connect Write each equation in slope-intercept form:
(116)

a. $y + 5 = x$ $y = x - 5$ **b.** $2x + y = 4$ $y = -2x + 4$

* **19.** Generalize Factor each algebraic expression:
(115)

a. $24xy^2$ (2)(2)(2)(3)xyy **b.** $3x^2 + 6xy - 9x$ $3x(x + 2y - 3)$

20. Find the area of a square with sides 5×10^3 mm long. Express the area
(83)

a. in scientific notation. 2.5×10^7 mm^2

b. as a standard numeral. 25,000,000 mm^2

21. Use two unit multipliers to convert the answer to problem **20b** to square meters. 25 m^2
(88)

22. Triangle ABC is a right triangle and is similar to triangles CAD and CBD.
(97)

a. Which side of $\triangle CBD$ corresponds to side BC of $\triangle ABC$? side BD

b. Which side of $\triangle CAD$ corresponds to side AC of $\triangle ABC$? side AD

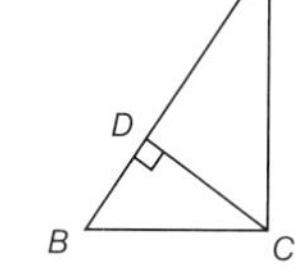

23. Refer to the figure below to find the length of segment BD. $\frac{5}{12}$
(7, 30)

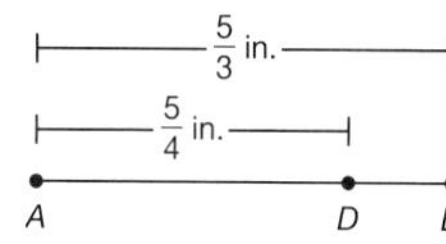

See Math Conversations in the sidebar.

3 Written Practice (Continued)

Math Conversations

Discussion opportunities are provided below.

Problem 17a Analyze

Discuss how students found the slope of the line. Ask a student who found it by inspection to describe the method.

Problem 18 Connect

"How do you know that an equation is in slope-intercept form?" Sample: The y term is by itself on the left side, and there is an x term and a number on the right side, but either one of those could be zero.

Problem 19 Generalize

Have students tell what type of polynomial each of the two expressions is. **a.** monomial; **b.** trinomial Then ask:

"How can you check your answers?" Samples: You can multiply and see if you get the original expression. If you are factoring a binomial or a trinomial, you check whether the factor after the GCF is also a binomial or trinomial.

Errors and Misconceptions

Problem 22

For students who get confused as they try to find corresponding sides, suggest that they first note which side of each triangle is the hypotenuse, the longer leg, and the shorter leg. Using different colored pencils to mark each triangle may help.

Problem 23

If students give answers such as $\frac{1}{2}$ in., $\frac{3}{8}$ in., or $\frac{7}{16}$ in., they have used a ruler to measure, rather than calculating. Have them do the problem without using a ruler by subtracting $\frac{5}{4}$ from $\frac{5}{3}$. Suggest that they find a common denominator first.

(continued)

3 Written Practice (Continued)

Math Conversations

Discussion opportunities are provided below.

Problems 26–30 Generalize

Point out that checking the answer is an important part of solving any problem, whether it is a simple exercise or a multistep problem. For each of these problems, discuss how students checked their answers. Sample: For problem 27, I redid the work without looking at what I did the first time and then checked that the answers were the same. They weren't, so I did it again.

Errors and Misconceptions

Problem 24

For students who do not get the correct answer, tell them that they first need to solve for x in an equation that has the sum of the two supplementary angles equal to 180°. After they find the value of x, they need to use it to determine the values of $3x$ and $x - 5$, and then find the value of y.

▶ **24.** (101) Find the measure of the angle marked y in the figure shown. 50°

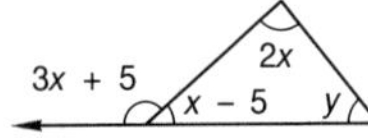

25. (102) Solve: $6w - 3w + 18 = 9(w - 4)$ 9

▶ Generalize Simplify:

* **26.** (96) $3x(x - 2y) + 2xy(x + 3)$ $3x^2 + 2x^2y$

* **27.** (57, 103, 105) $2^{-2} + 4^{-1} + \sqrt[3]{27} + (-1)^3$ $2\frac{1}{2}$

28. (85) $(-3) + (-2)[(-3)(-2) - (+4)] - (-3)(-4)$ -19

* **29.** (111) $\dfrac{1.2 \times 10^{-6}}{4 \times 10^3}$ 3×10^{-10}

30. (103) $\dfrac{36a^2b^3c}{12ab^2c}$ $3ab$

Early Finishers Activity *Math and Architecture*

The Great Pyramid of Giza was built by the Egyptian pharaoh Khufu in 2560 B.C. Its shape is a square pyramid with a base length of 756 feet and a height of 480 feet.

a. What is the perimeter of the pyramid's base? 3024 feet

b. What is the volume of the Great Pyramid? 91,445,760 ft^3

c. Approximately how much area does the floor and outer shell of the pyramid cover? Sample: 1,495,368 ft^2

824 **Saxon** Math Course 2

▶ See Math Conversations in the sidebar.

• Division by Zero

Objective

- Guard against division by zero.

Lesson Preparation

Materials

- **Power Up W** (in *Instructional Masters*)
- **Manipulative kit: inch rulers, protractors, compasses**
- **Teacher-provided material: calculators, graph paper** (2 per student)

Optional

- **Investigation Activity 13** (in *Instructional Masters*)

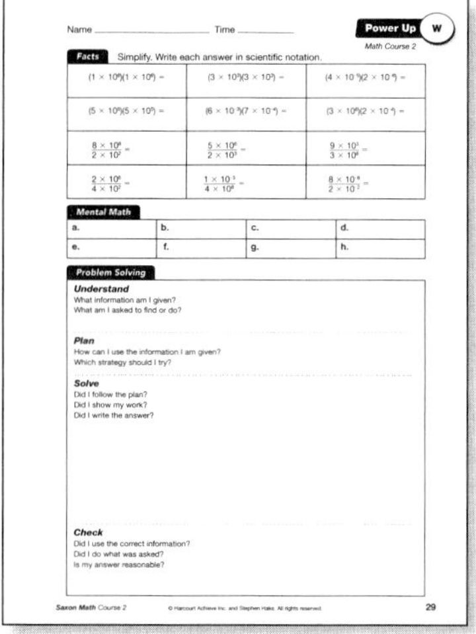

Name ______ Time ______

Power Up W

Math Course 2

Facts Simplify. Write each answer in scientific notation.

[illegible]	[illegible]	[illegible]
[illegible]	[illegible]	[illegible]
[illegible]	[illegible]	[illegible]
[illegible]	[illegible]	[illegible]

Mental Math

a.	b.	c.	d.
e.	f.	g.	h.

Problem Solving

Understand
What information am I given?
What am I asked to find or do?

Plan
How can I use the information I am given?
Which strategy should I try?

Solve
Did I follow the plan?
Did I show my work?
Did I write the answer?

Check
Did I use the correct information?
Did I do what was asked?
Is my answer reasonable?

Saxon Math Course 2 — — 29

Power Up W

Math Language

English Learners (ESL)
vertical

Technology Resources

Student eBook Complete student textbook in electronic format.

Resources and Planner CD Assessment, reteaching, and instructional masters, plus a pacing calendar with standards.

Test and Practice Generator CD Create additional practice sheets and custom-made tests.

www.SaxonPublishers.com Visit for more student activities and planning materials.

Inclusion

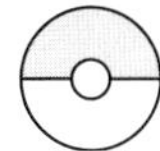

Adaptations CD Adapted lessons, investigations, practice and assessments.

Meeting Standards

National Council of Teachers of Mathematics (NCTM)

Numbers and Operations

NO.1a Work flexibly with fractions, decimals, and percents to solve problems

NO.2a Understand the meaning and effects of arithmetic operations with fractions, decimals, and integers

Algebra

AL.2a Develop an initial conceptual understanding of different uses of variables

Connections

CN.4a Recognize and use connections among mathematical ideas

Power-Up Discussion *For use with Power Up, p. 825*

Problem-Solving Strategy: Draw a Diagram/ Find a Pattern

A group of citizens meet to discuss improvements of a local park. If each person shakes hands with every other person at the meeting, and 28 handshakes take place altogether, how many citizens attended the meeting?

Understand **Understand the problem.**

"What information are we given?"

Every citizen at the meeting shook the hand of every other citizen at the meeting. There were 28 handshakes altogether.

"What are we asked to do?"

We are asked to determine how many citizens attended the meeting.

Plan **Make a plan.**

"What problem-solving strategy will we use?"

We will *draw a diagram* to help us *find a pattern* in the numbers of handshakes that take place between groups of people.

Solve **Carry out the plan.**

"How will we begin our diagram?"

We begin with two people and one handshake. We will then add a third person and their handshakes, a fourth person, and so on.

2 people
1 handshake

3 people
3 handshakes
(1 + **2** more)

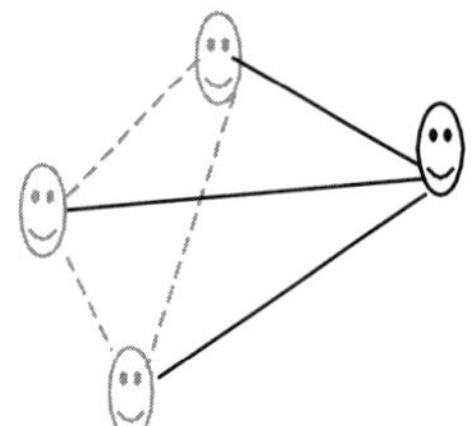

4 people
6 handshakes
(the previous 3 + **3** more)

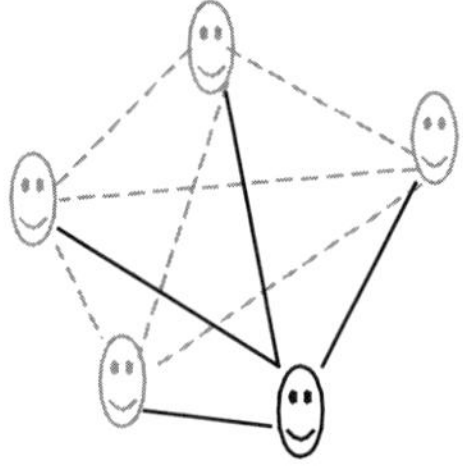

5 people
10 handshakes
(the previous 6 + **4** more)

"If a sixth person arrives, how many new handshakes will occur, and how many handshakes total will have taken place?"

The sixth person will shake hands 5 times, and a total of 15 handshakes will have taken place.

"How does the pattern continue?"

If there are 7 people, there are $15 + 6 = 21$ total handshakes. If there are 8 people, there are $21 + 7 = 28$ handshakes.

Check **Look back.**

"Did we do what we were asked to do?"

Yes, we found that there were 8 people at the meeting.

"How can we verify the solution is correct?"

We could draw a diagram of 8 people using dots and segments and count the number of handshakes that take place.

LESSON 118

• Division by Zero

Power Up — *Building Power*

facts Power Up W

mental math

a. **Positive/Negative:** $(-3)^2 + 3^{-2}$ $9\frac{1}{9}$

b. **Scientific Notation:** $(5 \times 10^{-6})(3 \times 10^{2})$ 1.5×10^{-3}

c. **Ratio:** $\frac{k}{33} = \frac{200}{300}$ 22

d. **Measurement:** Convert 7500 g to kg. 7.5 kg

e. **Percent:** 150% of $4000 $6000

f. **Percent:** $4000 increased 150% $10,000

g. **Geometry:** A triangle has a base of 6 ft and a height of 2 ft. What is the area of the triangle? 6 ft^2

h. **Rate:** At an average speed of 30 mph, how long will it take to drive 40 miles? 1 hr 20 min

problem solving A group of citizens meet to discuss improvements of a local park. If each person shakes hands with every other person at the meeting, and 28 handshakes take place altogether, how many citizens attended the meeting? 8 citizens

New Concept — *Increasing Knowledge*

When performing algebraic operations, it is necessary to guard against dividing by zero. For example, the following expression reduces to 2 only if x is not zero:

$$\frac{2x}{x} = 2 \quad \text{if } x \neq 0$$

Thinking Skill
Analyze
What is the value of $\frac{3x}{x}$ for all values of x except 0? 3

What is the value of this expression if x is zero?

$\frac{2x}{x}$	expression
$\frac{2 \cdot 0}{0}$	substituted 0 for x
$\frac{0}{0}$	multiplied $2 \cdot 0$

Facts Simplify. Write each answer in scientific notation.

$(1 \times 10^6)(1 \times 10^6) =$ 1×10^{12}	$(3 \times 10^3)(3 \times 10^3) =$ 9×10^6	$(4 \times 10^{-5})(2 \times 10^{-6}) =$ 8×10^{-11}
$(5 \times 10^5)(5 \times 10^5) =$ 2.5×10^{11}	$(6 \times 10^{-3})(7 \times 10^{-4}) =$ 4.2×10^{-6}	$(3 \times 10^6)(2 \times 10^{-4}) =$ 6×10^2
$\frac{8 \times 10^8}{2 \times 10^2} = 4 \times 10^6$	$\frac{5 \times 10^6}{2 \times 10^3} = 2.5 \times 10^3$	$\frac{9 \times 10^3}{3 \times 10^8} = 3 \times 10^{-5}$
$\frac{2 \times 10^6}{4 \times 10^2} = 5 \times 10^3$	$\frac{1 \times 10^{-3}}{4 \times 10^8} = 2.5 \times 10^{-12}$	$\frac{8 \times 10^{-8}}{2 \times 10^{-2}} = 4 \times 10^{-6}$

1 Power Up

Facts

Distribute **Power Up W** to students. See answers below.

Mental Math

Encourage students to share different ways to mentally compute these exercises. Strategies for exercises **c** and **g** are listed below.

c. Reduce First

$\frac{200}{300} = \frac{2}{3}$

$\frac{2}{3} \times \frac{11}{11} = \frac{22}{33}$

$k = 22$

Cross Multiply and Divide

$300k = 200 \times 33$

$k = \frac{200 \times 33}{300} = \frac{2 \times 33}{3}$

$k = \frac{66}{3} = 22$

g. Use Logical Thinking

The area is one half times the base times the height.

The height is 2, and half of 2 is 1.

The area is equal to the base, or 6 ft^2.

Use the Equation

$A = \frac{1}{2}(b \times h)$

$A = \frac{1}{2}(6 \times 2)$

$A = 6 \text{ ft}^2$

Problem Solving

Refer to **Power-Up Discussion,** p. 825B.

2 New Concepts

Instruction

Explain that the reason for including the expression *if* $x \neq 0$ is so that 0 will not be used as a divisor. The expression $\frac{2(0)}{0}$ does not equal 2, and the indicated division by 0 cannot be performed.

Students know that it is impossible to divide by zero, but presenting mathematical proofs helps them understand why this is so. Varied examples and illustrations reinforce this concept and remind them to guard against division by zero if it appears in their work.

(continued)

2 New Concepts (Continued)

Instruction

Help students explore the ideas presented in the first paragraph. Have them use calculators to try dividing zero and other numbers by zero. Knowing how their calculators respond to division by zero will help them avoid dividing by zero as they evaluate expressions.

Let students choose any number and use their calculators to divide by two or three numbers that are each closer to zero. Have them observe what happens to the quotient.

Use the *Discuss* question to help students understand what it means for a number to be closer to zero than another number.

Example 1

Instruction

Have students use calculators to work through this example. Some may want to use even smaller divisors to explore the change in the size of the quotient as the divisor grows smaller and closer to zero.

Instruction

The concept of infinity may seem simple but is very complex. It is easy to think that there is a greatest number, but that is not what infinity is. It is the idea of something greater than any possible value. Guide students through the discussion in the paragraph after example 1.

It may be easier for students to understand the reasoning for the impossibility of division by zero through the inverse relationship of multiplication and division.

continued

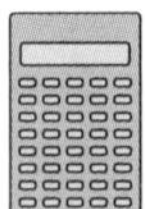

What is the value of $\frac{0}{0}$? How many zeros are in zero? Is the quotient 0? Is the quotient 1? Is the quotient some other number? Try the division with a calculator. What answer does the calculator display? Notice that the calculator displays an error message when division by zero is entered. The display is frozen and other calculations cannot be performed until the erroneous entry is cleared. In this lesson we will consider why division by zero is not possible.

Consider what happens to a quotient when a number is divided by numbers closer and closer to zero. As we know, zero lies on the number line between −1 and 1. Zero is also between −0.1 and 0.1, and between −0.01 and 0.01.

−0.01 0.01
−1 −0.1 0 0.1 1

In the following example, notice the quotients we get when we divide a number by numbers closer and closer to zero.

Discuss What are two other divisors that are closer to zero than −0.01 and 0.01. Sample: 0.001, −0.001

Example 1

Find each set of quotients. As the divisors become closer to zero, do the quotients become closer to zero or farther from zero?

a. $\frac{10}{1}, \frac{10}{0.1}, \frac{10}{0.01}$ **b.** $\frac{10}{-1}, \frac{10}{-0.1}, \frac{10}{-0.01}$

Solution

a. 10, 100, 1000 **b. −10, −100, −1000**

As the divisors become closer to zero, the quotients become farther from zero.

Notice from example 1a that as the divisors approach zero from the positive side, the quotients become greater and greater toward positive infinity ($+\infty$). However, in example 1b as the divisors approach zero from the negative side, the quotients become less and less toward negative infinity ($-\infty$).

In other words, as the divisors of a number approach zero from opposite sides of zero, the quotients do not become closer. Rather, the quotients grow infinitely far apart. As the divisor finally reaches zero, we might wonder whether the quotient would equal positive infinity or negative infinity! Considering this growing difference in quotients as divisors approach zero from opposite sides can help us understand why division by zero is not possible.

Another consideration is the relationship between multiplication and division. Recall that multiplication and division are inverse operations. The numbers that form a multiplication fact may be arranged to form two division facts. For the multiplication fact $4 \times 5 = 20$, we may arrange the numbers to form these two division facts:

$$\frac{20}{4} = 5 \quad \text{and} \quad \frac{20}{5} = 4$$

Inclusion

Some students may need to have a simple explanation along with the deeper meaning to divisibility of zero. Say:

"What does $\frac{0}{n}$ spell?" on

"What does $\frac{n}{0}$ spell?" no

"So the saying goes, when you have 0 divided by a number it's on and the answer is zero. For a number divided by 0 it's no and the answer is undefined!"

Math Background

What is infinity?

The word "infinity" comes from the Latin word *infinitus*, meaning boundless or unlimited. In mathematics, infinity is not a specific number, but is the concept of a quantity greater than any number. Infinity is not a number, so it cannot be odd or even, or prime or composite. Its symbol ∞ looks like two attached zeros or an 8 on its side.

Mathematicians think about infinity in many ways. On a number line, positive infinity is a concept that represents something that is greater than any number and negative infinity is a concept that represents something less than any number.

826 **Saxon** Math Course 2

No, the relationship does not apply. Although $0 \div 2$ is 0, it is not true that $0 \div 0$ is 2.

We see that if we divide the product of two factors by either factor, the result is the other factor.

$$\frac{\text{product}}{\text{factor}_1} = \text{factor}_2 \quad \text{and} \quad \frac{\text{product}}{\text{factor}_2} = \text{factor}_1$$

List Rearrange some other multiplication facts to form two division facts. See student work.

Predict Does the relationship between multiplication and division apply when zero is a factor? Try $2 \times 0 = 0$.

This relationship between multiplication and division breaks down when zero is one of the factors, as we see in example 2.

Example 2

The numbers in the multiplication fact $2 \times 3 = 6$ can be arranged to form two division facts.

$$\frac{6}{3} = 2 \quad \text{and} \quad \frac{6}{2} = 3$$

If we attempt to form two division facts for the multiplication fact $2 \times 0 = 0$, one of the arrangements is not a fact. Which arrangement is not a fact?

Solution

The product is 0 and the factors are 2 and 0. So the possible arrangements are these:

$$\underset{\text{fact}}{\frac{0}{2} = 0} \quad \text{and} \quad \underset{\text{not a fact}}{\frac{0}{0} = 2}$$

The arrangement **$0 \div 0 = 2$ is not a fact.**

The multiplication fact $2 \times 0 = 0$ does not imply $0 \div 0 = 2$ any more than $3 \times 0 = 0$ implies $0 \div 0 = 3$. This breakdown in the inverse relationship between multiplication and division when zero is one of the factors is another indication that division by zero is not possible.

Example 3

If we were asked to graph the following equation, what number could we not use in place of x when generating a table of ordered pairs?

$$y = \frac{12}{3 + x}$$

Solution

This equation involves division. Since division by zero is not possible, we need to guard against the divisor, $3 + x$, being zero. When x is 0, the expression $3 + x$ equals 3. So we may use 0 in place of x. However, when x is -3, the expression $3 + x$ equals zero.

2 New Concepts *(Continued)*

Instruction

As you discuss the *List* question, remind students that each set of multiplication and division facts should contain the same three numbers.

Example 2

Instruction

This example should solidify understanding of this concept. Being unable to use the inverse relationship of multiplication and division to write a set of related facts for a fact such as $2 \times 0 = 0$ clearly demonstrates that division by zero is impossible.

Example 3

Instruction

Help students understand that whenever the denominator of a fraction contains a variable, they must be on guard for values that will make the denominator equal zero.

(continued)

Teacher Tip

To **incorporate writing** in this lesson (and to get a picture of how well students understand this concept), have students use what they have learned so far to write a paragraph about why dividing by zero is impossible. Encourage them to write their paragraphs as if their intended audience did not know dividing by zero was not possible.

2 New Concepts (Continued)

Instruction

The *Discuss* question provides an opportunity to stress that the numerator of a fraction may have a value of 0, but that the denominator may never be equal to zero.

Practice Set

Problem b (Error Alert)

If students have difficulty with this problem, have them refer to example 2.

Problems c–h (Analyze)

Ask students to explain how they determined what number or numbers could not be used for the variable. Guide them to understand that they need only consider what the value of the denominator will be.

Problem h (Error Alert)

If students are having trouble with this problem, tell them that only one of the variables has an impossible value.

Problem i (Justify)

Have volunteers read their explanations. If they mention that they found two numbers that cannot be used in place of the variable but do not explain why there are two numbers, ask them to do so.

3 Written Practice

Math Conversations

Discussion opportunities are provided below.

Problem 3 (Explain)

Ask several students to read their explanations. For each explanation, ask others in the class to comment on a strong point of the explanation and to ask questions that would clarify or enhance the explanation. Sample: Joe, I think that your explanation of how the triangle would work is very clear, but I am wondering whether you mean 6, 8, and 10 meters or 6, 8, and 10 feet, or some other unit.

Errors and Misconceptions

Problem 2

Students whose answer is 0.15 m probably did not change 1 meter to 100 centimeters when they set up the proportion. Suggest that they do that, or that they change 40 centimeters to 0.04 meters. Point out that the units in the ratio need to be the same.

(continued)

$$y = \frac{12}{3 + x} \quad \text{equation}$$

$$y = \frac{12}{3 + (-3)} \quad \text{replaced } x \text{ with } -3$$

$$y = \frac{12}{0} \quad \text{not permitted}$$

Therefore, we may not use −3 in place of x in this equation. We can write our answer this way:

$$x \neq -3$$

Discuss If the numerator of the equation were $3 + x$ and the denominator were 12, could you use −3 in place of x? Why or why not?

Yes; Sample: It is okay for the numerator to equal zero as long as the denominator does not equal zero.

Practice Set

a. Use a calculator to divide several different numbers of your choosing by zero. Remember to clear the calculator before entering a new problem. What answers are displayed? A typical error message display is [E 0]. Error messages vary.

▸ b. The numbers in the multiplication fact $7 \times 8 = 56$ can be arranged to form two division facts. If we attempt to form two division facts for the multiplication fact $7 \times 0 = 0$, one of the arrangements is not a fact. Which arrangement is not a fact and why? $0 \div 0 = 7$ is not a fact, because division by zero is not possible.

▸ **Analyze** For the following expressions, find the number or numbers that may not be used in place of the variable.

c. $\frac{6}{w}$ $w \neq 0$

d. $\frac{3}{x - 1}$ $x \neq 1$

e. $\frac{4}{2w}$ $w \neq 0$

f. $\frac{y + 3}{y - 3}$ $y \neq 3$

g. $\frac{8}{x^2 - 4}$ $x \neq 2, -2$

h. $\frac{3ab}{c}$ $c \neq 0$

▸ i. **Justify** Explain your answer to **g.**

i. Sample: Squaring both 2 and −2 results in 4, and 4 − 4 = 0 so $x \neq 2$ and $x \neq -2$ since the denominator of a fraction cannot be zero.

Written Practice *Strengthening Concepts*

1. (92) The median home price in the county increased from $360,000 to $378,000 in one year. This was an increase of what percent? 5%

▸ 2. (97) To indirectly measure the height of a power pole, Teddy compared the lengths of the shadows of a vertical meterstick and of the power pole. When the shadow of the meterstick was 40 centimeters long, the shadow of the power pole was 6 meters long. About how tall was the power pole? about 15 meters

▸ * 3. (112) **Explain** Armando is marking off a grass field for a soccer game. He has a long tape measure and chalk for lining the field. Armando wants to be sure that the corners of the field are right angles. How can he use the tape measure to ensure that he makes right angles?

3. Armando can select a Pythagorean triplet like 3-4-5 to verify that he has formed a right angle. For example, he can measure and mark from a corner 3 meters along one line and 4 meters along a proposed perpendicular line. Then he can check to see whether it is 5 meters between the marks.

4. (50) Convert 15 meters to feet using the approximation 1 m ≈ 3.28 ft. Round the answer to the nearest foot. 49 ft

▸ See Math Conversations in the sidebar.

English Learners

Direct the students' attention to problem 2. Draw a **vertical** line on the board. Say:

"This is a vertical line."

Ask volunteers to come to the board and draw vertical lines.

5. The illustration below shows one room of a scale drawing of a house. One inch on the drawing represents a distance of 10 feet. Use a ruler to help calculate the actual area of the room. 225 ft^2
(98)

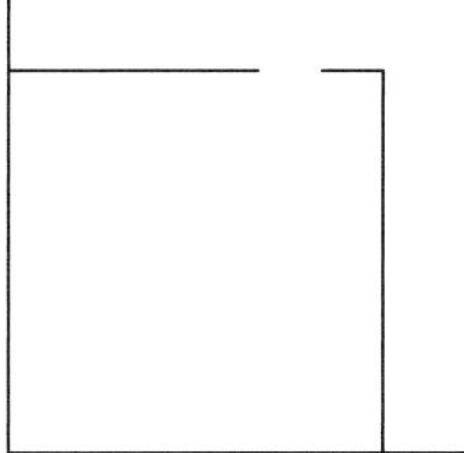

6. A pair of number cubes is rolled once.
(Inv. 8)

a. What is the probability of rolling a total of 9? $\frac{1}{9}$

b. What is the chance of rolling a total of 10? $8\frac{1}{3}\%$

c. What are the odds of rolling a total of 11? 1 to 17

7. Use the Pythagorean theorem to find the distance from (4, 6) to (−1, −6). 13 units
(99)

▶ *** 8.** Analyze A two-liter bottle filled with water
(114)

a. contains how many cubic centimeters of water? 2000 cubic centimeters

b. has a mass of how many kilograms? 2 kilograms

9. Write an equation to solve this problem: $\frac{1}{2}x - \frac{2}{3} = \frac{5}{6}$; 3
(101)

Two thirds less than half of what number is five sixths?

▶ *** 10.** Conclude In this figure lines m and n are parallel. If the sum of the measures of angles a and e is 200°, what is the measure of $\angle g$? 80°
(102)

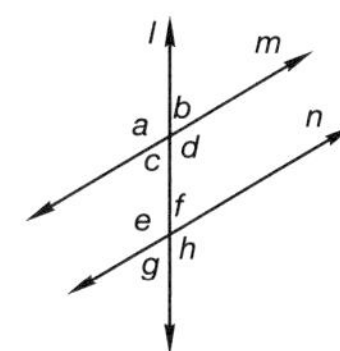

11. $y = -3x + 6$

▶ *** 11.** Connect Transform the equation $3x + y = 6$ into slope-intercept form. Then graph the equation on a coordinate plane. $y = -3x + 6$
(116)

▶ **12.** Explain Find the measure of the smallest angle of the triangle shown. Explain how you found your answer. 50°; Sample: Wrote the equation $3x + x + 30 + 2x = 180$; solved for x; found the measure of each angle and compared.
(101)

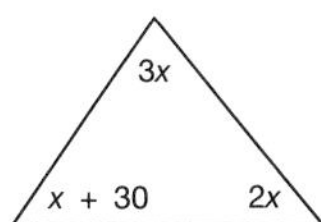

▶ See Math Conversations in the sidebar.

3 Written Practice (Continued)

Math Conversations

Discussion opportunities are provided below.

Problem 8 Analyze

"Suppose the bottle is used to fill a 1000 mL beaker to the line. How much water will be left in the bottle?" 1 liter or 1000 milliliters or the equivalent

"What is the mass of the water in the beaker?" 1 kilogram or 1000 grams or the equivalent

Problem 10 Conclude

Ask the students which angles in the figure measure 100°. angles a, d, e, and h Then ask which measure 80°. angles b, c, f, and g Finally have students name all pairs of supplementary angles in the figure. a and b, a and c, a and f, a and g; d and b, d and c, d and f, d and g; e and b, e and c, e and f, e and g; h and b, h and c, h and f, h and g

Ask if anyone can think of a way to be sure that all the supplementary angles have been found. Sample: If you use the Fundamental Counting Principle, you know that there are 4 ways to choose the 100° angle and 4 ways to choose the 80° angles, so there are 4 × 4, or 16 pairs of supplementary angles.

Problem 11 Connect

"How can you check that your graph represents this equation?" Sample: Choose an ordered pair on the line and see whether its coordinates satisfy the equation.

Problem 12 Explain

Have several volunteers read what they wrote. Then ask why you can't find the answer just by looking at the expressions that give the value of the expressions. Sample: You don't know whether x is greater or less than 30 so you can't tell.

(continued)

3 Written Practice (Continued)

Math Conversations

Discussion opportunities are provided below.

Problem 16 Estimate

"Is Lina's estimate greater or less than the actual surface area of the grapefruit? Explain your answer." Samples: It is probably less than the actual surface area, because 3 is less than the value of π. It would be greater than the actual surface area if her estimate of the diameter is greater than the actual diameter.

Problem 18a Analyze

Have students explain why they know that the slope is positive. Sample: The line rises from left to right.

Problem 18c Represent

Ask how students can tell whether $2y = x - 2$ is also represented by the line. Sample: We can check whether the same ordered pairs satisfy both equations.

Errors and Misconceptions

Problem 13

Some students may not be able to determine the height of the pyramid. Remind them that a cube has the same height everywhere so the height of the pyramid can be found by subtracting the length of an edge of the cube from the total height of the figure.

Problem 15

Students who have difficulty finding the proportions to use may find it easier if they sketch the three triangles separately all in the same orientation and label what parts they know. Then they can systematically find the unknown measures.

(continued)

▶* **13.** (113) A cube, 12 inches on edge, is topped with a pyramid so that the total height of the cube and pyramid is 20 inches. What is the total volume of the figure? 2112 cubic inches

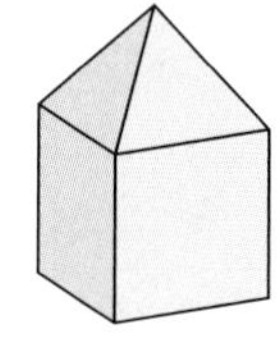

14. (101) The length of segment *BD* is 12. The length of segment *BA* is *c*. Using 12 and *c*, write an expression that indicates the length of segment *AD*. $AD = c - 12$

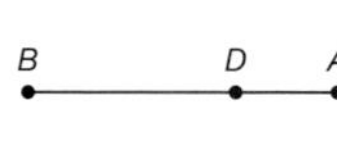

▶ **15.** (97) The three triangles in the figure shown are similar. The sum of *x* and *y* is 25. Use proportions to find *x* and *y*. $x = 16$; $y = 9$

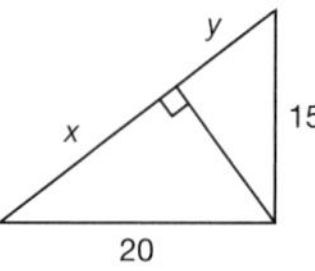

▶* **16.** (105) Estimate Lina needs to estimate the surface area of a grapefruit. She cut a grapefruit in half. (The flat surface formed is called a cross section.)

Lina estimated that the diameter of the grapefruit was 8 cm, and she used 3 in place of π. Using Lina's numbers, estimate the area of the whole grapefruit peel.
$A = 4\pi r^2 \approx 4 \times 3(4\text{ cm})^2 = 192\text{ cm}^2$

* **17.** (116) Write the equation $y - 2x + 5 = 1$ in slope-intercept form. Then graph the equation. $y = 2x - 4$

17. y=2x −4

* **18.** (116) Refer to the graph shown below to answer **a–c.**

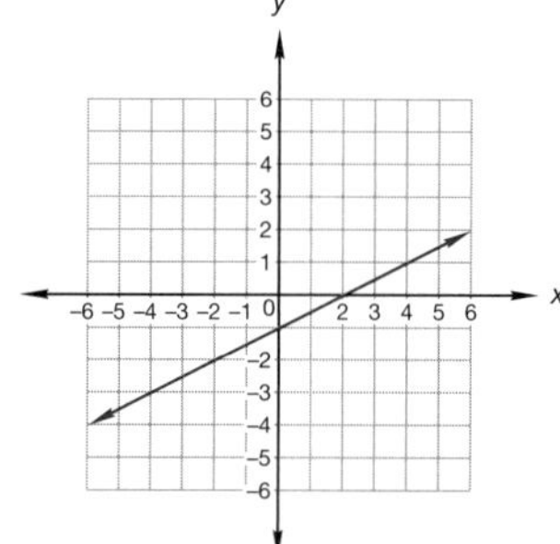

▶ **a.** Analyze What is the slope of the line? $\frac{1}{2}$

b. What is the *y*-intercept of the line? -1

▶ **c.** Represent What is the equation of the line in slope-intercept form?

c. $y = \frac{1}{2}x - 1$

▶ See Math Conversations in the sidebar.

▶* **19.** (96, 117) **Model** Draw an estimate of a 60° angle, and check your estimate with a protractor. Then set the protractor aside, and use a compass and straightedge to copy the angle. See student work.

20. (104) A semicircle with a 7-inch diameter was cut from a rectangular half sheet of paper. What is the perimeter of the resulting shape? (Use $\frac{22}{7}$ for π.) $34\frac{1}{2}$ in.

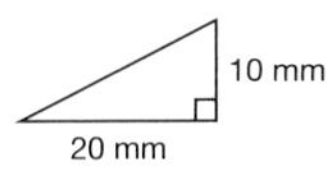

21. $\frac{1 \times 10^3}{1 \times 10^{-3}} =$ 1×10^6 dimes

▶* **21.** (111) **Analyze** A dime is about 1×10^{-3} m thick. A kilometer is 1×10^3 m. About how many dimes would be needed to make a stack of dimes one kilometer high? Express the answer in scientific notation.

▶* **22.** (117) **Generalize** Factor each algebraic expression:

a. $x^2 + x$ $x(x + 1)$

b. $12m^2n^3 + 18mn^2 - 24m^2n^2$ $6mn^2(2mn + 3 - 4m)$

Solve:

23. (93) $-2\frac{2}{3}w - 1\frac{1}{3} = 4$ -2

* **24.** (109) $5x^2 + 1 = 81$ $4, -4$

25. (57) $\left(\frac{1}{2}\right)^2 - 2^{-2}$ 0

26. (48) $66\frac{2}{3}\%$ of $\frac{5}{6}$ of 0.144 0.08 or $\frac{2}{25}$

27. (91) $[-3 + (-4)(-5)] - [-4 - (-5)(-2)]$ 31

Simplify:

28. (103) $\frac{(5x^2yz)(6xy^2z)}{10xyz}$ $3x^2y^2z$

29. (96) $x(x + 2) + 2(x + 2)$ $x^2 + 4x + 4$

▶ **30.** (100) The length of the hypotenuse of this right triangle is between which two consecutive whole numbers of millimeters? 22 mm and 23 mm

10 mm

20 mm

Early Finishers
Math Applications

Look at the three transformations below.

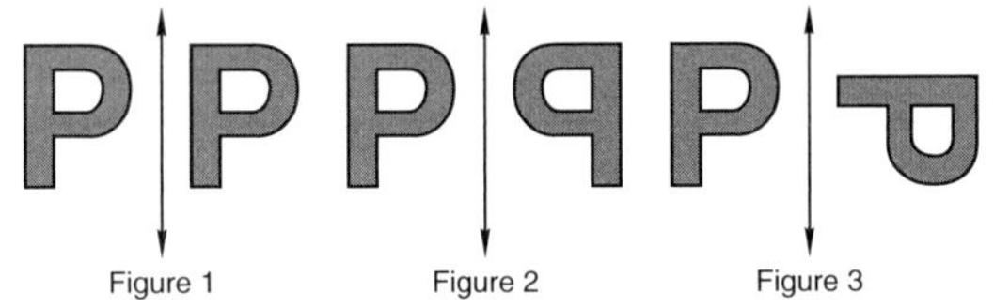

a. Name each transformation. Explain your reasoning for choosing each.

a. 1. translation. Sample: The P has been slid to the right.; 2. reflection, Sample: The P is flipped over the vertical line.; 3. rotation, Sample: The P is turned to the right.

b. Which figure shows a transformation that has a line of symmetry? Explain your answer. Figure 2; Sample: A line of symmetry divides a figure into mirror images. The Ps in Figure 2 are mirror images of each other.

▶ See Math Conversations in the sidebar.

3 Written Practice (Continued)

Math Conversations

Discussion opportunities are provided below.

Problem 19 Model

Have students tell how close the angles they drew were to 60°. Ask what they did to try to draw an angle close to 60°. Sample: I thought of the angle in an equilateral triangle and tried to do one like that.

Problem 21 Analyze

Let students predict how many dollars would be in the kilometer stack of dimes. Then have students calculate the value. Sample: I predict that there is \$10,000 in the stack. I calculated that there is \$100,000 in the stack.

Problem 22 Generalize

"How do you know that you have completely factored the expression?"

Sample: I check that no terms of the polynomial part have the same factor.

Errors and Misconceptions

Problem 30

If students seemed to be confused by how to answer this problem, remind them that consecutive numbers are numbers that follow one after the other. Suggest that they think about what two whole numbers the square root of 500 will come between. Since the square root of 400 is 20 and the square root of 900 is 30, they can tell that $\sqrt{500}$ will be between 20 and 30, and will be between 2 numbers that are closer to 20 than 30. They can use guess and check to find the numbers.

Graphing Area and Volume Formulas

Objective

- Graph area and volume formulas.

Lesson Preparation

Materials

- **Power Up V** (in *Instructional Masters*)
- **Investigation Activity 13** (in *Instructional Masters*) or **graph paper,** 3 per student
- **Manipulative kit: metric rulers, protractors, compasses, straightedges**

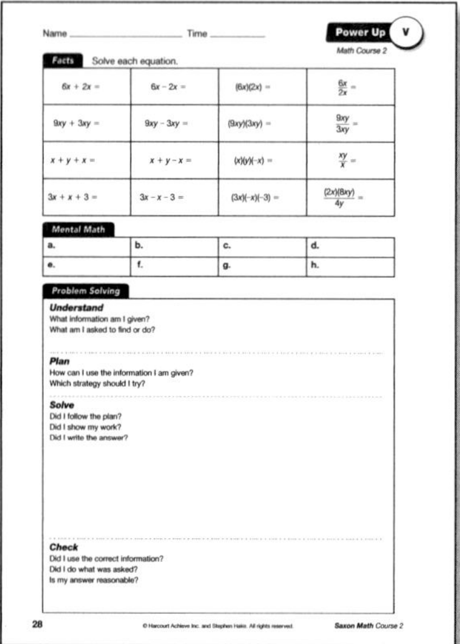
Power Up V

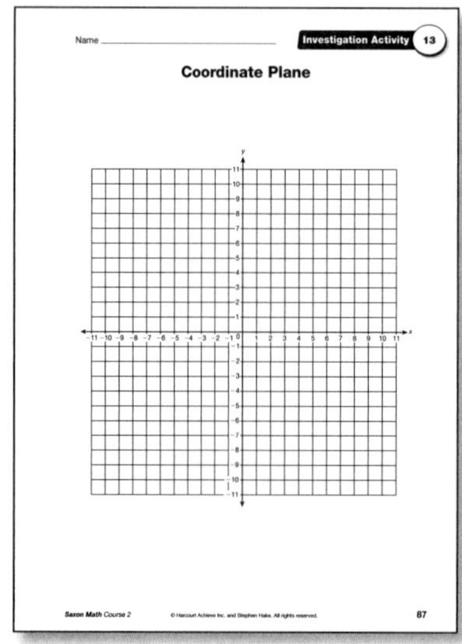
Investigation Activity 13

Technology Resources

Student eBook Complete student textbook in electronic format.

Resources and Planner CD Blackline masters, plus a pacing calendar with standards.

Test and Practice Generator CD Create additional practice sheets and custom-made tests.

www.SaxonPublishers.com Visit for more student activities and planning materials.

Inclusion

Adaptations CD Adapted lessons, investigations, practice and assessments.

Meeting Standards

National Council of Teachers of Mathematics (NCTM)

Algebra

AL.3a Model and solve contextualized problems using various representations, such as graphs, tables, and equations

Geometry

GM.4d Use geometric models to represent and explain numerical and algebraic relationships

Measurement

ME.2d Develop strategies to determine the surface area and volume of selected prisms, pyramids, and cylinders

Representation

RE.5a Create and use representations to organize, record, and communicate mathematical ideas

Power-Up Discussion

For use with Power Up, p. 832

Problem-Solving Strategy: Use Logical Reasoning

A paper cone is filled with water. Then the water is poured into a cylindrical glass beaker that has the same height and diameter as the paper cone. How many cones of water are needed to fill the beaker?

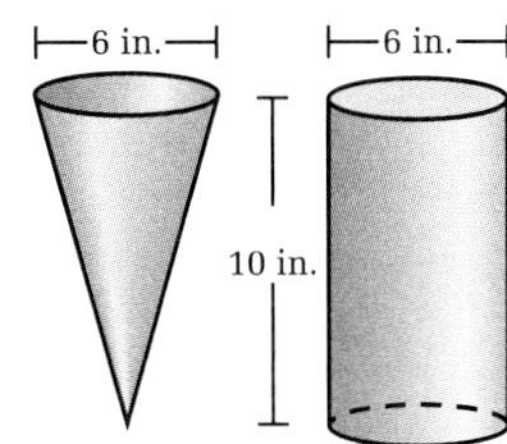

Understand ***Understand the problem.***

"What information are we given?"

A paper cone and a cylindrical beaker have the same height and diameter.

"What are we asked to do?"

We are asked to find how many cones of water are needed to fill the beaker.

Plan ***Make a plan.***

"What problem-solving strategy will we use?"

We will *use logical reasoning* to determine the number of cones needed.

Solve ***Carry out the plan.***

"In a previous lesson we learned that the volume of a cone is what fraction of the volume of a cylinder with the same height and diameter?"

$\frac{1}{3}$

"Therefore, how many cones of water will it take to fill the cone?"

three

Check ***Look back.***

"Did we do what we were asked to do?"

Yes, we found the number of cones of water it would take to fill the beaker.

1 Power Up

Facts

Distribute **Power Up V** to students. See answers below.

Mental Math

Encourage students to share different ways to mentally compute these exercises. Strategies for exercises **c** and **h** are listed below.

c. Subtract from Both Sides

$2y + \frac{1}{2} = \frac{1}{2}$

$2y + \frac{1}{2} - \frac{1}{2} = \frac{1}{2} - \frac{1}{2}$

$2y = 0$

$y = 0$

Use Logical Reasoning

I see $2y$ plus $\frac{1}{2}$ equals $\frac{1}{2}$.

$2y$ has to be 0.

So $y = 0$.

h. Change All to Fractions

$5 \text{ min} = \frac{1}{12} \text{ hr}$

$W_f = \frac{1}{3} - \frac{1}{12} = \frac{4}{12} - \frac{1}{12}$

$W_f = \frac{3}{12} = \frac{1}{4} \text{ hr}$

Change All to Minutes

$\frac{1}{3} \text{ hr} = 20 \text{ min}$

$20 \text{ min} - 5 \text{ min} = 15 \text{ min}$

$15 \text{ min} = \frac{1}{4} \text{ hr}$

Problem Solving

Refer to **Power-Up Discussion,** p. 832B.

2 New Concepts

Instruction

Sketch a pair of x and y axes on the board or overhead and draw a straight diagonal line on the graph. Ask:

"What operations might this graph represent?" addition, subtraction, multiplication, or division

"How many variables does it represent?" 2, x and y

"What are the exponents of these variables?" Both are understood to be 1.

Explain that the graphs drawn so far in class have been straight lines but that this lesson will cover graphs that are curves.

(continued)

LESSON **119**

• Graphing Area and Volume Formulas

Power Up *Building Power*

facts Power Up V

mental math

a. **Positive/Negative:** $(2^{-2})(-2)^2$ 1

b. **Scientific Notation:** $(1 \times 10^{-8}) \div (1 \times 10^{-4})$ 1×10^{-4}

c. **Algebra:** $2y + \frac{1}{2} = \frac{1}{2}$ 0

d. **Measurement:** Convert 5 cm² to mm². 500 mm²

e. **Percent:** $66\frac{2}{3}\%$ of \$600 \$400

f. **Percent:** \$600 reduced $33\frac{1}{3}\%$ \$400

g. **Geometry:** This pair of angles is A

A supplementary.

B complementary.

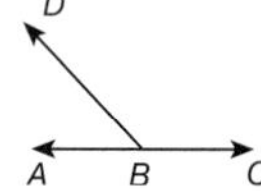

h. **Fractional Parts/Measurement:** What fraction of an hour is 5 minutes less than $\frac{1}{3}$ of an hour? $\frac{1}{4}$

problem solving

A paper cone is filled with water. Then the water is poured into a cylindrical glass beaker that has the same height and diameter as the paper cone. How many cones of water are needed to fill the beaker? 3 cones

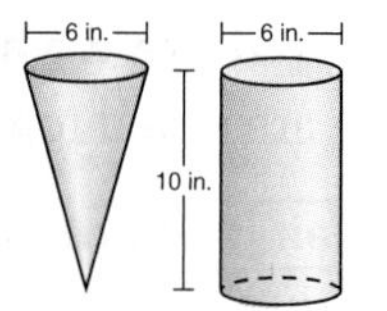

New Concept *Increasing Knowledge*

The graph of a function may be a curve. In the example below we graph the relationship between the length of the side of a square and its area.

Example 1

The formula for the area of a square is $A = s^2$. Graph this function.

Solution

We use the letter A and s to represent the area in square units and the side length of the square respectively.

Facts Solve each equation.

$6x + 2x = 8x$	$6x - 2x = 4x$	$(6x)(2x) = 12x^2$	$\frac{6x}{2x} = 3$
$9xy + 3xy = 12xy$	$9xy - 3xy = 6xy$	$(9xy)(3xy) = 27x^2y^2$	$\frac{9xy}{3xy} = 3$
$x + y + x = 2x + y$	$x + y - x = y$	$(x)(y)(-x) = -x^2y$	$\frac{xy}{x} = y$
$3x + x + 3 = 4x + 3$	$3x - x - 3 = 2x - 3$	$(3x)(-x)(-3) = 9x^2$	$\frac{(2x)(8xy)}{4y} = 4x^2$

Thinking Skill

Predict

Is it possible to tell by looking at the table if the function is nonlinear? Yes. If the slope, the change in A over the change in s, is not constant for all pairs, the function is nonlinear.

$A = s^2$

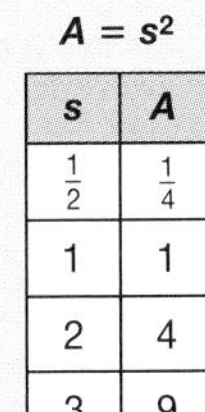

s	A
$\frac{1}{2}$	$\frac{1}{4}$
1	1
2	4
3	9

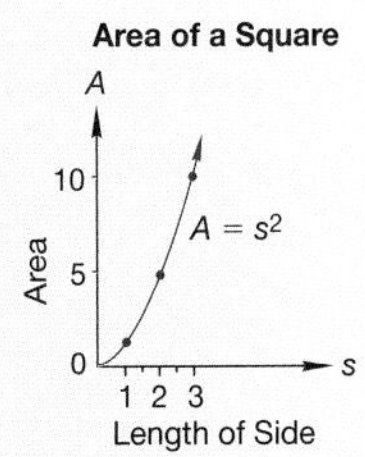

The dots on the graph of the function show the (s, A) pairs from the table. Other (s, A) pairs of numbers are represented by other points on the curve. Notice that the graph of the function rapidly becomes steeper as the side of the square becomes longer.

The graph relating the edge length to the volume of a cube grows steeper even more rapidly. In example 2, we use different vertical and horizontal scales to contain the graph for a few points that are easy to calculate.

Predict What could you do to the graph to plot more points? What would happen to the graph if you plotted more ordered pairs? Extend the axes. It would become steeper.

Example 2

The formula for the volume of a cube is $V = e^3$ in which V is volume and e is the length of an edge. Make a function table for this formula and describe how to graph the function.

Solution

The input is the length of the edge, the output is the volume. We use 0, 1, 2, 3 and 4 for edge lengths and calculate the volumes. To graph these points we need to space the intervals on the e-axis relatively far apart and reduce the interval length on the V-axis. Then we plot the points and draw a smooth curve.

$V = e^3$

e	V
0	0
1	1
2	8
3	27
4	64

Analyze Refer to the table. How do the values for V relate to the value for e?

In each case V is the cube of e. For instance, when $e = 2$, $V = 2^3$; $V = 2 \times 2 \times 2 = 8$

Practice Set

a.

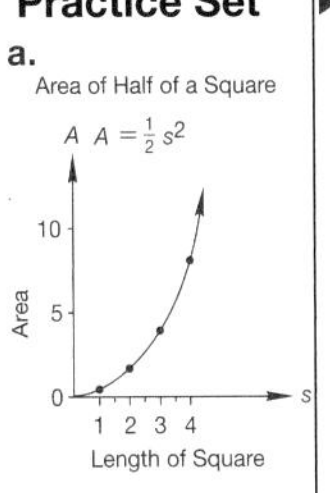

▸ a. Connect Half of the area of a square is shaded. As the square becomes larger, the area of the shaded region becomes greater, as indicated by the function table in which A represents the area of half of a square and s represents the length of a side of the square. Copy this table and find the missing numbers. Then graph the function.

$A = \frac{1}{2}s^2$

s	A
1	$\frac{1}{2}$
2	2
3	$4\frac{1}{2}$
4	8

▸ See Math Conversations in the sidebar.

Math Background

Are all graphs of area formulas curves?

Not all area formulas will produce the curved graph that the formula for the area of a square does. The length and height of a square are always equal, so if the size of a square is increased, it will always increase in two dimensions.

However, the length of a rectangle can increase without a corresponding increase in width. Because it is possible for the area of a rectangle to increase in only one dimension, graphing the area of a rectangle only in relation to its length does not necessarily produce a curved line.

The area of a circle, on the other hand, increases in two dimensions as its radius increases, and so a graph of the formula for the area of a circle would produce a curve similar to that of a square.

2 New Concepts *(Continued)*

Example 1

Instruction

Provide students with graph paper or a copy of **Investigation Activity 13** Coordinate Plane so they can follow along as you demonstrate graphing the function.

Explain that the curve becomes steeper as the length of a side increases. This is because the differences in the areas of the squares become greater as the length of a side increases. Continue the table to demonstrate this.

S	A	Difference
3	9	
4	16	$16 - 9 = 7$
5	25	$25 - 16 = 9$
6	36	$36 - 25 = 11$
7	49	$49 - 36 = 13$
8	64	$64 - 49 = 15$
9	81	$81 - 64 = 17$
10	100	$100 - 81 = 19$

While the difference in the length of the side has changed by 1 for each row of the table, the difference in area has increased by more than 1, and each difference in area is greater than the one before.

Example 2

Instruction

Ask students why there are no negative values for s and e in the tables for the two examples. It is impossible to have negative length.

As you discuss the *Analyze* question, you may want to ask students to describe how the e values increase compared to the V values. The e values increase slowly while the V values increase even more rapidly than the values in example 1.

You may want to add a column with the actual differences in volume so that students can see how they increase.

Practice Set

Problem a Connect

Ask students why the shape of this curve is similar to the one they drew in Example 1. Sample: The values for this function are half those for the other function.

(continued)

2 New Concepts (Continued)

Practice Set

Problem b Connect

Discuss why the scales on the axes are different. Sample: If the scales were the same, you could only graph a couple of points on a regular-size piece of graph paper. You would need a huge piece of graph paper, so instead you use a different scale for the volume because it grows faster.

Problem c Analyze

If you extended the chart when working on example 1, suggest that students refer to it as well as to the tables for problem a and example 1 as they answer this question. There are enough values that they can determine that doubling a side quadruples the volume, but examining more pairs helps to reinforce the concept. Ask students to name values that illustrate their answers. Samples:

side: 1 unit, area: 1 square unit
side: 2 units, area: 4 square units

side: 2 units, area: 4 square units
side: 4 units, area: 16 square units

side: 3 units, area: 9 square units
side: 6 units, area: 36 square units

3 Written Practice

Math Conversations

Discussion opportunities are provided below.

Problem 7 Generalize

Ask students to explain how they can be sure that their answer is written in scientific notation. Sample: I check that the whole number part is a number equal to or greater than 1, but less than 10, and that the decimal part is multiplied by a power of 10.

Errors and Misconceptions

Problem 3

A source of error for this problem is the use of solid dots or empty circles at the ends of the graph. When a number, such as -3 in this problem, is included in the inequality, a solid dot is used. When a number, such as 2 in this problem, is not included in the inequality, an empty circle is used.

(continued)

b.

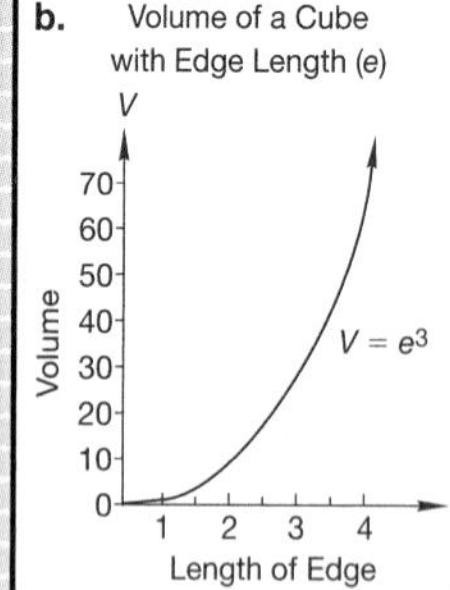

▸ **b.** Connect Graph the function $V = e^3$ using the function table from example 2. Make the scale on the axes is similar to the one shown here.

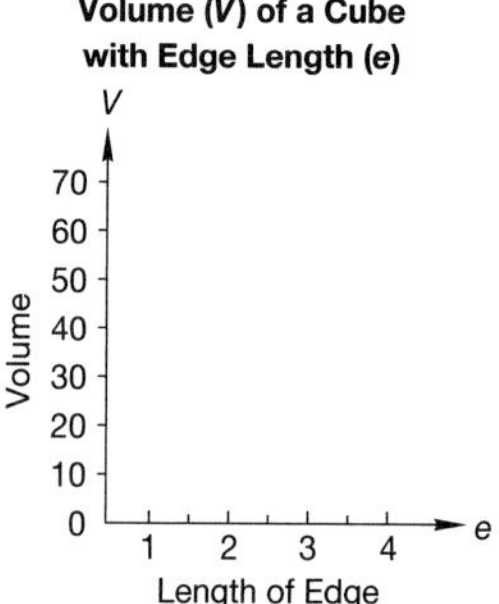

▸ **c.** Analyze Refer to **a.** What effect does doubling the side length of a square have on the area of the square? Sample: Doubling the side length of a square quadruples the area.

Written Practice *Strengthening Concepts*

1. (94) Lily is asked to select and hold 3 marbles from a bag of 52 marbles. Four of the marbles are green. If the first two marbles she selects are green, what is the chance that the third marble she selects will be one of the two remaining green marbles? 4%

2. (92) If Khalid saved \$5 by purchasing a box of blank CDs at a sale price of \$15, then the regular price was reduced by what percent? 25%

▸ **3.** (78) On a number line graph all real numbers that are both greater than or equal to -3 and less than 2. –4 –3 –2 –1 0 1 2 3

4. (89) What is the sum of the measures of the interior angles of any quadrilateral? 360°

5. (48) Complete the table.

Fraction	Decimal	Percent
a. $\frac{1}{200}$	**b.** 0.005	0.5%
$\frac{8}{9}$	**c.** $0.\overline{8}$	**d.** $88\frac{8}{9}\%$

6. a.

6. (17) **a.** Use a centimeter ruler and a protractor to draw a right triangle with legs 10 cm long.

b. What is the measure of each acute angle? 45°

c. Measure the length of the hypotenuse to the nearest centimeter. 14 cm

▸ * **7.** (111) Generalize Simplify. Write the answer in scientific notation. 4×10^7

$$\frac{(6 \times 10^5)(2 \times 10^6)}{(3 \times 10^4)}$$

▸ See Math Conversations in the sidebar.

▶ * **8.** (115) Generalize Factor each expression:

a. $2x^2 + x$ $x(2x + 1)$

b. $3a^2b - 12a^2 + 9ab^2$ $3a(ab - 4a + 3b^2)$

Analyze The figure at right was formed by stacking 1-cm cubes. Refer to the figure to answer problems **9** and **10**.

▶ **9.** (70) What is the volume of the figure? 18 cm^3

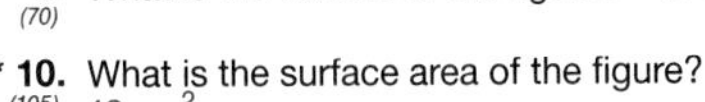

Thinking Skill

Analyze

How many cube faces are visible from each view (top, bottom, back, front, and sides)? top, bottom, front, and back views: 9 cube faces; side views: 6 cube faces.

▶* **10.** (105) What is the surface area of the figure? 48 cm^2

* **11.** (108) Transform the formula $A = \frac{1}{2}bh$ to solve for h. Then use the transformed formula to find h when A is 1.44 m^2 and b is 1.6 m. $h = \frac{2A}{b}$; 1.8 m

12. (66) If the ratio of blue T-shirts to white T-shirts is 3 to 5, then what percent of the T-shirts are blue? $37\frac{1}{2}\%$

▶* **13.** (112) Analyze If a 10-foot ladder is leaning against a wall so that the foot of the ladder is 6 feet from the base of the wall, how far up the wall will the ladder reach? 8 ft

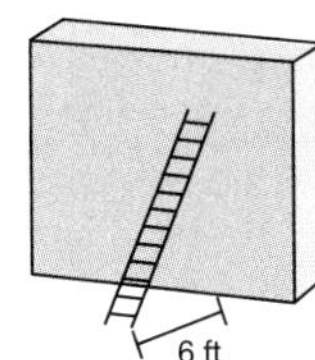

Connect The graph below shows line l perpendicular to line m. Refer to the graph to answer problems **14** and **15**.

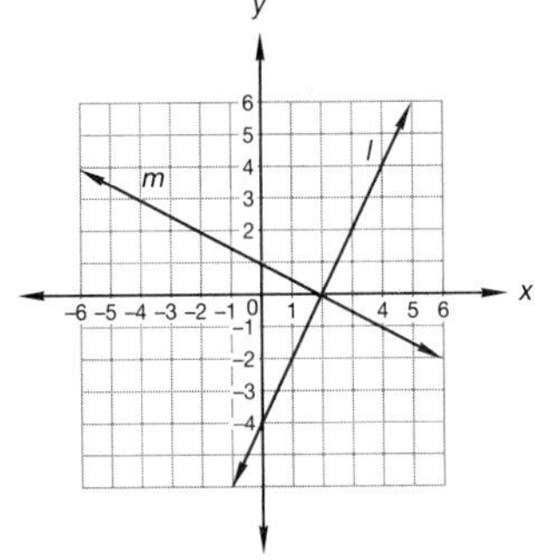

▶* **14.** (116) **a.** What is the equation of line l in slope-intercept form? $y = 2x - 4$

b. What is the equation of line m in slope-intercept form? $y = -\frac{1}{2}x + 1$

▶* **15.** (107) What is the product of the slopes of line l and line m? Why? The product of the slopes is -1. The slopes are negative reciprocals.

▶ See Math Conversations in the sidebar.

3 Written Practice (Continued)

Math Conversations

Discussion opportunities are provided below.

Problem 8 Generalize

Have volunteers describe what they did first to factor each expression and explain the reason for doing it. Sample: For problem **b**, I first looked for a common factor for the numerical part of each term, because the coefficient is written first in an expression.

Problems 9 and 10 Analyze

Extend the Problem

Tell students to imagine that the cubes could be held together temporarily so that the figure could be painted green on the entire outer surface. After the paint dries, the figure is pulled apart so that the 18 cubes are separated.

Then ask how many cubes have green paint

- on no sides 0
- on one side 2
- on two sides 6
- on three sides 6
- on four sides 4
- on five sides 0

Problem 13 Analyze

Ask how many students recognized that they could use a Pythagorean triplet to solve the problem. Let those who did not explain how they solved the problem. Sample: I used the equation $10^2 = 6^2 + x^2$, and found that $x = 8$.

Problem 14 Connect

Ask students what they notice about the slopes of the two lines. Samples: One slope is positive, the other is negative. The coefficients are reciprocals.

Problem 15 Connect

Extend the Problem

Point out that the two lines are perpendicular. Ask if either one is vertical. no Explain that their slopes are negative reciprocals and that the product of the slopes is -1.

Tell students that whenever two nonvertical lines are perpendicular, their slopes will be negative reciprocals and the product of the slopes will be -1. It is also true that if the product of the slopes of two nonvertical lines is -1, the two lines are perpendicular.

Errors and Misconceptions

Problem 10

Some students may simply multiply 6 cm^2 by 18 to get 108 cm^2. Have these students work, surface by surface, to see how many cube surfaces are included in the total surface area.

(continued)

3 Written Practice (Continued)

Math Conversations

Discussion opportunities are provided below.

Problem 18 Analyze

Have volunteers explain how they found the numbers that may not be used for the variable. Sample: I found the number that would make the denominator zero.

Problem 29 Generalize

Ask students what value may not be used for x, y, or z. 0

Errors and Misconceptions

Problem 20

Students may not have been able to solve this problem because they could not write a proportion to find the lengths needed to calculate the area. Help them to mark corresponding sides and write the proportions. Two proportions that could be used are $\frac{25}{20} = \frac{20}{x}$ and $\frac{25}{20} = \frac{15}{z}$. In this problem, $x = 16$ in., $y = 9$ in., $z = 12$ in.

Problem 28

Students who give an answer of $x^2 - 2x + 10$ did not multiply both terms in the parentheses by the factor in front of the parentheses. Explain that the number outside the parentheses must multiply all terms inside parentheses.

* **16.** (110) If $8000 is deposited in an account paying 6% interest compounded annually, then what is the total value of the account after four years? $10,099.82

17. (88) The Joneses are planning to carpet their home. The area to be carpeted is 1250 square feet. How many square yards of carpeting must be installed? Round the answer up to the next square yard.
139 square yards

▶* **18.** (118) Analyze In the following expressions, what number may not be used for the variable?

a. $\frac{12}{3w}$ $w \neq 0$ **b.** $\frac{12}{3 + m}$ $m \neq -3$

19. (101) In the figure shown, $\overline{BD}$ is x units long, and $\overline{BA}$ is c units long. Using x and c, write an expression that indicates the length of $\overline{DA}$.
$DA = c - x$

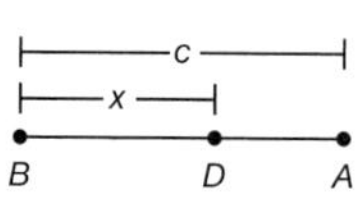

Thinking Skill
Analyze
Use what you know about similar triangles and the Pythagorean Theorem to find y and z.

▶ **20.** (97) In the figure at right, the three triangles are similar. Find the area of the smallest triangle. Dimensions are in inches. 54 in.^{2}

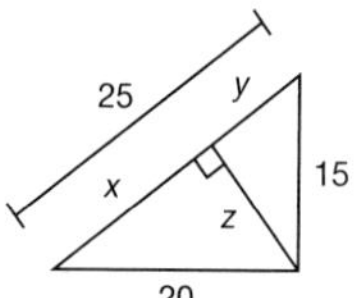

* **21.** (113) A sphere with a diameter of 30 cm has a volume of how many cubic centimeters? 14,130 cm^3

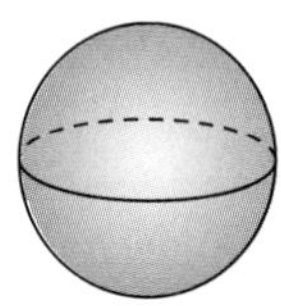

Use 3.14 for π.

22. (96, 117) Draw an estimate of a 45° angle. Then use a compass and straightedge to copy the angle. See student work.

Solve:

23. (93) $\frac{2}{3}m + \frac{1}{4} = \frac{7}{12}$ $\frac{1}{2}$

24. (102) $5(3 - x) = 55$ -8

25. (102) $x + x + 12 = 5x$ 4

26. (109) $10x^2 = 100$ $\sqrt{10}, -\sqrt{10}$

Simplify:

27. (20) $\sqrt{90{,}000}$ 300

▶ **28.** (96) $x(x + 5) - 2(x + 5)$ $x^2 + 3x - 10$

▶ **29.** (103) $\frac{(12xy^2z)(9x^2y^2z)}{36xyz^2}$ $3x^2y^3$

30. (48) $33\frac{1}{3}\%$ of 0.12 of $3\frac{1}{3}$
$\frac{2}{15}$ or $0.1\overline{3}$

▶ See Math Conversations in the sidebar.

Looking Forward

Graphing area and volume formulas prepares students for:

- **Lesson 120,** graphing nonlinear equations on the coordinate plane.

Graphing Nonlinear Equations

Objective

- Graph nonlinear equations.

Lesson Preparation

Materials

- **Power Up W** (in *Instructional Masters*)
- **Investigation Activity 13** (in *Instructional Masters*) or **graph paper,** 7 per student
- **Manipulative kit: metric rulers**

Optional

- **Teacher-provided material: calculators**

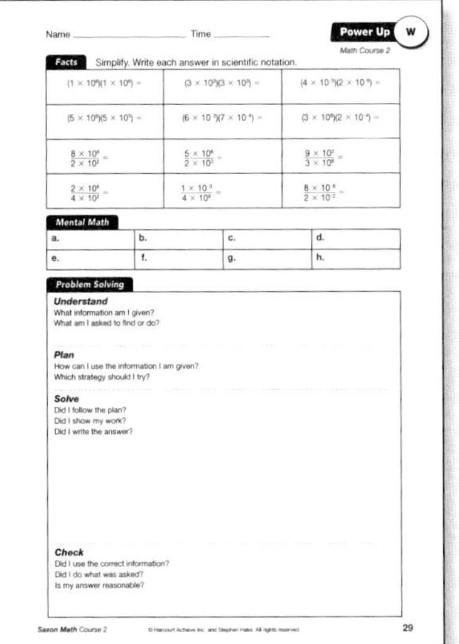
Name ______ Time ______ Power Up W

Math Course 2

Facts Simplify. Write each answer in scientific notation.

Mental Math

a.	b.	c.	d.
e.	f.	g.	h.

Problem Solving

Understand
What information am I given?
What am I asked to find or do?

Plan
How can I use the information I am given?
Which strategy should I try?

Solve
Did I follow the plan?
Did I show my work?
Did I write the answer?

Check
Did I use the correct information?
Did I do what was asked?
Is my answer reasonable?

Saxon Math Course 2 29

Power Up W

Name ______ Investigation Activity 13

Coordinate Plane

Saxon Math Course 2 87

Investigation Activity 13

Math Language

New	English Learners (ESL)
dependent variable	inverse variation
independent variable	
linear equations	
nonlinear equations	

Technology Resources

Student eBook Complete student textbook in electronic format.

Resources and Planner CD Blackline masters, plus a pacing calendar with standards.

Test and Practice Generator CD Create additional practice sheets and custom-made tests.

www.SaxonPublishers.com Visit for more student activities and planning materials.

Inclusion

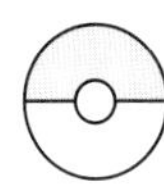

Adaptations CD Adapted lessons, investigations, practice and assessments.

Meeting Standards

National Council of Teachers of Mathematics (NCTM)

Algebra

AL.3a Model and solve contextualized problems using various representations, such as graphs, tables, and equations

Geometry

GM.4d Use geometric models to represent and explain numerical and algebraic relationships

Problem Solving

PS.1c Apply and adapt a variety of appropriate strategies to solve problems

Representation

RE.5a Create and use representations to organize, record, and communicate mathematical ideas

Power-Up Discussion *For use with Power Up, p. 837*

Problem-Solving Strategy: Use Logical Reasoning

Does $0.\overline{9} = 1$? Here are two arguments that say it is:

$$\begin{array}{rl} & \frac{1}{3} = 0.\overline{3} \\ + & \frac{2}{3} = 0.\overline{6} \\ \hline & \frac{3}{3} = 0.\overline{9} \\ & 1 = 0.\overline{9} \end{array}$$

$$\begin{array}{r} 0.9999 \\ 5\overline{)5.0000} \\ \underline{4\,5} \\ 5\,0 \\ \underline{4\,5} \\ 5\,0 \\ \underline{4\,5} \\ 5 \end{array}$$

Understand — Understand the problem.

"What information are we given?"

We are shown two arguments that "show" that $0.\overline{9} = 1$.

"What are we asked to do?"

We are asked to determine whether or not $0.\overline{9}$ actually equals 1.

Plan — Make a plan.

"What problem-solving strategy will we use?"

We will *use logical reasoning* to discuss why both of the arguments presented are incorrect.

Teacher's Note: Take an informal student poll to determine whether students accept or reject the arguments presented.

Solve — Carry out the plan.

"Why is the first argument invalid?"

The numbers $0.\overline{3}$ and $0.\overline{6}$ do not add to 1. The number $0.\overline{9}$ is very close to 1, but does not quite equal 1.

"Why is the second argument invalid?"

The remainder in each instance is equal to or greater than the divisor, which is improper when performing division.

Check — Look back

"Did we do what we were asked to do?"

Yes, we determined that 0.9 is very close to but does not equal 1.

LESSON 120

• Graphing Nonlinear Equations

Power Up

Building Power

facts Power Up W

mental math

a. **Positive/Negative:** $(10^2)(10^{-2})$ 1

b. **Scientific Notation:** $(5 \times 10^{-5})^2$ 2.5×10^{-9}

c. **Algebra:** $2x^2 = 32$ 4, −4

d. **Measurement:** Convert 0°C to Fahrenheit. 32°F

e. **Percent:** 10% of \$250 \$25

f. **Percent:** 10% more than \$250 \$275

g. **Probability:** The weather forecast stated that the chance of rain is 70%. What is the chance it will not rain? 30%

h. **Calculation:** $2 \times 12, + 1, \sqrt{\ }, \times 3, + 1, \sqrt{\ }, \times 2, + 1, \sqrt{\ }, + 1, \sqrt{\ }, - 1, \sqrt{\ }$ 1

problem solving

Does $0.\overline{9} = 1$? Here are two arguments that say it is:

$$\frac{1}{3} = 0.\overline{3}$$
$$+\frac{2}{3} = 0.\overline{6}$$
$$\frac{3}{3} = 0.\overline{9}$$
$$1 = 0.\overline{9}$$

$$\begin{array}{r} 0.9999 \\ 5\overline{)5.0000} \\ \underline{4\,5} \\ 50 \\ \underline{45} \\ 50 \\ \underline{45} \\ 5 \end{array}$$

Verify or refute each argument. See script for explanation.

New Concept

Increasing Knowledge

Equations whose graphs are lines are called **linear equations.** (Notice the word *line* in *linear.*) In Lesson 119 and in this lesson we graph equations whose graphs are not lines but are curves. These equations are called **nonlinear equations.** One way to graph nonlinear equations is to make a table of ordered pairs (a function table) and plot enough points to get an idea of the path of the curve.

Recall that the graphs in Lesson 119 were confined to the first quadrant. That is because we were graphing lengths and areas and volumes which are positive numbers. In this lesson we will graph functions whose variables may be negative, so we need to select some values for the input numbers that are negative as well as positive.

Facts Simplify. Write each answer in scientific notation.

$(1 \times 10^6)(1 \times 10^6) =$ 1×10^{12}	$(3 \times 10^3)(3 \times 10^3) =$ 9×10^6	$(4 \times 10^{-5})(2 \times 10^{-6}) =$ 8×10^{-11}
$(5 \times 10^5)(5 \times 10^5) =$ 2.5×10^{11}	$(6 \times 10^{-3})(7 \times 10^{-4}) =$ 4.2×10^{-6}	$(3 \times 10^6)(2 \times 10^{-4}) =$ 6×10^2
$\frac{8 \times 10^8}{2 \times 10^2} = 4 \times 10^6$	$\frac{5 \times 10^6}{2 \times 10^3} = 2.5 \times 10^3$	$\frac{9 \times 10^3}{3 \times 10^8} = 3 \times 10^{-5}$
$\frac{2 \times 10^6}{4 \times 10^2} = 5 \times 10^3$	$\frac{1 \times 10^{-3}}{4 \times 10^8} = 2.5 \times 10^{-12}$	$\frac{8 \times 10^{-8}}{2 \times 10^{-2}} = 4 \times 10^{-6}$

1 Power Up

Facts

Distribute **Power Up W** to students. See answers below.

Mental Math

Encourage students to share different ways to mentally compute these exercises. Strategies for exercises **d** and **e** are listed below.

d. From Memory

0°C = 32°F

Use the Formula

$F = \frac{9}{5}C + 32$

$F = \frac{9}{5} \times 0 + 32 = 32$

0°C = 32°F

e. Multiply by 10, Divide by 10

10% of \$250 = 100% of \$25 = \$25

Use a Fraction

10% of \$250 = $\frac{1}{10}$ × \$250 = \$25

Problem Solving

Refer to **Power-Up Discussion,** p. 837B.

2 New Concepts

Instruction

In this lesson, students will graph more nonlinear equations. It is helpful for students to have a brief introduction to such equations now, because they will learn more about them as they continue their study of mathematics.

(continued)

2 New Concepts (Continued)

Example 1

Instruction

Demonstrate each example in this lesson on the board or on an overhead projector. Be sure students have a copy of **Investigation Activity 13** Coordinate Plane or graph paper so that they can follow along by making tables, plotting points, and drawing curves for the examples.

Ask students to describe all the ordered pairs of x and y that satisfy this equation. The possible values for x include the set of all real numbers, and the possible values for y include numbers greater than or equal to zero, $y \geq 0$. Explain that although rational numbers can be used in this equation, it is usually easier to plot integer values.

Be sure that students understand the concept covered in the *Discuss* question. It is helpful for students to understand how and why the graph represents the mathematics.

(continued)

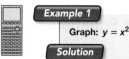

Visit www.SaxonPublishers.com/ActivitiesC2 *for a graphing calculator activity.*

Example 1

Graph: $y = x^2$

Solution

This equation is like the formula for the area of a square, except that y and x replace A and S respectively. We begin by making a table of ordered pairs. We think of numbers for x and then calculate y. We replace x with negative numbers as well. Remember that squaring a negative number results in a positive number.

$$y = x^2$$

x	y	(x, y)
0	0	(0, 0)
1	1	(1, 1)
2	4	(2, 4)
3	9	(3, 9)

x	y	(x, y)
−1	1	(−1, 1)
−2	4	(−2, 4)
−3	9	(−3, 9)

After generating several pairs of coordinates, we graph the points on a coordinate plane.

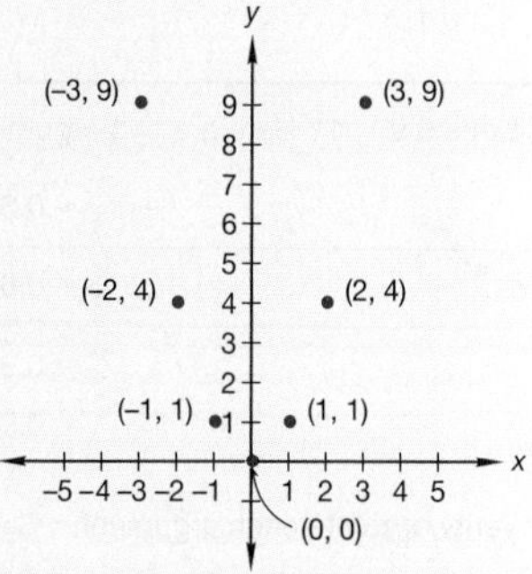

Discuss Would you expect to find an ordered pair that satisfies this equation in the third or fourth quadrant? Why or why not? No. Sample: In the third and fourth quadrants, the value for y is negative. Since y equals a number squared, y cannot be negative.

838 **Saxon** Math Course 2

We complete the graph by drawing a smooth curve through the graphed points.

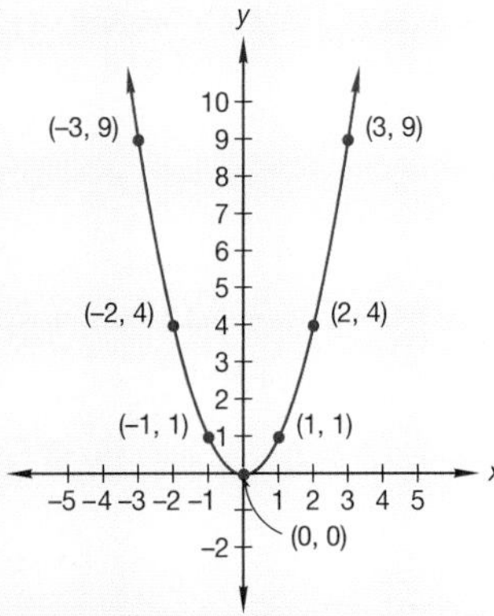

The coordinates of any point on the curve should satisfy the original equation.

Analyze What is a line of symmetry for this graph? the *y*-axis

In example 2 we graph another nonlinear equation using a table of ordered pairs. We have used the terms *input* and *output* to refer to variables when creating function tables. Mathematicians use the words **independent variable** and **dependent variable** respectively to refer to these variables.

The dependent variable is usually isolated on one side of the equation. In example 2 the dependent variable is *y*. We freely select numbers to substitute for the independent variable, which in example 2 is *x*. The value of *y* depends upon the number we select for the independent variable.

Example 2

Graph: $y = \frac{6}{x}$

Solution

We make a table of ordered pairs. For convenience we select *x* values that are factors of 6. We remember to select negative values as well. Note that we may not select zero for *x*.

$$y = \frac{6}{x}$$

x	y	(x, y)
1	6	(1, 6)
2	3	(2, 3)
3	2	(3, 2)
6	1	(6, 1)

x	y	(x, y)
−1	−6	(−1, −6)
−2	−3	(−2, −3)
−3	−2	(−3, −2)
−6	−1	(−6, −1)

Thinking Skill

Explain

Why can't you use zero in place of the variable *x*? Division by zero is not possible.

2 New Concepts (Continued)

Example 1 (continued)

Instruction

As you discuss the *Analyze* question, ask students how they can tell where the line of symmetry is. Sample: When I look at the graph, I can see that if I folded the paper along the *y*-axis the two sides of the curve would be together. So, the *y*-axis is the line of symmetry.

Instruction

Help students see that the value of the *independent variable* or the input can be chosen, either by the person making the table or graph or by the person who wrote the problem. The value of the *dependent variable* or output cannot be chosen, but is determined by the value of the independent variable and the function. The *y* variable is called the dependent value because its value depends on the value of *x*.

Example 2

Instruction

Ask why values that are factors of 6 were chosen for *x* in making the table. They will give integer values for *y*. Suggest that students analyze an equation briefly before choosing values to use for *x*. Explain that this can help make plotting the corresponding values of *y* easier.

Point out that neither *x* nor *y* will have the value of 0 for this equation since *x* is not allowed to be 0 and since the numerator of the fraction is 6, the value of *y* will not be 0.

(continued)

Teacher Tip

Students may forget to choose **negative values for the independent variable** in an equation. Stress the importance of using a range of numbers for the variable including zero and integers near zero. If students forget to do so, they may not have a clear idea of what the graph should look like.

2 New Concepts (Continued)

Instruction

Ask students to describe all the values for x and y that can be used to make ordered pairs for this function. The possible values for x include the set of all real numbers except 0. The possible values for y include the set of all real numbers except 0.

Once students have plotted the ordered pairs, discuss why there are no points in the second or fourth quadrants. Explain that for a point to be in either of these quadrants, its coordinates cannot have the same sign. All coordinate pairs that satisfy this equation must have the same sign.

Practice Set

Problems a–d Connect

When students complete their graphs, discuss how they are similar and different from the graphs in examples 1 and 2. Sample: The two curves for $y = \frac{12}{x}$ have the same shape as those in example 2 but are farther away from the axes.

Remind students to use both positive and negative numbers as values for the independent variables in these problems.

On a coordinate plane we graph the x, y pairs we found that satisfy the equation.

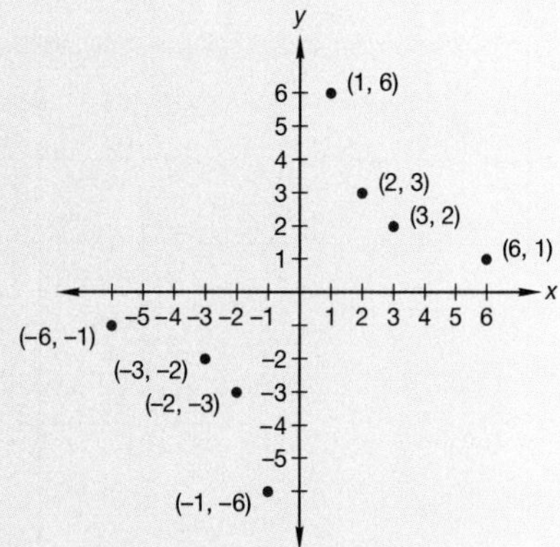

This arrangement of points on the coordinate plane suggests two curves that do not intersect.

We draw two smooth curves through the two sets of points.

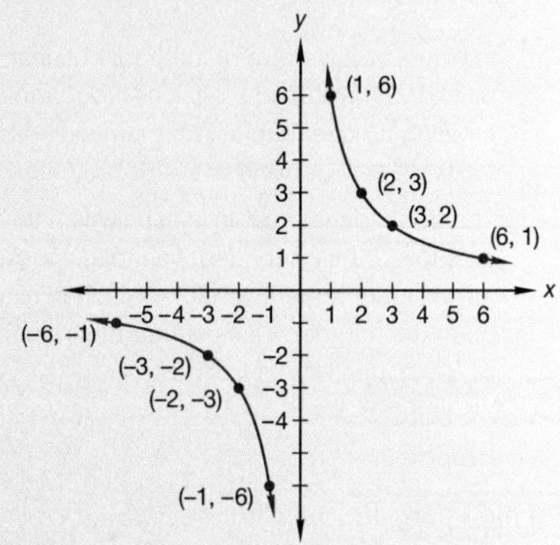

You might recall seeing this graph in Investigation 9 where we graphed $xy = 6$. Notice that $y = \frac{6}{x}$ is an alternate form of the same equation. Can you transform one equation into the other? The equation $y = \frac{6}{x}$ is an example of inverse variation.

Conclude Will either curve ever cross the x- or y-axis? Why or why not? No. Sample: Neither x nor y can ever equal zero.

Practice Set

Connect Graph each equation.

▸ **a.** $y = \frac{12}{x}$ Begin by creating a table of ordered pairs. Use 6, 4, 3, 2, −2, −3, −4, and −6 in place of x. See student work.

▸ **b.** $y = x^2 - 2$ Compare your graph to the graph in example 2. See student work.

▸ See Math Conversations in the sidebar.

English Learners

Below the last graph in the solution for example 2, review the meaning of **inverse variation.** Tell students:

"In an inverse variation, if one value increases, then the other value decreases at the same rate."

Direct the students' attention to the graph of example 2 in the book. Ask what happens to the value of y as the value of x increases?" It decreases.

▶ c. $y = \frac{10}{x}$ Compare your graph to the graph in example 1. See student work.

▶ d. $y = 2x^2$ Compare your graph to the graph in example 2. See student work.

Written Practice *Strengthening Concepts*

▶ **1.** *(Inv. 8)* Schuster was playing a board game with a pair of number cubes. He rolled a 7 three times in a row. What are the odds of Schuster getting a 7 with the next roll? 1 to 5

2. *(92)* If the total cost of a package of paper clips including 8% sales tax is $2.70, then what was the price before tax was added? $2.50

3. *(77)* In the year 2000, the population of the United States was about 280 million. In the election that year about 105 million people voted. About what percent of the population voted in the presidential election of 2000? about 38%

▶ **4.** *(58)* If a trapezoid has a line of symmetry and one of its angles measures 100°, what is the measure of each of its other angles? 100°; 80°; 80°

5. *(48)* Complete the table.

Fraction	Decimal	Percent
a. $\frac{1}{1000}$	**b.** 0.001	0.1%
$\frac{8}{5}$	**c.** 1.6	**d.** 160%

▶ * **6.** *(111)* **Generalize** Simplify. Write the answer in scientific notation. 3×10^{-12}

$$\frac{(4 \times 10^{-5})(6 \times 10^{-4})}{8 \times 10^3}$$

▶ * **7.** *(115)* **Generalize** Factor each expression:

a. $3y^2 - y$ $y(3y - 1)$

b. $6w^2 + 9wx - 12w$ $3w(2w + 3x - 4)$

The figure below shows a cylinder and a cone whose heights and diameters are equal. Refer to the figure to answer problems **8** and **9.**

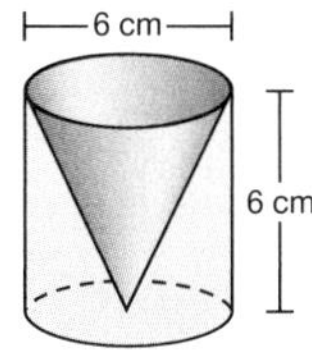

▶ * **8.** *(113)* **Analyze** What is the ratio of the volume of the cone to the volume of the cylinder? $\frac{1}{3}$

* **9.** *(105)* The lateral surface area of a cylinder is the area of the curved side and excludes the areas of the circular ends. What is the lateral surface area of the cylinder rounded to the nearest square centimeter? (Use 3.14 for π.) 113 cm^2

▶ See Math Conversations in the sidebar.

3 Written Practice

Math Conversations

Discussion opportunities are provided below.

Problem 1

Extend the Problem

"What are the odds starting out, before any cubes are rolled, of rolling four 7s in a row?" 1 to 1295

Problem 6 Generalize

"Why is the simplified expression less than the numerator of the unsimplified expression?" Sample: Think of this as a division problem with the numerator as the dividend and the denominator as the divisor. The simplified fraction will be the quotient. Since the divisor is greater than 1, the quotient will be less than the dividend.

Problem 7 Generalize

Discuss how to check that the expressions have been correctly factored. Samples: Multiply the factors in the answer and if the original expression is the product, then the answer is correct. Check that no similar factors remain in the terms of the polynomial part.

Problem 8 Analyze

Ask whether it is true that the ratio of the volume of a cone contained in a cylinder is always $\frac{1}{3}$. Sample: Yes, because the formula for the volume of the cone is $\frac{1}{3}$ the formula for the volume of the cylinder. Ask whether it would be true even if the cylinder and the cone did not have the same diameter and height. It would still be true.

Errors and Misconceptions

Problem 4

If students had difficulty determining the measures of the angles, they should first draw a trapezoid with a line of symmetry.

(continued)

3 Written Practice (Continued)

Math Conversations

Discussion opportunities are provided below.

Problem 11

Extend the Problem

Point out that the connection between mass and energy discovered by Albert Einstein is expressed in the equation, $E = mc^2$. In this equation, E represents energy, m represents mass, and c^2 is the square of the speed of light. Ask what the students know about Einstein.

Problem 13 Connect

Point out that the lines are perpendicular and ask whether it is their slopes or their intercepts that make them perpendicular. Samples: The slopes do it. The slopes are negative reciprocals and this makes the lines perpendicular. Then ask what the intercepts determine. Samples: The intercepts tell where the lines will cross the y-axis. The intercepts tell how far apart the lines are when they cross the y-axis.

Problem 15 Generalize

If students have calculators, ask them what will happen to the investment in 8 years and in 13 years. In 8 years, it more than quadruples, and in 13 years, it is more than 10 times its original value.

Errors and Misconceptions

Problem 17

Students whose answer is 4536 ft^3 most likely changed $\frac{1}{2}$ foot to 6 inches and multiplied $36 \times 21 \times 6$. Point out that the $\frac{1}{2}$ foot should stay as $\frac{1}{2}$ when doing this calculation.

(continued)

10. (99) The hypotenuse of this triangle is twice the length of the shorter leg.

2 cm, 1 cm

a. Use the Pythagorean theorem to find the length of the remaining side. $\sqrt{3}$ cm

b. Use a centimeter ruler to find the length of the unmarked side to the nearest tenth of a centimeter. 1.7 cm

▶* **11.** (106) Transform the formula $E = mc^2$ to solve for m. $m = \frac{E}{c^2}$

12. (54) If 60% of the students in the assembly were girls, what was the ratio of boys to girls in the assembly? $\frac{2}{3}$

The graph below shows $m \perp n$. Refer to the graph to answer problems **13** and **14**.

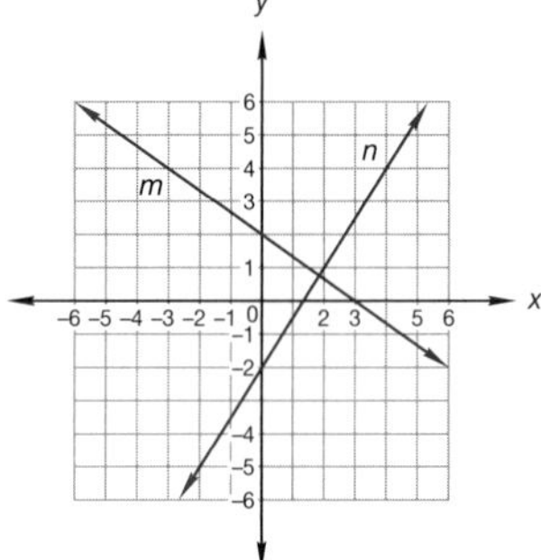

▶* **13.** (116) Connect What is the equation of each line in slope-intercept form? line m: $y = -\frac{2}{3}x + 2$; line n: $y = \frac{3}{2}x - 2$

14. (107) What is the product of the slopes of lines m and n? Why? The product of the slopes is -1. The slopes are negative reciprocals.

▶* **15.** (110) Generalize If a $1000 investment earns 20% interest compounded annually, then the investment will double in value in how many years? about 4 years

* **16.** (112) The stated size of a TV screen or computer monitor is its diagonal measure. A screen that is 17 in. wide and 12 in. tall would be described as what size of screen? Round the answer to the nearest inch. 21 in.

▶ **17.** (70, 88) Premixed concrete is sold by the cubic yard. The Jeffersons are pouring a concrete driveway that is 36 feet long, 21 feet wide, and $\frac{1}{2}$ foot thick.

a. Find the number of cubic feet of concrete needed. 378 cubic feet

b. Use three unit multipliers to convert answer **a** to cubic yards. 14 cubic yards

▶ See Math Conversations in the sidebar.

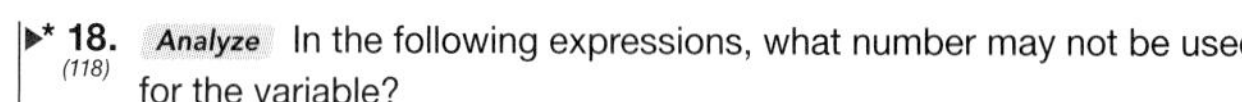

▶* **18.** (118) **Analyze** In the following expressions, what number may not be used for the variable?

a. $\frac{12}{4 - 2m}$ $m \neq 2$ **b.** $\frac{y - 5}{y + 5}$ $y \neq -5$

▶* **19.** (120) **Connect** Graph: $y = x^2 - 4$

19. $y = x^2 - 4$

20. (97) Refer to this drawing of three similar triangles to find the letter that completes the proportion below. y

$$\frac{c}{a} = \frac{a}{?}$$

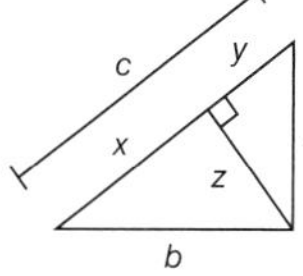

▶* **21.** (105) **Analyze** Recall that the surface area of a sphere is four times the area of its largest "cross section." What is the approximate surface area of a cantaloupe that is 6 inches in diameter? Round the answer to the nearest square inch. (Use 3.14 for π.) 113 in.^{2}

▶* **22.** (114) **Connect** A cup containing 250 cubic centimeters of water holds how many liters of water? 0.25 liter

Solve:

23. (102) $15 + x = 3x - 17$ 16

24. (93) $3\frac{1}{3}x - 16 = 74$ 27

25. (109) $\frac{m^2}{4} = 9$ 6, −6

26. (98) $\frac{1.2}{m} = \frac{0.04}{8}$ 240

Simplify:

27. (96) $x(x - 5) - 2(x - 5)$ $x^2 - 7x + 10$

28. (103) $\frac{(3xy)(4x^2y)(5x^2y^2)}{10x^3y^3}$ $6x^2y$

29. (91) $|-8| + 3(-7) - [(-4)(-5) - 3(-2)]$ −39

▶ **30.** (43, 45) $\frac{7\frac{1}{2} - \frac{2}{3}(0.9)}{0.03}$ 230

▶ See Math Conversations in the sidebar.

3 Written Practice (Continued)

Math Conversations

Discussion opportunities are provided below.

Problem 18 Analyze

"In part b, if y = 5, the numerator will have a value of 0. Can 5 be used as a value of y? Explain your answer." Sample: Yes, because it is the denominator that matters, and it cannot have a value of 0. The numerator may have any value, including 0.

Problem 19 Connect

Before students start to work on this problem, ask:

"Will this graph be a straight line? Why or why not?" Sample: No, because the equation has x^2 in it.

"Where will this graph intersect the y-axis?" at $x = -4$

Problem 21 Analyze

Discuss what approaches students used to solve this problem. Sample: I know the largest cross-section is a circle with the same diameter as the sphere, so its radius is 3 inches. Then I found the value of $4\pi r^2$ to be 113.04 and I rounded that to 113 in.^{2}

Problem 22 Connect

Make a connection between the metric and standard systems of measure. Ask what the mass of the water is. 250 g Then ask about how many ounces that would be. about 8.8 or 9 ounces Guide students to see that 250 grams is a little more than half a pound.

Errors and Misconceptions

Problem 30

To help students who were confused by trying to work with both fractions and decimals, explain that finding $\frac{2}{3}$ of 0.9 first is an easy way to start this problem. After doing that, using either fraction or decimal form works well.

Assessment

30–40 minutes *For use after Lesson 120*

Distribute **Cumulative Test 23** to each student. Two versions of the test are available in *Saxon Math Course 2 Course Assessments Book.* Have students complete the **Power-Up Test** first. Allow 10 minutes. Then have students work the 20 numbered items on the **Cumulative Test.** Students may use copies of the answer sheet to record their work. Track individual and class progress with the **Test Analysis** forms.

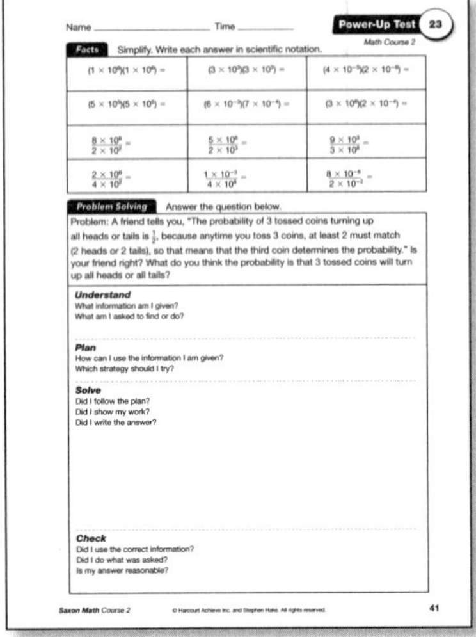
Name ______ Time ______ **Power-Up Test 23** *Math Course 2*

Facts Simplify. Write each answer in scientific notation.

(1 × 10[illegible])(1 × 10[illegible]) =	(3 × 10[illegible])(3 × 10[illegible]) =	(4 × 10[illegible])(2 × 10[illegible]) =
(5 × 10[illegible])(5 × 10[illegible]) =	(6 × 10[illegible])(7 × 10[illegible]) =	(3 × 10[illegible])(2 × 10[illegible]) =
(8 × 10[illegible]) / (2 × 10[illegible]) =	(5 × 10[illegible]) / (2 × 10[illegible]) =	(9 × 10[illegible]) / (3 × 10[illegible]) =
(2 × 10[illegible]) / (4 × 10[illegible]) =	(1 × 10[illegible]) / (4 × 10[illegible]) =	(8 × 10[illegible]) / (2 × 10[illegible]) =

Problem Solving Answer the question below.

Problem: A friend tells you, "The probability of 3 tossed coins turning up all heads or tails is $\frac{1}{2}$, because anytime you toss 3 coins, at least 2 must match (2 heads or 2 tails), so that means that the third coin determines the probability." Is your friend right? What do you think the probability is that 3 tossed coins will turn up all heads or all tails?

Understand What information am I given? What am I asked to find or do?

Plan How can I use the information I am given? Which strategy should I try?

Solve Did I follow the plan? Did I show my work? Did I write the answer?

Check Did I use the correct information? Did I do what was asked? Is my answer reasonable?

Saxon Math Course 2 © Harcourt Achieve Inc. and Stephen Hake. All rights reserved. 41

Power-Up Test 23

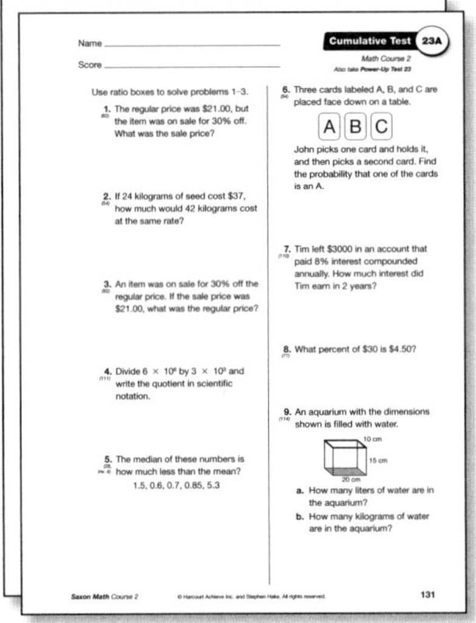
Name ______ Score ______ **Cumulative Test 23A** *Math Course 2* Also take Power-Up Test 23

Use ratio boxes to solve problems 1–3.

1. The regular price was $21.00, but the item was on sale for 30% off. What was the sale price?
2. If 24 kilograms of seed cost $37, how much would 42 kilograms cost at the same rate?
3. An item was on sale for 30% off the regular price. If the sale price was $21.00, what was the regular price?
4. Divide 6 × 10[illegible] by 3 × 10[illegible] and write the quotient in scientific notation.
5. The median of these numbers is how much less than the mean? 1.5, 0.6, 0.7, 0.85, 5.3
6. Three cards labeled A, B, and C are placed face down on a table. A B C John picks one card and holds it, and then picks a second card. Find the probability that one of the cards is an A.
7. Tim left $3000 in an account that paid 8% interest compounded annually. How much interest did Tim earn in 2 years?
8. What percent of $30 is $4.50?
9. An aquarium with the dimensions shown is filled with water. (10 cm, 15 cm, 20 cm)
 a. How many liters of water are in the aquarium?
 b. How many kilograms of water are in the aquarium?

Saxon Math Course 2 © Harcourt Achieve Inc. and Stephen Hake. All rights reserved. 131

Cumulative Test 23A

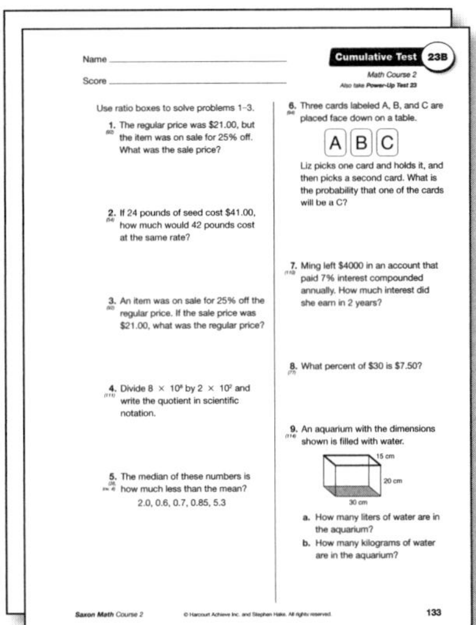
Name ______ Score ______ **Cumulative Test 23B** *Math Course 2* Also take Power-Up Test 23

Use ratio boxes to solve problems 1–3.

1. The regular price was $21.00, but the item was on sale for 25% off. What was the sale price?
2. If 24 pounds of seed cost $41.00, how much would 42 pounds cost at the same rate?
3. An item was on sale for 25% off the regular price. If the sale price was $21.00, what was the regular price?
4. Divide 8 × 10[illegible] by 2 × 10[illegible] and write the quotient in scientific notation.
5. The median of these numbers is how much less than the mean? 2.0, 0.6, 0.7, 0.85, 5.3
6. Three cards labeled A, B, and C are placed face down on a table. A B C Liz picks one card and holds it, and then picks a second card. What is the probability that one of the cards will be a C?
7. Ming left $4000 in an account that paid 7% interest compounded annually. How much interest did she earn in 2 years?
8. What percent of $30 is $7.50?
9. An aquarium with the dimensions shown is filled with water. (15 cm, 20 cm, 30 cm)
 a. How many liters of water are in the aquarium?
 b. How many kilograms of water are in the aquarium?

Saxon Math Course 2 © Harcourt Achieve Inc. and Stephen Hake. All rights reserved. 133

Alternative Cumulative Test 23B

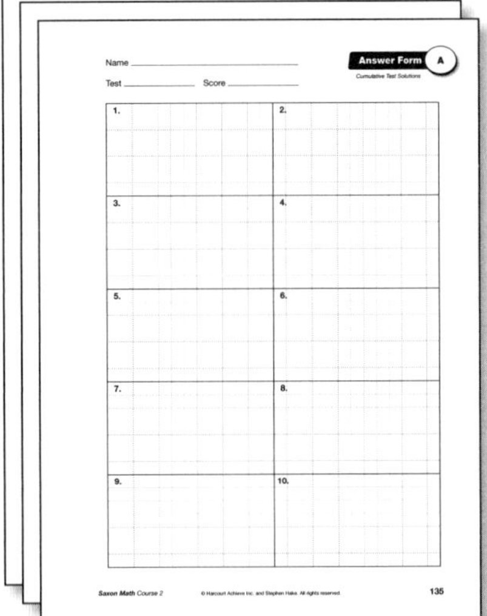
Name ______ **Answer Form A** *Cumulative Test Solutions*

Test ______ Score ______

1. 2. 3. 4. 5. 6. 7. 8. 9. 10.

Saxon Math Course 2 © Harcourt Achieve Inc. and Stephen Hake. All rights reserved. 135

Optional Answer Forms

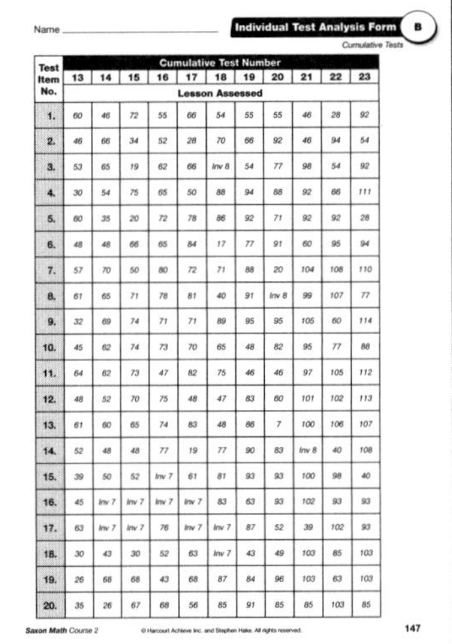
Name ______ **Individual Test Analysis Form B** *Cumulative Tests*

Test Item No.	Cumulative Test Number										
	13	14	15	16	17	18	19	20	21	22	23
	Lesson Assessed										
1.	60	46	72	55	66	54	55	55	46	28	92
2.	46	66	34	52	28	70	66	92	46	94	54
3.	53	65	19	62	66	Inv 8	54	77	98	54	92
4.	30	54	75	65	50	88	94	88	92	66	111
5.	60	35	20	72	78	86	92	71	92	92	28
6.	48	48	66	65	84	17	77	91	60	95	94
7.	57	70	50	80	72	71	88	20	104	108	110
8.	61	65	71	78	81	40	91	Inv 8	99	107	77
9.	32	69	74	71	71	89	95	95	105	60	114
10.	45	62	74	73	70	65	48	82	95	77	88
11.	64	62	73	47	82	75	46	46	97	105	112
12.	48	52	70	75	48	47	83	60	101	102	113
13.	61	60	65	74	83	48	86	7	100	106	107
14.	52	48	48	77	19	77	90	83	Inv 8	40	108
15.	39	50	52	Inv 7	61	81	93	93	100	98	40
16.	45	Inv 7	Inv 7	Inv 7	Inv 7	83	63	93	102	93	93
17.	63	Inv 7	Inv 7	76	Inv 7	Inv 7	87	52	39	102	93
18.	30	43	30	52	63	Inv 7	43	49	103	85	103
19.	26	68	68	43	68	87	84	96	103	63	103
20.	35	26	67	68	56	85	91	85	85	103	85

Saxon Math Course 2 © Harcourt Achieve Inc. and Stephen Hake. All rights reserved. 147

Individual Test Analysis Form

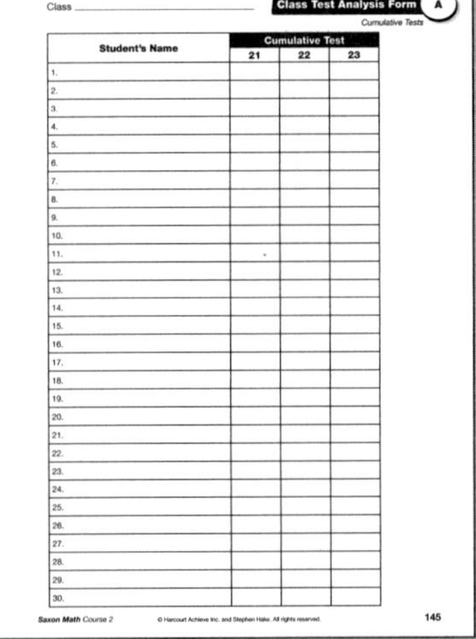
Class ______ **Class Test Analysis Form A** *Cumulative Tests*

	Student's Name	Cumulative Test 21	22	23
1.				
2.				
3.				
4.				
5.				
6.				
7.				
8.				
9.				
10.				
11.				
12.				
13.				
14.				
15.				
16.				
17.				
18.				
19.				
20.				
21.				
22.				
23.				
24.				
25.				
26.				
27.				
28.				
29.				
30.				

Saxon Math Course 2 © Harcourt Achieve Inc. and Stephen Hake. All rights reserved. 145

Class Test Analysis Form

Reteaching

Students who score below 80% on the assessment may be in need of reteaching. Look for the causes of student mistakes. If errors are conceptual, refer to the *Reteaching Masters* for reteaching.

Customized Benchmark Assessment

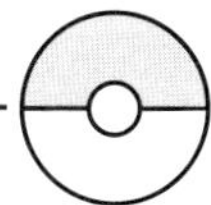

You can develop customized benchmark tests using the Test Generator located on the *Test and Practice Generator CD.*

This chart shows the lesson, the standard, and the test item question that can be found on the *Test and Practice Generator CD.*

LESSON	NEW CONCEPTS	LOCAL STANDARD	TEST ITEM ON CD
111	• Dividing in Scientific Notation		12.111.1
112	• Applications of the Pythagorean Theorem		12.112.1
113	• Volume of Pyramids, Cones, and Spheres		12.113.1
114	• Volume, Capacity, and Mass in the Metric System		12.114.1
115	• Factoring Algebraic Expressions		12.115.1
116	• Slope-Intercept Form of Linear Equations		12.116.1
117	• Copying Geometric Figures		12.117.1
118	• Division by Zero		12.118.1
119	• Graphing Area and Volume Formulas		12.119.1
120	• Graphing Nonlinear Equations		12.120.1

Using the Test Generator CD

- Develop tests in both English and Spanish.
- Choose from multiple-choice and free-response test items.
- Clone test items to create multiple versions of the same test.
- View and edit test items to make and save your own questions.
- Administer assessments through paper tests or over a school LAN.
- Monitor student progress through a variety of individual and class reports —for both diagnosing and assessing standards mastery.

Performance Task 23

Package Wooden Puzzles

Assign after Lesson 120 and Test 23

Objectives

- Draw a net of a cube.
- Determine the dimensions and calculate the volumes of 3-D figures.
- Find the largest 3-D figure that will fit in a cube of given size.
- Determine the effect on volume of doubling the edges of a cube.
- Communicate their ideas through writing.

Materials

Performance Tasks 23A and **23B**

Preparation

Make copies of **Performance Tasks 23A** and **23B.** (One each per student.)

Time Requirement

30–60 minutes; Begin in class and complete at home.

Task

Explain to students that for this task they will be responsible for the packaging of wood puzzles at The Wood Toy and Puzzle Company. They will make a net of a cube with a given surface area. They will find the dimensions of the largest pyramid, cylinder, sphere, and cone that will fit in a cube of that size. They will also find the volume of these figures. They will be required to give explanations for some of their answers and will write about the effect on volume of doubling the edges of a cube. Point out that all of the information students need is on **Performance Tasks 23A** and **23B.**

Criteria for Evidence of Learning

- Accurately draws a net for a cube with a surface area of 24 square inches.
- Accurately states the dimensions of the largest 3-D figures that will fit into a 2-inch cube.
- Accurately finds the volume of 3-D figures.
- Communicates ideas clearly through writing.

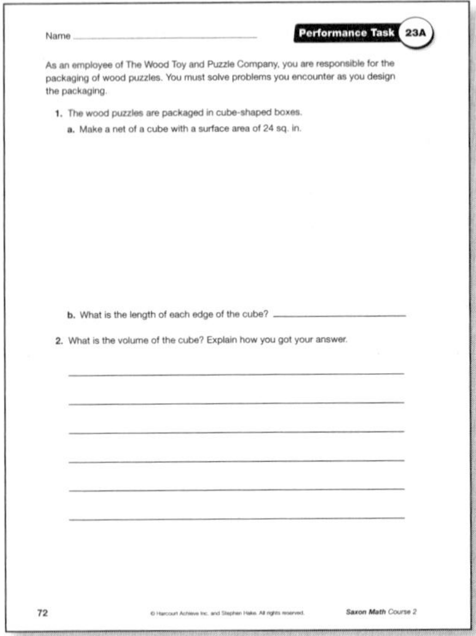

Name ______________ **Performance Task 23A**

As an employee of The Wood Toy and Puzzle Company, you are responsible for the packaging of wood puzzles. You must solve problems you encounter as you design the packaging.

1. The wood puzzles are packaged in cube-shaped boxes.
   a. Make a net of a cube with a surface area of 24 sq. in.

   b. What is the length of each edge of the cube? ______________
2. What is the volume of the cube? Explain how you got your answer.

72 © Harcourt Achieve Inc. and Stephen Hake. All rights reserved. *Saxon Math* Course 2

Performance Task 23A

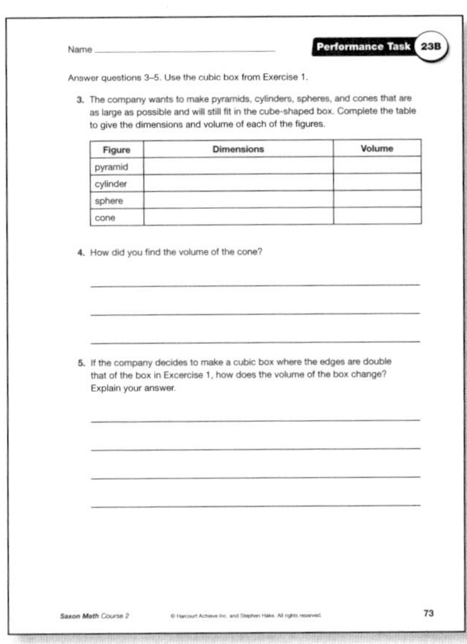

Name ______________ **Performance Task 23B**

Answer questions 3–5. Use the cubic box from Exercise 1.

3. The company wants to make pyramids, cylinders, spheres, and cones that are as large as possible and will still fit in the cube-shaped box. Complete the table to give the dimensions and volume of each of the figures.

Figure	Dimensions	Volume
pyramid		
cylinder		
sphere		
cone		

4. How did you find the volume of the cone?

5. If the company decides to make a cubic box where the edges are double that of the box in Excercise 1, how does the volume of the box change? Explain your answer.

Saxon Math Course 2 © Harcourt Achieve Inc. and Stephen Hake. All rights reserved. 73

Performance Task 23B

Meeting Standards

National Council of Teachers of Mathematics (NCTM)

Geometry

GM.4a Draw geometric objects with specified properties, such as side lengths or angle measures

GM.4b Use two–dimensional representations of three-dimensional objects to visualize and solve problems such as those involving surface area and volume

GM.4c Use visual tools such as networks to represent and solve problems

Problem Solving

PS.1b Solve problems that arise in mathematics and in other contexts

Communication

CM.3a Organize and consolidate their mathematical thinking through communication

Connections

CN.4a Recognize and use connections among mathematical ideas

Representation

RE.5a Create and use representations to organize, record, and communicate mathematical ideas

Focus on

• Platonic Solids

Objectives

- Identify and make models of the Platonic solids—tetrahedron, cube, octahedron, dodecahedron, and icosahedron.
- Identify the number of faces, vertices, and edges for each model created.

Lesson Preparation

Materials

- **Investigation Activities 26–28** (in *Instructional Masters*), one set per student pair
- **Manipulative kit: rulers**
- **Teacher-provided material: scissors, tape or glue**

Optional:

- **Manipulative kit: Relational Geosolids**

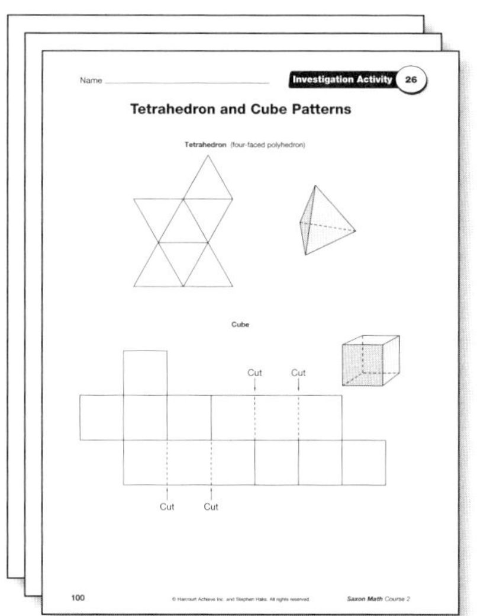
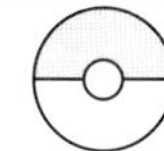

Investigation Activities 26–28

Math Language

New	Maintain
dodecahedron	cube
icosahedron	edge
octahedron	face
Platonic solids	polyhedron
tetrahedron	vertex

Technology Resources

Student eBook Complete student textbook in electronic format.

Resources and Planner CD Assessment, reteaching, and instructional masters, plus a pacing calendar with standards.

Test and Practice Generator CD Create additional practice sheets and custom-made tests.

www.SaxonPublishers.com Visit for more student activities and planning materials.

Inclusion

Adaptations CD Adapted lessons, investigations, practice and assessments.

Meeting Standards

National Council of Teachers of Mathematics (NCTM)

Geometry

GM.1a Precisely describe, classify, and understand relationships among types of two- and three-dimensional objects using their defining properties

GM.4b Use two-dimensional representations of three-dimensional objects to visualize and solve problems such as those involving surface area and volume

GM.4d Use geometric models to represent and explain numerical and algebraic relationships

INVESTIGATION 12

In this investigation, students will learn how to model polyhedrons and will study the properties of each one they create. They will also learn how to represent several polyhedrons as nets.

Polyhedrons

Instruction

Sketch an equilateral triangle, a square, and a regular pentagon on the board or an overhead projector. Identify each figure and point out that each is a regular polygon, so the sides and angles are equal. Tell students that the faces of the Platonic solids they will learn about in this investigation are either squares, equilateral triangles, or regular pentagons.

Point out to students that a tetrahedron is a special kind of triangular pyramid in which the faces are congruent equilateral triangles.

INVESTIGATION 12

Focus on

• Platonic Solids

Recall that polygons are closed, two-dimensional figures with straight sides. If every face of a solid figure is a polygon, then the solid figure is called a **polyhedron.** Thus polyhedrons do not have any curved surfaces. So rectangular prisms and pyramids are polyhedrons, but spheres and circular cylinders are not.

Remember also that regular polygons have sides of equal length and angles of equal measure. Just as there are regular polygons, so there are regular polyhedrons. A cube is one example of a regular polyhedron. All the edges of a cube are of equal length, and all the angles are of equal measure, so all the faces are congruent regular polygons.

There are five regular polyhedrons. These polyhedrons are known as the **Platonic solids,** named after the ancient Greek philosopher Plato. We illustrate the five Platonic solids below.

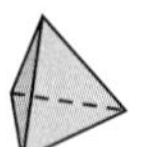
tetrahedron

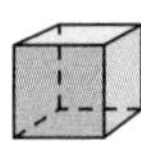
cube

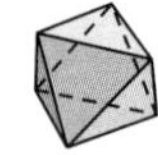
octahedron

dodecahedron

icosahedron

In this activity we will construct models of four of the Platonic solids.

Activity

Platonic Solids

Materials needed:

- copies of Investigation Activity 26 and Investigation Activity 27
- ruler
- scissors
- glue or tape

Working in pairs or small groups is helpful. Sometimes more than two hands are needed to fold and glue.

Beginning with the tetrahedron pattern, cut around the border of the pattern. The line segments in the pattern are fold lines. Do not cut these. The folds will become the edges of the polyhedron. The triangles marked with "T" are

Manipulative Use

Pass around the Relational GeoSolids from the manipulative kit. Instruct the students to touch the edges. Have them identify which objects have straight edges and which have curved edges.

"Which solids are polyhedrons? Explain." Sample: triangular prism; its edges are straight

"Which solids are not polyhedrons? Explain." Sample: sphere; there are no edges

Math Background

Why are regular polyhedrons also called Platonic solids?

Platonic solids are named after the Greek philosopher Plato, who described these regular polyhedrons in his writings over two thousand years ago. Plato thought that each regular polyhedron was the shape of one of the basic elements of the physical universe. In Plato's work, the tetrahedron represented fire, the cube represented earth, the octahedron represented water, the dodecahedron represented the material from which the constellations were made, and the icosahedron represented air.

tabs for gluing. These tabs are tucked inside the polyhedron and are hidden from view when the polyhedron is finished.

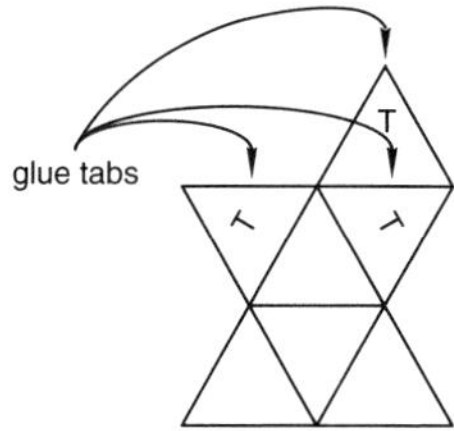

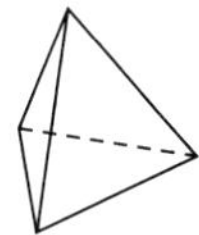
tetrahedron

Fold the pattern to make a pyramid with four faces. Glue the tabs or tape across the joining edges to hold the pattern in place.

When you have completed the tetrahedron, select another pattern to cut, fold, and form. All tabs are hidden when the pattern is properly folded, but all other polygons should be fully visible. When you have completed the models, copy this table and fill in the missing information by studying your models.

Thinking Skill

Generalize

For each polyhedron in this table, add together the number of faces (F) and vertices (V). Then find a relationship between this sum and the number of edges (E) in the polyhedron.

extensions

$F + V = E + 2$

Platonic Solid	Each Face is What Polygon?	How Many Faces?	How Many Vertices?	How Many Edges?
tetrahedron	equilateral triangle	4	4	6
cube	square	6	8	12
octahedron	triangle	8	6	12
dodecahedron	pentagon	12	20	30

a. This arrangement of four equilateral triangles was folded to make a model of a tetrahedron. Draw another arrangement of four adjoining equilateral triangles that can be folded to make a tetrahedron model. (Omit tabs.)

Activity

Instruction

Demonstrate how to cut, fold, and glue the pattern to create a tetrahedron. If necessary, help groups construct the cube, octahedron, and dodecahedron.

After students have completed the table, ask them to find a pattern that relates the sum of the faces and vertices to the number of edges. The number of edges is two less than the sum of the number of faces and vertices.

Tell students that many artists throughout history have used Platonic solids in their work. The artist M.C. Escher created a wood engraving called "Stars" in 1948 that contained several Platonic solids. Interested students can do an internet search for a copy of this engraving. Ask students to study the print and identify the different Platonic solids in it.

Investigation 12 **845**

Extensions

For extension **c,** distribute copies of **Investigation Activity 28,** scissors, and glue to pairs or small groups of students. After students have constructed the icosahedron model and answered the questions, have them compare all five of their models. Ask:

"Which Platonic solid has the greatest number of faces, edges, and vertices? Which has the least?" greatest: icosahedron; least: tetrahedron

Then ask:

"Which Platonic solids have equilateral triangles as faces?" tetahedron, octahedron, icosahedron

b. This arrangement of six squares was folded to make a model of a cube. How many other different patterns of six adjacent squares can you draw that can be folded to make a model of a cube? (Omit tabs.)

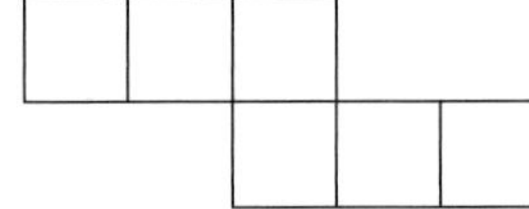

c. Using scissors and glue, cut out and construct the icosahedron model on **Instruction Activity 28** Icosahedon. Working in pairs or in small groups is helpful. We suggest pre-folding the pattern before making the cuts to separate the tabs. Remember that the triangles marked with a "T" are tabs and should be hidden from view when the model is finished.

Once you have constructed the model, hold it lightly between your thumb and forefinger. You should be able to rotate the icosahedron while it is in this position. Since your icosahedron is a regular polyhedron, you also should be able to reposition the model so that your fingers touch two different vertices but the appearance of the figure remains unchanged.

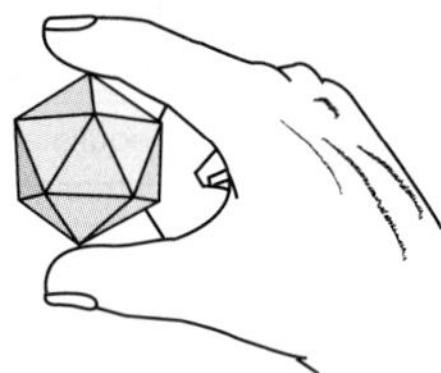

Holding the model as shown, your thumb and finger each touch a vertex. As you rotate the icosahedron, you can count the vertices. How many vertices are there in all? How many faces are there in all? What is the shape of each face?

846 ***Saxon*** *Math Course 2*

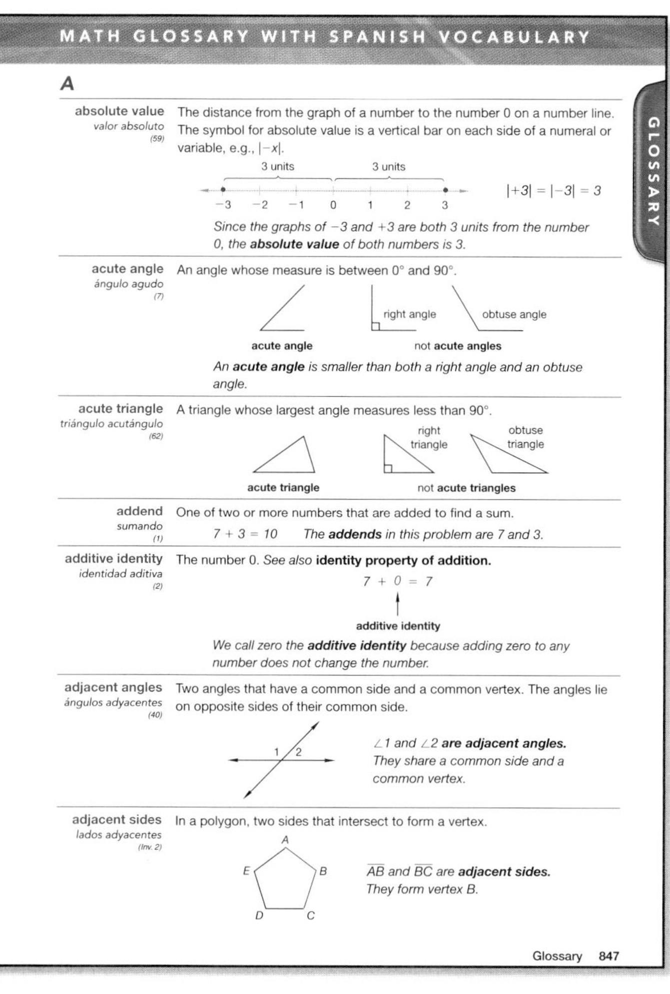

A

absolute value *valor absoluto* (59) — The distance from the graph of a number to the number 0 on a number line. The symbol for absolute value is a vertical bar on each side of a numeral or variable, e.g., $|-x|$.

*Since the graphs of −3 and +3 are both 3 units from the number 0, the **absolute value** of both numbers is 3.*

acute angle *ángulo agudo* (7) — An angle whose measure is between 0° and 90°.

*An **acute angle** is smaller than both a right angle and an obtuse angle.*

acute triangle *triángulo acutángulo* (62) — A triangle whose largest angle measures less than 90°.

addend *sumando* (1) — One of two or more numbers that are added to find a sum.

*7 + 3 = 10 The **addends** in this problem are 7 and 3.*

additive identity *identidad aditiva* (2) — The number 0. *See also* **identity property of addition.**

$7 + 0 = 7$

*We call zero the **additive identity** because adding zero to any number does not change the number.*

adjacent angles *ángulos adyacentes* (40) — Two angles that have a common side and a common vertex. The angles lie on opposite sides of their common side.

*∠1 and ∠2 **are adjacent angles.** They share a common side and a common vertex.*

adjacent sides *lados adyacentes* (Inv. 2) — In a polygon, two sides that intersect to form a vertex.

*$\overline{AB}$ and $\overline{BC}$ are **adjacent sides.** They form vertex B.*

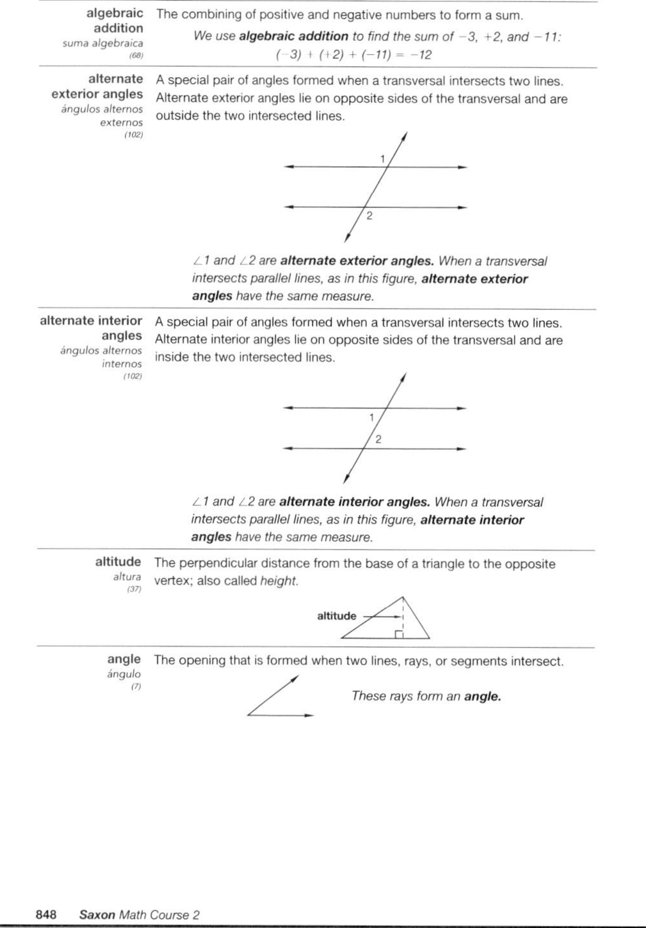

algebraic addition *suma algebraica* (68) — The combining of positive and negative numbers to form a sum.

*We use **algebraic addition** to find the sum of −3, +2, and −11:*

$(-3) + (+2) + (-11) = -12$

alternate exterior angles *ángulos alternos externos* (102) — A special pair of angles formed when a transversal intersects two lines. Alternate exterior angles lie on opposite sides of the transversal and are outside the two intersected lines.

*∠1 and ∠2 are **alternate exterior angles.** When a transversal intersects parallel lines, as in this figure, **alternate exterior angles** have the same measure.*

alternate interior angles *ángulos alternos internos* (102) — A special pair of angles formed when a transversal intersects two lines. Alternate interior angles lie on opposite sides of the transversal and are inside the two intersected lines.

*∠1 and ∠2 are **alternate interior angles.** When a transversal intersects parallel lines, as in this figure, **alternate interior angles** have the same measure.*

altitude *altura* (37) — The perpendicular distance from the base of a triangle to the opposite vertex; also called *height.*

angle *ángulo* (7) — The opening that is formed when two lines, rays, or segments intersect.

*These rays form an **angle.***

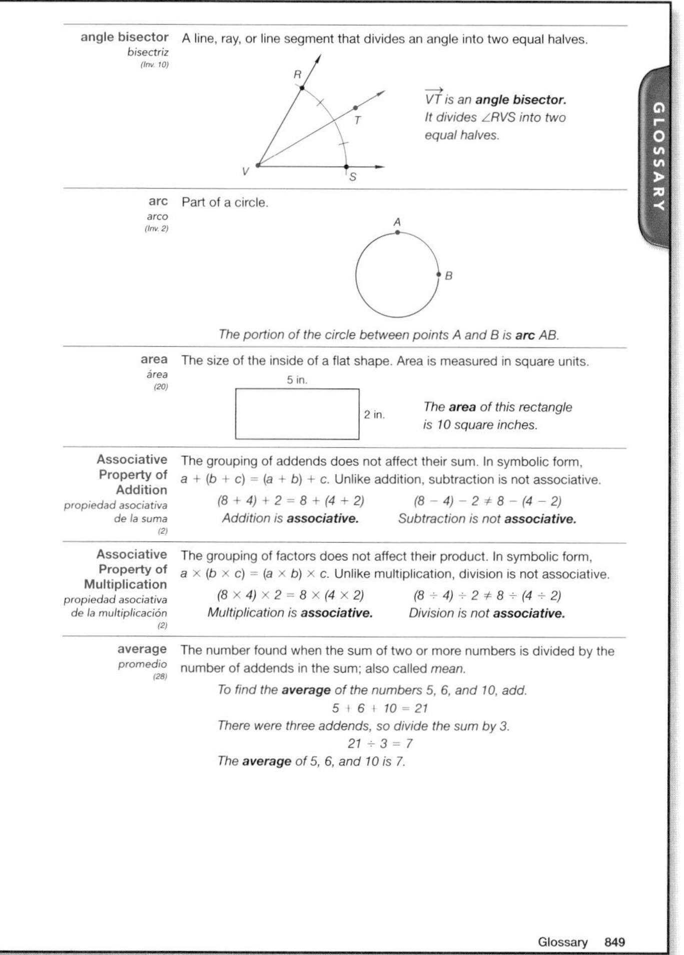

angle bisector *bisectriz* (Inv. 10) — A line, ray, or line segment that divides an angle into two equal halves.

*$\overrightarrow{VT}$ is an **angle bisector.** It divides ∠RVS into two equal halves.*

arc *arco* (Inv. 2) — Part of a circle.

*The portion of the circle between points A and B is **arc** AB.*

area *área* (20) — The size of the inside of a flat shape. Area is measured in square units.

*The **area** of this rectangle is 10 square inches.*

Associative Property of Addition *propiedad asociativa de la suma* (2) — The grouping of addends does not affect their sum. In symbolic form, $a + (b + c) = (a + b) + c$. Unlike addition, subtraction is not associative.

$(8 + 4) + 2 = 8 + (4 + 2)$	$(8 - 4) - 2 \neq 8 - (4 - 2)$
*Addition is **associative.***	*Subtraction is not **associative.***

Associative Property of Multiplication *propiedad asociativa de la multiplicación* (2) — The grouping of factors does not affect their product. In symbolic form, $a \times (b \times c) = (a \times b) \times c$. Unlike multiplication, division is not associative.

$(8 \times 4) \times 2 = 8 \times (4 \times 2)$	$(8 \div 4) \div 2 \neq 8 \div (4 \div 2)$
*Multiplication is **associative.***	*Division is not **associative.***

average *promedio* (28) — The number found when the sum of two or more numbers is divided by the number of addends in the sum; also called *mean.*

*To find the **average** of the numbers 5, 6, and 10, add.*

$5 + 6 + 10 = 21$

There were three addends, so divide the sum by 3.

$21 \div 3 = 7$

*The **average** of 5, 6, and 10 is 7.*

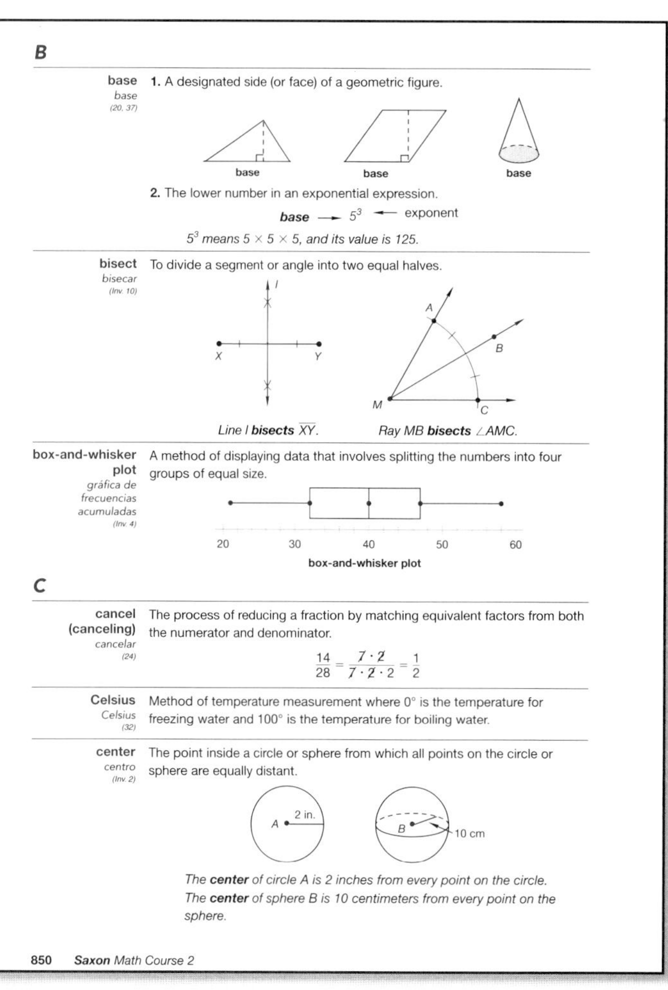

B

base *base* (20, 37) — **1.** A designated side (or face) of a geometric figure.

2. The lower number in an exponential expression.

5^3

5^3 means 5 × 5 × 5, and its value is 125.

bisect *bisecar* (Inv. 10) — To divide a segment or angle into two equal halves.

*Line l **bisects** $\overline{XY}$. Ray MB **bisects** ∠AMC.*

box-and-whisker plot *gráfica de frecuencias acumuladas* (Inv. 4) — A method of displaying data that involves splitting the numbers into four groups of equal size.

box-and-whisker plot

C

cancel (canceling) *cancelar* (24) — The process of reducing a fraction by matching equivalent factors from both the numerator and denominator.

$$\frac{14}{28} = \frac{\cancel{7} \cdot \cancel{2}}{\cancel{7} \cdot \cancel{2} \cdot 2} = \frac{1}{2}$$

Celsius *Celsius* (32) — Method of temperature measurement where 0° is the temperature for freezing water and 100° is the temperature for boiling water.

center *centro* (Inv. 2) — The point inside a circle or sphere from which all points on the circle or sphere are equally distant.

*The **center** of circle A is 2 inches from every point on the circle. The **center** of sphere B is 10 centimeters from every point on the sphere.*

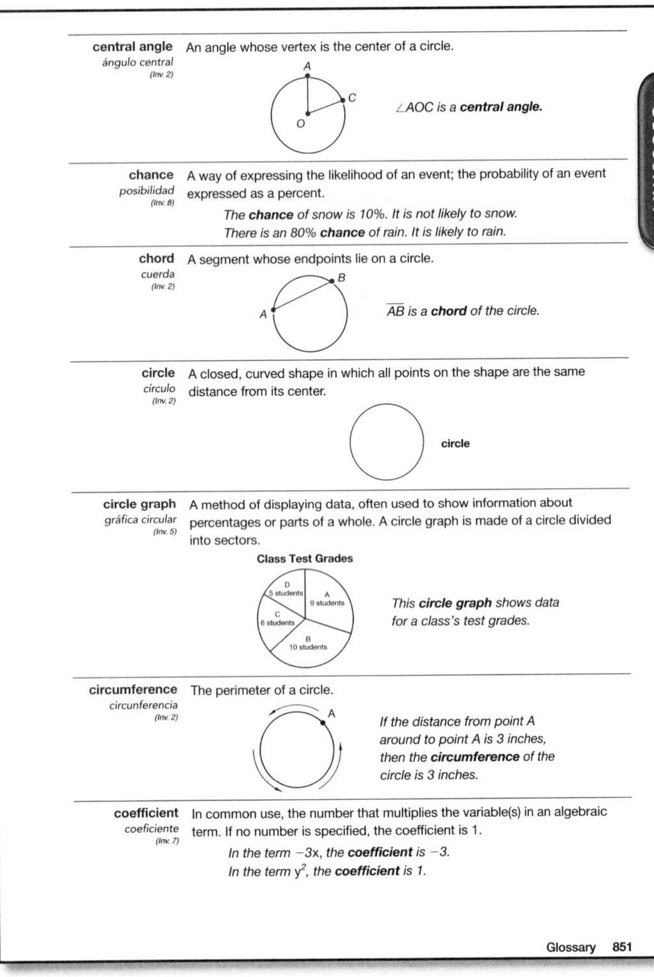

central angle *ángulo central* (Inv. 2) An angle whose vertex is the center of a circle.

∠AOC is a ***central angle.***

chance *posibilidad* (Inv. 8) A way of expressing the likelihood of an event; the probability of an event expressed as a percent.

The ***chance*** *of snow is 10%. It is not likely to snow.*
There is an 80% ***chance*** *of rain. It is likely to rain.*

chord *cuerda* (Inv. 2) A segment whose endpoints lie on a circle.

$\overline{AB}$ is a ***chord*** *of the circle.*

circle *círculo* (Inv. 2) A closed, curved shape in which all points on the shape are the same distance from its center.

circle

circle graph *gráfica circular* (Inv. 5) A method of displaying data, often used to show information about percentages or parts of a whole. A circle graph is made of a circle divided into sectors.

Class Test Grades

This ***circle graph*** *shows data for a class's test grades.*

circumference *circunferencia* (Inv. 2) The perimeter of a circle.

If the distance from point A around to point A is 3 inches, then the ***circumference*** *of the circle is 3 inches.*

coefficient *coeficiente* (Inv. 7) In common use, the number that multiplies the variable(s) in an algebraic term. If no number is specified, the coefficient is 1.

In the term $-3x$, the ***coefficient*** *is -3.*
In the term y^2, the ***coefficient*** *is 1.*

GLOSSARY

Glossary 851

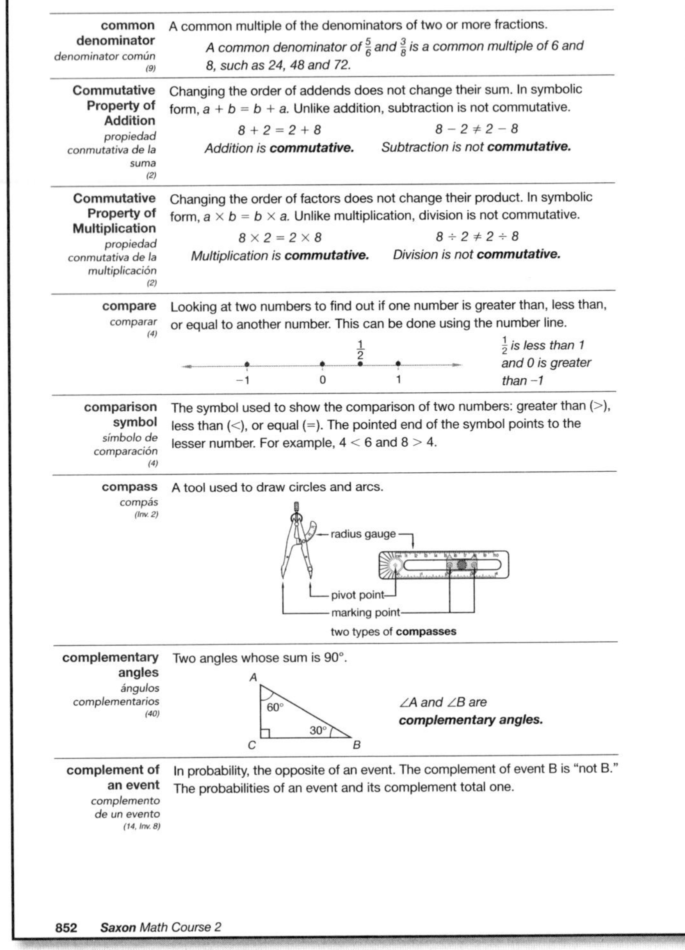

common denominator *denominador común* (9) A common multiple of the denominators of two or more fractions.

A common denominator of $\frac{5}{6}$ and $\frac{3}{8}$ is a common multiple of 6 and 8, such as 24, 48 and 72.

Commutative Property of Addition *propiedad conmutativa de la suma* (2) Changing the order of addends does not change their sum. In symbolic form, $a + b = b + a$. Unlike addition, subtraction is not commutative.

$8 + 2 = 2 + 8$ — *Addition is* ***commutative.***
$8 - 2 \neq 2 - 8$ — *Subtraction is not* ***commutative.***

Commutative Property of Multiplication *propiedad conmutativa de la multiplicación* (2) Changing the order of factors does not change their product. In symbolic form, $a \times b = b \times a$. Unlike multiplication, division is not commutative.

$8 \times 2 = 2 \times 8$ — *Multiplication is* ***commutative.***
$8 \div 2 \neq 2 \div 8$ — *Division is not* ***commutative.***

compare *comparar* (4) Looking at two numbers to find out if one number is greater than, less than, or equal to another number. This can be done using the number line.

$\frac{1}{2}$ is less than 1 and 0 is greater than -1

comparison symbol *símbolo de comparación* (4) The symbol used to show the comparison of two numbers: greater than (>), less than (<), or equal (=). The pointed end of the symbol points to the lesser number. For example, $4 < 6$ and $8 > 4$.

compass *compás* (Inv. 2) A tool used to draw circles and arcs.

two types of **compasses**

complementary angles *ángulos complementarios* (40) Two angles whose sum is 90°.

∠A and ∠B are ***complementary angles.***

complement of an event *complemento de un evento* (14, Inv. 8) In probability, the opposite of an event. The complement of event B is "not B." The probabilities of an event and its complement total one.

852 **Saxon** Math Course 2

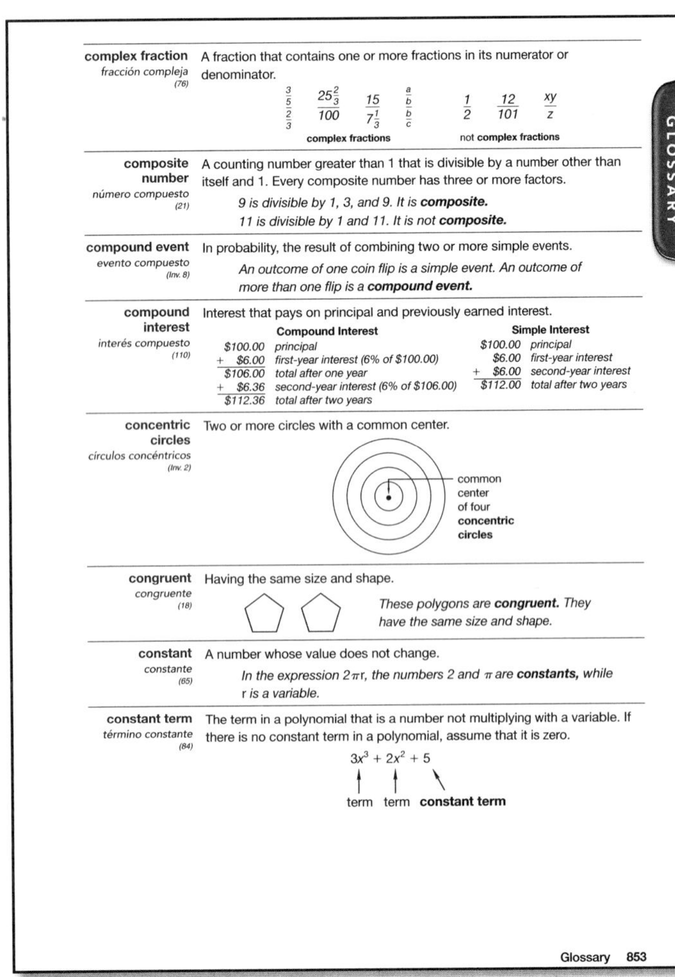

complex fraction *fracción compleja* (76) A fraction that contains one or more fractions in its numerator or denominator.

$\frac{\frac{3}{5}}{\frac{2}{3}}$ $\frac{25\frac{2}{3}}{100}$ $\frac{15}{7\frac{1}{3}}$ $\frac{\frac{a}{b}}{\frac{b}{c}}$ — **complex fractions**

$\frac{1}{2}$ $\frac{12}{101}$ $\frac{xy}{z}$ — **not complex fractions**

composite number *número compuesto* (21) A counting number greater than 1 that is divisible by a number other than itself and 1. Every composite number has three or more factors.

9 is divisible by 1, 3, and 9. It is ***composite.***
11 is divisible by 1 and 11. It is not ***composite.***

compound event *evento compuesto* (Inv. 8) In probability, the result of combining two or more simple events.

An outcome of one coin flip is a simple event. An outcome of more than one flip is a ***compound event.***

compound interest *interés compuesto* (110) Interest that pays on principal and previously earned interest.

Compound Interest

$100.00	principal
+ $6.00	first-year interest (6% of $100.00)
$106.00	total after one year
+ $6.36	second-year interest (6% of $106.00)
$112.36	total after two years

Simple Interest

$100.00	principal
$6.00	first-year interest
+ $6.00	second-year interest
$112.00	total after two years

concentric circles *círculos concéntricos* (Inv. 2) Two or more circles with a common center.

common center of four **concentric circles**

congruent *congruente* (18) Having the same size and shape.

These polygons are ***congruent.*** *They have the same size and shape.*

constant *constante* (65) A number whose value does not change.

In the expression $2\pi r$, the numbers 2 and π are ***constants,*** *while r is a variable.*

constant term *término constante* (84) The term in a polynomial that is a number not multiplying with a variable. If there is no constant term in a polynomial, assume that it is zero.

$3x^3 + 2x^2 + 5$

term term **constant term**

GLOSSARY

Glossary 853

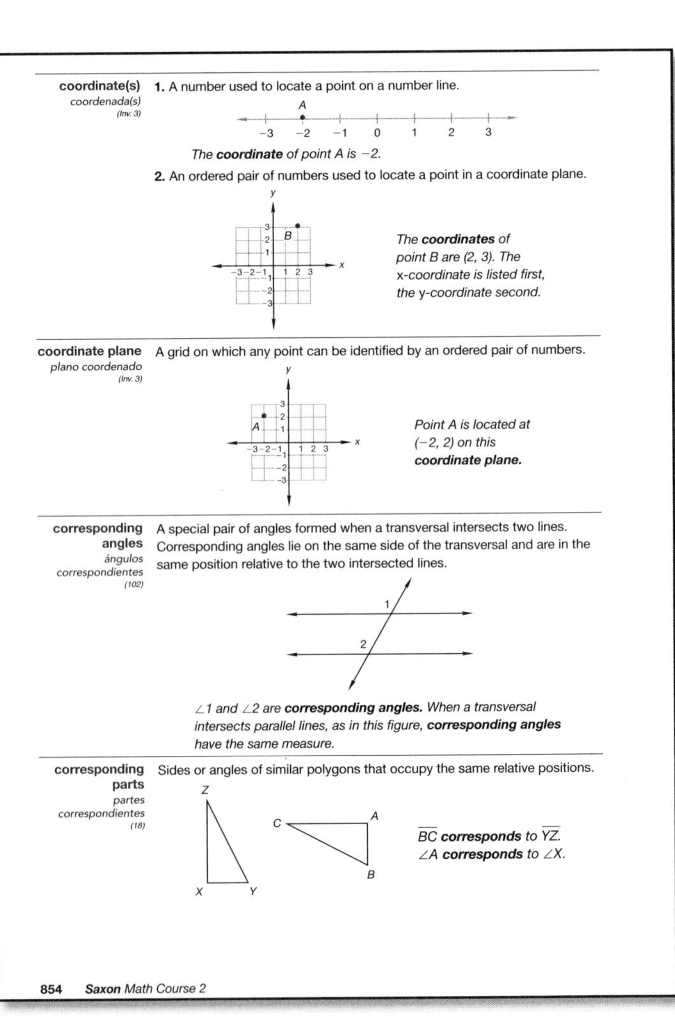

coordinate(s) *coordenada(s)* (Inv. 3) **1.** A number used to locate a point on a number line.

The ***coordinate*** *of point A is -2.*

2. An ordered pair of numbers used to locate a point in a coordinate plane.

The ***coordinates*** *of point B are (2, 3). The x-coordinate is listed first, the y-coordinate second.*

coordinate plane *plano coordenado* (Inv. 3) A grid on which any point can be identified by an ordered pair of numbers.

Point A is located at $(-2, 2)$ on this ***coordinate plane.***

corresponding angles *ángulos correspondientes* (102) A special pair of angles formed when a transversal intersects two lines. Corresponding angles lie on the same side of the transversal and are in the same position relative to the two intersected lines.

∠1 and ∠2 are ***corresponding angles.*** *When a transversal intersects parallel lines, as in this figure,* ***corresponding angles*** *have the same measure.*

corresponding parts *partes correspondientes* (18) Sides or angles of similar polygons that occupy the same relative positions.

$\overline{BC}$ corresponds *to $\overline{YZ}$.*
∠A corresponds *to ∠X.*

854 **Saxon** Math Course 2

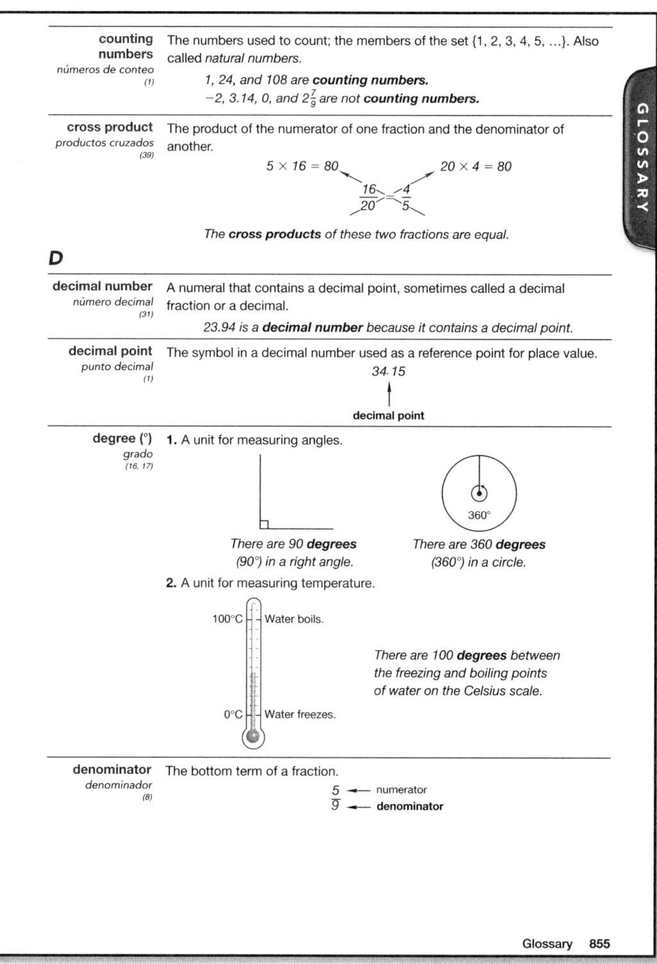

counting numbers *números de conteo* (1)
The numbers used to count; the members of the set {1, 2, 3, 4, 5, ...}. Also called *natural numbers.*

*1, 24, and 108 are **counting numbers.***
*−2, 3.14, 0, and $2\frac{7}{9}$ are not **counting numbers.***

cross product *productos cruzados* (39)
The product of the numerator of one fraction and the denominator of another.

$5 \times 16 = 80$ $\quad$ $20 \times 4 = 80$
$\frac{16}{20} = \frac{4}{5}$

*The **cross products** of these two fractions are equal.*

D

decimal number *número decimal* (31)
A numeral that contains a decimal point, sometimes called a decimal fraction or a decimal.

*23.94 is a **decimal number** because it contains a decimal point.*

decimal point *punto decimal* (1)
The symbol in a decimal number used as a reference point for place value.

34.15
decimal point

degree (°) *grado* (16, 17)
1. A unit for measuring angles.

*There are 90 **degrees** (90°) in a right angle.* $\quad$ *There are 360 **degrees** (360°) in a circle.*

2. A unit for measuring temperature.

*There are 100 **degrees** between the freezing and boiling points of water on the Celsius scale.*

denominator *denominador* (8)
The bottom term of a fraction.

$\frac{5}{9}$ ← numerator ← **denominator**

dependent events *eventos dependientes* (94)
In probability, events that are not independent because the outcome of one event affects the probability of the other event.

*If a bag contains 4 red marbles and 2 blue marbles and a marble is drawn from the bag twice without replacing the first draw, then the probabilities for the second draw is **dependent** upon the outcome of the first draw.*

dependent variable *variable dependiente* (120)
A variable whose value is determined by the value of one or more other variables.

In the equation y = 2x, the dependent variable is y because its value depends upon the value chosen for x.

diagonal *diagonal* (Inv. 6)
A line segment, other than a side, that connects two vertices of a polygon.

diameter *diámetro* (Inv. 2)
The distance across a circle through its center.

*The **diameter** of this circle is 3 inches.*

difference *diferencia* (1)
The result of subtraction.

*In 12 − 8 = 4, the **difference** is 4.*

digit *dígito* (5)
Any of the symbols used to write numbers: 0, 1, 2, 3, 4, 5, 6, 7, 8, 9.

*The last **digit** in the number 7862 is 2.*

direct variation *variación directa* (Inv. 9)
A relationship between two variables in which one variable is a constant multiple of the other, $y = kx$; also known as **direct proportion** because any two pairs of values form a proportion.

A graph of direct variation is a line or ray that intersects the origin. $\quad$ *A function table displays direct variation if the x- and y-values share a common ratio.*

x	y	$\frac{y}{x}$
1	2	$\frac{2}{1} = 2$
2	4	$\frac{4}{2} = 2$
3	6	$\frac{6}{3} = 2$
4	8	$\frac{8}{4} = 2$

direct proportion *proporción directa* (Inv. 9)
See **direct variation.**

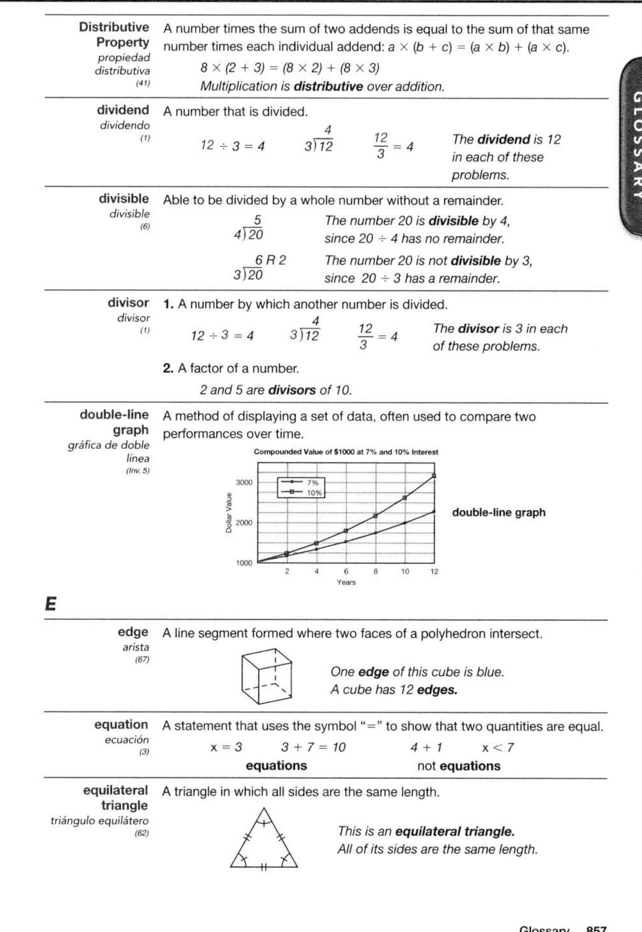

Distributive Property *propiedad distributiva* (41)
A number times the sum of two addends is equal to the sum of that same number times each individual addend: $a \times (b + c) = (a \times b) + (a \times c)$.

8 × (2 + 3) = (8 × 2) + (8 × 3)
*Multiplication is **distributive** over addition.*

dividend *dividendo* (1)
A number that is divided.

$12 \div 3 = 4$ $\quad$ $3\overline{)12}$ = 4 $\quad$ $\frac{12}{3} = 4$ $\quad$ *The **dividend** is 12 in each of these problems.*

divisible *divisible* (6)
Able to be divided by a whole number without a remainder.

$4\overline{)20}$ = 5 $\quad$ *The number 20 is **divisible** by 4, since 20 ÷ 4 has no remainder.*

$3\overline{)20}$ = 6 R 2 $\quad$ *The number 20 is not **divisible** by 3, since 20 ÷ 3 has a remainder.*

divisor *divisor* (1)
1. A number by which another number is divided.

$12 \div 3 = 4$ $\quad$ $3\overline{)12}$ = 4 $\quad$ $\frac{12}{3} = 4$ $\quad$ *The **divisor** is 3 in each of these problems.*

2. A factor of a number.

*2 and 5 are **divisors** of 10.*

double-line graph *gráfica de doble línea* (Inv. 5)
A method of displaying a set of data, often used to compare two performances over time.

double-line graph

E

edge *arista* (67)
A line segment formed where two faces of a polyhedron intersect.

*One **edge** of this cube is blue.*
*A cube has 12 **edges.***

equation *ecuación* (3)
A statement that uses the symbol "=" to show that two quantities are equal.

x = 3	3 + 7 = 10	4 + 1	x < 7
equations		not **equations**	

equilateral triangle *triángulo equilátero* (62)
A triangle in which all sides are the same length.

*This is an **equilateral triangle.***
All of its sides are the same length.

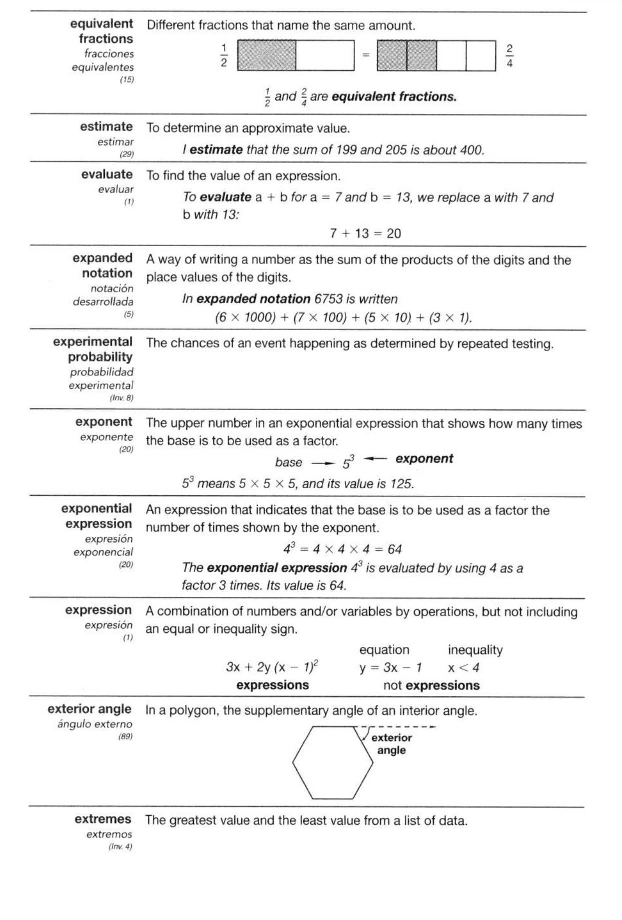

equivalent fractions *fracciones equivalentes* (15)
Different fractions that name the same amount.

$\frac{1}{2}$ = $\frac{2}{4}$

*$\frac{1}{2}$ and $\frac{2}{4}$ are **equivalent fractions.***

estimate *estimar* (29)
To determine an approximate value.

*I **estimate** that the sum of 199 and 205 is about 400.*

evaluate *evaluar* (1)
To find the value of an expression.

*To **evaluate** a + b for a = 7 and b = 13, we replace a with 7 and b with 13:*

7 + 13 = 20

expanded notation *notación desarrollada* (5)
A way of writing a number as the sum of the products of the digits and the place values of the digits.

*In **expanded notation** 6753 is written*
(6 × 1000) + (7 × 100) + (5 × 10) + (3 × 1).

experimental probability *probabilidad experimental* (Inv. 8)
The chances of an event happening as determined by repeated testing.

exponent *exponente* (20)
The upper number in an exponential expression that shows how many times the base is to be used as a factor.

base → 5^3 ← **exponent**

5^3 means 5 × 5 × 5, and its value is 125.

exponential expression *expresión exponencial* (20)
An expression that indicates that the base is to be used as a factor the number of times shown by the exponent.

$4^3 = 4 \times 4 \times 4 = 64$

*The **exponential expression** 4^3 is evaluated by using 4 as a factor 3 times. Its value is 64.*

expression *expresión* (1)
A combination of numbers and/or variables by operations, but not including an equal or inequality sign.

3x + 2y (x − 1)^2	equation y = 3x − 1	inequality x < 4
expressions	not **expressions**	

exterior angle *ángulo externo* (89)
In a polygon, the supplementary angle of an interior angle.

extremes *extremos* (Inv. 4)
The greatest value and the least value from a list of data.

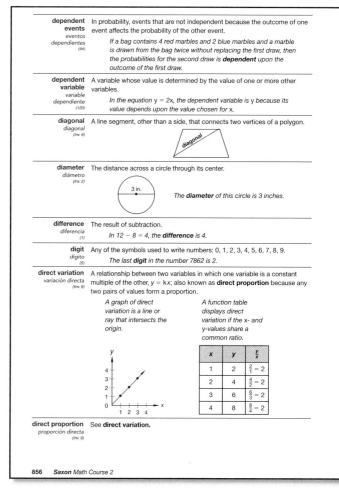

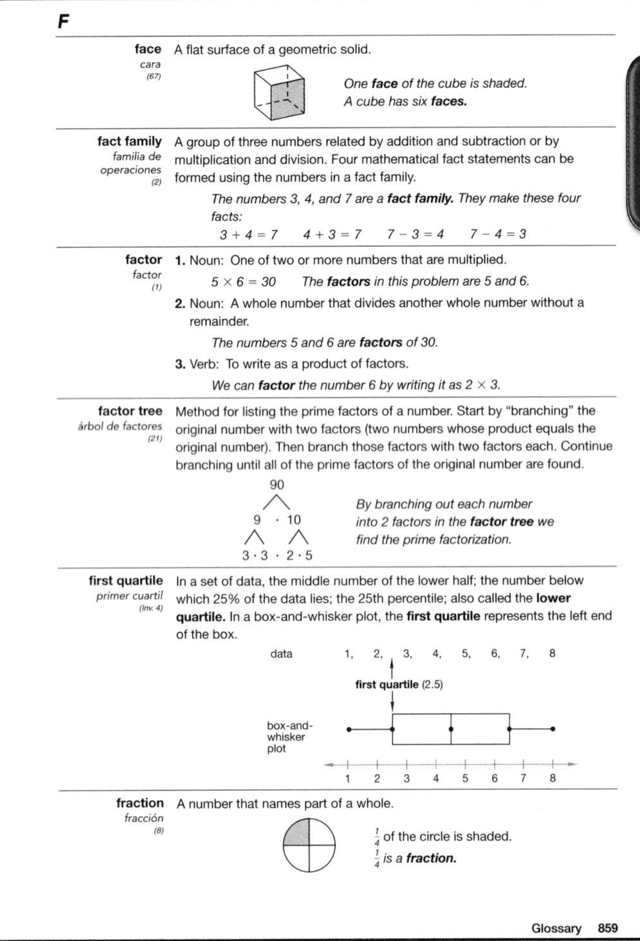

F

face
cara
(67)
A flat surface of a geometric solid.

*One **face** of the cube is shaded.*
*A cube has six **faces**.*

fact family
familia de operaciones
(2)
A group of three numbers related by addition and subtraction or by multiplication and division. Four mathematical fact statements can be formed using the numbers in a fact family.

*The numbers 3, 4, and 7 are a **fact family**. They make these four facts:*

$3 + 4 = 7 \quad 4 + 3 = 7 \quad 7 - 3 = 4 \quad 7 - 4 = 3$

factor
factor
(1)
1. Noun: One of two or more numbers that are multiplied.

$5 \times 6 = 30$ *The **factors** in this problem are 5 and 6.*

2. Noun: A whole number that divides another whole number without a remainder.

*The numbers 5 and 6 are **factors** of 30.*

3. Verb: To write as a product of factors.

*We can **factor** the number 6 by writing it as 2×3.*

factor tree
árbol de factores
(21)
Method for listing the prime factors of a number. Start by "branching" the original number with two factors (two numbers whose product equals the original number). Then branch those factors with two factors each. Continue branching until all of the prime factors of the original number are found.

90
9 · 10
3 · 3 · 2 · 5

*By branching out each number into 2 factors in the **factor tree** we find the prime factorization.*

first quartile
primer cuartil
(Inv. 4)
In a set of data, the middle number of the lower half; the number below which 25% of the data lies; the 25th percentile; also called the **lower quartile.** In a box-and-whisker plot, the **first quartile** represents the left end of the box.

fraction
fracción
(8)
A number that names part of a whole.

$\frac{1}{4}$ of the circle is shaded.
*$\frac{1}{4}$ is a **fraction**.*

Glossary 859

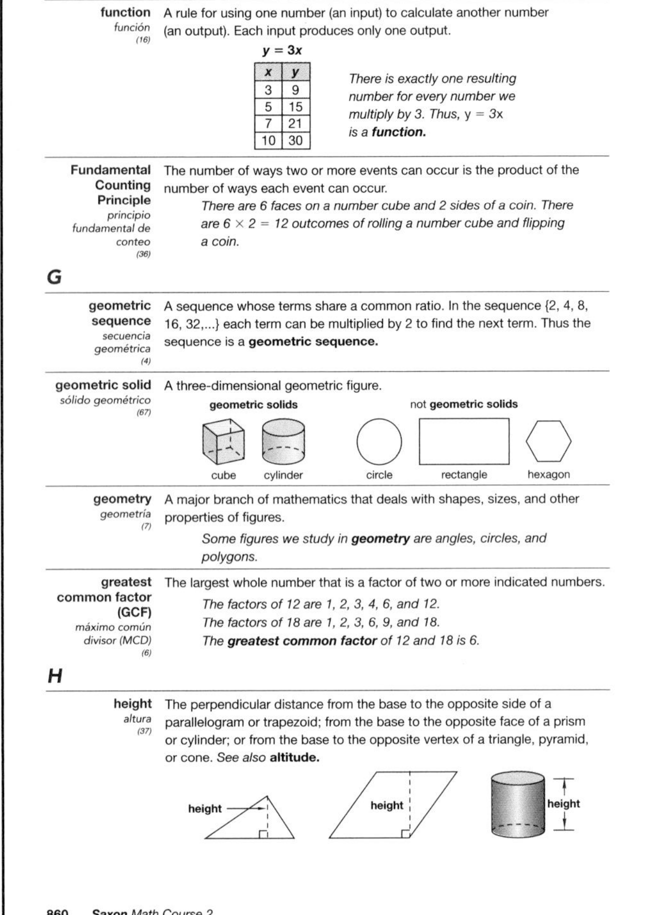

function
función
(16)
A rule for using one number (an input) to calculate another number (an output). Each input produces only one output.

y = 3x

x	y
3	9
5	15
7	21
10	30

*There is exactly one resulting number for every number we multiply by 3. Thus, y = 3x is a **function**.*

Fundamental Counting Principle
principio fundamental de conteo
(36)
The number of ways two or more events can occur is the product of the number of ways each event can occur.

There are 6 faces on a number cube and 2 sides of a coin. There are $6 \times 2 = 12$ outcomes of rolling a number cube and flipping a coin.

G

geometric sequence
secuencia geométrica
(4)
A sequence whose terms share a common ratio. In the sequence {2, 4, 8, 16, 32,...} each term can be multiplied by 2 to find the next term. Thus the sequence is a **geometric sequence.**

geometric solid
sólido geométrico
(67)
A three-dimensional geometric figure.

geometry
geometría
(7)
A major branch of mathematics that deals with shapes, sizes, and other properties of figures.

*Some figures we study in **geometry** are angles, circles, and polygons.*

greatest common factor (GCF)
máximo común divisor (MCD)
(6)
The largest whole number that is a factor of two or more indicated numbers.

The factors of 12 are 1, 2, 3, 4, 6, and 12.
The factors of 18 are 1, 2, 3, 6, 9, and 18.
*The **greatest common factor** of 12 and 18 is 6.*

H

height
altura
(37)
The perpendicular distance from the base to the opposite side of a parallelogram or trapezoid; from the base to the opposite face of a prism or cylinder; or from the base to the opposite vertex of a triangle, pyramid, or cone. *See also* **altitude.**

860 *Saxon Math Course 2*

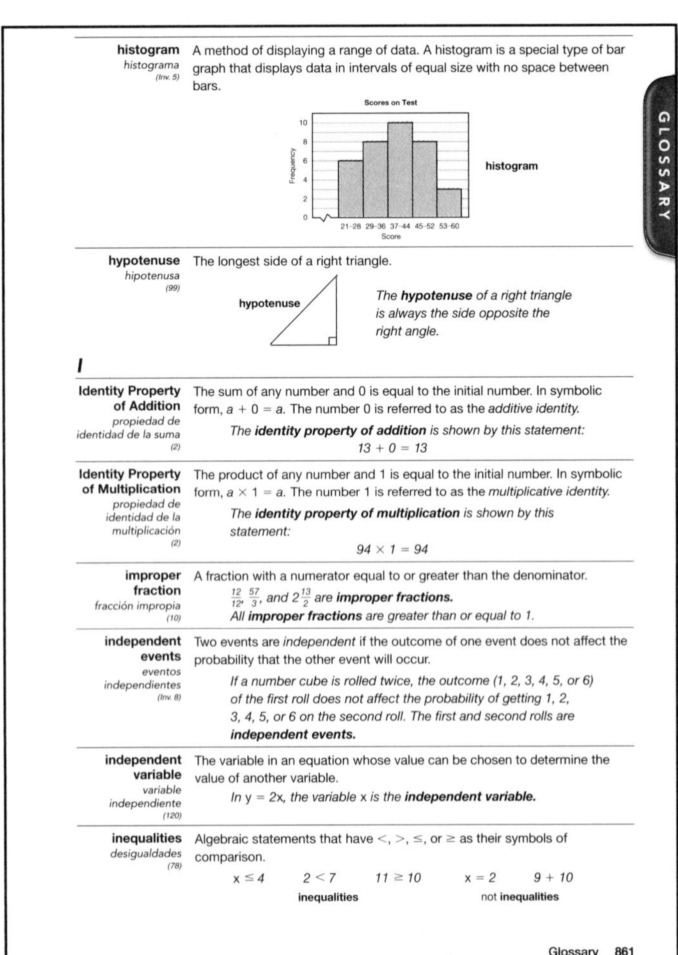

histogram
histograma
(Inv. 5)
A method of displaying a range of data. A histogram is a special type of bar graph that displays data in intervals of equal size with no space between bars.

hypotenuse
hipotenusa
(99)
The longest side of a right triangle.

*The **hypotenuse** of a right triangle is always the side opposite the right angle.*

I

Identity Property of Addition
propiedad de identidad de la suma
(2)
The sum of any number and 0 is equal to the initial number. In symbolic form, $a + 0 = a$. The number 0 is referred to as the *additive identity.*

*The **identity property of addition** is shown by this statement:*

$13 + 0 = 13$

Identity Property of Multiplication
propiedad de identidad de la multiplicación
(2)
The product of any number and 1 is equal to the initial number. In symbolic form, $a \times 1 = a$. The number 1 is referred to as the *multiplicative identity.*

*The **identity property of multiplication** is shown by this statement:*

$94 \times 1 = 94$

improper fraction
fracción impropia
(10)
A fraction with a numerator equal to or greater than the denominator.

*$\frac{12}{12}$, $\frac{57}{3}$, and $2\frac{13}{2}$ are **improper fractions.***
*All **improper fractions** are greater than or equal to 1.*

independent events
eventos independientes
(Inv. 8)
Two events are *independent* if the outcome of one event does not affect the probability that the other event will occur.

*If a number cube is rolled twice, the outcome (1, 2, 3, 4, 5, or 6) of the first roll does not affect the probability of getting 1, 2, 3, 4, 5, or 6 on the second roll. The first and second rolls are **independent events.***

independent variable
variable independiente
(120)
The variable in an equation whose value can be chosen to determine the value of another variable.

*In y = 2x, the variable x is the **independent variable.***

inequalities
desigualdades
(78)
Algebraic statements that have $<$, $>$, $\leq$, or $\geq$ as their symbols of comparison.

$x \leq 4 \quad 2 < 7 \quad 11 \geq 10$ — **inequalities**

$x = 2 \quad 9 + 10$ — not **inequalities**

Glossary 861

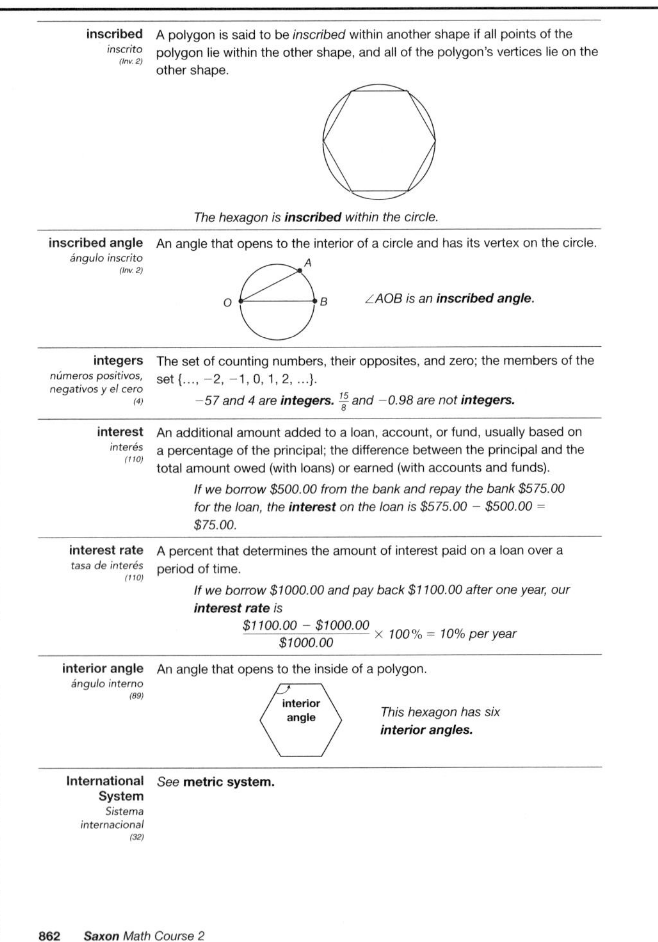

inscribed
inscrito
(Inv. 2)
A polygon is said to be *inscribed* within another shape if all points of the polygon lie within the other shape, and all of the polygon's vertices lie on the other shape.

*The hexagon is **inscribed** within the circle.*

inscribed angle
ángulo inscrito
(Inv. 2)
An angle that opens to the interior of a circle and has its vertex on the circle.

*$\angle AOB$ is an **inscribed angle.***

integers
números positivos, negativos y el cero
(4)
The set of counting numbers, their opposites, and zero; the members of the set {..., −2, −1, 0, 1, 2, ...}.

*−57 and 4 are **integers**. $\frac{15}{8}$ and −0.98 are not **integers.***

interest
interés
(110)
An additional amount added to a loan, account, or fund, usually based on a percentage of the principal; the difference between the principal and the total amount owed (with loans) or earned (with accounts and funds).

*If we borrow \$500.00 from the bank and repay the bank \$575.00 for the loan, the **interest** on the loan is \$575.00 − \$500.00 = \$75.00.*

interest rate
tasa de interés
(110)
A percent that determines the amount of interest paid on a loan over a period of time.

*If we borrow \$1000.00 and pay back \$1100.00 after one year, our **interest rate** is*

$$\frac{\$1100.00 - \$1000.00}{\$1000.00} \times 100\% = 10\% \text{ per year}$$

interior angle
ángulo interno
(89)
An angle that opens to the inside of a polygon.

*This hexagon has six **interior angles.***

International System
Sistema internacional
(32)
See **metric system.**

862 *Saxon Math Course 2*

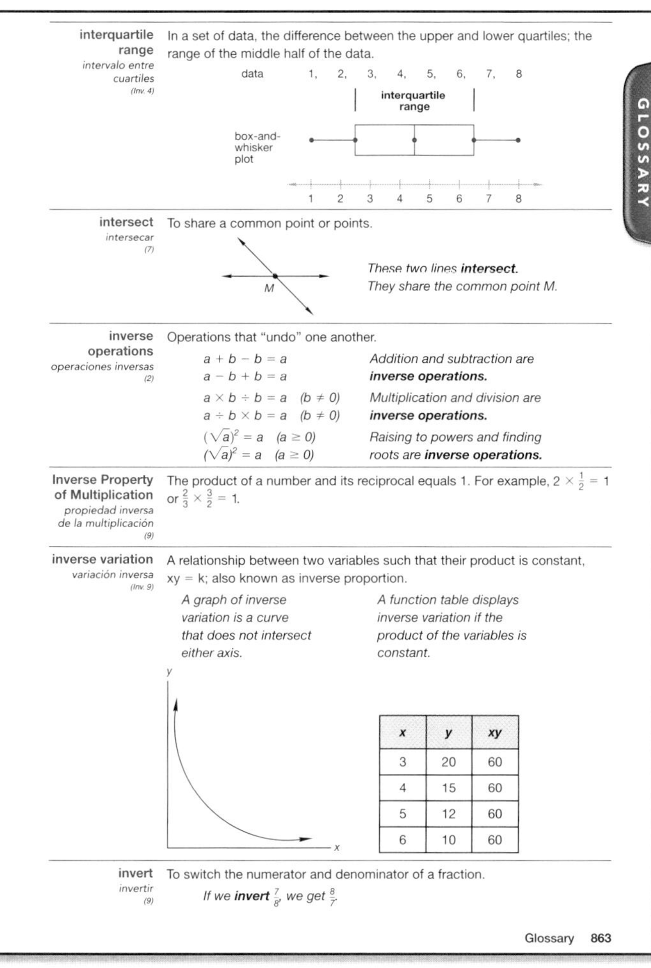

interquartile range *intervalo entre cuartiles* (Inv. 4) In a set of data, the difference between the upper and lower quartiles; the range of the middle half of the data.

intersect *intersecar* (7) To share a common point or points.

These two lines ***intersect.*** *They share the common point M.*

inverse operations *operaciones inversas* (2) Operations that "undo" one another.

$a + b - b = a$ / $a - b + b = a$ *Addition and subtraction are* ***inverse operations.***

$a \times b \div b = a \quad (b \neq 0)$ / $a \div b \times b = a \quad (b \neq 0)$ *Multiplication and division are* ***inverse operations.***

$(\sqrt{a})^2 = a \quad (a \geq 0)$ / $\sqrt{a^2} = a \quad (a \geq 0)$ *Raising to powers and finding roots are* ***inverse operations.***

Inverse Property of Multiplication *propiedad inversa de la multiplicación* (9) The product of a number and its reciprocal equals 1. For example, $2 \times \frac{1}{2} = 1$ or $\frac{2}{3} \times \frac{3}{2} = 1$.

inverse variation *variación inversa* (Inv. 9) A relationship between two variables such that their product is constant, xy = k; also known as inverse proportion.

A graph of inverse variation is a curve that does not intersect either axis. *A function table displays inverse variation if the product of the variables is constant.*

x	y	xy
3	20	60
4	15	60
5	12	60
6	10	60

invert *invertir* (9) To switch the numerator and denominator of a fraction.

If we ***invert*** $\frac{7}{8}$*, we get* $\frac{8}{7}$*.*

Glossary 863

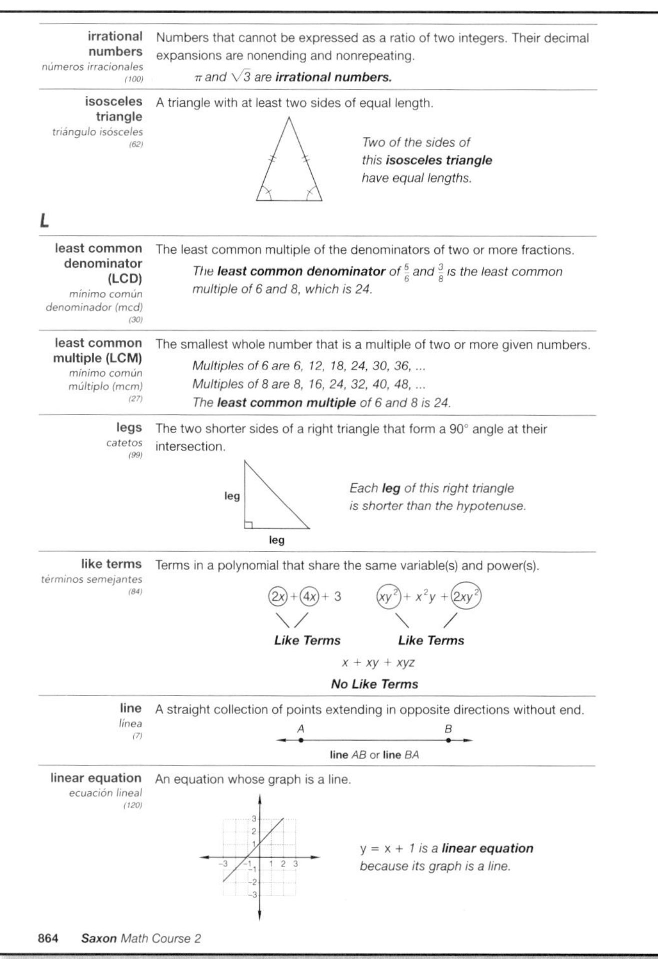

irrational numbers *números irracionales* (100) Numbers that cannot be expressed as a ratio of two integers. Their decimal expansions are nonending and nonrepeating.

π and $\sqrt{3}$ *are* ***irrational numbers.***

isosceles triangle *triángulo isósceles* (62) A triangle with at least two sides of equal length.

Two of the sides of this ***isosceles triangle*** *have equal lengths.*

L

least common denominator (LCD) *mínimo común denominador (mcd)* (30) The least common multiple of the denominators of two or more fractions.

The ***least common denominator*** *of* $\frac{5}{6}$ *and* $\frac{3}{8}$ *is the least common multiple of 6 and 8, which is 24.*

least common multiple (LCM) *mínimo común múltiplo (mcm)* (27) The smallest whole number that is a multiple of two or more given numbers.

Multiples of 6 are 6, 12, 18, 24, 30, 36, ...
Multiples of 8 are 8, 16, 24, 32, 40, 48, ...
The ***least common multiple*** *of 6 and 8 is 24.*

legs *catetos* (99) The two shorter sides of a right triangle that form a 90° angle at their intersection.

Each ***leg*** *of this right triangle is shorter than the hypotenuse.*

like terms *términos semejantes* (84) Terms in a polynomial that share the same variable(s) and power(s).

$2x + 4x + 3$ $\quad xy^2 + x^2y + 2xy^2$

Like Terms **Like Terms**

$x + xy + xyz$

No Like Terms

line *línea* (7) A straight collection of points extending in opposite directions without end.

linear equation *ecuación lineal* (120) An equation whose graph is a line.

$y = x + 1$ *is a* ***linear equation*** *because its graph is a line.*

864 *Saxon Math Course 2*

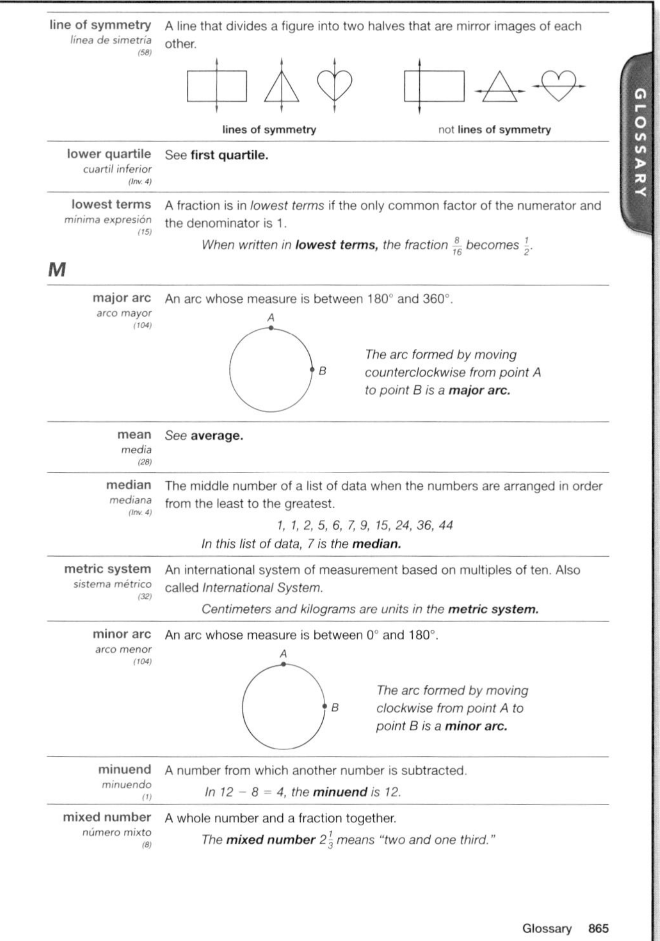

line of symmetry *línea de simetría* (58) A line that divides a figure into two halves that are mirror images of each other.

lower quartile *cuartil inferior* (Inv. 4) See **first quartile.**

lowest terms *mínima expresión* (15) A fraction is in *lowest terms* if the only common factor of the numerator and the denominator is 1.

When written in ***lowest terms,*** *the fraction* $\frac{8}{16}$ *becomes* $\frac{1}{2}$*.*

M

major arc *arco mayor* (104) An arc whose measure is between 180° and 360°.

The arc formed by moving counterclockwise from point A to point B is a ***major arc.***

mean *media* (28) See **average.**

median *mediana* (Inv. 4) The middle number of a list of data when the numbers are arranged in order from the least to the greatest.

1, 1, 2, 5, 6, 7, 9, 15, 24, 36, 44
In this list of data, 7 is the ***median.***

metric system *sistema métrico* (32) An international system of measurement based on multiples of ten. Also called *International System.*

Centimeters and kilograms are units in the ***metric system.***

minor arc *arco menor* (104) An arc whose measure is between 0° and 180°.

The arc formed by moving clockwise from point A to point B is a ***minor arc.***

minuend *minuendo* (1) A number from which another number is subtracted.

In 12 − 8 = 4, the ***minuend*** *is 12.*

mixed number *número mixto* (8) A whole number and a fraction together.

The ***mixed number*** $2\frac{1}{3}$ *means "two and one third."*

Glossary 865

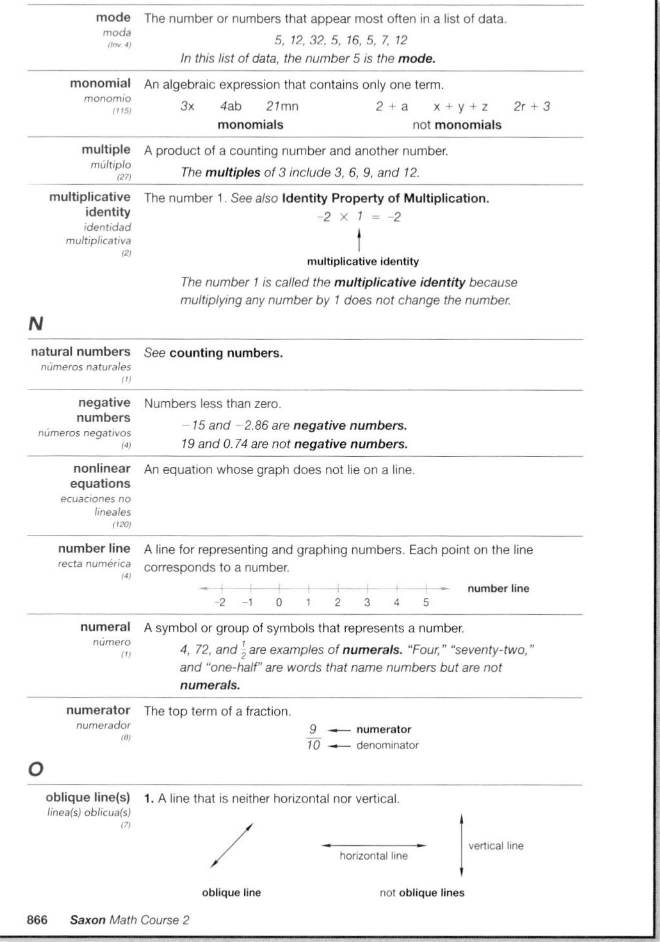

mode *moda* (Inv. 4) The number or numbers that appear most often in a list of data.

5, 12, 32, 5, 16, 5, 7, 12
In this list of data, the number 5 is the ***mode.***

monomial *monomio* (115) An algebraic expression that contains only one term.

3x 4ab 21mn — **monomials**
2 + a x + y + z 2r + 3 — not **monomials**

multiple *múltiplo* (27) A product of a counting number and another number.

The ***multiples*** *of 3 include 3, 6, 9, and 12.*

multiplicative identity *identidad multiplicativa* (2) The number 1. *See also* **Identity Property of Multiplication.**

$-2 \times 1 = -2$

multiplicative identity

The number 1 is called the ***multiplicative identity*** *because multiplying any number by 1 does not change the number.*

N

natural numbers *números naturales* (1) See **counting numbers.**

negative numbers *números negativos* (4) Numbers less than zero.

−15 and −2.86 are ***negative numbers.***
19 and 0.74 are not ***negative numbers.***

nonlinear equations *ecuaciones no lineales* (120) An equation whose graph does not lie on a line.

number line *recta numérica* (4) A line for representing and graphing numbers. Each point on the line corresponds to a number.

numeral *número* (1) A symbol or group of symbols that represents a number.

4, 72, and $\frac{1}{2}$ *are examples of* ***numerals.*** *"Four," "seventy-two," and "one-half" are words that name numbers but are not* ***numerals.***

numerator *numerador* (8) The top term of a fraction.

O

oblique line(s) *línea(s) oblicua(s)* (7) **1.** A line that is neither horizontal nor vertical.

866 *Saxon Math Course 2*

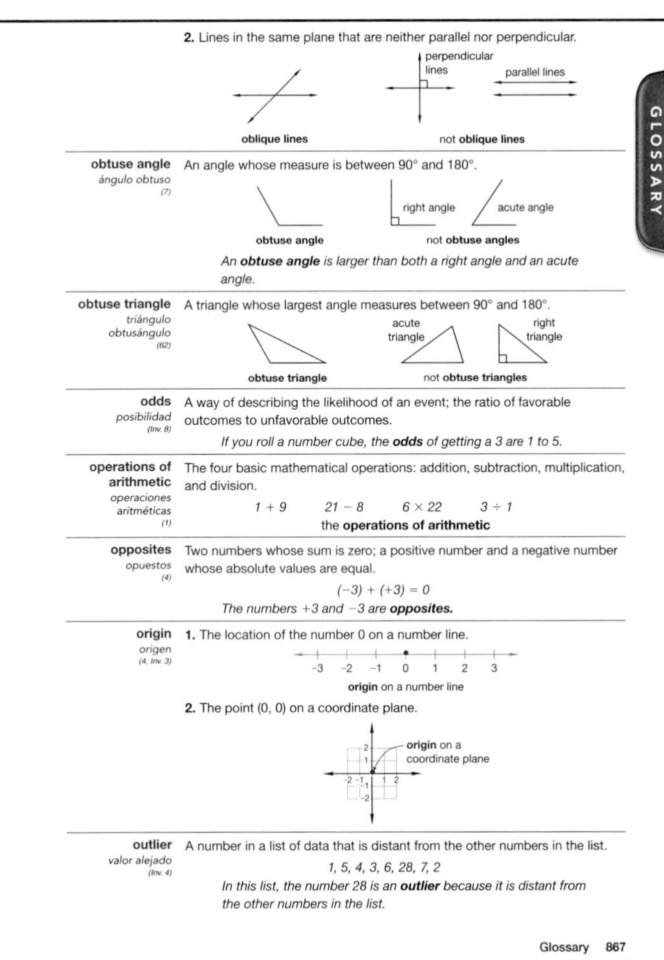

2. Lines in the same plane that are neither parallel nor perpendicular.

obtuse angle *ángulo obtuso* (7)
An angle whose measure is between 90° and 180°.

*An **obtuse angle** is larger than both a right angle and an acute angle.*

obtuse triangle *triángulo obtusángulo* (62)
A triangle whose largest angle measures between 90° and 180°.

odds *posibilidad* (Inv. 8)
A way of describing the likelihood of an event; the ratio of favorable outcomes to unfavorable outcomes.

*If you roll a number cube, the **odds** of getting a 3 are 1 to 5.*

operations of arithmetic *operaciones aritméticas* (1)
The four basic mathematical operations: addition, subtraction, multiplication, and division.

$1 + 9$ $21 - 8$ 6×22 $3 \div 1$

the **operations of arithmetic**

opposites *opuestos* (4)
Two numbers whose sum is zero; a positive number and a negative number whose absolute values are equal.

$(-3) + (+3) = 0$

*The numbers +3 and −3 are **opposites.***

origin *origen* (4, Inv. 3)
1. The location of the number 0 on a number line.

2. The point (0, 0) on a coordinate plane.

outlier *valor alejado* (Inv. 4)
A number in a list of data that is distant from the other numbers in the list.

1, 5, 4, 3, 6, 28, 7, 2

*In this list, the number 28 is an **outlier** because it is distant from the other numbers in the list.*

Glossary 867

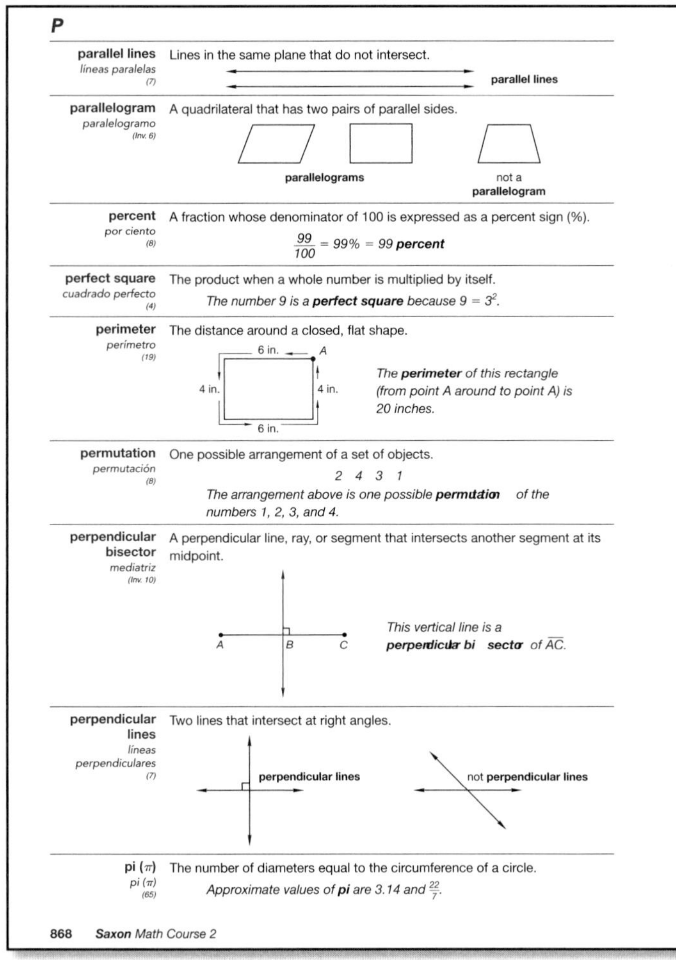

P

parallel lines *líneas paralelas* (7)
Lines in the same plane that do not intersect.

parallelogram *paralelogramo* (Inv. 6)
A quadrilateral that has two pairs of parallel sides.

percent *por ciento* (8)
A fraction whose denominator of 100 is expressed as a percent sign (%).

$\frac{99}{100} = 99\% = 99$ **percent**

perfect square *cuadrado perfecto* (4)
The product when a whole number is multiplied by itself.

*The number 9 is a **perfect square** because $9 = 3^2$.*

perimeter *perímetro* (19)
The distance around a closed, flat shape.

*The **perimeter** of this rectangle (from point A around to point A) is 20 inches.*

permutation *permutación* (8)
One possible arrangement of a set of objects.

2 4 3 1

*The arrangement above is one possible **permutation** of the numbers 1, 2, 3, and 4.*

perpendicular bisector *mediatriz* (Inv. 10)
A perpendicular line, ray, or segment that intersects another segment at its midpoint.

*This vertical line is a **perpendicular bisector** of $\overline{AC}$.*

perpendicular lines *líneas perpendiculares* (7)
Two lines that intersect at right angles.

pi (π) *pi (π)* (65)
The number of diameters equal to the circumference of a circle.

*Approximate values of **pi** are 3.14 and $\frac{22}{7}$.*

868 *Saxon Math Course 2*

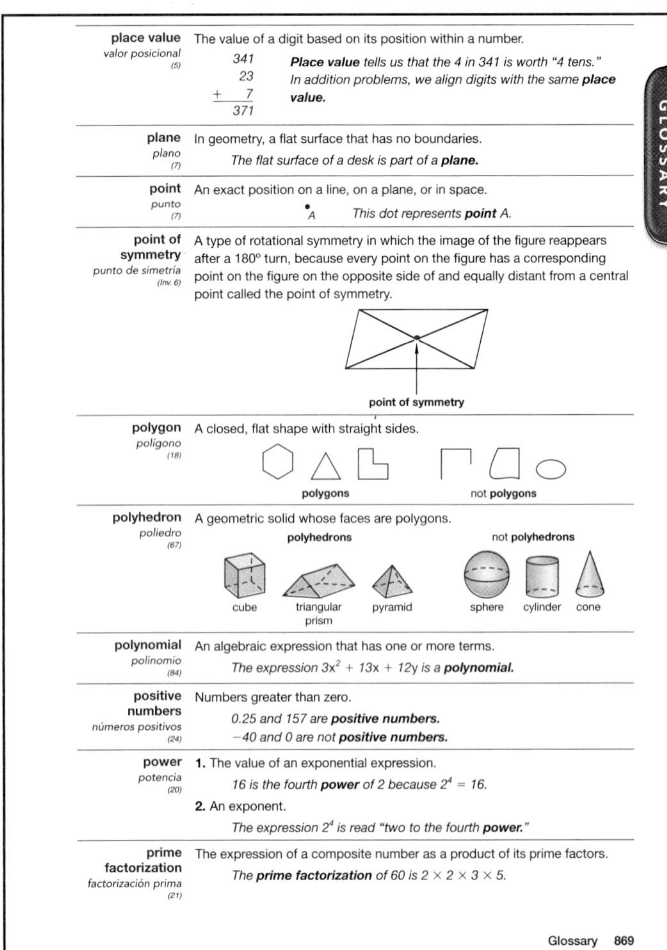

place value *valor posicional* (5)
The value of a digit based on its position within a number.

$$\begin{array}{r} 341 \\ 23 \\ +\ \ 7 \\ \hline 371 \end{array}$$

Place value** tells us that the 4 in 341 is worth "4 tens." In addition problems, we align digits with the same **place value.

plane *plano* (7)
In geometry, a flat surface that has no boundaries.

*The flat surface of a desk is part of a **plane.***

point *punto* (7)
An exact position on a line, on a plane, or in space.

*This dot represents **point** A.*

point of symmetry *punto de simetría* (Inv. 6)
A type of rotational symmetry in which the image of the figure reappears after a 180° turn, because every point on the figure has a corresponding point on the figure on the opposite side of and equally distant from a central point called the point of symmetry.

polygon *polígono* (18)
A closed, flat shape with straight sides.

polyhedron *poliedro* (67)
A geometric solid whose faces are polygons.

polynomial *polinomio* (84)
An algebraic expression that has one or more terms.

*The expression $3x^2 + 13x + 12y$ is a **polynomial.***

positive numbers *números positivos* (24)
Numbers greater than zero.

*0.25 and 157 are **positive numbers.***
*−40 and 0 are not **positive numbers.***

power *potencia* (20)
1. The value of an exponential expression.

*16 is the fourth **power** of 2 because $2^4 = 16$.*

2. An exponent.

*The expression 2^4 is read "two to the fourth **power.**"*

prime factorization *factorización prima* (21)
The expression of a composite number as a product of its prime factors.

*The **prime factorization** of 60 is $2 \times 2 \times 3 \times 5$.*

Glossary 869

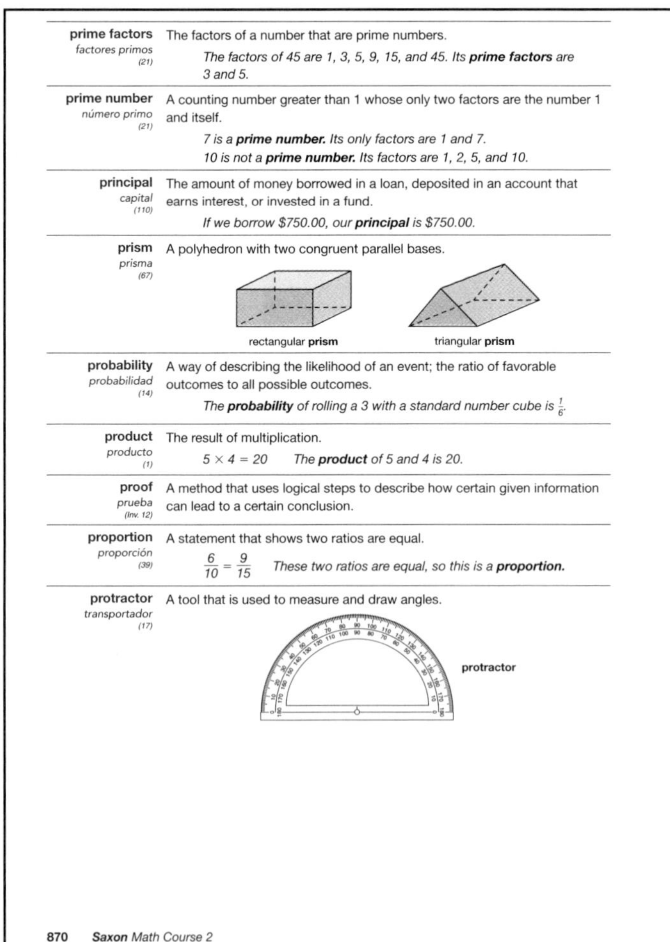

prime factors *factores primos* (21)
The factors of a number that are prime numbers.

*The factors of 45 are 1, 3, 5, 9, 15, and 45. Its **prime factors** are 3 and 5.*

prime number *número primo* (21)
A counting number greater than 1 whose only two factors are the number 1 and itself.

*7 is a **prime number.** Its only factors are 1 and 7.*
*10 is not a **prime number.** Its factors are 1, 2, 5, and 10.*

principal *capital* (110)
The amount of money borrowed in a loan, deposited in an account that earns interest, or invested in a fund.

*If we borrow \$750.00, our **principal** is \$750.00.*

prism *prisma* (67)
A polyhedron with two congruent parallel bases.

probability *probabilidad* (14)
A way of describing the likelihood of an event; the ratio of favorable outcomes to all possible outcomes.

*The **probability** of rolling a 3 with a standard number cube is $\frac{1}{6}$.*

product *producto* (1)
The result of multiplication.

*$5 \times 4 = 20$ The **product** of 5 and 4 is 20.*

proof *prueba* (Inv. 12)
A method that uses logical steps to describe how certain given information can lead to a certain conclusion.

proportion *proporción* (39)
A statement that shows two ratios are equal.

*$\frac{6}{10} = \frac{9}{15}$ These two ratios are equal, so this is a **proportion.***

protractor *transportador* (17)
A tool that is used to measure and draw angles.

870 *Saxon Math Course 2*

GLOSSARY

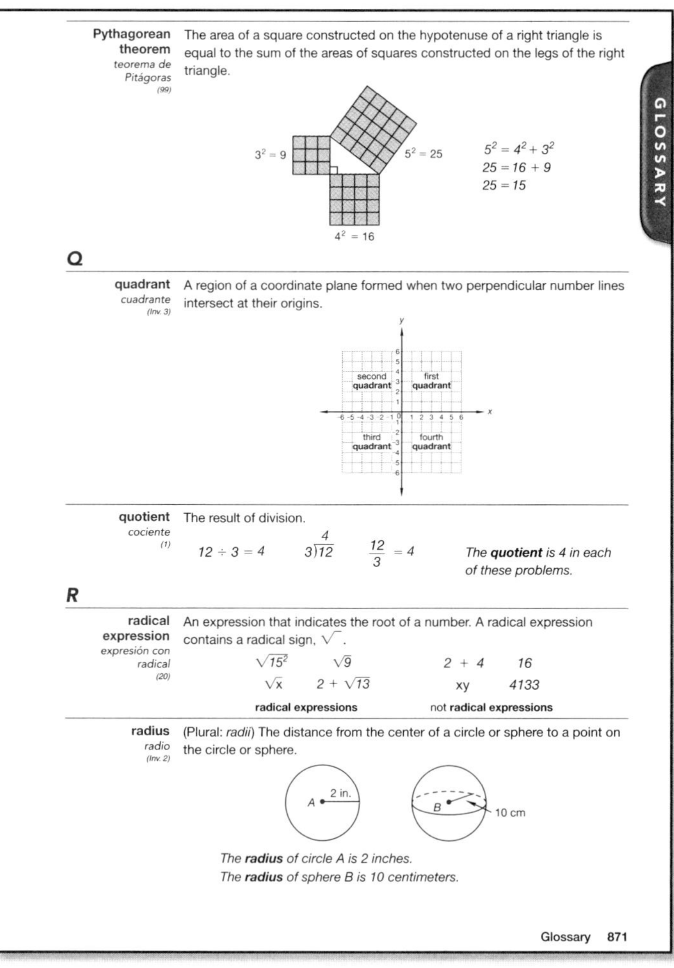

Pythagorean theorem *teorema de Pitágoras* (99) The area of a square constructed on the hypotenuse of a right triangle is equal to the sum of the areas of squares constructed on the legs of the right triangle.

Q

quadrant *cuadrante* (Inv. 3) A region of a coordinate plane formed when two perpendicular number lines intersect at their origins.

quotient *cociente* (1) The result of division.

$12 \div 3 = 4$ $\quad 3\overline{)12}$ = 4 $\quad \frac{12}{3} = 4$ *The **quotient** is 4 in each of these problems.*

R

radical expression *expresión con radical* (20) An expression that indicates the root of a number. A radical expression contains a radical sign, $\sqrt{\ }$.

radical expressions		not radical expressions	
$\sqrt{15^2}$	$\sqrt{9}$	2 + 4	16
$\sqrt{x}$	$2 + \sqrt{13}$	xy	4133

radius *radio* (Inv. 2) (Plural: *radii*) The distance from the center of a circle or sphere to a point on the circle or sphere.

*The **radius** of circle A is 2 inches.*
*The **radius** of sphere B is 10 centimeters.*

Glossary 871

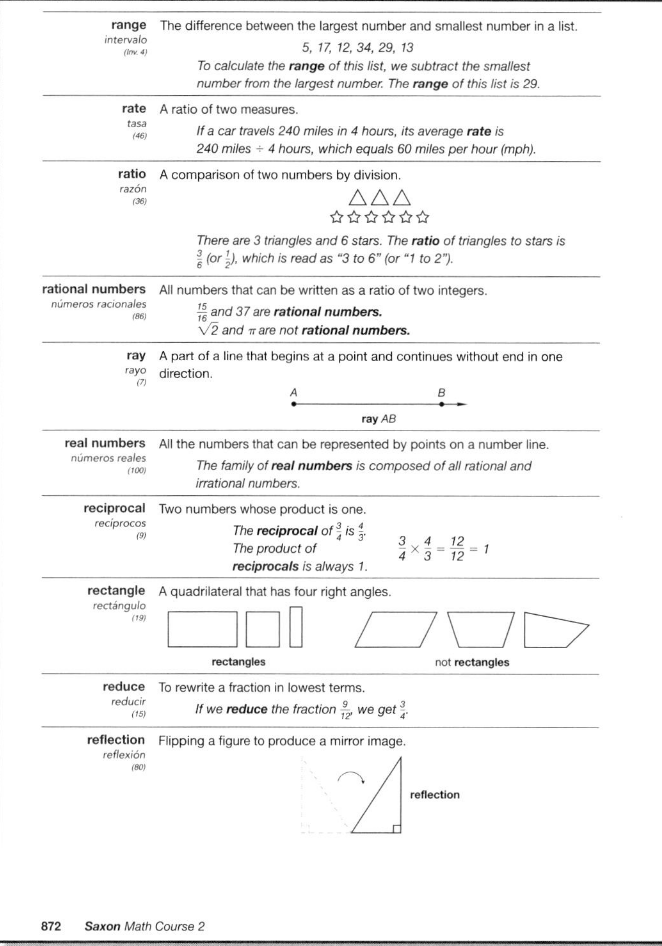

range *intervalo* (Inv. 4) The difference between the largest number and smallest number in a list.

5, 17, 12, 34, 29, 13

*To calculate the **range** of this list, we subtract the smallest number from the largest number. The **range** of this list is 29.*

rate *tasa* (46) A ratio of two measures.

*If a car travels 240 miles in 4 hours, its average **rate** is 240 miles ÷ 4 hours, which equals 60 miles per hour (mph).*

ratio *razón* (36) A comparison of two numbers by division.

*There are 3 triangles and 6 stars. The **ratio** of triangles to stars is $\frac{3}{6}$ (or $\frac{1}{2}$), which is read as "3 to 6" (or "1 to 2").*

rational numbers *números racionales* (86) All numbers that can be written as a ratio of two integers.

*$\frac{15}{16}$ and 37 are **rational numbers.***
*$\sqrt{2}$ and π are not **rational numbers.***

ray *rayo* (7) A part of a line that begins at a point and continues without end in one direction.

real numbers *números reales* (100) All the numbers that can be represented by points on a number line.

*The family of **real numbers** is composed of all rational and irrational numbers.*

reciprocal *recíprocos* (9) Two numbers whose product is one.

*The **reciprocal** of $\frac{3}{4}$ is $\frac{4}{3}$. The product of **reciprocals** is always 1.* $\quad \frac{3}{4} \times \frac{4}{3} = \frac{12}{12} = 1$

rectangle *rectángulo* (19) A quadrilateral that has four right angles.

reduce *reducir* (15) To rewrite a fraction in lowest terms.

*If we **reduce** the fraction $\frac{9}{12}$, we get $\frac{3}{4}$.*

reflection *reflexión* (80) Flipping a figure to produce a mirror image.

872 *Saxon Math Course 2*

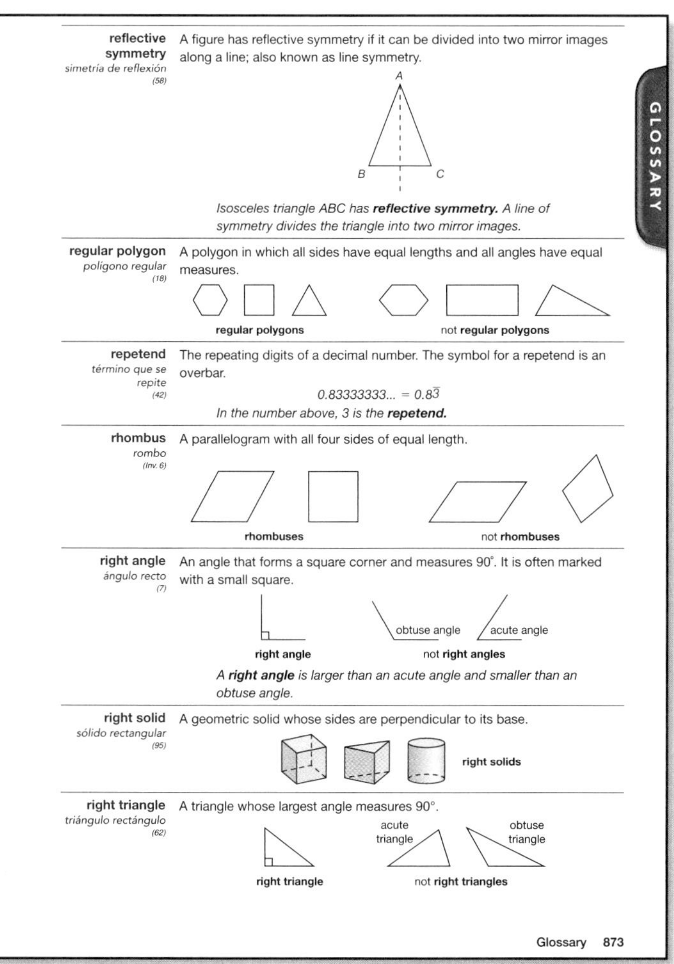

reflective symmetry *simetría de reflexión* (58) A figure has reflective symmetry if it can be divided into two mirror images along a line; also known as line symmetry.

*Isosceles triangle ABC has **reflective symmetry.** A line of symmetry divides the triangle into two mirror images.*

regular polygon *polígono regular* (18) A polygon in which all sides have equal lengths and all angles have equal measures.

repetend *término que se repite* (42) The repeating digits of a decimal number. The symbol for a repetend is an overbar.

$0.83333333... = 0.8\overline{3}$

*In the number above, 3 is the **repetend.***

rhombus *rombo* (Inv. 6) A parallelogram with all four sides of equal length.

right angle *ángulo recto* (7) An angle that forms a square corner and measures 90°. It is often marked with a small square.

*A **right angle** is larger than an acute angle and smaller than an obtuse angle.*

right solid *sólido rectangular* (95) A geometric solid whose sides are perpendicular to its base.

right triangle *triángulo rectángulo* (62) A triangle whose largest angle measures 90°.

Glossary 873

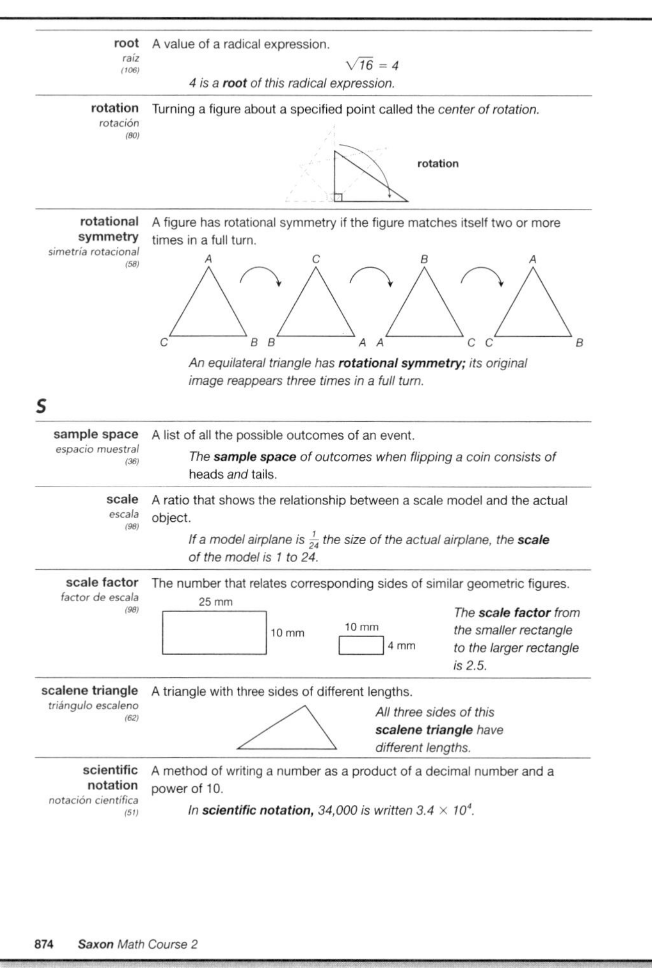

root *raíz* (106) A value of a radical expression.

$\sqrt{16} = 4$

*4 is a **root** of this radical expression.*

rotation *rotación* (80) Turning a figure about a specified point called the *center of rotation.*

rotational symmetry *simetría rotacional* (58) A figure has rotational symmetry if the figure matches itself two or more times in a full turn.

*An equilateral triangle has **rotational symmetry;** its original image reappears three times in a full turn.*

S

sample space *espacio muestral* (36) A list of all the possible outcomes of an event.

*The **sample space** of outcomes when flipping a coin consists of heads and tails.*

scale *escala* (98) A ratio that shows the relationship between a scale model and the actual object.

*If a model airplane is $\frac{1}{24}$ the size of the actual airplane, the **scale** of the model is 1 to 24.*

scale factor *factor de escala* (98) The number that relates corresponding sides of similar geometric figures.

*The **scale factor** from the smaller rectangle to the larger rectangle is 2.5.*

scalene triangle *triángulo escaleno* (62) A triangle with three sides of different lengths.

*All three sides of this **scalene triangle** have different lengths.*

scientific notation *notación científica* (51) A method of writing a number as a product of a decimal number and a power of 10.

*In **scientific notation,** 34,000 is written 3.4×10^4.*

874 *Saxon Math Course 2*

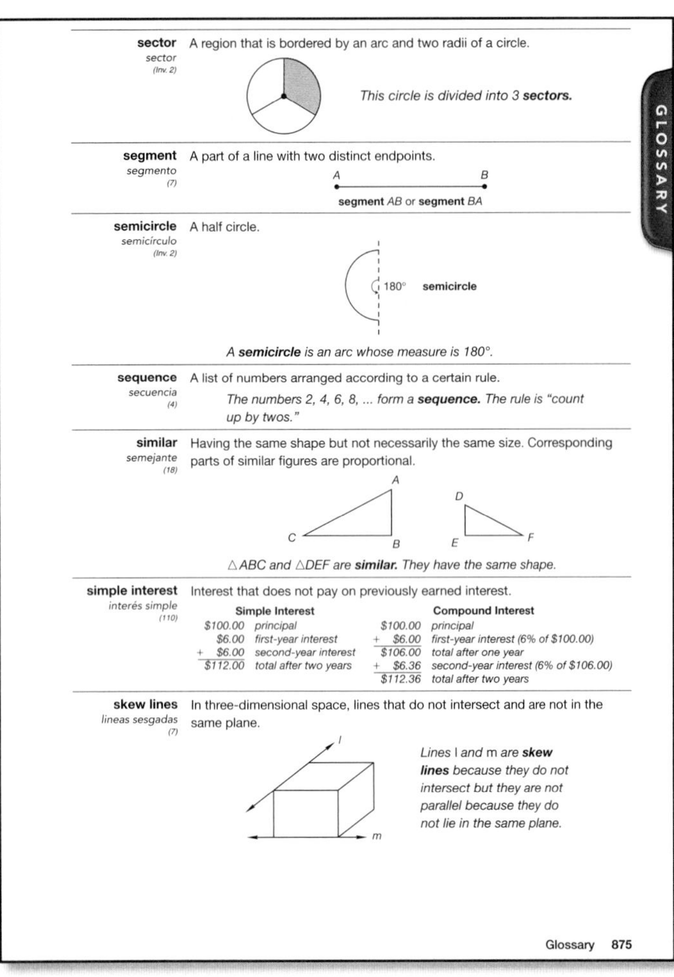

sector *sector* *(Inv. 2)* A region that is bordered by an arc and two radii of a circle.

This circle is divided into 3 ***sectors.***

segment *segmento* *(7)* A part of a line with two distinct endpoints.

A B

segment *AB* or **segment** *BA*

semicircle *semicírculo* *(Inv. 2)* A half circle.

180° **semicircle**

A ***semicircle*** *is an arc whose measure is 180°.*

sequence *secuencia* *(4)* A list of numbers arranged according to a certain rule.

The numbers 2, 4, 6, 8, ... form a ***sequence.*** *The rule is "count up by twos."*

similar *semejante* *(18)* Having the same shape but not necessarily the same size. Corresponding parts of similar figures are proportional.

A B C D E F

△ABC and △DEF are ***similar.*** *They have the same shape.*

simple interest *interés simple* *(110)* Interest that does not pay on previously earned interest.

Simple Interest		**Compound Interest**	
\$100.00	*principal*	*\$100.00*	*principal*
\$6.00	*first-year interest*	*+ \$6.00*	*first-year interest (6% of \$100.00)*
+ \$6.00	*second-year interest*	*\$106.00*	*total after one year*
\$112.00	*total after two years*	*+ \$6.36*	*second-year interest (6% of \$106.00)*
		\$112.36	*total after two years*

skew lines *líneas sesgadas* *(7)* In three-dimensional space, lines that do not intersect and are not in the same plane.

l m

Lines l and m are ***skew lines*** *because they do not intersect but they are not parallel because they do not lie in the same plane.*

GLOSSARY

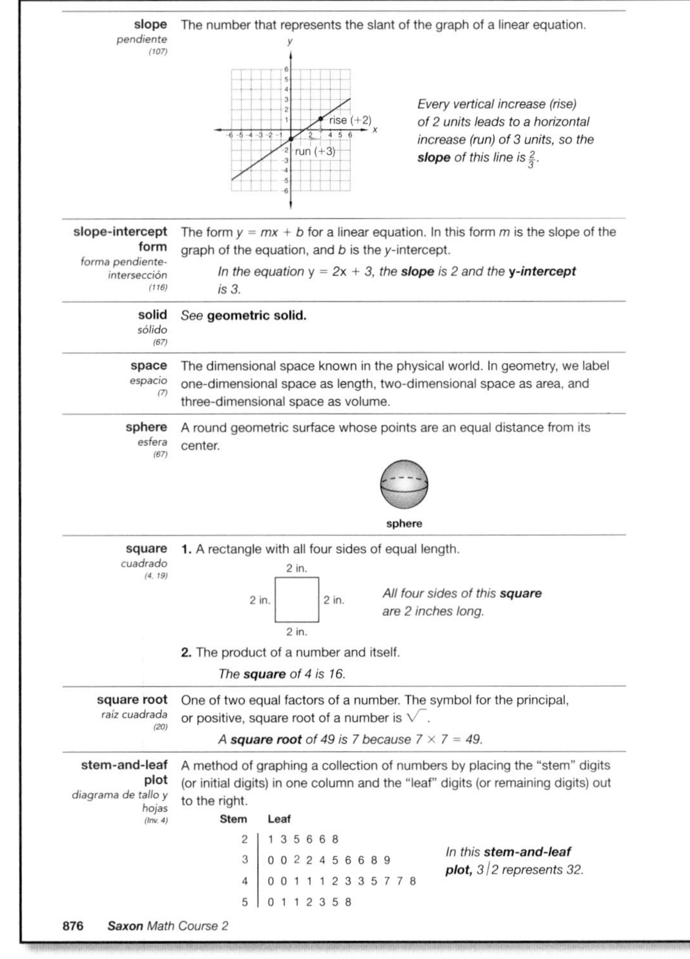

slope *pendiente* *(107)* The number that represents the slant of the graph of a linear equation.

Every vertical increase (rise) of 2 units leads to a horizontal increase (run) of 3 units, so the ***slope*** *of this line is $\frac{2}{3}$.*

slope-intercept form *forma pendiente-intersección* *(116)* The form $y = mx + b$ for a linear equation. In this form m is the slope of the graph of the equation, and b is the y-intercept.

In the equation y = 2x + 3, the ***slope*** *is 2 and the* ***y-intercept*** *is 3.*

solid *sólido* *(67)* See **geometric solid.**

space *espacio* *(7)* The dimensional space known in the physical world. In geometry, we label one-dimensional space as length, two-dimensional space as area, and three-dimensional space as volume.

sphere *esfera* *(67)* A round geometric surface whose points are an equal distance from its center.

sphere

square *cuadrado* *(4, 19)* **1.** A rectangle with all four sides of equal length.

2 in. 2 in. 2 in. 2 in.

All four sides of this ***square*** *are 2 inches long.*

2. The product of a number and itself.

The ***square*** *of 4 is 16.*

square root *raíz cuadrada* *(20)* One of two equal factors of a number. The symbol for the principal, or positive, square root of a number is $\sqrt{\ }$.

A ***square root*** *of 49 is 7 because 7 × 7 = 49.*

stem-and-leaf plot *diagrama de tallo y hojas* *(Inv. 4)* A method of graphing a collection of numbers by placing the "stem" digits (or initial digits) in one column and the "leaf" digits (or remaining digits) out to the right.

Stem	**Leaf**
2	1 3 5 6 6 8
3	0 0 2 2 4 5 6 6 8 9
4	0 0 1 1 1 2 3 3 5 7 7 8
5	0 1 1 2 3 5 8

In this ***stem-and-leaf plot,*** *3|2 represents 32.*

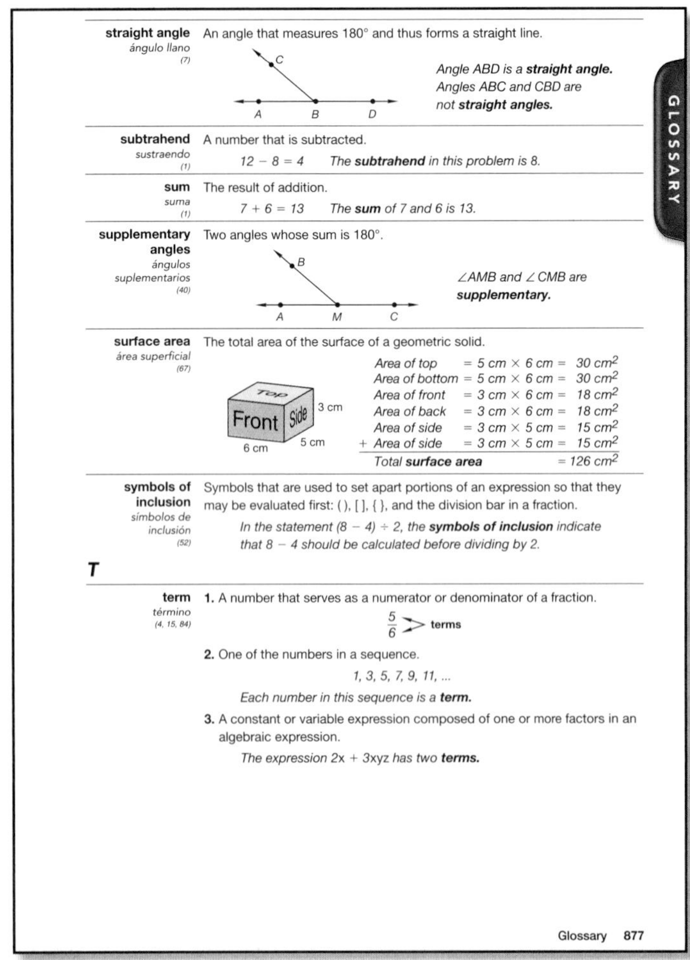

straight angle *ángulo llano* *(7)* An angle that measures 180° and thus forms a straight line.

C A B D

Angle ABD is a ***straight angle.*** *Angles ABC and CBD are not* ***straight angles.***

subtrahend *sustraendo* *(1)* A number that is subtracted.

12 − 8 = 4 The ***subtrahend*** *in this problem is 8.*

sum *suma* *(1)* The result of addition.

7 + 6 = 13 The ***sum*** *of 7 and 6 is 13.*

supplementary angles *ángulos suplementarios* *(40)* Two angles whose sum is 180°.

B A M C

∠AMB and ∠CMB are ***supplementary.***

surface area *área superficial* *(67)* The total area of the surface of a geometric solid.

Area of top	= 5 cm × 6 cm =	30 cm²
Area of bottom	= 5 cm × 6 cm =	30 cm²
Area of front	= 3 cm × 6 cm =	18 cm²
Area of back	= 3 cm × 6 cm =	18 cm²
Area of side	= 3 cm × 5 cm =	15 cm²
+ Area of side	= 3 cm × 5 cm =	15 cm²
Total ***surface area***		= 126 cm²

symbols of inclusion *símbolos de inclusión* *(52)* Symbols that are used to set apart portions of an expression so that they may be evaluated first: ( ), [ ], { }, and the division bar in a fraction.

In the statement (8 − 4) ÷ 2, the ***symbols of inclusion*** *indicate that 8 − 4 should be calculated before dividing by 2.*

T

term *término* *(4, 15, 84)* **1.** A number that serves as a numerator or denominator of a fraction.

$\frac{5}{6}$ **terms**

2. One of the numbers in a sequence.

1, 3, 5, 7, 9, 11, ...

Each number in this sequence is a ***term.***

3. A constant or variable expression composed of one or more factors in an algebraic expression.

The expression 2x + 3xyz has two ***terms.***

GLOSSARY

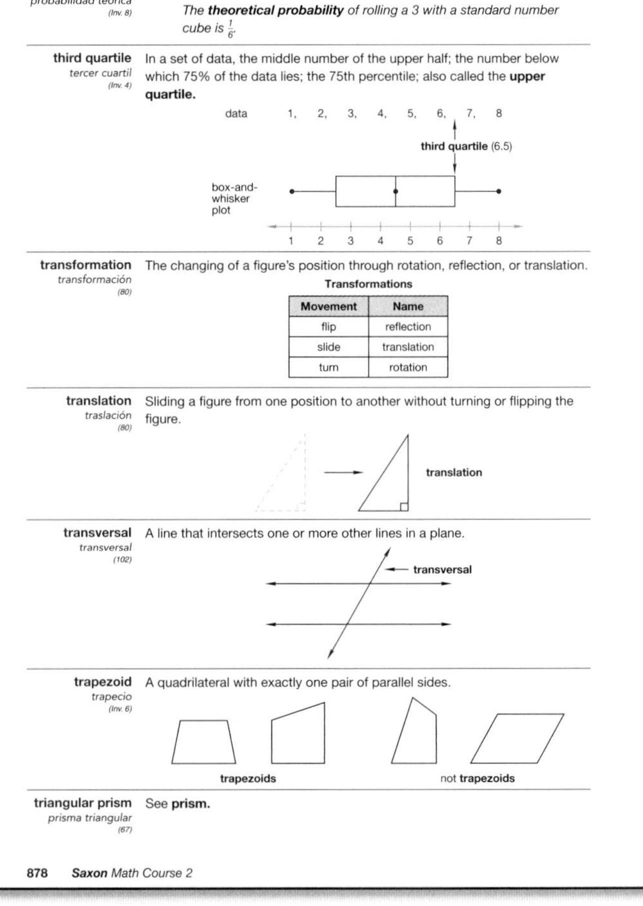

theoretical probability *probabilidad teórica* *(Inv. 8)* The probability that an event will occur as determined by analysis rather than by experimentation.

The ***theoretical probability*** *of rolling a 3 with a standard number cube is $\frac{1}{6}$.*

third quartile *tercer cuartil* *(Inv. 4)* In a set of data, the middle number of the upper half; the number below which 75% of the data lies; the 75th percentile; also called the **upper quartile.**

transformation *transformación* *(80)* The changing of a figure's position through rotation, reflection, or translation.

Transformations

Movement	Name
flip	reflection
slide	translation
turn	rotation

translation *traslación* *(80)* Sliding a figure from one position to another without turning or flipping the figure.

transversal *transversal* *(102)* A line that intersects one or more other lines in a plane.

trapezoid *trapecio* *(Inv. 6)* A quadrilateral with exactly one pair of parallel sides.

triangular prism *prisma triangular* *(67)* See **prism.**

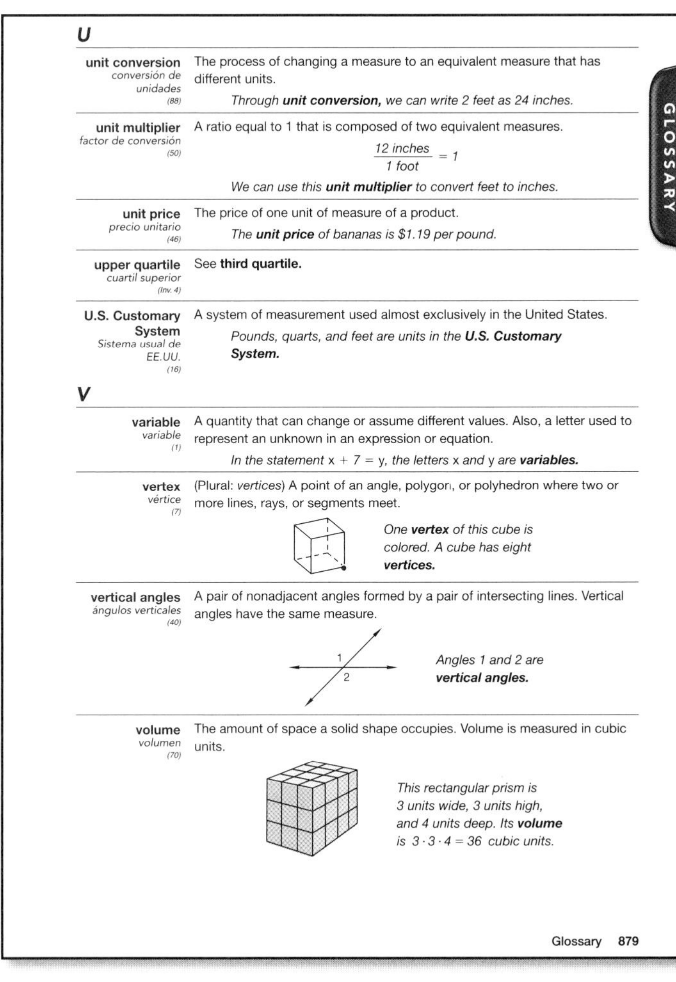

U

unit conversion *conversión de unidades* (88)
The process of changing a measure to an equivalent measure that has different units.
*Through **unit conversion,** we can write 2 feet as 24 inches.*

unit multiplier *factor de conversión* (50)
A ratio equal to 1 that is composed of two equivalent measures.

$$\frac{12 \text{ inches}}{1 \text{ foot}} = 1$$

*We can use this **unit multiplier** to convert feet to inches.*

unit price *precio unitario* (46)
The price of one unit of measure of a product.
*The **unit price** of bananas is $1.19 per pound.*

upper quartile *cuartil superior* (Inv. 4)
See **third quartile.**

U.S. Customary System *Sistema usual de EE.UU.* (16)
A system of measurement used almost exclusively in the United States.
*Pounds, quarts, and feet are units in the **U.S. Customary System.***

V

variable *variable* (1)
A quantity that can change or assume different values. Also, a letter used to represent an unknown in an expression or equation.
*In the statement x + 7 = y, the letters x and y are **variables.***

vertex *vértice* (7)
(Plural: *vertices*) A point of an angle, polygon, or polyhedron where two or more lines, rays, or segments meet.
*One **vertex** of this cube is colored. A cube has eight **vertices.***

vertical angles *ángulos verticales* (40)
A pair of nonadjacent angles formed by a pair of intersecting lines. Vertical angles have the same measure.
*Angles 1 and 2 are **vertical angles.***

volume *volumen* (70)
The amount of space a solid shape occupies. Volume is measured in cubic units.
*This rectangular prism is 3 units wide, 3 units high, and 4 units deep. Its **volume** is $3 \cdot 3 \cdot 4 = 36$ cubic units.*

Glossary 879

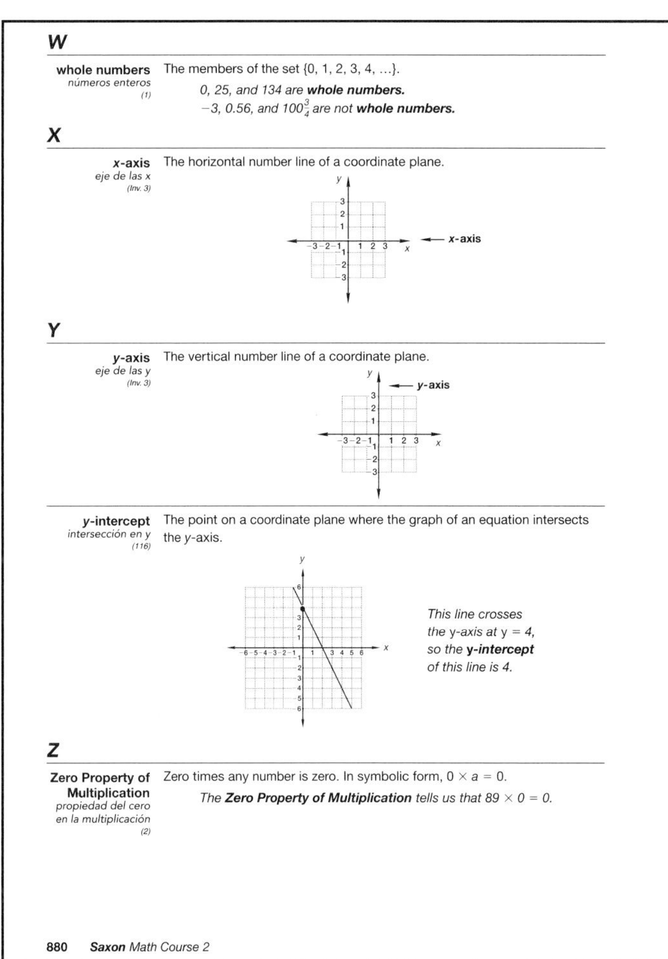

W

whole numbers *números enteros* (1)
The members of the set {0, 1, 2, 3, 4, ...}.
*0, 25, and 134 are **whole numbers.***
*-3, 0.56, and $100\frac{3}{4}$ are not **whole numbers.***

X

x-axis *eje de las x* (Inv. 3)
The horizontal number line of a coordinate plane.

Y

y-axis *eje de las y* (Inv. 3)
The vertical number line of a coordinate plane.

y-intercept *intersección en y* (116)
The point on a coordinate plane where the graph of an equation intersects the *y*-axis.
*This line crosses the y-axis at y = 4, so the **y-intercept** of this line is 4.*

Z

Zero Property of Multiplication *propiedad del cero en la multiplicación* (2)
Zero times any number is zero. In symbolic form, $0 \times a = 0$.
*The **Zero Property of Multiplication** tells us that $89 \times 0 = 0$.*

880 **Saxon** Math Course 2

A

References in color indicate content exclusive to the Teacher's Manual.

INDEX

D

E

F

INDEX

M

INDEX

N

O

P

INDEX

S

T

U

V

W

X

Y

Z

	COURSE 1	COURSE 2	COURSE 3
NUMBERS AND OPERATIONS			
Numeration			
digits	●		
read and write whole numbers and decimals	●	●	▲
place value to trillions	●	●	▲
place value to hundred trillions		●	▲
number line (integers, fractions)	●	●	▲
number line (rational and irrational numbers)		●	●
expanded notation	●	●	
comparison symbols ($=, <, >$)	●	●	▲
comparison symbols ($=, <, >, \leq, \geq$)		●	▲
compare and order rational numbers	●	●	▲
compare and order real numbers		●	●
scientific notation		●	●
Basic operations			
add, subtract, multiply, and divide integers	●	●	▲
add, subtract, multiply, and divide decimal numbers	●	●	▲
add, subtract, multiply, and divide fractions and mixed numbers	●	●	▲
add, subtract, multiply, and divide algebraic terms		●	●
add and subtract polynomials			●
add, subtract, multiply, and divide radical expressions			●
multiply binomials			●
mental math strategies	●	●	●
regrouping in addition, subtraction, and multiplication	●	●	▲
multiplication notations: $a \times b$, $a \cdot b$, $a(b)$	●	●	▲
division notations: division box, division sign, and division bar	●	●	▲
division with remainders	●	●	▲
Properties of numbers and operations			
even and odd integers	●	●	▲
factors, multiples, and divisibility	●	●	▲
prime and composite numbers	●	●	▲
greatest common factor (GCF)	●	●	▲
least common multiple (LCM)	●	●	▲
divisibility tests (2, 3, 5, 9, 10)	●	▲	▲
divisibility tests (4, 6, 8)		●	▲
prime factorization of whole numbers	●	▲	▲
positive exponents of whole numbers, decimals, fractions	●	●	▲
positive exponents of integers		●	▲
negative exponents of whole numbers		●	▲
negative exponents of rational numbers			●
square roots	●	●	●
cube roots		●	●
order of operations	●	●	▲
inverse operations	●	●	●

● Introduce and Develop
▲ Maintain and Apply

	COURSE 1	COURSE 2	COURSE 3
Estimation			
round whole numbers, decimals, mixed numbers	●	●	▲
estimate sums, differences, products, quotients	●	●	▲
estimate squares and square roots	●	●	●
determine reasonableness of solution	●	●	●
approximate irrational numbers		●	●
ALGEBRA			
Ratio and proportional reasoning			
fractional part of a whole, group, set, or number	●	●	▲
equivalent fractions	●	●	▲
convert between fractions, terminating decimals, and percents	●	●	▲
convert between fractions, repeating decimals, and percents		●	▲
reciprocals of numbers	●	●	▲
complex fractions involving one term in numerator/denominator		●	●
complex fractions involving two terms in numerator/denominator			●
identify/find percent of a whole, group, set, or number	●	●	▲
percents greater than 100%	●	●	▲
percent of change		●	●
solve proportions with unknown in one term	●	●	▲
find unit rates and ratios in proportional relationships	●	●	●
apply proportional relationships such as similarity, scaling, and rates	●	●	●
estimate and solve applications problems involving percent	●	●	●
estimate and solve applications problems involving proportional relationships such as similarity and rate		●	●
compare and contrast proportional and non-proportional linear relationships (direct and inverse variation)			●
Patterns, relations, and functions			
generate a different representation of data given another representation of data		●	●
use, describe, extend arithmetic sequence (with a constant rate of change)	●	●	●
input-output tables	●	●	●
analyze a pattern to verbalize a rule	●	●	▲
analyze a pattern to write an algebraic expression			●
evaluate an algebraic expression to extend a pattern		●	●
compare and contrast linear and nonlinear functions		●	●
Variables, expressions, equations, and inequalities			
solve equations using concrete and pictorial models	●	●	▲
formulate a problem situation for a given equation with one unknown variable		●	●
formulate an equation with one unknown variable given a problem situation	●	●	●
formulate an inequality with one unknown variable given a problem situation			●
solve one-step equations with whole numbers	●	▲	▲
solve one-step equations with fractions and decimals		●	▲
solve two-step equations with whole numbers	●	●	▲
solve two-step equations with fractions and decimals		●	●
solve equations with exponents			●

● Introduce and Develop
▲ Maintain and Apply

	COURSE 1	COURSE 2	COURSE 3
solve systems of equations with two unknowns by graphing			•
graph an inequality on a number line		•	•
graph pairs of inequalities on a number line			•
solve inequalities with one unknown		•	•
validate an equation solution using mathematical properties		•	•
GEOMETRY			
Describe basic terms			
point	•	•	▲
segment	•	•	▲
ray	•	•	▲
line	•	•	▲
angle	•	•	▲
plane	•	•	▲
Describe properties and relationships of lines			
parallel, perpendicular, and intersecting	•	•	•
horizontal, vertical, and oblique	•	•	•
slope		•	•
Describe properties and relationships of angles			
acute, obtuse, right	•	•	•
straight		•	•
complementary and supplementary	•	•	•
angles formed by transversals	•	•	•
angle bisector	•	•	
vertical angles		•	•
adjacent angles		•	•
calculate to find unknown angle measures	•	•	•
Describe properties and relationships of polygons			
regular	•	•	•
interior and exterior angles	•	•	
sum of angle measures	•	•	•
diagonals		•	•
effects of scaling on area		•	•
effects of scaling on volume		•	•
similarity and congruence	•	•	•
classify triangles	•	•	•
classify quadrilaterals	•	•	•
Use Pythagorean theorem to solve problems			
Pythagorean theorem involving whole numbers		•	•
Pythagorean theorem involving radicals			•
trigonometric ratios			•
3-Dimensional figures			
represent in 2-dimensional world using nets	•	•	•
draw 3-dimensional figures	•	•	•
Coordinate geometry			
name and graph ordered pairs	•	•	•
intercepts of a line		•	•
determine slope from the graph of line		•	•
formulate the equation of a line		•	•

• Introduce and Develop
▲ Maintain and Apply

	COURSE 1	COURSE 2	COURSE 3
identify reflections, translations, rotations, and symmetry	●	●	●
graph reflections across the horizontal or vertical axes	●	●	●
graph translations		●	●
graph rotations			●
graph dilations			●
graph linear equations		●	●
MEASUREMENT			
Measuring physical attributes			
use customary units of length, area, volume, weight, capacity	●	●	●
use metric units of length, area, volume, weight, capacity	●	●	●
use temperature scales: Fahrenheit, Celsius	●	●	●
use units of time	●	●	●
Systems of measurement			
convert units of measure	●	●	●
convert between systems	●	●	●
unit multipliers	●	●	●
Solving measurement problems			
perimeter of polygons, circles, complex figures	●	●	●
area of triangles, rectangles, and parallelograms	●	●	●
area of trapezoids		●	●
area of circles	●	●	●
area of semicircles and sectors		●	●
area of complex figures	●	●	●
surface area of right prisms and cylinders	●	●	●
surface area of spheres		●	●
surface area of cones and pyramids			●
estimate area	●	●	●
volume of right prisms, cylinders, pyramids, and cones	●	●	●
volume of spheres		●	●
estimate volume	●	●	●
Solving problems of similarity			
scale factor	●	●	●
similar triangles		●	●
indirect measurement		●	●
scale drawings: two-dimensional	●	●	●
scale drawings: three-dimensional			●
Use appropriate measurement instruments			
ruler (U.S. customary and metric)	●	●	▲
compass	●	●	●
protractor	●	●	●
thermometer	●	●	▲
DATA ANALYSIS AND PROBABILITY			
Data collection and representation			
collect and display data	●	●	●
tables and charts	●	●	▲

● Introduce and Develop
▲ Maintain and Apply

	COURSE 1	COURSE 2	COURSE 3
frequency tables	●	●	●
pictographs	●	●	
line graphs	●	●	▲
histograms	●	●	▲
bar graphs	●	●	▲
circle graphs	●	●	▲
Venn diagrams		●	●
scatter plots			●
line plots	●	●	▲
stem-and-leaf plots	●	●	▲
box-and-whisker plots		●	●
choose an appropriate graph	●	●	●
identify bias in data collection		●	▲
analyze bias in data collection			●
draw and compare different representations	●	●	●
Data set characteristics			
mean, median, mode, and range	●	●	▲
select the best measure of central tendency for a given situation		●	●
determine trends from data		●	●
predict from graphs		●	●
recognize misuses of graphical or numerical information		●	●
evaluate predictions and conclusions based on data analysis		●	●
Probability			
experimental probability	●	●	●
make predictions based on experiments	●	●	●
accuracy of predictions in experiments	●	●	●
theoretical probability	●	●	●
sample spaces	●	●	▲
simple probability	●	●	▲
probability of compound events	●	●	●
probability of the complement of an event	●	●	●
probability of independent events	●	●	●
probability of dependent events		●	●
select and use different models to simulate an event			●
PROBLEM SOLVING			
Connections			
identify and apply mathematics to everyday experiences	●	●	●
identify and apply mathematics to activities in and outside of school	●	●	●
identify and apply mathematics in other disciplines	●	●	●
identify and apply mathematics to other mathematical topics	●	●	●
Problem-solving skills and tools			
use a problem-solving plan	●	●	▲
evaluate for reasonableness	●	●	▲
use a proportion	●	●	▲
use a calculator	●	●	▲
use estimation	●	●	▲
use manipulatives	●	●	▲

● Introduce and Develop
▲ Maintain and Apply

	COURSE 1	COURSE 2	COURSE 3
use mental math	●	●	▲
use number sense	●	●	▲
use formulas	●	●	▲
Problem-solving strategies			
choose a strategy	●	●	▲
draw a picture or diagram	●	●	▲
find a pattern	●	●	▲
guess and check	●	●	▲
act it out	●	●	▲
make a table, chart, or graph	●	●	▲
work a simpler problem	●	●	▲
work backwards	●	●	▲
use logical reasoning	●	●	▲
write a number sentence or equation	●	●	▲
Communication			
relate mathematical language to everyday language	●	●	●
communicate mathematical ideas using efficient tools	●	●	●
communicate mathematical ideas with appropriate units	●	●	●
communicate mathematical ideas using graphical, numerical, physical, or algebraic mathematical models	●	●	●
evaluate the effectiveness of different representations to communicate ideas	●	●	●
Reasoning and proof			
justify answers	●	●	●
make generalizations	●	●	●
make conjectures from patterns	●	●	●
make conjectures from sets of examples and nonexamples	●	●	●
validate conclusions using mathematical properties and relationships	●	●	●
ALGEBRA TOPICS APPENDIX			
graph sequences			●
formulate the equation of a line with given characteristics			●
formulate the equation of a line parallel/perpendicular to a given line			●
solve proportions with an unknown in two terms			●
graph linear inequalities			●
factor quadratics			●
solve quadratic equations			●
solve systems of linear equations using substitution			●
solve systems of linear equations using elimination			●
formulate an equation with two unknown variables given a problem situation			●
solve systems of linear inequalities with two unknowns			●
graph systems of linear inequalities			●

● Introduce and Develop
▲ Maintain and Apply